CW00408076

Leveraging WMI Scripting

Leveraging WMI Scripting

Using Windows Management Instrumentation to
Solve Windows Management Problems

Alain Lissoir

Digital Press

An imprint of Elsevier Science
Amsterdam • Boston • London • New York • Oxford • Paris • San Diego
San Francisco • Singapore • Sydney • Tokyo

Digital Press is an imprint of Elsevier Science.

Copyright © 2003, Elsevier Science (USA). All rights reserved.

No part of this publication may be reproduced, stored in a retrieval system, or transmitted in any form or by any means, electronic, mechanical, photocopying, recording, or otherwise, without the prior written permission of the publisher.

 Recognizing the importance of preserving what has been written, Elsevier Science prints its books on acid-free paper whenever possible.

Library of Congress Cataloging-in-Publication Data

Lissoir, Alain.
    Leveraging WMI Scripting / Alain Lissoir.
       p. cm.
    Includes index.
    ISBN 1-55558-299-0
      1. Microsoft Windows (Computer file) 2. Operating systems (Computers) 3. Programming languages (Electronic computers)   I. Title.

    QA76.76.O63L55475 2003
    005.4'469--dc21   2003043552

British Library Cataloguing-in-Publication Data

A catalogue record for this book is available from the British Library.

The publisher offers special discounts on bulk orders of this book.
For information, please contact:

Manager of Special Sales
Elsevier Science
200 Wheeler Road
Burlington, MA 01803
Tel: 781-313-4700
Fax: 781-313-4882

For information on all Digital Press publications available, contact our World Wide Web home page at: http://www.digitalpress.com or http://www.bh.com/digitalpress

10 9 8 7 6 5 4 3 2 1

Printed in the United States of America

I dedicate this book to my friends and my family,
who didn't get the chance to see me a lot throughout
these 20 months of hard work. Things will change now!

Contents

Foreword   **xv**

Preface   **xvii**

Some Useful Scripts   **xxi**

Acknowledgments   **xxiii**

List of Figures   **xxix**

List of Samples   **xxxvii**

List of Tables   **xlvii**

I   The Windows WMI Providers Discovery   **I**

    I.I   Objective   I

    I.2   The WMI provider types   I

    I.3   WMI providers discovery   8

    I.4   Helpers for the discovery   20

    I.5   Summary   27

2   The Win32 Providers   **29**

    2.I   Objective   29

    2.2   The Win32 providers   29

    2.3   Computer system hardware classes   31

        2.3.I   Input device classes   31

        2.3.2   Mass storage classes   33

        2.3.3   Motherboard, controller, and port classes 40

        2.3.4   Networking device classes   49

        2.3.5   Power device classes   74

        2.3.6   Modem device classes   77

	2.3.7	Printing device classes	82
	2.3.8	Video and monitor classes	96
2.4	Operating System classes	105
	2.4.1	COM component classes	105
	2.4.2	Desktop information classes	113
	2.4.3	Driver classes	122
	2.4.4	File system classes	124
	2.4.5	Page file classes	139
	2.4.6	Multimedia audio/visual class	146
	2.4.7	Networking classes	147
	2.4.8	Operating System settings classes	154
	2.4.9	Process classes	171
	2.4.10	Registry class	183
	2.4.11	Job scheduler classes	183
	2.4.12	Service classes	191
	2.4.13	Share classes	197
	2.4.14	Start menu classes	201
	2.4.15	User account classes	202
2.5	Summary	209

3 The WMI Providers   **211**
3.1	Objective	211
3.2	The WMI providers	211
3.3	Core OS components providers	213
	3.3.1	The WBEM provider	213
	3.3.2	NT Event Log providers	218
	3.3.3	Registry providers	224
	3.3.4	Session providers	241
	3.3.5	Kernel Job providers	246
	3.3.6	TrustMon provider	251
	3.3.7	Windows Proxy provider	258
	3.3.8	Windows Product Activation provider	260
	3.3.9	Windows Installer provider	267
	3.3.10	Resultant Set of Policies (RSOP) providers	281
	3.3.11	The System Restore provider	309
3.4	Core OS components event providers	319
	3.4.1	The Clock provider	319
	3.4.2	Power management provider	323
	3.4.3	Shutdown provider	325
	3.4.4	Configuration Change provider	326

	3.4.5	Volume Change event provider	328
3.5		Core OS file system components providers	329
	3.5.1	Disk quota provider	329
	3.5.2	DFS provider	344
	3.5.3	Shadow Copy providers	352
3.6		Active Directory components providers	372
	3.6.1	Active Directory Service providers	372
	3.6.1.1	Creating and updating objects in Active Directory	378
	3.6.1.2	Searching in Active Directory	381
	3.6.1.3	Monitoring Active Directory group memberships	383
	3.6.1.4	Monitoring the FSMO roles	387
	3.6.1.5	Debugging Active Directory providers	391
	3.6.2	Active Directory Replication provider	394
3.7		Network components providers	405
	3.7.1	Ping provider	405
	3.7.2	Network Diagnostic provider	412
	3.7.3	IP routing provider	415
	3.7.4	DNS provider	423
	3.7.5	SNMP providers	450
	3.7.5.1	Accessing SNMP data	454
	3.7.5.2	Accessing SNMP private MIB information	463
	3.7.5.3	Organizing the SNMP data access	467
	3.7.5.4	Receiving SNMP traps	471
	3.7.5.5	Sending SNMP commands	480
	3.7.5.6	Debugging SNMP providers	485
3.8		Performance providers	486
	3.8.1	High-performance providers	486
	3.8.2	Performance Monitoring provider	502
3.9		Helper providers	508
	3.9.1	The View provider	508
	3.9.2	The Forwarding consumer provider	517
	3.9.3	The Event Correlator providers	525
3.10		Summary	526
3.11		Useful Internet URLs	527
4		**WMI Security Scripting**	**529**
4.1		Objective	529
4.2		The WMI security configuration	529
	4.2.1	The WMI connection security settings	530
	4.2.2	The group membership	530

4.3   WMI and Active Server Page (ASP)   536
    4.3.1   Authentication settings   536
    4.3.2   Customizing IIS 5.0 and above   539
4.4   WMI security descriptor management   544
    4.4.1   The security descriptor WMI representation   544
    4.4.2   How to access the security descriptor   546
    4.4.3   The security descriptor ADSI representation   547
    4.4.4   Which access technique to use? Which security descriptor
                 representation do we obtain?   549
4.5   The WMI Security provider   551
4.6   Connecting to the manageable entities   556
    4.6.1   Connecting to file and folder security descriptors   562
           4.6.1.1   Connecting to files and folders with WMI   562
           4.6.1.2   Connecting to files and folders with ADSI   565
    4.6.2   Connecting to file system share security descriptors   567
           4.6.2.1   Connecting to file system shares with WMI   567
           4.6.2.2   Connecting to file system shares with ADSI   569
    4.6.3   Connecting to Active Directory object security descriptors   571
           4.6.3.1   Connecting to Active Directory objects with WMI   571
           4.6.3.2   Connecting to Active Directory objects with ADSI   573
    4.6.4   Connecting to Exchange 2000 mailbox security descriptors   575
           4.6.4.1   Connecting to Exchange 2000 mailbox
                   security descriptor with WMI   576
           4.6.4.2   Connecting to Exchange 2000 mailbox
                   security descriptor with ADSI   578
           4.6.4.3   Connecting to Exchange 2000 mailbox
                   security descriptor with CDOEXM   579
    4.6.5   Connecting to registry keys security descriptor   581
           4.6.5.1   Connecting to registry keys with WMI   581
           4.6.5.2   Connecting to registry keys with ADSI   581
    4.6.6   Connecting to CIM repository namespace security descriptors   583
           4.6.6.1   Connecting to CIM repository namespaces with WMI   583
           4.6.6.2   Connecting to CIM repository namespaces with ADSI   585
4.7   Accessing the security descriptor set on manageable entities   585
    4.7.1   Retrieving file and folder security descriptors   585
           4.7.1.1   Retrieving file and folder security descriptors with WMI   585
           4.7.1.2   Retrieving file and folder security descriptors with ADSI   587
    4.7.2   Retrieving file system share security descriptors   592
           4.7.2.1   Retrieving file system share security descriptors with WMI 592
           4.7.2.2   Retrieving file system share security descriptors with ADSI 593
    4.7.3   Retrieving Active Directory object security descriptors   594

	4.7.3.1	Retrieving Active Directory object security descriptors with WMI	594
	4.7.3.2	Retrieving Active Directory object security descriptors with ADSI	596
4.7.4		Retrieving Exchange 2000 mailbox security descriptors	597
	4.7.4.1	Retrieving Exchange 2000 mailbox security descriptors with WMI	597
	4.7.4.2	Retrieving Exchange 2000 mailbox security descriptors with ADSI	598
	4.7.4.3	Retrieving Exchange 2000 mailbox security descriptors with CDOEXM	599
4.7.5		Retrieving registry key security descriptors with ADSI	600
4.7.6		Retrieving CIM repository namespace security descriptors with WMI	602

4.8 Creating a default security descriptor — 603

4.9 The security descriptor conversion — 607

4.10 Deciphering the security descriptor — 611
- 4.10.1 Deciphering the WMI security descriptor representation — 611
- 4.10.2 Deciphering the ADSI security descriptor representation — 616

4.11 Deciphering the security descriptor components — 619
- 4.11.1 Deciphering the Owner and Group properties — 619
- 4.11.2 Deciphering the security descriptor Control Flags — 620
- 4.11.3 Deciphering the Access Control Lists — 625
- 4.11.4 Deciphering the Access Control Entries — 626
  - 4.11.4.1 Deciphering the ACE Trustee property — 627
  - 4.11.4.2 Deciphering the ACE Type property — 627
  - 4.11.4.3 Deciphering the ACE Flags property — 632
  - 4.11.4.4 Deciphering the ACE FlagType property — 635
  - 4.11.4.5 Deciphering the ACE AccessMask property — 637
    - 4.11.4.5.1 The files and folders ACE AccessMask property — 637
    - 4.11.4.5.2 The File System share ACE AccessMask property — 644
    - 4.11.4.5.3 The Active Directory object ACE AccessMask property — 648
    - 4.11.4.5.4 The Exchange 2000 mailbox ACE AccessMask property — 680
    - 4.11.4.5.5 The registry key ACE AccessMask property — 684
    - 4.11.4.5.6 The CIM repository namespace ACE AccessMask property — 687

4.12 Modifying the security descriptor — 691
- 4.12.1 Updating the security descriptor Owner — 691
- 4.12.2 Updating the security descriptor Group — 694
- 4.12.3 Updating the security descriptor Control Flags — 696

4.12.4 Adding an ACE   699

    4.12.4.1 Adding an ACE in the ADSI object model   699

    4.12.4.2 Adding an ACE in the WMI object model   701

4.12.5 Removing an ACE   703

    4.12.5.1 Removing ACE in the ADSI object model   703

    4.12.5.2 Removing ACE in the WMI object model   707

4.12.6 Reordering ACEs   710

    4.12.6.1 Reordering ACEs in the ADSI object model   711

    4.12.6.2 Reordering ACEs in the WMI object model   713

4.13 Updating the security descriptor   715

  4.13.1 Updating file and folder security descriptors   715

    4.13.1.1 Updating file and folder security descriptors with WMI   715

    4.13.1.2 Updating file and folder security descriptors with ADSI 718

  4.13.2 Updating File System share security descriptors   719

    4.13.2.1 Updating share security descriptors with WMI   719

    4.13.2.2 Updating share security descriptors with ADSI   720

  4.13.3 Updating Active Directory object security descriptors   721

    4.13.3.1 Updating Active Directory object security descriptors
          with WMI   721

    4.13.3.2 Updating Active Directory object security descriptors
          with ADSI   723

  4.13.4 Updating Exchange 2000 mailbox security descriptors   724

    4.13.4.1 Updating Exchange 2000 mailbox security descriptors
          with WMI   726

    4.13.4.2 Updating Exchange 2000 mailbox security descriptors
          with ADSI   727

    4.13.4.3 Updating Exchange 2000 mailbox security descriptors
          with CDOEXM   728

  4.13.5 Updating registry key security descriptors with ADSI   729

  4.13.6 Updating CIM repository namespace security descriptors with WMI   730

4.14 How WMI scripters are affected by the Microsoft security push   731

  4.14.1 Asynchronous scripting   732

    4.14.1.1 How the lockdown mechanism of
          Windows Server 2003 works   735

  4.14.2 Setting the security descriptor of a CIM repository namespace   737

  4.14.3 The ADSI WMI Extension   737

  4.14.4 The Windows Authorizations Access Group (WAAG)   738

4.15 Summary   738

5 The Optional Windows Components and Application WMI Providers   741

5.1   Objective   741

5.2   WMI and some additional Windows services   741
      5.2.1   Network Load-Balancing service   741
      5.2.2   Cluster service   747
      5.2.3   Terminal Server service   749
              5.2.3.1   The Terminal Server configuration   752
              5.2.3.2   The Terminal Server connections configuration   755
                        5.2.3.2.1   Enabling/disabling the Terminal Server
                                    connections   755
                        5.2.3.2.2   The Terminal Services remote control settings   756
                        5.2.3.2.3   The Terminal Services network adapter
                                    and connection limit settings   757
                        5.2.3.2.4   The Terminal Services encryption and
                                    authentication settings   759
                        5.2.3.2.5   The Terminal Services client settings   760
                        5.2.3.2.6   The Terminal Services environment settings   764
                        5.2.3.2.7   The Terminal Services connection logon settings   766
                        5.2.3.2.8   The Terminal Services connection session settings   768
                        5.2.3.2.9   The Terminal Services connection
                                    permissions settings   770
      5.2.4   Windows Driver Model provider   771

5.3   WMI and some (server) products   776
      5.3.1   Internet Information Server provider   776
      5.3.2   Exchange 2000   785
              5.3.2.1   The Routing Table provider   786
              5.3.2.2   The Queue provider   789
              5.3.2.3   The Cluster provider   794
              5.3.2.4   The Message Tracking Logs provider   794
              5.3.2.5   The DSAccess provider   800
      5.3.3   SQL Server 2000   802

5.4   WMI and some Windows applications   809
      5.4.1   Microsoft Office   809
      5.4.2   Internet Explorer   811

5.5   WMI and some Enterprise Management software   813
      5.5.1   Insight Management Agents   814
      5.5.2   Microsoft Operation Manager   824
      5.5.3   HP OpenView Operations for Windows   825

5.6   WMI and the .NET Framework   843
        5.6.1   The .NET Framework WMI information access   844
        5.6.2   Accessing WMI information from Visual Studio.NET   846
        5.6.3   Accessing WMI information from a .NET language   850
5.7   Summary   858
5.8   Useful Internet URLs   858

6   A Look Into the Future of WMI Scripting   861
6.1   The .NET Framework and scripting   862
6.2   Windows scripting environments   864
6.3   Final thoughts   865

    Appendix   867

    Index   889

Foreword

Alain Lissoir's first book, *Understanding WMI Scripting*, did a fine job of setting the foundation for system administrators who want to come to grips with WMI and comprehend where WMI might be usefully deployed to solve management problems.

This book is different, because Alain now attempts to bring the reader on a journey where he demonstrates how to put WMI into practice. His approach is exhaustive, yet while the sheer number of examples might be off-putting to the casual reader, they represent a huge treasure trove of code, which can be employed by the administrator who really wants to put WMI to work.

For me, the most interesting parts of the book are those that address security and applications. Windows is a great operating system, but no operating system is much good if it is insecure or doesn't do a good job of supporting applications. Manageability is an important part of applications, so it's great to see that Microsoft and independent software vendors have invested to build WMI providers for applications, and it is even better that these can be combined together in a secure manner. There is no doubt that you can expect to see more applications added to the set that supports WMI in the future, so think of this part of the book as your entrée to an area that will expand.

To repeat some comments I made in the foreword of Alain's previous book, I don't have much time for those who insist on recreating the wheel. I think you'll find that you can do much more than you realized to extract data from applications, understand what's really happening on your servers, and get real work done as you dip into the depth of knowledge and Alain's experience of real-world problems found here.

I know Alain has worked very hard to bring this book together and build on the strong foundation set in the first book. Practical and straightforward advice is always valuable and this book—even on a standalone basis—is an asset that any enterprise Windows administrator can learn from.

Enjoy!

Tony Redmond
Chief Technology Officer
HP Consulting and Integration

Preface

This book is the second one dedicated to Windows Management Instrumentation (WMI) scripting. In the first book, *Understanding WMI Scripting* (ISBN 1555582664), we discovered the Windows scripting environment and the WMI architecture with its set of supported tools. We also learned the WMI Query Language (WQL) and the WMI COM Scripting API in order to understand the various WMI scripting techniques.

In this second book, which continues the WMI discovery started in the first book, we dive deeper into the WMI world to understand the real-world manageable entities of the Windows world. Basically, we discover in a structured way the most important WMI providers available from Windows NT 4.0 to Windows Server 2003 (including Windows 2000 and Windows XP). This discovery will extensively use the knowledge gathered throughout the first book to build real-world scripted management solutions. As with the first book, this second book dedicated to WMI is based on an important concept: learning by practice. Based on your previous experiences with WMI, if you understand the WMI concepts and have mastered the WMI scripting techniques related to the WMI data retrieval and WMI events monitoring, you can use this second book on a standalone basis. However, if you are new to the WMI world, I strongly recommend that you start with the first book to gather a base knowledge about WMI.

The information contained in this book is organized in six chapters.

- Chapter 1 covers the WMI providers discovery. The chapter explains how the WMI providers are registered in the CIM repository and how to locate them by scripts. This WMI providers discovery technique will be quite useful in understanding the WMI providers capabilities with the WMI classes they support. This technique will also allow you to discover any new future CIM extensions by yourself and to understand some aspects of the available WMI providers that are not always documented in the Software Developer Kits (SDK). Although we will not dive into the WMI providers implementation in depth, it is useful to understand their capabilities, since they also determine the behavior of the WMI classes they support.

- Chapter 2 covers everything that is related to the Win32 providers. In this chapter, and based on the knowledge acquired from the first book, we will discuss how to retrieve hardware information from the system, customize the page file, the operating system settings, and the system registry to name a few examples. Basically, we will discuss how to manage from WMI scripts everything that is related to the core operating system settings.

- Chapter 3 covers all WMI providers that are part of the core Operating System WMI installation. For instance, we will see how to script on top of the WMI classes supported by the Active Directory providers, the SNMP providers, the forwarding event providers, and the Trust monitoring providers, to name a few. By examining the provider capabilities and the classes they support, we will see how they can be used to develop WMI scripts directly applicable in the field for day-to-day management tasks.

- Chapter 4 is related to the WMI security enhancements and the WMI security scripting techniques. In this chapter, we will discuss how security descriptors are structured and how to script them to manage the security settings. This chapter is one of the most complex chapters, since it covers a difficult topic, which consists of manipulating Access Control Lists (ACL) and Access Control Entries (ACE) of the security descriptors protecting access to the manageable real-world entities. We will see how to retrieve, decipher, modify, and update from WMI and ADSI scripts the security descriptor of file system objects, Active Directory objects, Exchange 2000 mailbox, registry entries, and WMI namespaces created in the CIM repository. This chapter also contains some hints related to the Internet Information Server (IIS) configuration when running ASP WMI-enabled scripts. Last but not least, due the security push made by Microsoft in early 2002, we will see how Windows Server 2003 has been updated regarding the WMI security and how this initiative affects people scripting on top of WMI.

- Chapter 5 is related to the optional components of the Windows platform and Windows applications supporting WMI. Under Windows Server 2003, optional components, such as Terminal Services (TS) or Network Load Balancing (NLB), come with a WMI provider to extend their management capabilities from WMI. We will also consider the most common Windows applications, such as Internet Information Server (IIS) version 6.0, Exchange 2000, and SQL 2000. This chapter will also discuss the Enterprise Management Solutions that also offer some WMI support as providers and as consumers. This includes, for instance, HP OpenView Operation Manager for Windows (OVOW) version 7.0 or Microsoft Operation Manager (MOM) version 1.0. The chapter also considers the WMI support regarding the Microsoft .NET Framework. Because the scripting techniques are extensively described in the previous chapter, this last chapter will only focus on the functional aspects supported by the WMI providers with their related classes.

- Chapter 6 finishes this book by giving some hints about the WMI scripting future. What's coming up? What will the Windows management and scripting future look like? Of course, the goal is just to share a view of this possible future, since Microsoft could reconsider any features during the development phase.

Last but not least, this second book contains more than 250 script samples. They can be downloaded for free from http://www.LissWare.Net.

Now, let's dive further into the WMI discovery by examining how to locate and understand the WMI providers capabilities available under Windows.

Some Useful Scripts

In the first book, *Understanding WMI Scripting*, we have seen what WMI is and how to script on top of the WMI scripting API. Some of the scripts developed throughout this first book are available in the appendix of this second book for information completeness. Therefore, if some scripting techniques are referring to these script samples, the full listing is available for reference in the appendix. However, for more detailed explanations, I recommend that you refer to the first book, *Understanding WMI Scripting* (ISBN 1555582664). For those of you having strong WMI experience and who didn't read the first book, here is the list of the reused scripts with their respective purpose:

Sample 4.6, "Retrieving all instances of the Win32_Service class with their properties" called **InstancesOfObjectClassWithAPI.wsf.**

Sample 4.14, "Setting one read/write property of a Win32_Registry class instance directly" called **SetWin32_RegistrySizeWithAPI (Direct Properties).wsf.**

Sample 4.15, "Setting one read/write property of a Win32_Registry class instance indirectly" called **SetWin32_RegistrySizeWithAPI (Indirect Properties).wsf.**

Sample 4.30, "A generic routine to display the SWbemPropertySet object" called **DisplayInstanceProperties.vbs.**

Sample 4.31, "Browsing the namespaces to find class definitions" called **BrowseNameSpaceForClassWithAPI.wsf.**

Sample 4.32, "A Windows Script File self-documenting the CIM repository classes in an Excel sheet" called **LoadCIMinXL.wsf.**

Sample 6.14, "A generic script for synchronous event notification" called **GenericEventSyncConsumer.wsf.**

Sample 6.17, "A generic script for asynchronous event notification" called **GenericEventAsyncConsumer.wsf.**

Samples 6.18 through 6.21, "Monitoring, managing, and alerting script for the Windows services" called **ServiceMonitor.wsf.**

For reference, you will find the listing of these scripts in the appendix.

Acknowledgments

In 1997, when I joined Digital Equipment Corporation (DEC), I never imagined that one day I would complete a two volume book covering any area of technology. Like many other IT consultants, I was busy delivering IT solutions based on Microsoft technologies for various customer projects. Life has many surprises and the IT world is constantly changing—each change offering its own opportunities and challenges. In 1999, Compaq (which had taken over DEC and has since itself merged into HP) embarked on their Windows 2000 Academy program, and allowed Compaq consultants a great chance to meet colleagues from all over the world and learn a new set of Microsoft technologies. This time was also a great opportunity to share knowledge and increase our experience. In this context, Micky Balladelli and Jan De Clercq provided great motivation for me to start writing my first official publication for Compaq. I'm really grateful to them for supporting me and giving me the guts to start my first white paper. The first publication is always the hardest. In this context, I would also like to acknowledge Tony Redmond, Vice-President and Chief Technology Officer of HP Consultancy & Integration (HPCI), for all the support he has given me since 1999 when I was still working as a local consultant in Belgium. His trust, his support and all opportunities he gave me, such as working at Microsoft in Redmond during the Exchange 2000 development phase and being part of his team, the HPCI Technology Leadership Group (TLG), have built my confidence and my experience for a book project.

Working with a team like TLG is great. It is a team of talented people, a team implicitly showing you the way to follow and helping you to express capabilities that you never imagined you had. Today, I'm proud to be part of such a great team and I owe a great debt to each of my team mates for their support in creating this book on Windows Management Instrumentation. In this regard, I want to acknowledge each of the TLG members who worked with me at Compaq and HP. More specifically, I want to acknowledge the contribution of Aric Bernard (US) for giving me the marvelous chance to rebuild my lab almost every month with the new Windows.NET Server builds, Pierre Bijaoui (FR) for providing me some hardware resources and his advice about the book publishing and editing process, Jerry Cochran (US) for acting as a bridge between Microsoft in Redmond and myself in Brussels, Jan De Clercq (BE) for showing me the way to approach writing white papers, articles, and, last, a book, Olivier D'hose (BE) for his constant support, his carefulness, and the delicious northwest smoked salmon strips, Dung Hoang Khac (FR) for his help with the Chinese mafia, Kevin Laahs (SCO) for his thorough reviews, sharing loads and ideas about my ADCchecker project, Donald Livengood (US) for saving my life in a road bend in Lexington, Massachusetts, Kieran McCorry (IR) for the good laughs we had in Orlando, Emer McKenna (IR) for her thorough reviews and carefulness she gave me, Daragh Morrissey (IR) for sharing his insights about Microsoft clusters, John Rhoton (AT) for saving my life (once more!) in an incredible hailstorm in Nice on a beautiful day in September. All these people gave me, sometimes without even knowing it, invaluable help in completing this work.

I also want to acknowledge the TLG management for their support and for the understanding they always demonstrated during twenty months of work. Being part of TLG involves you in many activities, such as customer projects and workshops, knowledge-sharing activities, and delivering presentations at major IT industry events, such as Microsoft Exchange Conference (MEC), IT Forum, TechED, or DECUS, to name a few. This doesn't leave much time to write a book during normal work hours, so most writing is done during weekends, vacations, and airplane travels. Having management support is a great asset when you are trying to balance everything that's expected of you. Therefore, I want to acknowledge Don Vickers, Todd Rooke, and Tony Redmond for their trust and continuous support.

Of course, the people of TLG were not the only ones who contributed to this project. My colleagues around the world helped in many ways, too. Some people helped me simply by asking technical questions and exposing their problems in our technical discussion forums. This type of knowledge sharing represents an invaluable source of information for a book writer, as it brings to your desk the real-world problems and situations that people are trying to solve in the field around the world. The practical and concrete approach I tried to bring to these WMI books is inspired by these contributions. In this respect, I want to acknowledge Lyn Baird (US), Eric Bidonnet (BE), Andy Cederberg (US), Warren Cooley (US), Michel Cosman (NL), Henrik Damslund (DK), Vincent D'Haene (BE), Mike Dransfield (AU),

Ian Godfrey (UK), Guido Grillenmeier (DE), Gary Hall (CA), Juergen Hasslauer (DE), Ken Hendel (US), Mike Ireland (US), Henrik Joergensen (DK), John Johnson (US), Lasse Jokinen (FI), Andy Joyce (AU), Richard Joyce (IR), Patrick Kildea (US), Missy Koslosky (US), Ales Kostohryz (CZ), Stuart Ladd (US), André Larbière (BE), Carey Lee (US), Paul Loonen (BE), Paul Marshall (US), Susan McDonald (BE), John McManus (UK), Kim Mikkelsen (DK), Brendan Moon (US), Joseph Neubauer (US), Gary Olsen (US), Ken Punshon (UK), Ben Santing (IR), Rudy Schockaert (BE), Terry Storey (UK), Peter Struve (DK), Jason Trimble (CA), Peter Van Hees (BE), Marc Van Hooste (BE), Michael Vogt (CH), Filip Vranckx (BE), Raymond Warichet (BE), Randy Warrens (US), and Mats Weckstrom (FI).

It's hard to write a book about Microsoft technologies without the support of the Microsoft designers, program managers, and developers in Redmond. Again, in this respect, I'm more than grateful to many Microsoft people for their interest, their support, and their contribution to this project by sharing and reviewing information despite their other commitments. People who gave me help come from various development and service teams at Microsoft, such as the Exchange team, the WMI team, the Programmability team, the MOM team, the Support Server group team, and Microsoft Consultancy Service, to name a few. In this respect, I want to acknowledge Muhammad Arrabi, Jim Benton, J. C. Cannon, Andy Cheung, Max Ciccotosto, Andrew Clinick, Andi Comisioneru, Ahmed El-Shimi, Clark Gilder, Mary Gray, Keith Hageman, Andy Harjanto, Russ Herman, Vladimir Joanovic, Pat Kenny, Stuart Kwan, Eric Lippert, Jonathan Liu, Andreas Luther, Sergei Meleshchuk, Arun Nanda, Sasha Nosov, Ajay Ramachandran, Paul Reiner, Arkady Retik, Jan Shanahan, Barry Steinglass, Greg Stemp, Sanjay Tandon, Patrick Tousignant, Deun Dex Tsaltas, and Céline Van Maele.

I want to give very particular thanks to Mary Gray and Sergei Meleshchuk from Microsoft who supported me for more than 15 months via e-mail despite the heavy load of work they had. I'm even more grateful when I think that we didn't get the chance to meet for the first time until September 2002. They helped by answering questions and reviewing some of the chapters without even knowing each other. I really appreciate the trust they gave me throughout these months.

Reviewers are very important and they bring an enormous value to a book. I admire the commitment they demonstrated by reading carefully all chapters and correcting my English and technical mistakes in these two books despite their availability. I want to acknowledge Mary Gray, Kevin

Laahs, Susan McDonald, Emer McKenna, and Sergei Meleshchuk for their thorough reviews. I know they suffered a lot during the readings.

Beside the Microsoft people, I also want to thank some people of the HP OpenView team for their support in sharing the information related to HP OpenView Operations for Windows (OVOW) and WMI. I want to acknowledge Viher Bogdan (SI), Jonathan Cyr (US), Drew Dimmick (US), Jerry Estep (US), Angelika Hierath (DE), Roland Hofstetter (DE), Wilhelm Klenk (DE), Siegfried Link (DE), Reinhard Merle (AU), Juergen Riedlinger (DE), and Pradeep Tapadiya (US).

In the same way, I also want to acknowledge some people from the Compaq Insight Manager team who shared information about the Compaq Insight Management Agents. Thanks to Kevin Barnett (US), David Claypool (US), Brian R. Matthews (US), Mike Mckenna (US), Alan Minchew (US), Rich Purvis (US), Merriam Rudyard (US), Scott Shaffer (US), and Bernardo Tagariello (US).

Creating a book is not only about writing the technical content. The production of a book is also a long and tedious task. Having the full support of a publishing house like Digital Press is a very important aspect of the success of a book project. In this respect, I want to acknowledge Pam Chester, Theron Shreve, and Alan Rose—with particular thanks to Theron Shreve for his support when we decided to change the initial one book project to a two book project. I really appreciate his commitment and support in all the decisions we made during these twenty months.

Even if a book about Windows Management Instrumentation is purely technical, there is another form of contribution, which is almost as important as the technical contribution. In this respect, I want to acknowledge all my friends and family who supported me throughout these 20 months of hard work despite the frustration they had of not seeing me as much as they wanted. I spent weekends, vacations, and most evenings working on this project when I was not traveling for my TLG job. Without their support, their interest, and their understanding, I would never have been able to complete this long writing effort. During twenty months of hard work, having friends and family give you their best support "to get some rest" is a great asset. First of all, I want to acknowledge my mother who didn't see me a lot during these two last years. Despite the difficult moments, she always demonstrated courage and understanding with regard to the too small amount of time I dedicated to her. I also want to acknowledge all my friends: Elisa Araya for showing me how you can spend years writing a book between Louvain-La-Neuve in Belgium and Santiago de Chile, Caroline

Bonami for her discrete presence, her tenderness, carefulness, and interest in what I do, Véronique Burguet for her constant commitment of getting news from me, Pascale Caloens for her listening and close tenderness for so long, Christian Cambier for always bringing me a realistic view in life and his interest in what I do for 20 years, Isabelle Cliquet for her support, her listening, and carefulness she gave me despite her busy life, Caroline Criquilion for her complicity and tenderness combined with a great sensitivity and understanding during the long talks we had together, Paul Crompton for chasing down the funniest DVDs on the market for me while I was writing, Serena De Palo for constantly asking news about me from Italy, Angélique Deprez for acting like a sister, Olivia Deroux for acting like a mother, and Eric Henrard for showing me that you can have loads of stupid (not always that stupid, actually!) and annoying problems at work, Thierry Devroye for his friendship, his carefulness, and for cooking me the best French fries and T-bone steak meals from all over the world, Paul-Marie Fouquet who is my best hardware advisor and supplier, Nathalie and Emilio Imparato for showing me how to prepare a delicious salad when I was following a diet and didn't have sufficient time to prepare meals due to my writing commitment, Philippe Liemans for his constant support and interest despite the difficult moments he was living, Sophie Lowagie for her years of friendship, Benoît-Michel Morimont for his interest in what I do, Nathalie Pinet for her friendship and complicity for 30 years, France and Ivan Syemons for their interest in this project and the nice evenings we spent together.

The last category of people I would like to acknowledge are the people I was working with before I joined Digital Equipment Corporation (DEC) in 1997. Their continuous interest, support, and friendship for years were a great asset to my motivation. I want to thank Jean-Pierre Aerts, Philippe Foucart, Emmanuel Limage, André Mathy, Ounis Rachiq, Rudy Vanhaelen, and Jean-Michel Verheugen.

For twenty months, I had so many contacts with so many people around the world that I do apologize to people I inadvertently omitted. If you fall into that category, then please accept my apologies and know that I am eternally grateful for your contribution.

Without all these people behind me, it would have been impossible to complete these two books on Windows Management Instrumentation. I'm very grateful to them for being what they are to me and for simply been present before I started this, during these twenty months of work, and after.

If you have any comments or question about the material in this book, I would be happy to hear from you. You can contact me at the following email address: alain.lissoir@hp.com

Alain Lissoir
December 2002

List of Figures

Chapter 1: The Windows WMI Providers Discovery

Figure 1.1   The provider registration system classes.   2
Figure 1.2   The SNMP class provider registration.   2
Figure 1.3   The Registry instance provider registration.   3
Figure 1.4   The Registry property provider registration.   4
Figure 1.5   The Win32 method provider registration.   5
Figure 1.6   The NT Event Log event provider registration.   5
Figure 1.7   The Registry provider registration in the CIM repository and in the registry.   7
Figure 1.8   The provider qualifier of a class to determine the supported WMI provider.   9
Figure 1.9   The EventQueryList property of one __EventProviderRegistration instance.   10
Figure 1.10   The ConsumerClassNames property of one __EventConsumerProviderRegistration.   10

Chapter 2: The Win32 Providers

Figure 2.1   The Win32_LogicalDisk class associations.   34
Figure 2.2   Associated instances of one network adapter.   53
Figure 2.3   The static method qualifier.   70
Figure 2.4   The Win32_POTSModem class associations.   77
Figure 2.5   The Win32_Printer class associations.   83
Figure 2.6   Associated instances of one video controller.   100
Figure 2.7   The SNMP class provider COM information from the registry.   109
Figure 2.8   The WSHRemote settings modification.   111
Figure 2.9   The Win32_DCOMApplication class associations.   112
Figure 2.10   The Win32_Desktop class associations.   114
Figure 2.11   The CIM_Service class and its child classes.   122
Figure 2.12   The CIM_LogicalFile class and its child classes.   125

Figure 2.13   The Win32_DiskPartition class associations.   127
Figure 2.14   The CIM_LogicalDisk and its subclasses.   149
Figure 2.15   The Win32_MappedLogicalDisk class and its associations.   149
Figure 2.16   The Win32_LogonSession and its associations.   150
Figure 2.17   The Win32_NetworkAdapter class associations.   151
Figure 2.18   The Win32_ProcessStartup abstract class used only as a method
                  parameter class.   176
Figure 2.19   The associations of the Win32_LogicalProgramGroup class.   202
Figure 2.20   The Win32_LogicalProgramGroupOrItem superclass.   202
Figure 2.21   The Win32_Group class associations.   204
Figure 2.22   Associated instances of one group.   204

Chapter 3: The WMI Providers

Figure 3.1   The Win32_WMISetting class associations.   214
Figure 3.2   The Win32_NTLogEvent associations.   219
Figure 3.3   The Win32_Share and Win32_ServerConnection classes are
                  associated with the Win32_ConnectionShare association class.   242
Figure 3.4   The Win32_ServerSession and Win32_ServerConnection classes
                  are associated with the Win32_SessionConnection association class.   242
Figure 3.5   The Win32_NamedJobObject associations.   247
Figure 3.6   The Win32_WindowsProductActivation class is associated with the
                  Win32_ComputerSystem class.   261
Figure 3.7   Adding the Windows Installer provider under Windows Server 2003.   268
Figure 3.8   The classes associated with the Win32_Product class.   275
Figure 3.9   A WMI filter created for the Default Domain Controller Policy.   283
Figure 3.10   The RSOP subnamespaces.   286
Figure 3.11   The RSOP subnamespaces created during a CreateSession
                  method invocation.   287
Figure 3.12   The RSOP_PolicySetting superclass.   289
Figure 3.13   The RSOP_IEAKPolicySetting associated classes.   290
Figure 3.14   A GPO to enforce the automatic startup of the SNMP Windows
                  service at the organizational unit level.   291
Figure 3.15   A GPO to enforce the automatic startup of the SNMP Windows
                  service at the site level.   293
Figure 3.16   The RSOP_GPO association.   307
Figure 3.17   The System Restore wizard.   310

Figure 3.18 The Win32_CurrentTime class and its child classes.   320

Figure 3.19 The Win32_DiskQuota association class.   330

Figure 3.20 The Win32_QuotaSetting class associations.   330

Figure 3.21 The Windows Explorer quota management interface.   333

Figure 3.22 The Win32_DFSNodeTarget association class.   345

Figure 3.23 A DFS configuration example.   348

Figure 3.24 Managing the Shadow Copies of a volume from the user interface.   352

Figure 3.25 The Win32_Volume class and its associations.   355

Figure 3.26 The Active Directory WMI classes mapped to the Active Directory classes. 373

Figure 3.27 The WMI ads_user abstract class qualifiers.   374

Figure 3.28 The WMI ds_user dynamic instance class qualifiers.   375

Figure 3.30 The DS_LDAP_Class_Containment associations.   376

Figure 3.29 Some of the Active Directory classes as seen from WMI.   376

Figure 3.31 The DS_LDAP_Instance_Containment associations.   377

Figure 3.32 An Active Directory user created with WMI.   379

Figure 3.33 Querying Active Directory with LDAP from LDP.   383

Figure 3.34 The registry hive for the four WMI providers supporting activity logging. 392

Figure 3.35 The Win32_IP4RouteTable association.   417

Figure 3.36 The DNS server class is associated with the DNS domain class.   426

Figure 3.37 The DNS domain class is associated with itself.   426

Figure 3.38 The DNS domain class is associated with the DNS records superclass. 427

Figure 3.39 Adding the SNMP providers under Windows Server 2003.   451

Figure 3.40 The SNMP Module Information Repository classes in Root\SNMP\SMIR.   453

Figure 3.41 The SNMP service configuration.   454

Figure 3.42 The Root\SNMP\localhost namespace qualifier.   455

Figure 3.43 Enabling SNMP on your Cisco router.   458

Figure 3.44 The Cisco IOS loaded in the memory flash.   464

Figure 3.45 The Cisco Flash SNMP classes in the CIM repository.   466

Figure 3.46 Accessing SNMP data via the localhost namespace and the
SWBemNamedValueSet object.   468

Figure 3.47 Accessing SNMP data via a dedicated namespace on the localhost.   469

Figure 3.48 Accessing SNMP data through a remote WMI computer via a
dedicated namespace.   470

Figure 3.49 The NotificationMapper instances.   473

Figure 3.50 The SnmpV2Notification class and the varBindList property.   474

Figure 3.51   The SnmpVarBind class is an array of object instances.   474
Figure 3.52   The SNMP_OLD_CISCO_TS_MIB_lts class to send SNMP
              commands to a Cisco device (SNMP-enabled).   481
Figure 3.53   The tsMsgSend property qualifiers.   482
Figure 3.54   The Performance Monitor Process counters.   504
Figure 3.55   The Process counters of the Performance Counters available from WMI.   507
Figure 3.56   The new created Join View class.   512
Figure 3.57   The Win32_DiskQuota association class and the created
              Association View class.   516
Figure 3.58   The WMI Forwarding providers roles and locations.   519

Chapter 4: WMI Security Scripting

Figure 4.1   The default security settings on the Root namespace.   535
Figure 4.2   Granting all Scripting API permissions to the IIS account.   536
Figure 4.3   Setting the Windows Integrated Authentication.   537
Figure 4.5   Enabling remote access for remote users.   538
Figure 4.4   Setting the passport or digest authentication.   538
Figure 4.6   The three IIS locations where authentication can be defined.   539
Figure 4.8   Enabling anonymous access with IIS.   540
Figure 4.7   The isolated file system directory from the WWWRoot folder.   540
Figure 4.9   Ensuring WMI CIM repository access for the WMI-ASP
              dedicated account.   541
Figure 4.10   Viewing all Win32_Service instance states from the Web.   542
Figure 4.11   The security descriptor logical structure as seen from WMI.   545
Figure 4.12   The security descriptor logical structure as seen from ADSI.   548
Figure 4.13   The Win32_LogicalFileSecuritySetting class associations.   553
Figure 4.14   The owner and group associations.   554
Figure 4.15   The Win32_Account class and the Win32_SID class association.   554
Figure 4.16   Win32_LogicalShareSecuritySetting class associations.   555
Figure 4.17   The default share security descriptor.   604
Figure 4.18   The Control Flags bitwise values.   622
Figure 4.19   The files and folders security descriptor user interface.   638
Figure 4.20   The files and folders inheritance user interface.   643
Figure 4.21   The File System share security descriptor user interface   647
Figure 4.22   The Extended Rights enforced by Active Directory (left),
              enforced by applications (center), and enforced by the system (right).   654

Figure 4.23   The appliesTo GUID numbers of the "Personal Information"
Extended Right in liaison with the schemaIDGUID attribute of
the classSchema object.   655

Figure 4.24   Converting a GUID string to a GUID number and vice versa.   655

Figure 4.25   The appliesTo GUID numbers of the "Send As" Extended Right in
liaison with the schemaIDGUID attribute of the classSchema object.   656

Figure 4.26   The attributeSecurityGUID attribute of the attributeSchema
object contains the rightsGUID GUID number of the
"Personal Information" Extended Right.   656

Figure 4.27   The Extended Rights attributes links.   657

Figure 4.28   The ACE ObjectType property used to grant or deny the creation or
deletion of objects from a particular class.   669

Figure 4.29   ACE Inheritance to a specific object class.   678

Figure 4.30   The default Exchange 2000 mailbox security just after creation
from the MMC.   683

Figure 4.31   The registry hive security descriptor user interface.   687

Figure 4.32   The Root\CIMv2 namespace security descriptor user interface.   690

Figure 4.33   An Active Directory security descriptor owner.   695

Figure 4.34   The Control Flags configuration.   696

Figure 4.35   The effect of resetting the SE_DACL_PROTECTED flag twice.   697

Figure 4.36   A WMI client application performing an asynchronous operation.   733

Figure 4.37   A WMI client application performing an asynchronous operation
where UnSecApp.Exe is involved.   733

Figure 4.38   The registry activating the new lockdown mechanism of
Windows Server 2003.   735

Figure 4.39   A WMI client application performing an asynchronous
operation where UnSecApp.Exe is involved and when the
Windows Server 2003 lockdown mechanism is activated.   736

**Chapter 5: The Optional Windows Components and
Application WMI Providers**

Figure 5.1   The NLB network adapter user interface.   743

Figure 5.2   The NLB class associations.   746

Figure 5.3   The Node and Cluster classes.   747

Figure 5.4   The MSCluster_Cluster class associations.   750

Figure 5.5   The Terminal Services Configuration MMC.   752

Figure 5.6   The Terminal Services remote control configuration.   756

Figure 5.7   The Terminal Service connection limit settings.   758

Figure 5.8   The Terminal Services general connection settings.   759

Figure 5.9   The Terminal Services default client settings.   761

Figure 5.10   The Terminal Services connection environment settings.   764

Figure 5.11   The Terminal Services connection logon settings.   766

Figure 5.12   The Terminal Services connection session settings.   768

Figure 5.13   The Terminal Services connection permission settings.   770

Figure 5.14   The WMIBinaryMofResource class instances.   772

Figure 5.15   The WMIEvent extrinsic event class.   774

Figure 5.16   Detecting network cable disconnections with the
                    MSNdis_StatusMediaDisconnect extrinsic event class.   775

Figure 5.17   The IISWebServer class associations with their respective superclasses. 777

Figure 5.18   The ServerBindings property and ServerBinding instance.   778

Figure 5.19   The associations of the CIM_ManagedSystemElement superclass.   779

Figure 5.20   The associations of the CIM_Setting superclass.   780

Figure 5.21   The CIM_Component class with its references.   780

Figure 5.22   The CIM_ElementSetting class with its references.   781

Figure 5.23   The Exchange System Manager monitoring settings.   787

Figure 5.24   The Exchange System Manager showing the Exchange servers
                    and connectors state.   788

Figure 5.25   The IncreasingTime property behavior from the ExchangeLink
                    and ExchangeQueue classes.   791

Figure 5.26   The "Message Tracking" user interface.   797

Figure 5.27   The "DSAccess" user interface.   800

Figure 5.28   The Win32_Process View class in the Root\MicrosoftSQLServer
                    namespace.   808

Figure 5.29   The Insight Management Web-enabled Agents architecture of
                    CIM, version 7 SP1.   815

Figure 5.30   The Insight Management Agents information.   816

Figure 5.31   Some Insight Management Agents SNMP classes in the
                    CIM repository.   818

Figure 5.32   The CPQ_System_Performance superclass with its subclasses,
                    as shown in WMI CIM Studio.   823

Figure 5.33   The HP OpenView Operations for Windows console showing alerts.   827

Figure 5.34   The .NET Framework and the WMI architecture.   846

Figure 5.35 The WMI-based management extension to the
              Visual Studio.NET Server Explorer tool.   847
Figure 5.36 Browsing WMI namespaces for classes.   848
Figure 5.37 Event subscription from Visual Studio.NET.   849
Figure 5.38 Viewing events from Visual Studio.NET.   850

List of Samples

Chapter 1: The Windows WMI Providers Discovery

Sample 1.1   Locating WMI provider registration instances with their supported classes (Part I)   11

Sample 1.2   Locating WMI provider registration instances with their supported classes (Part II)   12

Sample 1.3   Locating WMI provider registration instances with their supported classes (Part III)   14

Sample 1.4   Listing a single instance of a class with its properties formatted   21

Sample 1.5   Listing all instances of a class with their properties formatted   22

Sample 1.6   The DisplayFormattedPropertyFunction.vbs function   24

Chapter 2: The Win32 Providers

Sample 2.1   Determine if a mouse is right or left hand configured   32

Sample 2.2   Alerting script when the free disk space decreases below 50 percent on a specific disk   34

Sample 2.3   Executing CHKDSK via WMI   37

Sample 2.4   Retrieving hardware resource information (Part I)   42

Sample 2.5   Retrieving hardware resource information (Part II)   44

Sample 2.6   Retrieving hardware resource information (Part III)   45

Sample 2.7   Retrieving hardware resource information (Part IV)   47

Sample 2.8   Retrieving network device information (Part I)   49

Sample 2.9   Retrieving network device information (Part II)   51

Sample 2.10   Retrieving network device information (Part III)   54

Sample 2.11   Retrieving network device information (Part IV)   55

Sample 2.12   Configuring a network adapter (Part I)   62

Sample 2.13   Configuring a network adapter (Part II)   66

Sample 2.14 Retrieving battery information   74

Sample 2.15 Retrieving modem information   78

Sample 2.16 Managing the printer drivers, the printers, and their related
print jobs (Part I)   85

Sample 2.17 Viewing printer drivers, printers, and job information (Part II) 87

Sample 2.18 Adding printers and printer connections (Part III)   90

Sample 2.19 Deleting, managing (test page, pause, resume, etc.) and renaming
printers (Part IV)   92

Sample 2.20 Adding and deleting printer drivers (Part V)   94

Sample 2.21 Managing printer jobs (pause, resume, and delete) (Part VI)   95

Sample 2.22 Retrieving the desktop monitor information   97

Sample 2.23 Retrieving the video adapter information   100

Sample 2.24 Locating the WMI provider registration instances with their
COM information   106

Sample 2.25 Retrieving DCOM application settings   109

Sample 2.26 Reading, creating, updating, and deleting environment variables (Part I) 116

Sample 2.27 Reading environment variables (Part II)   118

Sample 2.28 Creating environment variables (Part III)   119

Sample 2.29 Updating environment variables (Part IV)   120

Sample 2.30 Deleting environment variables (Part V)   121

Sample 2.31 Gathering disk partition, disk drive, and logical disk information (Part I) 127

Sample 2.32 Gathering disk partition information (Part II)   128

Sample 2.33 Gathering disk drive information (Part III)   129

Sample 2.34 Gathering logical disk information (Part IV)   130

Sample 2.35 Watching a file size   133

Sample 2.36 Copying, renaming, deleting, (un)compressing, and taking
ownership of files and directories.   136

Sample 2.37 Viewing, creating, updating, and deleting page files (Part I)   140

Sample 2.38 Viewing page files (Part II)   142

Sample 2.39 Creating page files (Part III)   144

Sample 2.40 Updating page files (Part IV)   144

Sample 2.41 Deleting page files (Part V)   145

Sample 2.42 Retrieving network device information (Part V)   150

Sample 2.43 Configuring the Operating System (Part I)   157

Sample 2.44 Viewing various Operating System properties (Part II)   159

Sample 2.45 Viewing Operating System QFE (Part III)   162

Sample 2.46 Joining and unjoining a domain or workgroup, and renaming a
workstation (Part IV)   163

Sample 2.47 Time zone, daylight savings, and startup options (Part V)   165

Sample 2.48 The Operating System recovery parameters (Part VI)   167

Sample 2.49 Setting application time slice, date and time, and rebooting the
Operating System (Part VII)   169

Sample 2.50 Viewing, creating, and killing processes (Part I)   172

Sample 2.51 Viewing processes (Part II)   174

Sample 2.52 Creating processes (Part II)   177

Sample 2.53 Killing processes (Part IV)   178

Sample 2.54 Viewing, creating, and killing processes (OnObjectReady sink
routine) (Part V)   179

Sample 2.55 Viewing, creating, and killing processes (OnCompleted sink
routine) (Part VI)   180

Sample 2.56 Viewing, creating, and deleting scheduled jobs (Part I)   185

Sample 2.57 Viewing the scheduled jobs (Part II)   189

Sample 2.58 Creating scheduled jobs (Part III)   190

Sample 2.59 Deleting scheduled jobs (Part IV)   191

Sample 2.60 Creating, updating, and deleting a Win32_Service (Part I)   193

Sample 2.61 Viewing the Win32_Service instances (Part II)   194

Sample 2.62 Creating a Win32_Service instance (Part III)   195

Sample 2.63 Modifying a Win32_Service instance (Part IV)   196

Sample 2.64 Deleting a Win32_Service instance (Part V)   197

Sample 2.65 Viewing, creating, updating, and deleting shares   199

Sample 2.66 Retrieving the group membership   205

Sample 2.67 Retrieving the SID from the UserID   207

Sample 2.68 Retrieving the UserID from the SID   208

Chapter 3: The WMI Providers

Sample 3.1 Updating the WMI settings   215

Sample 3.2 Viewing and updating the NT Event Log configuration and
clearing and backing up the NT Event Log information   221

Sample 3.3 Browsing, creating, deleting, searching, and replacing
information in the registry (Part I)   229

Sample 3.4 Browsing information in the registry (Part II)   232

Sample 3.5 Creating information in the registry (Part III)   233

Sample 3.6 Deleting information in the registry (Part IV)   234

Sample 3.7 Browsing, searching, and replacing information in the registry (Part V)   236

Sample 3.8 Browsing, searching, and replacing information in the registry (Part VI)   237

Sample 3.9 Creating or updating information in the registry (Part VII)   240

Sample 3.10 Viewing the active sessions with their associations   243

Sample 3.11 Viewing Job kernel instance associated with a process   248

Sample 3.12 Verifying trusts   254

Sample 3.13 Managing the Windows Proxy LAN settings   258

Sample 3.14 Windows Product Activation   263

Sample 3.15 Managing Windows Installer packages (Part I)   273

Sample 3.16 Managing Windows Installer packages (Part II)   277

Sample 3.17 Managing Windows Installer packages (Part III)   278

Sample 3.18 Retrieving RSOP information from an applied GPO (Part I)   295

Sample 3.19 Retrieving RSOP information from an applied GPO (Part II)   297

Sample 3.20 Retrieving RSOP information from an applied GPO (Part III)   299

Sample 3.21 Retrieving RSOP information from an applied GPO (Part IV)   300

Sample 3.22 Retrieving RSOP information from an applied GPO (Part V)   301

Sample 3.23 Retrieving RSOP information from an applied GPO (Part VI)   301

Sample 3.24 Retrieving RSOP information from an applied GPO (Part VII)   307

Sample 3.25 Exploiting the System Restore features from script (Part I)   312

Sample 3.26 Viewing the System Restore points (Part II)   313

Sample 3.27 Enabling/disabling disk monitoring (Part III)   314

Sample 3.28 Creating a restore point (Part IV)   315

Sample 3.29 Getting the last restore status (Part V)   317

Sample 3.30 Restoring a restore point (Part VI)   318

Sample 3.31 Updating the System Restore parameters (Part VII)   318

Sample 3.32 Getting the current time (UTC and local)   321

Sample 3.33 Retrieving Disk quota information for each logical disk   331

Sample 3.34 Viewing the default volume quotas (Part I)   334

Sample 3.35 Configuring the default volume quotas (Part II)   336

Sample 3.36 Viewing, creating, updating, and deleting volume quota per user (Part I)   339

Sample 3.37 Updating volume quota per user (Part II)   342

Sample 3.38 Deleting volume quota per user (Part III)   343

Sample 3.39 Viewing, creating, modifying, and deleting DFS nodes (Part I)   346

Sample 3.40 Viewing, creating, modifying, and deleting DFS nodes (Part II)   350

Sample 3.41 Managing disk services and shadow copies (Part I)   357

Sample 3.42 Viewing all Win32_ShadowCopy instances (Part II)   358

Sample 3.43 Creating new shadow copies (Part III)   359

Sample 3.44 Deleting shadow copies (Part IV)   360

Sample 3.45 Associating a shadow storage with a Win32_Volume instance (Part V)   361

Sample 3.46 Viewing the volumes with their related shadow storage and shadow
copies (Part VI)   362

Sample 3.47 Executing the Chkdsk Win32_Volume method (Part VII)   365

Sample 3.48 Executing the DefragAnalysis Win32_Volume method (Part VIII)   367

Sample 3.49 Executing the Defrag Win32_Volume method (Part IX)   368

Sample 3.50 Executing the Format Win32_Volume method (Part X)   369

Sample 3.51 Updating a Win32_ShadowStorage instance (Part XI)   371

Sample 3.52 Removing a Win32_ShadowStorage instance (Part XII)   371

Sample 3.53 Creating an Active Directory user object with WMI   378

Sample 3.54 Monitoring, managing, and alerting script for the Windows Group
modifications   384

Sample 3.55 Making the Configuration and Schema context accessible   387

Sample 3.56 Monitoring, managing, and alerting script for the FSMO role
modifications   388

Sample 3.57 Viewing and managing the Active Directory Replication state (Part I)   397

Sample 3.58 Viewing the inbound replication state information for a
Naming Context (Part II)   401

Sample 3.59 Triggering the KCC and forcing a Naming Context replication (Part III)   404

Sample 3.60 PINGing a system at regular time intervals (Part I)   408

Sample 3.61 PINGing a system at regular time intervals (Part II)   410

Sample 3.62 Testing connectivity with the Network Diagnostic provider   413

Sample 3.63 Viewing, adding, and deleting IP v4.0 routes (Part I)   418

Sample 3.64 Adding IP v4.0 routes (Part II)   420

Sample 3.65 Deleting IP v4.0 routes (Part III)   422

Sample 3.66 Managing the DNS server (Part I)   431

Sample 3.67 Viewing the DNS zones (Part IIa)   438

Sample 3.68 Managing the DNS zones (Part IIb)   440

Sample 3.69 Managing the DNS records (Part III)   446

Sample 3.70 Obtaining localhost IP addresses from WMI via SNMP   456

Sample 3.71 Obtaining remote device IP addresses from WMI via SNMP   458

Sample 3.72 A MOF file to create a dedicated namespace for an SNMP device   461

Sample 3.73 Creating a private MIB in the CIM repository   464

Sample 3.74 The updated DisplayProperties() function to display the SnmpVarBind instances — 477

Sample 3.75 The DisplaySNMPBindings() function to display the SnmpVarBind instances — 478

Sample 3.76 Sending SNMP commands — 483

Sample 3.77 Capturing performance counter values (raw or cooked) at regular time intervals (Part I) — 497

Sample 3.78 Capturing performance counter values (raw or cooked) at regular time intervals (Part II) — 501

Sample 3.79 The MOF file to register the Performance Monitoring provider — 503

Sample 3.80 A MOF file defining a class to retrieve Process counters from the Performance Monitor — 504

Sample 3.81 Viewing the Performance Monitor Process counters with a script — 506

Sample 3.82 Registering the View provider — 508

Sample 3.83 The Join View class — 510

Sample 3.84 The Union View class — 513

Sample 3.85 The Association View class — 514

Sample 3.86 A MOF file to forward WMI events — 519

Chapter 4: WMI Security Scripting

Sample 4.1 Viewing all Win32_Service instances with their status from a WMI-ASP script — 542

Sample 4.2 The WMIManageSD.Wsf framework to manage security descriptors from the command line — 558

Sample 4.3 Connecting to files and folders with WMI (Part I) — 562

Sample 4.4 Connecting to files and folders with ADSI (Part II) — 566

Sample 4.5 Connecting to shares with WMI (Part III) — 568

Sample 4.6 Connecting to shares with ADSI (Part IV) — 570

Sample 4.7 Connecting to Active Directory objects with WMI (Part V) — 572

Sample 4.8 Connecting to Active Directory objects with ADSI (Part VI) — 574

Sample 4.9 Connecting to Exchange 2000 mailbox information with WMI (Part VII) — 576

Sample 4.10 Connecting to Exchange 2000 mailbox information with ADSI (Part VIII) — 578

Sample 4.11 Connecting to Exchange 2000 mailbox information with CDOEXM (Part IX) — 580

Sample 4.12 Connecting to registry keys with ADSI (Part X) — 582

Sample 4.13 Connecting to CIM repository namespaces with WMI (Part XI) — 583

Sample 4.14 Retrieving file and folder security descriptors with WMI (Part I) — 586

Sample 4.15 Retrieving file and folder security descriptors with ADSI (Part II)   588

Sample 4.16 Retrieving file system share security descriptors with WMI (Part III)   593

Sample 4.17 Retrieving file system share security descriptors with ADSI (Part IV)   594

Sample 4.18 Retrieving Active Directory object security descriptors with WMI (Part V)   595

Sample 4.19 Retrieving Active Directory object security descriptors with ADSI (Part VI) 597

Sample 4.20 Retrieving Exchange 2000 mailbox security descriptors with WMI (Part VII)   598

Sample 4.21 Retrieving Exchange 2000 mailbox security descriptors with ADSI
(Part VIII)   599

Sample 4.22 Retrieving Exchange 2000 mailbox security descriptors with
CDOEXM (Part IX)   600

Sample 4.23 Retrieving registry key security descriptors with ADSI (Part X)   601

Sample 4.24 Retrieving CIM repository namespace security descriptors with
WMI (Part XI)   603

Sample 4.25 Create a default security descriptor for a share   605

Sample 4.26 Converting the binary security descriptor to an ADSI representation   608

Sample 4.27 Converting the ADSI security descriptor to a binary format   610

Sample 4.28 Deciphering a WMI security descriptor representation   612

Sample 4.29 Deciphering an ADSI security descriptor representation   616

Sample 4.30 Deciphering the security descriptor Control Flags property   622

Sample 4.31 Calculate the security descriptor controls value   624

Sample 4.32 Deciphering the ACE Type property   628

Sample 4.33 Deciphering the ACE Flags property   633

Sample 4.34 Deciphering the ACE FlagType property   635

Sample 4.35 Deciphering the ACE AccessMask property for files and folders   639

Sample 4.36 Deciphering the ACE AccessMask property for File System shares   645

Sample 4.37 Deciphering the ACE AccessMask property for Active Directory objects   648

Sample 4.38 Deciphering the ACE AccessMask property for Exchange 2000 mailboxes   681

Sample 4.39 Deciphering the ACE AccessMask property for registry keys   685

Sample 4.40 Deciphering the ACE AccessMask property for CIM repository namespaces   688

Sample 4.41 Updating the security descriptor owner   691

Sample 4.42 Creating a Win32_Trustee instance   692

Sample 4.43 Updating the security descriptor group   695

Sample 4.44 Updating the security descriptor control flags   698

Sample 4.45 Adding ACE in the ADSI object model (Part I)   700

Sample 4.46 Adding ACE in the WMI object model (Part II)   702

Sample 4.47 Removing ACE in the ADSI object model (Part I)   704

Sample 4.48 Removing ACE in the WMI object model (Part II)   707

Sample 4.49 Reordering ACE in the ADSI object model (Part I)   711

Sample 4.50 Reordering ACE in the WMI object model (Part II)   713

Sample 4.51 Updating file and folder security descriptors with WMI (Part I)   716

Sample 4.52 Updating file and folder security descriptors with ADSI (Part II)   718

Sample 4.53 Updating share security descriptors with WMI (Part III)   719

Sample 4.54 Updating share security descriptors with ADSI (Part IV)   721

Sample 4.55 Updating Active Directory object security descriptors with WMI (Part V)   722

Sample 4.56 Updating Active Directory object security descriptors with ADSI (Part VI) 723

Sample 4.57 Updating Exchange 2000 mailbox security descriptors with WMI (Part VII)   726

Sample 4.58 Updating Exchange 2000 mailbox security descriptors with ADSI (Part VIII) 727

Sample 4.59 Updating Exchange 2000 mailbox security descriptors with
             CDOEXM (Part IX)   728

Sample 4.60 Updating registry key security descriptors with ADSI (Part X)   729

Sample 4.61 Updating CIM repository namespace security descriptors with
             WMI (Part XI)   730

**Chapter 5:   The Optional Windows Components and
             Application WMI Providers**

Sample 5.1   Retrieving NLB network configuration settings   744

Sample 5.2   Changing the license mode   753

Sample 5.3   Changing the security mode   754

Sample 5.4   Changing the temporary folder settings   754

Sample 5.5   Enabling/disabling the Terminal Services connections   755

Sample 5.6   Configuring the Terminal Services remote control settings   757

Sample 5.7   Configuring the Terminal Services maximum connection settings   758

Sample 5.8   Configuring the Terminal Services encryption and authentication levels 760

Sample 5.9   Configuring the Terminal Services client connection policy settings 762

Sample 5.10 Configuring the Terminal Services client color depth policy settings 763

Sample 5.11 Configuring the Terminal Services client mapping settings   763

Sample 5.12 Configuring the Terminal Services connection environment settings   765

Sample 5.13 Configuring the Terminal Services connection logon settings   767

Sample 5.14 Configuring the Terminal Services connection session settings   769

Sample 5.15 Viewing the IISWebServer ServerBindings property with WMI   782

Sample 5.16 The script initialization phase   832

Sample 5.17 Retrieving a collection of OV_Message instances   834

Sample 5.18 Retrieving all properties of an OV_Message instance   838

Sample 5.19 Managing a specific OV_Message instance   840

Sample 5.20 Changing the OVOW message severity level   841

Sample 5.21 Retrieving the OVOW message annotation   842

Sample 5.22 Managing a series of OV_Message instances   843

Sample 5.23 Connecting and retrieving all Windows Services instances with
their properties with the System.Management classes with C#   851

Sample 5.24 Connecting and retrieving all Windows Services instances with
their properties with a WQL data query with the System.Management
classes with C#   853

Sample 5.25 Connecting and performing a WQL event query to display
Windows Services instances subject to a modification with the
System.Management classes with C#   854

Appendix

Sample 4.6 Retrieving all instances of the Win32_Service class with their properties   865

Sample 4.14 Setting one read/write property of a Win32_Registry class instance directly   866

Sample 4.15 Setting one read/write property of a Win32_Registry class
instance indirectly   867

Sample 4.30 A generic routine to display the SWbemPropertySet object   867

Sample 4.31 Browsing the namespaces to find class definitions   870

Sample 4.32 A Windows Script File self-documenting the CIM repository classes
in an Excel sheet   871

Sample 6.14 A generic script for synchronous event notification   880

Sample 6.17 A generic script for asynchronous event notification   881

Samples 6.18–6.21 Monitoring, managing, and alerting script for the Windows services   883

List of Tables

Chapter 1: The Windows WMI Providers Discovery

Table 1.1   The Most Important WMI Providers under the Windows Platforms
with Their Capabilities   16

Chapter 2: The Win32 Providers

Table 2.1   The Win32 Providers Capabilities   30
Table 2.2   The Input Devices Classes   31
Table 2.3   The Mass Storage Classes   33
Table 2.4   Motherboard, Controller, and Port Classes   41
Table 2.5   The Networking Device Classes   49
Table 2.6   The Connection Status Values   53
Table 2.7   The Win32_NetworkAdapterConfiguration Methods   58
Table 2.8   The Power Device Classes   74
Table 2.9   The Telephony Classes   78
Table 2.10   The Printing Device Classes   82
Table 2.11   The Video and Monitor Classes   97
Table 2.12   The COM Component Classes   105
Table 2.13   The Desktop Classes   113
Table 2.14   The Driver Classes   122
Table 2.15   The File System Classes   125
Table 2.16   The CIM_LogicalFile Methods   135
Table 2.17   The Page File Classes   140
Table 2.18   The Networking Classes   147
Table 2.19   The Operating System Settings Classes   155
Table 2.20   The DomainRole property of the Win32_ComputerSystem Class   160
Table 2.21   The Join and Unjoin Options   164

Table 2.22   The Operating System File Dump Values   169
Table 2.23   The Operating System Shutdown Values   170
Table 2.24   The Process Classes   171
Table 2.25   The Job Scheduler Classes   183
Table 2.26   The Service Classes   191
Table 2.27   The ServiceType, ErrorControl, and StartMode Parameters for a
              Windows Service Creation   195
Table 2.28   The Share Classes   197
Table 2.29   The "ShareType" Values   198
Table 2.30   The Start Menu Classes   201
Table 2.31   The User Account Classes   203

Chapter 3: The WMI Providers

Table 3.1   The WBEM Provider Classes   213
Table 3.2   The WBEM Provider Capabilities   214
Table 3.3   The NT Event Log Providers Capabilities   218
Table 3.4   The NT Event Log Providers Classes   219
Table 3.5   The OverWritePolicy and OverwriteOutDated Property Values 224
Table 3.7   The Registry Providers Classes   225
Table 3.6   The Registry Providers Capabilities   225
Table 3.8   The StdRegProv Methods   227
Table 3.9   The Session Provider Capabilities   241
Table 3.10   The Session Provider Classes   241
Table 3.11   The Kernel Job Object Providers Capabilities   246
Table 3.12   The Kernel Job Object Classes   247
Table 3.13   The TrustMon Provider Capabilities   252
Table 3.14   The TrustMon Provider Classes   252
Table 3.15   The TrustMon Check Levels   252
Table 3.16   The Windows Proxy Providers Capabilities   258
Table 3.17   The Windows Product Activation Providers Capabilities   260
Table 3.18   The Windows Product Activation Providers Classes   261
Table 3.19   The Windows Product Activation Providers Methods   261
Table 3.20   The Windows Installer Provider   268
Table 3.21   The Windows Installer WMI Classes   270
Table 3.22   The Win32_Product Class Methods   272
Table 3.23   The RSOP Providers   282

Table 3.24	The RSOP Classes and Their Methods	285
Table 3.25	The RSOP WMI Classes	287
Table 3.26	The Status Property of the RSOP_SecuritySettings Class	293
Table 3.27	The Logging Mode and Planning Mode Flag Values	298
Table 3.28	The Root\Policy Classes	306
Table 3.29	The SystemRestore Providers Capabilities	310
Table 3.30	The SystemRestore Providers Classes	311
Table 3.31	The RestorePointType Parameter	316
Table 3.32	The EventType Parameter	316
Table 3.33	The SystemRestoreConfig Properties	319
Table 3.34	The Win32ClockProvider Providers Capabilities	320
Table 3.35	The Win32ClockProvider Classes	320
Table 3.36	The Power Management Providers Capabilities	324
Table 3.37	The Power Management Event Type Values	325
Table 3.38	The Shutdown Providers Capabilities	325
Table 3.39	The Configuration Change Providers Capabilities	327
Table 3.40	The EventType Property Meaning	327
Table 3.41	The Volume Change Providers Capabilities	328
Table 3.42	The Disk Quota Providers Capabilities	329
Table 3.43	The Disk Quota Provider Classes	330
Table 3.44	The DFS Providers Capabilities	344
Table 3.45	The DFS Provider Classes	344
Table 3.46	The State Property Meaning of the Win32_DFSNode and Win32_Target Classes	352
Table 3.47	The Shadow Copy Providers Capabilities	353
Table 3.48	The Shadow Copy Providers Classes	353
Table 3.49	The Active Directory Providers Capabilities	372
Table 3.50	The Active Directory/WMI Syntax Mapping	375
Table 3.51	The Active Directory Providers Classes	377
Table 3.52	The Active FSMO Roles and Their Location in Active Directory	387
Table 3.53	Enabling the Trace Logging of a WMI Provider	391
Table 3.54	The Active Directory Replication Providers Capabilities	394
Table 3.55	The Active Directory Replication Providers Classes	394
Table 3.56	The ExecuteKCC Method Parameters	403
Table 3.57	The SyncNamingContext Method Parameters	404
Table 3.58	The Ping Providers Capabilities	406

Table 3.59	The Network Diagnostic Providers Capabilities	412
Table 3.60	The IP routing providers capabilities	415
Table 3.61	The IP routing Providers Classes	416
Table 3.62	The DNS Providers Capabilities	424
Table 3.63	The DNS Providers Classes	424
Table 3.64	Some DNS Server Property Values	437
Table 3.65	Some Zone Property Values	444
Table 3.66	The DNS Record Class Values	450
Table 3.67	The SNMP Providers Capabilities	451
Table 3.68	The SNMP Classes Available in the Root\SNMP\SMIR Namespaces	452
Table 3.69	The Proxy Namespace Qualifiers to Define SNMP Transport Characteristics	455
Table 3.70	The SMI2SMIR.Exe Command-Line Parameters	465
Table 3.71	The SNMP Debugging Output Level	485
Table 3.72	The High-Performance Providers Capabilities	486
Table 3.73	The Win32_PerfRawData Classes	487
Table 3.74	The Win32_PerfFormattedData Classes	489
Table 3.75	The __ADAPStatus System Class Properties	492
Table 3.76	The Win32_PerfFormattedData_Tcpip_NetworkInterface Properties	494
Table 3.77	The Miscellaneous Cooking Type	495
Table 3.78	The Performance Monitoring Providers Capabilities	503
Table 3.79	The View Providers Capabilities	509
Table 3.80	The View Provider Qualifiers	510
Table 3.81	The WMI Forwarding Consumer and Forwarding Event Providers Capabilities	517
Table 3.82	The WMI Forwarding Consumer and Forwarding Event Providers Classes	518
Table 3.83	The StatusCode Property Returned Values	524
Table 3.84	The Correlation WMI Providers	525

Chapter 4: WMI Security Scripting

Table 4.1	The WMI Privileges Required for Some Classes, Properties, or Methods	531
Table 4.2	The Default Right Settings on the WMI Root Namespace	535
Table 4.3	The WMI and ADSI Security Descriptor Exposed Methods and Properties	549
Table 4.4	The Security Descriptor Access Methods with their Representations	550
Table 4.5	The Security Provider Capabilities	552
Table 4.6	The Security Providers Classes	552

Table 4.7	The ADsSecurityUtility Constants	587
Table 4.8	The Security Descriptor Control Flags Values	621
Table 4.9	The Security Descriptor Inheritance Flags	632
Table 4.10	The Security Descriptor Inheritance Flags (Active Directory)	633
Table 4.11	The Files and Folders ACE AccessMask Values	638
Table 4.12	The Files and Folders ACE Flags Values	642
Table 4.13	The File System Share ACE AccessMask Values	645
Table 4.14	The Active Directory Object ACE AccessMask Values—Standard View	649
Table 4.15	The Active Directory Object ACE AccessMask Values—Advanced View	651
Table 4.16	The Active Directory Objects ACE Flags Values	652
Table 4.17	Extended Rights Available in Active Directory under Windows Server 2003 (Exchange 2000 Extended Rights Included)	658
Table 4.18	The schemaIDGUID GUID Number with iTs Class Names	671
Table 4.19	Summary of the GUID Number Origins for the ACE ObjectType Property	676
Table 4.20	The Exchange 2000 Mailbox ACE AccessMask Values	681
Table 4.21	The Exchange 2000 Mailbox ACE Flags Values	682
Table 4.22	The Registry Key ACE AccessMask Values	684
Table 4.23	The Registry Key ACE Flags Values	685
Table 4.24	The CIM Repository Namespace Key ACE AccessMask Values	688
Table 4.25	The CIM Repository Namespace Key ACE Flags Values	689
Table 4.26	The ChangeSecurityPermissionsEx Method Flags for the Security Descriptor Recursive Update	717

Chapter 5: The Optional Windows Components and Application WMI Providers

Table 5.1	The Network Load-Balancing Providers Capabilities	742
Table 5.2	The Network Load-Balancing Providers Classes	742
Table 5.3	The NlbsNic Class Static Methods	743
Table 5.4	The Cluster Providers Capabilities	748
Table 5.5	The Cluster Providers Classes	749
Table 5.6	The Terminal Server Providers Capabilities	750
Table 5.7	The Terminal Server Providers Classes	751
Table 5.8	The Win32_TerminalServiceSetting Customization Values	753
Table 5.9	The Terminal Services Remote Control Configuration Values	757
Table 5.10	The Terminal Services Encryption and Authentication Level Values	760

Table 5.11   The Terminal Services Default Client Settings Values   761
Table 5.12   The Terminal Services Connection Environment Policy Settings   765
Table 5.13   The Terminal Services Connection Logon Values   766
Table 5.14   The Terminal Services Connection Session Values   768
Table 5.15   The Terminal Services Permission Values and Masks   771
Table 5.16   The WDM Providers Capabilities   771
Table 5.17   The WDM Providers Classes   773
Table 5.18   The Internet Information Server Provider   776
Table 5.19   The Exchange 2000 WMI Providers   786
Table 5.20   The ExchangeServerState Class Properties   790
Table 5.21   The ExchangeLink Properties   795
Table 5.22   The ExchangeQueue Properties   796
Table 5.23   The ExchangeClusterResource Properties   796
Table 5.24   The Exchange_MessageTrackingEntry Class Properties   797
Table 5.25   The Exchange_MessageTrackingEntry EntryType Property Meaning   798
Table 5.26   The Exchange_DSAccessDC Class Properties   801
Table 5.27   The WMI SQL Provider Capabilities   803
Table 5.28   The WMI SQL Classes   804
Table 5.29   The Office Provider Capabilities   809
Table 5.30   The Office 2000 and Office XP Classes   810
Table 5.31   The Internet Explorer Provider Capabilities   812
Table 5.32   The Internet Explorer WMI Classes   812
Table 5.33   Insight SNMP MIB Files   817
Table 5.34   Insight Management Agents WMI Classes Created from the MIB Files   820
Table 5.35   The Insight Management Agents Performance Classes   822
Table 5.36   The OM_Alert Extrinsic Event Class with the MOM SP1 Classes   824
Table 5.37   The HP OpenView Providers Capabilities   826
Table 5.38   The OV_Message Class   829
Table 5.39   The OV_Message and OV_ManagedNode Property Value Meanings   836

I

The Windows WMI Providers Discovery

1.1   **Objective**

During the initial WMI discovery to illustrate the scripting technique, we used a very few number of classes from the CIM repository (see the first book about WMI, *Understanding WMI Scripting*). Mostly, we worked with the *Win32_Service* class, *Win32_WMISetting,* and *Win32_NTLogEvent* classes. We also examined the WMI event model and worked with some specific event classes. The standard WMI installation includes more than 600 classes that expose more than 3,000 properties. As we can see, we are a long way from completing our WMI discovery! Classes representing manageable entities of the real world have a direct relation with the WMI providers registered in the CIM repository. Although the Microsoft Platform SDK documents most of the WMI providers available, we discuss here how to retrieve information about the WMI providers and the class they support by extracting information from the CIM repository. This information will serve as the basis for subsequent chapters when discovering the most important WMI providers available with their classes and capabilities.

1.2   **The WMI provider types**

A WMI provider registered in the CIM repository is an instance of the *__Win32Provider* system class. Basically, the *__Win32Provider* system class registers information about a provider's physical implementation with WMI. So, requesting all instances of the *__Win32Provider* system class in a particular WMI namespace will list all registered providers in that particular namespace.

During the WMI discovery, we saw that a set of system classes is available to define the nature of the providers (see Figure 1.1).

Figure 1.1
*The provider
registration system
classes.*

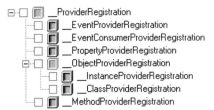

WMI defines a certain number of provider types, which determine the nature of the information delivered by the providers. These providers are as follows:

- **The class providers:** These providers supply applications with class definitions. They are rarely implemented, because classes are usually stored in the CIM repository. In most cases, the classes are slow-changing and finite. If classes need to be dynamically generated, then a class provider must be implemented, but this slows down the performance of information retrieval. This type of provider is registered in the CIM repository with an instance of the __*Win32Provider* system class, which has a reference to an instance of the __*Class-ProviderRegistration* system class (see Figure 1.2). The *Active Directory*

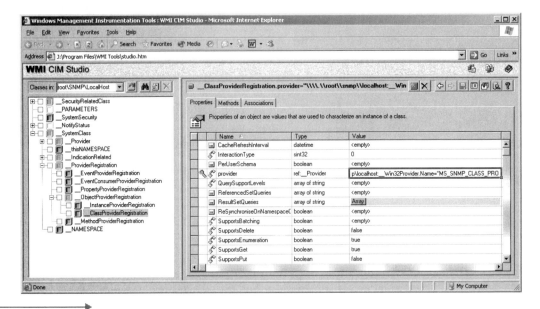

Figure 1.2   *The SNMP class provider registration.*

providers and the *SNMP* providers are two examples of providers that implement a class provider.

- **The instance providers:** These providers are the most common providers and supply instances of a given class. Usually, they provide services such as: instance retrieval, enumeration, modification, deletion, and query processing. This type of provider is registered in the CIM repository with an instance of the *__Win32Provider* system class, which has a reference to an instance of the *__Instance-ProviderRegistration* system class (see Figure 1.3). For instance, the *Win32* provider and the *Registry* provider are implemented as instance providers.

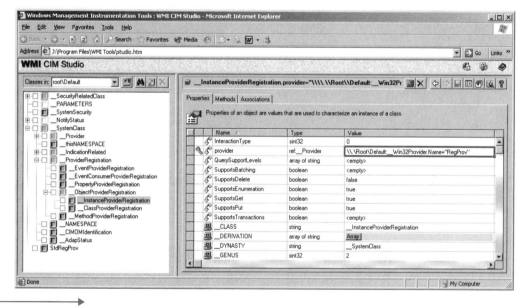

Figure 1.3   *The Registry instance provider registration.*

- **The property providers:** These providers can support the retrieval and the modification of individual property values. This type of provider is registered in the CIM repository with an instance of the *__Win32Provider* system class, which has a reference to an instance of the *__PropertyProviderRegistration* system class (see Figure 1.4). The *Registry* provider is also implemented as a property provider.

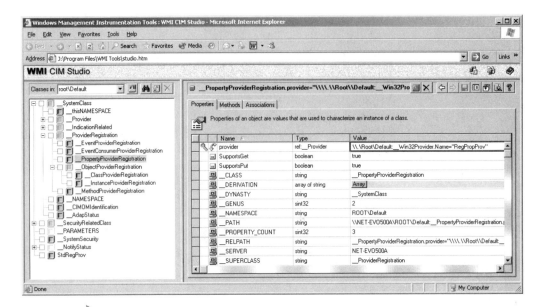

Figure 1.4   *The Registry property provider registration.*

- **The methods providers:** These providers implement the methods of one or more classes. This type of provider is registered in the CIM repository with an instance of the *__Win32Provider* system class, which has a reference to an instance of the *__Method-ProviderRegistration* system class (see Figure 1.5). For example, the *Win32* provider and the *Registry* provider are implemented as method providers as well.

- **The event providers:** These providers deliver event notifications to WMI. Next, WMI forwards the events to the appropriate event consumers (temporary or permanent, based on the consumer type). This type of provider is registered in the CIM repository with an instance of the *__Win32Provider* system class, which has a reference to an instance of the *__EventProviderRegistration* system class (see Figure 1.6). For instance, the *SNMP* provider, the *NT Event Log* provider, and the *Registry* provider are implemented as event providers.

- **The event consumer providers:** These providers were examined during the WMI discovery. They simply act as consumers of WMI events. This type of provider is registered in the CIM repository with an instance of the *__Win32Provider* system class, which has a reference to an instance of the *__EventConsumerProviderRegistration* system class.

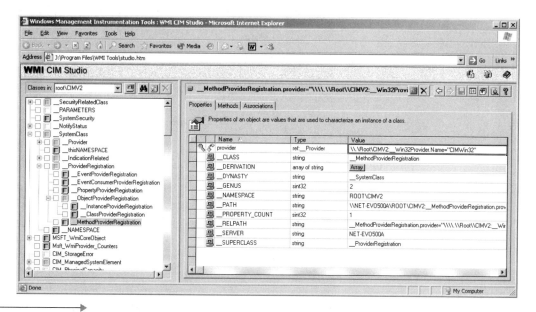

Figure 1.5   *The Win32 method provider registration.*

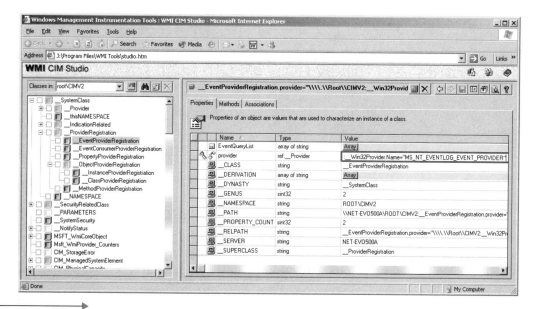

Figure 1.6   *The NT Event Log event provider registration.*

The *Command-Line* event consumer, the *SMTP* event consumer, and the *Active Script* event consumer are examples of event consumer providers (see Chapter 6 in *Understanding WMI Scripting*).

Among these provider types, WMI also supports high-performance providers. These providers greatly increase the speed at which WMI clients can obtain information from WMI. They are nothing more than instance providers implemented as Dynamic-Link Libraries (DLL). We will revisit this provider type later in this book when examining the *Performance Counter* provider and the *Cooked Counter* provider in Chapter 3, section 3.8.

Throughout *Understanding WMI Scripting*, we explain the difference between a class and an instance. While examining the properties exposed by some classes representing real-world manageable entities, we have seen that some classes only expose properties (i.e., *Win32_WMISetting* or *Win32_NTLogEvent* classes), while others expose both properties and methods (i.e., *Win32_Service* class). Because the characteristics implemented in the classes are nothing more than an object model representing the real-world manageable entities, it is clear that the primary role of the WMI provider is to provide the real-world information. This implies that a provider will be:

- An instance provider, if it provides instances of real-world manageable entities

- A property provider, if it provides properties

- A method provider, if it provides methods

Since the real-world entities can be instantiated with WMI to represent real-world objects, this also implies that methods can be invoked to perform some actions and that WMI events can be received to monitor modifications. Therefore, it is very common that a single provider combines different roles at the same time. For instance, the *Registry* provider is made of one single DLL called **STDPROV.DLL**, which exposes three COM objects. These three COM objects implement the four provider types used by WMI to manage the registry:

- The first COM object implements an instance and a method provider. It is called *RegProv*.

- The second COM object implements a property provider and is called *RegPropProv*.

- The third COM object implements an event provider and is called *RegistryEventProvider*.

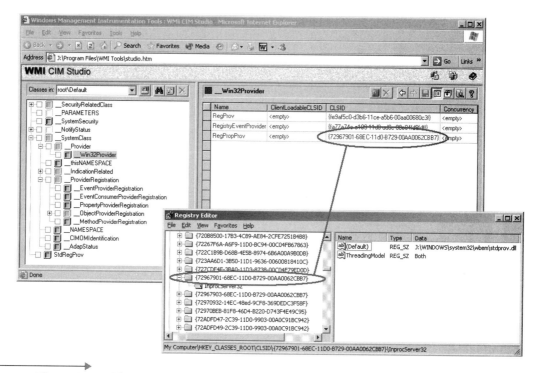

Figure 1.7   *The Registry provider registration in the CIM repository and in the registry.*

Therefore, the *Registry* provider must be registered accordingly in the CIM repository with:

- Three instances of the *__Win32Provider* system class for its physical implementation (**STDPROV.DLL**), where each instance contains the CLSID of the COM object registered in the registry (see Figure 1.7).

- An instance of the *__InstanceProviderRegistration* system class with a reference to its *__Win32Provider* instance.

- An instance of the *__MethodProviderRegistration* system class with a reference to its *__Win32Provider* instance.

- An instance of the *__EventProviderRegistration* system class with a reference to its *__Win32Provider* instance.

When we began the WMI discovery, we saw what a reference and an association are (please refer to Chapters 2, 3, and 4 in *Understanding WMI Scripting* for more information on this subject). We learned how to locate references and associations that exist with a class and an instance. This knowledge is useful, because this is the way to determine the provider type.

Each time an instance of the __Win32Provider system class is available, we have an instance of a WMI provider. By examining the references available from that instance, we determine the WMI provider type (Instance provider, Method provider, etc.). Doing so, we have created a WMI provider discovery technique that helps us to understand some of the WMI provider capabilities, which also determine the behavior of the WMI classes they support.

1.3   WMI providers discovery

Some of you may wonder why we need to discover the WMI provider existence with their classes when they are documented in the WMI SDK. First, not all providers available from WMI are documented in the WMI SDK, which implies that not all available WMI classes are documented. Mastering a discovery technique will allow you to understand how the CIM repository defines the existence of its providers and which class they support. The discovery will help to acquire knowledge about the WMI provider capabilities and get a better understanding about what it is possible to do when using their classes. This is why it is useful to have a WMI provider discovery technique. Moreover, if tomorrow a new application registers some new providers and adds new classes in the CIM repository, mastering the discovery technique immediately gives you the required information to develop an application or a script that leverages these new classes, even if they are not documented by the application developer (i.e., because the classes are intended for the application's internal use only).

As we have seen in the previous section, we know that every WMI provider registered in the CIM repository creates some instances from a set of system classes and that the set of system classes used depends on the WMI provider type. Sample 4.30 in the appendix shows how a script can browse the CIM repository to locate WMI instances across the namespaces. If we reuse that piece of code to locate the instances of the __Win32Provider system class used to register WMI providers across all existing namespaces, we will locate all registered WMI providers in the CIM repository. To be complete and determine the WMI provider type (Instance provider, Method provider, etc.), we must also check if each __Win32Provider instance has some associated references.

Listing the WMI providers with their types is only a piece of the desired information, because we want to know what classes are supported by the providers. This information is available in the class definition itself. The WMI provider that a class relates to depends on the provider type:

- For the class providers, the Instance providers, the Method providers, and the Property providers, the *provider* qualifier is set in the class definition, which determines the provider supporting the class (see Figure 1.8).

Figure 1.8
The provider qualifier of a class to determine the supported WMI provider.

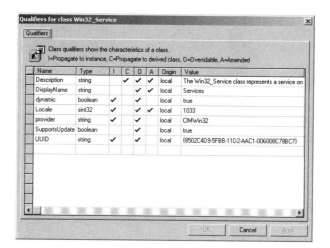

- For the event providers, the *__EventProviderRegistration* system class exposes a property called *EventQueryList*. This property contains a collection of the WQL queries supported by the event provider. In these WQL queries, the various classes supported by the event provider are mentioned (see Figure 1.9). These classes are categorized as intrinsic and extrinsic event classes.

- For the event consumer providers, the *__EventConsumerProvider-Registration* system class exposes a property called *ConsumerClass-Names*. This property contains a collection of classes supported by the event consumer provider (see Figure 1.10).

In *Understanding WMI Scripting*, Chapter 4, we saw how to retrieve the qualifiers of a class and enumerate a collection of properties. We can reuse this knowledge to develop script logic that retrieves the registered providers with the classes they provide. This logic is implemented in Samples 1.1 through 1.3.

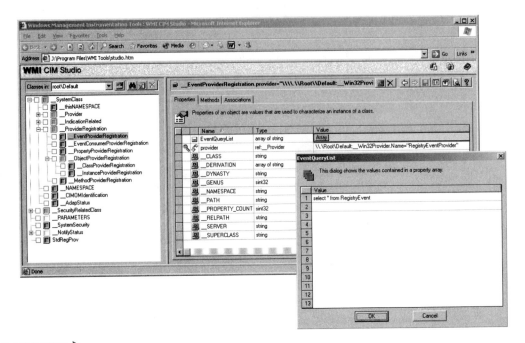

Figure 1.9   *The EventQueryList property of one __EventProviderRegistration instance.*

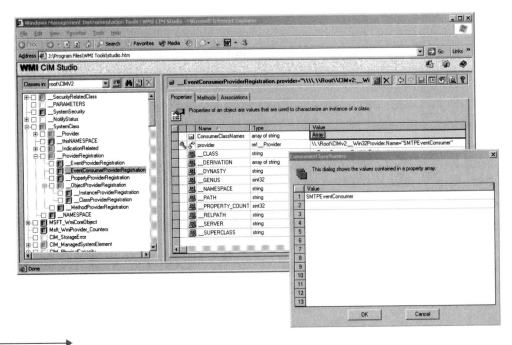

Figure 1.10   *The ConsumerClassNames property of one __EventConsumerProviderRegistration.*

Sample 1.1 *Locating WMI provider registration instances with their supported classes (Part I)*

```
 1:<?xml version="1.0"?>
 .:
 8:<package>
 9: <job>
..:
13:   <runtime>
14:     <named name="Machine" helpstring="determine the WMI system to connect to.
                (default=LocalHost)" required="false" type="string"/>
15:     <named name="User" helpstring="determine the UserID to perform the remote connection.
                (default=none)" required="false" type="string"/>
16:     <named name="Password" helpstring="determine the password to perform the remote connection.
                (default=none)" required="false" type="string"/>
17:   </runtime>
18:
19:   <script language="VBScript" src=".\Functions\DisplayInstanceProperties.vbs" />
20:   <script language="VBScript" src=".\Functions\TinyErrorHandler.vbs" />
21:
22:   <object progid="WbemScripting.SWbemLocator" id="objWMILocator" reference="true"/>
23:   <object progid="WbemScripting.SWbemDateTime" id="objWMIDateTime" />
24:
25:   <script language="VBscript">
26:   <![CDATA[
..:
30:   Const cComputerName = "LocalHost"
31:   Const cWMINameSpace = "Root"
32:   Const cWMINamespaceclass = "__NAMESPACE"
33:   Const cWMIclass = "__Win32provider"
..:
39:   ' ----------------------------------------------------------------------------
40:   ' Parse the command line parameters
41:   strUserID = WScript.Arguments.Named("User")
42:   If Len(strUserID) = 0 Then strUserID = ""
43:
44:   strPassword = WScript.Arguments.Named("Password")
45:   If Len(strPassword) = 0 Then strPassword = ""
46:
47:   strComputerName = WScript.Arguments.Named("Machine")
48:   If Len(strComputerName) = 0 Then strComputerName = cComputerName
49:
50:   DisplayNameSpaces cWMINameSpace, cWMIclass, strUserID, strPassword, strComputerName
51:
..:
..:
..:
```

Sample 1.1 contains the first part of the script. This part uses a structure that we have already seen many times in the first book, *Understanding WMI Scripting*. Lines 13 through 17 contain the parameter definitions that can be used from the command line. Next, the script processes the command-line parameters analysis (lines 39 through 48).

Once the command-line parameters analysis completes, the script calls the DisplayNameSpaces() function (line 50). Note that the parameters

passed to the function are the **Root** namespace (defined in line 31) and the
__Win32Provider system class (defined in line 33). The Display-
NameSpaces() function uses the same parameters as Sample 4.30 (see the
appendix) to browse the namespaces defined in the CIM repository.
Although the function is still using a recursive model, the internal logic has
been slightly modified to suit our needs. Sample 1.2 shows the updated version of this function.

Sample 1.2   *Locating WMI provider registration instances with their supported classes (Part II)*

```
..:
..:
..:
 51:
 52: ' --------------------------------------------------------------------
 53: Private Function DisplayNameSpaces (ByVal strWMINameSpace, _
 54:                                     ByVal strWMIclass, _
 55:                                     ByVal strUserID, _
 56:                                     ByVal strPassword, _
 57:                                     ByVal strComputerName)
..:
 66:    objWMILocator.Security_.AuthenticationLevel = wbemAuthenticationLevelDefault
 67:    objWMILocator.Security_.ImpersonationLevel = wbemImpersonationLevelImpersonate
 68:    Set objWMIServices = objWMILocator.ConnectServer(strComputerName, _
 69:                              strWMINameSpace, _
 70:                              strUserID, _
 71:                              strPassword)
 72:    If Err.Number Then ErrorHandler (Err)
 73:
 74:    Set objWMIInstances = objWMIServices.ExecQuery ("Select * From " & strWMIclass)
 75:    If Err.Number Then
 76:        Err.Clear
 77:    Else
 78:        WScript.Echo strWMINameSpace
 79:        For Each objWMIInstance in objWMIInstances
 80:
 81:            WScript.Echo " " & String (40, "-")
 82:            WScript.Echo objWMIInstance.Name
 83:
 84:            For Each objWMIReference in objWMIInstance.References_
 85:              WScript.Echo objWMIReference.Path_.class
 86:              Select Case LCase (objWMIReference.Path_.class)
 87:                  Case "__eventproviderregistration"
 88:                     DisplaySupportedQueryclasses (objWMIReference.EventQueryList)
 89:                  Case "__eventconsumerproviderregistration"
 90:                     DisplaySupportedConsumerclasses (objWMIReference.ConsumerclassNames)
 91:              End Select
 92:            Next
 93:
 94:            Displayproviderclasses objWMIServices, "", objWMIInstance.Name
 95:        Next
 96:        Set objWMIInstances = Nothing
 97:    End If
 98:
 99:    Set objWMINSInstances = objWMIServices.InstancesOf (cWMINamespaceclass, _
100:                              wbemQueryFlagShallow)
```

```
101:    For Each objWMINSInstance in objWMINSInstances
102:        DisplayNameSpaces strWMINameSpace & "/" & objWMINSInstance.Name, _
103:                strWMIclass, strUserID, strPassword, strComputerName
104:    Next
...:
109:  End Function
110:
...:
...:
...:
```

Once the DisplayNameSpaces() function is called, the code starts by establishing the WMI connection to the examined namespace (lines 66 through 72). Next, the script retrieves all instances of the WMI providers registered in the examined namespace (line 74). For this, it uses the _Win32Provider system class passed as a parameter of the DisplayNameSpaces() function (line 50). If no fault occurs, the code enumerates the retrieved collection (lines 79 through 95). The slight change concerns the logic encapsulated in this particular loop. Originally, the DisplayNameSpaces() function displayed the properties of the retrieved instances. Now, it shows the name of the WMI provider instance (line 82) and retrieves the references of the provider instance by using the _References_ property (line 84).

If the references point to an __EventProviderRegistration or an __EventConsumerProviderRegistration system class, the script locates the supported classes, as previously explained. For this, it calls the DisplaySupportedQueryClasses() (line 87) or DisplaySupportedConsumerClasses() (line 89) functions based on the system class type used by the reference (lines 85 through 91). These two functions simply enumerate the properties content visible in Figures 1.9 and 1.10.

For each reference found, the script shows the class reference (line 85). For instance, if the WMI provider is an instance provider and a method provider, it shows the __InstanceProviderRegistration and the __MethodProviderRegistration system classes, as shown in the following sample output (lines 9 and 10).

```
 1: C:\>Locateproviders.Wsf
 2: Microsoft (R) Windows Script Host Version 5.6
 3: Copyright (C) Microsoft Corporation 1996-2000. All rights reserved.
 4:
 5: Root
 6: Root/CIMV2
 7: ----------------------------------------
 8: CIMWin32
 9: __MethodproviderRegistration
10: __InstanceproviderRegistration
11: > CIM_LogicalFile
12: > CIM_DataFile
13: > Win32_CodecFile
```

```
14: > Win32_ShortcutFile
15: > Win32_PageFile
16: > Win32_Directory
17: > Win32_ComputerSystem
18: > Win32_DeviceMemoryAddress
19: > Win32_PortResource
20: > Win32_DMAChannel
21: > Win32_IRQResource
22: > Win32_Environment
23: > Win32_LogicalDisk
..:
..:
..:
```

At line 8 of the output, we see the name of the provider. This name is referenced by the *provider* qualifier of the classes supported by the examined WMI provider (shown in Figure 1.8 for the *Win32_Service* class). This element can be used to determine the classes that relate to a WMI provider (lines 11 through 23 and more). This is why, at line 94 of Sample 1.2, the script calls the DisplayProviderClasses() function (see Sample 1.3 for the function code). The function call passes the following parameters:

- The **SWBemServices** object created when establishing the connection to the examined WMI namespace

- The provider name (i.e., *CIMWin32*)

- An empty class name

The empty class name refers to the root class of the examined namespace. Sample 1.3 contains the code that searches the classes supported by the examined WMI provider from the top class hierarchy.

Sample 1.3 *Locating WMI provider registration instances with their supported classes (Part III)*

```
...:
...:
...:
110:
111: ' ----------------------------------------------------------------------------
112: Private Function Displayproviderclasses (ByVal objWMIServices, _
113:                                           ByVal strWMIclass, _
114:                                           ByVal strproviderName)
...:
121:     Set objWMIInstances = objWMIServices.SubclassesOf (strWMIclass, wbemQueryFlagDeep)
122:
123:     For Each objWMIInstance in objWMIInstances
124:         strProvqualifier = objWMIInstance.qualifiers_.item("provider")
125:         If Not Err.Number Then
126:             If Ucase (strproviderName) = Ucase (strProvqualifier) Then
127:                 WScript.Echo "> " & objWMIInstance.Path_.RelPath
128:             End If
129:         End If
130:         strProvqualifier = ""
131:     Next
132:
```

```
133:        Set objWMIInstances = Nothing
134:
135:    End Function
136:
137:    ' -----------------------------------------------------------------------------
138:    Private Function DisplaySupportedQueryclasses (ByVal arrayEventQueryList)
...:
144:        For Each strEventQuery in arrayEventQueryList
145:            WScript.Echo "> " & Mid (strEventQuery, _
146:                                     InStrRev (strEventQuery, " ", -1, vbTextCompare) + 1)
147:        Next
148:
149:    End Function
150:
151:    ' -----------------------------------------------------------------------------
152:    Private Function DisplaySupportedConsumerclasses (ByVal arrayConsumerclassList)
...:
158:      For Each strConsumerclass in arrayConsumerclassList
159:        WScript.Echo "> " & strConsumerclass
160:      Next
161:
162:    End Function
163:
164:    ]]>
165:    </script>
166:  </job>
167:</package>
```

In the DisplayProviderClasses() function, the code uses the *SubClassesOf* method of the **SWBemServices** object with the **wbemQueryFlagDeep** flag (line 121). This means that the script code retrieves all classes available in the namespace. Don't forget that we use a blank class (line 94) to force a search from the Root of the namespace. Next, the retrieved collection of classes is examined one by one in the **For Each** loop (lines 123 through 131). For each examined class in the collection, the function retrieves the *provider* qualifier (line 124) and compares its content (line 126) with the name of the provider passed during the function call (line 114). If there is a match, it means that the examined provider supports the class. In this case, the class name is displayed (line 127). The output is as follows:

```
..:
..:
..:
11:> CIM_LogicalFile
12:> CIM_DataFile
13:> Win32_CodecFile
14:> Win32_ShortcutFile
15:> Win32_PageFile
16:> Win32_Directory
17:> Win32_ComputerSystem
18:> Win32_DeviceMemoryAddress
19:> Win32_PortResource
20:> Win32_DMAChannel
21:> Win32_IRQResource
22:> Win32_Environment
23:> Win32_LogicalDisk
..:
..:
..:
```

Table 1.1   *The Most Important WMI Providers under the Windows Platforms with Their Capabilities*

Provider Name	Provider Classes	Class Provider	Instance Provider	Method Provider	Property Provider	Event Provider	Event Consumer Provider	Support Get	Support Put	Support Enumeration	Support Delete	Windows Server 2003	Windows XP	Windows 2000 Server	Windows 2000 Professional	Windows NT 4.0
ActiveScriptEventConsumer (Optional)	Root/subscription						X					X	X	X		
CommandLineEventConsumer (Optional)	Root/subscription						X					X	X	X		
EventViewerConsumer (Optional with the WMI Tools)	Root/CIMV2						X					X	X	X	X	X
LogFileEventConsumer (Optional)	Root/subscription						X					X	X	X		
Microsoft WMI Forwarding Consumer Provider	Root/subscription						X						X			
Microsoft WMI Forwarding Consumer Trace Event Provider						X										
Microsoft WMI Forwarding Event Provider	Root/CIMV2					X										
NTEventLogEventConsumer	Root/subscription						X					X	X	X		
SMTPEventConsumer (Optional)	Root/subscription						X					X	X	X		
CIMWin32	Root/CIMV2		X	X				X	X	X	X	X	X	X	X	X
CIMWin32A	Root/CIMV2		X	X				X	X	X	X	X	X	X	X	X
Cluster Event Provider	Root/MSCluster	X				X						X				
MS_CLUSTER_CLASS_PROVIDER	Root/MSCluster		X					X		X		X				
MS_CLUSTER_PROVIDER	Root/MSCluster		X	X				X	X	X	X	X				
DFSProvider	Root/CIMV2		X	X				X	X	X	X	X				
DskQuotaProvider	Root/CIMV2		X					X	X	X	X	X	X			
HiPerfCooker_v1	Root/WMI		X					X		X		X	X			
HiPerfCooker_v1	Root/CIMV2		X					X		X		X	X			
IeInfo5	Root/CIMV2/Applications/MicrosoftIE		X					X	X	X	X	X			X	
IIS_PROVIDER	Root/MicrosoftIISv2	X						X	X	X	X	X				
Microsoft|DSLDAPClassAssociationsProvider|V1.0	Root/directory/LDAP		X					X	X	X	X	X	X	X	X	
Microsoft|DSLDAPClassProvider|V1.0	Root/directory/LDAP	X						X		X		X	X	X	X	
Microsoft|DSLDAPInstanceProvider|V1.0	Root/directory/LDAP		X					X	X	X	X	X	X	X	X	
Microsoft NLB_Provider|V1.0	Root/MicrosoftNLB		X	X				X	X	X	X	X		X		
NlbsNicProv	Root/MicrosoftNLB		X	X				X	X	X	X	X				
MS_NT_DNS_PROVIDER	Root/MicrosoftDNS		X					X	X	X	X	X	X			

Table 1.1   *The Most Important WMI Providers under the Windows Platforms with Their Capabilities (continued)*

Provider Name	Provider Classes	Class Provider	Instance Provider	Method Provider	Property Provider	Event Provider	Event Consumer Provider	Support Get	Support Put	Support Enumeration	Support Delete	Windows Server 2003	Windows XP	Windows 2000 Server	Windows 2000 Professional	Windows NT 4.0
MS_NT_EVENTLOG_EVENT_PROVIDER	Root/CIMV2					X						X	X	X	X	X
MS_NT_EVENTLOG_PROVIDER	Root/CIMV2		X	X				X	X	X		X	X	X	X	X
MS_Power_Management_Event_Provider	Root/CIMV2					X						X	X	X	X	X
MS_Shutdown_Event_Provider	Root/CIMV2					X						X	X			
MS_SNMP_CLASS_PROVIDER (Optional)	Root/snmp/localhost	X						X		X		X		X	X	X
MS_SNMP_ENCAPSULATED_EVENT_PROVIDER (Optional)	Root/snmp/localhost					X				X		X		X	X	X
MS_SNMP_INSTANCE_PROVIDER (Optional)	Root/snmp/localhost		X					X	X	X	X	X		X	X	X
MS_SNMP_REFERENT_EVENT_PROVIDER (Optional)	Root/snmp/localhost					X				X		X		X	X	X
MS_VIEW_INSTANCE_PROVIDER	Root/MicrosoftIISv2		X	X				X	X	X	X	X		X	X	
MSIProv	Root/CIMV2		X	X				X	X	X	X	X		X	X	X
MSVDS_PROVIDER	Root/CIMV2		X	X				X	X	X	X	X				
MSVSS_PROVIDER	Root/CIMV2		X	X				X	X	X	X	X				
NamedJobObjectActgInfoProv	Root/CIMV2		X					X		X	X	X	X			
NamedJobObjectLimitSettingProv	Root/CIMV2		X					X	X	X	X	X	X			
NamedJobObjectProv	Root/CIMV2		X					X		X	X	X	X			
NamedJobObjectSecLimitSettingProv	Root/CIMV2		X					X	X	X	X	X	X			
NetDiagProv	Root/CIMV2		X	X				X	X	X	X	X	X			
NetFrameworkv1Provider	Root/NetFrameworkv1		X	X				X	X	X	X	X				
NT5_GenericPerfProvider_V1	Root/CIMV2		X					X		X		X		X	X	X
PolicSOM	Root/Policy		X					X	X		X	X	X			
PolicStatus	Root/Policy		X					X				X	X			
RegistryEventProvider	Root/DEFAULT					X						X	X	X	X	X
RegPropProv	Root/DEFAULT				X			X	X	X		X	X	X	X	X
RegProv	Root/DEFAULT		X	X				X	X	X		X	X	X	X	X
RegProv	Root/CIMV2		X	X				X	X	X		X	X	X	X	X

Table 1.1 *The Most Important WMI Providers under the Windows Platforms with Their Capabilities (continued)*

Provider Name	Provider Classes	Class Provider	Instance Provider	Method Provider	Property Provider	Event Provider	Event Consumer Provider	Support Get	Support Put	Support Enumeration	Support Delete	Windows Server 2003	Windows XP	Windows 2000 Server	Windows 2000 Professional	Windows NT 4.0
ReplProv1	Root/MicrosoftActiveDirectory		x	x				x		x		x				
RouteEventProvider	Root/CIMV2					x				x			x	x	x	x
RouteProvider	Root/CIMV2		x					x	x	x	x	x	x			
Rsop Logging Mode Provider	Root/RSOP			x				x	x	x	x	x	x			
Rsop Planning Mode Provider	Root/RSOP			x				x	x	x	x	x	x			
SECRCW32	Root/CIMV2		x	x				x	x	x	x	x	x	x	x	x
SessionProvider	Root/CIMV2		x	x				x	x	x	x	x	x			
SystemRestoreProv	Root/Default		x	x				x	x	x	x		x			
TrustPrv	Root/MicrosoftActiveDirectory		x					x		x		x				
VolumeChangeEvents	Root/CIMV2					x						x	x			
WBEMCORE	Root/CIMV2		x					x	x	x	x	x	x	x	x	x
Win32_WIN32_COMPUTERSYSTEMWINDOWSPRODUCTACTIVATIONSETTING_Prov	Root/CIMV2		x	x				x	x	x	x	x	x			
Win32_WIN32_WINDOWSPRODUCTACTIVATION_Prov	Root/CIMV2		x	x				x	x	x	x	x	x			
Win32_WIN32_PROXY_Prov	Root/CIMV2		x					x	x	x	x	x	x			

Table 1.1   *The Most Important WMI Providers under the Windows Platforms with Their Capabilities (continued)*

Provider Name	Provider Classes	Class Provider	Instance Provider	Method Provider	Property Provider	Event Provider	Event Consumer Provider	Support Get	Support Put	Support Enumeration	Support Delete	Windows Server 2003	Windows XP	Windows 2000 Server	Windows 2000 Professional	Windows NT 4.0
Win32_WIN32_TERMINAL_Prov	Root/CIMV2		x	x				x	x	x	x	x	x			
Win32_WIN32_TERMINALSERVICE_Prov	Root/CIMV2		x	x				x	x	x	x	x	x			
Win32_WIN32_TERMINALSERVICESETTING_Prov	Root/CIMV2		x	x				x	x	x	x	x	x			
Win32_WIN32_TERMINALSERVICETOSETTING_Prov	Root/CIMV2		x	x				x	x	x	x	x	x			
Win32_WIN32_TERMINALTERMINALSETTING_Prov	Root/CIMV2		x					x	x	x	x	x	x			
Win32_WIN32_TSACCOUNT_Prov	Root/CIMV2		x	x				x	x	x	x	x	x			
Win32_WIN32_TSCLIENTSETTING_Prov	Root/CIMV2		x	x				x	x	x	x	x	x			
Win32_WIN32_TSENVIRONMENTSETTING_Prov	Root/CIMV2		x	x				x	x	x	x	x	x			
Win32_WIN32_TSGENERALSETTING_Prov	Root/CIMV2		x	x				x	x	x	x	x	x			
Win32_WIN32_TSLOGONSETTING_Prov	Root/CIMV2		x	x				x	x	x	x	x	x			
Win32_WIN32_TSNETWORKADAPTERLISTSETTING_Prov	Root/CIMV2		x	x				x	x	x	x	x	x			
Win32_WIN32_TSNETWORKADAPTERSETTING_Prov	Root/CIMV2		x	x				x	x	x	x	x	x			
Win32_WIN32_TSPERMISSIONSSETTING_Prov	Root/CIMV2		x	x				x	x	x	x	x	x			
Win32_WIN32_TSREMOTECONTROLSETTING_Prov	Root/CIMV2		x	x				x	x	x	x	x	x			
Win32_WIN32_TSSESSIONDIRECTORY_Prov	Root/CIMV2		x	x				x	x	x	x	x	x			
Win32_WIN32_TSSESSIONDIRECTORYSETTING_Prov	Root/CIMV2		x	x				x	x	x	x	x	x			
Win32_WIN32_TSSESSIONSETTING_Prov	Root/CIMV2		x	x				x	x	x	x	x	x			
Win32ClockProvider	Root/CIMV2					x						x	x			
WMIEventProv	Root/WMI					x						x	x	x		
WMIEventProv	Root/MicrosoftNLB					x						x		x		
WMIPingProvider	Root/CIMV2		x					x		x		x	x			
WMIProv	Root/WMI	x	x	x				x	x	x	x	x	x	x		
WMIProv	Root/MicrosoftNLB	x	x	x				x	x	x	x	x		x	x	
Microsoft WMI Updating Consumer Assoc Provider	Root/subscription		x					x		x	x					
Microsoft WMI Updating Consumer Event Provider	Root/subscription					x									x	
Microsoft WMI Updating Consumer Provider	Root/subscription						x									
Microsoft WMI Template Association Provider	Root/subscription		x					x		x					x	x
Microsoft WMI Template Event Provider	Root/subscription					x									x	x
Microsoft WMI Template Provider	Root/subscription		x					x	x	x	x					
Microsoft WMI Transient Event Provider	Root/subscription					x							x			
Microsoft WMI Transient Provider	Root/subscription		x					x	x	x	x		x			
Microsoft WMI Transient Reboot Event Provider	Root/subscription					x							x			

However, because we use the *provider* qualifier, only the classes representing instances are located. This means that abstract classes, which are often used as parent templates to create subclasses, are not located. In practice, this has no impact on the information we are looking for, because abstract classes do not represent real-world manageable entities (or instances). Since we need to gather information about the classes that represent the real-world entities that we want managed, the abstract classes are useless for our purpose—even if it is good to know their existence in order to have a good knowledge of the implemented object model.

With this script, it is possible to locate all WMI registered providers across all existing namespaces in the CIM repository and find their supported classes. Doing so, the script self-documents the WMI providers available with their characteristics. If, in the future, some applications are adding new providers, a simple run of the script will provide the updated content of the CIM repository with their providers and supported classes.

Next, to gather more information about the classes, a simple run of the **LoadCIMinXL.wsf** script (see Sample 4.32 in the appendix) provides all the class details with its properties and methods.

The result of the script execution (Samples 1.1 through 1.3) under Windows Server 2003 is summarized in Table 1.1. This table shows the most important WMI providers registered in the CIM repository with their respective namespaces and their type (class provider, instance provider, property provider, etc.).

1.4   Helpers for the discovery

Discovering the class capabilities and the instances they provide is a long process. For this, you can use **WMI CIM Studio** or scripts such as those shown in Sample 1.4 ("Listing a single instance of a class with its properties formatted") and Sample 1.5 ("Listing all instances of a class with their properties formatted"). These samples expose some command-line parameters (class name, namespace, userid, and password) to be more generic and usable remotely. The next script, helping us in our discovery and called **GetSingleInstance.Wsf**, exposes the following command-line parameters:

```
C:\>GetSingleInstance.Wsf
Microsoft (R) Windows Script Host Version 5.6
Copyright (C) Microsoft Corporation 1996-2001. All rights reserved.

Usage: GetSingleInstance.wsf WMIclass WMIInstanceName [/Machine:value] [/
User:value] [/Password:value] [/NameSpace:value]
```

```
Options:

WMIclass : the WMI class to use.
WMIInstanceName : the WMI instance name.
Machine : determine the WMI system to connect to. (default=LocalHost)
User : determine the UserID to perform the remote connection.    (default=none)
Password : determine the password to perform the remote connection. (default=none)
NameSpace : determine the WMI namespace to connect to. (default=Root\CIMv2)
```

The listing of the script is given for information purposes only, since it is pretty simple.

──────────────►

Sample 1.4   *Listing a single instance of a class with its properties formatted*

```
 1:<?xml version="1.0"?>
 .:
 8:<package>
 9: <job>
..:
13:  <runtime>
..:
20:  </runtime>
21:
22:  <script language="VBScript" src=".\Functions\DisplayFormattedPropertyFunction.vbs" />
23:  <script language="VBScript" src=".\Functions\TinyErrorHandler.vbs" />
24:
25:  <object progid="WbemScripting.SWbemLocator" id="objWMILocator" reference="true"/>
26:  <object progid="WbemScripting.SWbemDateTime" id="objWMIDateTime" />
27:
28:  <script language="VBscript">
29:  <![CDATA[
..:
33:  Const cComputerName = "LocalHost"
34:  Const cWMINameSpace = "root/cimv2"
..:
49:  ' ---------------------------------------------------------------------------
50:  ' Parse the command line parameters
51:  If WScript.Arguments.Unnamed.Count = 0 Or WScript.Arguments.Unnamed.Count = 1 Then
52:     WScript.Arguments.ShowUsage()
53:     WScript.Quit
54:  Else
55:     strWMIclass = WScript.Arguments.Unnamed.Item(0)
56:     strWMIInstance = WScript.Arguments.Unnamed.Item(1)
57:  End If
58:
59:  strUserID = WScript.Arguments.Named("User")
60:  If Len(strUserID) = 0 Then strUserID = ""
61:
62:  strPassword = WScript.Arguments.Named("Password")
63:  If Len(strPassword) = 0 Then strPassword = ""
64:
65:  strComputerName = WScript.Arguments.Named("Machine")
66:  If Len(strComputerName) = 0 Then strComputerName = cComputerName
67:
68:  strWMINameSpace = WScript.Arguments.Named("NameSpace")
69:  If Len(strWMINameSpace) = 0 Then strWMINameSpace = cWMINameSpace
70:  strWMINameSpace = UCase (strWMINameSpace)
71:
```

```
72: objWMILocator.Security_.AuthenticationLevel = wbemAuthenticationLevelDefault
73: objWMILocator.Security_.ImpersonationLevel = wbemImpersonationLevelImpersonate
74:
75: Set objWMIServices = objWMILocator.ConnectServer(strComputerName, strWMINameSpace, _
76:                            strUserID, strPassword)
..:
79: Set objWMIInstance = objWMIServices.Get (strWMIclass & "=" & strWMIInstance)
..:
82: Set objWMIPropertySet = objWMIInstance.Properties_
83: For Each objWMIProperty In objWMIPropertySet
84:   DisplayFormattedProperty objWMIInstance, _
85:                   objWMIProperty.Name, _
86:                   objWMIProperty.Name, _
87:                   Null
88: Next
..:
94: ]]>
95: </script>
96: </job>
97:</package>
```

Sample 1.5 uses the same structure as Sample 1.4. Only the core code logic is displayed. The command-line parameters are:

```
C:\>GetCollectionOfInstances.Wsf
Microsoft (R) Windows Script Host Version 5.6
Copyright (C) Microsoft Corporation 1996-2001. All rights reserved.

Usage: GetCollectionOfInstances.wsf WMIclass [/Machine:value] [
User:value] [/Password:value] [/NameSpace:value]
Options:

WMIclass  : the WMI class to use.
Machine   : determine the WMI system to connect to. (default=LocalHost)
User   : determine the UserID to perform the remote connection. (default=none)
Password  : determine the password to perform the remote connection. (default=none)
NameSpace : determine the WMI namespace to connect to. (default=Root\CIMv2)
```

Sample 1.5   *Listing all instances of a class with their properties formatted*

```
 1:<?xml version="1.0"?>
 .:
 8:<package>
 9:  <job>
..:
13:    <runtime>
..:
19:    </runtime>
20:
21:    <script language="VBScript" src=".\Functions\DisplayFormattedPropertyFunction.vbs" />
22:    <script language="VBScript" src=".\Functions\TinyErrorHandler.vbs" />
23:
24:    <object progid="WbemScripting.SWbemLocator" id="objWMILocator" reference="true"/>
25:    <object progid="WbemScripting.SWbemDateTime" id="objWMIDateTime" />
26:
27:    <script language="VBscript">
28:    <![CDATA[
..:
```

```
 32:     Const cComputerName = "LocalHost"
 33:     Const cWMINameSpace = "root/cimv2"
 ..:
 72:     Set objWMIServices = objWMILocator.ConnectServer(strComputerName, strWMINameSpace, _
 73:                                                 strUserID, strPassword)
 74:     If Err.Number Then ErrorHandler (Err)
 75:
 76:     Set objWMIInstances = objWMIServices.InstancesOf (strWMIclass)
 77:     If Err.Number Then ErrorHandler (Err)
 78:
 79:     If objWMIInstances.Count Then
 80:        For Each objWMIInstance In objWMIInstances
 81:            WScript.Echo
 82:            Set objWMIPropertySet = objWMIInstance.Properties_
 83:            For Each objWMIProperty In objWMIPropertySet
 84:                DisplayFormattedProperty objWMIInstance, _
 85:                                   objWMIProperty.Name, _
 86:                                   objWMIProperty.Name, _
 87:                                   Null
 88:            Next
 89:            Set objWMIPropertySet = Nothing
 90:        Next
 91:     Else
 92:        WScript.Echo "No instance."
 93:     End If
 ..:
 98:     ]]>
 99:     </script>
100:   </job>
101:</package>
```

Instead of using the **DisplayInstanceProperties.vbs** script containing the DisplayInstanceProperties() function (see Sample 4.31 in the appendix), these scripts use the DisplayFormattedPropertyFunction() contained in the **DisplayFormattedPropertyFunction.vbs** script (line 13). This function has the exact same purpose as **DisplayInstanceProperties.vbs** developed previously, but it displays the property content in a different way. As an example:

```
 1:   C:\>GetSingleInstance Win32_Service "'SNMP'"
 2:   Microsoft (R) Windows Script Host Version 5.6
 3:   Copyright (C) Microsoft Corporation 1996-2001. All rights reserved.
 4:
 5:   AcceptPause: ........................... FALSE
 6:   AcceptStop: ............................ FALSE
 7:   Caption: ............................... SNMP Service
 8:   CheckPoint: ............................ 0
 9:   CreationclassName: ..................... Win32_Service
10:   Description: ........................... Enables Simple Network Management Protocol (SNMP)
                                                requests to be processed by this computer. If
                                                this service is stopped, the computer will be
                                                unable to process SNMP requests. If this service
                                                is disabled, any services that explicitly depend
                                                on it will fail to start.
11:   DesktopInteract: ....................... FALSE
12:   DisplayName: ........................... SNMP Service
13:   ErrorControl: .......................... Normal
14:   ExitCode: .............................. 1077
15:   *Name: ................................. SNMP
```

```
16:    PathName: ...............,.............. J:\WINDOWS\System32\snmp.exe
17:    ProcessId: ............................. 0
18:    ServiceSpecificExitCode: ............... 0
19:    ServiceType: ........................... Own Process
20:    Started: ............................... FALSE
21:    StartMode: ............................. Manual
22:    StartName: ............................. LocalSystem
23:    State: ................................. Stopped
24:    Status: ................................ OK
25:    SystemCreationclassName: ............... Win32_ComputerSystem
26:    SystemName: ............................ XP-DPEN6400
27:    TagId: ................................. 0
28:    WaitHint: .............................. 0
```

This display formatting is easier to read and can be used to display instance information in a manner similar to some command-line utilities.

The **DisplayFormattedPropertyFunction.vbs** accepts four parameters, as follows:

- The WMI instance object (line 38)

- Any string type that can be used as a label for the property (line 39)

- The property name to extract the value from (line 40)

- A second property name that could be displayed on the same line as the first property (line 41)

When set to null, the second property is not displayed. However, the function does not display the property syntax. In the same way, the property is skipped if its value is null. Moreover, if the property is an array, the function behaves accordingly and transparently. This function will greatly help and ease the display of any class properties for the next samples. The **DisplayFormattedPropertyFunction.vbs** code is given in Sample 1.6 for reference. The WMI scripting technique used was covered in *Understanding WMI Scripting*, Chapter 4.

Sample 1.6   *The DisplayFormattedPropertyFunction.vbs function*

```
.:
6:' --------------------------------------------------------------------------------
7:Function DisplayFormattedProperty (objWMIInstance, strText, strProperty1, strProperty2)
..:
16:    If Not IsNull (strProperty1) Then
17:       varValue1 = objWMIInstance.Properties_.Item (strProperty1)
18:       If Err.Number Then
19:          varValue1 = strProperty1
20:          Err.Clear
21:       Else
22:          If Ucase (strProperty1) = "TIME_CREATED" Then
23:             objWMIDateTime.SetFileTime (varValue1)
24:             varValue1 = objWMIDateTime.GetVarDate (True) & " (" & objWMIDateTime.Value & ")"
25:          Else
```

```
26:              Select Case objWMIInstance.Properties_.Item (strProperty1).CIMType
27:                 Case wbemCimtypeDatetime
28:                     objWMIDateTime.Value = varValue1
29:                     varValue1 = objWMIDateTime.GetVarDate (False)
30:                 Case wbemCimtypeBoolean
31:                     varValue1 = Ucase (varValue1)
32:                 Case wbemCimtypeObject
33:                     varValue1 = "<OBJECT>"
34:              End Select
35:          End If
36:
37:          boolCIMKey = _
38:              objWMIInstance.Properties_.Item (strProperty1).qualifiers_.Item("key").Value
39:          If Err.Number Then
40:              Err.Clear
41:              boolCIMKey = False
42:          End If
43:          If boolCIMKey Then
44:              If Mid (strText, 1, 1) = Chr (32) Then
45:                  intSpace = Len (strText) - Len(LTrim(strText))
46:                  strText = Space(intSpace) & "*" & Ltrim(strText)
47:              Else
48:                  strText = "*" & strText
49:              End If
50:          End If
51:      End If
52:  Else
53:      varValue1 = strProperty1
54:  End If
55:
56:  If Not IsNull (strProperty2) Then
57:      varValue2 = objWMIInstance.Properties_.Item (strProperty2)
58:      If Err.Number Then
59:          varValue2 = strProperty2
60:          Err.Clear
61:      Else
62:          If Ucase (strProperty2) = "TIME_CREATED" Then
63:              objWMIDateTime.SetFileTime (varValue2)
64:              varValue2 = objWMIDateTime.GetVarDate (True) & " (" & objWMIDateTime.Value & ")"
65:          Else
66:              Select Case objWMIInstance.Properties_.Item (strProperty2).CIMType
67:                  Case wbemCimtypeDatetime
68:                      objWMIDateTime.Value = varValue2
69:                      varValue2 = objWMIDateTime.GetVarDate (False)
70:                  Case wbemCimtypeBoolean
71:                      varValue2 = Ucase (varValue2)
72:                  Case wbemCimtypeObject
73:                      varValue2 = "<OBJECT>"
74:              End Select
75:          End If
76:      End If
77:  Else
78:      varValue2 = strProperty2
79:  End If
80:
81:  If Not IsNull (varValue1) Then
82:      If Not IsNull (varValue2) Then
83:          If IsArray (varValue1) Then
84:              For intIndice=0 To UBound(varValue1)
85:                  If intIndice = 0 Then
```

```
86:                    WScript.Echo strText & ": " & string (40 - Len(strText), ".") & _
87:                                " " & varValue1 (intIndice) & _
88:                                " " & varValue2 (intIndice)
89:                Else
90:                    WScript.Echo Space (42) & _
91:                                " " & varValue1 (intIndice) & _
92:                                " " & varValue2 (intIndice)
93:                End if
94:           Next
95:         Else
96:            WScript.Echo strText & ": " & string (40 - Len(strText), ".") & _
97:                        " " & varValue1 & _
98:                        " " & varValue2
99:         End IF
100:       Else
101:         If IsArray (varValue1) Then
102:            For intIndice=0 To UBound(varValue1)
103:                If intIndice = 0 Then
104:                    WScript.Echo strText & ": " & string (40 - Len(strText), ".") & _
105:                                " " & varValue1 (intIndice)
106:                Else
107:                    WScript.Echo Space (42) & _
108:                                " " & varValue1 (intIndice)
109:                End if
110:           Next
111:         Else
112:            WScript.Echo strText & ": " & string (40 - Len(strText), ".") & _
113:                        " " & varValue1
114:         End IF
115:       End IF
116:     End IF
117:
118:     Err.Clear
119:
120:End Function
```

For now, we have four scripts that can be used as utilities to help our understanding and WMI discovery:

- **LoadCIMinXL.wsf**: a Windows script file self-documenting the classes available from the CIM repository in an Excel sheet (see Sample 4.32 in the appendix).

- **LocateProviders.wsf**: to locate the WMI provider registration instances with the supported classes (Samples 1.1 through 1.3).

- **GetSingleInstance.wsf**: to list a single instance of a class with its properties formatted (Sample 1.4).

- **GetCollectionOfInstances.wsf**: to list all instances of a class with their properties formatted (Sample 1.5).

With the help of these scripts, our next purpose is to develop small utilities based on the WMI scripting techniques and the class capabilities.

1.5   Summary

Because a class is a template that represents a manageable entity from the real world, made accessible with a provider, mastering the provider capabilities with its classes is a determinant factor when developing applications on top of WMI.

Although our class classification is made by WMI providers, Microsoft, in its Platform SDK, classifies the classes by role. This classification regroups the classes that are related to the same parts of the system independently of the WMI provider supporting them. This difference comes from the fact that Microsoft estimates that it is not necessary to know and understand the provider implementation to work with the classes they support. This statement is true in a sense, but having a rough idea of the provider capabilities, such as determining if it is implemented as an event provider or an instance provider, can help people to determine how a WQL event query must be formulated (use of the **WITHIN** statement for dynamic instance classes or not using the **WITHIN** statement when an extrinsic event class is referenced in the query, as it is supported by an event provider).

When installing Windows Server 2003, WMI is part of the installation and it comes with an important number of WMI providers and classes. Although we can list the classes available from the providers, it is impossible to list each class properties in a single book, but the helper scripts (**Load-CIMinXL.wsf, LocateProviders.wsf, GetSingleInstance.wsf, GetCollectionOfInstances.wsf**) can be used as tools to complete the discovery. From a manageability perspective, Windows Server 2003 represents a major step for the Enterprise because it offers much more WMI management capabilities than Windows 2000. Besides the WMI functionalities part of the Operating System installation, Windows applications such as Exchange 2000, SQL Server 2000, and HP OpenView Operations for Windows (OVOW), to name a few, bring their own providers and enhance the WMI capabilities. This means that there is no limit to the WMI discovery, since each new piece of software can extend the WMI capabilities. This is where the helper scripts become interesting, since they can help you discover information not necessarily documented in an SDK.

In this chapter, we learned that the WMI provider discovery technique helps us to understand the WMI provider types available, to structure their roles and the classes they support, since each provider brings its own set of capabilities with a certain number of classes. Now, the next step is to examine each of them with their own set of classes with their capabilities. Therefore, in the next chapter, we will pursue the discovery by exploring the *Win32* providers, which serve as a great example since they support the largest number of classes available from WMI.

2

The Win32 Providers

2.1   **Objective**

Due to the huge number of classes, it is impossible to review all classes available from WMI, but we focus by category on the most important one. As before, we learn by practice and see how each interesting class can be used in a script. Because the *Win32* providers support a large number of classes, we start our discovery with these providers. In the next chapters we focus on the classes supported by other WMI providers available under Windows Server 2003 and methodically review their capabilities with their supported set of classes used in a script.

Due to the number of classes supported by the *Win32* providers, this chapter is divided into two sections: one section focusing on the *Win32* class related to the computer system hardware and a second section focusing on the *Win32* classes related to operating systems. All classes are organized by category in a way very similar to the Microsoft Platform SDK organization. For instance, we have a category for the "Video and Monitor" classes, a category for the "Printing devices" classes, and a category for the "Networking devices" classes. In this chapter, we cover more than 20 categories. Let's start the *Win32* providers discovery with their classes.

2.2   **The Win32 providers**

The *Win32* providers (called *WINCIM32* and *WINCIM32a*) are certainly the WMI providers supporting the biggest number of classes among all providers that come with WMI. All the *Win32* provider classes are available in the **Root\CIMv2** namespace.

The *Win32* providers are implemented as instance and method providers. They are not implemented as event providers, which means that the use of the **WITHIN** statement in the context of a WQL event query is required. They support Get, Put, Enumerations, and Delete operations. This means that it is possible to retrieve a single instance (get) with a WMI object path, modify a single instance (put), retrieve instances by enumeration, and delete instances (see Table 2.1). All these operations are also influenced by the class capabilities.

Table 2.1   *The Win32 Providers Capabilities*

Provider Name	Provider Namespace	Class Provider	Instance Provider	Method Provider	Property Provider	Event Provider	Event Consumer Provider	Support Get	Support Put	Support Enumeration	Support Delete	Windows Server 2003	Windows XP	Windows 2000 Server	Windows 2000 Professional	Windows NT 4.0
Win32 Providers																
CIMWin32	Root/CIMV2	X	X					X	X	X	X	X	X	X	X	X
Cimwin32A	Root/CIMV2	X	X					X	X	X	X	X	X			

The *Win32* provider classes are classified in two large categories: the "Computer System Hardware Classes" and "Operating System Classes."

The *Win32_Service* class used throughout the first book, *Understanding WMI Scripting*, is a class supported by the *Win32* providers. All classes supported by the *Win32* providers can be used in the same way as the *Win32_Service* class. Of course, the script must respect the properties and the methods exposed by the classes, but the scripting technique is exactly the same.

Once again, we cannot examine in detail all classes supported by the *Win32* providers. This would be a repeat of the information already available in the Platform SDK and the MSDN Library. However, it is highly recommended to explore the class instances with Sample 1.4 ("Listing a single instance of a class with its properties formatted") and Sample 1.5 ("Listing all instances of a class with their properties formatted") developed in the previous chapter. The class characteristics can be discovered with the **Load-CIMInXL.wsf** script previously developed (see Sample 4.32 in the appendix). All properties and methods exposed by the classes are retrieved with this script. By using the **LoadCIMInXL.wsf** script, even the classes not documented in the Microsoft Platform SDK are self-documented. Of course, you can also use the **WMI CIM Studio** as a discovery tool.

In the next sections, we examine, by category, some of the most interesting classes available from the *Win32* providers and how to use them in scripts directly applicable in the field.

2.3   Computer system hardware classes

2.3.1   Input device classes

The input device classes represent keyboards and pointing devices (see Table 2.2). The *Win32_Keyboard* and *Win32_PointingDevice* classes usually have one instance available, since a computer usually has one keyboard and one pointing device.

Table 2.2   *The Input Devices Classes*

Name	Description
Win32_Keyboard	Represents a keyboard installed on a Windows system.
Win32_PointingDevice	Represents an input device used to point to and select regions on the display of a Windows computer system.

However, the Key property of these classes is quite difficult to use (line 11 in the display output below). This is why it is easier to request all instances of the *Win32_Keyboard* and *Win32_PointingDevice* classes. The output obtained for the *Win32_Keyboard* class with Sample 1.5 ("Listing all instances of a class with their properties formatted") is as follows:

```
 1:    C:\>GetCollectionOfInstances.wsf Win32_Keyboard
 2:    Microsoft (R) Windows Script Host Version 5.6
 3:    Copyright (C) Microsoft Corporation 1996-2001. All rights reserved.
 4:
 5:
 6:    Caption: ............................... Enhanced (101- or 102-key)
 7:    ConfigManagerErrorCode: ................. 0
 8:    ConfigManagerUserConfig: ................ FALSE
 9:    CreationClassName: ...................... Win32_Keyboard
10:    Description: ............................ PC/AT Enhanced PS/2 Keyboard (101/102-Key)
11:    *DeviceID: ............................. ROOT\*PNP030B\1_0_22_0_32_0
12:    Layout: ................................ 00000813
13:    Name: .................................. Enhanced (101- or 102-key)
14:    NumberOfFunctionKeys: .................. 12
15:    PNPDeviceID: ........................... ROOT\*PNP030B\1_0_22_0_32_0
16:    PowerManagementSupported: .............. FALSE
17:    Status: ................................ OK
18:    SystemCreationClassName: ............... Win32_ComputerSystem
19:    SystemName: ............................ XP-DPEN6400
```

The output obtained for the *Win32_PointingDevice* class with Sample 1.5 ("Listing all instances of a class with their properties formatted") is as follows:

```
 1:    C:\>GetCollectionOfInstances.wsf Win32_PointingDevice
 2:    Microsoft (R) Windows Script Host Version 5.6
 3:    Copyright (C) Microsoft Corporation 1996-2001. All rights reserved.
 4:
 5:
```

```
 6:    Caption: ............................. Microsoft PS/2 Mouse
 7:    ConfigManagerErrorCode: .................. 0
 8:    ConfigManagerUserConfig: ................ FALSE
 9:    CreationClassName: ...................... Win32_PointingDevice
10:    Description: ............................ Microsoft PS/2 Mouse
11:    *DeviceID: ............................. ROOT\*PNP0F03\1_0_21_0_31_0
12:    DeviceInterface: ........................ 4
13:    DoubleSpeedThreshold: ................... 6
14:    Handedness: ............................. 2
15:    HardwareType: ........................... Microsoft PS/2 Mouse
16:    InfFileName: ............................ msmouse.inf
17:    InfSection: ............................. PS2_Inst
18:    Manufacturer: ........................... Microsoft
19:    Name: ................................... Microsoft PS/2 Mouse
20:    NumberOfButtons: ........................ 5
21:    PNPDeviceID: ............................ ROOT\*PNP0F03\1_0_21_0_31_0
22:    PointingType: ........................... 2
23:    PowerManagementSupported: ............... FALSE
24:    QuadSpeedThreshold: ..................... 10
25:    Status: ................................. OK
26:    SystemCreationClassName: ................ Win32_ComputerSystem
27:    SystemName: ............................. XP-DPEN6400
```

To show a practical application of the *Win32_PointingDevice* class, Sample 2.1 determines if a mouse is configured for a right hand or a left hand.

Sample 2.1 *Determine if a mouse is right or left hand configured*

```
 1:<?xml version="1.0"?>
 .:
 8:<package>
 9:  <job>
..:
13:    <script language="VBScript" src=".\Functions\TinyErrorHandler.vbs" />
14:
15:    <script language="VBscript">
16:    <![CDATA[
..:
20:    Const cComputerName = "LocalHost"
21:    Const cWMINameSpace = "root/cimv2"
22:    Const cWMIClass = "Win32_PointingDevice"
..:
29:    Set objWMIServices = GetObject("WinMgmts:{impersonationLevel=impersonate}!//" & _
30:                                   cComputerName & "/" & cWMINameSpace)
..:
33:    Set objWMIInstances = objWMIServices.InstancesOf (cWMIClass)
34:    If Err.Number Then ErrorHandler (Err)
35:
36:    For Each objWMIInstance In objWMIInstances
37:        Select Case objWMIInstance.Handedness
38:            Case 0
39:                WScript.Echo "The handedness for the " & _
40:                             objWMIInstance.Description & " is unknown."
41:            Case 1
42:                WScript.Echo "The handedness for the " & _
43:                             objWMIInstance.Description & " is not applicable."
```

```
44:              Case 2
45:                  WScript.Echo "The handedness for the " & _
46:                              objWMIInstance.Description & " is set for the right hand."
47:              Case 3
48:                  WScript.Echo "The handedness for the " & _
49:                              objWMIInstance.Description & " is set for the left hand."
50:      End Select
51:   Next
..:
56:   ]]>
57:   </script>
58:  </job>
59:</package>
```

The output is as follows:

```
C:\>IsMouseRightOrLeftHanded.wsf
Microsoft (R) Windows Script Host Version 5.6
Copyright (C) Microsoft Corporation 1996-2000. All rights reserved.

The Microsoft PS/2 mouse is set for the right hand.
```

2.3.2   Mass storage classes

The mass storage classes represent storage devices such as hard disk drives, CD-ROM drives, and tape drives. These classes are shown in Table 2.3.

Table 2.3   *The Mass Storage Classes*

Name	Description
Win32_AutochkSetting	Represents the settings for the autocheck operation of a disk.
Win32_CDROMDrive	Represents a CD-ROM drive on a Windows computer system.
Win32_DiskDrive	Represents a physical disk drive as seen by a computer running the Windows operating system.
Win32_FloppyDrive	Manages the capabilities of a floppy disk drive.
Win32_LogicalDisk	Represents a data source that resolves to an actual local storage device on a Windows system.
Win32_MappedLogicalDisk	Represents network storage devices that are mapped as logical disks on the computer system.
Win32_TapeDrive	Represents a tape drive on a Windows computer.

One very interesting class in this category is the *Win32_LogicalDisk* class. Besides the properties and the methods exposed by this class, it is important to note that this class is also associated with an interesting set of classes (see Figure 2.1). With the associations, we can see that some classes, such as *Win32_QuotaSettings*, are associated with *Win32_LogicalDisk*, which means that it is possible to retrieve the quota information when working with one instance of the *Win32_LogicalDisk* class. We discuss this feature later, when working with the *Disk Quota* provider in the next chapter.

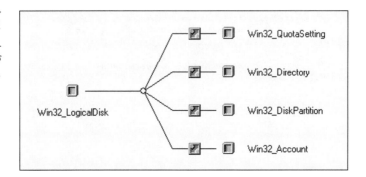

Figure 2.1
*The Win32_
LogicalDisk class
associations.*

Of course, besides the ability to retrieve information about the media,
which we made for the keyboard and the mouse, an interesting application
of the *Win32_LogicalDisk* class is to monitor the free space on hard disks.
Here we can reuse some of the scripts developed in the first book, *Understanding WMI Scripting*, Chapter 6, when we learned the WMI Event
scripting technique. Instead of reusing one of the generic scripts to monitor
WMI events (see Sample 6.14, "A generic script for synchronous event notification" and Sample 6.17, "A generic script for asynchronous event notification" in the appendix), which displays all properties of the event with its
associated instance, let's make a script that uses a customized logic and that
displays a message only when the free disk space falls below 50 percent for a
specific disk. This logic is shown in Sample 2.2.

Sample 2.2   *Alerting script when the free disk space decreases below 50 percent on a specific disk*

```
 1:<?xml version="1.0"?>
 .:
 8:<package>
 9:  <job>
..:
13:    <script language="VBScript" src=".\Functions\TinyErrorHandler.vbs" />
14:    <script language="VBScript" src=".\Functions\PauseScript.vbs" />
..:
18:    <script language="VBscript">
19:    <![CDATA[
..:
23:    ' -------------------------------------------------------------------------
24:    Const cComputerName = "LocalHost"
25:    Const cWMINameSpace = "root/cimv2"
26:    Const cWMIClass = "Win32_LogicalDisk"
27:    Const cWMIInstance = "'C:'"
28:    Const cPercentage = 50
..:
36:    Set objWMISink = WScript.CreateObject ("WbemScripting.SWbemSink", "SINK_")
37:
38:    Set objWMIServices = GetObject("WinMgmts:{impersonationLevel=impersonate}!//" & _
39:                                   cComputerName & "/" & cWMINameSpace)
```

```
..:
42:     strWQLQuery = "Select * From __InstanceModificationEvent Within 10 " & _
43:                   "Where TargetInstance ISA 'Win32_LogicalDisk' And " & _
44:                   "TargetInstance.DriveType=3 And " & _
45:                   "TargetInstance.DeviceID=" & cWMIInstance & " And " & _
46:                   "TargetInstance.FreeSpace < PreviousInstance.FreeSpace"
47:
48:     objWMIServices.ExecNotificationQueryAsync objWMISink, _
49:                                     strWQLQuery, _
50:                                     , _
51:                                     wbemFlagSendStatus
..:
54:     WScript.Echo "Waiting for events..."
55:
56:     PauseScript "Click on 'Ok' to terminate the script ..."
57:
58:     WScript.Echo vbCRLF & "Cancelling event subscription ..."
59:     objWMISink.Cancel
..:
64:     WScript.Echo "Finished."
65:
66:     ' -------------------------------------------------------------------------------------
67:     Sub SINK_OnObjectReady (objWbemObject, objWbemAsyncContext)
..:
74:         WScript.Echo FormatDateTime(Date, vbLongDate) & " at " & _
75:                      FormatDateTime(Time, vbLongTime) & "."
76:
77:         intPercentageFree = _
78:             objWbemObject.TargetInstance.FreeSpace / objWbemObject.TargetInstance.Size * 100
79:
80:         If cPercentage >= CLng(intPercentageFree) Then
81:             WScript.Echo "Warning, disk " & objWbemObject.TargetInstance.Name & " has " & _
82:                          objWbemObject.TargetInstance.FreeSpace & _
83:                          " bytes free on a total capacity of " & _
84:                          objWbemObject.TargetInstance.Size & _
85:                          " bytes (" & intPercentageFree & "% free)."
86:         End If
87:
88:     End Sub
89:
90:     ]]>
91:    </script>
92:   </job>
93:</package>
```

The trick to monitoring the disk space with the necessary conditions requires two things: the WQL query (lines 42 through 46) and the logic of the event sink routine (lines 77 and 80). For a logical disk C: defined on a hard disk, the WQL query is as follows:

```
1:   Select * From __InstanceModificationEvent Within 10
2:       Where TargetInstance ISA 'Win32_LogicalDisk' And
3:       TargetInstance.DriveType=3 And
4:       TargetInstance.DeviceID='C:' And
5:       TargetInstance.FreeSpace < PreviousInstance.FreeSpace"
```

The WQL query contains four conditions, based on:

- **The *TargetInstance* class type** (line 2): This condition makes sense, because the monitoring must be executed on an instance of the *Win32_LogicalDisk* class.

- **The *DriveType*** (line 3): Since the monitoring must be performed on a local hard disk, the drive type must be equal to 3 (0=Unknown, 1=No Root Directory, 2=Removable Disk, 3=Local Disk, 4=Network Drive, 5=Compact Disk, and 6=RAM Disk).

- **The *DeviceID*** (line 4): The device ID is the letter assigned to the logical drive. In this case, we evaluate the disk space on the C: drive.

- **The decreasing *FreeSpace*** (line 5): Since the requirement is to send an alert only when the free space decreases, the test evaluates the free space of the current instance with the value of the previous instance. If the current instance free space value is smaller, it means that the free disk space decreases.

The *Win32_LogicalDisk* class doesn't expose a property giving the percentage of free space, which means that the provider does not provide this value. The script must compute this value from the total disk size and current free space values (line 78). This percentage evaluation is done during the event sink execution (line 80).

```
..:
..:
..:
77:        intPercentageFree = _
78:            objWbemObject.TargetInstance.FreeSpace / objWbemObject.TargetInstance.Size * 100
79:
80:        If cPercentage >= Clng(intPercentageFree) Then
81:            WScript.Echo "Warning, disk " & objWbemObject.TargetInstance.Name & " has " & _
82:                        objWbemObject.TargetInstance.FreeSpace & _
..:
..:
..:
```

If the condition matches, the script will display messages as follows:

```
C:\>AlertWhenFreeSpaceLessThan50%.wsf
Microsoft (R) Windows Script Host Version 5.6
Copyright (C) Microsoft Corporation 1996-2001. All rights reserved.

Waiting for events...

Wednesday, 15 August, 2001 at 10:42:15.
Warning, disk C: has 415331128 bytes free on a total capacity of 843816448 bytes (49.2205% free).

Wednesday, 15 August, 2001 at 10:42:42.
Warning, disk C: has 353877210 bytes free on a total capacity of 843816448 bytes (41.9376% free).
```

Another interesting feature of the *Win32_LogicalDisk* class is the *Chkdsk* method. This method launches the CHKDSK utility. Because it executes in a WMI context, it is also possible to run CHKDSK on a remote computer. Sample 2.3 shows how to proceed.

Sample 2.3   *Executing CHKDSK via WMI*

```
 1:<?xml version="1.0"?>
 .:
 8:<package>
 9:  <job>
..:
13:    <runtime>
14:      <unnamed name="LogicalDisk" helpstring="the logical disk letter."
                    required="true" type="string" />
15:      <named name="FixErrors" helpstring="Indicates what should be done to errors found
                    on the disk. If true, then errors are fixed. The default is FALSE."
                    required="false" type="boolean" />
16:      <named name="VigorousIndexCheck" helpstring="If TRUE, a vigorous check of index entries
                    should be performed. The default is TRUE."
                    required="false" type="boolean" />
17:      <named name="SkipFolderCycle" helpstring="If TRUE, the folder cycle checking should be
                    skipped or not. The default is TRUE."
                    required="false" type="boolean" />
18:      <named name="ForceDismount" helpstring="If TRUE, the drive should be forced to dismount
                    before checking. The default is FALSE."
                    required="false" type="boolean" />
19:      <named name="RecoverBadSectors" helpstring="If TRUE, the bad sectors should be located
                    and the readable information should be recovered from these sectors.
                    The default is FALSE." required="false" type="boolean" />
20:      <named name="OKToRunAtBootUp" helpstring="If TRUE, the chkdsk operation should be
                    performed at next boot up time, in case the operation could not be
                    performed because the disk was locked at time the method was called.
                    The default is FALSE." required="false" type="boolean" />
21:      <named name="Machine" helpstring="determine the WMI system to connect to.
                    (default=LocalHost)" required="false" type="string"/>
22:      <named name="User" helpstring="determine the UserID to perform the remote connection.
                    (default=none)" required="false" type="string"/>
23:      <named name="Password" helpstring="determine the password to perform the remote
                    connection. (default=none)" required="false" type="string"/>
24:      <example>Example:
25:
26:      WMIChkdsk.wsf C: /FixErrors+ /VigorousIndexCheck+ /SkipFolderCycle+
27:      WMIChkdsk.wsf C: /ForceDismount+ /RecoverBadSectors+ /OKToRunAtBootUp+
28:      WMIChkdsk.wsf C:
29:      </example>
30:    </runtime>
31:
32:    <script language="VBScript" src=".\Functions\TinyErrorHandler.vbs" />
33:
34:    <object progid="WbemScripting.SWbemLocator" id="objWMILocator" reference="true"/>
35:
36:    <script language="VBscript">
37:    <![CDATA[
..:
41:    Const cComputerName = "LocalHost"
42:    Const cWMINameSpace = "root/cimv2"
```

```
 43:    Const cWMIClass = "Win32_LogicalDisk"
 ..:
 63:    ' ----------------------------------------------------------------------------
 64:    ' Parse the command line parameters
 65:    If WScript.Arguments.Unnamed.Count = 0 Then
 66:       WScript.Arguments.ShowUsage()
 67:       WScript.Quit
 68:    Else
 69:       strWMIInstance = WScript.Arguments.Unnamed.Item(0)
 70:    End If
 71:
 72:    boolFixErrors = WScript.Arguments.Named("FixErrors")
 73:    If Len(boolFixErrors) = 0 Then boolFixErrors = False
 74:
 75:    boolVigorousIndexCheck = WScript.Arguments.Named("VigorousIndexCheck")
 76:    If Len(boolVigorousIndexCheck) = 0 Then boolVigorousIndexCheck = True
 77:
 78:    boolSkipFolderCycle = WScript.Arguments.Named("SkipFolderCycle")
 79:    If Len(boolSkipFolderCycle) = 0 Then boolSkipFolderCycle = True
 80:
 81:    boolForceDismount = WScript.Arguments.Named("ForceDismount")
 82:    If Len(boolForceDismount) = 0 Then boolForceDismount = False
 83:
 84:    boolRecoverBadSectors = WScript.Arguments.Named("RecoverBadSectors")
 85:    If Len(boolRecoverBadSectors) = 0 Then boolRecoverBadSectors = False
 86:
 87:    boolOKToRunAtBootUp = WScript.Arguments.Named("OKToRunAtBootUp")
 88:    If Len(boolOKToRunAtBootUp) = 0 Then boolOKToRunAtBootUp = False
 89:
 90:    strUserID = WScript.Arguments.Named("User")
 91:    If Len(strUserID) = 0 Then strUserID = ""
 92:
 93:    strPassword = WScript.Arguments.Named("Password")
 94:    If Len(strPassword) = 0 Then strPassword = ""
 95:
 96:    strComputerName = WScript.Arguments.Named("Machine")
 97:    If Len(strComputerName) = 0 Then strComputerName = cComputerName
 98:
 99:    objWMILocator.Security_.AuthenticationLevel = wbemAuthenticationLevelDefault
100:    objWMILocator.Security_.ImpersonationLevel = wbemImpersonationLevelImpersonate
101:
102:    Set objWMIServices = objWMILocator.ConnectServer(strComputerName, cWMINameSpace, _
103:                                           strUserID, strPassword)
...:
106:    Set objWMIInstance = objWMIServices.Get (cWMIClass & "='" & strWMIInstance & "'")
...:
109:    If boolFixErrors Then
110:        WScript.Echo "Errors will be fixed."
111:    End If
112:
113:    If boolVigorousIndexCheck Then
114:        WScript.Echo "Vigorous check of index entries will be performed."
115:    End If
116:
117:    If boolSkipFolderCycle Then
118:        WScript.Echo "The folder cycle checking will be skipped."
119:    End If
120:
```

```
121:    If boolForceDismount Then
122:        WScript.Echo "The drive will be forced to dismount before checking."
123:    End If
124:
125:    If boolRecoverBadSectors Then
126:        WScript.Echo "The bad sectors will be located ... will be recovered from these sectors."
127:    End If
128:
129:    If boolOKToRunAtBootUp Then
130:        WScript.Echo "The chkdsk operation should be performed at next boot up time."
131:    End If
132:
133:    WScript.Echo
134:    WScript.Echo "Volume " & Ucase (objWMIInstance.DeviceID) & _
135:                 " has " & objWMIInstance.FreeSpace & _
136:                 " bytes free on a total of " & _
137:                 objWMIInstance.Size & " bytes."
138:    WScript.Echo "The type of the file system is " & _
139:                 objWMIInstance.FileSystem & "."
140:    WScript.Echo "Volume is " & objWMIInstance.VolumeName & "."
141:    WScript.Echo "Volume Serial Number is " & _
142:                 objWMIinstance.VolumeSerialNumber & "."
143:
144:    WScript.Echo "WMI chkdsk started ..."
145:    intRC = objWMIInstance.Chkdsk (boolFixErrors, _
146:                                   boolVigorousIndexCheck, _
147:                                   boolSkipFolderCycle, _
148:                                   boolForceDismount, _
149:                                   boolRecoverBadSectors, _
150:                                   boolOKToRunAtBootUp)
151:    If Err.Number Then ErrorHandler (Err)
152:
153:    Select Case intRC
154:          Case 0
155:              WScript.Echo "WMI chkdsk completed successfully."
156:          Case 1
157:              WScript.Echo "Locked and chkdsk scheduled on reboot."
158:          Case 2
159:              WScript.Echo "WMI chkdsk failure - Unknown file system."
160:          Case 3
161:              WScript.Echo "WMI chkdsk failure - Unknown error."
162:    End Select
...:
167:    ]]>
168:    </script>
169:  </job>
170:</package>
```

The script parses the *Win32_LogicalDisk Chkdsk* method parameters (lines 13 through 30 and lines 72 through 88) from the command line. After executing the WMI connection (lines 102 and 103), Sample 2.3 instantiates the desired logical disk (line 106). Before executing the CHKDSK utility, the script shows the actions to be executed (lines 109 through 131) with some information about the logical disk itself (lines 133 through 142). Next, the *Chkdsk* method is invoked (lines 145 through 150) with the given parameters. Once executed, the return code of the operation is interpreted (lines 151 through 162). The output produced by Sample 2.3 is as follows:

```
C:\>WMIChkdsk.wsf E: /Machine:Remote.LissWare.Net /User:Administrator /Password:password
Microsoft (R) Windows Script Host Version 5.6
Copyright (C) Microsoft Corporation 1996-2001. All rights reserved.

Vigorous check of index entries will be performed.
The folder cycle checking will be skipped.

Volume E: has 6418804736 bytes free on a total of 7229595648 bytes.
The type of the file system is NTFS.
Volume is Win2003.
Volume Serial Number is 84FC2438.
WMI chkdsk started ...
WMI chkdsk completed successfully.
```

2.3.3   Motherboard, controller, and port classes

The motherboard, controller, and port classes represent devices such as memory, hardware controllers (i.e., IDE, PCMCIA, floppy), BIOS, parallel and serial ports, and so on. The classes related to these hardware devices and supported by the *Win32* providers are shown in Table 2.4.

By using some of these classes, it is possible to create a script to collect information about the hardware devices and the resources they use (IRQ, DMA). For the script sample, we use some classes that represent devices that are available in all computers. This makes the script usable with all computer types. For instance, some hardware components that are common to any computer are:

- The processor represented by the *Win32_Processor* class

- The memory represented by the *Win32_PhysicalMemory* class

- The hardware resources, such as the IRQ and the DMA, respectively, represented by *Win32_IRQResource* and *Win32_DMAChannel* classes.

Many other classes from this category can be used to gather information about the hardware. All of them use the same logic. Samples 2.4 through 2.7 contain the script code to display the processor, the memory, and the hardware resources of a computer. This script can be easily extended to suit any other needs (i.e., displaying information about the PCMCIA controller with the *Win32_PCMCIAController* class).

Table 2.4   *Motherboard, Controller, and Port Classes*

Name	Description
Win32_1394Controller	Represents the capabilities and management of a 1394 controller.
Win32_1394ControllerDevice	Relates the high-speed serial bus (IEEE 1394 Firewire) Controller and the CIM_LogicalDevice instance connected to it.
Win32_AllocatedResource	Relates a logical device to a system resource.
Win32_AssociatedProcessorMemory	Relates a processor and its cache memory.
Win32_BaseBoard	Represents a baseboard (also known as a motherboard or systemboard).
Win32_BIOS	Represents the attributes of the computer system's basic input/output services (BIOS) that are installed on the computer.
Win32_Bus	Represents a physical bus as seen by a Windows operating system.
Win32_CacheMemory	Represents cache memory (internal and external) on a computer system.
Win32_ControllerHasHub	Represents the hubs downstream from the Universal Serial Bus (USB) controller.
Win32_DeviceBus	Relates a system bus and a logical device using the bus.
Win32_DeviceMemoryAddress	Represents a device memory address on a Windows system.
Win32_DeviceSettings	Relates a logical device and a setting that can be applied to it.
Win32_DMAChannel	Represents a direct memory access (DMA) channel on a Windows computer system.
Win32_FloppyController	Represents the capabilities and management capacity of a floppy disk drive controller.
Win32_IDEController	Represents the capabilities of an Integrated Drive Electronics (IDE) controller device.
Win32_IDEControllerDevice	Association class that relates an IDE controller and the logical device.
Win32_InfraredDevice	Represents the capabilities and management of an infrared device.
Win32_IRQResource	Represents an interrupt request line (IRQ) number on a Windows computer system.
Win32_MemoryArray	Represents the properties of the computer system memory array and mapped addresses.
Win32_MemoryArrayLocation	Relates a logical memory array and the physical memory array upon which it exists.
Win32_MemoryDevice	Represents the properties of a computer system's memory device along with its associated mapped addresses.
Win32_MemoryDeviceArray	Relates a memory device and the memory array in which it resides.
Win32_MemoryDeviceLocation	Association class that relates a memory device and the physical memory on which it exists.
Win32_MotherboardDevice	Represents a device that contains the central components of the Windows computer system.
Win32_OnBoardDevice	Represents common adapter devices built into the motherboard (system board).
Win32_ParallelPort	Represents the properties of a parallel port on a Windows computer system.
Win32_PCMCIAController	Manages the capabilities of a Personal Computer Memory Card Interface Adapter (PCMCIA) controller device.
Win32_PhysicalMemory	Represents a physical memory device located on a computer as available to the operating system.
Win32_PhysicalMemoryArray	Represents details about the computer system's physical memory.
Win32_PhysicalMemoryLocation	Relates an array of physical memory and its physical memory.
Win32_PNPAllocatedResource	Represents an association between logical devices and system resources.
Win32_PNPDevice	Relates a device (known to Configuration Manager as a PNPEntity), and the function it performs.
Win32_PNPEntity	Represents the properties of a Plug and Play device.
Win32_PortConnector	Represents physical connection ports, such as DB-25 pin male, Centronics, and PS/2.
Win32_PortResource	Represents an I/O port on a Windows computer system.
Win32_Processor	Represents a device capable of interpreting a sequence of machine instructions on a Windows computer system.
Win32_SCSIController	Represents a SCSI controller on a Windows system.
Win32_SCSIControllerDevice	Relates a Small Computer System Interface (SCSI) controller and the logical device (disk drive) connected to it.
Win32_SerialPort	Represents a serial port on a Windows system.
Win32_SerialPortConfiguration	Represents the settings for data transmission on a Windows serial port.
Win32_SerialPortSetting	Relates a serial port and its configuration settings.
Win32_SMBIOSMemory	Represents the capabilities and management of memory-related logical devices.
Win32_SoundDevice	Represents the properties of a sound device on a Windows computer system.
Win32_SystemBIOS	Relates a computer system (including data such as startup properties, time zones, boot configurations, or administrative passwords) and a system BIOS (services, languages, system management properties).

Table 2.4   *Motherboard, Controller, and Port Classes (continued)*

Name	Description
Win32_SystemDriverPNPEntity	Relates a Plug and Play device on the Windows computer system and the driver that supports the Plug and Play device.
Win32_SystemEnclosure	Represents the properties associated with a physical system enclosure.
Win32_SystemMemoryResource	Represents a system memory resource on a Windows system.
Win32_SystemSlot	Represents physical connection points including ports, motherboard slots and peripherals, and proprietary connections points.
Win32_USBController	Manages the capabilities of a Universal Serial Bus (USB) controller.
Win32_USBControllerDevice	Relates a USB controller and the CIM_LogicalDevice instances connected to it.
Win32_USBHub	Represents the management characteristics of a USB hub.

Sample 2.4   *Retrieving hardware resource information (Part I)*

```
 1:<?xml version="1.0"?>
 .:
 8:<package>
 9:  <job>
..:
13:    <runtime>
..:
17:    </runtime>
18:
19:    <script language="VBScript" src=".\Functions\DecodeDeviceAvailabilityFunction.vbs" />
20:    <script language="VBScript" src=".\Functions\DecodePwrManCapabilitiesFunction.vbs" />
21:    <script language="VBScript" src=".\Functions\TinyErrorHandler.vbs" />
22:
23:    <object progid="WbemScripting.SWbemLocator" id="objWMILocator" reference="true"/>
24:
25:    <script language="VBscript">
26:    <![CDATA[
..:
44:    ' -------------------------------------------------------------------------------
45:    ' Parse the command line parameters
46:    strUserID = WScript.Arguments.Named("User")
..:
58:    Set objWMIServices = objWMILocator.ConnectServer(strComputerName, cWMINameSpace, _
59:                                                     strUserID, strPassword)
..:
62:    ' -------------------------------------------------------------------------------
63:    WScript.Echo "--- Processors information " & String (60, "-")
64:    Set objWMIInstances = objWMIServices.InstancesOf ("Win32_Processor")
65:    If Err.Number Then ErrorHandler (Err)
66:
67:    If objWMIInstances.Count Then
68:       For Each objWMIInstance In objWMIInstances
69:           WScript.Echo objWMIInstance.DeviceID & " is an " & _
70:                        objWMIInstance.Name & " (" & _
71:                        objWMIInstance.Caption & ")."
72:           WScript.Echo "It is an " & objWMIInstance.AddressWidth & " bits CPU running at " & _
73:                        "an internal clock speed of " & _
74:                        objWMIInstance.CurrentClockSpeed & " Mhz."
75:           WScript.Echo "The external clock speed is " & objWMIInstance.ExtClock & " Mhz."
76:           WScript.Echo objWMIInstance.DeviceID & " is " & _
77:                        DeviceAvailability (objWMIInstance.Availability) & " and state is " & _
78:                        objWMIInstance.Status & "."
79:           WScript.Echo "The Second Level (L2) cache size is " & _
80:                        objWMIInstance.L2CacheSize & " KB and is running at a speed of " & _
81:                        objWMIInstance.L2CacheSpeed & " Mhz."
```

```
82:            WScript.Echo "This processor is manufactured by " & objWMIInstance.Manufacturer & _
83:                " and uses a " & objWMIInstance.SocketDesignation & " socket."
84:            WScript.Echo "The current revision level is " & objWMIInstance.Revision & _
85:                " stepping " & objWMIInstance.Stepping & "."
86:            WScript.Echo "The processor ID is " & objWMIInstance.ProcessorId & "."
87:            If objWMIInstance.PowerManagementSupported Then
88:                WScript.Echo "Power management capabilities are " & _
89:                    PwrManCapabilities(objWMIInstance.PowerManagementCapabilities) & "."
90:            Else
91:                WScript.Echo "Power management capabilities are not supported."
92:            End If
93:        Next
94:    Else
95:        WScript.Echo "No information available."
96:    End If
97:    WScript.Echo
98:
. . :
. . :
. . :
```

The script does not require any specific parameter. This is the reason why it only contains the traditional parameters to connect to a remote machine with some optional credentials (skipped lines 13 through 17). Next, the script includes two helper functions (lines 19 and 20):

- DecodeDeviceAvailabilityFunction.vbs

- DecodePwrManCapabilitiesFunction.vbs

These two functions convert values contained in the *PowerManagement-Capabilities* and the *Availability* properties into a readable text instead of showing their values. These two properties are not related to one specific class. Actually, many classes dealing with the hardware devices expose these properties. By using these functions, we simplify the hardware data reading and interpretation.

Once the command-line parameters are parsed and the WMI connection is established (lines 46 through 60), the script retrieves information about the processor (lines 63 through 97). The script requests the collection of processors available (line 64) and displays the most relevant properties (lines 69 through 92). The script outputs these properties in a readable text, as follows:

```
1:  C:\>GetHardwareResourceInfo.wsf
2:  Microsoft (R) Windows Script Host Version 5.6
3:  Copyright (C) Microsoft Corporation 1996-2001. All rights reserved.
4:
5:  --- Processors information ------------------------------------------------
6:  CPU0 is an Intel(R) Pentium(R) 4 CPU 1.50GHz (x86 Family 15 Model 1 Stepping 2).
7:  It is an 32 bits CPU running at an internal clock speed of 1495 Mhz.
8:  The external clock speed is 400 Mhz.
9:  CPU0 is Running/Full Power and its state is OK.
10: The Second Level (L2) cache size is 256 KB and is running at a speed of 1495 Mhz.
11: This processor is manufactured by GenuineIntel and uses a XU1 socket.
```

```
12:    The current revision level is 258 stepping 2.
13:    The processor ID is 3FEBFBFF00000F12.
14:    Power management capabilities are not supported.
15:
..:
..:
..:
```

Once the processor information is displayed, the script gathers information about the memory (see Sample 2.5). It follows the same logic. Only the
way the information is displayed is different. The script retrieves the memory chips available and takes their size into account to display the values in
KB or in MB (line 106).

Sample 2.5   *Retrieving hardware resource information (Part II)*

```
..:
..:
..:
99:    ' --------------------------------------------------------------------------------
100:   WScript.Echo "--- Memory information " & String (60, "-")
101:   Set objWMIInstances = objWMIServices.InstancesOf ("Win32_PhysicalMemory")
102:   If Err.Number Then ErrorHandler (Err)
103:
104:   If objWMIInstances.Count Then
105:       For Each objWMIInstance In objWMIInstances
106:           If (objWMIInstance.Capacity - 1024^2) < 0 Then
107:               WScript.Echo objWMIInstance.BankLabel & " is " & _
108:                            objWMIInstance.Capacity / (1024) & " KB chip size (" & _
109:                            objWMIInstance.DeviceLocator & ")."
110:           Else
111:               WScript.Echo objWMIInstance.BankLabel & " is " & _
112:                            objWMIInstance.Capacity / (1024^2) & " MB chip size (" & _
113:                            objWMIInstance.DeviceLocator & ")."
114:           End If
115:       Next
116:   Else
117:       WScript.Echo "No information available."
118:   End If
119:   WScript.Echo
120:
...:
...:
...:
```

The output obtained is as follows:

```
..:
..:
..:
15:
16:    --- Memory information ------------------------------------------------------
17:    Bank  0: J10 is 512 MB chip size (XMM1).
18:    Bank  1: J11 is 512 MB chip size (XMM2).
19:    ROM: XU15 is 512 KB chip size (XU15).
20:
..:
..:
..:
```

Next, the script retrieves information about the hardware resources used. Sample 2.6 retrieves information about the DMA resource usage, while Sample 2.7 retrieves information about the IRQ resource usage.

Sample 2.6 *Retrieving hardware resource information (Part III)*

```
...:
...:
...:
120:
121:   ' ----------------------------------------------------------------------------------
122:   WScript.Echo "--- DMA resource usage " & String (60, "-")
123:   Set objWMIInstances = objWMIServices.InstancesOf ("Win32_DMAChannel")
124:   If Err.Number Then ErrorHandler (Err)
125:
126:   If objWMIInstances.Count Then
127:       For Each objWMIInstance In objWMIInstances
128:           Set objAssoc1Instances = objWMIServices.ExecQuery _
129:                               ("Associators of {Win32_DMAChannel='" & _
130:                               objWMIInstance.DMAChannel & _
131:                               "'} Where AssocClass=Win32_PNPAllocatedResource")
132:
133:           If objAssoc1Instances.Count Then
134:               WScript.Echo objWMIInstance.Caption
135:               For Each objAssoc1Instance In objAssoc1Instances
136:                   If Len (objAssoc1Instance.Service) Then
137:                       WScript.Echo "  " & Trim (objAssoc1Instance.Name) & "."
138:                       WScript.Echo "  Service name is '" & UCase (objAssoc1Instance.Service) & _
139:                               "' and status is " & objAssoc1Instance.Status & "."
140:
141:                       Set objAssoc2Instances = objWMIServices.ExecQuery _
142:                               ("Associators of {Win32_PnPEntity='" & _
143:                               objAssoc1Instance.DeviceID & _
144:                               "'} Where ResultClass=Win32_PortResource " & _
145:                               "AssocClass=Win32_PNPAllocatedResource")
146:
147:                       For Each objAssoc2Instance In objAssoc2Instances
148:                           WScript.Echo "      Address range is " & objAssoc2Instance.Name
149:                       Next
150:
151:                   Else
152:                       WScript.Echo "  " & objAssoc1Instance.Name & "."
153:                   End If
154:               Next
155:           End If
156:       Next
157:   Else
158:       WScript.Echo "No information available."
159:   End If
160:   WScript.Echo
161:
...:
...:
...:
```

The script retrieves the number of DMA channels available by requesting the instances of the *Win32_DMAChannel* class (line 123). Next, it enumerates the DMA channels (lines 127 through 156) and, for each channel, the script requests the collection of instances associated with the examined DMA channel (lines 128 through 131). This collection of instances is nothing more than the devices using the DMA channel number. If the collection of associated instances contains at least one item (line 133), which is one device that uses the examined DMA channel, the script displays the DMA channel instance name (line 134) and enumerates each associated instance in the collection (lines 135 through 154). For each associated instance, the script displays its name and status (lines 138 and 139).

As a result, the device name and its state are displayed. Because the device could use some I/O port addresses, the script also retrieves the I/O port addresses used by requesting the list of I/O ports associated with the instance (lines 141 through 145). In such a case, the script retrieves a list of associated instances (the list of I/O ports used) from each associated instance (the device examined). Lines 147 through 149 display the I/O port collection.

To summarize, the script retrieves a collection of DMA channels used, and for each DMA channel examined the script retrieves the list of devices using that DMA channel. Next, for each device using the considered DMA channel the script retrieves the list of I/O ports used by that device. In WMI words, we have a collection of instances where each instance is associated with a collection of instances, which in turn are associated with a second collection of instances. As a result, the script generates the following output:

```
..:
..:
..:
20:
21:    --- DMA resource usage ---------------------------------------------------------
22:    Channel 4
23:      Direct memory access controller.
24:    Channel 2
25:      Standard floppy disk controller.
26:          Service name is 'FDC' and status is OK.
27:          Address range is 0x000003F0-0x000003F5
28:          Address range is 0x000003F7-0x000003F7
..:
..:
..:
```

Sample 2.7 uses the exact same logic as Sample 2.6. The only variation concerns the instance type retrieved. Sample 2.6 retrieves *Win32_DMAChannel* instances, while Sample 2.7 retrieves *Win32_IRQResource* instances (line 164).

Sample 2.7 *Retrieving hardware resource information (Part IV)*

```
...:
...:
...:
161:
162:  ' -----------------------------------------------------------------------------------------
163:  WScript.Echo "--- IRQ resource usage " & String (60, "-")
164:  Set objWMIInstances = objWMIServices.InstancesOf ("Win32_IRQResource")
165:  If Err.Number Then ErrorHandler (Err)
166:
167:  If objWMIInstances.Count Then
168:      For Each objWMIInstance In objWMIInstances
169:          Set objAssoc1Instances = objWMIServices.ExecQuery _
170:                                  ("Associators of {Win32_IRQResource='" & _
171:                                  objWMIInstance.IRQNumber & _
172:                                  "'} Where AssocClass=Win32_PNPAllocatedResource")
173:          If objAssoc1Instances.Count Then
174:              WScript.Echo objWMIInstance.Caption
175:              For Each objAssoc1Instance In objAssoc1Instances
176:                  If Len (objAssoc1Instance.Service) Then
177:                      WScript.Echo "  " & Trim (objAssoc1Instance.Name) & "."
178:                      WScript.Echo "  Service name is '" & UCase (objAssoc1Instance.Service) & _
179:                                  "' and status is " & objAssoc1Instance.Status & "."
180:
181:                      Set objAssoc2Instances = objWMIServices.ExecQuery _
182:                                  ("Associators of {Win32_PnPEntity='" & _
183:                                  objAssoc1Instance.DeviceID & _
184:                                  "'} Where ResultClass=Win32_PortResource " & _
185:                                  "AssocClass=Win32_PNPAllocatedResource")
186:
187:                      For Each objAssoc2Instance In objAssoc2Instances
188:                          WScript.Echo "     Address range is " & objAssoc2Instance.Name
189:                      Next
190:
191:                  Else
192:                      WScript.Echo "  " & objAssoc1Instance.Name & "."
193:                  End If
194:              Next
195:          End If
196:      Next
197:  Else
198:      WScript.Echo "No information available."
199:  End If
...:
204:  ]]>
205:  </script>
206:  </job>
207:</package>
```

As a result, the script displays the following information:

```
..:
..:
..:
29:
30:    --- IRQ resource usage -------------------------------------------------------
31:    IRQ 9
32:      Microsoft ACPI-Compliant System.
33:          Service name is 'ACPI' and status is OK.
34:    IRQ 18
35:      NVIDIA GeForce2 MX/MX 400.
36:          Service name is 'NV' and status is OK.
37:          Address range is 0x000003B0-0x000003BB
38:          Address range is 0x000003C0-0x000003DF
39:    IRQ 20
40:      Intel(R) PRO/100 VM Network Connection.
41:          Service name is 'E100B' and status is OK.
42:          Address range is 0x00001400-0x0000143F
43:    IRQ 21
44:      Adaptec AHA-2940AU PCI SCSI Controller.
45:          Service name is 'AIC78XX' and status is OK.
46:          Address range is 0x00001000-0x000010FF
47:    IRQ 22
48:      Creative SB Live! Basic (WDM).
49:          Service name is 'EMU10K' and status is OK.
50:          Address range is 0x00001440-0x0000145F
51:    IRQ 13
52:      Numeric data processor.
53:    IRQ 0
54:      System timer.
55:    IRQ 8
56:      System CMOS/real time clock.
57:    IRQ 12
58:      PS/2 Compatible Mouse.
59:          Service name is 'I8042PRT' and status is OK.
60:    IRQ 1
61:      Standard 101/102-Key or Microsoft Natural PS/2 Keyboard.
62:          Service name is 'I8042PRT' and status is OK.
63:          Address range is 0x00000060-0x00000060
64:          Address range is 0x00000064-0x00000064
65:    IRQ 4
66:      Communications Port (COM1).
67:          Service name is 'SERIAL' and status is OK.
68:          Address range is 0x000003F8-0x000003FF
69:    IRQ 3
70:      Communications Port (COM2).
71:          Service name is 'SERIAL' and status is OK.
72:          Address range is 0x000002F8-0x000002FF
73:    IRQ 6
74:      Standard floppy disk controller.
75:          Service name is 'FDC' and status is OK.
76:          Address range is 0x000003F0-0x000003F5
77:          Address range is 0x000003F7-0x000003F7
78:    IRQ 14
79:      Primary IDE Channel.
80:          Service name is 'ATAPI' and status is OK.
81:          Address range is 0x000001F0-0x000001F7
82:          Address range is 0x000003F6-0x000003F6
83:    IRQ 15
```

```
84:      Secondary IDE Channel.
85:          Service name is 'ATAPI' and status is OK.
86:          Address range is 0x00000170-0x00000177
87:          Address range is 0x00000376-0x00000376
88:      IRQ 19
89:      Intel(r) 82801BA/BAM USB Universal Host Controller - 2442.
90:          Service name is 'USBUHCI' and status is OK.
91:          Address range is 0x00002440-0x0000245F
```

2.3.4   **Networking device classes**

Even though a network device is listed in the previous sample output ("Intel[R] PRO/100 VM Network," lines 39 through 42) with the motherboard, controller, and the port classes, the sample does not show the network configuration of a network adapter. The classes used in Samples 2.4 through 2.7 do not allow the retrieval of such information. For this, WMI implements some other interesting classes to retrieve and set the network adapter configuration. These classes are listed in Table 2.5.

Table 2.5   *The Networking Device Classes*

Name	Description
Win32_NetworkAdapter	Represents a network adapter on a Windows system.
Win32_NetworkAdapterConfiguration	Represents the attributes and behaviors of a network adapter. The class is not guaranteed to be supported after the ratification of the Distributed Management Task Force (DMTF) CIM network specification.
Win32_NetworkAdapterSetting	Relates a network adapter and its configuration settings.

Besides the hardware information related to an adapter, with the help of these classes it is possible to gather information about the adapter protocol configuration (see Samples 2.8 through 2.11). Although the *Win32_NetworkAdapterConfiguration* class can retrieve IP and IPX network configurations, the script focuses on the IP configuration only (to retrieve the IPX configuration, the code sample can easily be extended by displaying some additional class properties).

As usual, Sample 2.8 starts with the command-line parameter definition (lines 13 through 19), continues with the command-line parsing (lines 56 through 75), and performs the WMI connection (lines 77 through 80).

Sample 2.8   *Retrieving network device information (Part I)*

```
1:<?xml version="1.0"?>
 .:
8:<package>
9:   <job>
..:
13:     <runtime>
14:        <unnamed name="AdapterName" helpstring="The name of the network adapter." required="true"
```

```
               type="string" />
15:      <named name="List" helpstring="Only list the adapter names." required="false"
               type="boolean" />
16:      <named name="Machine" helpstring="determine the WMI system to connect to.
               (default=LocalHost)" required="false" type="string"/>
17:      <named name="User" helpstring="determine the UserID to perform the remote connection.
               (default=none)" required="false" type="string"/>
18:      <named name="Password" helpstring="determine the password to perform the remote
               connection. (default=none)" required="false" type="string"/>
19:    </runtime>
20:
21:    <script language="VBScript" src=".\Functions\DecodeDeviceAvailabilityFunction.vbs" />
22:    <script language="VBScript" src=".\Functions\DecodeNetworkConnectionStatusFunction.vbs" />
23:
24:    <script language="VBScript" src=".\Functions\DisplayFormattedPropertyFunction.vbs" />
25:    <script language="VBScript" src=".\Functions\TinyErrorHandler.vbs" />
26:
27:    <object progid="WbemScripting.SWbemLocator" id="objWMILocator" reference="true"/>
28:    <object progid="WbemScripting.SWbemDateTime" id="objWMIDateTime" />
29:
30:    <script language="VBscript">
31:    <![CDATA[
..:
35:    Const cComputerName = "LocalHost"
36:    Const cWMINameSpace = "root/cimv2"
..:
54:    ' --------------------------------------------------------------------------
55:    ' Parse the command line parameters
56:    boolAdapterList = WScript.Arguments.Named("List")
57:    If Len(boolAdapterList) = 0 Then boolAdapterList = False
58:
59:    If WScript.Arguments.Unnamed.Count = 0 And boolAdapterList = False Then
60:        WScript.Arguments.ShowUsage()
61:        WScript.Quit
62:    Else
63:        If WScript.Arguments.Unnamed.Count Then
64:            strAdapterName = WScript.Arguments.Unnamed.Item(0)
65:        End If
66:    End If
67:
68:    strUserID = WScript.Arguments.Named("User")
69:    If Len(strUserID) = 0 Then strUserID = ""
70:
71:    strPassword = WScript.Arguments.Named("Password")
72:    If Len(strPassword) = 0 Then strPassword = ""
73:
74:    strComputerName = WScript.Arguments.Named("Machine")
75:    If Len(strComputerName) = 0 Then strComputerName = cComputerName
76:
77:    objWMILocator.Security_.AuthenticationLevel = wbemAuthenticationLevelDefault
78:    objWMILocator.Security_.ImpersonationLevel = wbemImpersonationLevelImpersonate
79:    Set objWMIServices = objWMILocator.ConnectServer(strComputerName, cWMINameSpace, _
80:                                                      strUserID, strPassword)
..:
82:
..:
..:
..:
```

Notice that the script has a Boolean parameter called **/List** (lines 15, 56, and 57). This parameter requests the list of adapters available in the system. To extract the network information from one specific network adapter, it is necessary to determine which *Win32_NetworkAdapter* Key property to use. Because the Key is an index representing the adapter number (called the *DeviceID*), it is easier to use the name of the network adapter. To do so, the script lists the network adapter names, as follows:

```
 1:   C:\>GetNetworkConfiguration.wsf /list+
 2:   Microsoft (R) Windows Script Host Version 5.6
 3:   Copyright (C) Microsoft Corporation 1996-2001. All rights reserved.
 4:
 5:   Compaq NC3121 Fast Ethernet NIC
 6:   RAS Async Adapter
 7:   WAN Miniport (L2TP)
 8:   WAN Miniport (PPTP)
 9:   WAN Miniport (PPPOE)
10:   Direct Parallel
11:   WAN Miniport (IP)
12:   WAN Miniport (Network Monitor)
13:   Microsoft Loopback Adapter
```

Because the *Win32_NetworkAdapter* class does not define the adapter *name* property as a Key property for the class, the script does not instantiate the adapter directly. Instead, the script creates a collection that lists all available adapters. The collection of adapters is retrieved in Sample 2.9 at line 83, while the existing adapter enumeration starts at line 85. If the **/List+** switch is specified, the script uses the same collection to list all adapter names available (lines 83 and 87). If the **/List+** switch is not specified, the script searches for a match between the name given on the command line and the existing adapter names (line 89). It was possible to use a WQL query to find the adapter name (with the *ExecQuery* method of the **SWBemServices** object), but because we usually have a few number of adapters in a computer system, the enumeration technique is acceptable. Moreover, the same loop (lines 85 through 314) is used to list adapters (line 87) or to select the adapter to work with (line 89).

Sample 2.9 *Retrieving network device information (Part II)*

```
..:
..:
..:
82:
83:     Set objWMIAdapterInstances = objWMIServices.InstancesOf ("Win32_NetworkAdapter")
84:
85:     For Each objWMIAdapterInstance in objWMIAdapterInstances
86:         If boolAdapterList Then
87:             WScript.Echo Mid (objWMIAdapterInstance.Caption, 12)
88:         Else
89:             If Ucase(Mid (objWMIAdapterInstance.Caption, 12)) = Ucase(strAdapterName) Then
```

```
 90:              DisplayFormattedProperty objWMIAdapterInstance, _
 91:                              "Adapter name", _
 92:                              "Name", _
 93:                              Null
 94:              DisplayFormattedProperty objWMIAdapterInstance, _
 95:                  "Device availability", _
 96:                  DeviceAvailability (objWMIAdapterInstance.Availability), _
 97:                              Null
 98:
 99:              If objWMIAdapterInstance.NetConnectionStatus = 0 Then
100:                  DisplayFormattedProperty objWMIAdapterInstance, _
101:                              "Adapter state", _
102:                              "DISABLED", _
103:                              Null
104:              Else
105:                  DisplayFormattedProperty objWMIAdapterInstance, _
106:                              "Adapter type", _
107:                              "AdapterType", _
108:                              Null
109:                  DisplayFormattedProperty objWMIAdapterInstance, _
110:                      "Adapter state", _
111:                      NetworkConnectionStatus (objWMIAdapterInstance.NetConnectionStatus), _
112:                              Null
113:                  DisplayFormattedProperty objWMIAdapterInstance, _
114:                              "MAC address is ", _
115:                              "MACAddress", _
116:                              Null
117:              End If
118:
119:              DisplayFormattedProperty objWMIAdapterInstance, _
120:                              "Adapter service name", _
121:                              "ServiceName", _
122:                              Null
123:              DisplayFormattedProperty objWMIAdapterInstance, _
124:                              "Last reset", _
125:                              "TimeOfLastReset", _
126:                              Null
127:
...:
...:
...:
```

Once a match is found, the script displays all adapter properties (lines 89 through 313). For instance, properties such as the adapter *name* (lines 90 through 93), *state* (lines 99 through 103), type (lines 105 through 108), and *MACAddress* are listed (lines 113 through 116).

You will notice at line 99 the test on the adapter *NetConnectionStatus* property. If the adapter is enabled, the adapter type, the network connection status, and the MAC address properties are displayed (lines 105 through 116). If the *NetConnectionStatus* property has a value of 0 (line 99), this means that the adapter is disabled (lines 100 through 103). Table 2.6 summarizes the connection status values resolved by the NetworkConnectionStatus() function included at line 22 and invoked at line 111.

Table 2.6 *The Connection Status Values*

Name	Values
Disconnected	0
Connecting	1
Connected	2
Disconnecting	3
Hardware Not Present	4
Hardware Disabled	5
Hardware Malfunction	6
Media Disconnected	7
Authenticating	8
Authentication Succeeded	9
Authentication Failed	10

Next, the script retrieves the hardware resource information used by the adapter: IRQ, DMA, I/O Port, and memory address (see Sample 2.10). The script bases its research on the associations defined in the CIM repository. For instance, Figure 2.2 shows the associated instances available for one network adapter. This should ease the understanding of the relationships that exist between the adapter and the hardware resources.

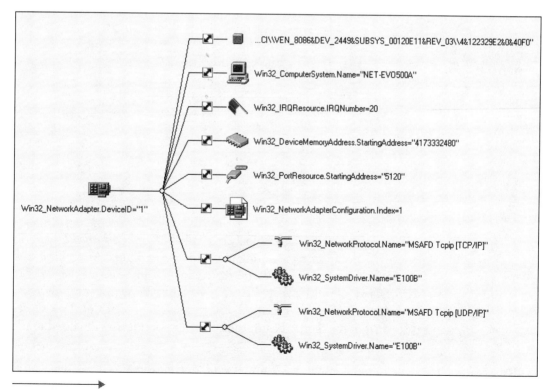

Figure 2.2 *Associated instances of one network adapter.*

Sample 2.10   *Retrieving network device information (Part III)*

```
...:
...:
...:
128:            Set objWMIAdapterResourceInstances = objWMIServices.ExecQuery _
129:                         ("Associators of {Win32_NetworkAdapter='" & _
130:                         objWMIAdapterInstance.Index & _
131:                         "'} Where AssocClass=Win32_AllocatedResource")
132:
133:       If objWMIAdapterResourceInstances.Count Then
134:          WScript.Echo
135:          For Each objWMIAdapterResourceInstance In objWMIAdapterResourceInstances
136:             Select Case objWMIAdapterResourceInstance.Path_.Class
137:                Case "Win32_IRQResource"
138:                   DisplayFormattedProperty objWMIAdapterResourceInstance, _
139:                                            "IRQ resource", _
140:                                            "IRQNumber", _
141:                                            Null
142:                Case "Win32_DMAChannel"
143:                   DisplayFormattedProperty objWMIAdapterResourceInstance, _
144:                                            "DMA channel", _
145:                                            "DMAChannel", _
146:                                            Null
147:                Case "Win32_PortResource"
148:                   DisplayFormattedProperty objWMIAdapterResourceInstance, _
149:                                            "I/O Port", _
150:                                            "Caption", _
151:                                            Null
152:                Case "Win32_DeviceMemoryAddress"
153:                   DisplayFormattedProperty objWMIAdapterResourceInstance, _
154:                                            "Memory address", _
155:                                            "Caption", _
156:                                            Null
157:             End Select
158:          Next
159:       End If
...:
...:
...:
```

The script uses an association class called *Win32_AllocatedResource* to retrieve the instances representing the hardware resources. As we have seen before, the hardware resources are represented by instances of the *Win32_IRQResource*, *Win32_DMAChannel*, *Win32_PortResource*, and *Win32_DeviceMemoryAddress* classes (lines 136 through 157). Each of these classes is classified in the motherboard, controller, and port classes discussed in the previous section.

To retrieve instances of the *Win32_AllocatedResource* class that correspond to the adapter (lines 128 through 131), the script uses the Key property (called *Index*) of the *Win32_NetworkAdapter* class with the index number of the adapter instance (line 130) previously retrieved in the script with the enumeration at line 85 (see Sample 2.9).

Once hardware resources are examined, the script starts to look at the IP protocol settings (see Sample 2.11). For this, it uses the *Win32_Network-AdapterConfiguration* class. This class exposes a large number of properties related to the DHCP settings (lines 188 through 204), IP address settings (lines 208 through 223), DNS settings (lines 226 through 249), WINS settings (lines 252 through 285), and IP Security/Filtering settings (lines 288 through 309).

To retrieve the instance of the *Win32_NetworkAdapterConfiguration* that corresponds to the adapter (lines 180 through 182 in Sample 2.11), the script uses the Key property (called *Index*) of the *Win32_NetworkAdapter-Configuration* class with the index number of the adapter instance (line 182) previously retrieved from the script with the enumeration at line 85 (see Sample 2.9).

You will note that Sample 2.10 jumps from line 159 to Sample 2.11 at line 180. Lines 160 through 179 are not discussed in this section, because they use the *Win32_NetworkProtocol* class. This class is explained in section 2.4.7 ("Networking classes") in this chapter (see also Sample 2.42).

Sample 2.11   *Retrieving network device information (Part IV)*

```
...:
...:
...:
180:              Set objWMIAdapterInstance = objWMIServices.Get _
181:                               ("Win32_NetworkAdapterConfiguration=" & _
182:                               objWMIAdapterInstance.Index)
183:
184:          If objWMIAdapterInstance.IPEnabled Then
185:              WScript.Echo
186:
187:              ' DHCP -------------------------------------------------------------------
188:              DisplayFormattedProperty objWMIAdapterInstance, _
189:                               "DHCP enabled", _
190:                               "DHCPEnabled", _
191:                               Null
192:              If objWMIAdapterInstance.DHCPEnabled Then
193:                  DisplayFormattedProperty objWMIAdapterInstance, _
194:                               "DHCP expires", _
195:                               "DHCPLeaseExpires", _
196:                               Null
...:
205:              End If
206:
207:              ' IP Addresses -----------------------------------------------------------
208:              DisplayFormattedProperty objWMIAdapterInstance, _
209:                               "IP address(es)", _
```

```
210:                                         "IPAddress", _
211:                                         "IPSubnet"
...:
216:            DisplayFormattedProperty objWMIAdapterInstance, _
217:                                     "Default Gateway(s) and metric", _
218:                                     "DefaultIPGateway", _
219:                                     "GatewayCostMetric"
...:
224:
225:            ' DNS --------------------------------------------------------------
226:            DisplayFormattedProperty objWMIAdapterInstance, _
227:                                     "DNS registration enabled", _
228:                                     "DomainDNSRegistrationEnabled", _
229:                                     Null
...:
246:            DisplayFormattedProperty objWMIAdapterInstance, _
247:                                     "DNS enabled for WINS resolution", _
248:                                     "DNSEnabledForWINSResolution", _
249:                                     Null
250:
251:            ' WINS -------------------------------------------------------------
252:            DisplayFormattedProperty objWMIAdapterInstance, _
253:                                     "Primary WINS Server", _
254:                                     "WINSPrimaryServer", _
255:                                     Null
...:
264:            DisplayFormattedProperty objWMIAdapterInstance, _
265:                                     "Enable LMHOSTS lookup", _
266:                                     "WINSEnableLMHostsLookup", _
267:                                     Null
268:
269:            Select Case objWMIAdapterInstance.TcpipNetbiosOptions
270:                    Case 0
271:                         DisplayFormattedProperty objWMIAdapterInstance, _
272:                                                  "NETBIOS over TCP/IP", _
273:                                                  "by DHCP", _
274:                                                  Null
275:                    Case 1
276:                         DisplayFormattedProperty objWMIAdapterInstance, _
277:                                                  "NETBIOS over TCP/IP", _
278:                                                  "ENABLED", _
279:                                                  Null
280:                    Case 2
281:                         DisplayFormattedProperty objWMIAdapterInstance, _
282:                                                  "NETBIOS over TCP/IP", _
283:                                                  "DISABLED", _
284:                                                  Null
285:            End Select
286:
287:            ' IP Security ------------------------------------------------------
288:            If objWMIAdapterInstance.IPFilterSecurityEnabled Then
289:               DisplayFormattedProperty objWMIAdapterInstance, _
290:                                        "IP filtering security enabled", _
291:                                        "ENABLED", _
292:                                        Null
...:
305:               DisplayFormattedProperty objWMIAdapterInstance, _
306:                                        "UDP ports allowed", _
307:                                        "IPSecPermitUDPPorts", _
308:                                        Null
```

```
309:                End If
310:              End If
311:              Set objWMIAdapterInstance = Nothing
312:            End If
313:          End If
314:    Next
315:    WScript.Echo
...:
320:    ]]>
321:    </script>
322:  </job>
323:</package>
```

When the script is executed, the output is as follows (the section between lines 17 and 63 is skipped, since it is provided by the *Win32_NetworkProtocol* class examined in section 2.4.7).

```
1:    C:\>"GetNetworkConfiguration (With NetProtocols).wsf" "Compaq NC3121 Fast Ethernet NIC"
2:    Microsoft (R) Windows Script Host Version 5.6
3:    Copyright (C) Microsoft Corporation 1996-2001. All rights reserved.
4:
5:    Adapter name: ......................... Compaq NC3121 Fast Ethernet NIC
6:    Device availability: .................. Running/Full Power
7:    Adapter type: ......................... Ethernet 802.3
8:    Adapter state: ........................ Connected
9:    MAC address is : ...................... 00:08:C7:A9:27:56
10:   Adapter service name: ................. N100
11:   Last reset: ........................... 21-10-2001 12:02:00
12:
13:   *IRQ resource: ........................ 10
14:   Memory address: ....................... 0x40300000-0x40300FFF
15:   Memory address: ....................... 0x40100000-0x401FFFFF
16:   I/O Port: ............................. 0x00002420-0x0000243F
17:
..:
..:
..:
63:
64:   DHCP enabled: ......................... FALSE
65:   IP address(es): ....................... 10.10.10.3 255.0.0.0
66:   IP connection metric: ................. 30
67:   Default Gateway(s) and metric: ........ 10.10.10.254 1
68:   Dead gateway detection enabled: ....... TRUE
69:   DNS registration enabled: ............. FALSE
70:   DNS FULL registration enabled: ........ TRUE
71:   DNS search order: ..................... 10.10.10.3
72:   DNS domain: ........................... LissWare.Net
73:   DNS enabled for WINS resolution: ...... FALSE
74:   WINS scope ID: ........................
75:   Enable LMHOSTS lookup: ................ FALSE
76:   NETBIOS over TCP/IP: .................. ENABLED
77:   IP filtering security enabled: ........ ENABLED
78:   IP permitted protocols: ............... 0
79:   TCP ports allowed: .................... 0
80:   UDP ports allowed: .................... 0
```

Note that for the "IP address" (line 65) and the "Default Gateway and metric" (line 67) properties are displayed on the same line. This piece of code (see Sample 2.11, lines 208 through 211 and lines 216 through 219) takes advantage of the DisplayFormattedProperty() function capabilities (see Sample 1.6, "The **DisplayFormattedPropertyFunction.vbs** function") to display two properties that are usually shown together:

- The IP address and its mask

- The Gateway address and its metric

This allows an output similar to the one obtained with the **IPConfig.Exe** utility.

The previous scripts are able to retrieve information from the real-world manageable entities (such as a network adapter), but at no time do the samples show how to modify the information retrieved. However, the *Win32_NetworkAdapterConfiguration* class exposes an important set of methods that allows the modification of the network adapter configuration. Table 2.7 lists the miscellaneous methods.

Table 2.7   *The Win32_NetworkAdapterConfiguration Methods*

Method name	Description
DisableIPSec	The DisableIPSec method is used to disable IP security on this TCP/IP-enabled network adapter.
EnableDHCP	The EnableDHCP method enables the Dynamic Host Configuration Protocol (DHCP) for service with this network adapter. DHCP allows IP addresses to be dynamic allocated.
EnableDNS	The EnableDNS method enables the Domain Name System (DNS) for service on this TCP/IP-bound network adapter.
EnableIPFilterSec	The EnableIPFilterSec method is used to enable IP security globally across all IP-bound network adapters. With security enabled, the operational security characteristics for any single network adapter can be controlled using the network adapter specific EnableIPSec method.
EnableIPSec	The EnableIPSec method is used to enable IP security on this specific TCP/IP-enabled network adapter. Ports are secured only when the IPFilterSecurityEnabled property is TRUE.
EnableStatic	The EnableStatic method enables static TCP/IP addressing for the target network adapter. As a result, DHCP for this network adapter is disabled.
EnableWINS	The EnableWINS method enables Windows Internet Naming Service (WINS) settings specific to TCP/IP, but independent of the network adapter.
ReleaseDHCPLease	The ReleaseDHCPLease method releases the IP address bound to a specific DHCP enabled network adapter. WARNING: If DHCP is enabled on this local computer system, the option disables TCP/IP on this specific network adapter. Unless you have an alternate path to the target system, that is, another TCP/IP bound network adapter, all TCP/IP communications will be lost.
ReleaseDHCPLeaseAll	The ReleaseDHCPLeaseAll method releases the IP addresses bound to all DHCP enabled network adapters. WARNING: If DHCP is enabled on this local computer system, the option will terminate all DHCP TCP/IP connections. The method returns an integer value that can be interpretted as follows: 0 - Successful completion, no reboot required.
RenewDHCPLease	The RenewDHCPLease method renews the IP address on specific DHCP-enabled network adapters. The lease for the IP address assigned via a DHCP server has an expiration date that the client must renew if it intends to continue use of the assigned IP address.
RenewDHCPLeaseAll	The RenewDHCPLeaseAll method renews the IP addresses on all DHCP-enabled network adapters. The lease for the IP address assigned via a DHCP server has an expiration date that the client must renew if it intends to continue use of the assigned IP address.
SetArpAlwaysSourceRoute	The SetArpAlwaysSourceRoute method is used to set the transmission of ARP queries by the TCP/IP.
SetArpUseEtherSNAP	The SetArpUseEtherSNAP method is used to enable Ethernet packets to use 802.3 SNAP encoding. By default, the stack transmits packets in Digital, Intel, Xerox(DIX) Ethernet format. It will always receive both formats.
SetDatabasePath	The SetDatabasePath method sets the path to the standard Internet database files (HOSTS, LMHOSTS, NETWORKS, PROTOCOLS). It is used by the Windows Sockets interface.

Table 2.7   *The Win32_NetworkAdapterConfiguration Methods (continued)*

Method name	Description
SetDeadGWDetect	The SetDeadGWDetect method is used to enable Dead Gateway detection. Setting this parameter to TRUE causes TCP to perform Dead Gateway Detection. With this feature enabled, TCP asks IP to change to a backup gateway if it retransmits a segment several times without receiving a response.
SetDefaultTOS	The SetDefaultTOS method is used to set the default Type of Service (TOS) value in the header of outgoing IP packets.
SetDefaultTTL	The SetDefaultTTL method is used to set the default Time to Live (TTL) value in the header of outgoing IP packets. The TTL specifies the number of routers an IP packet may pass through to reach its destination before being discarded. Each router decrements the TTL count of a packet by one and discards the packets with a TTL of 0. Default: 32, Valid Range: 1 - 255
SetDNSDomain	The SetDNSDomain method allows for the setting of the DNS domain. This is an instance dependent method call that applies on a per adapter basis. On Windows 2000 the setting applies to the targeted adapter. On NT4 this setting is global.
SetDNSServerSearchOrder	The SetDNSServerSearchOrder method allows for the setting of the server search order as an array of elements. This is an instance dependent method call that applies on a per adapter basis. On Windows 2000 the setting applies to the targeted adapter. On NT4 this setting is global.
SetDNSSuffixSearchOrder	The SetDNSSuffixSearchOrder method allows for the setting of the suffix search order as an array of elements. This is an instance independent method call that applies across all adapters. Windows NT only.
SetDynamicDNSRegistration	The SetDynamicDNSRegistration method is used to indicate dynamic DNS registration of IP addresses for this IP bound adapter.
SetForwardBufferMemory	The SetForwardBufferMemory method is used to specify how much memory IP allocates to store packet data in the router packet queue. When this buffer space is filled, the router begins discarding packets at random from its queue. Packet queue data buffers are 256 bytes in length, so the value of this parameter should be a multiple of 256. Multiple buffers are chained together for larger packets. The IP header for a packet is stored separately. This parameter is ignored and no buffers are allocated if the IP router is not enabled. The buffer size can range from the network MTU to the a value smaller than 0xFFFFFFFF. Default: 74240 (fifty 1480-byte packets, rounded to a multiple of 256).
SetGateways	The SetGateways method is used to specify a list of gateways for routing packets destined for a different subnet than the one this adapter is connected to. A more specific route should not exist for this subnet.
SetIGMPLevel	The SetIGMPLevel method is used to set the extent to which the system supports IP multicasting and participates in the Internet Group Management Protocol.
SetIPConnectionMetric	The SetIPConnectionMetric method is used to set the routing metric associated with this IP bound adapter.
SetIPUseZeroBroadcast	The SetIPUseZeroBroadcast method is used to set IP zero broadcast usage. If this parameter is set to TRUE, then IP will use zeros-broadcasts (0.0.0.0) instead of ones-broadcasts (255.255.255.255). Most systems use ones-broadcasts, but systems derived from BSD implementations use zeros-broadcasts. Systems that use different broadcasts will not interoperate on the same network. Default: FALSE.
SetIPXFrameTypeNetworkPairs	The SetIPXFrameTypeNetworkPairs method is used to set Internetworking Packet Exchange (IPX) network number/frame pairs for this network adapter. Windows 2000 and Windows NT 3.51 and higher use an IPX network number for routing purposes. It is assigned to each configured frame type/network adapter combination on your computer system. This number is sometimes referred to as the "external network number." It must be unique for each network segment. If the frame type is set to AUTO, the network number should to zero.
SetIPXVirtualNetworkNumber	The SetIPXVirtualNetworkNumber method is used to set the Internetworking Packet Exchange (IPX) virtual network number on the target computer system. Windows 2000 and Windows NT 3.51 or greater uses an internal network number for internal routing. The internal network number is also known as a virtual network number. It uniquely identifies the computer system on the network.
SetKeepAliveInterval	The SetKeepAliveInterval method is used to set the interval separating Keep Alive Retransmissions until a response is received. Once a response is received, the delay until the next Keep Alive Transmission is again controlled by the value of KeepAliveTime. The connection will be terminated after the number of retransmissions specified by TcpMaxDataRetransmissions have gone unanswered.
SetKeepAliveTime	The SetKeepAliveTime method is used to set how often TCP attempts to verify that an idle connection is still available by sending a Keep Alive packet. If the remote system is still reachable and functioning, it will acknowledge the Keep Alive transmission. Keep Alive packets are not sent by default. This feature may be enabled in a connection by an application.
SetMTU	The SetMTU method is used to set the default Maximum Transmission Unit (MTU) for a network interface. The MTU is the maximum packet size (in bytes) that the transport will transmit over the underlying network. The size includes the transport header. Note that an IP datagram may span multiple packets. Values larger than the default for the underlying network will result in the transport using the network default MTU. Values smaller than 68 will result in the transport using an MTU of 68.
SetNumForwardPackets	The SetNumForwardPackets method is used to set the number of IP packet headers allocated for the router packet queue. When all headers are in use, the router will begin to discard packets from the queue at random.

Table 2.7   *The Win32_NetworkAdapterConfiguration Methods (continued)*

Method name	Description
SetPMTUBHDetect	The SetPMTUBHDetect method is used to enable detection of Black Hole routers. Setting this parameter to TRUE causes TCP to try to detect Black Hole routers while doing Path MTU Discovery. A Black Hole router does not return the Internet Control Message Protocol (ICMP) Destination Unreachable messages when it needs to fragment an IP datagram with the Don't Fragment bit set. TCP depends on receiving these messages to perform Path MTU Discovery. With this feature enabled, TCP will try to send segments without the Don't Fragment bit set if several retransmissions of a segment go unacknowledged. If the segment is acknowledged as a result, the maximum segment size (MSS) will be decreased and the Don't Fragment bit will be set in future packets on the connection. Enabling Black Hole detection increases the maximum number of retransmissions performed for a given segment.
SetPMTUDiscovery	The SetPMTUDiscovery method is used to enable Maximum Transmission Unit (MTU) discovery. Setting this parameter to TRUE causes TCP to attempt to discover the MTU (or largest packet size) over the path to a remote host. By discovering the Path MTU and limiting TCP segments to this size, TCP can eliminate fragmentation at routers along the path that connect networks with different MTUs. Fragmentation adversely affects TCP throughput and network congestion. Setting this parameter to FALSE causes an MTU of 576 bytes to be used for all connections that are not connected to machines on the local subnet. Default: TRUE.
SetTcpipNetbios	The SetTcpipNetbios method is used to set the default operation of NetBIOS over TCP/IP. Windows 2000 only.
SetTcpMaxConnectRetransmissions	The SetTcpMaxConnectRetransmissions method is used to set the number of attempts TCP will retransmit a Connect Request before aborting. The initial retransmission timeout is 3 seconds and doubles for each attempt.
SetTcpMaxDataRetransmissions	The SetTcpMaxDataRetransmissions method is used to set the number of times TCP will retransmit an individual data segment before aborting the connection. The retransmission timeout doubles with each successive retransmission on a connection.
SetTcpNumConnections	The SetTcpNumConnections method is used to set the maximum number of connections that TCP may have open simultaneously.
SetTcpUseRFC1122UrgentPointer	The SetTcpUseRFC1122UrgentPointer method is used to specify whether TCP uses the RFC 1122 specification for urgent data, or the mode used by Berkeley Software Design (BSD) derived systems. The two mechanisms interpret the urgent pointer in the TCP header and the length of the urgent data differently. They are not interoperable. Windows 2000 and Windows NT version 3.51 or higher defaults to BSD mode.
SetTcpWindowSize	The SetTcpWindowSize method is used to set the maximum TCP Receive Window size offered by the system. The Receive Window specifies the number of bytes a sender can transmit without receiving an acknowledgment. In general, larger receive windows improve performance over high-delay and high-bandwidth networks. For efficiency, the receive window should be an even multiple of the TCP Maximum Segment Size (MSS).
SetWINSServer	The SetWINSServer method sets the primary and secondary Windows Internet Naming Service (WINS) servers on this TCP/IP-bound network adapter. This method is applied independently of the network adapter.

To gather more information about the parameters required by these methods, you can use the **LoadCIMInXL.wsf** script (see Sample 4.32 in the appendix) or refer to the Platform SDK. Because each method corresponds to a network setting, the command-line parameters required by the script represent the parameters required by each *Win32_NetworkAdapterConfiguration* method. Before diving into the script code (see Sample 2.12), let's examine the script parameters. This demonstrates the script capabilities in terms of network device configuration. The following output shows the script usage information with some command-line syntax samples at the end:

```
C:\>SetNetworkConfiguration.wsf
Microsoft (R) Windows Script Host Version 5.6
Copyright (C) Microsoft Corporation 1996-2001. All rights reserved.

Usage: SetNetworkConfiguration.wsf AdapterName
                        [List]
                        [EnableDHCP]
                        [ReleaseDHCPLease]
                        [ReleaseDHCPLeaseAll]
                        [RenewDHCPLease]
```

```
                                    [RenewDHCPLeaseAll]
                                    [EnableStatic]
                                    [SetIPConnectionMetric]
                                    [SetGateways]
                                    [SetDeadGWDetect]
                                    [SetDNSDomain]
                                    [SetDNSServerSearchOrder]
                                    [SetDNSSuffixSearchOrder]
                                    [SetDynamicDNSRegistration]
                                    [EnableWINS]
                                    [SetWINSServer]
                                    [SetTcpipNetbios]
                                    [EnableIPSec]
                                    [DisableIPSec]
                                    [EnableIPsecFilter]
                                    [/Machine:value]
                                    [/User:value]
                                    [/Password:value]
```

```
Options:

AdapterName                : Define the name of the network adapter to configure.
List                       : Only list the adapter names.
EnableDHCP                 : Enable DHCP for the given adapter.
ReleaseDHCPLease           : Release DHCP lease for the given adapter.
ReleaseDHCPLeaseAll        : Release DHCP lease for all adapters.
RenewDHCPLease             : Renew DHCP lease for the given adapter.
RenewDHCPLeaseAll          : Renew DHCP for all adapters.
EnableStatic               : Enable static IP address(es) for the given adapter.
SetIPConnectionMetric      : Set the IP connection metric for the given adapter.
SetGateways                : Set the Gateway IP address(es) for the given adapter.
SetDeadGWDetect            : Set dead gateway detection for the given adapter.
SetDNSDomain               : Set DNS domain for the given adapter.
SetDNSServerSearchOrder    : Set the DNS search order for the given adapter.
SetDNSSuffixSearchOrder    : Set the DNS suffix search order for the given adapter.
SetDynamicDNSRegistration  : Set the Dynamic DNS registration for the given adapter.
EnableWINS                 : Enable WINS for the given adapter.
SetWINSServer              : Set the WINS IP address(es) for the given adapter.
SetTcpipNetbios            : Set NETBIOS over TCP/IP state for the given adapter.
EnableIPSec                : Enable IPsec for all adapters.
DisableIPSec               : Disable IPsec for all adapters.
EnableIPsecFilter          : Enable IPsec filters for all adapters.
Machine                    : determine the WMI system to connect to. (default=LocalHost)
User                       : determine the UserID to perform the remote connection. (default=none)
Password                   : determine the password to perform the remote connection. (default=none)
Examples:


SetNetworkConfiguration.wsf "Compaq NC3121 Fast Ethernet NIC" EnableDHCP
SetNetworkConfiguration.wsf "Compaq NC3121 Fast Ethernet NIC" ReleaseDHCPLease
SetNetworkConfiguration.wsf "Compaq NC3121 Fast Ethernet NIC" ReleaseDHCPLeaseAll
SetNetworkConfiguration.wsf "Compaq NC3121 Fast Ethernet NIC" RenewDHCPLease
SetNetworkConfiguration.wsf "Compaq NC3121 Fast Ethernet NIC" RenewDHCPLeaseAll
SetNetworkConfiguration.wsf "Compaq NC3121 Fast Ethernet NIC"
                           EnableStatic="192.1.1.1/255.255.0.0,193.1.1.2/255.0.0.0"
SetNetworkConfiguration.wsf "Compaq NC3121 Fast Ethernet NIC" SetIPConnectionMetric=98
SetNetworkConfiguration.wsf "Compaq NC3121 Fast Ethernet NIC"
                           SetGateways="192.1.1.1m98,193.1.1.2m97"
SetNetworkConfiguration.wsf "Compaq NC3121 Fast Ethernet NIC" SetDeadGWDetect=True
SetNetworkConfiguration.wsf "Compaq NC3121 Fast Ethernet NIC" SetDNSDomain="LissWare.Net"
SetNetworkConfiguration.wsf "Compaq NC3121 Fast Ethernet NIC"
```

```
                                 SetDNSServerSearchOrder="192.10.10.1,10.10.10.3"
SetNetworkConfiguration.wsf "Compaq NC3121 Fast Ethernet NIC"
                                 SetDNSSuffixSearchOrder="MySub1.LissWare.Net,MySub2.LissWare.Net"
SetNetworkConfiguration.wsf "Compaq NC3121 Fast Ethernet NIC" SetDynamicDNSRegistration="True,True"
SetNetworkConfiguration.wsf "Compaq NC3121 Fast Ethernet NIC"
                                 EnableWINS="True,True,%SystemRoot%\System32\Drivers\Etc\LMHOSTS,"
SetNetworkConfiguration.wsf "Compaq NC3121 Fast Ethernet NIC" SetWINSServer="192.1.1.1,193.1.1.2"
SetNetworkConfiguration.wsf "Compaq NC3121 Fast Ethernet NIC" SetTcpipNetbios=Disable
SetNetworkConfiguration.wsf "Compaq NC3121 Fast Ethernet NIC" EnableIPSec="80;443,53;20;21,0;1"
SetNetworkConfiguration.wsf "Compaq NC3121 Fast Ethernet NIC" DisableIPSec
SetNetworkConfiguration.wsf "Compaq NC3121 Fast Ethernet NIC" EnableIPsecFilter=True
```

The biggest challenge of this script is to properly parse the command line. Sample 2.12 is 492 lines in length, but the command-line parsing easily takes 50 percent of the code (from line 160 through 319). This comes from the fact that the script exposes more than 20 command-line parameters, while some *Win32_NetworkAdapterConfiguration* class methods require one or more arrays as input parameters. On a command line, it is only possible to read strings. To work around this difficulty, Sample 2.12 includes a subroutine called **ConvertStringInArrayFunction.vbs** (line 65) and uses the SplitArrayInTwoArrays() function (lines 456 through 487). These two functions are helper functions to ease the command-line parsing and the string to array conversion required by some of the *Win32_NetworkAdapterConfiguration* class method parameters. Note that the command line only accepts keywords and does not make use of any keywords starting with a backslash. The script code configuring a network adapter is listed in Sample 2.12 (for the command-line parsing) and in Sample 2.13 (for the WMI network adapter configuration).

Sample 2.12   *Configuring a network adapter (Part I)*

```
 1:<?xml version="1.0"?>
 .:
 8:<package>
 9:  <job>
..:
13:     <runtime>
..:
62:     </runtime>
63:
64:     <script language="VBScript" src=".\Functions\DecodeWin32_NetAdapterConfigRCFunction.vbs" />
65:     <script language="VBScript" src=".\Functions\ConvertStringInArrayFunction.vbs" />
66:     <script language="VBScript" src=".\Functions\TinyErrorHandler.vbs" />
67:
68:     <object progid="WbemScripting.SWbemLocator" id="objWMILocator" reference="true"/>
69:     <object progid="WbemScripting.SWbemDateTime" id="objWMIDateTime" />
70:
71:     <script language="VBscript">
72:     <![CDATA[
..:
76:     Const cComputerName = "LocalHost"
77:     Const cWMINameSpace = "root/cimv2"
```

```
 78:    Const cWMIClass = "Win32_NetworkAdapterConfiguration"
...:
158:    ' -----------------------------------------------------------------------------
159:    ' Parse the command line parameters
160:    boolAdapterList = WScript.Arguments.Named("List")
161:    If Len(boolAdapterList) = 0 Then boolAdapterList = False
162:
163:    If (WScript.Arguments.Unnamed.Count = 0 And boolAdapterList = False) Or _
164:       (WScript.Arguments.Unnamed.Count <> 0 And boolAdapterList = True) Then
165:        WScript.Arguments.ShowUsage()
166:        WScript.Quit
167:    Else
168:        If WScript.Arguments.Unnamed.Count Then
169:            strAdapterName = WScript.Arguments.Unnamed.Item(0)
170:        End If
171:    End If
172:
173:    For intUnnamedIndice = 1 To WScript.Arguments.Unnamed.Count - 1
174:        varTemp = ConvertStringInArray (WScript.Arguments.Unnamed(intUnnamedIndice), cEqual)
175:        If Ubound (varTemp) = 0 Then
176:            strOperation = varTemp(0)
177:            strAssignment = ""
178:        Else
179:            strOperation = varTemp(0)
180:            strAssignment = varTemp(1)
181:        End If
182:
183:        Select Case Ucase(strOperation)
184:
185:            ' -----------------------------------------------------------------------------
186:            Case "ENABLEDHCP"
187:                boolEnableDHCP = True
188:            ' -----------------------------------------------------------------------------
189:            Case "RELEASEDHCPLEASE"
190:                boolReleaseDHCPLease = True
191:            ' -----------------------------------------------------------------------------
192:            Case "RELEASEDHCPLEASEALL"
193:                boolReleaseDHCPLeaseAll = True
194:            ' -----------------------------------------------------------------------------
195:            Case "RENEWDHCPLEASE"
196:                boolRenewDHCPLease = True
197:            ' -----------------------------------------------------------------------------
198:            Case "RENEWDHCPLEASEALL"
199:                boolRenewDHCPLeaseAll = True
200:            ' -----------------------------------------------------------------------------
201:            Case "ENABLESTATIC"
202:                If Len(strAssignment) Then
203:                    strAssignment = ConvertStringInArray (strAssignment, cComma)
204:                    SplitArrayInTwoArrays strAssignment, _
205:                                          arrayIPAddresses, _
206:                                          arrayIPMasks, _
207:                                          cSlash
208:                    boolIPAddresses = True
209:                End If
210:            ' -----------------------------------------------------------------------------
211:            Case "SETIPCONNECTIONMETRIC"
212:                If Len(strAssignment) Then
213:                    intIPConnectionMetric = Cint(strAssignment)
214:                    boolIPConnectionMetric = True
215:                End If
```

```
216:                  ' ----------------------------------------------------------------
217:                  Case "SETGATEWAYS"
218:                       If Len(strAssignment) Then
219:                          strAssignment = ConvertStringInArray (strAssignment, cComma)
220:                          SplitArrayInTwoArrays strAssignment, _
221:                                                arrayIPGateways, _
222:                                                arrayIPGatewayMetric, _
223:                                                cMletter
224:                          boolIPGateways = True
225:                       End If
226:                  ' ----------------------------------------------------------------
227:                  Case "SETDEADGWDETECT"
228:                       Select Case Ucase(strAssignment)
229:                             Case "TRUE"
230:                                   boolSetDeadGWDetectValue = True
231:                                   boolSetDeadGWDetect = True
232:                             Case "FALSE"
233:                                   boolSetDeadGWDetectValue = False
234:                                   boolSetDeadGWDetect = True
235:                             Case Else
236:                                   boolSetDeadGWDetect = False
237:                       End Select
238:                  ' ----------------------------------------------------------------
239:                  Case "SETDNSDOMAIN"
240:                       strDNSDomain = strAssignment
241:                       boolDNSDomain = True
242:                  ' ----------------------------------------------------------------
243:                  Case "SETDNSSERVERSEARCHORDER"
244:                       If Len (strAssignment) Then
245:                          arrayDNSServerSearchOrder = ConvertStringInArray (strAssignment, cComma)
246:                          boolDNSServerSearchOrder = True
247:                       End If
248:                  ' ----------------------------------------------------------------
249:                  Case "SETDNSSUFFIXSEARCHORDER"
250:                       arrayDNSSuffixSearchOrder = ConvertStringInArray (strAssignment, cComma)
251:                       boolDNSSuffixSearchOrder = True
252:                  ' ----------------------------------------------------------------
253:                  Case "SETDYNAMICDNSREGISTRATION"
254:                       If Len(strAssignment) Then
255:                          arrayDynamicDNSRegistration = ConvertStringInArray (strAssignment, cComma)
256:                          If Ubound(arrayDynamicDNSRegistration) Then
257:                             boolDynamicDNSRegistration = True
258:                          End If
259:                       End If
260:                  ' ----------------------------------------------------------------
261:                  Case "ENABLEWINS"
262:                       If Len(strAssignment) Then
263:                          arrayEnableWINS = ConvertStringInArray (strAssignment, cComma)
264:                          If Ubound(arrayEnableWINS) Then
265:                             boolEnableWINS = True
266:                          End If
267:                       End If
268:                  ' ----------------------------------------------------------------
269:                  Case "SETWINSSERVER"
270:                       If Len(strAssignment) Then
271:                          arrayWINSServer = ConvertStringInArray (strAssignment, cComma)
272:                       Else
273:                          Redim arrayWINSServer (1)
274:                          arrayWINSServer (0) = ""
275:                          arrayWINSServer (1) = ""
```

```
276:                    End If
277:                    boolWINSServer = True
278:             ' --------------------------------------------------------------------
279:             Case "SETTCPIPNETBIOS"
280:                 Select Case Ucase(strAssignment)
281:                    Case "BYDHCP"
282:                        intTcpipNetbios = 0
283:                        boolTcpipNetbios = True
284:                    Case "ENABLE"
285:                        intTcpipNetbios = 1
286:                        boolTcpipNetbios = True
287:                    Case "DISABLE"
288:                        intTcpipNetbios = 2
289:                        boolTcpipNetbios = True
290:                 End Select
291:             ' --------------------------------------------------------------------
292:             Case "ENABLEIPSEC"
293:                 If Len(strAssignment) Then
294:                     strAssignment = ConvertStringInArray (strAssignment, cComma)
295:                     arrayTCP = ConvertStringInArray (strAssignment(0), cSemiColumn)
296:                     arrayUDP = ConvertStringInArray (strAssignment(1), cSemiColumn)
297:                     arrayIP = ConvertStringInArray (strAssignment(2), cSemiColumn)
298:                     boolEnableIPSec = True
299:                 End If
300:             ' --------------------------------------------------------------------
301:             Case "DISABLEIPSEC"
302:                 boolDisableIPSec = True
303:             ' --------------------------------------------------------------------
304:             Case "ENABLEIPSECFILTER"
305:                 Select Case Ucase(strAssignment)
306:                        Case "TRUE"
307:                             boolEnableIPsecFilterValue = True
308:                             boolEnableIPsecFilter = True
309:                        Case "FALSE"
310:                             boolEnableIPsecFilterValue = False
311:                             boolEnableIPsecFilter = True
312:                        Case Else
313:                             boolEnableIPsecFilter = False
314:                 End Select
315:         End Select
316:     Next
317:
318:     strUserID = WScript.Arguments.Named("User")
319:     If Len(strUserID) = 0 Then strUserID = ""
...:
329:
...:
...:
...:
```

Each command-line parameter corresponds to a *Win32_Network-AdapterConfiguration* method and uses the name of the method. Although it is interesting to look at the code in detail, we do not examine every parameter because Sample 2.12 accepts more than 20 parameters. Once the most typical parameters are explained, all other parameters parsing use the same scripting logic. Moreover, the scripting technique and principles to analyze command-line parameters in the next samples are the same. This allows us to focus on the WMI coding only. For Sample 2.12, we examine the code corresponding to the following command-line parameters:

- EnableDHCP

- ReleaseDHCPLease

- ReleaseDHCPLeaseAll

- RenewDHCPLease

- RenewDHCPLeaseAll

- EnableStatic

- SetIPConnectionMetric

- SetGateways

- SetDeadGWDetect

- EnableIPSec

- DisableIPSec

- EnableIPSecFilter

For each of these parameters, we also examine the corresponding WMI coding shown in Sample 2.13. Before configuring settings on the desired network adapter, an instance of the considered network adapter is retrieved at line 334. At line 335, the script also retrieves an instance from the *Win32_NetworkAdapterConfiguration* class. We will see further during the script code analysis why we need to do this.

Sample 2.13   *Configuring a network adapter (Part II)*

```
...:
...:
...:
329:
330:    Set objWMIServices = objWMILocator.ConnectServer(strComputerName, cWMINameSpace, _
331:                                           strUserID, strPassword)
...:
334:    Set objWMIInstances = objWMIServices.InstancesOf (cWMIClass)
335:    Set objWMIClass = objWMIServices.Get (cWMIClass)
336:
337:    For Each objWMIInstance in objWMIInstances
338:        If boolAdapterList Then
339:            WScript.Echo Mid (objWMIInstance.Caption, 12)
340:        Else
341:            If Mid (objWMIInstance.Caption, 12) = strAdapterName Then
342:                WScript.Echo "Configuring '" & objWMIInstance.Description & _
343:                        "' adapter ..." & vbCRLF
344:
```

```
345:                   If boolEnableDHCP Then
346:                       intRC = objWMIInstance.EnableDHCP ()
347:                       WScript.Echo "EnableDHCP: " & Win32_NetAdapterConfigRC(intRC)
348:                   End If
349:
350:                   If boolReleaseDHCPLease Then
351:                       intRC = objWMIInstance.ReleaseDHCPLease ()
352:                       WScript.Echo "ReleaseDHCPLease: " & Win32_NetAdapterConfigRC(intRC)
353:                   End If
354:
355:                   If boolReleaseDHCPLeaseAll Then
356:                       intRC = objWMIClass.ReleaseDHCPLeaseAll ()
357:                       WScript.Echo "ReleaseDHCPLeaseAll: " & Win32_NetAdapterConfigRC(intRC)
358:                   End If
359:
360:                   If boolRenewDHCPLease Then
361:                       intRC = objWMIInstance.RenewDHCPLease ()
362:                       WScript.Echo "RenewDHCPLease: " & Win32_NetAdapterConfigRC(intRC)
363:                   End If
364:
365:                   If boolRenewDHCPLeaseAll Then
366:                       intRC = objWMIClass.RenewDHCPLeaseAll ()
367:                       WScript.Echo "RenewDHCPLeaseAll: " & Win32_NetAdapterConfigRC(intRC)
368:                   End If
369:
370:                   If boolIPAddresses Then
371:                       intRC = objWMIInstance.EnableStatic (arrayIPAddresses, arrayIPMasks)
372:                       WScript.Echo "EnableStatic: " & Win32_NetAdapterConfigRC(intRC)
373:                   End If
374:
375:                   If boolIPConnectionMetric Then
376:                       intRC = objWMIInstance.SetIPConnectionMetric (intIPConnectionMetric)
377:                       WScript.Echo "SetIPConnectionMetric: " & Win32_NetAdapterConfigRC(intRC)
378:                   End If
379:
380:                   If boolIPGateways Then
381:                       intRC = objWMIInstance.SetGateways (arrayIPGateways, arrayIPGatewayMetric)
382:                       WScript.Echo "SetGateways: " & Win32_NetAdapterConfigRC(intRC)
383:                   End If
384:
385:                   If boolSetDeadGWDetect Then
386:                       intRC = objWMIClass.SetDeadGWDetect (boolSetDeadGWDetectValue)
387:                       WScript.Echo "SetDeadGWDetect: " & Win32_NetAdapterConfigRC(intRC)
388:                   End If
389:
390:                   If boolDNSDomain Then
391:                       intRC = objWMIInstance.SetDNSDomain (strDNSDomain)
392:                       WScript.Echo "SetDNSDomain: " & Win32_NetAdapterConfigRC(intRC)
393:                   End If
394:
395:                   If boolDNSServerSearchOrder Then
396:                       intRC = objWMIInstance.SetDNSServerSearchOrder (arrayDNSServerSearchOrder)
397:                       WScript.Echo "SetDNSServerSearchOrder: " & Win32_NetAdapterConfigRC(intRC)
398:                   End If
399:
400:                   If boolDNSSuffixSearchOrder Then
401:                       intRC = objWMIClass.SetDNSSuffixSearchOrder (arrayDNSSuffixSearchOrder)
402:                       WScript.Echo "SetDNSSuffixSearchOrder: " & Win32_NetAdapterConfigRC(intRC)
403:                   End If
404:
```

```
405:            If boolDynamicDNSRegistration Then
406:                intRC = objWMIInstance.SetDynamicDNSRegistration _
407:                                        (arrayDynamicDNSRegistration (0), _
408:                                         arrayDynamicDNSRegistration(1))
409:                WScript.Echo "SetDynamicDNSRegistration: " & Win32_NetAdapterConfigRC(intRC)
410:            End If
411:
412:            If boolEnableWINS Then
413:                intRC = objWMIClass.EnableWINS (arrayEnableWINS(0), _
414:                                    arrayEnableWINS(1), _
415:                                    arrayEnableWINS(2), _
416:                                    arrayEnableWINS(3))
417:                WScript.Echo "EnableWINS: " & Win32_NetAdapterConfigRC(intRC)
418:            End If
419:
420:            If boolWINSServer Then
421:                intRC = objWMIInstance.SetWINSServer (arrayWINSServer(0), _
422:                                        arrayWINSServer(1))
423:                WScript.Echo "SetWINSServer: " & Win32_NetAdapterConfigRC(intRC)
424:            End If
425:
426:            If boolTcpipNetbios Then
427:                intRC = objWMIInstance.SetTcpipNetbios (intTCPIPNetbios)
428:                WScript.Echo "SetTcpipNetbios: " & Win32_NetAdapterConfigRC(intRC)
429:            End If
430:
431:            If boolEnableIPSec Then
432:                intRC = objWMIInstance.EnableIPSec (arrayTCP, arrayUDP, arrayIP)
433:                WScript.Echo "EnableIPSec: " & Win32_NetAdapterConfigRC(intRC)
434:            End If
435:
436:            If boolDisableIPSec Then
437:                intRC = objWMIInstance.DisableIPSec ()
438:                WScript.Echo "DisableIPSec: " & Win32_NetAdapterConfigRC(intRC)
439:            End If
440:
441:            If boolEnableIPsecFilter Then
442:                intRC = objWMIClass.EnableIPFilterSec (boolEnableIPsecFilterValue)
443:                WScript.Echo "EnableIPFilterSec: " & Win32_NetAdapterConfigRC(intRC)
444:            End If
445:
446:            Set objWMIInstance = Nothing
447:          End If
448:      End If
449:  Next
450:  WScript.Echo
...:
455:  ' --------------------------------------------------------------------------
456:  Function SplitArrayInTwoArrays (varTemp, array1, array2, strSeparator)
...:
487:  End Function
488:
489:  ]]>
490:  </script>
491:  </job>
492:</package>
```

The script code analysis is as follows:

- *EnableDHCP*: Once this keyword is given on the command line, the script configures the adapter as a DHCP client. The keyword presence is tested at line 186 and the DHCP configuration is performed from line 345 through 348. The *Win32_NetworkAdapterConfiguration EnableDHCP* method does not require a parameter (line 346).

- *ReleaseDHCPLease*: From a coding technique point of view, this command-line parameter works the same as the previous one. However, once the keyword is given on the command line, the script releases the adapter DHCP IP address. The keyword presence is tested at line 189 and the DHCP IP address release is performed from line 350 through 353. The *Win32_NetworkAdapterConfiguration ReleaseDHCPLease* method does not require a parameter (line 351).

- *ReleaseDHCPLeaseAll*: Again, from a coding technique point of view, this command-line parameter works the same as the previous ones. However, once the keyword is given, it releases the DHCP address on all network adapters available in the computer. The keyword presence is tested at line 192, and the DHCP IP address release is performed from line 355 through 358. Note that the method invocation is a bit unusual (line 356). Because the *ReleaseDHCPLeaseAll* method does not relate to a specific network adapter (since it releases the IP address of all network adapters in the computer), the method is not invoked from the network adapter instance but from the network adapter class instance (line 356). The network adapter class instance is created at line 335, while the network adapter instance is created at line 334.

All methods that relate to a network setting that is not specific to a network adapter must be invoked from the class instance instead of the network adapter instance. These methods are defined in the CIM repository as static methods and contain a specific qualifier called *static* set on True. This specific qualifier method can be viewed with **WMI CIM Studio**, as shown in Figure 2.3. In this figure, we clearly see that the *ReleaseDHCPLeaseAll* method contains the static qualifier, while the *ReleaseDHCPLease* method does not contain this qualifier.

The same rule applies for the following *Win32_NetworkAdapterConfiguration* methods, since these methods are not specific to an adapter but apply to all adapters available in the system:

- ReleaseDHCPLeaseAll (line 356)

- RenewDHCPLeaseAll (line 366)

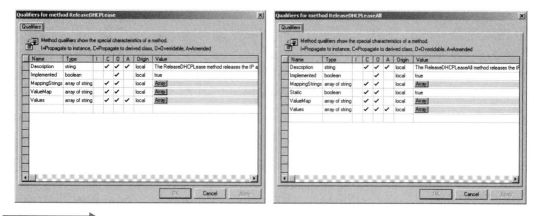

Figure 2.3   *The static method qualifier.*

- SetDeadGWDetect (line 386)

- SetDNSSuffixSearchOrder (line 401)

- EnableWINS (line 413)

- EnableIPFilterSec (line 442)

All these methods are static methods and must be invoked from a class instance. We see with further samples that there are other classes exposing static methods. This is not a peculiarity related to the *Win32_Network-AdapterConfiguration* class only. Classes exposing static methods must all be used in the same way. Let's continue with the remaining methods:

- *ReNewDHCPLease*: The *ReNewDHCPLease* keyword works in the exact same way as the *ReleaseDHCPLease* from a coding point of view. However, it requests a new DHCP IP address. The keyword presence is tested at line 195, and the DHCP renewal operation is performed from line 360 through 363. The *Win32_NetworkAdapterConfiguration ReNewDHCPLease* method does not require any parameter (line 361).

- *ReNewDHCPLeaseAll*: The *ReNewDHCPLeaseAll* keyword is coded in the exact same way as the *ReleaseDHCPLeaseAll*. However, it requests a new DHCP IP address for all DHCP-enabled network adapters. The keyword presence is tested at line 198 and the DHCP renewal operation is performed from line 365 through 368. The *Win32_NetworkAdapterConfiguration* method *ReNewDHCPLease* does not require any parameter (line 366). This method is a static method similar to the *ReleaseDHCPLeaseAll* method and is invoked from the *Win32_NetworkAdapterConfiguration* class instance created at line 335.

- *EnableStatic*: This command-line parameter requires two arrays as parameters. One array contains the IP addresses, while the second array contains the corresponding subnet masks. This keyword with its parameters must be given on the command line in the following format:

```
C:\>SetNetworkConfiguration.wsf "Compaq NC3121 Fast Ethernet NIC"
              EnableStatic="10.10.10.3/255.0.0.0,192.10.10.4/255.255.255.0"
```

  The keyword presence is tested at line 201, and the parameters are parsed and converted in two arrays from line 203 through 207. Note the comma to separate the IP addresses if the network adapter is multihosted. We clearly have a direct application of the ConvertStringInArray() and SplitArrayInTwoArrays() functions to help with the command-line conversion into two arrays (lines 203 and 204). The IP address configuration is performed from line 370 through 373. The *Win32_NetworkAdapterConfiguration* method *EnableStatic* uses the two arrays as parameters (line 371).

- *SetIPConnectionMetric*: This command-line parameter requires one parameter that contains the IP metric of the network adapter. The keyword must be given on the command line in the following format:

```
C:\>SetNetworkConfiguration.wsf "Compaq NC3121 Fast Ethernet NIC"
              SetIPConnectionMetric=0
```

  The keyword presence is tested at line 211, and the parameter value is parsed and converted to an integer from line 212 through 215. The metric configuration is performed from line 375 through 378.

- *SetGateways*: This command-line parameter requires two arrays as parameters. One array contains the gateway IP addresses, while the second array contains the corresponding gateway metrics. The keyword must be given on the command line in the following format:

```
C:\>SetNetworkConfiguration.wsf "Compaq NC3121 Fast Ethernet NIC"
              SetGateways="10.10.10.254m1,192.10.10.254m1"
```

  The keyword presence is tested at line 217, and the parameters are parsed and converted in two arrays from line 218 through 225. Note the "m" letter to separate the metric from the IP gateway address and the comma to separate the gateway IP addresses if several gateways are specified. Again, we clearly see the use of the ConvertStringInArray() and SplitArrayInTwoArrays() functions to help with the command-line conversion into two arrays (lines 219 through 220). The IP address configuration is performed from line 380 through 383. The

Win32_NetworkAdapterConfiguration method *SetGateways* uses the two created arrays as parameters (line 381).

- *SetDeadGWDetect*: This command-line parameter requires one parameter, which contains a Boolean value, to determine if the dead gateway detection mechanism must be enabled or disabled. The key-word must be given on the command line in the following format:

```
C:\>SetNetworkConfiguration.wsf "Compaq NC3121 Fast Ethernet NIC"
SetDeadGWDetect=True
```

The keyword presence is tested at line 227 and the parameter value is parsed from line 228 through 237. The dead gateway detection configuration is performed from line 385 through 388. Note the use of the static method, since the dead gateway detection mechanism does not relate to a specific network adapter.

- *EnableIPSec, DisableIPSec*, and *EnableIPSecFilter*: It is important to note that these methods are used to configure the IP filtering parameters of the network adapter. Therefore, these methods have no relationship with the configuration of the IPSec protocol, which is totally different. Usually, two of these three command-line parameters are used together. The *EnableIPSec* requires one parameter that contains three arrays. These arrays contain the IP port numbers to be filtered in the TCP/IP configuration. Setting the IP port numbers is not enough to activate the IP filtering. The IP filters are only enabled if the *EnableIPSecFilter* command-line parameter is specified. The *EnableIPSecFilter* accepts one parameter that contains a Boolean value to enable or disable the IP filters. The keywords must be given on the command line in the following format:

```
SetNetworkConfiguration.wsf "Compaq NC3121 Fast Ethernet NIC"
                    EnableIPSec="80;443,53;20;21,0;1"
                    EnableIPsecFilter=True
```

To parse the *EnableIPSec* parameters, the ConvertStringInArray() functions is used (lines 294 through 297). Notice that each array is separated on the command line by a comma (line 294), while a semicolumn separates each item in the array (lines 295 through 297). Each array corresponds to the TCP ports, UDP ports, and protocol filters, respectively. The execution of the *EnableIPSec* method is made in the script at the level of the adapter instance (line 432), while the *EnableIPsecFilter* static method is executed at the level of the *Win32_NetworkAdapterConfiguration* class instance (line 442). This implies that the activation of the IP filters is applied to any existing adapters in the system, while the IP filters are specific to one selected network adapter.

To disable the IP filters, the *EnableIPSecFilter* method is used with a Boolean parameter equal to False. To clear the IP filter values, the *DisableIPSec* command-line parameter is required. This parameter does not need any parameter, and its use is similar to the use of the *ReleaseDHCPLeaseAll* or *ReNewDHCPLeaseAll* command-line parameters. The keywords must be given on the command line in the following format:

```
SetNetworkConfiguration.wsf "Compaq NC3121 Fast Ethernet NIC"
                            DisableIPSec
                            EnableIPsecFilter=False
```

All other parameters and methods from the *Win32_NetworkAdapterConfiguration* use the same logic and the same set of routines to parse and execute the command-line parameters. Some small changes in the command-line syntax are required based on the IP parameter specified. The following command-line sample shows how to use Sample 2.12 to completely configure a network adapter IP address. The sample also contains the resulting output:

```
C:\>SetNetworkConfiguration.wsf "Compaq NC3121 Fast Ethernet NIC"
                            EnableStatic:"10.10.10.3/255.0.0.0"
                            SetIPConnectionMetric=0
                            SetGateways:"10.10.10.254m1"
                            SetDeadGWDetect=True
                            SetDNSDomain:"LissWare.Net"
                            SetDNSServerSearchOrder:"10.10.10.3"
                            SetDNSSuffixSearchOrder:""
                            EnableWINS:"False,False,,"
                            SetTcpipNetbios=Enable
                            DisableIPSec

Microsoft (R) Windows Script Host Version 5.6
Copyright (C) Microsoft Corporation 1996-2001. All rights reserved.

Configuring 'Compaq NC3121 Fast Ethernet NIC' adapter ...

EnableStatic: The method succeeded.
SetIPConnectionMetric: The method succeeded.
SetGateways: The method succeeded.
SetDeadGWDetect: The method completed successfully. However, the system must be
rebooted.
SetDNSDomain: The method succeeded.
SetDNSServerSearchOrder: The method succeeded.
SetDNSSuffixSearchOrder: The method succeeded.
EnableWINS: The method succeeded.
SetTcpipNetbios: The method succeeded.
DisableIPSec: The method completed successfully. However, the system must be
rebooted.
```

As we can see, it is also possible to specify several command-line parameters at the same time. This forces the script to execute the various *Win32_NetworkAdapterConfiguration* methods one by one.

2.3.5   **Power device classes**

The power device classes represent power supplies and batteries related to these devices. The classes in this category are listed in Table 2.8.

Table 2.8   *The Power Device Classes*

Name	Type	Description
Win32_PowerManagementEvent	Extrinsic event	Represents power management events resulting from power state changes.
Win32_Battery	Dynamic	Represents a battery connected to the computer system.
Win32_CurrentProbe	Dynamic	Represents the properties of a current monitoring sensor (ammeter).
Win32_PortableBattery	Dynamic	Represents the properties of a portable battery, such as one used for a notebook computer.
Win32_UninterruptiblePowerSupply	Dynamic	Represents the capabilities and management capacity of an uninterruptible power supply (UPS).
Win32_VoltageProbe	Dynamic	Represents the properties of a voltage sensor (electronic voltmeter).
Win32_AssociatedBattery	Association	Relates a logical device and the battery it is using.

It is important to make a clear distinction between the *Win32_Power-ManagementEvent* class and other classes. Although the *Win32_PowerMan-agementEvent* class is also related to power management aspects, this class is an extrinsic event class and relates to the *MS_Power_Management_Event_provider* event provider. Because this class requires the examination of another WMI provider, we examine it further in the next chapter when looking at the *MS_Power_Management_Event_provider* event provider.

Sample 2.14 retrieves information about the batteries available in a computer.

Sample 2.14   *Retrieving battery information*

```
1:<?xml version="1.0"?>
.:
8:<package>
9:  <job>
..:
13:    <runtime>
14:      <unnamed name="Portable" helpstring="Examine portable battery properties."
                            required="false" type="boolean" />
15:      <named name="Machine" helpstring="determine the WMI system to connect to.
                             (default=LocalHost)" required="false" type="string"/>
16:      <named name="User" helpstring="determine the UserID to perform the remote connection.
                             (default=none)" required="false" type="string"/>
17:      <named name="Password" helpstring="determine the password to perform the remote
                             connection. (default=none)" required="false" type="string"/>
18:    </runtime>
19:
20:    <script language="VBScript" src=".\Functions\DecodeDeviceAvailabilityFunction.vbs" />
21:    <script language="VBScript" src=".\Functions\DecodeCfgManErrCodeFunction.vbs" />
22:    <script language="VBScript" src=".\Functions\DecodeStatusInfoFunction.vbs" />
23:    <script language="VBScript" src=".\Functions\DecodePwrManCapabilitiesFunction.vbs" />
```

```
 24:
 25:     <script language="VBScript" src=".\Functions\DecodeBatteryStatusFunction.vbs" />
 26:     <script language="VBScript" src=".\Functions\DecodeBatteryChemistryFunction.vbs" />
 27:
 28:     <script language="VBScript" src=".\Functions\DisplayFormattedPropertyFunction.vbs" />
 29:     <script language="VBScript" src=".\Functions\TinyErrorHandler.vbs" />
 30:
 31:     <object progid="WbemScripting.SWbemLocator" id="objWMILocator" reference="true"/>
 32:     <object progid="WbemScripting.SWbemDateTime" id="objWMIDateTime" />
 33:
 34:     <script language="VBscript">
 35:     <![CDATA[
 ..:
 53:     ' -------------------------------------------------------------------------------
 54:     ' Parse the command line parameters
 55:     boolPortableBattery = WScript.Arguments.Named("Portable")
 56:     If Len(boolPortableBattery) = 0 Then boolPortableBattery = False
 ..:
 65:     If Len(strComputerName) = 0 Then strComputerName = cComputerName
 66:
 67:     objWMILocator.Security_.AuthenticationLevel = wbemAuthenticationLevelDefault
 68:     objWMILocator.Security_.ImpersonationLevel = wbemImpersonationLevelImpersonate
 69:
 70:     Set objWMIServices = objWMILocator.ConnectServer(strComputerName, cWMINameSpace, _
 71:                                    *                            strUserID, strPassword)
 ..:
 74:     Select Case boolPortableBattery
 75:         Case TRUE
 76:             Set objWMIInstances = objWMIServices.InstancesOf ("Win32_PortableBattery")
 77:         Case FALSE
 78:             Set objWMIInstances = objWMIServices.InstancesOf ("Win32_Battery")
 79:     End Select
 ..:
 82:     If objWMIInstances.Count Then
 83:        For Each objWMIInstance In objWMIInstances
 84:            DisplayFormattedProperty objWMIInstance, _
 85:                                    "Availability", _
 86:                                    DeviceAvailability (objWMIInstance.Availability), _
 87:                                    Null
 88:
 89:            If boolPortableBattery = False Then
 90:               DisplayFormattedProperty objWMIInstance, _
 91:                                        "Recharge time (min)", _
 92:                                        "BatteryRechargeTime", _
 93:                                        Null
 94:            End If
 95:
 96:            DisplayFormattedProperty objWMIInstance, _
 97:                                    "Battery status", _
 98:                                    BatteryStatus (objWMIInstance.BatteryStatus), _
 99:                                    Null
100:
101:            If boolPortableBattery = True Then
102:               DisplayFormattedProperty objWMIInstance, _
103:                                        "Capacity multiplier", _
104:                                        "CapacityMultiplier", _
105:                                        Null
106:            End If
107:
108:            DisplayFormattedProperty objWMIInstance, _
```

```
109:                                     "Chemistry", _
110:                                     BatteryChemistry (objWMIInstance.Chemistry), _
111:                                     Null
...:
148:          DisplayFormattedProperty objWMIInstance, _
149:                                    "Estimated run-time (min)", _
150:                                    "EstimatedRunTime", _
151:                                    Null
152:
153:          If boolPortableBattery = False Then
154:             DisplayFormattedProperty objWMIInstance, _
155:                                       "Expected battery life", _
156:                                       "ExpectedBatteryLife", _
157:                                       Null
158:          End If
159:
160:          DisplayFormattedProperty objWMIInstance, _
161:                                    "Expected life", _
162:                                    "ExpectedLife", _
163:                                    Null
...:
177:          If boolPortableBattery = True Then
178:             DisplayFormattedProperty objWMIInstance, _
179:                                       "Location", _
180:                                       "Location", _
181:                                       Null
...:
190:             DisplayFormattedProperty objWMIInstance, _
191:                                       "Max. battery error", _
192:                                       "MaxBatteryError", _
193:                                       Null
194:          End If
195:
196:          DisplayFormattedProperty objWMIInstance, _
197:                                    "Max. recharge time (min)", _
198:                                    "MaxRechargeTime", _
199:                                    Null
...:
224:          DisplayFormattedProperty objWMIInstance, _
225:                                    "Time to fullcharge (min)", _
226:                                    "TimeToFullCharge", _
227:                                    Null
228:       Next
229:    Else
230:       WScript.Echo "No information available."
231:    End If
...:
236:    ]]>
237:    </script>
238:  </job>
239:</package>
```

The script retrieves information about the battery and lists its properties. Besides listing the various properties, the script uses some external functions to convert the information to a suitable display format (lines 20 through 26). If specific information related to a laptop battery must be retrieved, the script accepts the **/Portable+** switch (lines 14, 55, and 56).

Once executed, the script displays the following information:

```
 1:   C:\>GetBatteryInformation.wsf /Machine:MyPortable.LissWare.Net
 2:   Microsoft (R) Windows Script Host Version 5.6
 3:   Copyright (C) Microsoft Corporation 1996-2001. All rights reserved.
 4:
 5:   Availability: .......................... Running/Full Power
 6:   Battery status: ........................ Fully Charged
 7:   Chemistry: ............................. Lithium-ion
 8:   Description: ........................... Portable Battery
 9:   Design capacity (milliwatt-hours): ..... 2700
10:   Design voltage (millivolts): ........... 14400
11:   *Device ID: ............................ Internal Battery
12:   Estimated charge remaining (%): ........ 100
13:   Status: ................................ OK
```

If executed with a laptop, the script displays the following information:

```
 1:   C:\>GetBatteryInformation.wsf /Machine:MyPortable.LissWare.Net /Portable+
 2:   Microsoft (R) Windows Script Host Version 5.6
 3:   Copyright (C) Microsoft Corporation 1996-2001. All rights reserved.
 4:
 5:   Availability: .......................... Running/Full Power
 6:   Battery status: ........................ Fully Charged
 7:   Capacity multiplier: ................... 1
 8:   Chemistry: ............................. Lithium-ion
 9:   Description: ........................... Portable Battery
10:   Design capacity (milliwatt-hours): ..... 2700
11:   Design voltage (millivolts): ........... 14400
12:   *Device ID: ............................ Internal Battery
13:   Estimated charge remaining (%): ........ 100
14:   Location: .............................. Left Hand Side
15:   Manufacturer: .......................... Compaq
16:   Manufacture date: ...................... 20001202010000.000000+060
17:   Max. battery error: .................... 0
18:   Status: ................................ OK
```

2.3.6   Modem device classes

The classes under this category represent the services and the characteristics of a Plain Old Telephone Service (POTS). This includes the plain old telephone modem devices with the associated serial port (see Figure 2.4).

Figure 2.4
*The Win32_*
POTSModem class
associations.

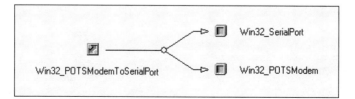

The classes available in this category are listed in Table 2.9.

Table 2.9   *The Telephony Classes*

Name	Type	Description
Win32_POTSModem	Dynamic	Represents the services and characteristics of a Plain Old Telephone Service (POTS) modem on a Windows system.
Win32_POTSModemToSerialPort	Association	Relates a modem and the serial port the modem uses.

Instead of simply listing the properties of the *Win32_POTSModem* class line by line (as in Sample 2.14), we optimize the properties enumeration. The purpose is to make the coding shorter and the logic more generic while maintaining the capability to display some properties in a converted format. Sample 2.15 contains the script code listing.

Sample 2.15   *Retrieving modem information*

```
 1:<?xml version="1.0"?>
 .:
 8:<package>
 9:  <job>
..:
13:    <runtime>
14:      <named name="Machine" helpstring="determine the WMI system to connect to.
                 (default=LocalHost)" required="false" type="string"/>
15:      <named name="User" helpstring="determine the UserID to perform the remote connection.
                 (default=none)" required="false" type="string"/>
16:      <named name="Password" helpstring="determine the password to perform the remote
                 connection. (default=none)" required="false" type="string"/>
17:    </runtime>
18:
19:    <script language="VBScript" src=".\Functions\DecodeDeviceAvailabilityFunction.vbs" />
20:    <script language="VBScript" src=".\Functions\DecodeCfgManErrCodeFunction.vbs" />
21:    <script language="VBScript" src=".\Functions\DecodeStatusInfoFunction.vbs" />
22:    <script language="VBScript" src=".\Functions\DecodePwrManCapabilitiesFunction.vbs" />
23:
24:    <script language="VBScript" src=".\Functions\ConvertArrayInOneStringFunction.vbs" />
25:    <script language="VBScript" src=".\Functions\DisplayFormattedPropertyFunction.vbs" />
26:    <script language="VBScript" src=".\Functions\TinyErrorHandler.vbs" />
27:
28:    <object progid="WbemScripting.SWbemLocator" id="objWMILocator" reference="true"/>
29:    <object progid="WbemScripting.SWbemDateTime" id="objWMIDateTime" />
30:
31:    <script language="VBscript">
32:    <![CDATA[
..:
36:    Const cComputerName = "LocalHost"
37:    Const cWMINameSpace = "root/cimv2"
38:    Const cWMIPOTSModemClass = "Win32_POTSModem"
..:
51:    ' -------------------------------------------------------------------------
52:    ' Parse the command line parameters
53:    strUserID = WScript.Arguments.Named("User")
54:    If Len(strUserID) = 0 Then strUserID = ""
55:
56:    strPassword = WScript.Arguments.Named("Password")
57:    If Len(strPassword) = 0 Then strPassword = ""
```

```
 58:
 59:     strComputerName = WScript.Arguments.Named("Machine")
 60:     If Len(strComputerName) = 0 Then strComputerName = cComputerName
 61:
 62:     objWMILocator.Security_.AuthenticationLevel = wbemAuthenticationLevelDefault
 63:     objWMILocator.Security_.ImpersonationLevel = wbemImpersonationLevelImpersonate
 64:
 65:     Set objWMIServices = objWMILocator.ConnectServer(strComputerName, cWMINameSpace, _
 66:                                                   strUserID, strPassword)
 ..:
 69:     Set objWMIInstances = objWMIServices.InstancesOf (cWMIPOTSModemClass)
 ..:
 72:     If objWMIInstances.Count Then
 73:         For Each objWMIInstance In objWMIInstances
 74:             Set objWMIPropertySet = objWMIInstance.Properties_
 75:             For Each objWMIProperty In objWMIPropertySet
 76:                 Select Case objWMIProperty.Name
 77:                     Case "Availability"
 78:                         DisplayFormattedProperty objWMIInstance, _
 79:                             objWMIProperty.Name, _
 80:                             DeviceAvailability (objWMIInstance.Availability), _
 81:                             Null
 82:                     Case "ConfigManagerErrorCode"
 83:                         DisplayFormattedProperty objWMIInstance, _
 84:                             objWMIProperty.Name, _
 85:                             CfgManErrCode (objWMIInstance.ConfigManagerErrorCode), _
 86:                                             Null
 87:                     Case "ConfigManagerUserConfig"
 88:                         DisplayFormattedProperty objWMIInstance, _
 89:                             objWMIProperty.Name, _
 90:                             UCase (objWMIInstance.ConfigManagerUserConfig), _
 91:                             Null
 92:                     Case "PowerManagementCapabilities"
 93:                         DisplayFormattedProperty objWMIInstance, _
 94:                             objWMIProperty.Name, _
 95:                             PwrManCapabilities (objWMIInstance.PowerMan...abilities), _
 96:                             Null
 97:                     Case "StatusInfo"
 98:                         DisplayFormattedProperty objWMIInstance, _
 99:                             objWMIProperty.Name, _
100:                             StatusInfo (objWMIInstance.StatusInfo), _
101:                             Null
102:                     Case "DCB"
103:                         DisplayFormattedProperty objWMIInstance, _
104:                             objWMIProperty.Name, _
105:                             ConvertArrayInOneString (objWMIInstance.DCB, ","), _
106:                             Null
107:                     Case "Default"
108:                         DisplayFormattedProperty objWMIInstance, _
109:                             objWMIProperty.Name, _
110:                             ConvertArrayInOneString (objWMIInstance.Default, ","), _
111:                             Null
112:                     Case "Properties"
113:                         DisplayFormattedProperty objWMIInstance, _
114:                             objWMIProperty.Name, _
115:                             ConvertArrayInOneString (objWMIInstance.Properties, ","), _
116:                             Null
117:                     Case "CreationClassName"
118:
119:                     Case "SystemCreationClassName"
120:
121:                     Case "SystemName"
122:
```

```
123:                    Case "Caption"
124:
125:                    Case "Name"
126:
127:                Case Else
128:                    DisplayFormattedProperty objWMIInstance, _
129:                        objWMIProperty.Name, _
130:                        objWMIProperty.Name, _
131:                        Null
132:            End Select
133:        Next
134:        Set objWMIPropertySet = Nothing
135:
136:        Set objWMIResourceInstances = objWMIServices.ExecQuery _
137:                        ("Associators of {" & cWMIPOTSModemClass & "='" &
138:                        objWMIInstance.DeviceID & _
139:                        "'} Where AssocClass=Win32_AllocatedResource")
140:
141:        If objWMIResourceInstances.Count Then
142:            WScript.Echo
143:            For Each objWMIResourceInstance In objWMIResourceInstances
144:                Select Case objWMIResourceInstance.Path_.Class
145:                    Case "Win32_IRQResource"
146:                        DisplayFormattedProperty objWMIResourceInstance, _
147:                            "IRQ resource", _
148:                            "IRQNumber", _
149:                            Null
150:                    Case "Win32_DMAChannel"
151:                        DisplayFormattedProperty objWMIResourceInstance, _
152:                            "DMA channel", _
153:                            "DMAChannel", _
154:                            Null
155:                    Case "Win32_PortResource"
156:                        DisplayFormattedProperty objWMIResourceInstance, _
157:                            "I/O Port", _
158:                            "Caption", _
159:                            Null
160:                    Case "Win32_DeviceMemoryAddress"
161:                        DisplayFormattedProperty objWMIResourceInstance, _
162:                            "Memory address", _
163:                            "Caption", _
164:                            Null
165:                End Select
166:            Next
167:        End If
168:        WScript.Echo
169:    Next
170:    Else
171:        WScript.Echo "No information available."
172:    End If
...:
177:    ]]>
178:    </script>
179: </job>
180:</package>
```

As usual, the script starts by defining and parsing the command-line parameters (lines 13 through 17 and 53 through 60). Once the WMI connection is established (lines 65 and 66), the script retrieves the instances of the *Win32_POTSModem* class (line 69). Next, and this where the new logic starts, instead of coding the property list one by one, the script enumerates all properties available from the instance (lines 75 through 133). The peculiarity is in the **Select Case** statement (lines 76 through 132), where the property name is tested. If the property must be displayed with a specific label, format, or converted value, or if the property must be skipped, the **Select Case** statement evaluates the property name and proceeds accordingly. Lines 77 through 116 display the properties that must be displayed with a specific label, format, or converted value, while lines 117 through 126 skip the properties. The default **Select Case** statement displays the property with its property name (lines 128 through 131). As a result, the following output is obtained when examining a Compaq Armada M700 internal modem device:

```
 1:   C:\>GetPOTSModemInformation.wsf /Machine:MyPortable.LissWare.Net
 2:   Microsoft (R) Windows Script Host Version 5.6
 3:   Copyright (C) Microsoft Corporation 1996-2001. All rights reserved.
 4:
 5:   AttachedTo: ............................ COM4
 6:   BlindOff: .............................. X4
 7:   BlindOn: ............................... X3
 8:   CompressionOff: ........................ %C0
 9:   CompressionOn: ......................... %C1
10:   ConfigManagerErrorCode: ................ This device is working properly.
11:   ConfigManagerUserConfig: ............... FALSE
12:   ConfigurationDialog: ................... modemui.dll
13:   CountrySelected: ....................... Belgium
14:   DCB: ................................... 28,0,0,0,0,194,1,0,21,32,0,0,0,0
15:   Default: ............................... 60,0,0,0,15,0,0,0,2,0
16:   Description: ........................... Compaq 56K (V.90) Mini PCI
17:   *DeviceID: ............................. PCI\VEN_11C1&DEV_04&SUBSYS_2086&REV_00\3&601&0&49
18:   DeviceType: ............................ Internal Modem
19:   DriverDate: ............................ 20000301******.******+***
20:   ErrorControlForced: .................... \N4
21:   ErrorControlOff: ....................... \N1
22:   ErrorControlOn: ........................ \N3
23:   FlowControlHard: ....................... &K3
24:   FlowControlOff: ........................ &K0
25:   FlowControlSoft: ....................... &K4
26:   InactivityScale: ....................... "3c000000"
27:   InactivityTimeout: ..................... 0
28:   Index: ................................. 0
29:   MaxBaudRateToPhone: .................... 56000
30:   MaxBaudRateToSerialPort: ............... 115200
31:   Model: ................................. Compaq 56K (V.90) Mini PCI
32:   ModemInfPath: .......................... oem5.inf
33:   ModemInfSection: ....................... Modem_PCI_DF
34:   ModulationBell: ........................ B1B16B2
35:   ModulationCCITT: ....................... B0B15B2
36:   PNPDeviceID: ........................... PCI\VEN_11C1&DEV_04&SUBSYS_2086&REV_00\3&601&0&49
37:   PortSubClass: .......................... "02"
38:   PowerManagementSupported: .............. FALSE
39:   Prefix: ................................ AT
40:   Properties: ............................ 192,1,0,0,255,0,0,0,255,0,0,0,7,0,0,0
41:   ProviderName: .......................... Lucent
42:   Pulse: ................................. P
```

```
43:   Reset: ............................ AT&F<cr>
44:   ResponsesKeyName: ................. Compaq 56K (V.90) Mini PCI::Lucent::Lucent
45:   SpeakerModeDial: .................. M1
46:   SpeakerModeOff: ................... M0
47:   SpeakerModeOn: .................... M2
48:   SpeakerModeSetup: ................. M3
49:   SpeakerVolumeHigh: ................ L3
50:   SpeakerVolumeLow: ................. L0
51:   SpeakerVolumeMed: ................. L2
52:   Status: ........................... OK
53:   StatusInfo: ....................... Enabled
54:   StringFormat: ..................... UNICODE string format
55:   Terminator: ....................... <cr>
56:   Tone: ............................. T
57:
58:   *IRQ resource: .................... 11
59:   Memory address: ................... 0x41300000-0x41300FFF
60:   I/O Port: ......................... 0x00003440-0x00003447
```

Since some properties contain arrays (*DCB* at line 103, *Default* at line 107, and *Properties* at line 112), we see an application of ConvertArrayIn-String() function. This function is the complementary function of the ConvertStringInArray() function developed for Sample 2.12 ("Configuring a network adapter").

Apart from this new way of enumerating and displaying the instance properties, there is no further commenting required regarding the POTS classes and this script sample.

2.3.7 Printing device classes

The printing category classes represent printers, printer configurations, and print jobs. The classes in this category are listed in Table 2.10.

Table 2.10   *The Printing Device Classes*

Name	Type	Description
Win32_Printer	Dynamic	Represents a device connected to a Windows computer system that is capable of reproducing a visual image on a medium.
Win32_PrinterConfiguration	Dynamic	Defines the configuration for a printer device.
Win32_PrinterController	Dynamic	Relates a printer and the local device to which the printer is connected.
Win32_PrinterDriver	Dynamic	Represents the drivers for a Win32_Printer Dynamic.
Win32_PrintJob	Dynamic	Represents a print job generated by a Windows application.
Win32_TCPIPPrinterPort	Dynamic	The Win32_TCPIPPrinterPort class represents a TCP//IP service access point, for example, a TCP/IP printer port.
Win32_DriverForDevice	Association	Relates a printer to a printer driver.
Win32_PrinterDriverDll	Association	Relates a local printer and its driver file (not the driver itself).
Win32_PrinterSetting	Association	Relates a printer and its configuration settings.

Instead of simply retrieving information about printers with their print jobs, it would be useful to perform some specific tasks. We should note that the *Win32_Printer* class has some interesting associations to exploit when searching for printer information (see Figure 2.5).

Figure 2.5
*The Win32_*
Printer class
associations.

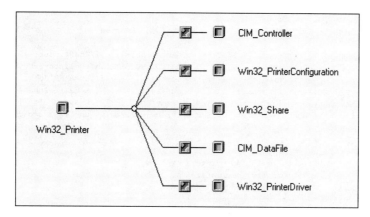

To configure printers, each task corresponds to a WMI class usage. The tasks and their related WMI classes are as follows:

- **Adding a printer driver:** requires the *Win32_PrinterDriver* class usage with its *AddPrinterDriver* method.

- **Adding a new printer:** requires the creation of a new instance with the *Win32_Printer* class.

- **Creating a new printer connection:** requires the *Win32_Printer* class usage with its *AddPrinterConnection* method.

- **Removing a printer:** requires the deletion of the *Win32_Printer* instance representing the printer.

- **Removing a printer driver:** requires the deletion of the *Win32_PrinterDriver* instance representing the printer driver.

- **Pausing and resuming a printer:** requires the *Win32_Printer* class usage with its *Pause* method or *Resume* method.

- **Pausing and resuming a job:** requires the *Win32_Printer*Job class usage with its *Pause* method or *Resume* method.

- **Canceling a job:** requires the deletion of the *Win32_Printer*Job instance representing the print job.

- **Canceling all jobs:** requires the *Win32_Printer* class usage with its *CancelAllJobs* method.

To support these operations, the script exposes a lot of command-line parameters. The command-line parameters displayed by the script are as follows:

```
C:\>WMIPrinters.Wsf
Microsoft (R) Windows Script Host Version 5.6
Copyright (C) Microsoft Corporation 1996-2001. All rights reserved.

Usage: WMIPrinters.wsf [/List:Value] [/AddPrinterConnection[+|-]] [/AddPrinter[+|-]]
                       [/DelPrinter[+|-]] [/AddPrinterDriver[+|-]] [/DelPrinterDriver[+|-]]
                       [/PrinterName[+|-]] [/PrintTestPage[+|-]] [/CancelAllJobs[+|-]]
                       [/PausePrinter[+|-]] [/ResumePrinter[+|-]] [/RenamePrinter[+|-]]
                       [/SetDefaultPrinter[+|-]] [/PauseJob[+|-]] [/ResumeJob[+|-]]
                       [/CancelJob[+|-]] [/Machine:value] [/User:value] [/Password:value]


Options:

List                  : List the existing printers or jobs.
                        Only [Drivers], [Printers] or [Jobs] are accepted.
AddPrinterConnection  : Add a printer connection.
AddPrinter            : Add a printer.
DelPrinter            : Remove a printer or a printer connection.
AddPrinterDriver      : Add a printer driver.
DelPrinterDriver      : Remove a printer driver.
PrinterName           : Printer name to work with.
PrintTestPage         : Print a test page.
CancelAllJobs         : Cancel all jobs in the printer.
PausePrinter          : Pause the printer.
ResumePrinter         : Resume the printer.
RenamePrinter         : Rename the printer.
SetDefaultPrinter     : Set the printer as the default printer.
PauseJob              : Pause a specific job.
ResumeJob             : Resume a specific job.
CancelJob             : Cancel a specific job.
Machine               : Determine the WMI system to connect to. (default=LocalHost)
User                  : Determine the UserID to perform the remote connection. (default=none)
Password              : Determine the password to perform the remote connection. (default=none)
Examples:

     WMIPrinters.Wsf /List:Drivers
     WMIPrinters.Wsf /List:Printers
     WMIPrinters.Wsf /List:Jobs

     WMIPrinters.Wsf /PrinterDriverName:"HP LaserJet 5" /AddPrinterDriver+
     WMIPrinters.Wsf /PrinterDriverName:"HP LaserJet 5" /DelPrinterDriver+

     WMIPrinters.Wsf /PrinterName:"My Printer" /PrinterDriverName:"HP LaserJet 5" /AddPrinter+
     WMIPrinters.Wsf /PrinterName:"My Printer" /DelPrinter+

     WMIPrinters.Wsf /PrinterName:\\MyServer\MyPrinter /AddPrinterConnection+
     WMIPrinters.Wsf /PrinterName:\\MyServer\MyPrinter /DelPrinter+

     WMIPrinters.Wsf /PrinterName:"MyPrinter" /PrintTestPage+
     WMIPrinters.Wsf /PrinterName:\\MyServer\MyPrinter /CancelAllJobs+
     WMIPrinters.Wsf /PrinterName:"MyPrinter" /PausePrinter+
     WMIPrinters.Wsf /PrinterName:"MyPrinter" /ResumePrinter+
     WMIPrinters.Wsf /PrinterName:\\MyServer\MyPrinter /SetDefaultPrinter+
     WMIPrinters.Wsf /PrinterName:\\MyServer\MyPrinter /RenamePrinter:NewPrinterName
     WMIPrinters.Wsf /PrinterName:\\MyServer\MyPrinter /PauseJob:MyDocument
     WMIPrinters.Wsf /PrinterName:\\MyServer\MyPrinter /ResumeJob:MyDocument
     WMIPrinters.Wsf /PrinterName:\\MyServer\MyPrinter /CancelJob:MyDocument
```

The script code is presented in Samples 2.16 through 2.21. Sample 2.16 starts with the command-line parameters definition (skipped lines 13 through 64, giving the previous result) and parsing (lines 162 through 252). This first part of the script also contains some constant declarations. These constants are used later in the script.

Sample 2.16   *Managing the printer drivers, the printers, and their related print jobs (Part I)*

```
  1:<?xml version="1.0"?>
  .:
  8:<package>
  9:  <job>
 ..:
 13:    <runtime>
 ..:
 64:    </runtime>
 ..:
 72:    <script language="VBScript" src="..\Functions\ConvertArrayInStringFunction.vbs" />
 73:    <script language="VBScript" src="..\Functions\DisplayFormattedPropertyFunction.vbs" />
 74:    <script language="VBScript" src="..\Functions\TinyErrorHandler.vbs" />
 75:
 76:    <object progid="WbemScripting.SWbemLocator" id="objWMILocator" reference="true"/>
 77:    <object progid="WbemScripting.SWbemDateTime" id="objWMIDateTime" />
 78:
 79:    <script language="VBscript">
 80:    <![CDATA[
 ..:
 84:    ' -------------------------------------------------------------------------------------
 85:    Const cComputerName = "LocalHost"
 86:    Const cWMINameSpace = "root/cimv2"
 87:
 88:    Const cWMIPrinterDriverClass = "Win32_PrinterDriver"
 89:    Const cWMIPrinterClass = "Win32_Printer"
 90:    Const cWMIJobClass = "Win32_PrintJob"
 91:
 92:    Const cPortName = "LPT1:"
 93:    Const cAttributes = 2624
 94:    Const cComment = ""
 95:    Const cDefaultPriority = 0
 96:    Const cDirect = False
 97:    Const cDoCompleteFirst = True
 98:    Const cEnableBIDI = True
 99:    Const cEnableDevQueryPrint = False
100:    Const cHidden = False
101:    Const cKeepPrintedJobs = False
102:    Const cLocal = True
103:    Const cLocation = ""
104:    Const cNetwork = False
105:    Const cParameters = ""
106:    Const cPrintJobDataType = "RAW"
107:    Const cPrintProcessor = "WinPrint"
108:    Const cPriority = 1
109:    Const cPublished = False
110:    Const cQueued = False
111:    Const cRawOnly = True
112:    Const cSeparatorFile = ""
113:    Const cShared = False
114:    Const cShareName = ""
```

```
115:     Const cStartTime = "********080000.000000+000"
116:     Const cUntilTime = "********200000.000000+000"
117:     Const cWorkOffline = False
...:
160:     ' ----------------------------------------------------------------------------
161:     ' Parse the command line parameters
162:     If WScript.Arguments.Named.Count = 0 Then
163:         WScript.Arguments.ShowUsage()
164:         WScript.Quit
165:     End If
166:
167:     strList = UCase (WScript.Arguments.Named("List"))
168:     If Len (strList) Then
169:         Select Case strList
170:                 Case "DRIVERS"
171:
172:                 Case "PRINTERS"
173:
174:                 Case "JOBS"
175:
176:                 Case Else
177:                         WScript.Echo "Invalid List argument. Only [Drivers], ...
178:                         WScript.Arguments.ShowUsage()
179:                         WScript.Quit
180:         End Select
181:     End If
182:
183:     boolAddPrnDriver = WScript.Arguments.Named("AddPrinterDriver")
184:     If Len(boolAddPrnDriver) = 0 Then boolAddPrnDriver = False
185:
186:     boolDelPrnDriver = WScript.Arguments.Named("DelPrinterDriver")
187:     If Len(boolDelPrnDriver) = 0 Then boolDelPrnDriver = False
188:
189:     boolAddPrn = WScript.Arguments.Named("AddPrinter")
190:     If Len(boolAddPrn) = 0 Then boolAddPrn = False
191:
192:     If boolAddPrnDriver Or boolDelPrnDriver Then
193:         strPrinterDriverName = WScript.Arguments.Named("PrinterDriverName")
194:         If Len (strPrinterDriverName) = 0 Then
195:            WScript.Echo "Invalid printer driver name." & vbCRLF
196:            WScript.Arguments.ShowUsage()
197:            WScript.Quit
198:         End If
199:     ElseIf boolAddPrn Then
200:         strPrinterDriverName = WScript.Arguments.Named("PrinterDriverName")
201:         strPrinterName = WScript.Arguments.Named("PrinterName")
202:         If Len (strPrinterDriverName) = 0 Or Len (strPrinterName) = 0 Then
203:            WScript.Echo "Invalid printer name or print driver name." & vbCRLF
204:            WScript.Arguments.ShowUsage()
205:            WScript.Quit
206:         End If
207:     Else
208:         strPrinterName = WScript.Arguments.Named("PrinterName")
209:         If Len (strPrinterName) = 0 And Len (strList) = 0 Then
210:            WScript.Echo "Invalid printer name." & vbCRLF
211:            WScript.Arguments.ShowUsage()
212:            WScript.Quit
213:         End If
214:     End If
215:
216:     boolAddPrnConnection = WScript.Arguments.Named("AddPrinterConnection")
217:     If Len(boolAddPrnConnection) = 0 Then boolAddPrnConnection = False
...:
```

```
...:
...:
243:    strCancelJob = WScript.Arguments.Named("CancelJob")
244:
245:    strUserID = WScript.Arguments.Named("User")
246:    If Len(strUserID) = 0 Then strUserID = ""
247:
248:    strPassword = WScript.Arguments.Named("Password")
249:    If Len(strPassword) = 0 Then strPassword = ""
250:
251:    strComputerName = WScript.Arguments.Named("Machine")
252:    If Len(strComputerName) = 0 Then strComputerName = cComputerName
253:
254:    objWMILocator.Security_.AuthenticationLevel = wbemAuthenticationLevelDefault
255:    objWMILocator.Security_.ImpersonationLevel = wbemImpersonationLevelImpersonate
256:
257:    Set objWMIServices = objWMILocator.ConnectServer(strComputerName, cWMINameSpace, _
...:
260:
...:
...:
...:
```

The command-line parsing is quite complex, because some switches are only required for some specific actions. For instance, when **/List:<value>** switch is used, no other command-line parameter is needed. However, when **/AddPrinter+** switch is used, some more command-line parameters are required. For instance, to install a printer driver, create a printer using the installed printer driver, make it the default printer, and print one test page, the following command lines must be used:

```
WMIPrinters.Wsf /PrinterDriverName:"HP LaserJet 5" /AddPrinterDriver+
WMIPrinters.Wsf /PrinterName:"My Printer" /PrinterDriverName:"HP LaserJet 5" /AddPrinter+
WMIPrinters.Wsf /PrinterName:\\MyServer\MyPrinter /SetDefaultPrinter+
WMIPrinters.Wsf /PrinterName:\\MyServer\MyPrinter /PrintTestPage+
```

Because the script performs many different tasks with the printers, it is divided into different sections. Each section is responsible for a specific action. Sample 2.17 shows the code to retrieve information about the installed printer drivers, printers, and jobs in the printer queue.

Sample 2.17   *Viewing printer drivers, printers, and job information (Part II)*

```
...:
...:
...:
260:
261:    ' LIST Printers or Jobs --------------------------------------------------------------
262:    If Len (strList) Then
263:
264:        If strList = "DRIVERS" Then
265:            Set objWMIInstances = objWMIServices.InstancesOf (cWMIPrinterDriverClass)
266:            If Err.Number Then ErrorHandler (Err)
267:            varTemp = "- Job "
268:        End If
```

```
269:
270:        If strList = "PRINTERS" Then
271:           Set objWMIInstances = objWMIServices.InstancesOf (cWMIPrinterClass)
272:           If Err.Number Then ErrorHandler (Err)
273:           varTemp = "- Printer "
274:        End If
275:
276:        If strList = "JOBS" Then
277:           Set objWMIInstances = objWMIServices.InstancesOf (cWMIJobClass)
278:           If Err.Number Then ErrorHandler (Err)
279:           varTemp = "- Job "
280:        End If
281:
282:        If objWMIInstances.Count Then
283:           For Each objWMIInstance in objWMIInstances
284:               If strList = "DRIVERS" Then
285:                  WScript.Echo "- Driver '" & objWMIInstance.Name & "' " & _
286:                               String (60, "-")
287:               End If
288:               If strList = "PRINTERS" Then
289:                  WScript.Echo "- Printer '" & objWMIInstance.Name & "' " & _
290:                               String (60, "-")
291:               End If
292:               If strList = "JOBS" Then
293:                  WScript.Echo "- Job '" & Ucase (objWMIInstance.Name) & _
294:                               "' (" & objWMIInstance.Document & _
295:                               ") " & String (60, "-")
296:               End If
297:
298:               Set objWMIPropertySet = objWMIInstance.Properties_
299:               For Each objWMIProperty In objWMIPropertySet
300:                   Select Case objWMIProperty.Name
301:                          Case "CreationClassName"
302:
303:                          Case "SystemCreationClassName"
...:
...:
...:
340:                          Case Else
341:                                 DisplayFormattedProperty objWMIInstance, _
342:                                                          objWMIProperty.Name, _
343:                                                          objWMIProperty.Name, _
344:                                                          Null
345:                   End Select
346:               Next
...:
349:               WScript.Echo
350:           Next
351:        Else
352:           WScript.Echo "No information available."
353:        End If
...:
357:     End If
358:
...:
...:
...:
```

To retrieve information about the printer drivers, printers, and print jobs, three classes are used:

- *Win32_PrinterDriver* class to display information about the installed printer drivers (lines 264 through 268).

- *Win32_Printer* class to display information about the printers (lines 270 through 274).

- *Win32_Printer*Job class to display information about the printer jobs (lines 276 through 280).

Because a collection of instances for the class is created, the script enumerates the collection and displays the properties with the help of the DisplayFormattedProperty() function (lines 283 through 350). Based on the instance examined, a message specific to the printer drivers, printers, or print jobs is created (lines 284 through 296). For instance, the following command-line parameters display information about the printers:

```
 1:   C:\>WMIPrinters.Wsf /List:Printers
 2:   Microsoft (R) Windows Script Host Version 5.6
 3:   Copyright (C) Microsoft Corporation 1996-2001. All rights reserved.
 4:
 5:   - Printer 'My Printer' ------------------------------------------------------
 6:   Attributes: ............................ 6724
 7:   AveragePagesPerMinute: .................. 0
 8:   Capabilities: ........................... 4
 9:                                             2
10:                                             3
11:                                             5
12:   CapabilityDescriptions: ................. Copies
13:                                             Color
14:                                             Duplex
15:                                             Collate
16:   Caption: ................................ My Printer
17:   Default: ................................ TRUE
18:   DefaultPriority: ........................ 0
19:   DetectedErrorState: ..................... 2
20:   *DeviceID: .............................. My Printer
21:   Direct: ................................. FALSE
22:   DoCompleteFirst: ........................ TRUE
23:   DriverName: ............................. HP LaserJet 5
24:   EnableBIDI: ............................. TRUE
25:   EnableDevQueryPrint: .................... FALSE
26:   ExtendedDetectedErrorState: ............. 2
27:   ExtendedPrinterStatus: .................. 8
28:   Hidden: ................................. FALSE
29:   HorizontalResolution: ................... 600
30:   JobCountSinceLastReset: ................. 0
31:   KeepPrintedJobs: ........................ FALSE
32:   Local: .................................. TRUE
33:   Name: ................................... My Printer
34:   Network: ................................ FALSE
35:   PaperSizesSupported: .................... 7,8,1,22,23,11,1,1,1,1
36:   PortName: ............................... LPT1:
37:   PrinterPaperNames: ...................... Letter
```

```
38:                                         Legal
39:                                         Executive
40:                                         A4
41:                                         A5
42:                                         Envelope #10
43:                                         Envelope DL
44:                                         Envelope C5
45:                                         Envelope B5
46:                                         Envelope Monarch
47:    PrinterState: ..........................  1
48:    PrinterStatus: .........................  Other
49:    PrintJobDataType: ......................  RAW
50:    PrintProcessor: ........................  WinPrint
51:    Priority: ..............................  1
52:    Published: .............................  FALSE
53:    Queued: ................................  FALSE
54:    RawOnly: ...............................  TRUE
55:    Shared: ................................  FALSE
56:    SpoolEnabled: ..........................  TRUE
57:    StartTime: .............................  ********080000.000000+000
58:    Status: ................................  OK
59:    SystemName: ............................  XP-DPEN6400
60:    UntilTime: .............................  ********200000.000000+000
61:    VerticalResolution: ....................  600
62:    WorkOffline: ...........................  FALSE
```

It is important to note that in this set of properties, some of them are modifiable. For instance, the *StartTime* and the *UntilTime* properties of the *Win32_Printer* class use a DMTF date/time value that is easily modifiable. In this sample script, most of these property values are defined as constants in the beginning of the script (lines 92 through 117). These constants are used in the next segment of code to create a new printer (see Sample 2.18).

Sample 2.18   *Adding printers and printer connections (Part III)*

```
...:
...:
...:
358:
359:    ' ADD PRINTER CONNECTION ------------------------------------------------------------
360:    If boolAddPrnConnection Then
361:        Set objWMIClass = objWMIServices.Get (cWMIPrinterClass)
362:        If Err.Number Then ErrorHandler (Err)
363:
364:        intRC = objWMIClass.AddPrinterConnection (strPrinterName)
...:
367:        WScript.Echo "Printer connection '" & strPrinterName & "' added (" & intRC & ")."
368:
369:        Set objWMIClass = Nothing
370:
371:    End If
372:
373:    ' ADD PRINTER ------------------------------------------------------------------------
374:    If boolAddPrn Then
375:        Set objWMIClass = objWMIServices.Get (cWMIPrinterClass)
...:
```

```
378:        Set objWMIInstance = objWMIClass.SpawnInstance_
379:
380:        objWMIInstance.DeviceID = strPrinterName
381:        objWMIInstance.DriverName = strPrinterDriverName
382:
383:        objWMIInstance.PortName = cPortName
384:        objWMIInstance.Comment = cComment
385:        objWMIInstance.DefaultPriority = cDefaultPriority
386:        objWMIInstance.Direct = cDirect
387:        objWMIInstance.DoCompleteFirst = cDoCompleteFirst
388:        objWMIInstance.EnableBIDI = cEnableBIDI
389:        objWMIInstance.EnableDevQueryPrint = cEnableDevQueryPrint
390:        objWMIInstance.Hidden = cHidden
391:        objWMIInstance.KeepPrintedJobs = cKeepPrintedJobs
392:        objWMIInstance.Local = cLocal
393:        objWMIInstance.Location = cLocation
394:        objWMIInstance.Network = cNetwork
395:        objWMIInstance.Parameters = cParameters
396:        objWMIInstance.PrintJobDataType = cPrintJobDataType
397:        objWMIInstance.PrintProcessor = cPrintProcessor
398:        objWMIInstance.Priority = cPriority
399:        objWMIInstance.Published = cPublished
400:        objWMIInstance.Queued = cQueued
401:        objWMIInstance.RawOnly = cRawOnly
402:        objWMIInstance.SeparatorFile = cSeparatorFile
403:        objWMIInstance.Shared = cShared
404:        objWMIInstance.ShareName = cShareName
405:        objWMIInstance.StartTime = cStartTime
406:        objWMIInstance.UntilTime = cUntilTime
407:        objWMIInstance.WorkOffline = cWorkOffline
408:
409:        objWMIInstance.Put_ (wbemChangeFlagCreateOrUpdate Or wbemFlagReturnWhenComplete)
...:
412:        WScript.Echo "Printer connection '" & strPrinterName & "' added."
...:
416:    End If
417:
...:
...:
...:
```

To create a new printer connection (lines 360 through 371), the script uses a method that is defined as a static method (line 364). In Sample 2.12 ("Configuring a network adapter"), we saw the difference between a static method and a dynamic method. We saw that the static method must be used from a class instance. So, to create a printer connection, Sample 2.18 creates an instance of the *Win32_Printer* class (line 361) and invokes the *AddPrinterConnection* method (line 364). The method requires one parameter, the printer name of the printer to install (i.e., "My Printer"), or the share name of the network printer to connect to (i.e., \\MyServer\MyPrinterShare).

To create a new printer (lines 374 through 416), the script spawns a new instance of the *Win32_Printer* class (lines 375 through 378). Next, it initializes the miscellaneous values defining the new printer (lines 380 through

407). Once the values are assigned to the properties, the script invokes the
*Put_* method of the **SWBemObject** object (line 409). Two of these properties are assigned from the command-line parameters: These are the printer
name and the printer driver name. All other properties come from constants
defined in the script header (see Sample 2.16, lines 92 through 117). We
proceed like this to minimize the number of parameters to specify from the
command line. Moreover, the constants are set on a value that suits the
requirement of a local printer. If needed, the script can be easily modified or
extended to expose some more command-line parameters.

The next task supported by this WMI script sample is the deletion of an
existing printer. The coding technique is presented in Sample 2.19, with
some extra code to pause, resume, and print a test page. We also see that it is
possible to rename a printer. All these tasks require an instance of the
printer to be managed (lines 427 and 428). This is the reason why this piece
of the code corresponds to many actions supported by WMI on a printer
instance (lines 419 through 425).

Sample 2.19   *Deleting, managing (test page, pause, resume, etc.) and renaming printers (Part IV)*

```
...:
...:
...:
417
418:    ' --------------------------------------------------------------------------------
419:    If boolDelPrn Or _
420:       boolTestPage Or _
421:       boolCancelAllJobs Or _
422:       boolPausePrinter Or _
423:       boolResumePrinter Or _
424:       boolSetDefaultPrinter Or _
425:       Len (strRenamePrinter) Then
426:
427:       Set objWMIInstance = objWMIServices.Get (cWMIPrinterClass & "='" & _
428:                                          strPrinterName & "'")
...:
431:       ' DELETE PRINTER & PRINTER CONNECTION ------------------------------------------
432:       If boolDelPrn Then
433:          objWMIInstance.Delete_
434:          If Err.Number Then ErrorHandler (Err)
435:          WScript.Echo "Printer '" & strPrinterName & "' deleted."
436:       End If
437:
438:       ' TEST PAGE --------------------------------------------------------------------
439:       If boolTestPage Then
440:          intRC = objWMIInstance.PrintTestPage
441:          If Err.Number Then ErrorHandler (Err)
442:          WScript.Echo "Test page for printer '" & strPrinterName & _
443:                   "' requested (" & intRC & ")."
444:       End If
445:
446:       ' CANCEL ALL JOBS --------------------------------------------------------------
```

```
447:        If boolCancelAllJobs Then
448:            intRC = objWMIInstance.CancelAllJobs
449:            If Err.Number Then ErrorHandler (Err)
450:            WScript.Echo "All jobs for printer '" & strPrinterName & _
451:                         "' cancelled (" & intRC & ")."
452:        End If
453:
454:        ' PAUSE PRINTER -------------------------------------------------------------------------
455:        If boolPausePrinter Then
456:            intRC = objWMIInstance.Pause
457:            If Err.Number Then ErrorHandler (Err)
458:            WScript.Echo "Printer '" & strPrinterName & "' paused (" & intRC & ")."
459:        End If
460:
461:        ' RESUME PRINTER ------------------------------------------------------------------------
462:        If boolResumePrinter Then
463:            intRC = objWMIInstance.Resume
464:            If Err.Number Then ErrorHandler (Err)
465:            WScript.Echo "Printer '" & strPrinterName & "' resumed (" & intRC & ")."
466:        End If
467:
468:        ' DEFAULT PRINTER -----------------------------------------------------------------------
469:        If boolSetDefaultPrinter Then
470:            intRC = objWMIInstance.SetDefaultPrinter
471:            If Err.Number Then ErrorHandler (Err)
472:            WScript.Echo "Printer '" & strPrinterName & _
473:                         "' set as default printer (" & intRC & ")."
474:        End If
475:
476:        ' RENAME PRINTER ------------------------------------------------------------------------
477:        If Len (strRenamePrinter) Then
478:            intRC = objWMIInstance.RenamePrinter (strRenamePrinter)
479:            If Err.Number Then ErrorHandler (Err)
480:            WScript.Echo "Printer '" & strPrinterName & "' renamed to '" & _
481:                         strRenamePrinter & "' (" & intRC & ")."
482:        End If
...:
485:    End If
486:
...:
...:
...:
```

Once the managed printer is instantiated (lines 427 and 428), based on the command-line parameters, the first possible action is the printer deletion. To do this, the script must simply delete the corresponding printer instance (line 433) by invoking the *Delete_* method of the **SWBemObject** object. Note that this delete operation can remove an existing printer connection or delete a local printer.

The subsequent operations (lines 438 through 482) use the method instance that corresponds to the task to be performed. It is possible to send a test page (line 440), to cancel all jobs (line 448), to pause (line 456) and resume (line 463) the printer, set the printer as the default printer (line 470), and rename the printer (line 478). Note that to rename the printer a specific command-line parameter is required, which is the new printer name (i.e., **/RenamePrinter:NewPrinterName**).

To add and delete printer drivers, the technique is very similar to that used previously. However, the script must use the *Win32_PrinterDriver* class. The code is shown in Sample 2.20.

Sample 2.20   *Adding and deleting printer drivers (Part V)*

```
...:
...:
...:
486:
487:    ' ADD PRINTER DRIVER -------------------------------------------------------------
488:    If boolAddPrnDriver Then
489:       Set objWMIPrnDrvClass = objWMIServices.Get (cWMIPrinterDriverClass)
...:
492:       Set objWMIPrnDrvInstance = objWMIPrnDrvClass.SpawnInstance_
493:       objWMIPrnDrvInstance.Name = strPrinterDriverName
494:
495:       Set objWMIClass = objWMIServices.Get (cWMIPrinterDriverClass)
...:
498:       intRC = objWMIClass.AddPrinterDriver (objWMIPrnDrvInstance)
...:
501:       WScript.Echo "Printer driver '" & strPrinterDriverName & "' added (" & intRC & ")."
...:
507:    End If
508:
509:    ' DELETE PRINTER DRIVER ----------------------------------------------------------
510:    If boolDelPrnDriver Then
511:       Set objWMIInstance = objWMIServices.Get (cWMIPrinterDriverClass & "='" & _
512:                                         strPrinterDriverName & "'")
513:       objWMIInstance.Delete_
514:       If Err.Number Then ErrorHandler (Err)
515:       WScript.Echo "Printer driver '" & strPrinterDriverName & "' Cancelled."
...:
518:    End If
519:
...:
...:
...:
```

To add a new printer driver, the script must use a specific method (called *AddPrinterDriver*), which is defined as a static method of the *Win32_PrinterDriver*s class (lines 495 through 498). Because *AddPrinterDriver* method requires one parameter, which is an instance of the *Win32_Printer* driver to install, the script first creates a printer driver instance with the name given on the command line (lines 489 through 493). For instance:

```
WMIPrinters.Wsf /PrinterDriverName:"HP LaserJet 5" /AddPrinterDriver+
```

To delete a printer driver, the following command line is used:

```
WMIPrinters.Wsf /PrinterDriverName:"HP LaserJet 5" /DelPrinterDriver+
```

The deletion is performed from line 511 through 516 and consists of the deletion of the printer driver instance by invoking the *Delete_* method of the **SWBemObject** object representing the printer driver.

The last type of task to be performed at the printer level is the print job management. WMI exposes the *Win32_PrintJob* class with some specific methods to manage the print jobs of a printer. This piece of code is shown in Sample 2.21.

Sample 2.21 *Managing printer jobs (pause, resume, and delete) (Part VI)*

```
...:
...:
...:
519:
520:    ' PAUSE JOB -----------------------------------------------------------------------
521:    If Len (strPauseJob) Then
522:       Set objWMIInstance = objWMIServices.Get (cWMIJobClass & "='" & strPauseJob & "'")
523:       intRC = objWMIInstance.Pause
524:       WScript.Echo "Job '" & strPauseJob & "' paused (" & intRC & ")."
525:       Set objWMIInstance = Nothing
526:    End If
527:
528:    ' RESUME JOB ----------------------------------------------------------------------
529:    If Len (strResumeJob) Then
530:       Set objWMIInstance = objWMIServices.Get (cWMIJobClass & "='" & strResumeJob & "'")
531:       intRC = objWMIInstance.Resume
532:       WScript.Echo "Job '" & strResumeJob & "' Resumed (" & intRC & ")."
533:       Set objWMIInstance = Nothing
534:    End If
535:
536:    ' CANCEL JOB ----------------------------------------------------------------------
537:    If Len (strCancelJob) Then
538:       Set objWMIInstance = objWMIServices.Get (cWMIJobClass & "='" & strCancelJob & "'")
539:       objWMIInstance.Delete_
540:       If Err.Number Then ErrorHandler (Err)
541:       WScript.Echo "Job '" & strCancelJob & "' Cancelled."
542:       Set objWMIInstance = Nothing
543:    End If
...:
547:    ]]>
548:    </script>
549:  </job>
550:</package>
```

The command-line parameters to manage print jobs require one parameter, which is the print job name itself. Since the print job name is not exactly the one visible from the user interface (an index is appended to the printer name), it is recommended that you use the **/List:PrintJobs** switch to display the print job name list. A sample output of the existing print jobs looks like this:

```
 1:   C:\>WMIPrinters.Wsf /List:Jobs
 2:   Microsoft (R) Windows Script Host Version 5.6
 3:   Copyright (C) Microsoft Corporation 1996-2001. All rights reserved.
 4:
 5:   - Job 'MY PRINTER, 3' (Microsoft Word - My Document.doc) -----------------------------------
 6:   Caption: ............................... My Printer, 3
 7:   DataType: .............................. RAW
 8:   Description: ........................... My Printer, 3
 9:   Document: .............................. Microsoft Word - My Document.doc
10:   DriverName: ............................ HP LaserJet 5
11:   ElapsedTime: ........................... 00000000000000.000000:000
12:   HostPrintQueue: ........................ \\XP-DPEN6400
13:   JobId: ................................. 3
14:   *Name: ................................. My Printer, 3
15:   Notify: ................................ Alain.Lissoir
16:   Owner: ................................. Alain.Lissoir
17:   PagesPrinted: .......................... 0
18:   PrintProcessor: ........................ WinPrint
19:   Priority: .............................. 1
20:   Size: .................................. 359
21:   StartTime: ............................. ********080000.000000+000
22:   Status: ................................ UNKNOWN
23:   StatusMask: ............................ 0
24:   TimeSubmitted: ......................... 01-11-2001 16:37:23
25:   TotalPages: ............................ 1
26:   UntilTime: ............................. ********200000.000000+000
```

To delete this print job, the following command line must be used:

```
C:\>WMIPrinters.Wsf /PrinterName:"My Printer" /CancelJob:"My Printer, 3"
Microsoft (R) Windows Script Host Version 5.6
Copyright (C) Microsoft Corporation 1996-2001. All rights reserved.

Job 'My Printer, 3' Cancelled.
```

From a scripting point of view, the job deletion is nothing more than the deletion of the instance representing the print job (lines 537 through 543) by invoking the *Delete_* method of the **SWBemObject** object.

2.3.8   Video and monitor classes

The video and monitor classes represent monitors, video cards, and their associated settings. The Microsoft classes in this category are listed in Table 2.11.

The *Win32_DisplayConfiguration*, the *Win32_DisplayControllerConfig-uration*, and the *Win32_VideoConfiguration* are obsolete classes and should not be used anymore. Moreover, the *Win32_DisplayControllerConfiguration*

Table 2.11   *The Video and Monitor Classes*

Name	Type	Description
Win32_DesktopMonitor	Dynamic	Represents the type of monitor or display device attached to the computer system.
Win32_DisplayConfiguration	Dynamic	Represents configuration information for the display device on a Windows system. This class is obsolete. In place of this class, you should use the properties in the Win32_VideoController, Win32_DesktopMonitor, and CIM_VideoControllerResolution classes.
Win32_DisplayControllerConfiguration	Dynamic	Represents the video adapter configuration information of a Windows system. This class is obsolete. In place of this class, you should use the properties in the Win32_VideoController, Win32_DesktopMonitor, and CIM_VideoControllerResolution classes.
Win32_VideoConfiguration	Dynamic	This class has been eliminated from Windows XP and later; attempts to use it will generate a fatal error. In place of this class, you should use the properties contained in the Win32_VideoController, Win32_DesktopMonitor, and CIM_VideoControllerResolution classes.
Win32_VideoController	Dynamic	Represents the capabilities and management capacity of the video controller on a Windows computer system.
Win32_VideoSettings	Association	Relates a video controller and video settings that can be applied to it.

contains a subset of information already available from the *Win32_Display-Configuration* class.

Sample 2.22 retrieves the desktop monitor information. The script is not different from Sample 2.15 ("Retrieving modem information") except for the fact that it uses the *Win32_DesktopMonitor* class.

Sample 2.22   *Retrieving the desktop monitor information*

```
 1:<?xml version="1.0"?>
 .:
 8:<package>
 9:   <job>
..:
13:     <runtime>
14:       <named name="Machine" helpstring="determine the WMI system to connect to.
                          (default=LocalHost)" required="false" type="string"/>
15:       <named name="User" helpstring="determine the UserID to perform the remote connection.
                          (default=none)" required="false" type="string"/>
16:       <named name="Password" helpstring="determine the password to perform the remote
                          connection. (default=none)" required="false" type="string"/>
17:     </runtime>
18:
19:     <script language="VBScript" src="..\Functions\DecodeDeviceAvailabilityFunction.vbs" />
20:     <script language="VBScript" src="..\Functions\DecodeCfgManErrCodeFunction.vbs" />
21:     <script language="VBScript" src="..\Functions\DecodeStatusInfoFunction.vbs" />
22:     <script language="VBScript" src="..\Functions\DecodePwrManCapabilitiesFunction.vbs" />
23:
24:     <script language="VBScript" src="..\Functions\DisplayFormattedPropertyFunction.vbs" />
25:     <script language="VBScript" src="..\Functions\TinyErrorHandler.vbs" />
26:
27:     <object progid="WbemScripting.SWbemLocator" id="objWMILocator" reference="true"/>
28:     <object progid="WbemScripting.SWbemDateTime" id="objWMIDateTime" />
29:
```

```
30:     <script language="VBscript">
31:     <![CDATA[
..:
35:     Const cComputerName = "LocalHost"
36:     Const cWMINameSpace = "root/cimv2"
..:
48:     ' --------------------------------------------------------------------------
49:     ' Parse the command line parameters
50:     strUserID = WScript.Arguments.Named("User")
51:     If Len(strUserID) = 0 Then strUserID = ""
52:
53:     strPassword = WScript.Arguments.Named("Password")
54:     If Len(strPassword) = 0 Then strPassword = ""
55:
56:     strComputerName = WScript.Arguments.Named("Machine")
57:     If Len(strComputerName) = 0 Then strComputerName = cComputerName
58:
59:     objWMILocator.Security_.AuthenticationLevel = wbemAuthenticationLevelDefault
60:     objWMILocator.Security_.ImpersonationLevel = wbemImpersonationLevelImpersonate
61:
62:     Set objWMIServices = objWMILocator.ConnectServer(strComputerName, cWMINameSpace, _
63:                                                       strUserID, strPassword)
..:
66:     Set objWMIInstances = objWMIServices.InstancesOf ("Win32_DesktopMonitor")
..:
69:     If objWMIInstances.Count Then
70:        For Each objWMIInstance In objWMIInstances
71:            Set objWMIPropertySet = objWMIInstance.Properties_
72:            For Each objWMIProperty In objWMIPropertySet
73:                Select Case objWMIProperty.Name
74:                    Case "Availability"
75:                        DisplayFormattedProperty objWMIInstance, _
76:                            objWMIProperty.Name, _
77:                            DeviceAvailability (objWMIInstance.Availability), _
78:                            Null
79:                    Case "ConfigManagerErrorCode"
80:                        DisplayFormattedProperty objWMIInstance, _
81:                            objWMIProperty.Name, _
82:                            CfgManErrCode (objWMIInstance.ConfigManagerErrorCode), _
83:                            Null
84:                    Case "ConfigManagerUserConfig"
85:                        DisplayFormattedProperty objWMIInstance, _
86:                            objWMIProperty.Name, _
87:                            UCase (objWMIInstance.ConfigManagerUserConfig), _
88:                            Null
89:                    Case "PowerManagementCapabilities"
90:                        DisplayFormattedProperty objWMIInstance, _
91:                            objWMIProperty.Name, _
92:                            PwrManCapabilities (objWMIInstance.Power...entCapabilities), _
93:                            Null
94:                    Case "StatusInfo"
95:                        DisplayFormattedProperty objWMIInstance, _
96:                            objWMIProperty.Name, _
97:                            StatusInfo (objWMIInstance.StatusInfo), _
98:                            Null
99:                    Case "CreationClassName"
100:
101:                    Case "SystemCreationClassName"
102:
```

```
103:                    Case "SystemName"
104:
105:                    Case "Caption"
106:
107:                    Case "Name"
108:
109:                    Case Else
110:                        DisplayFormattedProperty objWMIInstance, _
111:                                                  objWMIProperty.Name, _
112:                                                  objWMIProperty.Name, _
113:                                                  Null
114:              End Select
115:          Next
116:          Set objWMIPropertySet = Nothing
117:          WScript.Echo
118:       Next
119:    Else
120:       WScript.Echo "No information available."
121:    End If
...:
126:    ]]>
127:    </script>
128:    </job>
129:</package>
```

Once started, the script displays the following information:

```
1:    C:\>GetDesktopMonitorInformation.wsf
2:    Microsoft (R) Windows Script Host Version 5.6
3:    Copyright (C) Microsoft Corporation 1996-2001. All rights reserved.
4:
5:    Availability: ........................... Running/Full Power
6:    ConfigManagerErrorCode: ................. This device is working properly.
7:    ConfigManagerUserConfig: ................ FALSE
8:    Description: ............................ COMPAQ S700 Color Monitor
9:    *DeviceID: .............................. DesktopMonitor1
10:   MonitorManufacturer: .................... COMPAQ
11:   MonitorType: ............................ COMPAQ S700 Color Monitor
12:   PixelsPerXLogicalInch: .................. 96
13:   PixelsPerYLogicalInch: .................. 96
14:   PNPDeviceID: ............................ DISPLAY\CPQ1349\4&2E81F5BD&0&80000001&01&00
15:   ScreenHeight: ........................... 864
16:   ScreenWidth: ............................ 1152
17:   Status: ................................. OK
```

The two last classes of this category are *Win32_VideoController* and *Win32_VideoSettings*. The *Win32_VideoSettings* class is an association class, which can be used in the script to retrieve a complementary set of information coming from the *CIM_VideoControllerResolution* (see Figure 2.6). This last class contains the available video resolution.

Sample 2.23 shows how to retrieve the video adapter information with these classes.

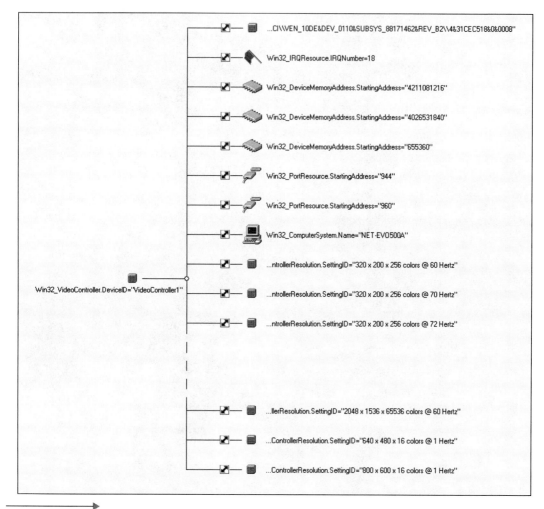

Figure 2.6   *Associated instances of one video controller.*

Sample 2.23   *Retrieving the video adapter information*

```
1:<?xml version="1.0"?>
 .:
8:<package>
9:  <job>
..:
13:    <runtime>
14:      <unnamed name="Resolutions" helpstring="Display available resolutions." required="false"
                 type="boolean" />
15:      <named name="Machine" helpstring="determine the WMI system to connect to.
                 (default=LocalHost)" required="false" type="string"/>
16:      <named name="User" helpstring="determine the UserID to perform the remote connection.
```

```
                           (default=none)" required="false" type="string"/>
17:        <named name="Password" helpstring="determine the password to perform the remote
                           connection. (default=none)" required="false" type="string"/>
18:        </runtime>
19:
20:        <script language="VBScript" src=".\Functions\DecodeDeviceAvailabilityFunction.vbs" />
21:        <script language="VBScript" src=".\Functions\DecodeCfgManErrCodeFunction.vbs" />
22:        <script language="VBScript" src=".\Functions\DecodeStatusInfoFunction.vbs" />
23:        <script language="VBScript" src=".\Functions\DecodePwrManCapabilitiesFunction.vbs" />
24:
25:        <script language="VBScript" src=".\Functions\ConvertArrayInOneStringFunction.vbs" />
26:        <script language="VBScript" src=".\Functions\DisplayFormattedPropertyFunction.vbs" />
27:        <script language="VBScript" src=".\Functions\TinyErrorHandler.vbs" />
28:
29:        <object progid="WbemScripting.SWbemLocator" id="objWMILocator" reference="true"/>
30:        <object progid="WbemScripting.SWbemDateTime" id="objWMIDateTime" />
31:
32:        <script language="VBscript">
33:        <![CDATA[
..:
37:        Const cComputerName = "LocalHost"
38:        Const cWMINameSpace = "root/cimv2"
..:
56:        ' -----------------------------------------------------------------------------
57:        ' Parse the command line parameters
58:        boolResolutionList = WScript.Arguments.Named("Resolutions")
59:        If Len(boolResolutionList) = 0 Then boolResolutionList = False
60:
61:        strUserID = WScript.Arguments.Named("User")
62:        If Len(strUserID) = 0 Then strUserID = ""
63:
64:        strPassword = WScript.Arguments.Named("Password")
65:        If Len(strPassword) = 0 Then strPassword = ""
66:
67:        strComputerName = WScript.Arguments.Named("Machine")
68:        If Len(strComputerName) = 0 Then strComputerName = cComputerName
69:
70:        objWMILocator.Security_.AuthenticationLevel = wbemAuthenticationLevelDefault
71:        objWMILocator.Security_.ImpersonationLevel = wbemImpersonationLevelImpersonate
72:
73:        Set objWMIServices = objWMILocator.ConnectServer(strComputerName, cWMINameSpace, _
74:                                                    strUserID, strPassword)
..:
77:        Set objWMIInstances = objWMIServices.InstancesOf ("Win32_VideoController")
..:
80:        If objWMIInstances.Count Then
81:            For Each objWMIInstance In objWMIInstances
82:                Set objWMIPropertySet = objWMIInstance.Properties_
83:                    For Each objWMIProperty In objWMIPropertySet
84:                        Select Case objWMIProperty.Name
85:                            Case "Availability"
86:                                DisplayFormattedProperty objWMIInstance, _
87:                                    objWMIProperty.Name, _
88:                                    DeviceAvailability (objWMIInstance.Availability), _
89:                                    Null
90:                            Case "ConfigManagerErrorCode"
91:                                DisplayFormattedProperty objWMIInstance, _
92:                                    objWMIProperty.Name, _
93:                                    CfgManErrCode (objWMIInstance.ConfigManagerErrorCode), _
94:                                    Null
```

```
 95:                    Case "ConfigManagerUserConfig"
 96:                        DisplayFormattedProperty objWMIInstance, _
 97:                            objWMIProperty.Name, _
 98:                            UCase (objWMIInstance.ConfigManagerUserConfig), _
 99:                            Null
100:                    Case "PowerManagementCapabilities"
101:                        DisplayFormattedProperty objWMIInstance, _
102:                            objWMIProperty.Name, _
103:                            PwrManCapabilities (objWMIInstance.PowerMan...abilities), _
104:                            Null
105:                    Case "StatusInfo"
106:                        DisplayFormattedProperty objWMIInstance, _
107:                            objWMIProperty.Name, _
108:                            StatusInfo (objWMIInstance.StatusInfo), _
109:                            Null
110:                    Case "CreationClassName"
111:
112:                    Case "SystemCreationClassName"
113:
114:                    Case "SystemName"
115:
116:                    Case "Caption"
117:
118:                    Case "Name"
119:
120:                    Case Else
121:                        DisplayFormattedProperty objWMIInstance, _
122:                            objWMIProperty.Name, _
123:                            objWMIProperty.Name, _
124:                            Null
125:                End Select
126:            Next
127:        Set objWMIPropertySet = Nothing
128:
129:        Set objWMIResourceInstances = objWMIServices.ExecQuery _
130:                                ("Associators of {Win32_VideoController='" & _
131:                                objWMIInstance.DeviceID & _
132:                                "'} Where AssocClass=Win32_AllocatedResource")
133:
134:        If objWMIResourceInstances.Count Then
135:            WScript.Echo
136:            For Each objWMIResourceInstance In objWMIResourceInstances
137:                Select Case objWMIResourceInstance.Path_.Class
138:                    Case "Win32_IRQResource"
139:                        DisplayFormattedProperty objWMIResourceInstance, _
140:                            "IRQ resource", _
141:                            "IRQNumber", _
142:                            Null
143:                    Case "Win32_DMAChannel"
144:                        DisplayFormattedProperty objWMIResourceInstance, _
145:                            "DMA channel", _
146:                            "DMAChannel", _
147:                            Null
148:                    Case "Win32_PortResource"
149:                        DisplayFormattedProperty objWMIResourceInstance, _
150:                            "I/O Port", _
151:                            "Caption", _
152:                            Null
153:                    Case "Win32_DeviceMemoryAddress"
154:                        DisplayFormattedProperty objWMIResourceInstance, _
```

```
155:                              "Memory address", _
156:                              "Caption", _
157:                              Null
158:                  End Select
159:           Next
160:       End If
161:
162:       If boolResolutionList Then
163:           Set objWMISettingInstances = objWMIServices.ExecQuery _
164:                              ("Associators of {Win32_VideoController='" & _
165:                              objWMIInstance.DeviceID & _
166:                              "'} Where AssocClass=Win32_VideoSettings")
167:
168:           If objWMISettingInstances.Count Then
169:               WScript.Echo
170:               intIndice = 0
171:               ReDim strVideoSetting(0)
172:               For Each objWMISettingInstance In objWMISettingInstances
173:                   ReDim Preserve strVideoSetting(intIndice)
174:                   strVideoSetting (intIndice) = objWMISettingInstance.SettingID
175:                   intIndice = intIndice + 1
176:               Next
177:               DisplayFormattedProperty objWMISettingInstances, _
178:                              "Available resolutions", _
179:                              strVideoSetting, _
180:                              Null
181:           End If
182:       End If
183:
184:       WScript.Echo
185:   Next
186:   Else
187:       WScript.Echo "No information available."
188:   End If
...:
193:   ]]>
194:   </script>
195:   </job>
196:</package>
```

Sample 2.23 uses the same logic as previous scripts and contains three main parts:

- A first part, which lists the *Win32_VideoController* properties (lines 81 through 126).

- A second part, which lists the hardware resources used by the video adapter (lines 128 through 159).

- A third part, which retrieves the available resolutions if the switch **/Resolutions+** is specified on the command line (lines 161 through 181).

Each of these parts uses a logic that we discovered in the previous samples. The new element in this script code is a combination of all the scripting techniques in one script. The obtained output is as follows:

```
 1:    C:\>GetVideoAdapterInformation.wsf /Machine:MyPortable.LissWare.Net /Resolutions+
 2:    Microsoft (R) Windows Script Host Version 5.6
 3:    Copyright (C) Microsoft Corporation 1996-2001. All rights reserved.
 4:
 5:    AdapterCompatibility: .................... ATI
 6:    AdapterDACType: .......................... ATI Internal DAC
 7:    AdapterRAM: .............................. 8388608
 8:    Availability: ............................ Running/Full Power
 9:    ConfigManagerErrorCode: .................. This device is working properly.
10:    ConfigManagerUserConfig: ................. FALSE
11:    CurrentBitsPerPixel: ..................... 32
12:    CurrentHorizontalResolution: ............. 1024
13:    CurrentNumberOfColors: ................... 4294967296
14:    CurrentNumberOfColumns: .................. 0
15:    CurrentNumberOfRows: ..................... 0
16:    CurrentRefreshRate: ...................... 60
17:    CurrentScanMode: ......................... 4
18:    CurrentVerticalResolution: ............... 768
19:    Description: ............................. ATI RAGE MOBILITY-P AGP (English)
20:    *DeviceID: ............................... VideoController1
21:    DeviceSpecificPens: ...................... -1
22:    DriverDate: .............................. 20-12-2000 12:36:46
23:    DriverVersion: ........................... 5.00.2195.4050
24:    InfFilename: ............................. oem14.inf
25:    InfSection: .............................. ati2mpab_ENU
26:    InstallDate: ............................. 20-12-2000 12:36:46
27:    InstalledDisplayDrivers: ................. ati2drab.dll
28:    MaxRefreshRate: .......................... 120
29:    MinRefreshRate: .......................... 58
30:    Monochrome: .............................. FALSE
31:    NumberOfColorPlanes: ..................... 1
32:    PNPDeviceID: ............................. PCI\VEN_12&DEV_4C4D&SUBSYS_B1E11&REV_64\4&4E&0&08
33:    Status: .................................. OK
34:    TimeOfLastReset: ......................... 20-12-2000 12:36:46
35:    VideoArchitecture: ....................... 5
36:    VideoMemoryType: ......................... 2
37:    VideoModeDescription: .................... 1024 x 768 x 4294967296 colors
38:    VideoProcessor: .......................... ATI RAGE Mobility P/M AGP 2X (A21/2)
39:
40:    *IRQ resource: ........................... 11
41:    Memory address: .......................... 0x40000000-0x410FFFFF
42:    Memory address: .......................... 0x41000000-0x41000FFF
43:    Memory address: .......................... 0xA0000-0xBFFFF
44:    I/O Port: ................................ 0x00002000-0x00002FFF
45:    I/O Port: ................................ 0x000003B0-0x000003BB
46:    I/O Port: ................................ 0x000003C0-0x000003DF
47:
48:    Available resolutions: ................... 320 x 200 x 256 colors @ 60 Hertz
..:
52:                                              320 x 200 x 65536 colors @ 75 Hertz
53:                                              320 x 200 x 65536 colors @ 85 Hertz
...:
160:                                             800 x 600 x 4294967296 colors @ 75 Hertz
161:                                             800 x 600 x 4294967296 colors @ 85 Hertz
162:                                             800 x 600 x 4294967296 colors @ 90 Hertz
163:                                             800 x 600 x 4294967296 colors @ 100 Hertz
164:                                             1024 x 768 x 256 colors @ 60 Hertz
165:                                             1024 x 768 x 256 colors @ 70 Hertz
166:                                             1024 x 768 x 256 colors @ 72 Hertz
167:                                             1024 x 768 x 256 colors @ 75 Hertz
```

```
168:                                          1024 x 768 x 256 colors @ 85 Hertz
...:
175:                                          1024 x 768 x 65536 colors @ 85 Hertz
176:                                          1024 x 768 x 65536 colors @ 90 Hertz
177:                                          1024 x 768 x 65536 colors @ 100 Hertz
178:                                          1024 x 768 x 16777216 colors @ 60 Hertz
179:                                          1024 x 768 x 16777216 colors @ 70 Hertz
...:
233:                                          1600 x 1200 x 4294967296 colors @ 66 Hertz
234:                                          1600 x 1200 x 4294967296 colors @ 70 Hertz
235:                                          1600 x 1200 x 4294967296 colors @ 75 Hertz
```

2.4   Operating System classes

2.4.1   COM component classes

Most of the classes examined in the previous samples were related to the hardware. With the COM components category, and the categories that we examine in the next sections, we start to examine classes that are related to the Operating System. The Operating System classes represent operating system–related objects. They describe the various configurations and settings that define a computing environment. Besides the COM component settings, this also includes the boot configuration, the desktop environment settings, the drivers, the security settings, the user settings, and the registry settings. Let's start with the COM component settings first. The classes related to the COM components are shown in Table 2.12.

Table 2.12   *The COM Component Classes*

Name	Type	Description
Win32_ClassicCOMClass	Dynamic	Represents the properties of a COM component.
Win32_COMApplication	Dynamic	Represents a COM application.
Win32_COMClass	Dynamic	Represents the properties of a Component Object Model (COM) component.
Win32_ComponentCategory	Dynamic	Represents a component category.
Win32_COMSetting	Dynamic	Represents the settings associated with a COM component or COM application.
Win32_DCOMApplication	Dynamic	Represents the properties of a DCOM application.
Win32_DCOMApplicationSetting	Dynamic	Represents the settings of a DCOM application.
Win32_ClassicCOMApplicationClasses	Association	Relates a DCOM application and a COM component grouped under it.
Win32_ClassicCOMClassSettings	Association	Relates a COM class and the settings used to configure Dynamics of the COM class.
Win32_ClientApplicationSetting	Association	Relates an executable and a DCOM application that contains the DCOM configuration options for the executable file.
Win32_COMApplicationClasses	Association	Relates a COM component and the COM application where it resides.
Win32_COMApplicationSettings	Association	Relates a DCOM application and its configuration settings.
Win32_ComClassAutoEmulator	Association	Relates a COM class and another COM class that it automatically emulates.
Win32_ComClassEmulator	Association	Relates two versions of a COM class.
Win32_DCOMApplicationAccessAllowedSetting	Association	Relates the Win32_DCOMApplication Dynamic and the user SIDs that can access it.
Win32_DCOMApplicationLaunchAllowedSetting	Association	Relates the Win32_DCOMApplication Dynamic and the user SIDs that can launch it.
Win32_ImplementedCategory	Association	Relates a component category and the COM class using its interfaces.

When working with WMI and real-world manageable entities, we always use WMI providers. As we have seen before, the WMI providers are implemented as COM components. In the previous chapter, we created a script retrieving information from instances of the *__Win32Provider* system class (see Samples 1.1 through 1.3, "Locating WMI provider registration instances with their exposed classes"). We can reuse the logic developed in these scripts to gather the COM information about the WMI providers. This is the purpose of Sample 2.24.

Sample 2.24 *Locating the WMI provider registration instances with their COM information*

```
 1:<?xml version="1.0"?>
 .:
 8:<package>
 9:  <job>
..:
13:    <runtime>
14:      <named name="Machine" helpstring="determine the WMI system to connect to.
                             (default=LocalHost)" required="false" type="string"/>
15:      <named name="User" helpstring="determine the UserID to perform the remote connection.
                             (default=none)" required="false" type="string"/>
16:      <named name="Password" helpstring="determine the password to perform the remote
                             connection. (default=none)" required="false" type="string"/>
17:    </runtime>
18:
19:    <script language="VBScript" src=".\Functions\DisplayFormattedPropertyFunction.vbs" />
20:    <script language="VBScript" src=".\Functions\TinyErrorHandler.vbs" />
21:
22:    <object progid="WbemScripting.SWbemLocator" id="objWMILocator" reference="true"/>
23:    <object progid="WbemScripting.SWbemDateTime" id="objWMIDateTime" />
24:
25:    <script language="VBscript">
26:    <![CDATA[
..:
30:    Const cComputerName = "LocalHost"
31:    Const cWMICIMv2NameSpace = "Root\CIMv2"
32:    Const cWMINameSpace = "Root"
33:    Const cWMINamespaceClass = "__NAMESPACE"
34:    Const cWMIClass = "__Win32Provider"
..:
42:    ' ---------------------------------------------------------------------------
43:    ' Parse the command line parameters
..:
51:    If Len(strComputerName) = 0 Then strComputerName = cComputerName
52:
53:    objWMILocator.Security_.AuthenticationLevel = wbemAuthenticationLevelDefault
54:    objWMILocator.Security_.ImpersonationLevel = wbemImpersonationLevelImpersonate
55:
56:    Set objWMICIMv2Services = objWMILocator.ConnectServer(strComputerName, _
57:                                            cWMICIMv2NameSpace, _
58:                                            strUserID, _
59:                                            strPassword)
..:
62:    DisplayNameSpaces cWMINameSpace, cWMIClass, strUserID, strPassword, strComputerName
63:
```

```
 64:     ' ---------------------------------------------------------------------------------
 65:     Private Function DisplayNameSpaces (ByVal strWMINameSpace, _
 66:                                         ByVal strWMIClass, _
 67:                                         ByVal strUserID, _
 68:                                         ByVal strPassword, _
 69:                                         ByVal strComputerName)
 ..:
 79:         objWMILocator.Security_.AuthenticationLevel = wbemAuthenticationLevelDefault
 80:         objWMILocator.Security_.ImpersonationLevel = wbemImpersonationLevelImpersonate
 81:         Set objWMIServices = objWMILocator.ConnectServer(strComputerName, _
 82:                                                          strWMINameSpace, _
 83:                                                          strUserID, _
 84:                                                          strPassword)
 ..:
 86:
 87:         Set objWMIProviderInstances = objWMIServices.InstancesOf (strWMIClass, _
 88:                                                                   wbemQueryFlagShallow)
 89:         If Err.Number Then
 90:            Err.Clear
 91:         Else
 92:            WScript.Echo strWMINameSpace
 93:            For Each objWMIProviderInstance In objWMIProviderInstances
 94:
 95:                WScript.Echo "  " & objWMIProviderInstance.Name
 96:
 97:                Set objCOMSettingInstance = objWMICIMv2Services.Get _
 98:                                        ("Win32_ClassicCOMClassSetting.ComponentId='" & _
 99:                                        objWMIProviderInstance.CLSID & "'")
100:
101:                Set objWMIPropertySet = objCOMSettingInstance.Properties_
102:                For Each objWMIProperty In objWMIPropertySet
103:                    DisplayFormattedProperty objCOMSettingInstance, _
104:                                        "    " & objWMIProperty.Name, _
105:                                        objWMIProperty.Name, _
106:                                        Null
107:                Next
...:
112:            Next
...:
114:        End If
115:
116:        Set objWMINSInstances = objWMIServices.InstancesOf (cWMINamespaceClass, _
117:                                                            wbemQueryFlagShallow)
118:        For Each objWMINSInstance in objWMINSInstances
119:           DisplayNameSpaces strWMINameSpace & "/" & objWMINSInstance.Name, _
120:                          strWMIClass, strUserID, strPassword, strComputerName
121:        Next
...:
126:     End Function
127:
128:     ]]>
129:     </script>
130:   </job>
131:</package>
```

Sample 2.24 is exactly the same as Samples 1.1 through 1.3 until line 93. From line 97 through 99, the script retrieves the COM instance of the examined WMI provider instance by using its class ID (CLSID). The class

ID is represented by the *ComponentID* property in the *__Win32Provider* class. This property can be used as selection criteria to locate the COM object instance, because the *Win32_ClassicCOMClassSettings* class uses this property as a key. Once the COM component instance is available, the script shows its properties (lines 101 through 107). Next, the script enumerates the rest of the collection (line 112) and locates the next WMI namespace (lines 116 through 121).

The output from Sample 2.24 is partially represented in the following code segment. The result is interesting, since it shows the file (.DLL or .Exe) implementing the COM component, which is the WMI provider (see lines 16, 25, 45, and 55).

```
 1:   C:\>LocateProvidersWithCOMInfo.wsf
 2:   Microsoft (R) Windows Script Host Version 5.6
 3:   Copyright (C) Microsoft Corporation 1996-2001. All rights reserved.
 4:
 5:   Root
 6:   Root/SECURITY
 7:   Root/RSOP
 8:     Rsop Planning Mode Provider
 9:       AppID: ............................. {6EBBFC6C-B721-4D10-9371-5D8E8C76D315}
10:       Caption: ........................... RsopPlanningModeProvider Class
11:       *ComponentId: ...................... {F0FF8EBB-F14D-4369-bd2e-d84fbf6122d6}
12:       Control: ........................... FALSE
13:       Description: ....................... RsopPlanningModeProvider Class
14:       Insertable: ........................ FALSE
15:       JavaClass: ......................... FALSE
16:       LocalServer32: ..................... %SystemRoot%\system32\rsopprov.exe
17:       ProgId: ............................ RSOPPROV.RsopPlanningModeProvider.1
18:       VersionIndependentProgId: .......... RSOPPROV.RsopPlanningModeProvider
19:
20:     Rsop Logging Mode Provider
21:       Caption: ........................... Rsop Logging Mode Provider
22:       *ComponentId: ...................... {B3FF88A4-96EC-4cc1-983F-72BE0EBB368B}
23:       Control: ........................... FALSE
24:       Description: ....................... Rsop Logging Mode Provider
25:       InprocServer32: .................... J:\WINDOWS\system32\USERENV.dll
26:       Insertable: ........................ FALSE
27:       JavaClass: ......................... FALSE
28:       ThreadingModel: .................... Both
29:
30:   Root/RSOP/User
31:   Root/RSOP/User/ms_409
32:   Root/RSOP/User/S_1_5_21_2025429265_507921405_1202660629_1112
33:   Root/RSOP/User/S_1_5_21_2025429265_507921405_1202660629_500
34:   Root/RSOP/User/S_1_5_21_2025429265_507921405_1202660629_1140
35:   Root/RSOP/Computer
36:   Root/RSOP/Computer/ms_409
37:   Root/Cli
38:   Root/snmp
39:   Root/snmp/localhost
40:     MS_SNMP_CLASS_PROVIDER
41:       Caption: ........................... Microsoft WBEM SNMP Class Provider
42:       *ComponentId: ...................... {70426720-F78F-11cf-9151-00AA00A4086C}
43:       Control: ........................... FALSE
```

```
44:       Description: ...................... Microsoft WBEM SNMP Class Provider
45:       InprocServer32: ................... J:\WINDOWS\System32\wbem\snmpincl.dll
46:       Insertable: ....................... FALSE
47:       JavaClass: ........................ FALSE
48:       ThreadingModel: ................... Both
49:
50:    MS_SNMP_ENCAPSULATED_EVENT_PROVIDER
51:       Caption: .......................... Microsoft WBEM SNMP Event Provider
52:       *ComponentId: ..................... {19C813AC-FEE7-11D0-AB22-00C04FD9159E}
53:       Control: .......................... FALSE
54:       Description: ...................... Microsoft WBEM SNMP Event Provider
55:       InprocServer32: ................... J:\WINDOWS\System32\wbem\snmpincl.dll
56:       Insertable: ....................... FALSE
57:       JavaClass: ........................ FALSE
58:       ThreadingModel: ................... Both
..:
..:
..:
```

You can compare the obtained output for the *SNMP* class provider (lines 41 through 48) with the registry data shown in Figure 2.7.

Figure 2.7
*The SNMP class
provider COM
information from
the registry.*

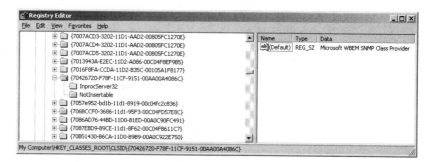

The *Win32_ClassicCOMClassSetting* class relates to the traditional COM object settings. However, by using the *Win32_DCOMApplication-Setting* class, it is possible to retrieve the settings of a DCOM application. In *Understanding WMI Scripting*, Chapter 1, when discovering WSH, we talk about a feature called WSH remote. This WSH feature is based on DCOM. If we use the *Win32_DCOMApplicationSetting* class, it is possible to retrieve the DCOM settings of this application. Sample 2.25 contains the code listing the *Win32_DCOMApplicationSetting* class settings.

Sample 2.25   *Retrieving DCOM application settings*

```
1:<?xml version="1.0"?>
.:
8:<package>
9:  <job>
..:
13:    <runtime>
14:      <unnamed name="DCOMAppsName" helpstring="the WMI instance name." required="true"
```

```
                                          type="string" />
15:      <named name="Machine" helpstring="determine the WMI system to connect to.
                                  (default=LocalHost)" required="false" type="string"/>
16:      <named name="User" helpstring="determine the UserID to perform the remote connection.
                                  (default=none)" required="false" type="string"/>
17:      <named name="Password" helpstring="determine the password to perform the remote
                                  connection. (default=none)" required="false" type="string"/>
18:      </runtime>
19:
20:      <script language="VBScript" src=".\Functions\DecodeDCOMAuthLevelFunction.vbs" />
21:
22:      <script language="VBScript" src=".\Functions\DisplayFormattedPropertyFunction.vbs" />
23:      <script language="VBScript" src=".\Functions\TinyErrorHandler.vbs" />
24:
25:      <object progid="WbemScripting.SWbemLocator" id="objWMILocator" reference="true"/>
26:      <object progid="WbemScripting.SWbemDateTime" id="objWMIDateTime" />
27:
28:      <script language="VBscript">
29:      <![CDATA[
..:
33:      Const cComputerName = "LocalHost"
34:      Const cWMINameSpace = "root/cimv2"
35:      Const cWMIClass = "Win32_DCOMApplicationSetting"
..:
48:      ' ---------------------------------------------------------------------------
49:      ' Parse the command line parameters
50:      If WScript.Arguments.Unnamed.Count = 0 Then
51:         WScript.Arguments.ShowUsage()
52:         WScript.Quit
53:      Else
54:         strWMIInstance = WScript.Arguments.Unnamed.Item(0)
55:      End If
..:
66:      objWMILocator.Security_.AuthenticationLevel = wbemAuthenticationLevelDefault
67:      objWMILocator.Security_.ImpersonationLevel = wbemImpersonationLevelImpersonate
68:
69:      Set objWMIServices = objWMILocator.ConnectServer(strComputerName, cWMINameSpace, _
70:                                          strUserID, strPassword)
..:
73:      Set objWMIInstances = objWMIServices.InstancesOf (cWMIClass)
..:
76:      For Each objWMIInstance in objWMIInstances
77:          If Ucase (objWMIInstance.Caption) = Ucase(strWMIInstance) Then
78:             Set objWMIPropertySet = objWMIInstance.Properties_
79:             For Each objWMIProperty In objWMIPropertySet
80:                 Select Case objWMIProperty.Name
81:                     Case "AuthenticationLevel"
82:                         DisplayFormattedProperty objWMIInstance, _
83:                             objWMIProperty.Name, _
84:                             DCOMAuthLevel (objWMIInstance.AuthenticationLevel), _
85:                                             Null
86:                     Case Else
87:                         DisplayFormattedProperty objWMIInstance, _
88:                             objWMIProperty.Name, _
89:                             objWMIProperty.Name, _
90:                             Null
91:                 End Select
92:             Next
..:
94:          End If
```

```
95:      Next
96:      WScript.Echo
..:
101:     ]]>
102:     </script>
103:  </job>
104:</package>
```

This sample simply lists the properties available from the *Win32_DCOMApplicationSetting* instance (lines 78 through 92). The instance is retrieved from the name given on the command line (lines 54 and 77). By default, the output obtained with the WSHRemote default settings is:

```
C:\>GetDCOMAppsSettings.wsf WSHRemote
Microsoft (R) Windows Script Host Version 5.6
Copyright (C) Microsoft Corporation 1996-2001. All rights reserved.

*AppID: ............................... {6F201542-B482-11D2-A250-00104BD35090}
AuthenticationLevel: .................... Default
Caption: ............................... WSHRemote
Description: ........................... WSHRemote
EnableAtStorageActivation: .............. FALSE
UseSurrogate: .......................... FALSE
```

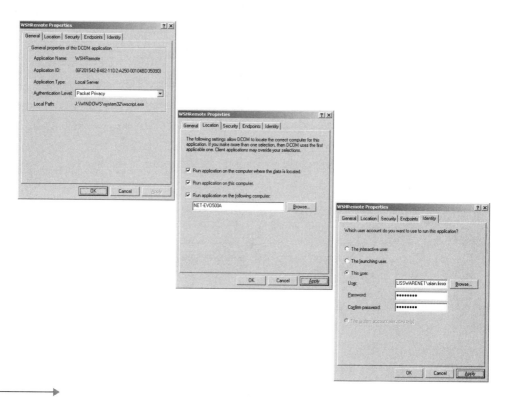

Figure 2.8   *The WSHRemote settings modification.*

If these settings are modified, as shown in Figure 2.8, the output is affected as follows:

```
C:\>GetDCOMAppsSettings.wsf WSHRemote
Microsoft (R) Windows Script Host Version 5.6
Copyright (C) Microsoft Corporation 1996-2001. All rights reserved.

*AppID: ............................... {6F201542-B482-11D2-A250-00104BD35090}
AuthenticationLevel: ................... Packet
                                         (authentication is performed on ...)
Caption: .............................. WSHRemote
Description: .......................... WSHRemote
EnableAtStorageActivation: ............ TRUE
RemoteServerName: ..................... XP-DPEP6400.LissWare.Net
RunAsUser: ............................ LISSWARENET\alain.lissoir
UseSurrogate: ......................... FALSE
```

Note that Figure 2.8 does not show the DCOM security settings. Even if these settings are modified, Sample 2.25 does not show the updated security settings. To show these DCOM rights we have to work with the

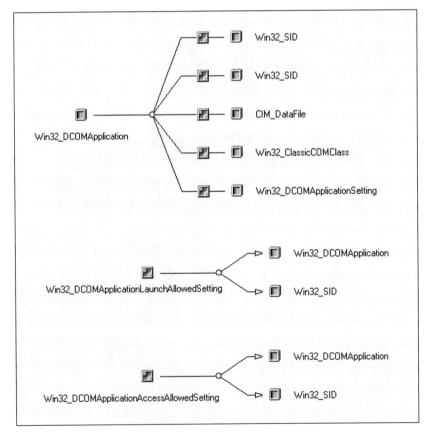

Figure 2.9
The Win32_DCOM-Application class associations.

Win32_DCOMApplicationAccessAllowedSetting and *Win32_DCOMApplicationLaunchAllowedSetting* association classes. These two classes are two association classes linking the *Win32_SID* class with the *Win32_DCOMApplication* class (see Figure 2.9).

2.4.2 Desktop information classes

The desktop information class category retrieves information about the user's desktop. This includes the current desktop settings, the environment variables, and the time zone. The classes included in this category are listed in Table 2.13.

Table 2.13 *The Desktop Classes*

Name	Type	Description
Win32_Desktop	Dynamic	Represents the common characteristics of a user's desktop.
Win32_Environment	Dynamic	Represents an environment or system environment setting on a Windows computer system.
Win32_TimeZone	Dynamic	Represents the time zone information for a Windows system.
Win32_UserDesktop	Association	Relates a user account and desktop settings that are specific to it.

Have you ever wanted to know if the profile of your users has the screen saver activated? Well, by using the *Win32_Desktop* class, you can determine if this is the case and which screen saver is selected. If we simply reuse Sample 1.5 ("Listing all instances of a class with their properties formatted") developed in the previous chapter, we can list the desktop settings located in every Windows NT profile stored on the system. The output is as follows:

```
 1:   C:\>GetCollectionOfInstances.wsf Win32_Desktop /MAchine:MyPortable.LissWare.Net
 2:   Microsoft (R) Windows Script Host Version 5.6
 3:   Copyright (C) Microsoft Corporation 1996-2001. All rights reserved.
 4:
 5:
 6:   BorderWidth: .......................... 1
 7:   CoolSwitch: ........................... TRUE
 8:   CursorBlinkRate: ...................... 530
 9:   DragFullWindows: ...................... TRUE
10:   GridGranularity: ...................... 0
11:   IconSpacing: .......................... 43
12:   IconTitleFaceName: .................... Tahoma
13:   IconTitleSize: ........................ 8
14:   IconTitleWrap: ........................ TRUE
15:   *Name: ................................ MYPORTABLE\Alain.Lissoir
16:   Pattern: .............................. (None)
17:   ScreenSaverActive: .................... TRUE
18:   ScreenSaverExecutable: ................ C:\WINNT\System32\ss3dfo.scr
19:   ScreenSaverSecure: .................... TRUE
20:   ScreenSaverTimeout: ................... 180
21:   Wallpaper: ............................ C:\WINNT\CompaqFlag.bmp
22:   WallpaperStretched: ................... FALSE
23:   WallpaperTiled: ....................... FALSE
```

```
24:
25:    BorderWidth: ............................ 1
26:    CoolSwitch: ............................. TRUE
27:    CursorBlinkRate: ........................ 530
28:    DragFullWindows: ........................ TRUE
29:    GridGranularity: ........................ 0
30:    IconSpacing: ............................ 43
31:    IconTitleFaceName: ...................... Tahoma
32:    IconTitleSize: .......................... 8
33:    IconTitleWrap: .......................... TRUE
34:    *Name: .................................. MYPORTABLE\Administrator
35:    Pattern: ................................ (None)
36:    ScreenSaverActive: ...................... FALSE
37:    ScreenSaverExecutable: .................. (NONE)
38:    ScreenSaverSecure: ...................... FALSE
39:    ScreenSaverTimeout: ..................... 900
40:    Wallpaper: .............................. C:\WINNT\Compaq.bmp
41:    WallpaperStretched: ..................... FALSE
42:    WallpaperTiled: ......................... FALSE
43:
44:    BorderWidth: ............................ 1
45:    CoolSwitch: ............................. TRUE
46:    CursorBlinkRate: ........................ 530
47:    DragFullWindows: ........................ FALSE
48:    GridGranularity: ........................ 0
49:    IconSpacing: ............................ 43
50:    IconTitleFaceName: ...................... Tahoma
51:    IconTitleSize: .......................... 8
52:    IconTitleWrap: .......................... TRUE
53:    *Name: .................................. .DEFAULT
54:    Pattern: ................................ (None)
55:    ScreenSaverActive: ...................... TRUE
56:    ScreenSaverExecutable: .................. logon.scr
57:    ScreenSaverSecure: ...................... FALSE
58:    ScreenSaverTimeout: ..................... 900
59:    Wallpaper: .............................. C:\WINNT\Compaq.bmp
60:    WallpaperStretched: ..................... FALSE
61:    WallpaperTiled: ......................... FALSE
```

As we see, the *name* property is the key property of the *Win32_Desktop* class and contains a Windows user account. The *Win32_Desktop* class is linked with the *Win32_UserAccount* class via the *Win32_UserDesktop* association class (see Figure 2.10).

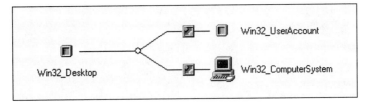

Figure 2.10
*The Win32_
Desktop class
associations.*

This link enables an application to retrieve information about the user account associated with a desktop. We revisit the *Win32_UserAccount* class later in this chapter (section 2.4.15, "User account classes").

In the same way, the *Win32_TimeZone* retrieves the current Time Zone settings. As before, if we use previous Sample 1.5 ("Listing all instances of a class with their properties formatted"), we get one instance that corresponds to the current time zone settings.

```
 1:   C:\>GetCollectionOfInstances.wsf Win32_TimeZone
 2:   Microsoft (R) Windows Script Host Version 5.6
 3:   Copyright (C) Microsoft Corporation 1996-2001. All rights reserved.
 4:
 5:
 6:   Bias: .................................. 60
 7:   Caption: .............................. (GMT+01:00) Brussels, Copenhagen, Madrid, Paris
 8:   DaylightBias: .......................... -60
 9:   DaylightDay: ........................... 5
10:   DaylightDayOfWeek: ..................... 0
11:   DaylightHour: .......................... 2
12:   DaylightMillisecond: ................... 0
13:   DaylightMinute: ........................ 0
14:   DaylightMonth: ......................... 3
15:   DaylightName: .......................... Romance Daylight Time
16:   DaylightSecond: ........................ 0
17:   DaylightYear: .......................... 0
18:   Description: .......................... (GMT+01:00) Brussels, Copenhagen, Madrid, Paris
19:   StandardBias: .......................... 0
20:   StandardDay: ........................... 5
21:   StandardDayOfWeek: ..................... 0
22:   StandardHour: .......................... 3
23:   StandardMillisecond: ................... 0
24:   StandardMinute: ........................ 0
25:   StandardMonth: ......................... 10
26:   *StandardName: ......................... Romance Standard Time
27:   StandardSecond: ........................ 0
28:   StandardYear: .......................... 0
```

Undoubtedly, the most interesting class in this category is the *Win32_Environment* class, which allows the manipulation of the environment variables. This class can be used to create, update, and delete user and system environment variables. Sample 2.26 is a script example that performs all these operations from the command line.

Before diving into the code, let's see the available command-line parameters.

```
C:\>WMIEnv.Wsf
Microsoft (R) Windows Script Host Version 5.6
Copyright (C) Microsoft Corporation 1996-2001. All rights reserved.

Environment variable with its value is missing.
```

```
Usage: WMIEnv.wsf [EnvVariable] /Env:value /Action:value [/Force[+|-]]
                  [/Machine:value] [/User:value] [/Password:value]

Options:

EnvVariable : The environment variable name with its value.
Env         : Specify the environment type: [system] for the system, [user] for the current
              user, [Domain\UserAccout] for any other user account.
Action      : Specify the operation to perform: [list] or [create] or [update] or [delete].
Force       : Force a creation if the update fails, force an update if the creation fails.
Machine     : Determine the WMI system to connect to. (default=LocalHost)
User        : Determine the UserID to perform the remote connection. (default=none)
Password    : Determine the password to perform the remote connection. (default=none)
Example:

    WMIEnv.wsf /Action:List
    WMIEnv.wsf MyVariable=MyValue /Env:LISSWARENET\Alain.Lissoir /Action:Create
    WMIEnv.wsf MyOtherVariable=MyValue /Env:SYSTEM /Action:Create
    WMIEnv.wsf MyOtherVariable /Env:SYSTEM /Action:Delete
```

As we can see, the script accepts four action types. Each action corresponds to the *Win32_Environment* operations supported. Basically, we have a first section to view the environment variables, a second section to create environment variables, a third section to update existing environment variables, and a fourth section to delete environment variables.

Sample 2.26   *Reading, creating, updating, and deleting environment variables (Part I)*

```
 1:<?xml version="1.0"?>
 .:
 8:<package>
 9:  <job>
..:
13:     <runtime>
..:
28:     </runtime>
29:
30:     <script language="VBScript" src="..\Functions\TinyErrorHandler.vbs" />
31:
32:     <object progid="WbemScripting.SWbemLocator" id="objWMILocator" reference="true"/>
33:     <object progid="Wscript.Network" id="WshNetwork" reference="true"/>
34:
35:     <script language="VBscript">
36:     <![CDATA[
..:
40:     Const cComputerName = "LocalHost"
41:     Const cWMINameSpace = "root/cimv2"
42:     Const cWMIClass = "Win32_Environment"
..:
67:     ' --------------------------------------------------------------------------
68:     ' Parse the command line parameters
69:     If WScript.Arguments.Named.Count Then
70:        Select Case Ucase(WScript.Arguments.Named("Action"))
71:           Case "LIST"
72:                 boolList = True
73:           Case "CREATE"
74:                 boolCreate = True
```

```
75:                Case "UPDATE"
76:                    boolUpdate = True
77:                Case "DELETE"
78:                    boolDelete = True
79:                Case Else
80:                    WScript.Echo "Invalid action type. Only ... are accepted." & vbCRLF
81:                    WScript.Arguments.ShowUsage()
82:                    WScript.Quit
83:        End Select
84:
85:        Select Case Ucase(WScript.Arguments.Named("Env"))
86:                Case "USER"
87:                    boolUserEnv = True
88:                Case "SYSTEM"
89:                    boolUserEnv = False
90:                Case Else
91:                    strUserEnv = WScript.Arguments.Named("Env")
92:                    If Len(strUserEnv) = 0 And Not boolList = True Then
93:                        WScript.Echo "Invalid ... type. Only ... are accepted." & vbCRLF
94:                        WScript.Arguments.ShowUsage()
95:                        WScript.Quit
96:                    End If
97:                    boolUserEnv = True
98:        End Select
99:    End If
100:
101:    If WScript.Arguments.Unnamed.Count = 0 And Not boolList = True Then
102:        WScript.Echo "Environment variable with its value is missing." & vbCRLF
103:        WScript.Arguments.ShowUsage()
104:        WScript.Quit
105:    Else
106:        If Not boolList = True Then
107:            strEnvVar = WScript.Arguments.Unnamed.Item(0)
108:            intEqualPosition = InStr (strEnvVar, "=")
109:            If intEqualPosition Then
110:                strEnvVarValue = Mid (strEnvVar, intEqualPosition + 1)
111:                strEnvVar = Mid (strEnvVar, 1, intEqualPosition - 1)
112:            Else
113:                If Not boolDelete = True Then
114:                    WScript.Echo "Invalid environment variable value." & vbCRLF
115:                    WScript.Arguments.ShowUsage()
116:                    WScript.Quit
117:                End If
118:            End If
119:        End If
120:    End If
121:
122:    boolForce = WScript.Arguments.Named("Force")
123:    If Len(boolForce) = 0 Then boolForce = False
124:
125:    strUserID = WScript.Arguments.Named("User")
126:    If Len(strUserID) = 0 Then strUserID = ""
127:
128:    strPassword = WScript.Arguments.Named("Password")
129:    If Len(strPassword) = 0 Then strPassword = ""
130:
131:    strComputerName = WScript.Arguments.Named("Machine")
132:    If Len(strComputerName) = 0 Then strComputerName = cComputerName
133:
134:    objWMILocator.Security_.AuthenticationLevel = wbemAuthenticationLevelDefault
```

```
135:    objWMILocator.Security_.ImpersonationLevel = wbemImpersonationLevelImpersonate
136:
137:    Set objWMIServices = objWMILocator.ConnectServer(strComputerName, cWMINameSpace, _
138:                                                      strUserID, strPassword)
139:    If Err.Number Then ErrorHandler (Err)
140:
...:
...:
...:
```

As usual, the script starts with the command-line parameters definition (skipped lines 13 through 28) and parsing (lines 69 through 132). The command-line parsing is a bit more complex, because some switches are only required for some specific actions. For instance, when **/Action:List** switch is used, no other command-line parameter is needed. However, when the **/Action:Create** switch is used, some more command-line parameters are required. In the case of the **/Action:Create** switch, the complete command line is as follows:

```
C:\WMIEnv MyVariable=MyValue /Action:Create /Env:Alain.Lissoir
```

When creating an environment variable, it is mandatory to specify the variable name with its value. Next, it is also necessary to specify the environment type where this new variable must be created (user or system). The parameters are verified from line 70 through 83 for the **/Action** switch, from line 85 through 98 for the **/Env** switch, and from line 106 through 119 for the variable name with its value. Once the command-line parameters are parsed and the WMI connection is executed, the corresponding environment variable action is executed accordingly (see Samples 2.27 through 2.30).

Each section of the script corresponds to a particular action. Sample 2.27 shows the code to read the environment variables.

Sample 2.27   *Reading environment variables (Part II)*

```
...:
...:
...:
140:
141:    ' -- LIST ----------------------------------------------------------------
142:    If boolList = True Then
143:        Set objWMIInstances = objWMIServices.InstancesOf (cWMIClass)
144:
145:        For Each objWMIInstance In objWMIInstances
146:            WScript.Echo objWMIInstance.Name
147:            WScript.Echo "  " & objWMIInstance.Name & "=" & objWMIInstance.VariableValue
148:            WScript.Echo "  PROFILE=" & objWMIInstance.UserName
149:            WScript.Echo "  SYSTEM=" & objWMIInstance.SystemVariable
150:        Next
151:
152:        WScript.Echo vbCRLF & "Completed."
```

```
153:
154:          Set objWMIInstance = Nothing
155:       End If
156:
...:
...:
...:
```

This code segment requests all instances of the *Win32_Environment* class (line 143). Once the collection is created, the script enumerates the variable name (line 146), its value (line 147), and its related profile and profile type (lines 148 and 149).

The environment variable creation is a bit more complex. The first point to note is that the *Win32_Environment* class does not expose any method to create an environment variable. The trick to create a new variable is to create a new instance of the *Win32_Environment* class by using the *Put_* method of a spawned **SWbemObject**. Sample 2.28 shows how this works.

Sample 2.28   *Creating environment variables (Part III)*

```
...:
...:
...:
156:
157:       ' -- CREATE ---------------------------------------------------------------
158:       If boolCreate = True Then
159:          Set objWMIClass = objWMIServices.Get (cWMIClass)
160:          Set objWMIInstance = objWMIClass.SpawnInstance_
161:
162:          If boolUserEnv = True Then
163:             If Len(strUserEnv) = 0 Then
164:                objWMIInstance.UserName = WshNetwork.UserDomain & "\" & WshNetwork.UserName
165:             Else
166:                objWMIInstance.UserName = strUserEnv
167:             End If
168:             objWMIInstance.SystemVariable = False
169:          Else
170:             objWMIInstance.UserName = "<SYSTEM>"
171:             objWMIInstance.SystemVariable = True
172:          End If
173:
174:          objWMIInstance.Name = strEnvVar
175:          objWMIInstance.VariableValue = strEnvVarValue
176:
177:          If boolForce = True Then
178:             objWMIInstance.Put_ (wbemChangeFlagCreateOrUpdate Or wbemFlagReturnWhenComplete)
179:          Else
180:             objWMIInstance.Put_ (wbemChangeFlagCreateOnly Or wbemFlagReturnWhenComplete)
181:          End If
...:
184:          WScript.Echo "Environment variable '" & strEnvVar & "' created."
...:
187:       End If
188:
...:
...:
...:
```

First, the script creates a new instance of the *Win32_Environment* class (lines 159 and 160). Based on the environment variable type (user or system), the script initializes the required properties (lines 162 through 172). Note that if the **/Env** switch has a value equal to "User," the script retrieves the name of the user running the script with some WSH objects (line 164). It is important to note that if you execute the script with a remote system, it is mandatory to explicitly specify the remote user name environment, since WSH only retrieves the local user name. Next, the variable name and its value are stored in the new instance (lines 174 and 175). At line 177, the script tests if the switch **/Force+** is specified on the command line. This switch allows the creation of a variable even if the environment variable already exists. Basically, the presence of the **/Force+** switch transforms the creation process into an update process if the environment variable already exists (with the **wbemChangeFlagCreateOrUpdate** constant at line 178 versus the **wbemChangeFlagCreateOnly** constant at line 180). The environment variable creation is executed with the *Put_* method of the new environment variable instance stored in an **SWBemObject**. Once the method executes, the code verifies that no error occurred during the creation (line 182). At that time, the new environment variable exists in the system or user environment. You can use the **/Action:List** switch to check its presence (or open a new command-line window and type the "set" command).

Sample 2.29   *Updating environment variables (Part IV)*

```
...:
...:
...:
188:
189:    ' -- UPDATE -----------------------------------------------------------------
190:    If boolUpdate = True Then
191:        If boolUserEnv = True Then
192:            If Len(strUserEnv) = 0 Then
193:                objWMIInstance.UserName = WshNetwork.UserDomain & "\" & WshNetwork.UserName
194:            Else
195:                objWMIInstance.UserName = strUserEnv
196:            End If
197:        Else
198:            strUserName = "<SYSTEM>"
199:        End If
200:
201:        Set objWMIInstance = objWMIServices.Get _
202:                (cWMIClass & ".Name='" & strEnvVar & "',UserName='" & strUserName & "'")
...:
205:        objWMIInstance.VariableValue = strEnvVarValue
206:
207:        objWMIInstance.Put_ (wbemChangeFlagUpdateOnly Or wbemFlagReturnWhenComplete)
...:
211:        WScript.Echo "Environment variable '" & strEnvVar & "' updated."
```

```
...:
214:      End If
215:
...:
...:
...:
```

The update process of the environment variable almost follows the same logic as the variable creation. Of course, since we are in an update process, the script retrieves an instance of the environment variable given on the command line (lines 201 and 202). Next, the script updates the variable value (line 205). Once completed, the updated instance is saved with the *Put_* method of the **SWbemObject** (line 207).

Sample 2.30   *Deleting environment variables (Part V)*

```
...:
...:
...:
215:
216:     ' -- DELETE -------------------------------------------------------------------
217:     If boolDelete = True Then
218:         If boolUserEnv = True Then
219:             If Len(strUserEnv) = 0 Then
220:                 objWMIInstance.UserName = WshNetwork.UserDomain & "\" & WshNetwork.UserName
221:             Else
222:                 objWMIInstance.UserName = strUserEnv
223:             End If
224:         Else
225:             strUserName = "<SYSTEM>"
226:         End If
227:
228:         Set objWMIInstance = objWMIServices.Get _
229:                 (cWMIClass & ".Name='" & strEnvVar & "',UserName='" & strUserName & "'")
...:
232:         objWMIInstance.Delete_
...:
235:         WScript.Echo "Environment variable '" & strEnvVar & "' deleted."
...:
238:     End If
...:
242:     ]]>
243:     </script>
244: </job>
245:</package>
237:</package>
```

To delete an environment variable, the script retrieves the existing *Win32_Environment* instance of the variable to be deleted (lines 228 and 229). Next, since the retrieved instance is stored in an **SWbemObject**, the *Delete_* method is executed to delete the environment variable (line 232). No particular difficulty here!

2.4.3   Driver classes

The driver category classes represent the virtual device drivers and system drivers for base services. There are two classes are in this category (see Table 2.14).

Table 2.14   *The Driver Classes*

Name	Description
Win32_DriverVXD	Represents a virtual device driver on a Windows computer system.
Win32_SystemDriver	Represents the system driver for a base service.

The *Win32_SystemDriver* class is a subclass of the *Win32_BaseService* class. If you remember, throughout the first book, *Understanding WMI Scripting*, we worked a lot with the *Win32_Service* class. We saw that the *Win32_Service* class is also a child of *Win32_BaseService* (see Figure 2.11).

Figure 2.11
The CIM_Service class and its child classes.

If you look at the properties inheritance, you see that most of the properties and methods come from the *Win32_BaseService* class. This means that both classes share the same set of properties and methods and that most of the things valid for the *Win32_Service* class are also valid for the *Win32_SystemDriver*. For reference, by using Sample 1.5 ("Listing all instances of a class with their properties formatted"), we obtain the following output:

```
 1:   C:\>GetCollectionOfInstances.wsf Win32_SystemDriver
 2:   Microsoft (R) Windows Script Host Version 5.6
 3:   Copyright (C) Microsoft Corporation 1996-2001. All rights reserved.
 4:
 5:
 6:   AcceptPause: ........................... FALSE
 7:   AcceptStop: ............................ FALSE
 8:   Caption: .............................. Abiosdsk
 9:   CreationClassName: ..................... Win32_SystemDriver
10:   Description: .......................... Abiosdsk
11:   DesktopInteract: ....................... FALSE
12:   DisplayName: .......................... Abiosdsk
13:   ErrorControl: ......................... Ignore
```

```
14:     ExitCode: ............................... 1077
15:     *Name: .................................. Abiosdsk
16:     ServiceSpecificExitCode: ................ 0
17:     ServiceType: ............................ Kernel Driver
18:     Started: ................................ FALSE
19:     StartMode: .............................. Disabled
20:     StartName: ..............................
21:     State: .................................. Stopped
22:     Status: ................................. OK
23:     SystemCreationClassName: ................ Win32_ComputerSystem
24:     SystemName: ............................. XP-DPEN6400
25:     TagId: .................................. 3
26:
27:     AcceptPause: ............................ FALSE
28:     AcceptStop: ............................. FALSE
29:     Caption: ................................ abp480n5
30:     CreationClassName: ...................... Win32_SystemDriver
31:     Description: ............................ abp480n5
32:     DesktopInteract: ........................ FALSE
33:     DisplayName: ............................ abp480n5
34:     ErrorControl: ........................... Normal
35:     ExitCode: ............................... 1077
36:     *Name: .................................. abp480n5
..:
..:
..:
```

Under Windows 95, 98, and Millennium, you will find instances of the *Win32_DriverVXD* class. With the same script, the output is as follows:

```
1:     C:\>GetCollectionOfInstances.wsf Win32_DriverVXD
2:     Microsoft (R) Windows Script Host Version 5.6
3:     Copyright (C) Microsoft Corporation 1996-2001. All rights reserved.
4:
5:
6:     Caption: ................................ VMM
7:     Control: ................................ c0002788
8:     Description: ............................ VMM
9:     DeviceDescriptorBlock: .................. c0011330
10:    InstallDate: ............................
11:    *Name: .................................. VMM
12:    OtherTargetOS: .......................... Win9X
13:    PM_API: ................................. c0002f30
14:    ServiceTableSize: ....................... 446
15:    *SoftwareElementID: ..................... VMM
16:    *SoftwareElementState: .................. 3
17:    Status: ................................. OK
18:    *TargetOperatingSystem: ................. 1
19:    V86_API: ................................ c0002f30
20:    *Version: ............................... 4,10
21:
22:    Caption: ................................ MTRR
23:    Control: ................................ c00403ec
24:    Description: ............................ MTRR
25:    DeviceDescriptorBlock: .................. c003f2a0
26:    InstallDate: ............................
27:    *Name: .................................. MTRR
28:    OtherTargetOS: .......................... Win9X
```

```
29:  PM_API: ...................................          0
30:  ServiceTableSize: ........................  4
31:  *SoftwareElementID: ......................  MTRR
32:  *SoftwareElementState: ...................  3
33:  Status: ..................................  OK
34:  *TargetOperatingSystem: ..................  1
35:  V86_API: .................................          0
36:  *Version: ................................  1,00
37:
38:  Caption: .................................  VCACHE
39:  Control: .................................  c004ddf4
40:  Description: .............................  VCACHE
41:  DeviceDescriptorBlock: ...................  c004eab8
42:  InstallDate: .............................
43:  *Name: ...................................  VCACHE
44:  OtherTargetOS: ...........................  Win9X
45:  PM_API: ..................................  c004e9c4
46:  ServiceTableSize: ........................  29
47:  *SoftwareElementID: ......................  VCACHE
48:  *SoftwareElementState: ...................  3
49:  Status: ..................................  OK
50:  *TargetOperatingSystem: ..................  1
51:  V86_API: .................................  c004e9c4
52:  *Version: ................................  3,01
53:
54:  Caption: .................................  DFS
55:  Control: .................................  c007ac67
56:  Description: .............................  DFS
57:  DeviceDescriptorBlock: ...................  c007ac0c
58:  InstallDate: .............................  20-12-1998 19:52:16
59:  *Name: ...................................  DFS
60:  OtherTargetOS: ...........................  Win9X
..:
..:
..:
```

2.4.4 **File system classes**

The file system category classes represent the way a hard disk is logically organized. This includes the type of file system used, the directory structure, and way the disk is partitioned. The classes included in this category are listed in Table 2.15.

As we can see, this category includes the *Win32_DiskQuota*, *Win32_QuotaSetting*, and *Win32_VolumeQuotaSetting* classes. These classes work in conjunction with the *Disk Quota* WMI provider, which is examined in the next chapter.

The *Win32_ShortcutFile* class is a subclass of the *CIM_DataFile* class. The *CIM_DataFile* class is a generic representation of a file. The *CIM_Data-File* class is also a superclass for classes such as *Win32_CodecFile*, *Win32_NTEventLogFile*, and *Win32_PageFile*. Note that the *Win32_NTEventLog-File* class is supported by the *MS_NT_EVENTLOG_PROVIDER* provider

Table 2.15 *The File System Classes*

Name	Type	Description
Win32_Directory	Dynamic	Represents a directory entry on a Windows computer system.
Win32_DirectorySpecification	Dynamic	Represents the directory layout for the product.
Win32_DiskPartition	Dynamic	Represents the capabilities and management capacity of a partitioned area of a physical disk on a Windows system.
Win32_QuotaSetting	Dynamic	Contains setting information for disk quotas on a volume.
Win32_ShortcutFile	Dynamic	Represents files that are shortcuts to other files, directories, and commands.
Win32_CIMLogicalDeviceCIMDataFile	Association	Relates logical devices and data files, indicating the driver files used by the device.
Win32_DiskDriveToDiskPartition	Association	Relates a disk drive and a partition existing on it.
Win32_DiskQuota	Association	Tracks disk space usage for NTFS volumes.
Win32_LogicalDiskRootDirectory	Association	Relates a logical disk and its directory structure.
Win32_LogicalDiskToPartition	Association	Relates a logical disk drive and the disk partition it resides on.
Win32_OperatingSystemAutochkSetting	Association	Represents the association between a CIM_ManagedSystemElement Dynamic and the settings defined for it.
Win32_SubDirectory	Association	Relates a directory (folder) and one of its subdirectories (subfolders).
Win32_SystemPartitions	Association	Relates a computer system and a disk partition on that system.
Win32_VolumeQuotaSetting	Association	Relates disk quota settings with a specific disk volume.

and will be examined in the next chapter, since this class is supported by a provider other than the *Win32* provider.

The *Win32_Directory* class is a subclass of the *CIM_Directory*. However, this class is the only subclass of *CIM_Directory* class. The *CIM_DataFile* relationships are shown in Figure 2.12.

Figure 2.12
The CIM_ LogicalFile class and its child classes.

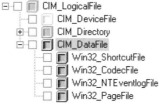

To gather information about a file, it is best to use the *CIM_DataFile* class, because it is the most generic file representation. The existing subclasses are too specific to a particular file type. Since there are thousands of files in a file system, it is better to retrieve a single instance of a file than a collection. For example, to retrieve information related to the BOOT.INI file, we can use Sample 1.4 ("Listing a single instance of a class with its properties formatted"):

```
1:   C:\>GetSingleInstance CIM_DataFile "'C:\Boot.Ini'"
2:   Microsoft (R) Windows Script Host Version 5.6
3:   Copyright (C) Microsoft Corporation 1996-2001. All rights reserved.
4:
5:   AccessMask: ........................... 18809343
6:   Archive: .............................. FALSE
```

```
 7:   Caption: ............................. c:\boot.ini
 8:   Compressed: .......................... FALSE
 9:   CreationClassName: ................... CIM_LogicalFile
10:   CreationDate: ........................ 03-05-2001 12:53:02
11:   CSCreationClassName: ................. Win32_ComputerSystem
12:   CSName: .............................. XP-DPEN6400
13:   Description: ......................... c:\boot.ini
14:   Drive: ............................... c:
15:   EightDotThreeFileName: ............... c:\boot.ini
16:   Encrypted: ........................... FALSE
17:   Extension: ........................... ini
18:   FileName: ............................ boot
19:   FileSize: ............................ 199
20:   FileType: ............................ Configuration Settings
21:   FSCreationClassName: ................. Win32_FileSystem
22:   FSName: .............................. NTFS
23:   Hidden: .............................. TRUE
24:   InstallDate: ......................... 03-05-2001 12:53:02
25:   LastAccessed: ........................ 20-10-2001 22:26:07
26:   LastModified: ........................ 20-10-2001 22:26:07
27:   *Name: ............................... c:\boot.ini
28:   Path: ................................ \
29:   Readable: ............................ TRUE
30:   Status: .............................. OK
31:   System: .............................. TRUE
32:   Writeable: ........................... TRUE
```

This output summarizes the typical properties of a file. Note at line 5 that the *AccessMask* property is a bit array representing the access rights to the given file held by the user or group on whose behalf the instance is returned. We revisit the access mask and the rights granted on the file system in Chapter 4, when we examine the *Security* WMI provider. The same operation can be repeated with the *CIM_Directory* class; the output is as follows:

```
 1:   C:\>GetSingleInstance CIM_Directory "'C:\Windows'"
 2:   Microsoft (R) Windows Script Host Version 5.6
 3:   Copyright (C) Microsoft Corporation 1996-2001. All rights reserved.
 4:
 5:   Archive: ............................. FALSE
 6:   Caption: ............................. C:\Windows
 7:   Compressed: .......................... FALSE
 8:   CreationClassName: ................... CIM_LogicalFile
 9:   CreationDate: ........................ 03-05-2001 03:44:03
10:   CSCreationClassName: ................. Win32_ComputerSystem
11:   CSName: .............................. XP-DPEN6400
12:   Description: ......................... C:\Windows
13:   Drive: ............................... j:
14:   EightDotThreeFileName: ............... C:\Windows
15:   Encrypted: ........................... FALSE
16:   Extension: ...........................
17:   FileName: ............................ windows
18:   FileType: ............................ File Folder
19:   FSCreationClassName: ................. Win32_FileSystem
20:   FSName: .............................. NTFS
21:   Hidden: .............................. FALSE
22:   InstallDate: ......................... 03-05-2001 03:44:03
23:   LastAccessed: ........................ 21-10-2001 14:37:08
24:   LastModified: ........................ 21-10-2001 12:08:30
```

```
25:   *Name:  ................................. C:\Windows
26:   Path:   ................................. \
27:   Readable:  .............................. TRUE
28:   Status:  ................................ OK
29:   System:  ................................ FALSE
30:   Writeable:  ............................. TRUE
```

Since we examine the file system, we must also examine the *Win32_DiskPartition* class, since a disk partition generally contains a file system. Examining the *Win32_DiskPartition* class implies the examination of some classes that have an association with the *Win32_DiskPartition* class, such as the *Win32_LogicalDisk* and *Win32_DiskDrive* classes examined previously in section 2.3.2 ("Mass storage classes"). Figure 2.13 represents the association relationship seen from the *Win32_DiskPartition* class.

Figure 2.13
*The Win32_
DiskPartition class
associations.*

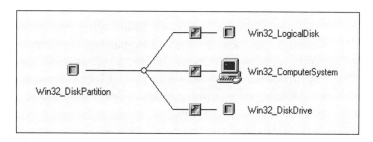

The purpose of Samples 2.31 through 2.34 is to retrieve information about these classes.

Sample 2.31   *Gathering disk partition, disk drive, and logical disk information (Part I)*

```
1:<?xml version="1.0"?>
.:
8:<package>
9:  <job>
..:
13:    <runtime>
..:
17:    </runtime>
18:
19:    <script language="VBScript" src="..\Functions\DecodeDeviceAvailabilityFunction.vbs" />
20:    <script language="VBScript" src="..\Functions\DecodeCfgManErrCodeFunction.vbs" />
21:    <script language="VBScript" src="..\Functions\DecodeStatusInfoFunction.vbs" />
22:    <script language="VBScript" src="..\Functions\DecodePwrManCapabilitiesFunction.vbs" />
23:    <script language="VBScript" src="..\Functions\DecodeDiskCapabilitiesFunction.vbs" />
24:
25:    <script language="VBScript" src="..\Functions\DisplayFormattedPropertyFunction.vbs" />
26:    <script language="VBScript" src="..\Functions\TinyErrorHandler.vbs" />
27:
28:    <object progid="WbemScripting.SWbemLocator" id="objWMILocator" reference="true"/>
29:    <object progid="WbemScripting.SWbemDateTime" id="objWMIDateTime" />
30:
31:    <script language="VBscript">
```

```
32:      <![CDATA[
..:
36:      Const cComputerName = "LocalHost"
37:      Const cWMINameSpace = "root/cimv2"
..:
52:      ' ---------------------------------------------------------------------------
53:      ' Parse the command line parameters
54:      strUserID = WScript.Arguments.Named("User")
..:
61:      If Len(strComputerName) = 0 Then strComputerName = cComputerName
..:
66:      Set objWMIServices = objWMILocator.ConnectServer(strComputerName, cWMINameSpace, _
67:                                                       strUserID, strPassword)
..:
69:
..:
..:
..:
```

Once again, the code starts by including the external functions (lines 19 through 26) and defining and parsing the command-line parameters (skipped lines 13 through 17 and 54 through 61) before establishing the WMI connection (lines 66 and 67). Once completed, the script examines the *Win32_DiskPartition* instances (see Sample 2.32).

Sample 2.32   *Gathering disk partition information (Part II)*

```
..:
..:
..:
69:
70:      Set objWMIInstances = objWMIServices.InstancesOf ("Win32_DiskPartition")
..:
73:      If objWMIInstances.Count Then
74:         For Each objWMIInstance In objWMIInstances
75:            WScript.Echo "- " & objWMIInstance.DeviceID & " " & String (61, "-")
76:
77:            Set objWMIPropertySet = objWMIInstance.Properties_
78:            For Each objWMIProperty In objWMIPropertySet
79:               Select Case objWMIProperty.Name
80:                   Case "Availability"
81:                       DisplayFormattedProperty objWMIInstance, _
82:                              " " & objWMIProperty.Name, _
83:                              DeviceAvailability (objWMIInstance.Availability), _
84:                              Null
...:
100:                  Case "StatusInfo"
101:                      DisplayFormattedProperty objWMIInstance, _
102:                             " " & objWMIProperty.Name, _
103:                             StatusInfo (objWMIInstance.StatusInfo), _
104:                             Null
105:                  Case "CreationClassName"
106:
107:                  Case "SystemCreationClassName"
108:
109:                  Case "SystemName"
```

```
110:
111:                    Case "Caption"
112:
113:                    Case "Name"
114:
115:                    Case Else
116:                        DisplayFormattedProperty objWMIInstance, _
117:                                  "   " & objWMIProperty.Name, _
118:                                  objWMIProperty.Name, _
119:                                  Null
120:               End Select
121:           Next
122:           Set objWMIPropertySet = Nothing
123:
...:
...:
...:
```

To explore the *Win32_DiskPartition* instances, the script contains nothing unusual compared with the previous script developed. Sample 2.32 is only provided for reference. However, since a disk partition is located on a disk drive, to gather information about the *Win32_DiskDrive* instance associated with the *Win32_DiskPartition* instance, the script retrieves the information by using the *Win32_DiskDrive*ToDiskPartition association class (see Figure 2.13). This code is available in Sample 2.33 from lines 124 through 127.

Sample 2.33 *Gathering disk drive information (Part III)*

```
...:
...:
...:
123:
124:           Set objWMIPhysicalDiskInstances = objWMIServices.ExecQuery _
125:                            ("Associators of {Win32_DiskPartition='" & _
126:                             objWMIInstance.DeviceID & _
127:                             "'} Where AssocClass=Win32_DiskDriveToDiskPartition")
128:
129:           If objWMIPhysicalDiskInstances.Count Then
130:              WScript.Echo
131:              WScript.Echo "  -- Physical disk information " & " " & String (53, "-")
132:              For Each objWMIPhysicalDiskInstance In objWMIPhysicalDiskInstances
133:                 Set objWMIPropertySet = objWMIPhysicalDiskInstance.Properties_
134:                 For Each objWMIProperty In objWMIPropertySet
135:                    Select Case objWMIProperty.Name
136:                        Case "Availability"
137:                            DisplayFormattedProperty objWMIPhysicalDiskInstance, _
138:                                "   " & objWMIProperty.Name, _
...:
156:                        Case "StatusInfo"
157:                            DisplayFormattedProperty objWMIPhysicalDiskInstance, _
158:                                "   " & objWMIProperty.Name, _
159:                                StatusInfo (objWMIPhysicalDiskInstance.StatusInfo), _
160:                                Null
161:                        Case "CreationClassName"
```

```
162:
163:                              Case "SystemCreationClassName"
164:
165:                              Case "SystemName"
166:
167:                              Case "Caption"
168:
169:                              Case "Name"
170:
171:                              Case "Capabilities"
172:                                    DisplayFormattedProperty objWMIPhysicalDiskInstance, _
173:                                          "  " & objWMIProperty.Name, _
...:
177:                              Case Else
178:                                    DisplayFormattedProperty objWMIPhysicalDiskInstance, _
179:                                          "  " & objWMIProperty.Name, _
180:                                          objWMIProperty.Name, _
181:                                          Null
182:                        End Select
183:                  Next
184:            Set objWMIPropertySet = Nothing
185:      Next
186:  End If
187:
188:  Set objWMIPhysicalDiskInstances = Nothing
189:
...:
...:
...:
```

Again, the display of the *Win32_DiskDrive* properties is executed as before. In the same way, since a disk partition hosts a logical disk, it is interesting to gather information about it. By using the *Win32_LogicalDisk*To-Partition association class, it is possible to retrieve the *Win32_LogicalDisk* instances for the *Win32_DiskPartition* (see Figure 2.13). Sample 2.34 executes this operation from lines 190 through 193. Next, the script displays the properties of the retrieved instances (lines 198 through 268).

Sample 2.34   *Gathering logical disk information (Part IV)*

```
...:
...:
...:
189:
190:      Set objWMILogicalDiskInstances = objWMIServices.ExecQuery _
191:            ("Associators of {Win32_DiskPartition='" & _
192:            objWMIInstance.DeviceID & _
193:            "'} Where AssocClass=Win32_LogicalDiskToPartition")
194:
195:      If objWMILogicalDiskInstances.Count Then
196:          WScript.Echo
197:          WScript.Echo "  -- Logical disk information " & " " & String (55, "-")
198:          For Each objWMILogicalDiskInstance In objWMILogicalDiskInstances
199:              Set objWMIPropertySet = objWMILogicalDiskInstance.Properties_
200:              For Each objWMIProperty In objWMIPropertySet
```

```
201:                    Select Case objWMIProperty.Name
202:                        Case "Availability"
203:                            DisplayFormattedProperty objWMILogicalDiskInstance, _
204:                                " " & objWMIProperty.Name, _
...:
232:
233:                        Case "Caption"
234:
235:                        Case "Name"
236:
237:                        Case Else
238:                            DisplayFormattedProperty objWMILogicalDiskInstance, _
239:                                " " & objWMIProperty.Name, _
240:                                objWMIProperty.Name, _
241:                                Null
242:                    End Select
243:                Next
244:                Set objWMIPropertySet = Nothing
245:
...:
...:
...:
267:
268:            Next
269:            Set objWMILogicalDiskInstances = Nothing
270:        End If
271:
272:        WScript.Echo
273:    Next
274: Else
275:    WScript.Echo "No information available."
276: End If
...:
281: ]]>
282: </script>
283: </job>
284:</package>
```

Notice that between lines 245 and 267 we have a certain number of lines missing. This part of the code examines the quotas set on the logical disk. We examine this code in the next chapter, since it relates to the use of the *Win32_DiskQuota*, *Win32_QuotaSetting*, and *Win32_VolumeQuotaSetting* classes supported by the *Disk Quota* WMI provider.

Once the script is started, you obtain the following output:

```
 1:  C:\>GetPartitionInformation.wsf
 2:  Microsoft (R) Windows Script Host Version 5.6
 3:  Copyright (C) Microsoft Corporation 1996-2001. All rights reserved.
 4:
 5:  - Disk #1, Partition #0 -------------------------------------------------------
 6:    BlockSize: ........................... 512
 7:    Description: ......................... MS-DOS V4 Huge
 8:    *DeviceID: ........................... Disk #1, Partition #0
 9:    DiskIndex: ........................... 1
10:    Index: ............................... 0
11:    InstallDate: ......................... 01-01-2000
```

```
12:    NumberOfBlocks: .......................... 4188177
13:    PrimaryPartition: ........................ FALSE
14:    Size: .................................... 2144346624
15:    StartingOffset: .......................... 32256
16:    Type: .................................... MS-DOS V4 Huge
17:
18:    -- Physical disk information  ----------------------------------------------------
19:    BytesPerSector: .......................... 512
20:    Capabilities: ............................ Random Access, Supports Writing
21:    ConfigManagerErrorCode: .................. This device is working properly.
22:    ConfigManagerUserConfig: ................. FALSE
23:    Description: ............................. Disk drive
24:    *DeviceID: ............................... \\.\PHYSICALDRIVE1
25:    Index: ................................... 1
26:    InstallDate: ............................. 01-01-2000
27:    InterfaceType: ........................... IDE
28:    Manufacturer: ............................ (Standard disk drives)
29:    MediaLoaded: ............................. TRUE
30:    MediaType: ............................... Fixed hard disk media
31:    Model: ................................... FUJITSU MPC310AT   E
32:    Partitions: .............................. 4
33:    PNPDeviceID: ............................. IDE\DSKFUJITSU_MPC310AT_E_CD05_\4&8F1A1C8&0&0.1.0
34:    SCSIBus: ................................. 0
35:    SCSILogicalUnit: ......................... 0
36:    SCSIPort: ................................ 0
37:    SCSITargetId: ............................ 1
38:    SectorsPerTrack: ......................... 63
39:    Signature: ............................... 2101398628
40:    Size: .................................... 10001940480
41:    Status: .................................. OK
42:    TotalCylinders: .......................... 1292
43:    TotalHeads: .............................. 240
44:    TotalSectors: ............................ 19535040
45:    TotalTracks: ............................. 310080
46:    TracksPerCylinder: ....................... 240
47:
48:    -- Logical disk information  -----------------------------------------------------
49:    Compressed: .............................. FALSE
50:    Description: ............................. Local Fixed Disk
51:    *DeviceID: ............................... D:
52:    DriveType: ............................... 3
53:    FileSystem: .............................. FAT
54:    FreeSpace: ............................... 497254400
55:    InstallDate: ............................. 01-01-2000
56:    MaximumComponentLength: .................. 255
57:    MediaType: ............................... 12
58:    Size: .................................... 2144043008
59:    SupportsDiskQuotas: ...................... FALSE
60:    SupportsFileBasedCompression: ........... FALSE
61:    VolumeDirty: ............................. FALSE
62:    VolumeName: .............................. APPS
63:    VolumeSerialNumber: ...................... 4C2002DB
..:
..:
..:
```

Instead of developing some passive scripts, we can use the classes in the
File System category differently. For instance, by using the *CIM_DataFile*
class, it is possible to watch the growth of a file. This is interesting if you

want to monitor the physical size of database files (i.e., Exchange 2000 Information Store size). In section 2.3.2, we developed a script that monitors the free disk space (see Sample 2.2, "Alerting script when the free disk space decreases below 50 percent on a specific disk"). We can develop the same kind of script, but instead of monitoring the free disk space diminutions, we can monitor the growth of a selected file. The code is shown in Sample 2.35.

Sample 2.35   *Watching a file size*

```
 1:<?xml version="1.0"?>
 . :
 8:<package>
 9:  <job>
 ..:
13:     <script language="VBScript" src="..\Functions\TinyErrorHandler.vbs" />
14:     <script language="VBScript" src="..\Functions\PauseScript.vbs" />
15:
16:     <reference object="WbemScripting.SWbemLocator"/>
17:
18:     <script language="VBscript">
19:     <![CDATA[
..:
23:     ' -------------------------------------------------------------------------------
24:     Const cComputerName = "LocalHost"
25:     Const cWMINameSpace = "root/cimv2"
26:     Const cWMIClass = "CIM_DataFile"
27:     Const cWMIInstance = "'E:\\TEST.TXT'"
28:     Const cFileSize = 10240
..:
36:     Set objWMISink = WScript.CreateObject ("WbemScripting.SWbemSink", "SINK_")
37:
38:     Set objWMIServices = GetObject("WinMgmts:{impersonationLevel=impersonate}!//" & _
39:                                     cComputerName & "/" & cWMINameSpace)
..:
42:     strWQLQuery = "Select * From __InstanceModificationEvent Within 10 " & _
43:                   "Where TargetInstance ISA '" & cWMIClass & "' And " & _
44:                   "TargetInstance.Name=" & cWMIInstance & " And " & _
45:                   "TargetInstance.FileSize > " & cFileSize & " And " & _
46:                   "TargetInstance.FileSize > PreviousInstance.FileSize"
47:
48:     objWMIServices.ExecNotificationQueryAsync objWMISink, _
49:                                                strWQLQuery, _
50:                                                , _
51:                                                wbemFlagSendStatus
..:
54:     WScript.Echo "Waiting for events..."
55:
56:     PauseScript "Click on 'Ok' to terminate the script ..."
57:
58:     WScript.Echo vbCRLF & "Cancelling event subscription ..."
59:     objWMISink.Cancel
..:
64:     WScript.Echo "Finished."
65:
66:     ' -------------------------------------------------------------------------------
67:     Sub SINK_OnObjectReady (objWbemObject, objWbemAsyncContext)
..:
```

```
73:            Wscript.Echo
74:            WScript.Echo FormatDateTime(Date, vbLongDate) & " at " & _
75:                         FormatDateTime(Time, vbLongTime) & "."
76:
77:            WScript.Echo "Warning, file " & UCase (objWbemObject.TargetInstance.Name) & " has " & _
78:                         objWbemObject.TargetInstance.FileSize & _
79:                         " bytes of size."
80:
81:      End Sub
82:
83:      ]]>
84:    </script>
85:  </job>
86:</package>
```

If Sample 2.35 is compared with Sample 2.2, it is almost the same script. The major difference resides in the WQL query (lines 42 through 46):

```
1:  Select * From __InstanceModificationEvent Within 10
2:       Where TargetInstance ISA 'CIM_DataFile' And
3:       TargetInstance.Name=" & 'E:\\TEST.TXT' And
4:       TargetInstance.FileSize > 10240 And
5:       TargetInstance.FileSize > PreviousInstance.FileSize
```

The WQL query contains four conditions, based on:

- **The *TargetInstance* class type** (line 2): This condition makes sense, since the monitoring must be executed on an instance of the *CIM_DataFile*.

- **The *Name*** (line 3): Because the monitoring must be done on a specific file name.

- **The *FileSize*** (line 4): The *FileSize* is the current size of the file instance. If we do not want the script to send an alert if the size is less than 10,240 bytes (10 K), this requirement must be included in the condition statement.

- **The file growth** (line 5): Since the requirement is to send an alert only when the file size increases, the test evaluates the size of the file instance with the value of the previous file instance. If the current instance size is greater, it means that the file size increases.

Once this WQL event query is submitted, and when the examined file meets these conditions, the event sink routine SINK_OnObjectReady() (lines 67 through 81) is called, and a message containing the file size information is displayed on the screen (lines 77 through 79).

If you look at the *CIM_DataFile* class and *CIM_Directory* class methods, you see that they share the same methods. These two classes are subclasses of the *CIM_LogicalFile* class, which is the CIM origin of the method definitions. Table 2.16 shows the *CIM_LogicalFile* methods.

Table 2.16 *The CIM_LogicalFile Methods*

Method name	Description
TakeOwnerShip	Class method that obtains ownership of the logical file specified in the object path.
ChangeSecurityPermissions	Class method that changes the security permissions for the logical file specified in the object path.
Copy	Class method that copies the logical file or directory specified in the object path to the location specified by the input parameter.
Rename	Class method that renames the logical file (or directory) specified in the object path.
Delete	Class method that deletes the logical file (or directory) specified in the object path.
Compress	Class method that compresses the logical file (or directory) specified in the object path.
Uncompress	Class method that uncompresses the logical file (or directory) specified in the object path.
TakeOwnerShipEx	Class method that obtains ownership of the logical file specified in the object path.
ChangeSecurityPermissionsEx	Class method that changes the security permissions for the logical file specified in the object path.
CopyEx	Class method that copies the logical file or directory specified in the object path to the location specified by the FileName parameter.
DeleteEx	Class method that deletes the logical file (or directory) specified in the object path.
CompressEx	Class method that compresses the logical file (or directory) specified in the object path.
UncompressEx	Class method that uncompresses the logical file (or directory) specified in the object path.
GetEffectivePermission	Class method that determines whether the caller has the aggregated permissions specified by the *Permission* argument not only on the file object, but on the share the file or directory resides on (if it is on a share).

By using these methods it is possible to copy, rename, delete, compress or decompress, and take ownership of any file or directory. Using the method at the level of the *CIM_LogicalFile* class permits the equal manipulation of files or directories. Sample 2.36 shows how to proceed. The command-line parameters required are:

```
C:\>WMIFileMan.Wsf
Microsoft (R) Windows Script Host Version 5.6
Copyright (C) Microsoft Corporation 1996-2001. All rights reserved.

Usage: WMIFileMan.wsf Operation Source [target] [/recursive[+|-]] [/Machine:value]
                                [/User:value] [/Password:value]


Options:

Operation : Operation to perform. Only [Copy], [Rename], [Delete], [Compress],
            [Uncompress] and [TakeOwnerShip] are accepted.
Source    : The source file name or directory.
target    : The target file name or directory (if required by the operation).
recursive : Perform the operation recursively (if supported by the operation).
Machine   : Determine the WMI system to connect to. (default=LocalHost)
User      : Determine the UserID to perform the remote connection. (default=none)
Password  : Determine the password to perform the remote connection. (default=none)
Examples:

    WMIFileMan Copy C:\BOOT.INI D:\BOOT.INI
    WMIFileMan Copy "C:\Program Files" "D:\Program Files" /Recursive+
    WMIFileMan Compress "D:\Program Files" /Recursive+
    WMIFileMan TakeOwnership "D:\Program Files"
    WMIFileMan Delete "D:\Program Files"
```

Sample 2.36   *Copying, renaming, deleting, (un)compressing, and taking ownership of files and directories.*

```
  1:<?xml version="1.0"?>
  .:
  8:<package>
  9:  <job>
 ..:
 13:    <runtime>
 ..:
 30:    </runtime>
 31:
 32:    <script language="VBScript" src="..\Functions\DecodeWin32_DirectoryRCFunction.vbs" />
 33:    <script language="VBScript" src="..\Functions\TinyErrorHandler.vbs" />
 34:
 35:    <object progid="WbemScripting.SWbemLocator" id="objWMILocator" reference="true"/>
 36:
 37:    <script language="VBscript">
 38:    <![CDATA[
 ..:
 42:    Const cComputerName = "LocalHost"
 43:    Const cWMINameSpace = "root/cimv2"
 44:    Const cWMIClass = "CIM_LogicalFile"
 ..:
 66:    ' ----------------------------------------------------------------------------
 67:    ' Parse the command line parameters
 68:    If WScript.Arguments.Unnamed.Count = 0 Then
 69:       WScript.Arguments.ShowUsage()
 70:       WScript.Quit
 71:    Else
 72:       strWMIOperation = Ucase(WScript.Arguments.Unnamed.Item(0))
 73:    End If
 74:
 75:    boolRecursive = WScript.Arguments.Named("Recursive")
 76:    If Len(boolRecursive) = 0 Then boolRecursive = False
 77:
 78:    Select Case strWMIOperation
 79:         Case "COPY"
 80:              If WScript.Arguments.Unnamed.Count < 3 Then
 ..:
 84:              Else
 85:                 strWMISourceInstance = WScript.Arguments.Unnamed.Item(1)
 86:                 strWMITargetInstance = WScript.Arguments.Unnamed.Item(2)
 87:              End If
 88:
 89:         Case "RENAME"
 90:              If WScript.Arguments.Unnamed.Count < 3 Then
 ..:
 94:              Else
 95:                 strWMISourceInstance = WScript.Arguments.Unnamed.Item(1)
 96:                 strWMITargetInstance = WScript.Arguments.Unnamed.Item(2)
 97:              End If
 98:
 99:         Case "DELETE"
100:              If WScript.Arguments.Unnamed.Count < 2 Then
...:
104:              Else
105:                 strWMISourceInstance = WScript.Arguments.Unnamed.Item(1)
```

```
106:                    End If
107:
108:            Case "COMPRESS"
109:                    If WScript.Arguments.Unnamed.Count < 2 Then
...:
113:                    Else
114:                       strWMISourceInstance = WScript.Arguments.Unnamed.Item(1)
115:                    End If
116:
117:            Case "UNCOMPRESS"
118:                    If WScript.Arguments.Unnamed.Count < 2 Then
...:
122:                    Else
123:                       strWMISourceInstance = WScript.Arguments.Unnamed.Item(1)
124:                    End If
125:
126:            Case "TAKEOWNERSHIP"
127:                    If WScript.Arguments.Unnamed.Count < 2 Then
...:
135:            Case Else
136:                    WScript.Echo "Invalid action. Only [Copy], [Rename],  ..." & vbCRLF
137:                    WScript.Arguments.ShowUsage()
138:                    WScript.Quit (1)
139:     End Select
140:
141:     strUserID = WScript.Arguments.Named("User")
...:
148:     If Len(strComputerName) = 0 Then strComputerName = cComputerName
...:
153:     Set objWMIServices = objWMILocator.ConnectServer(strComputerName, cWMINameSpace, _
154:                                         strUserID, strPassword)
...:
157:     Set objWMIInstance = objWMIServices.Get (cWMIClass & "='" & _
158:                                         strWMISourceInstance & "'")
159:     Select Case UCase(strWMIOperation)
160:            Case "COPY"
161:                    WScript.Echo strWMIOperation & " of '" & strWMISourceInstance & _
162:                               "' to '" & strWMITargetInstance & _
163:                               "' (Recursive=" & boolRecursive & ")."
164:                    WScript.Echo "Operation in progress on '" & _
165:                               strComputerName & "', please wait ..."
166:                    intRC = objWMIInstance.CopyEX (strWMITargetInstance, _
167:                                         strStopFileName, _
168:                                         strStartFileName, _
169:                                         boolRecursive)
170:            Case "RENAME"
171:                    WScript.Echo strWMIOperation & " of '" & strWMISourceInstance & _
172:                               "' to '" & strWMITargetInstance & "'."
173:                    WScript.Echo "Operation in progress on '" & _
174:                               strComputerName & "', please wait ..."
175:                    intRC = objWMIInstance.Rename (strWMITargetInstance)
176:            Case "DELETE"
177:                    WScript.Echo strWMIOperation & " of '" & strWMISourceInstance & "'."
178:                    WScript.Echo "Operation in progress on '" & _
179:                               strComputerName & "', please wait ..."
180:                    intRC = objWMIInstance.Delete (strStopFileName, _
181:                                         strStartFileName)
182:            Case "COMPRESS"
183:                    WScript.Echo strWMIOperation & " of '" & strWMISourceInstance & _
184:                               "' (Recursive=" & boolRecursive & ")."
```

```
185:                    WScript.Echo "Operation in progress on '" & _
186:                              strComputerName & "', please wait ..."
187:                    intRC = objWMIInstance.Compress (strStopFileName, _
188:                                                     strStartFileName, _
189:                                                     boolRecursive)
190:          Case "UNCOMPRESS"
191:                    WScript.Echo strWMIOperation & " of '" & strWMISourceInstance & _
192:                              "' (Recursive=" & boolRecursive & ")."
193:                    WScript.Echo "Operation in progress on '" & _
194:                              strComputerName & "', please wait ..."
195:                    intRC = objWMIInstance.UnCompress (strStopFileName, _
196:                                                       strStartFileName, _
197:                                                       boolRecursive)
198:          Case "TAKEOWNERSHIP"
199:                    WScript.Echo strWMIOperation & " of '" & strWMISourceInstance & _
200:                              "' (Recursive=" & boolRecursive & ")."
201:                    WScript.Echo "Operation in progress on '" & _
202:                              strComputerName & "', please wait ..."
203:                    intRC = objWMIInstance.TakeOwnerShipEx (strStopFileName, _
204:                                                            strStartFileName, _
205:                                                            boolRecursive)
206:    End Select
207:
208:    WScript.Echo UCase(strWMIOperation) & ": " & Win32_DirectoryRC(intRC)
209:    If intRC Then
210:       WScript.Echo "Failed " & UCase(strWMIOperation) & _
211:                " operation on '" & Ucase (strStopFileName) & "'."
212:    End If
...:
217:    ]]>
218:    </script>
219: </job>
220:</package>
```

As usual, the script defines and parses the command-line parameters (skipped lines 13 through 30 and 68 through 148). Next, based on the command-line parameters, the corresponding method is executed. Each method has its own set of parameters:

- *Copy* method (from line 160 through 169): The *CopyEx* method is invoked instead of the *Copy* method, because the *CopyEx* method exposes a parameter to perform recursive copies. This can be useful when copying a directory with its subdirectories. It is important to note that the copy operation is not supported if it overwrites an existing *Win32_LogicalFile* instance.

- *Rename* method (from line 170 through 175): The *Rename Win32_LogicalFile* class method renames a *Win32_LogicalFile* instance specified in the path. The rename is not supported if the destination is on another drive or if it overwrites an existing *Win32_LogicalFile* instance.

- *Delete* method (from line 176 through 181): This method simply deletes a *Win32_LogicalFile* instance. Note that in the case of a directory, if subdirectories exist, they will also be deleted.

- *Compress* method (from line 182 through 189): Again, the *CompressEx* method is used instead of the *Compress* method, because the *CompressEx* method exposes a parameter to perform the recursive compression. The same rule applies for the uncompress operation.

- *UnCompress* method (from line 190 through 197): See *Compress* method.

- *TakeOwnerShip* method (from line 198 through 205): The *TakeOwnerShip* method obtains ownership of the *Win32_LogicalFile* instance specified in the object path. If the logical file is a directory, and if the **/Recursive+** switch is given, then the *TakeOwnerShip* method acts recursively, taking ownership of all the files and subdirectories the directory contains. It is important to note that the user running the script becomes the owner. Currently, it is impossible to set the owner for another user account with this method. Even if the WMI connection is done with other credentials (**/User** and **/Password** switch), the user who starts the script is the one set as the owner. By editing the security descriptor, it is also possible to change the owner. We will see how to proceed when examining the *Security* provider in Chapter 4.

Because Sample 2.36 utilizes the extended methods of the *Win32_LogicalFile* class, it is possible, in case of error, to determine the name of the file or directory where the problem occurred. This information is displayed at lines 210 and 211. Note that by using a different script structure, it is possible to restart the operation by using the *StartFileName* method parameter to recover the execution of the *Win32_LogicalFile* method from the point of failure.

2.4.5 Page file classes

The page file information class category retrieves information about the page file settings. This includes the page file settings and usage. The classes included in this category are listed in Table 2.17.

More than simply retrieving the page file setting, the use of the *Win32_PageFile* class allows the creation, modification, and deletion of a page file. The technique is very similar to the script technique used in Samples 2.26 through 2.30 ("Reading, creating, updating, and deleting environment vari-

Table 2.17   *The Page File Classes*

Name	Type	Description
Win32_LogicalMemoryConfiguration	Dynamic	This class is obsolete and has been replaced by the Win32_OperatingSystem class.
Win32_PageFile	Dynamic	Represents the file used for handling virtual memory file swapping on a Windows system.
Win32_PageFileSetting	Dynamic	Represents the settings of a page file.
Win32_PageFileUsage	Dynamic	Represents the file used for handling virtual memory file swapping on a Windows system.
Win32_PageFileElementSetting	Association	Relates the initial settings of a page file and the state of those settings during normal use.
Win32_SystemLogicalMemoryConfiguration	Association	This class is obsolete, because the properties existing in the Win32_LogicalMemoryConfiguration class are now a part of the Win32_OperatingSystem class.

ables"). Of course, the set of parameters is different. Let's see what the parameters are.

```
C:\>WMIPageFile.wsf
Microsoft (R) Windows Script Host Version 5.6
Copyright (C) Microsoft Corporation 1996-2001. All rights reserved.

Usage: WMIPageFile.wsf PageFileName /Action:value [/SetInitialSize:value] [/SetMaximumSize:value]
                            [/Machine:value] [/User:value] [/Password:value]

Options:

PageFileName    : Define the name of the pagefile to configure.
Action          : specify the operation to perform: [create] or [update] or [delete].
SetInitialSize  : Set the initial size of the pagefile.
SetMaximumSize  : Set the maximum size of the pagefile.
Machine         : determine the WMI system to connect to. (default=LocalHost)
User            : determine the UserID to perform the remote connection. (default=none)
Password        : determine the password to perform the remote connection. (default=none)
Examples:

    WMIPageFile.wsf /Action:List
    WMIPageFile.wsf C:\PAGEFILE.SYS /SetInitialSize:128 /SetMaximumSize:256 /Action:Create
    WMIPageFile.wsf C:\PAGEFILE.SYS /SetInitialSize:256 /SetMaximumSize:512 /Action:Update
    WMIPageFile.wsf C:\PAGEFILE.SYS /Action:Delete
```

Basically, the usual four basic operations can be executed: viewing, creating, updating, and deleting. Since a page file has an initial and a maximum size, these parameters also can be set from the command line. Samples 2.37 through 2.41 show how to proceed.

Sample 2.37   *Viewing, creating, updating, and deleting page files (Part I)*

```
 1:<?xml version="1.0"?>
 .:
 8:<package>
 9:  <job>
..:
13:    <runtime>
..:
29:    </runtime>
```

```
30:
31:     <script language="VBScript" src=".\Functions\DisplayFormattedPropertyFunction.vbs" />
32:     <script language="VBScript" src=".\Functions\TinyErrorHandler.vbs" />
33:
34:     <object progid="WbemScripting.SWbemLocator" id="objWMILocator" reference="true"/>
35:     <object progid="WbemScripting.SWbemDateTime" id="objWMIDateTime" />
36:
37:     <script language="VBscript">
38:     <![CDATA[
..:
42:     Const cComputerName = "LocalHost"
43:     Const cWMINameSpace = "root/cimv2"
44:     Const cWMIPageFileClass = "Win32_PageFile"
45:     Const cWMIPageFileUsageClass = "Win32_PageFileUsage"
..:
73:     ' ---------------------------------------------------------------------------
74:     ' Parse the command line parameters
75:     If WScript.Arguments.Named.Count Then
76:        Select Case Ucase(WScript.Arguments.Named("Action"))
77:              Case "LIST"
78:                   boolList = True
79:              Case "CREATE"
80:                   boolCreate = True
81:              Case "UPDATE"
82:                   boolUpdate = True
83:              Case "DELETE"
84:                   boolDelete = True
85:              Case Else
86:                   WScript.Echo "Invalid action type. Only [list], ..." & vbCRLF
87:                   WScript.Arguments.ShowUsage()
88:                   WScript.Quit
89:        End Select
90:     End If
91:
92:     If (WScript.Arguments.Unnamed.Count = 0 And boolList = False) Or _
93:        (WScript.Arguments.Unnamed.Count <> 0 And boolList = True) Then
94:        WScript.Arguments.ShowUsage()
95:        WScript.Quit
96:     Else
97:        If WScript.Arguments.Unnamed.Count Then
98:           strWMIInstanceName = WScript.Arguments.Unnamed.Item(0)
99:        End If
100:    End If
101:
102:    longInitialSize = CLng(WScript.Arguments.Named("SetInitialSize"))
103:    If longInitialSize > 0 Then boolInitialSize = True
104:
105:    longMaximumSize = CLng(WScript.Arguments.Named("SetMaximumSize"))
106:    If longMaximumSize > 0 Then boolMaximumSize = True
107:
108:    strUserID = WScript.Arguments.Named("User")
...:
115:    If Len(strComputerName) = 0 Then strComputerName = cComputerName
116:
117:    objWMILocator.Security_.AuthenticationLevel = wbemAuthenticationLevelDefault
118:    objWMILocator.Security_.ImpersonationLevel = wbemImpersonationLevelImpersonate
119:    objWMILocator.Security_.Privileges.AddAsString "SeCreatePagefilePrivilege", True
120:
121:    Set objWMIServices = objWMILocator.ConnectServer(strComputerName, cWMINameSpace, _
122:                                                     strUserID, strPassword)
```

```
123:     If Err.Number Then ErrorHandler (Err)
124:
...:
...:
...:
```

This first part of the script is very common now. Nothing unusual, except a command-line definition (lines 13 through 29) and parsing (lines 74 through 115) adapted to the page file needs.

The first basic operation is coded in Sample 2.38. The purpose is to show the page file properties.

Sample 2.38   *Viewing page files (Part II)*

```
...:
...:
...:
124:
125:     ' -- LIST ----------------------------------------------------------------
126:     If boolList = True Then
127:         Set objWMIInstances = objWMIServices.InstancesOf (cWMIPageFileClass)
...:
130:         For Each objWMIInstance in objWMIInstances
131:             WScript.Echo "- " & Ucase(objWMIInstance.Name) & String (60, "-")
132:             Set objWMIPropertySet = objWMIInstance.Properties_
133:             For Each objWMIProperty In objWMIPropertySet
134:                 Select Case objWMIProperty.Name
135:                     Case "Caption"
...:
147:                     Case Else
148:                         DisplayFormattedProperty objWMIInstance, _
149:                                                  "   " & objWMIProperty.Name, _
150:                                                  objWMIProperty.Name, _
151:                                                  Null
152:                 End Select
153:             Next
154:             Set objWMIPropertySet = Nothing
155:
156:             WScript.Echo
157:
158:             Set objWMIPageFileUsage = objWMIServices.Get (cWMIPageFileUsageClass & "='" & _
159:                                                           objWMIInstance.Name & "'")
...:
162:             Set objWMIPropertySet = objWMIPageFileUsage.Properties_
163:             For Each objWMIProperty In objWMIPropertySet
164:                 Select Case objWMIProperty.Name
165:                     Case "AllocatedBaseSize"
...:
175:                     Case Else
176:                         DisplayFormattedProperty objWMIPageFileUsage, _
177:                                                  "   " & objWMIProperty.Name, _
178:                                                  objWMIProperty.Name, _
179:                                                  Null
180:                 End Select
181:             Next
```

```
...:
186:            WScript.Echo
187:        Next
188:
189:        Set objWMIInstances = Nothing
190:    End If
191:
...:
...:
...:
```

This piece of code has one peculiarity, since it not only shows the properties of the *Win32_PageFile* instances (lines 127 and 130 through 153) but also shows the page file usage for the corresponding instance (lines 158 and 159 and 162 through 181). The page file usage is available from an instance of the *Win32_PageFileUsage* class. This class uses the same property key as the *Win32_PageFile* class. This is why, at lines 158 and 159, the *Name* property of the *Win32_PageFile* class is used. Because these two classes have some properties in common, the loop (lines 163 through 181) skips some of the properties to avoid duplicated information. The obtained output is as follows:

```
1:    C:\>WMIPageFile.wsf /Action:List
2:    Microsoft (R) Windows Script Host Version 5.6
3:    Copyright (C) Microsoft Corporation 1996-2001. All rights reserved.
4:
5:    - J:\PAGEFILE.SYS--------------------------------------------------------
6:       Archive: ............................ TRUE
7:       Compressed: ......................... FALSE
8:       CreationDate: ....................... 28-11-2001 19:19:19
9:       CSName: ............................. NET-DPEN6400
10:      Drive: .............................. j:
11:      EightDotThreeFileName: .............. j:\pagefile.sys
12:      Encrypted: .......................... FALSE
13:      Extension: .......................... sys
14:      FileName: ........................... pagefile
15:      FileSize: ........................... 704643072
16:      FileType: ........................... System file
17:      FSName: ............................. NTFS
18:      Hidden: ............................. TRUE
19:      InitialSize: ........................ 672
20:      InstallDate: ........................ 28-11-2001 19:19:19
21:      LastAccessed: ....................... 10-02-2002 07:45:39
22:      LastModified: ....................... 10-02-2002 07:45:39
23:      MaximumSize: ........................ 1344
24:      Path: ............................... \
25:      Readable: ........................... TRUE
26:      Status: ............................. OK
27:      System: ............................. TRUE
28:      Writeable: .......................... TRUE
29:
30:      CurrentUsage: ....................... 26
31:      PeakUsage: .......................... 27
```

Sample 2.39   *Creating page files (Part III)*

```
...:
...:
...:
191:
192:      ' -- CREATE -----------------------------------------------------------------
193:      If boolCreate = True Then
194:          Set objWMIClass = objWMIServices.Get (cWMIPageFileClass)
...:
197:          Set objWMIInstance = objWMIClass.SpawnInstance_
198:
199:          objWMIInstance.Name = strWMIInstanceName
200:
201:          If boolInitialSize Then
202:              objWMIInstance.InitialSize = longInitialSize
203:          Else
204:              objWMIInstance.InitialSize = 0
205:          End If
206:
207:          If boolMaximumSize Then
208:              objWMIInstance.MaximumSize = longMaximumSize
209:          Else
210:              objWMIInstance.MaximumSize = 256
211:          End If
212:
213:          objWMIInstance.Put_ (wbemChangeFlagCreateOrUpdate Or wbemFlagReturnWhenComplete)
214:          If Err.Number Then ErrorHandler (Err)
215:
216:          WScript.Echo "Pagefile '" & Ucase (objWMIInstance.Name) & "' created (" & _
217:                       longInitialSize & "/" & longMaximumSize & ")."
...:
220:      End If
221:
...:
...:
...:
```

Creating a new page file creates a new *Win32_PageFile* instance. This logic is exactly the same as that used to create new environment variables (see Sample 2.28). The script creates an instance of the class (line 194); next, it creates a new page file instance (line 197). Based on the parameters given on the command line, it initializes the properties of the new page file (lines 199 through 211). Once completed, the created instance is saved (line 213).

Sample 2.40   *Updating page files (Part IV)*

```
...:
...:
...:
221:
222:      ' -- UPDATE -----------------------------------------------------------------
223:      If boolUpdate = True Then
224:          Set objWMIInstance = objWMIServices.Get (cWMIPageFileClass & "='" & _
225:                                          strWMIInstanceName & "'")
```

```
...:
228:        If boolInitialSize Then
229:            WScript.Echo "Current initial size is " & objWMIInstance.InitialSize & " MB."
230:            objWMIInstance.InitialSize = longInitialSize
231:        End If
232:
233:        If boolMaximumSize Then
234:            WScript.Echo "Current maximum size is " & objWMIInstance.MaximumSize & " MB."
235:            objWMIInstance.MaximumSize = longMaximumSize
236:        End If
237:
238:        objWMIInstance.Put_ (wbemChangeFlagUpdateOnly Or wbemFlagReturnWhenComplete)
239:        If Err.Number Then ErrorHandler (Err)
240:
241:        WScript.Echo
242:        WScript.Echo "Pagefile '" & Ucase (objWMIInstance.Name) & "' updated (" & _
243:                        longInitialSize & "/" & longMaximumSize & ")."
244:
245:        Set objWMIInstance = Nothing
246:    End If
247:
...:
...:
...:
```

To update page file settings, an instance of the page file is retrieved (lines 224 and 225). Once retrieved, the properties are initialized according to the parameters given on the command line (lines 228 through 236). Once modified, the changes are committed back (line 238). Notice the use of the **wbemChangeFlagUpdateOnly** flag to perform only an update operation. This code is very similar to that used to update an environment variable value (see Sample 2.29).

Sample 2.41   *Deleting page files (Part V)*

```
...:
...:
...:
247:
248:    ' -- DELETE ----------------------------------------------------------------
249:    If boolDelete = True Then
250:        Set objWMIInstance = objWMIServices.Get (cWMIPageFileClass & "='" & _
251:                                        strWMIInstanceName & "'")
...:
254:        objWMIInstance.Delete_
255:        If Err.Number Then ErrorHandler (Err)
256:
257:        WScript.Echo "Pagefile '" & Ucase (objWMIInstance.Name) & "' deleted."
258:
259:        Set objWMIInstance = Nothing
260:    End If
...:
264:    ]]>
265:    </script>
266:  </job>
267:</package>
```

The last operation uses the same tactic as deleting an environment variable (see Sample 2.30); once the instance is retrieved (lines 250 and 251), the *Delete_* method of the **SWBemObject** is executed to delete the page file instance (line 254).

2.4.6   Multimedia audio/visual class

This category contains only one class: the *Win32_CodecFile* class. This class has the same properties and methods as its parent class, the *CIM_DataFile* class (see Figure 2.12). There is only one new property defined at the level of the *Win32_CodecFile* class: the *Group* property. This *Group* property indicates the type of codec represented by the codec file instance. We can reuse the **GetCollectionOfInstances.wsf** sample developed previously (see Sample 1.5, "Listing all instances of a class with their properties formatted") to list the *Win32_CodecFile* instances.

```
 1:   C:\>GetCollectionOfInstances Win32_CodecFile
 2:   Microsoft (R) Windows Script Host Version 5.6
 3:   Copyright (C) Microsoft Corporation 1996-2001. All rights reserved.
 4:
 5:
 6:   AccessMask: ........................... 18809343
 7:   Archive: .............................. TRUE
 8:   Caption: .............................. j:\windows\system32\msadp32.acm
 9:   Compressed: ........................... FALSE
10:   CreationClassName: .................... Win32_CodecFile
11:   CreationDate: ......................... 12-08-2001 21:29:10
12:   CSCreationClassName: .................. Win32_ComputerSystem
13:   CSName: ............................... XP-DPEN6400
14:   Description: ..........................
15:   Drive: ................................ j:
16:   EightDotThreeFileName: ................ j:\windows\system32\msadp32.acm
17:   Encrypted: ............................ FALSE
18:   Extension: ............................ acm
19:   FileName: ............................. msadp32
20:   FileSize: ............................. 13312
21:   FileType: ............................. acm File
22:   FSCreationClassName: .................. Win32_FileSystem
23:   FSName: ............................... NTFS
24:   Group: ................................ Audio
25:   Hidden: ............................... FALSE
26:   InstallDate: .......................... 12-08-2001 21:29:10
27:   LastAccessed: ......................... 01-09-2001 17:25:23
28:   LastModified: ......................... 01-08-2001 16:00:00
29:   Manufacturer: ......................... Microsoft Corporation
30:   *Name: ................................ J:\WINDOWS\System32\MSADP32.ACM
31:   Path: ................................. \windows\system32\
32:   Readable: ............................. TRUE
33:   Status: ............................... OK
34:   System: ............................... FALSE
35:   Version: .............................. 5.1.3531.0 (main.010730-1811)
36:   Writeable: ............................ TRUE
37:
```

```
 . . :
 . . :
 . . :
102:    AccessMask: .......................... 18809343
103:    Archive: ............................. TRUE
104:    Caption: ............................. j:\windows\system32\iccvid.dll
105:    Compressed: .......................... FALSE
106:    CreationClassName: ................... Win32_CodecFile
107:    CreationDate: ........................ 12-08-2001 21:28:52
108:    CSCreationClassName: ................. Win32_ComputerSystem
109:    CSName: .............................. XP-DPEN6400
110:    Description: .........................
111:    Drive: ............................... j:
112:    EightDotThreeFileName: ............... j:\windows\system32\iccvid.dll
113:    Encrypted: ........................... FALSE
114:    Extension: ........................... dll
115:    FileName: ............................ iccvid
116:    FileSize: ............................ 110592
117:    FileType: ............................ Application Extension
118:    FSCreationClassName: ................. Win32_FileSystem
119:    FSName: .............................. NTFS
120:    Group: ............................... Video
 . . . :
 . . . :
 . . . :
```

2.4.7   Networking classes

The networking category class represents network connections, network clients, and network connection settings. The classes included in this category are shown in Table 2.18.

Table 2.18   *The Networking Classes*

Name	Type	Description
Win32_IP4RouteTableEvent	Extrinsic event	Represents IP route change events.
Win32_IP4PersistedRouteTable	Dynamic	Represents persisted IP routes.
Win32_IP4RouteTable	Dynamic	Represents information that governs the routing of network data packets.
Win32_NetworkClient	Dynamic	Represents a network client on a Windows system.
Win32_NetworkConnection	Dynamic	Represents an active network connection in a Windows environment.
Win32_NetworkProtocol	Dynamic	Represents a protocol and its network characteristics on a Windows computer system.
Win32_NTDomain	Dynamic	Represents a Windows NT domain.
Win32_PingStatus	Dynamic	Represents the values returned by the standard ping command.
Win32_ActiveRoute	Association	Relates the current IP4 route to the persisted IP route table.
Win32_ProtocolBinding	Association	Relates a system-level driver, network protocol, and network adapter.

Some of these classes are not supported by the *Win32* providers. The *Win32_ActiveRoute*,   *Win32_IP4PersistedRouteTable*,   *Win32_IP4Route-Table*, and *Win32_IP4RouteTable*Event classes are supported by the WMI *RouteProvider* provider. The *Win32_PingStatus* class is supported by the *WMIPingProvider* provider. Since the WMI *RouteProvider* and *WMIPingProvider* providers are discussed in the next chapter, we will not consider these classes in this section.

To retrieve information from the *Win32_NetworkClient* classes, we can reuse the **GetCollectionOfInstances.wsf** sample developed previously (see Sample 1.5, "Listing all instances of a class with their properties formatted") to list the properties of the *Win32_NetworkClient* class.

```
C:\>GetCollectionOfInstances Win32_NetworkClient
Microsoft (R) Windows Script Host Version 5.6
Copyright (C) Microsoft Corporation 1996-2001. All rights reserved.

Caption: ............................... Workstation
Description: ........................... Creates and maintains client network connections to
                                         remote servers. If this service is stopped, these
                                         connections will be unavailable. If this service is
                                         disabled, any services that explicitly depend on it will
                                         fail to start.
Manufacturer: .......................... Microsoft Corporation
*Name: ................................. Microsoft Windows Network
Status: ................................ OK

Caption: ............................... WebClient
Description: ........................... Enables Windows-based programs to create, access, and
                                         modify Internet-based files. If this service is stopped,
                                         these functions will not be available. If this service is
                                         disabled, any services that explicitly depend on it will
                                         fail to start.
Manufacturer: .......................... Microsoft Corporation
*Name: ................................. Web Client Network
Status: ................................ OK
```

The *Win32_NetworkConnection* retrieves the list of the network connections made in the system. Basically, retrieving the *Win32_NetworkConnection* instances is similar to a "Net Use" command. Here is sample output of a *Win32_NetworkConnection* instance:

```
C:\>GetCollectionOfInstances Win32_NetworkConnection
Microsoft (R) Windows Script Host Version 5.6
Copyright (C) Microsoft Corporation 1996-2001. All rights reserved.


Caption: ............................... RESOURCE CONNECTED
Comment: ...............................
ConnectionState: ....................... Connected
ConnectionType: ........................ Current Connection
Description: ........................... RESOURCE CONNECTED - Microsoft Windows Network
DisplayType: ........................... Share
LocalName: ............................. R:
*Name: ................................. \\MyXPServer\MyShare (R:)
Persistent: ............................ FALSE
ProviderName: .......................... Microsoft Windows Network
RemoteName: ............................ \\MyXPServer\MyShare
RemotePath: ............................ \\MyXPServer\MyShare
ResourceType: .......................... Disk
Status: ................................ OK
UserName: .............................. LISSWARENET\Alain.Lissoir
```

The *Win32_MappedLogicalDisk* class retrieves information in a manner similar to the *Win32_NetworkConnection* class. However, the *Win32_MappedLogicalDisk* class is derived from the *CIM_LogicalDisk* superclass, such as the *Win32_LogicalDisk*. (See Figure 2.14.)

Figure 2.14
The CIM_LogicalDisk and its subclasses.

The information displayed by this class when a connection is made via the R: drive letter is as follows:

```
C:\>GetCollectionOfInstances Win32_MappedLogicalDisk
Microsoft (R) Windows Script Host Version 5.6
Copyright (C) Microsoft Corporation 1996-2001. All rights reserved.


Caption: ............................... R:
Compressed: ............................ FALSE
*DeviceID: ............................. R:
FileSystem: ............................ NTFS
FreeSpace: ............................. 5447909376
InstallDate: ........................... 01-01-2000
MaximumComponentLength: ................ 255
Name: .................................. R:
*SessionID: ............................ 115643
Size: .................................. 20398661632
SupportsDiskQuotas: .................... FALSE
SupportsFileBasedCompression: .......... TRUE
SystemCreationClassName: ............... Win32_ComputerSystem
SystemName: ............................ NET-DPEN6400
VolumeName: ............................ Shared
VolumeSerialNumber: .................... 0837A458
```

The user-related information for this connection is not available from the class. However, the *Win32_MappedLogicalDisk* class is associated with the *Win32_LogonSession* (see Figure 2.15).

Figure 2.15
The Win32_MappedLogical-Disk class and its associations.

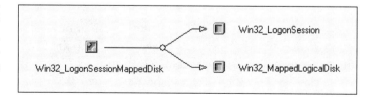

With the help of the *Win32_LogonSession*, it is possible to retrieve the user information, because this class is associated with the *Win32_Account* class, as shown in Figure 2.16.

Figure 2.16
*The Win32_*
LogonSession and
its associations.

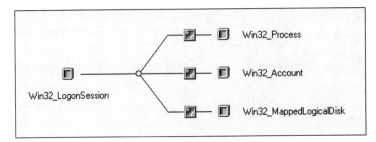

The *Win32_NetworkProtocol* class is used in Sample 2.8 ("Retrieving network device information [Part I]"). Sample 2.42 contains the previously skipped piece of code in Sample 2.8.

Sample 2.42   *Retrieving network device information (Part V)*

```
...:
...:
...:
160:
161:        Set objWMIProtocolInstances = objWMIServices.ExecQuery _
162:                        ("Associators of {Win32_NetworkAdapter='" & _
163:                        objWMIAdapterInstance.Index & _
164:                        "'} Where ResultClass=Win32_NetworkProtocol")
165:
166:        If objWMIProtocolInstances.Count Then
167:           For Each objWMIProtocolInstance In objWMIProtocolInstances
168:              WScript.Echo
169:              Set objWMIProperties = objWMIProtocolInstance.Properties_
170:              For Each objWMIProperty In objWMIProperties
171:                 DisplayFormattedProperty objWMIProtocolInstance, _
172:                                   objWMIProperty.Name, _
173:                                   objWMIProperty.Name, _
174:                                   Null
175:              Next
176:              Set objWMIProperties = Nothing
177:           Next
178:        End If
179:
...:
...:
...:
```

With the association mechanism, the script retrieves the list of *Win32_NetworkProtocol* instances linked to the examined *Win32_NetworkAdapter* instance (lines 161 through 164). Figure 2.17 shows this relationship at the class level. Figure 2.2 shows the associations at the instance level.

If the collection is not empty (line 166), the script displays the properties of each item. As a result, Sample 2.8 shows the complete set of information available from a *Win32_NetworkAdapter* instance. Note the presence of

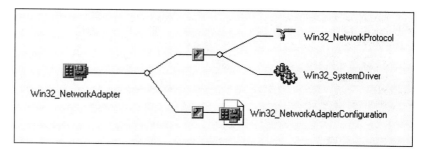

Figure 2.17
*The Win32_
NetworkAdapter
class associations.*

the TCP/IP protocol drivers: MSAFD Tcpip [TCP/IP] from line 18
through 39 and MSAFD Tcpip [UDP/IP] from line 41 through 62.

```
 1:   C:\>"GetNetworkConfiguration (With NetProtocols).wsf" "Compaq NC3121 Fast Ethernet NIC"
 2:   Microsoft (R) Windows Script Host Version 5.6
 3:   Copyright (C) Microsoft Corporation 1996-2001. All rights reserved.
 4:
 5:   Adapter name: .......................... Compaq NC3121 Fast Ethernet NIC
 6:   Device availability: .................... Running/Full Power
 7:   Adapter type: .......................... Ethernet 802.3
 8:   Adapter state: ......................... Connected
 9:   MAC address is : ....................... 00:08:C7:A9:27:56
10:   Adapter service name: .................. N100
11:   Last reset: ............................ 01-09-2001 18:02:30
12:
13:   *IRQ resource: ......................... 10
14:   Memory address: ........................ 0x40300000-0x40300FFF
15:   Memory address: ........................ 0x40100000-0x401FFFFF
16:   I/O Port: .............................. 0x00002420-0x0000243F
17:
18:   Caption: ............................... Tcpip
19:   ConnectionlessService: ................. FALSE
20:   Description: ........................... TCP/IP Protocol Driver
21:   GuaranteesDelivery: .................... TRUE
22:   GuaranteesSequencing: .................. TRUE
23:   InstallDate: ........................... 12-08-2001 21:29:47
24:   MaximumAddressSize: .................... 16
25:   MaximumMessageSize: .................... 0
26:   MessageOriented: ....................... FALSE
27:   MinimumAddressSize: .................... 16
28:   *Name: ................................. MSAFD Tcpip [TCP/IP]
29:   PseudoStreamOriented: .................. FALSE
30:   Status: ................................ OK
31:   SupportsBroadcasting: .................. FALSE
32:   SupportsConnectData: ................... FALSE
33:   SupportsDisconnectData: ................ FALSE
34:   SupportsEncryption: .................... FALSE
35:   SupportsExpeditedData: ................. TRUE
36:   SupportsGracefulClosing: ............... TRUE
37:   SupportsGuaranteedBandwidth: ........... FALSE
38:   SupportsMulticasting: .................. FALSE
39:   SupportsQualityofService: .............. FALSE
40:
41:   Caption: ............................... Tcpip
42:   ConnectionlessService: ................. TRUE
43:   Description: ........................... TCP/IP Protocol Driver
```

```
44:   GuaranteesDelivery: ..................... FALSE
45:   GuaranteesSequencing: ................... FALSE
46:   InstallDate: ............................ 12-08-2001 21:29:47
47:   MaximumAddressSize: ..................... 16
48:   MaximumMessageSize: ..................... 65467
49:   MessageOriented: ........................ TRUE
50:   MinimumAddressSize: ..................... 16
51:   *Name: .................................. MSAFD Tcpip [UDP/IP]
52:   PseudoStreamOriented: ................... FALSE
53:   Status: ................................. OK
54:   SupportsBroadcasting: ................... TRUE
55:   SupportsConnectData: .................... FALSE
56:   SupportsDisconnectData: ................. FALSE
57:   SupportsEncryption: ..................... FALSE
58:   SupportsExpeditedData: .................. FALSE
59:   SupportsGracefulClosing: ................ FALSE
60:   SupportsGuaranteedBandwidth: ............ FALSE
61:   SupportsMulticasting: ................... TRUE
62:   SupportsQualityofService: ............... FALSE
63:
64:   DHCP enabled: ........................... FALSE
65:   IP address(es): ......................... 10.10.10.3 255.0.0.0
66:   IP connection metric: ................... 30
67:   Default Gateway(s) and metric: .......... 10.10.10.254 1
68:   Dead gateway detection enabled: ......... TRUE
69:   DNS registration enabled: ............... FALSE
70:   DNS FULL registration enabled: .......... TRUE
71:   DNS search order: ....................... 10.10.10.3
72:   DNS domain: ............................. LissWare.Net
73:   DNS enabled for WINS resolution: ........ FALSE
74:   WINS scope ID: ..........................
75:   Enable LMHOSTS lookup: .................. FALSE
76:   NETBIOS over TCP/IP: .................... ENABLED
```

The class to use to gather information about the Domain is the *Win32_ NTDomain* class. Again, this class only displays information. The class does not offer methods or properties that can be changed. However, we will see later, with the *Win32_ComputerSystem* class, how to remove or join a domain from a Windows Server 2003 member server or a Windows XP client (currently, the *Win32_ComputerSystem* class under Windows 2000 does not contain any method to perform these operations). The property list obtained from the *Win32_NTDomain* class is as follows:

```
 1:   C:\>GetCollectionOfInstances Win32_NTDomain
 2:   Microsoft (R) Windows Script Host Version 5.6
 3:   Copyright (C) Microsoft Corporation 1996-2001. All rights reserved.
 4:
 5:
 6:   Caption: ................................ LISSWARENET
 7:   ClientSiteName: ......................... Brussels
 8:   CreationClassName: ...................... Win32_NTDomain
 9:   DcSiteName: ............................. Brussels
10:   Description: ............................ LISSWARENET
11:   DnsForestName: .......................... LissWare.Net
12:   DomainControllerAddress: ................ \\10.10.10.3
13:   DomainControllerAddressType: ............ 1
14:   DomainControllerName: ................... \\NET-DPEN6400
```

```
15:   DomainGuid: ........................... {CCA9C1AB-9500-4332-9237-EDEEA1057D46}
16:   DomainName: ........................... LISSWARENET
17:   DSDirectoryServiceFlag: ............... TRUE
18:   DSDnsControllerFlag: .................. FALSE
19:   DSDnsDomainFlag: ...................... FALSE
20:   DSDnsForestFlag: ...................... TRUE
21:   DSGlobalCatalogFlag: .................. TRUE
22:   DSKerberosDistributionCenterFlag: ....... TRUE
23:   DSPrimaryDomainControllerFlag: .......... TRUE
24:   DSTimeServiceFlag: .................... FALSE
25:   DSWritableFlag: ....................... TRUE
26:   *Name: ................................ Domain: LISSWARENET
27:   Status: ............................... OK
```

It is important to note some interesting information, such as the client (line 7) and Active Directory Domain Controller site location (line 9). Since the script runs on a Domain Controller, some extra information about the directory service is also available (lines 17 through 25). We see that the system is acting as a Directory Server (line 17), that the DC and the Domain name do not use a DNS name (lines 18 and 19), but the Forest does use a DNS name (line 20). The DC is a Global Catalog server, a Kerberos ticket distribution center, and a PDC for the Domain (lines 21 through 23). However, the system does not act as a *Time Service* provider (line 24). This output is obtained on a Windows Server 2003 acting as a Domain Controller. The output obtained on a Windows XP client is as follows:

```
1:    C:\>GetCollectionOfInstances Win32_NTDomain
2:    Microsoft (R) Windows Script Host Version 5.6
3:    Copyright (C) Microsoft Corporation 1996-2001. All rights reserved.
4:
5:
6:    Caption: .............................. XP-PRO01
7:    CreationClassName: .................... Win32_NTDomain
8:    Description: .......................... XP-PRO01
9:    *Name: ................................ Domain: XP-PRO01
10:   Status: ............................... Unknown
11:
12:   Caption: .............................. LISSWARENET
13:   ClientSiteName: ....................... Brussels
14:   CreationClassName: .................... Win32_NTDomain
15:   DcSiteName: ........................... Brussels
16:   Description: .......................... LISSWARENET
17:   DnsForestName: ........................ LissWare.Net
18:   DomainControllerAddress: .............. \\10.10.10.3
19:   DomainControllerAddressType: .......... 1
20:   DomainControllerName: ................. \\XP-DPEN6400
21:   DomainGuid: ........................... {CCA9C1AB-9500-4332-9237-EDEEA1057D46}
22:   DomainName: ........................... LISSWARENET
23:   DSDirectoryServiceFlag: ............... TRUE
24:   DSDnsControllerFlag: .................. FALSE
25:   DSDnsDomainFlag: ...................... FALSE
26:   DSDnsForestFlag: ...................... TRUE
27:   DSGlobalCatalogFlag: .................. FALSE
28:   DSKerberosDistributionCenterFlag: ....... TRUE
```

```
29:    DSPrimaryDomainControllerFlag: ...........  TRUE
30:    DSTimeServiceFlag: .....................  TRUE
31:    DSWritableFlag: ........................  TRUE
32:    *Name: .................................  Domain: LISSWARENET
33:    Status: ................................  OK
```

2.4.8   **Operating System settings classes**

The operating system settings classes category represents the Operating System and its settings. This category class exposes an important number of settings that can be modified from a WMI script. The classes included in this category and supported by the *Win32* WMI providers are listed in Table 2.19.

However, although related to the Operating System classes category, the extrinsic event classes listed in Table 2.19 are supported by a different set of WMI providers. We revisit these classes when examining the *MS_Shutdown_Event_provider*, *WMI Kernel Trace Event provider*, and *System-ConfigurationChangeEvents* WMI providers in the next chapter.

To customize the Operating System, it would be handy to have a script to configure the settings (dump file) and perform some typical Operating System operations (such as joining, unjoining a domain, renaming the computer, or rebooting the Operating System). This is the purpose of the next sample. For this, the script will make use of four classes. Each of them will be used for a specific set of tasks.

- The *Win32_ComputerSystem* class: This class is used to gather information about the computer, to rename the computer, and to join and unjoin a domain or workgroup. With the same class, it is also possible to modify the time zone, daylight savings time, and the system startup options of the BOOT.INI file.

- The *Win32_QuickFixEngineering* class: This class is used to retrieve the Quick Fix Engineering (QFE) installed in the Operating System.

- The *Win32_OperatingSystem* class: This class is used to gather information about the Operating System, shut down the Operating System (shut down, reboot, or log off), change the date and time, or modify the foreground application time slice.

- The *Win32_OSRecoveryConfiguration* class: This class is used to gather and set settings about system failure information, such as the auto reboot, the debug file path, the debug type desired, and if an Admin alert must be sent.

Table 2.19 *The Operating System Settings Classes*

Name	Type	Description
Win32_ComputerShutdownEvent	Extrinsic event	Represents computer shutdown events.
Win32_ComputerSystemEvent	Extrinsic event	Represents events related to a computer system.
Win32_DeviceChangeEvent	Extrinsic event	Represents device change events resulting from the addition, removal, or modification of devices on the computer system.
Win32_ModuleLoadTrace	Extrinsic event	Indicates that a process has loaded a new module.
Win32_ModuleTrace	Extrinsic event	Base event for module events.
Win32_ProcessStartTrace	Extrinsic event	Indicates that a new process has started.
Win32_ProcessStopTrace	Extrinsic event	Indicates that a process has terminated.
Win32_ProcessTrace	Extrinsic event	Base event for process events.
Win32_SystemConfigurationChangeEvent	Extrinsic event	Indicates that the device list on the system has been refreshed (a device has been added or removed, or the configuration changed).
Win32_SystemTrace	Extrinsic event	Base class for all system trace events, including module, process, and thread traces.
Win32_ThreadStartTrace	Extrinsic event	Indicates a new thread has started.
Win32_ThreadStopTrace	Extrinsic event	Indicates that a thread has stopped.
Win32_ThreadTrace	Extrinsic event	Base event class for thread events.
Win32_VolumeChangeEvent	Extrinsic event	Represents a network-mapped drive event resulting from the addition of a network drive letter or mounted drive on the computer system.
Win32_BootConfiguration	Dynamic	Represents the boot configuration of a Windows system.
Win32_ComputerSystem	Dynamic	Represents a computer system operating in a Windows environment.
Win32_ComputerSystemProduct	Dynamic	Represents a product.
Win32_LoadOrderGroup	Dynamic	Represents a group of system services that define execution dependencies.
Win32_LoadOrderGroupServiceDependencies	Dynamic	Represents an association between a base service and a load order group that the service depends on to start running.
Win32_OperatingSystem	Dynamic	Represents an operating system installed on a Windows computer system.
Win32_OSRecoveryConfiguration	Dynamic	Represents the types of information that will be gathered from memory when the operating system fails.
Win32_QuickFixEngineering	Dynamic	Represents system-wide Quick Fix Engineering (QFE) or updates that have been applied to the current operating system.
Win32_StartupCommand	Dynamic	Represents a command that runs automatically when a user logs on to the computer system.
Win32_ComputerSystemProcessor	Association	Relates a computer system and a processor running on that system.
Win32_DependentService	Association	Relates two interdependent base services.
Win32_LoadOrderGroupServiceMembers	Association	Relates a load order group and a base service.
Win32_OperatingSystemQFE	Association	Relates an operating system and product updates applied as represented in Win32_QuickFixEngineering.
Win32_SystemBootConfiguration	Association	Relates a computer system and its boot configuration.
Win32_SystemDesktop	Association	Relates a computer system and its desktop configuration.
Win32_SystemDevices	Association	Relates a computer system and a logical device installed on that system.
Win32_SystemLoadOrderGroups	Association	Relates a computer system and a load order group.
Win32_SystemNetworkConnections	Association	Relates a network connection and the computer system on which it resides.
Win32_SystemOperatingSystem	Association	Relates a computer system and its operating system.
Win32_SystemProcesses	Association	Relates a computer system and a process running on that system.
Win32_SystemProgramGroups	Association	Relates a computer system and a logical program group.
Win32_SystemResources	Association	Relates a system resource and the computer system it resides on.
Win32_SystemServices	Association	Relates a computer system and a service program that exists on the system.
Win32_SystemSetting	Association	Relates a computer system and a general setting on that system.

Before diving into the script code, let's see the command-line parameters exposed by this script sample:

```
C:\>WMIOSConfig.wsf
Microsoft (R) Windows Script Host Version 5.6
Copyright (C) Microsoft Corporation 1996-2001. All rights reserved.

Usage: WMIOSConfig.wsf [/List[+|-]] [/QFE[+|-]] [/Join:value] [/OU:value] [/UnJoin:value]
                       [/Rename:value] [/AccountName:value] [/AccountPassword:value]
                       [/SetDateTime:value] [/CurrentTimeZone:value]
                       [/EnableDaylightSavingsTime[+|-]] [/SystemStartupDelay:value]
                       [/SystemStartupOptions:value] [/SystemStartupSetting:value]
                       [/ForegroundApplicationBoost:value] [/Shutdown:value] [/DebugFilePath:value]
                       [/MiniDumpDirectory:value] [/DebugInfoType:value] [/AutoReboot[+|-]]
                       [/OverwriteExistingDebugFile[+|-]] [/SendAdminAlert[+|-]]
                       [/WriteToSystemLog[+|-]] [/Machine:value] [/User:value] [/Password:value]


Options:

List                        : View the Operating System configuration settings.
QFE                         : View the Operating System Quick Fix Engineering.
Join                        : Join computer systems to a domain or workgroup.
OU                          : Distinguished name of the OU where the computer account must
                              be created.
UnJoin                      : Un-Join or removes a computer system from a domain or workgroup.
Rename                      : Rename a computer. Must be local.
AccountName                 : Username to use for Join, Un-join or rename operation. Can be a UPN.
AccountPassword             : Password for the Join, Un-join or rename operation.
SetDateTime                 : Set the date and time of the system
CurrentTimeZone             : Set the system time zone.
EnableDaylightSavingsTime   : Active the day light saving time.
SystemStartupDelay          : Number of seconds to waut before booting.
SystemStartupOptions        : Set options for starting the computer.
SystemStartupSetting        : Set the index of the default start profile.
ForegroundApplicationBoost  : Increase the priority given to foreground applications. Must 0, 1 or 2.
Shutdown                    : Must be [Shutdown], [Reboot], [Logoff] or [PowerOff].
DebugFilePath               : Indicates the path to the debug file.
MiniDumpDirectory           : Indicates the directory where small memory dump files will be
                              recorded and accumulated.
DebugInfoType               : Indicates what type of debugging information is to be written saved.
                              Must be [None], [Complete], [Kernel] or [Small].
AutoReboot                  : Determines whether the system will automatically reboot during a
                              recovery operation.
OverwriteExistingDebugFile  : Indicates whether a new file will overwrite an existing one.
SendAdminAlert              : Indicates whether or not an alert message will be sent to the system
                              administrator.
WriteToSystemLog            : Indicates whether or not events will be written to a system log.
Machine                     : Determine the WMI system to connect to. (default=LocalHost)
User                        : Determine the UserID to perform the remote connection. (default=none)
Password                    : Determine the password to perform the remote connection. (default=none)
Examples:

     WMIOSConfig.wsf /List+
     WMIOSConfig.wsf /QFE+
     WMIOSConfig.wsf /Join:NewDomain /OU:OU=MyOU,DC=MyDomain,DC=Com
                     /AccountName:Administrator /AccountPassword:password
     WMIOSConfig.wsf /UnJoin+ /AccountName:Administrator /AccountPassword:password
     WMIOSConfig.wsf /Rename:NewName /AccountName:Administrator /AccountPassword:password
```

```
WMIOSConfig.wsf /SetDateTime:20010901231500.000000+120
WMIOSConfig.wsf /CurrentTimeZone:120
WMIOSConfig.wsf /EnableDaylightSavingsTime+

WMIOSConfig.wsf /SystemStartupDelay:30
WMIOSConfig.wsf /SystemStartupOptions:"'Microsoft Windows Server 2003, Enterprise' /fastdetect"
WMIOSConfig.wsf /SystemStartupSetting:0

WMIOSConfig.wsf /ForegroundApplicationBoost:1

WMIOSConfig.wsf /Shutdown:Reboot

WMIOSConfig.wsf /DebugFilePath:%SystemRoot%\MEMORY.DMP
WMIOSConfig.wsf /MiniDumpDirectory:%SystemRoot%\Minidump
WMIOSConfig.wsf /DebugInfoType:Small

WMIOSConfig.wsf /AutoReboot+
WMIOSConfig.wsf /OverwriteExistingDebugFile+
WMIOSConfig.wsf /SendAdminAlert+
WMIOSConfig.wsf /WriteToSystemLog+
```

This script, along with Sample 2.12 ("Configuring a network adapter"), exposes a huge number of parameters. Since the command-line parameters analysis uses the same functions and techniques as Sample 2.12, we do not examine this part of the code. Sample 2.43 is structured in the same way as before: an XML section to define the XML named parameters (skipped from line 13 through 78) and a code section to parse and format the command-line parameters (skipped from line 114 through 340).

Sample 2.43   *Configuring the Operating System (Part I)*

```
 1:<?xml version="1.0"?>
 .:
 8:<package>
 9:  <job>
..:
13:    <runtime>
..:
78:    </runtime>
79:
80:    <script language="VBScript" src="..\Functions\ConvertStringInArrayFunction.vbs" />
81:    <script language="VBScript" src="..\Functions\ReplaceByFunction.vbs" />
82:
83:    <script language="VBScript" src="..\Functions\DisplayFormattedPropertyFunction.vbs" />
84:    <script language="VBScript" src="..\Functions\TinyErrorHandler.vbs" />
85:
86:    <object progid="WbemScripting.SWbemLocator" id="objWMILocator" reference="true"/>
87:    <object progid="WbemScripting.SWbemDateTime" id="objWMIDateTime" />
88:
89:    <object progid="Wscript.Shell" id="WshShell" />
90:
91:    <script language="VBscript">
92:    <![CDATA[
..:
96:    Const cComputerName = "LocalHost"
97:    Const cWMINameSpace = "root/cimv2"
```

```
 98:
 99:     Const cWMIComputerSysClass = "Win32_ComputerSystem"
100:     Const cWMIOperaringSystemClass = "Win32_OperatingSystem"
101:     Const cWMIOSRecoveryConfigClass = "Win32_OSRecoveryConfiguration"
102:     Const cWMIQFEClass = "Win32_QuickFixEngineering"
103:
104:     Const cLogOff = 1
105:     Const cShutdown = 2
106:     Const cReboot = 3
107:     Const cPowerOff = 9
108:     Const cForcedLogOff = 5
109:     Const cForcedShutdown = 6
110:     Const cForcedReboot = 7
111:     Const cForcedPowerOff = 13
112:
113:     Const cJoinOptions = 39     ' Bit 0=On, 1=On, 2=On and 5=On
114:     Const cUnJoinOptions = 4    ' Bit 2=On
...:
...:
...:
333:     strUserID = WScript.Arguments.Named("User")
334:     If Len(strUserID) = 0 Then strUserID = ""
335:
336:     strPassword = WScript.Arguments.Named("Password")
337:     If Len(strPassword) = 0 Then strPassword = ""
338:
339:     strComputerName = WScript.Arguments.Named("Machine")
340:     If Len(strComputerName) = 0 Then strComputerName = cComputerName
341:
342:     objWMILocator.Security_.AuthenticationLevel = WbemAuthenticationLevelPktPrivacy
343:     objWMILocator.Security_.ImpersonationLevel = wbemImpersonationLevelImpersonate
344:     objWMILocator.Security_.Privileges.AddAsString "SeSystemtimePrivilege", True
345:     objWMILocator.Security_.Privileges.AddAsString "SeRemoteShutdownPrivilege", True
346:     objWMILocator.Security_.Privileges.AddAsString "SeShutdownPrivilege", True
347:
348:     Set objWMIServices = objWMILocator.ConnectServer(strComputerName, cWMINameSpace, _
349:                                          strUserID, strPassword)
...:
352:     Set objWMIComputerSysInstances = objWMIServices.InstancesOf (cWMIComputerSysClass)
...:
355:     Set objWMIOSInstances = objWMIServices.InstancesOf (cWMIOperaringSystemClass)
...:
358:     Set objWMIOSRecConfigInstances = objWMIServices.InstancesOf (cWMIOSRecoveryConfigClass)
...:
360:
...:
...:
...:
```

When the WMI connection is established, some required privileges are granted to change the system time (line 344) and reboot the computer (lines 345 and 346). Without these privileges, it is impossible to successfully execute these operations. Of course, it is always possible to add some logic to specify these rights if only the corresponding switches are given on the command line. Next, three collections of instances from the *Win32_ComputerSystem* (line 352), *Win32_OperatingSystem* (line 355), and

Win32_OSRecoveryConfiguration (line 358) classes are created. The *Win32_QuickFixEngineering* class is used later. Notice in the script header, the definition of some constants (lines 104 through 114). These constants are used later to perform some specific WMI Operating System operations. We revisit this later during the script analysis.

The first step consists of viewing all properties of the three collections of instances just created. This action corresponds to the **/List+** switch usage. The operation is executed in Sample 2.44 by performing an enumeration of the three collections: the *Win32_ComputerSystem* collection (lines 363 through 373), *Win32_OperatingSystem* collection (lines 378 through 388), and *Win32_OSRecoveryConfiguration* collection (lines 393 through 403).

Sample 2.44   *Viewing various Operating System properties (Part II)*

```
...:
...:
...:
360:
361:    If boolList Then
362:        If objWMIComputerSysInstances.Count = 1 Then
363:            For Each objWMIComputerSysInstance in objWMIComputerSysInstances
364:                WScript.Echo "- Computer System " & String (60, "-")
365:                Set objWMIPropertySet = objWMIComputerSysInstance.Properties_
366:                For Each objWMIProperty In objWMIPropertySet
367:                    DisplayFormattedProperty objWMIComputerSysInstance, _
368:                                             objWMIProperty.Name, _
369:                                             objWMIProperty.Name, _
370:                                             Null
371:                Next
372:                Set objWMIPropertySet = Nothing
373:            Next
374:            WScript.Echo
375:        End If
376:
377:        If objWMIOSInstances.Count = 1 Then
378:            For Each objWMIOSInstance in objWMIOSInstances
379:                WScript.Echo "- OS Settings " & String (60, "-")
380:                Set objWMIPropertySet = objWMIOSInstance.Properties_
381:                For Each objWMIProperty In objWMIPropertySet
382:                    DisplayFormattedProperty objWMIOSInstance, _
383:                                             objWMIProperty.Name, _
384:                                             objWMIProperty.Name, _
385:                                             Null
386:                Next
387:                Set objWMIPropertySet = Nothing
388:            Next
389:            WScript.Echo
390:        End If
391:
392:        If objWMIOSRecConfigInstances.Count = 1 Then
393:            For Each objWMIOSRecConfigInstance in objWMIOSRecConfigInstances
394:                WScript.Echo "- OS Recovery Settings " & String (60, "-")
395:                Set objWMIPropertySet = objWMIOSRecConfigInstance.Properties_
```

```
396:              For Each objWMIProperty In objWMIPropertySet
397:                  DisplayFormattedProperty objWMIOSRecConfigInstance, _
398:                                           objWMIProperty.Name, _
399:                                           objWMIProperty.Name, _
400:                                           Null
401:              Next
402:              Set objWMIPropertySet = Nothing
403:          Next
404:          WScript.Echo
405:      End If
406:  ElseIf boolQFE Then
...:
...:
...:
```

These three classes provide a rich set of information about the Operating System. Take a few minutes to review the listed properties with **WMI CIM Studio.**

Table 2.20   *The DomainRole property of the Win32_ComputerSystem Class*

Value	Description
0	Standalone Workstation
1	Member Workstation
2	Standalone Server
3	Member Server
4	Backup Domain Controller
5	Primary Domain Controller

The display output is given in the following code segment as reference. Information such as the domain role (line 18 and Table 2.20), infrared support capability (line 20), service pack level (line 63), and available memory (lines 50 and 98) are just a few examples.

```
 1:  C:\>WMIOSConfig.wsf /List+ /Machine:MyPortable /User:Administrator /Password:password
 2:  Microsoft (R) Windows Script Host Version 5.6
 3:  Copyright (C) Microsoft Corporation 1996-2001. All rights reserved.
 4:
 5:  - Computer System -------------------------------------------------------------
 6:  AdminPasswordStatus: ......... 0
 7:  AutomaticResetBootOption: .... TRUE
 8:  AutomaticResetCapability: .... TRUE
 9:  BootROMSupported: ............ TRUE
10:  BootupState: ................. Normal
11:  Caption: ..................... MYPORTABLE
12:  ChassisBootupState: .......... 3
13:  CreationClassName: ........... Win32_ComputerSystem
14:  CurrentTimeZone: ............. 60
15:  DaylightInEffect: ............ FALSE
16:  Description: ................. AT/AT COMPATIBLE
17:  Domain: ...................... WORKGROUP
18:  DomainRole: .................. 0
19:  FrontPanelResetStatus: ....... 2
20:  InfraredSupported: ........... TRUE
21:  KeyboardPasswordStatus: ...... 0
22:  Manufacturer: ................ Compaq
23:  Model: ....................... Armada     M700
```

```
24:   *Name: ...................... MYPORTABLE
25:   NetworkServerModeEnabled: .... TRUE
26:   NumberOfProcessors: .......... 1
27:   OEMStringArray: .............. www.compaq.com
28:   PauseAfterReset: ............. -1
29:   PowerOnPasswordStatus: ....... 0
30:   PowerState: .................. 0
31:   PowerSupplyState: ............ 3
32:   PrimaryOwnerName: ............ Alain Lissoir
33:   ResetCapability: ............. 1
34:   ResetCount: .................. -1
35:   ResetLimit: .................. -1
36:   Roles: ....................... LM_Workstation
37:                                  LM_Server
38:                                  NT
39:                                  Potential_Browser
40:                                  Master_Browser
41:   Status: ...................... OK
42:   SystemStartupDelay: .......... 30
43:   SystemStartupOptions: ........ "Microsoft Windows 2000 Professional" /fastdetect
44:                                  "Microsoft Windows 2000 Advanced Server (LABS)" /fastdetect
45:                                  "Microsoft Windows Server 2003 Advanced Server (LABS)" /fastdetect
46:                                  "Windows NT Workstation Version 4.00 (Recovery)"
47:   SystemStartupSetting: ........ 0
48:   SystemType: .................. X86-based PC
49:   ThermalState: ................ 3
50:   TotalPhysicalMemory: ......... 267894784
51:   UserName: .................... MYPORTABLE\Lissoir
52:   WakeUpType: .................. 6
53:
54:   - OS Settings -----------------------------------------------
55:   BootDevice: .................. \Device\Harddisk0\Partition1
56:   BuildNumber: ................. 2195
57:   BuildType: ................... Uniprocessor Free
58:   Caption: ..................... Microsoft Windows 2000 Professional
59:   CodeSet: ..................... 1252
60:   CountryCode: ................. 1
61:   CreationClassName: ........... Win32_OperatingSystem
62:   CSCreationClassName: ......... Win32_ComputerSystem
63:   CSDVersion: .................. Service Pack 2
64:   CSName: ...................... MYPORTABLE
65:   CurrentTimeZone: ............. 60
66:   Debug: ....................... FALSE
67:   Description: .................
68:   Distributed: ................. FALSE
69:   ForegroundApplicationBoost: .. 2
70:   FreePhysicalMemory: .......... 86996
71:   FreeSpaceInPagingFiles: ...... 281828
72:   FreeVirtualMemory: ........... 368824
73:   InstallDate: ................. 01-01-1999 07:49:30
74:   LastBootUpTime: .............. 28-10-2001 15:28:20
75:   LocalDateTime: ............... 29-10-2001 14:48:27
76:   Locale: ...................... 0409
77:   Manufacturer: ................ Microsoft Corporation
78:   MaxNumberOfProcesses: ........ -1
79:   MaxProcessMemorySize: ........ 2097024
80:   *Name: ....................... Microsoft Windows 2000 Professional|C:\WINNT|\Devic...
81:   NumberOfProcesses: ........... 48
82:   NumberOfUsers: ............... 1
83:   Organization: ................ Compaq Computer
84:   OSLanguage: .................. 1033
85:   OSType: ...................... 18
86:   Primary: ..................... TRUE
```

```
87:   QuantumLength: .............. 0
88:   QuantumType: ................ 0
89:   RegisteredUser: ............. Alain Lissoir
90:   SerialNumber: ............... 51873-005-0246414-09900
91:   ServicePackMajorVersion: ..... 2
92:   ServicePackMinorVersion: ..... 0
93:   SizeStoredInPagingFiles: ..... 435704
94:   Status: ..................... OK
95:   SystemDevice: ............... \Device\Harddisk0\Partition1
96:   SystemDirectory: ............ C:\WINNT\System32
97:   TotalVirtualMemorySize: ...... 697320
98:   TotalVisibleMemorySize: ...... 261616
99:   Version: .................... 5.0.2195
100:  WindowsDirectory: ........... C:\WINNT
101:
102:  - OS Recovery Settings -----------------------------------------
103:  AutoReboot: ................. TRUE
104:  DebugFilePath: .............. C:\WINNT\MEMORY.DMP
105:  KernelDumpOnly: ............. FALSE
106:  *Name: ...................... Microsoft Windows 2000 Professional|C:\WINNT|\Device\Hard...
107:  OverwriteExistingDebugFile: .. TRUE
108:  SendAdminAlert: ............. TRUE
109:  WriteDebugInfo: ............. FALSE
110:  WriteToSystemLog: ........... TRUE
```

Listing the Quick Fix Engineering (QFE) is not complicated. The logic is always the same. The code is shown in Sample 2.45. A collection of the QFE instances is created (line 407); next, an enumeration of the collection is performed (lines 411 through 420).

Sample 2.45   *Viewing Operating System QFE (Part III)*

```
...:
...:
...:
406:     ElseIf boolQFE Then
407:         Set objWMIQFEInstances = objWMIServices.InstancesOf (cWMIQFEClass)
...:
410:         If objWMIComputerSysInstances.Count = 1 Then
411:             For Each objWMIQFEInstance in objWMIQFEInstances
412:                 WScript.Echo "- Quick Fix Engineering" & " (" & _
413:                              objWMIQFEInstance.HotFixID & ") " & String (60, "-")
414:                 Set objWMIPropertySet = objWMIQFEInstance.Properties_
415:                 For Each objWMIProperty In objWMIPropertySet
416:                     DisplayFormattedProperty objWMIQFEInstance, _
417:                                              objWMIProperty.Name, _
418:                                              objWMIProperty.Name, _
419:                                              Null
420:                 Next
421:                 Set objWMIPropertySet = Nothing
422:                 WScript.Echo
423:             Next
424:         End If
...:
427:     Else
...:
...:
...:
```

The next parts of the script are the most interesting ones because this is where some Operating System operations are executed. We start with the *Win32_ComputerSystem* class operations. With this class, it is possible to join or unjoin a domain or a workgroup. Moreover, the computer can also be renamed. Note that under Windows 2000 and before, it is only possible to rename the computer. The WMI implementation under Windows 2000 and before does not contain a *Win32_ComputerSystem* class definition that exposes a method to join and unjoin from a domain or a workgroup. Sample 2.46 shows how to proceed.

Sample 2.46   *Joining and unjoining a domain or workgroup, and renaming a workstation (Part IV)*

```
...:
...:
...:
427:    Else
428:        If objWMIComputerSysInstances.Count = 1 Then
429:            For Each objWMIComputerSysInstance in objWMIComputerSysInstances
430:                If Len(strJoin) Then
431:                    intRC = objWMIComputerSysInstance.JoinDomainOrWorkGroup (strJoin, _
432:                                                        strAccountPassword, _
433:                                                        strAccountName, _
434:                                                        strJoinOU, _
435:                                                        cJoinOptions)
436:                    WScript.Echo "Join completed (" & intRC & ")."
437:                End If
438:
439:                If boolUnJoin Then
440:                    intRC = objWMIComputerSysInstance.UnJoinDomainOrWorkGroup (strAccountPassword,
441:                                                        strAccountName, _
442:                                                        cUnJoinOptions)
443:                    WScript.Echo "UnJoin completed (" & intRC & ")."
444:                End If
445:
446:                If Len(strRename) Then
447:                    intRC = objWMIComputerSysInstance.Rename (strRename, _
448:                                                        strAccountPassword, _
449:                                                        strAccountName)
450:                    WScript.Echo "Rename completed (" & intRC & ")."
451:                End If
452:
453:
...:
...:
...:
```

If the **/Join** switch, for example, is specified with a domain name to join, lines 430 through 437 are executed. The *JoinDomainOrWorkGroup* method of the *Win32_ComputerSystem* instance accepts five parameters. The first parameter is the domain or workgroup name to join and is contained in the *strJoin* variable (line 431). Because joining a domain or workgroup can't

usually be made without specific credentials, the next two parameters are
the account name and the password to use (lines 432 and 433). During the
join operation, a computer object can be created (based on the flags given in
the last parameter). If the computer account is created, it can be created in a
specific OU of Active Directory. This fourth parameter contains the **distinguishedName** of the OU targeted for the computer account creation. If the
default container must be used, this parameter must be set to Null. Last,
but not least, the fifth parameter is the join options parameter. It contains a
set of bit flags defining the join options. The bit flag meaning is shown in
Table 2.21.

Table 2.21   *The Join and Unjoin Options*

Join options		
Bit	**Action**	**Description**
0	Join Domain	If set (value=1), it joins the computer to a domain. If this bit flag equals 0, it joins the computer to a workgroup.
1	Acct Create	If set (value=2), it creates the account on the domain.
2	Acct Delete	If set (value=4), it deletes the account when a domain is left.
4	Win9X Upgrade	If set (value=16), the join operation is occurring as part of an upgrade of Windows 95/98 to Windows NT/Windows 2000.
5	Domain join if already joined	If set (value=32), it allows a join to a new domain even if the computer is already joined to a domain.
6	Join unsecure	If set (value=64), it performs an unsecured join.
7	Machine password passed	If set (value=128), it indicates that the machine (not user) password is passed. This option is only valid for unsecure joins.
8	Deferred SPN Set	If set (value=256), it specifies that writing service principal name (SPN) and DnsHostName attributes on the computer object should be deferred until the rename that will follow the join.
18	Install Invocation	If set (value=262144), the APIs were invoked during install.
Unjoin options		
Bit	**Action**	**Description**
2	Acct Delete	If set (value=4), it deletes the computer account when a domain is left. Actually, the account is disabled when the unjoin occurs.

In the script header, at line 113, a constant called *cJoinOptions* is defined
with a value equal to 39. This value corresponds to the bit flags 0, 1, 2, and
5 set to 1 (1 + 2 + 4 + 32 = 39). This default value is used by the script at
line 435 and corresponds to the most suitable value to use for the script
purpose. Based on the script context usage (i.e., during an upgrade to Windows XP), it is necessary to adapt the value. Once the method is executed, it
returns a 0 if the join is successful (line 436).

If the **/UnJoin+** switch is specified, lines 439 through 444 are executed.
The *UnJoinDomainOrWorkGroup* method of the *Win32_ComputerSystem*
instance accepts three parameters: the account with the password for the
unjoin operation (lines 440 and 441) and the unjoin options parameter
(line 442) defined at line 114 of Sample 2.43. The unjoin is made up of one
bit flag, listed in Table 2.21. Once the method executes, it returns a 0 if the
unjoin is successful (line 443). When bit 2 is set to ON (Value = 4), the
unjoined domain must be reachable, since the computer account is dis-

abled. If the domain you quit is not available anymore, ensure that bit 2 is OFF (Value = 0); otherwise, you won't be able to leave the domain.

If the **/Rename** switch is specified with the new computer name, lines 446 through 451 are executed. The *Rename* method of the *Win32_ComputerSystem* instance accepts three parameters: the new computer name (line 447) and the account with the password for the rename operation (lines 447 and 448). Once the method executes, it returns a 0 if the rename is successful (line 443). However, the computer must be rebooted to get the new name in effect. We see later, in the same script, how to reboot the computer.

The next piece of code, presented in Sample 2.47, modifies some properties of the *Win32_ComputerSystem* instance.

Sample 2.47   *Time zone, daylight savings, and startup options (Part V)*

```
. . . :
. . . :
. . . :
453:            If intCurrentTimeZone <> - 1 Then
454:                objWMIComputerSysInstance.CurrentTimeZone = intCurrentTimeZone
455:                WScript.Echo "CurrentTimeZone set."
456:            End If
457:
458:            If Len (boolDaylightSavingsTime) Then
459:                objWMIComputerSysInstance.EnableDaylightSavingsTime = boolDaylightSavingsTime
460:                If boolDaylightSavingsTime Then
461:                    WScript.Echo "EnableDaylightSavingsTime set."
462:                Else
463:                    WScript.Echo "EnableDaylightSavingsTime unset."
464:                End If
465:            End If
466:
467:            If intSysStartupDelay <> -1 Then
468:                objWMIComputerSysInstance.SystemStartupDelay = intSysStartupDelay
469:                WScript.Echo "SystemStartupDelay set."
470:            End If
471:
472:            If IsArray (arraySysStartupOptions) Then
473:                objWMIComputerSysInstance.SystemStartupOptions = arraySysStartupOptions
474:                WScript.Echo "SystemStartupOptions set."
475:            End If
476:
477:            If intSysStartupSetting <> - 1 Then
478:                objWMIComputerSysInstance.SystemStartupSetting = intSysStartupSetting
479:                WScript.Echo "SystemStartupSetting set."
480:            End If
481:
482:            objWMIComputerSysInstance.Put_ (wbemChangeFlagUpdateOnly Or _
483:                                            wbemFlagReturnWhenComplete)
484:            If Err.Number Then ErrorHandler (Err)
485:        Next
486:    End If
487:
. . . :
. . . :
. . . :
```

This piece of code modifies the computer time zone, as well as the daylight savings time and the startup options. The computer time zone is a boundary value of 60 and comprised between −720 and +780 (lines 453 through 456). For daylight savings time, it is a Boolean value set on True to enable daylight savings time (lines 458 through 465).

The rest of the code (from line 467) changes the system startup parameters encoded in the **Boot.Ini** file. If we consider the following **Boot.INI**:

```
[boot loader]
timeout=30
default=multi(0)disk(0)rdisk(0)partition(2)\WINDOWS
[operating systems]
multi(0)disk(0)rdisk(0)partition(2)\WINDOWS="MS Windows 2003 " /fastdetect
multi(0)disk(0)rdisk(1)partition(2)\WINDOWS="MS Windows XP" /fastdetect
```

If the switch:

```
/SystemStartupDelay:120
```

is used, the *timeout* parameter of the Boot.Ini is set to 120 seconds. However, when changing the other two startup options, some care must be taken. As we can see in the code at line 473, the *SystemStartupOptions* property accepts an array to specify the startup options. The array only contains the assigned information to the partition pointers, which are:

```
"MS Windows 2003" /fastdetect
"MS Windows XP" /fastdetect
```

It is important to respect the order of the items in the array. In the **Boot.INI** sample, the line defining the Windows Server 2003 boot partition is the first one, while the second line defines the Windows XP boot partition. This means that to respect the **Boot.INI** items ordering, while updating it, element 0 of the array must contain:

```
"MS Windows Server 2003" /fastdetect /debug
```

while element 1 of the array must contain:

```
"MS Windows XP" /fastdetect /debug
```

If the elements 0 and 1 are inverted in the array, this will result in an incorrect assignment of the partition pointers. In such a case, the Boot.Ini will look like:

```
[boot loader]
timeout=30
default=multi(0)disk(0)rdisk(0)partition(2)\WINDOWS
[operating systems]
multi(0)disk(0)rdisk(0)partition(2)\WINDOWS="MS Windows XP" /fastdetect /debug
multi(0)disk(0)rdisk(1)partition(2)\WINDOWS="MS Windows Server 2003" /fastdetect /debug
```

which is obviously wrong since the multi(0)disk(0)rdisk(0)parti-
tion(2)\WINDOWS partition physically contains the Windows Server
2003 and the multi(0)disk(0)rdisk(1)partition(2)\WINDOWS partition
physically contains Windows XP. Although not a disaster, this may intro-
duce some confusion when manipulating the startup options.

Because this information contains some double quotes, which can cause
some trouble when specified from the command line, the script accepts single quotes from the command line and converts them into double quotes
before assignment (during the command-line parameters parsing). This is
the reason why the function ReplaceBy() is included at the beginning of the
script in Sample 2.43 (line 81). So, the command line for this switch must
look like:

```
WMIOSConfig.wsf /SystemStartupOptions:"'MS Windows Server 2003' /fastdetect,'MS Windows XP' /fastdetect"
```

Note the order of the items to match **Boot.INI** items' ordering and the
use of the comma to separate each item in the array. The last startup option
is modified with the **/SystemStartupSetting** switch (lines 477 through
480). This parameter is an index that corresponds to the items ordering in
the **Boot.INI** file. If the startup options must be set to boot Windows
Server 2003 by default, the following command line will be used (based on
the original **Boot.INI**):

```
WMIOSConfig.wsf /SystemStartupSetting:0
```

If Windows XP must be booted by default, the following command line
must be used:

```
WMIOSConfig.wsf /SystemStartupSetting:1
```

The use of the startup options implies knowledge of the item ordering in
the **Boot.INI**. This is very important in order to modify the **Boot.INI** correctly. To commit the changes, the *Put_* method of the **SWBemObject**
object (which contains the *Win32_ComputerSystem* instance) is invoked
(lines 482 and 483).

The next piece of code modifies some more Operating System parameters with the help of the *Win32_OSRecoveryConfiguration* class.

Sample 2.48   *The Operating System recovery parameters (Part VI)*

```
...:
...:
...:
487:
488:       If objWMIOSRecConfigInstances.Count = 1 Then
489:          For Each objWMIOSRecConfigInstance in objWMIOSRecConfigInstances
490:             If Len (strDebugFilePath) Then
```

```
491:                    objWMIOSRecConfigInstance.DebugFilePath = strDebugFilePath
492:                    objWMIOSRecConfigInstance.ExpandedDebugFilePath = strExpDebugFilePath
493:                    WScript.Echo "DebugFilePath set."
494:                End If
495:
496:                If Len (strMiniDumpDirectory) Then
497:                    objWMIOSRecConfigInstance.MiniDumpDirectory = strMiniDumpDirectory
498:                    objWMIOSRecConfigInstance.ExpandedMiniDumpDirectory = strExpMiniDumpDirectory
499:                    WScript.Echo "MiniDumpDirectory set."
500:                End If
501:
502:                If intDebugInfoType Then
503:                    objWMIOSRecConfigInstance.DebugInfoType = intDebugInfoType - 1
504:                    WScript.Echo "DebugInfoType set."
505:                End If
506:
507:                If Len (boolAutoReboot) Then
508:                    objWMIOSRecConfigInstance.AutoReboot = boolAutoReboot
509:                    If boolAutoReboot Then
510:                        WScript.Echo "AutoReboot set."
511:                    Else
512:                        WScript.Echo "AutoReboot unset."
513:                    End If
514:                End If
515:
516:                If Len (boolOverwriteDebugFile) Then
517:                    objWMIOSRecConfigInstance.OverwriteExistingDebugFile = boolOverwriteDebugFile
518:                    If boolOverwriteDebugFile Then
519:                        WScript.Echo "OverwriteExistingDebugFile set."
520:                    Else
521:                        WScript.Echo "OverwriteExistingDebugFile unset."
522:                    End If
523:                End If
524:
525:                If Len (boolSendAdminAlert) Then
526:                    objWMIOSRecConfigInstance.SendAdminAlert = boolSendAdminAlert
527:                    If boolSendAdminAlert Then
528:                        WScript.Echo "SendAdminAlert set."
529:                    Else
530:                        WScript.Echo "SendAdminAlert unset."
531:                    End If
532:                End If
533:
534:                If Len (boolWriteToSystemLog) Then
535:                    objWMIOSRecConfigInstance.WriteToSystemLog = boolWriteToSystemLog
536:                    If boolWriteToSystemLog Then
537:                        WScript.Echo "WriteToSystemLog set."
538:                    Else
539:                        WScript.Echo "WriteToSystemLog unset."
540:                    End If
541:                End If
542:
543:                objWMIOSRecConfigInstance.Put_ (wbemChangeFlagUpdateOnly Or _
544:                                                wbemFlagReturnWhenComplete)
545:                If Err.Number Then ErrorHandler (Err)
546:            Next
547:        End If
548:
...:
...:
...:
```

The change of the Operating System recovery options is pretty easy and does not contain any tricks. Each property is assigned with the value specified from the command line. For instance, from line 490 through 494, the debugging file path is set, and from line 496 through 500, the minidump directory is set. Lines 502 through 505 assign a value that corresponds to the dump type desired. The values and the corresponding dump type are presented in Table 2.22.

Table 2.22   *The Operating System File Dump Values*

Value	Description
0	None
1	Complete
2	Kernel
3	Small

The changes are committed with the *Put_* method of the **SWBemObject** object, which contains the *Win32_OSRecoveryConfiguration* instance (lines 543 and 544).

The last piece of code concerning the Operating System operations is shown in Sample 2.49 and modifies the application time slice, the system date and time, and also can reboot the computer.

Sample 2.49   *Setting application time slice, date and time, and rebooting the Operating System (Part VII)*

```
...:
...:
...:
548:
549:        If objWMIOSInstances.Count = 1 Then
550:           For Each objWMIOSInstance in objWMIOSInstances
551:
552:              If intForeAppsBoost <> - 1 Then
553:                 objWMIOSInstance.ForegroundApplicationBoost = intForeAppsBoost
554:                 WScript.Echo "ForegroundApplicationBoost set."
555:              End If
556:
557:              If Len (strDateTime) Then
558:                 intRC = objWMIOSInstance.SetDateTime (strDateTime)
559:                 WScript.Echo "SetDateTime (" & intRC & ")."
560:              End If
561:
562:              If intShutdownValue Then
563:                 intRC = objWMIOSInstance.Win32Shutdown (intShutdownValue - 1)
564:                 WScript.Echo "Shutdown (" & intRC & ")."
565:              End If
566:
567:              objWMIOSInstance.Put_ (wbemChangeFlagUpdateOnly Or _
568:                                     wbemFlagReturnWhenComplete)
```

```
569:                If Err.Number Then ErrorHandler (Err)
570:         Next
571:      End If
572:    End If
...:
580:    ]]>
581:    </script>
582:  </job>
583:</package>
```

When the **/ForegroundApplicationBoost** switch is used with a value between 0 and 2, it modifies the priority given to the foreground application (lines 552 through 555). On computer systems running Windows NT 4.0 and Windows 2000 and beyond, application boost is implemented by giving an application more execution time slices, called the quantum lengths. A value of 0 boosts the quantum length by 6. If the value is set to 1, the system boosts the quantum length by 12, and if set to 2, the system boosts the quantum by 18. The default value is 2. On Windows NT 3.51 and earlier, application boost is implemented by increasing the scheduling priority. For these systems, the scheduling priority is increased by the value of this property.

To change the date and time of the computer, the **/SetDateTime** switch must be used with one parameter that contains a date and time value in DMTF format. Once specified, lines 557 through 560 are executed.

To reboot the computer, the script uses the *Win32Shutdown* method of the *Win32_OperatingSystem* instance (lines 562 through 565). This method accepts one parameter, which contains a set of bit flags. Table 2.23 contains the different values with their corresponding actions.

Table 2.23   *The Operating System Shutdown Values*

Value	Description
0	Log Off
0 + 4	Forced Log Off
1	Shutdown
1 + 4	Forced Shutdown
2	Reboot
2 + 4	Forced Reboot
8	Power Off
8 + 4	Forced Power Off

The script header contains some constants (see Sample 2.43, from line 104 through 110) that define the miscellaneous values. The command-line parsing converts the command-line keyword to the corresponding value passed to the *Win32Shutdown* method. For instance, to reboot a computer with the script, the following command line must be used:

```
WMIOSConfig.wsf /Shutdown:Reboot
```

To shut down the computer, the following command line must be used:

```
WMIOSConfig.wsf /Shutdown:Shutdown
```

2.4.9 Process classes

The process category classes represent the system processes and threads. The classes supported by the *Win32* providers and included in this category are listed in Table 2.24.

Table 2.24   *The Process Classes*

Name	Description
Win32_Process	Represents a sequence of events on a Windows system.
Win32_ProcessStartup	Represents the startup configuration of a Windows process.
Win32_Thread	Represents a thread of execution.

These classes are not the only classes referring to the processes. For instance, the *Win32_NamedJobObject* class also provides some information about the processes. We revisit the Job Kernel–related classes when examining the *Job Kernel* providers in the next chapter.

The *Win32_NamedJobObject* class represents a kernel object that is used to group processes for the sake of controlling the life and resources of the processes within the job object. Only the job objects that have been named are instrumented.

With the *Win32_Process* class, it is possible to gather information about the running processes, create new processes, and kill processes. The next script sample performs these tasks. The command-line parameter syntax is as follows:

```
C:\>WMIProcess.wsf
Microsoft (R) Windows Script Host Version 5.6
Copyright (C) Microsoft Corporation 1996-2001. All rights reserved.

Usage: WMIProcess.wsf /Action:value [/Executable[+|-]] [/CurrentDirectory:value]
                      [/TerminateCode:value] [/PauseBeforeTerminate:value] [/ProcessID:value]
                      [/Title:value] [/FillAttribute:value] [/PriorityClass:value]
                      [/ShowWindow:value]
                      [/X:value] [/XCountChars:value] [/XSize:value]
                      [/Y:value] [/YCountChars:value] [/YSize:value]
                      [/Machine:value] [/User:value] [/Password:value]

Options:

Action               : specify the operation to perform: [List] or [Create] or [Kill].
Executable           : The name of the executable to start.
CurrentDirectory     : The directory where the process must be executed. (Default=C:\)
TerminateCode        : Return code of the ended process.
PauseBeforeTerminate : Pause before ending the started process (Default=10 s).
```

```
ProcessID          : Process ID of the process to Kill.
Title              : Contains the string displayed in the title bar if a new console window
                     is created.
FillAttribute      : Specifies the initial text and background colors if a new console window
                     is created.
PriorityClass      : Used to determine the scheduling priorities of the threads in the process.
ShowWindow         : Specifies how the window is to be displayed to the user.
X                  : Specifies the x offset, in pixels, of the upper left corner of a window
                     if a new window is created.
XCountChars        : Used for processes creating a console window, specifies the screen buffer
                     width in character columns.
XSize              : Specifies the width, in pixels, of the window if a new window is created.
Y                  : Specifies the y offset, in pixels, of the upper left corner of a window
                     if a new window is created.
YCountChars        : Used for processes creating a console window, specifies the screen buffer
                     height in character rows.
YSize              : Specifies the height, in pixels, of the window if a new window is created.
Machine            : Determine the WMI system to connect to. (default=LocalHost)
User               : Determine the UserID to perform the remote connection. (default=none)
Password           : Determine the password to perform the remote connection. (default=none)
Examples:

    WMIProcess.wsf /Action:List
    WMIProcess.wsf /Action:List /Executable:NotePad.Exe

    WMIProcess.wsf /Action:Create /Executable:NotePad.Exe /CurrentDirectory:C:\
                   /PauseBeforeTerminate:4000 /TerminateCode:0
    WMIProcess.wsf /Executable:NotePad.Exe /CurrentDirectory:C:\ /PauseBeforeTerminate:2000
    WMIProcess.wsf /Executable:NotePad.Exe /CurrentDirectory:C:\ /TerminateCode:0
    WMIProcess.wsf /Executable:CMD.Exe /FillAttribute:12 /PriorityClass:32 /ShowWindow:1
                   /X:150 /XCountChars:40 /XSize:1024
                   /Y:150 /YCountChars:10 /YSize:500
    WMIProcess.wsf /Executable:CMD.Exe /Machine:RemoteSystem.LissWare.Net

    WMIProcess.wsf /Action:Kill /ProcessID:1252 /TerminateCode:0
    WMIProcess.wsf /Action:Kill /ProcessID:412  /TerminateCode:0
                   /Machine:RemoteSystem.LissWare.Net
```

To change the scripting technique used in the previous script samples, the next sample creates and kills processes asynchronously. From a global perspective, this does not change anything about the class usage, but the script structure and the scripting technique change significantly. The code is presented in Sample 2.50 through 2.55. As usual, the script starts with the command-line parameters definition and parsing. Since the command-line parameters parsing code is structured in the same way as previously, it is omitted (lines 13 through 49 and 126 through 264) in the sample code visible below.

Sample 2.50   *Viewing, creating, and killing processes (Part I)*

```
1:<?xml version="1.0"?>
 .:
8:<package>
9:  <job>
..:
```

```
 13:    <runtime>
 ..:
 49:    </runtime>
 50:
 51:    <script language="VBScript" src="..\Functions\DisplayFormattedPropertyFunction.vbs" />
 52:    <script language="VBScript" src="..\Functions\TinyErrorHandler.vbs" />
 53:
 54:    <object progid="WbemScripting.SWbemLocator" id="objWMILocator" reference="true"/>
 55:    <object progid="WbemScripting.SWbemNamedValueSet" id="objWMIMethodSinkContext" />
 56:    <object progid="WbemScripting.SWbemDateTime" id="objWMIDateTime" />
 57:
 58:    <script language="VBscript">
 59:    <![CDATA[
 ..:
 63:    ' -------------------------------------------------------------------------------
 64:    Const cComputerName = "LocalHost"
 65:    Const cWMINameSpace = "root/cimv2"
 66:    Const cWMIProcClass = "Win32_Process"
 67:    Const cWMIProcStartupClass = "Win32_ProcessStartup"
 68:
 69:    Const cWMITerminateCode = 0
 70:    Const cPauseBeforeTerminate = 10000
 71:
 72:    Const cFillAttribute = 12
 73:    Const cPriorityClass = 32
 74:    Const cShowWindow = 1
 75:    Const cX = 100
 76:    Const cXCountChars = 1000
 77:    Const cXSize = 400
 78:    Const cY = 100
 79:    Const cYCountChars = 120
 80:    Const cYSize = 300
...:
124:    ' ----------------------------------------------------------------------------
125:    ' Parse the command line parameters
126:    varTemp = WScript.Arguments.Named("TerminateCode") ...:
...:
264:    If Len(strComputerName) = 0 Then strComputerName = cComputerName
265:
266:    Set objWMISink = WScript.CreateObject ("WbemScripting.SWbemSink", "SINK_")
267:
268:    objWMILocator.Security_.AuthenticationLevel = wbemAuthenticationLevelDefault
269:    objWMILocator.Security_.ImpersonationLevel = wbemImpersonationLevelImpersonate
270:
271:    Set objWMIServices = objWMILocator.ConnectServer(strComputerName, cWMINameSpace, _
272:                                        strUserID, strPassword)
...:
274:
...:
...:
...:
```

The header of the script contains some constants (lines 69 through 80) that are used as default values when creating a new process. These constants are used later.

Sample 2.51 gathers information about the running processes. First, the script creates a collection of the process instances (line 284). Next, it enu-

merates the collection (lines 289 through 334) with all properties available
from each instance (lines 292 through 312). Because many processes can
run at the same time, the script uses the optional **/Executable** switch only to
display information about the given executable name. However, because the
executable name is not used as a key property of the *Win32_Process* class,
the script queries for an instance using a *name* property that matches the
executable name given (lines 278 through 281). As mentioned, the **/Execut-
able** switch is optional; if no executable name is given (line 277), all
instances will be listed.

Sample 2.51   *Viewing processes (Part II)*

```
...:
...:
...:
274:
275:   ' - LIST ---------------------------------------------------------------------------
276:   If boolList Then
277:       If Len (strExecutable) Then
278:           Set objWMIProcInstances = objWMIServices.ExecQuery ("Select * From " & _
279:                                                                cWMIProcClass & _
280:                                                                " Where Name='" & _
281:                                                                strExecutable & "'")
282:           If Err.Number Then ErrorHandler (Err)
283:       Else
284:           Set objWMIProcInstances = objWMIServices.InstancesOf (cWMIProcClass)
285:           If Err.Number Then ErrorHandler (Err)
286:       End If
287:
288:       If objWMIProcInstances.Count Then
289:           For Each objWMIProcInstance in objWMIProcInstances
290:               WScript.Echo "- " & Ucase(objWMIProcInstance.Name) & String (60, "-")
291:               Set objWMIPropertySet = objWMIProcInstance.Properties_
292:               For Each objWMIProperty In objWMIPropertySet
293:                   Select Case objWMIProperty.Name
294:                           Case "Caption"
295:
296:                           Case "Description"
297:
298:                           Case "Name"
299:
300:                           Case "CSCreationClassName"
301:
302:                           Case "OSCreationClassName"
303:
304:                           Case "CreationClassName"
305:
306:                           Case Else
307:                               DisplayFormattedProperty objWMIProcInstance, _
308:                                                        "  " & objWMIProperty.Name, _
309:                                                        objWMIProperty.Name, _
310:                                                        Null
311:                   End Select
312:               Next
...:
```

```
315:            WScript.Echo
316:
317:            intRC = objWMIProcInstance.GetOwner (strOwnerUser, strOwnerDomain)
318:            If intRC = 0 Then
319:               DisplayFormattedProperty objWMIProcInstance, _
320:                                        " Process owner", _
321:                                        strOwnerDomain, _
322:                                        strOwnerUser
323:            End If
324:
325:            intRC = objWMIProcInstance.GetOwnerSid (strOwnerSID)
326:            If intRC = 0 Then
327:               DisplayFormattedProperty objWMIProcInstance, _
328:                                        " Process owner SID", _
329:                                        strOwnerSID, _
330:                                        Null
331:            End If
332:
333:            WScript.Echo
334:         Next
335:      Else
336:         WScript.Echo "No information available."
337:      End If
...:
340:
...:
...:
...:
```

The *Win32_Process* class exposes two methods to retrieve information about the process owner. The *GetOwner* method (lines 317 through 323) retrieves the domain name and user name of the process owner, while the *GetOwnerSID* method (lines 325 through 331) retrieves the SID of the process owner. If you run the script to view process information about **NotePad.Exe,** you receive the following output:

```
 1:  C:\>WMIProcess.wsf /Action:List /Executable:Notepad.Exe
 2:  Microsoft (R) Windows Script Host Version 5.6
 3:  Copyright (C) Microsoft Corporation 1996-2001. All rights reserved.
 4:
 5:  - NOTEPAD.EXE----------------------------------------------------------
 6:    CommandLine: ......................... "J:\WINDOWS\System32\Notepad.Exe" WMIProcessN.wsf
 7:    CreationDate: ........................ 31-10-2001 16:32:22
 8:    CSName: .............................. XP-DPEN6400
 9:    ExecutablePath: ...................... J:\WINDOWS\System32\Notepad.Exe
10:    *Handle: ............................. 3532
11:    HandleCount: ......................... 22
12:    InstallDate: ......................... 31-10-2001 16:32:22
13:    KernelModeTime: ...................... 37754288
14:    MaximumWorkingSetSize: ............... 1413120
15:    MinimumWorkingSetSize: ............... 204800
16:    OSName: .............................. Microsoft Windows .NET Enterprise Server ...
17:    OtherOperationCount: ................. 44
18:    OtherTransferCount: .................. 432
19:    PageFaults: .......................... 776
20:    PageFileUsage: ....................... 692224
21:    ParentProcessId: ..................... 288
```

```
22:     PeakPageFileUsage: .................... 692224
23:     PeakVirtualSize: ...................... 30711808
24:     PeakWorkingSetSize: ................... 3121152
25:     Priority: ............................ 8
26:     PrivatePageCount: .................... 692224
27:     ProcessId: ........................... 3532
28:     QuotaNonPagedPoolUsage: .............. 1680
29:     QuotaPagedPoolUsage: ................. 26672
30:     QuotaPeakNonPagedPoolUsage: .......... 1760
31:     QuotaPeakPagedPoolUsage: ............. 33136
32:     ReadOperationCount: .................. 0
33:     ReadTransferCount: ................... 0
34:     SessionId: ........................... 0
35:     TerminationDate: ..................... 31-10-2001 16:32:22
36:     ThreadCount: ......................... 1
37:     UserModeTime: ........................ 3404896
38:     VirtualSize: ......................... 24297472
39:     WindowsVersion: ...................... 5.1.3553
40:     WorkingSetSize: ...................... 3121152
41:     WriteOperationCount: ................. 0
42:     WriteTransferCount: .................. 0
43:
44:     Process owner: ....................... LISSWARENET Alain.Lissoir
45:     Process owner SID: ................... S-1-5-21-2025429265-507921405-1202660629-1140
```

Note that none of the listed properties displays information about the process CPU usage. This information is available from the performance counters. We discuss how to retrieve this in the next chapter.

To create a process, the *Create* method of the *Win32_Process* class is used (see Sample 2.52). It is important to note that the *Create* method is a static method for the class. This implies that a static qualifier is set on the *Create* method definition, which means that the method invocation must be made from an instance of the *Win32_Process* class (line 343). We have already seen this peculiarity when we worked with Sample 2.12 ("Configuring a network adapter"). Next, when creating a new process, it is possible to specify a series of parameters for the created process. These parameters are stored in a class instance of the *Win32_ProcessStartup* class (lines 346 through 349). The *Win32_ProcessStartup* class is a bit unusual, because it is defined as an abstract class. (See Figure 2.18.)

Figure 2.18
*The Win32_
ProcessStartup
abstract class used
only as a method
parameter class.*

The *Win32_ProcessStartup* is a child class of the *Win32_MethodParameter-Class* class. The classes defined as a subclass of the *Win32_MethodParameter-*

Class class are only used to create an instance used as a method parameter. The
Win32_ProcessStartup properties set by the script are only applicable if the
created process is a console application (lines 351 through 360).

Sample 2.52   *Creating processes (Part II)*

```
...:
...:
...:
340:
341:     ' - CREATE -----------------------------------------------------------------------
342:     ElseIf boolCreate Then
343:         Set objWMIProcClass = objWMIServices.Get (cWMIProcClass)
...:
346:         Set objWMIProcStartupClass = objWMIServices.Get (cWMIProcStartupClass)
...:
349:         Set objWMIProcStartupInstance = objWMIProcStartupClass.SpawnInstance_
350:
351:         objWMIProcStartupInstance.FillAttribute = intFillAttribute
352:         objWMIProcStartupInstance.PriorityClass = intPriorityClass
353:         objWMIProcStartupInstance.ShowWindow = intShowWindow
354:         objWMIProcStartupInstance.Title = strTitle
355:         objWMIProcStartupInstance.X = intX
356:         objWMIProcStartupInstance.XCountChars = intXCountChars
357:         objWMIProcStartupInstance.XSize = intXSize
358:         objWMIProcStartupInstance.Y = intY
359:         objWMIProcStartupInstance.YCountChars = intYCountChars
360:         objWMIProcStartupInstance.YSize = intYSize
361:
362:         objWMIMethodSinkContext.Add "WMIMethod", "Create"
363:         Set objWMIMethod = objWMIProcClass.Methods_("Create")
364:         Set objWMIInParameters = objWMIMethod.InParameters
365:
366:         objWMIInParameters.Properties_.Item("CommandLine") = strExecutable
367:         objWMIInParameters.Properties_.Item("CurrentDirectory") = strCurrentDirectory
368:         objWMIInParameters.Properties_.Item("ProcessStartupInformation") = _
369:                                             objWMIProcStartupInstance
370:
371:         objWMIProcClass.ExecMethodAsync_ objWMISink, _
372:                                     "Create", _
373:                                     objWMIInParameters, _
374:                                     wbemFlagDontSendStatus, _
375:                                     '_
376:                                     objWMIMethodSinkContext
...:
384:         Do While (boolEndScript = False)
385:             WScript.Sleep (500)
386:         Loop
387:
388:         objWMISink.Cancel
389:
...:
...:
...:
```

Next, since the script is executed asynchronously, the sink routine context is defined (line 362) and the *Create* method parameters are set (lines
363 through 369). Line 366 sets the executable to be started, line 367

defines the default directory for the new process, and line 368 stores the
Win32_ProcessStartup instance that contains the optional parameters for a
console application. Once completed, the method execution is invoked
asynchronously (lines 371 through 376). Next, the script waits for the end
of the asynchronous operation (lines 384 through 386).

Before diving into the sink subroutines, since the kill process operation
is also asynchronously executed with the same set of sink routines, let's see
how the *Terminate* method of the *Win32_Process* class is invoked with Sample 2.53. This method is not a static method and relates to an instance of an
existing process. This is the reason why the script first retrieves the process
instance by using its process ID, which is used as a key property for the
Win32_Process class (line 392). The process ID is retrieved during the asynchronous execution of the process creation (line 438 and following). Next, a
context is defined for the asynchronous method invocation. This context is
used later during the sink routine's execution.

Because it is possible to specify a termination code, the script makes use
of the **/TerminateCode** switch and assigns the given value at line 399. Next,
the method is asynchronously invoked (lines 400 through 405). As previously, the script waits for the end of the asynchronous operation (lines 410
through 412).

Sample 2.53   *Killing processes (Part IV)*

```
...:
...:
...:
389:
390:    ' - KILL -------------------------------------------------------------------------
391:    ElseIf boolKill Then
392:        Set objWMIProcInstance = objWMIServices.Get (cWMIProcClass & "='" & intProcID & "'")
393:        If Err.Number Then ErrorHandler (Err)
394:
395:        objWMIMethodSinkContext.Add "WMIMethod", "Terminate"
396:        Set objWMIMethod = objWMIProcInstance.Methods_("Terminate")
397:        Set objWMIInParameters = objWMIMethod.InParameters
398:
399:        objWMIInParameters.Properties_.Item("Reason") = intTerminateCode
400:        objWMIProcInstance.ExecMethodAsync_ objWMISink, _
401:                                            "Terminate", _
402:                                            objWMIInParameters, _
403:                                            wbemFlagDontSendStatus, _
404:                                            , _
405:                                            objWMIMethodSinkContext
...:
410:        Do While (boolEndScript = False)
411:            WScript.Sleep (500)
412:        Loop
413:
414:        objWMISink.Cancel
```

```
415:    End If
...:
421:
...:
...:
...:
```

The asynchronous sink routines are shown in Sample 2.54. Two event sinks are used: the SINK_OnCompleted() (lines 423 through 457) and SINK_OnObjectReady() (lines 460 through 531).

Sample 2.54 *Viewing, creating, and killing processes (OnObjectReady sink routine) (Part V)*

```
...:
...:
...:
421:
422:    ' ----------------------------------------------------------------------
423:    Sub SINK_OnObjectReady (objWMIInstance, objWMIAsyncContext)
...:
429:        Wscript.Echo
430:        Wscript.Echo "BEGIN - OnObjectReady."
431:
432:        Set objContextItem = objWMIAsyncContext.Item ("WMIMethod")
...:
435:        Select Case objContextItem.Value
436:            Case "Create"
437:                If objWMIInstance.ReturnValue = 0 Then
438:                    intProcID = objWMIInstance.ProcessID
439:                    WScript.Echo "Process ID " & intProcID & " created."
440:                Else
441:                    Wscript.Echo "Asynchronous method execution failed (" & _
442:                                      objWMIInstance.ReturnValue & ")."
443:                End If
444:            Case "Terminate"
445:                If objWMIInstance.ReturnValue = 0 Then
446:                    WScript.Echo "Process ID " & intProcID & " terminated."
447:                Else
448:                    Wscript.Echo "Asynchronous method execution failed (" & _
449:                                      objWMIInstance.ReturnValue & ")."
450:                End If
451:        End Select
...:
455:        Wscript.Echo "END - OnObjectReady."
456:
457:    End Sub
458:
...:
...:
...:
```

When a *Win32_Process* method is executed asynchronously (i.e., for the *Create* or *Terminate* methods), the code first determines its context (lines 432 and 435). If a process is created (lines 436 through 443), the Process ID of the newly created process is saved in a variable at line 438. This variable is used later to retrieve the instance of the process to kill, as well as during the SINK_OnCompleted() sink routine once the process is successfully killed. In the context *Terminate* method execution, the return value of the *Terminate* method is tested, and a message is displayed accordingly (lines 444 through 450).

Once the asynchronous operation is completed, the SINK_OnCompleted() sink routine is called. This routine contains some extra logic based on the command-line parameters given.

Sample 2.55   *Viewing, creating, and killing processes (OnCompleted sink routine) (Part VI)*

```
...:
...:
...:
458:
459:    ' --------------------------------------------------------------------------------
460:    Sub SINK_OnCompleted (intHResult, objWMILastError, objWMIAsyncContext)
...:
467:        Wscript.Echo
468:        Wscript.Echo "BEGIN - OnCompleted."
469:
470:        Set objContextItem = objWMIAsyncContext.Item ("WMIMethod")
...:
473:        If intHResult = 0 Then
474:            WScript.Echo "'" & objContextItem.Value & _
475:                        "' WMI Scripting API Asynchronous call successful " & _
476:                        "(" & intHResult & ")."
477:
478:        Select Case objContextItem.Value
479:                Case "Create"
480:                    If intTerminateCode <> -1 And intProcID <> 0 Then
481:                        WScript.Echo "Pausing script execution for " & _
482:                                    intPauseBeforeTerminate / 1000 & _
483:                                    " seconds before ending procees ID " & _
484:                                    intProcID & " ..."
485:                        WScript.Sleep (intPauseBeforeTerminate)
486:
487:                        Set objWMIProcInstance = objWMIServices.Get (cWMIProcClass & "='" & _
488:                                                    intProcID & "'")
...:
491:                        objWMIMethodSinkContext.Add "WMIMethod", "Terminate"
492:                        Set objWMIMethod = objWMIProcInstance.Methods_("Terminate")
493:                        Set objWMIInParameters = objWMIMethod.InParameters
494:
495:                        objWMIInParameters.Properties_.Item("Reason") = intTerminateCode
496:                        objWMIProcInstance.ExecMethodAsync_ objWMISink, _
497:                                                    "Terminate", _
498:                                                    objWMIInParameters, _
499:                                                    wbemFlagDontSendStatus, _
500:                                                    ' _
501:                                                    objWMIMethodSinkContext
...:
505:                    Else
506:                        boolEndScript = True
507:                    End If
508:                Case "Terminate"
509:                    boolEndScript = True
```

```
510:            End Select
511:        Else
512:            WScript.Echo String (60, "-")
513:
514:            WScript.Echo "'" & objContextItem.Value & _
515:                    "' WMI Scripting API Asynchronous call failed " & _
516:                    "(" & intHResult & ")."
517:
518:            WScript.Echo vbCRLF & "SWbemLastError content:"
519:            Set objWMIPropertySet = objWMILastError.Properties_
520:            For Each objWMIProperty In objWMIPropertySet
521:                WScript.Echo "  " & objWMIProperty.Name & "=" & objWMIProperty.Value
522:            Next
523:            Set objWMIPropertySet = Nothing
524:            WScript.Echo String (60, "-")
525:        End If
...:
529:        Wscript.Echo "END   - OnCompleted."
530:
531:    End Sub
532:
533:    ]]>
534:    </script>
535:  </job>
536:</package>
```

At line 470, the script first determines the context of the WMI asynchronous operation (*Create* or *Terminate* method execution). Based on its result (line 473), the script displays an informational message (lines 474 and 475 or 512 through 524). If the asynchronous context operation corresponds to a process creation (lines 480 through 507), the code performs some extra tests. These tests are done with the variables that contain information given on the command line. Let's take an example. To create a process, the following command line can be given:

```
WMIProcess.wsf /Action:Create /Executable:NotePad.Exe /CurrentDirectory:C:\
```

This command line creates a process called **NotePad.Exe** with a default directory of C:\. Once the process is created, the script terminates properly. The obtained output is as follows:

```
C:\>WMIProcess.wsf /Action:Create /Executable:NotePad.Exe /CurrentDirectory:C:\
Microsoft (R) Windows Script Host Version 5.6
Copyright (C) Microsoft Corporation 1996-2001. All rights reserved.


BEGIN - OnObjectReady.
Process ID 4092 created.
END - OnObjectReady.

BEGIN - OnCompleted.
'Create' WMI Scripting API Asynchronous call successful (0).
END   - OnCompleted.
```

However, with the logic implemented in the SINK_OnCompleted() sink routine it is also possible to start a process for a defined period of time,

and, once this time elapses, the created process is automatically killed by the
script itself. The command line to use, and the output obtained, is as follows:

```
C:\>WMIProcess.wsf /Action:Create /Executable:NotePad.Exe /CurrentDirectory:C:\
                             /PauseBeforeTerminate:4000 /TerminateCode:0
Microsoft (R) Windows Script Host Version 5.6
Copyright (C) Microsoft Corporation 1996-2001. All rights reserved.


BEGIN - OnObjectReady.
Process ID 3596 created.
END - OnObjectReady.

BEGIN - OnCompleted.
'Create' WMI Scripting API Asynchronous call successful (0).
Pausing script execution for 4 seconds before ending procees ID 3596 ...
END   - OnCompleted.

BEGIN - OnObjectReady.
Process ID 3596 terminated.
END - OnObjectReady.

BEGIN - OnCompleted.
'Terminate' WMI Scripting API Asynchronous call successful (0).
END   - OnCompleted.
```

The fact that the **/TerminateCode** is given on the command line with
the **/Action:Create** switch forces the script to kill the newly created process
before ending. The **/PauseBeforeTerminate** switch forces a pause of four
seconds. If the **/PauseBeforeTerminate** switch is not given, a default pause
of ten seconds is made. This default timeout is defined in the constant
defined in the script header (see Sample 2.50, line 70).

From a coding point of view, the value given with the **/TerminateCode**
switch is tested to determine if the new process must be killed. This test is
made at line 480. On the same line the Process ID value saved during the
SINK_OnObjectReady() sink routine (see Sample 2.54) is reused. If the
test evaluation is successful (line 480), it means that a pause must be performed (line 485). Once the pause ends, the script retrieves an instance of
the created process (lines 487 and 488). Next, we retrieve the same logic as
before to kill a process asynchronously (lines 491 through 501).

If the **/Terminate** switch is not given, the script sets a Boolean variable
to True (line 506) to terminate the loop waiting for the end of the asynchronous operation (see Sample 2.52, lines 384 through 386). If the **/Terminate**
switch is given, and once the newly created process is killed, the SINK_
OnCompleted() sink routine is called a second time for the *Terminate*
method asynchronous execution. In the same way, the script sets the Boolean variable to True (line 509) to terminate the loop waiting for the end of
the asynchronous operation (see Sample 2.52, lines 384 through 386).

When the script is used to kill a process based on its process ID, the following command line is used:

```
WMIProcess.wsf /Action:Kill /ProcessID:412  /TerminateCode:0
```

In this case, the dedicated piece of code executed is located between lines 444 and 450 in the SINK_OnObjectReady() sink routine and line 509 in the SINK_OnCompleted() sink routine. At line 509, you will notice the Boolean variable value set on True to stop the loop waiting for the end of the asynchronous operation (see Sample 2.53, lines 410 through 412).

2.4.10 Registry class

The class in the registry category represents the settings of the Windows registry. There is only one class, called *Win32_Registry*. It is important to avoid confusion between this class and the classes exposed by the WMI *Registry* provider. The *Win32_Registry* class represents the Windows registry settings, such as the registry size, while the WMI *Registry* provider exposes classes and methods that allow access and event monitoring of the Windows registry data. We examine the WMI *Registry* provider, its related classes, and how to manipulate the registry content in the next chapter.

When we learned the WMI scripting technique in *Understanding WMI Scripting*, Chapter 4, we used the *Win32_Registry* class. Instead of reproducing one of these samples, you can refer to the appendix for Sample 4.14 ("Setting one read/write property of a *Win32_Registry* class instance directly") and Sample 4.15 ("Setting one read/write property of a *Win32_ Registry* class instance indirectly"). The *Win32_Registry* class exposes only one read/write property, called *ProposedSize*. All other properties are read-only, and there is no method available from the class.

2.4.11 Job scheduler classes

The job scheduler classes category represents scheduled job settings. This category contains only two classes, listed in Table 2.25.

Table 2.25 *The Job Scheduler Classes*

Name	Type	Description
Win32_CurrentTime	Abstract	Represents as Dynamic in time as component seconds, minutes, day of the week, and so on.
Win32_ScheduledJob	Dynamic	Represents a job scheduled using the Windows NT schedule service.

The *Win32_ScheduledJob* class with its two methods implements the necessary features to develop a script equivalent to the **AT.Exe** command. With this class, it is possible to view, create, and delete scheduled jobs. Even if the *Win32_CurrentTime* class is categorized in the Jobs Scheduler category in the Microsoft Platform SDK, it is important to note that this class is supported by the *Win32Clockprovider* WMI provider and not by the *Win32* providers. We examine this provider and its related *Win32_CurrentTime* class in the next chapter.

As in previous scripts, the next sample supports a set of command-line parameters. Each of the switches corresponds to one of the features supported by the classes. The command-line parameters supported are:

```
C:\>WMIScheduledJob.wsf
Microsoft (R) Windows Script Host Version 5.6
Copyright (C) Microsoft Corporation 1996-2001. All rights reserved.

Usage: WMIScheduledJob.wsf [/List[+|-]] [/Create:value] [/StartTime:value] [/RunRepeatedly[+|-]]
                           [/DaysOfWeek:value] [/DaysOfMonth:value] [/InteractWithDesktop[+|-]]
                           [/Delete:value] [/GetTime[+|-]] [/Machine:value] [/User:value]
                           [/Password:value]


Options:

List                  : List the existing scheduled jobs.
Create                : The name of the executable to start.
StartTime             : Represents the UTC time to run the job.
RunRepeatedly         : Indicates whether the scheduled job should run repeatedly on the days that
                        the job is scheduled.
DaysOfWeek            : Indicates the days of the week when the job is scheduled to run
                        (used with RunRepeatedly).
DaysOfMonth           : Indicates the days of the month when the job is scheduled to run
                        (used with RunRepeatedly).
InteractWithDesktop : Indicates whether the specified job should be interactive.
Delete                : Deletes a scheduled job.
GetTime               : Get the current time in UTC format.
Machine               : Determine the WMI system to connect to. (default=LocalHost)
User                  : Determine the UserID to perform the remote connection. (default=none)
Password              : Determine the password to perform the remote connection. (default=none)
Examples:

    WMIScheduledJob.wsf /GetTime+
    WMIScheduledJob.wsf /List+
    WMIScheduledJob.wsf /Create:MyJob.Exe /StartTime:********180000.000000+120
                        /DaysOfWeek:Mon,Tue,Wed,Thu,Fri,Sat,Sun
                        /DaysOfMonth:1,2,3,4,24
    WMIScheduledJob.wsf /Delete:9,15,17,18,23
    WMIScheduledJob.wsf /Delete:14
```

The complete script code is shown in Samples 2.56 through 2.59. As with all previous scripts, Sample 2.56 starts with the command-line parameters definition (skipped lines 13 through 37) and parsing (lines 96 through 183). Although very similar to the command-line parsing technique used in the previous scripts, we will briefly examine this piece of code, because it requires some special care to build two required parameters of the *Create* method exposed by the *Win32_ScheduledJob* class. These two parameters are *DaysOfWeek* and *DaysOfMonth*.

Sample 2.56   *Viewing, creating, and deleting scheduled jobs (Part I)*

```
 1:<?xml version="1.0"?>
 .:
 8:<package>
 9:  <job>
..:
13:    <runtime>
..:
37:    </runtime>
38:
39:    <script language="VBScript" src="..\Functions\DecodeDaysOfWeekFunction.vbs" />
40:    <script language="VBScript" src="..\Functions\DecodeDaysOfMonthFunction.vbs" />
41:
42:    <script language="VBScript" src="..\Functions\ConvertStringInArrayFunction.vbs" />
43:    <script language="VBScript" src="..\Functions\DisplayFormattedPropertyFunction.vbs" />
44:    <script language="VBScript" src="..\Functions\TinyErrorHandler.vbs" />
45:
46:    <object progid="WbemScripting.SWbemLocator" id="objWMILocator" reference="true"/>
47:    <object progid="WbemScripting.SWbemDateTime" id="objWMIDateTime" />
48:
49:    <script language="VBscript">
50:    <![CDATA[
..:
54:    ' -------------------------------------------------------------------------------
55:    Const cComputerName = "LocalHost"
56:    Const cWMINameSpace = "root/cimv2"
57:
58:    Const cWMIScheduledJobClass = "Win32_ScheduledJob"
..:
94:    ' -------------------------------------------------------------------------------
95:    ' Parse the command line parameters
96:    If WScript.Arguments.Named.Count = 0 Then
97:       WScript.Arguments.ShowUsage()
98:       WScript.Quit
99:    End If
100:
101:    boolList = WScript.Arguments.Named("List")
102:    If Len(boolList) = 0 Then boolList = False
103:
104:    boolGetTime = WScript.Arguments.Named("GetTime")
105:    If Len(boolGetTime) = 0 Then boolGetTime = False
106:
107:    varTemp = WScript.Arguments.Named("Delete")
108:    If Len (varTemp) Then
109:       arrayJobIDToDelete = ConvertStringInArray (varTemp, ",")
110:       boolJobIDToDelete = True
111:    Else
112:       boolJobIDToDelete = False
113:    End If
114:
115:    strJobToCreate = WScript.Arguments.Named("Create")
116:    If Len (strJobToCreate) = 0 And _
```

```
117:        boolList = False And _
118:        boolGetTime = False And _
119:        boolJobIDToDelete = False Then
120:        WScript.Arguments.ShowUsage()
121:        WScript.Quit
122:    End If
123:
124:    strStartTime = WScript.Arguments.Named("StartTime")
125:    If Len (strStartTime) = 0 And _
126:        boolList = False And _
127:        boolGetTime = False And _
128:        boolJobIDToDelete = False Then
129:        WScript.Arguments.ShowUsage()
130:        WScript.Quit
131:    End If
132:
133:    boolRunRepeatedly = WScript.Arguments.Named("RunRepeatedly")
134:    If Len(boolRunRepeatedly) = 0 Then boolRunRepeatedly = False
135:
136:    varTemp = WScript.Arguments.Named("DaysOfWeek")
137:    If Len (varTemp) Then
138:        arrayDaysOfWeek = ConvertStringInArray (varTemp, ",")
139:        For Each strDayOfWeek In arrayDaysOfWeek
140:            Select Case Ucase (strDayOfWeek)
141:                Case "MON"
142:                    intIndice = 0
143:                Case "TUE"
144:                    intIndice = 1
145:                Case "WED"
146:                    intIndice = 2
147:                Case "THU"
148:                    intIndice = 3
149:                Case "FRI"
150:                    intIndice = 4
151:                Case "SAT"
152:                    intIndice = 5
153:                Case "SUN"
154:                    intIndice = 6
155:                Case Else
156:                    WScript.Echo "Invalid day of week. Only Mon, Tue, ..." & vbCRLF
157:                    WScript.Arguments.ShowUsage()
158:                    WScript.Quit
159:            End Select
160:            intDaysOfWeek = intDaysOfWeek + 2^intIndice
161:        Next
162:    Else
163:        intDaysOfWeek = 0
164:    End If
165:
166:    varTemp = WScript.Arguments.Named("DaysOfMonth")
167:    If Len (varTemp) Then
168:        arrayDaysOfMonth = ConvertStringInArray (varTemp, ",")
169:        For Each intIndice In arrayDaysOfMonth
170:            If intIndice < 1 Or intIndice > 31 Then
171:                WScript.Echo "Invalid day of month. Only numbers from to 1 to 31 ..." & vbCRLF
172:                WScript.Arguments.ShowUsage()
173:                WScript.Quit
174:            Else
175:                intDaysOfMonth = intDaysOfMonth + 2^(intIndice - 1)
176:            End If
```

```
177:        Next
178:    Else
179:        intDaysOfMonth = 0
180:    End If
181:
182:    boolInteractWithDesktop = WScript.Arguments.Named("InteractWithDesktop")
183:    If Len(boolInteractWithDesktop) = 0 Then boolInteractWithDesktop = False
...:
194:    objWMILocator.Security_.AuthenticationLevel = wbemAuthenticationLevelDefault
195:    objWMILocator.Security_.ImpersonationLevel = wbemImpersonationLevelImpersonate
196:
197:    Set objWMIServices = objWMILocator.ConnectServer(strComputerName, cWMINameSpace, _
198:                                        strUserID, strPassword)
...:
200:
...:
...:
...:
```

Most of the command-line parameters are easily parsed and checked in a few lines, as shown previously. However, regarding the *DaysOfWeek* and *DaysOfMonth* parameters, the string given on the command line must be converted to a specific value, which represents the days of the week (lines 136 through 164) or the days of the month (lines 166 through 180). For the days of the week, each bit of the value represents a specific day of the week (from bit 0 to 6):

- Bit 0—Monday, which defines a value of 1 to activate the job on Monday.

- Bit 1—Tuesday, which defines a value of 2 to activate the job on Tuesday.

- Bit 2—Wednesday, which defines a value of 4 to activate the job on Wednesday.

- Bit 3—Thursday, which defines a value of 8 to activate the job on Thursday.

- Bit 4—Friday, which defines a value of 16 to activate the job on Friday.

- Bit 5—Saturday, which defines a value of 32 to activate the job on Saturday.

- Bit 6—Sunday, which defines a value of 64 to activate the job on Sunday.

So, to activate a job on Monday, Wednesday, and Friday, the command line to use is:

```
C:\>WMIScheduledJob.wsf /Create:MyJob.Exe /StartTime:********180000.000000+120
                        /DaysOfWeek:Mon,Wed,Fri
```

The resulting value is 1 + 4 + 16 = 21. When the **/DaysOfWeek** switch is read, the abbreviation of the days given in a comma-delimited string is converted in an array with the help of the ConvertStringInArray() function, included at line 42. Next, this array is enumerated, and, for each day found, a corresponding bit value is used to calculate the value of the day (lines 139 through 161).

For the days of the month, the principle is exactly the same as for the days of the week. The command line to use is:

```
WMIScheduledJob.wsf /Create:MyJob.Exe /StartTime:********180000.000000+120
                    /DaysOfMonth:3,5,10,25,30
```

Each bit corresponds to a day of the month, and the value uses 31 bits to cover a complete month (from bit 0 to 30).

- Bit 0—1st day of the month, which defines a value of 1 to activate the job the 1st day.

- Bit 1—2nd day of the month, which defines a value of 2 to activate the job the 2nd day.

- Bit 2—3rd day of the month, which defines a value of 4 to activate the job the 3rd day.

    . . .

- Bit 29—30th day of the month, which defines a value of 536 870 912 to activate the job the 30th day.

- Bit 30—31st day of the month, which defines a value of 1 073 741 824 to activate the job the 31st day.

So, to activate a job on the 3rd, 5th, 10th, 25th, and 30th days of the month, the resulting value must be 4 + 16 + 512 + 16 777 216 + 536 870 912 = 553 648 660.

Based on the day numbers given with the **/DaysOfMonth** switch, lines 168 through 177 are used to calculate the value. These two calculated values are used when a scheduled job is created.

When the **/List+** switch is given on the command line, the portion of code available in Sample 2.57 is executed. This code does not contain anything unusual. It creates a collection of instances from the *Win32_ScheduledJob* class (line 203). This collection represents the list of scheduled jobs available in the computer. Next, this collection is enumerated with each property of the *Win32_ScheduledJob* class (lines 207 through 232). Note the conversion of the *DaysOfTheWeek* (line 221) and *DaysOfTheMonth* (line 216) properties.

Sample 2.57   *Viewing the scheduled jobs (Part II)*

```
...:
...:
...:
200:
201:    ' LIST --------------------------------------------------------------------------------
202:    If boolList Then
203:        Set objWMIInstances = objWMIServices.InstancesOf (cWMIScheduledJobClass)
...:
206:        If objWMIInstances.Count Then
207:            For Each objWMIInstance in objWMIInstances
208:                WScript.Echo "- Scheduled jobs (" & objWMIInstance.JobID & _
209:                             ") " & String (60, "-")
210:                Set objWMIPropertySet = objWMIInstance.Properties_
211:                For Each objWMIProperty In objWMIPropertySet
212:                    Select Case objWMIProperty.Name
213:                           Case "DaysOfMonth"
214:                                DisplayFormattedProperty objWMIInstance, _
215:                                                         objWMIProperty.Name, _
216:                                                         DaysOfMonth (objWMIProperty.Value), _
217:                                                         Null
218:                           Case "DaysOfWeek"
219:                                DisplayFormattedProperty objWMIInstance, _
220:                                                         objWMIProperty.Name, _
221:                                                         DaysOfWeek (objWMIProperty.Value), _
222:                                                         Null
223:                           Case Else
224:                                DisplayFormattedProperty objWMIInstance, _
225:                                                         objWMIProperty.Name, _
226:                                                         objWMIProperty.Name, _
227:                                                         Null
228:                    End Select
229:                Next
230:                Set objWMIPropertySet = Nothing
231:                WScript.Echo
232:            Next
233:        Else
234:            WScript.Echo "No scheduled job."
235:        End If
236:    End If
237:
...:
...:
...:
```

The creation of a new scheduled job can be made with the following command lines:

```
C:\>WMIScheduledJob.wsf /Create:MyJob.Exe /StartTime:********180000.000000+120
```

or:

```
C:\>WMIScheduledJob.wsf /Create:MyJob.Exe /StartTime:********180000.000000+120
                        /DaysOfWeek:Mon,Tue,Wed,Thu,Fri,Sat,Sun
```

or:

```
C:\>WMIScheduledJob.wsf /Create:MyJob.Exe /StartTime:********180000.000000+120
                        /DaysOfMonth:1,2,3,4,24
```

or:

```
C:\>WMIScheduledJob.wsf /Create:MyJob.Exe /StartTime:********180000.000000+120
                        /DaysOfWeek:Mon,Tue,Wed,Thu,Fri,Sat,Sun /DaysOfMonth:1,2,3,4,24
```

Once the command-line parameters are parsed (as explained previously), the scheduled job is created with the use of the *Create* method exposed by the *Win32_ScheduledJob* class. This portion of the code is shown in Sample 2.58. Again, as seen in some of the previous samples, the method is defined in the CIM repository as a static method. Doing so, the script must invoke the method from a *Win32_ScheduledJob* class instance (lines 240 through 243).

Sample 2.58   *Creating scheduled jobs (Part III)*

```
...:
...:
...:
237:
238:   ' CREATE --------------------------------------------------------------------------
239:   If Len (strJobToCreate) Then
240:       Set objWMIClass = objWMIServices.Get (cWMIScheduledJobClass)
241:       If Err.Number Then ErrorHandler (Err)
242:
243:       intRC = objWMIClass.Create (strJobToCreate, _
244:                                   strStartTime, _
245:                                   boolRunRepeatedly, _
246:                                   intDaysOfWeek, _
247:                                   intDaysOfMonth, _
248:                                   boolInteractWithDesktop, _
249:                                   intJobID)
250:       If Err.Number Then ErrorHandler (Err)
251:
252:       WScript.Echo "Schedule job " & intJobID & " created (" & intRC & ")."
253:
254:       Set objWMIInstance = Nothing
255:
256:   End If
257:
...:
...:
...:
```

A scheduled job is simply deleted by invoking the *Delete_* method of the **SWBemObject** representing the instance of the scheduled job (see Sample 2.59). For this, an instance of the job must first be retrieved (lines 261 and 262). Next, the retrieved instance is deleted (line 265). Note that the deletion is made in a loop, because the **/Delete** switch accepts several job IDs.

This allows the deletion of several scheduled jobs in one script execution. For instance, the command-line parameter for such an operation is as follows:

```
C:\>WMIScheduledJob.wsf /Delete:9,15,17,18,23
```

Sample 2.59   *Deleting scheduled jobs (Part IV)*

```
...:
...:
...:
257:
258:    ' DELETE -------------------------------------------------------------------------
259:    If boolJobIDToDelete Then
260:       For intIndice = 0 To Ubound (arrayJobIDToDelete)
261:          Set objWMIInstance = objWMIServices.Get (cWMIScheduledJobClass & "=" & _
262:                                                    arrayJobIDToDelete(intIndice))
263:          If Err.Number Then ErrorHandler (Err)
264:
265:          objWMIInstance.Delete_
266:          If Err.Number Then ErrorHandler (Err)
267:
268:          WScript.Echo "Scheduled Job " & arrayJobIDToDelete(intIndice) & " deleted."
269:
270:          Set objWMIInstance = Nothing
271:       Next
272:    End If
273:
...:
...:
...:
```

2.4.12   Service classes

The service classes category represents the Windows services and base services. There are only two classes in this category: *Win32_BaseService* and *Win32_Service* (see Table 2.26).

Table 2.26   *The Service Classes*

Name	Description
Win32_BaseService	Represents executable objects that are installed in a registry database maintained by the Service Control Manager.
Win32_Service	Represents a service on a Windows computer system.

The *Win32_BaseService* is a superclass for the *Win32_Service* class. We examined these classes in a different context throughout the first book, *Understanding WMI Scripting*, and are familiar with them. However, the *Create*, *Change*, and *Delete* methods exposed by the *Win32_Service* method were not used previously. Samples 2.60 through 2.64 illustrate the use of

these methods, and the command-line parameters from the script are as follows:

```
C:\>WMIServices.Wsf
Microsoft (R) Windows Script Host Version 5.6
Copyright (C) Microsoft Corporation 1996-2001. All rights reserved.

Usage: WMIServices.wsf /Action:value /Name:value /DisplayName:value /PathName:value
                       /ServiceType:value /ErrorControl:value /StartMode:value
                       [/DesktopInteract[+|-]] [/StartName:value] [/StartPassword:value]
                       [/LoadOrderGroup:value] [/LoadOrderGroupDependencies:value]
                       [/ServiceDependencies:value] [/Machine:value] [/User:value]
                       [/Password:value]

Options:

Action                       : Specify the operation to perform. Only [list], [create], [update] or
                               [delete] are accepted.
Name                         : Name of the service to install.
DisplayName                  : Display name of the service.
PathName                     : Fully-qualified path to the executable file that implements
                               the service.
ServiceType                  : 1=Kernel Driver, 2=File System Driver, 4=Adapter, 8=Recognizer Driver,
                               16=Own Process, 32=Share Process, 256=Interactive Process
ErrorControl                 : 0=User is not notified, 1=User is notified, 2=System is restarted with
                               last-known-good configuration, 3=System attempts to start with a good
                               configuration.
StartMode                    : Start mode of the service. Only [Boot], [System], [Automatic], [Manual]
                               or [Disabled] are accepted.
DesktopInteract              : If TRUE, the service can create or communicate with windows on the
                               desktop.
StartName                    : Account name under which the service runs. If empty, the LocalSystem
                               account is used.
StartPassword                : Password to the account name specified by the StartName parameter.
LoadOrderGroup               : Group name associated with the new service.
LoadOrderGroupDependencies : List of load-ordering groups that must start before this service.
ServiceDependencies          : List containing names of services that must start before this service
                               starts.
Machine                      : Determine the WMI system to connect to. (default=LocalHost)
User                         : Determine the UserID to perform the remote connection. (default=none)
Password                     : Determine the password to perform the remote connection. (default=none)
Example:

    WMIServices.Wsf /Action:Create /Name:"MySNMP" /DisplayName:"My SNMP Service"
                    /PathName:"J:\WINDOWS\System32\snmp.exe" /ServiceType:16
                    /ErrorControl:1 /StartMode:"Manual"
    WMIServices.Wsf /Action:Update /Name:"MySNMP" /DisplayName:"My SNMP Service"
                    /PathName:"J:\WINDOWS\System32\snmp.exe" /ServiceType:16 /ErrorControl:1
                    /StartMode:"Automatic"
    WMIServices.Wsf /Action:Delete /Name:"MySNMP"
```

The creation of a service requires many parameters. However, the command-line parsing continues to use the same logic and scripting techniques
(omitted lines 13 through 40 and lines 92 through 179). (See Sample 2.60.)

Sample 2.60   *Creating, updating, and deleting a Win32_Service (Part I)*

```
1:<?xml version="1.0"?>
 .:
8:<package>
9:  <job>
..:
13:    <runtime>
..:
40:    </runtime>
41:
42:    <script language="VBScript" src="..\Functions\ConvertStringInArrayFunction.vbs" />
43:    <script language="VBScript" src="..\Functions\DisplayFormattedPropertyFunction.vbs" />
44:    <script language="VBScript" src="..\Functions\TinyErrorHandler.vbs" />
45:
46:    <object progid="WbemScripting.SWbemLocator" id="objWMILocator" reference="true"/>
47:    <object progid="WbemScripting.SWbemDateTime" id="objWMIDateTime" />
48:
49:    <script language="VBscript">
50:    <![CDATA[
..:
54:    Const cComputerName = "LocalHost"
55:    Const cWMINameSpace = "root/cimv2"
56:    Const cWMIClass = "Win32_Service"
..:
90:    ' -----------------------------------------------------------------------------
91:    ' Parse the command line parameters
92:    If WScript.Arguments.Named.Count Then
93:       Select Case Ucase(WScript.Arguments.Named("Action"))
94:            Case "LIST"
95:                 boolList = True
96:            Case "CREATE"
97:                 boolCreate = True
98:            Case "UPDATE"
99:                 boolUpdate = True
100:            Case "DELETE"
101:                 boolDelete = True
102:            Case Else
103:                 WScript.Echo "Invalid action type. Only [List], [Create], ..." & vbCRLF
104:                 WScript.Arguments.ShowUsage()
105:                 WScript.Quit
106:       End Select
...:
178:    strComputerName = WScript.Arguments.Named("Machine")
179:    If Len(strComputerName) = 0 Then strComputerName = cComputerName
180:
181:    objWMILocator.Security_.AuthenticationLevel = wbemAuthenticationLevelDefault
182:    objWMILocator.Security_.ImpersonationLevel = wbemImpersonationLevelImpersonate
183:
184:    Set objWMIServices = objWMILocator.ConnectServer(strComputerName, cWMINameSpace, _
185:                                                      strUserID, strPassword)
186:    If Err.Number Then ErrorHandler (Err)
187:
...:
...:
...:
```

The code of Sample 2.61 lists the Windows services available in a system. This routine is included in the script for functionality completeness. There is no need to make any particular comments on the code presented in Sample 2.61, since the scripting technique is very well known.

Sample 2.61   *Viewing the Win32_Service instances (Part II)*

```
...:
...:
...:
187:
188:    ' -- LIST ------------------------------------------------------------------
189:    If boolList = True Then
190:        Set objWMIInstances = objWMIServices.InstancesOf (cWMIClass)
191:
192:        For Each objWMIInstance In objWMIInstances
193:            WScript.Echo "- " & objWMIInstance.DisplayName & _
194:                          " (" & objWMIInstance.Name & ") " & _
195:                          String (60, "-")
196:            Set objWMIPropertySet = objWMIInstance.Properties_
197:            For Each objWMIProperty In objWMIPropertySet
198:                Select Case objWMIProperty.Name
199:                    Case ""

201:                    Case Else
202:                        DisplayFormattedProperty objWMIInstance, _
203:                                                 objWMIProperty.Name, _
204:                                                 objWMIProperty.Name, _
205:                                                 Null
206:                End Select
207:            Next
208:            Set objWMIPropertySet = Nothing
209:            WScript.Echo
210:        Next
211:
212:        WScript.Echo vbCRLF & "Completed."
...:
215:    End If
216:
...:
...:
...:
```

To create, modify, and delete a Windows service, the script uses the three methods defined at the level of the *Win32_BaseService* class. The *Create* method requires 12 parameters. Although most of the parameters to use with the script sample are obvious, the *ServiceType*, *ErrorControl*, and *Start-Mode* parameters are summarized in Table 2.27.

As shown in Sample 2.62, the *Create* method is invoked from the *Win32_Service* class instance (line 219 and lines 222 through 233), since it is a static method. Even if the method requires 12 parameters, not all of

Table 2.27   *The ServiceType, ErrorControl, and StartMode Parameters for a Windows Service Creation*

ServiceType	
Value	**Description**
1	Kernel Driver
2	File System Driver
4	Adapter
8	Recognizer Driver
16	Own Process
32	Share Process
256	Interactive Process

ErrorControl	
Value	**Description**
0	User is not notified.
1	User is notified.
2	System is restarted with last-known-good configuration.
3	System attempts to start with a good configuration.

StartMode	
Value	**Description**
Boot	Device driver started by the operating system loader. This value is valid only for driver services.
System	Device driver started by the **IoInitSystem** method. This value is valid only for driver services.
Automatic	Service to be started automatically by the service control manager during system startup.
Manual	Service to be started by the service control manager when a process calls the **StartService** method.
Disabled	Service that can no longer be started.

them must be given. For instance, the following command line is sufficient to create a Windows service:

```
C:\>WMIServices.Wsf /Action:Create /Name:"MySNMP" /DisplayName:"My SNMP Service"
                    /PathName:"J:\WINDOWS\System32\snmp.exe" /ServiceType:16
                    /ErrorControl:1 /StartMode:"Manual"
Microsoft (R) Windows Script Host Version 5.6
Copyright (C) Microsoft Corporation 1996-2001. All rights reserved.

Service name 'MySNMP' created (0).
```

Note the value specified with the **/ServiceType** switch. This value defines the service type to be created (see Table 2.27). The code that corresponds to the previous output is shown in Sample 2.62.

Sample 2.62   *Creating a Win32_Service instance (Part III)*

```
...:
...:
...:
216:
217:    ' -- CREATE ------------------------------------------------------------
218:    If boolCreate = True Then
219:        Set objWMIClass = objWMIServices.Get (cWMIClass)
...:
222:        intRC = objWMIClass.Create (strServiceName, _
223:                                    strDisplayName, _
224:                                    strPathName, _
225:                                    intServiceType, _
226:                                    intErrorControl, _
227:                                    strStartMode, _
228:                                    boolDesktopInteract, _
```

```
229:                              strStartName, _
230:                              strStartPassword, _
231:                              strLoadOrderGroup, _
232:                              arrayLoadOrderGroupDependencies, _
233:                              arrayServiceDependencies)
234:
235:        WScript.Echo "Service name '" & strServiceName & "' created (" & intRC & ")."
...:
238:    End If
239:
...:
...:
...:
```

To update an existing Windows service, the corresponding Windows
service instance must be retrieved (line 242). Once retrieved, the *Change*
method can be invoked (lines 245 through 255). This method requires 11
parameters, one less than the *Create* method. This makes sense, since the
service name is not required by the method anymore. However, the service
name is used to retrieve the Windows service instance (line 242).

Sample 2.63   *Modifying a Win32_Service instance (Part IV)*

```
...:
...:
...:
239:
240:    ' -- UPDATE ---------------------------------------------------------------
241:    If boolUpdate = True Then
242:        Set objWMIInstance = objWMIServices.Get (cWMIClass & ".Name='" & strServiceName & "'")
...:
245:        intRC = objWMIInstance.Change (strDisplayName, _
246:                                  strPathName, _
247:                                  intServiceType, _
248:                                  intErrorControl, _
249:                                  strStartMode, _
250:                                  boolDesktopInteract, _
251:                                  strStartName, _
252:                                  strStartPassword, _
253:                                  strLoadOrderGroup, _
254:                                  arrayLoadOrderGroupDependencies, _
255:                                  arrayServiceDependencies)
256:
257:        WScript.Echo "Service name '" & strServiceName & "' updated (" & intRC & ")."
...:
260:    End If
261:
...:
...:
...:
```

Last but not least, if we are able to create Windows services, we should
be able to delete Windows service instances. This operation is probably the
easiest one to implement. After retrieving the Windows service instance to

be deleted (line 264), the *Delete* method is invoked. Note that the *Delete* method invoked is the one defined at the level of the *Win32_BaseService* class and not the one defined at the level of the created **SWBemObject** (called *Delete_*). Invoking the deletion from the **SWBemObject** could also work, but since the class exposes a specific method for it, it is best to use the class method. The **SWBemObject** method is generic for the deletion of any instance represented by an **SWBemObject**. The methods implemented at the level of the class are specific to the object represented by the class. (See Sample 2.64.)

Sample 2.64   *Deleting a Win32_Service instance (Part V)*

```
...:
...:
...:
261:
262:    ' -- DELETE -----------------------------------------------------------------
263:    If boolDelete = True Then
264:        Set objWMIInstance = objWMIServices.Get (cWMIClass & ".Name='" & strServiceName & "'")
...:
267:        intRC = objWMIInstance.Delete
268:
269:        WScript.Echo "Service name '" & strServiceName & "' deleted (" & intRC & ")."
...:
272:    End If
...:
276:    ]]>
277:    </script>
278:  </job>
279:</package>
```

2.4.13   **Share classes**

The share classes category represents details of shared resources, such as printers and folders. This category includes the classes listed in Table 2.28.

Table 2.28   *The Share Classes*

Name	Type	Description
Win32_ServerConnection	Dynamic	Represents the connections made from a remote computer to a shared resource on the local computer.
Win32_ServerSession	Dynamic	Represents the sessions that have been established with the local computer, by users on a remote computer.
Win32_Share	Dynamic	Represents a shared resource on a Windows system.
Win32_ConnectionShare	Association	Relates a shared resource on the computer and the connection made to the shared resource.
Win32_PrinterShare	Association	Relates a local printer and the share that represents it as it is viewed over a network.
Win32_SessionConnection	Association	Represents an association between a session established with the local server, by a user on a remote machine, and the connections that depend on the session.
Win32_SessionProcess	Association	Represents an association between a logon session and the processes associated with that session.
Win32_ShareToDirectory	Association	Relates a shared resource on the computer system and the directory to which it is mapped.

The *Win32_Share* class also exposes methods to create, update, and delete shares. Performing these operations with shares is no more complicated than viewing, creating, updating, and deleting Windows services. Although there is no common point between a share and a Windows service, the WMI abstraction of these two real-world entities makes the scripting technique very similar. The *Win32_Share* class methods are called *Create, SetShareInfo,* and *Delete.* Sample 2.65 shows how to script with the *Win32_Share* class. Its command-line parameters are as follows:

```
C:\>WMIShares.Wsf
Microsoft (R) Windows Script Host Version 5.6
Copyright (C) Microsoft Corporation 1996-2001. All rights reserved.

Usage: WMIShares.wsf [ShareName] /Action:value /ShareType:value [/ShareAdmin[+|-]]
                     [/MaximumAllowed:value] [/Description:value] [/SharePassword:value]
                     [/Machine:value] [/User:value] [/Password:value]


Options:

ShareName       : The share name with its physical path.
Action          : Specify the operation to perform: [list] or [create] or [update] or [delete].
ShareType       : Specify the share type: [Disk], [PrintQ], [Device] or [IPC].
ShareAdmin      : Specify if the share is an admin share.
MaximumAllowed  : Specify the maximum number of simultaneous connections.
Description     : Specify the description for the share.
SharePassword   : Specify the password for the share.
Machine         : Determine the WMI system to connect to. (default=LocalHost)
User            : Determine the UserID to perform the remote connection. (default=none)
Password        : Determine the password to perform the remote connection. (default=none)
Example:

    WMIShare.wsf /Action:List
    WMIShare.wsf MyShare=C:\MyDirectory /ShareType:Disk /MaximumAllowed:10
                 /Description:"This is my share" /Action:Create
    WMIShare.wsf MyOtherShare=C:\MyOtherDirectory /ShareType:Disk /MaximumAllowed:1
                 /ShareAdmin+ /Action:Create
    WMIShare.wsf MyOtherShare=C:\MyOtherDirectory /ShareType:Disk /MaximumAllowed:5
                 /Description:"This is my admin share" /Action:Update
    WMIShare.wsf MyPrinterShare="My Printer,LocalsplOnly" /ShareType:PrintQ /Action:Create
    WMIShare.wsf MyShare /Action:Delete
```

To create a share, seven parameters are required. Most of them are easy to understand, based on Sample 2.65. The only unusual parameter is the the *ShareType* parameter. Its values are shown in Table 2.29.

Table 2.29   *The "ShareType" Values*

Value	Description
0	Disk Drive
1	Print Queue
2	Device
3	IPC
0x80000000	Disk Drive Admin
0x80000001	Print Queue Admin
0x80000002	Device Admin
0x80000003	IPC Admin

Sample 2.65 is structured and uses the same logic as Samples 2.60 through 2.64 ("Creating, updating, and deleting a *Win32_Service*").

Sample 2.65   *Viewing, creating, updating, and deleting shares*

```
 1:<?xml version="1.0"?>
 .:
 8:<package>
 9:  <job>
..:
13:    <runtime>
..:
33:    </runtime>
34:
35:    <script language="VBScript" src="..\Functions\DecodeShareTypeFunction.vbs" />
36:    <script language="VBScript" src="..\Functions\DisplayFormattedPropertyFunction.vbs" />
37:    <script language="VBScript" src="..\Functions\TinyErrorHandler.vbs" />
38:
39:    <object progid="WbemScripting.SWbemLocator" id="objWMILocator" reference="true"/>
40:    <object progid="WbemScripting.SWbemDateTime" id="objWMIDateTime" />
41:
42:    <script language="VBscript">
43:    <![CDATA[
..:
47:    Const cComputerName = "LocalHost"
48:    Const cWMINameSpace = "root/cimv2"
49:    Const cWMIClass = "Win32_Share"
..:
79:    ' ---------------------------------------------------------------------------
80:    ' Parse the command line parameters
81:    If WScript.Arguments.Named.Count Then
82:       Select Case Ucase(WScript.Arguments.Named("Action"))
83:             Case "LIST"
84:                   boolList = True
85:             Case "CREATE"
86:                   boolCreate = True
87:             Case "UPDATE"
88:                   boolUpdate = True
89:             Case "DELETE"
90:                   boolDelete = True
91:             Case Else
92:                   WScript.Echo "Invalid action type. Only [List], [Create]..." & vbCRLF
93:                   WScript.Arguments.ShowUsage()
94:                   WScript.Quit
95:       End Select
...:
...:
151:    strComputerName = WScript.Arguments.Named("Machine")
152:    If Len(strComputerName) = 0 Then strComputerName = cComputerName
153:
154:    objWMILocator.Security_.AuthenticationLevel = wbemAuthenticationLevelDefault
155:    objWMILocator.Security_.ImpersonationLevel = wbemImpersonationLevelImpersonate
156:
157:    Set objWMIServices = objWMILocator.ConnectServer(strComputerName, cWMINameSpace, _
158:                                          strUserID, strPassword)
...:
161:    ' -- LIST -----------------------------------------------------------------
162:    If boolList = True Then
```

```
163:        Set objWMIInstances = objWMIServices.InstancesOf (cWMIClass)
164:
165:        For Each objWMIInstance In objWMIInstances
166:            WScript.Echo "- " & Ucase (objWMIInstance.Name) & " " & String (60, "-")
167:            Set objWMIPropertySet = objWMIInstance.Properties_
168:            For Each objWMIProperty In objWMIPropertySet
169:                Select Case objWMIProperty.Name
170:                    Case "Type"
171:                        DisplayFormattedProperty objWMIInstance, _
172:                                                 objWMIProperty.Name, _
173:                                                 ShareType (objWMIProperty.Value), _
174:                                                 Null
175:
176:                    Case Else
177:                        DisplayFormattedProperty objWMIInstance, _
178:                                                 objWMIProperty.Name, _
179:                                                 objWMIProperty.Name, _
180:                                                 Null
181:                End Select
182:            Next
183:            Set objWMIPropertySet = Nothing
184:            WScript.Echo
185:        Next
186:
187:        WScript.Echo vbCRLF & "Completed."
...:
190:    End If
191:
192:    ' -- CREATE ------------------------------------------------------------------
193:    If boolCreate = True Then
194:        Set objWMIClass = objWMIServices.Get (cWMIClass)
195:        If Err.Number Then ErrorHandler (Err)
196:
197:        intRC = objWMIClass.Create (strSharePath, _
198:                                    strShareName, _
199:                                    intShareType, _
200:                                    intMaximumAllowed, _
201:                                    strDescription, _
202:                                    strSharePassword, _
203:                                    Null)
204:
205:        WScript.Echo "Share name '" & strShareName & "' created (" & intRC & ")."
...:
208:    End If
209:
210:    ' -- UPDATE ------------------------------------------------------------------
211:    If boolUpdate = True Then
212:        Set objWMIInstance = objWMIServices.Get (cWMIClass & ".Name='" & strShareName & "'")
213:        If Err.Number Then ErrorHandler (Err)
214:
215:        intRC = objWMIInstance.SetShareInfo (intMaximumAllowed, _
216:                                             strDescription, _
217:                                             Null)
218:
219:        WScript.Echo "Share name '" & strShareName & "' updated (" & intRC & ")."
...:
222:    End If
223:
224:    ' -- DELETE ------------------------------------------------------------------
```

```
225:    If boolDelete = True Then
226:        Set objWMIInstance = objWMIServices.Get (cWMIClass & ".Name='" & strShareName & "'")
227:        If Err.Number Then ErrorHandler (Err)
228:
229:        intRC = objWMIInstance.Delete
230:
231:        WScript.Echo "Share name '" & strShareName & "' deleted (" & intRC & ")."
...:
234:    End If
...:
238:    ]]>
239:    </script>
240:  </job>
241:</package>
```

In the share classes category, there are also two interesting classes to consider: *Win32_ServerConnection* and *Win32_ServerSession*. These two classes are supported by the *Session* provider (discussed in the next chapter) and allow the review of the current connections (*Win32_ServerConnection*) and sessions (*Win32_ServerSession*) established with a server. The instances of these classes can be enumerated and deleted as well. Last but not least, with the *Win32_Share* class, it is possible to define the security on a share by using the *SetShareInfo* method and its *Access* parameter. This will be examined in Chapter 4, "WMI Security Scripting."

2.4.14   **Start menu classes**

The start menu classes category represents program groups from the start menu. The classes in this category are listed in Table 2.30.

Table 2.30   *The Start Menu Classes*

Name	Type	Description
Win32_LogicalProgramGroup	Dynamic	Represents a program group in a Windows system.
Win32_LogicalProgramGroupItem	Dynamic	Represents an element contained by a Win32_ProgramGroup Dynamic that is not itself another Win32_ProgramGroup Dynamic.
Win32_ProgramGroup	Dynamic	Deprecated.
Win32_ProgramGroupOrItem	Dynamic	Represents a logical grouping of programs on the user's Start|Programs menu.
Win32_UserAccount	Dynamic	Represents information about a user account on a Windows system.
Win32_LogicalProgramGroupDirectory	Association	Relates logical program groups (groupings in the start menu) and the file directories in which they are stored.
Win32_LogicalProgramGroupItemDataFile	Association	Relates the program group items of the start menu and the files in which they are stored.
Win32_ProgramGroupContents	Association	Relates a program group order and an individual program group or item contained in it.

The use of these classes is strictly limited to a read-only mode. For instance, currently the WMI providers do not support the creation of a *Win32_LogicalProgramGroup* instance to create a new "Start Menu" group.

Figure 2.19 shows the associations that are in place for the *Win32_LogicalProgramGroup* class.

Figure 2.19
*The associations
of the Win32_
LogicalProgram-
Group class.*

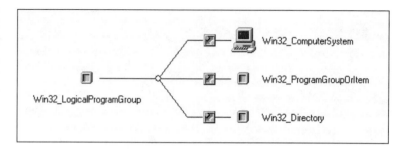

Figure 2.19 shows that the *Win32_LogicalProgramGroup* class is associated with the *Win32_LogicalProgramGroup*OrItem class. Actually, the *Win32_LogicalProgramGroup*OrItem class is a superclass for the *Win32_LogicalProgramGroup*Item class and the *Win32_LogicalProgramGroup* class (Figure 2.20).

Figure 2.20
*The Win32_
LogicalProgram-
GroupOrItem
superclass.*

A group in the "Start Menu" may contain a shortcut (*Win32_LogicalProgramGroup*Item) or another group (*Win32_LogicalProgramGroup*).

2.4.15   User account classes

The user account classes category represents user account information, such as group membership details. The classes in this category are listed in Table 2.31.

To retrieve information about user accounts and groups, it is possible to use the *Win32_Account*. This class is used as a superclass for three other classes: *Win32_UserAccount, Win32_SystemAccount,* and *Win32_Group.*

The *Win32_UserAccount* and *Win32_Group* classes expose a *rename* method, which allows the rename of a Windows account. To show an example of information available from the *Win32_UserAccount* class, by reusing Sample 1.5 ("Listing all instances of a class with their properties formatted"), we obtain the following output:

```
 1:   C:\>GetCollectionOfinstances Win32_Account
 2:   Microsoft (R) Windows Script Host Version 5.6
 3:   Copyright (C) Microsoft Corporation 1996-2001. All rights reserved.
 4:
 5:
 6:   Caption: ............................... XP-DPEN6400\Administrators
 7:   Description: ........................... Administrators have complete ...
 8:   *Domain: .............................. XP-DPEN6400
 9:   LocalAccount: ......................... TRUE
10:   *Name: ................................ Administrators
11:   SID: .................................. S-1-5-32-544
12:   SIDType: .............................. 4
13:   Status: ............................... OK
14:
...:
...:
...:
222:   Caption: ............................... LISSWARENET\Domain Users
223:   Description: ........................... All domain users
224:   *Domain: .............................. LISSWARENET
225:   LocalAccount: ......................... FALSE
226:   *Name: ................................ Domain Users
227:   SID: .................................. S-1-5-21-2025429265-507921405-1202660629-513
228:   SIDType: .............................. 2
229:   Status: ............................... OK
...:
...:
...:
609:   AccountType: .......................... 512
610:   Caption: .............................. LISSWARENET\alain.lissoir
611:   Description: ..........................
612:   Disabled: ............................. FALSE
613:   *Domain: .............................. LISSWARENET
614:   FullName: ............................. LISSOIR Alain
615:   LocalAccount: ......................... FALSE
616:   Lockout: .............................. FALSE
617:   *Name: ................................ alain.lissoir
618:   PasswordChangeable: ................... TRUE
619:   PasswordExpires: ...................... FALSE
620:   PasswordRequired: ..................... TRUE
621:   SID: .................................. S-1-5-21-2025429265-507921405-1202660629-1140
622:   SIDType: .............................. 1
623:   Status: ............................... OK
...:
...:
...:
```

Table 2.31   *The User Account Classes*

Name	Type	Description
Win32_Account	Dynamic	Represents information about user accounts and group accounts known to the Windows system.
Win32_Group	Dynamic	Represents data about a group account.
Win32_LogonSession	Dynamic	Describes the logon session or sessions associated with a user logged on to Windows NT or Windows 2000.
Win32_LogonSessionMappedDisk	Dynamic	Represents the mapped logical disks associated with the session.
Win32_NetworkLoginProfile	Dynamic	Represents the network login information of a particular user on a Windows system.
Win32_SystemAccount	Dynamic	Represents a system account.
Win32_UserAccount	Dynamic	Represents information about a user account on a Windows system.
Win32_GroupInDomain	Association	Identifies the group accounts associated with a Windows NT domain.
Win32_GroupUser	Association	Relates a group and an account that is a member of that group.
Win32_UserInDomain	Association	Relates a user account and a Windows NT domain.

Because the *Win32_Account* class is associated with the *Win32_Group* class, it is possible to retrieve the user group membership. In the same way, from a *Win32_Group* instance, it is possible to retrieve members of a group by using the associations in place. Figure 2.21 shows the associations available for *Win32_Group* class.

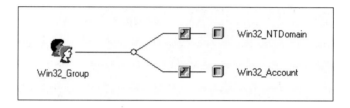

Figure 2.21   *The Win32_Group class associations.*

Figure 2.22 shows an example of existing associations for a particular user.

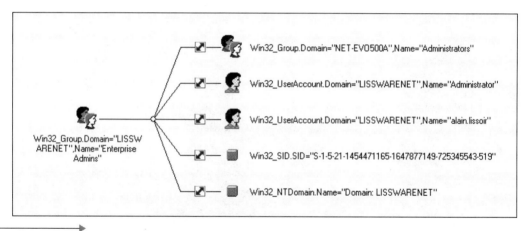

Figure 2.22   *Associated instances of one group.*

We can benefit from these relationships by using a specific WQL Query. In the first book, *Understanding WMI Scripting*, we saw how to retrieve miscellaneous associations from classes and instances with WQL, and we put that in practice with some sample scripts in this chapter (e.g., Samples 2.4 through 2.7, "Retrieving hardware resource information"). For example, from an "Enterprise Admins" group instance, if we want to retrieve the members of the group, we must use the following WQL query:

```
Associators of {Win32_Group.Domain='LISSWARENET',Name='Enterprise Admins'}
                        Where AssocClass=Win32_GroupUser Role=GroupComponent
```

In the same way, to retrieve the inclusion of the "Enterprise Admins" group in any other group (MemberOf), we must use the following WQL query:

```
Associators of {Win32_Group.Domain='LISSWARENET',Name='Enterprise Admins'}
                        Where AssocClass=Win32_GroupUser Role=PartComponent
```

Sample 2.66 implements these two WQL queries in a script. This script requests a group name as a command-line parameter. Once started, the script retrieves the group instance (lines 73 and 74) and displays its properties (lines 82 through 92). Next, based on the *Win32_Group* associations, the script retrieves the group membership information. At line 99 through 103, we recognize the first WQL query (Members) and at line 118 through 122, we recognize the second WQL query (MemberOf).

Sample 2.66   *Retrieving the group membership*

```
 1:<?xml version="1.0"?>
 .:
 8:<package>
 9:  <job>
..:
13:    <runtime>
..:
19:    </runtime>
20:
21:    <script language="VBScript" src="..\Functions\DisplayFormattedPropertyFunction.vbs" />
22:    <script language="VBScript" src="..\Functions\TinyErrorHandler.vbs" />
23:
24:    <object progid="WbemScripting.SWbemLocator" id="objWMILocator" reference="true"/>
25:    <object progid="WbemScripting.SWbemDateTime" id="objWMIDateTime" />
26:
27:    <script language="VBscript">
28:    <![CDATA[
..:
32:    Const cComputerName = "LocalHost"
33:    Const cWMINameSpace = "root/cimv2"
..:
47:    ' --------------------------------------------------------------------------
48:    ' Parse the command line parameters
49:    If WScript.Arguments.UnNamed.Count = 0 Then
50:       WScript.Arguments.ShowUsage()
51:       WScript.Quit
52:    End If
53:
54:    strGroupName = WScript.Arguments.UnNamed(0)
..:
65:    objWMILocator.Security_.AuthenticationLevel = wbemAuthenticationLevelDefault
66:    objWMILocator.Security_.ImpersonationLevel = wbemImpersonationLevelImpersonate
67:
68:    Set objWMIServices = objWMILocator.ConnectServer(strComputerName, cWMINameSpace, _
69:                                          strUserID, strPassword)
..:
72:    ' --------------------------------------------------------------------------
```

```
 73:        Set objWMIInstances = objWMIServices.ExecQuery ("Select * From Win32_Group " & _
 74:                                              "Where Name='" & strGroupName & "'")
 ..:
 77:        If objWMIInstances.Count Then
 78:           For Each objWMIInstance In objWMIInstances
 79:               WScript.Echo "- '" & Ucase (objWMIInstance.Domain) & "\" & _
 80:                         objWMIInstance.Name & "' " & String (60, "-")
 81:               Set objWMIPropertySet = objWMIInstance.Properties_
 82:               For Each objWMIProperty In objWMIPropertySet
 83:                   Select Case objWMIProperty.Name
 84:                       Case ""
 85:
 86:                       Case Else
 87:                           DisplayFormattedProperty objWMIInstance, _
 88:                                                    objWMIProperty.Name, _
 89:                                                    objWMIProperty.Name, _
 90:                                                    Null
 91:                   End Select
 92:               Next
 93:               WScript.Echo
...:
 97:               ' Members -------------------------------------------------------------
 98:               WScript.Echo " - Members: " & String (60, "-")
 99:               Set objAssocInstances = objWMIServices.ExecQuery _
100:                                  ("Associators of {Win32_Group.Domain='" & _
101:                                  objWMIInstance.Domain & "',Name='" & _
102:                                  objWMIInstance.Name & _
103:                                  "'} Where AssocClass=Win32_GroupUser Role=GroupComponent")
104:
105:               If objAssocInstances.Count Then
106:                  For Each objAssocInstance In objAssocInstances
107:                      WScript.Echo "  " & objAssocInstance.Domain & "\" & objAssocInstance.Name
108:                  Next
109:               Else
110:                  WScript.Echo "  No 'Members' available."
111:               End If
112:               WScript.Echo
...:
116:               ' MemberOf -------------------------------------------------------------
117:               WScript.Echo " - MemberOf: " & String (60, "-")
118:               Set objAssocInstances = objWMIServices.ExecQuery _
119:                                  ("Associators of {Win32_Group.Domain='" & _
120:                                  objWMIInstance.Domain & "',Name='" & _
121:                                  objWMIInstance.Name & _
122:                                  "'} Where AssocClass=Win32_GroupUser Role=PartComponent")
123:
124:               If objAssocInstances.Count Then
125:                  For Each objAssocInstance In objAssocInstances
126:                      WScript.Echo "  " & objAssocInstance.Domain & "\" & objAssocInstance.Name
127:                  Next
128:               Else
129:                  WScript.Echo "  No 'memberOf' available."
130:               End If
131:               WScript.Echo
...:
134:        Next
135:
136:        WScript.Echo "Completed."
...:
```

```
139:     Else
140:         WScript.Echo "No group available."
141:     End If
142:     WScript.Echo
...:
147:     ]]>
148:     </script>
149: </job>
150:</package>
```

Once executed, we obtain the following output:

```
C:\>GetGroupInfo "Enterprise Admins"
Microsoft (R) Windows Script Host Version 5.6
Copyright (C) Microsoft Corporation 1996-2001. All rights reserved.

- 'LISSWARENET\Enterprise Admins' ------------------------------------------------------------
Caption: ............................... LISSWARENET\Enterprise Admins
Description: ........................... Designated administrators of the enterprise
*Domain: ............................... LISSWARENET
LocalAccount: .......................... FALSE
*Name: ................................. Enterprise Admins
SID: ................................... S-1-5-21-2025429265-507921405-1202660629-519
SIDType: ............................... 2
Status: ................................ OK

  - Members: -------------------------------------------------------------
  LISSWARENET\Administrator
  LISSWARENET\alain.lissoir

  - MemberOf: ------------------------------------------------------------
  XP-DPEN6400\Administrators

Completed.
```

Another useful and immediate application of the *Win32_UserAccount* class is the conversion of the user name to a SID and vice versa. The principle is very simple. It consists of a WQL data query. To retrieve the SID from the UserID, the following WQL query can be used:

```
Select SID From Win32_Account Where Name='Alain.Lissoir'
```

Sample 2.67 is a function making use of this WQL data query. This function is called GetSIDFromUserID() and can perform a WMI connection (lines 16 through 20) with a specific set of credentials.

Sample 2.67   *Retrieving the SID from the UserID*

```
 .:
 .:
 .:
 8:' -------------------------------------------------------------------------------
 9:Function GetSIDFromUserID (strUserAccount, strComputerName, strUserID, strPassword)
...:
16:     objWMILocator.Security_.AuthenticationLevel = wbemAuthenticationLevelDefault
17:     objWMILocator.Security_.ImpersonationLevel = wbemImpersonationLevelImpersonate
```

```
18:
19:     Set objWMIServices = objWMILocator.ConnectServer(strComputerName, "Root\CIMv2", _
20:                                                       strUserID, strPassword)
..:
23:     Set objWMIInstances = objWMIServices.ExecQuery ("Select SID From Win32_Account Where" & _
24:                                                      "Name='" & strUserAccount & "'")
..:
27:     If objWMIInstances.Count = 1 Then
28:        For Each objWMIInstance In objWMIInstances
29:            GetSIDFromUserID = objWMIInstance.SID
30:        Next
31:     Else
32:            GetSIDFromUserID = ""
33:     End If
..:
39:End Function
```

The WMI connection with a set of different credentials is not mandatory to retrieve the SID; however, this makes the function totally independent of the caller context. The only required parameters are the system and the credentials to use for the WMI connection with the UserID to be resolved as a SID (line 9). Next, the routine makes use of the *ExecQuery* method of the **SWBemServices** object to run the WQL data query (lines 23 and 24). Since a query always returns a collection, the routine expects to have one instance of the *Win32_UserAccount* class stored in a collection (line 27) and extracts the SID from the *SID* property accordingly (line 29).

To retrieve the UserID from the SID, the following WQL query can be used:

```
Select Name From Win32_Account Where SID='S-1-5-21-1935655697-839522115-1708537768-1003'
```

Sample 2.68 uses the exact same logic as Sample 2.67, but, instead, it accepts a SID as a parameter and returns a UserID as a result.

Sample 2.68   *Retrieving the UserID from the SID*

```
.:
.:
.:
8:' --------------------------------------------------------------------------------
9:Function GetUserIDFromSID (strSID, strComputerName, strUserID, strPassword)
..:
16:     objWMILocator.Security_.AuthenticationLevel = wbemAuthenticationLevelDefault
17:     objWMILocator.Security_.ImpersonationLevel = wbemImpersonationLevelImpersonate
18:
19:     Set objWMIServices = objWMILocator.ConnectServer(strComputerName, "Root\CIMv2", _
20:                                                       strUserID, strPassword)
..:
23:     Set objWMIInstances = objWMIServices.ExecQuery ("Select Name From Win32_Account" & _
24:                                                      "Where SID='" & strSID & "'")
..:
```

```
27:     If objWMIInstances.Count = 1 Then
28:         For Each objWMIInstance In objWMIInstances
29:             GetUserIDFromSID = objWMIInstance.Name
30:         Next
31:     Else
32:             GetUserIDFromSID = ""
33:     End If
..:
39:End Function
```

2.5   Summary

This chapter continues to use the scripting techniques revealed in *Understanding WMI Scripting*, Chapters 4, 5, and 6, and applied to some real-world scenarios. For instance, we have seen how to manage the environment variables, the Operating System processes, and the printer devices. These scripting management techniques combine knowledge of the WMI scripting API, asynchronous scripting techniques (i.e., the script sample managing processes), and WMI event techniques (i.e., the script watching the free disk space and file size). From the simple information retrieval up to the complete utility to configure a network adapter from the command line, we really discovered the WMI capabilities. It is important to note that the WMI capabilities do not only cover system customization; they also cover system monitoring.

Now that we know the possibilities of the *Win32* providers, let's see what we can do with the other WMI providers available in Windows NT 4.0, Windows 2000, Windows XP, and Window Server 2003. We use the same learning techniques and structure. However, based on the WMI provider purpose, the scripts perform different types of tasks in the system customization and monitoring areas.

The WMI Providers

3.1 Objective

Although the *Win32* provider class capabilities cover a lot of material, we haven't examined WMI providers that support various components and applications, which are part of Windows Server 2003 and the previous Windows platforms. Under Windows Server 2003, WMI comes with more than 40 other providers supporting a specific set of classes. We must make a clear distinction between the providers that are part of the system installation and the ones that can be added during an optional software component installation. In this chapter, we will only focus on the WMI providers provided with the Windows Server 2003 installation. For example, this includes providers such as the *IP routing* providers, the *DNS* providers, the *Active Directory* providers, and the *Resultant Set of Policies* (RSOP) providers, to name a few. WMI providers related to optional Windows Server 2003 components or applications, such as *Internet Information Server* (IIS) provider, *Network Load Balancing* (NLB) provider, and the *Cluster Service* provider, will be examined later in the book, as will certain WMI-enabled applications such as Exchange 2000, HP OpenView Operations for Windows, Microsoft Operation Manager, and the Windows Server 2003 Framework.

3.2 The WMI providers

Each of the providers examined in this chapter can be considered as specialized providers. Some of them provide functionality about system components not supported by the *Win32* providers, such as the *Windows Product Activation* provider and the *Active Directory Trust Monitoring* provider. On the other hand, some providers complement functionality supported by the *Win32* providers. For example, in the previous chapter, when we examined the classes related to the file system, we saw that the *CIM_DataFile* class is supported by the *Win32* provider. Even if the *CIM_DataFile* class is a superclass of the *Win32_NTEventLogFile* class, the *Win32_NTEventLogFile* class is supported by a set of specialized providers, which are designed to manage the Windows NT Event Log files: the *NT Event Log* providers.

All WMI providers are designed to manage a particular Windows Server 2003 component and therefore implement some capabilities relevant to that component. For example, the *Ping* provider is implemented as an instance provider and retrieves the ping command status code when pinging a host. The *DNS* provider is implemented as an instance provider to manipulate DNS zones and DNS records stored in these zones. Another example is the *Power management* provider, which is able to trigger an event when the power state of the system changes.

To ease the discovery of the WMI providers available, they are classified in different categories, which will be examined section by section in this chapter. These categories are:

- **Core OS components providers:** This category contains WMI providers that manage Operating System components such as the NT Event Logs, the registry, and the trusts.

- **Core OS components event providers:** This category contains WMI providers that trigger events when something occurs in the Operating System. The *Power management* and the *Shutdown* WMI event providers are just two examples of providers in this category.

- **Core OS file system components providers:** This category contains providers managing specific features of the file system, such as disk quotas or the Distributed File System (DFS).

- **Active Directory components providers:** The WMI providers in this category only support features related to Active Directory. For example, accessing objects in Active Directory or monitoring Active Directory Replication are two features offered by the WMI providers of this category.

- **Network components providers:** This category only contains the providers supporting features related to network components. For example, in this category we find WMI providers that manage DNS, the IP routing table, and SNMP devices.

- **Performance providers:** This category contains providers giving access to performance counter information. Performance counters exist for applications as well as the Operating System, but we will only focus on the latter in this category.

- **Helper providers:** The providers included in this category are the specialized WMI providers that are not directly managing real-world entities but are helping to access some information in the CIM repository from a local or a remote system. The *View* provider and the *Forwarding* consumer provider are in this category.

Note that some of the providers examined in this chapter are also available under Windows 2000 and Windows NT! During the WMI provider discussion, we will mention in which operating system they are available.

Let's start the WMI providers discovery!

3.3   Core OS components providers

3.3.1   The WBEM provider

The *WBEM* provider exposes the WMI configuration parameters. The three classes supported by this provider are listed in Table 3.1.

Table 3.1   *The WBEM Provider Classes*

Name	Type	Comments
Win32_WMISetting	Dynamic (Singleton)	Contains the operational parameters for the WMI service.
Win32_WMIElementSetting	Association	Association between a service running in the Win32 system, and the WMI settings it can use.
Win32_MethodParameterClass	Abstract	Abstract, base class that implements method parameters derived from this class.

You can use the **LoadCIMInXL.wsf** script (see Sample 4.32 in the appendix) or the **WMI CIM Studio** of the Platform SDK to gather more information about the class properties. In the Platform SDK, these classes are classified as the WMI System Management classes.

The *WBEM* provider classes are available in the **Root\CIMv2** namespace. Basically, the *Win32_WMISetting* class gives access to the WMI settings available from the WMI Control MMC (in the Computer Management MMC). Since there is one installation of WMI per system, there is only one instance of the *Win32_WMISetting* class. This is the reason why this class has no Key property defined in its properties and is therefore defined as a singleton class.

Because this class relates to one WMI installation in one system, the *Win32_WMIElementSetting* class associates the *Win32_WMISetting* with the *Win32_Service* class (see Figure 3.1). The *Win32_WMISetting* has one Windows associated service instance: the **WinMgmt.Exe** service.

Figure 3.1
*The Win32_
WMISetting class
associations.*

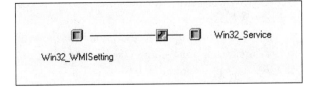

The *Win32_MethodParameterClass* class is an abstract class, which means that no instance can be retrieved from the class. This class is used as a template for classes used as parameters when invoking specific methods. The *Win32_MethodParameterClass* is a superclass for the *Win32_Security-Descriptor, Win32_ACE, Win32_Trustee,* and *Win32_ProcessStartup* classes. For example, when executing the *Create* method of the *Win32_Process* class (see Sample 2.53 in Chapter 2), we create a *Win32_ProcessStartup* instance to define some process parameters used for its creation.

The *WBEM* provider is an instance provider only. If the *Win32_WMISetting* class must be used in the context of a WQL event query, the **WITHIN** statement must be used, because the provider is not implemented as an event provider. For example, a valid WQL query for the *WBEM* provider would be:

```
Select * From __InstanceModificationEvent Within 10 Where TargetInstance ISA 'Win32_WMISetting'
```

The *WBEM* instance provider supports the Get, Put, and Enumeration operations (see Table 3.2). This means that it is possible to retrieve a single instance (get) with its WMI object path, modify a single instance (put), and retrieve a collection of instances (enumeration).

Table 3.2   *The WBEM Provider Capabilities*

Provider Name	Provider Namespace	Class Provider	Instance Provider	Method Provider	Property Provider	Event Provider	Event Consumer Provider	Support Get	Support Put	Support Enumeration	Support Delete	Windows Server 2003	Windows XP	Windows 2000 Server	Windows 2000 Professional	Windows NT 4.0
WBEM core Provider																
WBEMCORE	Root/CIMV2	X						X	X	X		X	X	X	X	X

The next script sample is able to change some of the WMI settings from the command line. The WMI settings that can be changed are available from the script command-line help.

```
C:\>WMISettings.wsf
Microsoft (R) Windows Script Host Version 5.6
Copyright (C) Microsoft Corporation 1996-2001. All rights reserved.

Usage: WMISettings.wsf /Action:value [/ASPScriptDefaultNamespace:value] [/ASPScriptEnabled[+|-]]
                       [/BackupInterval:value] [/EnableEvents[+|-]] [/LoggingDirectory:value]
                       [/LoggingLevel:value] [/MaxLogFileSize:value]
                       [/Machine:value] [/User:value] [/Password:value]

Options:

Action                       : Specify the operation to perform: [List] or [Config].
ASPScriptDefaultNamespace : Defines the namespace used by calls from the scripting API if none is
                             specified by the caller.
ASPScriptEnabled             : Indicates whether WMI scripting can be used on Active Server Pages
                             (ASP). This property is valid on Windows NT 4.0 systems only.
BackupInterval               : Specifies the length of time that will elapse between backups of the WMI
                             database.
EnableEvents                 : Indicates whether the WMI event subsystem should be enabled.
LoggingDirectory             : Specifies the directory path containing the location of the WMI system
                             log files.
LoggingLevel                 : Indicates whether event logging is enabled and the verbosity level of
                             logging used.
MaxLogFileSize               : Indicates the maximum size of the log files produced by the WMI service.
Machine                      : Determine the WMI system to connect to. (default=LocalHost)
User                         : Determine the UserID to perform the remote connection. (default=none)
Password                     : Determine the password to perform the remote connection. (default=none)
Examples:

    WMISettings.wsf /Action:List
    WMISettings.wsf /Action:Config /ASPScriptDefaultNamespace:Root\CIMv2
    WMISettings.wsf /Action:Config /ASPScriptEnabled+
    WMISettings.wsf /Action:Config /BackupInterval:30
    WMISettings.wsf /Action:Config /EnableEvents+
    WMISettings.wsf /Action:Config /LoggingDirectory:C:\WINDOWS\System32\Wbem\Logs
    WMISettings.wsf /Action:Config /LoggingLevel:ErrorsOnly
    WMISettings.wsf /Action:Config /MaxLogFileSize:65535
```

The *Win32_WMISetting* class exposes more properties than the ones that can be modified by the script. However, this sample can be easily extended to cater to any additional WMI settings that need to be modified. The purpose of the script is to view the *Win32_WMISetting* singleton instance and update some of its properties. From a scripting technique point of view, there is nothing new compared with all scripts previously developed. The segment of code changing some WMI settings is shown in Sample 3.1.

Sample 3.1   *Updating the WMI settings*

```
 1:<?xml version="1.0"?>
 . :
 8:<package>
 9:  <job>
 ..:
13:     <runtime>
```

```
..:
38:     </runtime>
39:
40:     <script language="VBScript" src="..\Functions\DisplayFormattedPropertyFunction.vbs" />
41:     <script language="VBScript" src="..\Functions\TinyErrorHandler.vbs" />
42:
43:     <object progid="WbemScripting.SWbemLocator" id="objWMILocator" reference="true"/>
44:     <object progid="WbemScripting.SWbemDateTime" id="objWMIDateTime" />
45:
46:     <script language="VBscript">
47:     <![CDATA[
..:
51:     Const cComputerName = "LocalHost"
52:     Const cWMINameSpace = "Root/cimv2"
53:     Const cWMIClass = "Win32_WMISetting"
..:
77:     ' ---------------------------------------------------------------------------
78:     ' Parse the command line parameters
79:     If WScript.Arguments.Named.Count = 0 Then
80:        WScript.Arguments.ShowUsage()
81:        WScript.Quit
82:     End If
...:
131:    If Len(strComputerName) = 0 Then strComputerName = cComputerName
132:
133:    objWMILocator.Security_.AuthenticationLevel = wbemAuthenticationLevelDefault
134:    objWMILocator.Security_.ImpersonationLevel = wbemImpersonationLevelImpersonate
135:
136:    Set objWMIServices = objWMILocator.ConnectServer(strComputerName, cWMINameSpace, _
137:                                                      strUserID, strPassword)
...:
140:    Set objWMIInstance = objWMIServices.Get (cWMIClass & "=@")
...:
143:    ' -- LIST ---------------------------------------------------------------------
144:    If boolList = True Then
145:       Set objWMIPropertySet = objWMIInstance.Properties_
146:       For Each objWMIProperty In objWMIPropertySet
147:           DisplayFormattedProperty objWMIInstance, _
148:                                    " " & objWMIProperty.Name, _
149:                                    objWMIProperty.Name, _
150:                                    Null
151:       Next
152:       Set objWMIPropertySet = Nothing
153:       WScript.Echo
154:    End If
155:
156:    ' -- CONFIG -------------------------------------------------------------------
157:    If boolConfig = True Then
158:
159:       If Len (strASPScriptDefaultNamespace) Then
160:          objWMIInstance.ASPScriptDefaultNamespace = strASPScriptDefaultNamespace
161:       End If
162:
163:       If Len (boolASPScriptEnabled) Then
164:          objWMIInstance.ASPScriptEnabled = boolASPScriptEnabled
165:       End If
166:
167:       If intBackupInterval <> 0 Then
168:          objWMIInstance.BackupInterval = intBackupInterval
169:       End If
170:
```

```
171:        If Len (boolEnableEvents) Then
172:            objWMIInstance.EnableEvents = boolEnableEvents
173:        End If
174:
175:        If Len (strLoggingDirectory) Then
176:            objWMIInstance.LoggingDirectory = strLoggingDirectory
177:        End If
178:
179:        If longMaxLogFileSize  <> 0 Then
180:            objWMIInstance.MaxLogFileSize = longMaxLogFileSize
181:        End If
182:
183:        If Len (strLoggingLevel) Then
184:            objWMIInstance.LoggingLevel = intLoggingLevel
185:        End If
186:
187:        objWMIInstance.Put_ (wbemChangeFlagUpdateOnly Or _
188:                             wbemFlagReturnWhenComplete)
...:
191:        WScript.Echo "WMI Settings updated."
192:
193:    End If
...:
199:    ]]>
200:    </script>
201:  </job>
202:</package>
```

As previously mentioned, the *Win32_WMISetting* class is a singleton class; this means that:

- Only one instance is available per system.

- There is no Key property.

Note that a particular syntax is used to create an instance of the *Win32_WMISetting* singleton class (line 140). The WMI settings are updated from line 157 through 193. Only the specified settings are modified. Once the desired WMI properties are updated, the script commits the changes back to the system (lines 187 and 188).

The Sample 3.1 output obtained with the **/Action:List** switch is as follows:

```
1:    C:\>WMISettings.wsf /Action:List
2:    Microsoft (R) Windows Script Host Version 5.6
3:    Copyright (C) Microsoft Corporation 1996-2001. All rights reserved.
4:
5:    ASPScriptDefaultNamespace: ............... Root\cimv2
6:    ASPScriptEnabled: ........................ TRUE
7:    AutorecoverMofs: ......................... J:\WINDOWS\system32\WBEM\cimwin32.mof
8:                                               J:\WINDOWS\system32\WBEM\cimwin32.mfl
9:                                               J:\WINDOWS\system32\WBEM\system.mof
10:                                              J:\WINDOWS\system32\WBEM\wmipcima.mof
11:                                              J:\WINDOWS\system32\WBEM\wmipcima.mfl
..:
..:
..:
```

```
62:                                          J:\WINDOWS\system32\WBEM\snmpsmir.mof
63:                                          J:\WINDOWS\system32\WBEM\snmpreg.mof
64:                                          J:\WINDOWS\System32\Wbem\RSoP.mof
65:                                          J:\WINDOWS\System32\Wbem\RSoP.mfl
66:                                          J:\WINDOWS\System32\Wbem\SceRsop.mof
67:                                          J:\WINDOWS\system32\wbem\iiswmi.mfl
68:                                          J:\WINDOWS\system32\wbem\ADStatus\TrustMon.mof
69:                                          J:\WINDOWS\System32\replprov.mof
70:   BackupInterval: ........................ 30
71:   BuildVersion: .......................... 3663.0000
73:   EnableEvents: .......................... TRUE
74:   EnableStartupHeapPreallocation: ........ FALSE
75:   HighThresholdOnClientObjects: .......... 20000000
76:   HighThresholdOnEvents: ................. 20000000
77:   InstallationDirectory: ................. J:\WINDOWS\system32\WBEM
78:   LoggingDirectory: ...................... J:\WINDOWS\system32\WBEM\Logs\
79:   LoggingLevel: .......................... 1
80:   LowThresholdOnClientObjects: ........... 10000000
81:   LowThresholdOnEvents: .................. 10000000
82:   MaxLogFileSize: ........................ 65536
83:   MaxWaitOnClientObjects: ................ 60000
84:   MaxWaitOnEvents: ....................... 2000
85:   MofSelfInstallDirectory: ............... J:\WINDOWS\system32\WBEM\MOF
```

Among this list of properties, the output shows the list of MOF files to recompile when recovering the CIM repository (lines 7 through 69), the backup interval (line 70), and the WMI logging level (line 79).

3.3.2   NT Event Log providers

The *NT Event Log* providers consist of two WMI providers: one WMI event provider and one instance and method provider, which support the *get, put,* and *enumeration* operations (see Table 3.3).

Table 3.3   *The NT Event Log Providers Capabilities*

Provider Name	Provider Namespace	Class Provider	Instance Provider	Method Provider	Property Provider	Event Provider	Event Consumer Provider	Support Get	Support Put	Support Enumeration	Support Delete	Windows Server 2003	Windows XP	Windows 2000 Server	Windows 2000 Professional	Windows NT 4.0
Event Log Providers																
MS_NT_EVENTLOG_EVENT_PROVIDER	Root/CIMV2					X						X	X	X	X	X
MS_NT_EVENTLOG_PROVIDER	Root/CIMV2		X	X				X	X	X		X	X	X	X	X

These providers are designed to expose information stored in the Windows NT Event Log files, view the configuration settings related to the Windows NT Event Log files, and perform some specific actions, such as clearing or backing up the NT Event Log. The classes supported by these providers are listed in Table 3.4.

Table 3.4   *The NT Event Log Providers Classes*

Name	Type	Comments
Win32_NTEventlogFile	Dynamic	Represents settings of a Windows NT/Windows 2000 Event Log file
Win32_NTLogEvent	Dynamic	Represents data stored in a Windows NT/Windows 2000 log file.
Win32_NTLogEventComputer	Association	Relates instances of Win32_NTLogEvent and Win32_ComputerSystem.
Win32_NTLogEventLog	Association	Relates instances of Win32_NTLogEvent and Win32_NTEventlogFile classes.
Win32_NTLogEventUser	Association	Relates instances of Win32_NTLogEvent and Win32_UserAccount.

These classes are available in the **Root\CIMv2** namespace. The *Win32_NTLogEvent* class is shown in Figure 3.2.

Figure 3.2
*The Win32_
NTLogEvent
associations.*

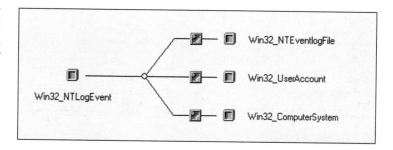

Since there is an *NT Event Log* event provider, there is no need to use the **WITHIN** statement in a WQL event query. In such a case, a valid WQL query would be as follows:

- To capture any WMI event corresponding to a record addition to any NT Event Log:

```
Select * From __InstanceCreationEvent Where TargetInstance ISA 'Win32_NTLogEvent'
```

- To capture any WMI event corresponding to a record addition to the Directory Service Event Log:

```
Select * From __InstanceCreationEvent Where TargetInstance ISA 'Win32_NTLogEvent'
And TargetInstance.LogFile='Directory Service'"
```

It is important to note that the *NT Event Log* event provider only supports the intrinsic event *__InstanceCreationEvent* class. The generic asynchronous script to capture events from a WQL event query passed on the command line (see Sample 6.17, "A generic script for asynchronous event notification" in the appendix) can be used with the following command line. The output will be as follows when a new Event Log record is created:

```
 1:   C:\>GenericEventAsyncConsumer.wsf "Select * From __InstanceCreationEvent
 2:                                     Where TargetInstance ISA 'Win32_NTLogEvent' And
 3:                                     TargetInstance.EventCode=1013"
 4:   Microsoft (R) Windows Script Host Version 5.6
 5:   Copyright (C) Microsoft Corporation 1996-2001. All rights reserved.
 6:
 7:   Waiting for events...
 8:
 9:   BEGIN - OnObjectReady.
10:   Sunday, 11 November, 2001 at 16:51:01: '__InstanceCreationEvent' has been triggered.
11:
12:      - __InstanceCreationEvent ----------------------------------------------------
13:      SECURITY_DESCRIPTOR: .................. 1,0,4,128,84,1,0,0,96,1,0,0,0,0,0,20,...
14:
15:         - Win32_NTLogEvent --------------------------------------------------------
16:         Category: .......................... 1
17:         CategoryString: .................... Knowledge Consistency Checker
18:         ComputerName: ...................... NET-DPEN6400A
19:         EventCode: ......................... 1013
20:         EventIdentifier: ................... 1073742837
21:         EventType: ......................... 3
22:         *Logfile: .......................... Directory Service
23:         Message: ........................... Internal event: The replication topology ...
24:         *RecordNumber: ..................... 72
25:         SourceName: ........................ NTDS KCC
26:         TimeGenerated: ..................... 11-11-2001 16:50:39
27:         TimeWritten: ....................... 11-11-2001 16:50:39
28:         Type: .............................. information
29:         User: .............................. NT AUTHORITY\ANONYMOUS LOGON
30:
31:      TIME_CREATED: ......................... 11-11-2001 15:50:40 (20011111145040.276894+060)
32:
33:   END - OnObjectReady.
34:
35:   Cancelling event subscription ...
36:
37:   BEGIN - OnCompleted.
38:   END   - OnCompleted.
39:   Finished.
```

The second interesting class supported by the *NT Event Log* providers is the *Win32_NTEventlogFile* class. In addition to being able to review and configure various NT Event Log configuration settings (i.e., Maximum Size, overwrite policy) you can also clear and back up any NT Event Log. The next script sample illustrates how to achieve this. Its command-line parameters are as follows:

```
C:\>WMIEventLog.Wsf
Microsoft (R) Windows Script Host Version 5.6
Copyright (C) Microsoft Corporation 1996-2001. All rights reserved.

Usage: WMIEventLog.wsf /Action:value [/EventLog:value] [/MaxFileSize:value]
                       [/OverwriteOutDated:value] [/Machine:value] [/User:value] [/Password:value]

Options:

Action              : Specify the operation to perform: [List], [Config], [Clear] and [Backup].
```

```
EventLog            : Specify the Log name (All means all available Event Logs).
MaxFileSize         : Set the maximum size of the Event Log file (in Kb).
OverwriteOutDated : Overwrites events policy [WhenNeeded], [Never] or a value 1 and 365.
Machine             : Determine the WMI system to connect to. (default=LocalHost)
User                : Determine the UserID to perform the remote connection. (default=none)
Password            : Determine the password to perform the remote connection. (default=none)
Examples:

    WMIEventLog.wsf /Action:List
    WMIEventLog.wsf /Action:Clear /EventLog:All
    WMIEventLog.wsf /Action:Clear /EventLog:NTDS
    WMIEventLog.wsf /Action:Backup /EventLog:DNSEvent
    WMIEventLog.wsf /Action:Backup /EventLog:NTFRS
    WMIEventLog.wsf /Action:Config /EventLog:SecEvent /MaxFileSize:5120
    WMIEventLog.wsf /Action:Config /EventLog:SysEvent /OverwriteOutDated:7
    WMIEventLog.wsf /Action:Config /EventLog:All /OverwriteOutDated:WhenNeeded
    WMIEventLog.wsf /Action:Config /EventLog:AppEvent /OverwriteOutDated:Never
    WMIEventLog.wsf /Action:Config /EventLog:All /MaxFileSize:5120 /OverwriteOutDated:WhenNeeded
```

The script code using the *Win32_NTEventLogFile* class capabilities is shown in Sample 3.2. As usual, the script uses the same structure to define (skipped lines 13 through 35) and parse the command-line parameters (skipped lines 78 through 142) and to list the instance properties available from this class (lines 159 through 173).

Sample 3.2   *Viewing and updating the NT Event Log configuration and clearing and backing up the NT Event Log information*

```
 1:<?xml version="1.0"?>
 .:
 8:<package>
 9: <job>
..:
13:    <runtime>
..:
35:    </runtime>
36:
37:    <script language="VBScript" src="..\Functions\DisplayFormattedPropertyFunction.vbs" />
38:    <script language="VBScript" src="..\Functions\TinyErrorHandler.vbs" />
39:
40:    <object progid="WbemScripting.SWbemLocator" id="objWMILocator" reference="true"/>
41:    <object progid="WbemScripting.SWbemDateTime" id="objWMIDateTime" />
42:
43:    <script language="VBscript">
44:    <![CDATA[
..:
48:    Const cComputerName = "LocalHost"
49:    Const cWMINameSpace = "Root/cimv2"
50:    Const cWMIClass = "Win32_NTEventLogFile"
..:
77:    ' -------------------------------------------------------------------------
78:    ' Parse the command line parameters
79:    If WScript.Arguments.Named.Count = 0 Then
80:       WScript.Arguments.ShowUsage()
81:       WScript.Quit
82:    Else
```

```
 83:        Select Case Ucase(WScript.Arguments.Named("Action"))
 ..:
 96:        End Select
 97:     End If
...:
116:     If Len(strOverWriteOutDated) Then
117:        Select Case Ucase (strOverWriteOutDated)
118:             Case "WHENNEEDED"
119:                   intOverWriteOutDated = 0
120:                   strOverWriteOutDated = "WhenNeeded"
121:             Case "NEVER"
122:                   intOverWriteOutDated = 4294967295          '  2^32 - 1
123:                   strOverWriteOutDated = "Never"
124:             Case Else
125:                   intOverWriteOutDated = Cint (strOverWriteOutDated)
126:                   If intOverWriteOutDated < 1 Or intOverWriteOutDated > 365 Then
127:                      WScript.Echo "Invalid overwrite outdated parameter." & vbCRLF
128:                      WScript.Arguments.ShowUsage()
129:                      WScript.Quit
130:                   End If
131:                   strOverWriteOutDated = "OutDated"
132:        End Select
133:     End If
...:
142:     If Len(strComputerName) = 0 Then strComputerName = cComputerName
143:
144:     objWMILocator.Security_.AuthenticationLevel = wbemAuthenticationLevelDefault
145:     objWMILocator.Security_.ImpersonationLevel = wbemImpersonationLevelImpersonate
146:     objWMILocator.Security_.Privileges.AddAsString "SeBackupPrivilege", True
147:     objWMILocator.Security_.Privileges.AddAsString "SeSecurityPrivilege", True
148:
149:     Set objWMIServices = objWMILocator.ConnectServer(strComputerName, cWMINameSpace, _
150:                                                 strUserID, strPassword)
...:
153:     Set objWMIInstances = objWMIServices.InstancesOf (cWMIClass, wbemFlagUseAmendedQualifiers)
...:
156:     For Each objWMIInstance in objWMIInstances
157:
158:         ' -- LIST -------------------------------------------------------------------
159:         If boolList = True Then
160:            WScript.Echo "- " & objWMIInstance.LogfileName & " Event Log " & _
161:                         "(" & Ucase (objWMIInstance.FileName) & _
162:                         ") " & String (60, "-")
163:
164:            Set objWMIPropertySet = objWMIInstance.Properties_
165:            For Each objWMIProperty In objWMIPropertySet
166:                DisplayFormattedProperty objWMIInstance, _
167:                                    " " & objWMIProperty.Name, _
168:                                    objWMIProperty.Name, _
169:                                    Null
170:            Next
171:            Set objWMIPropertySet = Nothing
172:            WScript.Echo
173:         End If
174:
175:         If UCase (objWMIInstance.FileName) = strEventLogName Or _
176:            strEventLogName = "ALL" Then
177:            ' -- CONFIG ----------------------------------------------------------------
178:            If boolConfig = True Then
179:
```

```
180:                  If intMaxFileSize <> 0 Then
181:                      objWMIInstance.MaxFileSize = intMaxFileSize * 1024
182:                  End If
183:
184:                  If Len (strOverWriteOutDated) Then
185:                      objWMIInstance.OverwriteOutDated = intOverWriteOutDated
186:                      objWMIInstance.OverWritePolicy = strOverWriteOutDated
187:                  End If
188:
189:                  objWMIInstance.Put_ (wbemChangeFlagUpdateOnly Or _
190:                                       wbemFlagReturnWhenComplete Or _
191:                                       wbemFlagUseAmendedQualifiers)
192:                  If Err.Number Then ErrorHandler (Err)
193:
194:                  If intMaxFileSize <> 0 Then
195:                      varTemp = objWMIInstance.LogfileName & _
196:                               " Event Log maximum size is set on " & _
197:                               intMaxFileSize & " Kb. "
198:                  Else
199:                      varTemp = objWMIInstance.LogfileName & _
200:                               " Event Log overwrite policy configured. "
201:                  End If
202:
203:                  Select Case Ucase (strOverWriteOutDated)
204:                         Case "WHENNEEDED"
205:                              WScript.Echo varTemp & "Events are overwritten as needed."
206:                         Case "NEVER"
207:                              WScript.Echo varTemp & "Events are never overwritten."
208:                         Case "OUTDATED"
209:                              WScript.Echo varTemp & "Events older than " & _
210:                                           intOverWriteOutDated & _
211:                                           " day(s) are overwritten."
212:                         Case Else
213:                              WScript.Echo varTemp
214:                  End Select
...:
217:              End If
218:
219:              ' -- CLEAR -------------------------------------------------------------
220:              If boolClear = True Then
221:                  intRC = objWMIInstance.ClearEventlog
222:                  If Err.Number Then ErrorHandler (Err)
223:
224:                  WScript.Echo objWMIInstance.LogfileName & _
225:                           " Event Log is cleared (" & intRC & ")."
...:
228:              End If
229:
230:              ' -- BACKUP ------------------------------------------------------------
231:              If boolBackup = True Then
232:                  intRC = objWMIInstance.BackupEventlog (objWMIInstance.Name & ".Bak")
233:                  If Err.Number Then ErrorHandler (Err)
234:
235:                  WScript.Echo objWMIInstance.LogfileName & " Event Log is backuped to '" & _
236:                           Ucase (objWMIInstance.Name) & ".Bak' (" & intRC & ")."
...:
239:              End If
240:
241:          End If
242:      Next
```

```
...:
248:    ]]>
249:    </script>
250:  </job>
251:</package>
```

The most interesting part of this script resides in the NT Event Log settings configuration (lines 178 through 217) and the method invocations (lines 220 through 228 for clearing and lines 231 through 239 for backup). The script is structured in such a way that it can manage all NT Event Logs in one single run. For this, the script gets the collection of all NT Event Logs available (line 153) and performs an enumeration (lines 156 through 242). Then, the script uses a special NT Event Log name called "All" (as defined in the script at line 176) to determine if the operation concerns a specific NT Event Log name or all the collection (lines 175 and 176). This script uses the "All" label to differentiate the scope of the requested operation.

An interesting NT Event Log setting is the overwrite policy. To set the overwrite policy (lines 185 and 186) two properties of the NT Event Log instance must be set up. The two property values are determined during the command-line parameters parsing (lines 117 through 132). The command-line parsing for this setting ensures that correct values are set. It is important to note that both property values must be set up as shown in Table 3.5.

Table 3.5   *The OverWritePolicy and OverwriteOutDated Property Values*

	WhenNeeded	Never	OutDated
OverWritePolicy	0	4294967295	1 < Value > 365
OverwriteOutDated	WhenNeeded	Never	OutDated

Last but not least, some privileges at the WMI level must be specified (lines 146 and 147) to ensure transparent access to the Security NT Event Log (line 146) and perform the backup operation (line 147).

3.3.3   Registry providers

There are three WMI providers in this category: one instance and method provider (*RegProv*), one property provider (*RegPropProv*), and one event provider (*RegistryEvent*Provider). The providers capabilities are summarized in Table 3.6.

Table 3.6 *The Registry Providers Capabilities*

Provider Name	Provider Namespace	Class Provider	Instance Provider	Method Provider	Property Provider	Event Provider	Event Consumer Provider	Support Get	Support Put	Support Enumeration	Support Delete	Windows Server 2003	Windows XP	Windows 2000 Server	Windows 2000 Professional	Windows NT 4.0
Registry Providers																
RegistryEventProvider	Root/DEFAULT					X						X	X	X	X	X
RegPropProv	Root/DEFAULT				X			X	X			X	X	X	X	X
RegProv	Root/DEFAULT	X	X					X	X	X		X	X	X	X	X

These providers are designed to expose information stored in the Windows NT Registry. The classes supported by these providers are listed in Table 3.7.

Table 3.7 *The Registry Providers Classes*

Name	Type	Comments
StdRegProv	Dynamic	The StdRegProv class only contains methods that interact with the system registry. You can use these methods to verify the access permissions for a user, create, enumerate, and delete registry keys; create, enumerate, and delete named values; and read, write, and delete data values.
RegistryValueChangeEvent	Extrinsic event	Represents a registry extrinsic event that corresponds to a registry value modification.
RegistryKeyChangeEvent	Extrinsic event	Represents a registry extrinsic event that corresponds to a registry key modification.
RegistryTreeChangeEvent	Extrinsic event	Represents a registry extrinsic event that corresponds to a registry tree modification.

These classes are available in the **Root\Default** namespace. The *StdReg-Prov* class only exposes methods; it does not expose any property and has no association.

The *Registry* event provider allows a process to receive a notification when a registry change occurs. For this, three extrinsic event classes are supported (see Table 3.7). Each of these classes corresponds to a particular modification made in the registry. For example, imagine that you would like to monitor the registry key value that enables Active Directory schema changes. The key value is named "Schema Update Allowed" and is located in the following registry key hive:

```
HKLM\SYSTEM\CurrentControlSet\Services\NTDS\Parameters
```

To detect any change made on that key value, the following WQL event query must be used:

```
Select * FROM RegistryValueChangeEvent Where Hive='HKEY_LOCAL_MACHINE' AND
              KeyPath='SYSTEM\\CurrentControlSet\\Services\\NTDS\\Parameters' AND
              ValueName='Schema Update Allowed'
```

Now, if you want to detect all changes made to any key values below the same registry key hive, the following WQL Event query must be used:

```
Select * FROM RegistryKeyChangeEvent Where Hive='HKEY_LOCAL_MACHINE' AND
              KeyPath='SYSTEM\\CurrentControlSet\\Services\\NTDS\\Parameters'
```

If you want to detect all changes made to any key values under the following registry key hive and all child registry entries, use the following:

```
HKLM\SYSTEM\CurrentControlSet\Services\NTDS
```

The following WQL event query must be used:

```
Select * FROM RegistryTreeChangeEvent Where Hive='HKEY_LOCAL_MACHINE' AND
              RootPath='SYSTEM\\CurrentControlSet\\Services\\NTDS'
```

To summarize:

- The extrinsic *RegistryValueChangeEvent* class focuses the change detection on a particular key value.

- The extrinsic *RegistryKeyChangeEvent* class focuses the change detection on all key values below a given registry key hive.

- The extrinsic *RegistryTreeChangeEvent* class focuses the change detection on all key values in a given registry key hive, as shown in the example below.

If we reuse the generic asynchronous script to capture events from a WQL event query (see Sample 6.17, "A generic script for asynchronous event notification" in the appendix) with the last WQL Event query sample, the output will be as follows:

```
 1:   C:\>GenericEventAsyncConsumer.wsf "Select * FROM RegistryTreeChangeEvent Where
 2:                          Hive='HKEY_LOCAL_MACHINE' AND
 3:                          RootPath='SYSTEM\\CurrentControlSet\\Services\\NTDS'"
 4:                          /NameSpace:Root\Default
 5:   Microsoft (R) Windows Script Host Version 5.6
 6:   Copyright (C) Microsoft Corporation 1996-2001. All rights reserved.
 7:
 8:   Waiting for events...
 9:
10:   BEGIN - OnObjectReady.
11:   Monday, 19 November, 2001 at 13:27:29: 'RegistryTreeChangeEvent' has been triggered.
12:
13:      - RegistryTreeChangeEvent -----------------------------------------------------
14:      Hive: ............................... HKEY_LOCAL_MACHINE
15:      RootPath: ........................... SYSTEM\CurrentControlSet\Services\NTDS
16:      TIME_CREATED: ....................... 19-11-2001 12:27:29 (20011119112729.796836+060)
17:
18:   END - OnObjectReady.
```

Even if we get a notification, it is important to note that we do not get the registry value associated with the change in the instance representing the notification.

Besides the registry key monitoring, the methods exposed by the *StdReg-Prov* class allow the enumeration of registry keys and values. It is also possible to create new registry keys, read and update registry key values, and delete registry keys and values. These methods are summarized in Table 3.8.

Table 3.8   *The StdRegProv Methods*

Method name	Description
CheckAccess	Verifies that the user possesses the specified access permissions.
CreateKey	Creates a subkey.
DeleteKey	Deletes a subkey.
DeleteValue	Deletes a named value.
EnumKey	Enumerates subkeys.
EnumValues	Enumerates the named values of a key.
GetBinaryValue	Gets the binary data value of a named value.
GetDWORDValue	Gets the DWORD data value of a named value.
GetExpandedStringValue	Gets the expanded string data value of a named value.
GetMultiStringValue	Gets the multiple string data values of a named value.
GetStringValue	Gets the string data value of a named value.
SetBinaryValue	Sets the binary data value of a named value.
SetDWORDValue	Sets the DWORD data value of a named value.
SetExpandedStringValue	Sets the expanded string data value of a named value.
SetMultiStringValue	Sets the multiple string values of a named value.
SetStringValue	Sets the string value of a named value.

Sample 3.3 illustrates the use of these methods. Its command-line parameters are as follows:

```
C:\>WMIRegistry
Microsoft (R) Windows Script Host Version 5.6
Copyright (C) Microsoft Corporation 1996-2001. All rights reserved.

Usage: WMIRegistry.wsf [RegistryKeyValue] /BaseKey:value /Action:value [/DisplayRegValues[+|-]]
                       [/KeyType:value] [/SearchString:value]
                       [/ReplaceString:value] [/Machine:value]
                       [/User:value] [/Password:value]


Options:

RegistryKeyValue : The registry key name with its value.
BaseKey          : Specify the base registry.
Action           : Specify the operation to perform: [list], [Search], [Replace], [create], [update] or
[delete].
DisplayRegValues : Display the registry key values (default=TRUE)
KeyType          : Specify the registry value type.
SearchString     : String to search in the registry.
ReplaceString    : String to replace in the registry.
Machine          : Determine the WMI system to connect to. (default=LocalHost)
User             : Determine the UserID to perform the remote connection. (default=none)
Password         : Determine the password to perform the remote connection. (default=none)
Examples:
```

```
WMIRegistry.wsf /BaseKey:HKLM\Software\MyKeys /Action:Create
WMIRegistry.wsf MyStringValue=XYW /KeyType:REG_SZ /BaseKey:HKLM\Software\MyKeys /Action:Create
WMIRegistry.wsf MyMultiStringValue=RST,STU,TUV,UVW,VWX,WXY,XYZ /KeyType:REG_MULTI_SZ
                /BaseKey:HKLM\Software\MyKeys /Action:Create
WMIRegistry.wsf MyExpandedStringValue=%SystemRoot%\System32\Wbem /KeyType:REG_EXPAND_SZ
                /BaseKey:HKLM\Software\MyKeys /Action:Create
WMIRegistry.wsf MyDWordValue=436327632 /KeyType:REG_DWORD
                /BaseKey:HKLM\Software\MyKeys /Action:Create
WMIRegistry.wsf MyBinaryValue=03,04,255,78,34,23 /KeyType:REG_BINARY
                /BaseKey:HKLM\Software\MyKeys /Action:Create

WMIRegistry.wsf /BaseKey:HKLM\Software /Action:List /DisplayRegValues-
WMIRegistry.wsf /BaseKey:HKLM\Software /Action:List /DisplayRegValues+
WMIRegistry.wsf /BaseKey:HKLM\SOFTWARE\MyKeys /Action:Search /SearchString:String
WMIRegistry.wsf /BaseKey:HKLM\SOFTWARE\MyKeys /Action:Replace
                /SearchString:String /ReplaceString:MyString

WMIRegistry.wsf MyBinaryValue /BaseKey:HKLM\Software\MyKeys /Action:Delete
WMIRegistry.wsf /BaseKey:HKLM\Software\MyKeys /Action:Delete
```

With this script it is possible to manage the Windows registry from the command line. Other than simply browsing or updating the registry, it is also capable of performing search and replace operations in the registry. This script is shown in Samples 3.3 through 3.9. Careful use of the replace feature is recommended, since it is very easy to mess up a working system!

To perform the command-line definition (skipped lines 13 through 42) and parsing (lines 111 through 244), the script reuses the same structure as seen in the previous script samples. Next, it reuses most of the functions previously developed (lines 46 through 48). Only two new functions, SearchString() (line 44) and ReplaceString() (line 45), are added to support the search and replace capabilities. We will come back to the use of these functions later, along with the script discovery (see Samples 3.3 through 3.9).

Some very important constants are also defined in the script header. These constants are used to identify the registry hive type (lines 61 through 66) and the registry key value type (lines 68 through 72). These constants will be used later in the script.

Before diving into the code, it is important to note that the logic used for the search and replace capabilities is a particular case of the script logic used to browse the registry. We will see this further, but this peculiarity is reflected during the command-line parameter parsing (lines 117 through 135) where the "List," "Search," and "Replace" actions define a different browse level value (List=0, Search=1, Replace=2).

Sample 3.3   *Browsing, creating, deleting, searching, and replacing information in the registry (Part I)*

```
  1:<?xml version="1.0"?>
  .:
  8:<package>
  9:  <job>
 ..:
 13:    <runtime>
 ..:
 42:    </runtime>
 43:
 44:    <script language="VBScript" src="..\Functions\SearchStringFunction.vbs" />
 45:    <script language="VBScript" src="..\Functions\ReplaceStringFunction.vbs" />
 46:    <script language="VBScript" src="..\Functions\ConvertStringInArrayFunction.vbs" />
 47:    <script language="VBScript" src="..\Functions\ConvertArrayInStringFunction.vbs" />
 48:    <script language="VBScript" src="..\Functions\TinyErrorHandler.vbs" />
 49:
 50:    <object progid="WbemScripting.SWbemLocator" id="objWMILocator" reference="true"/>
 51:
 52:    <script language="VBscript">
 53:    <![CDATA[
 ..:
 57:    Const cComputerName = "LocalHost"
 58:    Const cWMINameSpace = "Root/default"
 59:    Const cWMIClass = "StdRegProv"
 60:
 61:    Const HKEY_CLASSES_ROOT = &h80000000
 62:    Const HKEY_CURRENT_USER = &h80000001
 63:    Const HKEY_LOCAL_MACHINE = &h80000002
 64:    Const HKEY_USERS = &h80000003
 65:    Const HKEY_CURRENT_CONFIG = &h80000005
 66:    Const HKEY_DYN_DATA = &h80000006
 67:
 68:    Const REG_SZ = 1
 69:    Const REG_EXPAND_SZ = 2
 70:    Const REG_BINARY = 3
 71:    Const REG_DWORD = 4
 72:    Const REG_MULTI_SZ = 7
 73:
 74:    Const cBrowse = 0
 75:    Const cSearch = 1
 76:    Const cReplace = 2
...:
109:    ' -------------------------------------------------------------------------
110:    ' Parse the command line parameters
111:    If WScript.Arguments.Named.Count = 0 Then
112:       WScript.Arguments.ShowUsage()
113:       WScript.Quit
114:    End If
115:
116:    If WScript.Arguments.Named.Count Then
117:       Select Case Ucase(WScript.Arguments.Named("Action"))
118:              Case "LIST"
119:                   boolList = True
120:                   intBrowseLevel = cBrowse
121:              Case "SEARCH"
122:                   boolList = True
```

```
123:                        intBrowseLevel = cSearch
124:             Case "REPLACE"
125:                   boolList = True
126:                   intBrowseLevel = cReplace
127:             Case "CREATE"
128:                   boolCreate = True
129:             Case "DELETE"
130:                   boolDelete = True
131:             Case Else
132:                   WScript.Echo "Invalid action type. Only [List], [Search], ..." & vbCRLF
133:                   WScript.Arguments.ShowUsage()
134:                   WScript.Quit
135:        End Select
136:
137:        strBaseKey = WScript.Arguments.Named("BaseKey")
138:        If Len(strBaseKey) = 0 Then
139:           WScript.Echo "Invalid registry key path." & vbCRLF
140:           WScript.Arguments.ShowUsage()
141:           WScript.Quit
142:        Else
143:           intDelimiterPosition = InStr (strBaseKey, "\")
144:           If intDelimiterPosition Then
145:              strHiveType = Mid (strBaseKey, 1, intDelimiterPosition - 1)
146:              strBaseKey = Mid (strBaseKey, intDelimiterPosition + 1)
147:           Else
148:              If boolList Then
149:                 strHiveType = strBaseKey
150:                 strBaseKey = ""
151:              Else
152:                 WScript.Echo "Invalid registry key base." & vbCRLF
153:                 WScript.Arguments.ShowUsage()
154:                 WScript.Quit
155:              End If
156:           End If
157:
158:           Select Case Ucase (strHiveType)
159:                Case "HKCLS"
160:                     intHiveType = HKEY_CLASSES_ROOT
161:                Case "HKCU"
162:                     intHiveType = HKEY_CURRENT_USER
163:                Case "HKLM"
164:                     intHiveType = HKEY_LOCAL_MACHINE
165:                Case "HKUSERS"
166:                     intHiveType = HKEY_USERS
167:                Case "HKCONFIG"
168:                     intHiveType = HKEY_CURRENT_CONFIG
169:                Case "HKDYN"
170:                     intHiveType = HKEY_DYN_DATA
171:                Case Else
172:                     WScript.Echo "Invalid hive type. Only [HKCLS], [HKCU], ..." & vbCRLF
173:                     WScript.Arguments.ShowUsage()
174:                     WScript.Quit
175:           End Select
176:        End If
177:     End If
178:
179:     If WScript.Arguments.Unnamed.Count = 1 Then
180:        strKeyName = WScript.Arguments.Unnamed.Item(0)
181:        intDelimiterPosition = InStr (strKeyName, "=")
182:        If intDelimiterPosition Then
```

```
183:             varKeyNameValue = Mid (strKeyName, intDelimiterPosition + 1)
184:             strKeyName = Mid (strKeyName, 1, intDelimiterPosition - 1)
185:        Else
186:           If Not boolDelete = True Then
187:              WScript.Echo "Invalid registry key value." & vbCRLF
188:              WScript.Arguments.ShowUsage()
189:              WScript.Quit
190:           End If
191:        End If
192:        If boolDelete = False Then
193:           Select Case Ucase (WScript.Arguments.Named("KeyType"))
194:                Case "REG_SZ"
195:                     intKeyType = REG_SZ
196:                     boolKeyValue = True
197:                Case "REG_MULTI_SZ"
198:                     varKeyNameValue = ConvertStringInArray (varKeyNameValue, ",")
199:                     intKeyType = REG_MULTI_SZ
200:                     boolKeyValue = True
201:                Case "REG_EXPAND_SZ"
202:                     intKeyType = REG_EXPAND_SZ
203:                     boolKeyValue = True
204:                Case "REG_BINARY"
205:                     varKeyNameValue = ConvertStringInArray (varKeyNameValue, ",")
206:                     intKeyType = REG_BINARY
207:                     boolKeyValue = True
208:                Case "REG_DWORD"
209:                     varKeyNameValue = CLng (varKeyNameValue)
210:                     intKeyType = REG_DWORD
211:                     boolKeyValue = True
212:                Case Else
213:                     WScript.Echo "Invalid key type. Only [REG_SZ], ..." & vbCRLF
214:                     WScript.Arguments.ShowUsage()
215:                     WScript.Quit
216:           End Select
217:        End If
218:     End If
219:
220:     strStringToSearch = WScript.Arguments.Named("SearchString")
221:     If Len(strStringToSearch) = 0 And intBrowseLevel = 1 Then
222:        WScript.Echo "Invalid search string."
223:        WScript.Arguments.ShowUsage()
224:        WScript.Quit
225:     End If
226:
227:     strStringToReplace = WScript.Arguments.Named("ReplaceString")
228:     If Len(strStringToSearch) = 0 And Len(strStringToReplace) = 0 And intBrowseLevel = 2 Then
229:        WScript.Echo "Invalid search or replace string."
230:        WScript.Arguments.ShowUsage()
231:        WScript.Quit
232:     End If
233:
234:     If intBrowseLevel = 0 Then boolDisplayRegValues=WScript.Arguments.Named("DisplayRegValues")
235:     If Len(boolDisplayRegValues) = 0 Then boolDisplayRegValues = True
236:
237:     strUserID = WScript.Arguments.Named("User")
238:     If Len(strUserID) = 0 Then strUserID = ""
239:
240:     strPassword = WScript.Arguments.Named("Password")
241:     If Len(strPassword) = 0 Then strPassword = ""
242:
```

```
243:    strComputerName = WScript.Arguments.Named("Machine")
244:    If Len(strComputerName) = 0 Then strComputerName = cComputerName
245:
246:    objWMILocator.Security_.AuthenticationLevel = wbemAuthenticationLevelDefault
247:    objWMILocator.Security_.ImpersonationLevel = wbemImpersonationLevelImpersonate
248:
249:    Set objWMIServices = objWMILocator.ConnectServer(strComputerName, cWMINameSpace, _
250:                                                      strUserID, strPassword)
...:
253:    Set objWMIClass = objWMIServices.Get (cWMIClass)
...:
255:
...:
...:
...:
```

From line 137 through 176, the script parses the **/BaseKey** switch. Basically, it separates the complete registry key path given on the command line into two parts: the registry hive (i.e., HKLM) and the tree path (i.e., SOFTWARE\Microsoft). The registry hive is converted to its corresponding value (lines 158 through 175) based on the constants given in the script header. This value is required for the methods exposed by the *StdRegProv* class.

Lines 179 through 218 parse the registry key name (line 183), its value assignment (line 184), and its type (lines 193 through 216). The logic developed is very similar to the one used to parse the environment variable assignment developed in the previous chapter (see Sample 2.26, "Reading, creating, updating, and deleting environment variables").

After establishing the WMI connection (lines 249 and 250), the *StdRegProv* class is instantiated. Note that a class instance is created (line 253), since the *StdRegProv* class is defined as a static class (*Static* qualifier).

Based on the command-line parameters, the browse operation is started in Sample 3.4. There is nothing unusual in this piece of code, since the browsing logic is encapsulated in a subfunction (line 261).

Sample 3.4   *Browsing information in the registry (Part II)*

```
...:
...:
...:
255:
256:    ' -- LIST --------------------------------------------------------------
257:    If boolList = True Then
258:        intCounterValue = 0
259:        intCounterValueName = 0
260:
261:        BrowseRegistry objWMIClass, intHiveType, strBaseKey
262:
263:        Select Case intBrowseLevel
264:            Case cBrowse
265:
```

```
266:              Case cSearch
267:                  WScript.Echo
268:                  WScript.Echo intCounterValue & " registry value(s) found."
269:                  WScript.Echo intCounterValueName & " registry value name(s) found."
270:              Case cReplace
271:                  WScript.Echo
272:                  WScript.Echo intCounterValue & " registry value(s) replaced."
273:                  WScript.Echo intCounterValueName & " registry value name(s) replaced."
274:       End Select
275:
276:       WScript.Echo vbCRLF & "Completed."
277:
278:    End If
279:
...:
...:
...:
```

Once the browse operation completes, and based on the browse type (simply browsing, searching, or replacing), an output message is displayed to show the number of matches during a search (lines 268 and 269) or a replace (lines 272 and 273). We will examine the BrowseRegistry() function in Samples 3.7 and 3.8.

Sample 3.5   *Creating information in the registry (Part III)*

```
...:
...:
...:
279:
280:    ' -- CREATE -------------------------------------------------------------------
281:    If boolCreate = True Then
282:       If boolKeyValue Then
283:          intRC = SetRegistryValue (objWMIClass, intHiveType, _
284:                                     strBaseKey, intKeyType, _
285:                                     strKeyName, varKeyNameValue)
286:          If intRC Then
287:             WScript.Echo "Cannot create registry key value '" & strKeyName & _
288:                          "' under '" & strBaseKey & "' (" & intRC & ")."
289:          Else
290:             WScript.Echo "Registry key value '" & strKeyName & "' under '" & _
291:                          strBaseKey & "' created."
292:          End If
293:       Else
294:          intRC = objWMIClass.CreateKey(intHiveType, strBaseKey)
295:          If intRC Then
296:             WScript.Echo "Cannot create registry key '" & strBaseKey & "' (" & intRC & ")."
297:          Else
298:             WScript.Echo "Registry key '" & strBaseKey & "' created."
299:          End If
300:       End If
301:    End If
302:
...:
...:
...:
```

To create registry information (see Sample 3.5), two different cases must be considered:

- **The registry tree is already created and a registry key value must be created:** This case corresponds to the logic coded from line 282 through 292. This portion of code sets the registry key value. If the key exists, it is updated; if the key does not exist, it is created. The key value creation or update is encapsulated in the SetRegistryValue() function (line 283). This operation is encapsulated in a subfunction, because a particular *StdRegProv* class method must be invoked based on the registry key type (i.e., REG_SZ, REG_DWORD). This function will also be reused during the replace operation. This case corresponds to the following command-line parameters:

```
C:\>WMIRegistry.wsf MyStringValue=XYW /KeyType:REG_SZ
/BaseKey:HKLM\Software\MyKeys /Action:Create
```

- **The registry tree does not exist and it must be created:** This case corresponds to the logic coded from line 294 through 299. This portion of code creates a registry tree by using the *CreateKey* method exposed by the *StdRegProv* class (line 294). This piece of code is only executed when no registry key assignment is given on the command line (line 282). This case corresponds to the following command-line parameters:

```
C:\>WMIRegistry.wsf /BaseKey:HKLM\Software\MyKeys /Action:Create
```

Sample 3.6   *Deleting information in the registry (Part IV)*

```
...:
...:
...:
302:
303:     ' -- DELETE -------------------------------------------------------------
304:     If boolDelete = True Then
305:         If Len (strKeyName) Then
306:             intRC = objWMIClass.DeleteValue (intHiveType, strBaseKey, strKeyName)
307:             If intRC Then
308:                 WScript.Echo "Cannot delete registry key value '" & strKeyName & _
309:                             "' under '" & strBaseKey & "' (" & intRC & ")."
310:             Else
311:                 WScript.Echo "Registry key value '" & strKeyName & "' under '" & _
312:                             strBaseKey & "' deleted."
313:             End If
314:         Else
315:             intRC = objWMIClass.DeleteKey(intHiveType, strBaseKey)
316:             If intRC Then
317:                 WScript.Echo "Cannot delete registry key '" & strBaseKey & "' (" & intRC & ")."
318:             Else
319:                 WScript.Echo "Registry key '" & strBaseKey & "' deleted."
```

```
320:            End If
321:        End If
322:    End If
...:
327:
...:
...:
...:
```

To delete some registry data (see Sample 3.6), two different cases must be considered:

- **A registry value must be deleted:** This case corresponds to the logic coded from line 305 through 313. This portion of code deletes the registry value by using the *DeleteValue* method exposed by the *StdRegProv* class (line 306). This piece of code is only executed when registry key name is given on the command line (line 305). This corresponds to the following command-line parameters:

```
C:\>WMIRegistry.wsf MyStringValue /BaseKey:HKLM\Software\MyKeys /Action:Delete
```

- **A registry key must be deleted:** This case corresponds to the logic coded from line 315 through 321. This portion of code deletes the registry key by using the *DeleteKey* method exposed by the *StdRegProv* class (line 315). Note that it is not possible to delete a complete registry tree with this method. If subkeys exist below the selected registry key, they must be deleted first. This piece of code is only executed when no registry key name is given on the command line (line 305). This case corresponds to the following command-line parameters:

```
C:\>WMIRegistry.wsf /BaseKey:HKLM\Software\MyKeys /Action:Delete
```

When a registry browse operation, search operation, or replace operation is requested, the BrowseRegistry() function is invoked (see Sample 3.7). This case corresponds to the following command-line parameters:

```
C:\>WMIRegistry.wsf /BaseKey:HKLM\Software /Action:List /DisplayRegValues-
C:\>WMIRegistry.wsf /BaseKey:HKLM\Software /Action:List /DisplayRegValues+
C:\>WMIRegistry.wsf /BaseKey:HKLM\SOFTWARE\MyKeys /Action:Search /SearchString:String
C:\>WMIRegistry.wsf /BaseKey:HKLM\SOFTWARE\MyKeys /Action:Replace /SearchString:String
                    /ReplaceString:MyString
```

Displaying registry values occurs by default with a search or replace operation but not with a browse operation. To enable the values to be displayed during a browse, you must supply the **/DisplayRegValue+** switch. The BrowseRegistryValues() function is invoked to browse the existing registry values (line 340). We will review the BrowseRegistryValues() function when discussing Sample 3.8.

Sample 3.7   *Browsing, searching, and replacing information in the registry (Part V)*

```
...:
...:
...:
327:
328:    ' -------------------------------------------------------------------------------
329:    Function BrowseRegistry (objWMIClass, intHiveType, strBaseKey)
...:
338:        WScript.Echo strBaseKey
339:        If boolDisplayRegValues Then
340:            BrowseRegistryValues objWMIClass, intHiveType, strBaseKey
341:        End If
342:
343:        If Len (strBaseKey) Then
344:            strBackSlash = "\"
345:        Else
346:            strBackSlash = ""
347:        End If
348:
349:        intRC = objWMIClass.EnumKey (intHiveType, strBaseKey, strSubKeys)
350:        If intRC = 0 Then
351:            If IsNull (strSubKeys) = False Then
352:                If Ubound (strSubKeys) <> -1 Then
353:                    For intIndice = 0 To Ubound (strSubKeys)
354:                        BrowseRegistry objWMIClass, intHiveType, _
355:                                        strBaseKey & strBackSlash & strSubKeys (intIndice)
356:                    Next
357:                End If
358:            End If
359:        End If
360:
361:    End Function
362:
...:
...:
...:
```

Sample 3.7 retrieves from the base key the list of subkeys available (line 349). The list is returned in an array, called **strSubKeys**, passed as a parameter of the *EnumKey* method of the *StdRegProv* class (line 349). If the array is properly initialized, the BrowseRegistry() function is recursively invoked and the new base key is passed by concatenating the current base key with each subkey found in the array (line 355).

If the registry values in a key are browsed, the BrowseRegistryValues() function is invoked (line 340). The BrowseRegistryValues() function code is shown in Sample 3.8.

Sample 3.8   *Browsing, searching, and replacing information in the registry (Part VI)*

```
...:
...:
...:
362:
363:     ' -------------------------------------------------------------------------------------
364:     Function BrowseRegistryValues (objWMIClass, intHiveType, strKeyPath)
...:
383:        intRC = objWMIClass.EnumValues (intHiveType, strKeyPath, strKeyNames, intKeyTypes)
384:        If intRC = 0 Then
385:           If IsArray (strKeyNames) Then
386:              For intIndiceKeyName = 0 To Ubound (strKeyNames)
387:                 Select Case intKeyTypes (intIndiceKeyName)
388:                       Case REG_SZ
389:                             strKeyType = " (REG_SZ) "
390:                             intRC = objWMIClass.GetStringValue (intHiveType, strKeyPath, _
391:                                                    strKeyNames (intIndiceKeyName), _
392:                                                    varKeyValue)
393:                       Case REG_EXPAND_SZ
394:                             strKeyType = " (REG_EXPAND_SZ) "
395:                             intRC = objWMIClass.GetExpandedStringValue (intHiveType, _
396:                                                    strKeyPath, _
397:                                                    strKeyNames (intIndiceKeyName), _
398:                                                    varKeyValue)
399:                       Case REG_MULTI_SZ
400:                             strKeyType = " (REG_MULTI_SZ) "
401:                             intRC = objWMIClass.GetMultiStringValue (intHiveType, strKeyPath,
402:                                                    strKeyNames (intIndiceKeyName), _
403:                                                    varKeyValue)
404:                       Case REG_BINARY
405:                             strKeyType = " (REG_BINARY) "
406:                             intRC = objWMIClass.GetBinaryValue (intHiveType, strKeyPath, _
407:                                                    strKeyNames (intIndiceKeyName), _
408:                                                    varKeyValue)
409:                       Case REG_DWORD
410:                             strKeyType = " (REG_DWORD) "
411:                             intRC = objWMIClass.GetDWORDValue (intHiveType, strKeyPath, _
412:                                                    strKeyNames (intIndiceKeyName), _
413:                                                    varKeyValue)
414:              End Select
415:
416:              If intRC = 0 Then
417:                 boolDisplay = False
418:                 boolDisplayDeleted = False
419:
420:                 Select Case intBrowseLevel
421:                       Case cBrowse
422:                             boolDisplay = True
423:                       Case csearch
424:                             boolFoundInName = SearchString(strKeyNames(intIndiceKeyName),
425:                                                    strStringToSearch)
426:                             boolFoundInValue = SearchString(varKeyValue, _
427:                                                    strStringToSearch)
428:                             If boolFoundInValue Then
429:                                intCounterValue = intCounterValue + 1
430:                                boolDisplay = True
431:                             End If
```

```
432:                            If boolFoundInName Then
433:                                intCounterValueName = intCounterValueName + 1
434:                                boolDisplay = True
435:                            End If
436:                        Case cReplace
437:                            strOriginalKeyName = strKeyNames (intIndiceKeyName)
438:
439:                            boolFoundInValue = ReplaceString (varKeyValue, _
440:                                                              strStringToSearch, _
441:                                                              strStringToReplace)
442:                            boolFoundInName = ReplaceString(strKeyNames(intIndiceKeyName), _
443:                                                            strStringToSearch, _
444:                                                            strStringToReplace)
445:                            If (boolFoundInName Or boolFoundInValue) Then
446:                                intRC = SetRegistryValue (objWMIClass, intHiveType, _
447:                                                          strKeyPath, _
448:                                                          intKeyTypes(intIndiceKeyName), _
449:                                                          strKeyNames(intIndiceKeyName), _
450:                                                          varKeyValue)
451:                                If intRC = 0 Then
452:                                    boolDisplay = True
453:                                End If
454:                                If boolFoundInValue Then
455:                                    intCounterValue = intCounterValue + 1
456:                                End If
457:                                If boolFoundInName Then
458:                                    intCounterValueName = intCounterValueName + 1
459:                                    intRC = objWMIClass.DeleteValue(intHiveType, _
460:                                                                    strKeyPath, _
461:                                                                    strOriginalKeyName)
462:                                    If intRC = 0 Then
463:                                        boolDisplayDeleted = True
464:                                    End If
465:                                End If
466:                            End If
467:                End Select
468:
469:                If Len (strKeyNames (intIndiceKeyName)) = 0 Then
470:                    strDisplayKeyName = "<DEFAULT>"
471:                Else
472:                    strDisplayKeyName = strKeyNames (intIndiceKeyName)
473:                End If
474:
475:                If boolDisplay Then
476:                    Select Case intKeyTypes (intIndiceKeyName)
477:                            Case REG_MULTI_SZ
478:                                WScript.Echo strKeyType & _
479:                                            strDisplayKeyName & _
480:                                            "=" & ConvertArrayInString (varKeyValue, _
481:                                                                        ",", _
482:                                                                        False)
483:                            Case REG_BINARY
484:                                WScript.Echo strKeyType & _
485:                                            strDisplayKeyName & _
486:                                            "=" & ConvertArrayInString (varKeyValue, _
487:                                                                        ",", _
488:                                                                        True)
489:                            Case REG_DWORD
490:                                WScript.Echo strKeyType & _
491:                                            strDisplayKeyName & _
```

```
492:                                                    "=&h" & Hex(varKeyValue)
493:                              Case Else
494:                                  WScript.Echo strKeyType & _
495:                                              strDisplayKeyName & _
496:                                              "=" & varKeyValue
497:                          End Select
498:
499:                          If boolDisplayDeleted Then
500:                              WScript.Echo "  Deleting" & strKeyType & _
501:                                          strOriginalKeyName & _
502:                                          " ... "
503:                          End If
504:
505:                      End If
506:                  End If
507:              Next
508:          End If
509:      End If
510:
511:  End Function
512:
...:
...:
...:
```

This function can be divided into three parts:

- **The registry value reading** (lines 383 through 414): This piece of code extracts the collection of values with the *EnumValues* method of the *StdRegProv* class (line 383). This method returns in two arrays the key value name (**strKeyNames**) and its corresponding type (**intKey-Types**). If the arrays are properly initialized, each array element is examined in a loop (lines 386 through 507) containing the two other portions of code (see the next two bullets). Based on the key value type (i.e., REG_SZ, REG_BINARY), the value is extracted from the registry with the *StdRegProv* method corresponding to the registry value type (lines 387 through 414).

- **The registry value parsing for a search or a replace operation** (lines 416 through 467): Once the value is extracted, the desired browse operation is executed. If it is a simple browse operation to display the registry tree with its key values, the process forces a display of the value by setting a Boolean variable to True (line 422). For a search operation, the code invokes the SearchString() function for the examined key name (line 424) with its value (line 426). If a match is found, the matching value will be displayed later and a Boolean variable is set to True (lines 430 and 434). For a replace operation, first the code saves the original key name in a temporary variable (line 437). Next, the code invokes the ReplaceString() function for the examined key name (line 442) with its value (line 439). It is important to note that the ReplaceString() function automatically replaces the variable content of the key name ("**strKeyNames (intIndiceKey-Name)**") with its value ("**varKeyValue**") if there is a match. If there is no match, no change to the original content of the variables is made. If a match is found, a new key is created with the updated content of the variables by invoking the SetRegistryValue() function. If the key name is modified by the replace operation, it means that the key with the original name still exists in the registry. This is why the script deletes the original key name by using the temporary variable initialized at line 437. The delete operation is executed at line 459.

■ **The registry value display** (lines 469 through 503): To display the key value with its name, the script checks if the key name is not blank. In such a case, it means that the key has no name and corresponds to a default registry value for the key (line 470). Next, the registry key value is converted according to its type (lines 476 through 497) for a suitable display.

Creating or updating a registry key value in the registry is pretty straightforward. The *StdRegProv* method corresponding to the registry key type (i.e., REG_SZ, REG_BINARY) must be invoked. This logic is shown in Sample 3.9 in lines 521 through 547.

Sample 3.9   *Creating or updating information in the registry (Part VII)*

```
...:
...:
...:
512:
513:     ' ---------------------------------------------------------------------------------
514:     Function SetRegistryValue (objWMIClass, intHiveType, _
515:                               strBaseKey, intKeyType, _
516:                               strKeyName, varKeyNameValue)
...:
521:         Select Case intKeyType
522:             Case REG_SZ
523:                 intRC = objWMIClass.SetStringValue (intHiveType, _
524:                                                     strBaseKey, _
525:                                                     strKeyName, _
526:                                                     varKeyNameValue)
527:             Case REG_MULTI_SZ
528:                 intRC = objWMIClass.SetMultiStringValue (intHiveType, _
529:                                                          strBaseKey, _
530:                                                          strKeyName, _
531:                                                          varKeyNameValue)
532:             Case REG_EXPAND_SZ
533:                 intRC = objWMIClass.SetExpandedStringValue (intHiveType, _
534:                                                             strBaseKey, _
535:                                                             strKeyName, _
536:                                                             varKeyNameValue)
537:             Case REG_BINARY
```

```
538:                          intRC = objWMIClass.SetBinaryValue (intHiveType, _
539:                                                     strBaseKey, _
540:                                                     strKeyName, _
541:                                                     varKeyNameValue)
542:              Case REG_DWORD
543:                          intRC = objWMIClass.SetDWORDValue (intHiveType, _
544:                                                     strBaseKey, _
545:                                                     strKeyName, _
546:                                                     varKeyNameValue)
547:          End Select
548:
549:          SetRegistryValue = intRC
550:
551:      End Function
552:
553:      ]]>
554:      </script>
555:    </job>
556:</package>
```

3.3.4   Session providers

The *Session* provider enables the management of network sessions and connections. The provider is implemented as an instance and method provider, as shown in Table 3.9.

Table 3.9   *The Session Provider Capabilities*

Provider Name	Provider Namespace	Class Provider	Instance Provider	Method Provider	Property Provider	Event Provider	Event Consumer Provider	Support Get	Support Put	Support Enumeration	Support Delete	Windows Server 2003	Windows XP	Windows 2000 Server	Windows 2000 Professional	Windows NT 4.0
Session Provider																
SessionProvider	Root/CIMV2	X	X					X	X	X	X	X	X			

Available in the **Root\CIMv2** namespace, the classes it supports are listed in Table 3.10.

Table 3.10   *The Session Provider Classes*

Name	Type	Comments
Win32_ServerConnection	Dynamic	Represents the connections made from a remote computer to a shared resource on the local computer.
Win32_ServerSession	Dynamic	Represents the sessions that have been established with the local computer, by users on a remote computer.
Win32_SessionConnection	Association	Represents an association between a session established with the local server, by a user on a remote machine, and the connections that depend on the session.
Win32_ConnectionShare	Association	Relates a shared resource on the computer and the connection made to the shared resource.

On one hand, the *Win32_ServerConnection* is associated with the *Win32_Share* class (with the help of the *Win32_ConnectionShare* association class), and on the other hand the *Win32_ServerConnection* is associated with the *Win32_ServerSession* class (with the help of the *Win32_SessionConnection*). These associations are shown in Figures 3.3 and 3.4, respectively.

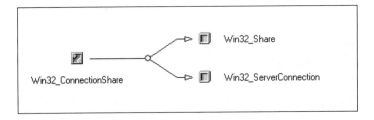

Figure 3.3 *The Win32_Share and Win32_ServerConnection classes are associated with the Win32_ConnectionShare association class.*

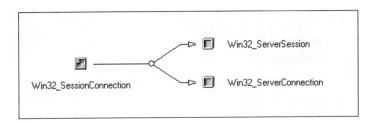

Figure 3.4 *The Win32_ServerSession and Win32_ServerConnection classes are associated with the Win32_SessionConnection association class.*

The next sample demonstrates the code logic to retrieve the session information with its associated instances. This script sample doesn't expect any switch by default. So, if a machine with the IP address 192.10.10.3 has a connection established by the administrator on a share called "MyShare" and resides on the computer where the script is launched, the output would be as follows:

```
 1:   C:\>WMISessions.Wsf
 2:   Microsoft (R) Windows Script Host Version 5.6
 3:   Copyright (C) Microsoft Corporation 1996-2001. All rights reserved.
 4:
 5:   - \\192.10.10.3\MYSHARE (ADMINISTRATOR) -----------------------------------------
 6:   ActiveTime: ........................... 443
 7:   *ComputerName: ........................ 192.10.10.3
 8:   ConnectionID: ......................... 174
 9:   InstallDate: .......................... 01-01-2000
10:   NumberOfFiles: ........................ 0
11:   NumberOfUsers: ........................ 1
12:   *ShareName: ........................... MYSHARE
13:   *UserName: ............................ ADMINISTRATOR
```

```
14:
15:      -- Session connection information  ------------------------------------------
16:      ActiveTime: .......................... 443
17:      ClientType: .......................... Windows .NET 3718
18:      *ComputerName: ....................... 192.10.10.3
19:      IdleTime: ............................ 8
20:      InstallDate: ......................... 01-01-2000
21:      ResourcesOpened: ..................... 0
22:      SessionType: ......................... 2
23:      TransportName: ....................... \Device\NetbiosSmb
24:      *UserName: ........................... ADMINISTRATOR
25:
26:      -- Share connection information  -------------------------------------------
27:      AllowMaximum: ........................ TRUE
28:      Caption: ............................. MYSHARE
29:      Description: .........................
30:      InstallDate: ......................... 01-01-2000
31:      *Name: ............................... MYSHARE
32:      Path: ................................ J:\MYDIR
33:      Status: .............................. OK
34:      Type: ................................ Disk
```

First, the script retrieves the *Win32_ServerConnection* instances (lines 5 through 13); next, it retrieves the *Win32_ServerSession* associated instances (lines 15 through 24) with some basic information about the *Win32_Share* associated instance (lines 26 and 27).

It is also possible to delete a session based on the computer name. The command line will be as follows:

```
C:\>WMISessions.Wsf /Delete:192.10.10.3
Microsoft (R) Windows Script Host Version 5.6
Copyright (C) Microsoft Corporation 1996-2001. All rights reserved.
Session '192.10.10.3' deleted.
Completed.
```

The code is shown in Sample 3.10. Since the command-line parameters definition and parsing are pretty simple and use the same logic as previous samples, they have been skipped. Right after the WMI connection (lines 69 through 73), the script checks if a computer name is specified with the **/Delete** switch. If not, it processes the display of the session information (lines 78 through 150). If a computer name is specified, it processes the deletion of the sessions established from the given computer name (lines 153 through 167).

Sample 3.10   *Viewing the active sessions with their associations*

```
1:<?xml version="1.0"?>
 .:
8:<package>
9:  <job>
..:
13:    <runtime>
```

```
..:
24:     </runtime>
25:
26:     <script language="VBScript" src="..\Functions\DecodeShareTypeFunction.vbs" />
27:     <script language="VBScript" src="..\Functions\DisplayFormattedPropertyFunction.vbs" />
28:     <script language="VBScript" src="..\Functions\TinyErrorHandler.vbs" />
29:
30:     <object progid="WbemScripting.SWbemLocator" id="objWMILocator" reference="true"/>
31:     <object progid="WbemScripting.SWbemDateTime" id="objWMIDateTime" />
32:
33:     <script language="VBscript">
34:     <![CDATA[
..:
38:     Const cComputerName = "LocalHost"
39:     Const cWMINameSpace = "Root/cimv2"
40:     Const cWMIConnClass = "Win32_ServerConnection"
41:     Const cWMISessionClass = "Win32_ServerSession"
..:
56:     ' ---------------------------------------------------------------------------
..:
69:     objWMILocator.Security_.AuthenticationLevel = wbemAuthenticationLevelDefault
70:     objWMILocator.Security_.ImpersonationLevel = wbemImpersonationLevelImpersonate
71:
72:     Set objWMIServices = objWMILocator.ConnectServer(strComputerName, cWMINameSpace, _
73:                                                 strUserID, strPassword)
..:
76:     If Len(strComputer) = 0 Then
77:         ' -- LIST -------------------------------------------------------------
78:         Set objWMIInstances = objWMIServices.InstancesOf (cWMIConnClass)
..:
81:         If objWMIInstances.Count Then
82:             For Each objWMIInstance In objWMIInstances
83:                 WScript.Echo "- \\" & Ucase (objWMIInstance.ComputerName) & _
84:                             "\" & Ucase (objWMIInstance.ShareName) & _
85:                             " (" & Ucase (objWMIInstance.UserName) & _
86:                             ") " & String (60, "-")
87:                 Set objWMIPropertySet = objWMIInstance.Properties_
88:                 For Each objWMIProperty In objWMIPropertySet
89:                     DisplayFormattedProperty objWMIInstance, _
90:                             objWMIProperty.Name, _
91:                             objWMIProperty.Name, _
92:                             Null
93:             Next
..:
96:                 Set objWMIAssocInstances = objWMIServices.ExecQuery _
97:                             ("Associators of {" & objWMIInstance.Path_.RelPath & _
98:                             "} Where AssocClass=Win32_SessionConnection")
...:
101:             If objWMIAssocInstances.Count Then
102:                 WScript.Echo
103:                 WScript.Echo " -- Session connection information " & " " & String (53, "-")
104:                 For Each objWMIAssocInstance In objWMIAssocInstances
105:                     Set objWMIPropertySet = objWMIAssocInstance.Properties_
106:                     For Each objWMIProperty In objWMIPropertySet
107:                         DisplayFormattedProperty objWMIAssocInstance, _
108:                                 "   " & objWMIProperty.Name, _
109:                                 objWMIProperty.Name, _
110:                                 Null
111:                     Next
112:                     Set objWMIPropertySet = Nothing
```

```
113:                    Next
114:                End If
115:
116:                Set objWMIAssocInstances = objWMIServices.ExecQuery _
117:                            ("Associators of {" & objWMIInstance.Path_.RelPath & _
118:                            "} Where AssocClass=Win32_ConnectionShare")
...:
121:                If objWMIAssocInstances.Count Then
122:                    WScript.Echo
123:                    WScript.Echo "  -- Share connection information " & " " & String (53, "-")
124:                    For Each objWMIAssocInstance In objWMIAssocInstances
125:                        Set objWMIPropertySet = objWMIAssocInstance.Properties_
126:                        For Each objWMIProperty In objWMIPropertySet
127:                            Select Case objWMIProperty.Name
128:                                Case "Type"
129:                                    DisplayFormattedProperty objWMIAssocInstance, _
130:                                        "  " & objWMIProperty.Name, _
131:                                        ShareType (objWMIProperty.Value), _
132:                                        Null
133:
134:                                Case Else
135:                                    DisplayFormattedProperty objWMIAssocInstance, _
136:                                        "  " & objWMIProperty.Name, _
137:                                        objWMIProperty.Name, _
138:                                        Null
139:                            End Select
140:                        Next
141:                        Set objWMIPropertySet = Nothing
142:                    Next
143:                End If
144:                WScript.Echo
...:
147:            Next
148:        Else
149:            WScript.Echo "No session." & vbCRLF
150:        End If
151:    Else
152:        ' -- Delete -------------------------------------------------------------------
153:        Set objWMIInstances = objWMIServices.ExecQuery ("Select * From " & cWMISessionClass & _
154:                            " Where ComputerName='" & strComputer & "'")
...:
157:        If objWMIInstances.Count Then
158:            For Each objWMIInstance In objWMIInstances
159:                objWMIInstance.Delete_
...:
162:                WScript.Echo "Session '" & objWMIInstance.ComputerName & "' deleted."
163:            Next
164:            WScript.Echo
165:        End If
...:
168:    End If
169:
170:    WScript.Echo "Completed."
...:
176:    ]]>
177:    </script>
178:  </job>
179:</package>
```

When the script displays session information, it retrieves a collection of *Win32_ServerConnection* instances (line 78). For each instance (lines 82 through 147), the script displays the instance properties (lines 87 through 93) with the existing associated instances. As we have seen in Figures 3.3 and 3.4, two associated instances with their properties can be retrieved:

■ The *Win32_ServerSession* instances associated with the *Win32_SessionConnection* association class (lines 96 through 114)

■ The *Win32_Share* instances associated with the *Win32_ConnectionShare* association class (lines 116 through 143).

Once completed, the script terminates its execution.

With the **/Delete** switch, sessions established by a specific computer can be deleted (lines 153 through 167). Instead of retrieving a specific session, based on the command-line parameters, the script retrieves all sessions available for the given computer (lines 153 and 154) and deletes them (line 159) in a loop (lines 158 through 163).

3.3.5   Kernel Job providers

Installed on Windows XP and Windows Server 2003, the *Kernel Job Object* provider enables access to data on named kernel job objects. This provider does not report unnamed kernel job objects. The *Kernel Job Object* providers capabilities are listed in Table 3.11.

Table 3.11   *The Kernel Job Object Providers Capabilities*

Provider Name	Provider Namespace	Class Provider	Instance Provider	Method Provider	Property Provider	Event Provider	Event Consumer Provider	Support Get	Support Put	Support Enumeration	Support Delete	Windows Server 2003	Windows XP	Windows 2000 Server	Windows 2000 Professional	Windows NT 4.0
Job Object Providers																
NamedJobObjectActgInfoProv	Root/CIMV2		X					X	X	X	X	X	X			
NamedJobObjectLimitSettingProv	Root/CIMV2		X					X	X	X	X	X	X			
NamedJobObjectProv	Root/CIMV2		X					X	X	X	X	X	X			
NamedJobObjectSecLimitSettingProv	Root/CIMV2		X					X	X	X	X	X	X			

The classes supported by these providers are available in the **Root\CIMv2** namespace and summarized in Table 3.12.

Table 3.12   *The Kernel Job Object Classes*

Name	Type	Comments
Win32_NamedJobObject	Dynamic	Represents a kernel object that is used to group processes for the sake of controlling the life and resources of the processes within the job object.
Win32_NamedJobObjectActgInfo	Dynamic	Represents the I/O accounting information for a job object.
Win32_NamedJobObjectLimitSetting	Dynamic	Represents the limit settings for a job object.
Win32_NamedJobObjectSecLimitSetting	Dynamic	Represents the security limit settings for a job object.
Win32_SIDandAttributes	Dynamic	Represents a security identifier (SID) and its attributes.
Win32_NamedJobObjectProcess	Association Aggregation	Relates a job object and the process contained in the job object.
Win32_CollectionStatistics	Association	Relates a managed system element collection and the class representing statistical information about the collection.
Win32_NamedJobObjectLimit	Association	Represents an association between a job object and the job object limit settings.
Win32_NamedJobObjectSecLimit	Association	Relates a job object and the job object security limit settings.
Win32_NamedJobObjectStatistics	Assocation	Represents an association between a job object and the job object I/O accounting information class.
Win32_LUID	Abstract	Represents a locally unique identifier (LUID)
Win32_LUIDandAttributes	Abstract	Represents a LUID and its attributes.
Win32_TokenGroups	Abstract	Represents information about the group SIDs in an access token.
Win32_TokenPrivileges	Abstract	Represents information about a set of privileges for an access token.

The *Win32_NamedJobObject* class represents a kernel object that is used to group processes for the sake of controlling the life and resources of the processes within the job object. Figure 3.5 shows the associations in place.

Figure 3.5
*The Win32_
NamedJobObject
associations.*

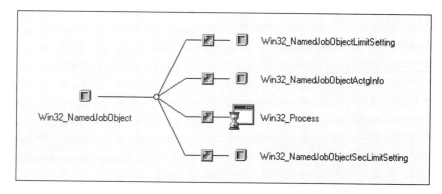

As we can see in Figure 3.5, the *Win32_NamedJobObject* has an association with the *Win32_Process*. In the previous chapter, we developed a script using the *Win32_Process* (see Sample 2.50, "Viewing, creating, and killing processes"). We can easily extend this previous sample to show the information available from the associations shown in Figure 3.5. We won't review the complete script. Only the portion of the code showing the process information will be examined. Until line 333, the script is exactly the same as Sample 2.50. The portion of code is included from line 335 through 389 and is executed for each *Win32_Process* instance examined during the loop (lines 289 through 386).

Sample 3.11   *Viewing Job kernel instance associated with a process*

```
...:
...:
...:
275:    ' - LIST -------------------------------------------------------------------------------
276:    If boolList Then
277:        If Len (strExecutable) Then
278:            Set objWMIProcInstances = objWMIServices.ExecQuery ("Select * From " & _
279:                                                                cWMIProcClass & _
280:                                                                " Where Name='" & _
281:                                                                strExecutable & "'")
282:            If Err.Number Then ErrorHandler (Err)
283:        Else
284:            Set objWMIProcInstances = objWMIServices.InstancesOf (cWMIProcClass)
285:            If Err.Number Then ErrorHandler (Err)
286:        End If
287:
288:        If objWMIProcInstances.Count Then
289:            For Each objWMIProcInstance in objWMIProcInstances
290:                WScript.Echo "- " & Ucase(objWMIProcInstance.Name) & String (60, "-")
291:                Set objWMIPropertySet = objWMIProcInstance.Properties_
292:                For Each objWMIProperty In objWMIPropertySet
293:                    Select Case objWMIProperty.Name
294:                           Case "Caption"
295:
296:                           Case "Description"
297:
298:                           Case "Name"
299:
300:                           Case "CSCreationClassName"
301:
302:                           Case "OSCreationClassName"
303:
304:                           Case "CreationClassName"
305:
306:                           Case Else
307:                               DisplayFormattedProperty objWMIProcInstance, _
308:                                                        "   " & objWMIProperty.Name, _
309:                                                        objWMIProperty.Name, _
310:                                                        Null
311:                    End Select
312:                Next
313:                Set objWMIPropertySet = Nothing
314:
315:                WScript.Echo
316:
317:                intRC = objWMIProcInstance.GetOwner (strOwnerUser, strOwnerDomain)
318:                If intRC = 0 Then
319:                    DisplayFormattedProperty objWMIProcInstance, _
320:                                             " Process owner", _
321:                                             strOwnerDomain, _
322:                                             strOwnerUser
323:                End If
324:
325:                intRC = objWMIProcInstance.GetOwnerSid (strOwnerSID)
326:                If intRC = 0 Then
327:                    DisplayFormattedProperty objWMIProcInstance, _
328:                                             " Process owner SID", _
329:                                             strOwnerSID, _
330:                                             Null
331:                End If
```

```
332:
333:                WScript.Echo
334:
335:                Set objWMIJobInstances = objWMIServices.ExecQuery _
336:                                    ("Associators of {" & _
337:                                     objWMIProcInstance.Path_.RelPath & _
338:                                     "} Where AssocClass=" & _
339:                                     "Win32_NamedJobObjectProcess")
340:
341:                If objWMIJobInstances.Count Then
342:                   For Each objWMIJobInstance in objWMIJobInstances
343:                      WScript.Echo "  - " & Ucase(objWMIJobInstance.CollectionID) & _
344:                                   " " & String (60, "-")
345:                      Set objWMIPropertySet = objWMIJobInstance.Properties_
346:                      For Each objWMIProperty In objWMIPropertySet
347:                         DisplayFormattedProperty objWMIJobInstance, _
348:                                              "    " & objWMIProperty.Name, _
349:                                              objWMIProperty.Name, _
350:                                              Null
351:                      Next
352:                      Set objWMIPropertySet = Nothing
353:
354:                      WScript.Echo
355:
356:                      For Each strAssocClass In Array ("Win32_NamedJobObjectLimit", _
357:                                                       "Win32_NamedJobObjectSecLimit", _
358:                                                       "Win32_NamedJobObjectStatistics")
359:
360:                         Set objWMIJobAssocInstances = objWMIServices.ExecQuery _
361:                                              ("Associators of {" & _
362:                                               objWMIJobInstance.Path_.RelPath & _
363:                                               "} Where AssocClass=" & _
364:                                               strAssocClass)
365:
366:                         If objWMIJobAssocInstances.Count Then
367:                            For Each objWMIJobAssocInstance in objWMIJobAssocInstances
368:                               WScript.Echo "    - " & _
369:                                            Ucase(objWMIJobAssocInstance.Path_.Class) & _
370:                                            " " & String (60, "-")
371:                               Set objWMIPropertySet = objWMIJobAssocInstance.Properties_
372:                               For Each objWMIProperty In objWMIPropertySet
373:                                  DisplayFormattedProperty objWMIJobAssocInstance, _
374:                                                 "      " & objWMIProperty.Name, _
375:                                                 objWMIProperty.Name, _
376:                                                 Null
377:                               Next
378:                               Set objWMIPropertySet = Nothing
379:
380:                               WScript.Echo
381:                            Next
382:                         End If
383:                      Next
384:                   Next
385:                End If
386:             Next
387:          Else
388:             WScript.Echo "No information available."
389:          End If
...:
...:
...:
```

At line 335, the script retrieves the *Win32_NamedJobObject* instances associated with the *Win32_NamedObjectProcess* association class. If instances of the *Win32_NamedJobObject* class are available (line 341), the script displays their properties (lines 345 through 352). Next, for each instance of the *Win32_NamedJobObject* class, the script retrieves three associated instances (lines 356 through 383):

- The *Win32_NamedJobObjectLimitSetting* instances with the *Win32_NamedJobObjectLimit* association class.

- The *Win32_NamedJobObjectActgInfo* instances with the *Win32_NamedJobObjectActgInfo* association class.

- The *Win32_NamedJobObjectSecLimitSetting* instances with the *Win32_NamedJobObjectSecLimitSetting* association class.

The obtained output for the WMI process is as follows:

```
 1:  C:\>WMIProcess /Action:List /Executable:wmiprvse.exe
 2:  Microsoft (R) Windows Script Host Version 5.6
 3:  Copyright (C) Microsoft Corporation 1996-2001. All rights reserved.
 4:
 5:  - WMIPRVSE.EXE-------------------------------------------------------
 6:    CreationDate: ......................... 09-02-2002 07:18:37
 7:    CSName: ............................... NET-DPEN6400A
 8:    *Handle: .............................. 2712
 9:    HandleCount: .......................... 175
10:    InstallDate: .......................... 09-02-2002 07:18:37
11:    KernelModeTime: ....................... 24234848
12:    OSName: ............................... Microsoft Windows .NET Enterprise Serv...
13:    OtherOperationCount: .................. 4967
14:    OtherTransferCount: ................... 44708
15:    PageFaults: ........................... 10974
16:    PageFileUsage: ........................ 3674112
17:    ParentProcessId: ...................... 696
18:    PeakPageFileUsage: .................... 3977216
19:    PeakVirtualSize: ...................... 29556736
20:    PeakWorkingSetSize: ................... 7913472
21:    Priority: ............................. 8
22:    PrivatePageCount: ..................... 3674112
23:    ProcessId: ............................ 2712
24:    QuotaNonPagedPoolUsage: ............... 5656
25:    QuotaPagedPoolUsage: .................. 25264
26:    QuotaPeakNonPagedPoolUsage: ........... 7744
27:    QuotaPeakPagedPoolUsage: .............. 26268
28:    ReadOperationCount: ................... 2846
29:    ReadTransferCount: .................... 938974
30:    SessionId: ............................ 0
31:    TerminationDate: ...................... 09-02-2002 07:18:37
32:    ThreadCount: .......................... 9
33:    UserModeTime: ......................... 60887552
34:    VirtualSize: .......................... 27336704
35:    WindowsVersion: ....................... 5.1.3590
36:    WorkingSetSize: ....................... 7864320
37:    WriteOperationCount: .................. 2383
```

```
38:     WriteTransferCount: .................. 144244
39:
40:     Process owner: ....................... NT AUTHORITY NETWORK SERVICE
41:     Process owner SID: ................... S-1-5-20
42:
43:     - \WMI\PROVIDER\SUB\SYSTEM\HOST\JOB ----------------------------------------------
44:       BasicUIRestrictions: ............... 0
45:       *CollectionID: ..................... \wmi\provider\sub\system\host\job
46:
47:       - WIN32_NAMEDJOBOBJECTLIMITSETTING -------------------------------------------
48:         ActiveProcessLimit: .............. 32
49:         Affinity: ........................ 0
50:         JobMemoryLimit: .................. 1073741824
51:         LimitFlags: ...................... 11016
52:         MaximumWorkingSetSize: ........... 0
53:         MinimumWorkingSetSize: ........... 0
54:         PerJobUserTimeLimit: ............. 0
55:         PerProcessUserTimeLimit: ......... 0
56:         PriorityClass: ................... 32
57:         ProcessMemoryLimit: .............. 134217728
58:         SchedulingClass: ................. 5
59:         *SettingID: ...................... \wmi\provider\sub\system\host\job
60:
61:       - WIN32_NAMEDJOBOBJECTSECLIMITSETTING ----------------------------------------
62:         PrivilegesToDelete: .............. <OBJECT>
63:         RestrictedSIDs: .................. <OBJECT>
64:         SecurityLimitFlags: .............. 0
65:         *SettingID: ...................... \wmi\provider\sub\system\host\job
66:         SIDsToDisable: ................... <OBJECT>
67:
68:       - WIN32_NAMEDJOBOBJECTACTGINFO ----------------------------------------------
69:         ActiveProcesses: ................. 1
70:         *Name: ........................... \wmi\provider\sub\system\host\job
71:         OtherOperationCount: ............. 4975
72:         OtherTransferCount: .............. 44708
73:         PeakJobMemoryUsed: ............... 3977216
74:         PeakProcessMemoryUsed: ........... 4136960
75:         ReadOperationCount: .............. 2885
76:         ReadTransferCount: ............... 941298
77:         ThisPeriodTotalKernelTime: ....... 24935856
78:         ThisPeriodTotalUserTime: ......... 62790288
79:         TotalKernelTime: ................. 24935856
80:         TotalPageFaultCount: ............. 11105
81:         TotalProcesses: .................. 1
82:         TotalTerminatedProcesses: ........ 0
83:         TotalUserTime: ................... 62790288
84:         WriteOperationCount: ............. 2422
85:         WriteTransferCount: .............. 146912
```

3.3.6 TrustMon provider

Only available under Windows Server 2003, the *TrustMon* provider is an instance provider that only supports the "Get" and "Enumeration" operations (Table 3.13).

Table 3.13   *The TrustMon Provider Capabilities*

Provider Name	Provider Namespace	Class Provider	Instance Provider	Method Provider	Property Provider	Event Provider	Event Consumer Provider	Support Get	Support Put	Support Enumeration	Support Delete	Windows Server 2003	Windows XP	Windows 2000 Server	Windows 2000 Professional	Windows NT 4.0
Trust Monitoring Providers																
TrustPrv	Root/ActiveDirectory		X					X	X	X		X	X	X		

Supporting three classes available in the **Root\MicrosoftActiveDirectory** namespace (Table 3.14), the provider purpose is to verify the state of the existing trust relationships between domains.

Table 3.14   *The TrustMon Provider Classes*

Name	Type	Comments
Microsoft_TrustProvider	Dynamic (Singleton)	Provider parameterization class.
Microsoft_DomainTrustStatus	Dynamic	Trust enumerator class.
Microsoft_LocalDomainInfo	Dynamic (Singleton)	Local domain information class.

The *Microsoft_TrustProvider* class is a singleton class and includes properties that control how domains will be enumerated with the *Microsoft_DomainTrustStatus* class. The *TrustMon* provider caches the last trust enumeration (default ListLifeTime = 20 min) and the last request for the trust status (default *StatusLifeTime* = 3 min). It is also possible to define the trust check level (Table 3.15), if only the trusting domains must be returned (without the trusted domains).

Table 3.15   *The TrustMon Check Levels*

Meaning	Values
Enumerate only	0
Enumerate with SC_QUERY	1
Enumerate with password check	2
Enumerate with SC_RESET	3

The *Microsoft_LocalDomainInfo* class is used to gather information about the domain, while the last class, the *Microsoft_DomainTrustStatus* class, is used to enumerate the trust status. The verification of the trusts is made during the enumeration of the *Microsoft_DomainTrustStatus* class based on the parameters given at the level of the *Microsoft_TrustProvider* instance. It is important to note that the effectiveness of the updated parameters is not immediate, even if the *Microsoft_TrustProvider* instance is updated immediately before the trust enumeration. The only way to immediately change the provider parameters is to update the settings stored in the repository and stopping/restarting the WMI service **WinMgmt.Exe**. Based on this information, Sample 3.12 has the following command-line parameters:

```
C:\>WMITrust.Wsf
Microsoft (R) Windows Script Host Version 5.6
Copyright (C) Microsoft Corporation 1996-2001. All rights reserved.

Usage: WMITrust.wsf /Check:value [/ListLifeTime:value] [/StatusLifeTime:value] [/TrustingOnly[+|-]]
                        [/DomainInfo[+|-]] [/Machine:value] [/User:value] [/Password:value]

Options:

Check           : Specify the verification to perform: [EnumOnly], [EnumQuery],
                  [EnumPwdCheck] or [EnumReset].
ListLifeTime    : Time in minutes to cache the last trust enumeration.
StatusLifeTime  : Time in minutes to cache the last request for status.
TrustingOnly    : If TRUE, enumerations return trusting as well as trusted domains.
DomainInfo      : Provide information about the domain on which this instance of
                  the trust monitor is running.
Machine         : Determine the WMI system to connect to. (default=LocalHost)
User            : Determine the UserID to perform the remote connection. (default=none)
Password        : Determine the password to perform the remote connection. (default=none)
Examples:

    WMITrust /DomainInfo+
    WMITrust /Check:EnumOnly /StatusLifeTime:3 /ListLifeTime:20 /TrustingOnly+
    WMITrust /Check:EnumQuery /ListLifeTime:20 /TrustingOnly+
    WMITrust /Check:EnumPwdCheck /StatusLifeTime:3 /TrustingOnly+
    WMITrust /Check:EnumReset /TrustingOnly+
```

Requesting the domain information will also show the *TrustMon* provider parameters. For example, the following command line would give:

```
C:\>WMITrust /DomainInfo+
Microsoft (R) Windows Script Host Version 5.6
Copyright (C) Microsoft Corporation 1996-2001. All rights reserved.

- Local Domain information ------------------------------------------------------
  DCname: ............................ NET-DPEN6400A
  DNSname: ........................... LissWare.NET
  FlatName: .......................... LISSWARENET
  SID: .............................. S-1-5-21-1935655697-839522115-1708537768
  TreeName: .......................... LissWare.Net

- Trust provider parameters -----------------------------------------------------
  ReturnAll: ......................... TRUE
  TrustCheckLevel: ................... 2
  TrustListLifetime: ................. 0
  TrustStatusLifetime: ............... 0
```

While the following command line would give:

```
C:\>WMITrust /Check:EnumPwdCheck /TrustingOnly-
Microsoft (R) Windows Script Host Version 5.6
Copyright (C) Microsoft Corporation 1996-2001. All rights reserved.

   FlatName: ........................... EMEA
   SID: ................................ S-1-5-21-1708537768-854245398-1957994488
   TrustAttributes: .................... 0
   TrustDirection: ..................... Bi-directional
   TrustedDCName: ......................
   TrustedDomain: ...................... Emea.LissWare.Net
   TrustIsOk: .......................... False
   TrustStatus: ........................ 1355
   TrustStatusString: .................. The specified domain either does not exist
                                         or could not be contacted.
   TrustType: .......................... Uplevel

   FlatName: ........................... MYNT40DOMAIN
   SID: ................................ S-1-5-21-42165204-196285673-1159422225
   TrustAttributes: .................... 0
   TrustDirection: ..................... Inbound
   TrustedDCName: ......................
   TrustedDomain: ...................... HOME
   TrustIsOk: .......................... True
   TrustStatus: ........................ 0
   TrustStatusString: .................. Inbound-only trusts are verified from the trusting side.
   TrustType: .......................... Downlevel
```

Sample 3.12 shows the code logic developed on top of the *TrustMon* provider. The command-line parameter definitions and parsing follow the same structure as previous script samples.

Sample 3.12   *Verifying trusts*

```
 1:<?xml version="1.0"?>
 .:
 8:<package>
 9:  <job>
..:
13:    <runtime>
..:
31:    </runtime>
32:
33:    <script language="VBScript" src="..\Functions\DecodeTrustsFunction.vbs" />
34:
35:    <script language="VBScript" src="..\Functions\DisplayFormattedPropertyFunction.vbs" />
36:    <script language="VBScript" src="..\Functions\TinyErrorHandler.vbs" />
37:
38:    <object progid="WbemScripting.SWbemLocator" id="objWMILocator" reference="true"/>
39:    <object progid="WbemScripting.SWbemDateTime" id="objWMIDateTime" />
40:
41:    <script language="VBscript">
42:    <![CDATA[
..:
46:    Const cComputerName = "LocalHost"
47:    Const cWMINameSpace = "Root\MicrosoftActiveDirectory"
```

```
 48:    Const cWMITrustProvClass = "Microsoft_TrustProvider"
 49:    Const cWMIDomTrustClass = "Microsoft_DomainTrustStatus"
 50:    Const cWMIDomInfoClass = "Microsott_LocalDomainInfo"
 ..:
 72:    ' -----------------------------------------------------------------------------
 73:    ' Parse the command line parameters
 74:    If WScript.Arguments.Named.Count = 0 Then
 75:       WScript.Arguments.ShowUsage()
 76:       WScript.Quit
 77:    End If
 ..:
122:    If Len(strComputerName) = 0 Then strComputerName = cComputerName
123:
124:    objWMILocator.Security_.AuthenticationLevel = wbemAuthenticationLevelDefault
125:    objWMILocator.Security_.ImpersonationLevel = wbemImpersonationLevelImpersonate
126:
127:    Set objWMIServices = objWMILocator.ConnectServer(strComputerName, cWMINameSpace, _
128:                                                     strUserID, strPassword)
...:
131:    If boolDomainInfo = True Then
132:       ' -----------------------------------------------------------------------------------
133:       WScript.Echo "- Local Domain information " & String (60, "-")
134:
135:       Set objWMIInstance = objWMIServices.Get (cWMIDomInfoClass & "=@")
136:       If Err.Number Then ErrorHandler (Err)
137:
138:       Set objWMIPropertySet = objWMIInstance.Properties_
139:       For Each objWMIProperty In objWMIPropertySet
140:           DisplayFormattedProperty objWMIInstance, _
141:                               "  " & objWMIProperty.Name, _
142:                               objWMIProperty.Name, _
143:                               Null
144:       Next
145:
146:       WScript.Echo
147:       WScript.Echo "- Trust provider parameters " & String (60, "-")
148:
149:       Set objWMIInstance = objWMIServices.Get (cWMITrustProvClass & "=@")
...:
152:       Set objWMIPropertySet = objWMIInstance.Properties_
153:       For Each objWMIProperty In objWMIPropertySet
154:           DisplayFormattedProperty objWMIInstance, _
155:                               "  " & objWMIProperty.Name, _
156:                               objWMIProperty.Name, _
157:                               Null
158:       Next
...:
162:    Else
163:       ' -----------------------------------------------------------------------------------
164:       Set objWMIInstance = objWMIServices.Get (cWMITrustProvClass & "=@")
...:
167:       objWMIInstance.TrustCheckLevel = intCheckLevel
168:
169:       If intStatusLifeTime <> - 1 Then
170:           objWMIInstance.TrustStatusLifetime = intStatusLifeTime
171:       End If
172:       If intListLifeTime <> - 1 Then
173:           objWMIInstance.TrustListLifetime = intListLifeTime
174:       End If
175:       If Len(boolTrustingOnly) Then
```

```
176:            objWMIInstance.ReturnAll = Not boolTrustingOnly
177:        End If
178:
179:        objWMIInstance.Put_ (wbemChangeFlagUpdateOnly Or wbemFlagReturnWhenComplete)
...:
184:        ' --------------------------------------------------------------------------------
185:        Set objWMIInstances = objWMIServices.InstancesOf (cWMIDomTrustClass)
...:
188:        For Each objWMIInstance in objWMIInstances
189:            Set objWMIPropertySet = objWMIInstance.Properties_
190:            For Each objWMIProperty In objWMIPropertySet
191:                Select Case objWMIProperty.Name
192:                    Case "TrustDirection"
193:                        DisplayFormattedProperty objWMIInstance, _
194:                            " " & objWMIProperty.Name, _
195:                            DecodeTrustDirection (objWMIProperty.Value), _
196:                            Null
197:                    Case "TrustType"
198:                        DisplayFormattedProperty objWMIInstance, _
199:                            " " & objWMIProperty.Name, _
200:                            DecodeTrustType (objWMIProperty.Value), _
201:                            Null
202:                    Case "TrustAttributes"
203:                        DisplayFormattedProperty objWMIInstance, _
204:                            " " & objWMIProperty.Name, _
205:                            DecodeTrustAttributes (objWMIProperty.Value), _
206:                            Null
207:                    Case Else
208:                        DisplayFormattedProperty objWMIInstance, _
209:                            " " & objWMIProperty.Name, _
210:                            objWMIProperty.Value, _
211:                            Null
212:                End Select
213:            Next
...:
216:        Next
...:
219:    End If
...:
223:    ]]>
224:    </script>
225:  </job>
226:</package>
```

When the **/DomainInfo+** switch is supplied on the command line, the script gets the *Microsoft_LocalDomainInfo* (lines 135 through 144) and *Microsoft_TrustProvider* instances (lines 149 through 158) to display their properties. If the **/DomainInfo** switch is not supplied, the script updates the *Microsoft_TrustProvider* instance with the command-line parameters (lines 164 through 179) and enumerates the list of trusts in place (lines 185 through 216).

To detect a trust status change, a WQL event query can be used. Since the *TrustMon* provider is not implemented as an event provider, the WQL event query must use the **WITHIN** statement. For example, a valid WQL would be as follows:

```
 1:   C:\>GenericEventAsyncConsumer.wsf "Select * FROM __InstanceModificationEvent Within 5
                                       Where TargetInstance ISA 'Microsoft_DomainTrustStatus'"
                                       /NameSpace:Root\MicrosoftActiveDirectory
 2:   Microsoft (R) Windows Script Host Version 5.6
 3:   Copyright (C) Microsoft Corporation 1996-2001. All rights reserved.
 4:
 5:   Waiting for events...
 6:
 7:   BEGIN - OnObjectReady.
 8:   Monday, 10 June, 2002 at 12:11:12: '__InstanceModificationEvent' has been triggered.
 9:     PreviousInstance (wbemCimtypeObject)
10:       FlatName (wbemCimtypeString) = EMEA
11:       SID (wbemCimtypeString) = S-1-5-21-1060284298-484763869-1343024091
12:       TrustAttributes (wbemCimtypeUint32) = 0
13:       TrustDirection (wbemCimtypeUint32) = 3
14:       TrustedDCName (wbemCimtypeString) = \\net-dpep6400a.Emea.LissWare.NET
15:       *TrustedDomain (wbemCimtypeString) = Emea.LissWare.NET
16:       TrustIsOk (wbemCimtypeBoolean) = True
17:       TrustStatus (wbemCimtypeUint32) = 0
18:       TrustStatusString (wbemCimtypeString) = The secure channel was reset and the trust is OK.
19:       TrustType (wbemCimtypeUint32) = 2
20:     SECURITY_DESCRIPTOR (wbemCimtypeUint8) = (null)
21:     TargetInstance (wbemCimtypeObject)
22:       FlatName (wbemCimtypeString) = EMEA
23:       SID (wbemCimtypeString) = S-1-5-21-1060284298-484763869-1343024091
24:       TrustAttributes (wbemCimtypeUint32) = 0
25:       TrustDirection (wbemCimtypeUint32) = 3
26:       TrustedDCName (wbemCimtypeString) = \\net-dpep6400a.Emea.LissWare.NET
27:       *TrustedDomain (wbemCimtypeString) = Emea.LissWare.NET
28:       TrustIsOk (wbemCimtypeBoolean) = False
29:       TrustStatus (wbemCimtypeUint32) = 1311
30:       TrustStatusString (wbemCimtypeString) = There are currently no logon servers
                                                   available to service the logon request.
31:       TrustType (wbemCimtypeUint32) = 2
32:     TIME_CREATED (wbemCimtypeUint64) = (null)
33:
34:   END - OnObjectReady.
35:
36:   BEGIN - OnObjectReady.
37:   Monday, 10 June, 2002 at 12:11:12: '__InstanceModificationEvent' has been triggered.
38:     PreviousInstance (wbemCimtypeObject)
39:       FlatName (wbemCimtypeString) = EMEA
40:       SID (wbemCimtypeString) = S-1-5-21-1060284298-484763869-1343024091
41:       TrustAttributes (wbemCimtypeUint32) = 0
42:       TrustDirection (wbemCimtypeUint32) = 3
43:       TrustedDCName (wbemCimtypeString) = \\net-dpep6400a.Emea.LissWare.NET
44:       *TrustedDomain (wbemCimtypeString) = Emea.LissWare.NET
45:       TrustIsOk (wbemCimtypeBoolean) = False
46:       TrustStatus (wbemCimtypeUint32) = 1311
47:       TrustStatusString (wbemCimtypeString) = There are currently no logon servers
                                                   available to service the logon request.
48:       TrustType (wbemCimtypeUint32) = 2
49:     SECURITY_DESCRIPTOR (wbemCimtypeUint8) = (null)
50:     TargetInstance (wbemCimtypeObject)
51:       FlatName (wbemCimtypeString) = EMEA
52:       SID (wbemCimtypeString) = S-1-5-21-1060284298-484763869-1343024091
53:       TrustAttributes (wbemCimtypeUint32) = 0
54:       TrustDirection (wbemCimtypeUint32) = 3
55:       TrustedDCName (wbemCimtypeString) = \\net-dpep6400a.Emea.LissWare.NET
56:       *TrustedDomain (wbemCimtypeString) = Emea.LissWare.NET
```

```
57:        TrustIsOk (wbemCimtypeBoolean) = False
58:        TrustStatus (wbemCimtypeUint32) = 1355
59:        TrustStatusString (wbemCimtypeString) = The specified domain either does not exist
                                                   or could not be contacted.
60:        TrustType (wbemCimtypeUint32) = 2
61:      TIME_CREATED (wbemCimtypeUint64) = (null)
62:
63:    END - OnObjectReady.
```

From line 7 through 34, the trust status changes from 0 to 1311 (line 17 versus line 29), generating an error message at line 30. From line 36 through 63, the trust status changes from 1311 to 1355 (line 46 versus line 58), generating a different error message at line 59.

3.3.7 Windows Proxy provider

The *Windows Proxy* provider supports one single class called *Win32_Proxy* and is located in the **Root\CIMv2** namespace. This provider is implemented as an instance and a method provider (Table 3.16) and manages the Windows Proxy LAN settings.

Table 3.16   *The Windows Proxy Providers Capabilities*

Provider Name	Provider Namespace	Class Provider	Instance Provider	Method Provider	Property Provider	Event Provider	Event Consumer Provider	Support Get	Support Put	Support Enumeration	Support Delete	Windows Server 2003	Windows XP	Windows 2000 Server	Windows 2000 Professional	Windows NT 4.0
Proxy Provider																
Win32_WIN32_PROXY_Prov	Root/CIMv2		X	X				X	X	X	X	X	X			

The information exposed by the *Win32_Proxy* class is similar to the information exposed by the *MicrosoftIE_LanSettings* class in **Root/CIMV2/Applications/MicrosoftIE** namespace. However, the *MicrosoftIE_LanSettings* class uses the *IEINFO5* provider. With the *SetProxySetting* method exposed by the *Win32_Proxy* class, it is possible to update the Proxy LAN settings. Sample 3.13 shows how to proceed.

Sample 3.13   *Managing the Windows Proxy LAN settings*

```
1:<?xml version="1.0"?>
 .:
8:<package>
9:  <job>
..:
13:    <runtime>
..:
```

```
26:    </runtime>
27:
28:    <script language="VBScript" src="..\Functions\DisplayFormattedPropertyFunction.vbs" />
29:    <script language="VBScript" src="..\Functions\TinyErrorHandler.vbs" />
30:
31:    <object progid="WbemScripting.SWbemLocator" id="objWMILocator" reference="true"/>
32:    <object progid="WbemScripting.SWbemDateTime" id="objWMIDateTime" />
33:
34:    <script language="VBscript">
35:    <![CDATA[
..:
39:    Const cComputerName = "LocalHost"
40:    Const cWMINameSpace = "Root\CIMv2"
41:    Const cWMIClass = "Win32_Proxy"
..:
62:    ' -----------------------------------------------------------------------------
63:    ' Parse the command line parameters
64:    If WScript.Arguments.Named.Count = 0 Then
65:       WScript.Arguments.ShowUsage()
66:       WScript.Quit
67:    End If
..:
99:    strComputerName = WScript.Arguments.Named("Machine")
100:   If Len(strComputerName) = 0 Then strComputerName = cComputerName
101:
102:   objWMILocator.Security_.AuthenticationLevel = wbemAuthenticationLevelDefault
103:   objWMILocator.Security_.ImpersonationLevel = wbemImpersonationLevelImpersonate
104:
105:   Set objWMIServices = objWMILocator.ConnectServer(strComputerName, cWMINameSpace, _
106:                                                     strUserID, strPassword)
...:
109:   Set objWMIInstances = objWMIServices.InstancesOf (cWMIClass)
...:
112:   If objWMIInstances.Count > 0 Then
113:      For Each objWMIInstance In objWMIInstances
114:          If boolViewProxy Then
115:              Set objWMIPropertySet = objWMIInstance.Properties_
116:              For Each objWMIProperty In objWMIPropertySet
117:                  DisplayFormattedProperty objWMIInstance, _
118:                                           " " & objWMIProperty.Name, _
119:                                           objWMIProperty.Name, _
120:                                           Null
121:              Next
...:
124:          End If
125:
126:          If boolSetProxy Then
127:              intRC = objWMIInstance.SetProxySetting (strProxyAddress, intProxyPort)
128:              If Err.Number Then ErrorHandler (Err)
129:
130:              If intRC = 0 Then
131:                  WScript.Echo "Proxy settings successfuly udpated."
132:              Else
133:                  WScript.Echo "Failed to update Proxy settings (" & intRC & ")."
134:              End If
135:          End If
136:      Next
137:   End If
...:
143:   ]]>
144:   </script>
145: </job>
146:</package>
```

Once command-line parsing completes (lines 62 through 100) and the WMI connection is executed (lines 102 through 106), the script retrieves all instances of the *Win32_Proxy* class (line 109). Since this class is not a singleton class, and because it uses the proxy settings as Key properties, the easiest way to retrieve the information is to start an enumeration of the available instances.

When the **/ViewProxy+** switch is used, the script shows the current Windows Proxy settings (lines 114 through 124). This portion of code enumerates and displays all properties available from the *Win32_Proxy* class (lines 115 through 121). Once executed, the output will be as follows:

```
C:\>WMIProxy.Wsf /ViewProxy+
Microsoft (R) Windows Script Host Version 5.6
Copyright (C) Microsoft Corporation 1996-2001. All rights reserved.

   ProxyPortNumber: ...................... 8080
   ProxyServer: ......................... http://proxy.LissWare.Net
   *ServerName: ......................... net-dpen6400a.LissWare.Net
```

When the **/ProxyAddress** switch is supplied, the script invokes the *Set-ProxySetting* method of the *Win32_Proxy* class to configure the Windows Proxy LAN settings (line 127). This script is not really complicated; it simply takes advantage of the *Win32_Proxy* class capabilities.

3.3.8   Windows Product Activation provider

These providers manage the information related to the *Windows Product Activation* (WPA). The providers are implemented as instance and method providers (Table 3.17). Available for Windows XP and Windows Server 2003, the WPA is not supported on 64-bit Windows and previous Windows platforms.

Table 3.17   *The Windows Product Activation Providers Capabilities*

Provider Name	Provider Namespace	Class Provider	Instance Provider	Method Provider	Property Provider	Event Provider	Event Consumer Provider	Support Get	Support Put	Support Enumeration	Support Delete	Windows Server 2003	Windows XP	Windows 2000 Server	Windows 2000 Professional	Windows NT 4.0
Performance Monitoring Provider																
Win32_WIN32_COMPUTERSYSTEMWINDOWSPRODUCTACTIVATIONSETTING_Prov	Root/CIMV2		X	X				X	X	X	X	X	X			
Win32_WIN32_WINDOWSPRODUCTACTIVATION_Prov	Root/CIMV2		X	X				X	X	X	X	X	X			

Two classes are supported by the WMI providers and expose methods to perform Windows product activation. Table 3.18 lists the class names available, while Table 3.19 shows the methods exposed by the *Win32_Windows-ProductActivation* class.

Table 3.18   *The Windows Product Activation Providers Classes*

Name	Type	Comments
Win32_WindowsProductActivation	Dynamic	The Win32_WindowsProductActivation class contains properties and methods that relate to Windows Product Activation, such as: activation state, grace period, and provides the ability to activate the machine online and offline.
Win32_ComputerSystemWindowsProductActivationSetting	Association	This class represents an association between Win32_ComputerSystem and Win32_WindowsProductActivation

Table 3.19   *The Windows Product Activation Providers Methods*

Name	Comments
ActivateOffline	This function is a scriptable equivalent to manual telephone activation. It permits offline activation using the Confirmation ID provided by the Microsoft Clearinghouse. In order to complete offline activation, the InstallationID for the machine must be retrieved by querying for the property. The method returns 0 on success and an error code otherwise.
ActivateOnline	The ActivateOnline method exchanges license-related data with the Microsoft Clearinghouse server and, if successful, completes system activation. It requires that the target machine be able to communicate through the Internet using the HTTPS protocol. If necessary, the SetProxySetting method should first be used to connect through a firewall. The method returns 0 on success and an error code otherwise.
GetInstallationID	GetInstallationID gets the InstallationID property and comprises the Product ID and Hardware ID, and is identical to the Installation ID displayed on the telephone activation page. Installation ID must be provided to the Microsoft Clearinghouse to obtain the corresponding Confirmation ID, which is required for the ActivateOffline method.
SetNotification	SetNotification is a function that enables or disables Windows Product Activation Notification reminders. The method returns 0 on success (or if activation is not pending) and an error code otherwise. Notification reminders are enabled by default. Note that this method does not affect Logon or event log reminders, nor does it alter the need to activate the computer.
SetProductKey	SetProductKey permits a computer's Product Key (and therefore its ProductID) to be changed or corrected. Only Product Keys that are valid for the media type (i.e., retail, volume licensing, OEM) will be accepted. The method can only be used while ActivationRequired is 1. Product KeyProduct Key is a 25-character alphanumeric string formatted in groups of five characters separated by dashes.

Note that all methods are only usable if the Windows product is not activated. Once the activation is completed, none of the methods can be used. Because WPA relates to a single computer, the *Win32_WindowsProductActivation* class is associated with the *Win32_ComputerSystem* class, as shown in Figure 3.6.

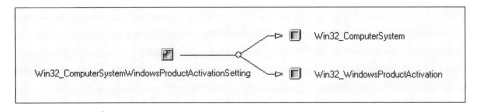

Figure 3.6   *The Win32_WindowsProductActivation class is associated with the Win32_ComputerSystem class.*

It is important to understand that WPA can be executed on line or off line. While on-line activation executes via the Internet, off-line activation is executed on the phone with a Microsoft representative. In this case, the customer must provide an installation ID. Sample 3.14 implements the script logic to perform both activation types. The command-line parameters exposed by this script are as follows:

```
C:\>WMIWPA.wsf
Microsoft (R) Windows Script Host Version 5.6
Copyright (C) Microsoft Corporation 1996-2001. All rights reserved.

Usage: WMIWPA.wsf [/ViewProxy[+|-]] [/ProxyAddress:value] [/ProxyPort:value] [/ViewWPA[+|-]]
                  [/ActivateOffLine:value] [/ActivateOnLine:value] [/GetInstallationID:value]
                  [/SetProductKey:value] [/SetNotification:value] [/Machine:value] [/User:value]
                  [/Password:value]


Options:

ViewProxy           : View the proxy settings.
ProxyAddress        : Name of the proxy server to configure.
ProxyPort           : Port number configured on the computer for access to the proxy server specified.
ViewWPA             : View the Windows Product Activation (WPA) settings.
ActivateOffLine     : Activates the system offline using the confirmation ID provided by the Microsoft
                      Clearinghouse license server.
ActivateOnLine      : Exchanges license-related data with the Microsoft Clearinghouse license server;
                      if the method succeeds, it activates the system.
GetInstallationID   : Retrieves the installation ID which is required to activate a system offline.
SetProductKey       : Updates the system product key for a computer.
SetNotification     : Enable the notification of Number of days remaining before activation of the
                      system is required.
Machine             : Determine the WMI system to connect to. (default=LocalHost)
User                : Determine the UserID to perform the remote connection. (default=none)
Password            : Determine the password to perform the remote connection. (default=none)
Examples:

    WMIWPA.Wsf /ViewProxy+
    WMIWPA.Wsf /ProxyAddress:proxy.LissWare.Net /ProxyPort:8080

    WMIWPA.Wsf /ViewWPA+
    WMIWPA.Wsf /ActivateOffLine:[ConfirmationID]
    WMIWPA.Wsf /ActivateOnLine
    WMIWPA.Wsf /GetInstallationID
    WMIWPA.Wsf /SetProductKEY:VVVVV-WWWWW-XXXXX-YYYYY-ZZZZZ
    WMIWPA.Wsf /SetNotification+
```

Because proxy settings could be required for an on-line activation, the script also uses the *Win32_Proxy* class to configure the Windows Proxy LAN settings. As we have previously seen in Sample 3.13, this portion of the code is skipped in Sample 3.14 (skipped lines 153 through 186).

Sample 3.14 *Windows Product Activation*

```
 1:<?xml version="1.0"?>
 .:
 8:<package>
 9:  <job>
 ..:
13:    <runtime>
..:
40:    </runtime>
41:
42:    <script language="VBScript" src="..\Functions\DisplayFormattedPropertyFunction.vbs" />
43:    <script language="VBScript" src="..\Functions\TinyErrorHandler.vbs" />
44:
45:    <object progid="WbemScripting.SWbemLocator" id="objWMILocator" reference="true"/>
46:    <object progid="WbemScripting.SWbemDateTime" id="objWMIDateTime" />
47:
48:    <script language="VBscript">
49:    <![CDATA[
..:
53:    Const cComputerName = "LocalHost"
54:    Const cWMINameSpace = "Root\CIMv2"
55:    Const cWMIProxyClass = "Win32_Proxy"
56:    Const cWMIWPAClass = "Win32_WindowsProductActivation"
..:
89:    ' ----------------------------------------------------------------------------
90:    ' Parse the command line parameters
91:    If WScript.Arguments.Named.Count = 0 Then
92:       WScript.Arguments.ShowUsage()
93:       WScript.Quit
94:    End If
...:
145:    strComputerName = WScript.Arguments.Named("Machine")
146:    If Len(strComputerName) = 0 Then strComputerName = cComputerName
147:
148:    objWMILocator.Security_.AuthenticationLevel = wbemAuthenticationLevelDefault
149:    objWMILocator.Security_.ImpersonationLevel = wbemImpersonationLevelImpersonate
150:
151:    Set objWMIServices = objWMILocator.ConnectServer(strComputerName, cWMINameSpace, _
152:                                            strUserID, strPassword)
...:
186:
187:    ' ----------------------------------------------------------------------------
188:    Set objWMIInstances = objWMIServices.InstancesOf (cWMIWPAClass)
...:
191:    If objWMIInstances.Count = 1 Then
192:       For Each objWMIInstance In objWMIInstances
193:          If boolViewWPA Then
194:          Set objWMIPropertySet = objWMIInstance.Properties_
195:             For Each objWMIProperty In objWMIPropertySet
196:                DisplayFormattedProperty objWMIInstance, _
197:                                  "  " & objWMIProperty.Name, _
198:                                  objWMIProperty.Name, _
199:                                  Null
200:          Next
...:
203:          End If
```

```
204:            If boolGetInstallationID Then
205:                If objWMIInstance.ActivationRequired = 1 Then
206:                    intRC = objWMIInstance.GetInstallationID (strInstallationID)
...:
209:                    If intRC = 0 Then
210:                        WScript.Echo "Installation ID is '" & strInstallationID & "'."
211:                    Else
212:                        WScript.Echo "Failed to get Installation ID (" & intRC & ")."
213:                    End If
214:                Else
215:                    WScript.Echo "Unable to get the Installation ID " & _
216:                                 "as the Windows activation is already completed."
217:                End If
218:            End If
219:            If boolActivateOffLine Then
220:                If objWMIInstance.ActivationRequired = 1 Then
221:                    intRC = objWMIInstance.ActivateOffline (strConfirmationID)
...:
224:                    If intRC = 0 Then
225:                        WScript.Echo "Windows successfuly activated (off-line)."
226:                    Else
227:                        WScript.Echo "Failed (" & intRC & ")."
228:                    End If
229:                Else
230:                    WScript.Echo "Unable to acticate Windows " & _
231:                                 "as the Windows activation is already completed."
232:                End If
233:            End If
234:            If boolActivateOnLine Then
235:                If objWMIInstance.ActivationRequired = 1 Then
236:                    intRC = objWMIInstance.ActivateOnline()
...:
239:                    If intRC = 0 Then
240:                        WScript.Echo "Windows successfuly activated (on-line)."
241:                    Else
242:                        WScript.Echo "Failed to activate Windows (" & intRC & ")."
243:                    End If
244:                Else
245:                    WScript.Echo "Unable to acticate Windows " & _
246:                                 "as the Windows activation is already completed."
247:                End If
248:            End If
249:            If boolSetProductKEY Then
250:                If objWMIInstance.ActivationRequired = 1 Then
251:                    intRC = objWMIInstance.SetProductKey (strProductKey)
...:
254:                    If intRC = 0 Then
255:                        WScript.Echo "'" & strProductKey & "' product key successfuly set."
256:                    Else
257:                        WScript.Echo "Failed setting '" & strProductKey & _
258:                                     "' product key (" & intRC & ")."
259:                    End If
260:                Else
261:                    WScript.Echo "Unable to set the Product Key " & _
262:                                 "as the Windows activation is already completed."
263:                End If
264:            End If
265:            If Len (boolSetNotification) Then
266:                intRC = objWMIInstance.SetNotification (intSetNotificationWPA)
...:
```

```
269:                    If intRC = 0 Then
270:                        If boolSetNotification Then
271:                            WScript.Echo "WPA Notification enabled."
272:                        Else
273:                            WScript.Echo "WPA Notification disabled."
274:                        End If
275:                    Else
276:                        WScript.Echo "Failed to set WPA notification (" & intRC & ")."
277:                    End If
278:                End If
279:        Next
280:    End If
...:
286:    ]]>
287:    </script>
288:  </job>
289:</package>
```

Once the command-line parameter definitions (lines 13 through 40) and parsing (lines 89 through 146) with the WMI connection are completed (lines 148 through 152), the script executes the various operations supported by the *Win32_WindowsProductActivation* class (lines 188 through 280). First, independently of the WPA operation performed, the script retrieves all instances of the *Win32_WindowsProductActivation* class (line 188). This class is not implemented as a singleton class, but since we only have one instance of the WPA in a computer system, the script only considers the first instance available (line 191). The first supported script action displays the WPA information with the following command line:

```
 1:   C:\>WMIWPA.Wsf /ViewWPA+
 2:   Microsoft (R) Windows Script Host Version 5.6
 3:   Copyright (C) Microsoft Corporation 1996-2001. All rights reserved.
 4:
 5:      ActivationRequired: ................... 1
 6:      IsNotificationOn: ..................... 1
 7:      ProductID: ........................... 55039-986-4602466-00615
 8:      RemainingEvaluationPeriod: ........... 185
 9:      RemainingGracePeriod: ................ 14
10:      *ServerName: ......................... NET-DPEP6400
```

The script logic is shown from line 194 through 200 and does not contain any particular coding that we haven't seen before.

The next WPA-supported action is the retrieval of the *InstallationID*. When performing an off-line activation, the customer must provide an *InstallationID* to the Microsoft representative over the phone. The *InstallationID* can be retrieved with the following command line:

```
C:\>WMIWPA.Wsf /GetInstallationID
Microsoft (R) Windows Script Host Version 5.6
Copyright (C) Microsoft Corporation 1996-2001. All rights reserved.

Installation ID is '0045005297308353269457996674329602164103448469537O'.
```

The script logic is available from line 204 through 217. It is important to note that the script tests the state of the activation by verifying the value contained in the *ActivationRequired* property (line 205). This verification is made for every WPA action, since the *Win32_WindowsProductActivation* methods are only executable when the product is not activated (lines 220, 235, and 250). Next, the *GetInstallationID* method is invoked. When the execution is successful (line 209), the parameter passed during the method invocation (line 206) contains the *InstallationID* required by the Microsoft representative.

In exchange, the Microsoft representative will provide another number, which is a *ConfirmationID*, that is required to perform the off-line activation. This is the next action supported by Sample 3.14. The following command line must be used:

```
C:>WMIWPA.Wsf /ActivateOffLine:[ConfirmationID]
Microsoft (R) Windows Script Host Version 5.6
Copyright (C) Microsoft Corporation 1996-2001. All rights reserved.

Windows successfuly activated (off-line).
```

The script logic is available from line 219 through 233. Although the script follows the same logic as before, it invokes the *ActiveOffLine* method, which requires the *ConfirmationID* as parameter (line 221).

The next WPA action performs the on-line Product Activation. In this case the command line to use is:

```
C:\>WMIWPA.Wsf /ActivateOnLine
Microsoft (R) Windows Script Host Version 5.6
Copyright (C) Microsoft Corporation 1996-2001. All rights reserved.

Windows successfuly activated (on-line).
```

The script logic is available from line 234 through 248. Again, the logic is exactly the same as before. However, the *ActiveOnLine* method does not require any parameter (line 236).

While the product key is given at installation time, the *SetProductKey* method of the *Win32_WindowsProductActivation* class allows the modification of the product key before activation. The following command line must be used with a valid product key:

```
C:\>WMIWPA.Wsf /SetProductKEY:[VVVV-WWWWW-XXXXX-YYYYY-ZZZZZ]
Microsoft (R) Windows Script Host Version 5.6
Copyright (C) Microsoft Corporation 1996-2001. All rights reserved.

'VVVV-WWWWW-XXXXX-YYYYY-ZZZZZ' product key successfuly set.
```

The script logic is available from line 249 through 264. The *SetProduct-Key* method requires the product key as a parameter (line 251).

If the product is not activated, the system sends notification of the remaining days before activation is mandatory. It is possible to enable or disable this notification with the script by using the following command line:

```
C:\>WMIWPA.Wsf /SetNotification+
Microsoft (R) Windows Script Host Version 5.6
Copyright (C) Microsoft Corporation 1996-2001. All rights reserved.

WPA Notification enabled.
```

Here again, the script logic for this action is exactly the same as the previous WPA operation (lines 265 through 278). The method to configure the notification is invoked at line 266. This method requests an integer value as parameter. A value of 0 means "disable" and a value of 1 means "enable."

3.3.9   Windows Installer provider

The *Windows Installer* provider is not always available by default for all Windows platforms! To install this provider, you should perform the following tasks:

- **For Windows XP:** It is included in the system installation by default.

- **For Windows Server 2003:** From Control Panel, select Add/Remove Programs. Next, select Add/Remove Windows Components; then, in the Windows Components Wizard, select Management and Monitoring Tools (see Figure 3.7).

   Finally, select WMI *Windows Installer* provider, and then click OK. Follow the steps in the wizard to complete the installation.

- **For Windows 2000 and Windows NT 4.0:** The Windows Installer package for Windows NT 4.0 and 2000 is available at http://www.microsoft.com/downloads/release.asp?releaseid=32832.

The WMI *Windows Installer* provider allows WMI-enabled scripts or applications to access information collected from Windows Installer–compliant applications. The provider mirrors the functionality of the Windows Installer. It can read any property of a software product installation. In addition, due to the WMI architecture, the *Windows Installer* provider makes available to remote users the set of procedures that the Windows Installer

Figure 3.7
*Adding the
Windows Installer
provider under
Windows Server
2003.*

makes available to local users. This provider is implemented as an instance
and a method provider (Table 3.20).

Table 3.20   *The Windows Installer Provider*

Provider Name	Provider Namespace	Class Provider	Instance Provider	Method Provider	Property Provider	Event Provider	Event Consumer Provider	Support Get	Support Put	Support Enumeration	Support Delete	Windows Server 2003	Windows XP	Windows 2000 Server	Windows 2000 Professional	Windows NT 4.0
Windows Installer Provider																
MSIProv	Root/CIMV2		X	X				X	X	X	X	X	X	X	X	X

The Windows Installer supports more than 50 classes. Unfortunately, it
is beyond the scope of this book to review all the classes. Instead, we will
give an overview of the most important classes available with their capabilities. The classes supported by the WMI *Windows Installer* provider can be
classified into six categories.

■ **Actions:** This category contains the classes derived from the *CIM_
Action* abstract class and represents actions performed during installation, upgrade, uninstall, or application maintenance.

- **Associations:** This category contains the association classes that represent references to other WMI *Windows Installer* provider classes.

- **Checks:** This category contains the classes derived from the *CIM_ Check* abstract class and represents conditions that should be met when a software feature or element is installed.

- **Core Classes:** This category contains the most important classes, because it provides most of the software installation features.

- **External Associations:** This category contains the association classes that represent the references to **Win32** classes beyond the scope of the *Windows Installer* provider classes.

- **Settings:** This category contains the classes that represent instances of settings containing additional information about installations or their components.

Table 3.21 summarizes by category the WMI classes related to the Windows Installer.

The easiest way to get an immediate benefit from the Windows Installer via WMI is to work with the *Win32_Product* class. This class represents the Windows Installer–compliant products installed in a system. This class exposes seven methods with some parameters (Table 3.22).

Samples 3.15 through 3.17 illustrate the use of the *Win32_Product* methods. The script exposes the following command-line parameters:

```
C:\>WMIMSI.Wsf
Microsoft (R) Windows Script Host Version 5.6
Copyright (C) Microsoft Corporation 1996-2001. All rights reserved.

Usage: WMIMSI.wsf [/Action:value] [/SoftwareFeature[+|-]] [/PackageLocation:value] [/Options:value]
                  [/AllUsers[+|-]] [/TargetLocation:value] [/ReInstallMode:value]
                  [/PackageName:value] [/PackageVersion:value]
                  [/Machine:value] [/User:value] [/Password:value]

Options:

Action            : Windows Installer action to perform. Only [View], [Install], [Admin], [Advertise],
                    [ReInstall], [UnInstall] or [Upgrade]is accepted.
SoftwareFeature   : View software features associated with the Windows Installer package
                    (View action only).
PackageLocation   : Defines the Windows Installer package source path
                    (Install, Admin, Advertise and Upgrade actions only).
Options            : Command line options for the installation.
AllUsers          : Specifies if the package is installed for All Users
                    (Install and Advertise actions only).
TargetLocation    : Defines the Windows Installer package admin installation path target
                    (Admin action only).
ReInstallMode     : Defines the package reinstallation mode (Reinstall action only).
PackageName       : Name of the package (Reinstall, Upgrade and Uninstall action only).
PackageVersion    : Version of the package (Reinstall, Upgrade and Uninstall action only).
```

```
Machine          : Determine the WMI system to connect to. (default=LocalHost)
User             : Determine the UserID to perform the remote connection. (default=none)
Password         : Determine the password to perform the remote connection. (default=none)
Examples:

    WMIMSI.Wsf /Action:View
    WMIMSI.Wsf /Action:View /SoftwareFeature+
    WMIMSI.Wsf /Action:Install /PackageLocation:L:\SUPPORT\TOOLS\SUPTOOLS.MSI /AllUsers+
    WMIMSI.Wsf /Action:Admin /PackageLocation:L:\SUPPORT\TOOLS\SUPTOOLS.MSI
                        /TargetLocation:"E:\SUPTOOLS"
    WMIMSI.Wsf /Action:Advertise /PackageLocation:L:\SUPPORT\TOOLS\SUPTOOLS.MSI /AllUsers+
    WMIMSI.Wsf /Action:ReInstall /ReinstallMode:Shortcut /PackageName:"Windows Support Tools"
                        /PackageVersion:"5.1.2510.0"
    WMIMSI.Wsf /Action:Upgrade /PackageLocation:L:\SUPPORT\TOOLS\SUPTOOLS.MSI
                        /PackageName:"Windows Support Tools" /PackageVersion:"5.1.2510.0"
    WMIMSI.Wsf /Action:UnInstall /PackageName:"Windows Support Tools" /PackageVersion:"5.1.2510.0"
```

Table 3.21   *The Windows Installer WMI Classes*

Name	Comments
Actions	
Win32_BindImageAction	The BindImage action binds each executable that needs to be bound to the DLLs imported by it by computing the virtual address of each function that is imported from all DLLs. The computed virtual address is then saved in the importing image's Import Address Table (IAT). The action works on each file installed locally.
Win32_ClassInfoAction	The RegisterClassInfo action manages the registration of COM class information with the system. In the Advertise mode the action registers all COM classes for which the corresponding feature is enabled. Else the action registers COM classes for which the corresponding feature is currently selected to be installed.
Win32_CreateFolderAction	The CreateFolder action creates empty folders for components set to be installed locally. The removal of these folders is handled by the RemoveFolders action. When a folder is newly-created, it is registered with the appropriate component identifier.
Win32_DuplicateFileAction	The DuplicateFileAction allows the author to make one or more duplicate copies of files installed by the InstallFiles executable action, either to a directory different from the original file, or to the same directory, but with a different name.
Win32_ExtensionInfoAction	The ExtensionInfoAction manages the registration of extension-related information with the system. The action registers the extension servers for which the corresponding feature is currently selected to be uninstalled.
Win32_FontInfoAction	The RegisterFonts action registers installed fonts with the system. It maps the Font.FontTitle to the path of the font file installed. The RegisterFonts action is triggered when the Component to which the Font.File_ belongs is selected for install. This implies that fonts can be made private, shared or system by making the Components to which they belong so.
Win32_MIMEInfoAction	The RegisterMIMEInfo action registers the MIME-related registry information with the system. In the Advertise mode the action registers all MIME info for servers for which the corresponding feature is enabled. Else the action registers MIME info for servers for which the corresponding feature is currently selected to be installed.
Win32_MoveFileAction	The MoveFiles action allows the author to locate files that already exist on the user's machine, and move or copy those files to a new location.
Win32_PublishComponentAction	The PublishComponents action manages the advertisement of the components that may be faulted in by other products with the system. In the Advertise mode the action publishes the all components for which the corresponding feature is enabled. Else the action publishes components for which the corresponding feature is currently selected to be installed.
Win32_RegistryAction	The WriteRegistryValues action sets up registry information that the application desires in the system Registry. The registry information is gated by the Component class. A registry value is written to the system registry if the corresponding component has been set to be installed either locally or run from source.
Win32_RemoveFileAction	The RemoveFiles action uninstalls files previously installed by the InstallFiles action. Each of these files is 'gated' by a link to an entry in the Component class; only those files whose components are resolved to the iisAbsent Action state, or the iisSource Action state state IF the component is currently installed locally, will be removed. The RemoveFiles action can also remove specific author-specified files that weren't installed by the InstallFiles action. Each of these files is 'gated' by a link to an entry in the Component class; those files whose components are resolved to any 'active' Action state (i.e. not in the 'off', or NULL, state) will be removed (if the file exists in the specified directory, of course). This implies that removal of files will be attempted when the gating component is first installed, during a reinstall, and again when the gating component is removed.
Win32_RemoveIniAction	The RemoveIniValues action deletes .INI file information that the application desires to delete from .INI files. The deletion of the information is gated by the Component class. An .INI value is deleted if the corresponding component has been set to be installed either locally or run from source.
Win32_SelfRegModuleAction	The SelfRegModules action processes all the modules in the SelfReg to register the modules, if installed.
Win32_ShortcutAction	The CreateShortcuts action manages the creation of shortcuts. In the Advertise mode, the action creates shortcuts to the key files of components of features that are enabled. Advertised shortcuts are those for which the Target property is the feature of the component and the directory of the shortcut is one of the Shell folders or below one. Advertised shortcuts are created with a Microsoft installer technology Descriptor as the target. Non-advertised shortcuts are those for which the Target column in the Shortcut class is a property or the directory of the shortcut is not one of the Shell folders or below one. Advertised shortcuts are created with a Microsoft installer technology Descriptor as the target. In the non-advertise mode (normal install) the action creates shortcuts to the key files of components of features that are selected for install as well as non-advertised shortcuts whose component is selected for install.

Table 3.21 *The Windows Installer WMI Classes (continued)*

Name	Comments
Actions	
Win32_TypeLibraryAction	The RegisterTypeLibraries action registers type libraries with the system. The action works on each file referenced which is triggered to be installed.
Associations	
Win32_ActionCheck	This association relates an MSI action with any locational information it requires. This location is in the form of a file and/or directory specification.
Win32_ApplicationCommandLine	The ApplicationCommandLine association allows one to to identify connection between an application and its command-line access point.
Win32_CheckCheck	This association relates a MSI Check with any locational information it requires. The location is in the form of a file and/or directory specification.
Win32_ODBCDriverSoftwareElement	Since software elements in a ready to run state cannot transition into another state, the value of the phase property is restricted to in-state for CIM_SoftwareElement objects in a ready to run state.
Win32_ProductCheck	This association relates instances of CIM_Check and Win32_Product.
Win32_ProductResource	This association relates instances of Win32_Product and Win32_MSIResource.
Win32_ProductSoftwareFeatures	The CIM_ProductSoftwareFeatures association identifies the software features for a particular product.
Win32_SettingCheck	This association relates an Installer check with any setting information it requires.
Win32_ShortcutSAP	This association relates the connection between an application access point and the corresponding shortcut.
Win32_SoftwareElementAction	This association relates an MSI software element with an action that accesses the element.
Win32_SoftwareElementCheck	This association relates an MSI element with any condition or locational information that a feature may require.
Win32_SoftwareElementResource	This association relates an MSI feature with an action used to register and/or publish the feature.
Win32_SoftwareFeatureAction	This association relates an MSI feature with an action used to register and/or publish the feature.
Win32_SoftwareFeatureCheck	This association relates an MSI feature with any condition or locational information that a feature may require.
Win32_SoftwareFeatureParent	A generic association to establish dependency relationships between objects.
Win32_SoftwareFeatureSoftwareElements	CIM_Component is a generic association used to establish 'part of relationships between Managed System Elements. For example, the SystemComponent association defines parts of a System.
Core	
Win32_Product	Instances of this class represent products as they are installed by MSI. A product generally correlates to a single installation package.
Win32_SoftwareElement	SoftwareFeatures and SoftwareElements: A 'SoftwareFeature' is a distinct subset of a Product, consisting of one or more 'SoftwareElements'. Each SoftwareElement is defined in a Win32_SoftwareElement instance, and the association between a feature and its SoftwareFeature(s) is defined in the Win32_SoftwareFeatureSoftwareElement Association. Any component can be 'shared' between two or more SoftwareFeatures. If two or more features reference the same component, that component will be selected for installation if any of these features are selected.
Win32_SoftwareFeature	SoftwareFeatures and SoftwareElements: A 'SoftwareFeature' is a distinct subset of a Product, consisting of one or more 'SoftwareElements'. Each SoftwareElement is defined in a Win32_SoftwareElement instance, and the association between a feature and its SoftwareFeature(s) is defined in the Win32_SoftwareFeatureSoftwareElement Association. Any component can be 'shared' between two or more SoftwareFeatures. If two or more features reference the same component, that component will be selected for installation if any of these features are selected.
Checks	
Win32_Condition	The Condition class can be used to modify the selection state of any entry in the Feature class, based on a conditional expression. If Condition evaluates to True, the corresponding Levelvalue in the Feature class will be set to the value specified in the Condition class's Level column. Using this mechanism, any feature can be permanently disabled (by setting the Level to 0), set to be always installed (by setting the Level to 1), or set to a different install priority (by setting Level to an intermediate value). The Level may be set based upon any conditional statement, such as a test for platform, operating system, a particular property setting, etc.
Win32_DirectorySpecification	This class represents the directory layout for the product. Each instance of the class represents a directory in both the source image and the destination image. Directory resolution is performed during the CostFinalize action and is done as follows: Root destination directories: Root directories entries are those with a null Directory_Parent value or a irectory_Parent value identical to the Directory value. The value in the Directory property is interpreted as the name of a property defining the location of the destination directory. If the property is defined, the destination directory is resolved to the property's value. If the property is undefined, the ROOTDRIVE property is used instead to resolve the path. Root source directorires: The value of the DefaultDir column for root entries is interpreted as the name of a property defining the source location of this directory. This property must be defined or an error will occur. Non-root destination directories: The Directory value for a non-root directory is also interpreted as the name of a property defining the location of the destination. If the property is defined, the destination directory is resolved to the property's value. If the property is not defined, the destination directory is resolved to a sub-directory beneath the resolved destination directory for the Directory_Parent entry. The DefaultDir value defines the name of the sub-directory. Non-root source directories: The source directory for a non-root directory is resolved to a sub-directory of the resolved source directory for the Directory_Parent entry. Again, the DefaultDirvalue defines the name of the sub-directory.
Win32_EnvironmentSpecification	Instances of this class contain information about any environment variables that may need to be registered for their associated products installation.
Win32_FileSpecification	Each instance of this class represents a source file with itsvarious attributes, ordered by a unique, nonlocalized identifier. For uncompressed files, the File property is ignored, and the FileName column is used for both the source and destination file name. You must set the 'Uncompressed' bit of the Attributes column for any file that is not compressed in a cabinet.
Win32_IniFileSpecification	This class contains the .INI information that the application needs to set in an .INI file. The .INI file information is written out when the corresponding component has been selected to be installed, either locally or run from source.
Win32_LaunchCondition	The LaunchCondition class is used by the LaunchConditions action. It contains a list of conditions, all of which must be satisfied for the action to succeed.

Table 3.21   *The Windows Installer WMI Classes (continued)*

Name	Comments
Checks	
Win32_ODBCDataSourceSpecification	This association relates an MSI check with any setting information it requires.
Win32_ODBCDriverSpecification	This class represents any ODBC drivers that are to be installed as part of a particular product.
Win32_ODBCTranslatorSpecification	Instances of this class represent any ODBC Translators that are included as part of a products installation.
Win32_ProgIDSpecification	Instances of this class represent and ProgIDs that need to be registered durring a given installation.
Win32_ReserveCost	This optional class allows the author to 'reserve' a specified amount of disk space in any directory, depending on the installation state of a component. Reserving cost in this way could be useful for authors who want to ensure that a minimum amount of disk space will be available after the installation is completed. For example, this disk space might be reserved for user documents, or for application files (such as index files) that are created only after the application is launched following installation. The ReserveCost class also allows custom actions to specify an approximate cost for any files, registry entries, or other items, that the custom action might install.
Win32_ServiceSpecification	Instances of this class represent the services that are to be installed along with an associated package.
Win32_SoftwareElementCondition	Instances of this class represent conditional checks that must be evaluated to TRUE before their associated Win32_SoftwareElement can be installed.
External Associations	
Win32_InstalledSoftwareElement	The InstalledSoftwareElement association allows one to to identify the Computer System a particular Software element is installed on.
Win32_ServiceSpecificationService	Represents instances of Win32_ServiceSpecification and Win32_Service.
Settings	
Win32_Binary	Instances of this class represent binary information (such as bitmaps, icons, executables, etc.) that are used by an installation.
Win32_MSIResource	Represents any resources that are used by the Installer during the course of an installation, patch, or upgrade.
Win32_ODBCAttribute	The Setting class represents configuration-related and operational parameters for one or more ManagedSystemElement(s). A ManagedSystemElement may have multiple Setting objects associated with it. The current operational values for an Element's parameters are reflected by properties in the Element itself or by properties in its associations. These properties do not have to be the same values present in the Setting object. For example, a modem may have a Setting baud rate of 56Kb/sec but be operating at 19.2Kb/sec.
Win32_ODBCSourceAttribute	The Setting class represents configuration-related and operational parameters for one or more ManagedSystemElement(s). A ManagedSystemElement may have multiple Setting objects associated with it. The current operational values for an Element's parameters are reflected by properties in the Element itself or by properties in its associations. These properties do not have to be the same values present in the Setting object. For example, a modem may have a Setting baud rate of 56Kb/sec but be operating at 19.2Kb/sec.
Win32_Patch	Instances of this class represent individual patches that are to be applied to a particular file and whose source resides at a specified location.
Win32_PatchPackage	The PatchPackage class describes all patch packages that have been applied to this product. For each patch package, the unique identifier for the patch is provided, along with information about the media image the on which the patch is located.
Win32_Property	This table contains the property names and values for all defined properties in the installation. Properties with Null values are not present in the table.
Win32_ServiceControl	Instances of this class represent instructions for controlling both installed and uninstalled services.

Table 3.22   *The Win32_Product Class Methods*

Method name	Comments
Admin	
PackageLocation	The path to the package that is to be administrated.
TargetLocation	The location for the administrative image to be installed.
Options	The command-line options for the upgrade.
Advertise	
PackageLocation	The path to the package that is to be administrated.
Options	The command-line options for the upgrade.
AllUsers	Indicates whether the operation should be applied to the current user (FALSE) or all users on the machine (TRUE).
Configure	
InstallState	Default, Local, Source
InstallLevel	Default, Minimum, Maximum
Install	
PackageLocation	The path to the package that is to be administrated.
Options	The command-line options for the upgrade.
AllUsers	Indicates whether the operation should be applied to the current user (FALSE) or all users on the machine (TRUE).
Reinstall	
ReinstallMode	Perform the package installation in the specified mode. The mode can be one of the following values: FileMissing (1), FileOlderVersion (2), FileEqualVersion (3), FileExact (4), FileVerify (5), FileReplace (6), UserData (7), MachineData(8), Shortcut (9), Package (10).
Uninstall	
-	
Upgrade	
PackageLocation	The command-line options for the upgrade.
Options	Indicates whether the operation should be applied to the current user (FALSE) or all users on the machine (TRUE).

The first portion of the script is shown in Sample 3.15. Written in Jscript, and similar to previous scripts, this sample starts with the command-line parameter definitions (skipped lines 13 through 39) and parsing (skipped lines 92 through 246). Next, it contains the coding logic to display information about the installed Windows Installer–compliant applications (lines 263 through 359).

Sample 3.15   *Managing Windows Installer packages (Part I)*

```
  1:<?xml version="1.0"?>
  .:
  8:<package>
  9:  <job>
 ..:
 13:    <runtime>
 ..:
 39:    </runtime>
 40:
 41:    <script language="VBScript" src="..\Functions\DecodeInstallStateFunction.vbs" />
 42:
 43:    <script language="VBScript" src="..\Functions\DisplayFormattedPropertyFunction.vbs" />
 44:    <script language="VBScript" src="..\Functions\TinyErrorHandler.vbs" />
 45:
 46:    <object progid="WbemScripting.SWbemLocator" id="objWMILocator" reference="true"/>
 47:    <object progid="WbemScripting.SWbemDateTime" id="objWMIDateTime" />
 48:
 49:    <script language="JScript">
 50:    <![CDATA[
 51:
 52:    var cComputerName = "LocalHost";
 53:    var cWMINameSpace = "Root/CIMv2";
 54:    var cWMIClass = "Win32_Product";
 55:
 56:    var cVIEW = 1;
 57:    var cADMIN = 2;
 58:    var cADVERTISE = 3;
 59:    var cINSTALL = 4;
 60:    var cREINSTALL = 5;
 61:    var cUNINSTALL = 6;
 62:    var cUPGRADE = 7;
 ..:
 92:    // ----------------------------------------------------------------------------
 93:    // Parse the command line parameters
 94:    if (WScript.Arguments.Named.Count == 0)
 95:        {
 96:        WScript.Arguments.ShowUsage();
 97:        WScript.Quit();
 98:        }
...:
242:    strComputerName = WScript.Arguments.Named("Machine");
243:    if (strComputerName == null)
244:        {
245:        strComputerName = cComputerName;
246:        }
247:
248:    objWMILocator.Security_.AuthenticationLevel = wbemAuthenticationLevelDefault;
249:    objWMILocator.Security_.ImpersonationLevel = wbemImpersonationLevelImpersonate;
250:
251:    try
```

```
252:      {
253:      objWMIServices = objWMILocator.ConnectServer(strComputerName, cWMINameSpace,
254:                                          strUserID, strPassword);
255:      }
...:
261:   switch (intAction)
262:         {
263:         // VIEW -------------------------------------------------------------------
264:         case cVIEW:
265:              try
266:                {
267:                objWMIInstances = objWMIServices.InstancesOf (cWMIClass);
268:                }
...:
274:              enumWMIInstances = new Enumerator (objWMIInstances);
275:              for (;! enumWMIInstances.atEnd(); enumWMIInstances.moveNext())
276:                  {
277:                  objWMIInstance = enumWMIInstances.item();
278:
279:                  WScript.Echo ("- " + objWMIInstance.Caption + " " + strDashes);
280:                  objWMIPropertySet = objWMIInstance.Properties_;
281:                  enumWMIPropertySet = new Enumerator (objWMIPropertySet);
282:                  for (;! enumWMIPropertySet.atEnd(); enumWMIPropertySet.moveNext())
283:                      {
284:                      objWMIProperty = enumWMIPropertySet.item();
285:
286:                      switch (objWMIProperty.Name)
287:                          {
288:                          case "Caption":
289:                               break;
290:
291:                          case "InstallState":
292:                               DisplayFormattedProperty (objWMIInstance,
293:                                      "  " + objWMIProperty.Name,
294:                                      InstallState (objWMIProperty.Value),
295:                                      null);
296:                               break;
297:                          default:
298:                               DisplayFormattedProperty (objWMIInstance,
299:                                      "  " + objWMIProperty.Name,
300:                                      objWMIProperty.Name,
301:                                      null);
302:                          }
303:                      }
304:
305:                  if (boolSoftwareFeature)
306:                      {
307:                      try
308:                        {
309:                        objWMIAssocInstances = objWMIServices.ExecQuery
310:                                      ("Associators of {" +
311:                                      objWMIInstance.Path_.RelPath + "} Where " +
312:                                      "ResultClass=Win32_SoftwareFeature");
313:                        }
...:
319:                      if (objWMIAssocInstances.Count != 0)
320:                          {
321:                          enumWMIAssocInstances = new Enumerator (objWMIAssocInstances);
322:                          for(;!enumWMIAssocInstances.atEnd();enumWMIAssocInstances.moveNext())
323:                              {
324:                              objWMIAssocInstance = enumWMIAssocInstances.item();
325:
326:                              WScript.Echo ("\n - Software feature for '" +
```

```
327:                                    objWMIInstance.Caption + "' " + strDashes);
328:                          objWMIPropertySet = objWMIAssocInstance.Properties_;
329:                          enumWMIPropertySet = new Enumerator (objWMIPropertySet);
330:                      for(;! enumWMIPropertySet.atEnd(); enumWMIPropertySet.moveNext())
331:                              {
332:                                  objWMIProperty = enumWMIPropertySet.item();
333:
334:                              switch (objWMIProperty.Name)
335:                                  {
336:                                  case "Caption":
337:                                      break;
338:
339:                                  case "InstallState":
340:                                      DisplayFormattedProperty (objWMIAssocInstance,
341:                                          "  " + objWMIProperty.Name,
342:                                          InstallState (objWMIProperty.Value),
343:                                          null);
344:                                      break;
345:                                  default:
346:                                      DisplayFormattedProperty (objWMIAssocInstance,
347:                                          "  " + objWMIProperty.Name,
348:                                          objWMIProperty.Name,
349:                                          null);
350:                                  }
351:                              }
352:                          }
353:                      }
354:                  }
355:
356:              WScript.Echo();
357:              }
358:
359:          break;
...:
...:
...:
```

Although Jscript is used, the logic from a WMI standpoint is exactly the same as used in many previous scripts. The script requests the collection of instances available from the *Win32_Product* class (line 267). Next, it creates an enumerator object to display properties of each *Win32_Product* instance (lines 280 through 303). If the **/SoftwareFeature+** switch is given on the command line, the script displays some extra information from the *Win32_SoftwareFeature* class, which is associated with the *Win32_Product* class (Figure 3.8).

Figure 3.8
The classes associated with the Win32_Product class.

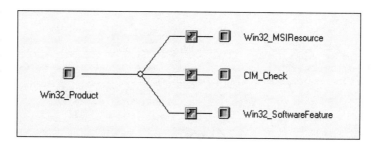

Once the collection of associated instances is created, the properties of each associated instance available in the collection are displayed (lines 306 through 354).

The result obtained for the Microsoft Support Tools Windows Installer package is as follows:

```
 1:   C:\>WMIMSI.Wsf /Action:View /SoftwareFeature+ /Machine:MyRemoteSystem.LissWare.Net
 2:   Microsoft (R) Windows Script Host Version 5.6
 3:   Copyright (C) Microsoft Corporation 1996-2001. All rights reserved.
 4:
 5:   - Windows Support Tools ------------------------------------------------------------
 6:     Description: ......................... Windows Support Tools
 7:     *IdentifyingNumber: ................... {8398B542-3CC4-44D9-83DF-696CCE70124B}
 8:     InstallDate: ......................... 20020127
 9:     InstallDate2: ........................ 27-01-2002
10:     InstallState: ........................ Installed
11:     *Name: ............................... Windows Support Tools
12:     PackageCache: ........................ C:\WINDOWS\Installer\566eb2.msi
13:     Vendor: .............................. Microsoft Corporation
14:     *Version: ............................ 5.1.2510.0
15:
16:     - Software feature for 'Windows Support Tools' -------------------------------------
17:       Accesses: ............................ 0
18:       Attributes: .......................... 17
19:       Description: ......................... Minimum tools that would be installed.
20:       *IdentifyingNumber: ................... {8398B542-3CC4-44D9-83DF-696CCE70124B}
21:       InstallDate: ......................... 27-01-2002
22:       InstallState: ........................ Local
23:       LastUse: ............................. 19800000******.000000+***
24:       *Name: ............................... FeRequired
25:       *ProductName: ........................ Windows Support Tools
26:       Vendor: .............................. Microsoft Corporation
27:       *Version: ............................ 5.1.2510.0
28:
29:     - Software feature for 'Windows Support Tools' -------------------------------------
30:       Accesses: ............................ 0
31:       Attributes: .......................... 17
32:       Description: ......................... Windows Support Tools
33:       *IdentifyingNumber: ................... {8398B542-3CC4-44D9-83DF-696CCE70124B}
34:       InstallState: ........................ Local
35:       LastUse: ............................. 19800000******.000000+***
36:       *Name: ............................... FeFullKit
37:       *ProductName: ........................ Windows Support Tools
38:       Vendor: .............................. Microsoft Corporation
39:       *Version: ............................ 5.1.2510.0
40:
41:     - Software feature for 'Windows Support Tools' -------------------------------------
42:       Accesses: ............................ 0
43:       Attributes: .......................... 17
44:       Description: ......................... These are all optional tools.
45:       *IdentifyingNumber: ................... {8398B542-3CC4-44D9-83DF-696CCE70124B}
46:       InstallState: ........................ Absent
47:       LastUse: ............................. 19800000******.000000+***
48:       *Name: ............................... FeOptional
49:       *ProductName: ........................ Windows Support Tools
50:       Vendor: .............................. Microsoft Corporation
51:       *Version: ............................ 5.1.2510.0
```

Because WMI is DCOM based, it is possible to access the information available from a remote Windows Installer instance. This remains valid for any methods exposed by the *Win32_Product* class. The next portion of the script sample (Sample 3.16) addresses the Installation, the Admin Installation, and the Advertisement of a Windows Installer–compliant application. The use of these methods in combination with the **/Machine** switch and the **/User** and **/Password** switches allows the installation of the Windows Installer package on a remote computer from the command line. This is exactly where WMI leverages the power of the Windows Installer, since the Windows Installer is local only.

Sample 3.16   *Managing Windows Installer packages (Part II)*

```
...:
...:
...:
359:            break;
360:        // INSTALL ----------------------------------------------------------------
361:        case cINSTALL:
362:            objWMIClass = objWMIServices.Get (cWMIClass);
363:            WScript.Echo ("Installing ...");
364:
365:            intRC = objWMIClass.Install (strPackageLocation,
366:                                         strOptions,
367:                                         boolAllUsers);
368:            if (intRC == 0)
369:                {
370:                WScript.Echo ("Package '" + strPackageLocation + " successfuly installed.");
371:                }
372:            else
373:                {
374:                WScript.Echo ("Failed to install package '" + strPackageLocation +
375:                        "' (" + intRC + ").");
376:                }
377:
378:            break;
379:        // ADMIN ------------------------------------------------------------------
380:        case cADMIN:
381:            objWMIClass = objWMIServices.Get (cWMIClass);
382:            WScript.Echo ("Installing ...");
383:
384:            intRC = objWMIClass.Admin (strPackageLocation,
385:                                       strTargetLocation,
386:                                       strOptions);
387:            if (intRC == 0)
388:                {
389:                WScript.Echo ("Admin installation of package '" + strPackageLocation +
390:                        "' successfuly completed.");
391:                }
392:            else
393:                {
394:                WScript.Echo ("Failed to install package '" + strPackageLocation +
395:                        "' (" + intRC + ").");
396:                }
397:
398:            break;
399:        // ADVERTISE --------------------------------------------------------------
```

```
400:            case cADVERTISE:
401:                objWMIClass = objWMIServices.Get (cWMIClass);
402:                WScript.Echo ("Advertising ...");
403:
404:                intRC = objWMIClass.Advertise (strPackageLocation,
405:                                               strTargetLocation,
406:                                               boolAllUsers);
407:                if (intRC == 0)
408:                   {
409:                    WScript.Echo ("Package '" + strPackageLocation +
410:                                  "' successfuly advertised.");
411:                   }
412:                else
413:                   {
414:                    WScript.Echo ("Failed to advertise package '" + strPackageLocation +
415:                                  "' (" + intRC + ").");
416:                   }
417:
418:                break;
...:
...:
...:
```

Because these three operations do not relate to a specific application package, the three *Win32_Product* methods ("Install," "Admin," and "Advertise") are defined in the CIM repository as static methods (*Static* qualifier). This justifies the class instance creation at line 362 for the Installation, at line 381 for the Admin Installation, and at line 401 for the Advertisement. For these three operations, the script logic is exactly the same in each case. Based on the command-line parameters given, the corresponding method with its set of parameters is invoked. Note that the **/Options** command-line parameter corresponds to some optional command-line parameters specific to the Windows Installer–compliant package (see Table 3.22).

The last portion of the script is shown in Sample 3.17 and shows the script logic to use the *Reinstall,* the *Uninstall,* and the *Upgrade* methods of the *Win32_Product* class. Note that these methods are specific to a *Win32_Product* instance. This is why the script starts by retrieving the Windows Installer application that corresponds to the **/PackageName** and **/Package-Version** command-line switches (lines 423 through 426 for the "Reinstall," lines 467 through 470 for the "Uninstall," and lines 511 through 514 for the "Upgrade").

Sample 3.17   *Managing Windows Installer packages (Part III)*

```
...:
...:
...:
418:                break;
419:            // REINSTALL --------------------------------------------------------------
420:            case cREINSTALL:
421:                try
422:                   {
```

```
423:                    objWMIInstances = objWMIServices.ExecQuery
424:                                        ("Select * From " + cWMIClass +
425:                                         " Where Name='" + strPackageName +
426:                                         "' And Version='" + strPackageVersion + "'");
427:                    }
...:
433:                if (objWMIInstances.Count != 0)
434:                    {
435:                    WScript.Echo ("Found package '" + strPackageName +
436:                                    "' (" + strPackageVersion + ") ... Reinstalling ...");
437:
438:                    enumWMIInstances = new Enumerator (objWMIInstances);
439:                    for (;! enumWMIInstances.atEnd(); enumWMIInstances.moveNext())
440:                        {
441:                        objWMIInstance = enumWMIInstances.item();
442:
443:                        intRC = objWMIInstance.ReInstall (intReinstallMode);
444:                        if (intRC == 0)
445:                            {
446:                            WScript.Echo ("Package '" + strPackageName +
447:                                            "' successfuly reinstalled.");
448:                            }
449:                        else
450:                            {
451:                            WScript.Echo ("Failed to reinstall package '" + strPackageName +
452:                                            "' (" + intRC + ").");
453:                            }
454:                        }
455:                    }
456:                else
457:                    {
458:                    WScript.Echo ("Package '" + strPackageName +
459:                                    "' (" + strPackageVersion + ") not found.");
460:                    }
461:
462:                break;
463:            // UNINSTALL -----------------------------------------------------------------
464:            case cUNINSTALL:
465:                try
466:                    {
467:                    objWMIInstances = objWMIServices.ExecQuery
468:                                        ("Select * From " + cWMIClass +
469:                                         " Where Name='" + strPackageName +
470:                                         "' And Version='" + strPackageVersion + "'");
471:                    }
...:
477:                if (objWMIInstances.Count != 0)
478:                    {
479:                    WScript.Echo ("Found package '" + strPackageName +
480:                                    "' (" + strPackageVersion + ") ... Uninstalling ...");
481:
482:                    enumWMIInstances = new Enumerator (objWMIInstances);
483:                    for (;! enumWMIInstances.atEnd(); enumWMIInstances.moveNext())
484:                        {
485:                        objWMIInstance = enumWMIInstances.item();
486:
487:                        intRC = objWMIInstance.UnInstall();
488:                        if (intRC == 0)
489:                            {
490:                            WScript.Echo ("Package '" + strPackageName +
491:                                            "' successfuly uninstalled.");
492:                            }
493:                        else
```

```
494:                              {
495:                                  WScript.Echo ("Failed to uninstall package '" + strPackageName +
496:                                            "' (" + intRC + ").");
497:                              }
498:                        }
499:                  }
500:            else
501:                  {
502:                  WScript.Echo ("Package '" + strPackageName +
503:                            "' (" + strPackageVersion + ") not found.");
504:                  }
505:
506:            break;
507:            // UPGRADE -----------------------------------------------------------------
508:            case cUPGRADE:
509:                  try
510:                        {
511:                        objWMIInstances = objWMIServices.ExecQuery
512:                                          ("Select * From " + cWMIClass +
513:                                           " Where Name='" + strPackageName +
514:                                           "' And Version='" + strPackageVersion + "'");
515:                        }
...:
521:                  if (objWMIInstances.Count != 0)
522:                        {
523:                        WScript.Echo ("Found package '" + strPackageName +
524:                                  "' (" + strPackageVersion + ") ... Upgrading ...");
525:
526:                        enumWMIInstances = new Enumerator (objWMIInstances);
527:                        for (;! enumWMIInstances.atEnd(); enumWMIInstances.moveNext())
528:                              {
529:                              objWMIInstance = enumWMIInstances.item();
530:
531:                              intRC = objWMIInstance.Upgrade (strPackageLocation,
532:                                                  strOptions);
533:                              if (intRC == 0)
534:                                    {
535:                                    WScript.Echo ("Package '" + strPackageLocation +
536:                                              "' successfuly upgraded.");
537:                                    }
538:                              else
539:                                    {
540:                                    WScript.Echo ("Failed to upgrade package '" + strPackageName +
541:                                              "' (" + intRC + ").");
542:                                    }
543:                              }
544:                        }
545:                  else
546:                        {
547:                        WScript.Echo ("Package '" + strPackageName +
548:                                  "' (" + strPackageVersion + ") not found.");
549:                        }
550:                  }
...:
552:      ]]>
553:      </script>
554:  </job>
555:</package>
```

Whether the requested Windows Installer action is to reinstall, uninstall, or upgrade an existing package, the script always uses the same technique. It is important to note that the *Win32_Product* key uses three properties as a key. The following output shows the three keys (lines 7, 11, and 14):

```
 1:  C:\>WMIMSI.Wsf /Action:View /SoftwareFeature+ /Machine:MyRemoteSystem.LissWare.Net
 2:  Microsoft (R) Windows Script Host Version 5.6
 3:  Copyright (C) Microsoft Corporation 1996-2001. All rights reserved.
 4:
 5:  - Windows Support Tools --------------------------------------------------------------
 6:    Description: ......................... Windows Support Tools
 7:    *IdentifyingNumber: ................... {8398B542-3CC4-44D9-83DF-696CCE70124B}
 8:    InstallDate: ......................... 20020127
 9:    InstallDate2: ........................ 27-01-2002
10:    InstallState: ........................ Installed
11:    *Name: ............................... Windows Support Tools
12:    PackageCache: ........................ C:\WINDOWS\Installer\566eb2.msi
13:    Vendor: .............................. Microsoft Corporation
14:    *Version: ............................ 5.1.2510.0
```

Although it is possible to supply the three keys on the command line to locate the corresponding *Win32_Product* instance, you will note that the *IdentifyingNumber* property key is not really easy to type from a command line (GUID number). For the script user facility, the code requests only the *Name* and the *Version* property key of the package. By using a WQL query, the script locates the corresponding Windows Installer application (lines 423 through 426 for an install, lines 467 through 470 for an uninstall, and lines 511 through 514 for an upgrade). For these three operations, the script logic is exactly the same in each case. Based on the supplied command-line parameters, the corresponding method with its set of parameters is invoked.

Since WMI is event driven, it is, of course, possible to monitor a package installation with the use of an appropriate WQL event query. Since this provider is not implemented as an event provider, the WQL event query requires the use of the **WITHIN** statement. The principle to detect the installation of a software product is quite easy, since it consists of tracking down the creation of the *Win32_Product* instances. For example, the WQL query to use would be as follows:

```
Select * From __InstanceCreationEvent Within 10 Where TargetInstance ISA 'Win32_Product'
```

3.3.10 Resultant Set of Policies (RSOP) providers

Have you ever dreamed of how good it would be to know if a specific Group Policy Object (GPO) is applied in the user or computer environment? Well, with the WMI implementation of the *Resultant Set of Policies* (RSOP), this is possible. The RSOP is the set of GPOs effectively applied to a particular user, once logged on, or computer, once booted. The rules that determine if a particular GPO will be applied to a specific user or computer environment are complex. Briefly, the rules are determined by:

- The GPO container location in the Active Directory hierarchy (Local, Site, Domain, or Organizational Unit)

- The rights granted on the GPO for the object being considered for application of the considered GPO

- The WMI filter that applies for the GPO in question

- The order of the GPO at the container level, since one container may contain several GPO definitions or links (the one at the bottom of the list is the one with the highest priority)

As a consequence, the end result of the GPO application can vary widely. To discover the GPO that is applied or could be applied (simulation) to a particular object, the Windows XP and Windows Server 2003 Operating Systems contain two WMI providers that calculate the RSOP (see Table 3.23). Next, two additional providers expose complementary information about the GPO itself. They are not directly related to RSOP providers, but we will see that they can be useful in an RSOP context as well.

Table 3.23   *The RSOP Providers*

Provider Name	Provider Namespace	Class Provider	Instance Provider	Method Provider	Property Provider	Event Provider	Event Consumer Provider	Support Get	Support Put	Support Enumeration	Support Delete	Windows Server 2003	Windows XP	Windows 2000 Server	Windows 2000 Professional	Windows NT 4.0
Resultant Set Of Policies Providers																
Rsop Planning Mode Provider	Root/RSOP			X								X	X			
Rsop Logging Mode Provider	Root/RSOP			X								X	X			
PolicSOM provider	Root/Policy							X	X		X	X	X			
PolicStatus provider	Root/Policy							X				X	X			

The two RSOP providers are located in the **Root\RSOP** namespace and are implemented as method providers. The two providers enabling complementary information about the GPO are located in the **Root\Policy** namespace. We will come back to these two providers later while examining the next script sample.

Before examining any methods or classes available, it is interesting to note that under Windows Server 2003, WMI is utilized at two different levels for the GPO.

- First, a WQL query can be used to filter the GPO appliance. Under Windows 2000, the only way to filter GPO is to create specific rights on the GPO Active Directory object. Based on the granted rights or the group memberships, the GPO is applied to a considered object. Although this way of filtering GPO is still available in Windows Server 2003, it is also possible to filter the GPO by creating a WQL query, called a WMI filter. WMI filters are nothing other than WQL data queries used to verify if there are items in the system matching the specified query. If the query result is positive, the GPO will be applied on the computer or user in question. Obviously, the knowledge of WQL is quite useful in creating these WMI filters. Figure 3.9 shows a WMI filter example for the Default Domain Controller Policy.

In Figure 3.9, we see that the WQL data query searches for systems that have the Windows SNMP service installed. With such a

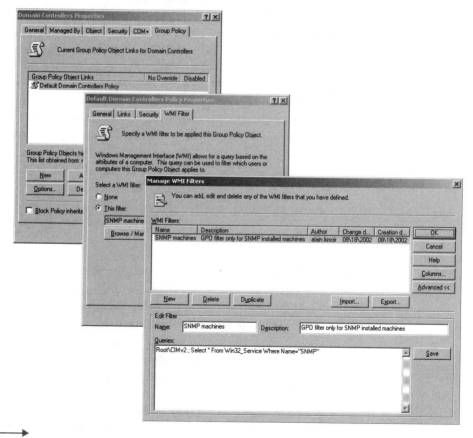

Figure 3.9   *A WMI filter created for the Default Domain Controller Policy.*

query, only the systems that have the SNMP service installed will have the Default Domain Controller Policy applied. You will note the particular syntax, which combines the WMI namespace and WQL data query separated by a semicolumn. This syntax is not WQL specific but is just the way the information is stored in the GPO infrastructure.

- Second, WMI can be used to calculate the RSOP. Out of the box, Windows Server 2003 and Windows XP offer an MMC snap-in to analyze the RSOP. This MMC snap-in is called the "Resultant Set of Policies" snap-in. Basically this snap-in uses the two WMI providers presented in Table 3.23. In parallel to this MMC snap-in included in Windows Server 2003, Microsoft is currently developing another MMC snap-in to centrally manage the Group Policies. This MMC is called *Group Policies Management Console* (GPMC) and offers interesting functionalities to manage policies from one single interface despite the fact that GPOs are coming from different Sites, Domains or Forests. GPMC also makes use of the *RSOP* WMI providers to calculate the Resultant Set Of Policies. Beyond these functionalities, GPMC also implements an object model to manage the GPO from scripts. However, this scriptable object model has no relationship with WMI. At writing time, GPMC is still under development, therefore, more information is available through the Microsoft beta program (although GPMC is supposed to be widely available when Windows Server 2003 is released). With the help of these *RSOP* providers, and based on the GPO structure, we will see how we can develop a script to retrieve the GPO information and how to determine if some specific GPOs are applied in a specific environment.

It is important to understand that the *RSOP* providers can be used in two modes, as follows:

- **The Planning mode:** Supported by the *RSOP Planning mode* provider, this mode simulates a snapshot of the policy data that could be present on a computer or user environment by using data from Active Directory. This provider supports one single class called the *RsopPlanningModeProvider* class. This class consists of two methods, as shown in Table 3.24. The *RsopCreateSession* method creates a simulated snapshot of the policy data from a particular container (Site, Domain, or Organizational Unit) for a particular user or computer. For the simulation, it is also possible to specify a group membership and a WMI filter for the considered user or computer. The RSOP MMC snap-in, mentioned before, comes with a wizard to collect the various parameters. Behind the scene, the snap-in uses the *RsopCreateSession* method to produce a Planning mode RSOP result. Of course, we can develop a script to produce an RSOP simulated result, but the script will simply duplicate the functionality provided by the MMC snap-in. Although technically feasible, from a management perspective, writing such a script will not provide any added value compared with the MMC snap-in.

Table 3.24   *The RSOP Classes and Their Methods*

Name	Type	Comments
RsopPlanningModeProvider		
RsopCreateSession	Static Method	Takes a snapshot of actual policy data for display by the RSoP UI.
RsopDeleteSession	Static Method	Deletes the snapshot of policy data made by RsopCreateSession when the data is no longer required by the RSoP UI.
RsopEnumerateUsers	Static Method	Returns the list of users whose policy data is available in logging mode.
RsopPlanningModeProvider		
RsopCreateSession	Static Method	Generates planning mode policy data.
RsopDeleteSession	Static Method	Deletes planning mode policy data.

- **The Logging mode:** Supported by the *RSOP Logging mode* provider, this mode takes a snapshot of the policy data that is present on a computer or user environment. This provider supports a single class called the *RsopLoggingModeProvider* class. This class consists of three methods, as shown in Table 3.24. The *RsopCreateSession* method takes a snapshot of the policy data, which allows any application to display the RSOP data before the system overwrites or deletes it during a refresh of the policy. This mode is the most interesting one from a scripting perspective.

To understand how to work with the RSOP data, it is important to know how it is stored. We saw that the two classes for the Logging and Planning mode are available from the **Root\RSOP** namespace. To examine Logging mode RSOP data in a Windows XP or Windows Server 2003 computer, we must look at another specific namespace. Here we must make a clear distinction between two types of Logging mode RSOP data, as follows:

- The RSOP data as is once the user is logged on or when the computer is booted. In such a case, the RSOP data is available from some precreated WMI namespaces in the CIM repository. The first namespace available is the **Root\RSOP\Computer** namespace, which exposes information about the GPOs applied on the computer. Other namespaces available include the **Root\RSOP\User\<SID>** namespace, which exposes information about the GPOs applied to users who logged on to the computer system. As you can see, the namespace uses the SID of the user in its name! The **Root\RSOP\User\<SID>**

namespace is created only during the user profile creation. If the namespace is deleted, it will not be recreated until the user profile is recreated, which means that the user profile must be deleted to recreate this namespace. However, once the namespace is created, the namespace is accordingly updated at logon time to reflect the GPOs applied on the user profile. Note that when the user profile is deleted, the **RSOP** namespace corresponding to the deleted user profile is also deleted. Figure 3.10 shows an example of the namespaces available.

Figure 3.10
The RSOP subnamespaces.

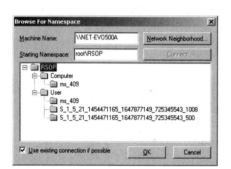

- The RSOP data that will be applied during the next policy refresh, which does not necessarily represent the applied GPO after boot or logon. The resulting *RSOP* data, as it will look after the next refresh, can be created with the *RsopCreateSession* method. The RSOP information will be stored in a dedicated namespace especially created for that purpose. To create the RSOP data for a user, it is important that the selected user has already logged on to the system. This implies that a namespace, **Root\RSOP\User\<SID>**, already exists. In such a case, the *CreateSession* method of the *RsopLoggingModeProvider* class can be invoked. Basically, when you execute the MMC *RSOP* snap-in in Logging mode, the snap-in invokes the *CreateSession* method of the *RsopLoggingModeProvider* class. The requested information will be available from this dedicated namespace. Figure 3.11 shows an example of the namespaces available.

Compared with Figure 3.10, a new namespace, called **NS1C0CCE73_BF05_41C9_935F_C12435CF9196**, is created. The subnamespaces of this namespace contain the requested information for each environment (Computer and User).

In both cases, these namespaces contain a collection of classes that represents the set of GPOs that are applied or will be applied during the next refresh cycle. Requesting instances of these classes show if a particular GPO

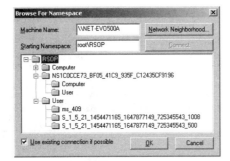

Figure 3.11
*The RSOP
subnamespaces
created during a
CreateSession
method invocation.*

is, or will be, effectively applied in the specified environment. The RSOP classes available are summarized in Table 3.25.

Table 3.25   *The RSOP WMI Classes*

Name		Comments
Group Policy Core Classes		
RSOP_ExtensionEventSource	Dynamic	Represents client-side extensions' event log message sources.
RSOP_ExtensionEventSourceLink	Dynamic	Represents the association between a client-side extension's event log message source and the extension's status.
RSOP_ExtensionStatus	Dynamic	Provides information about the overall status a client-side extension's processing of policy.
RSOP_GPO	Dynamic	Provides information about a GPO.
RSOP_Session	Dynamic	Represents an RSoP session. There can be only one instance of this class per namespace.
RSOP_SOM	Dynamic	Represents a scope of management (SOM) which can be a site, domain, organizational unit, or local scope.
RSOP_GPLink	Association	Represents the links from a site, domain, organizational unit, or local scope, to one or more GPOs.
Policy Setting Template Classes		
RSOP_PolicySetting	Dynamic	The class from which client-side extensions' policy objects are inherited. An instance of this class corresponds to a specific policy setting.
RSOP_PolicySettingStatus	Dynamic	Provides a link to an event in the event log that corresponds to an error that occurred while applying a specific policy setting.
RSOP_PolicySettingLink	Association	Represents the association between a policy setting and the setting's status.
Registry Policy Classes		
RSOP_AdministrativeTemplateFile	Dynamic	Represents an administrative template (.adm) file.
RSOP_RegistryPolicySetting	Dynamic	Represents the policy object for registry or administrative template extension.
Application Management Policy Classes		
RSOP_ApplicationManagementCategory	Dynamic	Represents the list of programs in the Add or Remove Programs Control Panel utility.
RSOP_ApplicationManagementPolicySetting	Dynamic	Represents the policy data for application management extension.
Folder Redirection and Script Policy Classes		
RSOP_FolderRedirectionPolicySetting	Dynamic	Provides information about a folder-redirection extension.
RSOP_ScriptCmd	Dynamic	Represents a script command and its parameters.
RSOP_ScriptPolicySetting	Dynamic	Represents a script setting.
Security Policy Classes (Only available in the Computer RSOP namespace)		
RSOP_AuditPolicy	Dynamic	Represents the security setting for a local group policy that relates to the auditing of an event type. Events can include, among others, system events and account management events.
RSOP_File	Dynamic	Represents a security policy setting that defines the access permissions and audit settings for a securable file system object.
RSOP_RegistryKey	Dynamic	Represents a security policy setting that defines the access permissions and audit settings for a particular registry key.
RSOP_RegistryValue	Dynamic	Represents specific security-related registry values.
RSOP_RestrictedGroup	Dynamic	Represents a security policy setting that defines the members of a restricted (security-sensitive) group.
RSOP_SecurityEventLogSettingBoolean	Dynamic	Represents a security policy setting that determines whether or not guests can access the system, application and security event logs.
RSOP_SecurityEventLogSettingNumeric	Dynamic	Represents a security policy setting that determines numeric properties related to the system, application and security event logs. Properties include the number of days to retain entries and maximum log size.

Table 3.25   *The RSOP WMI Classes (continued)*

Name		Comments
Security Policy Classes (Only available in the Computer RSOP namespace)		
RSOP_SecuritySettingBoolean	Dynamic	Represents the Boolean security setting for an account policy. Account policies include password policies and account lockout policies.
RSOP_SecuritySettingNumeric	Dynamic	Represents the numeric security setting for an account policy. Account policies include password policies, account lockout policies, and Kerberos-related policies.
RSOP_SecuritySettings	Dynamic	Abstract class from which other RSoP security classes derive. Instances of this class are not logged. RSOP_SecuritySettings derives from the RSOP_PolicySetting class.
RSOP_SecuritySettingString	Dynamic	Represents the string security setting for an account policy.
RSOP_SystemService	Dynamic	Represents the security policy setting that defines the start-up mode and access permissions for a particular system service.
RSOP_UserPrivilegeRight	Dynamic	Represents the security setting for a local group policy that relates to the assignment of a particular user privilege.
IEAK Policy Classes		
RSOP_IEAdministrativeTemplateFile	Dynamic	Represents the abstraction for an administrative template (.adm) file for Microsoft Internet Explorer.
RSOP_IEAKPolicySetting	Dynamic	Represents the policy data for general settings related to management and customization of Internet Explorer.
RSOP_IEAuthenticodeCertificate	Dynamic	Represents the details of customized settings for Internet Explorer that designate software publishers and credentials agencies as trustworthy.
RSOP_IEConnectionDialUpCredentials	Dynamic	Represents the settings used by the RasDial function when establishing a dial-up (remote access) connection to the Internet using Internet Explorer.
RSOP_IEConnectionDialUpSettings	Dynamic	Contains the details of a phone-book entry for connecting to the Internet; corresponds to the RASENTRY structure.
RSOP_IEConnectionSettings	Dynamic	Represents the details of an Internet connection made using Internet Explorer, including details related to auto-configuration.
RSOP_IEConnectionWinINetSettings	Dynamic	Represents the settings used by the RasDial function to establish a remote access connection to the Internet using the Microsoft Win32® Internet (WinInet) application programming interface (API).
RSOP_IEFavoriteItem	Dynamic	Represents an item or folder in a user's Internet Explorer Favorites list.
RSOP_IEFavoriteOrLinkItem	Dynamic	Parent class from which Internet Explorer Favorites, Favorite folders, and Link toolbar items (Links) are inherited.
RSOP_IELinkItem	Dynamic	Represents an Internet Explorer Links bar item (a Link).
RSOP_IEPrivacySettings	Dynamic	Represents the privacy settings imported for the Internet security zone.
RSOP_IEProgramSettings	Dynamic	Contains details about the imported programs to use for Internet Explorer.
RSOP_IEProxySettings	Dynamic	Represents the details of a proxy server connection for Internet Explorer.
RSOP_IERegistryPolicySetting	Dynamic	Represents the abstraction for registry extension policy data for Internet Explorer.
RSOP_IESecurityContentRatings	Dynamic	Represents customized settings or attributes related to security content ratings that should be used with Internet Explorer.
RSOP_IESecurityZoneSettings	Dynamic	Represents customized settings or attributes to use with Internet Explorer for a particular security zone.
RSOP_IEToolbarButton	Dynamic	Represents the toolbar button object for Internet Explorer.
RSOP_IEConnectionDialUpCredentialsLink	Association	Represents the association between an Internet Explorer Administration Kit (IEAK) policy setting and the dial-up credentials for a given Internet Explorer Internet connection.
RSOP_IEConnectionDialUpSettingsLink	Association	Represents the association between an IEAK policy setting and its imported dial-up settings for a specific connection of Internet Explorer to the Internet.
RSOP_IEConnectionSettingsLink	Association	Represents the association between an IEAK policy setting and the policy's Internet connection settings.
RSOP_IEConnectionWinINetSettingsLink	Association	Represents the association between an IEAK policy setting and WinInet connection settings for a remote access connection to the Internet.
RSOP_IEFavoriteItemLink	Association	Represents the association between an IEAK policy setting and an item or folder in a user's Internet Explorer Favorites list.
RSOP_IEImportedProgramSettings	Association	Represents the association between an IEAK policy setting and its imported program settings for Internet Explorer.
RSOP_IELinkItemLink	Association	Represents the association between an IEAK policy setting and an item in a user's Internet Explorer Links bar.
RSOP_IEToolbarButtonLink	Association	Represents the association between an IEAK policy setting and a custom Internet Explorer toolbar button.
Access Method Classes		
RsopLoggingModeProvider	Dynamic	Contains methods that the RSoP UI calls to take a snapshot of actual policy data in the logging mode.
RsopPlanningModeProvider	Dynamic	Contains methods that the RSoP UI calls to create resultant policy data in a what-if (planning mode) scenario.

Note that the Security Policy classes are only available from the **Root\RSOP\Computer** namespace. The easiest way to verify whether a particular GPO is applied to a User or a Computer is to check if we have instances of the *RSOP_PolicySetting* class or one of its child classes (see Figure 3.12). This is due to the fact that an instance of the *RSOP_PolicySetting* class corresponds to a specific GPO setting.

Figure 3.12
*The RSOP_*
PolicySetting
superclass.

Since some of these classes are associated with other classes that represent the specific settings of the GPO, by using the WMI associations in place it is possible to retrieve any type of information related to the applied GPO. For example, the *RSOP_IEAKPolicySetting*, which represents the GPO for the general settings related to management and customization of Internet Explorer, is associated with the collection of classes shown in Figure 3.13.

Now let's see how we script with the *RSOP* providers and the RSOP classes. The following scripts (Samples 3.18 through 3.24) retrieve the RSOP instances from a chosen RSOP class. If one or more instances of the *RSOP_PolicySetting* (or one of its child classes) are available, the script will display the GPO information available from the RSOP data. If the given class does not have any instance, it means that the selected GPO class is not applied for that particular environment. The following script sample supports these command-line parameters:

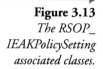

Figure 3.13
*The RSOP_
IEAKPolicySetting
associated classes.*

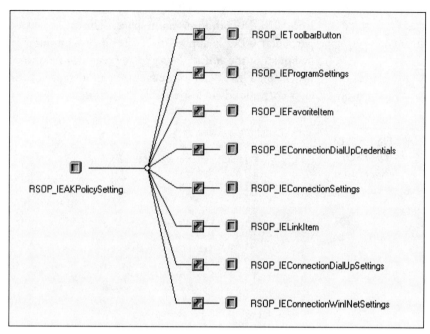

```
C:\>WMIRSOP.wsf
Microsoft (R) Windows Script Host Version 5.6
Copyright (C) Microsoft Corporation 1996-2001. All rights reserved.

Usage: WMIRSOP.wsf /GPOClass:value [/UserRSOP:value] [/UserRSOPOnly[+|-]] [/ComputerRSOPOnly[+|-]]
                  [/GPOFullInfo[+|-]] [/NewRSOPSession[+|-]]
                  [/Machine:value] [/User:value] [/Password:value]

Options:

GPOClass          : WMI class name of the GPO to retrieve from RSOP.
UserRSOP          : Specifies User RSOP data to retrieve.
UserRSOPOnly      : Retrieve applied User GPO only.
ComputerRSOPOnly  : Retrieve applied Computer GPO only.
GPOFullInfo       : Display all GPO information.
NewRSOPSession    : Retrieve GPO information from a new RSOP session in logging mode.
Machine           : Determine the WMI system to connect to. (default=LocalHost)
User              : Determine the UserID to perform the remote connection. (default=none)
Password          : Determine the password to perform the remote connection. (default=none)
Examples:

    WMIRSOP.Wsf /GPOClass:RSOP_SystemService /UserRSOP:Alain.Lissoir
                /SIDResolutionDC:MyDC.LissWare.Net
    WMIRSOP.Wsf /GPOClass:RSOP_SystemService /UserRSOP:Alain.Lissoir /GPOFullInfo+
                /SIDResolutionDC:MyDC.LissWare.Net
    WMIRSOP.Wsf /GPOClass:RSOP_IEAKPolicySetting /UserRSOP:Alain.Lissoir /UserRSOPOnly+
                /SIDResolutionDC:MyDC.LissWare.Net
    WMIRSOP.Wsf /GPOClass:RSOP_IEAKPolicySetting /UserRSOP:Alain.Lissoir /UserRSOPOnly+
                /GPOFullInfo+ /SIDResolutionDC:MyDC.LissWare.Net
    WMIRSOP.Wsf /GPOClass:RSOP_SystemService /ComputerRSOPOnly+
                /SIDResolutionDC:MyDC.LissWare.Net
```

```
WMIRSOP.Wsf /GPOClass:RSOP_SystemService /ComputerRSOPOnly+ /GPOFullInfo+
            /SIDResolutionDC:MyDC.LissWare.Net
WMIRSOP.Wsf /GPOClass:RSOP_SystemService /NewRSOPSession+ /UserRSOP:Alain.Lissoir
            /SIDResolutionDC:MyDC.LissWare.Net
WMIRSOP.Wsf /GPOClass:RSOP_SystemService /NewRSOPSession+ /UserRSOP:Alain.Lissoir
            /GPOFullInfo+ /SIDResolutionDC:MyDC.LissWare.Net
WMIRSOP.Wsf /GPOClass:RSOP_IEAKPolicySetting /NewRSOPSession+ /UserRSOP:Alain.Lissoir
            /UserRSOPOnly+ /SIDResolutionDC:MyDC.LissWare.Net
WMIRSOP.Wsf /GPOClass:RSOP_IEAKPolicySetting /NewRSOPSession+ /UserRSOP:Alain.Lissoir
            /UserRSOPOnly+ /GPOFullInfo+ /SIDResolutionDC:MyDC.LissWare.Net
WMIRSOP.Wsf /GPOClass:RSOP_SystemService /NewRSOPSession+ /ComputerRSOPOnly+
            /SIDResolutionDC:MyDC.LissWare.Net
WMIRSOP.Wsf /GPOClass:RSOP_SystemService /NewRSOPSession+ /ComputerRSOPOnly+ /GPOFullInfo+
            /SIDResolutionDC:MyDC.LissWare.Net
```

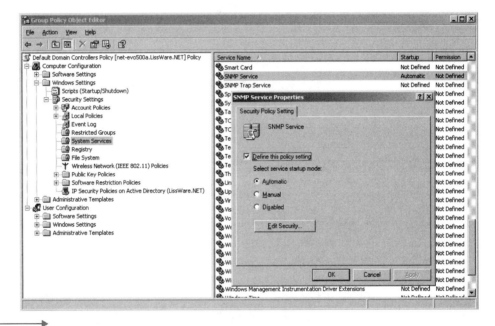

Figure 3.14 *A GPO to enforce the automatic startup of the SNMP Windows service at the organizational unit level.*

If a GPO is created to enforce the automatic startup of the SNMP Windows service, as shown in Figure 3.14, and if the script is started with the following command line, the obtained output would be as follows:

```
1:   C:\>WMIRSOP.Wsf /GPOClass:RSOP_SystemService /UserRSOP:Alain.Lissoir
                                                  /SIDResolutionDC:MyDC.LissWare.Net
2:   Microsoft (R) Windows Script Host Version 5.6
3:   Copyright (C) Microsoft Corporation 1996-2001. All rights reserved.
4:
5:   - GPO for Brussels Site (RSOP_SystemService) -----------------------------------------------
6:     creationTime: ........................ 01-01-2000
7:     ErrorCode: ........................... 0
8:     GPOID: ............................... CN={A252ACD2-2F93-44B5-ACBF-7948EC5B7080},
```

```
 9:                                                 CN=Policies,CN=System,DC=LissWare,DC=Net
10:     id: ..................................... {244AD6A8-5315-43ED-9810-E6C55FA15127}
11:     name: .................................
12:     *precedence: .......................... 2
13:     SDDLString: ........................... D:AR(A;;CCDCLCSWRPWPDTLOCRSDRCWDWO;;;BA)
14:                                                 (A;;CCDCLCSWRPWPDTLOCRSDRCWDWO;;;SY)
15:                                                 (A;;CCLCSWLOCRRC;;;IU)S:
16:                                                 (AU;FA;CCDCLCSWRPWPDTLOCRSDRCWDWO;;;WD)
17:     *Service: ............................. SNMP
18:     SOMID: ................................ 2
19:     StartupMode: .......................... 2
20:     Status: ............................... 0
21:
22:   - Default Domain Controllers Policy (RSOP_SystemService) --------------------------------
23:     creationTime: ......................... 01-01-2000
24:     ErrorCode: ............................ 0
25:     GPOID: ................................ CN={6AC1786C-016F-11D2-945F-00C04fB984F9},
26:                                                 CN=Policies,CN=System,DC=LissWare,DC=Net
27:     id: ................................... {83884976-3D07-4983-83A8-D115ADF7C777}
28:     name: .................................
29:     *precedence: .......................... 1
30:     SDDLString: ........................... D:AR(A;;CCDCLCSWRPWPDTLOCRSDRCWDWO;;;BA)
31:                                                 (A;;CCDCLCSWRPWPDTLOCRSDRCWDWO;;;SY)
32:                                                 (A;;CCLCSWLOCRRC;;;IU)
33:                                                 S:(AU;FA;CCDCLCSWRPWPDTLOCRSDRCWDWO;;;WD)
34:     *Service: ............................. SNMP
35:     SOMID: ................................ 4
36:     StartupMode: .......................... 2
37:     Status: ............................... 1
38:
39:   The 'RSOP_SystemService' GPO class does not exist in the User RSOP data.
```

Several remarks must be made about this output. First, we note that two GPOs are listed (from lines 5 and 22) instead of one. Actually, Figure 3.14 only shows the GPO settings of the "Default Domain Controllers Policy," but, in reality, a second policy exists at the Brussels site level, as shown in Figure 3.15.

Next, we see that the GPO applied at the site level has a precedence of 2 (line 12), while the same GPO applied at the OU level has a precedence of 1. This means that the GPO at the organizational unit (OU) level (highest priority) overwrites the one at the site level (lowest priority). Keep in mind that the last applied GPO is the winner. With this in mind, it makes sense, since the GPO application order is the Local GPO first, the Site GPO next, the Domain GPO, and finally the OU GPO.

Next, we see that the *StartupMode* property (lines 19 and 36) has a value of 2, which means an automatic service startup (2=Automatic, 3=Manual, and 4=Disabled) for this particular policy. This property is defined at the level of the *RSOP_SystemService* class (look at the WMI origin definition of the property in the CIM repository).

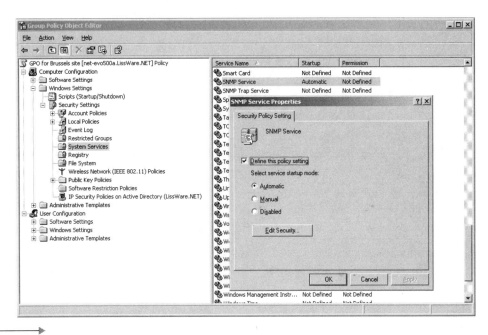

Figure 3.15   *A GPO to enforce the automatic startup of the SNMP Windows service at the site level.*

Based on the GPO application order, we know that only the GPO at the OU level is applied. This information is seen by looking at the *Status* property. The GPO at the site level has a status of 0 (line 20), while the GPO at the OU level has a status of 1 (line 37). By looking at the CIM origin definition of the *Status* property, we know that this property is defined at the level of the *RSOP_SecuritySettings* class. The *Status* property can take several values, as summarized in Table 3.26.

Table 3.26   *The Status Property of the RSOP_SecuritySettings Class*

Value	Comments
0	The system did not attempt to configure the setting.
1	The system successfully applied the policy setting for the specific item.
3	The system attempted to configure a specific policy setting but the configuration was not successful.
4	The system attempted to configure the child of a specific policy setting, but the configuration was not successful. Note that this value is valid only for configuration of file system or registry ACLs.

Based on Table 3.26, we see that the *Status* property reflects the GPO application, since the only GPO with a status of 1 (successfully applied) is the one at the OU level.

It is interesting to note that the *RSOP_SystemService* class is not available from the User environment. This makes sense, since this GPO is a Computer GPO only (line 39).

Now, if we delete the GPO SNMP Windows service setting at the OU level, the only remaining GPO is the one at the site level. Once the GPO has been refreshed, the same script execution will show the following output:

```
 1:   C:\>WMIRSOP.Wsf /GPOClass:RSOP_SystemService /UserRSOP:Alain.Lissoir
                                          /SIDResolutionDC:MyDC.LissWare.Net
 2:   Microsoft (R) Windows Script Host Version 5.6
 3:   Copyright (C) Microsoft Corporation 1996-2001. All rights reserved.
 4:
 5:   - GPO for Brussels Site (RSOP_SystemService) ------------------------------------------
 6:      creationTime: ........................ 01-01-2000
 7:      ErrorCode: ........................... 0
 8:      GPOID: ............................... CN={A252ACD2-2F93-44B5-ACBF-7948EC5B7080},
 9:                                             CN=Policies,CN=System,DC=LissWare,DC=Net
10:      id: .................................. {0F317256-2812-48AB-B3F5-B4C49943BF54}
11:      name: ...............................
12:      *precedence: ......................... 1
13:      SDDLString: .......................... D:AR(A;;CCDCLCSWRPWPDTLOCRSDRCWDWO;;;BA)
14:                                             (A;;CCDCLCSWRPWPDTLOCRSDRCWDWO;;;SY)
15:                                             (A;;CCLCSWLOCRRC;;;IU)
16:                                             S:(AU;FA;CCDCLCSWRPWPDTLOCRSDRCWDWO;;;WD)
17:      *Service: ............................ SNMP
18:      SOMID: ............................... 2
19:      StartupMode: ......................... 2
20:      Status: .............................. 1
21:
22:   The 'RSOP_SystemService' GPO class does not exist in the User RSOP data.
```

We clearly see that the status of the GPO at the site level has changed from 0 to 1 (line 20) and that the precedence has changed from 2 to 1 (line 12).

There are many other properties available from the RSOP classes, and each of these will vary with the GPO. The purpose of this book is not to reproduce the information contained in the Microsoft SDK. Fortunately, the Microsoft SDK gives all the required information about these classes and their properties, but note that the WMI RSOP information is not available from the WMI SDK section. You must look in the "Group Policy Reference" of the "Policies and Profiles" section, in the "Setup and System Administration" general section. During the script sample discussion, we will review some of the characteristics of these classes.

Samples 3.18 through 3.24 contain the full script working with the *RSOP Logging mode* provider. As with the previous script samples, it starts with the command-line definition (skipped lines 13 through 40) and parsing (lines 101 through 153). However, the WMI connection is a bit unsual, since the script must deal with several namespaces (lines 155 through 241).

Sample 3.18   *Retrieving RSOP information from an applied GPO (Part I)*

```
  1:<?xml version="1.0"?>
  .:
  8:<package>
  9:  <job>
 ..:
 13:    <runtime>
 ..:
 40:    </runtime>
 41:
 42:    <script language="VBScript" src="..\Functions\GetSIDFromUserIDFunction.vbs" />
 43:    <script language="VBScript" src="..\Functions\GetUserIDFromSIDFunction.vbs" />
 44:    <script language="VBScript" src="..\Functions\ReplaceStringFunction.vbs" />
 45:    <script language="VBScript" src="..\Functions\DisplayFormattedPropertyFunction.vbs" />
 46:    <script language="VBScript" src="..\Functions\DisplayFormattedPropertiesFunction.vbs" />
 47:    <script language="VBScript" src="..\Functions\TinyErrorHandler.vbs" />
 48:
 49:    <object progid="WbemScripting.SWbemLocator" id="objWMILocator" reference="true"/>
 50:    <object progid="WbemScripting.SWbemDateTime" id="objWMIDateTime" />
 51:
 52:    <script language="VBscript">
 53:    <![CDATA[
 ..:
 57:    Const cComputerName = "LocalHost"
 58:    Const cWMIRSOPNameSpace = "Root\RSOP"
 59:    Const cWMIPolicyNameSpace = "Root\Policy"
 60:    Const cWMIRSOPUserNameSpace = "Root\RSOP\User"
 61:    Const cWMIRSOPComputerNameSpace = "Root\RSOP\Computer"
 62:    Const cWMIADNameSpace = "Root\Directory\LDAP"
 63:    Const cWMIRSOPLoggingModeClass = "RsopLoggingModeProvider"
 64:
 65:    ' Diagnostic mode provider flags
 66:    Const cFLAG_NO_USER = &h00000001          ' Don't get any user data
 67:    Const cFLAG_NO_COMPUTER = &h00000002      ' Don't get any machine data
 68:    Const cFLAG_FORCE_CREATENAMESPACE = &h00000004  ' Recreate the namespace for this snapshot.
 ..:
101:    ' ----------------------------------------------------------------------------
102:    ' Parse the command line parameters
103:    If WScript.Arguments.Named.Count = 0 Then
104:       WScript.Arguments.ShowUsage()
105:       WScript.Quit
106:    End If
...:
149:    strComputerName = WScript.Arguments.Named("Machine")
150:    If Len(strComputerName) = 0 Then strComputerName = cComputerName
151:
152:    strSIDResolutionDC = WScript.Arguments.Named("SIDResolutionDC")
153:    If Len(strSIDResolutionDC) = 0 Then strSIDResolutionDC = strComputerName
154:
155:    objWMILocator.Security_.AuthenticationLevel = wbemAuthenticationLevelDefault
156:    objWMILocator.Security_.ImpersonationLevel = wbemImpersonationLevelImpersonate
157:
158:    ' Connect to Root\RSOP namespace to invoke RSOP Query available or create new one.
159:    Set objWMIRSOPServices = objWMILocator.ConnectServer(strComputerName, _
```

```
160:                                                   cWMIRSOPNameSpace, _
161:                                                   strUserID, _
162:                                                   strPassword)
...:
165:      ' Connect to Root\Policy namespace to gather more information about SOM
166:      Set objWMIPolicyServices = objWMILocator.ConnectServer(strComputerName, _
167:                                                   cWMIPolicyNameSpace, _
168:                                                   strUserID, _
169:                                                   strPassword)
...:
172:      Set objWMIRSOPClass = objWMIRSOPServices.Get (cWMIRSOPLoggingModeClass)
...:
175:      ' Verify the correct User RSOP namespaces -------------------------------------------
176:      If boolComputerRSOPOnly = False Then
177:          strUserSIDRSOP = GetSIDFromUserID (strUserRSOP, _
178:                                             strSIDResolutionDC, _
179:                                             strUserID, _
180:                                             strPassword)
181:          If CheckIfRSOPLoggingModeData (objWMIRSOPClass, strUserSIDRSOP) = False Then
182:              WScript.Echo "Requested RSOP data for '" & strUserRSOP & _
183:                           "' user is not available."
184:
185:              objWMIRSOPClass.RsopEnumerateUsers arrayUserSID, intRC
...:
188:              If intRC = 0 Then
189:                  WScript.Echo vbCRLF & "Only the following users are " & _
190:                              "available for RSOP Logging mode:" & vbCRLF
191:                  For Each strUserSID In arrayUserSID
192:                      WScript.Echo "  " & GetUserIDFromSID (strUserSID, _
193:                                                          strSIDResolutionDC, _
194:                                                          strUserID, _
195:                                                          strPassword) & _
196:                                                          " -> " & strUserSID
197:                  Next
198:              End If
199:
200:              WScript.Quit
201:          End If
202:      End If
203:
...:
...:
...:
```

The WMI connection is first established with the **Root\RSOP** namespace. This allows access to the various methods of the *RsopLogging-ModeProvider* class (lines 155 through 162). Next, a second WMI connection is established with the WMI **Root\Policy** namespace (lines 165 through 169). This namespace exposes classes that contain some relevant information about the Scope of Management (SOM), which will be discussed later. Next, the script retrieves an instance of the *RsopLogging-ModeProvider* class (line 172). It is interesting to note that an instance of the class must be created, since the exposed methods are static methods (*Static* qualifier).

Once the *RsopLoggingModeProvider* class instance is retrieved, the script verifies that the user name given on the command line with the **/UserRSOP** switch has a corresponding **Root\RSOP\<SID>** namespace (lines 175 through 202). To perform this verification, the script first retrieves the SID of the given user with the GetSIDFromUserID() function (lines 177 through 180). The GetSIDFromUserID() and the GetSIDFromUserID() functions were developed when examining the *Win32_UserAccount* class (see Sample 2.67, "Retrieving the SID from the UserID," and Sample 2.68, "Retrieving the UserID from the SID"). Because these functions can establish a WMI connection to another system to perform the UserID to SID and SID to UserID resolution, the script accepts the **/SIDResolutionDC** switch to select the DC to use. If this switch is not given, the **/Machine** switch value is used, which is the accessed system for the RSOP information.

Once the SID is known, the script invokes the CheckIfRSOPLogging-ModeData() function to check if the **Root\RSOP\<SID>** namespace exists. This function is based on the *RsopEnumerateUsers* method of the *RsopLoggingModeProvider* class (Table 3.24). We will examine this function in Sample 3.24. If the given user has no corresponding **Root\RSOP\<SID>** namespace, the script retrieves the list of namespaces available with the *RsopEnumerateUsers* method (line 185) and displays these namespaces with their corresponding user names (lines 189 through 197).

However, if a **Root\RSOP\<SID>** namespace corresponds to the given user, the script continues its execution (Sample 3.19). The next step creates a new *RSOP* session if the switch **/NewRSOPSession+** is given on the command line.

Sample 3.19 *Retrieving RSOP information from an applied GPO (Part II)*

```
...:
...:
...:
203:
204:    ' Build the correct RSOP namespaces ------------------------------------------------------
205:    If boolNewRSOPSession Then
206:        If boolUserRSOPOnly = True And boolComputerRSOPOnly = False Then
207:            intFlags = cFLAG_FORCE_CREATENAMESPACE Or cFLAG_NO_COMPUTER
208:        End If
209:        If boolUserRSOPOnly = False And boolComputerRSOPOnly = True Then
210:            intFlags = cFLAG_FORCE_CREATENAMESPACE Or cFLAG_NO_USER
211:        End If
212:        If boolUserRSOPOnly = False And _
213:            boolComputerRSOPOnly = False Then
214:            intFlags = cFLAG_FORCE_CREATENAMESPACE
215:        End If
216:
```

```
217:        WScript.Echo "Creating new RSOP Logging mode session ..."
218:
219:        objWMIRSOPClass.RsopCreateSession intFlags, _
220:                                          strUserSIDRSOP, _
221:                                          strTempNameSpace, _
222:                                          intRC, _
223:                                          intExtendedInfo
...:
226:        If intRC = 0 Then
227:            WScript.Echo "New RSOP Logging mode session created." & vbCRLF
228:
229:            strWMIRSOPUserNameSpace = strTempNameSpace & "\User"
230:            strWMIRSOPComputerNameSpace = strTempNameSpace & "\Computer"
231:        Else
232:            WScript.Echo "Unable to create a new RSOP Logging mode session. " & _
233:                         "(0x" & Hex(IntRC) & ")."
234:            WScript.Quit
235:        End If
236:    Else
237:        strWMIRSOPUserNameSpace = cWMIRSOPUserNameSpace & "\" & strUserSIDRSOP
238:        ReplaceString strWMIRSOPUserNameSpace, "-", "_"
239:
240:        strWMIRSOPComputerNameSpace = cWMIRSOPComputerNameSpace
241:    End If
242:
...:
...:
...:
```

In this case, based on the presence of the **/ComputerRSOPOnly+** and the **/UserRSOPOnly+** switches, the script will determine the flags to use for the *RsopCreateSession* method invocation. Table 3.27 summarizes the various flag values. By default, if none of these switches is given on the command line, the script will request both User and Computer RSOP information.

Table 3.27   *The Logging Mode and Planning Mode Flag Values*

Name	Value	Description
Loggin mode provider flags		
FLAG_NO_USER	0x1	Don't get any user data
FLAG_NO_COMPUTER	0x2	Don't get any machine data
FLAG_FORCE_CREATENAMESPACE	0x4	Delete and recreate the namespace for this snapshot.
Planning mode provider flags		
FLAG_NO_GPO_FILTER	0x80000000	GPOs are not filtered, implies FLAG_NO_CSE_INVOKE
FLAG_NO_CSE_INVOKE	0x40000000	Only GP processing done for planning mode
FLAG_ASSUME_SLOW_LINK	0x20000000	Planning mode RSoP assumes slow link
FLAG_LOOPBACK_MERGE	0x10000000	Planning mode RSoP assumes merge loop back
FLAG_LOOPBACK_REPLACE	0x8000000	Planning mode RSoP assumes replace loop back
FLAG_ASSUME_USER_WQLFILTER_TRUE	0x4000000	Planning mode RSoP assumes all comp filters to be true
FLAG_ASSUME_COMP_WQLFILTER_TRUE	0x2000000	Planning mode RSoP assumes all user filters to be true
Error codes		
RSOP_USER_ACCESS_DENIED	0x1	User accessing the RSoP provider doesn't have access to user data.
RSOP_COMPUTER_ACCESS_DENIED	0x2	User accessing the RSoP provider doesn't have access to computer data.
RSOP_TEMPNAMESPACE_EXISTS	0x4	This user is an interactive nonadmin user, the temp snapshot namespace already exists, and the FLAG_FORCE_CREATENAMESPACE was not passed in.

When creating a new *RSOP* session, it is possible to select the *RSOP* information for only the user or for only the computer environment. The flag combination determines the *RSOP* data requested (lines 206 through 215). Because a new *RSOP* session creates a temporary namespace (see Figure 3.11), the temporary namespace name is returned in one of the method parameters (line 221). If the method invocation is successful (line 226), the temporary namespaces for the User (line 229) and the Computer RSOP data are initialized (line 230).

If the **/NewRSOPSession+** switch is not supplied on the command line, the script initializes the namespace names in order to work with the RSOP data available in the **Root\RSOP\Computer** and **Root\RSOP\User\<SID>** namespaces (lines 237 through 240). Note the replacement of the dash (-), which exists in the SID by an underscore (_) (line 238). This character replacement must be done, because WMI uses the SID of the user with underscores instead of dashes to name the namespace.

Once completed, the script is ready to connect to the required **RSOP** namespaces to examine the User and/or the Computer RSOP data in Logging mode from the current session or from a new session, since the namespace names are initialized accordingly (Sample 3.20).

Sample 3.20   *Retrieving RSOP information from an applied GPO (Part III)*

```
...:
...:
...:
242:
243:    ' Get the RSOP Computer data --------------------------------------------------------
244:    If boolUserRSOPOnly = False Then
245:        ' Connect to RSOP computer namespace
246:        Set objWMIRSOPComputerServices = objWMILocator.ConnectServer(strComputerName, _
247:                                                     strWMIRSOPComputerNameSpace, _
248:                                                     strUserID, _
249:                                                     strPassword)
...:
252:        Set objWMIRSOPInstances = objWMIRSOPComputerServices.InstancesOf (strWMIGPOClass)
...:
255:        If objWMIRSOPInstances.Count Then
256:            If Err.Number Then
257:                WScript.Echo "The '" & strWMIGPOClass & "' GPO class does not " & _
258:                        "exist in the computer RSOP data." & vbCRLF
259:                Err.Clear
260:            Else
261:                DisplayRSOPInstances objWMIPolicyServices, _
262:                                objWMIRSOPComputerServices, _
263:                                objWMIRSOPInstances, _
264:                                boolGPOFullInfo
265:            End If
266:        Else
267:            WScript.Echo "No computer RSOP data the '" & strWMIGPOClass & _
```

```
268:                         "' GPO class." & vbCRLF
269:          End If
...:
274:      End If
275:
...:
...:
...:
```

To examine the RSOP Computer information, the principle is quite simple. First, the script connects to the corresponding namespace (lines 246 through 249). Next, it requests all instances available from the RSOP class given on the command line (line 252). If there is at least one instance available (line 255), it means that a GPO exists for this class. Next, the related information is displayed (lines 261 through 264) via the DisplayRSOPInstances() function. This function will be examined in Sample 3.23.

To retrieve the RSOP User information, the principle is exactly the same as the RSOP Computer information. Only the namespace is different (Sample 3.21).

Sample 3.21   *Retrieving RSOP information from an applied GPO (Part IV)*

```
...:
...:
...:
275:
276:    ' Get the RSOP User data -----------------------------------------------------------
277:    If boolComputerRSOPOnly = False Then
278:        ' Connect to RSOP user namespace
279:        Set objWMIRSOPUserServices = objWMILocator.ConnectServer(strComputerName, _
280:                                                    strWMIRSOPUserNameSpace, _
281:                                                    strUserID, _
282:                                                    strPassword)
...:
285:        Set objWMIRSOPInstances = objWMIRSOPUserServices.InstancesOf (strWMIGPOClass)
...:
288:        If objWMIRSOPInstances.Count Then
289:            If Err.Number Then
290:                WScript.Echo "The '" & strWMIGPOClass & "' GPO class does not " & _
291:                         "exist in the User RSOP data." & vbCRLF
292:                Err.Clear
293:            Else
294:                DisplayRSOPInstances objWMIPolicyServices, _
295:                             objWMIRSOPUserServices, _
296:                             objWMIRSOPInstances, _
297:                             boolGPOFullInfo
298:            End If
299:        Else
300:            WScript.Echo "No user RSOP data for the '" & strWMIGPOClass & _
301:                         "' GPO class." & vbCRLF
302:        End If
303:
304:        Set objWMIRSOPInstances = Nothing
305:
```

```
306:          Set objWMIRSOPUserServices = Nothing
307:     End If
308:
...:
...:
...:
```

Before completion, if a new RSOP session was created, the script deletes the temporary namespace to ensure that the CIM repository is cleaned up (Sample 3.22). The *RsopDeleteSession* method of the *RsopLoggingModeProvider* class will delete the temporary namespace (line 311).

Sample 3.22   *Retrieving RSOP information from an applied GPO (Part V)*

```
...:
...:
...:
308:
309:     ' Delete new session RSOP namespace -------------------------------------------------------
310:     If boolNewRSOPSession Then
311:         objWMIRSOPClass.RsopDeleteSession strTempNameSpace, _
312:                                           intRC
...:
315:         If intRC = 0 Then
316:             WScript.Echo "New RSOP Logging mode session deleted."
317:         Else
318:             WScript.Echo "Unable to delete the new RSOP " & _
319:                          "Logging mode session. (0x" & Hex(IntRC) & ")."
320:         End If
321:     End If
322:
...:
...:
...:
```

For each RSOP data (Computer and User), the DisplayRSOPInstances() is invoked (Sample 3.23). To display the RSOP information, the script uses an enumeration technique (lines 345 through 462), since the RSOP instances are retrieved as a collection of instances.

Sample 3.23   *Retrieving RSOP information from an applied GPO (Part VI)*

```
...:
...:
...:
329:
330:     ' -------------------------------------------------------------------------------------------
331:     Function DisplayRSOPInstances (objWMIPolicyServices, _
332:                                    objWMIRSOPServices, _
333:                                    objWMIRSOPInstances, _
334:                                    boolGPOFullInfo)
...:
345:         For Each objWMIRSOPInstance In objWMIRSOPInstances
346:             Set objWMIGPOInstance = objWMIRSOPServices.Get ("RSOP_GPO.id='" & _
347:                                                             objWMIRSOPInstance.GPOID & "'")
```

```
...:
350:             WScript.Echo "- " & objWMIGPOInstance.Name & _
351:                          " (" & objWMIRSOPInstance.Path_.Class & ") " & _
352:                          String (60, "-")
353:
354:             Set objWMIPropertySet = objWMIRSOPInstance.Properties_
355:             For Each objWMIProperty In objWMIPropertySet
356:                DisplayFormattedProperty objWMIRSOPInstance, _
357:                                         "   " & objWMIProperty.Name, _
358:                                         objWMIProperty.Name, _
359:                                         Null
360:             Next
...:
363:             Set objWMIAssocInstances = objWMIRSOPServices.ExecQuery _
364:                                        ("Associators of {" & _
365:                                         objWMIRSOPInstance.Path_.RelPath & "}")
366:
367:             For Each objWMIAssocInstance In objWMIAssocInstances
368:                WScript.Echo vbCRLF & "  - " & objWMIAssocInstance.Path_.Class & _
369:                             "  " & String (60, "-")
370:                Set objWMIPropertySet = objWMIAssocInstance.Properties_
371:                For Each objWMIProperty In objWMIPropertySet
372:                   DisplayFormattedProperty objWMIAssocInstance, _
373:                                            "   " & objWMIProperty.Name, _
374:                                            objWMIProperty.Name, _
375:                                            Null
376:                Next
...:
378:             Next
...:
382:             If boolGPOFullInfo Then
383:                WScript.Echo vbCRLF & "  - Complementary GPO information (" & _
384:                             objWMIGPOInstance.Path_.Class & ") " & String (60, "-")
385:
386:                Set objWMIPropertySet = objWMIGPOInstance.Properties_
387:                For Each objWMIProperty In objWMIPropertySet
388:                   Select Case objWMIProperty.Name
389:                        Case "securityDescriptor"
390:
391:                        Case Else
392:                           DisplayFormattedProperty objWMIGPOInstance, _
393:                                                    "   " & objWMIProperty.Name, _
394:                                                    objWMIProperty.Name, _
395:                                                    Null
396:                   End Select
397:                Next
...:
400:                If Len (objWMIGPOInstance.filterId) Then
401:                   Set objWMIFilterInstance=objWMIPolicyServices.Get(objWMIGPOInstance.filterId)
...:
403:                   WScript.Echo vbCRLF & "   - GPO Filter (" & _
404:                                objWMIFilterInstance.Path_.Class & ") " & String (60, "-")
405:                   Set objWMIPropertySet = objWMIFilterInstance.Properties_
406:                   For Each objWMIProperty In objWMIPropertySet
407:                      If objWMIProperty.CIMType = wbemCimtypeObject Then
408:                         For Each varElement In objWMIProperty.Value
409:                            DisplayFormattedProperties varElement, 6
410:                         Next
411:                      Else
412:                         DisplayFormattedProperty objWMIFilterInstance, _
```

```
413:                                         "      " & objWMIProperty.Name, _
414:                                     objWMIProperty.Name, _
415:                                     Null
416:               End If
417:            Next
...:
419:        End If
420:
421:        Set objWMIAssocInstances = objWMIRSOPServices.ExecQuery _
422:                               ("Associators of {" & _
423:                               objWMIGPOInstance.Path_.RelPath & "}")
424:
425:        For Each objWMIAssocInstance In objWMIAssocInstances
426:           WScript.Echo vbCRLF & "  - GPO Scope of Domain (" & _
427:                      objWMIAssocInstance.Path_.Class & ") " & String (60, "-")
428:           Set objWMIPropertySet = objWMIAssocInstance.Properties_
429:           For Each objWMIProperty In objWMIPropertySet
430:              DisplayFormattedProperty objWMIAssocInstance, _
431:                                     "      " & objWMIProperty.Name, _
432:                                     objWMIProperty.Name, _
433:                                     Null
434:           Next
...:
436:        Next
...:
440:        Set objWMIAssocInstances = objWMIRSOPServices.ExecQuery _
441:                               ("References of {" & _
442:                               objWMIGPOInstance.Path_.RelPath & "}")
443:
444:        For Each objWMIAssocInstance In objWMIAssocInstances
445:           WScript.Echo vbCRLF & "  - GPO link (" & _
446:                      objWMIAssocInstance.Path_.Class & ") " & String (60, "-")
447:           Set objWMIPropertySet = objWMIAssocInstance.Properties_
448:           For Each objWMIProperty In objWMIPropertySet
449:              DisplayFormattedProperty objWMIAssocInstance, _
450:                                     "      " & objWMIProperty.Name, _
451:                                     objWMIProperty.Name, _
452:                                     Null
453:           Next
...:
455:        Next
...:
458:        End If
459:        WScript.Echo
...:
462:     Next
...:
466:  End Function
467:
...:
...:
...:
```

For each RSOP instance, a different level of information is retrieved:

- **Information about the RSOP instance** (lines 346 through 360): First, an instance of the *RSOP_GPO* class is retrieved. This class includes information about a GPO. To retrieve this information, the

script uses the *GPOID* property of the RSOP class (lines 346 and
347). This instance is useful to display the GPO container name (line
350). If more details about the GPO are requested by the **/GPOFull-
Info+** switch, this instance will be used again. Next, the script displays the properties of the RSOP instance coming from the class
given on the command line (lines 354 through 360).

- **Information about the RSOP associated instances** (lines 363 through
  378): If there are some instances associated with the RSOP instance,
  the WQL query executed in this portion of the code (lines 363
  through 365) will return a collection of instances. Next, the returned
  collection is enumerated (lines 367 through 378) and the information
  displayed (lines 370 through 376). For example, if instances of the
  RSOP_IEAKPolicySetting class are examined, it is likely that some associated instances will be available (see Figure 3.13).

Next, the script enters in a code portion, which is only executed if the
/GPOFullInfo+ switch is specified (lines 382 through 458). In such a case,
the output obtained would be as follows:

```
 1:   C:\>WMIRSOP.Wsf /GPOClass:RSOP_SystemService /UserRSOP:Alain.Lissoir /GPOFullInfo+
 2:   Microsoft (R) Windows Script Host Version 5.6
 3:   Copyright (C) Microsoft Corporation 1996-2001. All rights reserved.
 4:
 5:   - GPO for Brussels Site (RSOP_SystemService) -----------------------------------------
 6:      creationTime: ........................ 01-01-2000
 7:      ErrorCode: ........................... 0
 8:      GPOID: ............................... CN={A252ACD2-2F93-44B5-ACBF-7948EC5B7080},
 9:                                             CN=Policies,CN=System,DC=LissWare,DC=Net
10:      id: .................................. {6562C1CD-B998-44C4-85A8-3BB1F780E1D9}
11:      name: ...............................
12:      *precedence: ......................... 1
13:      SDDLString: .......................... D:AR(A;;CCDCLCSWRPWPDTLOCRSDRCWDWO;;;BA)
14:                                             (A;;CCDCLCSWRPWPDTLOCRSDRCWDWO;;;SY)
15:                                             (A;;CCLCSWLOCRRC;;;IU)
16:                                             S:(AU;FA;CCDCLCSWRPWPDTLOCRSDRCWDWO;;;WD)
17:      *Service: ............................ SNMP
18:      SOMID: ............................... 2
19:      StartupMode: ......................... 2
20:      Status: .............................. 1
21:
22:   - Complementary GPO information (RSOP_GPO) ------------------------------------------
23:      accessDenied: ........................ FALSE
24:      enabled: ............................. TRUE
25:      fileSystemPath: ...................... \\LissWare.Net\SysVol\
26:                                             LissWare.Net\Policies\
27:                                             {A252ACD2-2F93-44B5-ACBF-7948EC5B7080}\Machine
28:      filterAllowed: ....................... TRUE
29:      filterId: ............................ MSFT_SomFilter.ID=
30:                                             "{C455EC3F-A9BF-4EA0-B224-571CA683B11C}",
31:                                             Domain="LissWare.Net"
32:      guidName: ............................ {A252ACD2-2F93-44B5-ACBF-7948EC5B7080}
33:      *id: ................................. CN={A252ACD2-2F93-44B5-ACBF-7948EC5B7080},
34:                                             CN=Policies,CN=System,DC=LissWare,DC=Net
```

```
35:      name: ............................. GPO for Brussels Site
36:      version: ........................... 65537
37:
38:      - GPO Filter (MSFT_SomFilter) -------------------------------------------------
39:      Author: ........................... Alain.Lissoir
40:      ChangeDate: ....................... 25-01-2002 14:46:38
41:      CreationDate: ..................... 01-01-2002 14:55:53
42:      Description: ...................... Only applied SNMP
43:      *Domain: .......................... LissWare.Net
44:      *ID: .............................. {C455EC3F-A9BF-4EA0-B224-571CA683B11C}
45:      Name: ............................. Only for SNMP machines
46:
47:        - MSFT_Rule -------------------------------------------------------------------
48:      Query: ............................ Select * From Win32_Service Where Name="SNMP"
49:      QueryLanguage: .................... WQL
50:      TargetNameSpace: .................. Root\cimv2
51:
52:    - GPO Scope of Domain (RSOP_SOM) ---------------------------------------------------
53:      blocked: .......................... FALSE
54:      blocking: ......................... FALSE
55:      *id: .............................. CN=Brussels,CN=Sites,CN=Configuration,
56:                                          DC=LissWare,DC=Net
57:      *reason: .......................... 1
58:      SOMOrder: ......................... 2
59:      type: ............................. 2
60:
61:    - GPO link (RSOP_GPLink) -----------------------------------------------------------
62:      appliedOrder: ..................... 2
63:      enabled: .......................... TRUE
64:      *GPO: ............................. RSOP_GPO.id=
65:                                          "CN={A252ACD2-2F93-44B5-ACBF-7948EC5B7080},
66:                                          CN=Policies,CN=System,DC=LissWare,DC=Net"
67:      linkOrder: ........................ 2
68:      noOverride: ....................... FALSE
69:      *SOM: ............................. RSOP_SOM.id="CN=Brussels,CN=Sites,
70:                                          CN=Configuration,DC=LissWare,DC=Net",reason=1
71:      *somOrder: ........................ 1
72:
73:  The 'RSOP_SystemService' GPO class does not exist in the User RSOP data.
```

The supplementary information displayed by the presence of the /GPO-FullInfo+ switch starts at line 22.

This portion of the script (Sample 3.23, lines 378 through 452) also retrieves different levels of information about the GPO:

- **Information about the *RSOP_GPO* instance** (lines 383 through 397): This instance is retrieved earlier in the script code (lines 346 and 347), but its related information is only displayed if the **/GPOFullInfo+** switch is specified (lines 386 through 397).

- **Information about the list of rules**, expressed as WMI queries, which are evaluated on the target machine (lines 400 through 419): This portion of the code makes use of the *RSOP_GPO* instance previously retrieved (lines 346 and 347) and the namespace **Root\Policy** connection established at lines 166 through 169. It exploits the *FilterID* property displayed in the output sample at lines 29 through 31, which contains a WMI path of a GPO filter corresponding to an instance of the *MSFT_SomFilter* class:

```
MSFT_SomFilter.ID="{C455EC3F-A9BF-4EA0-B224-571CA683B11C}",Domain="LissWare.Net"
```

The classes available in the **Root\Policy** namespace are listed in Table 3.28.

Table 3.28   *The Root\Policy Classes*

Name	Type	Comments
MSFT_SomFilterStatus	Dynamic	Represents client-side extensions' event log message sources.
MSFT_Rule	Dynamic	Represents the association between a client-side extension's event log message source and the extension's status.
MSFT_SomFilter	Dynamic	Provides information about the overall status of a client-side extension's processing of policy.

Once the instance of the WMI path is retrieved (line 401), the script displays its properties (lines 405 through 417). The output is available from line 38 through 45. It is important to note that the *Rules* property of the *MSFT_SomFilter* class contains an array of objects (embedded objects). The purpose of the syntax evaluation at line 407 is to determine if an object is contained in the property. If the test is positive, the array containing objects is enumerated (lines 408 through 410), and the properties of each object are displayed with the help of the DisplayFormattedProperties() function (line 409). The output is available from line 47 through 50. You will recognize the WMI filter displayed in Figure 3.9.

For completeness, since WMI filters are stored in Active Directory, it is possible to retrieve the filters by executing a WQL query in the **Root\directory\LDAP** namespace:

```
Select * From ads_msWMI_Som  Where DS_cn="{C455EC3F-A9BF-4EA0-B224-571CA683B11C}"
```

The WMI filters use the *ID* property of the *MSFT_SomFilter* WMI class as the CN of the Active Directory object. The Active Directory object representing a WMI filter uses an **msWMI-Som** Active Directory class. In section 3.6, we see in more depth how to work with the *Active Directory* providers.

■ **Information about the Scope of Management** (SOM) (lines 421 through 436): Because we have an instance of the *RSOP_GPO* class (lines 346 and 347), it is interesting to exploit a new association not yet mentioned. This association is shown in Figure 3.16.

Figure 3.16
The RSOP_GPO
association.

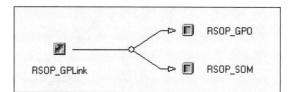

With this association, we retrieve instances of the *RSOP_SOM* class. This class contains information about the SOM, which could be Local, a Site, a Domain, or an OU. This information is displayed in the output example from line 52 through 59. Some relevant information is available from this class:

- The "blocked" state (line 53), which is a flag that indicates whether this SOM is blocked by a SOM lower in the hierarchy of Sites, Domains, and OUs.
- The "blocking" state (line 54), which is a flag that indicates whether this SOM blocks inheritance of policy from other SOMs higher in the hierarchy.
- The SOM (line 55) itself, which is the Brussels site in this case.

- **Information about the GPO link** (lines 440 through 455): Since we have an association in place, an association class is used with its references (lines 440 through 442). In this case, the class is the *RSOP_GPLink* class. By retrieving the instances available from this class, we can get some interesting information about the GPO (lines 61 through 71 in the output sample). For example, we can see if the GPO is enabled (line 63) and its override state (line 68).

The last piece of code of this script sample simply contains the CheckIf-RSOPLoggingModeData() function, which was used earlier (line 181). The script code makes use of this routine to test if the **Root\RSOP\User\<SID>** namespace is available for the User name given on the command line. This function compares (line 482) the SID of the user (passed as a parameter) with the list of SIDs available from the **RSOP User** namespaces (line 474). If there is a match, it means that the namespace exists.

Sample 3.24 *Retrieving RSOP information from an applied GPO (Part VII)*

```
...:
...:
...:
467:
468:     ' --------------------------------------------------------------------
469:     Function CheckIfRSOPLoggingModeData (objWMIRSOPClass, strUserSIDRSOP)
...:
```

```
477:          CheckIfRSOPLoggingModeData = False
478:
479:          objWMIRSOPClass.RsopEnumerateUsers arrayUserSID, intRC
...:
482:          If intRC Then
483:              Exit Function
484:          End If
485:
486:          For Each strUserSID In arrayUserSID
487:              If strUserSID = strUserSIDRSOP Then
488:                  CheckIfRSOPLoggingModeData = True
489:                  Exit Function
490:              End If
491:          Next
492:
493:      End Function
494:
495:      ]]>
496:      </script>
497:  </job>
498:</package>
```

We now have an understanding of how an RSOP is represented by WMI. To monitor the appearance or the deletion of a specific GPO during a refresh cycle, WQL event queries can be submitted in the appropriate namespaces (i.e., **Root\RSOP\Computer**). If a Windows service GPO is applied to a computer, the following WQL event query should be used:

```
Select * From __InstanceCreationEvent Within 5 Where TargetInstance ISA 'RSOP_SystemService'
```

If the same GPO is removed, the following WQL event query should be used:

```
Select * From __InstanceDeletionEvent Within 5 Where TargetInstance ISA 'RSOP_SystemService'
```

Note the presence of the **WITHIN** statement, since the RSOP providers are not implemented as event providers.

If we reuse Sample 6.17 ("A generic script for asynchronous event notification") presented in the appendix, we can easily track the GPO creation and deletion. For example, for a GPO deletion, we will have:

```
1:    C:\>GenericEventAsyncConsumer.wsf "Select * From __InstanceDeletionEvent Within 5
                Where TargetInstance ISA 'RSOP_SystemService'" /NameSpace:Root\RSOP\Computer
2:    Microsoft (R) Windows Script Host Version 5.6
3:    Copyright (C) Microsoft Corporation 1996-2001. All rights reserved.
4:
5:    Waiting for events...
6:
7:    BEGIN - OnObjectReady.
8:    Sunday, 03 February, 2002 at 13:01:42: '__InstanceDeletionEvent' has been triggered.
9:      SECURITY_DESCRIPTOR (wbemCimtypeUint8) = (null)
10:     TargetInstance (wbemCimtypeObject)
11:       creationTime (wbemCimtypeDatetime) = (null)
12:       ErrorCode (wbemCimtypeUint32) = 0
```

```
13:         GPOID (wbemCimtypeString) = CN={6AC1786C-016F-11D2-945F-00C04fB984F9},
14:                                     CN=Policies,CN=System,DC=LissWare,DC=Net
15:         id (wbemCimtypeString) = {25127460-F569-4D2C-95FB-69D47F0294B5}
16:         name (wbemCimtypeString) =
17:         *precedence (wbemCimtypeUint32) = 1
18:         SDDLString (wbemCimtypeString) = D:AR(A;;CCDCLCSWRPWPDTLOCRSDRCWDWO;;;BA)
19:                                     (A;;CCDCLCSWRPWPDTLOCRSDRCWDWO;;;SY)
20:                                     (A;;CCLCSWLOCRRC;;;IU)
21:                                     S:(AU;FA;CCDCLCSWRPWPDTLOCRSDRCWDWO;;;WD)
22:         *Service (wbemCimtypeString) = SNMP
23:         SOMID (wbemCimtypeString) = 4
24:         StartupMode (wbemCimtypeUint32) = 2
25:         Status (wbemCimtypeUint32) = 1
26:       TIME_CREATED (wbemCimtypeUint64) = 03-02-2002 12:01:42 (20020203120142.177488+060)
27:
28:   END - OnObjectReady.
```

In this sample output, we recognize the properties of the *RSOP_System-Service* class discussed in this section. Of course, as with any WQL query, it can be generalized with the use of a parent class to capture any GPO type creation and deletion. This means we have a mechanism to monitor any updates on any systems.

Since the GPO mechanism is quite complex, there is no better way than to play with the script to understand the underlying mechanisms. This is key for a good understanding of this technology.

3.3.11   **The System Restore provider**

To undo harmful changes to a computer, Windows XP includes a feature called *System Restore*. *System Restore* returns the Operating System to an earlier situation (called a restore point) without causing the loss of all recent work. Any changes that *System Restore* makes are completely reversible. Windows XP automatically creates restore points (called system checkpoints), but it is also possible to create your own restore points. This is useful if you are about to make a major change to your system, such as installing a new program or changing your registry. The *System Restore* wizard, located in the System Tools folder of the Start Menu, allows you to perform *System Restore* operations (see Figure 3.17).

When a restore point is created, *System Restore* archives the states of a core set of system and application files with a full snapshot of the registry and some dynamic system files. To function properly, *System Restore* requires a minimum of 200 MB of free disk space on the system drive. If the free disk space falls below 50 MB on any drive, *System Restore* switches to standby mode and stops creating restore points. In such a case, all restore points are deleted. If you recover 200 MB of free disk space, the *System Restore* resumes and continues to create restore points. The set of files that is

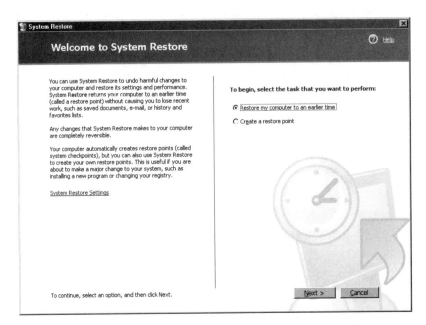

Figure 3.17
*The System Restore
wizard.*

monitored or excluded by *System Restore* is specified in an XML file called
FILELIST.XML and located in the %windir%\System32\Restore folder.
When a user is not actively using the Windows XP system, *System Restore*
compresses the registry and any file copies made.

Although restore points can be created with the *System Restore* wizard
(see Figure 3.17), it is also possible to perform the exact same operation
from a script by using the *SystemRestore* class supported by the *System Restore*
WMI provider. Only available under Windows XP and registered under the
Root\Default namespace, the *System Restore* WMI provider is implemented
as an instance and method provider (see Table 3.29).

Table 3.29   *The SystemRestore Providers Capabilities*

Provider Name	Provider Namespace	Class Provider	Instance Provider	Method Provider	Property Provider	Event Provider	Event Consumer Provider	Support Get	Support Put	Support Enumeration	Support Delete	Windows Server 2003	Windows XP	Windows 2000 Server	Windows 2000 Professional	Windows NT 4.0
System Restore Provider																
System Restore Provider	Root/Default		X	X				X	X	X			X			

The *System Restore* provider supports two WMI classes (see Table 3.30).

Table 3.30   *The SystemRestore Providers Classes*

Name	Type	Comments
SystemRestore	Dynamic	Provides methods for disabling and enabling monitoring, listing available restore points, and initiating a restore on the local system.
SystemRestoreConfig	Dynamic	Provides properties for controlling the frequency of scheduled restore point creation and the amount of disk space consumed on each drive.

The class supporting *System Restore* operations from a script is the *SystemRestore* class. Basically, this class supports five methods implementing the five typical *System Restore* operations. As with the wizard, it is possible to create new restore points, to enable or disable the *System Restore* monitoring for all disks or per disk, get the last *System Restore* status, and restore a specific restore point with this class. To configure the various intervals and the percentage of disk space used by *System Restore*, the *SystemRestoreConfig* class must be used. The logic making use of these classes is implemented in Samples 3.25 through 3.31. The code is written in Jscript and is called **WMISystemRestore.Wsf**. This sample exposes a set of command-line parameters corresponding to methods exposed by the *SystemRestore* class and properties exposed by the *SystemRestoreConfig* class.

```
C:\>WMISystemRestore.wsf
Microsoft (R) Windows Script Host Version 5.6
Copyright (C) Microsoft Corporation 1996-2001. All rights reserved.

Usage: WMISystemRestore.wsf /Action:value [/Volume:value] [/Description:value]
                    [/RestoreSequence[+|-]] [/DiskPercentage[+|-]] [/GlobalInterval[+|-]]
                    [/LifeInterval[+|-]] [/SessionInterval[+|-]]
                    [/Machine:value] [/User:value] [/Password:value]
Options:

Action          : Specify the operation to perform: [List], [Disable], [Enable],
                  [CreateRestorePoint], [LastRestoreStatus], [Restore] and [Update].
Volume          : Specify the System Resstore volume (i.e., C:\ or * for all volumes).
Description     : Description for the new restore point.
RestoreSequence : Sequence number of the restore point.
DiskPercentage  : Maximum amount of disk space on each drive that can be used by System Restore.
GlobalInterval  : Absolute time interval at which scheduled system checkpoints are created (hours).
LifeInterval    : Time interval for which restore points are preserved (hours).
SessionInterval : Time interval at which scheduled system checkpoints are created
                  during the session (hours)
Machine         : Determine the WMI system to connect to. (default=LocalHost)
User            : Determine the UserID to perform the remote connection. (default=none)
Password        : Determine the password to perform the remote connection. (default=none)
Examples:

    WMISystemRestore.wsf /Action:List
    WMISystemRestore.wsf /Action:Disable /Volume:D:\
    WMISystemRestore.wsf /Action:Enable /Volume:D:\
    WMISystemRestore.wsf /Action:Disable /Volume:*
    WMISystemRestore.wsf /Action:Enable /Volume:*
```

```
WMISystemRestore.wsf /Action:CreateRestorePoint /Description:"My System Restore"
WMISystemRestore.wsf /Action:LastRestoreStatus
WMISystemRestore.wsf /Action:Restore /RestoreSequence:28 /Volume:C:
WMISystemRestore.wsf /Action:Update /DiskPercentage:12 /GlobalInterval:72
                                    /LifeInterval:120 /SessionInterval:120
```

As with other script samples, the **WMISystemRestore.Wsf** script (see Sample 3.25) starts with the command-line parameter definition (skipped lines 13 through 37), the inclusion of some external functions (lines 39 through 45), the command-line parsing (skipped lines 49 through 147), and the WMI connection (lines 148 through 159).

Sample 3.25   *Exploiting the System Restore features from script (Part I)*

```
  1:<?xml version="1.0"?>
  .:
  8:<package>
  9:  <job>
...:
 13:    <runtime>
...:
 37:    </runtime>
 38:
 39:    <script language="VBScript" src="..\Functions\DecodeSystemRestoreFunction.vbs" />
 40:
 41:    <script language="VBScript" src="..\Functions\DisplayFormattedPropertyFunction.vbs" />
 42:    <script language="VBScript" src="..\Functions\TinyErrorHandler.vbs" />
 43:
 44:    <object progid="WbemScripting.SWbemLocator" id="objWMILocator" reference="true"/>
 45:    <object progid="WbemScripting.SWbemDateTime" id="objWMIDateTime" />
 46:
 47:    <script language="Jscript">
 48:    <![CDATA[
 49:    var cComputerName = "LocalHost";
 50:    var cWMINameSpace = "Root/Default";
 51:
...:
147:
148:    objWMILocator.Security_.AuthenticationLevel = wbemAuthenticationLevelDefault;
149:    objWMILocator.Security_.ImpersonationLevel = wbemImpersonationLevelImpersonate;
150:
151:    try
152:      {
153:      objWMIServices = objWMILocator.ConnectServer(strComputerName, cWMINameSpace,
154:                                          strUserID, strPassword);
155:      }
156:    catch (Err)
157:      {
158:      ErrorHandler (Err);
159:      }
160:
...:
...:
...:
```

To view the restore points available, Sample 3.26 retrieves all instances of the *SystemRestore* class (line 166). The scripting technique is quite easy, since it simply consists of an enumeration of all instances (lines 173 through 218) with all their properties (lines 183 through 216).

Sample 3.26   *Viewing the System Restore points (Part II)*

```
...:
...:
...:
160:
161:    // -- LIST ---------------------------------------------------------------
162:    if (boolList == true)
163:       {
164:       try
165:          {
166:          objWMIInstances = objWMIServices.InstancesOf ("SystemRestore")
167:          }
168:       catch (Err)
169:          {
170:          ErrorHandler (Err)
171:          }
172:
173:       enumWMIInstances = new Enumerator (objWMIInstances);
174:       for (;! enumWMIInstances.atEnd(); enumWMIInstances.moveNext())
175:          {
176:          objWMIInstance = enumWMIInstances.item();
177:
178:          objWMIDateTime.Value = objWMIInstance.CreationTime;
179:          WScript.Echo ("- " + objWMIInstance.Description + " (" +
180:                       objWMIDateTime.GetVarDate (false) + ")" +
181:                       "----------------------------------------------------");
182:
183:          objWMIPropertySet = objWMIInstance.Properties_
184:          enumWMIPropertySet = new Enumerator (objWMIPropertySet);
185:          for (;! enumWMIPropertySet.atEnd(); enumWMIPropertySet.moveNext())
186:             {
187:             objWMIProperty = enumWMIPropertySet.item()
188:
189:             switch (objWMIProperty.Name)
190:                {
191:                case "RestorePointType":
192:                    DisplayFormattedProperty (objWMIInstance,
193:                        "  " + objWMIProperty.Name,
194:                        DecodeRestorePointType (objWMIProperty.Value),
195:                        null);
196:                    break;
197:                case "EventType":
198:                    DisplayFormattedProperty (objWMIInstance,
199:                        "  " + objWMIProperty.Name,
200:                        DecodeEventType (objWMIProperty.Value),
201:                        null);
202:                    break;
203:                case "CreationTime":
204:                    DisplayFormattedProperty (objWMIInstance,
205:                        "  " + objWMIProperty.Name,
206:                        objWMIDateTime.GetVarDate (false),
```

```
207:                              null);
208:                         break;
209:                default:
210:                         DisplayFormattedProperty (objWMIInstance,
211:                              " " + objWMIProperty.Name,
212:                              objWMIProperty.Name,
213:                              null);
214:                         break;
215:                    }
216:                }
217:            WScript.Echo();
218:            }
219:        }
220:
...:
...:
...:
```

To enable or disable the *System Restore* disk monitoring, the scripting technique is pretty simple. Sample 3.27 retrieves an instance of the *System-Restore* class (lines 224 and 250). Because these *Disable* and *Enable* methods do not relate to a particular dynamic instance, they are defined as static methods (Static qualifier set to true) in the CIM repository. Actually, the logical disk for which the *System Restore* monitoring must be enabled or disabled must be specified as a parameter of the methods (lines 224 and 250). If a drive letter is specified on the command line (in the form "C:\" or "D:\"), the method will be related to the specified disk (lines 232 and 258). If an asterisk is given on the command line, the method will apply to all disks (lines 226 and 252). In this case, the disk letter will be an empty string when passing the parameter to the method (lines 228 and 254). Interestingly, the disk is not managed via a WMI instance stored in an **SWBemObject,** which represents the real disk. Instead, it is managed by an instance of the class where parameters specify the disk to manage (lines 228 and 254). This implementation is totally dependent on how the WMI provider and its supported classes are designed.

Sample 3.27   *Enabling/disabling disk monitoring (Part III)*

```
...:
...:
...:
220:
221:    // -- ENABLE -----------------------------------------------------------------
222:    if (boolEnable == true)
223:        {
224:        objWMIClass = objWMIServices.Get ("SystemRestore")
225:
226:        if (strDeviceID == "*")
227:            {
228:            intRC = objWMIClass.Enable ("", true)
229:            }
230:        else
```

```
231:              {
232:                  intRC = objWMIClass.Enable (strDeviceID, true)
233:              }
234:
235:          if (intRC)
236:              {
237:              WScript.Echo ("Failed to enable SystemRestore on " +
238:                          strDeviceID + " drive (" + intRC + ")")
239:              }
240:          else
241:              {
242:              WScript.Echo ("SystemRestore on " + strDeviceID +
243:                          " drive successfully enabled.")
244:              }
245:          }
246:
247:      // -- DISABLE ----------------------------------------------------------------
248:      if (boolDisable == true)
249:          {
250:          objWMIClass = objWMIServices.Get ("SystemRestore")
251:
252:          if (strDeviceID == "*")
253:              {
254:              intRC = objWMIClass.Disable ("")
255:              }
256:          else
257:              {
258:              intRC = objWMIClass.Disable (strDeviceID)
259:              }
260:
261:          if (intRC)
262:              {
263:              WScript.Echo ("Failed to disable SystemRestore on " +
264:                          strDeviceID + " drive (" + intRC + ")")
265:              }
266:          else
267:              {
268:              WScript.Echo ("SystemRestore on " + strDeviceID +
269:                          " drive successfully disabled.")
270:              }
271:          }
272:
...:
...:
...:
```

To create a restore point, the same logic applies as enabling or disabling a disk (see Sample 3.28). An instance of the *SystemRestore* class is first retrieved (line 276). Next, the *CreateRestorePoint* method is invoked (lines 278 through 280).

Sample 3.28 *Creating a restore point (Part IV)*

```
...:
...:
...:
272:
273:      // -- CreateRestorePoint --------------------------------------------------------
274:      if (boolCreateRestorePoint == true)
275:          {
```

```
276:        objWMIClass = objWMIServices.Get ("SystemRestore")
277:
278:        intRC = objWMIClass.CreateRestorePoint (strDescription,
279:                                                 APPLICATION_INSTALL,
280:                                                 BEGIN_SYSTEM_CHANGE)
281:
282:        if (intRC)
283:            {
284:            WScript.Echo ("Failed to create a new system restore point (" + intRC + ")")
285:            }
286:        else
287:            {
288:            WScript.Echo ("System restore point successfully created.")
289:            }
290:        }
291:
...:
...:
...:
```

The three parameters passed along the method invocation are as follows:

- **Description:** The *Description* parameter is a string used to identify the restore point.

- **RestorePointType:** The *RestorePointType* is an integer defining the type of restore point. The various values that can be specified with this parameter are summarized in Table 3.31.

Table 3.31   *The RestorePointType Parameter*

Name	Value	Comments
APPLICATION_INSTALL	0	An application has been installed.
APPLICATION_UNINSTALL	1	An application has been uninstalled.
DEVICE_DRIVER_INSTALL	10	A device driver has been installed.
MODIFY_SETTINGS	12	An application has had features added or removed.
CANCELLED_OPERATION	13	An application needs to delete the restore point it created. For example, an application would use this flag when a user cancels an installation.

- **EventType:** The *EventType* is an integer defining the type of event for the restore point. The various values that can be specified with this parameter are summarized in Table 3.32.

Table 3.32   *The EventType Parameter*

Name	Value	Comments
BEGIN_NESTED_SYSTEM_CHANGE	102	A system change has begun. A subsequent nested call does not create a new restore point. Subsequent calls must use END_NESTED_SYSTEM_CHANGE, not END_SYSTEM_CHANGE.
BEGIN_SYSTEM_CHANGE	100	A system change has begun.
END_NESTED_SYSTEM_CHANGE	103	A system change has ended.
END_SYSTEM_CHANGE	101	A system change has ended.

Getting the last restore status from the script is a very simple operation (see Sample 3.29). The *GetLastRestoreStatus* method is a static method and is therefore executed from an instance of the *SystemRestore* class (lines 295 through 297). The last restore status is returned as a result of the method execution.

Sample 3.29   *Getting the last restore status (Part V)*

```
...:
...:
...:
291:
292:    // -- LastRestoreStatus ----------------------------------------------------
293:    if (boolRestoreStatus == true)
294:        {
295:        objWMIClass = objWMIServices.Get ("SystemRestore")
296:
297:        intRC = objWMIClass.GetLastRestoreStatus ()
298:
299:        WScript.Echo ("Last restore status: " + intRC)
300:        }
301:
...:
...:
...:
```

To restore a restore point, the coding is no more complicated than getting the last restore status (see Sample 3.30). The *Restore* static method must still be executed from an instance of *SystemRestore* class. The only required input parameter to execute the *Restore* method is the restore point sequence number. The restore point sequence number can be found by executing the **WMISystemRestore.Wsf** script with the **/Action:List** command-line parameter. A sample output will look as follows:

```
1:    C:\>WMISystemRestore.wsf /Action:List
2:    Microsoft (R) Windows Script Host Version 5.6
3:    Copyright (C) Microsoft Corporation 1996-2001. All rights reserved.
4:
5:    - System Checkpoint (Fri Oct 11 10:33:16 UTC+0200 2002)------------------------------------
6:        CreationTime: ......................... 11-10-2002 10:33:16
7:        Description: .......................... System Checkpoint
8:        EventType: ............................ BEGIN_SYSTEM_CHANGE
9:        RestorePointType: ..................... APPLICATION_INSTALL
10:       *SequenceNumber: ...................... 45
11:
12:    - Windows Update V4 (Fri Oct 11 21:38:54 UTC+0200 2002)------------------------------------
13:        CreationTime: ......................... 11-10-2002 21:38:54
14:        Description: .......................... Windows Update V4
15:        EventType: ............................ BEGIN_SYSTEM_CHANGE
16:        RestorePointType: ..................... APPLICATION_INSTALL
17:       *SequenceNumber: ...................... 46
18:
```

```
19:    - System Checkpoint (Sun Oct 13 07:50:20 UTC+0200 2002)-------------------------------
20:      CreationTime: ......................... 13-10-2002 07:50:20
21:      Description: .......................... System Checkpoint
22:      EventType: ........................... BEGIN_SYSTEM_CHANGE
23:      RestorePointType: .................... APPLICATION_INSTALL
24:      *SequenceNumber: ..................... 47
```

As we can see, the sequence number is a key property of the *SystemRestore* instances (lines 10, 17, and 24).

Sample 3.30   *Restoring a restore point (Part VI)*

```
...:
...:
...:
301:
302:    // -- Restore ---------------------------------------------------------------------
303:    if (boolCreateRestorePoint == true)
304:       {
305:       objWMIClass = objWMIServices.Get ("SystemRestore")
306:
307:       intRC = objWMIClass.Restore(intSequenceNumber)
308:
309:       if (intRC)
310:          {
311:          WScript.Echo ("Failed to create a new system restore point (" + intRC + ")")
312:          }
313:       else
314:          {
315:          WScript.Echo ("System restore point successfully created.")
316:          }
317:       }
318:
...:
...:
...:
```

To manage the properties controlling the frequency of the scheduled restore point creation and the amount of disk space consumed on each drive, the *SystemRestoreConfig* class must be used, as shown in Sample 3.31.

Sample 3.31   *Updating the System Restore parameters (Part VII)*

```
...:
...:
...:
318:
319:    // -- Update ----------------------------------------------------------------------
320:    if (boolUpdate == true)
321:       {
322:       objWMIInstance = objWMIServices.Get ("SystemRestoreConfig.MyKey='SR'");
323:
324:       if (intDiskPercentage != -1) objWMIInstance.DiskPercent=intDiskPercentage;
325:       if (intGlobalInterval != -1) objWMIInstance.RPGlobalInterval=intGlobalInterval*3600;
```

```
326:        if (intLifeInterval != -1) objWMIInstance.RPLifeInterval=intLifeInterval*3600;
327:        if (intSessionInterval != -1) objWMIInstance.RPSessionInterval=intSessionInterval*3600;
328:
329:        try
330:          {
331:          objWMIInstance.Put_ (wbemChangeFlagUpdateOnly | wbemFlagReturnWhenComplete);
332:          }
333:        catch (Err)
334:          {
335:          ErrorHandler (Err);
336:          }
337:
338:        WScript.Echo ("System restore point parameters updated.")
339:        }
340:    ]]>
341:    </script>
342:  </job>
343:</package>
```

The only instance available from the *SystemRestoreConfig* class is the **SR**
instance (line 322). That instance exposes the disk percentage in the *Disk-
Percent* property and the three frequency properties in *RPGlobalFrequency,*
RPLifeInterval, and *RPSessionInterval,* respectively (lines 324 through 327).
The meaning of these properties is summarized in Table 3.33. Note that the
script accepts the schedule parameters in hours, while the *SystemRestoreConfig* class exposes these properties in seconds. That's why the script code mul-
tiplies the values by 3,600 during the property assignment (lines 324
through 327).

Table 3.33   *The SystemRestoreConfig Properties*

Name	Comments
DiskPercent	Maximum amount of disk space on each drive that can be used by System Restore. This value is specified as a percentage of the total drive space. The default value is 12 percent.
RPGlobalInterval	Absolute time interval at which scheduled system checkpoints are created, in seconds. The default value is 86,400 (24 hours).
RPLifeInterval	Time interval for which restore points are preserved, in seconds. When a restore point becomes older than this specified interval, it is deleted. The default age limit is 90 days.
RPSessionInterval	Time interval at which scheduled system checkpoints are created during the session, in seconds. The default value is zero, indicating that the feature is turned off.

3.4   Core OS components event providers

3.4.1   The Clock provider

The *Win32 Clock* provider is an instance and an event provider. The provider capabilities are summarized in Table 3.34.

Table 3.34   *The Win32ClockProvider Providers Capabilities*

Provider Name	Provider Namespace	Class Provider	Instance Provider	Method Provider	Property Provider	Event Provider	Event Consumer Provider	Support Get	Support Put	Support Enumeration	Support Delete	Windows XP	Windows Server 2003	Windows 2000 Professional	Windows 2000 Server
Clock Provider															
Win32ClockProvider	Root/CIMV2	X			X			X		X		X	X		

As shown in Table 3.35, this provider supports two classes: the *Win32_LocalTime* and *Win32_UTCTime* classes.

Table 3.35   *The Win32ClockProvider Classes*

Name	Type	Comments
Win32_LocalTime	Dynamic (Singleton)	Represents an instance of the local time
Win32_UTCTime	Dynamic (Singleton)	Represents an instance of the UTC time

These two classes are created from the *Win32_CurrentTime* superclass (see Figure 3.18). All classes are singleton classes. There is no particular event class, since the *Clock* provider works with the *__InstanceModificationEvent* intrinsic event class.

Figure 3.18
The Win32_CurrentTime class and its child classes.

Because this provider is implemented as an event provider, it is possible to formulate a WQL query without the **WITHIN** statement. For example, the following query:

```
Select * From __InstanceModificationEvent Where TargetInstance ISA 'Win32_LocalTime'
```

will trigger a notification every time the local time changes. We can obtain the same result by performing a WQL event query with the *Win32_UTCTime*:

```
Select * From __InstanceModificationEvent Where TargetInstance ISA 'Win32_UTCTime'
```

Now, if we want to get a notification every new minute for the UTC time, we can use the following query:

```
Select * From __InstanceModificationEvent Where TargetInstance ISA 'Win32_UTCTime' AND
                          TargetInstance.Second=0
```

In *Understanding WMI Scripting*, Chapter 6, when we talked about the Timer Events, we saw how to use the interval timer event with its corresponding *__IntervalTimerInstruction* class. This last WQL event query could represent a good alternative to the interval timer event.

With the help of the *Win32_CurrentTime* class, it is possible to get the current system time. In the previous chapter, we wrote a script to manage scheduled jobs. This script makes use of the *Win32_CurrentTime* class, but we didn't examine this part of the code (see Samples 2.56 through 2.59). When we schedule jobs, it is sometimes useful to retrieve the current system time, especially when these jobs are scheduled on a remote computer. Because the *Win32_CurrentTime* class is a superclass for the *Win32_UTCTime* and *Win32_LocalTime* classes, it is possible to retrieve the current time in two forms: UTC and localized.

The portion of code retrieving the system time is shown in Sample 3.32 (lines 275 and 319) and is an extract of Samples 2.56 through 2.59.

Sample 3.32   *Getting the current time (UTC and local)*

```
 1:<?xml version="1.0"?>
 .:
 8:<package>
 9:  <job>
..:
13:    <runtime>
..:
37:    </runtime>
38:
39:    <script language="VBScript" src="..\Functions\DecodeDaysOfWeekFunction.vbs" />
40:    <script language="VBScript" src="..\Functions\DecodeDaysOfMonthFunction.vbs" />
41:
42:    <script language="VBScript" src="..\Functions\ConvertStringInArrayFunction.vbs" />
43:    <script language="VBScript" src="..\Functions\DisplayFormattedPropertyFunction.vbs" />
44:    <script language="VBScript" src="..\Functions\TinyErrorHandler.vbs" />
45:
46:    <object progid="WbemScripting.SWbemLocator" id="objWMILocator" reference="true"/>
47:    <object progid="WbemScripting.SWbemDateTime" id="objWMIDateTime" />
48:
49:    <script language="VBscript">
50:    <![CDATA[
..:
54:    ' -------------------------------------------------------------------------------
55:    Const cComputerName = "LocalHost"
56:    Const cWMINameSpace = "Root/cimv2"
```

```
 57:
 58:     Const cWMIScheduledJobClass = "Win32_ScheduledJob"
 59:     Const cWMICurrentTimeClass = "Win32_CurrentTime"
 ..:
 94:     ' ------------------------------------------------------------------------------
 95:     ' Parse the command line parameters
 96:     If WScript.Arguments.Named.Count = 0 Then
 97:        WScript.Arguments.ShowUsage()
 98:        WScript.Quit
 99:     End If
...:
...:
...:
273:
274:     ' TIME ------------------------------------------------------------------------------------
275:     If boolGetTime Then
276:        Set objWMIInstances = objWMIServices.InstancesOf (cWMICurrentTimeClass)
...:
279:        For Each objWMIInstance in objWMIInstances
280:           objWMIDateTime.Year = objWMIInstance.Year
281:           objWMIDateTime.YearSpecified = True
282:           objWMIDateTime.Month = objWMIInstance.Month
283:           objWMIDateTime.MonthSpecified = True
284:           objWMIDateTime.Day = objWMIInstance.Day
285:           objWMIDateTime.DaySpecified = True
286:
287:           objWMIDateTime.Hours = objWMIInstance.Hour
288:           objWMIDateTime.HoursSpecified = True
289:           objWMIDateTime.Minutes = objWMIInstance.Minute
290:           objWMIDateTime.MinutesSpecified = True
291:           objWMIDateTime.Seconds = objWMIInstance.Second
292:           objWMIDateTime.SecondsSpecified = True
293:
294:           objWMIDateTime.IsInterval = False
295:           If objWMIInstance.Path_.Class = "Win32_UTCTime" Then
296:              WScript.Echo "- UTC " & String (70, "-")
297:              WScript.Echo "Current date/time is: " & _
298:                           objWMIDateTime.GetVarDate (False) & _
299:                           " (" & objWMIDateTime.Value & ")."
300:           Else
301:              WScript.Echo "- Local " & String (68, "-")
302:              WScript.Echo "Current date/time is: " & _
303:                           objWMIDateTime.GetVarDate (False) & _
304:                           " (" & objWMIDateTime.Value & ")."
305:           End If
306:
307:           Set objWMIPropertySet = objWMIInstance.Properties_
308:           For Each objWMIProperty In objWMIPropertySet
309:              DisplayFormattedProperty objWMIInstance, _
310:                                       objWMIProperty.Name, _
311:                                       objWMIProperty.Name, _
312:                                       Null
313:           Next
...:
316:           WScript.Echo
317:        Next
318:        WScript.Echo
319:     End If
...:
```

```
324:   ]]>
325:   </script>
326:   </job>
327:</package>
```

Because we want the script to show the time type (UTC or local), it retrieves the collection available from the *Win32_CurrentTime* (line 276). This collection is made up of the *Win32_UTCTime* singleton instance and the *Win32_LocalTime* singleton instance. Next, it enumerates the collection (lines 279 through 317), and, for each instance found, the script stores the time result in an **SWBemDateTime** object (lines 280 through 292). Based on the class name of the retrieved time (*Win32_LocalTime* or *Win32_UTC-Time* at line 295), the script displays the corresponding time message with the class properties. Once executed, we get the following output:

```
 1:   C:\>WMIScheduledJob.wsf /GetTime+
 2:   Microsoft (R) Windows Script Host Version 5.6
 3:   Copyright (C) Microsoft Corporation 1996-2001. All rights reserved.
 4:
 5:   - Local ------------------------------------------------------------
 6:   Current date/time is: 01-11-2001 19:35:54 (20011101193554.000000+000).
 7:   Day: ................................... 1
 8:   DayOfWeek: ............................. 4
 9:   Hour: .................................. 19
10:   Minute: ................................ 35
11:   Month: ................................. 11
12:   Quarter: ............................... 4
13:   Second: ................................ 54
14:   WeekInMonth: ........................... 1
15:   Year: .................................. 2001
16:
17:   - UTC --------------------------------------------------------------
18:   Current date/time is: 01-11-2001 18:35:54 (20011101183554.000000+000).
19:   Day: ................................... 1
20:   DayOfWeek: ............................. 4
21:   Hour: .................................. 18
22:   Minute: ................................ 35
23:   Month: ................................. 11
24:   Quarter: ............................... 4
25:   Second: ................................ 54
26:   WeekInMonth: ........................... 1
27:   Year: .................................. 2001
```

3.4.2 Power management provider

The *power management* provider consists of only one event provider (see Table 3.36) supporting one event class.

This provider is designed to trigger a WMI event notification to every event consumer who has subscribed to receive power management event notifications. The *Win32_PowerManagementEvent* class is the only class supported and is an extrinsic event class available in the **Root\CIMv2**

Table 3.36 *The Power Management Providers Capabilities*

Provider Name	Provider Namespace	Class Provider	Instance Provider	Method Provider	Property Provider	Event Provider	Event Consumer Provider	Support Get	Support Put	Support Enumeration	Support Delete	Windows Server 2003	Windows XP	Windows 2000 Server	Windows 2000 Professional	Windows NT 4.0
Power Management Provider																
MS_Power_Management_Event_Provider	Root/CIMV2					X						X	X	X	X	X

namespace. This provider is not an instance or property provider and therefore does not expose information about the power devices themselves. To gather information about the power devices, you must refer to the previous chapter (section 2.3.5), and work with one of the following classes: *Win32_Battery, Win32_CurrentProbe, Win32_PortableBattery, Win32_UninterruptiblePowerSupply,* or *Win32_VoltageProbe.* The WQL event query to receive all power management events is as follows:

```
Select * From Win32_PowerManagementEvent
```

The easiest way to test this WQL event query with a script is to execute Sample 6.17 ("A generic script for asynchronous event notification"), available in the appendix on a laptop. For example, once you have started the script with the following command line, you can switch the laptop to standby mode. Note that if you switch your laptop to hibernate mode, you should obtain the same result. The output would be as follows:

```
1:    C:\>GenericEventAsyncConsumer.wsf "Select * From Win32_PowerManagementEvent"
2:    Microsoft (R) Windows Script Host Version 5.6
3:    Copyright (C) Microsoft Corporation 1996-2001. All rights reserved.
4:
5:    Waiting for events...
6:
7:    BEGIN - OnObjectReady.
8:    Tuesday, 20 November, 2001 at 15:41:27: 'Win32_PowerManagementEvent' has been triggered.
9:      EventType (wbemCimtypeUint16) = 4
10:     OEMEventCode (wbemCimtypeUint16) = (null)
11:   END - OnObjectReady.
12:
13:   BEGIN - OnObjectReady.
14:   Tuesday, 20 November, 2001 at 15:41:56: 'Win32_PowerManagementEvent' has been triggered.
15:     EventType (wbemCimtypeUint16) = 18
16:     OEMEventCode (wbemCimtypeUint16) = (null)
17:   END - OnObjectReady.
18:
19:   BEGIN - OnObjectReady.
20:   Tuesday, 20 November, 2001 at 15:41:56: 'Win32_PowerManagementEvent' has been triggered.
21:     EventType (wbemCimtypeUint16) = 7
22:     OEMEventCode (wbemCimtypeUint16) = (null)
23:   END - OnObjectReady.
```

Each time a power management event occurs (lines 7, 13, and 19), the script receives the event represented by a *Win32_PowerManagementEvent* instance. This class exposes a property called *EventType,* and its value corresponds to the power management event type (lines 9, 15, and 21). The meaning of the values is shown in Table 3.37.

Table 3.37   *The Power Management Event Type Values*

Meaning	Values
Entering Suspend	4
Resume from Suspend	7
Power Status Change	10
OEM Event	11
Resume Automatic	18

In the sample output, the *OEMEventCode* property is always set to Null, because there is no OEM event reported. Note that if you remove the power supply of the laptop, it will switch on the battery and this will trigger power management event 10 ("Power Status Change").

This event type can be useful for applications that must perform specific tasks when the power status of the computer changes.

3.4.3   Shutdown provider

As with the *power management* provider, the *shutdown* provider is also made up of one event provider supporting only one single extrinsic event class, which is called *Win32_ComputerShutdownEvent* (see Table 3.38.)

Table 3.38   *The Shutdown Providers Capabilities*

Provider Name	Provider Namespace	Class Provider	Instance Provider	Method Provider	Property Provider	Event Provider	Event Consumer Provider	Support Get	Support Put	Support Enumeration	Support Delete	Windows Server 2003	Windows XP	Windows 2000 Server	Windows 2000 Professional	Windows NT 4.0
Shutdown Provider																
MS_Shutdown_Event_Provider	Root/CIMV2					X						X	X			

This event class represents events when a computer has begun the process of shutting down. To receive a computer shutdown notification, the following WQL event query must be used:

```
Select * From Win32_ComputerShutdownEvent
```

Again by reusing Sample 6.17 ("A generic script for asynchronous event notification") available in the appendix, we obtain the following output:

```
1:   C:\>GenericEventAsyncConsumer.wsf "Select * From Win32_ComputerShutdownEvent"
2:   Microsoft (R) Windows Script Host Version 5.6
3:   Copyright (C) Microsoft Corporation 1996-2001. All rights reserved.
4:
5:   Waiting for events...
6:
7:   BEGIN - OnObjectReady.
8:   Tuesday, 20 November, 2001 at 16:46:33: 'Win32_ComputerShutdownEvent' has been triggered.
9:
10:     - Win32_ComputerShutdownEvent -------------------------------------------------
11:     MachineName: ......................... NET-DPEN6400A
12:     TIME_CREATED: ......................... 20-11-2001 14:44:22 (20011120134422.849164+060)
13:     Type: ................................ 0
14:
15:   END - OnObjectReady.
16:
17:   BEGIN - OnObjectReady.
18:   Tuesday, 20 November, 2001 at 16:46:39: 'Win32_ComputerShutdownEvent' has been triggered.
19:
20:     - Win32_ComputerShutdownEvent -------------------------------------------------
21:     MachineName: ......................... NET-DPEN6400A
22:     TIME_CREATED: ......................... 20-11-2001 14:44:28 (20011120134428.717603+060)
23:     Type: ................................ 1
24:
25:
```

The output sample is obtained when a server reboot or shutdown is requested. You will notice two events: the first event (lines 11 through 13) corresponds to a Logoff (value 0 of the *type* property at line 13); the second event (lines 21 through 23) corresponds to a shutdown or reboot (value 1 of the *type* property at line 23). From this output, it is interesting to note that this provider notifies any Logoff event to the subscribed consumers in addition to detecting Operating System shutdowns.

As with the power management event, this event type can be useful for an application that must perform some specific tasks when a user logoff or machine shutdown is invoked.

3.4.4   Configuration Change provider

The *Configuration Change* provider is implemented as an event provider (Table 3.39). Only available under Windows XP or Windows Server 2003, this provider indicates with the *Win32_SystemConfigurationChangeEvent* extrinsic event class that the device list on the system has been refreshed. This means that a device has been added, removed, or reconfigured.

Table 3.39 *The Configuration Change Providers Capabilities*

Provider Name	Provider Namespace	Class Provider	Instance Provider	Method Provider	Property Provider	Event Provider	Event Consumer Provider	Support Get	Support Put	Support Enumeration	Support Delete	Windows Server 2003	Windows XP	Windows 2000 Server	Windows 2000 Professional	Windows NT 4.0
Configuration Change Provider																
SystemConfigurationChangeEvents	Root/CIMV2					X						X	X			

The *Win32_SystemConfigurationChangeEvent* event class is the only class supported by the *Configuration Change* provider. The change to the device list is not contained in the event and therefore an application or a script is required to refresh its knowledge of the device list in order to obtain the current system settings. Configuration changes can be anything related to the system configuration, such as IRQ settings, COM ports, and BIOS version, to name a few. For example, in the previous chapter, we developed a script to retrieve the hardware resource information (see Samples 2.4 through 2.7, "Retrieving hardware resource information"). This script can be easily reused and expanded to determine the updated configuration. The only relevant information contained in the extrinsic event is the event type, which is contained in the *EventType* property. This property indicates the type of device change notification event that has occurred (Table 3.40).

Table 3.40 *The EventType Property Meaning*

Meaning	Values
Configuration Changed	1
Device Arrival	2
Device Removal	3
Docking	4

If we reuse Sample 6.17 ("A generic script for asynchronous event notification") in the appendix, and if you connect a USB device to your Windows Server 2003 or Windows XP system, you may get an output similar to the following one:

```
1:  C:\>GenericEventAsyncConsumer.wsf "Select * From Win32_SystemConfigurationChangeEvent"
2:  Microsoft (R) Windows Script Host Version 5.6
3:  Copyright (C) Microsoft Corporation 1996-2001. All rights reserved.
4:
5:  Waiting for events...
6:
7:  BEGIN - OnObjectReady.
8:  Sunday, 17 Feb, 2002 at 11:01:00: 'Win32_SystemConfigurationChangeEvent' has been triggered.
```

```
 9:     EventType (wbemCimtypeUint16) = 1
10:     SECURITY_DESCRIPTOR (wbemCimtypeUint8) = (null)
11:     TIME_CREATED (wbemCimtypeUint64) = 17-02-2002 10:01:00 (20020217100100.359920+060)
12:
13:  END - OnObjectReady.
14:
15:  BEGIN - OnObjectReady.
16:  Sunday, 17 Feb, 2002 at 11:01:00: 'Win32_SystemConfigurationChangeEvent' has been triggered.
17:     EventType (wbemCimtypeUint16) = 1
18:     SECURITY_DESCRIPTOR (wbemCimtypeUint8) = (null)
19:     TIME_CREATED (wbemCimtypeUint64) = 17-02-2002 10:01:00 (20020217100100.460064+060)
20:
21:  END - OnObjectReady.
```

Based on Table 3.40, we clearly see that the WMI event corresponds to a configuration change (lines 9 and 17).

3.4.5   Volume Change event provider

The *Volume Change* event provider supports only one extrinsic event class available in the **Root\CIMv2** namespace (Table 3.41). Its purpose is to detect the addition or the removal of a drive letter or mounted/dismounted drive on the computer system.

Table 3.41   *The Volume Change Providers Capabilities*

Provider Name	Provider Namespace	Class Provider	Instance Provider	Method Provider	Property Provider	Event Provider	Event Consumer Provider	Support Get	Support Put	Support Enumeration	Support Delete	Windows Server 2003	Windows XP	Windows 2000 Server	Windows 2000 Professional	Windows NT 4.0
Volume Change Provider																
VolumeChangeEvents	Root/CIMV2					X						X	X			

The *Win32_VolumeChangeEvent* event class represents a local drive event resulting from the change. Network drives are not currently supported. The *Win32_VolumeChangeEvent* event class is generally used in a WQL event query:

```
Select * From Win32_VolumeChangeEvent
```

If we reuse Sample 6.17 ("A generic script for asynchronous event notification") in the appendix, and if we change the drive letter of volume E: to Z: in a Windows Server 2003 or Windows XP system, we may get an output similar to the following one:

```
C:\>GenericEventAsyncConsumer.wsf "Select * From Win32_VolumeChangeEvent"
Microsoft (R) Windows Script Host Version 5.6
Copyright (C) Microsoft Corporation 1996-2001. All rights reserved.

Waiting for events...

BEGIN - OnObjectReady.
Wednesday, 14 August, 2002 at 17:23:56: 'Win32_VolumeChangeEvent' has been triggered.
  DriveName (wbemCimtypeString) = E:
  EventType (wbemCimtypeUint16) = 3
  SECURITY_DESCRIPTOR (wbemCimtypeUint8) = (null)
  TIME_CREATED (wbemCimtypeUint64) = 14-08-2002 15:23:56 (20020814152356.796875+120)

END - OnObjectReady.

BEGIN - OnObjectReady.
Wednesday, 14 August, 2002 at 17:23:57: 'Win32_VolumeChangeEvent' has been triggered.
  DriveName (wbemCimtypeString) = Z:
  EventType (wbemCimtypeUint16) = 2
  SECURITY_DESCRIPTOR (wbemCimtypeUint8) = (null)
  TIME_CREATED (wbemCimtypeUint64) = 14-08-2002 15:23:56 (20020814152356.984375+120)

END - OnObjectReady.
```

The *Win32_VolumeChangeEvent* class exposes an *EventType* property. You can refer to Table 3.40 for more information about this property.

3.5   Core OS file system components providers

3.5.1   Disk quota provider

The *Disk quota* provider is made up of only one instance provider (see Table 3.42) supporting three classes. This provider is designed to expose information about quota settings configured on NTFS volumes.

Table 3.42   *The Disk Quota Providers Capabilities*

Provider Name	Provider Namespace	Class Provider	Instance Provider	Method Provider	Property Provider	Event Provider	Event Consumer Provider	Support Get	Support Put	Support Enumeration	Support Delete	Windows Server 2003	Windows XP	Windows 2000 Server	Windows 2000 Professional	Windows NT 4.0
Disk Quota Provider																
DskQuotaProvider	Root/CIMV2		X					X	X	X	X	X	X			

It supports one dynamic instance class and two association classes, as shown in Table 3.43.

Table 3.43   *The Disk Quota Provider Classes*

Name	Type	Comments
Win32_QuotaSetting	Dynamic	Contains setting information for disk quotas on a volume.
Win32_DiskQuota	Association	Tracks disk space usage for NTFS volumes.
Win32_VolumeQuotaSetting	Association	Relates disk quota settings with a specific disk volume.

These classes are available in the **Root\CIMv2** namespace. The *Win32_DiskQuota* association class associates the *Win32_LogicalDisk* class with the *Win32_Account* (see Figure 3.19).

Figure 3.19
The Win32_DiskQuota association class.

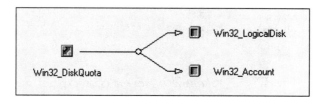

With this association, it is possible to view and configure different quotas per user. We will exploit this capability in the next script sample. On the other hand, the *Win32_QuotaSetting* class is associated with the *Win32_LogicalDisk* class via the *Win32_VolumeQuotaSetting* class (Figure 3.20).

Figure 3.20
The Win32_QuotaSetting class associations.

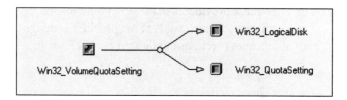

With this association, it is possible to view and configure the default quota settings for each NTFS volume. In the previous chapter, when we examined the File System, we saw how to use the *Win32_LogicalDisk* class. To illustrate its use, we developed Samples 2.31 through 2.34 ("Gathering disk partition, disk drive, and logical disk information"). However, we skipped some lines (lines 245 through 267), because this piece of code was related to the disk quota information. These lines are presented in Sample 3.33.

Sample 3.33   *Retrieving Disk quota information for each logical disk*

```
...:
...:
...:
245:
246:                   Set objWMIQuotaInstances = objWMIServices.ExecQuery _
247:                             ("Associators of {Win32_LogicalDisk='" & _
248:                             objWMILogicalDiskInstance.DeviceID & _
249:                             "'} Where AssocClass=Win32_VolumeQuotaSetting")
250:
251:                   If objWMIQuotaInstances.Count Then
252:                      WScript.Echo
253:                      WScript.Echo "  -- Quota information " & " " & String (63, "-")
254:                      For Each objWMIQuotaInstance In objWMIQuotaInstances
255:                         Set objWMIPropertySet = objWMIQuotaInstance.Properties_
256:                         For Each objWMIProperty In objWMIPropertySet
257:                            DisplayFormattedProperty objWMIQuotaInstance, _
258:                                                    "  " & objWMIProperty.Name, _
259:                                                    objWMIProperty.Name, _
260:                                                    Null
261:                         Next
262:                         Set objWMIPropertySet = Nothing
263:                      Next
264:                   End If
265:
266:                   Set objWMIQuotaInstances = Nothing
267:
...:
...:
...:
```

In this sample, we use the association class *Win32_VolumeQuotaSetting* to retrieve the *Win32_QuotaSetting* instances associated with the *Win32_LogicalDisk* (lines 246 through 249). Once the collection of instances is available, the script displays the disk quota information (lines 253 through 263). The quota information is available between lines 70 and 77 in the following output:

```
1:  C:\>GetPartitionInformation.wsf
2:  Microsoft (R) Windows Script Host Version 5.6
3:  Copyright (C) Microsoft Corporation 1996-2001. All rights reserved.
4:
5:  - Disk #0, Partition #0 -----------------------------------------------
6:    BlockSize: ........................... 512
7:    Bootable: ............................ TRUE
..:
15:   PrimaryPartition: .................... TRUE
16:   Size: ................................ 843816960
17:   StartingOffset: ...................... 874782720
18:   Type: ................................ MS-DOS V4 Huge
19:
20:   -- Physical disk information  -----------------------------------------
21:   BytesPerSector: ...................... 512
22:   Capabilities: ........................ Random Access, Supports Writing
..:
```

```
44:     TotalCylinders: ...................... 555
45:     TotalHeads: .......................... 240
46:     TotalSectors: ....................... 8391600
47:     TotalTracks: ........................ 133200
48:     TracksPerCylinder: .................. 240
49:
50:     -- Logical disk information  ---------------------------------------------
51:     Compressed: .......................... FALSE
52:     Description: ......................... Local Fixed Disk
..:
60:     QuotasDisabled: ...................... FALSE
61:     QuotasIncomplete: .................... FALSE
62:     QuotasRebuilding: .................... FALSE
63:     Size: ............................... 843816448
64:     SupportsDiskQuotas: .................. TRUE
65:     SupportsFileBasedCompression: ......... TRUE
66:     VolumeDirty: ......................... FALSE
67:     VolumeName: .......................... Whistler
68:     VolumeSerialNumber: .................. 988BD271
69:
70:     -- Quota information  ----------------------------------------------------
71:     Caption: ............................ C:
72:     DefaultLimit: ....................... 1073741824
73:     DefaultWarningLimit: ................. 134217728
74:     ExceededNotification: ................ TRUE
75:     State: .............................. 1
76:     *VolumePath: ........................ C:\
77:     WarningExceededNotification: ......... FALSE
```

As mentioned previously, it is possible to configure a default quota per volume and a quota per user. To configure a default quota per volume, we must work with the *Win32_QuotaSetting* class. To configure a quota per user, we must work with the *Win32_DiskQuota* and exploit the associations in place (see Figure 3.19). Let's start with the default quota per volume first! The command-line parameters of the next script sample are as follows:

```
C:\>WMIQuotaSetting.wsf
Microsoft (R) Windows Script Host Version 5.6
Copyright (C) Microsoft Corporation 1996-2001. All rights reserved.

Usage: WMIQuotaSetting.wsf /Action:value /Volume:value [/DefaultLimit:value]
                    [/DefaultWarningLimit[+|-]] [/ExceededNotification[+|-]]
                    [/WarningExceededNotification[+|-]]
                    [/Machine:value] [/User:value] [/Password:value]

Options:

Action                          : Specify the operation to perform: [List], [Disabled],
                                  [Tracked] and [Enforced].
Volume                          : Set the volume associated with the quota.
DefaultLimit                    : Set the default limit for the quota in MB.
DefaultWarningLimit             : Set the default warning limit for the quota in MB.
ExceededNotification            : Log event when a user exceeds quota limit.
WarningExceededNotification : Log event when a user exceeds warning level.
Machine                         : Determine the WMI system to connect to. (default=LocalHost)
User                            : Determine the UserID to perform the remote connection. (default=none)
```

```
Password                          : Determine the password to perform the remote
                                    connection. (default=none)
Examples:

   WMIQuotaSetting.wsf /Action:List
   WMIQuotaSetting.wsf /Volume:C: /Action:Disabled
   WMIQuotaSetting.wsf /Volume:C: /Action:Tracked
   WMIQuotaSetting.wsf /Volume:C: /Action:Enforced
   WMIQuotaSetting.wsf /Volume:C: /Action:Enforced /DefaultWarningLimit:128 /DefaultLimit:256
   WMIQuotaSetting.wsf /Volume:C: /Action:Enforced /DefaultWarningLimit:256 /DefaultLimit:NoLimit
   WMIQuotaSetting.wsf /Volume:C: /Action:Enforced /DefaultWarningLimit:NoLimit /DefaultLimit:512
   WMIQuotaSetting.wsf /Volume:C: /Action:Enforced /DefaultWarningLimit:128 /DefaultLimit:256
                       /ExceededNotification+
   WMIQuotaSetting.wsf /Volume:C: /Action:Enforced /DefaultWarningLimit:128 /DefaultLimit:256
                       /WarningExceededNotification+
```

Each parameter exposed by the script corresponds exactly to the settings exposed by the Windows Explorer graphical interface to manage the default quota settings, as shown in Figure 3.21. By using the script, the configuration of Figure 3.21 can be obtained with the following command line:

```
C:\>WMIQuotaSetting.wsf /Volume:C: /Action:Tracked
```

Figure 3.21
The Windows Explorer quota management interface.

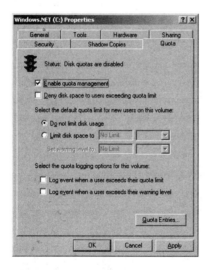

To configure all settings available, the following command line can be used:

```
C:\>WMIQuotaSetting.wsf /Volume:C: /Action:Enforced /DefaultWarningLimit:128 /DefaultLimit:256
                        /ExceededNotification+ /WarningExceededNotification+
```

This command line will enforce the quota settings to a maximum default limit of 256 MB with a default warning limit at 128 MB. Each time a user uses a quota higher than the warning limit or the maximum limit, an event log recod will be created in the system NT Event Log. Let's see how to script in Jscript the default quota configuration with Samples 3.34 and 3.35.

Sample 3.34   *Viewing the default volume quotas (Part I)*

```
1:<?xml version="1.0"?>
 .:
8:<package>
9:  <job>
..:
13:    <runtime>
..:
36:    </runtime>
37:
38:    <script language="VBScript" src="..\Functions\DecodeVolumeQuotaStatusFunction.vbs" />
39:
40:    <script language="VBScript" src="..\Functions\DisplayFormattedPropertyFunction.vbs" />
41:    <script language="VBScript" src="..\Functions\TinyErrorHandler.vbs" />
42:
43:    <object progid="WbemScripting.SWbemLocator" id="objWMILocator" reference="true"/>
44:
45:    <script language="Jscript">
46:    <![CDATA[
47:    var cComputerName = "LocalHost";
48:    var cWMINameSpace = "Root/cimv2";
49:    var cWMIQuotaSettingClass = "Win32_QuotaSetting";
50:
51:    var cQuotaNoLimit = "18446744073709551615";
..:
77:    // ----------------------------------------------------------------------------
78:    // Parse the command line parameters
79:    if ((WScript.Arguments.Named.Count == 0) || (WScript.Arguments.Named("Action") == null))
80:       {
81:       WScript.Arguments.ShowUsage();
82:       WScript.Quit();
83:       }
...:
112:    varDefaultLimit = WScript.Arguments.Named("DefaultLimit");
113:    if (varDefaultLimit != null)
114:       if (varDefaultLimit.toUpperCase() == "NOLIMIT")
115:          {
116:          varDefaultLimit = cQuotaNoLimit;
117:          }
118:       else
119:          {
120:          varDefaultLimit = varDefaultLimit.valueOf() * 1024 * 1024;
121:          }
122:
123:    varDefaultWarningLimit = WScript.Arguments.Named("DefaultWarningLimit");
124:    if (varDefaultWarningLimit != null)
125:       if (varDefaultWarningLimit.toUpperCase() == "NOLIMIT")
126:          {
127:          varDefaultWarningLimit = cQuotaNoLimit;
128:          }
129:       else
130:          {
131:          varDefaultWarningLimit = varDefaultWarningLimit.valueOf() * 1024 * 1024;
132:          }
```

```
...:
154:
155:     objWMILocator.Security_.AuthenticationLevel = wbemAuthenticationLevelDefault;
156:     objWMILocator.Security_.ImpersonationLevel = wbemImpersonationLevelImpersonate;
157:
158:     try
159:       {
160:       objWMIServices = objWMILocator.ConnectServer(strComputerName, cWMINameSpace,
161:                                                     strUserID, strPassword);
162:       }
...:
168:     // -- LIST -----------------------------------------------------------------
169:     if (boolList == true)
170:       {
171:       try
172:         {
173:         objWMIInstances = objWMIServices.InstancesOf (cWMIQuotaSettingClass)
174:         }
...:
180:       enumWMIInstances = new Enumerator (objWMIInstances);
181:       for (;! enumWMIInstances.atEnd(); enumWMIInstances.moveNext())
182:           {
183:           objWMIInstance = enumWMIInstances.item();
184:
185:           WScript.Echo ("- " + objWMIInstance.Caption + " " +
186:                         "--------------------------------------------------");
187:
188:           objWMIPropertySet = objWMIInstance.Properties_
189:           enumWMIPropertySet = new Enumerator (objWMIPropertySet);
190:           for (;! enumWMIPropertySet.atEnd(); enumWMIPropertySet.moveNext())
191:               {
192:               objWMIProperty = enumWMIPropertySet.item()
193:
194:               switch (objWMIProperty.Name)
195:                   {
196:                   case "State":
197:                       DisplayFormattedProperty (objWMIInstance,
198:                                                 "   " + objWMIProperty.Name,
199:                                                 VolumeQuotaStatus (objWMIInstance.State),
200:                                                 null);
201:                       break;
202:                   case "DefaultLimit":
203:                       if (objWMIInstance.DefaultLimit == cQuotaNoLimit)
204:                           {
205:                           varDefaultLimit = "No Limit";
206:                           }
207:                       else
208:                           {
209:                           varDefaultLimit = objWMIInstance.DefaultLimit;
210:                           }
211:                       DisplayFormattedProperty (objWMIInstance,
212:                                                 "   DefaultLimit (bytes)",
213:                                                 varDefaultLimit,
214:                                                 null);
215:                       break;
216:                   case "DefaultWarningLimit":
217:                       if (objWMIInstance.DefaultWarningLimit == cQuotaNoLimit)
218:                           {
219:                           varDefaultWarningLimit = "No Limit";
220:                           }
```

```
221:                              else
222:                                  {
223:                                  varDefaultWarningLimit = objWMIInstance.DefaultWarningLimit;
224:                                  }
225:                              DisplayFormattedProperty (objWMIInstance,
226:                                               " DefaultWarningLimit (bytes)",
227:                                               varDefaultWarningLimit,
228:                                               null);
229:                          break;
230:                      default:
231:                              DisplayFormattedProperty (objWMIInstance,
232:                                               "  " + objWMIProperty.Name,
233:                                               objWMIProperty.Name,
234:                                               null);
235:                          break;
236:                      }
237:                  }
238:          WScript.Echo();
239:          }
240:      }
241:
...:
...:
...:
```

Once the command-line parameter definition (lines 13 through 36) and parsing (lines 77 through 154) are completed, followed by the WMI connection (lines 155 through 162), the first portion of code allows the display of the current default quota settings (lines 169 through 240). Although the Jscript language is used in this example, you will easily recognize the traditional structure to display all available instances (lines 180 through 239) with their properties (lines 188 through 237). Every volume able to support disk quotas will be displayed. We will obtain the same information as obtained from Samples 2.31 through 2.34 but without any related disk, partition, or volume information, since we are not working with the associations in this example. The most interesting part of this sample concerns the scripting logic used to enable the disk quotas and to set the miscellaneous settings. This portion of the code is shown in Sample 3.35.

Sample 3.35   *Configuring the default volume quotas (Part II)*

```
...:
...:
...:
241:
242:    // -- UPDATE -------------------------------------------------------------------
243:    if (intState > 0)
244:        {
245:        try
246:            {
247:            objWMIInstance = objWMIServices.Get ("Win32_QuotaSetting.VolumePath='" +
248:                                     strDeviceID + "\\'");
249:            }
```

```
...:
255:        if (varDefaultLimit == null)
256:          {
257:            varDefaultLimit = objWMIInstance.DefaultLimit;
258:          }
259:        else
260:          {
261:            objWMIInstance.DefaultLimit = varDefaultLimit;
262:          }
263:
264:        if (varDefaultWarningLimit == null)
265:          {
266:            varDefaultWarningLimit = objWMIInstance.DefaultWarningLimit;
267:          }
268:        else
269:          {
270:            objWMIInstance.DefaultWarningLimit = varDefaultWarningLimit;
271:          }
272:
273:        if (boolExceededNotification == null)
274:          {
275:            boolExceededNotification = objWMIInstance.ExceededNotification;
276:          }
277:        else
278:          {
279:            objWMIInstance.ExceededNotification = boolExceededNotification;
280:          }
281:
282:        if (boolWarningExceededNotification == null)
283:          {
284:            boolWarningExceededNotification = objWMIInstance.WarningExceededNotification;
285:          }
286:        else
287:          {
288:            objWMIInstance.WarningExceededNotification = boolWarningExceededNotification;
289:          }
290:
291:        objWMIInstance.State = (intState - 1);
292:
293:        try
294:          {
295:            objWMIInstance.Put_ (wbemChangeFlagUpdateOnly | wbemFlagReturnWhenComplete);
296:          }
...:
302:        if (varDefaultLimit == cQuotaNoLimit)
303:          {
304:            varDefaultLimit = "No Limit";
305:          }
306:        if (varDefaultWarningLimit == cQuotaNoLimit)
307:          {
308:            varDefaultWarningLimit = "No Limit";
309:          }
310:
311:        WScript.Echo ("Default quota setting on '" + strDeviceID + "' updated.");
312:        WScript.Echo ("Quota is '" + VolumeQuotaStatus (objWMIInstance.State) + "' (" +
313:                      varDefaultWarningLimit + " (bytes) / " +
314:                      varDefaultLimit + " (bytes)).");
315:      }
316:
317:    ]]>
```

```
318:    </script>
319:  </job>
320:</package>
```

Because NTFS volumes are the only ones supporting quotas, a *Win32_QuotaSetting* instance is always available when the selected volume is an NTFS volume. Therefore, there is no need to create a *Win32_QuotaSetting* instance for a volume. However, the script must be able to update that *Win32_QuotaSetting* instance accordingly with the parameters given on the command line. This means that if only some parameters are given, other values must not be destroyed. For example, if the following command line is given:

```
1:    C:\>WMIQuotaSetting.wsf /Volume:C: /Action:Enforced /DefaultWarningLimit:256
                             /WarningExceededNotification+
2:    Microsoft (R) Windows Script Host Version 5.6
3:    Copyright (C) Microsoft Corporation 1996-2001. All rights reserved.
4:
5:    Default quota setting on 'C:' updated.
6:    Quota is 'Enforced' (268435456 (bytes) / No Limit (bytes)).
```

The warning limit will be fixed to 256 MB, and an NT Event Log trace will be created once this warning limit is reached. However, the hard limit is not specified on the command line and, as Figure 3.21 shows, there is no hard limit configured. The script takes care of this missing parameter and does not change its existing value. This logic is implemented by testing the miscellaneous variables assigned by the command-line parameters. If the command-line parameter was given, the variable contains a value; otherwise, the variable is equal to Null (see lines 255, 264, 273, and 282). If the variable is Null, the current property instance value is assigned to the variable (lines 257, 266, 275, and 284). If the variable has a value, the new value is assigned to the corresponding property instance (lines 261, 270, 279, and 288).

It is important to note that when no quota limit is set the assigned value is equal to 18446744073709551615 ($2^{64} - 1$). This value is defined in the script header at line 51. If the keyword "NoLimit" is assigned, the command-line parsing code assigns the correct value to reflect the "No Limit" configuration setting (lines 112 through 132). The WMI *state* property (line 291) determines if the quota management must be disabled, tracked, or enforced. Each of these states corresponds to a value of the *state* property: 0=Disabled, 1=Tracked, and 2=Enforced.

Once the examined instance is modified, the changes must be committed back to the system. This update is executed at lines 293 through 296. Once completed, the script displays a message showing the current configuration.

To configure a quota per user, as mentioned previously, the *Win32_Disk-Quota* with its associations must be used. This is the purpose of the next sample, also written in Jscript. Its command-line parameters are as follows:

```
C:\>WMIQuota.wsf
Microsoft (R) Windows Script Host Version 5.6
Copyright (C) Microsoft Corporation 1996-2001. All rights reserved.

Usage: WMIQuota.wsf /Action:value /Account:value /Volume:value [/Limit:value]
                    [/WarningLimit:value] [/Machine:value] [/User:value] [/Password:value

Options:

Action       : Specify the operation to perform: [List], [Create], [Update] and [Delete].
Account      : Set the account associated with the quota.
Volume       : Set the volume associated with the quota.
Limit        : Set the limit for the quota in MB.
WarningLimit : Set the warning limit for the quota in MB.
Machine      : Determine the WMI system to connect to. (default=LocalHost)
User         : Determine the UserID to perform the remote connection. (default=none)
Password     : Determine the password to perform the remote connection. (default=none)
Examples:

     WMIQuota.wsf /Action:List
     WMIQuota.wsf /Account:LISSWARENET\Alain.Lissoir /Volume:C: /Limit:512 /WarningLimit:256
                  /Action:Create
     WMIQuota.wsf /Account:LISSWARENET\Alain.Lissoir /Volume:C: /Limit:NoLimit /WarningLimit:256
                  /Action:Create
     WMIQuota.wsf /Account:LISSWARENET\Alain.Lissoir /Volume:C: /Limit:512 /WarningLimit:NoLimit
                  /Action:Create
     WMIQuota.wsf /Account:LISSWARENET\Alain.Lissoir /Volume:C: /Limit:1024 /Action:Update
     WMIQuota.wsf /Account:LISSWARENET\Alain.Lissoir /Volume:C: /Limit:NoLimit /Action:Update
     WMIQuota.wsf /Account:LISSWARENET\Alain.Lissoir /Volume:C: /WarningLimit:512 /Action:Update
     WMIQuota.wsf /Account:LISSWARENET\Alain.Lissoir /Volume:C: /WarningLimit:NoLimit
                  /Action:Update
     WMIQuota.wsf /Account:LISSWARENET\Alain.Lissoir /Volume:C: /Action:Delete
```

Because the command-line parameters and parsing always use the same structure, Sample 3.36 does not show this portion of the code. We also skipped the portion of the code showing all available instances with their properties, since it also uses a script logic used many times now (lines 203 through 316). The first interesting piece of code in Sample 3.36 concerns the user quota creation (lines 319 through 389).

Sample 3.36   *Viewing, creating, updating, and deleting volume quota per user (Part I)*

```
 1:<?xml version="1.0"?>
 .:
 8:<package>
 9:  <job>
..:
13:    <runtime>
..:
35:    </runtime>
36:
```

```
37:    <script language="VBScript" src="..\Functions\DecodeQuotaStatusInfoFunction.vbs" />
38:    <script language="VBScript" src="..\Functions\ExtractUserIDFunction.vbs" />
39:    <script language="VBScript" src="..\Functions\ExtractUserDomainFunction.vbs" />
40:
41:    <script language="VBScript" src="..\Functions\DisplayFormattedPropertyFunction.vbs" />
42:    <script language="VBScript" src="..\Functions\TinyErrorHandler.vbs" />
43:
44:    <object progid="WbemScripting.SWbemLocator" id="objWMILocator" reference="true"/>
45:    <object progid="WbemScripting.SWbemDateTime" id="objWMIDateTime" />
46:
47:    <script language="Jscript">
48:    <![CDATA[
49:
50:    var cComputerName = "LocalHost";
51:    var cWMINameSpace = "Root/cimv2";
52:    var cWMIDiskQuotaClass = "Win32_DiskQuota";
53:    var cWMIAccountClass = "Win32_Account";
54:    var cWMILogicalDiskClass = "Win32_LogicalDisk";
55:
56:    var cQuotaNoLimit = "18446744073709551615";
...:
189:   objWMILocator.Security_.AuthenticationLevel = wbemAuthenticationLevelDefault;
190:   objWMILocator.Security_.ImpersonationLevel = wbemImpersonationLevelImpersonate;
191:
192:   try
193:     {
194:     objWMIServices = objWMILocator.ConnectServer(strComputerName, cWMINameSpace,
195:                                                  strUserID, strPassword);
196:     }
...:
201:
202:   // -- LIST ----------------------------------------------------------------
203:   if (boolList == true)
204:     {
...:
316:     }
317:
318:   // -- CREATE --------------------------------------------------------------
319:   if (boolCreate == true)
320:     {
321:     try
322:       {
323:       objWMIClass = objWMIServices.Get (cWMIDiskQuotaClass);
324:       }
...:
329:
330:     objWMIInstance = objWMIClass.SpawnInstance_();
331:
332:     try
333:       {
334:       objWMIUserInstance = objWMIServices.Get (cWMIAccountClass + ".Domain='" +
335:                                       strDomain + "',Name='" + strName + "'");
336:       }
...:
342:     try
343:       {
344:       objWMIDiskInstance = objWMIServices.Get (cWMILogicalDiskClass + "='" +
345:                                       strDeviceID + "'");
346:       }
...:
```

```
352:        objWMIInstance.User = objWMIUserInstance.Path_.RelPath;
353:        objWMIInstance.QuotaVolume = objWMIDiskInstance.Path_.RelPath;
354:
355:        if (varLimit == null)
356:            {
357:            varLimit = cQuotaNoLimit;
358:            }
359:
360:        if (varWarningLimit == null)
361:            {
362:            varWarningLimit = cQuotaNoLimit;
363:            }
364:
365:        objWMIInstance.Limit = varLimit;
366:        objWMIInstance.WarningLimit = varWarningLimit;
367:
368:        try
369:          {
370:          objWMIInstance.Put_ (wbemChangeFlagCreateOrUpdate | wbemFlagReturnWhenComplete);
371:          }
...:
377:        if (objWMIInstance.Limit == cQuotaNoLimit)
378:            {
379:            varLimit = "No Limit";
380:            }
381:        if (objWMIInstance.WarningLimit == cQuotaNoLimit)
382:            {
383:            varWarningLimit = "No Limit";
384:            }
385:
386:        WScript.Echo ("Quota on '" + strDeviceID + "' for '" +
387:                      strDomain + "\\" + strName + "' created (" +
388:                      varWarningLimit + " (bytes) / " + varLimit + " (bytes)).");
389:        }
...:
...:
...:
```

Because the *Win32_DiskQuota* class is an association class, its creation is a bit unusual, because it is made up of references. First, a new instance of the *Win32_DiskQuota* is created (lines 321 through 330) and because the class is an association class that associates a *Win32_UserAccount* and a *Win32_LogicalDisk*, the code must retrieve these associated instances by using the information given on the command-line parameters (**/Account** and **/Volume** switches). This operation is executed from line 332 through 336 for the *Win32_Account* instance and from line 342 through 346 for the *Win32_LogicalDisk* instance. Once these two instances are available, their WMI paths are assigned to the *Win32_DiskQuota* references (lines 352 and 353). If there is no quota limit specified for the user quota creation, by default the script does not define a limit (lines 355 through 363). Next, the script commits the changes to the system (lines 368 through 371).

Besides the user quota creation, the script is also able to handle existing user quota modifications. This portion of the code is shown in Sample 3.37.

Sample 3.37   *Updating volume quota per user (Part II)*

```
...:
...:
...:
390:
391:    // -- UPDATE -------------------------------------------------------------------
392:    if (boolUpdate == true)
393:       {
394:        try
395:          {
396:           objWMIInstance = objWMIServices.Get ("Win32_DiskQuota.QuotaVolume=\"" +
397:                                      "Win32_LogicalDisk.DeviceID='" +
398:                                      strDeviceID + "'\"" +
399:                                      ",User=\"" + "Win32_Account.Domain='" +
400:                                      strDomain + "',Name='" + strName + "'\"");
401:          }
...:
407:        if (varLimit == null)
408:           {
409:            varLimit = objWMIInstance.Limit;
410:           }
411:        else
412:           {
413:            objWMIInstance.Limit = varLimit;
414:           }
415:
416:        if (varWarningLimit == null)
417:           {
418:            varWarningLimit = objWMIInstance.WarningLimit;
419:           }
420:        else
421:           {
422:            objWMIInstance.WarningLimit = varWarningLimit;
423:           }
424:
425:        try
426:          {
427:           objWMIInstance.Put_ (wbemChangeFlagUpdateOnly | wbemFlagReturnWhenComplete)
428:          }
...:
434:        if (objWMIInstance.Limit == cQuotaNoLimit)
435:           {
436:            varLimit = "No Limit";
437:           }
438:        if (objWMIInstance.WarningLimit == cQuotaNoLimit)
439:           {
440:            varWarningLimit = "No Limit";
441:           }
442:
443:        WScript.Echo ("Quota on '" + strDeviceID + "' for '" +
444:                      strDomain + "\\" + strName + "' updated (" +
445:                      varWarningLimit + " (bytes) / " + varLimit + " (bytes)).");
```

```
446:            }
447:
...:
...:
...:
```

To update a user quota, we must first retrieve the user quota instance. This is done from line 396 through 400. The WMI path of a *Win32_Disk-Quota* instance is made up of the Key properties. This is why it is a bit more complex to code. For example, a *Win32_DiskQuota* path will be coded as follows:

```
Win32_DiskQuota.QuotaVolume="Win32_LogicalDisk.DeviceID=\"C:\"",
                User="Win32_Account.Domain=\"NET-DPEN6400A\",
                Name=\"Administrators\""
```

Once the *Win32_DiskQuota* instance is retrieved, the miscellaneous settings will be configured based on the command-line parameters given (lines 407 through 423) and committed back to the system (lines 425 through 428). The logic used here is exactly the same as in Sample 3.35—it takes care of the parameters not specified on the command line.

The last supported operation is the deletion of a user quota (see Sample 3.38). This operation has nothing unusual about it. It retrieves the user quota instance to delete (lines 453 through 457), and then deletes that instance with the *Delete_* method of the **SWBemObject** (lines 464 through 467).

Sample 3.38   *Deleting volume quota per user (Part III)*

```
...:
...:
...:
447:
448:    // -- DELETE ---------------------------------------------------------------
449:    if (boolDelete == true)
450:        {
451:        try
452:            {
453:        objWMIInstance = objWMIServices.Get ("Win32_DiskQuota.QuotaVolume=\"" +
454:                                             "Win32_LogicalDisk.DeviceID='" +
455:                                             strDeviceID + "'\"" +
456:                                             ",User=\"" + "Win32_Account.Domain='" +
457:                                             strDomain + "',Name='" + strName + "'\"");
458:            }
...:
464:        try
465:            {
466:        objWMIInstance.Delete_();
467:            }
...:
473:        WScript.Echo ("Quota on '" + strDeviceID + "' for '" +
474:                        strDomain + "\\" + strName + "' deleted.");
```

```
475:        }
476:
477:    ]]>
478:    </script>
479:  </job>
480:</package>
```

3.5.2   DFS provider

Distributed File System (DFS) is the ability to logically group shares from multiple servers and to link these shares transparently. All the linked shares appear in a treelike structure within a single Root. The *DFS* provider supports the configuration and the management of DFS in Windows Server 2003. Table 3.44 shows the *DFS* provider capabilities.

Table 3.44   *The DFS Providers Capabilities*

Provider Name	Provider Namespace	Class Provider	Instance Provider	Method Provider	Property Provider	Event Provider	Event Consumer Provider	Support Get	Support Put	Support Enumeration	Support Delete	Windows Server 2003	Windows XP	Windows 2000 Server	Windows 2000 Professional	Windows NT 4.0
DFS Provider																
DFSProvider	Root/CIMV2	X	X					X	X	X	X	X				

Table 3.45 summarizes the classes supported by the *DFS* provider. All classes are available in the **Root\CIMv2** namespace.

Table 3.45   *The DFS Provider Classes*

Name	Type	Comments
Win32_DfsTarget	Dynamic	The DfsTarget class represents a target of a DFS link.
Win32_DfsNode	Dynamic	The Win32_DfsNode class represents a root or a link of a domain based or a standalone distributed file system (DFS).
Win32_DfsNodeTarget	Association	The Win32_DfsNodeTarget class associates a DFS node to one of its targets.

With this provider it is possible to create DFS nodes and use associations to represent the connections between nodes, shares, and servers linked to the nodes. Figure 3.22 represents this association.

A DFS Root can be defined at the domain level for domain-based operation or at the server level for standalone operation. Domain-based DFS can have multiple Roots in the domain but only one Root on each server. The *Create* method of the *Win32_DfsNode* can be used to create new nodes.

Figure 3.22
*The Win32_*
DFSNodeTarget
association class.

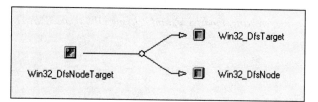

Sample 3.39 and 3.40 show how to retrieve, create, update, and delete DFS nodes. The script exposes the following command-line parameters:

```
C:\>WMIDFS.Wsf
Microsoft (R) Windows Script Host Version 5.6
Copyright (C) Microsoft Corporation 1996-2001. All rights reserved.

Usage: WMIDfs.wsf /Action:value /Share:value /Server:value /RootDFS:value
                  [/LinkState:value] [/TimeOut:value] [/Description:value]
                  [/Machine:value] [/User:value] [/Password:value]

Options:

Action      : Specify the operation to perform: [ViewRootNodes], [ViewNodes], [Create],
              [Update] and [Delete].
Share       : The ShareName indicates the name of the share that the link references.
Server      : The ServerName indicates the name of the server that the link references.
RootDFS     : The Root DFS Node that represents a link of a domain based or a standalone DFS.
LinkState   : Indicates the state of the DFS link. Only [Offline], [Online] or
              [Active] are accepted.
TimeOut     : Indicates the time in seconds for which the client caches the referral of a node.
Description : Textual description of a Node.
Machine     : Determine the WMI system to connect to. (default=LocalHost)
User        : Determine the UserID to perform the remote connection. (default=none)
Password    : Determine the password to perform the remote connection. (default=none)
Examples:

    WMIDFS.Wsf /Action:ViewRootNodes
    WMIDFS.Wsf /Action:ViewNodes
    WMIDFS.Wsf /Action:Create /Share:SubDirectory_9 /Server:NET-DPEN6400A.LissWare.Net
               /RootDFS:\\LISSWARENET\MyDFSRoot /Description:"DFS Node to SubDirectory_1"
    WMIDFS.Wsf /Action:Update /Share:SubDirectory_9 /Server:NET-DPEN6400A.LissWare.Net
               /RootDFS:\\LISSWARENET\MyDFSRoot /Timeout:10
    WMIDFS.Wsf /Action:Update /Share:SubDirectory_9 /Server:NET-DPEN6400A.LissWare.Net
               /RootDFS:\\LISSWARENET\MyDFSRoot /LinkState:OffLine
    WMIDFS.Wsf /Action:Update /Share:SubDirectory_9 /Server:NET-DPEN6400A.LissWare.Net
               /RootDFS:\\LISSWARENET\MyDFSRoot /LinkState:OnLine
    WMIDFS.Wsf /Action:Update /Share:SubDirectory_9 /Server:NET-DPEN6400A.LissWare.Net
               /RootDFS:\\LISSWARENET\MyDFSRoot /LinkState:Active
    WMIDFS.Wsf /Action:Delete /Share:SubDirectory_9 /Server:NET-DPEN6400A.LissWare.Net
               /RootDFS:\\LISSWARENET\MyDFSRoot
```

The first part of the script (Sample 3.39) defines and parses the command-line parameters (skipped lines 13 through 36 and lines 86 through 160). Next, after the WMI connection (lines 162 through 165), based on the value of the **/Action** switch, the script retrieves the *Win32_DFSNode* instances (lines 169 through 239).

Sample 3.39   *Viewing, creating, modifying, and deleting DFS nodes (Part I)*

```
1:<?xml version="1.0"?>
 .:
8:<package>
9:  <job>
..:
13:    <runtime>
..:
36:    </runtime>
37:
38:    <script language="VBScript" src="..\Functions\DecodeDFSStateFunction.vbs" />
39:
40:    <script language="VBScript" src="..\Functions\DisplayFormattedPropertyFunction.vbs" />
41:    <script language="VBScript" src="..\Functions\TinyErrorHandler.vbs" />
42:
43:    <object progid="WbemScripting.SWbemLocator" id="objWMILocator" reference="true"/>
44:    <object progid="WbemScripting.SWbemDateTime" id="objWMIDateTime" />
45:
46:    <script language="VBscript">
47:    <![CDATA[
..:
51:    Const cComputerName = "LocalHost"
52:    Const cWMINameSpace = "Root/cimv2"
53:    Const cWMIDfsNodeClass = "Win32_DfsNode"
54:    Const cWMIDfsTargetClass = "Win32_DfsTarget"
..:
84:    ' --------------------------------------------------------------------------
85:    ' Parse the command line parameters
86:    If WScript.Arguments.Named.Count = 0 Then
87:        WScript.Arguments.ShowUsage()
88:        WScript.Quit
89:    End If
90:
91:    Select Case Ucase(WScript.Arguments.Named("Action"))
92:            Case "VIEWROOTNODES"
93:                boolList = True
94:                boolDFSRootNodes = True
95:            Case "VIEWNODES"
96:                boolList = True
97:                boolDFSRootNodes = False
98:            Case "CREATE"
99:                boolCreate = True
100:           Case "UPDATE"
101:                boolUpdate = True
102:           Case "DELETE"
103:                boolDelete = True
104:           Case Else
105:                WScript.Echo "Invalid action type. Only [List], [Create], [Update] ...
106:                WScript.Arguments.ShowUsage()
107:                WScript.Quit
108:    End Select
...:
159:    strComputerName = WScript.Arguments.Named("Machine")
160:    If Len(strComputerName) = 0 Then strComputerName = cComputerName
161:
162:    objWMILocator.Security_.AuthenticationLevel = wbemAuthenticationLevelDefault
163:    objWMILocator.Security_.ImpersonationLevel = wbemImpersonationLevelImpersonate
```

```
164:
165:    Set objWMIServices = objWMILocator.ConnectServer(strComputerName, cWMINameSpace, _
166:                                                     strUserID, strPassword)
...:
169:    ' -- LIST ---------------------------------------------------------------------
170:    If boolList = True Then
171:
172:        Set objWMIInstances = objWMIServices.InstancesOf (cWMIDfsNodeClass)
...:
175:        If objWMIInstances.Count Then
176:            For Each objWMIInstance in objWMIInstances
177:                If boolDFSRootNodes = objWMIInstance.Root Then
178:                    WScript.Echo "- Node: " & objWMIInstance.Name & String (60, "-")
179:
180:                    Set objWMIPropertySet = objWMIInstance.Properties_
181:                    For Each objWMIProperty In objWMIPropertySet
182:                        Select Case objWMIProperty.Name
183:                            Case "Caption"
184:
185:                            Case "State"
186:                                DisplayFormattedProperty objWMIInstance, _
187:                                    " " & objWMIProperty.Name, _
188:                                    DecodeDFSNodeState (objWMIProperty.Value), _
189:                                    Null
190:                            Case Else
191:                                DisplayFormattedProperty objWMIInstance, _
192:                                    " " & objWMIProperty.Name, _
193:                                    objWMIProperty.Value, _
194:                                    Null
195:                        End Select
196:                    Next
...:
199:                    Set objWMIAssocInstances = objWMIServices.ExecQuery _
200:                                                    ("Associators of {" & _
201:                                                    objWMIInstance.Path_.RelPath & "}")
202:
203:                    For Each objWMIAssocInstance In objWMIAssocInstances
204:                        WScript.Echo vbCRLF & " - Target Link: \\" & _
205:                                        objWMIAssocInstance.ServerName & _
206:                                        "\" & objWMIAssocInstance.ShareName & _
207:                                        " " & String (60, "-")
208:                        Set objWMIPropertySet = objWMIAssocInstance.Properties_
209:                        For Each objWMIProperty In objWMIPropertySet
210:                            Select Case objWMIProperty.Name
211:                                Case "Caption"
212:
213:                                Case "State"
214:                                    DisplayFormattedProperty objWMIInstance, _
215:                                        " " & objWMIProperty.Name, _
216:                                        DecodeDFSTargetState (objWMIProperty.Value), _
217:                                        Null
218:                                Case Else
219:                                    DisplayFormattedProperty objWMIInstance, _
220:                                        " " & objWMIProperty.Name, _
221:                                        objWMIProperty.Value, _
222:                                        Null
223:                            End Select
224:                        Next
...:
226:                    Next
```

```
...:
230:                    WScript.Echo
231:                End If
232:            Next
233:        Else
234:            WScript.Echo "No DFS nodes available."
235:        End If
...:
239:    End If
240:
...:
...:
...:
```

At line 172, the script retrieves all instances from the *Win32_DFSNode* class. Next, it uses the usual scripting technique to display the *Win32_DFS-Node* instance properties (lines 176 through 232). The **/Action:ViewRoot-Nodes** or **/Action:ViewNodes** switches determine if the DFS node Root instances must be displayed by performing a comparison of the switch value with the *Root* property of the *Win32_DFSNode* instance (line 177). Next, it displays the properties of the instance accordingly (lines 180 through 196).

As shown in Figure 3.22, the *Win32_DFSNode* class is associated with the *Win32_DFSTarget* by the *Win32_DfsNodeTarget* association class. The script takes advantage of this association (lines 199 through 201) to display information about the *Win32_DFSTarget* instances (lines 203 through 224).

Figure 3.23
A DFS configuration example.

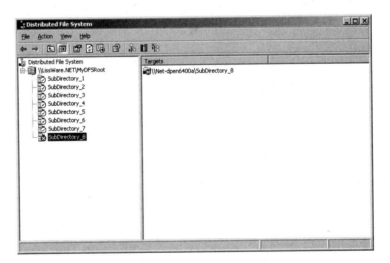

For a configuration similar to the one shown in Figure 3.23, the script execution with the **/Action:ViewRootNodes** switch will produce an output similar to the following one:

```
1:    C:\>WMIDFS.Wsf /Action:ViewRootNodes
2:    Microsoft (R) Windows Script Host Version 5.6
3:    Copyright (C) Microsoft Corporation 1996-2001. All rights reserved.
4:
5:    - Node: \\LISSWARENET\MyDFSRoot-------------------------------------------------
6:      Description: .......................... My Domain DFS Root
7:      Name: ................................. \\LISSWARENET\MyDFSRoot
8:      Root: ................................. True
9:      State: ................................ Ok
10:     Timeout: .............................. 30
11:
12:     - Target Link: \\NET-DPEN6400A\MyDFSRoot -----------------------------------------
13:       LinkName: ........................... \\LISSWARENET\MyDFSRoot
14:       ServerName: ......................... NET-DPEN6400A
15:       ShareName: .......................... MyDFSRoot
16:       State: .............................. OnLine.
```

From line 5 through 10, we see the *Win32_DFSNode* instance properties and from line 12 through 16, we see the *Win32_DFSTarget* instance properties associated with it.

The script execution with the **/Action:ViewNodes** switch will produce an output similar to the following one:

```
1:    C:\>WMIDFS.Wsf /Action:ViewNodes
2:    Microsoft (R) Windows Script Host Version 5.6
3:    Copyright (C) Microsoft Corporation 1996-2001. All rights reserved.
4:
5:    - Node: \\LISSWARENET\MyDFSRoot\SubDirectory_3-----------------------------------------
6:      Description: .......................... SubDirectory_3
7:      Name: ................................. \\LISSWARENET\MyDFSRoot\SubDirectory_3
8:      Root: ................................. False
9:      State: ................................ OnLine
10:     Timeout: .............................. 10
11:
12:     - Target Link: \\NET-DPEN6400A.LissWare.Net\SubDirectory_3 ----------------------------
13:       LinkName: ........................... \\LISSWARENET\MyDFSRoot\SubDirectory_3
14:       ServerName: ......................... NET-DPEN6400A.LissWare.Net
15:       ShareName: .......................... SubDirectory_3
16:       State: .............................. OnLine.
17:
18:     - Node: \\LISSWARENET\MyDFSRoot\SubDirectory_8-----------------------------------------
19:       Description: ........................ SubDirectory_8
20:       Name: .............................. \\LISSWARENET\MyDFSRoot\SubDirectory_8
21:       Root: .............................. False
22:       State: ............................. OnLine
23:       Timeout: ........................... 10
24:
25:       - Target Link: \\NET-DPEN6400A.LissWare.Net\SubDirectory_8 --------------------------
26:         LinkName: ......................... \\LISSWARENET\MyDFSRoot\SubDirectory_8
27:         ServerName: ....................... NET-DPEN6400A.LissWare.Net
28:         ShareName: ........................ SubDirectory_8
29:         State: ............................ OffLine.
..:
..:
..:
```

The output is similar to the previous one. However, only *Win32_DFS-Node* non-Root instances are displayed. You will notice that the state of the "SubDirectory_8" is off line (line 29), as shown in Figure 3.23.

Sample 3.40, which is the second part of the script, creates (lines 242 through 259), modifies (lines 262 through 290), and deletes (lines 293 through 304) existing *Win32_DFSNode* instances.

Sample 3.40   *Viewing, creating, modifying, and deleting DFS nodes (Part II)*

```
...:
...:
...:
240:
241:    ' -- CREATE ------------------------------------------------------------
242:    If boolCreate = True Then
243:        Set objWMIClass = objWMIServices.Get (cWMIDfsNodeClass)
...:
246:        intRC = objWMIClass.Create (strRootDFS & "\" & strShare, _
247:                                    strServer, _
248:                                    strShare, _
249:                                    strDescription)
250:
251:        If intRC = 0 Then
252:            WScript.Echo "DFS node '" & strRootDFS & "\" & strShare & "' successfully created."
253:        Else
254:            WScript.Echo "Failed to create DFS node '" & strRootDFS & "\" & _
255:                         strShare & "' (0x" & Hex (IntRC) & ")."
256:        End If
...:
259:    End If
260:
261:    ' -- UPDATE ------------------------------------------------------------
262:    If boolUpdate = True Then
263:        if intTimeout Then
264:            Set objWMIInstance = objWMIServices.Get (cWMIDfsNodeClass & "='" & _
265:                                                     strRootDFS & "\" & strShare & "'")
...:
268:            objWMIInstance.Timeout = intTimeout
269:
270:            objWMIInstance.Put_ (wbemChangeFlagUpdateOnly Or wbemFlagReturnWhenComplete)
...:
272:        End If
273:
274:        If intLinkState Then
275:            Set objWMIInstance = objWMIServices.Get (cWMIDfsTargetClass & ".LinkName='" & _
276:                                                     strRootDFS & "\" & strShare & _
277:                                                     "',ServerName='" & strServer & _
278:                                                     "',ShareName='" & strShare & "'")
...:
281:            objWMIInstance.State = intLinkState - 1
282:
283:            objWMIInstance.Put_ (wbemChangeFlagUpdateOnly Or wbemFlagReturnWhenComplete)
...:
285:        End If
286:
287:        WScript.Echo "DFS Node '" & strRootDFS & "\" & strShare & "' successfully updated."
```

```
...:
290:    End If
291:
292:    ' -- DELETE ----------------------------------------------------------------
293:    If boolDelete = True Then
294:        Set objWMIInstance = objWMIServices.Get (cWMIDfsNodeClass & "=" & _
295:                                         strRootDFS & "\" & strShare & "'")
...:
298:        objWMIInstance.Delete_
...:
301:        WScript.Echo "DFS Node '" & strRootDFS & "\" & strShare & "' successfully deleted."
...:
304:    End If
...:
308:    ]]>
309:    </script>
310:    </job>
311:</package>
```

The creation of a *Win32_DFSNode* instance is performed with the *Create* static method exposed by the *Win32_DFSNode* class. This method requires four parameters, as follows:

- The DFS path parameter, which specifies the path of the DFS Root (which comes from the command line with the **/RootDFS** switch).

- The Server *name* parameter, which specifies the name of the server that hosts the share to which the DFS link is associated (which comes from the command line with the **/Server** switch).

- The *ShareName* parameter, which specifies the name of the share to which the DFS link is associated (which comes from the command line with the **/Share** switch).

- The *Description* parameter, which specifies a comment describing the DFS node (which comes from the command line with the **/Description** switch).

The *Win32_DFSNode* instance creation is executed at line 246. Next, the script tests if the *Create* method returned a value different from zero. Any value returned from the execution of this method states that an error occurred. These values correspond to the **Win32** errors (where corresponding messages are available with a "Net HelpMsg <value>" command).

The *Win32_DFSNode* class and the *Win32_DFSTarget* class allow the modification of some properties of the instances they represent. The *Win32_DFSNode* exposes a *Timeout* property to indicate the time in seconds for which the client caches the referral of this node. The script can modify this property (lines 264 through 270) by retrieving the corresponding *Win32_DFSNode* instance in an **SWBemObject** object (lines 264 and 265) and invoking the *Put_* method (line 270).

In the same way, it is possible to modify the state of a *Win32_DFSTarget* instance by changing the value of the *State* property (lines 274 through 285). The State property indicates the state of the DFS target. Note that both *Win32_DFSNode* and *Win32_DFSTarget* classes expose a *State* property. Table 3.46 shows the meaning of the different values for each class.

Table 3.46   *The State Property Meaning of the Win32_DFSNode and Win32_Target Classes*

Win32_DFSNode State property values	
Meaning	**Values**
Ok	0
Inconsistent	1
OnLine	2
OffLine	3

Win32_DFSTarget State property values	
Meaning	**Values**
OffLine	0
OnLine	1
Active	4

To delete a *Win32_DFSNode* instance, the script retrieves an instance of a DFS node (lines 294 and 295) and invokes the *Delete_* method of the **SWBemObject** representing the *Win32_DFSNode* instance (line 298).

3.5.3   Shadow Copy providers

The *Shadow Copy* providers provide management capabilities to the Windows Server 2003 shadow copy services. The user interface exposing information related to this new feature is available by right-clicking on a volume,

Figure 3.24
Managing the Shadow Copies of a volume from the user interface.

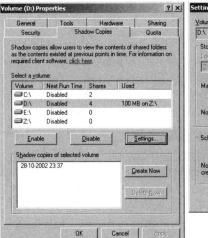

selecting properties, and clicking again on the Shadow Copies pane (see Figure 3.24). Bear in mind that this feature is only available under Windows Server 2003.

The set of properties and actions available from the user interface is also accessible from WMI. The *Shadow Copy* providers supporting these features are registered in the **Root\CIMv2** namespace of the CIM repository (see Table 3.47).

Table 3.47   *The Shadow Copy Providers Capabilities*

Provider Name	Provider Namespace	Class Provider	Instance Provider	Method Provider	Property Provider	Event Provider	Event Consumer Provider	Support Get	Support Put	Support Enumeration	Support Delete	Windows Server 2003	Windows XP	Windows 2000 Server	Windows 2000 Professional	Windows NT 4.0
Shadow Copy Providers																
MSVSS__PROVIDER	Root/CIMV2	X	X					X	X	X	X	X				
MSVDS__PROVIDER	Root/CIMV2	X	X					X	X	X	X	X				

These providers support a set of classes exposing properties and methods to perform most of the Shadow Copy tasks (see Table 3.48). The most relevant classes to use from a scripting point of view are the *Win32_Volume*, *Win32_ShadowCopy*, and *Win32_ShadowStorage* classes.

Table 3.48   *The Shadow Copy Providers Classes*

Name	Type	Comments
Win32_ShadowCopy	Dynamic	The Win32_ShadowCopy class is a storage extent that represents a duplicate copy of the original volume at some previous time.
Win32_ShadowProvider	Dynamic	The Win32_ShadowProvider class represents a component, typically a combination of user-mode and kernel/firmware implementation, that will perform the work involved in creating and representing volume shadow copies.
Win32_Volume	Dynamic	The Win32_Volume class represents an area of storage on a hard disk. The class returns local volumes that are formatted, unformatted, mounted, or offline. A volume is formatted by using a file system, such as FAT or NTFS, and may have a drive letter assigned to it. A single hard disk can have multiple volumes, and volumes can also span multiple disks.
Win32_MountPoint	Association	The mount point associates a volume to the directory at which it is mounted.
Win32_ShadowBy	Association	The association between a shadow copy and the provider that created the shadow copy.
Win32_ShadowDiffVolumeSupport	Association	The association between a shadow copy provider and a volume supported for differential storage area.
Win32_ShadowFor	Association	The association between a shadow copy and the volume for which the shadow was created.
Win32_ShadowOn	Association	The association between a shadow copy and the volume on which differential data is written.
Win32_ShadowStorage	Association	The association between the volume for which a shadow copy is made and the volume to which the differential data is written.
Win32_ShadowVolumeSupport	Association	The association between a shadow copy provider and a supported volume.
Win32_VolumeQuota	Association	The Win32_VolumeQuota association relates a volume to the per volume quota settings.
Win32_VolumeUserQuota	Association	The Win32_VolumeUserQuota association relates per user quotas to quota-enabled volumes. System administrators can configure Windows to prevent further disk space use and log an event when a user exceeds a specified disk space limit. They can also log an event when a user exceeds a specified disk space warning level. Note that disk quotas cannot be set for the Administrator accounts themselves.

It is interesting to note that the *Win32_Volume* class is quite similar to the *Win32_LogicalDisk* class. For instance, it is possible to invoke the *Chkdsk* method from the *Win32_Volume* class, as we did in Sample 2.3 with the *Win32_LogicalDisk* class. Both *Chkdsk* method implementations expose the exact same input parameters. However, the *Win32_Volume* class exposes some extra properties and methods especially related to the Shadow Copy features. Actually, during the design phase of the Shadow Copy object model, it had been noted that the current *Win32_LogicalDisk* class was not providing enough information to suit the requirements. Therefore, Microsoft decided to create the *Win32_Volume* class to suit its needs. That's why this class implements some methods of the *Win32_LogicalDisk* class (i.e., *Chkdsk*, *ExcludeFromAutoChk*, *ScheduleAutoChk*) with some new methods and functionalities to request information about the defragmentation analysis, perform a defragmentation, format a volume (i.e., *Defrag*, *DefragAnalysis*, *Format*), mount or dismount a volume, and manage shadow copies. However, there are sseveral noteworthy differences between *Win32_LogicalDisk* and *Win32_Volume* classes. These are as follows:

- The *Win32_Volume* class does not manage floppy disk drives.

- The *Win32_Volume* class can be used to change the volume drive letter, while the *Win32_LogicalDisk* does not support this.

- *Win32_Volume* class enumerates all volumes, not just those with drive letters similar to the *Win32_LogicalDisk* class.

- The *Win32_Volume* class does not enumerate network shares that are mapped to drive letters similar to the *Win32_LogicalDisk* class.

Besides the *Win32_Volume* class, another very interesting class is the *Win32_ShadowCopy* class. Instances of this class represent the shadow copies of the original volume at some previous time. The *Win32_Volume* and *Win32_ShadowCopy* classes are associated with the *Win32_ShadowFor* and *Win32_ShadowOn* association classes (see Figure 3.25). The *Win32_ShadowCopy* class exposes the *Create* method to create shadow copies, which corresponds to the "Create Now" button shown in Figure 3.24.

The final, most relevant class is the *Win32_ShadowStorage* class. This class is an association class linking the *Win32_Volume* class with the *Win32_Volume* class itself. The purpose of this association class is to expose some properties visible in the user interface (see Figure 3.24—i.e., used space, allocated space, and the maximum space) and create an association between a volume that contains information to be shadowed and a volume containing the shadows. Some interesting properties of the *Win32_Shad-*

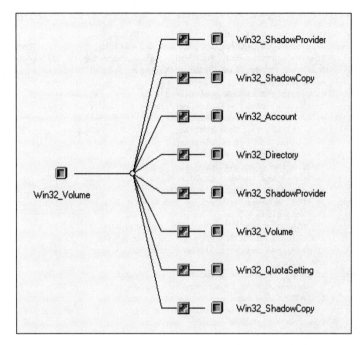

Figure 3.25
*The Win32_
Volume class and
its associations.*

owStorage class are, for example, *AllocatedSpace*, *MaxSpace*, and *UsedSpace*, where *MaxSpace* can be updated.

A very interesting aspect of the Shadow Copy object model is the existence of associations between the *Win32_Volume* class and the *Win32_QuotaSetting* class (see Figure 3.25). Similar to the *Win32_LogicalDisk* class, by managing the volumes with the *Win32_Volume* class, it is possible to retrieve and manage disk quota information. However, we will not cover the disk quota management in the next script sample, since the logic and coding technique are exactly the same as samples working with the *Win32_LogicalDisk* and *Win32_QuotaSettings* classes (see Samples 3.33 through 3.38).

Samples 3.41 through 3.52 illustrate how to work with these three Shadow Copy classes. The command-line parameters supported by the script expose most methods and manageable properties of the classes.

```
C:\>WMIDiskSvc.wsf /?
Microsoft (R) Windows Script Host Version 5.6
Copyright (C) Microsoft Corporation 1996-2001. All rights reserved.

Usage: WMIDiskSvc.wsf Volume [/Action:value] [/ShadowCopy[+|-]] [/Force[+|-]] [/FileSystem:value]
                             [/ClusterSize:value] [/Label:value] [/Compression[+|-]]
                             [/FixErrors[+|-]] [/VigorousIndexCheck[+|-]] [/SkipFolderCycle[+|-]]
                             [/ForceDismount[+|-]] [/RecoverBadSectors[+|-]] [/OKToRunAtBootUp[+|-]]
                             [/MaxSpace:value] [/ShadowStorage:value] [/ShadowCopyID:value]
                             [/Machine:value] [/User:value] [/Password:value]
```

```
Options:

Volume             : The logical disk letter (i.e., C: or D:).
Action             : Determines the action to perform. Only [List], [Format], [DefragAnalysis],
                     [Defrag], [Dismount], [Chkdsk], [CreateShadowCopy], [DeleteShadowCopy],
                     [CreateShadowStorage], [UpdateShadowStorage] or [DeleteShadowStorage] is
                     accepted.
ShadowCopy         : Only list the shadow copies available on the system.
Force              : Forces the defrag even if free space on the disk is low.
FileSystem         : Determines the filesystem to use for the formatted volume.
                     Only [NTFS], [FAT] or [FAT32].
ClusterSize        : Determines the volume cluster size to use.
Label              : Determines the volume label.
Compression        : Enables the compression on the formatted volume.
FixErrors          : Indicates what should be done to errors found on the disk. If true, then errors
                     are fixed. The default is FALSE.
VigorousIndexCheck : If TRUE, a vigorous check of index entries should be performed.
                     The default is TRUE.
SkipFolderCycle    : If TRUE, the folder cycle checking should be skipped or not.
                     The default is TRUE.
ForceDismount      : If TRUE, the drive should be forced to dismount before checking.
                     The default is FALSE.
RecoverBadSectors  : If TRUE, the bad sectors should be located and the readable information should
                     be recovered from these sectors. The default is FALSE.
OKToRunAtBootUp    : If TRUE, the chkdsk operation should be performed at next boot up time,
                     in case the operation could not be performed because the disk was locked at
                     time the method was called. The default is FALSE.
MaxSpace           : Determines the maximum space to be used on the Shadow Storage.
ShadowStorage      : Determines the volume to use to store the Shadows.
ShadowCopyID       : Specifies the shadow copy ID to delete.
Machine            : Determines the WMI system to connect to. (default=LocalHost)
User               : Determines the UserID to perform the remote connection. (default=none)
Password           : Determines the password to perform the remote connection. (default=none)
Example:

    WMIDiskSvc.wsf /Action:List
    WMIDiskSvc.wsf /Action:List /ShadowCopy+

    WMIDiskSvc.wsf C: /Action:DefragAnalysis
    WMIDiskSvc.wsf C: /Action:Defrag /Force+

    WMIDiskSvc.wsf C: /Action:Format /FileSystem:NTFS
                      /QuickFormat+ /ClusterSize:4096 /Label:"MyDisk" /Compression+

    WMIDiskSvc.wsf C: /Action:Chkdsk /FixErrors+ /VigorousIndexCheck+ /SkipFolderCycle+
    WMIDiskSvc.wsf C: /Action:Chkdsk /ForceDismount+ /RecoverBadSectors+ /OKToRunAtBootUp+

    WMIDiskSvc.wsf C: /Action:CreateShadowStorage /MaxSpace:850 /ShadowStorage:Z:
    WMIDiskSvc.wsf C: /Action:UpdateShadowStorage /MaxSpace:Unlimited
    WMIDiskSvc.wsf C: /Action:DeleteShadowStorage

    WMIDiskSvc.wsf C: /Action:CreateShadowCopy
    WMIDiskSvc.wsf /Action:DeleteShadowCopy /ShadowCopyID:{a2e1d5d6-4bab-4bd8-b133-dad5798ec9ff}
```

As usual, the first part of the script defines (skipped lines 13 through 59) and parses (skipped lines 130 through 274) the command-line parameters. Next, it executes the WMI connection (lines 276 through 280).

Sample 3.41 *Managing disk services and shadow copies (Part I)*

```
  1:<?xml version="1.0"?>
  .:
  8:<package>
  9:  <job>
 ..:
 13:    <runtime>
 ..:
 59:    </runtime>
 60:
 61:    <script language="VBScript" src="..\Functions\DisplayFormattedPropertiesFunction.vbs" />
 62:    <script language="VBScript" src="..\Functions\DisplayFormattedPropertyFunction.vbs" />
 63:    <script language="VBScript" src="..\Functions\TinyErrorHandler.vbs" />
 64:
 65:    <object progid="WbemScripting.SWbemLocator" id="objWMILocator" reference="true"/>
 66:    <object progid="WbemScripting.SWbemDateTime" id="objWMIDateTime" />
 67:
 68:    <script language="VBscript">
 69:    <![CDATA[
 ..:
 73:    Const cComputerName = "LocalHost"
 74:    Const cWMINameSpace = "root/cimv2"
 75:
 76:    Const cUnlimitedMaxSpace = "18446744073709551615"
...:
130:    ' -----------------------------------------------------------------------------
131:    ' Parse the command line parameters
132:    strAction = WScript.Arguments.Named("Action")
133:    Select Case UCase (strAction)
134:          Case "LIST"
135:                boolShadowCopy = WScript.Arguments.Named("ShadowCopy")
136:                If Len(boolShadowCopy) = 0 Then boolShadowCopy = False
137:
138:                boolList = True
139:
140:          Case "CHKDSK"
...:
267:    strUserID = WScript.Arguments.Named("User")
268:    If Len(strUserID) = 0 Then strUserID = ""
269:
270:    strPassword = WScript.Arguments.Named("Password")
271:    If Len(strPassword) = 0 Then strPassword = ""
272:
273:    strComputerName = WScript.Arguments.Named("Machine")
274:    If Len(strComputerName) = 0 Then strComputerName = cComputerName
275:
276:    objWMILocator.Security_.AuthenticationLevel = wbemAuthenticationLevelDefault
277:    objWMILocator.Security_.ImpersonationLevel = wbemImpersonationLevelImpersonate
278:
279:    Set objWMIServices = objWMILocator.ConnectServer(strComputerName, cWMINameSpace, _
280:                                                     strUserID, strPassword)
...:
282:
...:
...:
...:
```

The first feature supported by the script is the ability to list all shadow copies available on a system. This feature requires a very basic scripting technique, since it simply requests all instances of the *Win32_ShadowCopy* class and displays all properties of each instance. This capability will be useful when we will need to delete a shadow copy with WMI. Actually, the key property to retrieve a *Win32_ShadowCopy* instance is a GUID number exposed by the *ID* property. This is why it is interesting to implement a function listing all *Win32_ShadowCopy* instances with their properties (see Sample 3.42).

Sample 3.42   *Viewing all Win32_ShadowCopy instances (Part II)*

```
...:
...:
...:
282:
283:    ' -- List Shadow Copy -----------------------------------------------------------
284:    If boolList = True And boolShadowCopy = True Then
285:        Set objWMIInstances = objWMIServices.InstancesOf ("Win32_ShadowCopy")
...:
288:        If objWMIInstances.Count Then
289:            For Each objWMIInstance In objWMIInstances
290:                objWMIDateTime.Value = objWMIInstance.InstallDate
291:
292:                WScript.Echo "- Shadow Copy: (" & objWMIDateTime.GetVarDate (False) & _
293:                            ") " & String (60, "-")
294:
295:                Set objWMIPropertySet = objWMIInstance.Properties_
296:                For Each objWMIProperty In objWMIPropertySet
297:                    DisplayFormattedProperty objWMIInstance, _
298:                            objWMIProperty.Name, _
299:                            objWMIProperty.Name, _
300:                            Null
301:                Next
...:
304:            Next
305:        Else
306:            WScript.Echo "No shadow copy available."
307:        End If
308:    End If
309:
...:
...:
...:
```

As an example, the script will display the following information:

```
 1:    C:\>WMIDiskSvc.wsf /Action:List /ShadowCopy+
 2:    Microsoft (R) Windows Script Host Version 5.6
 3:    Copyright (C) Microsoft Corporation 1996-2001. All rights reserved.
 4:
 5:    - Shadow Copy: (28-10-2002 22:37:09) ------------------------------------------
 6:    ClientAccessible: ....................... TRUE
 7:    Count: .................................. 1
 8:    DeviceObject: ........................... \\?\GLOBALROOT\Device\HarddiskVolumeShadowCopy13
 9:    Differential: ........................... FALSE
10:    ExposedLocally: ......................... FALSE
```

```
11:   ExposedRemotely: ......................... FALSE
12:   HardwareAssisted: ........................ FALSE
13:   *ID: ..................................... {2f26b83b-d583-461d-b773-e6cd024f9710}
14:   Imported: ................................ FALSE
15:   InstallDate: ............................. 28-10-2002 22:37:09
16:   NoAutoRelease: ........................... TRUE
17:   NotSurfaced: ............................. FALSE
18:   NoWriters: ............................... TRUE
19:   OriginatingMachine: ...................... net-dpep6400a.Emea.LissWare.NET
20:   Persistent: .............................. TRUE
21:   Plex: .................................... FALSE
22:   ProviderID: .............................. {b5946137-7b9f-4925-af80-51abd60b20d5}
23:   ReadWrite: ............................... FALSE
24:   ServiceMachine: .......................... net-dpep6400a.Emea.LissWare.NET
25:   SetID: ................................... {238304a1-3df0-4d0e-9f16-d143abe87a29}
26:   State: ................................... 12
27:   Transportable: ........................... FALSE
28:   VolumeName: .............................. \\?\Volume{3eed7424-a3b2-11d6-a5f4-806e6f6e6963}\
```

Of course, if we are able to list the shadow copies available in a system, it is possible to create new shadow copies by using the *Win32_ShadowCopy* class and its *Create* method, as shown in Sample 3.43. It is interesting to note that the *Create* method is a static method. Therefore, the method does not relate to a particular *Win32_ShadowCopy* dynamic instance. Instead, an instance of the class must be created to invoke the method (line 314). From line 316 through 318, the method requests two input parameters (the drive letter and the context used by the WMI provider to create the shadow, which is always "Client Accessible") and returns one output parameter (which is the ID of the created shadow) displayed at line 324.

Sample 3.43   *Creating new shadow copies (Part III)*

```
...:
...:
...:
309:
310:   ' -- CreateShadowCopy -------------------------------------------------------------
311:   If boolCreateShadowCopy = True Then
312:       WScript.Echo "Creating shadow copy ..."
313:
314:       Set objWMIClass = objWMIServices.Get ("Win32_ShadowCopy")
315:
316:       intRC = objWMIClass.Create (strWMIDriverLetter & "\", _
317:                                   "ClientAccessible", _
318:                                   strShadowCopyID)
...:
321:       If intRC Then
322:           WScript.Echo "Shadow copy creation error (" & intRC & ")."
323:       Else
324:           WScript.Echo "Shadow copy '" & strShadowCopyID & "' successfully created."
325:       End If
326:   End If
327:
...:
...:
...:
```

To create a shadow copy, the following command line must be used:

```
1:    C:\>WMIDiskSvc.wsf D: /Action:CreateShadowCopy
2:    Microsoft (R) Windows Script Host Version 5.6
3:    Copyright (C) Microsoft Corporation 1996-2001. All rights reserved.
4:
5:    Creating shadow copy ...
6:    Shadow copy '{2f26b83b-d583-461d-b773-e6cd024f9710}' successfully created.
```

To delete shadow copies, the scripting technique is a little bit different from the creation technique. Instead of using a method exposed by the *Win32_ShadowCopy* class, the script (see Sample 3.44) retrieves the *Win32_ShadowCopy* instance to be deleted by referring the ID passed on the command-line parameters with the **/ShadowCopyID** switch (lines 332 and 333). Once the instance is retrieved, the script invokes the *Delete_* method exposed by the **SWBemObject** object (line 336) representing the *Win32_ShadowCopy* instance. The following command line will execute the routine shown in Sample 3.44:

```
1:    C:\>WMIDiskSvc.wsf /Action:DeleteShadowCopy /ShadowCopyID:{2f26b83b-d583-461d-b773-e6cd024f9710}
2:    Microsoft (R) Windows Script Host Version 5.6
3:    Copyright (C) Microsoft Corporation 1996-2001. All rights reserved.
4:
5:    Deleting shadow copy ...
6:    Shadow Copy '{2f26b83b-d583-461d-b773-e6cd024f9710}' successfully deleted.
```

Sample 3.44   *Deleting shadow copies (Part IV)*

```
...:
...:
...:
327:
328:    ' -- DeleteShadowCopy -----------------------------------------------------------------
329:    If boolDeleteShadowCopy = True Then
330:        WScript.Echo "Deleting shadow copy ..."
331:
332:        Set objWMIInstance = objWMIServices.Get ("Win32_ShadowCopy='" & _
333:                                         strShadowCopyID & "'")
...:
336:        objWMIInstance.Delete_
...:
339:        WScript.Echo "Shadow Copy '" & strShadowCopyID & "' successfully deleted."
...:
342:    End If
343:
...:
...:
...:
```

A shadow storage is an association between two volumes (which is simply an association between two *Win32_Volume* instances). To create a shadow storage, the script uses the *Create* static method exposed by the

Win32_ShadowStorage association class (see Sample 3.45, lines 352 through 354).

Sample 3.45   *Associating a shadow storage with a Win32_Volume instance (Part V)*

```
...:
...:
...:
343:
344:     ' -- Create Shadow Storage ------------------------------------------------------------
345:     If boolCreateShadowStorage = True Then
346:         If Len (strShadowStorage) Then
347:             WScript.Echo "Defining Shadow Storage area for volume '" & _
348:                             strWMIDriverLetter & "' on volume '" & _
349:                             strShadowStorage & "'..."
350:
351:             Set objWMIClass = objWMIServices.Get ("Win32_ShadowStorage")
352:             intRC = objWMIClass.Create (strWMIDriverLetter & "\", _
353:                                         strShadowStorage & "\", _
354:                                         varMaxSpace)
355:             If intRC Then
356:                 WScript.Echo "Shadow Storage creation error (" & intRC & ")."
357:             Else
358:                 WScript.Echo "Shadow Storage '" & strWMIDriverLetter & _
359:                         "' successfully defined for volume '" & _
360:                         strShadowStorage & "'."
361:             End If
...:
363:         End If
364:     Else
...:
...:
...:
```

The *Create* method exposes three parameters: the drive letter of the volume containing the data to shadow, the driver letter of the volume used to store the shadows, and the maximum disk space to allocate on that volume. Once the method execution successfully completes, the *Win32_ShadowStorage* association instance is created. The command line to use for this operation is:

```
1:    C:\>WMIDiskSvc.wsf D: /Action:CreateShadowStorage /MaxSpace:850 /ShadowStorage:Z:
2:    Microsoft (R) Windows Script Host Version 5.6
3:    Copyright (C) Microsoft Corporation 1996-2001. All rights reserved.
4:
5:    Defining Shadow Storage area for volume 'D:' on volume 'Z:'...
6:    Shadow Storage 'D:' successfully defined for volume 'Z:'.
```

Samples 3.46 through 3.52 relate to different operations regarding the *Win32_Volume* instances. Sample 3.46 shows how to list all *Win32_Volume* instances with their associated *Win32_ShadowStorage* and *Win32_Shadow-Copy* instances. Actually, the script exploits the associations illustrated in Figure 3.25.

Sample 3.46   *Viewing the volumes with their related shadow storage and shadow copies (Part VI)*

```
...:
...:
...:
364:    Else
365:        Set objWMIInstances = objWMIServices.InstancesOf ("Win32_Volume")
...:
368:        For Each objWMIInstance In objWMIInstances
369:
370:            ' -- List -------------------------------------------------------------------
371:            If boolList = True And boolShadowCopy = False Then
372:                WScript.Echo "- " & objWMIInstance.DriveLetter & " " & _
373:                             String (60, "-")
374:
375:                Set objWMIPropertySet = objWMIInstance.Properties_
376:                For Each objWMIProperty In objWMIPropertySet
377:                    DisplayFormattedProperty objWMIInstance, _
378:                            objWMIProperty.Name, _
379:                            objWMIProperty.Name, _
380:                            Null
381:                Next
...:
384:                Set objWMIAssociatedInstances = objWMIServices.ExecQuery _
385:                        ("References of {" & _
386:                         objWMIInstance.Path_.RelPath & _
387:                         "} Where Role=Volume " & _
388:                         "ResultClass=Win32_ShadowStorage")
...:
391:                For Each objWMIAssociatedInstance In objWMIAssociatedInstances
392:
393:                    WScript.Echo vbCRLF & "  - Shadow Storage: " & String (60, "-")
394:
395:                    Set objWMIPropertySet = objWMIAssociatedInstance.Properties_
396:                    For Each objWMIProperty In objWMIPropertySet
397:                        DisplayFormattedProperty objWMIAssociatedInstance, _
398:                                "  " & objWMIProperty.Name, _
399:                                objWMIProperty.Name, _
400:                                Null
401:                    Next
...:
403:                Next
404:
405:                Set objWMIAssociatedInstances = objWMIServices.ExecQuery _
406:                        ("Associators of {" & _
407:                         objWMIInstance.Path_.RelPath & _
408:                         "} Where AssocClass=Win32_ShadowFor")
...:
411:                For Each objWMIAssociatedInstance In objWMIAssociatedInstances
412:
413:                    WScript.Echo vbCRLF & "  - Shadow Copy: " & _
414:                            objWMIAssociatedInstance.ID & _
415:                            " " & String (20, "-")
416:
417:                    Set objWMIPropertySet = objWMIAssociatedInstance.Properties_
418:                    For Each objWMIProperty In objWMIPropertySet
419:                        DisplayFormattedProperty objWMIAssociatedInstance, _
420:                                "  " & objWMIProperty.Name, _
```

```
421:                           objWMIProperty.Name, _
422:                           Null
423:                 Next
...:
425:             Next
426:
427:             WScript.Echo
428:         Else
...:
...:
...:
```

First, Sample 3.46 requests all instances of the *Win32_Volume* class (line 365) and performs a loop (Sample 3.46, line 368, through Sample 3.52, line 596) to show the properties of each instance found in the collection (lines 372 through 382). Actually, this loop embraces many more operations than simply showing all instances of the *Win32_Volume* class. It is also used to find a specific instance of the *Win32_Volume* class when one *Win32_Volume* instance must be retrieved to perform a specific operation, such as a check disk or a defragmentation (Sample 3.47, line 429).

But let's come back to Sample 3.46 and how the associated classes are retrieved (lines 384 through 388 and lines 405 through 408). During the loop listing all *Win32_Volume* instances, Sample 3.46 retrieves the associated shadow storage instance (lines 384 through 388). The shadow storage is materialized in the CIM repository by an instance of the *Win32_ShadowStorage* association class. Usually, there is always one *Win32_ShadowStorage* association instance per *Win32_Volume* instance. Therefore, the script uses the following WQL data query to retrieve the *Win32_ShadowStorage* instance (lines 384 through 388):

```
References of {Win32_Volume.DeviceID="\\\\?\\Volume{3eed7424-a3b2-11d6-a5f4-806e6f6e6963}\\"}
        Where Role=Volume ResultClass=Win32_ShadowStorage
```

This query is directly inspired by the relationship that exists between the *Win32_Volume* class and the *Win32_ShadowStorage* association class (see Figure 3.25).

In the same way, to retrieve the *Win32_ShadowCopy* instances associated with the *Win32_Volume* instance, the script uses another WQL data query (lines 405 through 408):

```
Associators of {Win32_Volume.DeviceID="\\\\?\\Volume{3eed7424-a3b2-11d6-a5f4-806e6f6e6963}\\"}
        Where AssocClass=Win32_ShadowFor
```

Another interesting question, but not implemented in the current script, concerns the volumes using a specific volume for shadow storage. This question can be answered by using the following query:

```
Associators of {Win32_Volume.DeviceID="\\\\?\\Volume{3eed7424-a3b2-11d6-a5f4-806e6f6e6963}\\"}
                Where AssocClass=Win32_ShadowStorage ResultRole=Volume"
```

For each instance retrieved by the WQL data queries, the script displays all properties. A sample output would be as follows:

```
 1:   C:\>WMIDiskSvc.wsf /Action:List
 2:   Microsoft (R) Windows Script Host Version 5.6
 3:   Copyright (C) Microsoft Corporation 1996-2001. All rights reserved.
 4:
 5:   - C: ------------------------------------------------------------
 6:   Automount: .............................. TRUE
 7:   BlockSize: .............................. 2048
 8:   Capacity: ............................... 2144376832
 9:   Caption: ................................ C:\
10:   Compressed: ............................. FALSE
11:   *DeviceID: .............................. \\?\Volume{3eed7422-a3b2-11d6-a5f4-806e6f6e6963}\
12:   DirtyBitSet: ............................ FALSE
13:   DriveLetter: ............................ C:
14:   DriveType: .............................. 3
15:   FileSystem: ............................. NTFS
16:   FreeSpace: .............................. 782168064
17:   IndexingEnabled: ........................ TRUE
18:   InstallDate: ............................ 01-01-2000
19:   Label: .................................. Windows Server 2003
20:   MaximumFileNameLength: ..................255
21:   Name: ................................... C:\
22:   QuotasEnabled: .......................... FALSE
23:   QuotasIncomplete: ....................... FALSE
24:   QuotasRebuilding: ....................... FALSE
25:   SerialNumber: ........................... 615808770
26:   SupportsDiskQuotas: ..................... TRUE
27:   SupportsFileBasedCompression: ........... TRUE
28:   SystemName: ............................. NET-DPEP6400A
29:
30:   - D: ------------------------------------------------------------
31:   Automount: .............................. TRUE
32:   BlockSize: .............................. 4096
33:   Capacity: ............................... 7222730752
..:
50:   SerialNumber: ........................... 821048372
51:   SupportsDiskQuotas: ..................... TRUE
52:   SupportsFileBasedCompression: ........... TRUE
53:   SystemName: ............................. NET-DPEP6400A
54:
55:     - Shadow Storage: ------------------------------------------------------
56:     AllocatedSpace: ....................... 104857600
57:     *DiffVolume: .......................... Win32_Volume.DeviceID=
                                                "\\\\?\\Volume{3eed7423-a3b2-11d6-a5f4-806e6f6e6963}\\"
58:     MaxSpace: ............................. 891289600
59:     UsedSpace: ............................ 1064960
60:     *Volume: .............................. Win32_Volume.DeviceID=
                                                "\\\\?\\Volume{3eed7424-a3b2-11d6-a5f4-806e6f6e6963}\\"
61:
62:     - Shadow Copy: {2f26b83b-d583-461d-b773-e6cd024f9710} --------------------
63:     ClientAccessible: ..................... TRUE
64:     Count: ................................ 1
65:     DeviceObject: ......................... \\?\GLOBALROOT\Device\HarddiskVolumeShadowCopy13
66:     Differential: ......................... FALSE
```

```
67:          ExposedLocally: ...................... FALSE
68:          ExposedRemotely: ..................... FALSE
69:          HardwareAssisted: .................... FALSE
70:          *ID: ................................. {2f26b83b-d583-461d-b773-e6cd024f9710}
71:          Imported: ............................ FALSE
72:          InstallDate: ......................... 28-10-2002 22:37:09
73:          NoAutoRelease: ....................... TRUE
74:          NotSurfaced: ......................... FALSE
75:          NoWriters: ........................... TRUE
76:          OriginatingMachine: .................. net-dpep6400a.Emea.LissWare.NET
77:          Persistent: .......................... TRUE
78:          Plex: ................................ FALSE
79:          ProviderID: .......................... {b5946137-7b9f-4925-af80-51abd60b20d5}
80:          ReadWrite: ........................... FALSE
81:          ServiceMachine: ...................... net-dpep6400a.Emea.LissWare.NET
82:          SetID: ............................... {238304a1-3df0-4d0e-9f16-d143abe87a29}
83:          State: ............................... 12
84:          Transportable: ....................... FALSE
85:          VolumeName: .......................... \\?\Volume{3eed7424-a3b2-11d6-a5f4-806e6f6e6963}\
86:
87:    - E: ---------------------------------------------------------
88:    Automount: ............................ TRUE
89:    BlockSize: ............................ 4096
90:    Capacity: ............................. 7222759424
91:    Caption: .............................. E:\
92:    Compressed: ........................... FALSE
93:    *DeviceID: ............................ \\?\Volume{3eed7425-a3b2-11d6-a5f4-806e6f6e6963}\
..:
..:
..:
```

Sample 3.47 shows how to use the *Chkdsk* method exposed by the *Win32_Volume* class. This method is not a static method and therefore relates to a specific *Win32_Volume* instance. This is the reason why the method invocation is executed inside the loop (Sample 3.46, line 368, and Sample 3.52, line 596) and for a specific *Win32_Volume* instance (Sample 3.47, line 429). The method parameters and usage are exactly the same as the *Win32_LogicalDisk* method (see Sample 2.3).

Sample 3.47   *Executing the Chkdsk Win32_Volume method (Part VII)*

```
...:
...:
...:
428:         Else
429:            If Ucase (objWMIInstance.DriveLetter) = Ucase (strWMIDriverLetter) Then
430:
431:               ' -- Chkdsk --------------------------------------------------------
432:               If boolChkdsk Then
433:                  If boolFixErrors Then
434:                     WScript.Echo "Errors will be fixed."
435:                  End If
436:
437:                  If boolVigorousIndexCheck Then
438:                     WScript.Echo "Vigorous check of index entries will be performed."
```

```
439:                    End If
440:
441:                    If boolSkipFolderCycle Then
442:                        WScript.Echo "The folder cycle checking will be skipped."
443:                    End If
444:
445:                    If boolForceDismount Then
446:                        WScript.Echo "The drive will be forced to dismount before checking."
447:                    End If
448:
449:                    If boolRecoverBadSectors Then
450:                        WScript.Echo "The bad sectors will be ... recovered from these sectors."
451:                    End If
452:
453:                    If boolOKToRunAtBootUp Then
454:                        WScript.Echo "The chkdsk ... performed at next boot up time."
455:                    End If
456:
457:                    WScript.Echo
458:                    WScript.Echo "Volume " & Ucase (objWMIInstance.DriveLetter) & _
459:                                 " has " & objWMIInstance.FreeSpace & _
460:                                 " bytes free on a total of " & _
461:                                 objWMIInstance.Capacity & " bytes."
462:                    WScript.Echo "The type of the file system is " & _
463:                                 objWMIInstance.FileSystem & "."
464:                    WScript.Echo "Volume is " & objWMIInstance.Label & "."
465:                    WScript.Echo "Volume Serial Number is " & _
466:                        Right ("0000" & Hex(int (objWMIinstance.SerialNumber / 65536)), 4) & _
467:                        "-" & _
468:                        Right ("0000" & Hex(objWMIinstance.SerialNumber And 65535), 4)  & _
469:                        "."
470:
471:                    WScript.Echo "WMI chkdsk started ..."
472:                    intRC = objWMIInstance.Chkdsk (boolFixErrors, _
473:                                                   boolVigorousIndexCheck, _
474:                                                   boolSkipFolderCycle, _
475:                                                   boolForceDismount, _
476:                                                   boolRecoverBadSectors, _
477:                                                   boolOKToRunAtBootUp)
...:
480:                    Select Case intRC
481:                         Case 0
482:                              WScript.Echo "WMI chkdsk completed successfully."
483:                         Case 1
484:                              WScript.Echo "Locked and chkdsk scheduled on reboot."
485:                         Case 2
486:                              WScript.Echo "WMI chkdsk failure - Unknown file system."
487:                         Case 3
488:                              WScript.Echo "WMI chkdsk failure - Unknown error."
489:                    End Select
490:                End If
491:
...:
...:
...:
```

A small difference to note is the data type of the volume serial number. The *Win32_LogicalDisk* class exposes the volume serial number in the *VolumeSerialNumber* property in a hexadecimal string, while the *Win32_Vol-*

ume class exposes the serial number in the *SerialNumber* property as a 32-bit integer. This is why Sample 3.47 includes some extra logic to display the volume serial number in a hexadecimal format (lines 466 through 469).

Sample 3.48 *Executing the DefragAnalysis Win32_Volume method (Part VIII)*

```
...:
...:
...:
491:
492:        ' -- Defragmentation Analysis ------------------------------------------------
493:        If boolDefragAnalysis = True Then
494:            WScript.Echo "Defragmentation analysis started ..."
495:
496:            intRC = objWMIInstance.DefragAnalysis (boolDefragRecommended, _
497:                                                   objDefragAnalysis)
...:
500:            If intRC Then
501:                WScript.Echo "Defragmentation analysis error (" & inRC & ")."
502:            Else
503:                If boolDefragRecommended Then
504:                    WScript.Echo vbCRLF & "Defragmentation is recommended."
505:                Else
506:                    WScript.Echo vbCRLF & "Defragmentation is NOT recommended."
507:                End If
508:                DisplayFormattedProperties objDefragAnalysis, 0
509:            End If
510:        End If
511:
...:
...:
...:
```

The ability to request the defragmentation statistics and perform a defragmentation is a very interesting feature of the *Win32_Volume* class (see Sample 3.48 and 3.49). Both methods are very easy to use. Each of them relates to a specific instance of the *Win32_Volume* class. The *DefragAnalysis* method exposes two output parameters (lines 496 and 497): a Boolean variable informing if the defragmentation is recommended and an **SWbemObject** made from the *Win32_DefragAnalysis* class to return defragmentation statistics. The command line to use and the output obtained are as follows:

```
C:\>WMIDiskSvc.wsf D: /Action:DefragAnalysis
Microsoft (R) Windows Script Host Version 5.6
Copyright (C) Microsoft Corporation 1996-2001. All rights reserved.

Defragmentation analysis started ...

Defragmentation is NOT recommended.

- Win32_DefragAnalysis -----------------------------------------------------
AverageFileSize: ........................ 141980
AverageFragmentsPerFile: ................ 1
```

```
ClusterSize: ............................ 4096
ExcessFolderFragments: .................. 0
FilePercentFragmentation: ............... 0
FragmentedFolders: ...................... 1
FreeSpace: .............................. 1724788736
FreeSpacePercent: ....................... 23
FreeSpacePercentFragmentation: .......... 2
MFTPercentInUse: ........................ 84
MFTRecordCount: ......................... 55029
PageFileSize: ........................... 0
TotalExcessFragments: ................... 360
TotalFiles: ............................. 52188
TotalFolders: ........................... 2790
TotalFragmentedFiles: ................... 12
TotalMFTFragments: ...................... 2
TotalMFTSize: ........................... 66368512
TotalPageFileFragments: ................. 0
TotalPercentFragmentation: .............. 1
UsedSpace: .............................. 5497942016
VolumeSize: ............................. 7222730752
```

Sample 3.49   *Executing the Defrag Win32_Volume method (Part IX)*

```
...:
...:
...:
511:
512:            ' -- Defragmentation ------------------------------------------------------
513:          If boolDefrag = True Then
514:             WScript.Echo "Defragmentation started ..."
515:
516:             intRC = objWMIInstance.Defrag (boolForce, objDefragAnalysis)
...:
519:             If intRC Then
520:                WScript.Echo "Defragmentation error (" & inRC & ")."
521:             Else
522:                DisplayFormattedProperties objDefragAnalysis, 0
523:             End If
524:          End If
525:
...:
...:
...:
```

The invocation of the *Win32_Volume Defrag* method follows the same coding technique as the *DefragAnalysis* method (see Sample 3.49). The only difference resides in the method parameters, where one input parameter is required to eventually force the volume defragmentation and one output parameter is available to return the defragmentation analysis information (line 516). The execution of this code portion of the script is made with the following command line:

```
C:\>WMIDiskSvc.wsf D: /Action:Defrag
Microsoft (R) Windows Script Host Version 5.6
Copyright (C) Microsoft Corporation 1996-2001. All rights reserved.
```

```
Defragmentation started ...

- Win32_DefragAnalysis --------------------------------------------------------------
AverageFileSize: ........................ 141980
AverageFragmentsPerFile: ................ 1
ClusterSize: ............................ 4096
ExcessFolderFragments: .................. 0
FilePercentFragmentation: ............... 0
FragmentedFolders: ...................... 1
FreeSpace: .............................. 1724788736
FreeSpacePercent: ....................... 23
FreeSpacePercentFragmentation: .......... 2
MFTPercentInUse: ........................ 84
MFTRecordCount: ......................... 55029
PageFileSize: ........................... 0
TotalExcessFragments: ................... 16
TotalFiles: ............................. 52188
TotalFolders: ........................... 2790
TotalFragmentedFiles: ................... 1
TotalMFTFragments: ...................... 2
TotalMFTSize: ........................... 66368512
TotalPageFileFragments: ................. 0
TotalPercentFragmentation: .............. 1
UsedSpace: .............................. 5497942016
VolumeSize: ............................. 7222730752
```

With the *Format* method of the *Win32_Volume* class, it is possible to format a volume (see Sample 3.50). Basically, this method implements the functionality of the **FORMAT.COM** command. The *Format* method accepts five input parameters: the file system type (NTFS, FAT, or FAT32), a Boolean variable defining the formatting mode (true=quick or false=normal), the cluster size (by default 4,096), the volume label, and a Boolean variable to enable the compression (lines 530 through 534). The latter is actually not implemented, even if it is required to invoke the method.

Sample 3.50   *Executing the Format Win32_Volume method (Part X)*

```
...:
...:
...:
525:
526:                    ' -- Format --------------------------------------------------------------
527:                    If boolFormat = True Then
528:                        WScript.Echo "Format started ..."
529:
530:                        intRC = objWMIInstance.Format (strFileSystem, _
531:                                                       boolQuickFormat, _
532:                                                       intClusterSize, _
533:                                                       strLabel, _
534:                                                       boolCompression)
...:
537:                        If intRC Then
538:                            WScript.Echo "Format error (" & intRC & ")."
539:                        Else
540:                            WScript.Echo "Format completed successfully."
```

```
541:                    End If
542:            End If
543:
...:
...:
...:
```

If a shadow storage volume is associated with a *Win32_Volume* instance, it is possible to update the maximum disk space that can be allocated to the shadow copies. To do so, it is necessary to retrieve the association instance made from the *Win32_ShadowStorage* class (see Sample 3.51). The execution of a WQL data query from the *Win32_Volume* instance representing the disk containing the information to shadow will retrieve the association *Win32_ShadowStorage* instance (lines 549 through 552). The WQL data query will be as follows for a given *Win32_Volume* instance:

```
References of {Win32_Volume.DeviceID="\\\\?\\Volume{3eed7424-a3b2-11d6-a5f4-806e6f6e6963}\\"}
Where ResultClass=Win32_ShadowStorage
```

To create a *Win32_ShadowStorage* instance, Sample 3.45 ("Associating a shadow storage with a *Win32_Volume* instance [Part V]") requests a drive letter and a disk space allocated to the shadows. Actually, the disk space value can be updated after the *Win32_ShadowStorage* instance creation by examining the *MaxSpace* property of the corresponding *Win32_ShadowStorage* instance (see Sample 3.51). This *Win32_ShadowStorage* instance can be retrieved with a WQL data query similar to the previous one (lines 549 through 552). As mentioned previously, there is only one instance of the *Win32_ShadowStorage* class per *Win32_Volume* instance. This is the reason why the script tests the number of results at line 555. Because a WQL data query returns the result in a collection, by enumerating the collection (lines 556 through 562), it is possible to update the *MaxSpace* property of the *Win32_ShadowStorage* instances (line 557). From the user interface (see Figure 3.24), it is possible to set no limit on the space allocated to the shadows. The script supports this as well by using the **Unlimited** keyword from the command line:

```
1:    C:\>WMIDiskSvc.wsf D: /Action:UpdateShadowStorage /MaxSpace:Unlimited
2:    Microsoft (R) Windows Script Host Version 5.6
3:    Copyright (C) Microsoft Corporation 1996-2001. All rights reserved.
4:
5:    Updating maximum space for the shadow volume ...
6:    Maximum space for Shadow Storage successfully updated.
```

Actually, the **Unlimited** keyword sets the *MaxSpace* property to a value equal to 18446744073709551615 (which corresponds to $2^{64} - 1$) defined as a constant at line 76 of Sample 3.51.

Sample 3.51   *Updating a Win32_ShadowStorage instance (Part XI)*

```
...:
...:
...:
543:
544:            ' -- Update Shadow Storage ----------------------------------------------
545:            If boolUpdateShadowStorage = True Then
546:               If varMaxSpace <> -1 Then
547:                  WScript.Echo "Updating maximum space for the shadow volume ..."
548:
549:                  Set objWMIAssociatedInstances = objWMIServices.ExecQuery _
550:                          ("References of {" & _
551:                              objWMIInstance.Path_.RelPath & _
552:                              "} Where ResultClass=Win32_ShadowStorage")
...:
555:                  If objWMIAssociatedInstances.Count = 1 Then
556:                     For Each objWMIAssociatedInstance In objWMIAssociatedInstances
557:                         objWMIAssociatedInstance.MaxSpace = varMaxSpace
558:
559:                         objWMIAssociatedInstance.Put_ (wbemChangeFlagCreateOrUpdate Or _
560:                                                        wbemFlagReturnWhenComplete)
...:
562:                     Next
563:
564:                     WScript.Echo "Maximum space for Shadow Storage successfully updated."
565:                  Else
566:                     WScript.Echo "No Shadow Storage for volume '" & strWMIDriverLetter
567:                  End If
568:               End If
569:            End If
570:
...:
...:
...:
```

If we can create and update the *Win32_ShadowStorage* instances, it is possible to delete a *Win32_ShadowStorage* instance. The scripting technique is exactly the same as the update process, with the exception that the instance is deleted by invoking the *Delete_* method of the **SWBemObject** object representing the *Win32_ShadowStorage* instance (see Sample 3.52).

Sample 3.52   *Removing a Win32_ShadowStorage instance (Part XII)*

```
...:
...:
...:
570:
571:            ' -- Delete -----------------------------------------------------------
572:            If boolDeleteShadowStorage = True Then
573:               WScript.Echo "Reseting Shadow Storage area on default volume '" & _
574:                        strWMIDriverLetter & "'."
575:
576:               Set objWMIAssociatedInstances = objWMIServices.ExecQuery _
577:                       ("References of {" & _
```

```
578:                            objWMIInstance.Path_.RelPath & _
579:                            "} Where ResultClass=Win32_ShadowStorage")
...:
582:                    If objWMIAssociatedInstances.Count = 1 Then
583:                       For Each objWMIAssociatedInstance In objWMIAssociatedInstances
584:                            objWMIAssociatedInstance.Delete_
...:
586:                       Next
587:
588:                       WScript.Echo "Shadow Storage successfully reset."
589:                    Else
590:                       WScript.Echo "No Shadow Storage other than the default for volume '" & _
591:                            strWMIDriverLetter & "'."
592:                    End If
593:                 End If
594:              End If
595:           End If
596:        Next
597:     End If
...:
602:     ]]>
603:     </script>
604:     </job>
605:</package>
```

With the Shadow Copy classes, it is possible to perform all tasks available from the user interface and update almost all properties exposed by the user interface (see Figure 3.24). The only setting that is not manageable from WMI is the schedule information.

3.6   Active Directory components providers

3.6.1   Active Directory Service providers

There are three *Active Directory* providers, as shown in Table 3.49.

Table 3.49   *The Active Directory Providers Capabilities*

Provider Name	Provider Namespace	Class Provider	Instance Provider	Method Provider	Property Provider	Event Provider	Event Consumer Provider	Support Get	Support Put	Support Enumeration	Support Delete	Windows Server 2003	Windows XP	Windows 2000 Server	Windows 2000 Professional	Windows NT 4.0
Active Directory LDAP Providers																
Microsoft|DSLDAPClassAssociationsProvider|V1.0	Root/directory/LDAP		X					X	X			X	X	X	X	
Microsoft|DSLDAPClassProvider|V1.0	Root/directory/LDAP	X						X	X			X	X	X	X	
Microsoft|DSLDAPInstanceProvider|V1.0	Root/directory/LDAP		X					X	X	X	X	X	X	X	X	

To work with these providers, it is best to have an understanding of the Active Directory Schema, since WMI reflects its logical structure. All classes provided by the *Active Directory* class provider are mapped from the Active Directory schema classes. By accessing the **Root\Directory\LDAP** namespace, it is possible to reference any class and object in the Active Directory. Basically, we can say that the *Active Directory* providers mirror classes and instances from the Active Directory into this specific CIM repository namespace. To perform this mapping, the Active Directory Service providers follow naming rules to preserve the relationships that exist between the Active Directory classes and instances. Two mappings are realized: one for the Active Directory classes and one for the Active Directory instances.

Figure 3.26
The Active Directory WMI classes mapped to the Active Directory classes.

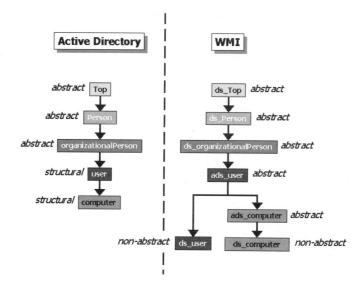

Let's take the Active Directory **user** class as an example. Defined in the Active Directory schema, the Active Directory **user** class is created from a class hierarchy starting from a Root class called **top** (see Figure 3.26, on the left side). To obtain the **user** class, several subclasses are created. This creation is called a derivation of classes, where the parent class is called a superclass. First, the **top** class is derived to obtain the **person** class. Next, the **person** class is derived to obtain the **organizationalPerson** class, which is in turn also derived to obtain the **user** class. Each class brings its set of Active Directory attributes. Each subclass inherits the set of attributes from the superclasses.

In Active Directory, the **user** class is defined as a structural class, which allows the creation of user instances from it. However, the **top, person,** and **organizationalPerson** classes are abstract classes in Active Directory and are used as parent templates to create their respective subclasses. As mentioned previously, classes in Active Directory are mapped to their equivalent WMI classes in the **Root\Directory\LDAP** namespace. In case of an abstract class, the WMI equivalent abstract class always uses the LDAP display name of the Active Directory class starting with the "*ds_*" prefix (Figure 3.26, on the right side). For example, for the Active Directory **organizationalPerson** class, we will have a corresponding *ds_organizationalPerson* WMI class. Since this Active Directory class is an abstract class, the WMI equivalent class is also an abstract class and has the *abstract* WMI qualifier set. When the Active Directory class is a non-abstract class (such as the **user** class, which is a structural class), the mapping is made to two WMI classes:

- A first class prefixed with the "*ads_*" prefix and implemented as a WMI abstract class (*abstract* qualifier is set). For the **user** class, we will have an *ads_user* WMI abstract class.

Figure 3.27
The WMI ads_user abstract class qualifiers.

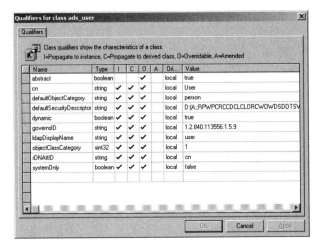

- A second class prefixed with the "*ds_*" prefix and implemented as a WMI dynamic instance class (provider qualifier is set). For the **user** class, we will have a *ds_user* WMI dynamic instance class.

In both Figures 3.27 and 3.28, you will notice the presence of other qualifiers representing Active Directory attributes defined in the schema and used to create the **user** class definition (i.e., **governsID, objectClass-Category, lDAPDisplayName,** etc.). In the same way, the syntax used by

Figure 3.28
*The WMI ds_user
dynamic instance
class qualifiers.*

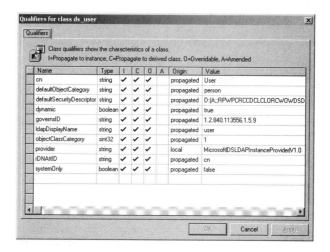

Active Directory is also mapped to WMI. Table 3.50 shows the syntax mapping.

Table 3.50   *The Active Directory/WMI Syntax Mapping*

Active Directory syntax	WMI data type	WMI property value
Access-Point	CIM_STRING	Mapped from the value of the string.
Boolean	CIM_BOOLEAN	Mapped directly to the appropriate Boolean value.
Case Insensitive String	CIM_STRING	Mapped from the value of the string.
Case Sensitive String	CIM_STRING	Mapped from the value of the string.
Distinguished Name	CIM_STRING	Mapped from the value of the string.
DN-Binary	Embedded object of class DN_With_Binary	Mapped to instances of the DN_With_Binary class.
DN-String	Embedded object of class DN_With_String	Mapped to instances of the DN_With_String class.
Enumeration	CIM_SINT32	Mapped directly to the integer value.
IA5-String	CIM_STRING	Mapped from the value of the string.
Integer	CIM_SINT32	Mapped directly to the integer value.
NT Security Descriptor	Embedded object of Class Uint8Array	Mapped to instances of the Uint8Array class.
Numeric String	CIM_STRING	Mapped from the value of the string.
Object Id	CIM_STRING	Mapped from the string representation of the OID; for example, "1.3.3.4."
Octet String	Embedded object of Class Uint8Array	Mapped to instances of the Uint8Array class.
OR Name	CIM_STRING	Mapped from the value of the string.
Presentation-Address	CIM_STRING	Mapped from the value of the string.
Print Case String	CIM_STRING	Mapped from the value of the string.
Replica Link	Embedded object of class Uint8Array	Mapped to instances of the Uint8Array class..
SID	Embedded object of Class Uint8Array	Mapped to instances of the Uint8Array class.
Time	CIM_DATETIME	Converted to the CIM_DATETIME representation and mapped.
Undefined	N/A	N/A
Unicode String	CIM_STRING	Mapped from the value of the string.
UTC Coded Time	CIM_DATETIME	Converted to the CIM_DATETIME representation and mapped.

The end result is that WMI exposes Active Directory classes as WMI classes (see Figure 3.29).

When a user object is created in Active Directory, it is always created in a container. The default container for user objects is the "Users" container, but it could be any other supported container, such as an organizational unit or a domain. In the Active Directory schema, the containers that can

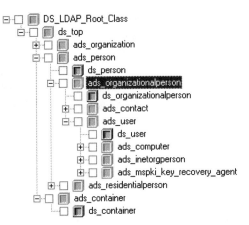

Figure 3.29
*Some of the Active
Directory classes as
seen from WMI.*

hold user objects are defined with the **possSuperiors** and **systemPossSuperiors** attributes of the Active Directory **user** class definition. These attributes reference the class (with their names) representing the supported containers—for example, the **domainDNS** class for the domain container or the **builtinDomain** class for the Users container. We see here that there is a relationship between the **user** class and the supported Active Directory container class definition. WMI represents this relationship with the *DS_LDAP_Class_Containment* association class (see Figure 3.30).

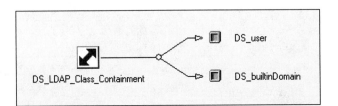

Figure 3.30
*The DS_LDAP_
Class_
Containment
associations.*

In the same way, once user objects are instantiated, they are contained in an existing container. We will retrieve the same kind of relationship between the user objects and the containers but at the instance level instead of the class level. WMI represents this relation with the use of the *DS_LDAP_Instance_Containment* association class. (See Figure 3.31.)

These two association classes, along with the *RootDSE* WMI class, are listed in Table 3.51. The *RootDSE* WMI class represents the **RootDSE** LDAP object available from any LDAP v3 directory.

Every WMI instance representing an Active Directory object uses the Active Directory ADSI path of the object. The ADSI path is represented in the WMI class definition with the *ADSIPath* WMI Key property. For exam-

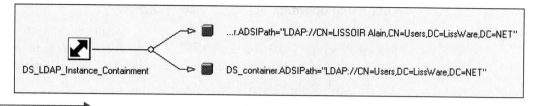

Figure 3.31   *The DS_LDAP_Instance_Containment associations.*

ple, the *ADSIPath* property for a user object called "LISSOIR Alain" and located in the "Users" containers of an Active Directory domain called Liss-Ware.Net will be:

```
LDAP://CN=LISSOIR Alain,CN=Users,DC=LissWare,DC=Net
```

There is one exception for the *RootDSE* WMI class, since it provides information about the capabilities of an LDAP server. This WMI class is a singleton class, since the **RootDSE** LDAP object is unique per LDAP server.

Everything we said about the **user** class and its WMI equivalents *ads_user* and *ds_user* WMI classes can be applied to any other class defined in the Active Directory schema. The logic is always the same. This is why a good understanding of the Active Directory schema mechanisms and definitions is helpful to navigate the WMI representation.

As seen in Table 3.49, the *Microsoft|DSLDAPInstanceProvider|V1.0* supports the "Get," "Put," "Enumeration," and "Delete" operations. This clearly means that we can manipulate Active Directory object instances through WMI. With the previous script samples, we have seen how to create, update, and delete existing WMI instances. To manipulate the WMI Active Directory object instances there are no exceptions; the rules and the scripting techniques are exactly the same. However, because the *Microsoft|DSLDAPClassProvider|V1.0* only supports "Get" and "Enumeration" operations, it is not possible to create new classes in Active Directory with WMI. Therefore, it means we must create all Active Directory schema extensions with the Active Directory Service Interfaces (ADSI).

Table 3.51   *The Active Directory Providers Classes*

Name	Type	Comments
DS_LDAP_Class_Containment	Association	This class models the possible superiors of a DS class.
DS_LDAP_Instance_Containment	Association	This class models the parent-child container relationship of instances in the DS.
RootDSE	Dynamic	This is the class used to model the LDAP RootDSE object.

3.6.1.1   *Creating and updating objects in Active Directory*

Although technically feasible with WMI to create, update, or delete Active Directory object instances, it is more efficient to use ADSI to perform these typical operations. As a basic example, we can create an Active Directory user with WMI, as illustrated in Sample 3.53.

Sample 3.53   *Creating an Active Directory user object with WMI*

```
1:<?xml version="1.0"?>
. :
8:<package>
9:  <job>
..:
13:     <script language="VBScript" src="..\Functions\TinyErrorHandler.vbs" />
14:
15:     <object progid="WbemScripting.SWbemLocator" id="objWMILocator" reference="true"/>
16:     <object progid="WbemScripting.SWbemNamedValueSet" id="objWMINamedValueSet" />
17:
18:     <script language="VBscript">
19:     <![CDATA[
..:
23:     Const cUserID = "WMIUser"
24:     Const cComputerName = "LocalHost"
25:     Const cWMINameSpace = "Root/directory/LDAP"
26:     Const cWMIClass = "ds_user"
27:
28:     Const ADS_UF_ACCOUNTDISABLE = &h000002
..:
36:     objWMILocator.Security_.AuthenticationLevel = wbemAuthenticationLevelDefault
37:     objWMILocator.Security_.ImpersonationLevel = wbemImpersonationLevelImpersonate
38:     Set objWMIServices = objWMILocator.ConnectServer(cComputerName, cWMINameSpace, "", "")
..:
41:     Set objWMIClass = objWMIServices.Get (cWMIClass)
..:
44:     Set objWMIInstance = objWMIClass.SpawnInstance_
45:
46:     objWMIInstance.DS_sAMAccountName = cUserID
47:     objWMIInstance.ADSIPath = "LDAP://CN=" & cUserID & ",CN=Users,DC=LissWare,DC=Net"
48:
49:     objWMIInstance.Put_ (wbemChangeFlagCreateOrUpdate Or wbemFlagReturnWhenComplete)
..:
52:     WScript.Echo "Active Directory user successfully created."
53:
54:     objWMIInstance.Refresh_
55:
56:     objWMINamedValueSet.Add "__PUT_EXTENSIONS", True
57:     objWMINamedValueSet.Add "__PUT_EXT_CLIENT_REQUEST", True
58:     objWMINamedValueSet.Add "__PUT_EXT_PROPERTIES", Array ("DS_userAccountControl", _
59:                                                    "DS_description")
60:
61:     objWMIInstance.DS_userAccountControl = objWMIInstance.DS_userAccountControl And _
62:                              (NOT ADS_UF_ACCOUNTDISABLE)
63:     objWMIInstance.DS_description = Array ("Active Directory user created with WMI.")
64:
65:     objWMIInstance.Put_ wbemChangeFlagUpdateOnly Or wbemFlagReturnWhenComplete, _
66:                     objWMINamedValueSet
```

```
..:
69:    WScript.Echo "Active Directory user successfully updated."
..:
75:    ]]>
76:    </script>
77:  </job>
78:</package>
```

The technique to create a user instance in Active Directory with WMI is the same as any other instance creation. However, to completely demonstrate the instance creation and update techniques, Sample 3.53 is divided into two parts:

- The first part (lines 41 through 52) creates the WMI instance representing the Active Directory **user** object. As with any other instance creation, the code creates a new instance of the desired class (lines 41 and 44). Next, it assigns various properties required to create the new Active Directory **user** instance (lines 46 and 47). Although the *ADSIPath* property is mandatory to create the new instance (since *Adsipath* is defined as a Key property of the *DS_user* WMI class in the CIM repository), the *DS_sAMAccountName* property is not required by WMI to create the new **user** instance. This may look amazing, since it is a mandatory attribute of the Active Directory **user** class, but, actually, if the *DS_sAMAccountName* value assignment is missing in the script, WMI generates a random value for it, as shown in Figure 3.32.

Figure 3.32
An Active Directory user created with WMI.

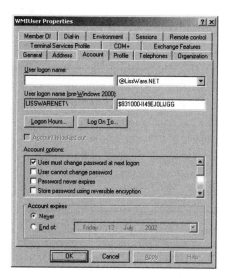

- The second part (lines 54 through 69) updates the previously created Active Directory **user** object. To update the existing Active Directory user, the script refreshes the instance information in order to get the latest information available from Active Directory (line 54), since some attributes are updated during the object creation (i.e., **modify-TimeStamp**, **userAccountControl**, **objectGUID**, **objectSID**, etc.). Under Windows 2000, since the *Refresh_* method is not available from an **SWBemObject** object, it is necessary to retrieve the created instance instead. Next, Sample 3.53 initializes an **SWBemNamedValueSet** object to perform a partial-instance update (lines 56 through 59). This partial-instance update updates two specific Active Directory attributes: the **userAccountControl** attribute (to enable the user object, since by default newly created users in Active Directory are disabled) and the **description** attribute (lines 61 through 63). The partial-instance update is mandatory, because saving the complete instance back to Active Directory will attempt to set some attributes that can only be set by the system, which means that the WMI call will fail to update the existing **user** object (lines 65 and 66). Once completed, the updated attributes are committed back by WMI to Active Directory.

The end result is the creation of an enabled Active Directory user with a specific description. Note that it is possible to commit the **description** attribute during the user creation (during the first part of the script). However, to enable the user, it is always necessary to create the user first and change its state by modifying the **userAccountControl** attribute next.

Although an Active Directory user creation is possible with WMI, it is clear that the ADSI scripting technique is more suitable for this type of task. However, there are situations where it could be useful to use the WMI technique to update a WMI instance representing an Active Directory object. As an example, this could be the case during WMI events notifying Active Directory objects creation. Once a user is created, WMI could detect its creation with a WQL event query and update the created Active Directory object with some information coming from a database (i.e., **telephoneNumber**, **postalAddress**, etc.). In such a case, the WQL query would be as follows:

```
1:   C:\>GenericEventAsyncConsumer.wsf "Select * From __InstanceCreationEvent Within 5
                      Where TargetInstance ISA 'DS_user'" /NameSpace:Root\Directory\LDAP
2:   Microsoft (R) Windows Script Host Version 5.6
3:   Copyright (C) Microsoft Corporation 1996-2001. All rights reserved.
4:
5:   Waiting for events...
6:
```

```
 7:   BEGIN - OnObjectReady.
 8:   Tuesday, 11 June, 2002 at 15:47:04: '__InstanceCreationEvent' has been triggered.
 9:     SECURITY_DESCRIPTOR (wbemCimtypeUint8) = (null)
10:     TargetInstance (wbemCimtypeObject)
11:       *ADSIPath (wbemCimtypeString) = LDAP://CN=Alain LISSOIR,CN=Users,DC=LissWare,DC=NET
12:       DS_accountExpires (wbemCimtypeSint64) = 9223372036854775807
..:
33:       DS_badPasswordTime (wbemCimtypeSint64) = 0
34:       DS_badPwdCount (wbemCimtypeSint32) = 0
..:
41:       DS_cn (wbemCimtypeString) = Alain LISSOIR
..:
62:       DS_displayName (wbemCimtypeString) = Alain LISSOIR
63:       DS_displayNamePrintable (wbemCimtypeString) = (null)
64:       DS_distinguishedName (wbemCimtypeString) = CN=Alain LISSOIR,CN=Users,DC=LissWare,DC=NET
65:       DS_division (wbemCimtypeString) = (null)
66:       DS_dLMemDefault (wbemCimtypeSint32) = (null)
67:       DS_dLMemRejectPerms (wbemCimtypeString) = (null)
68:       DS_dLMemRejectPermsBL (wbemCimtypeString) = (null)
69:       DS_dLMemSubmitPerms (wbemCimtypeString) = (null)
70:       DS_dLMemSubmitPermsBL (wbemCimtypeString) = (null)
..:
..:
..:
```

3.6.1.2   *Searching in Active Directory*

To query Active Directory via LDAP, four key elements are required to formulate the query:

- The base object in which the search will start: This could be an object container in the Active Directory, such as an **organizationalUnit**

  ```
  OU=Brussels,DC=LissWare,DC=Net
  ```

  or a naming context, such as the **defaultNamingContext**, **SchemaNamingContext**.

  ```
  CN=Configuration,DC=LissWare,DC=Net
  CN=Schema,CN=Configuration,DC=LissWare,DC=Net
  ```

- The filter determines which elements have to be selected (based on conditions) from the Active Directory. Any accessible characteristics of an object can be used to make a query. Some examples are:

  ```
  (|(objectClass=domainDNS)(objectClass=organizationalUnit))
  ```

  This will return the list of all objects using the class **domainDNS** or **organizationalUnit**. Note the "|" sign for the "or" statement.

  ```
  (&(objectClass=user)(objectCategory=person))
  ```

  This will return the list of all objects using the class **user** for which the **objectCategory** is equal to **person**. Actually, this will provide a list of all users available in the selected naming context. In this example, the objects of the class **contact** will be discarded, even if they are also using an **objectCategory** equal to **person**. Note the "&" sign for the "And" statement. To get both **contact** and **user** objects, the following syntax can be used:

```
(&(|(objectClass=user)(objectClass=contact))(objectCategory=person))
```

or, to make things simpler (because an object class **user** or **contact** is an object category equal to **person**), use:

```
(objectCategory=person)
```

In the first version note the possibility to combine search conditions "|" and "&."

- The attributes of the retrieved objects that are required. This can be any attribute associated with the retrieved objects (**cn**, **name**, **given-Name**, **sn**, etc.).

- How deep the search has to run in the Active Directory.

Base:	A **Base** search is limited to the base object selected. If the base object has children, they will not be included in the search. Only elements that are direct members of the base object are examined.
OneLevel:	A **OneLevel** search is restricted to the immediate children of a base object but excludes the base object itself. This scope is perfectly adapted for a search inside the **schemaNamingContext**.
SubTree:	A **SubTree** search includes the entire subtree below the base object.

To locate users residing in the Organizational Unit called "Brussels," having a first name (**givenName**) equal to "Alain," the following LDAP query filter must be used:

```
(&(objectclass=user)(givenName=Alain))
```

with the following base search:

```
OU=Brussels,DC=LissWare,DC=Net
```

and the following search level:

```
OneLevel
```

This LDAP query operation can be executed with the **LDP.Exe** utility available from the Windows 2000 or Windows Server 2003 Support Tools. The query result can be seen in Figure 3.33.

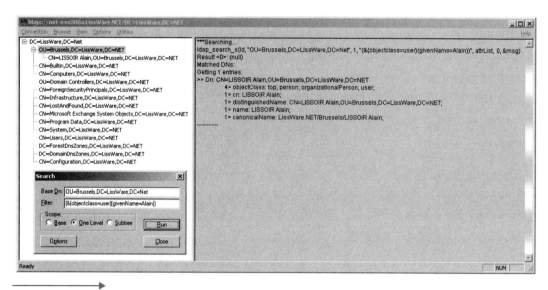

Figure 3.33   *Querying Active Directory with LDAP from LDP.*

Because WMI is connected to Active Directory, it is possible to obtain a similar result with a WQL data query:

```
Select * From DS_user Where DS_givenName='Alain'
```

However, there is no way to specify a base search. In this case, the search will be executed from the top of the domain tree (DC=LissWare,DC=Net). If a search must be performed in a context other than the Active Directory domain context (i.e., Configuration context), a *DN_Class* instance must be created. We will examine this technique later in this book, when monitoring the FSMO roles (see Sample 3.55, "Making the Configuration and Schema context accessible").

3.6.1.3   *Monitoring Active Directory group memberships*

Everybody knows the importance of Active Directory group memberships, right? It is clear that some Active Directory groups are more sensitive than others from a security point of view. For example, you wouldn't want to see just anyone added to the "Enterprise Admins" group without appropriate control, would you? No, of course you wouldn't! Well, with the *Active Directory* provider and a WQL event query, it is possible to get a WMI event notification when a modification is made to a group or any other object of Active Directory. The WQL event query to use should be as follows:

```
Select * From __InstanceModificationEvent Within 10 Where TargetInstance ISA 'ds_group' AND
                                TargetInstance.ds_name='Enterprise Admins'
```

Directly inspired from Samples 6.18 through 6.21 ("Monitoring, managing, and alerting script for the Windows services") in the appendix, Sample 3.54 is an immediate application of this WQL Event query example.

Sample 3.54 *Monitoring, managing, and alerting script for the Windows Group modifications*

```
 1:<?xml version="1.0"?>
 .:
 8:<package>
 9:  <job>
..:
13:    <runtime>
..:
18:    </runtime>
19:
20:    <script language="VBScript" src="..\Functions\TinyErrorHandler.vbs" />
21:    <script language="VBScript" src="..\Functions\PauseScript.vbs" />
22:    <script language="VBScript" src="..\Functions\GenerateHTML.vbs" />
23:    <script language="VBScript" src="..\Functions\SendMessageExtendedFunction.vbs" />
24:
25:    <object progid="WbemScripting.SWbemLocator" id="objWMILocator" reference="true"/>
26:    <object progid="WbemScripting.SWbemNamedValueSet" id="objWMIInstanceSinkContext"/>
27:    <object progid="WbemScripting.SWbemDateTime" id="objWMIDateTime" />
28:
29:    <script language="VBscript">
30:    <![CDATA[
..:
34:    ' -----------------------------------------------------------------------------------
35:    Const cComputerName = "LocalHost"
36:    Const cWMINameSpace = "Root/Directory/LDAP"
37:    Const cWMIQuery = "Select * From __InstanceModificationEvent Within 10
                                              Where TargetInstance ISA 'ds_group' "
38:
39:    Const cTargetRecipient = "Alain.Lissoir@LissWare.Net"
40:    Const cSourceRecipient = "WMISystem@LissWare.Net"
41:
42:    Const cSMTPServer = "10.10.10.3"
43:    Const cSMTPPort = 25
44:    Const cSMTPAccountName = ""
45:    Const cSMTPSendEmailAddress = ""
46:    Const cSMTPAuthenticate = 0' 0=Anonymous, 1=Basic, 2=NTLM
47:    Const cSMTPUserName = ""
48:    Const cSMTPPassword = ""
49:    Const cSMTPSSL = False
50:    Const cSMTPSendUsing = 2              ' 1=Pickup, 2=Port, 3=Exchange WebDAV
..:
67:    ' -----------------------------------------------------------------------------
68:    ' Parse the command line parameters
69:    If WScript.Arguments.Unnamed.Count = 0 Then
70:       WScript.Arguments.ShowUsage()
71:       WScript.Quit
72:    Else
73:       For intIndice = 0 To WScript.Arguments.Unnamed.Count - 1
74:            ReDim Preserve strGroupName(intIndice)
75:            strGroupName(intIndice) = Ucase (WScript.Arguments.Unnamed.Item(intIndice))
76:       Next
77:    End If
```

```
78:
79:    strUserID = WScript.Arguments.Named("User")
80:    If Len(strUserID) = 0 Then strUserID = ""
81:
82:    strPassword = WScript.Arguments.Named("strPassword")
83:    If Len(strPassword) = 0 Then strPassword = ""
84:
85:    strComputerName = WScript.Arguments.Named("Machine")
86:    If Len(strComputerName) = 0 Then strComputerName = cComputerName
87:
88:    Set objWMISink = WScript.CreateObject ("WbemScripting.SWbemSink", "SINK_")
89:
90:    objWMILocator.Security_.AuthenticationLevel = wbemAuthenticationLevelDefault
91:    objWMILocator.Security_.ImpersonationLevel = wbemImpersonationLevelImpersonate
92:    Set objWMIServices = objWMILocator.ConnectServer(strComputerName, cWMINameSpace, _
93:                                           strUserID, strPassword)
..:
96:    For intIndice = 0 To UBound (strGroupName)
97:        If Len(strWMIQuery) = 0 Then
98:            strWMIQuery = "TargetInstance.ds_name='" & strGroupName(intIndice) & "'"
99:        Else
100:           strWMIQuery = strWMIQuery & " Or " & _
101:                        "TargetInstance.ds_name='" & _
102:                        strGroupName(intIndice) & "'"
103:       End If
104:
105:       WScript.Echo "Adding '" & strGroupName(intIndice) & _
106:                    "' to subscription to monitor this Active Directory group."
107:   Next
108:
109:   strWMIQuery = cWMIQuery & " And (" & strWMIQuery & ")"
110:
111:   objWMIServices.ExecNotificationQueryAsync objWMISink, strWMIQuery
...:
114:   WScript.Echo vbCRLF & "Waiting for events..."
115:
116:   PauseScript "Click on 'Ok' to terminate the script ..."
117:
118:   WScript.Echo vbCRLF & "Cancelling event subscription ..."
119:   objWMISink.Cancel
...:
124:   WScript.Echo "Finished."
125:
126:   ' -------------------------------------------------------------------------------
127:   Sub SINK_OnObjectReady (objWbemObject, objWbemAsyncContext)
...:
133:       Wscript.Echo
134:       Wscript.Echo "BEGIN - OnObjectReady."
135:       WScript.Echo FormatDateTime(Date, vbLongDate) & " at " & _
136:                    FormatDateTime(Time, vbLongTime) & ": '" & _
137:                    objWbemObject.Path_.Class & "' has been triggered."
138:
139:       Select Case objWbemObject.Path_.Class
140:              Case "__InstanceModificationEvent"
141:                   Set objWMIInstance = objWbemObject
142:              Case "__AggregateEvent"
143:                   Set objWMIInstance = objWbemObject.Representative
144:              Case Else
145:                   Set objWMIInstance = Null
146:       End Select
```

```
147:
148:         If Not IsNull (objWMIInstance) Then
149:             If SendMessage (cTargetRecipient, _
150:                             cSourceRecipient, _
151:                             "'" & objWMIInstance.TargetInstance.ds_name & _
152:                             "' group modification - " & _
153:                                 FormatDateTime(Date, vbLongDate) & _
154:                                 " at " & _
155:                                 FormatDateTime(Time, vbLongTime), _
156:                             GenerateHTML (objWMIInstance.PreviousInstance, _
157:                                           objWMIInstance.TargetInstance) , _
158:                             "") Then
159:                 WScript.Echo "Failed to send email to '" & cTargetRecipient & "' ..."
160:             End If
161:         End If
...:
165:         Wscript.Echo "END - OnObjectReady."
166:
167:     End Sub
168:
169:     ]]>
170:    </script>
171:   </job>
172: </package>
```

As usual, the script structure is always the same. The script starts with the command-line parameter definitions (skipped lines 13 through 18) and parsing (lines 69 through 86). The script requires only one parameter on the command line, which lists one or more Active Directory group names to monitor. For example, to monitor modifications on the "Enterprise Admins" and "Domain Admins" group, the command line will be:

```
C:\>GroupMonitor.Wsf "Enterprise Admins" "Domain Admins"
```

The groups given on the command line are stored in an array (lines 75 through 78). Once the WMI connection is established (lines 90 through 93), the WQL query is constructed in a loop between lines 96 and 107. For the two sample groups given on the command line, the resulting WQL query will be:

```
Select * From __InstanceModificationEvent Within 10 Where TargetInstance ISA 'ds_group' And
        (TargetInstance.ds_name='Enterprise Admins' Or TargetInstance.ds_name='Domain Admins')
```

Next, the WQL query is submitted for asynchronous notifications (line 111), and the script enters an idle state. Once a modification is made to one of the given groups, the event sink routine (lines 127 through 167) is invoked, and the script immediately sends an email alert by reusing the SendMessage() function (included at line 23) and the GenerateHTML() function (included at line 22). The *PreviousInstance* and the *TargetInstance* properties containing object instances are formatted in HTML and stored in a MIME body mail message.

3.6.1.4   *Monitoring the FSMO roles*

By using the event instrumentation provided by WMI, it is also possible to monitor the Domain Controllers Flexible Single Master Operations (FSMO) role modifications. However, this monitoring requires a small setup at the level of the **Root\directory\LDAP** namespace. By default, the *Active Directory* provider accesses any Active Directory object instances located in the default naming context, which is the Windows Domain where the accessed Domain Controller resides. However, to monitor all FSMO roles, it is necessary to access the Active Directory Configuration and Schema naming contexts, since the attributes containing the relevant information are spread among the different Active Directory naming contexts. Table 3.52 lists the different FSMO roles and their respective naming context locations.

Table 3.52   *The Active FSMO Roles and Their Location in Active Directory*

FSMO Role	Naming Context	WMI Class	Object distinguishedName	WMI Property
PDC Emulator	Domain	ds_domaindns	DC=LissWare,DC=Net	ds_fSMORoleOwner
Infrastructure Master	Domain	ds_infrastructureupdate	CN=Infrastructure,DC=LissWare,DC=Net	ds_fSMORoleOwner
RID Master	Domain	ds_ridmanager	CN=RID Manager$,CN=System,DC=LissWare,DC=Net	ds_fSMORoleOwner
Domain Naming	Configuration	ds_crossrefcontainer	CN=Partitions,CN=Configuration,DC=LissWare,DC=Net	ds_fSMORoleOwner
Schema owner	Schema	ds_dmd	CN=Schema,CN=Configuration,DC=LissWare,DC=Net	ds_fSMORoleOwner

To enable access from WMI to the *ds_crossRefContainer* Active Directory object instance located in the Configuration naming context and to the *ds_dMD* Active Directory object instance located in the Schema naming context, an instance of the *DN_class* and the *DSClass_To_DNInstance* WMI classes first must be created in the **Root\directory\LDAP** namespace. This can be done with the help of a MOF file, as illustrated in Sample 3.55.

Sample 3.55   *Making the Configuration and Schema context accessible*

```
 1:   #pragma namespace("\\\\.\\Root\\directory\\ldap")
 2:
 3:   Instance of DN_Class
 4:
 5:       {
 6:       DN = "LDAP://CN=Configuration,DC= LissWare,DC=Net";
 7:       };
 8:
 9:   Instance of DSClass_To_DNInstance
10:
11:       {
12:       DSClass = "ds_crossRefContainer";
13:
14:       RootDNForSearchAndQuery = "DN_Class.DN=\"LDAP://CN=Configuration,DC= LissWare,DC=Net\"";
15:       };
16:
```

```
17:
18:    Instance of DN_Class
19:
20:        {
21:        DN = "LDAP://CN=Schema,CN=Configuration,DC= LissWare,DC=Net";
22:        };
23:
24:    Instance of DSClass_To_DNInstance
25:
26:        {
27:        DSClass = "ds_dMD";
28:
29:        RootDNForSearchAndQuery =
30:            "DN_Class.DN=\"LDAP://CN=Schema,CN=Configuration,DC=LissWare,DC=Net\"";
31:        };
```

The *DSClass_To_DNInstance* is an association class performing the association of an instance defining an Active Directory naming context and a WMI class representing the Active Directory class of the object instance to locate in that naming context. For example, to locate a *ds_crossRefContainer* instance in the Active Directory Configuration naming context, an instance of the *DSClass_To_DNInstance* association class must be created (lines 9 through 15) with its properties initialized as follows:

- The *DSClass* property is assigned with the *ds_crossRefContainer* class instance name (line 12).

- The *RootDNForSearchAndQuery* property is assigned with the WMI path of the WMI instance representing the Active Directory Configuration context (line 14). The instance representing the Active Directory Configuration context is created with the *DN_Class* WMI class (lines 3 through 7).

The same rule applies for the *ds_dMD* class, which has its instance located in the Active Directory Schema naming context (lines 18 through 31). Once the MOF file is loaded in the CIM repository with **MOF-COMP.EXE**, the monitoring of the FSMO roles can take place. The logic is implemented in Sample 3.56.

Sample 3.56   *Monitoring, managing, and alerting script for the FSMO role modifications*

```
 1:<?xml version="1.0"?>
 .:
 8:<package>
 9:  <job>
..:
13:    <runtime>
..:
17:    </runtime>
18:
19:    <script language="VBScript" src="..\Functions\TinyErrorHandler.vbs" />
20:    <script language="VBScript" src="..\Functions\PauseScript.vbs" />
```

```
 21:   <script language="VBScript" src="..\Functions\GenerateHTML.vbs" />
 22:   <script language="VBScript" src="..\Functions\SendMessageExtendedFunction.vbs" />
 23:
 24:   <object progid="WbemScripting.SWbemLocator" id="objWMILocator" reference="true"/>
 25:   <object progid="WbemScripting.SWBemNamedValueSet" id="objPDCFSMOSinkContext"/>
 26:   <object progid="WbemScripting.SWBemNamedValueSet" id="objINFFSMOSinkContext"/>
 27:   <object progid="WbemScripting.SWBemNamedValueSet" id="objRIDFSMOSinkContext"/>
 28:   <object progid="WbemScripting.SWBemNamedValueSet" id="objDOMFSMOSinkContext"/>
 29:   <object progid="WbemScripting.SWBemNamedValueSet" id="objSCHFSMOSinkContext"/>
 30:   <object progid="WbemScripting.SWbemDateTime" id="objWMIDateTime" />
 31:
 32:   <script language="VBscript">
 33:   <![CDATA[
 ..:
 72:   ' ---------------------------------------------------------------------------
 73:   ' Parse the command line parameters
 74:   strUserID = WScript.Arguments.Named("User")
 75:   If Len(strUserID) = 0 Then strUserID = ""
 76:
 77:   strPassword = WScript.Arguments.Named("strPassword")
 78:   If Len(strPassword) = 0 Then strPassword = ""
 79:
 80:   strComputerName = WScript.Arguments.Named("Machine")
 81:   If Len(strComputerName) = 0 Then strComputerName = cComputerName
 82:
 83:   Set objWMISink = WScript.CreateObject ("WbemScripting.SWbemSink", "SINK_")
 84:
 85:   objWMILocator.Security_.AuthenticationLevel = wbemAuthenticationLevelDefault
 86:   objWMILocator.Security_.ImpersonationLevel = wbemImpersonationLevelImpersonate
 87:   Set objWMIServices = objWMILocator.ConnectServer(strComputerName, cWMINameSpace, _
 88:                                                     strUserID, strPassword)
 ..:
 91:   objPDCFSMOSinkContext.Add "FSMO", "PDC"
 92:   objWMIServices.ExecNotificationQueryAsync objWMISink, _
 93:                                     cPDCFSMOWMIQuery, _
 94:                                               ' _
 95:                                               ' _
 96:                                               ' _
 97:                                     objPDCFSMOSinkContext
 98:   If Err.Number Then ErrorHandler (Err)
 99:   WScript.Echo "Monitoring PDC FSMO role ..."
100:
101:   objINFFSMOSinkContext.Add "FSMO", "INFRASTRUCTURE"
102:   objWMIServices.ExecNotificationQueryAsync objWMISink, _
103:                                     cINFFSMOWMIQuery, _
104:                                               ' _
105:                                               ' _
106:                                               ' _
107:                                     objINFFSMOSinkContext
108:   If Err.Number Then ErrorHandler (Err)
109:   WScript.Echo "Monitoring INFRASTRUCTURE FSMO role ..."
110:
111:   objRIDFSMOSinkContext.Add "FSMO", "RID"
112:   objWMIServices.ExecNotificationQueryAsync objWMISink, _
113:                                     cRIDFSMOWMIQuery, _
114:                                               ' _
115:                                               ' _
116:                                               ' _
117:                                     objRIDFSMOSinkContext
118:   If Err.Number Then ErrorHandler (Err)
```

```
119:     WScript.Echo "Monitoring RID FSMO role ..."
120:
121:     objDOMFSMOSinkContext.Add "FSMO", "DOMAIN NAMING"
122:     objWMIServices.ExecNotificationQueryAsync objWMISink, _
123:                                 cDOMFSMOWMIQuery, _
124:                                 ' _
125:                                 ' _
126:                                 ' _
127:                                 objDOMFSMOSinkContext
128:     If Err.Number Then ErrorHandler (Err)
129:     WScript.Echo "Monitoring DOMAIN NAMING FSMO role ..."
130:
131:     objSCHFSMOSinkContext.Add "FSMO", "SCHEMA"
132:     objWMIServices.ExecNotificationQueryAsync objWMISink, _
133:                                 cSCHFSMOWMIQuery, _
134:                                 ' _
135:                                 ' _
136:                                 ' _
137:                                 objSCHFSMOSinkContext
138:     If Err.Number Then ErrorHandler (Err)
139:     WScript.Echo "Monitoring SCHEMA FSMO role ..."
140:
141:     WScript.Echo vbCRLF & "Waiting for events..."
142:
143:     PauseScript "Click on 'Ok' to terminate the script ..."
144:
145:     WScript.Echo vbCRLF & "Cancelling event subscription ..."
146:     objWMISink.Cancel
...:
151:     WScript.Echo "Finished."
152:
153:     ' --------------------------------------------------------------------------------
154:     Sub SINK_OnObjectReady (objWbemObject, objWbemAsyncContext)
...:
203:     End Sub
204:
205:     ]]>
206:     </script>
207:     </job>
208:   </package>
```

The logic and structure of Sample 3.56 is basically the same as Sample 3.54 ("Monitoring, managing, and alerting script for the Windows Group modifications"). However, instead of executing one WQL event query, Sample 3.56 executes five WQL event queries (one per FSMO role):

For the PDC Emulator FSMO:

```
Select * From __InstanceModificationEvent Within 10
        Where TargetInstance ISA 'ds_domaindns' And
        PreviousInstance.DS_fSMORoleOwner <> TargetInstance.DS_fSMORoleOwner"
```

For the Infrastructure Master FSMO:

```
Select * From __InstanceModificationEvent Within 10
        Where TargetInstance ISA 'ds_infrastructureupdate' And
        PreviousInstance.DS_fSMORoleOwner <> TargetInstance.DS_fSMORoleOwner"
```

For the RID Master FSMO:

```
Select * From __InstanceModificationEvent Within 10
        Where TargetInstance ISA 'ds_ridmanager' And
        PreviousInstance.DS_fSMORoleOwner <> TargetInstance.DS_fSMORoleOwner"
```

For the Domain Naming Master FSMO:

```
Select * From __InstanceModificationEvent Within 10
        Where TargetInstance ISA 'ds_crossrefcontainer' And
        PreviousInstance.DS_fSMORoleOwner <> TargetInstance.DS_fSMORoleOwner"
```

For the Schema Owner FSMO:

```
Select * From __InstanceModificationEvent Within 10
        Where TargetInstance ISA 'ds_dmd' And
        PreviousInstance.DS_fSMORoleOwner <> TargetInstance.DS_fSMORoleOwner"
```

Once the WMI connection is established (lines 85 through 88), the five WQL event queries are submitted to WMI (lines 91 through 139). Note that each WQL query makes use of a WMI context, since the same event sink subroutine is used to capture all WMI events. This routine has the exact same logic and structure as Sample 3.54 ("Monitoring, managing, and alerting script for the Windows Group modifications").

3.6.1.5   *Debugging Active Directory providers*

If you experience trouble managing Active Directory objects with the WMI *Active Directory* providers, it is possible to trace the provider's activity in a log file. The configuration of a registry key set activates the trace logging. The registry keys are located at:

```
HKLM\SOFTWARE\Microsoft\WBEM\PROVIDERS\Logging\DSProvider
```

Table 3.53   *Enabling the Trace Logging of a WMI Provider*

Key names	Description
File	Full path and file name of the log file. The default value is %windir%\system32\wbem\logs. The *Type* named value must be set to "File" for this named value to be used.
Level	A 32-bit logical mask that defines the type of debugging output generated by the provider. This value is provider-dependent. The default value is 0 (zero).
MaxFileSize	Maximum file size (in bytes) of the log file. This integer value must be in the range 1024 to 2^32-1. When the file size exceeds this value, the file is renamed to ~*filename* and a new, empty log file is created. The disk space required for the log file is twice the value of *MaxFileSize*. The default value is 65,535.
Type	Can be set to "File" or "Debugger". If set to "File", the trace information is written to the log file specified in the *File* named value. The default value is "File."

Note that other WMI providers, such as *SNMP* providers, also support activity trace logging (see Table 3.53). They use the same set of registry key names but from a different registry hive, as shown in Figure 3.34; the *SNMP* providers use the "WBEMSNMP" hive.

Figure 3.34
The registry hive for the four WMI providers supporting activity logging.

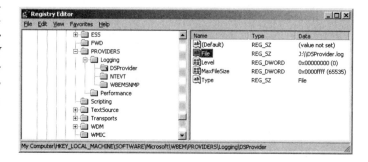

Once the *Active Directory* WMI providers logging is started, the **DSProvider.LOG** file contains trace information and error messages for the *Directory Service* providers. The *Level* registry key is set to zero by default and can remain zero for the *Active Directory* providers. However, the tracing of other providers (i.e., *SNMP* providers) may require some values. Actually, the required values are determined by the provider implementation. To give a simple trace example, if the script (Sample 3.53, "Creating an Active Directory **user** object with WMI") is executed a second time, it will return an error, since the user already exists. The output will be as follows:

```
C:\>CreateADUser.wsf
Microsoft (R) Windows Script Host Version 5.6
Copyright (C) Microsoft Corporation 1996-2001. All rights reserved.


------------------------------------------------------------
Error: &h80041001

Generic failure
------------------------------------------------------------
```

From a WMI perspective, the returned error message "Generic Failure" is not enough to determine the source of the problem. Of course, it is always possible to instantiate an **SWBemLastError** object, but in this particular case it will not give much more information about the problem. However, by looking at the **DSProvider.LOG**, it shows the following information:

```
1:   CDSClassProvider :: GetClassFromCacheOrADSI()
     Could not find class in Authenticated list for ds_user. Going to ADSI
2:   CDSClassProvider :: GetObjectAsync() called for ADS_user
3:   CDSClassProvider :: GetClassFromCacheOrADSI()
     Could not find class in Authenticated list for ADS_user. Going to ADSI
4:   CDSClassProvider :: GetObjectAsync() called for ADS_organizationalPerson
5:   CDSClassProvider :: GetClassFromCacheOrADSI()
     Could not find class in Authenticated list for ADS_organizationalPerson. Going to ADSI
6:   CDSClassProvider :: GetObjectAsync() called for ADS_person
7:   CDSClassProvider :: GetClassFromCacheOrADSI()
     Could not find class in Authenticated list for ADS_person. Going to ADSI
8:   CDSClassProvider :: GetObjectAsync() called for DS_top
```

```
 9:   CDSClassProvider :: GetClassFromCacheOrADSI()
      Could not find class in Authenticated list for DS_top. Going to ADSI
10:   CWbemCache :: AddClass() Added a class DS_top to cache
11:   CDSClassProvider :: GetClassFromCacheOrADSI()
      GetClassFromADSI succeeded for DS_top Added it to cache
12:   CDSClassProvider :: GetClassFromCacheOrADSI() Also added to Authenticated list : DS_top
13:   CWbemCache :: AddClass() Added a class ADS_person to cache
14:   CDSClassProvider :: GetClassFromCacheOrADSI()
      GetClassFromADSI succeeded for ADS_person Added it to cache
15:   CDSClassProvider :: GetClassFromCacheOrADSI()
      Also added to Authenticated list : ADS_person
16:   CWbemCache :: AddClass() Added a class ADS_organizationalPerson to cache
17:   CDSClassProvider :: GetClassFromCacheOrADSI()
      GetClassFromADSI succeeded for ADS_organizationalPerson Added it to cache
18:   CDSClassProvider :: GetClassFromCacheOrADSI()
      Also added to Authenticated list : ADS_organizationalPerson
19:   CWbemCache :: AddClass() Added a class ADS_user to cache
20:   CDSClassProvider :: GetClassFromCacheOrADSI()
      GetClassFromADSI succeeded for ADS_user Added it to cache
21:   CDSClassProvider :: GetClassFromCacheOrADSI() Also added to Authenticated list : ADS_user
22:   CWbemCache :: AddClass() Added a class ds_user to cache
23:   CDSClassProvider :: GetClassFromCacheOrADSI()
      GetClassFromADSI succeeded for ds_user Added it to cache
24:   CDSClassProvider :: GetClassFromCacheOrADSI() Also added to Authenticated list : ds_user
25:   CDSClassProvider :: GetObjectAsync() called for ds_user
26:   CDSClassProvider :: GetClassFromCacheOrADSI() Found class in Authenticated list for ds_user
27:   CDSClassProvider :: GetClassFromCacheOrADSI() Found class in cache for ds_user
28:   CDSClassProvider :: GetObjectAsync() called for ads_user
29:   CDSClassProvider :: GetClassFromCacheOrADSI() Found class in Authenticated list for ads_user
30:   CDSClassProvider :: GetClassFromCacheOrADSI() Found class in cache for ads_user
31:   CDSInstanceProviderClassFactory::CreateInstance() called
32:   CLDAPInstanceProvider :: CONSTRUCTOR
33:   CLDAPInstanceProvider :: Got Top Level Container as : DC=LissWare,DC=Net
34:   CLDAPInstanceProvider :: PutInstanceAsync() called
35:   CLDAPInstanceProvider :: PutInstanceAsync()
      calledfor ds_user.ADSIPath="LDAP://CN=WMIUser,CN=Users,DC=LissWare,DC=Net"
36:   CLDAPInstanceProvider :: The 362 attributes being put are:
37:   accountExpires
38:   accountNameHistory
39:   aCSPolicyName
...:
395:  whenCreated
396:  wWWHomePage
397:  x121Address
398:  x500uniqueIdentifier
399:  CLDAPInstanceProvider :: SetObjectAttributes FAILED with 80072035
400:  CLDAPInstanceProvider :: PutInstanceAsync()
      ModifyExistingInstance FAILED for LDAP://CN=WMIUser,CN=Users,DC=LissWare,DC=Net
      with 80072035
```

From line 1 through 30, we see the activity generated by the *Active Directory* provider to create the *ds_user* instance. At line 31, we see the instance creation followed by the *Put_* method invocation (lines 34 and 35). From line 36 through 398, we see the list of attributes that will be set. Because the user instance already exists in Active Directory, trying to set all these attributes will generate an error, since some attributes can only be set by the system itself (see section 3.6.1.1, "Creating and updating objects in Active Directory"). The end result is an error number 80072035 (line 399). By looking in the Active Directory platform SDK, we can determine that an error 8007* is a **Win32** Error. In such a case the rightmost part of the error number must be converted to a decimal value, which gives 8,245 in decimal (from 2,035 in hexadecimal). If we run the command "NET HELPMSG 8245" from the command line, we will get the informational message: "The server is unwilling to process the request." This makes sense, since the script tries to perform an illegal Active Directory operation, which is an update of all attributes available from the existing user object (even with the ones that can only be updated by the system).

3.6.2   Active Directory Replication provider

The *Active Directory Replication* provider allows the management of the replication. With this provider and its supported classes, it is possible to retrieve information about the replication state. The provider is implemented as an instance and method provider (see Table 3.54).

Table 3.54   *The Active Directory Replication Providers Capabilities*

Provider Name	Provider Namespace	Class Provider	Instance Provider	Method Provider	Property Provider	Event Provider	Event Consumer Provider	Support Get	Support Put	Support Enumeration	Support Delete	Windows Server 2003	Windows XP	Windows 2000 Server	Windows 2000 Professional	Windows NT 4.0
Active Directory Replication provider																
ReplProv1	Root/MicrosoftActiveDirectory		X	X				X	X		X					

The *Active Directory Replication* provider is located in the **Root\MicrosoftActiveDirectory** namespace of the CIM repository and supports five classes, as listed in Table 3.55.

Table 3.55   *The Active Directory Replication Providers Classes*

Name	Comments
MSAD_ReplPendingOp	Describes a replication task currently executing or pending execution on the DC.
MSAD_NamingContext	Various properties of the current Naming Context.
MSAD_ReplCursor	Contains inbound replication state information with respect to all replicas of a given Naming Context. This state information indicates up to what USN X the destination server has seen all changes <= USN X originated by the source server with the given invocation ID.
MSAD_DomainController	The current domain controller properties.
MSAD_ReplNeighbor	Inbound replication state information for a Naming Context & source server pair.

Since the *Active Directory Replication* provider is not implemented as an event provider, there is no extrinsic event class available. This also means that the use of the **WITHIN** statement in a WQL event query is mandatory. For example, the *MSAD_DomainController* class exposes Boolean values that determine if a domain controller is registered in the Dynamic DNS or if the replicated SYSVOL volume is ready for use. To capture any modification made in an *MSAD_DomainController* instance that represents a domain controller, the following WQL event query can be used:

```
 1:  C:>GenericEventAsyncConsumer.wsf "Select * From __InstanceModificationEvent Within 10
 2:                          Where TargetInstance ISA 'MSAD_DomainController'"
 3:                          /namespace:Root\MicrosoftActiveDirectory
 4:  Microsoft (R) Windows Script Host Version 5.6
 5:  Copyright (C) Microsoft Corporation 1996-2001. All rights reserved.
 6:
 7:  Waiting for events...
 8:
 9:  BEGIN - OnObjectReady.
10:  Sunday, 16 December, 2001 at 10:07:11: '__InstanceModificationEvent' has been triggered.
11:
12:     - __InstanceModificationEvent -----------------------------------------------------
13:
14:     - MSAD_DomainController ----------------------------------------------------------
15:     CommonName: ......................... NET-DPEN6400A
16:     *DistinguishedName: ................. CN=NTDS Settings,CN=NET-DPEN6400A,CN=Servers,
17:                                           CN=Brussels,CN=Sites,CN=Configuration,
18:                                           DC=LissWare,DC=Net
19:     IsAdvertisingToLocator: ............. TRUE
20:     IsGC: ............................... TRUE
21:     IsNextRIDPoolAvailable: ............. FALSE
22:     IsRegisteredInDNS: .................. FALSE
23:     IsSysVolReady: ...................... TRUE
24:     NTDsaGUID: .......................... 8b231f02-43e1-43f9-94c4-c8545e4b6d2b
25:     PercentOfRIDsLeft: .................. 98
26:     SiteName: ........................... Brussels
27:     TimeOfOldestReplAdd: ................ 01-01-1601
28:     TimeOfOldestReplDel: ................ 01-01-1601
29:     TimeOfOldestReplMod: ................ 01-01-1601
30:     TimeOfOldestReplSync: ............... 01-01-1601
31:     TimeOfOldestReplUpdRefs: ............ 01-01-1601
32:
33:
34:     - MSAD_DomainController ----------------------------------------------------------
35:     CommonName: ......................... NET-DPEN6400A
36:     *DistinguishedName: ................. CN=NTDS Settings,CN=NET-DPEN6400A,CN=Servers,
37:                                           CN=Brussels,CN=Sites,CN=Configuration,
38:                                           DC=LissWare,DC=Net
39:     IsAdvertisingToLocator: ............. TRUE
40:     IsGC: ............................... TRUE
41:     IsNextRIDPoolAvailable: ............. FALSE
42:     IsRegisteredInDNS: .................. TRUE
43:     IsSysVolReady: ...................... TRUE
44:     NTDsaGUID: .......................... 8b231f02-43e1-43f9-94c4-c8545e4b6d2b
45:     PercentOfRIDsLeft: .................. 98
46:     SiteName: ........................... Brussels
47:     TimeOfOldestReplAdd: ................ 01-01-1601
```

```
48:         TimeOfOldestReplDel: ................ 01-01-1601
49:         TimeOfOldestReplMod: ................ 01-01-1601
50:         TimeOfOldestReplSync: ............... 01-01-1601
51:         TimeOfOldestReplUpdRefs: ............ 01-01-1601
52:
53:
54:    END - OnObjectReady.
```

In this output sample, we can see that the DNS registration state has passed from False (line 22) to True (line 42).

Samples 3.57 through 3.59 make use of the other classes supported by the *Active Directory Replication* provider (see Table 3.55). The script exposes the following command-line parameters:

```
C:\>WMIADRepl.wsf
Microsoft (R) Windows Script Host Version 5.6
Copyright (C) Microsoft Corporation 1996-2001. All rights reserved.

Usage: WMIADRepl.wsf [/ReplPendingOp[+|-]] [/NC[+|-]] [/ReplCsr[+|-]] [/DC[+|-]]
                     [/ReplNeighbor:value] [/ExecuteKCC[+|-]] [/SyncNC:value]
                     [/Machine:value] [/User:value] [/Password:value]


Options:

ReplPendingOp : View the replication tasks currently executing or pending execution on the DC.
NC            : View the properties of the current Naming Contexts.
ReplCsr       : View inbound replication state information with respect to all replicas
                of a each Naming Context.
DC            : View current domain controller properties.
ReplNeighbor  : View inbound replication state information for a Naming Context
                and source server pair.
ExecuteKCC    : Invokes the Knowledge Consistency Checker in order to verify
                the replication topology.
SyncNC        : Synchronizes a destination Naming Context with one of its sources.
Machine       : Determine the WMI system to connect to. (default=LocalHost)
User          : Determine the UserID to perform the remote connection. (default=none)
Password      : Determine the password to perform the remote connection. (default=none)
Example:

    WMIADRepl.wsf /ReplPendingOp+
    WMIADRepl.wsf /NC+
    WMIADRepl.wsf /ReplCsr+
    WMIADRepl.wsf /DC+
    WMIADRepl.wsf /ReplNeighbor
    WMIADRepl.wsf /ReplNeighbor:CN=Configuration,DC=LissWare,DC=Net
    WMIADRepl.wsf /ReplNeighbor:CN=Schema,CN=Configuration,DC=LissWare,DC=Net
    WMIADRepl.wsf /ReplNeighbor:DC=ForestDnsZones,DC=LissWare,DC=Net
    WMIADRepl.wsf /ReplNeighbor:DC=Emea,DC=LissWare,DC=Net
    WMIADRepl.wsf /ExecuteKCC+
    WMIADRepl.wsf /SyncNC:CN=Configuration,DC=LissWare,DC=Net
    WMIADRepl.wsf /SyncNC:CN=Schema,CN=Configuration,DC=LissWare,DC=Net
    WMIADRepl.wsf /SyncNC:DC=ForestDnsZones,DC=LissWare,DC=Net
    WMIADRepl.wsf /SyncNC:DC=Emea,DC=LissWare,DC=Net
```

Basically, the script enumerates the various instances of the classes.

Sample 3.57 *Viewing and managing the Active Directory Replication state (Part I)*

```
 1:<?xml version="1.0"?>
 .:
 8:<package>
 9: <job>
..:
13:   <runtime>
..:
42:   </runtime>
43:
44:   <script language="VBScript" src="..\Functions\DisplayFormattedPropertyFunction.vbs" />
45:   <script language="VBScript" src="..\Functions\TinyErrorHandler.vbs" />
46:
47:   <object progid="WbemScripting.SWbemLocator" id="objWMILocator" reference="true"/>
48:   <object progid="WbemScripting.SWbemDateTime" id="objWMIDateTime" />
49:
50:   <script language="VBscript">
51:   <![CDATA[
..:
55:   Const cComputerName = "LocalHost"
56:   Const cWMINameSpace = "Root/MicrosoftActiveDirectory"
57:
58:   Const cExecKCCTaskID = 0
59:   Const cExecKCCFlags = 0
60:   Const cSyncNCOptions = 16
..:
87:   ' ----------------------------------------------------------------------------
88:   ' Parse the command line parameters
89:   If WScript.Arguments.Named.Count = 0 Then
90:      WScript.Arguments.ShowUsage()
91:      WScript.Quit
92:   End If
...:
121:   strComputerName = WScript.Arguments.Named("Machine")
122:   If Len(strComputerName) = 0 Then strComputerName = cComputerName
123:
124:   objWMILocator.Security_.AuthenticationLevel = wbemAuthenticationLevelDefault
125:   objWMILocator.Security_.ImpersonationLevel = wbemImpersonationLevelImpersonate
126:
127:   Set objWMIServices = objWMILocator.ConnectServer(strComputerName, cWMINameSpace, _
128:                                              strUserID, strPassword)
...:
131:   ' -- ReplPendingOp ----------------------------------------------------------
132:   If boolReplPendingOp Then
133:      Set objWMIInstances = objWMIServices.InstancesOf ("MSAD_ReplPendingOp")
134:      If Err.Number Then ErrorHandler (Err)
135:
136:      If objWMIInstances.Count Then
137:
138:         WScript.Echo "- " & objWMIInstance.NamingContextDN & " " & String (60, "-")
139:
140:         For Each objWMIInstance In objWMIInstances
141:            Set objWMIPropertySet = objWMIInstance.Properties_
142:            For Each objWMIProperty In objWMIPropertySet
143:               DisplayFormattedProperty objWMIInstance, _
144:                        objWMIProperty.Name, _
```

```
145:                           objWMIProperty.Name, _
146:                           Null
147:             Next
148:             Set objWMIPropertySet = Nothing
149:             WScript.Echo
150:          Next
151:       Else
152:          WScript.Echo "No information available." & vbCRLF
153:       End If
154:    End If
155:
156:    ' -- NC -------------------------------------------------------------------------
157:    If boolNC Then
158:       Set objWMIInstances = objWMIServices.InstancesOf ("MSAD_NamingContext")
159:       If Err.Number Then ErrorHandler (Err)
160:
161:       WScript.Echo "EXISTING NAMING CONTEXT "  & String (84, "=") & vbCRLF
162:       WScript.Echo Space (36) & "Naming Context    Full replica"
163:       WScript.Echo String (98, "-")
164:
165:       For Each objWMIInstance In objWMIInstances
166:           WScript.Echo String (50 - Len (objWMIInstance.DistinguishedName), " ") & _
167:                        objWMIInstance.DistinguishedName & " " & _
168:                        String (15 - Len (objWMIInstance.IsFullReplica), " ") & _
169:                        objWMIInstance.IsFullReplica
170:       Next
171:       WScript.Echo
172:    End If
173:
174:    ' -- ReplCsr -------------------------------------------------------------------
175:    If boolReplCsr Then
176:       Set objWMIInstances = objWMIServices.InstancesOf ("MSAD_ReplCursor")
177:       If Err.Number Then ErrorHandler (Err)
178:
179:       If objWMIInstances.Count Then
180:          For Each objWMIInstance In objWMIInstances
181:              WScript.Echo "- " & objWMIInstance.NamingContextDN & " " & String (60, "-")
182:
183:              Set objWMIPropertySet = objWMIInstance.Properties_
184:              For Each objWMIProperty In objWMIPropertySet
185:                  DisplayFormattedProperty objWMIInstance, _
186:                          objWMIProperty.Name, _
187:                          objWMIProperty.Name, _
188:                          Null
189:              Next
190:              Set objWMIPropertySet = Nothing
191:              WScript.Echo
192:          Next
193:       Else
194:          WScript.Echo "No information available." & vbCRLF
195:       End If
196:    End If
197:
198:    ' -- DC -------------------------------------------------------------------------
199:    If boolDC Then
200:       Set objWMIInstances = objWMIServices.InstancesOf ("MSAD_DomainController")
201:       If Err.Number Then ErrorHandler (Err)
202:
203:       If objWMIInstances.Count Then
204:          For Each objWMIInstance In objWMIInstances
```

```
205:                    Set objWMIPropertySet = objWMIInstance.Properties_
206:                    For Each objWMIProperty In objWMIPropertySet
207:                        DisplayFormattedProperty objWMIInstance, _
208:                                objWMIProperty.Name, _
209:                                objWMIProperty.Name, _
210:                                Null
211:                    Next
212:                    Set objWMIPropertySet = Nothing
213:                    WScript.Echo
214:                Next
215:            Else
216:                WScript.Echo "No information available." & vbCRLF
217:            End If
218:        End If
219:
...:
...:
...:
```

Once the command-line parameters are parsed (lines 87 through 122) and the WMI connection established (lines 124 through 128), the script retrieves miscellaneous instances based on the command-line parameters. If the command line includes the **/ReplPendingOp+** switch, the section from line 132 through 154 is executed (see Sample 3.58). This section retrieves information about the replication tasks currently executing or pending execution on the Domain Controller by requesting all instances of the *MSAD_ReplPendingOp* class (line 133). Next, the script retrieves the properties of each instance (lines 140 through 150).

The script proceeds exactly in the same way for all classes supported by the *Active Directory Replication* provider. The script uses:

- The *MSAD_NamingContext* class to retrieve properties of the current Naming Context available (lines 157 through 172). A sample output would be:

```
 1:   C:\>WMIADRepl.wsf /NC+
 2:   Microsoft (R) Windows Script Host Version 5.6
 3:   Copyright (C) Microsoft Corporation 1996-2001. All rights reserved.
 4:
 5:   EXISTING NAMING CONTEXT ========================================================
 6:
 7:                                 Naming Context     Full replica
 8:   --------------------------------------------------------------------------------
 9:            DC=DomainDnsZones,DC=LissWare,DC=Net             True
10:            DC=ForestDnsZones,DC=LissWare,DC=Net             True
11:      CN=Schema,CN=Configuration,DC=LissWare,DC=Net          True
12:             CN=Configuration,DC=LissWare,DC=Net             True
13:                         DC=LissWare,DC=Net                  True
14:                 DC=Emea,DC=LissWare,DC=Net                  False
15:
16:   Completed.
```

- The *MSAD_ReplCursor* class to retrieve inbound replication state information with respect to all replicas of a given Naming Context (lines 175 through 196). A sample output would be:

```
 1:  C:\>WMIADRepl.wsf /ReplCsr+
 2:  Microsoft (R) Windows Script Host Version 5.6
 3:  Copyright (C) Microsoft Corporation 1996-2001. All rights reserved.
 4:
 5:  - DC=DomainDnsZones,DC=LissWare,DC=Net ------------------------------------------
 6:  *NamingContextDN: ...................... DC=DomainDnsZones,DC=LissWare,DC=Net
 7:  SourceDsaDN: ........................... CN=NTDS Settings,CN=NET-DPEN6400A,CN=Servers,
 8:                                           CN=Brussels,CN=Sites,CN=Configuration,
 9:                                           DC=LissWare,DC=Net
10:  *SourceDsaInvocationID: ................ 8b231f02-43e1-43f9-94c4-c8545e4b6d2b
11:  TimeOfLastSuccessfulSync: .............. 16-12-2001 17:26:48
12:  USNAttributeFilter: .................... 12212
13:
14:  - DC=ForestDnsZones,DC=LissWare,DC=Net ------------------------------------------
15:  *NamingContextDN: ...................... DC=ForestDnsZones,DC=LissWare,DC=Net
16:  SourceDsaDN: ........................... CN=NTDS Settings,CN=NET-DPEN6400A,CN=Servers,
17:                                           CN=Brussels,CN=Sites,
18:                                           CN=Configuration,DC=LissWare,DC=Net
19:  *SourceDsaInvocationID: ................ 8b231f02-43e1-43f9-94c4-c8545e4b6d2b
20:  TimeOfLastSuccessfulSync: .............. 16-12-2001 17:26:48
21:  USNAttributeFilter: .................... 12212
```

- The *MSAD_DomainController* class to retrieve the domain controller properties (lines 199 through 218). A sample output would be:

```
 1:  C:\>WMIADRepl.wsf /DC+
 2:  Microsoft (R) Windows Script Host Version 5.6
 3:  Copyright (C) Microsoft Corporation 1996-2001. All rights reserved.
 4:
 5:  CommonName: ............................ NET-DPEN6400A
 6:  *DistinguishedName: .................... CN=NTDS Settings,CN=NET-DPEN6400A,CN=Servers,
 7:                                           CN=Brussels,CN=Sites,CN=Configuration,
 8:                                           DC=LissWare,DC=Net
 9:  IsAdvertisingToLocator: ................ TRUE
10:  IsGC: .................................. TRUE
11:  IsNextRIDPoolAvailable: ................ FALSE
12:  IsRegisteredInDNS: ..................... TRUE
13:  IsSysVolReady: ......................... TRUE
14:  NTDsaGUID: ............................. 8b231f02-43e1-43f9-94c4-c8545e4b6d2b
15:  PercentOfRIDsLeft: ..................... 98
16:  SiteName: .............................. Brussels
17:  TimeOfOldestReplAdd: ................... 01-01-1601
18:  TimeOfOldestReplDel: ................... 01-01-1601
19:  TimeOfOldestReplMod: ................... 01-01-1601
20:  TimeOfOldestReplSync: .................. 01-01-1601
21:  TimeOfOldestReplUpdRefs: ............... 01-01-1601
22:
23:  Completed.
```

You will notice the presence of several Boolean values, which indicate the state of the examined domain controller (i.e., *IsAdvertisingToLocator, IsGC, IsNextRIDPoolAvailable, IsRegisteredInDNS, IsSysVolReady*).

Sample 3.58 displays information from the *MSAD_ReplNeighbor* class. It retrieves the inbound replication state information for a Naming Context and source server pair.

Sample 3.58 *Viewing the inbound replication state information for a Naming Context (Part II)*

```
...:
...:
...:
219:
220:    ' -- ReplNeighbor -------------------------------------------------------------
221:    If boolReplNeighbor Then
222:        If Len (strReplNeighbor) Then
223:            Set objWMIInstances = objWMIServices.ExecQuery("Select * From MSAD_ReplNeighbor " & _
224:                                                  "Where NamingContextDN='" & _
225:                                                  strReplNeighbor & "'")
226:            If Err.Number Then ErrorHandler (Err)
227:
228:            If objWMIInstances.Count = 1 Then
229:                For Each objWMIInstance In objWMIInstances
230:
231:                    WScript.Echo "- " & objWMIInstance.NamingContextDN & " " & String (60, "-")
232:
233:                    Set objWMIPropertySet = objWMIInstance.Properties_
234:                    For Each objWMIProperty In objWMIPropertySet
235:                        DisplayFormattedProperty objWMIInstance, _
236:                                objWMIProperty.Name, _
237:                                objWMIProperty.Name, _
238:                                Null
239:                    Next
240:                    Set objWMIPropertySet = Nothing
241:                    WScript.Echo
242:                Next
243:            Else
244:                WScript.Echo "No information available." & vbCRLF
245:            End If
246:        Else
247:            Set objWMIInstances = objWMIServices.InstancesOf ("MSAD_ReplNeighbor")
248:            If Err.Number Then ErrorHandler (Err)
249:
250:            If objWMIInstances.Count Then
251:                WScript.Echo "INBOUND REPLICATION STATE" & String (188, "=") & vbCRLF
252:                WScript.Echo "                                    Naming Context" & _
253:                             "        Source DSA          Site SyncProg" & _
254:                             " SyncNext IsDeleted LastSync ModSyncFailures SyncFailure" & _
255:                             "      TimeOfLastSync     TimeOfLastSuccess" & _
256:                             "  USNAttr USNObject"
257:                WScript.Echo String (213, "-")
258:
259:                For Each objWMIInstance In objWMIInstances
260:                    objWMIDateTime.Value = objWMIInstance.TimeOfLastSyncAttempt
261:                    strTimeOfLastSyncAttempt = objWMIDateTime.GetVarDate (False)
262:                    objWMIDateTime.Value = objWMIInstance.TimeOfLastSyncSuccess
263:                    strTimeOfLastSyncSuccess = objWMIDateTime.GetVarDate (False)
264:
265:                    WScript.Echo String (50-Len(objWMIInstance.NamingContextDN)," ") & _
266:                        objWMIInstance.NamingContextDN & " " & _
```

```
267:                      String (20-Len(objWMIInstance.SourceDsaCN)," ") & _
268:                      objWMIInstance.SourceDsaCN & " " & _
269:                      String (15-Len(objWMIInstance.SourceDsaSite)," ") & _
270:                      objWMIInstance.SourceDsaSite & " " & _
271:                      String (8-Len(objWMIInstance.FullSyncInProgress)," ") & _
272:                      objWMIInstance.FullSyncInProgress & " " & _
273:                      String (-Len(objWMIInstance.FullSyncNextPacket)," ") & _
274:                      objWMIInstance.FullSyncNextPacket & " " & _
275:                      String (9-Len(objWMIInstance.IsDeletedSourceDsa)," ") & _
276:                      objWMIInstance.IsDeletedSourceDsa & " " & _
277:                      String (8-Len(objWMIInstance.LastSyncResult)," ") & _
278:                      objWMIInstance.LastSyncResult & " " & _
279:                      String(15-Len(objWMIInstance.ModifiedNumConsecutiveSyncFailures)," ") & _
280:                      objWMIInstance.ModifiedNumConsecutiveSyncFailures & " " & _
281:                      String (11-Len(objWMIInstance.NumConsecutiveSyncFailures)," ") & _
282:                      objWMIInstance.NumConsecutiveSyncFailures & " " & _
283:                      String (20-Len(strTimeOfLastSyncAttempt)," ") & _
284:                      strTimeOfLastSyncAttempt  & " " & _
285:                      String (20-Len(strTimeOfLastSyncSuccess)," ") & _
286:                      strTimeOfLastSyncSuccess & " " & _
287:                      String (8-Len(objWMIInstance.USNAttributeFilter)," ") & _
288:                      objWMIInstance.USNAttributeFilter & " " & _
289:                      String (9-Len(objWMIInstance.USNLastObjChangeSynced)," ") & _
290:                      objWMIInstance.USNLastObjChangeSynced
291:              Next
292:              WScript.Echo
293:          Else
294:              WScript.Echo "No information available." & vbCRLF
295:          End If
296:      End If
297:  End If
298:
...:
...:
...:
```

The script can display the information in two different ways. If no specific naming context is specified with the **/ReplNeighbor** switch, the script displays the information for all naming contexts available (lines 247 through 296). If a naming context is given on the command line, only the information related to that naming context is displayed (lines 223 through 245). A sample output would be:

```
1:   C:\>WMIADRepl.wsf /ReplNeighbor:CN=Configuration,DC=LissWare,DC=Net
2:   Microsoft (R) Windows Script Host Version 5.6
3:   Copyright (C) Microsoft Corporation 1996-2001. All rights reserved.
4:
5:   - CN=Configuration,DC=LissWare,DC=Net -----------------------------------------------
6:   AsyncIntersiteTransportObjGuid: .......... 00000000-0000-0000-0000-000000000000
7:   CompressChanges: ......................... TRUE
8:   DisableScheduledSync: .................... FALSE
9:   Domain: .................................. LissWare.Net
10:  DoScheduledSyncs: ........................ TRUE
11:  FullSyncInProgress: ...................... FALSE
12:  FullSyncNextPacket: ...................... FALSE
13:  IgnoreChangeNotifications: ............... FALSE
14:  IsDeletedSourceDsa: ...................... FALSE
15:  LastSyncResult: .......................... 0
```

```
16:   ModifiedNumConsecutiveSyncFailures: ...... 0
17:   *NamingContextDN: ....................... CN=Configuration,DC=LissWare,DC=Net
18:   NamingContextObjGuid: ................... ba172143-2bc0-4d55-be69-711a8f927419
19:   NeverSynced: ............................ FALSE
20:   NoChangeNotifications: .................. TRUE
21:   NumConsecutiveSyncFailures: ............. 0
22:   ReplicaFlags: ........................... 805306448
23:   SourceDsaAddress: ....................... 14612935-967d-402f-b5b1-0ae412edaec4.
24:                                             _msdcs.LissWare.Net
25:   SourceDsaCN: ............................ NET-DPEP6400
26:   SourceDsaDN: ............................ CN=NTDS Settings,CN=NET-DPEP6400,CN=Servers,
27:                                             CN=Seattle,CN=Sites,CN=Configuration,
28:                                             DC=LissWare,DC=Net
29:   SourceDsaInvocationID: .................. 905e62c2-6f20-4333-ae8b-c6829e12d5b9
30:   *SourceDsaObjGuid: ...................... 14612935-967d-402f-b5b1-0ae412edaec4
31:   SourceDsaSite: .......................... Seattle
32:   SyncOnStartup: .......................... FALSE
33:   TimeOfLastSyncAttempt: .................. 16-12-2001 17:38:05
34:   TimeOfLastSyncSuccess: .................. 16-12-2001 17:38:05
35:   TwoWaySync: ............................. FALSE
36:   UseAsyncIntersiteTransport: ............. FALSE
37:   USNAttributeFilter: ..................... 5810
38:   USNLastObjChangeSynced: ................. 5810
39:   Writeable: .............................. TRUE
40:
41:   Completed.
```

The class *MSAD_DomainController* exposes an interesting method called *ExecuteKCC*, which forces the execution of the Knowledge Consistency Checker (KCC). The *MSAD_DomainController* class exposing the *ExecuteKCC* method is a wrapper of the DsReplicaConsistencyCheck() API. Therefore, its method uses the same parameters as the API (see Table 3.56). These parameters are defined in constants at lines 58 and 59 (see Sample 3.57).

Table 3.56   *The ExecuteKCC Method Parameters*

Parameter name	Values	Description
TaskID		
DS_KCC_TASKID_UPDATE_TOPOLOGY	0	Identifies the task the KCC should execute. DS_KCC_TASKID_UPDATE_TOPOLOGY is the only supported value at this time.
Flags		
DS_KCC_FLAG_ASYNC_OP	1	DS_KCC_FLAG_ASYNC_OP. If specified, the server returns immediately, rather than waiting for the consistency check to complete.

To force the KCC execution, the script command line would be as follows:

```
1:    C:\>WMIADRepl.wsf /ExecuteKCC+
2:    Microsoft (R) Windows Script Host Version 5.6
3:    Copyright (C) Microsoft Corporation 1996-2001. All rights reserved.
4:
5:    KCC execution requested.
6:
7:    Completed.
```

Another interesting method is the *SyncNamingContext* method exposed by the *MSAD_ReplNeighbor* class. With this method it is possible to force the replication of a specific Active Directory naming context. The *MSAD_ReplNeighbor* class exposing the *SyncNamingContext* method is a wrapper of the DsReplicaSync() API. Therefore, the method requires the same parameters as the API (see Table 3.57). These parameters are defined in constants at line 60 (see Sample 3.57).

Table 3.57   *The SyncNamingContext Method Parameters*

Parameter name	Values	Description
Options		
DS_REPSYNC_ASYNCHRONOUS_OPERATION	0x1	Perform this operation asynchronously. Required when using DS_REPSYNC_ALL_SOURCES
DS_REPSYNC_WRITEABLE	0x2	Writeable replica. Otherwise, read-only.
DS_REPSYNC_PERIODIC	0x4	This is a periodic sync request as scheduled by the admin.
DS_REPSYNC_INTERSITE_MESSAGING	0x8	Use intersite messaging.
DS_REPSYNC_ALL_SOURCES	0x10	Sync from all sources.
DS_REPSYNC_FULL	0x20	Sync starting from scratch (i.e., at the first USN).
DS_REPSYNC_URGENT	0x40	This is a notification of an update that was marked urgent.
DS_REPSYNC_NO_DISCARD	0x80	Don't discard this synchronization request, even if a similar sync is pending.
DS_REPSYNC_FORCE	0x100	Sync even if link is currently disabled.
DS_REPSYNC_ADD_REFERENCE	0x200	Causes the source DSA to check if a reps-to is present for the local DSA source sends change notifications (aka the destination). If not, one is added. This ensures that source sends change notifications.

To force a naming context replication, the script command line would be as follows:

```
C:\>WMIADRepl.wsf /SyncNC:CN=Configuration,DC=LissWare,DC=Net
Microsoft (R) Windows Script Host Version 5.6
Copyright (C) Microsoft Corporation 1996-2001. All rights reserved.

Naming Context 'CN=Configuration,DC=LissWare,DC=Net' synchronization requested.

Completed.
```

The use of these two methods is shown in Sample 3.59. Lines 300 through 312 illustrate the *ExecuteKCC* method invocation, while lines 315 through 329 show the *SyncNamingContext* method invocation.

Sample 3.59   *Triggering the KCC and forcing a Naming Context replication (Part III)*

```
...:
...:
...:
298:
299:     ' - ExecuteKCC -------------------------------------------------------------
300:     If boolExecuteKCC Then
301:         Set objWMIInstances = objWMIServices.InstancesOf ("MSAD_DomainController")
...:
304:         If objWMIInstances.Count = 1 Then
305:             For Each objWMIInstance In objWMIInstances
306:                 objWMIInstance.ExecuteKCC cExecKCCTaskID, cExecKCCFlags
```

```
307:          Next
308:              WScript.Echo "KCC execution requested." & vbCRLF
309:          Else
310:              WScript.Echo "No information available." & vbCRLF
311:          End If
312:      End If
313:
314:      ' -- Sync ----------------------------------------------------------------
315:      If boolSyncNC Then
316:          Set objWMIInstances = objWMIServices.ExecQuery ("Select * From MSAD_ReplNeighbor " & _
317:                                          "Where NamingContextDN='" & _
318:                                          strSyncNC & "'")
...:
321:          If objWMIInstances.Count = 1 Then
322:              For Each objWMIInstance In objWMIInstances
323:                  objWMIInstance.SyncNamingContext cSyncNCOptions
324:              Next
325:              WScript.Echo "Naming Context '" & strSyncNC & "' synchronization requested." & vbCRLF
326:          Else
327:              WScript.Echo "No corresponding context to synchronize." & vbCRLF
328:          End If
329:      End If
330:
331:      WScript.Echo "Completed."
...:
337:      ]]>
338:      </script>
339: </job>
340:</package>
```

Note the scripting technique used to retrieve the naming context to synchronize (lines 316 through 318). The script executes a WQL data query with the naming context given on the command line to locate its corresponding WMI instance.

3.7   Network components providers

3.7.1   Ping provider

The *Ping* provider is a bit unusual, because it only supports the "Get" operation. Trying an "enumeration" operation makes no sense, since this provider reflects the result of the PING command execution. This provider only supports one class: the *Win32_PingStatus* class. (See Table 3.58.)

Creating an instance of the *Win32_PingStatus* class to ping a host is not really useful, but combining this functionality with some other WMI capabilities can produce a useful tool to determine if a system is still alive on the network. If we use a script code to create and delete an Interval Timer, combined with some asynchronous event notifications, we can develop a script that will ping a selected host on a regular time interval basis. Moreover, we can send an email alert to the Administrator if the PING reply is not suc-

Table 3.58   *The Ping Providers Capabilities*

Provider Name	Provider Namespace	Class Provider	Instance Provider	Method Provider	Property Provider	Event Provider	Event Consumer Provider	Support Get	Support Put	Support Enumeration	Support Delete	Windows Server 2003	Windows XP	Windows 2000 Server	Windows 2000 Professional	Windows NT 4.0
PING Provider																
WMIPingProvider	Root/CIMv2	X						X		X		X	X			

cessful by reusing some of the function previously developed (i.e., Send-Alert() function). The script reflects the **PING.Exe** command-line utility with some extra parameters specific to the script functionalities. The script command-line parameters are as follows:

```
C:\>WMIPingMonitor.wsf
Microsoft (R) Windows Script Host Version 5.6
Copyright (C) Microsoft Corporation 1996-2001. All rights reserved.

Usage: WMIPingMonitor.wsf host [/a[+|-]] [/l:value] [/f[+|-]] [/i:value] [/v:value] [/r:value]
                          [/s:value] [/j:value] [/k:value] [/w:value] [/interval:value]
                          [/verbose[+|-]] [/Alert[+|-]] [/Machine:value] [/User:value]
                          [/Password:value]

Options:

host     : IP Address or host name of the system to ping.
a        : Resolve addresses to hostnames.
l        : Send buffer size (size).
f        : Set Don't Fragment flag in packet.
i        : Time To Live (TTL).
v        : Type Of Service (TOS) (0=default, 2=Minimize Monetary Cost,
           4=Maximize Reliability, 8=Maximize Throughput, 16=Minimize Delay).
r        : Record route for count hops (count).
s        : Timestamp for count hops (count).
j        : Loose source route along host-list (host-list).
k        : Strict source route along host-list (host-list).
w        : Timeout in milliseconds to wait for each reply (timeout).
interval : Time interval between PING commands (in seconds).
verbose  : Show all Win32_PingStatus properties.
Alert    : Send an email in case of PING failure.
Machine  : Determine the WMI system to connect to. (default=LocalHost)
User     : Determine the UserID to perform the remote connection. (default=none)
Password : Determine the password to perform the remote connection. (default=none)
Examples:

    WMIPingMonitor.wsf 10.10.10.1
    WMIPingMonitor.wsf 10.10.10.1 /a+ /l:32 /f+ /i:80 /v:4 /r:2 /s:1
    WMIPingMonitor.wsf 10.10.10.1 /a+ /l:32 /f+ /i:80 /v:4 /r:5 /s:1 /Interval:10
    WMIPingMonitor.wsf 10.10.10.1 /a+ /l:32 /f+ /i:80 /v:4 /r:6 /s:1 /Interval:10 /Verbose+
    WMIPingMonitor.wsf 10.10.10.1 /a+ /l:32 /f+ /i:80 /v:4 /r:6 /s:1 /Verbose+ /Alert-
    WMIPingMonitor.wsf 10.10.10.1 /j "10.10.10.254,192.1.1.1"
```

```
WMIPingMonitor.wsf 10.10.10.1 /k "10.10.10.254,192.1.1.1"
WMIPingMonitor.wsf 10.10.10.1 /a+ /w:10000
WMIPingMonitor.wsf 10.10.10.1 /a+ /Machine:NET-DPEN6400A.LissWare.Net
                        /Account:LISSWARENET\Administrator /Password:password
```

If we use the following command-line parameters:

```
C:\>WMIPingMonitor.wsf 16.174.12.1 /a+ /l:32 /f+ /i:80 /v:4 /r:3 /s:1 /verbose+
```

we will ping a host with the 16.174.12.1 IP address, request a host name
resolution (**/a+**), use a packet size of 32 bytes (**/l:32**), ensure that the packet
is not fragmented (**/f+**), request a time to live (TTL) of 80 seconds, request
a service for a maximum reliability (**/v:4**), limit the record route for count
hops to 3 (**/r:3**) and the timestamp for count hops to 1 (**/s:1**). The presence
of the **/Verbose+** switch forces the script to display all properties of the
Win32_PingStatus class. The obtained output would be as follows:

```
 1:   C:\>WMIPingMonitor.wsf 16.174.12.1 /a+ /l:32 /f+ /i:80 /v:4 /r:3 /s:1 /verbose+
 2:   Microsoft (R) Windows Script Host Version 5.6
 3:   Copyright (C) Microsoft Corporation 1996-2001. All rights reserved.
 4:
 5:   PING timer created.
 6:   Waiting for events...
 7:
 8:   Sunday, 09 December, 2001 at 18:38:29.
 9:      WMIPING host '16.174.12.1' started ...
10:      Host '16.174.12.1' successfully contacted.
11:
12:      - Win32_PingStatus ----------------------------------------------------------
13:      *Address: ........................... 16.174.12.1
14:      *BufferSize: ........................ 32
15:      *NoFragmentation: ................... TRUE
16:      PrimaryAddressResolutionStatus: ........ 0
17:      ProtocolAddress: ..................... 16.174.12.1
18:      ProtocolAddressResolved: ............. NET-DPEP6400A.Emea.LissWare.Net
19:      *RecordRoute: ....................... 3
20:      ReplyInconsistency: ................. FALSE
21:      ReplySize: .......................... 32
22:      *ResolveAddressNames: ............... TRUE
23:      ResponseTime: ....................... 44
24:      ResponseTimeToLive: ................. 125
25:      RouteRecord: ........................ 16.183.44.1
26:                                          16.183.16.1
27:                                          16.174.12.1
28:      RouteRecordResolved: ................ NET-DPEN6400A
29:                                          16.183.16.1
30:                                          NET-DPEP6400A.Emea.LissWare.Net
31:      *SourceRoute: .......................
32:      *SourceRouteType: ................... 0
33:      StatusCode: ......................... 0
34:      *Timeout: ........................... 4000
35:      TimeStampRecord: .................... -1513502205
36:      TimeStampRecordAddress: ............. 16.183.44.1
37:      TimeStampRecordAddressResolved: ........ NET-DPEN6400A
38:      *TimestampRoute: .................... 1
```

```
39:     *TimeToLive: ........................ 80
40:     *TypeofService: ..................... 80
41:
42:     WMIPING host '16.174.12.1' ended.
```

The *Win32_PingStatus* class is only available from the Windows XP and Windows Server 2003 platforms. Therefore, it is possible to request a PING from one of these platforms to any other host on the network. Note that you can perform a WMI remote connection from any WMI-enabled system to a Windows XP or a Windows Server 2003 platform. From there the host targeted by the PING command can be any TCP/IP host. The key point is to instantiate the *Win32_PingStatus* class from a Windows XP or Windows Server 2003 platform. In this case, we obtain a PING command that is remotely executed—an interesting feature compared with the traditional PING command-line utility, which is, by default, executed locally.

The *Win32_PingStatus* class usage with an asynchronous event timer is shown in Sample 3.60. The command-line parameter definition and parsing sections are skipped, since they continue to use the same logic.

Sample 3.60   *PINGing a system at regular time intervals (Part I)*

```
 1:<?xml version="1.0"?>
 .:
 8:<package>
 9:  <job>
..:
13:    <runtime>
..:
44:    </runtime>
45:
46:    <script language="VBScript" src="..\Functions\DecodeWinSockAPIErrorsFunction.vbs" />
47:    <script language="VBScript" src="..\Functions\DecodePINGStatusCodeFunction.vbs" />
48:
49:    <script language="VBScript" src="..\Functions\DisplayFormattedPropertiesFunction.vbs" />
50:    <script language="VBScript" src="..\Functions\DisplayFormattedPropertyFunction.vbs" />
51:    <script language="VBScript" src="..\Functions\TinyErrorHandler.vbs" />
52:    <script language="VBScript" src="..\Functions\PauseScript.vbs" />
53:    <script language="VBScript" src="..\Functions\SendAlertFunction.vbs" />
54:    <script language="VBScript" src="..\Functions\SendMessageExtendedFunction.vbs" />
55:
56:    <object progid="WbemScripting.SWbemLocator" id="objWMILocator" reference="true"/>
57:    <object progid="WbemScripting.SWbemDateTime" id="objWMIDateTime" />
58:    <object progid="Microsoft.XMLDom" id="objXML" />
59:    <object progid="Microsoft.XMLDom" id="objXSL" />
60:
61:    <script language="VBscript">
62:    <![CDATA[
..:
66:    Const cComputerName = "LocalHost"
67:    Const cWMINameSpace = "Root/cimv2"
68:    Const cWMITimerClass = "__IntervalTimerInstruction"
69:    Const cPINGTimerID = "MyPINGTimerEvent"
```

```
 70:    Const cWMIPINGEventQuery = "Select * From __TimerEvent Where TimerID='MyPINGTimerEvent'"
 71:    Const cWMIPingStatusClass = "Win32_PingStatus"
 72:
 73:    Const cTargetRecipient = "Alain.Lissoir@LissWare.Net"
 74:    Const cSourceRecipient = "WMISystem@LissWare.Net"
 75:
 76:    Const cXSLFile = "PathLevel0Win32_PingStatus.XSL"
 77:
 78:    Const cSMTPServer = "relay.LissWare.Net"
 79:    Const cSMTPPort = 25
 80:    Const cSMTPAccountName = ""
 81:    Const cSMTPSendEmailAddress = ""
 82:    Const cSMTPAuthenticate = 0' 0=Anonymous, 1=Basic, 2=NTLM
 83:    Const cSMTPUserName = ""
 84:    Const cSMTPPassword = ""
 85:    Const cSMTPSSL = False
 86:    Const cSMTPSendUsing = 2              ' 1=Pickup, 2=Port, 3=Exchange WebDAV
...:
115:    ' -----------------------------------------------------------------------------
116:    ' Parse the command line parameters
117:    If WScript.Arguments.UnNamed.Count <> 1 Then
118:       WScript.Arguments.ShowUsage()
119:       WScript.Quit
120:    End If
121:
122:    strHost = WScript.Arguments.Unnamed.Item(0)
123:    If Len(strHost) = 0 Then
124:       WScript.Echo "Missing host address!"
125:       WScript.Arguments.ShowUsage()
126:       WScript.Quit
127:    End If
128:
129:    boolResolveAddressNames = WScript.Arguments.Named("a")
130:    If Len (boolResolveAddressNames) = 0 Then boolResolveAddressNames = False
131:
...:
177:    strComputerName = WScript.Arguments.Named("Machine")
178:    If Len(strComputerName) = 0 Then strComputerName = cComputerName
179:
180:    Set objWMISink = WScript.CreateObject ("WbemScripting.SWbemSink", "SINK_")
181:
182:    objWMILocator.Security_.AuthenticationLevel = wbemAuthenticationLevelDefault
183:    objWMILocator.Security_.ImpersonationLevel = wbemImpersonationLevelImpersonate
184:
185:    Set objWMIServices = objWMILocator.ConnectServer(strComputerName, cWMINameSpace, _
186:                                         strUserID, strPassword)
...:
189:    ' -----------------------------------------------------------------------------
190:    Set objWMIClass = objWMIServices.Get (cWMITimerClass)
191:
192:    Set objWMIInstance = objWMIClass.SpawnInstance_
193:    objWMIInstance.TimerID = cPINGTimerID
194:    objWMIInstance.IntervalBetweenEvents = intInterval * 1000
195:    objWMIInstance.Put_ (wbemChangeFlagCreateOrUpdate Or wbemFlagReturnWhenComplete)
196:    If Err.Number Then ErrorHandler (Err)
197:
198:    WScript.Echo "PING timer created."
199:
200:    ' -----------------------------------------------------------------------------
201:    objWMIServices.ExecNotificationQueryAsync objWMISink, cWMIPINGEventQuery
```

```
202:    If Err.Number Then ErrorHandler (Err)
203:
204:    WScript.Echo "Waiting for events..."
205:
206:    PauseScript "Click on 'Ok' to terminate the script ..."
207:
208:    WScript.Echo vbCRLF & "Cancelling event subscription ..."
209:    objWMISink.Cancel
210:
211:    ' ----------------------------------------------------------------------------
212:    objWMIInstance.Delete_
213:    If Err.Number Then ErrorHandler (Err)
214:
215:    WScript.Echo "PING timer deleted."
216:
217:    Set objWMIServices = Nothing
218:    Set objWMISink = Nothing
219:
220:    WScript.Echo "Finished."
221:
...:
...:
...:
```

Once the WMI connection is established (lines 182 through 186), the script creates an interval timer instance (lines 190 through 198). During the command-line parameters parsing, the default interval is set to ten seconds if it is not specified. Next, the script submits the WQL event query (line 201) and enters an idle state while waiting for events (line 206).

When the script is stopped, the event subscription is canceled (lines 208 and 209), and the timer interval event is deleted (lines 212 and 213).

Sample 3.61   *PINGing a system at regular time intervals (Part II)*

```
...:
...:
...:
221:
222:        ' ----------------------------------------------------------------------------
223:    Sub SINK_OnObjectReady (objWbemObject, objWbemAsyncContext)
...:
229:        Wscript.Echo
230:        WScript.Echo FormatDateTime(Date, vbLongDate) & " at " & _
231:                     FormatDateTime(Time, vbLongTime) & "." & vbCRLF & _
232:                     "  WMIPING host '" & strHost & "' started ..."
233:
234:        ' -- PING --------------------------------------------------------------------
235:        Set objWMIInstance = objWMIServices.Get _
236:                     (cWMIPingStatusClass & ".Address='" & strHost & "'," & _
237:                      "ResolveAddressNames=" & boolResolveAddressNames & "," & _
238:                      "BufferSize=" & intBufferSize & "," & _
239:                      "NoFragmentation=" & boolNoFragmentation & "," & _
240:                      "TimeToLive=" & intTimeToLive & "," & _
241:                      "TypeofService=" & intTypeofService & "," & _
242:                      "RecordRoute=" & intRecordRoute & "," & _
```

```
243:                          "TimestampRoute=" & intTimestampRoute & "," & _
244:                          "SourceRoute='" & strSourceRoute & "'," & _
245:                          "SourceRouteType=" & intSourceRouteType & "," & _
246:                          "Timeout=" & intTimeout)
...:
249:              If objWMIInstance.PrimaryAddressResolutionStatus Then
250:                  WScript.Echo Space (2) & _
251:                        DecodeWinSockAPIErrors (objWMIInstance.PrimaryAddressResolutionStatus)
252:                     If boolHasFailed = False And boolSendAlert Then
253:                        SendAlert objWMIInstance, _
254:                         "WMIPing failed: " & _
255:                         "From " & objWMIInstance.SystemProperties_.Item("__SERVER") & " '" & _
256:                         DecodeWinSockAPIErrors(objWMIInstance.PrimaryAddressResolutionStatus) &_
257:                         & "' - " & FormatDateTime(Date, vbLongDate) & _
258:                         " at " & _
259:                         FormatDateTime(Time, vbLongTime)
260:                        boolHasFailed = True
261:                     End If
262:              Else
263:                  If objWMIInstance.StatusCode Then
264:                      WScript.Echo Space (2) & _
265:                            DecodePINGStatusCode (objWMIInstance.StatusCode)
266:                     If boolHasFailed = False And boolSendAlert Then
267:                        SendAlert objWMIInstance, _
268:                         "WMIPing failed: " & _
269:                         "From " & objWMIInstance.SystemProperties_.Item("__SERVER") & " '" & _
270:                         DecodePINGStatusCode (objWMIInstance.StatusCode) & "' - " & _
271:                         FormatDateTime(Date, vbLongDate) & _
272:                         " at " & _
273:                         FormatDateTime(Time, vbLongTime)
274:                        boolHasFailed = True
275:                     End If
276:                  Else
277:                      WScript.Echo "  Host '" & strHost & "' successfully contacted."
278:                        boolHasFailed = False
279:                  End If
280:              End If
281:
282:              If boolVerbose Then
283:                  DisplayFormattedProperties objWMIInstance, 2
284:                  WScript.Echo
285:              End If
...:
289:              WScript.Echo "  WMIPING host '" & strHost & "' ended."
290:
291:      End Sub
292:
293:      ]]>
294:      </script>
295:   </job>
296:</package>
```

When the timer event notification occurs, the event sink routine is invoked (lines 223 through 291). Based on the parameters given on the command line (or the default parameters established during the command-line parsing operation), the script gets a *Win32_PingStatus* instance (lines 235 through 246). The properties of this instance reflect the results of the

PING command-line utility, which is displayed at line 283 if the verbose mode is requested.

If the PING naming resolution (line 249) or the PING status (line 263) failed, the script displays an error message (lines 250 and 251 or lines 264 and 265) and sends an email alert by reusing the SendAlert() function previously developed (lines 253 through 260 or lines 267 through 273). It is important to note that the script sends the email alert only one time. This is why a Boolean value is set to true once the alert has been sent (line 260 or 274). The next time the PING echo is successful, the Boolean value is reset to False (line 278).

3.7.2   Network Diagnostic provider

The *Network Diagnostic* provider exposes methods to test the IP connectivity to a particular host with eventually a specific port IP number. The provider is implemented as an instance and method provider, as shown in Table 3.59.

Table 3.59   *The Network Diagnostic Providers Capabilities*

Provider Name	Provider Namespace	Class Provider	Instance Provider	Method Provider	Property Provider	Event Provider	Event Consumer Provider	Support Get	Support Put	Support Enumeration	Support Delete	Windows Server 2003	Windows XP	Windows 2000 Server	Windows 2000 Professional	Windows NT 4.0
Network Diagnostic Provider																
NetDiagProv	Root/CIMV2	X	X					X	X	X	X		X			

This provider only supports one single class called *NetDiagnostics*, which is a singleton class. Available in the Windows XP release, this class has been removed from the Windows Server 2003 platform during the beta program. This class also exposes information about the proxy settings, such as the *Win32_Proxy* class. Since the *Win32_Proxy* class is especially designed to manage the proxy settings, it is the recommended class to work with. However, the *NetDiagnostics* class is quite interesting to use to test the TCP/IP port connectivity between two hosts. This is the purpose of Sample 3.62. This script sample is quite easy to use.

```
C:\>WMINetDiag.wsf
Microsoft (R) Windows Script Host Version 5.6
Copyright (C) Microsoft Corporation 1996-2001. All rights reserved.
```

```
Usage: WMINetDiag.wsf [/PingAddress:value] [/PingPort:value]
                      [/Machine:value] [/User:value] [/Password:value]

Options:

PingAddress : IP or host name to connect to.
PingPort    : Port number to connect to.
Machine     : Determine the WMI system to connect to. (default=LocalHost)
User        : Determine the UserID to perform the remote connection. (default=none)
Password    : Determine the password to perform the remote connection. (default=none)
Examples:

    WMINetDiag /PingAddress:proxy.LissWare.Net
    WMINetDiag /PingAddress:proxy.LissWare.Net /PingPort:8080
```

Sample 3.62 shows how to script with this *NetDiagnostics* class.

Sample 3.62 *Testing connectivity with the Network Diagnostic provider*

```
 1:<?xml version="1.0"?>
 .:
 8:<package>
 9:  <job>
..:
13:    <runtime>
..:
25:    </runtime>
26:
27:    <script language="VBScript" src="..\Functions\ReplaceStringFunction.vbs" />
28:    <script language="VBScript" src="..\Functions\TinyErrorHandler.vbs" />
29:
30:    <object progid="WbemScripting.SWbemLocator" id="objWMILocator" reference="true"/>
31:
32:    <script language="VBscript">
33:    <![CDATA[
..:
37:    Const cComputerName = "LocalHost"
38:    Const cWMINameSpace = "Root\CIMv2"
39:    Const cWMIClass = "NetDiagnostics"
..:
59:    ' --------------------------------------------------------------------------
60:    ' Parse the command line parameters
61:    If WScript.Arguments.Named.Count = 0 Then
62:       WScript.Arguments.ShowUsage()
63:       WScript.Quit
64:    End If
..:
89:    strComputerName = WScript.Arguments.Named("Machine")
90:    If Len(strComputerName) = 0 Then strComputerName = cComputerName
91:
92:    objWMILocator.Security_.AuthenticationLevel = wbemAuthenticationLevelDefault
93:    objWMILocator.Security_.ImpersonationLevel = wbemImpersonationLevelImpersonate
94:
95:    Set objWMIServices = objWMILocator.ConnectServer(strComputerName, cWMINameSpace, _
96:                                            strUserID, strPassword)
..:
```

```
 99:    Set objWMIInstance = objWMIServices.Get (cWMIClass & "=@")
...:
102:    If boolPing Then
103:        If intPingPort <> -1 Then
104:            boolRC = objWMIInstance.ConnectToPort (strPingAddress, intPingPort, strMessageOut)
105:            varTemp = "PINGing address '" & strPingAddress & ":" & intPingPort & "'"
106:        Else
107:            boolRC = objWMIInstance.Ping (strPingAddress, strMessageOut)
108:            varTemp = "PINGing address '" & strPingAddress & "'"
109:        End If
110:
111:        If boolRC Then
112:            WScript.Echo varTemp & " is successful."
113:        Else
114:            WScript.Echo varTemp & " has failed."
115:        End If
116:
117:        If Len (strMessageOut) Then
118:            ReplaceString strMessageOut, "<br>", vbCRLF
119:            WScript.Echo vbCRLF & "Message:" & vbCRLF & vbCRLF & strMessageOut
120:        End If
121:    End If
...:
127:    ]]>
128:    </script>
129:  </job>
130:</package>
```

Once the command line is parsed (lines 60 through 90) and the WMI connectivity is established (lines 92 through 96), the script retrieves the singleton instance of the *NetDiagnostics* class (line 99). If the /**PingAddress** switch is given, a ping to the given IP address is executed with the *Ping* method (lines 107 and 108). If the ping is successful, the following output message is returned:

```
C:\>WMINetDiag /PingAddress:proxy.LissWare.Net
Microsoft (R) Windows Script Host Version 5.6
Copyright (C) Microsoft Corporation 1996-2001. All rights reserved.

PINGing address 'proxy.LissWare.Net' is successful.

Message:

pinging (proxy.LissWare.Net)
64 bytes from 10.10.10.254: icmp_seq = 0.  time: 380 ms
64 bytes from 10.10.10.254: icmp_seq = 1.  time: 421 ms
64 bytes from 10.10.10.254: icmp_seq = 2.  time: 400 ms
64 bytes from 10.10.10.254: icmp_seq = 3.  time: 401 ms
```

Basically, this method performs the same task as the *Win32_PingStatus* class. However, none of the parameters to ping a host exposed by the *Win32_PingStatus* class is available from the *NetDiagnostics* class, which makes the *Win32_PingStatus* class more suitable to use. The message returned from the *Ping* method (line 107) contains an HTML carriage return <BR>; the message is parsed at line 118 with the ReplaceString() function included at line 27. Every occurrence of the
 HTML tag will be replaced with a carriage return and a line feed (line 118).

If the **/PingPort** switch is given, the *ConnectToPort* method is executed (line 104). Instead of performing a simple ping, the method tries to establish a connection with the given host at the specified port number. The obtained output is the following:

```
C:\>WMINetDiag /PingAddress:proxy.LissWare.Net /PingPort:8080
Microsoft (R) Windows Script Host Version 5.6
Copyright (C) Microsoft Corporation 1996-2001. All rights reserved.

PINGing address 'proxy.LissWare.Net:8080' is successful.
```

The method return code is tested to determine if there is an execution failure (line 111) and an appropriate message (built at line 105 or 108) is displayed (lines 112 through 114).

```
C:\>WMINetDiag /PingAddress:proxy.LissWare.Net /PingPort:8081
Microsoft (R) Windows Script Host Version 5.6
Copyright (C) Microsoft Corporation 1996-2001. All rights reserved.

PINGing address 'proxy.LissWare.Net:8081' has failed.
```

3.7.3   **IP routing provider**

The *IP routing* providers give access to the IP version 4.0 routing table. They allow the examination and the modification of the IP routing table of a particular system. There are two *IP routing* providers: one instance provider, which gives access to the routing table information (called *RouteProvider*), and one event provider (called *RouteEventProvider*) able to trigger WMI events in case of modification of the routing table (see Table 3.60).

Table 3.60   *The IP routing providers capabilities*

Provider Name	Provider Namespace	Class Provider	Instance Provider	Method Provider	Property Provider	Event Provider	Event Consumer Provider	Support Get	Support Put	Support Enumeration	Support Delete	Windows Server 2003	Windows XP	Windows 2000 Server	Windows 2000 Professional	Windows NT 4.0
IP Route Provider																
RouteEventProvider	Root/CIMV2					X						X	X			
RouteProvider	Root/CIMV2	X						X	X	X	X	X	X			

These providers are available in the **Root\CIMv2** namespace and support the classes listed in Table 3.61.

Table 3.61   *The IP routing Providers Classes*

Name	Type	Comments
Win32_IP4RouteTable	Dynamic	The IP4RouteTable class information governs where network data packets are routed (e.g., usually Internet packets are sent to a gateway, and local packets may be routed directly by the client's machine). Administrators can use this information to trace problems associated with misrouted packets, and also direct a computer to a new gateway as necessary. This class deals specifically with IP4 and does not address IPX or IP6. It is only intended to model the information revealed when typing the 'Route Print' command from the command prompt.
Win32_IP4PersistedRouteTable	Dynamic	The IP4PersistedRouteTable class contains IP routes that are persisted. By default, the routes you add to the routing table aren't permanent. You lose these routes when you reboot your computer. However, if you use the command route -p add, Windows NT makes them permanent, so you won't lose the route when you reboot your computer. Persistent entries are automatically reinserted in your route table each time your computer's route table is rebuilt. Windows NT stores persistent routes in the Registry. This class deals specifically with IP4 and does not address IPX or IP6.
Win32_ActiveRoute	Association	The ActiveRoute class associtiates the current IP4 Route being used with the persisted IP route table.
Win32_IP4RouteTableEvent	Event (Extrinsic)	The Win32_IP4RouteTableEvent class represents IP route change events resulting from the addition, removal, or modification of IP routes on the computer system.

Three classes work with the instance provider and one with the event provider. The *Win32_IP4RouteTableEvent* is an extrinsic class, which only provides timestamp information when an IP routing table modification occurs. To subscribe to this type of event, the following WQL event query must be used:

```
Select * From Win32_IP4RouteTableEvent
```

Once executed, the event returns the following information:

```
 1:   C:\GenericEventAsyncConsumer.wsf "Select * From Win32_IP4RouteTableEvent"
 2:   Microsoft (R) Windows Script Host Version 5.6
 3:   Copyright (C) Microsoft Corporation 1996-2001. All rights reserved.
 4:
 5:   Waiting for events...
 6:
 7:   BEGIN - OnObjectReady.
 8:   Saturday, 15 December, 2001 at 13:41:29: 'Win32_IP4RouteTableEvent' has been triggered.
 9:
10:      - Win32_IP4RouteTableEvent ------------------------------------------------
11:      TIME_CREATED: ......................... 15-12-2001 12:41:29 (20011215124129.409259+060)
12:
13:   END - OnObjectReady.
```

The routing table is a collection of instances from the *Win32_IP4RouteTable* class. However, each time a route is a persistent route, an association exists with the *Win32_IP4PersistedRouteTable* class. The association class used to link these two classes together is the *Win32_ActiveRoute* class (see Figure 3.35).

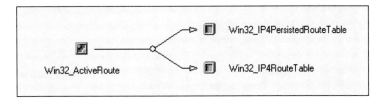

Figure 3.35
*The Win32_*
IP4RouteTable
association.

We will take advantage of this association to determine if a route is a persistent route or to create a new persistent route. The purpose of Samples 3.63 through 3.65 is to illustrate the scripting logic to use to view, add, and delete IP routes (persistent routes or not).

The command-line parameters exposed by the script are as follows:

```
C:\>WMIIP4Route.wsf
Microsoft (R) Windows Script Host Version 5.6
Copyright (C) Microsoft Corporation 1996-2001. All rights reserved.

Usage: WMIIP4Route.wsf Action Destination MASK Mask NextHop [METRIC Metric] [IF IfNumber]
                 [/Persistent[+|-]] [/Machine:value] [/User:value] [/Password:value]

Options:

Action        : Specify the operation to perform: [Print] or [Add] or [Delete].
Destination   : IP network destination.
MASK Mask     : Mask used by the specified IP network.
NextHop       : IP address of the gateway to access the specified IP network.
METRIC Metric : Specify the metric used.
IF IfNumber   : Specify the Network Interface Number to use.
Persistent    : Make the specified route persistent.
Machine       : Determine the WMI system to connect to. (default=LocalHost)
User          : Determine the UserID to perform the remote connection. (default=none)
Password      : Determine the password to perform the remote connection. (default=none)
Example:

    WMIIP4Route.wsf PRINT
    WMIIP4Route.wsf ADD 205.10.10.0 MASK 255.255.255.0 10.10.10.253 METRIC 30 IF 2
    WMIIP4Route.wsf ADD 205.10.10.0 MASK 255.255.255.0 10.10.10.253 METRIC 30 IF 2 /Persistent+
    WMIIP4Route.wsf DELETE 204.10.10.0 MASK 255.255.255.0 10.10.10.253
```

First, you will note that the script accepts commands that are similar to the **ROUTE.Exe** command-line utility. This will make the user more familiar with the script usage. Before diving into the code, let's see what the output of the script PRINT command looks like.

```
C:\>WMIIP4Route PRINT
Microsoft (R) Windows Script Host Version 5.6
Copyright (C) Microsoft Corporation 1996-2001. All rights reserved.

ACTIVE ROUTES ================================================================================

     Destination            Mask        NextHop     Metric  IfNumber  Protocol      Type  Persistent
------------------------------------------------------------------------------------------------
         0.0.0.0         0.0.0.0   10.10.10.254        30         2   Netmgmt   Indirect      -
        10.0.0.0       255.0.0.0     10.10.10.3        30         2    Local     Direct       -
    10.10.10.3 255.255.255.255      127.0.0.1        30         1    Local     Direct       -
10.255.255.255 255.255.255.255     10.10.10.3        30         2    Local     Direct       -
       127.0.0.0       255.0.0.0      127.0.0.1         1         1    Local     Direct       -
    192.10.10.0   255.255.255.0   10.10.10.253         1         2    10010   Indirect      Y
    193.10.10.0   255.255.255.0   10.10.10.253         1         2    10010   Indirect      Y
    194.10.10.0   255.255.255.0   10.10.10.253         1         2    10010   Indirect      Y
    195.10.10.0   255.255.255.0   10.10.10.253         1         2    10010   Indirect      Y
    200.10.10.0   255.255.255.0   10.10.10.253         1         2    10010   Indirect      Y
    205.10.10.0   255.255.255.0   10.10.10.253        30         2   Netmgmt   Indirect      Y
       224.0.0.0       240.0.0.0     10.10.10.3        30         2    Local     Direct       -
255.255.255.255 255.255.255.255     10.10.10.3         1         2    Local     Direct       -

Completed.
```

As you can see, the output is quite similar to the one obtained with the
ROUTE.Exe PRINT command. Let's see how the code producing this output works by looking at the first part of the script shown in Sample 3.63. As usual, the lines defining and parsing the command-line parameters are skipped.

Sample 3.63   *Viewing, adding, and deleting IP v4.0 routes (Part I)*

```
 1:<?xml version="1.0"?>
 .:
 8:<package>
 9:  <job>
..:
13:    <runtime>
..:
32:    </runtime>
33:
34:
35:    <script language="VBScript" src="..\Functions\DecodeIPRouteFunction.vbs" />
36:    <script language="VBScript" src="..\Functions\TinyErrorHandler.vbs" />
37:
38:    <object progid="WbemScripting.SWbemLocator" id="objWMILocator" reference="true"/>
39:    <object progid="Wscript.Network" id="WshNetwork" reference="true"/>
40:
41:    <script language="VBscript">
42:    <![CDATA[
..:
46:    Const cComputerName = "LocalHost"
47:    Const cWMINameSpace = "Root/cimv2"
48:    Const cWMIIP4RouteClass = "Win32_IP4RouteTable"
49:    Const cWMIIPPersistedRouteClass = "Win32_IP4PersistedRouteTable"
50:    Const cWMIActiveRouteClass = "Win32_ActiveRoute"
```

```
 51:
 52:      Const cNotFound = &h80041002
...:
159:      strComputerName = WScript.Arguments.Named("Machine")
160:      If Len(strComputerName) = 0 Then strComputerName = cComputerName
161:
162:      objWMILocator.Security_.AuthenticationLevel = wbemAuthenticationLevelDefault
163:      objWMILocator.Security_.ImpersonationLevel = wbemImpersonationLevelImpersonate
164:
165:      Set objWMIServices = objWMILocator.ConnectServer(strComputerName, cWMINameSpace, _
166:                                           strUserID, strPassword)
...:
169:      ' -- PRINT -------------------------------------------------------------------
170:      If boolPrint = True Then
171:         Set objWMIIP4RouteInstances = objWMIServices.InstancesOf (cWMIIP4RouteClass)
172:
173:         WScript.Echo "ACTIVE ROUTES " & String (84, "=") & vbCRLF
174:         WScript.Echo "   Destination            Mask         NextHop" & _
175:                      "  Metric IfNumber Protocol     Type  Persistent"
176:         WScript.Echo String (98, "-")
177:
178:         For Each objWMIIP4RouteInstance In objWMIIP4RouteInstances
179:            strIPProtocol = DecodeIPProtocolCode (objWMIIP4RouteInstance.Protocol)
180:            strIP4RouteType = DecodeIPRouteType (objWMIIP4RouteInstance.Type)
181:
182:            Set objWMIPersistentInstances = objWMIServices.ExecQuery _
183:                                        ("Associators of {" & _
184:                                         objWMIIP4RouteInstance.Path_.RelPath & _
185:                                         "} Where AssocClass=Win32_ActiveRoute")
...:
188:            If objWMIPersistentInstances.Count = 1 Then
189:               strPersistent = "         Y"
190:            Else
191:               strPersistent = "         -"
192:            End If
...:
196:            WScript.Echo String (15 - Len (objWMIIP4RouteInstance.Destination), " ") & _
197:                         objWMIIP4RouteInstance.Destination & " " & _
198:                         String (15 - Len (objWMIIP4RouteInstance.Mask), " ") & _
199:                         objWMIIP4RouteInstance.Mask & _
200:                         String (15 - Len (objWMIIP4RouteInstance.NextHop), " ") & _
201:                         objWMIIP4RouteInstance.NextHop & _
202:                         String (10 - Len (objWMIIP4RouteInstance.Metric1), " ") & _
203:                         objWMIIP4RouteInstance.Metric1 & _
204:                         String (10 - Len (objWMIIP4RouteInstance.InterfaceIndex), " ") & _
205:                         objWMIIP4RouteInstance.InterfaceIndex & _
206:                         String (10 - Len (strIPProtocol), " ") & _
207:                         strIPProtocol & _
208:                         String (10 - Len (strIP4RouteType), " ") & _
209:                         strIP4RouteType & "   " & _
210:                         strPersistent
211:         Next
212:
213:         WScript.Echo vbCRLF & "Completed."
...:
216:      End If
217:
...:
...:
...:
```

To print the routing table information, the basic principle is quite easy, since it consists of the retrieval of all instances available from the *Win32_IP4RouteTable* class (line 171). Next, the script enumerates in a loop all instances available (lines 178 through 211). Before displaying the properties of each IP route instance, the script checks if an association exists with an instance of the *Win32_IP4PersistedRouteTable* class (lines 182 through 192). If this is the case, it means that the examined IP route instance is a persistent route (line 189). The output is constructed in the loop (lines 196 through 210). Because some properties of *Win32_IP4RouteTable* class contain numbers having a particular meaning, the script includes the **Decode-IPRouteFunction.vbs** file (line 35), which contains several functions to decode the value of some properties (lines 179 and 180).

The *Win32_IP4RouteTable* class does not expose any method to add a new IP route. The creation of a new IP route is made by the creation of a new *Win32_IP4RouteTable* instance, as shown in Sample 3.64. However, the creation of the new instance is only made if there is no existing instance of the IP route to be added. This logic is implemented by trying first to retrieve an existing instance of the IP route to be added (lines 220 through 223). If the route exists, it will be updated with the new parameters. If the route does not exist (line 223), a new IP route will be created (lines 225 and 226). Next, independently of a route addition or update, the route parameters are set from line 234 through 240. Then the route is created or updated by using the *Put_* method of the **SWBemObject** representing the IP route instance (lines 242 and 243).

Sample 3.64   *Adding IP v4.0 routes (Part II)*

```
...:
...:
...:
217:
218:     ' -- Add ---------------------------------------------------------------
219:     If boolAdd = True Then
220:         Set objWMIIP4RouteInstance = objWMIServices.Get _
221:                 (cWMIIP4RouteClass & ".Destination='" & strDestination & _
222:                 "',NextHop='" & strNextHop & "'")
223:         If Err.Number = cNotFound Then
224:             Err.Clear
225:             Set objWMIClass = objWMIServices.Get (cWMIIP4RouteClass)
226:             Set objWMIIP4RouteInstance = objWMIClass.SpawnInstance_
227:             If Err.Number Then
228:                 ErrorHandler (Err)
229:             End If
...:
232:         End If
233:
234:         objWMIIP4RouteInstance.Destination = strDestination
235:         objWMIIP4RouteInstance.Mask = strMask
236:         objWMIIP4RouteInstance.NextHop = strNextHop
```

```
237:         objWMIIP4RouteInstance.Metric1 = intMetric
238:         objWMIIP4RouteInstance.InterfaceIndex = intIntNumber
239:         objWMIIP4RouteInstance.Protocol = intIPProtocol
240:         objWMIIP4RouteInstance.Type = intRouteType
241:
242:         objWMIIP4RouteInstance.Put_ (wbemChangeFlagCreateOrUpdate Or _
243:                                     wbemFlagReturnWhenComplete)
...:
246:         If boolPersistent Then
247:            Set objWMIPersistentInstance = objWMIServices.Get _
248:                    (cWMIIPPersistedRouteClass & _
249:                     ".Destination='" & strDestination & _
250:                     "',Mask='" & strMask & _
251:                     "',Metric1='" & intMetric & _
252:                     "',NextHop='" & strNextHop & "'")
253:            If Err.Number = cNotFound Then
254:               Err.Clear
255:               Set objWMIClass = objWMIServices.Get (cWMIIPPersistedRouteClass)
256:               Set objWMIPersistentInstance = objWMIClass.SpawnInstance_
...:
262:            End If
263:
264:            objWMIPersistentInstance.Destination = strDestination
265:            objWMIPersistentInstance.Mask = strMask
266:            objWMIPersistentInstance.NextHop = strNextHop
267:            objWMIPersistentInstance.Metric1 = intMetric
268:
269:            objWMIPersistentInstance.Put_ (wbemChangeFlagCreateOrUpdate Or _
270:                                           wbemFlagReturnWhenComplete)
...:
273:            Set objWMIAssocInstance = objWMIServices.Get _
274:                    (cWMIActiveRouteClass & ".SameElement='" & _
275:                     objWMIPersistentInstance.Path_.Path & _
276:                     "',SystemElement='" & _
277:                     objWMIIP4RouteInstance.Path_.Path & "'")
278:            If Err.Number = cNotFound Then
279:               Err.Clear
280:               Set objWMIClass = objWMIServices.Get (cWMIIPPersistedRouteClass)
281:               Set objWMIAssocInstance = objWMIClass.SpawnInstance_
...:
288:            objWMIAssocInstance.SameElement = objWMIPersistentInstance.Path_.Path
289:            objWMIAssocInstance.SystemElement = objWMIIP4RouteInstance.Path_.Path
290:
291:            objWMIAssocInstance.Put_ (wbemChangeFlagCreateOrUpdate Or _
292:                                      wbemFlagReturnWhenComplete)
...:
295:            End If
...:
300:            WScript.Echo "IP route " & strDestination & _
301:                         " MASK " & strMask & " " & _
302:                         strNextHop & " added as a persistent route."
303:
304:         Else
305:            WScript.Echo "IP route " & strDestination & _
306:                         " MASK " & strMask & " " & _
307:                         strNextHop & " added."
308:         End If
...:
311:     End If
312:
...:
...:
...:
```

Next, if the **/Persistent+** switch is specified on the command line, the script creates the association that must be in place to make the route persistent (lines 247 through 303). Along these lines two instances are created, as follows:

- One instance is made from the *Win32_IP4PersistedRouteTable* class (lines 247 through 270): The creation of this instance follows logic similar to the *Win32_IP4RouteTable* instance. The script checks first if no instance exists by trying to retrieve the instance (lines 247 through 252); if this operation fails (line 253), then a new instance is created (lines 255 and 256). Next, the instance properties are set (lines 264 through 267) and the information is saved in the CIM repository (lines 269 and 270).

- One association instance is made from the *Win32_ActiveRoute* class (lines 273 through 292): Here, again, the instance logic creation is the same. The script verifies first if a *Win32_ActiveRoute* instance exists (lines 273 through 277) and if not, a new *Win32_ActiveRoute* instance is created (lines 280 and 281). To create or update the *Win32_ActiveRoute* association instance, the script reuses the WMI path of the two previous instances: the *Win32_IP4RouteTable* instance path (line 289) and the *Win32_IP4PersistedRouteTable* instance (line 288). Next, the information is committed into the CIM repository (lines 291 and 292).

The deletion of a *Win32_IP4RouteTable* instance is much easier. The logic is shown in Sample 3.65.

Sample 3.65   *Deleting IP v4.0 routes (Part III)*

```
...:
...:
...:
312:
313:    ' -- DELETE ------------------------------------------------------------------
314:    If boolDelete = True Then
315:       Set objWMIIP4RouteInstance = objWMIServices.Get _
316:             (cWMIIP4RouteClass & ".Destination='" & strDestination & _
317:             "',NextHop='" & strNextHop & "'")
...:
320:       Set objWMIPersistentInstances = objWMIServices.ExecQuery _
321:                                  ("Associators of {" & _
322:                                  objWMIIP4RouteInstance.Path_.RelPath & _
323:                                  "} Where AssocClass=Win32_ActiveRoute")
...:
326:       If objWMIPersistentInstances.Count = 1 Then
327:          Set objWMIPersistentInstance = objWMIServices.Get _
```

```
328:                         (cWMIIPPersistedRouteClass  & _
329:                          ".Destination='" & objWMIIP4RouteInstance.Destination & _
330:                          "',Mask='" & objWMIIP4RouteInstance.Mask & _
331:                          "',Metric1='" & objWMIIP4RouteInstance.Metric1 &  _
332:                          "',NextHop='" & objWMIIP4RouteInstance.NextHop & "'")
...:
335:            objWMIPersistentInstance.Delete_
...:
339:        End If
...:
343:        objWMIIP4RouteInstance.Delete_
...:
346:        WScript.Echo "IP route " & strDestination & _
347:                     " MASK " & strMask & " " & _
348:                     strNextHop & " deleted."
...:
351:        End If
...:
355:        ]]>
356:        </script>
357:    </job>
358:</package>
```

First, the script retrieves the *Win32_IP4RouteTable* instance to delete (lines 315 through 317). Next, before executing the deletion of the retrieved instance, it is important to verify if there is an association with a *Win32_IP4PersistedRouteTable* instance. This verification is performed from line 320 through 326. If there is an association, the *Win32_IP4PersistedRouteTable* instance must also be retrieved (lines 327 through 332). Once all instances are retrieved, the script deletes each of them (lines 335 and 343). It is important to delete the associated instance, because, if a similar route is recreated, this route will be considered as a persistent route even if the **/Persistent+** switch is not specified. The simple existence of a *Win32_IP4PersistedRouteTable* instance matching the *Win32_IP4Route-Table* information will make the route persistent.

3.7.4 DNS provider

The *DNS* provider supports the management of the DNS server, the DNS zones, and the DNS records. It is made up of one provider, which is both an instance provider and a method provider. Only available under Windows Server 2003 by default, the *DNS* provider was also available for Windows 2000 at ftp://ftp.microsoft.com/reskit/win2000/dnsprov.zip. With this provider it is possible to retrieve ("Get" and "Enumeration"), modify ("Put"), and delete ("Delete") DNS information. The provider capabilities are summarized in Table 3.62.

Table 3.62 *The DNS Providers Capabilities*

Provider Name	Provider Namespace	Class Provider	Instance Provider	Method Provider	Property Provider	Event Provider	Event Consumer Provider	Support Get	Support Put	Support Enumeration	Support Delete	Windows Server 2003	Windows XP	Windows 2000 Server	Windows 2000 Professional	Windows NT 4.0
DNS Provider																
MS_NT_DNS_PROVIDER	Root/MicrosoftDNS	X	X					X	X	X	X	X		X		

The *DNS* provider is available in the **Root\MicrosoftDNS** WMI namespace. It supports more than 30 classes, where most of them represent the various DNS records. Each DNS manageable component is represented with a corresponding WMI class, as shown in Table 3.63.

Table 3.63 *The DNS Providers Classes*

Name	Type	Comments
MicrosoftDNS_Cache	Dynamic	This class describes a cache existing on a DNS server. It shouldn't be confused with a Cache file which contains root hints. This class simplifies visualizing the containment of DNS objects, rather than representing a real object. The class, MicrosoftDNS_Cache, is a container for the resource records cached by the DNS server. Every instance of the class MicrosoftDNS_Cache must be assigned to one and only one DNS server. It may be associated with (or more intuitively 'may contain') any number of instances of the classes, MicrosoftDNS_Domain and/or MicrosoftDNS_ResourceRecord.
MicrosoftDNS_Domain	Dynamic	This class represents a Domain in a DNS hierarchy tree.
MicrosoftDNS_ResourceRecord	Dynamic	This class represents the general properties of a DNS Resource Record.
MicrosoftDNS_RootHints	Dynamic	This class describes the Root Hints stored in a Cache file on a DNS server. This class simplifies visualizing the containment of DNS objects, rather than representing a real object. Class MicrosoftDNS_RootHints is a container for the resource records stored by the DNS server in a Cache file. Every instance of the class MicrosoftDNS_RootHints must be assigned to one and only one DNS server. It may be associated with (or more intuitively 'may contain') any number of instances of class MicrosoftDNS_ResourceRecord.
MicrosoftDNS_Server	Dynamic	This class describes a DNS server. Every instance of this class may be associated with (or more intuitively 'may contain') one instance of class MicrosoftDNS_Cache, one instance of class MicrosoftDNS_RootHints and multiple instances of class MicrosoftDNS_Zone.
MicrosoftDNS_Statistic	Dynamic	A single DNS Server statistic.
MicrosoftDNS_Zone	Dynamic	This class describes a DNS Zone. Every instance of the class MicrosoftDNS_Zone must be assigned to one and only one DNS server. Zones may be associated with (or more intuitively 'may contain') any number of instances of the classes MicrosoftDNS_Domain and/or MicrosoftDNS_ResourceRecord.
MicrosoftDNS_DomainDomainContainment	Association	Domains may contain other Domains. (Every instance of the MicrosoftDNS_Domain class may contain multiple other instances of MicrosoftDNS_Domain.) An instance of a MicrosoftDNS_Domain object is directly contained in (at most) one higher-level MicrosoftDNS_Domain.
MicrosoftDNS_DomainResourceRecordContainment	Association	Every instance of the class MicrosoftDNS_Domain may contain multiple instances of the class, MicrosoftDNS_ResourceRecord. Every instance of the class MicrosoftDNS_ResourceRecord belongs to a single instance of the class MicrosoftDNS_Domain and is defined to be weak to that instance.
MicrosoftDNS_ServerDomainContainment	Association	Every instance of the class MicrosoftDNS_Server may contain multiple instances of the class MicrosoftDNS_Domain. Every instance of the class MicrosoftDNS_Domain belongs to a single instance of the class MicrosoftDNS_Server and is defined to be weak to that server.

Table 3.63   *The DNS Providers Classes (continued)*

Name	Type	Comments
MicrosoftDNS_AAAAType	Dynamic	A subclass of MicrosoftDNS_ResourceRecord that represents a Type AAAA record.
MicrosoftDNS_AFSDBType	Dynamic	A subclass of MicrosoftDNS_ResourceRecord that represents a Type AFSDB record.
MicrosoftDNS_ATMAType	Dynamic	A subclass of MicrosoftDNS_ResourceRecord that represents a Type ATMA record.
MicrosoftDNS_AType	Dynamic	A subclass of MicrosoftDNS_ResourceRecord that represents a Type A record.
MicrosoftDNS_CNAMEType	Dynamic	A subclass of MicrosoftDNS_ResourceRecord that represents a Type CNAME record.
MicrosoftDNS_HINFOType	Dynamic	A subclass of MicrosoftDNS_ResourceRecord that represents a Type HINFO record.
MicrosoftDNS_ISDNType	Dynamic	A subclass of MicrosoftDNS_ResourceRecord that represents a Type ISDN record.
MicrosoftDNS_KEYType	Dynamic	A subclass of MicrosoftDNS_ResourceRecord that represents a Type KEY record.
MicrosoftDNS_MBType	Dynamic	A subclass of MicrosoftDNS_ResourceRecord that represents a Type MB record.
MicrosoftDNS_MDType	Dynamic	A subclass of MicrosoftDNS_ResourceRecord that represents a Type MD record.
MicrosoftDNS_MFType	Dynamic	A subclass of MicrosoftDNS_ResourceRecord that represents a Type MF record.
MicrosoftDNS_MGType	Dynamic	A subclass of MicrosoftDNS_ResourceRecord that represents a Type MG record.
MicrosoftDNS_MINFOType	Dynamic	A subclass of MicrosoftDNS_ResourceRecord that represents a Type MINFO record.
MicrosoftDNS_MRType	Dynamic	A subclass of MicrosoftDNS_ResourceRecord that represents a Type MR record.
MicrosoftDNS_MXType	Dynamic	A subclass of MicrosoftDNS_ResourceRecord that represents a Type MX record.
MicrosoftDNS_NSType	Dynamic	A subclass of MicrosoftDNS_ResourceRecord that represents a Type NS record.
MicrosoftDNS_NXTType	Dynamic	A subclass of MicrosoftDNS_ResourceRecord that represents a Type NXT record.
MicrosoftDNS_PTRType	Dynamic	A subclass of MicrosoftDNS_ResourceRecord that represents a Type PRT record.
MicrosoftDNS_RPType	Dynamic	A subclass of MicrosoftDNS_ResourceRecord that represents a Type RPT record.
MicrosoftDNS_RTType	Dynamic	A subclass of MicrosoftDNS_ResourceRecord that represents a Type RTT record.
MicrosoftDNS_SIGType	Dynamic	A subclass of MicrosoftDNS_ResourceRecord that represents a Type SIG record.
MicrosoftDNS_SOAType	Dynamic	A subclass of MicrosoftDNS_ResourceRecord that represents a Type SOA record.
MicrosoftDNS_SRVType	Dynamic	A subclass of MicrosoftDNS_ResourceRecord that represents a Type SRVrecord.
MicrosoftDNS_TXTType	Dynamic	A subclass of MicrosoftDNS_ResourceRecord that represents a Type TXT record.
MicrosoftDNS_WINSRType	Dynamic	A subclass of MicrosoftDNS_ResourceRecord that represents a Type WINSR record.
MicrosoftDNS_WINSType	Dynamic	A subclass of MicrosoftDNS_ResourceRecord that represents a Type WINS C12record.
MicrosoftDNS_WKSType	Dynamic	A subclass of MicrosoftDNS_ResourceRecord that represents a Type WKS record.
MicrosoftDNS_X25Type	Dynamic	A subclass of MicrosoftDNS_ResourceRecord that represents a Type X25 record.

It is important to note that the *DNS* provider is not implemented as a WMI event provider, which forces you to use the **WITHIN** statement in a WQL event query. For example, to monitor the A record modifications made in the LissWare.Net domain, the following WQL event query would be used:

```
Select * From __InstanceCreationEvent Within 10 Where TargetInstance ISA 'MicrosoftDNS_AType'
                And TargetInstance.DomainName='LissWare.Net'
```

When modifying an existing record, it is important to note that no
_InstanceModificationEvent intrinsic event is returned. A DNS record update
corresponds to a DNS record deletion followed by a DNS record creation.
This is the reason why the WQL event query sample uses the _Instance-
CreationEvent intrinsic event class instead of the _InstanceModificationEvent
intrinsic event class.

Because there is no direct relationship between the DNS server host
name and the domain definitions that it could contain, the DNS CIM representation defines an association class called MicrosoftDNS_ServerDomain-
Containment to associate the MicrosoftDNS_Server and the MicrosoftDNS_
Domain classes, as shown in Figure 3.36.

Figure 3.36
*The DNS server
class is associated
with the DNS
domain class.*

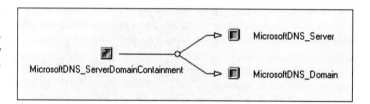

In the same way, because a DNS domain may contain another DNS
domain, an association class called MicrosoftDNS_DomainDomainContain-
ment establishes the relationship with the MicrosoftDNS_Domain class
itself, as shown in Figure 3.37. The MicrosoftDNS_Domain is a superclass
used for the definition of three subclasses called the MicrosoftDNS_Root-
Hints class, the MicrosoftDNS_Cache class, and the MicrosoftDNS_Zone. It
is interesting to note that a DNS domain delegation will be represented as
an association of two MicrosoftDNS_Domain instances.

Figure 3.37
*The DNS domain
class is associated
with itself.*

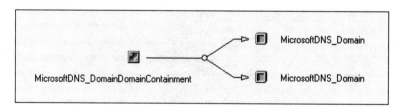

Last but not least, because a DNS domain usually contains DNS
records, an association class called MicrosoftDNS_DomainResourceRecord-
Containment establishes the relationship between the MicrosoftDNS_
Domain superclass and the MicrosoftDNS_ResourceRecord superclass, as
shown in Figure 3.38.

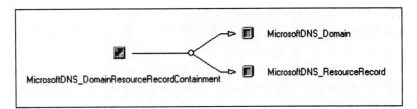

Figure 3.38
The DNS domain class is associated with the DNS records superclass.

The *MicrosoftDNS_ResourceRecord* class is used as a superclass because it is used as a parent class for all record-specific classes listed in Table 3.63.

These associations can be exploited to retrieve items contained in various DNS containers. For example, to retrieve the list of domains hosted in a DNS server called NET-DPEN6400A in the LissWare.Net domain, we will use the following WQL data query:

```
Associators of {MicrosoftDNS_Server.Name="net-dpen6400a.LissWare.Net"} Where
        AssocClass=MicrosoftDNS_ServerDomainContainment
```

The *MicrosoftDNS_Server* class is using only one key property, which is the Fully Qualified Domain Name (FQDN) of the DNS server. Thus, the WQL query only requires the name of the server for the selection.

In the same way, to retrieve the list of records that exist in a zone called LissWare.Net hosted in a server called NET-DPEN6400A, which is part of the LissWare.Net domain, the following WQL data query will be used:

```
Associators of {MicrosoftDNS_Zone.ContainerName="LissWare.Net",
        DnsServerName="net-dpen6400a.LissWare.Net",
        Name="LissWare.Net"} Where
        AssocClass=MicrosoftDNS_DomainResourceRecordContainment
```

Because the *MicrosoftDNS_Zone* has three key properties, the WQL query specifies the three key properties for the selection. This makes the WQL query quite complex to formulate in order to retrieve the DNS record list for a specific zone. Because the *MicrosoftDNS_ResourceRecord* class exposes a property that contains the container name, which is the domain name, it is possible to use the following WQL query instead:

```
Select * From MicrosoftDNS_ResourceRecord Where ContainerName='LissWare.Net'
```

Of course, in this case we do not exploit the associations in place. However, we use the fact that the *MicrosoftDNS_ResourceRecord* class is a superclass to simplify the WQL query.

The next script sample, shown in Samples 3.66 through 3.69, utilizes the *DNS* provider capabilities to manage the DNS server, the DNS zones, and DNS records from the command-line. It also exploits some of the characteristics we have seen regarding the DNS association classes. Due to the huge number of configurable parameters exposed by the DNS classes, the command-line parameters syntax is especially adapted. For example, to create an Active Directory integrated zone, the command would be as follows:

```
C:\>WMIDNS.Wsf Zone Create Name=LissWare.Net ZType=ADIntegrated
                      AdminEmailName=Administrator@LissWare.Net
Microsoft (R) Windows Script Host Version 5.6
Copyright (C) Microsoft Corporation 1996-2001. All rights reserved.

Zone 'LissWare.Net' created.
```

Once the zone is created, it is possible to create some records—for example, an A record. In this case, the command line would be as follows:

```
C:\>WMIDNS.Wsf Record Create RType=A DomainName=LissWare.Net Host=Net-dpen6400a
                      Class=IN TTL=3600 HostAddress=10.10.10.7
Microsoft (R) Windows Script Host Version 5.6
Copyright (C) Microsoft Corporation 1996-2001. All rights reserved.

'A' record for 'Net-dpen6400a.LissWare.Net' created.
```

And to create a DNS alias for the previously created A record, the command would be as follows:

```
C:\>WMIDNS.Wsf Record Create RType=CNAME DomainName=LissWare.Net Host=www
                      Class=IN TTL=7200 HostAddress=Net-dpen6400a.LissWare.Net
Microsoft (R) Windows Script Host Version 5.6
Copyright (C) Microsoft Corporation 1996-2001. All rights reserved.

'CNAME' record for 'www.LissWare.Net' created.
```

The following is a complete list of command-line parameters supported by the next sample script.

```
C:\>WMIDNS.Wsf
Microsoft (R) Windows Script Host Version 5.6
Copyright (C) Microsoft Corporation 1996-2001. All rights reserved.

Usage: WMIDNS.wsf DNS component [SERVER View] [SERVER Start] [SERVER Stop] [SERVER Scavenging]
                               [ZONE View] [ZONE Create] [ZONE Update] [ZONE AgeAllRecords]
                               [ZONE Refresh] [ZONE Pause] [ZONE Reload]

Options:

DNS component              : Select the DNS item to customize. Can be [Server],
                             [Zone], [Cache], [RootHints], [Record]
SERVER View                : Views the DNS Server properties.
SERVER Start               : Starts the DNS Service.
SERVER Stop                : Stops the DNS Service.
SERVER Scavenging          : Scavenging of stale records in the zones subjected to scavenging.
SERVER BootMethod          : Defines the boot method. Only [File], [Registry] or [AD] is accepted.
SERVER EventLogLevel       : Defines the logging level. Only [None], [Errors],
                             [ErrorsAndWarnings] or [All] is accepted.
SERVER Forwarders          : Defines the IP address list used as fowarders.
SERVER IsSlave             : Defines if the DNS server acts as a slave server.
                             Only [True] or [False] is accepted.
```

```
SERVER NoRecursion          : Defines the recursion usage. Only [Disable] or [Enable] is accepted.
SERVER RoundRobin           : Define the round robin usage. Only [True] or [False] is accepted.
SERVER ListenAddresses      : Define the IP address used to listen DNS requests.
ZONE View                   : Views the Zone properties.
ZONE Create                 : Creates a DNS new zone.
ZONE Update                 : Updates an existing DNS zone.
ZONE AgeAllRecords          : Enables aging for some or all non-NS and non SOA records in a zone.
ZONE Refresh                : Forces the DNS server to check the master server of a secondary
                              zone for updates.
ZONE Pause                  : Pauses the zone.
ZONE Reload                 : Reloads the zone.
ZONE ResetSecondaries       : Resets the secondary IP addresses.
ZONE Resume                 : Resumes the zone.
ZONE UpdateFromDS           : Forces an update of the zone from the DS. This method is
                              only valid for DS-integrated zones.
ZONE WriteBackZone          : Saves the zone's data to persistent storage.
ZONE Delete                 : Deletes a zone
   Name                     : Name of the zone to manage.
   ZType                    : Zone type. Can be [ADIntegrated], [Primary], [Secondary] or [Stub]
   DataFile                 : Zone file containing the zone data.
   AdminEmailName           : Zone administrator email address.
   IPAddresses              : Secondary DNS servers IP addresses.
   SecondaryServers         : IP addresses of the secondary servers.
   SecureSecondaries        : Secondary DNS zone transfer mode. Only [AnyServers], [OnlyNSServers],
                              [OnlyListedServers] or [None] is accepted.
   NotifyServers            : IP addresses of the secondary servers to notify.
   Notify                   : Notify mode. Only [OnlyNSServers], [OnlyListedServers]
                              or [None] is accepted.
CACHE Clear                 : Clears the DNS cache.
ROOTHINTS WriteBackDataFile : Saves the RootHints' zone data to persistent storage.
RECORD View                 : View DNS records for a given zone.
RECORD Create               : Create DNS records in a given zone.
RECORD Delete               : Delete DNS records from a given zone.
   RType                    : Record Type. Can be [A], [CNAME], [NS], ... or any
                              record type supported.
   DomainName               : Record's domain name
   Host                     : Corresponding host to the record.
   Class                    : Class of the record.
   TTL                      : Time to Live of the record.
   HostAddress              : HostAddress of the record (Could be an IP address or a host
                              name based on the record type).
Machine                     : determine the WMI system to connect to. (default=LocalHost)
User                        : determine the UserID to perform the remote connection. (default=none)
Password                    : determine the password to perform the remote
                              connection. (default=none)
Examples:

     WMIDNS.Wsf Server View
     WMIDNS.Wsf Server Start
     WMIDNS.Wsf Server Stop
     WMIDNS.Wsf Server Scavenging
     WMIDNS.Wsf Server BootMethod=Registry
     WMIDNS.Wsf Server EventLogLevel=ErrorsAndWarnings
     WMIDNS.Wsf Server Forwarders=10.10.10.1,172.16.23.1
     WMIDNS.Wsf Server IsSlave=True
     WMIDNS.Wsf Server NoRecursion=Disabled
     WMIDNS.Wsf Server RoundRobin=True
     WMIDNS.Wsf Server ListenAddresses=10.10.10.3,10.10.10.4
     WMIDNS.Wsf Server ListenAddresses=10.10.10.3 RoundRobin=True Forwarders=10.10.10.1
                       BootMethod=Registry EventLogLevel=ErrorsAndWarnings
```

```
WMIDNS.Wsf Zone View
WMIDNS.Wsf Zone View Name=LissWare.Net
WMIDNS.Wsf Zone Create Name=LissWare.Net ZType=ADIntegrated
                       AdminEmailName=Administrator@LissWare.Net
WMIDNS.Wsf Zone Create Name=LissWare.Net ZType=Primary DataFile=LissWare.Net.Dns
                       AdminEmailName=Administrator@LissWare.Net
WMIDNS.Wsf Zone Create Name=LissWare.Net ZType=Secondary DataFile=LissWare.Net.Dns
                       AdminEmailName=Administrator@LissWare.Net IPAddresses=10.10.10.3
WMIDNS.Wsf Zone Create Name=LissWare.Net ZType=Stub DataFile=LissWare.Net.Dns
                       AdminEmailName=Administrator@LissWare.Net IPAddresses=10.10.10.3
WMIDNS.Wsf Zone Update Name=LissWare.Net ZType=ADIntegrated
                       AdminEmailName=Administrator@LissWare.Net
WMIDNS.Wsf Zone Update Name=LissWare.Net ZType=Primary DataFile=LissWare.Net.Dns
                       AdminEmailName=Administrator@LissWare.Net
WMIDNS.Wsf Zone Update Name=LissWare.Net ZType=Primary DataFile=LissWare.Net.Dns
                       AdminEmailName=Administrator@LissWare.Net ZUpdate=NotAllowed
WMIDNS.Wsf Zone Update Name=LissWare.Net ZType=Secondary DataFile=LissWare.Net.Dns
                       AdminEmailName=Administrator@LissWare.Net IPAddresses=10.10.10.3
WMIDNS.Wsf Zone Update Name=LissWare.Net ZUpdate=NotAllowed
WMIDNS.Wsf Zone Update Name=LissWare.Net ZUpdate=AllowUpdates
WMIDNS.Wsf Zone Update Name=LissWare.Net ZUpdate=AllowSecureUpdates
WMIDNS.Wsf Zone Refresh Name=LissWare.Net
WMIDNS.Wsf Zone Pause Name=LissWare.Net
WMIDNS.Wsf Zone Reload Name=LissWare.Net
WMIDNS.Wsf Zone ResetSecondaries Name=LissWare.Net SecondaryServers=10.10.10.4,10.10.10.5
                                 SecureSecondaries=OnlyListedServers
                                 NotifyServers=10.10.10.4,10.10.10.5 Notify=OnlyListedServers
WMIDNS.Wsf Zone Resume Name=LissWare.Net
WMIDNS.Wsf Zone UpdateFromDS Name=LissWare.Net
WMIDNS.Wsf Zone WriteBackZone Name=LissWare.Net
WMIDNS.Wsf Zone Delete Name=LissWare.Net

WMIDNS.Wsf Cache Clear
WMIDNS.Wsf RootHints WriteBackDataFile

WMIDNS.Wsf Record View RType=A DomainName=LissWare.Net
WMIDNS.Wsf Record Create RType=A DomainName=LissWare.Net Host=Net-dpen6400a Class=IN
                         TTL=3600 HostAddress=10.10.10.7
WMIDNS.Wsf Record Create RType=CNAME DomainName=LissWare.Net Host=www Class=IN
                         TTL=7200 HostAddress=Net-dpen6400a.LissWare.Net
WMIDNS.Wsf Record Delete RType=A DomainName=LissWare.Net Host=Net-dpen6400a Class=IN
                         TTL=3600 HostAddress=10.10.10.7
WMIDNS.Wsf Record Delete RType=CNAME DomainName=LissWare.Net Host=www Class=IN
                         TTL=7200 HostAddress=Net-dpen6400a.LissWare.Net.
```

Note that Samples 3.66 through 3.69 make use of the most important parameters exposed by the DNS classes. To simplify the script coding and focus on the DNS class usage, the script performs a very limited syntax checking. However, if you require a stronger syntax checking and some properties supported by the DNS classes that are not currently implemented in Samples 3.66 through 3.69, the script is very easy to extend, since its logic is quite linear. Although a smarter scripting technique is possible to make the script smaller, this linear logic has the advantage of being easy to follow and understand, which is the primary purpose.

We can split Samples 3.66 through 3.69 into the following three parts:

- A portion to manage the DNS server, shown in Sample 3.66

- A portion to manage the DNS zones, shown in Samples 3.67 and 3.68

- A portion to manage the DNS records, shown in Sample 3.69

Once the WMI connection is established in the **Root\MicrosoftDNS** namespace (lines 569 through 573), the script retrieves the name of the DNS server available in the system (lines 576 through 582). Normally, we only have one DNS server per system, which means that we may expect the *MicrosoftDNS_Server* class to be defined as a singleton class. However, the class definition is not made that way, since it uses a key property called *name*, which contains the FQDN of the DNS server (line 580). The FQDN of the server is retrieved at the beginning of the script, simply because its name will be used to manage the server, the zones, and the records.

The rest of the script makes use of some of the *MicrosoftDNS_Server* methods and properties (lines 587 through 757).

Sample 3.66 *Managing the DNS server (Part I)*

```
  1:<?xml version="1.0"?>
  .:
  8:<package>
  9: <job>
 ..:
 13:     <runtime>
...:
108:     </runtime>
109:
110:     <script language="VBScript" src="..\Functions\DecodeDNSFunction.vbs" />
111:     <script language="VBScript" src="..\Functions\DisplayFormattedPropertyFunction.vbs" />
112:
113:     <script language="VBScript" src="..\Functions\ConvertStringInArrayFunction.vbs" />
114:     <script language="VBScript" src="..\Functions\TinyErrorHandler.vbs" />
115:
116:     <object progid="WbemScripting.SWbemLocator" id="objWMILocator" reference="true"/>
117:     <object progid="WbemScripting.SWbemDateTime" id="objWMIDateTime" />
118:
119:     <script language="VBscript">
120:     <![CDATA[
...:
124:     Const cComputerName = "LocalHost"
125:     Const cWMINameSpace = "Root/MicrosoftDNS"
...:
569:     objWMILocator.Security_.AuthenticationLevel = wbemAuthenticationLevelDefault
570:     objWMILocator.Security_.ImpersonationLevel = wbemImpersonationLevelImpersonate
571:
572:     Set objWMIServices = objWMILocator.ConnectServer(strComputerName, cWMINameSpace, _
```

```
573:                                                      strUserID, strPassword)
...:
576:     Set objWMIInstances = objWMIServices.InstancesOf ("MicrosoftDNS_Server")
577:
578:     If objWMIInstances.Count = 1 Then
579:        For Each objWMIInstance In objWMIInstances
580:            strDNSServerName = objWMIInstance.Name
581:        Next
582:     End If
...:
586:     ' --------------------------------------------------------------------------------
587:     If boolSRVView Then
588:        Set objWMIInstance = objWMIServices.Get ("MicrosoftDNS_Server.Name='" & _
589:                                       strDNSServerName & "'")
...:
592:        WScript.Echo "- " & objWMIInstance.Name & " " & String (60, "-")
593:        Set objWMIPropertySet = objWMIInstance.Properties_
594:        For Each objWMIProperty In objWMIPropertySet
595:            DisplayFormattedProperty objWMIInstance, _
596:                            " " & objWMIProperty.Name, _
597:                            objWMIProperty.Name, _
598:                            Null
599:        Next
...:
602:        WScript.Echo
603:
604:        WScript.Echo "- Hosted zones " & String (60, "-")
605:
606:        Set objWMIAssocInstances = objWMIServices.ExecQuery _
607:                            ("Associators of {" & _
608:                             objWMIInstance.Path_.RelPath & _
609:                             "} Where AssocClass=" & _
610:                             "MicrosoftDNS_ServerDomainContainment")
611:        For Each objWMIAssocInstance In objWMIAssocInstances
612:            If objWMIAssocInstance.Path_.Class = "MicrosoftDNS_Zone" Then
613:                WScript.Echo "  " & objWMIAssocInstance.Name
614:            End If
615:        Next
...:
619:     End If
620:     If boolSRVStart Then
621:        Set objWMIInstance = objWMIServices.Get ("MicrosoftDNS_Server.Name='" & _
622:                                       strDNSServerName & "'")
...:
625:        objWMIInstance.StartService()
...:
628:        WScript.Echo "DNS Server started."
...:
631:     End If
632:     If boolSRVStop Then
633:        Set objWMIInstance = objWMIServices.Get ("MicrosoftDNS_Server.Name='" & _
634:                                       strDNSServerName & "'")
...:
637:        objWMIInstance.StopService()
...:
640:        WScript.Echo "DNS Server stopped."
...:
643:     End If
644:     If boolSRVScavenging Then
645:        Set objWMIInstance = objWMIServices.Get ("MicrosoftDNS_Server.Name='" & _
```

```
646:                                        strDNSServerName & "'")
...:
648:        objWMIInstance.StartScavenging()
...:
650:        WScript.Echo "DNS Server Scavenging requested."
...:
652:    End If
653:    If boolBootMethod Then
654:        Set objWMIInstance = objWMIServices.Get ("MicrosoftDNS_Server.Name='" & _
655:                                        strDNSServerName & "'")
...:
658:        objWMIInstance.bootMethod = intBootMethod
659:
660:        objWMIInstance.Put_ (wbemChangeFlagUpdateOnly Or _
661:                        wbemFlagReturnWhenComplete)
...:
664:        WScript.Echo "DNS Server boot method updated."
...:
667:    End If
668:    If boolEventLogLevel Then
669:        Set objWMIInstance = objWMIServices.Get ("MicrosoftDNS_Server.Name='" & _
670:                                        strDNSServerName & "'")
...:
673:        objWMIInstance.EventLogLevel = intEventLogLevel
674:
675:        objWMIInstance.Put_ (wbemChangeFlagUpdateOnly Or _
676:                        wbemFlagReturnWhenComplete)
...:
679:        WScript.Echo "DNS Server event log level updated."
...:
682:    End If
683:    If boolForwarders Then
684:        Set objWMIInstance = objWMIServices.Get ("MicrosoftDNS_Server.Name='" & _
685:                                        strDNSServerName & "'")
...:
688:        objWMIInstance.Forwarders = arrayForwarders
689:
690:        objWMIInstance.Put_ (wbemChangeFlagUpdateOnly Or _
691:                        wbemFlagReturnWhenComplete)
...:
694:        WScript.Echo "DNS Server fowarders updated."
...:
697:    End If
698:    If boolSlave Then
699:        Set objWMIInstance = objWMIServices.Get ("MicrosoftDNS_Server.Name='" & _
700:                                        strDNSServerName & "'")
...:
703:        objWMIInstance.IsSlave = boolIsSlave
704:
705:        objWMIInstance.Put_ (wbemChangeFlagUpdateOnly Or _
706:                        wbemFlagReturnWhenComplete)
...:
709:        WScript.Echo "DNS Server slave updated."
...:
712:    End If
713:    If boolUpdateRecursion Then
714:        Set objWMIInstance = objWMIServices.Get ("MicrosoftDNS_Server.Name='" & _
715:                                        strDNSServerName & "'")
...:
718:        objWMIInstance.NoRecursion = boolRecursion
```

```
719:
720:           objWMIInstance.Put_ (wbemChangeFlagUpdateOnly Or _
721:                                 wbemFlagReturnWhenComplete)
...:
724:           WScript.Echo "DNS Server recursion updated."
...:
727:    End If
728:    If boolUpdateRoundRobin Then
729:        Set objWMIInstance = objWMIServices.Get ("MicrosoftDNS_Server.Name='" & _
730:                                 strDNSServerName & "'")
...:
733:           objWMIInstance.RoundRobin = boolRoundRobin
734:
735:           objWMIInstance.Put_ (wbemChangeFlagUpdateOnly Or _
736:                                 wbemFlagReturnWhenComplete)
...:
739:           WScript.Echo "DNS Server round robin updated."
...:
742:    End If
743:    If boolIPAddresses Then
744:        Set objWMIInstance = objWMIServices.Get ("MicrosoftDNS_Server.Name='" & _
745:                                 strDNSServerName & "'")
...:
748:           objWMIInstance.ListenAddresses = arrayIPAddresses
749:
750:           objWMIInstance.Put_ (wbemChangeFlagUpdateOnly Or _
751:                                 wbemFlagReturnWhenComplete)
...:
754:           WScript.Echo "DNS Server listen IP addresses updated."
...:
757:    End If
758:
...:
...:
...:
```

To manage, view, and update the DNS server information, the script
always retrieves the DNS server instance first. Sample 3.66 contains several
subportions, which are dedicated to a particular management task that can
be performed with the DNS server. The tasks are the following:

- **Viewing the DNS information** (lines 587 through 619): These lines
  retrieve the DNS server instance and show all properties by using the
  DisplayFormattedProperty() function previously developed (lines
  593 through 599). Because it is interesting to see the domain zones
  hosted on the DNS server, the script uses the associations in place to
  retrieve the domain list available from this server (lines 606 through
  615). The following command-line would give an output such as:

```
1:   C:\>WMIDNS.Wsf Server View
2:   Microsoft (R) Windows Script Host Version 5.6
3:   Copyright (C) Microsoft Corporation 1996-2001. All rights reserved.
4:
5:   - net-dpen6400a.LissWare.Net -------------------------------------------
6:     AddressAnswerLimit: .................... 0
```

```
 7:       AllowUpdate: .......................... 2
 8:       AutoCacheUpdate: ...................... FALSE
 9:       AutoConfigFileZones: .................. 1
10:       BindSecondaries: ...................... TRUE
11:       BootMethod: ........................... 2
12:       DefaultAgingState: .................... FALSE
13:       DefaultNoRefreshInterval: ............. 168
14:       DefaultRefreshInterval: ............... 168
15:       DisableAutoReverseZones: .............. FALSE
16:       DisjointNets: ......................... FALSE
17:       DsAvailable: .......................... TRUE
18:       DsPollingInterval: .................... 300
19:       DsTombstoneInterval: .................. 604800
20:       EDnsCacheTimeout: ..................... 86400
21:       EnableDirectoryPartitions: ............ TRUE
22:       EnableDnsSec: ......................... 1
23:       EnableEDnsProbes: ..................... TRUE
24:       EventLogLevel: ........................ 2
25:       ForwardDelegations: ................... 0
26:       Forwarders: ........................... 10.10.10.1
27:       ForwardingTimeout: .................... 5
28:       InstallDate: .......................... 01-01-2000
29:       IsSlave: .............................. FALSE
30:       ListenAddresses: ...................... 10.10.10.3
31:       LocalNetPriority: ..................... TRUE
32:       LogFileMaxSize: ....................... 500000000
33:       LogLevel: ............................. 0
34:       LooseWildcarding: ..................... FALSE
35:       MaxCacheTTL: .......................... 86400
36:       MaxNegativeCacheTTL: .................. 900
37:       *Name: ................................ net-dpen6400a.LissWare.Net
38:       NameCheckFlag: ........................ 2
39:       NoRecursion: .......................... FALSE
40:       RecursionRetry: ....................... 3
41:       RecursionTimeout: ..................... 15
42:       RoundRobin: ........................... TRUE
43:       RpcProtocol: .......................... -1
44:       ScavengingInterval: ................... 0
45:       SecureResponses: ...................... TRUE
46:       SendPort: ............................. 0
47:       ServerAddresses: ...................... 10.10.10.3
48:       Started: .............................. TRUE
49:       StartMode: ............................ Automatic
50:       Status: ............................... OK
51:       StrictFileParsing: .................... FALSE
52:       UpdateOptions: ........................ 783
53:       Version: .............................. 235274501
54:       WriteAuthorityNS: ..................... FALSE
55:       XfrConnectTimeout: .................... 30
56:
57:  - Hosted zones ------------------------------------------------------------
58:       _msdcs.LissWare.Net
59:       0.in-addr.arpa
60:       10.in-addr.arpa
61:       127.in-addr.arpa
62:       255.in-addr.arpa
63:       LissWare.Net
64:       LissWare.Net
```

We see the *MicrosoftDNS_Server* class properties from line 6 through 55 and the *MicrosoftDNS_Zone* associated instances from line 58 through 64.

- **Starting the DNS server service** (lines 620 through 631): The *MicrosoftDNS_Server* class is derived from the *CIM_Service* class. We have seen that this standard class exposes methods to start and stop a service. With the class inheritance mechanism of the CIM repository, the *MicrosoftDNS_Server* class also exposes these methods. This portion of the code makes use of the *StartService* method to start the DNS service (line 625).

- **Stopping the DNS server service** (lines 632 through 643): This portion of the code makes use of the *StopService* method coming from the *CIM_Service* class to stop the DNS service (line 637).

- **Scavenging the DNS server** (lines 644 through 652): Scavenging is the mechanism to perform cleanup and removal of stale DNS resource records, which can accumulate in zone data over time. By invoking the *StartScavenging* method of the *MicrosoftDNS_Server* class, it is possible to launch this cleanup process (line 648).

- **Setting the DNS boot method** (lines 653 through 667): A DNS server can be booted from a data file, the Windows Registry (default), or Active Directory. The *BootMethod* property defines the boot method to use (line 658). The boot method values are shown in Table 3.64.

- **Setting the DNS log level** (lines 668 through 682): The event logging level can be changed by setting the *EventLogLevel* property (line 673). The logging level values are also shown in Table 3.64. Do not confuse the event logging level with the debug logging level, for which values are also shown in Table 3.64.

- **Setting the DNS forwarders** (lines 683 through 697): Because several forwarders can be defined for one single DNS server, the *Forwarders* property accepts an array of IP addresses that correspond to the forwarder list (line 688).

- **Setting the DNS server as a slave** (lines 698 through 712): If the server must act as a slave, the *IsSlave* property of the *MicrosoftDNS_Server* class must be set to True (line 703).

- **Setting the DNS server recursion** (lines 713 through 727): To disable the recursion for the naming resolution, the *NoRecursion* prop-

Table 3.64   *Some DNS Server Property Values*

Server boot	Value
File	1
Registry	2
Active Directory & Registry	3
Server Events Log Level	**Value**
None	0
Errors only	1
Errors & Warnings	2
All events	7
Debug Log Level	**Value**
Query	1
Notify	16
Update	32
Nonquery transactions	254
Questions	256
Answers	512
Send	4096
Receive	8192
UDP	16384
TCP	32768
All packets	65535
NT Directory Service write transaction	65536
NT Directory Service update transaction	131072
Full Packets	16777216
Write Through	2147483648

erty of the *MicrosoftDNS_Server* class must be set to True (line 718). This property corresponds to one of the advanced server options. Note that it is impossible to set forwarders when the recursion is disabled.

■ **Setting the DNS server round-robin** (lines 728 through 742): If the DNS server must use the round-robin algorithm, which implements a load-balancing mechanism to share and distribute network resource loads, the *RoundRobin* property of the *MicrosoftDNS_Server* class must be set to True (line 733). This property corresponds to one of the advanced server options.

■ **Setting the DNS server listening IP addresses** (lines 743 through 757): To define the IP address interfaces on which the DNS server must listen for DNS requests, the *ListenAddresses* property accepts an array of IP addresses that correspond to the interface IP address list (line 748).

The next portion of the script manages the DNS zones. This portion is divided into two subportions: the first one displays all details related to one specific zone (lines 762 through 802); the second one displays an information summary about all zones available in a DNS server (lines 804 through 831).

Sample 3.67   *Viewing the DNS zones (Part IIa)*

```
...:
...:
...:
758:
759:    ' ---------------------------------------------------------------------------------
760:    If boolZONEView Then
761:        If Len (strZoneName) Then
762:            Set objWMIInstance = objWMIServices.Get ("MicrosoftDNS_Zone." & _
763:                                    "ContainerName='" & strZoneName & _
764:                                    "',DnsServerName='" & strDNSServerName & _
765:                                    "',Name='" & strZoneName & "'")
...:
768:            WScript.Echo "- " & objWMIInstance.Name & " " & String (60, "-")
769:            Set objWMIPropertySet = objWMIInstance.Properties_
770:            For Each objWMIProperty In objWMIPropertySet
771:                Select Case objWMIProperty.Name
772:                    Case "AllowUpdate"
773:                        DisplayFormattedProperty objWMIInstance, _
774:                                    " " & objWMIProperty.Name, _
775:                                    DecodeZoneUpdate (objWMIProperty.Value), _
776:                                    Null
777:                    Case "Notify"
778:                        DisplayFormattedProperty objWMIInstance, _
779:                                    " " & objWMIProperty.Name, _
780:                                    DecodeZoneNotify (objWMIProperty.Value), _
781:                                    Null
782:                    Case "SecureSecondaries"
783:                        DisplayFormattedProperty objWMIInstance, _
784:                                    " " & objWMIProperty.Name, _
785:                                    DecodeZoneTransfer (objWMIProperty.Value), _
786:                                    Null
787:                    Case "ZoneType"
788:                        DisplayFormattedProperty objWMIInstance, _
789:                                    " " & objWMIProperty.Name, _
790:                                    DecodeZoneType (objWMIProperty.Value, _
791:                                    objWMIInstance.DsIntegrated), _
792:                                    Null
793:                    Case Else
794:                        DisplayFormattedProperty objWMIInstance, _
795:                                    " " & objWMIProperty.Name, _
796:                                    objWMIProperty.Name, _
797:                                    Null
798:                End Select
799:            Next
...:
802:            WScript.Echo
803:        Else
804:            Set objWMIInstances = objWMIServices.InstancesOf ("MicrosoftDNS_Zone")
...:
807:            WScript.Echo "                    Zone Name              Type              Updates" & _
808:                        "          Transfer          Notify list  Reverse Zone     Paused"
809:            WScript.Echo String (124, "-")
810:            For Each objWMIInstance In objWMIInstances
811:                strZoneType = DecodeZoneType (objWMIInstance.ZoneType, _
812:                                    objWMIInstance.DsIntegrated)
```

```
813:                    strZoneTransfer = DecodeZoneTransfer (objWMIInstance.SecureSecondaries)
814:                    strZoneNotify = DecodeZoneNotify (objWMIInstance.Notify)
815:                    strZoneUpdate = DecodeZoneUpdate (objWMIInstance.AllowUpdate)
816:
817:                    WScript.Echo String (25 - Len (objWMIInstance.Name), " ") & _
818:                                  objWMIInstance.Name & _
819:                                  String (15 - Len (strZoneType), " ") & _
820:                                  strZoneType & _
821:                                  String (20 - Len (strZoneUpdate), " ") & _
822:                                  strZoneUpdate & _
823:                                  String (20 - Len (strZoneTransfer), " ") & _
824:                                  strZoneTransfer & _
825:                                  String (20 - Len (strZoneNotify), " ") & _
826:                                  strZoneNotify & _
827:                                  String (14 - Len (objWMIInstance.Reverse), " ") & _
828:                                  objWMIInstance.Reverse & _
829:                                  String (10 - Len (objWMIInstance.Paused), " ") & _
830:                                  objWMIInstance.Paused
831:            Next
...:
834:        End If
835:    End If
...:
...:
...:
```

Let's start with the second portion of the code, since it shows a zone information summary (lines 804 through 831). This part of the code is only executed when no specific zone name is given on the command line (line 761). For example, the following command line would give:

```
C:\>WMIDNS.Wsf Zone View
Microsoft (R) Windows Script Host Version 5.6
Copyright (C) Microsoft Corporation 1996-2001. All rights reserved.
```

Zone	Name	Type	Updates	Transfer	Notify list ...
_msdcs.LissWare.Net	AD Integrated	Only secure updates	To any servers	Only NS servers ...
0.in-addr.arpa	Primary	Not allowed	To any servers	Only NS servers ...
10.in-addr.arpa	Primary	Not allowed	None	Only listed servers ...
127.in-addr.arpa	Primary	Not allowed	To any servers	Only NS servers ...
255.in-addr.arpa	Primary	Not allowed	To any servers	Only NS servers ...
LissWare.Net	Primary	Not allowed	None	Only listed servers ...
LissWare.Net	AD Integrated	Only secure updates	To any servers	Only NS servers ...

In opposition to the technique used to retrieve the existing zone list at the DNS server level (see Sample 3.66, lines 606 through 615), the script logic requests the list of all instances made from the *MicrosoftDNS_Zone* class (line 804). Of course, both methods are valid! This simply shows another scripting technique to retrieve the same information.

If the zone name is given on the command line, the script will retrieve all properties of the corresponding *MicrosoftDNS_Zone* instance. The output would be as follows:

```
 1:    C:\>WMIDNS.Wsf Zone View Name=LissWare.Net
 2:    Microsoft (R) Windows Script Host Version 5.6
 3:    Copyright (C) Microsoft Corporation 1996-2001. All rights reserved.
 4:
 5:    - LissWare.Net -------------------------------------------------------
 6:      Aging: ............................... TRUE
 7:      AllowUpdate: ......................... Only secure updates
 8:      AutoCreated: ......................... FALSE
 9:      AvailForScavengeTime: ................ 3515052
10:      *ContainerName: ...................... LissWare.Net
11:      *DnsServerName: ...................... net-dpen6400a.LissWare.Net
12:      DsIntegrated: ........................ TRUE
13:      ForwarderSlave: ...................... FALSE
14:      ForwarderTimeout: .................... 0
15:      InstallDate: ......................... 01-01-2000
16:      LastSuccessfulSoaCheck: .............. 0
17:      LastSuccessfulXfr: ................... 0
18:      *Name: ............................... LissWare.Net
19:      NoRefreshInterval: ................... 168
20:      Notify: .............................. Only NS servers
21:      Paused: .............................. FALSE
22:      RefreshInterval: ..................... 168
23:      Reverse: ............................. FALSE
24:      SecureSecondaries: ................... To any servers
25:      Shutdown: ............................ FALSE
26:      UseWins: ............................. FALSE
27:      ZoneType: ............................ AD Integrated
```

More than simply retrieving information available from the existing zones, the script is also capable of performing the usual zone management tasks, such as creating a zone, updating the zone properties, and deleting a zone. These tasks are implemented in Sample 3.68.

Sample 3.68   *Managing the DNS zones (Part IIb)*

```
...:
...:
...:
835:    End If
836:    If boolZONECreate Then
837:        Set objWMIClass = objWMIServices.Get ("MicrosoftDNS_Zone")
...:
840:        Select Case intZoneType
841:            Case 1
842:                objWMIClass.CreateZone strZoneName, _
843:                                    0, _
844:                                    True, , , strAdminEmailName
845:            Case 2
846:                objWMIClass.CreateZone strZoneName, _
847:                                    0, _
848:                                    False, _
849:                                    strZoneDataFile, _
850:                                    , _
851:                                    strAdminEmailName
852:            Case 3
853:                objWMIClass.CreateZone strZoneName, _
854:                                    1, _
```

```
855:                                           False, _
856:                                           strZoneDataFile, _
857:                                           arrayIpAddresses,  _
858:                                           strAdminEmailName
859:            Case 4
860:                    objWMIClass.CreateZone strZoneName, _
861:                                           2, _
862:                                           False, _
863:                                           strZoneDataFile, _
864:                                           arrayIpAddresses, _
865:                                           strAdminEmailName
866:       End Select
...:
869:       WScript.Echo "Zone '" & strZoneName &  "' created."
...:
872:   End If
873:   If boolZONEChange Then
874:       Set objWMIInstance = objWMIServices.Get ("MicrosoftDNS_Zone." & _
875:                               "ContainerName='" & strZoneName & _
876:                               "',DnsServerName='" & strDNSServerName & _
877:                               "',Name='" & strZoneName & "'")
...:
880:       Select Case intZoneType
881:            Case 1
882:                    objWMIInstance.ChangeZoneType 0, True, , , strAdminEmailName
883:            Case 2
884:                    objWMIInstance.ChangeZoneType 0, _
885:                                                  False, _
886:                                                  strZoneDataFile, _
887:                                                  , _
888:                                                  strAdminEmailName
889:            Case 3
890:                    objWMIInstance.ChangeZoneType 1, _
891:                                                  False, _
892:                                                  strZoneDataFile, _
893:                                                  arrayIpAddresses, _
894:                                                  strAdminEmailName
895:            Case 4
896:                    objWMIInstance.ChangeZoneType 2, _
897:                                                  False, _
898:                                                  strZoneDataFile, _
899:                                                  arrayIpAddresses, _
900:                                                  strAdminEmailName
901:       End Select
...:
904:       objWMIInstance.AllowUpdate = intZoneUpdate
905:
906:       objWMIInstance.Put_ (wbemChangeFlagUpdateOnly Or _
907:                            wbemFlagReturnWhenComplete)
...:
910:       WScript.Echo "Zone '" & strZoneName &  "' updated."
...:
913:   End If
914:   If boolZONEDelete Then
915:       Set objWMIInstance = objWMIServices.Get ("MicrosoftDNS_Zone." & _
916:                               "ContainerName='" & strZoneName & _
917:                               "',DnsServerName='" & strDNSServerName & _
918:                               "',Name='" & strZoneName & "'")
...:
921:       objWMIInstance.Delete_
```

```
...:
924:        WScript.Echo "Zone '" & strZoneName &  "' deleted."
...:
927:    End If
928:    If boolZONERefresh Then
929:        Set objWMIInstance = objWMIServices.Get ("MicrosoftDNS_Zone." & _
930:                             "ContainerName='" & strZoneName & _
931:                             "',DnsServerName='" & strDNSServerName & _
932:                             "',Name='" & strZoneName & "'")
...:
935:        objWMIInstance.ForceRefresh()
...:
938:        WScript.Echo "Zone '" & strZoneName &  "' refreshed."
...:
941:    End If
942:    If boolZONEPause Then
943:        Set objWMIInstance = objWMIServices.Get ("MicrosoftDNS_Zone." & _
944:                             "ContainerName='" & strZoneName & _
945:                             "',DnsServerName='" & strDNSServerName & _
946:                             "',Name='" & strZoneName & "'")
...:
949:        objWMIInstance.PauseZone()
...:
952:        WScript.Echo "Zone '" & strZoneName &  "' paused."
...:
955:    End If
956:    If boolZONEReLoad Then
957:        Set objWMIInstance = objWMIServices.Get ("MicrosoftDNS_Zone." & _
958:                             "ContainerName='" & strZoneName & _
959:                             "',DnsServerName='" & strDNSServerName & _
960:                             "',Name='" & strZoneName & "'")
...:
963:        objWMIInstance.ReloadZone()
...:
966:        WScript.Echo "Zone '" & strZoneName &  "' reloaded."
...:
969:    End If
970:    If boolZONEReset2 Then
971:        Set objWMIInstance = objWMIServices.Get ("MicrosoftDNS_Zone." & _
972:                             "ContainerName='" & strZoneName & _
973:                             "',DnsServerName='" & strDNSServerName & _
974:                             "',Name='" & strZoneName & "'")
...:
977:        objWMIInstance.ResetSecondaries arraySecondaryServers, _
978:                                        intSecureSecondaries, _
979:                                        arrayNotifyServers, _
980:                                        intZoneNotify
...:
983:        WScript.Echo "Secondaries of zone '" & strZoneName &  "' reset."
...:
986:    End If
987:    If boolZONEResume Then
988:        Set objWMIInstance = objWMIServices.Get ("MicrosoftDNS_Zone." & _
989:                             "ContainerName='" & strZoneName & _
990:                             "',DnsServerName='" & strDNSServerName & _
991:                             "',Name='" & strZoneName & "'")
...:
994:        objWMIInstance.ResumeZone()
...:
997:        WScript.Echo "Zone '" & strZoneName &  "' resumed."
```

```
....:
1000:      End If
1001:      If boolZONEUpdate Then
1002:         Set objWMIInstance = objWMIServices.Get ("MicrosoftDNS_Zone." & _
1003:                              "ContainerName='" & strZoneName & _
1004:                              "',DnsServerName='" & strDNSServerName & _
1005:                              "',Name='" & strZoneName & "'")
....:
1008:         objWMIInstance.UpdateFromDS()
....:
1011:         WScript.Echo "Zone '" & strZoneName &  "' updated from DS."
....:
1014:      End If
1015:      If boolZONEWrite Then
1016:         Set objWMIInstance = objWMIServices.Get ("MicrosoftDNS_Zone." & _
1017:                              "ContainerName='" & strZoneName & _
1018:                              "',DnsServerName='" & strDNSServerName & _
1019:                              "',Name='" & strZoneName & "'")
....:
1022:         objWMIInstance.WriteBackZone()
....:
1025:         WScript.Echo "Zone '" & strZoneName &  "' WriteBack completed."
....:
1028:      End If
1029:      If boolCACHEClear Then
1030:         Set objWMIInstance = objWMIServices.Get ("MicrosoftDNS_Cache." & _
1031:                              "ContainerName='..Cache" & _
1032:                              "',DnsServerName='" & strDNSServerName & _
1033:                              "',Name='..Cache'")
....:
1036:         objWMIInstance.ClearCache()
....:
1039:         WScript.Echo "DNS cache cleared."
....:
1042:      End If
1043:      If boolROOTHWrite Then
1044:         Set objWMIInstance = objWMIServices.Get ("MicrosoftDNS_RootHints." & _
1045:                              "ContainerName='..RootHints" & _
1046:                              "',DnsServerName='" & strDNSServerName & _
1047:                              "',Name='..RootHints'")
....:
1050:         objWMIInstance.WriteBackRootHintDatafile()
....:
1053:         WScript.Echo "Roothints WriteBack completed."
....:
1056:      End If
1057:
....:
....:
....:
```

Here again, this portion can be divided into several subportions. Each portion corresponds to a management task that can be performed with a specific DNS zone. The tasks are as follows:

- **Creating a new zone** (lines 836 through 872): To create a zone we use the *CreateZone* method exposed by the *MicrosoftDNS_Zone* class. This method is invoked from the class instance (line 837), since the

CreateZone method is defined as a static method (you can check the *static* qualifier present in the method qualifiers). It is interesting to note that based on the zone type to be created, not all method parameters are required. When an Active Directory integrated zone is created, only the zone name (line 842), the value defining the zone type (line 843), the Boolean value setting the zone as an Active Directory Integrated zone (True), and the zone administrator's email address must be given. When a standard primary zone is created, we have the same set of parameters, but the Active Directory Integrated Boolean value is set to False (line 848) and the zone data file name is added (line 849) in the parameter list. For a secondary zone, again, we have the same set of parameters as for a primary zone creation, but the zone type value is different (line 854) and the primary IP address from which to transfer the zone is added (line 857). Basically, for a stub zone, the parameters are the same as for a secondary zone creation. Only the zone type is different (line 861). The values for the zone type are shown in Table 3.65.

Table 3.65   *Some Zone Property Values*

Zone type	Value
Primary or AD Integrated	0
Secondary	1
Stub	2
Zone transfer	**Value**
To any servers	0
Only NS servers	1
Only listed servers	2
No zone transfer	3
Zone notify	**Value**
No notification	0
Only NS servers	1
Only listed servers	2
Zone update	**Value**
Not allowed	0
Allow updates	1
Allow only secure updates	2

- **Updating the zone type** and its related information (lines 873 through 913): To update an existing zone, the script uses the *ChangeZoneType* method exposed by the *MicrosoftDNS_Zone* class. Basically, the method follows the same rules as the *CreateZone* method in the sense that not all method parameters are required, based on the zone type update to perform (lines 880 through 901). However, the method must be invoked from an instance representing the zone to be updated (lines 874 through 877). For example, this method can be used to convert an Active Directory integrated zone into a standard primary zone. It is interesting to note that the *ChangeZoneType* method does not modify the zone update mode for the DNS dynamic updates. This property is stored in a specific property called *AllowUpdate*, which is updated after the method invocation in the script code (lines 904 through 907).

- **Deleting a zone** (lines 914 through 927): To delete a zone from a DNS server, there is no specific method to use. The scripting technique simply retrieves the zone instance (lines 915 through 918) and invokes the *Delete_* method of the **SWBemObject** representing the zone instance (line 921).

- **Forcing the refresh of a zone** (lines 928 through 941): To refresh a DNS zone, the instance representing the zone must be retrieved (lines 929 through 932); next, the *ForceRefresh* method of the *Microsoft-DNS_Zone* instance must be invoked (line 935).

- **Pausing a zone** (lines 942 through 955): In the same way as with the zone refresh, to pause a DNS zone, the *PauseZone* method must be invoked (line 949) from an instance representing the zone to be paused.

- **Reloading a zone** (lines 956 through 969): To reload a zone, the technique is exactly the same. The script retrieves an instance of the zone (lines 957 through 960) and invokes the *ReloadZone* method (line 963).

- **Reconfiguring the secondary IP addresses** (lines 970 through 986): To update the configuration related to the secondary IP addresses, a specific method must be used. This method is called *ResetSecondaries* and allows the modification of several secondary server parameters. The first parameter accepted by the method contains the list of IP addresses representing the secondary servers (line 977). Next, the second method parameter defines how the zone transfer must be performed (line 978). The third method parameter contains a list of IP addresses that represents the servers to be notified for the zone updates (line 979). The final method parameter contains a value defining how the notification must be made (line 980). The various values used by this method are summarized in Table 3.65.

- **Resuming a zone** (lines 987 through 1000): Resuming a zone is the same as pausing a zone; the scripting technique is exactly the same.

- **Forcing a zone update** (lines 1001 through 1014): In the same way, from a scripting technique point of view, forcing a zone update is the same as reloading a zone.

- **Saving the zone back to the persistent storage** (lines 1015 through 1028): By invoking the *WriteBackZone* method, it is possible to force a save of the DNS zone information in a persistent storage. The persistent storage can be a zone file or Active Directory, based on the zone type.

- **Clearing the cache** (lines 1029 through 1042): The DNS cache is represented with the *MicrosoftDNS_Cache* class. The container name for the DNS cache is "..cache" (line 1031). By invoking the *ClearCache* method of the *MicrosoftDNS_Cache* instance, it is possible to clear the DNS cache content.

- **Saving the Root Hints to the used storage** (lines 1043 through 1056): The Root Hints are represented with *the MicrosoftDNS_RootHints* class. The container name for the DNS Root Hints zone is called "..RootHints" (line 1045). By invoking the *WriteBackRootHintDatafile* method of the *MicrosoftDNS_Zone* class, it is possible to save the Root Hints to the Root Hints data file.

By using the specific classes representing DNS records, it is possible to manage the records contained in the DNS zones. This is the purpose of Sample 3.69. The first operation is to retrieve the records contained in a zone. This operation is executed from line 1059 through 1098.

Sample 3.69   *Managing the DNS records (Part III)*

```
....:
....:
....:
1057:
1058:    ' -------------------------------------------------------------------------------------
1059:    If boolRECView Then
1060:        Set objWMIInstances = objWMIServices.ExecQuery ("Select * From " & _
1061:                                       strWMIClassRecordType & _
1062:                                       " Where ContainerName='" & _
1063:                                       strDomainName & "'")
....:
1066:        WScript.Echo "All '" & DecodeRecordClassString (strWMIClassRecordType) & _
1067:                     "' records of domain '" & _
1068:                     strDomainName & _
1069:                     "'." & vbCRLF
1070:
1071:        For Each objWMIInstance In objWMIInstances
1072:          Set objWMIPropertySet = objWMIInstance.Properties_
1073:          For Each objWMIProperty In objWMIPropertySet
1074:              Select Case objWMIProperty.Name
1075:                      Case "ContainerName"
1076:                      Case "TextRepresentation"
1077:                      Case "InstallDate"
1078:                      Case "DomainName"
1079:                      Case "RecordData"
```

```
1080:                       Case "RecordClass"
1081:                           DisplayFormattedProperty objWMIInstance, _
1082:                               "  " & objWMIProperty.Name, _
1083:                               DecodeRecordClass (objWMIProperty.Value), _
1084:                               Null
1085:                       Case Else
1086:                           DisplayFormattedProperty objWMIInstance, _
1087:                               "  " & objWMIProperty.Name, _
1088:                               objWMIProperty.Name, _
1089:                               Null
1090:               End Select
1091:           Next
1092:           WScript.Echo
....:
1095:       Next
....:
1098:     End If
1099:     If boolRECCreate Then
1100:        Set objWMIClass = objWMIServices.Get (strWMIClassRecordType)
....:
1103:        objWMIClass.CreateInstanceFromPropertyData strDNSServerName, _
1104:                                         strDomainName,  _
1105:                                         strHostOwner &  _
1106:                                         "." & strDomainName,  _
1107:                                         intRecordClass,  _
1108:                                         intTTL,  _
1109:                                         strHostAddress
....:
1112:        WScript.Echo "'" & strRecordType &  "' record for '" &  _
1113:                 strHostOwner & "." & strDomainName & "' created."
....:
1116:     End If
1117:     If boolRECDelete Then
1118:        Set objWMIInstance = objWMIServices.Get (strWMIClassRecordType & _
1119:                     ".ContainerName='" & strDomainName & _
1120:                     "',DnsServerName='" & strDNSServerName & _
1121:                     "',DomainName='" & strDomainName & _
1122:                     "',OwnerName='" & strHostOwner & "." & strDomainName & _
1123:                     "',RecordClass=" & intRecordClass & _
1124:                     ",RecordData='" & strHostAddress & "'")
....:
1127:        objWMIInstance.Delete_
....:
1130:        WScript.Echo "'" & strRecordType &  "' record for '" &  _
1131:                 strHostOwner & "." & strDomainName & "' deleted."
....:
1134:     End If
1135:
1136:     ]]>
1137:    </script>
1138:   </job>
1139:</package>
```

To retrieve the records available in a zone, the script performs a WQL query with some criteria to ensure that only the records of the given zone are retrieved (lines 1060 through 1063). We see in the query that the WMI record class name is stored in a variable (line 1061). If the Rtype parameter given on the command-line is an asterisk (*), then the class name used is the

MicrosoftDNS_ResourceRecord class. Because the *MicrosoftDNS_Resource-Record* class is a superclass for all record type classes, the use of this class in the WQL query will retrieve all records available in the zone. If the Rtype parameter given on the command-line corresponds to a specific record type (i.e., A record or CNAME record), then only this record type will be viewed, and the class used in the WQL query will be the one corresponding to the record type (see Table 3.63 to get a list of the record type WMI classes). This class selection, based on the record type, is made during the command-line parameters parsing. The following command line will list all A records available in the LissWare.Net domain:

```
 1:   C:\>WMIDNS.Wsf Record View RType=A DomainName=LissWare.Net
 2:   Microsoft (R) Windows Script Host Version 5.6
 3:   Copyright (C) Microsoft Corporation 1996-2001. All rights reserved.
 4:
 5:   All 'A' records of domain 'LissWare.Net'.
 6:
 7:      *DnsServerName: ....................... net-dpen6400a.LissWare.Net
 8:       IPAddress: ........................... 10.10.10.3
 9:      *OwnerName: .......................... LissWare.Net
10:       RecordClass: ......................... IN
11:       TTL: ................................. 600
12:
13:      *DnsServerName: ....................... net-dpen6400a.LissWare.Net
14:       IPAddress: ........................... 10.10.10.253
15:      *OwnerName: .......................... Cisco-Brussels.LissWare.Net
16:       RecordClass: ......................... IN
17:       TTL: ................................. 3600
18:
19:      *DnsServerName: ....................... net-dpen6400a.LissWare.Net
20:       IPAddress: ........................... 10.10.10.3
21:      *OwnerName: .......................... DomainDnsZones.LissWare.Net
22:       RecordClass: ......................... IN
23:       TTL: ................................. 600
24:
25:      *DnsServerName: ....................... net-dpen6400a.LissWare.Net
26:       IPAddress: ........................... 10.10.10.3
27:      *OwnerName: .......................... ForestDnsZones.LissWare.Net
28:       RecordClass: ......................... IN
29:       TTL: ................................. 600
30:
31:      *DnsServerName: ....................... net-dpen6400a.LissWare.Net
32:       IPAddress: ........................... 192.10.10.3
33:      *OwnerName: .......................... ForestDnsZones.LissWare.Net
34:       RecordClass: ......................... IN
35:       TTL: ................................. 600
36:
37:      *DnsServerName: ....................... net-dpen6400a.LissWare.Net
38:       IPAddress: ........................... 10.10.10.3
39:      *OwnerName: .......................... net-dpen6400a.LissWare.Net
40:       RecordClass: ......................... IN
41:       TTL: ................................. 3600
42:
43:      *DnsServerName: ....................... net-dpen6400a.LissWare.Net
44:       IPAddress: ........................... 192.10.10.3
45:      *OwnerName: .......................... net-dpep6400.Emea.LissWare.Net
```

```
46:        RecordClass: ......................... IN
47:        TTL: ................................. 3600
48:
49:        *DnsServerName: ...................... net-dpen6400a.LissWare.Net
50:        IPAddress: ........................... 10.10.10.100
51:        *OwnerName: .......................... XP-PRO01.LissWare.Net
52:        RecordClass: ......................... IN
53:        TTL: ................................. 1200
```

To create a new DNS record, the *CreateInstanceFromPropertyData* method is used in the script code (lines 1099 through 1116). This method is specific to the DNS record type and is not available at the level of the *MicrosoftDNS_ResourceRecord* class. Note that it is possible to use a text representation of the record to create a new record in the DNS zone. In such a case, the *CreateFromTextRepresentation* method of the *MicrosoftDNS_ResourceRecord* class can be used. Using one method or the other will always create a DNS record. However, based on the situation, one method will be easier than the other. By using the generic *CreateFromTextRepresentation* method of the *MicrosoftDNS_ResourceRecord* class, it is possible to create any record type with one single parameter, which is the text representation of the record type. This makes the scripting technique easier, since only one method with one single parameter must be used. However, the correct text representation must be passed to the method. As an example, we have the text representation of an A record and a CNAME record:

```
Net-dpen6400a.LissWare.Net IN A 10.10.10.3
```

```
www.LissWare.Net IN CNAME Net-dpen6400a.LissWare.Net.
```

The second method, called *CreatInstanceFromPropertyData,* requires specific parameters determined by the record type to be created. In such a case, the scripting technique becomes specific to the record type but does not require the DNS record string representation. Currently, the script uses the *CreatInstanceFromPropertyData* method defined at the level of the *MicrosoftDNS_Atype* class. Because the *MicrosoftDNS_CNAMEType* class exposes the same method name with the same number of parameters, it is possible to create transparently with the *CreatInstanceFromPropertyData* method A and CNAME records, provided that the correct parameters are passed to the method. Although the number of parameters is the same, the meaning of all parameters between an A record and a CNAME record is not exactly the same. The two following command-line samples show the parameter difference:

```
C:\>WMIDNS.Wsf Record Create RType=A DomainName=LissWare.Net Host=Net-dpen6400a Class=IN
               TTL=3600 HostAddress=10.10.10.7
```

```
C:\>WMIDNS.Wsf Record Create RType=CNAME DomainName=LissWare.Net Host=www Class=IN
               TTL=7200 HostAddress=Net-dpen6400a.LissWare.Net.
```

We see that most parameters are the same. However, we notice that the *HostAddress* is an IP address when creating an A record and that *HostAddress* is an FQDN when creating a CNAME record. The record class remains the same in both cases. The values used to define the record class during the *CreatInstanceFromPropertyData* method invocation are listed in Table 3.66.

Table 3.66   *The DNS Record Class Values*

Record class	Value
IN (INTERNET)	1
CS (CSNET)	2
CH (CHAOS)	3
HS (HESIOD)	4

The scripting technique to delete a record is very similar to the technique used to delete a zone. The first step is to retrieve an instance of the record (lines 1118 through 1124) and then to invoke the *Delete_* method of the **SWBemObject** representing the record instance (line 1127). To delete a DNS record, the following command-line parameter can be used:

```
C:>\WMIDNS.Wsf Record Delete RType=A DomainName=LissWare.Net Host=Net-dpen6400a Class=IN
                 TTL=3600 HostAddress=10.10.10.7
```

3.7.5   SNMP providers

The WMI *SNMP* providers are designed to integrate the Simple Network Management Protocol (SNMP) management information in WMI, which means that it is possible to seamlessly manage SNMP devices from WMI. By default, none of the *SNMP* providers is installed on any Windows platform! So, to install these providers, you should perform the following tasks:

- **For Windows XP and Windows Server 2003:** From the control panel, select Add/Remove Programs. Next, select Add/Remove Windows Components, and then in the Windows Components Wizard, select Management and Monitoring Tools (see Figure 3.39).

  Finally, select WMI *SNMP* providers, then click OK. Follow the steps in the wizard to complete the installation.

- **For Windows 2000:** Run the *SNMP* provider Setup program, **Wbemsnmp.exe**, from the System32\wbem directory or the \i386 directory of the Windows 2000 installation CD.

- **For Windows NT 4.0:** Install the *SNMP* provider when installing the WMI core component or from the Internet at http://www.microsoft.com/downloads/details.aspx?FamilyID=f8130806-2589-46b3-b472-26b816776f31&DisplayLang=en.

Figure 3.39
Adding the SNMP providers under Windows Server 2003.

Note that under Windows 95, 98, and Millennium, the WMI *SNMP* provider cannot be installed or run on this operating system.

The *SNMP* providers are made up of one instance provider, one class provider, and two event providers. (See Table 3.67.)

Table 3.67   *The SNMP Providers Capabilities*

Provider Name	Provider Namespace	Class Provider	Instance Provider	Method Provider	Property Provider	Event Provider	Event Consumer Provider	Support Get	Support Put	Support Enumeration	Support Delete	Windows Server 2003	Windows XP	Windows 2000 Server	Windows 2000 Professional	Windows NT 4.0
SNMP Providers																
MS_SNMP_CLASS_PROVIDER	Root/snmp/localhost	X						X	X			X	X	X	X	X
MS_SNMP_ENCAPSULATED_EVENT_PROVIDER	Root/snmp/localhost					X						X	X	X	X	X
MS_SNMP_INSTANCE_PROVIDER	Root/snmp/localhost		X					X	X	X	X	X	X	X	X	X
MS_SNMP_REFERENT_EVENT_PROVIDER	Root/snmp/localhost					X						X	X	X	X	X

Once the *SNMP* providers are installed, by default two new namespaces are created: the **Root\SNMP\SMIR** and the **Root\SNMP\LocalHost**. The **Root\SNMP\SMIR** namespace contains the SNMP schema database, which is called the SNMP Module Information Repository (SMIR). SNMP definitions, called the Structure of Management Information (SMI), are available from Management Information Base (MIB) files and represent the real-world manageable entities as defined by SNMP. MIB files use a standard notation (Abstract Syntax Notation 1 or ASN.1) and a number of macro definitions that serve as templates to describe real-world manageable entities. We will not go into the syntax details of MIB files, but it is important to realize that MIB files are the primary source of information used by WMI to represent these real-world SNMP manageable entities in the CIM repository. By default, the WMI installation only loads MIB definitions from the RFC 1213 and RFC 1215 MIB files that define standard MIB to manage IP networks. (See Table 3.68.)

Table 3.68   *The SNMP Classes Available in the Root\SNMP\SMIR Namespaces*

Name	Type	Comments
SNMP_RFC1213_MIB_atTable	Dynamic	The Address Translation tables contain the NetworkAddress to `physical' address equivalences. Some interfaces do not use translation tables for determining address equivalences (e.g., DDN-X.25 has an algorithmic method); if all interfaces are of this type, then the Address Translation table is empty (i.e., has zero entries).
SNMP_RFC1213_MIB_egp	Dynamic	The Exterior Gateway Protocol (EGP) group represents information about: The number of EGP messages received without error, the number of EGP messages received that proved to be in error, the total number of locally generated EGP messages, and the number of locally generated EGP messages not sent due to resource limitations within an EGP entity.
SNMP_RFC1213_MIB_egpNeighTable	Dynamic	The Exterior Gateway Protocol (EGP) neighbor table contains information about this entity's EGP neighbors.
SNMP_RFC1213_MIB_icmp	Dynamic	The ICMP group represents information about ICMP messages (number of messages, errors, unreachable destinations, exceeded time, redirections, etc.).
SNMP_RFC1213_MIB_ifTable	Dynamic	A list of interface entries. The number of entries is given by the value of ifNumber.
SNMP_RFC1213_MIB_interfaces	Dynamic	Represent the number of network interfaces (regardless of their current state) present on this system (ifNumber).
SNMP_RFC1213_MIB_ip	Dynamic	The IP group represents information about IP Forwarding, IP TTL, IP traffic, IP errors, Datagrams, packets discarded, etc.
SNMP_RFC1213_MIB_ipAddrTable	Dynamic	The table of addressing information relevant to this entity's IP addresses.
SNMP_RFC1213_MIB_ipNetToMediaTable	Dynamic	The IP Address Translation table used for mapping from IP addresses to physical addresses.
SNMP_RFC1213_MIB_ipRouteTable	Dynamic	The entity's IP Routing table.
SNMP_RFC1213_MIB_snmp	Dynamic	The entity's SNMP information.
SNMP_RFC1213_MIB_system	Dynamic	The entity's system information (contact, location, etc.).
SNMP_RFC1213_MIB_tcp	Dynamic	The TCP group represents information about TCP stack (open connections, errors, packet transmit and receive, etc.).
SNMP_RFC1213_MIB_tcpConnTable	Dynamic	Table containing active TCP connections information.
SNMP_RFC1213_MIB_udp	Dynamic	The UDP group represent information about UDP stack (datagrams, errors, packet transmit and receive, etc.)
SNMP_RFC1213_MIB_udpTable	Dynamic	Table containing UDP listener information.
SnmpV1ExtendedNotification	Extrinsic (Enterprise non-specific)	SNMP version 1 Enterprise nonspecific events.
SnmpV1Notification	Extrinsic (Enterprise non-specific)	SNMP version 1 Enterprise nonspecific events.
SnmpV2ExtendedNotification	Extrinsic (Enterprise non-specific)	SNMP version 2 Enterprise nonspecific events.
SnmpV2Notification	Extrinsic (Enterprise non-specific)	SNMP version 2 Enterprise nonspecific events.
SnmpAuthenticationFailureExtendedNotification	Extrinsic (Generic)	Notification representing an authentication failure.
SnmpAuthenticationFailureNotification	Extrinsic (Generic)	Notification representing an authentication failure.
SnmpColdStartExtendedNotification	Extrinsic (Generic)	Notification representing an SNMP device cold start.
SnmpColdStartNotification	Extrinsic (Generic)	Notification representing an SNMP device cold start.
SnmpEGPNeighborLossExtendedNotification	Extrinsic (Generic)	Notification representing an Exterior Gateway Protocol (EGP) neighbor loss.
SnmpEGPNeighborLossNotification	Extrinsic (Generic)	Notification representing an Exterior Gateway Protocol (EGP) neighbor loss.
SnmpExtendedNotification	Extrinsic (Generic)	The SnmpExtendedNotification class is the base class for any class mapped from the NOTIFICATION-TYPE macro to a CIM class by the SNMP Provider.
SnmpLinkDownExtendedNotification	Extrinsic (Generic)	Notification representing an interface link down.
SnmpLinkDownNotification	Extrinsic (Generic)	Notification representing an interface link down.
SnmpLinkUpExtendedNotification	Extrinsic (Generic)	Notification representing an interface link up.
SnmpLinkUpNotification	Extrinsic (Generic)	Notification representing an interface link up.
SnmpNotification	Extrinsic (Generic)	The SnmpNotification class is the base class for any class mapped from the NOTIFICATION-TYPE macro to an encapsulated CIM class by the SNMP Provider.
SnmpWarmStartExtendedNotification	Extrinsic (Generic)	Notification representing an SNMP device warm start.
SnmpWarmStartNotification	Extrinsic (Generic)	Notification representing an SNMP device warm start.

Both RFC 1213 and RFC 1215 MIB are loaded in the SNMP Module Information Repository (**Root\SNMP\SMIR**) namespace and are represented in the form of WMI classes, as shown in Figure 3.40.

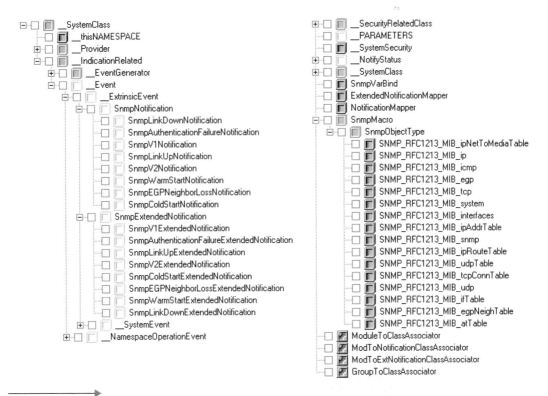

Figure 3.40 *The SNMP Module Information Repository classes in Root\SNMP\SMIR.*

Of course, since these classes represent SNMP information, we leave the world of WMI to go into the world of SNMP. Although some class names reflect very well the information they provide, you can refer to RFC 1213 and RFC 1215 to get more information (see http://www.faqs.org/rfcs/rfc1213.html and http://www.faqs.org/rfcs/rfc1215.html). We have dynamic classes, which are used to represent SNMP instances from RFC 1213 (left side of Figure 3.40), and extrinsic event classes, which represent SNMP event classes from RFC 1215, usually called SNMP traps or notifications (right side of Figure 3.40).

The *SNMP* dynamic class provider uses the SNMP Module Information Repository to create and retrieve class definitions. It is important to note that the **SMIR** namespace does not contain the *SNMP* provider registration instances (made from the *__Win32Provider* class). This namespace is just

used as a repository containing the SNMP MIB definitions to be used by
WMI. Of course, there are a lot of things to say about the WMI *SNMP*
providers and their integration with WMI. However, in the context of this
book, instead of doing long theoretical descriptions, we will show you how
you can take advantage of this integration. And by practicing, you will
understand how things work together.

3.7.5.1   Accessing SNMP data

To access SNMP information available from a Windows system, ensure that
the SNMP service is properly configured and running, since it implements
the SNMP agent contacted to provide information (see Figure 3.41).

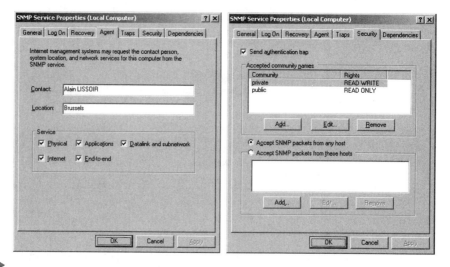

Figure 3.41   *The SNMP service configuration.*

Next, we can use the **Root\SNMP\Localhost** namespace created during
the installation of the WMI *SNMP* providers. This namespace is an SNMP
proxy namespace and contains registration instances of the WMI *SNMP*
providers (made from the __Win32Provider class). By default, all WMI
SNMP providers are available from this namespace (instance, class, and
event providers).

Each SNMP proxy WMI namespace has a set of qualifiers that describe
the transport characteristics for communicating with an SNMP agent. In
the case of the local system, there is one qualifier, called *AgentAddress,* defining the host name of the system, which in this case is the localhost (see Figure 3.42).

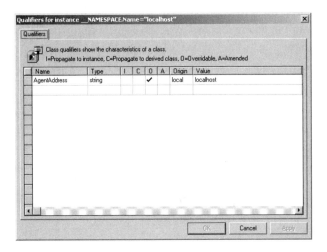

Figure 3.42
*The
Root\SNMP\local-
host namespace
qualifier.*

The *AgentAddress* is the only mandatory qualifier; however, there are other qualifiers defining other SNMP communication parameters. Table 3.69 summarizes the available qualifiers.

Table 3.69   *The Proxy Namespace Qualifiers to Define SNMP Transport Characteristics*

AgentAddress	CIM_STRING	Mandatory	Transport address associated with the SNMP agent, such as an IP address or DNS name. AgentAddress should be set to a valid unicast host address or a domain host name that can be resolved through the operating system's domain-name resolution process. There is no default value.
AgentTransport	CIM_STRING	Optional	Transport protocol used to communicate with the SNMP agent. Currently the only valid values are Internet Protocol (IP) and Internet Packet Exchange (IPX). The default value is IP.
AgentReadCommunityName	CIM_STRING	Optional	Variable-length octet string that is used by the SNMP agent to authenticate an SNMP Protocol Data Unit (PDU) during a read operation (SNMP GET/GET NEXT requests). The community name must be mapped to a Unicode string and is limited to alphanumeric characters. The default value is public.
AgentWriteCommunityName	CIM_STRING	Optional	Variable-length octet string that is used by the SNMP agent to authenticate an SNMP Protocol Data Unit (PDU) during a read operation (SNMP SET request). The community name must be mapped to a Unicode string and is limited to alphanumeric characters. The default value is public.
AgentRetryCount	CIM_SINT32	Optional	Number of times a single SNMP request can be retried when there is no response from the SNMP agent before the request is deemed to have failed. AgentRetryCount must be set to an integer between 0 and 2^32-1. The default value is 1.
AgentRetryTimeout	CIM_SINT32	Optional	Time in milliseconds before the SNMP Protocol Data Unit (PDU) is considered to have been dropped. This is the number of milliseconds to wait for a response to an SNMP request sent to the SNMP agent. AgentRetryTimeout must be set to an integer between 0 and 2^32-1. The default value is 500.
AgentVarBindsPerPdu	CIM_SINT32	Optional	Maximum number of variable bindings contained within a single SNMP PDU. Every SNMP request sent to the SNMP agent contains one or more SNMP variables. This parameter specifies the largest number of variables that can be included in a single request. AgentVarBindsPerPdu can be set to 0 to cause the implementation to determine the optimal variable bindings or to an integer between 1 and 2^32-1. Note that while increasing this value can improve performance, some agents and networks cannot deal with the resulting request. The default value is 10.
AgentFlowControlWindowSize	CIM_SINT32	Optional	Maximum number of concurrently outstanding SNMP requests that can be sent to this agent while a response has not yet been received. An SNMP request is considered outstanding until a PDU response has been received or it has timed out. A large window size generally improves performance, but some agents might not work well under a heavy load. AgentFlowControlWindowSize can be set to 0 to indicate an infinite window size or to an integer between 1 and 2^32-1. The default value is 10.
AgentSNMPVersion	CIM_SINT32	Optional	Version of the SNMP protocol to be used when communicating with the SNMP agent. Currently, the only valid values are 1 (for SNMPv1) and 2C (for SNMPv2C). The default value is 1.
Correlated	CIM_BOOLEAN	Optional	Set to True, defines the set of classes that a given SNMP agent is known to support at the time the enumeration occurs. Set to False, enumeration returns all classes present within the SMIR namespace (noncorrelated), regardless of whether the agent device supports them or not.

As you can see, you can use the *AgentReadCommunityName* to define the SNMP community string (public by default) or the *AgentTransport* to define the protocol type (IP by default, but it can be IPX). Let's take an example where a computer is using the following IP address and mask settings:

```
C:\>ipconfig

Windows 2000 IP Configuration

Ethernet adapter Local Area Connection:

        Connection-specific DNS Suffix  . :
        IP Address. . . . . . . . . . . : 10.10.10.3
        Subnet Mask . . . . . . . . . . : 255.0.0.0
        Default Gateway . . . . . . . . : 10.10.10.254
```

By using Sample 3.70, we can obtain from WMI and via SNMP the same type of information.

Sample 3.70   *Obtaining localhost IP addresses from WMI via SNMP*

```
 1:<?xml version="1.0"?>
 .:
 8:<package>
 9:  <job>
10:
11:     <?job error="True" debug="True" ?>
12:
13:     <script language="VBScript" src="..\Functions\DisplayFormattedPropertiesFunction.vbs" />
14:     <script language="VBScript" src="..\Functions\DisplayFormattedPropertyFunction.vbs" />
15:
16:     <object progid="WbemScripting.SWbemLocator" id="objWMILocator" reference="true"/>
17:     <object progid="WbemScripting.SWbemDateTime " id="objWMIDateTime" />
18:
19:     <script language="VBscript">
20:     <![CDATA[
..:
24:     Const cComputerName = "LocalHost"
25:     Const cWMINameSpace = "Root/SNMP/LocalHost"
26:     Const cWMIClass = "SNMP_RFC1213_MIB_ipAddrTable"
..:
33:     objWMILocator.Security_.AuthenticationLevel = wbemAuthenticationLevelDefault
34:     objWMILocator.Security_.ImpersonationLevel = wbemImpersonationLevelImpersonate
35:     Set objWMIServices = objWMILocator.ConnectServer(cComputerName, cWMINameSpace, "", "")
36:
37:     Set objWMIInstances = objWMIServices.InstancesOf(cWMIClass)
38:
39:     For Each objWMIInstance In objWMIInstances
40:         DisplayFormattedProperties objWMIInstance, 0
41:         WScript.Echo
42:     Next
..:
47:     ]]>
48:     </script>
49:  </job>
50:</package>
```

Sample 3.70 contains nothing complicated from a scripting point of view. We developed this script throughout the first book, *Understanding WMI Scripting*, when discovering the WMI Scripting API (see Sample 4.6 in the appendix). This demonstrates how transparent SNMP access is from WMI. We just need to access the appropriate WMI namespace (line 25) and request the *SNMP_RFC1213_MIB_ipAddrTable* class, which represents the requested SNMP information (line 26). The output would be as follows:

```
 1:   C:\>GetSingleInstanceWithAPI.wsf
 2:   Microsoft (R) Windows Script Host Version 5.6
 3:   Copyright (C) Microsoft Corporation 1996-2001. All rights reserved.
 4:
 5:
 6:   - SNMP_RFC1213_MIB_ipAddrTable -----------------------------------------------
 7:   *ipAdEntAddr: .......................... 10.10.10.3
 8:   ipAdEntBcastAddr: ...................... 1
 9:   ipAdEntIfIndex: ........................ 33554434
10:   ipAdEntNetMask: ........................ 255.0.0.0
11:   ipAdEntReasmMaxSize: ................... 65535
12:
13:
14:   - SNMP_RFC1213_MIB_ipAddrTable -----------------------------------------------
15:   *ipAdEntAddr: .......................... 127.0.0.1
16:   ipAdEntBcastAddr: ...................... 1
17:   ipAdEntIfIndex: ........................ 1
18:   ipAdEntNetMask: ........................ 255.0.0.0
19:   ipAdEntReasmMaxSize: ................... 65535
```

Accessing standard SNMP information from the local system is pretty straightforward, but how do you access SNMP information from a system other than the local host? We have two solutions: We can modify Sample 3.70 and make use of an **SWBemNamedValueSet** object, or we can create a new proxy namespace for that particular device or host. For this exercise, we will access via SNMP, a Cisco router 2503 loaded with the Cisco Internetwork Operating System (IOS) Software version 11.2(3)P. If you plan to use another SNMP-enabled device, please refer to the device specifications to determine if it supports RFC 1213 and RFC 1215. For the Cisco IOS, these RFCs are supported from version 10.2 or later.

First, the Cisco router must be SNMP enabled. If you are not familiar with Cisco devices, please contact your network administrator to get some help for the Cisco configuration. Figure 3.43 shows the basic commands that are required to SNMP enable a Cisco router 2500. The router can be easily configured via a TELNET session, assuming it is preconfigured for TELNET access and you have the required credentials.

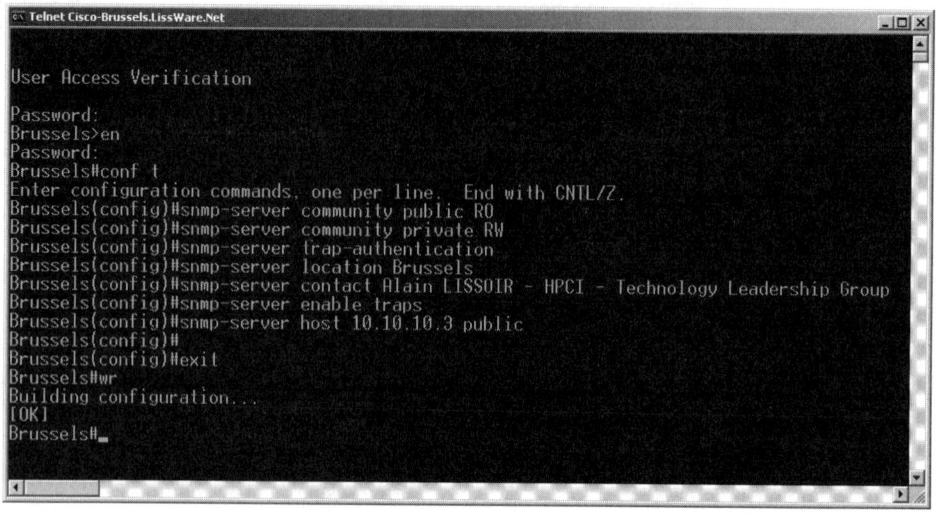

Figure 3.43   *Enabling SNMP on your Cisco router.*

As you can see in Figure 3.43, you can easily recognize the SNMP community string for the read-only operations (RO=public) and read/write operations (RW=private). Make sure that you use the correct community string for the SNMP agent; otherwise, you won't be able to access the Cisco router. Note that the read/write community string is optional in this example (actually, we will also send SNMP commands to the device in section 3.7.5.5, "Sending SNMP commands"). Again, request the help of your network administrator to correctly configure the SNMP information in your Cisco router, and, if you configure this in production, make sure that you respect the security policies of your company.

To access a remote SNMP device, we mentioned two options:

- Using an **SWBemNamedValueSet** object

- Creating a new WMI namespace

Let's start with the first one by using an **SWBemNamedValueSet** object. In this case, we do not create a dedicated namespace for the device as for the localhost. However, we reuse the existing namespace created for the localhost. This logic is shown in Sample 3.71.

Sample 3.71   *Obtaining remote device IP addresses from WMI via SNMP*

```
1:<?xml version="1.0"?>
.:
8:<package>
9:   <job>
```

```
..:
13:    <script language="VBScript" src="..\Functions\DisplayFormattedPropertiesFunction.vbs" />
14:    <script language="VBScript" src="..\Functions\DisplayFormattedPropertyFunction.vbs" />
15:
16:    <object progid="WbemScripting.SWbemLocator" id="objWMILocator" reference="true"/>
17:    <object progid="WbemScripting.SWBemNamedValueSet" id="objWMINamedValueSet" />
18:    <object progid="WbemScripting.SWbemDateTime " id="objWMIDateTime" />
19:
20:    <script language="VBscript">
21:    <![CDATA[
..:
25:    Const cComputerName = "LocalHost"
26:    Const cWMINameSpace = "Root/SNMP/LocalHost"
27:    Const cWMIClass = "SNMP_RFC1213_MIB_ipAddrTable"
..:
34:    objWMILocator.Security_.AuthenticationLevel = wbemAuthenticationLevelDefault
35:    objWMILocator.Security_.ImpersonationLevel = wbemImpersonationLevelImpersonate
36:    Set objWMIServices = objWMILocator.ConnectServer(cComputerName, cWMINameSpace, "", "")
37:
38:    objWMINamedValueSet.Add "Correlate", True
39:    objWMINamedValueSet.Add "AgentAddress", "Cisco-Brussels.LissWare.Net"
40:    objWMINamedValueSet.Add "AgentFlowControlWindowSize", 3
41:    objWMINamedValueSet.Add "AgentReadCommunityName", "public"
42:    objWMINamedValueSet.Add "AgentRetryCount", 1
43:    objWMINamedValueSet.Add "AgentRetryTimeout", 500
44:    objWMINamedValueSet.Add "AgentVarBindsPerPdu", 10
45:    objWMINamedValueSet.Add "AgentWriteCommunityName", "private"
46:
47:    Set objWMIInstances = objWMIServices.InstancesOf(cWMIClass, _
48:                                                    , _
49:                                                    objWMINamedValueSet)
50:
51:    For Each objWMIInstance In objWMIInstances
52:        DisplayFormattedProperties objWMIInstance, 0
53:        WScript.Echo
54:    Next
..:
59:    ]]>
60:    </script>
61:    </job>
62:</package>
```

The script code is almost the same as Sample 3.70; only the initialization of the **SWBemNamedValueSet** is new (lines 38 through 45). The **SWBemNamedValueSet** object instantiated at line 17 is initialized with the qualifiers listed in Table 3.69. Note that the script uses all supported qualifiers. This is, of course, not mandatory, but it shows the complete coding technique. Passing the **SWBemNamedValueSet** object when requesting the collection of instances (line 49) supersedes the qualifiers defined at the **Root\SNMP\Localhost** namespace level (see Figure 3.42).

We can see that the *AgentAddress* qualifier is set with the Fully Qualified Domain Name (FQDN) of the Cisco router (line 39), but it can also be the IP address. Depending on the Cisco router configuration, the output will look as follows:

```
 1:   C:\>GetSingleInstanceWithAPI2.wsf
 2:   Microsoft (R) Windows Script Host Version 5.6
 3:   Copyright (C) Microsoft Corporation 1996-2001. All rights reserved.
 4:
 5:
 6:   - SNMP_RFC1213_MIB_ipAddrTable ------------------------------------------------
 7:   *ipAdEntAddr: .......................... 10.10.10.253
 8:   ipAdEntBcastAddr: ...................... 1
 9:   ipAdEntIfIndex: ........................ 1
10:   ipAdEntNetMask: ........................ 255.0.0.0
11:   ipAdEntReasmMaxSize: ................... 18024
12:
13:
14:   - SNMP_RFC1213_MIB_ipAddrTable ------------------------------------------------
15:   *ipAdEntAddr: .......................... 192.10.10.253
16:   ipAdEntBcastAddr: ...................... 1
17:   ipAdEntIfIndex: ........................ 1
18:   ipAdEntNetMask: ........................ 255.255.255.0
19:   ipAdEntReasmMaxSize: ................... 18024
20:
21:
22:   - SNMP_RFC1213_MIB_ipAddrTable ------------------------------------------------
23:   *ipAdEntAddr: .......................... 193.10.10.253
24:   ipAdEntBcastAddr: ...................... 1
25:   ipAdEntIfIndex: ........................ 1
26:   ipAdEntNetMask: ........................ 255.255.255.0
27:   ipAdEntReasmMaxSize: ................... 18024
28:
29:
30:   - SNMP_RFC1213_MIB_ipAddrTable ------------------------------------------------
31:   *ipAdEntAddr: .......................... 194.10.10.253
32:   ipAdEntBcastAddr: ...................... 1
33:   ipAdEntIfIndex: ........................ 1
34:   ipAdEntNetMask: ........................ 255.255.255.0
35:   ipAdEntReasmMaxSize: ................... 18024
36:
37:
38:   - SNMP_RFC1213_MIB_ipAddrTable ------------------------------------------------
39:   *ipAdEntAddr: .......................... 195.10.10.253
40:   ipAdEntBcastAddr: ...................... 1
41:   ipAdEntIfIndex: ........................ 2
42:   ipAdEntNetMask: ........................ 255.255.255.0
43:   ipAdEntReasmMaxSize: ................... 18024
44:
45:
46:   - SNMP_RFC1213_MIB_ipAddrTable ------------------------------------------------
47:   *ipAdEntAddr: .......................... 200.10.10.1
48:   ipAdEntBcastAddr: ...................... 1
49:   ipAdEntIfIndex: ........................ 4
50:   ipAdEntNetMask: ........................ 255.255.255.0
51:   ipAdEntReasmMaxSize: ................... 18024
```

The second solution is to create a dedicated namespace to access the Cisco router. This namespace can be created with a MOF file. In the %SystemRoot%\System32\WBEM directory, there is a MOF file called **SNMPREG.MOF**. By using this MOF file as a template, it is very easy to obtain another MOF file to create the dedicated namespace to access the Cisco router. We will call this new namespace the **Root\SNMP\CiscoBrussels** namespace. The MOF file creating this namespace with the required qualifiers is shown in Sample 3.72. From line 10 through 32, the MOF file creates the **Root\SNMP\CiscoBrussels** namespace with the SNMP qualifiers defining the communication parameters (lines 13 through 26). Next, the subsequent lines are the exact copy of the information coming from the **SNMPREG.MOF** and define the registration information of the *SNMP* providers for the dedicated Cisco router namespace (lines 36 through 101).

Sample 3.72 *A MOF file to create a dedicated namespace for an SNMP device*

```
1:#pragma autorecover
2:
3:#pragma namespace("\\\\.\\Root")
4:
5:instance of __Namespace
6:{
7:    Name = "SNMP" ;
8:} ;
9:
10:#pragma namespace("\\\\.\\Root\\snmp")
11:
12:[
13:// IP address or DNS name.
14:AgentAddress ("Cisco-Brussels.LissWare.Net"),
15:// SNMP community name for SNMP GET/GETNEXT requests.
16:AgentReadCommunityName ("public"),
17:// SNMP community name for SNMP SET requests.
18:AgentWriteCommunityName ("private"),
19:// Number of SNMP PDU retries before transmission
20:AgentRetryCount (1),
21:// detects a 'No Response' from device.
22:AgentRetryTimeout (500),
23:// Maximum number of variable bindings contained within a single SNMP PDU.
24:AgentVarBindsPerPdu (10),
25:// Maximum number of outstanding SNMP PDUs that can be transmitted to an SNMP agent.
26:AgentFlowControlWindowSize (3)
27:]
28:
29:instance of __Namespace
30:{
31:    Name = "CiscoBrussels" ;
32:} ;
33:
34:#pragma namespace("\\\\.\\Root\\snmp\\CiscoBrussels")
35:
36:instance of __Win32Provider as $PClass
37:{
38:    Name = "MS_SNMP_CLASS_PROVIDER";
39:    Clsid = "{70426720-F78F-11cf-9151-00AA00A4086C}";
40:    HostingModel = "NetworkServiceHost";
41:};
42:
43:instance of __ClassProviderRegistration
44:{
```

```
45:     Provider = $PClass;
46:     SupportsGet = TRUE;
47:     SupportsPut = FALSE;
48:     SupportsDelete = FALSE;
49:     SupportsEnumeration = TRUE;
50:
51:     QuerySupportLevels = NULL ;
52:
53:     ResultSetQueries = { "Select * From meta_class Where __this isa \"SnmpMacro\"",
54:                     "Select * From meta_class Where __this isa \"SnmpNotification\"",
55:                     "Select * From meta_class Where __this isa \"SnmpExtendedNotification\""
56:                         } ;
57:} ;
58:
59:instance of __Win32Provider as $PInst
60:{
61:     Name = "MS_SNMP_INSTANCE_PROVIDER";
62:     Clsid = "{1F517A23-B29C-11cf-8C8D-00AA00A4086C}";
63:     HostingModel = "NetworkServiceHost";
64:};
65:
66:instance of __InstanceProviderRegistration
67:{
68:     Provider = $PInst;
69:     SupportsGet = TRUE;
70:     SupportsPut = TRUE;
71:     SupportsDelete = TRUE;
72:     SupportsEnumeration = TRUE;
73:
74:     QuerySupportLevels = { "WQL:UnarySelect" } ;
75:};
76:
77:instance of __Win32Provider as $EventProv
78:{
79:     Name = "MS_SNMP_REFERENT_EVENT_PROVIDER";
80:     ClsId = "{9D5BED16-0765-11d1-AB2C-00C04FD9159E}";
81:     HostingModel = "LocalSystemHost";
82:};
83:
84:instance of __EventProviderRegistration
85:{
86:     Provider = $EventProv;
87:     EventQueryList = {"select * from SnmpExtendedNotification"} ;
88:};
89:
90:instance of __Win32Provider as $EncapEventProv
91:{
92:     Name = "MS_SNMP_ENCAPSULATED_EVENT_PROVIDER";
93:     ClsId = "{19C813AC-FEE7-11D0-AB22-00C04FD9159E}";
94:     HostingModel = "LocalSystemHost";
95:};
96:
97:instance of __EventProviderRegistration
98:{
99:     Provider = $EncapEventProv;
100:     EventQueryList = {"select * from SnmpNotification"};
101:};
```

We compile this MOF file with **MOFCOMP.EXE**, as follows:

```
C:\>MOFCOMP.Exe Cisco-Brussels-snmpreg.mof
Microsoft (R) 32-bit MOF Compiler Version 1.50.1085.0007
Copyright (c) Microsoft Corp. 1997-1999. All rights reserved.

Parsing MOF file: Cisco-Brussels-snmpreg.mof
MOF file has been successfully parsed
Storing data in the repository...
Done!
```

Next, we can simply edit Sample 3.70 ("Obtaining localhost IP addresses from WMI via SNMP") and change line 25:

```
25:    Const cWMINameSpace = "Root/SNMP/LocalHost"
```

to the following line:

```
25:    Const cWMINameSpace = "Root/SNMP/CiscoBrussels"
```

and we will obtain the exact same output as Sample 3.71 ("Obtaining remote device IP addresses from WMI via SNMP"), which was using an **SWBemNamedValueSet** object to pass the SNMP parameters.

3.7.5.2   *Accessing SNMP private MIB information*

Because we access a Cisco router, it is clear that we may find some specific SNMP information that is not defined in the standard RFC 1213. This SNMP information is called the private MIB information and is defined in other MIB files published by Cisco. You can get the Cisco MIB files from http://www.cisco.com/public/sw-center/netmgmt/cmtk/mibs.shtml. To access the private MIB information from WMI, it is necessary to load the MIB file information into the CIM repository. This can be done with the MIB compiler delivered with WMI, called **SMI2SMIR.Exe**, which basically converts the Structure of Management Information (SMI) format to the Structure of Management Information Repository (SMIR) format. Simply said, this utility converts a MIB file into a MOF file loadable in the CIM repository. To locate the information you are interested in, it must be clear that the challenge is not about WMI anymore but is a pure SNMP issue. Knowing the SNMP representation of the device you want to manage is key!

A Cisco router has a lot of private MIB information. So let's take a very easy example of private MIB information. For those of you who are not familiar with the Cisco routers, you should know that the device contains a flash memory, which contains the Cisco Internetwork Operating System (IOS). The IOS is nothing but a binary file stored in this flash memory. If you execute a TELNET session on the Cisco router and execute the **show flash** command, you will see the IOS binary file loaded in the flash (see Figure 3.44).

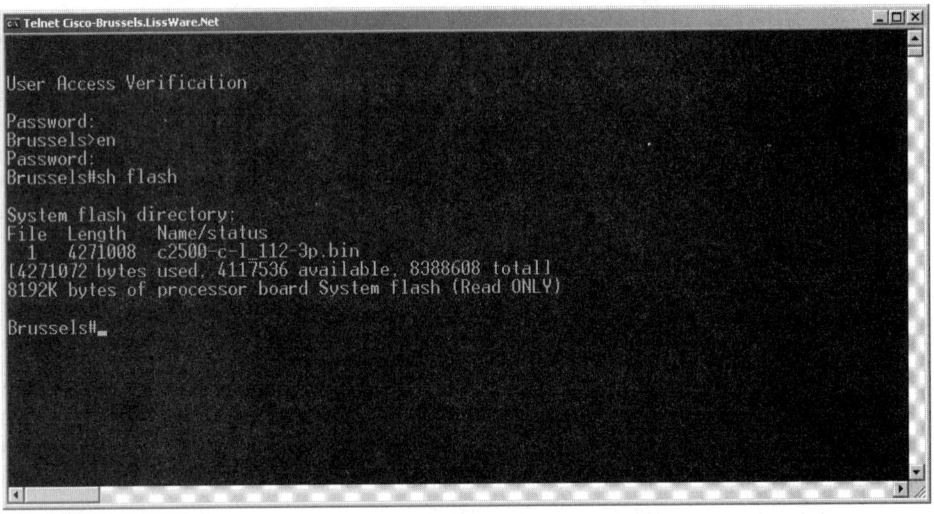

Figure 3.44   *The Cisco IOS loaded in the memory flash.*

As we can see in Figure 3.44, we have an IOS binary file, called "c2500-c-l_112-3p.bin," of 4,271,008 bytes (4,171 KB) size. The flash memory card has a total size of 8,388,608 bytes (8 MB). To retrieve this information from WMI via SNMP, we must a use a private Cisco MIB file. This MIB file is called **CISCO-FLASH-MIB.my** and is available from the Cisco Web site for download. To successfully convert the MIB file into a MOF file, we also need the **CISCO-SMI.my** MIB file, since it contains definitions used in **CISCO-FLASH-MIB.my**. The conversion to a MOF file can be created, as shown in Sample 3.73.

Sample 3.73   *Creating a private MIB in the CIM repository*

```
C:\>smi2smir /m 0 /g CISCO-FLASH-MIB.my CISCO-SMI.my > CISCO-FLASH-MIB.MOF

smi2smir : Version 1.50.1085.0000 : MIB definitions compiled from "CISCO-FLASH-MIB.my"

smi2smir : Syntax Check successful on "CISCO-FLASH-MIB.my"

smi2smir : Version 1.50.1085.0000 : MIB definitions compiled from "CISCO-SMI.my"

smi2smir : Syntax Check successful on "CISCO-SMI.my"
```

```
smi2smir : Semantic Check successful on "CISCO-FLASH-MIB.my"

smi2smir: Generated MOF successfully
```

Note the presence of the redirection ">" character on the command line. **SMI2SMIR.Exe** outputs the generated MOF on the screen. So, if you want this in a file, you must redirect the output. Table 3.70 shows the complete list of command-line parameters for **SMI2SMIR.Exe**.

Table 3.70   *The SMI2SMIR.Exe Command-Line Parameters*

smi2smir [<DiagnosticArgs>] [<VersionArgs>] [<IncludeDirs>] <CommandArgs> <MIB file> [<Import Files>]	
smi2smir [<DiagnosticArgs>] <RegistryArgs> [<Directory>]	
smi2smir <ModuleInfoArgs> <MIB file>	
smi2smir <HelpArgs>	
DiagnosticArgs:	
/m <diagnostic level>	Specifies the kind of diagnostics to display: 0 (silent), 1 (fatal), 2 (fatal and warning), or 3 (fatal, warning, and information messages).
/c <count>	Specifies the maximum number of fatal and warning messages to display.
VersionArgs:	
/v1	Specifies strict conformance to the SNMPv1 SMI.
/v2c	Specifies strict conformance to the SNMPv2 SMI.
CommandArgs:	
/d	Deletes the specified module from the SMIR.
/p	Deletes all modules in the SMIR.
/l	Lists all modules in the SMIR.
/lc	Performs a local syntax check on the module.
/ec [<CommandModifier>]	Performs local and external checks on the module.
/a [<CommandModifier>]	Performs local and external checks and loads the module into the SMIR.
/sa [<CommandModifier>]	Same as /a, but works silently.
/g [<CommandModifier>]	Generates a SMIR MOF file that can be loaded later into CIMOM (using the MOF compiler). Used by the SNMP class provider to dynamically provide classes to one or more namespaces.
/gc [<CommandModifier>]	Generates a static MOF file that can be loaded later into CIMOM as static classes for a particular namespace.
CommandModifiers:	
/ch	Generates context information (date, time, host, user, etc.) in the MOF file header. Use with /g and /gc.
/t	Also generates SnmpNotification classes. Use with /a, /sa, and /g.
/ext	Also generates SnmpExtendedNotification classes. Use with /a, /sa, and /g.
/t /o	Generates only SnmpNotification classes. Use with /a, /sa, and /g.
/ext /o	Generates only SnmpExtendedNotification classes. Use with /a, /sa, and /g.
/s	Does not map the text of the DESCRIPTION clause. Use with /a, /sa, /g, and /gc.
/auto	Rebuilds the MIB lookup table before completing <CommandArg> switch. Use with /ec, /a, /g, and /gc.
IncludeDirs:	
/i <directory>	Specifies a directory to be searched for dependent MIB modules. Use with /ec, /a, /sa, /g, and /gc.
RegistryArgs:	
/pa	Adds the specified directory to the registry (Default is current directory).
/pd	Deletes the specified directory from the registry (Default is current directory).
/pl	Lists the MIB lookup directories in the registry.
/r	Rebuilds the entire MIB lookup table.
ModuleInfoArgs:	
/n	Returns the ASN.1 name of the specified module.
/ni	Returns the ASN.1 names of all imports modules referenced by the input module.
HelpArgs:	
/h	Displays this usage information.
/?	Displays this usage information.

For auto-detection of dependent MIBs, the following values of type REG_MULTI_SZ must be set under the root key HKEY_LOCAL_MACHINE\SOFTWARE\Microsoft\WBEM\Providers\SNMP\Compiler:
  "File Path" : An ordered list of directory names where MIBs are located.
  "File Suffixes" : An ordered list of file extensions for MIB files.	

Once the MOF file generated, it is ready to be loaded in the CIM repository, as follows:

```
C:\>MOFCOMP.Exe CISCO-FLASH-MIB.MOF
Microsoft (R) 32-bit MOF Compiler Version 1.50.1085.0007
Copyright (c) Microsoft Corp. 1997-1999. All rights reserved.

Parsing MOF file: CISCO-FLASH-MIB.MOF
MOF file has been successfully parsed
Storing data in the repository...
Done!
```

Note that the MOF file will be loaded in the **Root\SNMP\SMIR** namespace. Once completed, the **Root\SNMP\CiscoBrussels** namespace should show WMI classes representing the Cisco Flash SNMP information, as shown in Figure 3.45. Ensure that the Cisco router is available on the network during this operation. If the Cisco router defined in the *AgentAddress* qualifier is not reachable, it is likely that the private MIB information stored in the MOF file will be improperly displayed.

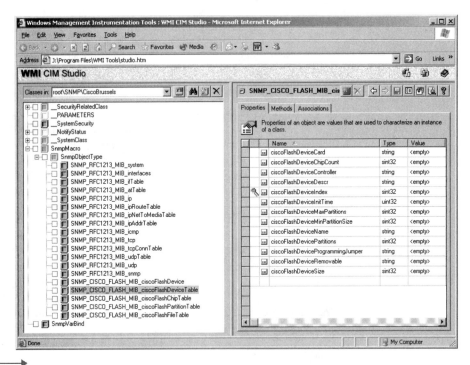

Figure 3.45   *The Cisco Flash SNMP classes in the CIM repository.*

If we reuse Sample 3.71 ("Obtaining remote device IP addresses from WMI via SNMP") and change line 27:

```
27:     Const cWMIClass = "SNMP_RFC1213_MIB_ipAddrTable"
```

to:

```
27:     Const cWMIClass = "SNMP_CISCO_FLASH_MIB_ciscoFlashFileTable"
```

we should obtain an output similar to this one:

```
 1:   C:\>GetSingleInstanceWithAPI2.wsf
 2:   Microsoft (R) Windows Script Host Version 5.6
 3:   Copyright (C) Microsoft Corporation 1996-2001. All rights reserved.
 4:
 5:
 6:   - SNMP_CISCO_FLASH_MIB_ciscoFlashFileTable -------------------------------------
 7:   *ciscoFlashDeviceIndex: ................. 1
 8:   ciscoFlashFileChecksum: .................. 3078424434
 9:   *ciscoFlashFileIndex: .................... 1
10:   ciscoFlashFileName: ...................... c2500-c-1_112-3p.bin
11:   ciscoFlashFileSize: ...................... 4271008
12:   ciscoFlashFileStatus: .................... valid
13:   *ciscoFlashPartitionIndex: ............... 1
```

We recognize the Cisco IOS binary file name (line 10) with its size (line 11), because we saw it in Figure 3.45. However, we do not see the flash memory size, because another WMI class, called *SNMP_CISCO_FLASH_MIB_ciscoFlashPartitionTable,* provides this information.

If the WMI classes representing the SNMP information are not shown, it is likely due to a feature part of the *SNMP* WMI providers called the correlation. Correlation might prevent you from seeing all classes that are actually supported by a device. In such a case, it could be wise to turn the correlation OFF. The side effect of turning correlation OFF is that many classes not supported by a device may appear in the SMIR. When correlation is turned ON, the *SNMP* provider causes an enumeration of device-supported classes, similar to the result of running an SNMP MIB walk operation. This could produce a performance cost in using correlation, because the device is queried to see what classes it supports. To set the correlation OFF, the *Correlate* parameter (or qualifier, if you use a dedicated namespace) set in the **SWbemNamedValueSet** object must be set to FALSE (OFF) or TRUE (ON). This value is set in Sample 3.71, line 38.

3.7.5.3   *Organizing the SNMP data access*

As we can see, based on the fact that the SNMP device is local or remote, uses a private MIB (i.e., Cisco device), and is WMI enabled (i.e., Windows computer), there are different options to access SNMP data. These various options can be quite confusing, since we have different ways of organizing the SNMP data in WMI and different protocols to access that information (i.e., RPC and SNMP). Let's try to summarize this with three figures showing the various options (see Figures 3.46 through 3.48).

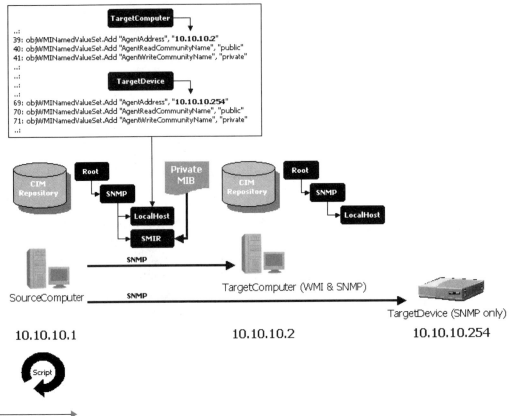

Figure 3.46   *Accessing SNMP data via the localhost namespace and the SWBemNamedValueSet object.*

The first option is the easiest one, since it consists of using the default SNMP CIM repository configuration and overriding some settings (i.e., *AgentAddress*) with an **SWBemNamedValueSet** object (see Figure 3.46) from the script. This technique gives the ability to access any SNMP device from any WMI computer in a Windows network, since no particular CIM repository customization is required. The developed script code can be run on any WMI computer. However, if some private MIB information must be accessed, it is necessary to load the related MIB information on a specific WMI system and connect the script to the WMI system where the private

MIB information is loaded. An important point to note in this scenario is that SNMP is the only protocol used to access the desired information across the network.

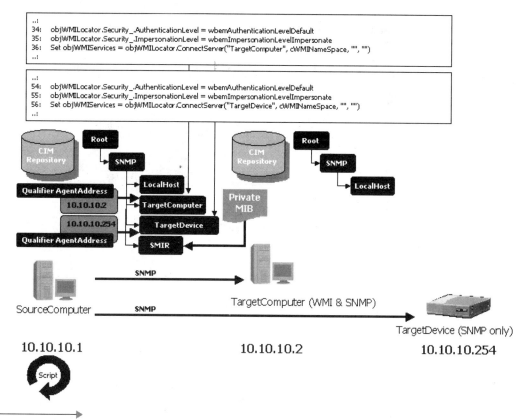

Figure 3.47   *Accessing SNMP data via a dedicated namespace on the localhost.*

The second technique consists of the creation of dedicated namespaces for each SNMP computer or device that must be accessed (see Figure 3.47). This technique requires a specific customization of the CIM repository and links the script to the system hosting the namespaces. Creating a dedicated namespace has the advantage of enabling the SNMP access to any tool running on top of WMI, since no specific logic is required to create an **SWBemNamedValueSet** object. Since all SNMP parameters are stored in the Qualifiers of the dedicated namespaces, any tool enumerating instances of the classes available in these namespaces will retrieve the SNMP information. As in the first case, the protocol used on the network is SNMP only. If some private MIB information must be accessed, the private MIB files must be loaded in the CIM repository.

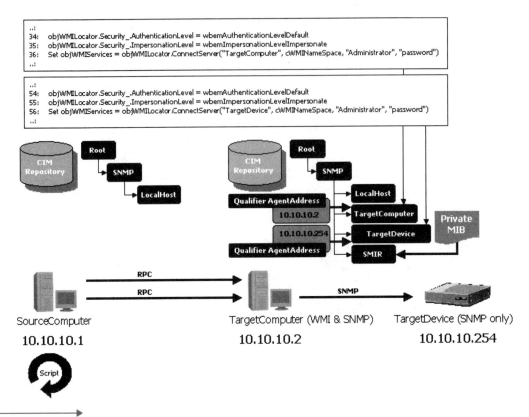

```
..:
34:   objWMILocator.Security_.AuthenticationLevel = wbemAuthenticationLevelDefault
35:   objWMILocator.Security_.ImpersonationLevel = wbemImpersonationLevelImpersonate
36:   Set objWMIServices = objWMILocator.ConnectServer("TargetComputer", cWMINameSpace, "Administrator", "password")
..:
```

```
..:
54:   objWMILocator.Security_.AuthenticationLevel = wbemAuthenticationLevelDefault
55:   objWMILocator.Security_.ImpersonationLevel = wbemImpersonationLevelImpersonate
56:   Set objWMIServices = objWMILocator.ConnectServer("TargetDevice", cWMINameSpace, "Administrator", "password")
..:
```

Figure 3.48   *Accessing SNMP data through a remote WMI computer via a dedicated namespace.*

The third technique is very similar to the second one (see Figure 3.48). However, in this case, the script code is run on a system where the dedicated namespaces are not available. Since WMI is COM/DCOM based, it is possible, by using the WMI scripting API (i.e., *ConnectServer* method of the **SWBemServices** object), to access a remote WMI host, which contains the dedicated namespace for the SNMP devices. Of course, as in the first technique, it is always possible to override the namespaces SNMP communication parameters in the remote hosts (Qualifiers) with an **SWBem-NamedValueSet** object. The interesting feature in this last case is that you must authenticate to the remote WMI system first (on top of the COM/DCOM mechanisms, which are RPC based) and then access the SNMP devices, as done previously (via the SNMP protocol). If some private MIB information must be accessed, the private MIB files must be loaded in the CIM repository of the remote WMI system.

3.7.5.4   Receiving SNMP traps

With the WMI *SNMP* providers it is possible to receive SNMP traps or notifications in addition to simply retrieving SNMP information. If you remember, in the beginning of this section, we mentioned that the *SNMP* providers are also implemented as event providers. We must distinguish two event provider types:

- **SNMP Encapsulated Event provider (SEEP):** The encapsulated provider means that the event instance has simple properties describing the information mapped directly from the SNMP trap. This corresponds to the *SnmpNotification* parent class with its subclasses.

- **SNMP Referent Event provider (SREP):** The referent provider abstracts the information present within the SNMP trap so that properties that share the same class and instance are presented as embedded objects. This allows for the unique instance, with which the trap is associated, to be retrieved after the receipt of the event, using the SNMP *__RELPATH*. This corresponds to the *SnmpExtendedNotification* parent class with its subclasses.

In both cases, the same information is provided. Only the manner in which this information is presented and structured is different.

Figure 3.40 shows the event classes (left pane) supported by the *SNMP* event provider. The *SNMP* event providers support three types of traps or notifications:

- **Generic:** These traps correspond to events such as link up and cold start. These traps are listed in Table 3.68. These classes are subclasses of the *SnmpNotification* and *SnmpExtendedNotification* classes.

- **Enterprise specific:** These traps correspond to events that are represented by a WMI class that is not a subclass of the *SnmpNotification* and *SnmpExtendedNotification* classes. To support enterprise-specific traps and notifications, an event consumer must define classes in the CIM repository by compiling MIB definitions using the SNMP MIB compiler (such as that made for the Cisco device to retrieve private MIB information about the memory flash but related to traps or notifications).

- **Enterprise nonspecific:** These traps do not correspond to any of the generic event types or enterprise-specific event types. Nonenterprise-specific traps and notifications do not have their MIB definitions compiled into the SMIR. These traps are listed in Table 3.68.

We can use the Cisco router to show how to capture traps sent by the device at startup. To monitor SNMP traps, we will reuse Sample 6.17 ("A generic script for asynchronous event notification") in the appendix). This would generate the following result:

```
 1:   C:\>GenericEventAsyncConsumer.wsf "Select * From SnmpColdStartNotification
                         Where AgentAddress='10.10.10.253'" /Namespace:Root\SNMP\CiscoBrussel
 2:   Microsoft (R) Windows Script Host Version 5.6
 3:   Copyright (C) Microsoft Corporation 1996-2001. All rights reserved.
 4:
 5:   Waiting for events...
 6:
 7:   BEGIN - OnObjectReady.
 8:   Saturday, 02 February, 2002 at 16:05:16: 'SnmpColdStartNotification' has been triggered.
 9:
10:       - SnmpColdStartNotification ----------------------------------------------------
11:       AgentAddress: ......................... 10.10.10.253
12:       AgentTransportAddress: ................ 10.10.10.253
13:       AgentTransportProtocol: .............. IP
14:       Community: ........................... public
15:       Identification: ...................... 1.3.6.1.6.3.1.1.5.1
16:       TIME_CREATED: ........................ 02-02-2002 15:05:16 (20020202150516.010497+060)
17:       TimeStamp: ........................... 1096
18:
19:   END - OnObjectReady.
20:
21:   BEGIN - OnObjectReady.
22:   Saturday, 02 February, 2002 at 16:05:18: 'SnmpColdStartNotification' has been triggered.
23:
24:       - SnmpColdStartNotification ----------------------------------------------------
25:       AgentAddress: ......................... 10.10.10.253
26:       AgentTransportAddress: ................ 10.10.10.253
27:       AgentTransportProtocol: .............. IP
28:       Community: ........................... public
29:       Identification: ...................... 1.3.6.1.6.3.1.1.5.1
30:       TIME_CREATED: ........................ 02-02-2002 15:05:18 (20020202150518.010497+060)
31:       TimeStamp: ........................... 1096
32:
33:   END - OnObjectReady.
```

Since the purpose is to receive traps related to the device startup, the WQL event query uses the *SnmpColdStartNotification* event class. We see in the previous output sample that the Cisco device sends two traps (lines 7 through 19 and lines 21 through 33). Because the *SnmpColdStartNotification* class is a generic trap representation coming from RFC 1215, we get the strict minimum information about the Cisco device itself. The dotted number contained in the *Identification* property (line 29) is the OID number used by the SNMP trap *coldStart*.

To get the SNMP trap-specific information without searching for the corresponding Cisco MIB (enterprise-specific traps), we can use a trick. This trick is not the ideal solution (the ideal solution will be the use of the specific Cisco MIB file), but when we must deal with a device for which very little information is available, this work-around can save a lot of time while giving a fairly usable solution. For this we must modify a definition made in the CIM repository in the **Root\SNMP\SMIR** namespace and enhance a portion of the script code.

In the **Root\SNMP\SMIR** namespace, there is a class called the *NotificationMapper* class. This class has several instances that correspond to the SNMP event standard classes. As we can see in Figure 3.49, among several instances, we have an instance with the OID number 1.3.6.1.6.3.1.1.5.1 in correspondence with the *SnmpColdStartNotification* event class.

Figure 3.49
The Notification-Mapper instances.

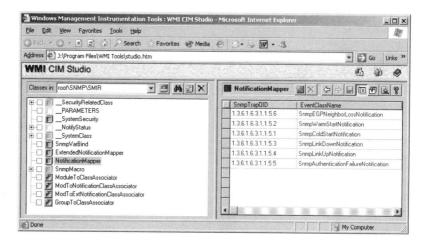

If a trap is received by WMI for which there is no corresponding SNMP event class for the received OID number, then WMI triggers an extrinsic event with the *SnmpV1Notification* or *SnmpV2Notification* event class. This corresponds to an enterprise nonspecific trap. If we delete the instance using the OID number 1.3.6.1.6.3.1.1.5.1, then WMI will not be able to map the received trap to the generic *SnmpColdStartNotification* event class. In such a case, as explained, WMI will map the trap to the *SnmpV1Notification* or *SnmpV2Notification* event class. Now, if we take a closer look at the *SnmpV1Notification* or *SnmpV2Notification* classes (Figure 3.50), we see the *VarBindList* property, which is an array of *SnmpVarBind* objects.

The *SnmpVarBind* class is shown in Figure 3.51.

As we can see, this class exposes three properties, called *Encoding*, *Object-Identifier*, and *Value*, where the *Value* property is an array of integers. This is an important detail and we will see how to read this information when examining Sample 3.75.

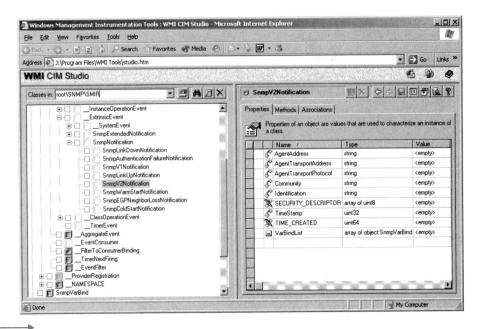

Figure 3.50   *The SnmpV2Notification class and the varBindList property.*

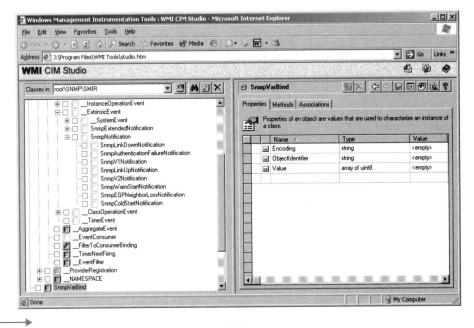

Figure 3.51   *The SnmpVarBind class is an array of object instances.*

Now that the *NotificationMapper* instance using the OID number 1.3.6.1.6.3.1.1.5.1 is deleted and before examining the code, let's see the result when the Cisco router sends the same traps as before (*coldStart*).

```
 1:   C:\>GenericEventAsyncConsumer.wsf "Select * From SnmpV2Notification
                       Where AgentAddress='10.10.10.253'" /Namespace:Root\SNMP\CiscoBrussels
 2:   Microsoft (R) Windows Script Host Version 5.6
 3:   Copyright (C) Microsoft Corporation 1996-2001. All rights reserved.
 4:
 5:   Waiting for events...
 6:
 7:   BEGIN - OnObjectReady.
 8:   Saturday, 02 February, 2002 at 17:47:38: 'SnmpV2Notification' has been triggered.
 9:      AgentAddress (wbemCimtypeString) = 10.10.10.253
10:      AgentTransportAddress (wbemCimtypeString) = 10.10.10.253
11:      AgentTransportProtocol (wbemCimtypeString) = IP
12:      Community (wbemCimtypeString) = public
13:      Identification (wbemCimtypeString) = 1.3.6.1.6.3.1.1.5.1
14:      SECURITY_DESCRIPTOR (wbemCimtypeUint8) = (null)
15:      TIME_CREATED (wbemCimtypeUint64) = 02-02-2002 16:47:38 (20020202164738.823428+060)
16:      TimeStamp (wbemCimtypeUint32) = 1096
17:      1.3.6.1.2.1.1.3.0 (TimeTicks) = 1095
18:      1.3.6.1.4.1.9.2.1.2.0 (OCTET STRING) = reload
19:      1.3.6.1.3.1057.1 (IpAddress) = 10.10.10.253
20:      1.3.6.1.6.3.1.1.4.3.0 (OBJECT IDENTIFIER) = 1.3.6.1.4.1.9.1.19
21:
22:   END - OnObjectReady.
23:
24:   BEGIN - OnObjectReady.
25:   Saturday, 02 February, 2002 at 17:47:39: 'SnmpV2Notification' has been triggered.
26:      AgentAddress (wbemCimtypeString) = 10.10.10.253
27:      AgentTransportAddress (wbemCimtypeString) = 10.10.10.253
28:      AgentTransportProtocol (wbemCimtypeString) = IP
29:      Community (wbemCimtypeString) = public
30:      Identification (wbemCimtypeString) = 1.3.6.1.6.3.1.1.5.1
31:      SECURITY_DESCRIPTOR (wbemCimtypeUint8) = (null)
32:      TIME_CREATED (wbemCimtypeUint64) = 02-02-2002 16:47:39 (20020202164739.013702+060)
33:      TimeStamp (wbemCimtypeUint32) = 1100
34:      1.3.6.1.2.1.1.3.0 (TimeTicks) = 1099
35:      1.3.6.1.4.1.9.2.1.2.0 (OCTET STRING) = reload
36:      1.3.6.1.3.1057.1 (IpAddress) = 10.10.10.253
37:      1.3.6.1.6.3.1.1.4.3.0 (OBJECT IDENTIFIER) = 1.3.6.1.4.1.9.1.19
38:
39:   END - OnObjectReady.
```

The result now displays the information contained in the *SnmpVarBind* instances, which are themselves contained in the *varBindList* array made of a collection of instances. For example, at lines 18 and 35, we see the OID number 1.3.6.1.4.1.9.2.1.2.0. This number corresponds to specific Cisco private MIB information. If you examine the Cisco documentation, you will discover that this SNMP information shows the reason for the last device reboot. In this case, since we used the Cisco **reload** command, we see the text "reload" (lines 18 and 35). To translate Cisco MIB OID numbers

to a readable form (1.3.6.1.4.1.9.2.1.2.0 to *whyReload*), you can also use the
following URL: http://jaguar.ir.miami.edu/%7Emarcus/snmptrans.html.

The script we use to display this information is still Sample 6.17 ("A
generic script for asynchronous event notification") in the appendix. However, at line 112 (see the following extract), this script invokes the Display-
Properties() function from the sink routine (the DisplayProperties()
function is available in Sample 4.30, "A generic routine to display the
SWbemPropertySet object" in the appendix).

```
1:<?xml version="1.0"?>
 .:
8:<package>
9:  <job>
10:
11:    <?job error="True" debug="True" ?>
12:
13:    <runtime>
..:
19:    </runtime>
20:
21:    <script language="VBScript" src=".\Functions\DisplayInstanceProperties (With SNMP).vbs" />
22:    <script language="VBScript" src=".\Functions\TinyErrorHandler.vbs" />
23:    <script language="VBScript" src=".\Functions\PauseScript.vbs" />
24:
25:    <object progid="WbemScripting.SWbemLocator" id="objWMILocator" reference="true"/>
26:    <object progid="WbemScripting.SWbemDateTime" id="objWMIDateTime" />
27:
28:    <script language="VBscript">
29:    <![CDATA[
..:
33:    ' -----------------------------------------------------------------------------
34:    Const cComputerName = "LocalHost"
35:    Const cWMINameSpace = "Root/cimv2"
...:
103:    ' -----------------------------------------------------------------------------
104:    Sub SINK_OnObjectReady (objWbemObject, objWbemAsyncContext)
105:
106:        Wscript.Echo
107:        Wscript.Echo "BEGIN - OnObjectReady."
108:        WScript.Echo FormatDateTime(Date, vbLongDate) & " at " & _
109:                     FormatDateTime(Time, vbLongTime) & ": '" & _
110:                     objWbemObject.Path_.Class & "' has been triggered."
111:
112:        DisplayProperties objWbemObject, 2
113:        Wscript.Echo
114:
115:        Wscript.Echo "END - OnObjectReady."
116:
117:    End Sub
118:
...:
127:
128:    ]]>
129:    </script>
130:  </job>
131:</package>
```

To display the *SnmpVarBind* instances, we updated the DisplayProperties() function accordingly. The code is shown in Sample 3.74. The code of this updated subroutine starts as the original one (lines 14 through 30). The only change made in the DisplayProperties() function concerns the test of the property name (line 31) and the invocation of the DisplaySNMPBindings() function (line 32), if the property is the *VarBindList* property exposed by the *SnmpV1Notification* or *SnmpV2Notification* classes.

Sample 3.74   *The updated DisplayProperties() function to display the SnmpVarBind instances*

```
 .:
 6:' -----------------------------------------------------------------------------------------
 7:Function DisplayProperties (objWMIInstance, intIndent)
..:
14:      Set objWMIPropertySet = objWMIInstance.Properties_
15:      For Each objWMIProperty In objWMIPropertySet
16:
17:          boolCIMKey = objWMIProperty.Qualifiers_.Item("key").Value
18:          If Err.Number Then
19:             Err.Clear
20:             boolCIMKey = False
21:          End If
22:          If boolCIMKey Then
23:             strCIMKey = "*"
24:          Else
25:             strCIMKey = ""
26:          End If
27:
28:          If Not IsNull (objWMIProperty.Value) Then
29:             If objWMIProperty.CIMType = wbemCimtypeObject Then
30:                If objWMIProperty.IsArray Then
31:                   If objWMIProperty.Name = "VarBindList" Then
32:                      DisplaySNMPBindings objWMIProperty, intIndent
33:                   Else
34:                      For Each varElement In objWMIProperty.Value
35:                         WScript.Echo Space (intIndent) & strCIMKey & objWMIProperty.Name & _
36:                                      " (" & GetCIMSyntaxText (objWMIProperty.CIMType) & ")"
37:                         DisplayProperties varElement, intIndent + 2
38:                      Next
39:                   End If
40:                Else
41:                   WScript.Echo Space (intIndent) & strCIMKey & objWMIProperty.Name & _
42:                                " (" & GetCIMSyntaxText (objWMIProperty.CIMType) & ")"
43:                   DisplayProperties objWMIProperty.Value, intIndent + 2
44:                End If
45:             Else
..:
75:             End If
76:          Else
..:
79:          End If
80:      Next
..:
83:End Function
84:
..:
..:
..:
```

Next, if the property matches the *varBindList* property, Sample 3.75, which contains the DisplaySNMPBindings() function, is executed.

Sample 3.75   *The DisplaySNMPBindings() function to display the SnmpVarBind instances*

```
 ..:
 ..:
 ..:
 84:
 85:' ----------------------------------------------------------------------------------------
 86:Function DisplaySNMPBindings (varBindList, intIndent)
 ..:
 96:     For Each varBindElement In varBindList.Value
 97:         Set objWMIPropertySet = varBindElement.Properties_
 98:
 99:         varSNMPValue = ""
100:
101:         For Each objWMIProperty In objWMIPropertySet
102:             Select Case objWMIProperty.Name
103:                 Case "Encoding"
104:                     strSNMPEncoding = objWMIProperty.Value
105:
106:                 Case "ObjectIdentifier"
107:                     strSNMPOID = objWMIProperty.Value
108:
109:                 Case "Value"
110:                     Select Case strSNMPEncoding
111:                         Case "TimeTicks"
112:                             varSNMPValue = objWMIProperty.Value(0) + _
113:                                 objWMIProperty.Value(1) * 256 + _
114:                                 objWMIProperty.Value(2) * 256 * 256 + _
115:                                 objWMIProperty.Value(3) * 256 * 256 * 256
116:                         Case "INTEGER"
117:                             varSNMPValue = objWMIProperty.Value(0) + _
118:                                 objWMIProperty.Value(1) * 256 + _
119:                                 objWMIProperty.Value(2) * 256 * 256 + _
120:                                 objWMIProperty.Value(3) * 256 * 256 * 256
121:                         Case "OCTET STRING"
122:                             For Each varElement In objWMIProperty.Value
123:                                 varSNMPValue = varSNMPValue & Chr(varElement)
124:                             Next
125:                         Case "IpAddress"
126:                             For Each varElement In objWMIProperty.Value
127:                                 If Len (varSNMPValue) = 0 Then
128:                                     varSNMPValue = varElement
129:                                 Else
130:                                     varSNMPValue = varSNMPValue & "." & varElement
131:                                 End If
132:                             Next
133:                         Case "OBJECT IDENTIFIER"
134:                             For intIndice=0 to Ubound (objWMIProperty.Value) Step 4
135:                                 varElement = objWMIProperty.Value(0 + intIndice) + _
136:                                     objWMIProperty.Value(1 + intIndice) * 256 + _
137:                                     objWMIProperty.Value(2 + intIndice) * 256 * 256 + _
138:                                     objWMIProperty.Value(3 + intIndice) * 256 * 256 * 256
139:                                 If Len (varSNMPValue) = 0 Then
140:                                     varSNMPValue = varElement
141:                                 Else
```

```
142:                                        varSNMPValue = varSNMPValue & "." & varElement
143:                                End If
144:                            Next
145:                    Case Else
146:                        varSNMPValue "<unknown coding>"
147:
148:                End Select
149:
150:            Case Else
151:
152:        End Select
153:        Next
154:        Set objWMIPropertySet = Nothing
155:
156:        WScript.Echo strSNMPOID & " (" & strSNMPEncoding & ") = " & varSNMPValue
157:
158:    Next
159:
160:End Function
...:
...:
...:
```

Because the *VarBindList* property is an array, the values of this property are enumerated (lines 96 through 158). Next, since each of these values is an object made from the *SnmpVarBind* class, the script extracts the properties of the examined *SnmpVarBind* instance (line 97). As we have done many times now, each property is enumerated in a loop for further examination (lines 101 through 153). Based on the property name of the *Snmp-VarBind* instance (line 102), the value of the property is retrieved accordingly (lines 103, 106, and 109). To retrieve the value of the *Value* property, some special care must be taken. Because the *SnmpVarBind* properties enumeration retrieves the encoding type of the *Value* property from the *Encoding* property (line 104), the script uses an appropriate decoding technique based on the value of the *Encoding* property (lines 110 through 148). Four encoding types are considered:

- **TIMETICKS:** The TIMETICKS encoding is a value made up of 4 bytes. Lines 112 through 115 calculate the corresponding value.

- **INTEGER:** The INTEGER encoding is an integer. Lines 117 through 120 calculate the corresponding value.

- **OCTET STRING:** The OCTET STRING is an array of bytes. Lines 112 through 124 concatenate each byte of the array in one single string.

- **IpAddress:** The IpAddress is an array of bytes. Lines 126 through 131 concatenate each byte of the array in one single dotted string to represent a well-formatted IP address.

- **OBJECT IDENTIFIER**: The OBJECT IDENTIFIER is an array of bytes, where each 4 bytes represent an integer. Lines 134 through 144 calculate the value of the integer and concatenate each value in one single dotted string to represent a well-formatted OID number.

Once the value extraction and formatting are completed, the script displays the SNMP information in a readable form (line 156).

3.7.5.5 *Sending SNMP commands*

If it is possible to read SNMP data from an SNMP-enabled device, it is also possible to write some information via SNMP. Of course, the device managed with SNMP must support a set of SNMP commands. Again, we need the SNMP knowledge and information available from the device itself. For example, with the Cisco router we used in the previous examples, it is possible to send an SNMP command to reload the device. Of course, the router must be configured properly at the SNMP level to accept such a command for obvious security reasons. Figure 3.43 ("Enabling SNMP on your Cisco router") shows the Cisco router SNMP configuration to access the device via SNMP. However, in order to make the Cisco router accept an SNMP reload command, it is necessary to add the following statements:

```
1:   snmp-server community private RW
2:   snmp-server system-shutdown
```

Line 1 is already part of the configuration shown in Figure 3.43 and defines the community string for SNMP write operations. However, line 2 is mandatory to reboot the Cisco router via SNMP. Of course, the primary goal is not to demonstrate how to reboot active network devices via SNMP but to show how, from a script written on top of WMI, it is possible to send an SNMP command to an SNMP-enabled device, where the SNMP command is defined in a private MIB of a manufacturer. The overall principle will always be the same despite the device used.

First of all, because the **Reboot** command is defined in a private MIB of Cisco, it is necessary to convert the desired MIB to a MOF file. The SNMP **reload** command definition is defined in the **OLD-CISCO-TS-MIB.My** MIB. This MIB, similar to the one we used previously, is also available from the Cisco Web site. As we did previously, the MIB file must be converted to a MOF file with the following command line:

```
C:\>smi2smir /g OLD-CISCO-TS-MIB.My CISCO-SMI.my > OLD-CISCO-TS-MIB.Mof
```

Next, in order to make this SNMP information available to WMI, the generated MOF file must be loaded in the CIM repository with **MOF-COMP.EXE**:

```
C:\>MOFCOMP OLD-CISCO-TS-MIB.Mof
Microsoft (R) 32-bit MOF Compiler Version 5.1.3590.0
Copyright (c) Microsoft Corp. 1997-2001. All rights reserved.
Parsing MOF file: OLD-CISCO-TS-MIB.Mof
MOF file has been successfully parsed
Storing data in the repository...
Done!
```

Figure 3.52 shows the WMI class result obtained from the private MIB conversion.

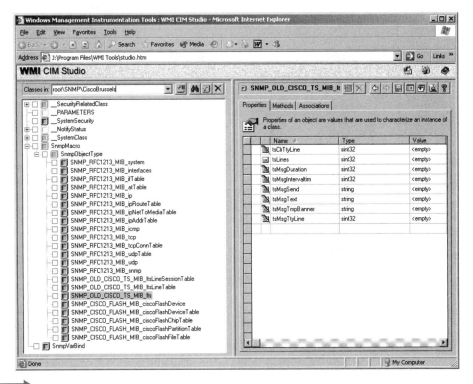

Figure 3.52   *The SNMP_OLD_CISCO_TS_MIB_lts class to send SNMP commands to a Cisco device (SNMP-enabled).*

The SNMP class to send SNMP commands to the device is called *SNMP_OLD_CISCO_TS_MIB_lts*. This class exposes a property called *tsMsgSend*. Basically, by looking at the MIB file, the *tsMsgSend* supports four parameters:

```
tsMsgSend OBJECT-TYPE
    SYNTAX  INTEGER {
        nothing(1),
        reload(2),
        messagedone(3),
        abort(4)
```

```
        }
        ACCESS   read-write
        STATUS   mandatory
        DESCRIPTION
                "Sends the message. The value determines what
                to do after the message has completed."
        ::= { lts 9 }
```

These parameters are also shown in the MOF file generated from the
SMI2SMIR.EXE conversion or from **WMI CIM Studio** by looking at the
enumeration qualifier (see Figure 3.53). The interesting parameter for our
purpose is the *Reload* parameter.

Figure 3.53
*The tsMsgSend
property qualifiers.*

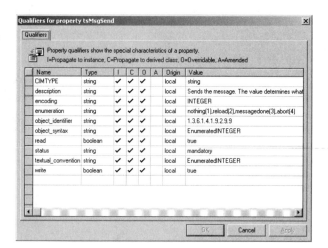

Of course, it must be clear that a perfect knowledge of the SNMP capabilities of the device is a requirement to find out which information to use
to perform the desired management tasks. As mentioned previously, you
must refer to your device manufacturer if you need support to locate the
desired information.

How to proceed? In theory, the goal is simple: A script must create an
instance of the *SNMP_OLD_CISCO_TS_MIB_lts* class and store the
"Reload" value into the *tsMsgSend* property. Next, the script will commit
the updated instance back to the CIM repository. The end result will create an SNMP write operation to the corresponding MIB property, which
will reload the Cisco router. In practice, things are less simple, since some
details must be taken into consideration, especially when saving the
updated instance back to the CIM repository. The logic is implemented in
Sample 3.76.

Sample 3.76 *Sending SNMP commands*

```
 1:<?xml version="1.0"?>
 .:
 8:<package>
 9:  <job>
..:
13:    <script language="VBScript" src="..\Functions\TinyErrorHandler.vbs" />
14:
15:    <object progid="WbemScripting.SWbemLocator" id="objWMILocator" reference="true"/>
16:    <object progid="WbemScripting.SWBemNamedValueSet" id="objWMINamedValueSet" />
17:
18:    <script language="VBscript">
19:    <![CDATA[
..:
23:    Const cComputerName = "LocalHost"
24:    Const cWMINameSpace = "Root/SNMP/CiscoBrussels"
25:    Const cWMIClass = "SNMP_OLD_CISCO_TS_MIB_lts"
..:
33:    objWMILocator.Security_.AuthenticationLevel = wbemAuthenticationLevelDefault
34:    objWMILocator.Security_.ImpersonationLevel = wbemImpersonationLevelImpersonate
35:    Set objWMIServices = objWMILocator.ConnectServer(cComputerName, cWMINameSpace, "", "")
..:
38:    objWMINamedValueSet.Add "Correlate", True
39:    objWMINamedValueSet.Add "AgentAddress", "Cisco-Brussels.LissWare.Net"
40:    objWMINamedValueSet.Add "AgentFlowControlWindowSize", 3
41:    objWMINamedValueSet.Add "AgentReadCommunityName", "public"
42:    objWMINamedValueSet.Add "AgentRetryCount", 1
43:    objWMINamedValueSet.Add "AgentRetryTimeout", 500
44:    objWMINamedValueSet.Add "AgentVarBindsPerPdu", 10
45:    objWMINamedValueSet.Add "AgentWriteCommunityName", "private"
46:
47:    Set objWMISNMPInstance = objWMIServices.Get(cWMIClass & "=@")
..:
50:    objWMISNMPInstance.tsMsgSend = "Reload"
51:
52:    objWMINamedValueSet.Add "__PUT_EXTENSIONS", True
53:    objWMINamedValueSet.Add "__PUT_EXT_CLIENT_REQUEST", True
54:    objWMINamedValueSet.Add "__PUT_EXT_PROPERTIES", Array ("tsMsgSend")
55:
56:    objWMISNMPInstance.Put_ wbemChangeFlagUpdateOnly Or wbemFlagReturnWhenComplete, _
57:                       objWMINamedValueSet
58:    If Err.Number Then
59:       WScript.Echo "0x" & Hex(Err.Number) & " - " & Err.Description & vbCRLF
60:
61:       Set objWMILastError = CreateObject("wbemscripting.swbemlasterror")
62:       WScript.Echo "Description: " & objWMILastError.Description
63:       WScript.Echo "Operation: " & objWMILastError.Operation
64:       WScript.Echo "ParameterInfo: " & objWMILastError.ParameterInfo
65:       WScript.Echo "ProviderName: " & objWMILastError.ProviderName
66:       WScript.Echo "SnmpStatusCode: 0x" & Hex (objWMILastError.SnmpStatusCode)
67:       WScript.Echo "StatusCode: 0x" & Hex(objWMILastError.StatusCode)
68:       WScript.Echo "Operation: " & objWMILastError.Operation
69:       WScript.Echo "ParameterInfo: " & objWMILastError.ParameterInfo
70:       WScript.Echo "ProviderName: " & objWMILastError.ProviderName
..:
73:       WScript.Quit (1)
74:    End If
```

```
75:
76:    WScript.Echo "Cisco router successfully reloaded."
..:
81:    ]]>
82:    </script>
83:   </job>
84:</package>
```

From line 33 through 35, Sample 3.76 executes the WMI connection to
the CIM repository. Next, from line 38 through 45, it sets up an **SWBem-
NamedValueSet** object defining the SNMP connection parameters (as
shown in Sample 3.71). Note the assignment of the *AgentWriteCommuni-
tyName* property (line 45) with a valid community string to perform an
SNMP write operation. Next, the *SNMP_OLD_CISCO_TS_MIB_lts*
instance is created (line 47) and the "Reload" value is assigned to the *tsMsg-
Send* property (line 50). The important and interesting point concerns the
scripting technique used to save the updated instance back to the CIM
repository (lines 52 through 57). This technique uses the partial-instance
update technique previously used in section 3.6.1.1, "Creating and updating objects in Active Directory." It is mandatory to commit the change in
this way to the CIM repository, because only the *tsMsgSend* property must
be written. Note that trying to save the complete instance to the CIM
repository will make the *Put_* method invocation fail. If an SNMP error
occurs, it is possible to retrieve some extra information by using the
SWbemLastError object, discussed in Chapter 5 of the first book, *Understanding WMI Scripting*. For example, if the statement "snmp-server system-
shutdown" is omitted in the Cisco configuration, the error returned will be
as follows:

```
1:    C:\>ReloadCisco.Wsf
2:    Microsoft (R) Windows Script Host Version 5.6
3:    Copyright (C) Microsoft Corporation 1996-2001. All rights reserved.
4:
5:    0x80041001 - Generic failure
6:
7:    Description: Agent reported Bad Value for property 'tsMsgSend'
8:    Operation: PutInstance
9:    ParameterInfo:
10:   ProviderName: MS_SNMP_INSTANCE_PROVIDER
11:   SnmpStatusCode: 0x80041030
12:   StatusCode: 0x80041001
13:   Operation: PutInstance
14:   ParameterInfo:
15:   ProviderName: MS_SNMP_INSTANCE_PROVIDER
```

If everything is properly set up, the SNMP command will be sent to the
Cisco device, which will be reloaded. Note that the Cisco router sends an
SNMP trap after receiving this SNMP command. It is always possible to

enhance Sample 3.76 to capture the SNMP trap message confirming the successful reload of the router.

3.7.5.6   *Debugging SNMP providers*

In the previous example we saw that the **SWbemLastError** object provides some extra information about the last WMI error. However, when working with SNMP devices, it is not always easy to troubleshoot the installation to determine the cause of the problem. A nice feature coming with the WMI SNMP implementation is the ability to trace the *SNMP* provider activity. Basically, the tracing activity setup is the same as the *Active Directory* providers' tracing activity. It uses the same registry key values (see Table 3.53, "Enabling the Trace Logging of a WMI Provider") but in a different registry hive:

```
HKLM\SOFTWARE\Microsoft\WBEM\PROVIDERS\Logging\WBEMSNMP
```

The value to use for the *Level* registry key takes an integer value from 0 through $2^{32} - 1$. The value is a logical mask consisting of 32 bits. Table 3.71 shows the bit masks to define the type of debugging output to be generated. By default, the information is contained in the **SWBEM-SNMP.LOG** file.

Table 3.71   *The SNMP Debugging Output Level*

Bits	Description
0	SNMP class provider **SWbemServices** object method invocations
1	SNMP class provider implementation
2	SNMP instance provider **SWbemServices** object method invocations
3	SNMP instance provider implementation
4	SNMP class library
5	SNMP SMIR
6	SNMP correlator
7	SNMP type mapping code
8	SNMP threading code
9	SNMP event provider interfaces and implementation

With a *Level* value of 35 when executing Sample 3.76 ("Sending SNMP commands"), the resulting trace is as follows:

```
 1: CImpClasProv::GetObjectAsync ( (SNMP_OLD_CISCO_TS_MIB_lts) )
 2: SnmpClassGetAsyncEventObject :: SnmpClassGetAsyncEventObject ()
 3: SnmpClassGetAsyncEventObject :: Process ()
 4: SnmpClassGetEventObject :: ProcessClass ( WbemSnmpErrorObject &a_errorObject )
 5: SnmpClassGetAsyncEventObject :: ReceiveClass ( IWbemClassObject *classObject )
 6: Returning from SnmpClassGetEventObject :: ProcessClass ( WbemSnmpErrorObject &a_errorObject (0))
 7: SnmpClassGetAsyncEventObject :: ReceiveComplete ()
 8: Reaping Task
 9: Deleting (this)
10: Returning from SnmpClassGetAsyncEventObject :: Receive4 ()
11: Returning from SnmpClassGetAsyncEventObject :: Process ()
12: WbemSnmpErrorObject :: SetMessage ( () )
```

```
13: SnmpClassGetAsyncEventObject :: ~SnmpClassGetAsyncEventObject ()
14: Sending Status
15: Returning from SnmpClassGetAsyncEventObject :: ~SnmpClassGetAsyncEventObject ()
16: Returning from CImpClasProv::GetObjectAsync ( (SNMP_OLD_CISCO_TS_MIB_lts) ) with Result = (0)
```

3.8   Performance providers

3.8.1   High-performance providers

High-performance providers are implemented as instance providers. However, without going into the implementation details of *High-performance* providers, the major difference from standard instance providers is that they run as an in-process component of WMI or an application. (See Table 3.72.) The aim of a *High-performance* provider is to monitor data sent to the System Monitor of Windows 2000 or later. Having a *High-performance* provider has the advantage of not having WMI call the *Performance Counter* provider, which in turn, calls the performance library to collect the data. Basically, *High-performance* providers remove that layer, which greatly improves performance.

Table 3.72   *The High-Performance Providers Capabilities*

Provider Name	Provider namespace	Class Provider	Instance Provider	Method Provider	Property Provider	Event Provider	Event Consumer Provider	Support Get	Support Put	Support Enumeration	Support Delete	Windows Server 2003	Windows XP	Windows 2000 Server	Windows 2000 Professional	Windows NT 4.0
High Performance Providers																
HiPerfCooker_v1	Root/WMI		X					X		X		X	X			
HiPerfCooker_v1	Root/CIMV2		X					X		X		X	X			
NT5_GenericPerfProvider_V1	Root/CIMV2		X					X		X		X	X	X	X	

We must distinguish between two different *High-performance* providers in Windows:

- The *Performance Counter* provider, which provides access to the raw counters data. This provider is only available in Windows 2000 and later. Its name is *NT5_GenericPerfProvider_V1*. It is available in the **Root\CIMv2** namespace. The *Performance Counter* provider supports a set of classes derived from the *Win32_PerfRawData* class (see Table 3.73).

- The *Cooked Counter* provider, which provides calculated counter data. This provider is only available under Windows XP or Windows

Table 3.73   *The Win32_PerfRawData Classes*

Name	Comments
Win32_PerfRawData_PerfProc_JobObjectDetails	% Job object Details shows detailed performance information about the active processes that make up a Job object.
Win32_PerfRawData_ASPNET_ASPNETApplications	ASP.NET Application performance counters
Win32_PerfRawData_ASPNET_ASPNET	ASP.NET global performance counters
Win32_PerfRawData_ASPNET_10321514_ASPNETAppsv10321514	ASP.NET v1.0.3215.14 application performance counters
Win32_PerfRawData_ASPNET_10321514_ASPNETv10321514	ASP.NET v1.0.3215.14 global performance counters
Win32_PerfRawData_NTDS_NTDS	CIM_StatisticalInformation is a root class for any arbitrary collection of statistical data and/or metrics applicable to one or more managed system elements.
Win32_PerfRawData_ESE_Database	Database provides performance statistics for each process using the ESE high-performance embedded database management system.
Win32_PerfRawData_Spooler_PrintQueue	Displays performance statistics about a Print Queue.
Win32_PerfRawData_FileReplicaConn_FileReplicaConn	Displays Performance statistics of the REPLICACONN object.
Win32_PerfRawData_MSExchangeMTA_MSExchangeMTAConnections	Each instance describes a single known entity.
Win32_PerfRawData_ESE_DatabaseInstances	Instances in this process
Win32_PerfRawData_MSDTC_DistributedTransactionCoordinator	Microsoft Distributed Transaction Coordinator performance counters
Win32_PerfRawData_MSExchangeAL_MSExchangeAL	Microsoft Exchange Address List Service
Win32_PerfRawData_MSExchangeIS_MSExchangeIS	Microsoft Exchange Information Store performance data
Win32_PerfRawData_MSExchangeIS_MSExchangeISMailbox	Microsoft Exchange Mailbox Store performance data
Win32_PerfRawData_MSExchangeIS_MSExchangeISPublic	Microsoft Exchange Public Folder Store performance data
Win32_PerfRawData_MSExchangeSA_MSExchangeSANSPIProxy	NSPI Proxy used by Microsoft Exchange System Attendant
Win32_PerfRawData_MSExchangeMTA_MSExchangeMTA	Only one instance : global MTA performance data.
Win32_PerfRawData_PerfProc_JobObject	Reports the accounting and processor usage data collected by each active named Job object.
Win32_PerfRawData_RSVP_RSVPInterfaces	RSVP Interfaces performance counters.
Win32_PerfRawData_RSVP_RSVPService	RSVP service performance counters.
Win32_PerfRawData_TermService_TerminalServicesSession	Terminal Services per-session resource monitoring.
Win32_PerfRawData_TermService_TerminalServices	Terminal Services summary information.
Win32_PerfRawData_ASP_ActiveServerPages	The Active Server Pages Object Type handles the Active Server Pages device on your system.
Win32_PerfRawData_PerfNet_Browser	The Browser performance object consists of counters that measure the rates of announcements, enumerations, and other Browser transmissions.
Win32_PerfRawData_PerfOS_Cache	The Cache performance object consists of counters that monitor the file system cache, an area of physical memory that stores recently used data as long as possible to permit access to the data without having to read from the disk. Because applications typically use the cache, the cache is monitored as an indicator of application I/O operations. When memory is plentiful, the cache can grow, but when memory is scarce, the cache can become too small to be effective.
Win32_PerfRawData_SMTPSVC_SMTPServer	The counters specific to the SMTP Server.
Win32_PerfRawData_PerfProc_FullImage_Costly	The Full Image performance object consists of counters that monitor the virtual address usage of images executed by processes on the computer. Full Image counters are the same counters as contained in Image object with the only difference being the instance name. In the Full Image object, the instance name includes the full file path name of the loaded modules, while in the Image object only the filename is displayed.
Win32_PerfRawData_Tcpip_ICMP	The ICMP performance object consists of counters that measure the rates at which messages are sent and received by using ICMP protocols. It also includes counters that monitor ICMP protocol errors.
Win32_PerfRawData_PerfProc_Image_Costly	The Image performance object consists of counters that monitor the virtual address usage of images executed by processes on the computer.
Win32_PerfRawData_InetInfo_InternetInformationServicesGlobal	The Internet Information Services Global object includes counters that monitor Internet Information Services (the Web service and the FTP service) as a whole.
Win32_PerfRawData_Tcpip_IP	The IP performance object consists of counters that measure the rates at which IP datagrams are sent and received by using IP protocols. It also includes counters that monitor IP protocol errors.
Win32_PerfRawData_PerfDisk_LogicalDisk	The Logical Disk performance object consists of counters that monitor logical partitions of a hard or fixed disk drives. Performance Monitor identifies logical disks by their a drive letter, such as C.
Win32_PerfRawData_PerfOS_Memory	The Memory performance object consists of counters that describe the behavior of physical and virtual memory on the computer. Physical memory is the amount of random access memory on the computer. Virtual memory consists of the space in physical memory and on disk. Many of the memory counters monitor paging, which is the movement of pages of code and data between disk and physical memory. Excessive paging, a symptom of a memory shortage, can cause delays which interfere with all system processes.
Win32_PerfRawData_MSExchangeSRS_MSExchangeSRS	The MSExchangeSRS Object Type handles the Microsoft Exchange Site Replication service on your system.
Win32_PerfRawData_Tcpip_NBTConnection	The NBT Connection performance object consists of counters that measure the rates at which bytes are sent and received over the NBT connection between the local computer and a remote computer. The connection is identified by the name of the remote computer.

Table 3.73   *The Win32_PerfRawData Classes (continued)*

Name	Comments
Win32_PerfRawData_Tcpip_NetworkInterface	The Network Interface performance object consists of counters that measure the rates at which bytes and packets are sent and received over a TCP/IP network connection. It includes counters that monitor connection errors.
Win32_PerfRawData_NntpSvc_NNTPCommands	The NNTP Commands object includes counters for all NNTP commands processed by the NNTP service.
Win32_PerfRawData_NntpSvc_NNTPServer	The NNTP Server object type includes counters specific to the NNTP Server service.
Win32_PerfRawData_PerfOS_Objects	The Object performance object consists of counters that monitor logical objects in the system, such as processes, threads, mutexes, and semaphores. This information can be used to detect the unnecessary consumption of computer resources. Each object requires memory to store basic information about the object.
Win32_PerfRawData_PerfOS_PagingFile	The Paging File performance object consists of counters that monitor the paging file(s) on the computer. The paging file is a reserved space on disk that backs up committed physical memory on the computer.
Win32_PerfRawData_PerfDisk_PhysicalDisk	The Physical Disk performance object consists of counters that monitor hard or fixed disk drive on a computer. Disks are used to store file, program, and paging data and are read to retrieve these items, and written to record changes to them. The values of physical disk counters are sums of the values of the logical disks (or partitions) into which they are divided.
Win32_PerfRawData_PerfProc_ProcessAddressSpace_Costly	The Process Address Space performance object consists of counters that monitor memory allocation and use for a selected process.
Win32_PerfRawData_PerfProc_Process	The Process performance object consists of counters that monitor running application program and system processes. All the threads in a process share the same address space and have access to the same data.
Win32_PerfRawData_PerfOS_Processor	The Processor performance object consists of counters that measure aspects of processor activity. The processor is the part of the computer that performs arithmetic and logical computations, initiates operations on peripherals, and runs the threads of processes. A computer can have multiple processors. The processor object represents each processor as an instance of the object.
Win32_PerfRawData_RemoteAccess_RASTotal	The RAS performance object consists of counters that combine values for all ports of the Remote Access Service (RAS) device on the computer.
Win32_PerfRawData_RemoteAccess_RASPort	The RAS performance object consists of counters that monitor individual Remote Access Service ports of the RAS device on the computer.
Win32_PerfRawData_PerfNet_Redirector	The Redirector performance object consists of counters that monitor network connections originating at the local computer.
Win32_PerfRawData_PerfNet_Server	The Server performance object consists of counters that measure communication between the local computer and the network.
Win32_PerfRawData_PerfNet_ServerWorkQueues	The Server Work Queues performance object consists of counters that monitor the length of the queues and objects in the queues.
Win32_PerfRawData_PerfOS_System	The System performance object consists of counters that apply to more than one instance of a component processors on the computer.
Win32_PerfRawData_Tcpip_TCP	The TCP performance object consists of counters that measure the rates at which TCP Segments are sent and received by using the TCP protocol. It includes counters that monitor the number of TCP connections in each TCP connection state.
Win32_PerfRawData_TapiSrv_Telephony	The Telephony System
Win32_PerfRawData_PerfProc_ThreadDetails_Costly	The Thread Details performance object consists of counters that measure aspects of thread behavior that are difficult or time-consuming or collect. These counters are distinguished from those in the Thread object by their high overhead.
Win32_PerfRawData_PerfProc_Thread	The Thread performance object consists of counters that measure aspects of thread behavior. A thread is the basic object that executes instructions on a processor. All running processes have at least one thread.
Win32_PerfRawData_Tcpip_UDP	The UDP performance object consists of counters that measure the rates at which UDP datagrams are sent and received by using the UDP protocol. It includes counters that monitor UDP protocol errors.
Win32_PerfRawData_W3SVC_WebServiceCache	The Web Service Cache Counters object includes cache counters specific to the World Wide Web Publishing Service.
Win32_PerfRawData_W3SVC_WebService	The Web Service object includes counters specific to the World Wide Web Publishing Service.
Win32_PerfRawData_NTFSDRV_SMTPNTFSStoreDriver	This object represents global counters for the Exchange NTFS Store driver.

Server 2003. Its name is *HiPerfCooker_v1*. It is available in both the **Root\CIMv2** namespace and the **Root\WMI** namespace. The *Cooked Counter* provider supports a set of classes derived from the *Win32_PerfFormattedData* class (see Table 3.74).

Table 3.74 *The Win32_PerfFormattedData Classes*

Name	Win32_PerfRawData class	Comments
Win32_PerfFormattedData_ESE_Database	Win32_PerfRawData_ESE_Database	Database provides performance statistics for each process using the ESE high performance embedded database management system.
Win32_PerfFormattedData_ESE_DatabaseInstances	Win32_PerfRawData_ESE_DatabaseInstances	Instances in this process
Win32_PerfFormattedData_FileReplicaConn_FileReplicaConn	Win32_PerfRawData_FileReplicaConn_FileReplicaConn	Displays Performance statistics of the REPLICACONN Object.
Win32_PerfFormattedData_MSDTC_DistributedTransactionCoordinator	Win32_PerfRawData_MSDTC_DistributedTransactionCoordinator	Microsoft Distributed Transaction Coordinator performance counters
Win32_PerfFormattedData_MSExchangeAL_MSExchangeAL	Win32_PerfRawData_MSExchangeAL_MSExchangeAL	Microsoft Exchange Address List Service
Win32_PerfFormattedData_MSExchangeIS_MSExchangeIS	Win32_PerfRawData_MSExchangeIS_MSExchangeIS	Microsoft Exchange Information Store performance data
Win32_PerfFormattedData_MSExchangeIS_MSExchangeISMailbox	Win32_PerfRawData_MSExchangeIS_MSExchangeISMailbox	Microsoft Exchange Mailbox Store performance data
Win32_PerfFormattedData_MSExchangeIS_MSExchangeISPublic	Win32_PerfRawData_MSExchangeIS_MSExchangeISPublic	Microsoft Exchange Public Folder Store performance data
Win32_PerfFormattedData_MSExchangeMTA_MSExchangeMTA	Win32_PerfRawData_MSExchangeMTA_MSExchangeMTA	Only one instance : global MTA performance data.
Win32_PerfFormattedData_MSExchangeMTA_MSExchangeMTAConnections	Win32_PerfRawData_MSExchangeMTA_MSExchangeMTAConnections	Each instance describes a single known entity.
Win32_PerfFormattedData_MSExchangeSA_MSExchangeSANSPIProxy	Win32_PerfRawData_MSExchangeSA_MSExchangeSANSPIProxy	NSPI Proxy used by Microsoft Exchange System Attendant
Win32_PerfFormattedData_MSExchangeSRS_MSExchangeSRS	Win32_PerfRawData_MSExchangeSRS_MSExchangeSRS	The MSExchangeSRS Object Type handles the Microsoft Exchange Site Replication service on your system.
Win32_PerfFormattedData_NTDS_NTDS	Win32_PerfRawData_NTDS_NTDS	CIM_StatisticalInformation is a root class for any arbitrary collection of statistical data and/or metrics applicable to one or more managed system elements.
Win32_PerfFormattedData_NTFSDRV_SMTPNTFSStoreDriver	Win32_PerfRawData_NTFSDRV_SMTPNTFSStoreDriver	This object represents global counters for the Exchange NTFS Store driver
Win32_PerfFormattedData_PerfDisk_LogicalDisk	Win32_PerfRawData_PerfDisk_LogicalDisk	The Logical Disk performance object consists of counters that monitor logical partitions of a hard or fixed disk drives. Performance Monitor identifies logical disks by their a drive letter, such as C.
Win32_PerfFormattedData_PerfDisk_PhysicalDisk	Win32_PerfRawData_PerfDisk_PhysicalDisk	The Physical Disk performance object consists of counters that monitor hard or fixed disk drive on a computer. Disks are used to store file, program, and paging data and are read to retrieve these items, and written to record changes to them. The values of physical disk counters are sums of the values of the logical disks (or partitions) into which they are divided.
Win32_PerfFormattedData_PerfNet_Browser	Win32_PerfRawData_PerfNet_Browser	The Browser performance object consists of counters that measure the rates of announcements, enumerations, and other Browser transmissions.
Win32_PerfFormattedData_PerfNet_Redirector	Win32_PerfRawData_PerfNet_Redirector	The Redirector performance object consists of counter that monitor network connections originating at the local computer.
Win32_PerfFormattedData_PerfNet_Server	Win32_PerfRawData_PerfNet_Server	The Server performance object consists of counters that measure communication between the local computer and the network.
Win32_PerfFormattedData_PerfNet_ServerWorkQueues	Win32_PerfRawData_PerfNet_ServerWorkQueues	The Server Work Queues performance object consists of counters that monitor the length of the queues and objects in the queues.
Win32_PerfFormattedData_PerfOS_Cache	Win32_PerfRawData_PerfOS_Cache	The Cache performance object consists of counters that monitor the file system cache, an area of physical memory that stores recently used data as long as possible to permit access to the data without having to read from the disk. Because applications typically use the cache, the cache is monitored as an indicator of application I/O operations. When memory is plentiful, the cache can grow, but when memory is scarce, the cache can become too small to be effective.
Win32_PerfFormattedData_PerfOS_Memory	Win32_PerfRawData_PerfOS_Memory	The Memory performance object consists of counters that describe the behavior of physical and virtual memory on the computer. Physical memory is the amount of random access memory on the computer. Virtual memory consists of the space in physical memory and on disk. Many of the memory counters monitor paging, which is the movement of pages of code and data between disk and physical memory. Excessive paging, a symptom of a memory shortage, can cause delays which interfere with all system processes.

Table 3.74 The *Win32_PerfFormattedData Classes* (continued)

Name	Win32_PerfRawData class	Comments
Win32_PerfFormattedData_PerfOS_Objects	Win32_PerfRawData_PerfOS_Objects	The Object performance object consists of counters that monitor logical objects in the system, such as processes, threads, mutexes, and semaphores. This information can be used to detect the unnecessary consumption of computer resources. Each object requires memory to store basic information about the object.
Win32_PerfFormattedData_PerfOS_PagingFile	Win32_PerfRawData_PerfOS_PagingFile	The Paging File performance object consists of counters that monitor the paging file(s) on the computer. The paging file is a reserved space on disk that backs up committed physical memory on the computer.
Win32_PerfFormattedData_PerfOS_Processor	Win32_PerfRawData_PerfOS_Processor	The Processor performance object consists of counters that measure aspects of processor activity The processor is the part of the computer that performs arithmetic and logical computations, initiates operations on peripherals, and runs the threads of processes. A computer can have multiple processors. The processor object represents each processor as an instance of the object.
Win32_PerfFormattedData_PerfOS_System	Win32_PerfRawData_PerfOS_System	The System performance object consists of counters that apply to more than one instance of a component processors on the computer.
Win32_PerfFormattedData_PerfProc_FullImage_Costly	Win32_PerfRawData_PerfProc_FullImage_Costly	The Full Image performance object consists of counters that monitor the virtual address usage of images executed by processes on the computer. Full Image counters are the same counters as contained in Image object with the only difference being the instance name. In the Full Image object, the instance name includes the full file path name of the loaded modules, while in the Image object only the filename is displayed.
Win32_PerfFormattedData_PerfProc_Image_Costly	Win32_PerfRawData_PerfProc_Image_Costly	The Image performance object consists of counters that monitor the virtual address usage of images executed by processes on the computer.
Win32_PerfFormattedData_PerfProc_JobObject	Win32_PerfRawData_PerfProc_JobObject	Reports the accounting and processor usage data collected by each active named Job object.
Win32_PerfFormattedData_PerfProc_JobObjectDetails	Win32_PerfRawData_PerfProc_JobObjectDetails	% Job object Details shows detailed performance information about the active processes that make up a Job object.
Win32_PerfFormattedData_PerfProc_Process	Win32_PerfRawData_PerfProc_Process	The Process performance object consists of counters that monitor running application program and system processes. All the threads in a process share the same address space and have access to the same data.
Win32_PerfFormattedData_PerfProc_ProcessAddressSpace_Costly	Win32_PerfRawData_PerfProc_ProcessAddressSpace_Costly	The Process Address Space performance object consists of counters that monitor memory allocation and use for a selected process.
Win32_PerfFormattedData_PerfProc_Thread	Win32_PerfRawData_PerfProc_Thread	The Thread performance object consists of counters that measure aspects of thread behavior. A thread is the basic object that executes instructions on a processor. All running processes have at least one thread.
Win32_PerfFormattedData_PerfProc_ThreadDetails_Costly	Win32_PerfRawData_PerfProc_ThreadDetails_Costly	The Thread Details performance object consists of counters that measure aspects of thread behavior that are difficult or time-consuming or collect. These counters are distinguished from those in the Thread object by their high overhead.
Win32_PerfFormattedData_RemoteAccess_RASPort	Win32_PerfRawData_RemoteAccess_RASPort	The RAS performance object consists of counters that monitor individual Remote Access Service ports of the RAS device on the computer.
Win32_PerfFormattedData_RemoteAccess_RASTotal	Win32_PerfRawData_RemoteAccess_RASTotal	The RAS performance object consists of counters that combine values for all ports of the Remote Access service (RAS) device on the computer.
Win32_PerfFormattedData_RSVP_RSVPInterfaces	Win32_PerfRawData_RSVP_RSVPInterfaces	RSVP Interfaces performance counters.
Win32_PerfFormattedData_RSVP_RSVPService	Win32_PerfRawData_RSVP_RSVPService	RSVP service performance counters.
Win32_PerfFormattedData_Spooler_PrintQueue	Win32_PerfRawData_Spooler_PrintQueue	Displays performance statistics about a Print Queue.
Win32_PerfFormattedData_TapiSrv_Telephony	Win32_PerfRawData_TapiSrv_Telephony	The Telephony System

Table 3.74   *The Win32_PerfFormattedData Classes (continued)*

Name	Win32_PerfRawData class	Comments
Win32_PerfFormattedData_Tcpip_ICMP	Win32_PerfRawData_Tcpip_ICMP	The ICMP performance object consists of counters that measure the rates at which messages are sent and received by using ICMP protocols. It also includes counters that monitor ICMP protocol errors.
Win32_PerfFormattedData_Tcpip_IP	Win32_PerfRawData_Tcpip_IP	The IP performance object consists of counters that measure the rates at which IP datagrams are sent and received by using IP protocols. It also includes counters that monitor IP protocol errors.
Win32_PerfFormattedData_Tcpip_NBTConnection	Win32_PerfRawData_Tcpip_NBTConnection	The NBT Connection performance object consists of counters that measure the rates at which bytes are sent and received over the NBT connection between the local computer and a remote computer. The connection is identified by the name of the remote computer.
Win32_PerfFormattedData_Tcpip_NetworkInterface	Win32_PerfRawData_Tcpip_NetworkInterface	The Network Interface performance object consists of counters that measure the rates at which bytes and packets are sent and received over a TCP/IP network connection. It includes counters that monitor connection errors.
Win32_PerfFormattedData_Tcpip_TCP	Win32_PerfRawData_Tcpip_TCP	The TCP performance object consists of counters that measure the rates at which TCP Segments are sent and received by using the TCP protocol. It includes counters that monitor the number of TCP connections in each TCP connection state.
Win32_PerfFormattedData_Tcpip_UDP	Win32_PerfRawData_Tcpip_UDP	The UDP performance object consists of counters that measure the rates at which UDP datagrams are sent and received by using the UDP protocol. It includes counters that monitor UDP protocol errors.
Win32_PerfFormattedData_TermService_TerminalServices	Win32_PerfRawData_TermService_TerminalServices	Terminal Services summary information.
Win32_PerfFormattedData_TermService_TerminalServicesSession	Win32_PerfRawData_TermService_TerminalServicesSession	Terminal Services per-session resource monitoring.

Both class types (raw and cooked) follow the same naming convention, which is of the form:

- *Win32_PerfRawData_*<service_name>_<object_name>

- *Win32_PerfFormattedData_*<service_name>_<object_name>

When dealing with TCP/IP information at the level of the network interface, we will have a class name such as *Win32_PerfRawData_Tcpip_NetworkInterface* for the raw data counters and *Win32_PerfFormattedData_Tcpip_NetworkInterface* for the cooked data counters.

The WMI AutoDiscovery/AutoPurge (ADAP) process transfers performance counter objects registered in the performance counter libraries into *Win32_PerfRawData* and *Win32_PerfFormattedData* classes in the WMI repository. When a new performance library is found, ADAP then adds a related performance object to the CIM repository. When an application is deinstalled, the deleted performance library is also detected by ADAP and it updates the CIM repository accordingly. So, basically, the ADAP process parses the performance libraries to build the *Win32_PerfRawData* and *Win32_PerfFormattedData* classes in the CIM repository.

You can look for errors generated by ADAP in two places: the NT Application Event Log (with the Event Viewer) and the WMI application event logs (in Windows\System32\Wbem\Logs\Wmiadap.log).

With the *__ADAPStatus* system class, it is possible to determine the status of the last ADAP execution. This system class exposes three read-only properties, described in Table 3.75. The *__ADAPStatus* system class is a singleton class located in the **Root\Default** namespace. The information exposed by the instance of the *__ADAPStatus* system class provides data about the most recent run of ADAP.

Table 3.75   *The __ADAPStatus System Class Properties*

Name	Type	Comments
LastStartTime	datetime	Last time the ADAP process started.
LastStopTime	datetime	Last time the ADAP process completed.
Status	uint32	Defines the current state of the ADAP process. 0 Process has never run on this computer. 1 Process is currently running. 2 Process is processing a performance library. 3 Process is updating and committing changes to WMI. 4 Process has finished.

Although started automatically, it is always possible to force a synchronization of the performance counters with the CIM repository content by using, for Windows 2000:

```
C:\>Winmgmt /resyncperf <PID_of_WINMGMT.EXE>
```

For Windows XP and Windows Server 2003, use the following:

```
C:\Winmgmt /resyncperf
```

In WMI, the *Win32_PerfFormattedData* is a calculated performance counter coming from the corresponding *Win32_PerfRawData* class representing the raw counter performance. The correspondence between the cooked class and the raw class is defined with the *AutoCook_RawClass* qualifier set on the same-named *Win32_PerfFormattedData* class. Table 3.74 shows the corresponding classes. Note that all *Win32_PerfFormattedData* classes have a corresponding *Win32_PerfRawData* class. For example, the *Win32_PerfFormattedData_Tcpip_NetworkInterface* has the *AutoCook_RawClass* qualifier set with a value equal to the name of the *Win32_PerfRawData_Tcpip_NetworkInterface* class.

Because the *Win32_PerfFormattedData_Tcpip_NetworkInterface* properties data is calculated from the *Win32_PerfRawData_Tcpip_NetworkInterface* properties data, this implies the use of a formula for each of the properties exposed by the *Win32_PerfFormattedData_Tcpip_NetworkInterface* class. The formula type is defined in a property qualifier for each calculated property of the *Win32_PerfFormattedData_Tcpip_NetworkInterface* class. This qualifier is called the *CookingType* qualifier and contains a cooking type identifier. Table 3.76 lists the *Win32_PerfFormattedData_Tcpip_NetworkInterface* properties exposing cooked counter information with the associated formula.

Table 3.77 lists the various cooking types available (for more details, you can refer to the **WinPerf.h** file, which comes with the Platform SDK installation).

The biggest challenge when working with the *Win32_PerfFormattedData* classes is not to extract information from the counters but to correctly interpret the meaning of the collected numbers. This is why it is important to explore in detail the miscellaneous *Win32_PerfFormattedData* derived classes with their properties. This information can be retrieved with the **LoadCIMInXL.wsf** script developed at the end of Chapter 4 of the first book, *Understanding WMI Scripting*, and available in the appendix. However, because a great number of details are provided in the qualifiers, it is best to run the script with a maximum of requested details. The command line to use would be as follows:

```
C:\>LoadCIMInXL.Wsf Win32_PerfFormattedData_Tcpip_NetworkInterface /Level:6
```

Table 3.76   *The Win32_PerfFormattedData_Tcpip_NetworkInterface Properties*

Name	Type	Cooking Type	Comments
BytesReceivedPersec	uint32	PERF_COUNTER_COUNTER	Bytes Received/sec is the rate at which bytes are received over each network adapter, including framing characters. Network Interface\\Bytes Received/sec is a subset of Network Interface\\Bytes Total/sec.
BytesSentPersec	uint32	PERF_COUNTER_COUNTER	Bytes Sent/sec is the rate at which bytes are sent over each network adapter, including framing characters. Network Interface\\Bytes Sent/sec is a subset of Network Interface\\Bytes Total/sec.
BytesTotalPersec	uint64	PERF_COUNTER_BULK_COUNT	Bytes Total/sec is the rate at which bytes are sent and received over each network adapter, including framing characters. Network Interface\\Bytes Received/sec is a sum of Network Interface\\Bytes Received/sec and Network Interface\\Bytes Sent/sec.
CurrentBandwidth	uint32	PERF_COUNTER_RAWCOUNT	Current Bandwidth is an estimate of the current bandwidth of the network interface in bits per second (BPS). For interfaces that do not vary in bandwidth or for those where no accurate estimation can be made, this value is the nominal bandwidth.
OutputQueueLength	uint32	PERF_COUNTER_RAWCOUNT	Output Queue Length is the length of the output packet queue (in packets). If this is longer than two, there are delays and the bottleneck should be found and eliminated, if possible. Since the requests are queued by the Network Driver Interface Specification (NDIS) in this implementation, this will always be 0.
PacketsOutboundDiscarded	uint32	PERF_COUNTER_RAWCOUNT	Packets Outbound Discarded is the number of outbound packets that were chosen to be discarded even though no errors had been detected to prevent transmission. One possible reason for discarding packets could be to free up buffer space.
PacketsOutboundErrors	uint32	PERF_COUNTER_RAWCOUNT	Packets Outbound Errors is the number of outbound packets that could not be transmitted because of errors.
PacketsPersec	uint32	PERF_COUNTER_COUNTER	Packets/sec is the rate at which packets are sent and received on the network interface.
PacketsReceivedDiscarded	uint32	PERF_COUNTER_RAWCOUNT	Packets Received Discarded is the number of inbound packets that were chosen to be discarded even though no errors had been detected to prevent their delivery to a higher-layer protocol. One possible reason for discarding packets could be to free up buffer space.
PacketsReceivedErrors	uint32	PERF_COUNTER_RAWCOUNT	Packets Received Errors is the number of inbound packets that contained errors preventing them from being deliverable to a higher-layer protocol.
PacketsReceivedNonUnicastPersec	uint32	PERF_COUNTER_COUNTER	Packets Received Non-Unicast/sec is the rate at which non-Unicast (subnet broadcast or subnet multicast) packets are delivered to a higher-layer protocol.
PacketsReceivedPersec	uint32	PERF_COUNTER_COUNTER	Packets Received/sec is the rate at which packets are received on the network interface.
PacketsReceivedUnicastPersec	uint32	PERF_COUNTER_COUNTER	Packets Received Unicast/sec is the rate at which (subnet) Unicast packets are delivered to a higher-layer protocol.
PacketsReceivedUnknown	uint32	PERF_COUNTER_RAWCOUNT	Packets Received Unknown is the number of packets received through the interface that were discarded because of an unknown or unsupported protocol.
PacketsSentNonUnicastPersec	uint32	PERF_COUNTER_COUNTER	Packets Sent Non-Unicast/sec is the rate at which packets are requested to be transmitted to non-Unicast (subnet broadcast or subnet multicast) addresses by higher-level protocols. The rate includes the packets that were discarded or not sent.
PacketsSentPersec	uint32	PERF_COUNTER_COUNTER	Packets Sent/sec is the rate at which packets are sent on the network interface.
PacketsSentUnicastPersec	uint32	PERF_COUNTER_COUNTER	Packets Sent Unicast/sec is the rate at which packets are requested to be transmitted to subnet-Unicast addresses by higher-level protocols. The rate includes the packets that were discarded or not sent.

Once loaded, all information related to the *Win32_PerfFormattedData_Tcpip_NetworkInterface* class with its properties and all associated qualifiers will be available in an Excel sheet.

Now that we have everything in our hands to understand what these raw and cooked counters are, the last step is to collect the counter information. Extracting a snapshot of a counter set is nice but not always relevant. The biggest interest in these classes is to monitor some counters over time and see

Table 3.77   *The Miscellaneous Cooking Type*

Noncomputational Counter Types		
PERF_COUNTER_TEXT	2816	This counter type shows a variable-length text string in Unicode. It does not display calculated values.
PERF_COUNTER_RAWCOUNT	65536	Raw counter value requiring no further calculations and representing a single sample, which is the last observed value only.
PERF_COUNTER_LARGE_RAWCOUNT	65792	Same as PERF_COUNTER_RAWCOUNT but a 64-bit representation for larger values.
PERF_COUNTER_RAWCOUNT_HEX	0	Most recently observed value in hexadecimal format. It does not display an average.
PERF_COUNTER_LARGE_RAWCOUNT	256	Same as PERF_COUNTER_RAWCOUNT_HEX but a 64-bit representation in hexadecimal for use with large values.
Basic Algorithm Counter Types		
PERF_RAW_FRACTION	537003008	Ratio of a subset to its set as a percentage. This counter type displays the current percentage only, not an average over time.
PERF_SAMPLE_FRACTION	549585920	Average ratio of hits to all operations during the last two sample intervals. This counter type requires a base property with the PERF_SAMPLE_BASE counter type.
PERF_COUNTER_DELTA	4195328	This counter type shows the change in the measured attribute between the two most recent sample intervals.
PERF_COUNTER_LARGE_DELTA	4195584	Same as PERF_COUNTER_DELTA but a 64-bit representation for larger values.
PERF_ELAPSED_TIME	807666944	Total time between when the process started and the time when this value is calculated.
Counter Algorithm Counter Types		
PERF_AVERAGE_BULK	1073874176	Number of items processed, on average, during an operation. This counter type displays a ratio of the items processed (such as bytes sent) to the number of operations completed, and requires a base property with PERF_AVERAGE_BASE as the counter type.
PERF_COUNTER_COUNTER	272696320	Average number of operations completed during each second of the sample interval.
PERF_SAMPLE_COUNTER	4260864	Average number of operations completed in one second. This counter type requires a base property with the counter type PERF_SAMPLE_BASE.
PERF_COUNTER_BULK_COUNT	272696576	Average number of operations completed during each second of the sample interval. This counter type is the same as the PERF_COUNTER_COUNTER type, but it uses larger fields to accommodate larger values.
Timer Algorithm Counter Types		
PERF_COUNTER_TIMER	541132032	Average time that a component is active as a percentage of the total sample time.
PERF_COUNTER_TIMER_INV	557909248	Average percentage of time observed during sample interval that the object is not active. This counter type is the same as PERF_100NSEC_TIMER_INV except that it measures time in units of ticks of the system performance timer rather than in 100ns units.
PERF_AVERAGE_TIMER	805438464	Average time to complete a process or operation. This counter type displays a ratio of the total elapsed time of the sample interval to the number of processes or operations completed during that time. Requires a base property with PERF_AVERAGE_BASE as the counter type.
PERF_100NSEC_TIMER	542180608	Active time of one component as a percentage of the total elapsed time in units of 100ns of the sample interval.
PERF_100NSEC_TIMER_INV	592512256	Percentage of time the object was not in use. This counter type is the same as PERF_COUNTER_TIMER_INV except that it measures time in 100ns units rather than in system performance timer ticks.
PERF_COUNTER_MULTI_TIMER	574686464	Active time of one or more components as a percentage of the total time of the sample interval. Differs from PERF_100NSEC_MULTI_TIMER in that it measures time in units of ticks of the system performance timer, rather than in 100ns units. Requires a base property with the PERF_COUNTER_MULTI_BASE counter type.
PERF_COUNTER_MULTI_TIMER_INV	591463680	Inactive time of one or more components as a percentage of the total time of the sample interval. Differs from PERF_100NSEC_MULTI_TIMER_INV in that it measures time in units of ticks of the system performance timer rather than in 100ns units. Requires a base property with the PERF_COUNTER_MULTI_BASE counter type.
PERF_100NSEC_MULTI_TIMER	575735040	This counter type shows the active time of one or more components as a percentage of the total time (100ns units) of the sample interval. Requires a base property with the PERF_COUNTER_MULTI_BASE counter type.
PERF_100NSEC_MULTI_TIMER_INV	592512256	Inactive time of one or more components as a percentage of the total time of the sample interval. Counters of this type measure time in 100ns units. Requires a base property with the PERF_COUNTER_MULTI_BASE counter type.
PERF_OBJ_TIME_TIMER		A 64-bit timer in object-specific units.
Precision Timer Algorithm Counter Types		
PERF_PRECISION_SYSTEM_TIMER	541525248	Similar to PERF_COUNTER_TIMER except that it uses a counter defined time base instead of the system timestamp.
PERF_PRECISION_100NS_TIMER	542573824	Similar to PERF_100NSEC_TIMER except that it uses a 100ns counter defined time base instead of the system 100ns timestamp.

Table 3.77   *The Miscellaneous Cooking Type (continued)*

Queue-length Algorithm Counter Types		
PERF_COUNTER_QUEUELEN_TYPE	4523008	Average length of a queue to a resource over time. It shows the difference between the queue lengths observed during the last two sample intervals divided by the duration of the interval.
PERF_COUNTER_LARGE_QUEUELEN_TYPE	4523264	Average length of a queue to a resource over time. Counters of this type display the difference between the queue lengths observed during the last two sample intervals, divided by the duration of the interval.
PERF_COUNTER_100NS_QUEUELEN_TYPE	5571840	Average length of a queue to a resource over time in 100 nanosecond units.
PERF_COUNTER_OBJECT_TIME_QUEUELEN_TYPE	6620416	Time an object is in a queue.
Base Counter Types		
PERF_AVERAGE_BASE	1073939458	Base value used in calculation of PERF_AVERAGE_TIMER and PERF_AVERAGE_BULK counter types.
PERF_COUNTER_MULTI_BASE	1107494144	Base value used in calculation of PERF_COUNTER_MULTI_TIMER, PERF_COUNTER_MULTI_TIMER_INV, PERF_100NSEC_MULTI_TIMER, PERF_100NSEC_MULTI_TIMER_INV counter types.
PERF_LARGE_RAW_BASE	1073939715	Base value found in calculation of PERF_RAW_FRACTION. 64 bits.
PERF_RAW_BASE	1073939459	Base value used in calculation of the PERF_RAW_FRACTION counter type.
PERF_SAMPLE_BASE	1073939457	Base value used in calculation of the PERF_SAMPLE_COUNTER and PERF_SAMPLE_FRACTION counter types.

the evolution of the miscellaneous values. For example, we can save a set of counters for a particular performance class instance and repeat the operation at a regular time interval. To do this, we can reuse some of the WMI features shown in the previous samples.

Samples 3.77 and 3.78 show how to retrieve one or more performance counter instances and save the snapshot taken at a regular time interval in a .CSV file for later review and analysis. For example, you may wish to use Excel to generate graphics from the captured data.

```
C:\>WMICounterMonitor.wsf
Microsoft (R) Windows Script Host Version 5.6
Copyright (C) Microsoft Corporation 1996-2001. All rights reserved.

Usage: WMICounterMonitor.wsf /CounterName:value /Instance:value [/interval:value] [/Raw[+|-]]
                            [/Machine:value] [/User:value] [/Password:value]

Options:

CounterName : List of counter names to capture.
Instance    : List of instance corresponding to the counter name
interval    : Time interval between counter reads (in seconds).
Raw         : Determine if the raw performance counter must be taken instead of the formatted one.
Machine     : Determine the WMI system to connect to. (default=LocalHost)
User        : Determine the UserID to perform the remote connection. (default=none)
Password    : Determine the password to perform the remote connection. (default=none)
Examples:

      WMICounterMonitor.wsf /CounterName:Tcpip_NetworkInterface
                          /Instance:"Compaq NC3121 Fast Ethernet NIC"
      WMICounterMonitor.wsf /CounterName:Tcpip_NetworkInterface
                          /Instance:"Compaq NC3121 Fast Ethernet NIC" /Log+
      WMICounterMonitor.wsf /CounterName:Spooler_PrintQueue
                          /Instance:"Lexmark 4039 Plus PS" /Interval:10
      WMICounterMonitor.wsf /CounterName:"Spooler_PrintQueue,Tcpip_NetworkInterface"
                          /Instance:"Lexmark 4039 Plus PS,Compaq NC3121 Fast Ethernet NIC"
                          /Interval:10
      WMICounterMonitor.wsf /CounterName:PerfOS_Processor /Instance:"_Total" /Interval:10
```

The script usage is pretty simple. Basically, it requires two mandatory command-line parameters:

- The **/CounterName** switch: It represents the name (<service_name>_ <object_name>) used to form the WMI performance class name. For example, with the *Win32_PerfFormattedData_Tcpip_NetworkInterface* class, the name given on the command line is "Tcpip_NetworkInterface."

- The **/InstanceName** switch: It represents the instance name of the requested counter instance. All performance classes (raw and cooked) are using a unique Key property called *name* or are singleton classes. For example, with the *Win32_PerfFormattedData_Tcpip_NetworkInterface* class, the instance name given on the command line could be "Compaq NC3121 Fast Ethernet NIC."

As a result, the complete command line would be as follows:

```
C:\>WMICounterMonitor.wsf /CounterName:"Tcpip_NetworkInterface"
                          /Instance:"Compaq NC3121 Fast Ethernet NIC"
```

It is possible to combine several performance classes with their respective instances. In such a case, the command line to use would be as follows:

```
C:\>WMICounterMonitor.wsf /CounterName:"Tcpip_NetworkInterface,Tcpip_NBTConnection,PerfNet_Browser"
                          /Instance:"Compaq NC3121 Fast Ethernet NIC,_Total,@"
```

In such a case, the script will retrieve all properties of:

- An instance called "Compaq NC3121 Fast Ethernet NIC" for the *Win32_PerfFormattedData_Tcpip_NetworkInterface* class.

- An instance called "_Total" for the *Win32_PerfFormattedData_ Tcpip_NBTConnection* class.

- An instance of the singleton *Win32_PerfFormattedData_PerfNet_ Browser* class. Its name is "@," since the class is a singleton class

Let's see how Samples 3.77 and 3.78 work. The script is using an asynchronous event notification. Sample 3.77 contains the initialization process of the event notification. Sample 3.78 contains the event sink routine handling the event notifications.

Sample 3.77 *Capturing performance counter values (raw or cooked) at regular time intervals (Part I)*

```
1:<?xml version="1.0"?>
 .:
8:<package>
9:  <job>
..:
13:    <runtime>
```

```
 ..:
 30:    </runtime>
 31:
 32:    <script language="VBScript" src="..\Functions\CreateTextFileFunction.vbs" />
 33:    <script language="VBScript" src="..\Functions\ConvertStringInArrayFunction.vbs" />
 34:    <script language="VBScript" src="..\Functions\TinyErrorHandler.vbs" />
 35:    <script language="VBScript" src="..\Functions\PauseScript.vbs" />
 36:
 37:    <object progid="WbemScripting.SWbemRefresher" id="objWMIRefresher" />
 38:    <object progid="WbemScripting.SWbemLocator" id="objWMILocator" reference="true"/>
 39:    <object progid="WbemScripting.SWbemDateTime" id="objWMIDateTime" />
 40:    <script language="VBscript">
 41:    <![CDATA[
 ..:
 45:    Const cComputerName = "LocalHost"
 46:    Const cWMINameSpace = "Root/cimv2"
 47:    Const cWMITimerClass = "__IntervalTimerInstruction"
 48:    Const cTimerID = "MyTimerEvent"
 49:    Const cWMITimerQuery = "Select * From __TimerEvent Where TimerID='MyTimerEvent'"
 50:    Const cWMIPerfFormattedClass = "Win32_PerfFormattedData"
 51:    Const cWMIPerfRawClass = "Win32_PerfRawData"
...:
119:    Set objWMISink = WScript.CreateObject ("WbemScripting.SWbemSink", "SINK_")
120:
121:    objWMILocator.Security_.AuthenticationLevel = wbemAuthenticationLevelDefault
122:    objWMILocator.Security_.ImpersonationLevel = wbemImpersonationLevelImpersonate
123:
124:    Set objWMIServices = objWMILocator.ConnectServer(strComputerName, cWMINameSpace, _
125:                                                     strUserID, strPassword)
...:
128:    ' ----------------------------------------------------------------------------
129:    ReDim objLogFileName (Ubound(arrayCounterName))
130:    For intIndice = 0 To UBound (arrayCounterName)
131:        If boolRaw Then
132:            strWMIPerfClass = cWMIPerfRawClass & "_" & _
133:                              arrayCounterName(intIndice)
134:        Else
135:            strWMIPerfClass = cWMIPerfFormattedClass & "_" & _
136:                              arrayCounterName(intIndice)
137:        End If
138:
139:        Set objWMIClass = objWMIServices.Get (strWMIPerfClass)
140:        If Err.Number Then ErrorHandler (Err)
141:
142:        boolSingleton = objWMIClass.Qualifiers_.Item("Singleton").Value
143:        If Err.Number Then
144:           Err.Clear
145:           boolSingleton = False
146:        End If
147:
148:        If boolSingleton Then
149:            objWMIRefresher.Add objWMIServices, _
150:                                strWMIPerfClass & "=@"
151:        Else
152:            objWMIRefresher.Add objWMIServices, _
153:                                strWMIPerfClass & ".Name='" & _
154:                                arrayInstanceName(intIndice) & "'"
155:        End If
...:
158:        ' ----------------------------------------------------------------------------
159:        strLogFileName = strWMIPerfClass & "_" & _
160:                         Year(Date) & _
161:                         Right ("0" & Month(Date), 2) & _
```

```
162:                                    Right ("0" & Day(Date), 2) & "-" & _
163:                                    Right ("0" & Hour(Time), 2) & _
164:                                    Right ("0" & Minute(Time), 2) & _
165:                                    Right ("0" & Second(Time), 2) & ".CSV"
166:
167:         Set objLogFileName(intIndice) = CreateTextFile (strLogFileName)
168:
169:         varTemp = objWMIClass.Path_.RelPath
170:         Set objWMIPropertySet = objWMIClass.Properties_
171:         For Each objWMIProperty In objWMIPropertySet
172:             Select Case objWMIProperty.Name
173:                     Case "Caption"
174:                     Case "Description"
175:                     Case "Name"
176:                     Case Else
177:                             varTemp = varTemp & "," & objWMIProperty.Name
178:             End Select
179:         Next
...:
184:         WriteToFile objLogFileName(intIndice), varTemp
185:     Next
186:
187:     objWMIRefresher.AutoReconnect = True
188:     objWMIRefresher.Refresh
189:
190:     ' --------------------------------------------------------------------------------
191:     Set objWMIClass = objWMIServices.Get (cWMITimerClass)
192:
193:     Set objWMITimerInstance = objWMIClass.SpawnInstance_
194:     objWMITimerInstance.TimerID = cTimerID
195:     objWMITimerInstance.IntervalBetweenEvents = intInterval * 1000
196:     objWMITimerInstance.Put_ wbemChangeFlagCreateOrUpdate Or _
197:                              wbemFlagReturnWhenComplete
...:
200:     WScript.Echo "Counter timer created."
201:
202:     ' --------------------------------------------------------------------------------
203:     objWMIServices.ExecNotificationQueryAsync objWMISink, cWMITimerQuery
204:     If Err.Number Then ErrorHandler (Err)
205:
206:     WScript.Echo "Waiting for events..."
207:
208:     PauseScript "Click on 'Ok' to terminate the script ..."
209:
210:     WScript.Echo vbCRLF & "Cancelling event subscription ..."
211:     objWMISink.Cancel
212:
213:     ' --------------------------------------------------------------------------------
214:     objWMITimerInstance.Delete_
...:
217:     WScript.Echo vbCRLF & "Counter timer deleted."
218:
219:     For intIndice = 0 To UBound (arrayCounterName)
220:         CloseTextFile objLogFileName (intIndice)
221:     Next
...:
226:     WScript.Echo "Finished."
227:
...:
...:
...:
```

Once the command-line parameters are defined and parsed, the script executes the WMI connection (lines 121 through 125). Right after the WMI connection, the script enters a loop (lines 130 through 185) to create several items used by the script:

- Based on the **/Raw** command-line parameter value, the script builds the class name to be used (lines 131 through 137). If the **/Raw** switch is set to False, the class name will be a *Win32_PerfFormattedData* class. If the **/Raw** switch is set to True, the class name will be a *Win32_PerfRawData* class. The counter name given on the command line and the desired class name are combined to give the performance class name used to retrieve performance counter instance values.

- From the performance class name, the script verifies if the *Singleton* qualifier is set to determine how the performance counter instance will be retrieved (lines 139 through 146).

- If the class is a singleton class, the script uses the appropriate syntax to retrieve the unique instance from the given singleton class (lines 149 and 150). If the class is not a singleton class, it retrieves the performance counter instance with the name given with the **/InstanceName** switch (lines 152 through 154). It is important to note that the performance counter instances are not immediately stored in an **SWBemObject** instance. Instead, they are stored in **SWbemRefresher** object. This will give us the facility, later in the script, to refresh all instances stored in the **SWbemRefresher** object. This will improve the performance in retrieving the counter information, since a refresh operation is faster than an object instantiation. We have seen how the **SWbemRefresher** object can be used in Chapter 5 of *Understanding WMI Scripting*.

- Once the performance counter class is instantiated and saved in the **SWbemRefresher** object, the script prepares the .CSV file name (lines 159 through 167). Once the .CSV file is created, the file header is also created from the various properties available from the class (lines 169 through 184).

Each of these operations is repeated in a loop for every performance counter specified with the **/CounterName** switch (lines 130 through 185). Next, the script initializes the **SWbemRefresher** object and ensures that it automatically attempts to reconnect to a remote provider if the connection is broken (lines 187 and 188).

To gather performance counter data at regular time intervals, the script creates an __IntervalTimerInstruction_ instance. We already used a similar technique in previous samples (Samples 3.60 and 3.61, "PINGing a system at regular time intervals"). From line 191 through 200, the __IntervalTim-erInstruction_ instance is created. Next, at line 203, the WQL event query is submitted to WMI to receive timer event notifications in the event sink (lines 229 through 274). The corresponding **SWbemSink** object is created at line 119. Next, as in any previous asynchronous event notification sample in this book, the script is paused (line 208). Once the script is resumed, the timer event notification is canceled (line 211), and the timer event instance is deleted from the CIM repository (lines 214 through 217). Before ending the script execution, every .CSV file created for each performance counter is closed (lines 219 through 221).

What happens in the event sink routine? The answer is shown in Sample 3.78.

Sample 3.78   *Capturing performance counter values (raw or cooked) at regular time intervals (Part II)*

```
...:
...:
...:
227:
228:    ' -------------------------------------------------------------------------------------------------
229:    Sub SINK_OnObjectReady (objWbemObject, objWbemAsyncContext)
...:
238:        intCounter = intCounter + 1
239:
240:        Wscript.Echo
241:        WScript.Echo FormatDateTime(Date, vbLongDate) & " at " & _
242:                     FormatDateTime(Time, vbLongTime) & _
243:                     " sample #" & intCounter & "."
244:
245:        objWMIRefresher.Refresh
246:
247:        For intIndice = 1 To objWMIRefresher.Count
248:            Set objWMIRefresherItem = objWMIRefresher.Item(intIndice * 2)
249:            Set objWMIInstance = objWMIRefresherItem.Object
250:
251:            varTemp = FormatDateTime(Date, vbShortDate) & " " & _
252:                      FormatDateTime(Time, vbLongTime)
253:            Set objWMIPropertySet = objWMIInstance.Properties_
254:            For Each objWMIProperty In objWMIPropertySet
255:                Select Case objWMIProperty.Name
256:                    Case "Caption"
257:                    Case "Description"
258:                    Case "Name"
259:                    Case Else
260:                        varTemp = varTemp & "," & objWMIProperty.Value
261:                End Select
262:            Next
```

```
...:
268:                WriteToFile objLogFileName(intIndice - 1), varTemp
269:
270:                WScript.Echo "  WMICounter '" & arrayCounterName(intIndice - 1) & _
271:                             "' saved."
272:            Next
273:
274:        End Sub
275:
276:        ]]>
277:    </script>
278:  </job>
279:</package>
```

First, the sink routine increments a counter (line 238) used to display the number of performance counter samples already taken (lines 241 through 243). Next, the script refreshes the performance instances stored in the **SWbemRefresher** object (line 245). For each instance available in the **SWbemRefresher** object, the script executes a loop (lines 247 through 272) to save the performance counter instance data (lines 251 through 268). Each property (lines 254 through 262) of the performance counter is properly formatted into a .CSV format (line 260). Next, the counter data is appended to the corresponding .CSV file (line 268).

Note that the timer event is defaulted to ten seconds. The command-line definition exposes a switch, called **/Interval**, to redefine the timer event interval. Although a smaller value can be used, it is important to avoid too small intervals, because they will create huge .CSV files and generate a lot of network traffic if the monitored system is remote. In the same way as the performance data capture is executed during the timer event sink execution, if the timer interval is small, the refreshed instances data may not correspond to the instance state at the timer event triggering. WMI sends the event notifications to the consumer when they are available. However, it is likely that the consumer processes the event notification more slowly than the event notifications arrive. In such a case, waiting requests are queued. In such circumstances, it is likely that event notifications are not immediately processed when they are triggered. This is the reason why the script takes the time of the __*IntervalTimerInstruction* system class stored in the *TIME_ CREATED* property exposed by the __*TimerEvent* system class (lines 252 and 253) and not the date and time of the event sink execution (lines 242 and 243).

3.8.2   **Performance Monitoring provider**

The *Performance Monitoring* provider is an instance and property provider that returns the same data seen in the System Monitor application. However, since it is not a *High-performance* provider, it lacks the speed and capabilities available through *High-performance* providers. (See Table 3.78.)

Table 3.78   *The Performance Monitoring Providers Capabilities*

Provider Name	Provider Namespace	Class Provider	Instance Provider	Method Provider	Property Provider	Event Provider	Event Consumer Provider	Support Get	Support Put	Support Enumeration	Support Delete	Windows Server 2003	Windows XP	Windows 2000 Server	Windows 2000 Professional	Windows NT 4.0
Performance Monitoring Provider																
PerfProv	Root/PerfMON	X						X	X			X	X	X	X	
PerfPropProv	Root/PerfMON			X				X				X	X	X	X	

The *Performance Monitoring* provider is not automatically registered in the Operating System. The main reason is that Microsoft does not encourage its use anymore and suggests the use of the *High-performance* providers instead. Therefore, if it is necessary to access system performance data using this provider, it must be registered first. (See Sample 3.79.)

Sample 3.79   *The MOF file to register the Performance Monitoring provider*

```
 1:    #pragma namespace("\\\\.\\Root")
 2:
 3:    instance of __Namespace
 4:    {
 5:        Name = "PerfMON";
 6:    };
 7:
 8:    #pragma namespace("\\\\.\\Root\\PerfMON")
 9:
10:    instance of __Win32Provider as $PMPInst
11:    {
12:        Name  = "PerfProv";
13:        ClsId = "{f00b4404-f8f1-11ce-a5b6-00aa00680c3f}";
14:    };
15:
16:    instance of __InstanceProviderRegistration
17:    {
18:        Provider = "__Win32Provider.Name=\"PerfProv\"";
19:        SupportsPut = FALSE;
20:        SupportsGet = TRUE;
21:        SupportsDelete = FALSE;
22:        SupportsEnumeration = TRUE;
23:    };
24:
25:    instance of __Win32Provider as $PMPProp
26:    {
27:        Name = "PerfPropProv";
28:        Clsid = "{72967903-68EC-11d0-B729-00AA0062CBB7}";
29:    };
```

```
30:
31:    instance of __PropertyProviderRegistration
32:    {
33:        Provider = $PMPProp;
34:        SupportsGet = TRUE;
35:        SupportsPut = FALSE;
36:    };
37:
```

Briefly, this MOF file registers the instance provider (lines 10 through 23) and the property provider (lines 25 through 36). This MOF file comes from the WMI section in the Microsoft Platform SDK. The only additions are lines 1 through 8 to ensure the registration of the provider in a dedicated namespace, in this case called PerfMON.

Once the provider is registered, it is also necessary to create the classes and the instances that will receive information from the provider. So, this provider is not usable out of the box and does not expose any classes by default. The classes must be created from a MOF file. For example, to retrieve all the Performance Monitor Counters related to the processes (as shown in Figure 3.54), the MOF file shown in Sample 3.80 must be loaded in the CIM repository.

Figure 3.54
The Performance Monitor Process counters.

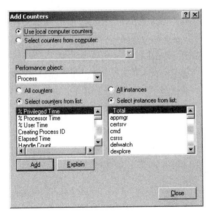

Sample 3.80   *A MOF file defining a class to retrieve Process counters from the Performance Monitor*

```
1:    #pragma namespace("\\\\.\\Root")
2:
3:    instance of __Namespace
4:    {
5:        Name = "PerfMON";
6:    };
7:
8:    #pragma namespace("//./Root/PerfMON")
9:
```

```
10:    [dynamic, provider("PerfProv"), ClassContext("local|Process")]
11:    class NTProcess
12:    {
13:        [key]
14:          String Process;
15:
16:        [PropertyContext("% Privileged Time")]
17:            uint32 PercentagePrivilegedTime;
18:        [PropertyContext("% Processor Time")]
19:            uint32 PercentageProcessTime;
20:        [PropertyContext("% User Time")]
21:            uint32 PercentageUserTime;
22:        [PropertyContext("Create Process ID")]
23:            uint32 CreateProcessID;
24:        [PropertyContext("Elapsed Time")]
25:            uint32 ElapsedTime;
26:        [PropertyContext("Handle Count")]
27:            uint32 HandleCount;
28:        [PropertyContext("ID Process")]
29:            uint32 ID;
30:        [PropertyContext("IO Data Bytes/sec")]
31:            uint32 IODataBytesPersec;
32:        [PropertyContext("IO Data Operations/sec")]
33:            uint32 IODataOperationsPersec;
34:        [PropertyContext("IO Other Bytes/sec")]
35:            uint32 IOOtherBytesPersec;
36:        [PropertyContext("IO Other Operations/sec")]
37:            uint32 IOOtherOperationsPersec;
38:        [PropertyContext("IO Read Bytes/sec")]
39:            uint32 IOReadBytesPersec;
40:        [PropertyContext("IO Read Operations/sec")]
41:            uint32 IOReadOperationsPersec;
42:        [PropertyContext("IO Write Bytes/sec")]
43:            uint32 IOWriteBytesPersec;
44:        [PropertyContext("IO Write Operations/sec")]
45:            uint32 IOWriteOperationsPersec;
46:        [PropertyContext("Page Faults/sec")]
47:            uint32 PageFaultsPersec;
48:        [PropertyContext("Page File Bytes")]
49:            uint32 PageFileBytes;
50:        [PropertyContext("Page File Bytes Peak")]
51:            uint32 PageFileBytesPeak;
52:        [PropertyContext("Pool Nonpaged Bytes")]
53:            uint32 PoolNonpagedBytes;
54:        [PropertyContext("Pool Paged Bytes")]
55:            uint32 PoolPagedBytes;
56:        [PropertyContext("Priority Base")]
57:            uint32 PriorityBase;
58:        [PropertyContext("Private Bytes")]
59:            uint32 PrivateBytes;
60:        [PropertyContext("Thread Count")]
61:            uint32 ThreadCount;
62:        [PropertyContext("Virtual Bytes")]
63:            uint32 VirtualBytes;
64:        [PropertyContext("Virtual Bytes Peak")]
65:            uint32 VirtualBytesPeak;
66:        [PropertyContext("Working Set")]
67:            uint32 WorkingSet;
68:        [PropertyContext("Working Set Peak")]
69:            uint32 WorkingSetPeak;
70:    };
```

From line 1 through 8, the MOF file creates the **Root\PerfMON** namespace. It also creates the Performance Monitor *NTProcess* class (lines 10 through 69). The class and properties creations require three qualifiers specific to the *Performance Monitor* provider usage:

- *Provider* qualifier: This qualifier specifies the *Performance Monitoring* provider as the dynamic provider responsible for managing the data for the new class. This provider is specified at the class level (line 10).

- *ClassContext* qualifier: This qualifier specifies information needed by the *Performance Monitoring* provider to access the requested counter. The format of the *ClassContext* qualifier is:

  ```
  machine | perfobject
  ```

  where **machine** is the machine name and **perfobject** is the name of the performance object shown in System Monitor in Performance Monitoring (see Figure 3.55). In Sample 3.80, a value of "local | Process" indicates processes on the local machine in a class defined to hold counter data about the processes.

- *PropertyContext* qualifier: This qualifier identifies the display name of each counter. This is the name appearing in the Performance Monitoring tool (see Figure 3.53). This qualifier is specified for each property created for the class and accessing a specific Performance Monitor Counter (even lines 16 through 68).

Once compiled, **WMI CIM Studio** will show the screen seen in Figure 3.55.

Now, we are ready to access the Process counters from the Performance Monitor tool with a script. This last part has nothing unusual, since the script follows the traditional scripting techniques. It is available for your information in the Jscript Sample 3.81.

Sample 3.81   *Viewing the Performance Monitor Process counters with a script*

```
 1:<?xml version="1.0"?>
 .:
 8:<package>
 9:  <job>
 ..:
13:    <script language="VBScript" src="..\Functions\DisplayFormattedPropertyFunction.vbs" />
14:
15:    <object progid="WbemScripting.SWbemLocator" id="objWMILocator" reference="true"/>
16:    <object progid="WbemScripting.SWbemDateTime" id="objWMIDateTime" />
17:
18:    <script language="JScript">
19:    <![CDATA[
20:
```

```
21:    var cComputerName = "LocalHost";
22:    var cWMINameSpace = "Root/PerfMON";
23:    var cWMIClass = "NTProcess";
..:
29:    objWMILocator.Security_.AuthenticationLevel = wbemAuthenticationLevelDefault;
30:    objWMILocator.Security_.ImpersonationLevel = wbemImpersonationLevelImpersonate;
31:    objWMIServices = objWMILocator.ConnectServer(cComputerName, cWMINameSpace, "", "");
32:    objWMIInstances = objWMIServices.InstancesOf (cWMIClass);
33:
34:    enumWMIInstances = new Enumerator (objWMIInstances);
35:    for (;! enumWMIInstances.atEnd(); enumWMIInstances.moveNext())
36:        {
37:        objWMIInstance = enumWMIInstances.item();
38:
39:        objWMIPropertySet = objWMIInstance.Properties_
40:        enumWMIPropertySet = new Enumerator (objWMIPropertySet);
41:        for (;! enumWMIPropertySet.atEnd(); enumWMIPropertySet.moveNext())
42:            {
43:            objWMIProperty = enumWMIPropertySet.item()
44:
45:            DisplayFormattedProperty (objWMIInstance,
46:                                      objWMIProperty.Name,
47:                                      objWMIProperty.Name,
48:                                      null);
49:            }
50:        WScript.Echo ();
51:        }
52:
53:    ]]>
54:    </script>
55:  </job>
56:</package>
```

Figure 3.55
*The Process
counters of the
Performance
Counters available
from WMI.*

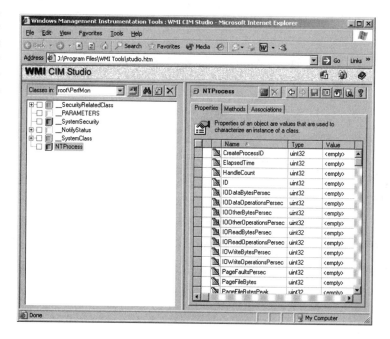

3.9   Helper providers

Until now, each time we worked with a WMI provider, it collected information about a specific managed object in a computer. WMI also comes with a collection of providers designed to support some WMI internal features. In this section, we will examine the two most useful features from a WMI consumer perspective: the *View* provider to support the concept of views and the *Forwarding consumer* provider to perform events forwarding. We will also briefly examine the event Correlator providers.

3.9.1   The View provider

The main capability of the *View* provider is its ability to take properties from different source classes, different namespaces, and different computers and combine all information in one single class. Basically, the concept of the *View* provider looks very similar to the concept of views developed for the relational database. Of course, this comparison must be limited here, since its implementation is totally different. To take advantage of the *View* provider, it must first be registered in the CIM repository. The registration can be done with the **MOFCOMP.EXE** tool and the MOF file shown in Sample 3.82.

Sample 3.82   *Registering the View provider*

```
 1:#pragma namespace("\\\\.\\Root")
 2:
 3:Instance of __Namespace
 4:{
 5:  Name = "View";
 6:};
 7:
 8:#pragma namespace("\\\\.\\ROOT\\View")
 9:
10:Instance of __Win32Provider as $DataProv
11:{
12:  Name = "MS_VIEW_INSTANCE_PROVIDER";
13:  ClsId = "{AA70DDF4-E11C-11D1-ABB0-00C04FD9159E}";
14:  ImpersonationLevel = 1;
15:  PerUserInitialization = "True";
16:  HostingModel = "NetworkServiceHost";
17:};
18:
19:Instance of __InstanceProviderRegistration
20:{
21:  Provider = $DataProv;
22:  SupportsPut = TRUE;
23:  SupportsGet = TRUE;
24:  SupportsDelete = TRUE;
25:  SupportsEnumeration = TRUE;
```

```
26:   QuerySupportLevels = {"WQL:UnarySelect"};
27:};
28:
29:Instance of __MethodProviderRegistration
30:{
31:   Provider = $DataProv;
32:};
```

You will note that the MOF file creates a new namespace for the provider (lines 3 through 6). This new namespace is not mandatory, since the registration can be done in any existing namespace. However, using a dedicated namespace clarifies the CIM repository organization, since only the classes created for the *View* provider will be available from this namespace. By default, there are few classes in the CIM repository supported by the *View* provider. These created classes are called the View classes. For example, the WMI information about the Internet Information Server (IIS) takes advantage of the *View* provider by accessing the *Win32_Service* instances in the **Root\CIMv2** namespace from the **Root\MicrosoftIISv2** namespace. The *View* provider is the component handling the cross-namespace access. As shown in Table 3.79, the *View* provider is implemented as an instance and a method provider.

Table 3.79   *The View Providers Capabilities*

Provider Name	Provider Namespace	Class Provider	Instance Provider	Method Provider	Property Provider	Event Provider	Event Consumer Provider	Support Get	Support Put	Support Enumeration	Support Delete	Windows Server 2003	Windows XP	Windows 2000 Server	Windows 2000 Professional	Windows NT 4.0
View Provider																
ViewProv	Not defined	X	X					X	X	X	X	X	X	X	X	X

As we will see, the *View* provider and the creation of the View classes are not directly related to the WMI scripting. However, once the View classes are created, any script can benefit from their existence.

We distinguish three types of view classes:

- The **Join view classes:** These classes represent the instances of different classes connected by a common property value.

- The **Union view classes:** These classes represent the union of one or more classes across the namespace boundary.

- The **Association view classes:** These classes represent views of existing association classes across the namespace boundary.

Because the View classes have these specific purposes, they use some specific qualifiers for their creation (see Table 3.80).

Table 3.80 *The View Provider Qualifiers*

Qualifier	Comments
Direct	Data type: Boolean Used with view association properties to prevent association references from being mapped to a view reference.
HiddenDefault	Data type: Boolean Default value for a view class property based on a source class property with a different default value. The underlying source class is implied by the view.
JoinOn	Data type: string Defines how source class instances should be joined in join view classes. The following example shows how to use the JoinOn qualifier to join two source classes from the Performance Monitoring Provider.
MethodSource	Data type: string array Source method to execute for the view method. For similar syntax, see PropertySources Qualifier. The signature of the method must match the signature of the source class exactly. Copy the method signature from the MOF file that defines the source class. This qualifier is only valid when it is used with union views.
PostJoinFilter	Data type:string WQL query to filter instances after they have been joined in a join class.
PropertySources	Data type: string array Source properties from which a view class property gets data.
Union	Data type: Boolean Indicates whether you are defining a union class. Union views contain instances based on the union of source instances. For example, you might declare the following.
ViewSources	Data type: string array Set of WMI Query Language (WQL) queries that define the source instances and properties used in a specific view class. Positional correspondence of all the array qualifiers is important.
ViewSpaces	Data type: string array Namespaces where the source instances are located.

Sample 3.83 shows a MOF file creating a Join view class. In this sample, the *View* provider joins the *Win32_PerfRawData_PerfProc_Process* class with the *Win32_PerfRawData_PerfProc_Thread* class. Because the join requires a common property value between the two classes, the *IDProcess* property is used as the common property.

Sample 3.83 *The Join View class*

```
 1:#pragma namespace("\\\\.\\Root\\View")
 2:
 3:[
 4: JoinOn("Win32_PerfRawData_PerfProc_Process.IDProcess=
                            Win32_PerfRawData_PerfProc_Thread.IDProcess"),
 5: ViewSources{
 6:         "SELECT Name, IDProcess, PriorityBase
                            FROM Win32_PerfRawData_PerfProc_Process" ,
 7:         "SELECT Name, IDProcess, ThreadState, PriorityCurrent
                            FROM Win32_PerfRawData_PerfProc_Thread"
 8:            },
 9: ViewSpaces{
10:            "\\\\.\\Root\\cimv2",
11:            "\\\\.\\Root\\cimv2"
12:            },
13: dynamic: ToInstance,
14: provider("MS_VIEW_INSTANCE_PROVIDER")
15:]
16:
17:class JoinedProcessThread
```

```
18:{
19: [read, PropertySources{"IDProcess",    "IDProcess"}] Uint32 ProcessID;
20: [read, PropertySources{"Name",         ""}] String ProcessName;
21: [read, PropertySources{"",             "Name"}, key] String ThreadName;
22: [read, PropertySources{"",             "ThreadState"}] Uint32 State;
23: [read, PropertySources{"PriorityBase", ""}] Uint32 BasePriority;
24: [read, PropertySources{"",             "PriorityCurrent"}] Uint32 CurrentPriority;
25:};
```

At line 4, we see the *JoinOn* qualifier stating the link between the two classes on the *IDProcess* property. Because the MOF file links two instances coming from two different classes, lines 5 through 8 use the *ViewSources* qualifier to locate each instance coming from each respective class. This qualifier contains the WQL queries to locate instances of each class. Since every instance must be located in its respective namespaces, the *ViewSpaces* qualifier contains the WMI namespaces in which to look. At line 13, the View class is defined as a dynamic View class with the *Dynamic* qualifier. Next, the provider qualifier defines the *View* provider to support this new class definition.

From line 17 through 25, the class itself is defined. Each property of the class definition uses the *PropertySources* qualifier to map the desired property of the original class to a property of the View class. Note that in this example, each qualifier supported by the *View* provider is an array containing two items, where each of them corresponds to information related to the original classes. Once the MOF file is loaded in the CIM repository, the *JoinedProcessThread* class will be accessible from the **Root\View** namespace (see Figure 3.56).

We can reuse the script developed in Chapter 1 (Sample 1.5, "Listing all instances of a class with their properties formatted") to display instances of this View class:

```
 1:   C:\>GetCollectionOfInstances.wsf JoinedProcessThread /NameSpace:Root\View
 2:   Microsoft (R) Windows Script Host Version 5.6
 3:   Copyright (C) Microsoft Corporation 1996-2001. All rights reserved.
 4:
 5:
 6:   BasePriority: ........................... 0
 7:   CurrentPriority: ........................ 0
 8:   ProcessName: ............................ Idle
 9:   ProcessID: .............................. 0
10:   State: .................................. 2
11:   *ThreadName: ............................ Idle/0
12:
13:   BasePriority: ........................... 0
14:   CurrentPriority: ........................ 0
15:   ProcessName: ............................ Idle
16:   ProcessID: .............................. 0
17:   State: .................................. 0
18:   *ThreadName: ............................ _Total/_Total
19:
```

```
20:    BasePriority: ........................... 8
21:    CurrentPriority: ........................ 0
22:    ProcessName: ............................ System
23:    ProcessID: .............................. 4
24:    State: .................................. 1
25:    *ThreadName: ............................ System/0
26:
27:    BasePriority: ........................... 8
28:    CurrentPriority: ........................ 13
29:    ProcessName: ............................ System
30:    ProcessID: .............................. 4
31:    State: .................................. 5
32:    *ThreadName: ............................ System/1
33:
34:    BasePriority: ........................... 8
35:    CurrentPriority: ........................ 13
36:    ProcessName: ............................ System
  ..:
  ..:
  ..:
```

If you compare the properties of each original class with the content of the MOF file sample, you will see that each instance contains a mix of the properties coming from the *Win32_PerfRawData_PerfProc_Process* and *Win32_PerfRawData_PerfProc_Thread* classes joined by the *IDProcess* property. In other words, you consolidate the data from two different instances into one.

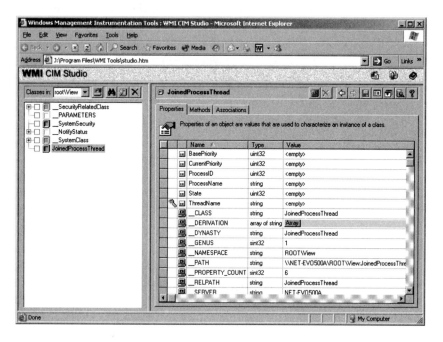

Figure 3.56   *The new created Join View class.*

The second View class type is the Union class. Sample 3.84 shows a MOF file example to create a Union View class.

Sample 3.84   *The Union View class*

```
 1:#pragma namespace("\\\\.\\Root\\View")
 2:
 3:[
 4: Union,
 5: ViewSources{
 6:            "SELECT * From Win32_LogicalDisk Where DeviceID='C:'",
 7:            "SELECT * From Win32_LogicalDisk Where DeviceID='C:'"
 8:            },
 9: ViewSpaces{
10:            "\\\\net-dpen6400a.LissWare.Net\\Root\\CIMv2",
11:            "\\\\net-dpep6400.Emea.LissWare.Net\\Root\\CIMv2"
12:            },
13: dynamic: ToInstance,
14: provider("MS_VIEW_INSTANCE_PROVIDER")
15:]
16:
17:Class UnionDrives_C
18:{
19: [read, PropertySources{"Description", "Description"}] string Description;
20: [read, PropertySources{"DeviceID", "DeviceID"}, key] String DeviceID;
21: [read, PropertySources{"VolumeSerialNumber", "VolumeSerialNumber"}, key] string VolumeSN;
22: [read, PropertySources{"FileSystem", "FileSystem"}] String FileSystem;
23: [read, PropertySources{"FreeSpace", "FreeSpace"}] uint64 FreeSpace;
24: [read, PropertySources{"VolumeName", "VolumeName"}, key] String VolumeName;
25: [read, PropertySources{"__SERVER", "__SERVER"}, key] String Server;
26:};
```

The *Union* qualifier doesn't use any parameter. However, it also works in conjunction with the *ViewSources* and the *ViewSpaces* qualifiers (lines 5 and 9). Although the *ViewSources* qualifier continues to use a WQL statement to locate the required instances (lines 5 through 8), it is important to note the following:

- The *ViewSources* qualifier selects the "C:" drive instances only (see WQL data query).

- The *ViewSpaces* qualifier locates these instances in the same namespaces but on two different systems (lines 9 through 12).

As a result, the *UnionDrives_C* class (defined from line 17 through 25) will list a collection of two "C:" drive instances coming from the two different systems defined in the *ViewSpaces* qualifier. Note the presence of the *__SERVER* system property, exposed as the "server" Key property (line 25), and the definition of the *VolumeSerialNumber* property as another Key property to distinguish each View class instance (line 24). Originally, the Key property of the *Win32_LogicalDisk* source class was the *DeviceID* property, which is the drive letter of the logical disk. Now, because the View class

retrieves a collection of "C:" drive instances, the *DeviceID* property can't be
used, since it is the only Key property originally used to distinguish the various instances. This means that other uniqueness criteria must be created.
This is why the *server* and the *VolumeSerialNumber* properties are also
defined as Key properties. The output would be as follows:

```
 1:   C:\>GetCollectionOfInstances.wsf UnionDrives_C /NameSpace:Root\View
 2:   Microsoft (R) Windows Script Host Version 5.6
 3:   Copyright (C) Microsoft Corporation 1996-2001. All rights reserved.
 4:
 5:
 6:   Description: ........................... Local Fixed Disk
 7:   *DeviceID: ............................. C:
 8:   FileSystem: ........................... NTFS
 9:   FreeSpace: ............................ 827183616
10:   Server: ............................... NET-DPEN6400A
11:   *VolumeName: .......................... Windows 2003
12:   *VolumeSerialNumber: .................. 988BD271
13:
14:   Description: ........................... Local Fixed Disk
15:   *DeviceID: ............................. C:
16:   FileSystem: ........................... NTFS
17:   FreeSpace: ............................ 725999616
18:   Server: ............................... NET-DPEP6400
19:   *VolumeName: .......................... Windows 2003
20:   *VolumeSerialNumber: .................. 74052931
```

By addressing one single class from one namespace, we get a collection
of instances coming from two different systems. However, it looks like this
information is coming from the local system. It must be clear that the credentials used to connect to the **Root\View** namespace must also be valid to
connect to the remote **Root\CIMv2** namespaces!

The last View class type supported by the *View* provider is the Association view class. Basically, what we did before with the previous classes (see
Sample 3.84) can be done with the association classes. This class creation is
illustrated in Sample 3.85.

Sample 3.85   *The Association View class*

```
 1:#pragma namespace("\\\\.\\Root\\View")
 2:
 3:[
 4: Union,
 5: ViewSources{
 6:          "SELECT * From Win32_LogicalDisk Where DeviceID='C:'"
 7:          },
 8: ViewSpaces{
 9:          "\\\\.\\Root\\CIMv2"
10:          },
11: dynamic,
12: provider("MS_VIEW_INSTANCE_PROVIDER")
```

```
13:]
14:
15:Class UnionDrive_C
16:{
17: [read, PropertySources{"Description"}] string Description;
18: [read, PropertySources{"DeviceID"}, key] String DeviceID;
19: [read, PropertySources{"VolumeSerialNumber"}, key] string VolumeSerialNumber;
20: [read, PropertySources{"FileSystem"}] String FileSystem;
21: [read, PropertySources{"FreeSpace"}] uint64 FreeSpace;
22: [read, PropertySources{"VolumeName"}, key] String VolumeName;
23: [read, PropertySources{"__SERVER"}, Key] String Server;
24:
25: [Implemented,
26:  MappingStrings{"Fmifs.dll | Method ChkDskExRoutine"}: ToSubClass,
27:  MethodSource{"Chkdsk"}] uint32 ViewChkdsk([in] boolean FixErrors = FALSE,
28:                                            [in] boolean VigorousIndexCheck = TRUE,
29:                                            [in] boolean SkipFolderCycle = TRUE,
30:                                            [in] boolean ForceDismount = FALSE,
31:                                            [in] boolean RecoverBadSectors = FALSE,
32:                                            [in] boolean OkToRunAtBootUp = FALSE);
33:};
34:
35:[
36: Association,
37: ViewSources {
38:            "SELECT * FROM Win32_DiskQuota"
39:            },
40: ViewSpaces {
41:            "\\\\.\\Root\\CIMv2"
42:            },
43: dynamic,
44: provider("MS_VIEW_INSTANCE_PROVIDER")
45:]
46:
47:class Association_UnionOfDriveQuota
48:{
49:    [key, PropertySources{"QuotaVolume"}]
50:    UnionDrive_C ref Drive;
51:
52:    [Direct, key, PropertySources{"User"}]
53:    Win32_Account ref User;
54:};
```

The MOF file sample contains two main parts:

- A Union View class creation, made from the *Win32_LogicalDisk* class (lines 3 through 33). Basically, this Union View class creation follows the same rules as Sample 3.84. However, the instances of this class are coming from one single namespace in one single computer (lines 8 through 10). So, this technique maps a class from one namespace (**Root\CIMv2**) to make it available to another namespace (**Root\View**). The Association View class created in the second part of the MOF file references this Union class.

The interesting addition in this Union class is the mapping of the *Chkdsk* method defined in the *Win32_LogicalDisk* class. In the previous sample, we only mapped some properties. In this example, we also map a method with the help of the *MethodSource* qualifier. Note that it is important to use a method definition in the View Class that exactly matches the method definition in the original class, which is, in this example, the *Win32_LogicalDisk* class. The best method is to take a MOF file export of this class, cut the method definition from this exported MOF file, and paste it into your MOF file. As a result, the *Chkdsk* method is mapped to the View class as the *ViewChkdsk* method (lines 27 through 32).

■ An Association View class, made from the *Win32_DiskQuota* association class, associates the previously created *UnionDrive_C* View class with the *Win32_Account* class. The link with the *Win32_Account* class is defined with the *User* reference originally coming from the *Win32_DiskQuota* class (lines 35 through 54). If you go back to the *Win32_DiskQuota* association class and look at what this class associates, you will see that two classes are linked together:

   ■ The *Win32_LogicalDisk* class with the *QuotaVolume* reference
   ■ The *Win32_Account* class with the *User* reference

However, the *QuotaVolume* reference is overwritten by the *Drive* reference defined in the association View class, while the *User* reference is kept intact in the *Win32_DiskQuota* association class by the presence of the *Direct* qualifier. You can compare the *Association_UnionOfDriveQuota* association View class with the *Win32_DiskQuota* association class shown in Figure 3.57.

Figure 3.57
The Win32_DiskQuota association class and the created Association View class.

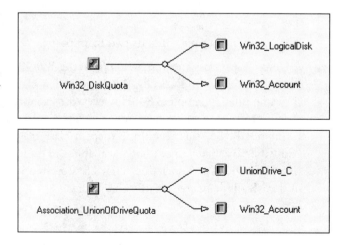

From a scripting perspective, we obtain the following output for the newly created Association View class:

```
1:   C:\>GetCollectionOfInstances.wsf Association_UnionOfDriveQuota /NameSpace:Root\View
2:   Microsoft (R) Windows Script Host Version 5.6
3:   Copyright (C) Microsoft Corporation 1996-2001. All rights reserved.
4:
5:
6:   *Drive: .............................. \\NET-DPEN6400A\Root\VIEW:UnionDrive_C.DeviceID=
              "C:",Server="NET-DPEN6400A",VolumeName="Windows 2003",VolumeSerialNumber="988BD271"
7:   *User: ............................... Win32_Account.Domain=
                                             "NET-DPEN6400A",Name="Administrators"
```

This last example illustrates how it is possible to associate classes from different namespaces with the *View* provider.

3.9.2 The Forwarding consumer provider

The *Microsoft WMI Forwarding consumer* provider is available under Windows XP.

Registered in the **Root\Subscription** namespace, it allows local WMI events to be forwarded to remote systems. In remote systems the *Microsoft WMI Forwarding event* provider, registered in the **Root\CIMv2** namespace, triggers the received forwarded event as an instance of the *MSFT_ForwardedEvent* extrinsic event class. To trace the *Microsoft WMI Forwarding consumer* provider activity, the *Microsoft WMI Forwarding Consumer Trace* event provider, also registered in the **Root\Subscription** namespace, generates WMI events with a specific set of extrinsic event classes to any WMI consumers subscribing to these event notifications.

Table 3.81 *The WMI Forwarding Consumer and Forwarding Event Providers Capabilities*

Provider Name	Provider Name Space	Class Provider	Instance Provider	Method Provider	Property Provider	Event Provider	Event Consumer Provider	Support Get	Support Put	Support Enumeration	Support Delete	Windows Server 2003	Windows XP	Windows 2000 Server	Windows 2000 Professional	Windows NT 4.0
Microsoft WMI Forwarding Consumer Provider																
FwdProv	Root/Subscription						X						X			
Microsoft WMI Forwarding Consumer Trace Event Provider																
FwdProv	Root/Subscription						X						X			
Microsoft WMI Forwarding Event Provider																
FwdProv	Root/CIMV2					X							X			

Table 3.81 summarizes the characteristics of the *Microsoft WMI Forwarding Consumer, Microsoft WMI Forwarding Event,* and *Microsoft WMI*

Forwarding Consumer Trace event providers. Table 3.82 lists classes supported by these three providers implemented in one single DLL (**Fwd-Prov.DLL**).

Table 3.82   *The WMI Forwarding Consumer and Forwarding Event Providers Classes*

Microsoft WMI Forwarding Consumer Provider class	
Name	**Description**
MSFT_ForwardingConsumer	Represents an event consumer that forwards messages to target computer(s).
Microsoft WMI Forwarding Consumer Trace Event Provider classes	
Name	**Description**
Select * From MSFT_FCTraceEventBase	
MSFT_FCTraceEventBase	Base class for all forwarding consumer trace events.
MSFT_FCExecutedTraceEvent	Represents an execution of the forwarding consumer.
MSFT_FCTargetTraceEvent	Represents an attempt to forward a message to a target.
Microsoft WMI Forwarding Event Provider class	
Name	**Description**
MSFT_ForwardedMessageEvent	Base class for all forwarded messages.
MSFT_ForwardedEvent	Indicates the arrival of a forwarded event.

Event forwarding involves at the minimum two systems: a source machine and a target machine. Figure 3.58 illustrates the logical organization of the various elements involved in event forwarding.

The source machine is the machine where the original WMI event notification occurs (i.e., SourceComputer01). This is also the machine that forwards the event. To do so, it is necessary to create an instance of the *MSFT_ForwardingConsumer* class supported by the *Microsoft WMI Forwarding consumer* provider. Basically, this instance determines which event notification will be forwarded and to which target machines it must be forwarded. Therefore, the *Microsoft WMI Forwarding consumer* provider consumes a specific WMI event notification to be forwarded to the target machine, as defined in the *MSFT_ForwardingConsumer* instance. At the other end, the target machine (i.e., TargetComputer01) is the system receiving the event forwarded by the *Microsoft WMI Forwarding consumer* provider in the source machine. The *Microsoft WMI Forwarding event* provider is in charge of receiving the forwarded event and triggering an event notification as an instance of the *MSFT_ForwardedEvent* extrinsic event class. Any WMI consumer who subscribed to receive the forwarded event will get a notification. More than simply notifying that an event has been forwarded, the subscriber will also find information inside the *MSFT_ForwardedEvent* about the instances (located in the source machine) subject to the event notification.

To configure this mechanism, the first step is to create an instance of the *MSFT_ForwardingConsumer* class with its __*EventFilter* associated class.

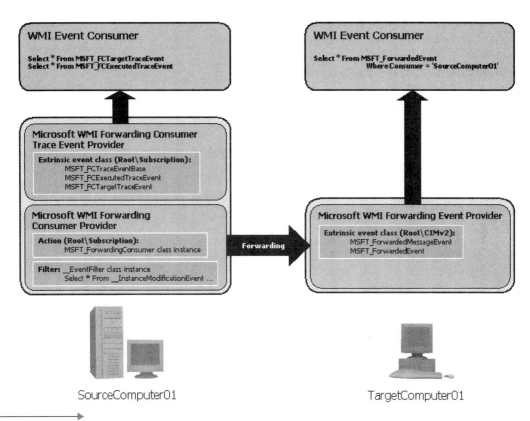

Figure 3.58   *The WMI Forwarding providers roles and locations.*

This can be done with a MOF file (see Sample 3.86). Of course, a script can create these instances as well.

Sample 3.86   *A MOF file to forward WMI events*

```
1:#pragma namespace ("\\\\.\\Root\\Subscription")
2:
3:Instance of MSFT_ForwardingConsumer as $SRCComputer01Consumer
4:
5:{
6:    // Indicates whether to include authentication information when forwarding the message.
7:        Authenticate = "True";
8:
9:    // Indicates whether to encrypt the message before forwarding.
10:       Encryption = "False";
11:
12:   // The Quality-of-Service used to forward the message (0=Synchronous).
13:       ForwardingQoS = 0;
14:
15:   // Indicates whether to send schema information for the event to be forwarded.
16:       IncludeSchema = "False";
```

```
17:
18:    // Name of the computer from which the message originates (inherited property).
19:    // MachineName =
20:
21:    // Maximum size of the queue in bytes.
22:    // MaximumQueueSize =
23:
24:    // A string uniquely identifying this consumer.
25:       Name = "SourceComputer01";
26:
27:    // An array of addresses to forward the messages to.
28:    // The forwarding consumer will try to forward the message, in order,
29:    // to each address in the list until it successfully sends it to one of them.
30:       Targets = {"NET-DPEN6400A.LissWare.NET"};
31:
32:    // A security descriptor, in SDDL format, that is attached to the
33:    // forwarded event when it is raised on the receiving end.
34:    // This security descriptor indicates to the receiver which security
35:    // identitiers are allowed to consume the forwarded event.
36:    // TargetSD = "";
37:};
38:
39:Instance of __EventFilter as $SRCComputer01Filter
40:
41:{
42:    Name = "Forward all Win32_Service instance modifications";
43:    Query = "Select * From __InstanceModificationEvent Within 5 "
44:                        "Where TargetInstance ISA 'Win32_Service'";
45:    QueryLanguage = "WQL";
46:    EventNamespace = "Root\\CIMv2";
47:};
48:
49:Instance of __FilterToConsumerBinding
50:
51:{
52:    Consumer=$SRCComputer01Consumer;
53:    Filter=$SRCComputer01Filter;
54:};
```

As with any WMI consumer providers, Sample 3.86 creates:

- An instance of the *MSFT_ForwardingConsumer* class (derived from the *__EventConsumer* superclass) supported by the WMI consumer (lines 3 through 37)

- An instance of the *__EventFilter* system class to define the WMI event notification to subscribe to (lines 39 through 47)

- An instance of the *__FilterToConsumerBinding* association class to link the consumer with the WQL event notification filter (lines 49 through 54)

In this particular example, we are interested in the *MSFT_Forwarding-Consumer* instance creation, since it contains all parameters related to the forwarding mechanism.

- **Authenticate** (line 7): **Authenticate** indicates whether to include authentication information when forwarding the message. Is there a reason not to include the authentication information? Well, in some situations, it could be necessary to forward events between Active Directory Forests, where no trust exists between Forests. In such a case, it is necessary to set the **Authenticate** parameter to False. However, this is not enough to get this working. Since the authentication information is not contained in the message, to avoid an access-denied error message and ensure that the *Microsoft WMI Forwarding Event* in the target machine effectively triggers the event notification, it is necessary to set the *AllowUnauthenticatedEvents* registry key located in the HKLM\SOFTWARE\Microsoft\WBEM\FWD hive to 1. This will ensure that the *Microsoft WMI Forwarding event* provider accepts unauthenticated events. Note that if you change this registry key value, it is necessary to restart the **WinMgmt.Exe** service to make the change effective.

- **Encryption** (line 10): **Encryption** indicates that packets between the source and the target machine are encrypted. The encryption is based on the COM Packet Privacy encryption mechanism. Note that by default, under Windows XP, the encryption is set to False.

- **ForwardingQoS** (line 13): This property is not used, but it is reserved for future use and extensions. Its default value must be zero.

- **IncludeSchema** (line 16): The **IncludeSchema** purpose is to send a CIM repository definition (which exists in the source machine) of the instances subject to the event. This ensures that the target machine understands the structure of the *TargetInstance* and *PreviousInstance* properties containing objects returned by the event forwarding notification in case these class definitions do not exist in the target machine. Keep in mind that setting **IncludeSchema** to True will represent a big overhead for the network. Therefore, it is best to set **IncludeSchema** to False for performance reasons. Note that setting **IncludeSchema** to False always includes the schema information for the first event with the condition that events are from the same source and class.

- **MaximumQueueSize** (line 22): This property is reserved for future use and extensions. It should not be defined (the line is commented out in Sample 3.86).

- **Targets** (line 30): **Targets** contain the list of computers that must be contacted as targets. This property acts as a "try list," which means that the forwarding consumer will try to forward the message, in order, to each address in the list until it successfully sends it to one of them. If you want to forward the same event to several computers, you must register several instances of the Forwarding Consumer (one per target). On the other hand, it is important to note that target machines, consuming forwarded events, are able to process *MSFT_ForwardedEvent* events from multiple computers and networks.

- **TargetSD** (line 36): **TargetSD** represents a security descriptor in security descriptor definition language (SDDL) format (see http:// msdn.microsoft.com/library/en-us/security/Security/security_ descriptor_string_format.asp for more information about SDDL). This security descriptor is attached to the forwarded event when it is raised on the target machine. It indicates to the receiver which security identifiers are allowed to consume the forwarded event.

Once the MOF file in Sample 3.86 is loaded with **MOFCOMP.EXE** in the CIM repository of the source machine, any *Win32_Service* instance modification events will be forwarded to the target machine. The only thing to do on the target machine is to run a WMI consumer subscribing to the event forwarding notification. In this example, we can reuse the **GenericEventAsyncConsumer.wsf** script (see Sample 6.17, "A generic script for asynchronous event notification" in the appendix). The WQL event query to formulate on the target machine must be as follows:

```
1:   C:\>GenericEventAsyncConsumer.wsf "Select * From MSFT_ForwardedEvent
                                        Where Consumer = 'SourceComputer01'"
2:   Microsoft (R) Windows Script Host Version 5.6
3:   Copyright (C) Microsoft Corporation 1996-2001. All rights reserved.
4:
5:   Waiting for events...
6:
7:   BEGIN - OnObjectReady.
8:   Thursday, 11 July, 2002 at 15:12:10: 'MSFT_ForwardedEvent' has been triggered.
9:      Account (wbemCimtypeUint8) = 1
10:     Account (wbemCimtypeUint8) = 5
11:     Account (wbemCimtypeUint8) = 0
..:
34:     Account (wbemCimtypeUint8) = 3
35:     Account (wbemCimtypeUint8) = 0
36:     Account (wbemCimtypeUint8) = 0
37:     Authenticated (wbemCimtypeBoolean) = True
38:     Consumer (wbemCimtypeString) = SourceComputer01
39:     Event (wbemCimtypeObject)
40:        PreviousInstance (wbemCimtypeObject)
41:           AcceptPause (wbemCimtypeBoolean) = False
42:           AcceptStop (wbemCimtypeBoolean) = False
43:           Caption (wbemCimtypeString) = SNMP Service
```

```
44:       CheckPoint (wbemCimtypeUint32) = 0
45:       CreationClassName (wbemCimtypeString) = Win32_Service
46:       Description (wbemCimtypeString) = Enables Simple Network Management ...
..:
60:       State (wbemCimtypeString) = Stopped
61:       Status (wbemCimtypeString) = OK
62:       SystemCreationClassName (wbemCimtypeString) = Win32_ComputerSystem
63:       SystemName (wbemCimtypeString) = NET-DPEP6400A
64:       TagId (wbemCimtypeUint32) = 0
65:       WaitHint (wbemCimtypeUint32) = 0
66:     SECURITY_DESCRIPTOR (wbemCimtypeUint8) = (null)
67:     TargetInstance (wbemCimtypeObject)
68:       AcceptPause (wbemCimtypeBoolean) = False
69:       AcceptStop (wbemCimtypeBoolean) = True
70:       Caption (wbemCimtypeString) = SNMP Service
71:       CheckPoint (wbemCimtypeUint32) = 0
72:       CreationClassName (wbemCimtypeString) = Win32_Service
73:       Description (wbemCimtypeString) = Enables Simple Network Management ...
..:
87:       State (wbemCimtypeString) = Running
88:       Status (wbemCimtypeString) = OK
89:       SystemCreationClassName (wbemCimtypeString) = Win32_ComputerSystem
90:       SystemName (wbemCimtypeString) = NET-DPEP6400A
91:       TagId (wbemCimtypeUint32) = 0
92:       WaitHint (wbemCimtypeUint32) = 0
93:     TIME_CREATED (wbemCimtypeUint64) = (null)
94:   Machine (wbemCimtypeString) = NET-DPEP6400A
95:   Namespace (wbemCimtypeString) = ROOT\subscription
96:   SECURITY_DESCRIPTOR (wbemCimtypeUint8) = (null)
97:   Time (wbemCimtypeDatetime) = 11-07-2002 15:12:10 (20020711131210.000000+000)
98:   TIME_CREATED (wbemCimtypeUint64) = 11-07-2002 13:12:10 (20020711131210.953590+120)
99:
100:  END - OnObjectReady.
```

There are two levels of information received:

- The information about the forwarded event itself (lines 9 through 38 and lines 94 through 98)

- The information about the instances subject to the event triggered in the source machine (lines 39 through 93), which is divided into two parts: the *PreviousInstance* (lines 40 through 65) and *TargetInstance* (lines 67 through 92)

In the source machine, with the help of the *Microsoft WMI Forwarding Consumer Trace* event provider and its set of supported classes, it is possible to trace the execution of the *Microsoft WMI Forwarding consumer* provider. By using a simple WMI consumer subscribing to the *MSFT_FCExecutedTraceEvent* or the *MSFT_FCTargetTraceEvent* extrinsic event classes, it is possible to gather information about an event forwarding execution. We can reuse the **GenericEventAsyncConsumer.wsf** script shown in Sample 6.17 ("A generic script for asynchronous event notification") in the appendix to catch this event in the source machine:

```
 1:   C:\>GenericEventAsyncConsumer.wsf "Select * From MSFT_FCTargetTraceEvent"
                                                   /Namespace:Root\Subscription
 2:   Microsoft (R) Windows Script Host Version 5.6
 3:   Copyright (C) Microsoft Corporation 1996-2001. All rights reserved.
 4:
 5:   Waiting for events...
 6:
 7:   BEGIN - OnObjectReady.
 8:   Friday, 12 July, 2002 at 11:35:26: 'MSFT_FCTargetTraceEvent' has been triggered.
 9:      Consumer (wbemCimtypeObject)
10:         Authenticate (wbemCimtypeBoolean) = True
11:         CreatorSID (wbemCimtypeUint8) = 1
12:         CreatorSID (wbemCimtypeUint8) = 2
13:         CreatorSID (wbemCimtypeUint8) = 0
14:         CreatorSID (wbemCimtypeUint8) = 0
15:         CreatorSID (wbemCimtypeUint8) = 0
16:         CreatorSID (wbemCimtypeUint8) = 0
17:         CreatorSID (wbemCimtypeUint8) = 0
18:         CreatorSID (wbemCimtypeUint8) = 5
19:         CreatorSID (wbemCimtypeUint8) = 32
20:         CreatorSID (wbemCimtypeUint8) = 0
21:         CreatorSID (wbemCimtypeUint8) = 0
22:         CreatorSID (wbemCimtypeUint8) = 0
23:         CreatorSID (wbemCimtypeUint8) = 32
24:         CreatorSID (wbemCimtypeUint8) = 2
25:         CreatorSID (wbemCimtypeUint8) = 0
26:         CreatorSID (wbemCimtypeUint8) = 0
27:         Encryption (wbemCimtypeBoolean) = False
28:         ForwardingQoS (wbemCimtypeSint32) = 0
29:         IncludeSchema (wbemCimtypeBoolean) = False
30:         MachineName (wbemCimtypeString) = (null)
31:         MaximumQueueSize (wbemCimtypeUint32) = 65535
32:        *Name (wbemCimtypeString) = SourceComputer01
33:         Targets (wbemCimtypeString) = NET-DPEN6400A.LissWare.NET
34:         TargetSD (wbemCimtypeString) = (null)
35:      ExecutionId (wbemCimtypeString) = {F7EF6E36-FBAD-4C80-8196-BCC3B9A3A895}
36:      SECURITY_DESCRIPTOR (wbemCimtypeUint8) = (null)
37:      StatusCode (wbemCimtypeUint32) = 0
38:      Target (wbemCimtypeString) = 7879E40D-9FB5-450a-
                                  8A6D-00C89F349FCE@ncacn_ip_tcp:NET-DPEN6400A.LissWare.NET
39:      TIME_CREATED (wbemCimtypeUint64) = 12-07-2002 09:35:26 (20020712093526.907875+120)
40:   END - OnObjectReady.
```

The *MSFT_FCTargetTraceEvent* extrinsic event class represents an attempt to forward a message to a target machine, while the *MSFT_FCExecutedTraceEvent* extrinsic event class represents an execution of the forward-

Table 3.83   *The StatusCode Property Returned Values*

	Value	Description
WMIMSG_E_AUTHFAILURE	0x80042101	There was a problem in attaching authentication info with the forwarded event.
WMIMSG_E_ENCRYPTFAILURE	0x80042102	There was a problem in encrypting the forwarded event.
WMIMSG_E_INVALIDADDRESS	0x80042105	The target address specified for the forwarded event is invalid.
WMIMSG_E_TARGETNOTFOUND	0x80042106	The machine for the specified target address was not found.
WMIMSG_E_INVALIDMESSAGE	0x80042108	A receiver has received an invalid / corrupt message.
WMIMSG_E_REQSVCNOTAVAIL	0x80042109	A requested service is not available.
WMIMSG_E_TARGETNOTLISTENING	0x80042113	The target is valid but it is not listening for forwarded events.

ing consumer. Therefore, the latter contains information about instances related to the WQL event filter associated with the *MSFT_ForwardingConsumer* instance. In both cases, the most important property is the *StatusCode* property (line 37), since this value contains a return code determining if the event forwarding was successful (see Table 3.83).

3.9.3   The Event Correlator providers

The *Event Correlator* providers are available under Windows XP. The goal of this provider set is to correlate different events and send an alert or provide information only if a sequence of WMI events or a combination of an expected WMI data set is available from the system. For instance, monitoring a system and sending an alert only when the disk usage is at 50 percent and when the CPU usage has been higher than 80 percent in the last ten minutes for a period of two minutes is an example of correlation.

Although available in Windows XP, it is very important to note that today Microsoft does not encourage the use of these WMI correlation providers. This is the reason why Microsoft doesn't plan to make this provider available under Windows Server 2003 (although it was available during the beta program of Windows Server 2003).

Table 3.84   *The Correlation WMI Providers*

Provider Name	Provider Name Space	Class Provider	Instance Provider	Method Provider	Property Provider	Event Provider	Event Consumer Provider	Support Get	Support Put	Support Enumeration	Support Delete	Windows Server 2003	Windows XP	Windows 2000 Server	Windows 2000 Professional	Windows NT 4.0
The Updating consumers																
Microsoft WMI Updating Consumer Assoc Provider	Root/subscription		X					X	X	X	X		X			
MSFT_UCScenarioAssociation																
Microsoft WMI Updating Consumer Event Provider	Root/subscription					X							X			
Select * From MSFT_UCTraceEventBase																
Select * From MSFT_UCEventBase																
Microsoft WMI Updating Consumer Provider	Root/subscription						X						X			
MSFT_UpdatingConsumer																
MSFT_UCScenarioControl																
The Template providers																
Microsoft WMI Template Association Provider	Root/subscription		X					X		X			X			
Microsoft WMI Template Event Provider	Root/subscription					X							X			
Select * From __InstanceOperationEvent WHERE TargetInstance ISA "MSFT_TemplateBase"																
Microsoft WMI Template Provider	Root/subscription		X					X	X	X	X		X			
The Transient providers																
Microsoft WMI Transient Event Provider	Root/subscription					X							X			
Select * From MSFT_TransientEggTimerEvent																
Select * From __InstanceOperationEvent where TargetInstance isa "MSFT_TransientStateBase"																
Microsoft WMI Transient Provider	Root/subscription		X					X	X	X	X		X			
Microsoft WMI Transient Reboot Event Provider	Root/subscription					X							X			
Select * From MSFT_TransientRebootEvent																

Actually, Microsoft does not recommend any time and development investment in this feature due to the complexity of the current correlation implementation and some upcoming architectural changes regarding the future of the Windows management. Microsoft does not plan to enhance and support these WMI providers in the future and plans to provide a new correlation architecture, which will be .NET based with the next version of its operating system. You can check Chapter 5, section 5.8, "A Look into the Future of WMI Scripting," for a view of the WMI Scripting future.

Therefore, we will not cover these providers and their related classes. However, since it is available in Windows XP, for greater details it is recommended that you refer to the platform SDK. For your information, Table 3.84 contains the list of correlation providers with their related classes as is right after installation.

3.10   Summary

In this chapter, we continued to use the same scripting techniques (enumeration, WQL queries, sink routines, etc.) as previously. However, at this stage, we clearly realize that the challenge is not limited to knowledge of the WMI Scripting API with the CIM repository classes. The challenge expands to the knowledge of the WMI provider capabilities with their classes, which determines the features available (i.e., instance provider versus event provider). In this case, the main concern is to understand the underlying technology the providers are managing. The WMI *SNMP* providers are a good example of providers that require a fair understanding of the SNMP MIBs before scripting on top of the WMI classes representing SNMP information. Moreover, if some private SNMP information must be added to the CIM repository, the knowledge of the managed device from an SNMP point of view is determinant.

Although the real-world managed entities vary throughout the chapter, the scripting technique remains a constant whatever the managed component is. This is exactly where we get the benefit of the abstraction made by WMI and the CIM repository. However, the management information nature, its interpretation, and its representation become the focus of the WMI development.

Now that we have a fair understanding of the core WMI providers under Windows Server 2003, there is still one aspect of WMI that we haven't yet examined: the WMI Security scripting. This is the purpose of the next chapter.

3.11   Useful Internet URLs

Windows Installer provider:

```
http://www.microsoft.com/downloads/release.asp?releaseid=32832
```

SNMP providers for Windows NT 4.0:

```
http://www.microsoft.com/downloads/details.aspx?FamilyID=f8130806-2589-46b3-b472-
26b816776f31&DisplayLang=en
```

RFC1213:

```
http://www.faqs.org/rfcs/rfc1213.html
```

RFC1215:

```
http://www.faqs.org/rfcs/rfc1215.html
```

Cisco Private MIB files:

```
http://www.cisco.com/public/sw-center/netmgmt/cmtk/mibs.shtml
```

Cisco MIB OID numbers translation:

```
http://jaguar.ir.miami.edu/%7Emarcus/snmptrans.html
```

Security Descriptor String Format

```
http://msdn.microsoft.com/library/en-us/security/Security/security_descriptor_
string_format.asp
```

WMI Security Scripting

4.1   Objective

Previously, we discovered how to manage various components of Windows. In some cases, we saw that the security configuration is part of the component management. In this chapter, we will discover the WMI capabilities to manage the security settings of various Windows components, such as files, folders, and shares on the file system; Active Directory objects; and CIM repository namespaces. Although quite specific, the manipulation of the security settings, defined by security descriptors, is one of the most complex tasks to script. This chapter will explain the security descriptor components, their roles, and how to decipher them. One of the goals is to help you navigate between the various challenges that you face when automating and maintaining the security configuration under Windows. Beyond that, we will also see the security implication when developing ASP WMI-enabled scripts for Internet Information Server and how the Microsoft security push initiative in early 2002 affects WMI scripting under Windows Server 2003.

4.2   The WMI security configuration

Any manageable object we discussed in the previous chapters can be accessed under some security conditions. The WMI access is defined by three methods:

- During the WMI connection, the entity accessing a system must provide an authentication method and some privileges to perform specific tasks (i.e., system reboot) or access some specific manageable objects (i.e., security event log).

- The entity accessing the manageable object is granted access to a CIM repository namespace and allowed to perform some specific operations. The entity in question could also be part of an authorized group.

- The manageable object is restricted in access in a namespace by the means of a security descriptor. A security descriptor is nothing other than a representation, in the form of a list, of the access rights granted or denied to entities for the purpose of accessing a secured object in the system.

4.2.1 The WMI connection security settings

The establishment of a WMI connection always includes an authentication method, an impersonation level, and some optional privileges definition. Throughout the first book, *Understanding WMI Scripting*, we talk about this aspect when we explain how to perform a WMI connection. You can refer to Chapter 4 of the first book, sections 4.3.3, "The security settings of the moniker," and 4.1, "Establishing the WMI connection," for more information about the WMI connection scripting technique and the various connection settings.

However, it is important to determine the type of privileges required for a specific WMI operation. Table 4.1 lists the WMI classes that require some specific privileges at the class level, the property level, or the method level.

4.2.2 The group membership

By default, every CIM repository namespace is secured from the **Root** namespace, while subnamespaces inherit the security settings from the **Root** (see Figure 4.1).

By default, only two built-in groups are configured to access a CIM repository namespace: *Administrators* and *Everyone*. While the *Administrators* group has full access to any CIM repository namespace by default, the *Everyone* group is restricted to a limited number of accesses, such as reading some configuration data from the local system.

Table 4.2 summarizes the access type granted to the default groups for the **Root** namespace. Each of these rights is stored in the CIM repository in the form of a security descriptor.

Table 4.1 *The WMI Privileges Required for Some Classes, Properties, or Methods*

Namespace	WMI Class	CIM Element	Name	Privileges	Description
ROOT/CIMV2	Win32_PageFileUsage	Class		SeCreatePagefilePrivilege	The Win32_PageFileUsage class represents the file used for handling virtual memory file swapping on a Win32 system. Information contained within objects instantiated from this class specify the runtime state of the page file. **Note:** The SE_CREATE_PAGEFILE privilege is required for Windows XP and Windows Server 2003.
		Property	ExecutablePath	SeDebugPrivilege	The ExecutablePath property indicates the path to the executable file of the process.
		Property	MaximumWorkingSetSize	SeDebugPrivilege	The MaximumWorkingSetSize property indicates the maximum working set size of a process. The working set of a process is the set of memory pages currently visible to the process in physical RAM. These pages are resident and available for an application to use without triggering a page fault.
ROOT/CIMV2	Win32_Process	Property	MinimumWorkingSetSize	SeDebugPrivilege	The MinimumWorkingSetSize property indicates the minimum working set size of a process. The working set of a process is the set of memory pages currently visible to the process in physical RAM. These pages are resident and available for an application to use without triggering a page fault.
		Method	Create	SeIncreaseQuotaPrivilege	The Create method creates a new process.
		Method	Terminate	SeDebugPrivilege	The Terminate method terminates a process and all of its threads.
		Property	SystemStartupDelay	SeSystemEnvironmentPrivilege	The SystemStartupDelay property indicates the time to delay before starting the operating system. **Note:** The SE_SYSTEM_ENVIRONMENT privilege is required on IA64bit machines. This privilege is not required for 32-bit systems.
ROOT/CIMV2	Win32_ComputerSystem	Property	SystemStartupOptions	SeSystemEnvironmentPrivilege	The SystemStartupOptions property array indicates the options for starting up the computer system. Note that this property is not writable on IA64-bit machines. Constraints: Must have a value. **Note:** The SE_SYSTEM_ENVIRONMENT privilege is required for IA64-bit machines. This privilege is not required for other systems.
		Property	SystemStartupSetting	SeSystemEnvironmentPrivilege	The SystemStartupSetting property indicates the index of the default start profile. This value is 'calculated' so that it usually returns zero (0) because at write-time, the profile string is physically moved to the top of the list. (This is how Windows NT determines which value is the default.) **Note:** The SE_SYSTEM_ENVIRONMENT privilege is required on IA64bit machines. This privilege is not required for 32-bit systems.

Table 4.1   *The WMI Privileges Required for Some Classes, Properties, or Methods (continued)*

Namespace	WMI Class	CIM Element	Name	Privileges	Description
ROOT/CIMV2	Win32_OperatingSystem	Method	Reboot	SeShutdownPrivilege	The Reboot method shuts down the computer system, then restarts it. On computers running Windows NT/2000, the calling process must have the SE_SHUTDOWN_NAME privilege. The method returns an integer value that can be interpreted as follows: 0 - Successful completion. Other - For integer values other than those listed above, refer to Win32 error code documentation.
		Method	Shutdown	SeShutdownPrivilege	The Shutdown method unloads programs and DLLs to the point where it is safe to turn off the computer. All file buffers are flushed to disk, and all running processes are stopped. On computer systems running Windows NT/2000, the calling process must have the SE_SHUTDOWN_NAME privilege. The method returns an integer value that can be interpreted as follows: 0 - Successful completion. Other - For integer values other than those listed above, refer to Win32 error code documentation.
		Method	Win32Shutdown	SeShutdownPrivilege	The Win32Shutdown method provides the full set of shutdown options supported by Win32 operating systems. The method returns an integer value that can be interpreted as follows: 0 - Successful completion. Other - For integer values other than those listed above, refer to Win32 error code documentation.
		Method	SetDateTime	SeSystemTimePrivilege	The SetDateTime method sets the current system time on the computer. On computer systems running Windows NT/2000, the calling process must have the SE_SYSTEMTIME_NAME privilege. The method returns an integer value that can be interpreted as follows: 0 - Successful completion. Other - For integer values other than those listed above, refer to Win32 error code documentation.
ROOT/CIMV2	CIM_LogicalFile	Method	GetEffectivePermission	SeSecurityPrivilege	The GetEffectivePermission method determines whether the caller has the aggregated permissions specified by the Permission argument not only on the file object, but on the share the file or directory resides on (if it is on a share).
ROOT/CIMV2	CIM_DeviceFile	Method	GetEffectivePermission	SeSecurityPrivilege	The GetEffectivePermission method determines whether the caller has the aggregated permissions specified by the Permission argument not only on the file object, but on the share the file or directory resides on (if it is on a share).
ROOT/CIMV2	CIM_Directory	Method	GetEffectivePermission	SeSecurityPrivilege	The GetEffectivePermission method determines whether the caller has the aggregated permissions specified by the Permission argument not only on the file object, but on the share the file or directory resides on (if it is on a share).
ROOT/CIMV2	Win32_Directory	Method	GetEffectivePermission	SeSecurityPrivilege	The GetEffectivePermission method determines whether the caller has the aggregated permissions specified by the Permission argument not only on the file object, but on the share the file or directory resides on (if it is on a share).
ROOT/CIMV2	CIM_DataFile	Method	GetEffectivePermission	SeSecurityPrivilege	The GetEffectivePermission method determines whether the caller has the aggregated permissions specified by the Permission argument not only on the file object, but on the share the file or directory resides on (if it is on a share).

Table 4.1 *The WMI Privileges Required for Some Classes, Properties, or Methods (continued)*

Namespace	WMI Class	CIM Element	Name	Privileges	Description
ROOT/CIMV2	Win32_ShortcutFile	Method	GetEffectivePermission	SeSecurityPrivilege	The GetEffectivePermission method determines whether the caller has the aggregated permissions specified by the Permission argument not only on the share but on the file or directory resides on (if it is on a share).
ROOT/CIMV2	Win32_CodecFile	Method	GetEffectivePermission	SeSecurityPrivilege	The GetEffectivePermission method determines whether the caller has the aggregated permissions specified by the Permission argument not only on the file but on the share the file or directory resides on (if it is on a share).
		Method	GetEffectivePermission	SeSecurityPrivilege	The GetEffectivePermission method determines whether the caller has the aggregated permissions specified by the Permission argument not only on the file object, but on the share the file or directory resides on (if it is on a share).
ROOT/CIMV2	Win32_NTEventlogFile	Method	ClearEventlog	SeBackupPrivilege	Clears the specified event log, and optionally saves the current copy of the logfile to a backup file. The method returns an integer value that can be interpreted as follows: 0 - Successful completion. 8 - The user does not have adequate privileges. 21 - Invalid parameter. Other - For integer values other than those listed above, refer to Win32 error code documentation.
		Method	BackupEventlog	SeBackupPrivilege	Saves the specified event log to a backup file. The method returns an integer value that can be interpreted as follows: 0 - Successful completion. 8 - The user does not have adequate privileges. 21 - Invalid parameter. 183 - Archive file name already exists. Cannot create file. Other - For integer values other than those listed above, refer to Win32 error code documentation.
ROOT/CIMV2	Win32_PageFile	Class		SeCreatePagefilePrivilege	The Win32_PageFile class has been Deprecated in favor of the Win32_PageFileUsage and Win32_PageFileSetting. These classes respectively correspond to the runtime and persisted states of pagefiles. The Win32_PageFile represents the file used for handling virtual memory file swapping on a Win32 system. Note: The SE_CREATE_PAGEFILE privilege is required for Windows XP and Windows Server 2003.
		Method	GetEffectivePermission	SeSecurityPrivilege	The GetEffectivePermission method determines whether the caller has the aggregated permissions specified by the Permission argument not only on the file object, but on the share the file or directory resides on (if it is on a share).
ROOT/CIMV2	Win32_NTLogEvent	Class		SeSecurityPrivilege	This class is used to translate instances from the NT Eventlog.
ROOT/CIMV2	Win32_SecuritySetting	Method	GetSecurityDescriptor	SeRestorePrivilege	Retrieves a structural representation of the object's security descriptor
		Method	SetSecurityDescriptor	SeRestorePrivilege	Sets security descriptor to the specified structure
ROOT/CIMV2	Win32_LogicalFileSecuritySetting	Method	GetSecurityDescriptor	SeRestorePrivilege	Retrieves a structural representation of the object's security descriptor.
		Method	SetSecurityDescriptor	SeRestorePrivilege	Sets security descriptor to the specified structure.

Table 4.1   *The WMI Privileges Required for Some Classes, Properties, or Methods (continued)*

Namespace	WMI Class	CIM Element	Name	Privileges	Description
ROOT/CIMV2	Win32_LogicalShareSecuritySetting	Method	GetSecurityDescriptor	SeRestorePrivilege	Retrieves a structural representation of the object's security descriptor. The method returns an integer value that can be interpreted as follows: 0 - Successful completion. 2 - The user does not have access to the requested information. 8 - Unknown failure. 9 - The user does not have adequate privileges. 21 - The specified parameter is invalid. Other - For integer values other than those listed above, refer to Win32 error code documentation.
		Method	SetSecurityDescriptor	SeRestorePrivilege	Sets security descriptor to the specified structure. The method returns an integer value that can be interpreted as follows: 0 - Successful completion. 2 - The user does not have access to the requested information. 8 - Unknown failure. 9 - The user does not have adequate privileges. 21 - The specified parameter is invalid. Other - For integer values other than those listed above, refer to Win32 error code documentation.
ROOT/CIMV2	Win32_PageFileSetting	Class		SeCreatePagefilePrivilege	The Win32_PageFileSetting class represents the settings of a page file. Information contained within objects instantiated from this class specify the page file parameters used when the file is created at system startup. The properties in this class can be modified and deferred until startup. These settings are different from the run time state of a page file expressed through the associated class Win32_PageFileUsage. **Note:** The SE_CREATE_PAGEFILE privilege is required for Windows XP and Windows Server 2003.
ROOT/CIMV2	Win32_NTLogEventLog	Class		SeSecurityPrivilege	The Win32_NTLogEventLog class represents an association between an NT log event and the log file that contains the event.
ROOT/CIMV2	CIM_ProcessExecutable	Class		SeDebugPrivilege	A link between a process and a data file indicating that the file participates in the execution of the process. **Note:** In order to receive all possible instances of this class, the SE_DEBUG PRIVILEGE should be enabled.
ROOT/CIMV2	Win32_NTLogEventUser	Class		SeSecurityPrivilege	The Win32_NTLogEventUser class represents an association between an NT log event and the active user at the time the event was logged.
ROOT/CIMV2	Win32_NTLogEventComputer	Class		SeSecurityPrivilege	The Win32_NTLogEventComputer class represents an association between an NT log event and the computer from which the event was generated.

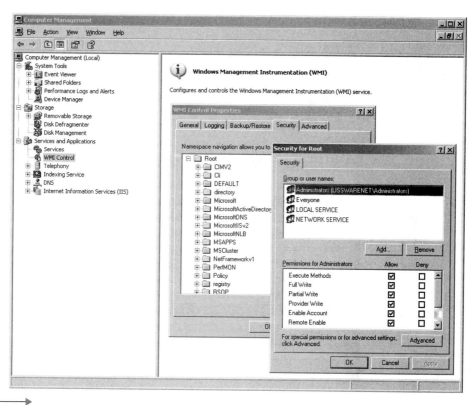

Figure 4.1   *The default security settings on the Root namespace.*

Table 4.2   *The Default Right Settings on the WMI Root Namespace*

	Administrators	Everyone	Local Service	Network Service
Execute Methods	X	X	X	X
Full Write	X			
Partial Write	X			
Provider Write	X	X	X	X
Enable Account	X	X	X	X
Remote Enable	X			
Read Security	X			
Edit Security	X			

4.3   WMI and Active Server Page (ASP)

Most of the scripting techniques we learned in previous chapters are applicable to Active Server Page (ASP) scripts. However, to run a WMI script from an Active Server Page (ASP) script, it is important to note two important points, where security is the main aspect to consider when developing WMI-ASP solutions. This is why we cover this information in this chapter. The two points to remember are:

1.   The asynchronous scripting technique cannot be used within an ASP script, because the VBScript *CreateObject* statement does not support the connection to a sink routine, such as the *CreateObject* statement used with WSH (i.e., *Wscript.CreateObject* statement).

2.   Regarding the security settings: Some parameters must be carefully considered regarding the platform the ASP script is run from.

4.3.1   Authentication settings

Authentication settings are as follows:

- **Security configuration under Windows NT 4.0:** To run a WMI-ASP script under the Windows NT 4.0 platform, a registry key must be modified to grant the Scripting API all of the permissions of the account running Internet Information Services (IIS). If not, then the browser client must contain the necessary permissions and security settings. The registry key to be modified is located in the *HKLM\Software\Microsoft\WBEM\Scripting* registry hive, where the DWORD value *Enable for ASP* must be set to 1 (see Figure 4.2). Of

Figure 4.2
Granting all Scripting API permissions to the IIS account.

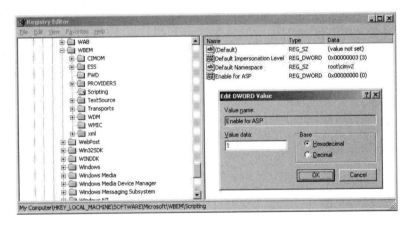

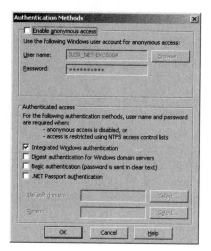

Figure 4.3
Setting the Windows Integrated Authentication.

course, changing this registry key is granting all privileges to the account running IIS, which represents some danger, since you will be granting all privileges without any further considerations. We will see later in this section that different approaches can be used to minimize such a risk.

- **Security configuration under Windows 2000 and above:** Under Windows 2000 and above, there are several ways to customize the IIS security. Of course, since a WMI-ASP script can perform some critical tasks, it is important to request the user to authenticate. Therefore, the recommended approach is to disable the anonymous access for the authentication protocol used. As we will see, the authentication method used will impact the WMI security configuration. Under Windows 2000 and above, you have a choice:

  - **The Windows Integrated Authentication:** As we can see in Figure 4.3, the Windows Integrated Authentication (WIA) is enabled for ASP, while the anonymous access is disabled. This security setting doesn't require any specific WMI security configuration. Enabling the Windows Integrated Authentication implies the use of Kerberos or NTLM.

  - **Passport or digest authentication:** The passport or digest authentications (see Figure 4.4) require that the CIM repository namespace *Remote Enable* privilege be granted to accounts authenticated by one of these protocols, since the user access is treated as a remote user access. For instance, creating a Windows Security Global Group and including the users authorized to remote access

Figure 4.4
*Setting the passport
or digest
authentication.*

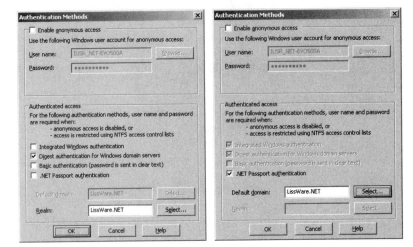

a selected namespace is a good practice (see Figure 4.5). Note that
with the digest authentication, passwords are still wrapped in a
password encryption key, but they are not hashed.

■ **Anonymous and basic authentications:** For obvious security reasons, it is recommended not using the anonymous and basic
authentications, which are a clear-text authentication without
encryption. Obviously, anonymous basically means "no authentication," which is not a recommended approach. However, the
Remote Enable privilege is not required for these two authentication methods if they are used.

Figure 4.5
*Enabling remote
access for remote
users.*

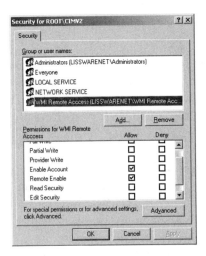

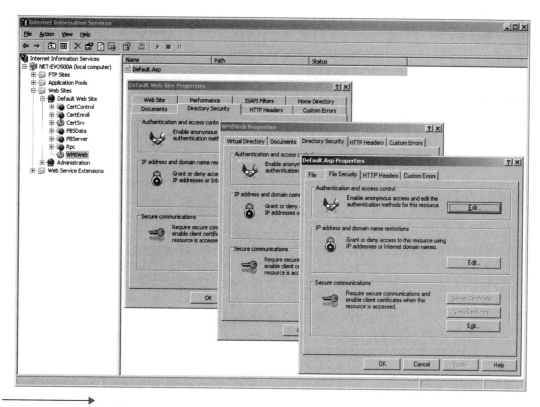

Figure 4.6   *The three IIS locations where authentication can be defined.*

4.3.2   Customizing IIS 5.0 and above

Regarding the security configuration under Internet Information Server (IIS) 5.0 and above, the authentication settings previously reviewed are not the only things to consider when setting up an IIS server running WMI-ASP scripts. Actually, the location of the authentication-level definitions is also very important. IIS can enforce the authentication at the Web Server level, the virtual directory, or the file level (see Figure 4.6).

Moreover, for WMI-dedicated security, it is a good practice to create an independent directory structure, which contains all HTML pages and WMI-ASP scripts (see Figure 4.7). This organization allows you to customize specific security settings independently from the rest of the server security. For example, Figure 4.7 shows that the *WMI-ASP Script* folder is not under the *WWWRoot* folder, which allows the creation of specific access rights on the file system to access the WMI-ASP scripts.

Figure 4.7
The isolated file system directory from the WWWRoot folder.

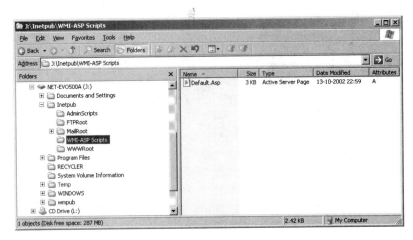

In order to increase the WMI-ASP script security, it is a good idea to disable the anonymous access and enable the Windows Integrated Authentication (WIA), as shown in Figure 4.3.

However, there are some situations where anonymous access is required. By default, Web clients accessing IIS are using the IIS logon identity (i.e., IUSR_<machine_name>). Therefore, it is a good idea for a more secure approach to create a new interactive user account. This allows you to define security settings that suit the *WMI-ASP Scripts* virtual Web site requirements without impacting the overall IIS security (unless you modify the security at the server level). From the directory security tab of the virtual directory properties, you can define the new logon identifier and enter the

Figure 4.8
Enabling anonymous access with IIS.

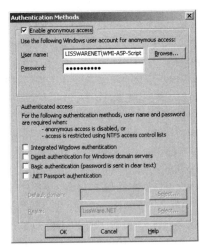

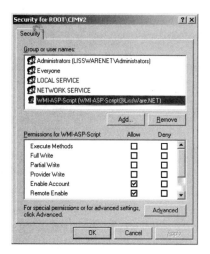

Figure 4.9
Ensuring WMI CIM repository access for the WMI-ASP dedicated account.

appropriate password in the authentication methods user interface, as shown in Figure 4.8.

Note that to secure applications, IIS 5.0 also has the ability to isolate applications in different security contexts. IIS 6.0 uses the concept of application pools to implement the same functionality. You can refer to the IIS documentation for more information about these security features.

Of course, since a different user account for the virtual Web site identity is used, you must make sure that this user account has access to the CIM repository accessed by the WMI-ASP script. For instance, if the WMI-ASP script uses the *Win32_Service* class located in the **Root\CIMv2** namespace, the *WMI-ASP-Script* user must be enabled and have remote access granted on that namespace. Even if everything is executed locally, the remote access must be granted, since the user account is treated by IIS as a remote user access (see Figure 4.9).

From a scripting point of view, developing WMI logics in ASP pages is the same as developing WMI logics in WSH (the exception, as mentioned in the beginning of this section, is that asynchronous calls are not supported). Of course, since the scripting environment is different, the output of information must be handled in respect to the ASP context and must make use of HTML tags.

Sample 4.1 shows an example of an ASP script listing the state of all Windows services in an HTML page (see Figure 4.10). To get this ASP script running, make sure that the IIS security settings are set accordingly, as explained previously, in regard to the operating system and IIS version used.

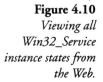

Figure 4.10
Viewing all
Win32_Service
instance states from
the Web.

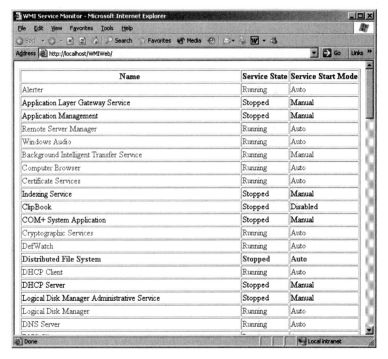

Sample 4.1   *Viewing all Win32_Service instances with their status from a WMI-ASP script*

```
 1:<%@ LANGUAGE="VBSCRIPT"%>
 2:
 3:<html>
 4: <head>
 5:  <title>WMI Service Monitor</title>
 6: </head>
 7:
 8: <body>
 9: <%
10:   Dim objWMIServices
11:   Dim objWMIInstance, objWMIInstances
12:
13:   Set objWMILocator = CreateObject("WbemScripting.SWbemLocator")
14:   Set objWMIServices = objWMILocator.ConnectServer(cComputerName, cWMINameSpace)
15:
16:   If Err.Number = 0 Then
17:      Set objWMIInstances = objWMIServices.InstancesOf ("Win32_Service")
18: %>
19:      <table BORDER="1">
20:      <tr>
21:       <th>Name</th>
22:       <th>Service State</th>
23:       <th>Service Start Mode</th>
24:      </tr>
25: <%
26:      For Each objWMIInstance in objWMIInstances
```

```
27:             If objWMIInstance.Started = False And objWMIInstance.StartMode = "Auto" Then
28: %>
29:                 <tr>
30:                  <td>
31:                   <font color="#FF0000"><b>
32:                    <%=objWMIInstance.DisplayName%>
33:                   </b></font>
34:                  </td>
35:                  <td>
36:                   <font color="#FF0000"><b>
37:                    <%=objWMIInstance.State%>
38:                   </b></font>
39:                  </td>
40:                  <td>
41:                   <font color="#FF0000"><b>
42:                    <%=objWMIInstance.StartMode%>
43:                   </b></font>
44:                  </td>
45:                 </tr>
46: <%
47:          Else
48:             If objWMIInstance.Started = True Then
49: %>
50:                 <tr>
51:                  <td>
52:                   <font color="#008000">
53:                    <%=objWMIInstance.DisplayName%>
54:                   </font>
55:                  </td>
56:                  <td>
57:                   <font color="#008000">
58:                    <%=objWMIInstance.State%>
59:                   </font>
60:                  </td>
61:                  <td>
62:                   <font color="#008000">
63:                    <%=objWMIInstance.StartMode%>
64:                   </font>
65:                  </td>
66:                 </tr>
67: <%
68:             Else
69: %>
70:                 <tr>
71:                  <td>
72:                   <%=objWMIInstance.DisplayName%>
73:                  </td>
74:                  <td>
75:                   <%=objWMIInstance.State%>
76:                  </td>
77:                  <td>
78:                   <%=objWMIInstance.StartMode%>
79:                  </td>
80:                 </tr>
81: <%
82:             End If
83:          End If
84:       Next
85: %>
86:       </table>
```

```
87: <%
88:   Else
89: %>
90:     <table>
91:      <tr>
92:       <td>Error - <%=Err.description%>, <%=Err.number%>, <%=Err.Source%></td>
93:      </tr>
94:     </table>
95: <%
96:   End If
97: %>
98: </body>
99:</html>
```

4.4   WMI security descriptor management

4.4.1   The security descriptor WMI representation

Under Windows, for the purposes of scripting, the security descriptor structure is abstracted by a collection of COM objects. For instance, the Active Directory Service Interfaces (ADSI) have their own collection of COM objects to represent a security descriptor. In the same way, WMI also has its own way to represent the security descriptor structure. In this particular case, WMI uses three classes to represent the security descriptor:

- *Win32_SecurityDescriptor*

- *Win32_ACE*

- *Win32_Trustee*

Note that security descriptors are not dedicated to Windows. Each operating system has its own way of structuring the content of a security descriptor and its own interfaces for manipulating the security descriptor content.

Before looking at classes exposing security information, we will first take a quick look at the security descriptor logical structure, as seen from WMI (see Figure 4.11). This will help us to understand the class purposes.

The security descriptor is made up of several components, which expose properties, which in turn may contain subcomponents. From a WMI point of view, the security descriptor is an **SWBemObject** object, which is an instance of the *Win32_SecurityDescriptor* class. Basically, a security descriptor as represented by WMI is made up of four properties, which contain other objects:

- **Owner:** It identifies the owner of the security descriptor. The owner is represented by an instance of the *Win32_Trustee* class.

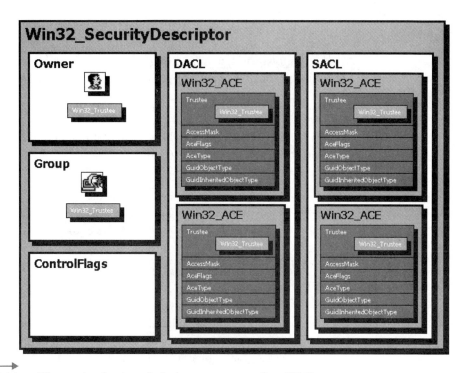

Figure 4.11 *The security descriptor logical structure as seen from WMI.*

- **Group:** It identifies the primary group of the security descriptor. The group is represented by an instance of the *Win32_Trustee* class. This property contains the SID for the owner's primary group. This information is only used by the POSIX subsystem of Windows and is ignored by other Windows subsystems (i.e., Win32). Therefore, the Group property is only present for compatibility purposes regarding the POSIX applications.

- **Control:** It is a set of bit flags that describes a security descriptor and/ or its components. It is mainly used to determine the presence of the Discretionary ACL (DACL) and the System ACL (SACL) and the effect of the inherited Access Control Entries (ACE) on the security descriptor. We will see in section 4.11.2 ("Deciphering the security descriptor *Control Flags*") how to decipher this value.

- **ACL:** The Access Control List (ACL) is an array holding Access Control Entries (ACE). An ACE object is represented by an instance of the *Win32_ACE* class, which defines, on a per user basis, what the user is authorized to do. This is the smallest data element defining the user privileges and permissions of an object.

There are two kinds of ACLs: the Discretionary ACL (DACL) and the System ACL (SACL). The DACL handles access control on objects. The SACL handles the system auditing on objects. To define each privilege and permission for a given user, an ACE has several properties. An ACE is composed of:

- **Trustee:** A trustee is a user, a group, or a computer with access rights to an object (i.e., DomainName\UserName). As for the owner and the group element of the security descriptor, a trustee is represented by an instance of the *Win32_Trustee* class.

- **AccessMask:** The access mask is a sequence of bits turned ON or OFF to activate specific rights. Note that the bit values are not the same for all securable objects. For instance, the bit sequence defining rights on a file is different from the bit sequence defining rights on an Active Directory object. In section 4.11.4.5 ("Deciphering the *ACE AccessMask* property"), we will see which bit sequence to use in regard to the secured object.

- **AceFlags:** This entry contains the inheritance control flags. As for the AccessMask, the bit sequence defining the inheritance may vary from one secured object to another. In section 4.11.4.3 ("Deciphering the *ACE Flags* property"), we will see which bit sequence to use in regard to the managed object.

- **AceType:** The value assigned to this ACE property determines the type of permissions granted for the corresponding access mask (Allowed, Denied, Audit).

- **GuidObjectType:** This property indicates what object class or Active Directory attribute set an ACE refers to. It takes a GUID as a value. Usually, this property is set when referring to an Active Directory Extended Right or to an Active Directory class.

- **GuidInheritedObjectType:** This property specifies the GUID of an object class whose instances will inherit the ACE.

4.4.2   How to access the security descriptor

The structural view of the security descriptor is the same for any object in a Windows system (i.e., share or file system objects such as files and folders). However, not all WMI classes representing manageable entities provide an access method to retrieve the security descriptor. The WMI provider capabilities related to a manageable entity and the classes it supports are determinant. For instance, as we will see further in section 4.7.1.1 ("Retrieving file and folder security descriptors with WMI"), the *Win32_LogicalFileSecuritySetting* class, supported by the WMI *Security* provider, exposes the *GetSecurityDescriptor* method to retrieve the security descriptor set on a file or a folder.

Unfortunately, it is not always easy or possible to retrieve a security descriptor from a secured object with WMI. In some cases, a more suitable COM abstraction layer such as ADSI must be used. When doing so, it is important to consider the secured object type to be managed when choosing an access method. For instance, the technique to access a security descriptor on a file or a folder will not necessarily be the same as the technique used to access the security descriptor on a registry key. Here, we totally rely on the COM abstraction layer capabilities (i.e., WMI versus ADSI).

Actually, we must clearly distinguish two things:

- **The technique for accessing and updating the security descriptor:** This relies on the WMI provider and class capabilities. If there is no WMI class method or properties exposing the desired security descriptor, it is possible that another technique not implemented by WMI must be used. In such a case, if ADSI offers some capabilities, we will use it to retrieve the security descriptor from a secured object.

- **The format of the security descriptor:** Once the security descriptor is read, its representation is not always in the form of a *Win32_SecurityDescriptor* instance. From a WMI perspective, some methods or properties return the security descriptor as a *Win32_SecurityDescriptor* instance; others return the security descriptor in a raw form (a binary array). If the security descriptor is accessed with ADSI, then its representation will be available in the ADSI object model, which is totally different from the *Win32_SecurityDescriptor* class representation supported by WMI.

4.4.3   The security descriptor ADSI representation

Because we will require help from ADSI, it is important to have a look at the security descriptor representation made by ADSI (Figure 4.12).

Although the security descriptor structure remains globally the same as the one shown in Figure 4.11, only the names of the components representing a security descriptor with their properties are slightly different.

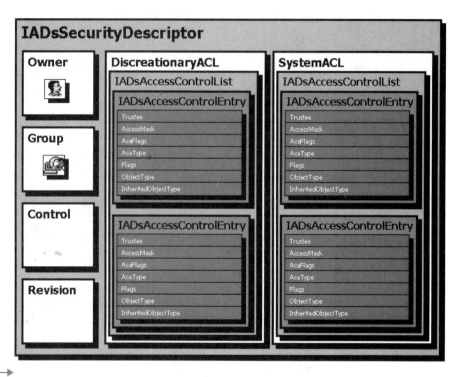

Figure 4.12   *The security descriptor logical structure as seen from ADSI.*

However, the information they contain is identical. Table 4.3 presents a short comparison of the properties exposed by both object models.

As we can see, WMI uses three classes to represent a security descriptor and its components (*Win32_SecurityDescriptor, Win32_ACE,* and *Win32_Trustee*). We clearly see in Figure 4.11 and Table 4.3 that WMI does not represent an ACL as an object. WMI represents an ACL as an array containing a series of ACEs exposed by the DACL or SACL properties. On the other hand, ADSI exposes the same information type, but it is organized differently. First, a **SecurityDescriptor** object (exposed by the **IADsSecurityDescriptor** ADSI COM interface) represents a security descriptor. Next, the *DiscretionaryACL* or the *SystemACL* properties expose the ACL in an **AccessControlList** object (exposed by the **IADsAccessControlList** ADSI COM interface), which, in turn, contains a collection of ACEs represented by **AccessControlEntry** objects (exposed by the **IADsAccessControlEntry** ADSI COM interface).

The only extra information we get from ADSI is the revision level of the security descriptor and some flags that are turned ON when values are set in

Table 4.3   *The WMI and ADSI Security Descriptor Exposed Methods and Properties*

WMI		ADSI	
Win32_SecurityDescriptor		**IADsSecurityDescriptor**	
Properties		**Properties**	
Owner	object:Win32_Trustee	Owner	string
Group	object:Win32_Trustee	Group	string
ControlFlags	unit32	Control	long
DACL	array of object:Win32_ACE	DiscretionaryACL	object:IADsAccessControlList
SACL	array of object:Win32_ACE	SystemACL	object:IADsAccessControlList
N/A		Revision	long
Methods		**Methods**	
N/A		CopySecurityDescriptor()	
		IADsAccessControlList	
Properties		**Properties**	
N/A		AclRevision	long
		AceCount	long
Methods		**Methods**	
N/A		AddAce (objACE)	
		RemoveAce (objACE)	
		CopyAccessList()	
		(Enumeration)	collection of object:IADsAccessControlEntry
Win32_ACE		**IADsAccessControlEntry**	
Properties		**Properties**	
Trustee	object:Win32_Trustee	Trustee	string
AccessMask	unit32	AccessMask	long
AceFlags	unit32	AceFlags	long
AceType	unit32	AceType	long
N/A		Flags	long
GUIDObjectType	string	ObjectType	string
GUIDInheritedObjectType	string	InheritedObjectType	string
Methods		**Methods**	
N/A		N/A	

the *ACE ObjectType* and *ACE InheritedObjectType* properties. In sections 4.11.4.5.3.1 ("Understanding the ACE ObjectType property") and 4.11.4.5.3.2 ("Understanding the ACE InheritedObjectType property"), we will see how to use these properties when working with Active Directory security descriptors.

4.4.4   Which access technique to use? Which security descriptor representation do we obtain?

As mentioned previously, based on the secured object type we access, it is important to determine the access methods available and the security descriptor format associated with the access method. Table 4.4 helps us understand which access method can be used and which security descriptor representation format is obtained, based on the security descriptor origin.

It is interesting to note that sometimes it is possible to use both WMI and ADSI to retrieve a security descriptor. For instance, this is the case for a security descriptor from a file or a folder. In some other cases, only WMI or ADSI can be used. This is the case for a security descriptor from a registry key, which only uses an ADSI access method. It is the same for a security

Table 4.4   *The Security Descriptor Access Methods with their Representations*

		File		Folder		Share		AD object		E2K mailbox			Registry key		WMI namespace	
		ADSI	WMI	ADSI	WMI	ADSI	WMI	ADSI	WMI	ADSI	CDOEXM	WMI	ADSI	WMI	ADSI	WMI
Source	**READ**	FS	FS	FS	FS	FS	FS	AD	AD	AD	E2K Store	AD	REG	-	-	CIM
SD retrieval technique		ADSI[1]	WMI	ADSI[1]	WMI	ADSI[3]	WMI	ADSI	WMI	ADSI	CDOEXM[8]	WMI	ADSI[1]	-	-	WMI
SD format		ADSI	WMI	ADSI	WMI	ADSI	WMI	ADSI	Raw	ADSI	ADSI	Raw	ADSI	-	-	Raw
SD conversion (raw->)		-	-	-	-	-	-	-	ADSI[5]	-	-	ADSI[5]	-	-	-	ADSI[5]
SD object model		ADSI	WMI	ADSI	WMI	ADSI	WMI	ADSI	ADSI	ADSI	ADSI	ADSI	ADSI	-	-	ADSI
Owner available?		Y	Y	Y	Y	-	-	Y	Y	Y	Y	Y	Y	-	-	Y
Group available?		Y	Y	Y	Y	-	-	Y	Y	Y	Y	Y	Y	-	-	Y
Security Descriptor revision?		Y	N	Y	N	Y	N	Y	-	Y	Y	Y	Y	-	-	-
DiscretionaryACL available?		Y	Y	Y	Y	Y	Y	Y	Y	Y	Y	Y	Y	-	-	Y
SystemACL available?		Y[2]	Y	Y[2]	Y	-	-	Y[4]	N[6]	Y[4]	Y	N[6]	Y[2]	-	-	-
SD object model	**WRITE**	ADSI	WMI	ADSI	WMI	ADSI	WMI	ADSI	ADSI	ADSI	ADSI	ADSI	ADSI	-	-	ADSI
SD conversion (-> raw)		-	-	-	-	-	-	-	ADSI[5]	-	-	ADSI[5]	-	-	-	ADSI[5]
SD format		ADSI	WMI	ADSI	WMI	ADSI	WMI	ADSI	Raw	ADSI	ADSI	Raw	ADSI	-	-	Raw
SD update technique		ADSI[1]	WMI	ADSI[1]	WMI	ADSI[3]	WMI	ADSI	WMI	ADSI	CDOEXM[8]	WMI	ADSI[1]	-	-	WMI
Target		FS	FS	FS	FS	FS	FS	AD	AD	AD[7]	E2K Store	AD[7]	REG	-	-	CIM

(1) **Windows NT 4.0/Windows 2000:** Requires **ADsSecurity.DLL** from the ADSI Resource Kit
    Windows XP/Windows Server 2003: Requires ADSI **ADsSecurityUtility** object.

(2) **Windows NT 4.0/Windows 2000:** SystemACL is not available.
    Windows XP/Windows Server 2003: By design SystemACL is only available with the **ADsSecurityUtility** object with statement:

```
objADsSecurity.SecurityMask = ADS_SECURITY_INFO_OWNER Or _
                              ADS_SECURITY_INFO_GROUP Or _
                              ADS_SECURITY_INFO_DACL Or _
                              ADS_SECURITY_INFO_SACL
```

    Warning: Unfortunately, a bug in the **ADsSecurityUtility** object prevents the retrieval of the SystemACL. Microsoft doesn't plan to fix this bug in the RTM code for timing issues (WMI offers an acceptable work-around for file and folders only. For the registry key, there is no work-around available).

(3) **Windows XP/Windows Server 2003:** Requires ADSI **ADsSecurityUtility** object. Not supported under Windows 2000.

(4) **Windows 2000 and Windows XP/Windows Server 2003:** Requires statement:

```
objADObject.SetOption ADS_OPTION_SECURITY_MASK, ADS_SECURITY_INFO_OWNER Or _
                      ADS_SECURITY_INFO_GROUP Or _
                      ADS_SECURITY_INFO_DACL Or _
                      ADS_SECURITY_INFO_SACL
```

(5) **Windows XP/Windows Server 2003:** Security descriptor conversion can done with **ADsSecurityUtility** object or ADSI legacy interfaces.
    Windows NT 4.0/Windows 2000: Security descriptor conversion can done with ADSI legacy interfaces.

(6) **Windows NT 4.0/Windows 2000/Windows XP/Windows Server 2003:** SystemACL is not available.

(7) Only if the mailbox is NOT yet created in the Exchange 2000 Web Store.

(8) Requires Exchange 2000 Service Pack 2 (or above) and Exchange System Manager installation for CDOEXM installation.

descriptor from a CIM repository namespace, which only uses a WMI access method. There is one particular case concerning the Exchange 2000 mailbox security descriptor. We see that we can get the security descriptor by using ADSI, WMI, or Collaboration Data Objects for Exchange Management (CDOEXM). Of course, each technique has its own peculiarities, which must be considered. We will examine this in section 4.7 ("Accessing the security descriptor set on manageable entities").

However, not all access methods retrieve security descriptors in the same format. It makes sense to think that an ADSI access method will retrieve the security descriptor in the ADSI object model and a WMI access method will retrieve the security descriptor in a *Win32_SecurityDescriptor* instance. However, there are exceptions. For instance, it is possible to retrieve a security descriptor from an Active Directory object with ADSI or with WMI. The ADSI access method will expose the security descriptor in the ADSI object model, while the WMI access method retrieves the security descriptor in binary form. In the latter case, the security descriptor needs to be converted to a structural representation. The conversion of a binary array representing a security descriptor to a *Win32_SecurityDescriptor* instance is not simple. This may require some advanced programming techniques on top of the Win32 API to decipher the security descriptor. Obviously, we leave the world of scripting to enter the world of API programming. Hopefully, with ADSI, it is possible to convert the binary array to a **SecurityDescriptor** object. We will see in section 4.9 ("The security descriptor conversion") how to proceed. This means that in some cases, we can access the security descriptor with WMI and manipulate its content with the ADSI object model. Although slightly more complex, this method works well and keeps programming in the space of the scripting world.

Last but not least, not all access methods retrieve all security descriptor properties. As seen before, ADSI shows the revision level of the security descriptor, while WMI does not. Most importantly, the System ACL is also subject to some exceptions. As we can see in Table 4.4, based on the security descriptor origin (file, share, Active Directory, etc.) and the access method used to read the security descriptor, the System ACL is not always available. For instance, this is the case for an Active Directory object retrieved with WMI, where the SystemACL is missing its ADSI representation. The Operating System platform also influences this, since the File System share security descriptor ADSI access method is not available under Windows 2000 or any earlier platforms.

4.5   **The WMI Security provider**

Since WMI implements some security scripting capabilities, it is interesting to examine closely the WMI *Security* provider capabilities. Available under Windows NT, Windows 2000, Windows XP, and Windows Server 2003, and registered in the **Root\CIMv2** namespace, the WMI *Security* provider is implemented as an instance and a method provider. It allows you to

Table 4.5   *The Security Provider Capabilities*

Provider Name	Provider Namespace	Class Provider	Instance Provider	Method Provider	Property Provider	Event Provider	Event Consumer Provider	Support Get	Support Put	Support Enumeration	Support Delete	Windows Server 2003	Windows XP	Windows 2000 Server	Windows 2000 Professional	Windows NT 4.0
WMI security Provider																
SECRCW32	Root/CIMV2	X	X					X	X	X	X	X	X	X	X	X

retrieve or change security settings that control ownership, auditing, and access rights to the files, directories, and shares. Table 4.5 summarizes the WMI *Security* provider capabilities.

The WMI *Security* provider supports several WMI classes representing the security settings on files, folders, and shares. These classes are listed in Table 4.6.

Since the WMI *Security* provider retrieves security settings from the file system, it is clear that an association exists between the CIM representation of the file system object (i.e., file, directory, or share) and its security settings CIM representation. We can see this association in Figure 4.13A, where the *CIM_LogicalFile* class is associated with the *Win32_Logical-FileSecuritySetting* class by the *Win32_SecuritySettingOfLogicalFile* Association class. Remember that the *CIM_LogicalFile* is a superclass for the *CIM_DataFile* and *CIM_Directory* classes (see Chapter 2, Figure 2.12, "The *CIM_LogicalFile* class and its child classes." It is interesting to note

Table 4.6   *The Security Providers Classes*

Name	Type	Comments
Win32_Ace	Dynamic	Specifies an access control entry (ACE). An ACE grants permission to execute a restricted operation, such as writing to a file or formatting a disk. ACEs particular to WMI allow logons, remote access, method execution, and writing to the WMI repository.
Win32_LogicalFileSecuritySetting	Dynamic	Represents security settings for a logical file.
Win32_LogicalShareSecuritySetting	Dynamic	Represents security settings for a logical file.
Win32_SecurityDescriptor	Dynamic	Represents a security descriptor structure.
Win32_SID	Dynamic	Represents an arbitrary security identifier (SID). This property cannot be enumerated.
Win32_Trustee	Dynamic	Specifies a trustee. Either a name or a SID (byte array) can be used.
Win32_AccountSID	Association	Relates a security account instance with a security descriptor instance.
Win32_LogicalFileAccess	Association	Relates the security settings of a file/directory and one member of its DACL.
Win32_LogicalFileAuditing	Association	Relates the security settings of a file/directory and one member of its SACL.
Win32_LogicalFileGroup	Association	Relates the security settings of a file/directory and its group.
Win32_LogicalFileOwner	Association	Relates the security settings of a file/directory and its owner.
Win32_LogicalShareAccess	Association	Relates the security settings of a share and one member of its DACL.
Win32_LogicalShareAuditing	Association	Relates the security settings of a share and one member of its SACL.
Win32_SecuritySettingOfLogicalFile	Association	Represents security settings of a file or directory object.
Win32_SecuritySettingOfLogicalShare	Association	Relates the security settings of a share object with the object.

that the *Win32_LogicalFileSecuritySetting* class represents the exact same file system object as the *CIM_LogicalFile* superclass and that both classes use the same key property to locate their corresponding instances, which is the path of the file or the folder they represent. However, the set of properties exposed by both classes is different. Basically, the *CIM_LogicalFile* class exposes information purely related to the file system settings (i.e., creation date, size, attribute settings, etc.), while the *Win32_LogicalFileSecuritySetting* class represents some security settings (control flags, owner permissions). You can use **WMI CIM Studio** or the **LoadCIMInXL.Wsf** script shown in Sample 4.32 in the appendix to examine and compare the properties exposed by both classes.

As mentioned before (see Figure 4.11), a security descriptor contains a Discretionary ACL (to define access settings) and a System ACL (to define auditing settings). Therefore, a file system object has relationships with the *Win32_SID* class representing the granted entities at the Discretionary ACL and System ACL levels. These relationships are represented in Figures 4.13B and 4.13C.

Figure 4.13
*The Win32_
LogicalFileSecurity
Setting class
associations.*

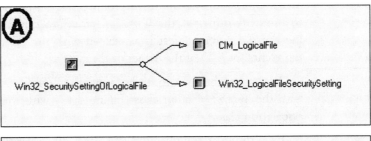

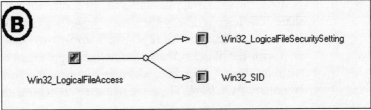

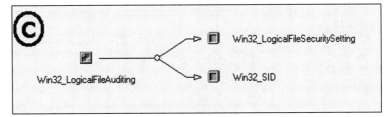

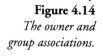
Figure 4.14
The owner and group associations.

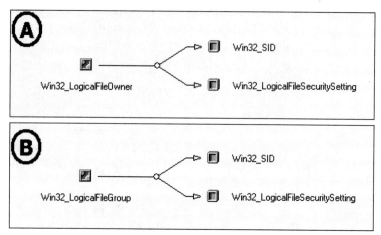

We also mentioned that a security descriptor contains an owner and a group. This implies that a file system object also has relationships with the WMI classes representing the owner and the group coming from the security descriptor. These relationships are represented in Figure 4.14A for the owner and Figure 4.14B for the group. Since a user and a group correspond to a security principal, the *Win32_LogicalFileSecuritySetting* class representing the file system object is associated with the *Win32_SID* class, which represents the SID of the owner or the group.

To resolve the SID to an account, the *Win32_SID* class is associated with the *Win32_Account* class (Figure 4.15) with the *Win32_AccountSID* association class.

Everything that applies for a file or a directory is also applicable for a share. The logic is exactly the same. However, since a share doesn't have any owner or group, the *Win32_LogicalShareSecuritySetting* class is only associated with the *Win32_Share* class, which represents the share instance, and with the *Win32_SID* class, which represents the granted entities at the Discretionary ACL level. These relationships are represented in Figure 4.16.

Figure 4.15
The Win32_ Account class and the Win32_SID class association.

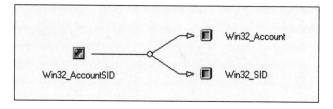

Figure 4.16
Win32_Logical-
ShareSecurity-
Setting class
associations.

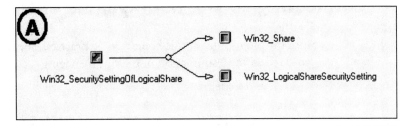

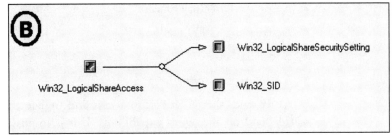

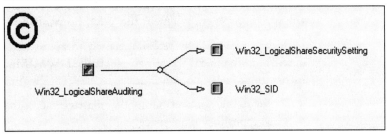

By using all these relationships, we decipher the security descriptor content by using the abstraction layer of the CIM repository. However, at no time do we look at the security descriptor directly. We always look at the security descriptor information through the relations defined in the CIM repository between different classes representing some items of its logical structure.

Another solution is to retrieve a security descriptor in a *Win32_Security-Descriptor* instance. This solution is the best approach, because it provides a closer look at the security descriptor content. Moreover, this technique allows the implementation of a deciphering technique applicable to any security descriptor (i.e., file, Active Directory, registry key, etc.) and therefore applicable to any security descriptor access method.

4.6   Connecting to the manageable entities

Since the philosophy of this book is to be practical, the rest of this chapter is dedicated to the examination of a script managing security descriptors of:

- A file or a folder
- A share
- An Active Directory object
- An Exchange 2000 mailbox
- A registry key
- A CIM repository namespace

As we said, the technique to access and update the security descriptor will depend on the WMI capabilities. If it is impossible to get a security descriptor via WMI, and if ADSI represents a valid alternative to WMI, we will use ADSI to complement the WMI functionality.

Independent of the technique used to access and manage the security descriptor, the next script sample (called **WMIManageSD.Wsf**) implements the following operations:

- Perform the connection to the manageable entity (i.e., file, share, CIM repository namespace, etc.).
- Retrieve the security descriptor of that manageable entity (via WMI and/or ADSI).
- Convert the security descriptor to an ADSI structural representation if necessary.
- Decipher the security descriptor structural representation to view the security settings on the manageable entity.
- Update the security descriptor owner.
- Update the security descriptor group.
- Update the security descriptor control flags.
- Add Access Control Entries in the Access Control List.
- Remove Access Control Entries in the Access Control List.
- Reorder the Access Control Entries in the Access Control List.
- Update the security descriptor back to the manageable entity.

These various operations are implemented in Samples 4.2 through 4.61.

As we discover the script, we will see the techniques used to manage the various security descriptors. As with all scripts we have seen in previous chapters, this script will follow the same philosophy by exposing various command-line parameters to manage the security descriptors. The script exposes the following command-line parameters:

```
C:\>WMIManageSD.Wsf
Microsoft (R) Windows Script Host Version 5.6
Copyright (C) Microsoft Corporation 1996-2001. All rights reserved.

Usage: WMIManageSD.Wsf [/FileSystem:value] [/Share:value] [/ADObject:value] [/E2KMailbox:value]
                       [/E2KStore[+|-]] [/RegistryKey:value] [/WMINameSpace:value]
                       [/ViewSD[+|-]]
                       [/Owner:value] [/Group:value] [/SDControls:value]
                       [/AddAce[+|-]] [/DelAce[+|-]]
                       [/Trustee:value] [/ACEMask:value] [/ACEType:value] [/ACEFlags:value]
                       [/ObjectType:value] [/InheritedObjectType:value]
                       [/SACL[+|-]] [/Decipher[+|-]] [/ADSI[+|-]] [/SIDResolutionDC[+|-]]
                       [/Machine:value] [/User:value] [/Password:value]


Options:

FileSystem          : Get the security descriptor of the specified file or directory path.
Share               : Get the security descriptor of the specified share name.
ADObject            : Get the security descriptor of the specified distinguished name AD object.
E2KMailbox          : Get the security descriptor of the Exchange 2000 mailbox
                      specified by AD user distinguished name.
E2KStore            : Specify if the security descriptor must come from the Exchange 2000 store.
RegistryKey         : Get the security descriptor of the specified registry key.
WMINameSpace        : Get the security descriptor of the specified WMI Name space.
ViewSD              : Decipher the security descriptor.
Owner               : Set the security descriptor owner.
Group               : Set the security descriptor group.
SDControls          : Set the security descriptor control flags.
AddAce              : Add a new ACE to the ACL.
DelAce              : Remove an existing ACE from the ACL.
Trustee             : Specify the ACE mask (granted user, group or machine account).
ACEMask             : Specify the ACE mask (granted rights).
ACEType             : Specify the ACE type (allow or deny the ACE mask).
ACEFlags            : Specify the ACE flags (ACE mask inheritance).
ObjectType          : Specify which object type, property set, or property an ACE refers to.
InheritedObjectType : Specify the GUID of an object that will inherit the ACE.
SACL                : Manage the System ACL (auditing) (default=Discretionary ACL).
Decipher            : Decipher the security descriptor.
ADSI                : Retrieve the security descriptor with ADSI.
SIDResolutionDC     : Domain Controller to use for SID resolution.
Machine             : Determine the WMI system to connect to. (default=LocalHost)
User                : Determine the UserID to perform the remote connection. (default=none)
Password            : Determine the password to perform the remote connection. (default=none)
```

The switch use is determined by the nature of the managed entity. During the script discovery, we will also examine the various command-line parameters to properly access, decipher, and update the respective security descriptors.

As usual, Sample 4.2 starts with the command-line parameters definition (skipped lines 13 through 153) and parsing (skipped lines 261 through
505). It is important to note that the script is initially written for Windows
XP and Windows Server 2003. However, it is easily adaptable for Windows
2000 and Windows NT 4.0. The lines that must be used for Windows
2000 (and earlier versions) are commented out in the code. If you plan to
use this script under Windows 2000, you must comment out the lines
pointed to by a "Windows Server 2003 only" comment and remove the
comment character of the lines pointed to by a "Windows 2000 only" comment. For instance, lines 188 through 192 and 199 through 203 illustrate
the script adaptability to Windows 2000. We will see some more comments
like this in the code, especially in the functions reading and updating the
security descriptor. If you run under Windows NT 4.0, make sure that the
latest update of WSH, WMI, and ADSI are installed on the managed systems. Once done, the script will use the same techniques under Windows
NT 4.0 as under Windows 2000.

Sample 4.2   *The WMIManageSD.Wsf framework to manage security descriptors from the command
line*

```
  1:<?xml version="1.0"?>
  .:
  8:<package>
  9:  <job>
 ..:
 13:    <runtime>
...:
153:    </runtime>
154:
155:    <script language="VBScript" src="..\Functions\SecurityInclude.vbs" />
156:    <script language="VBScript" src="..\Functions\GetSDFunction.vbs" />
157:    <script language="VBScript" src="..\Functions\SetSDFunction.vbs" />
158:    <script language="VBScript" src="..\Functions\DecipherWMISDFunction.vbs" />
159:    <script language="VBScript" src="..\Functions\DecipherADSISDFunction.vbs" />
160:
161:    <script language="VBScript" src="..\Functions\SetSDOwnerFunction.vbs" />
162:    <script language="VBScript" src="..\Functions\SetSDGroupFunction.vbs" />
163:
164:    <script language="VBScript" src="..\Functions\DecipherSDControlFlagsFunction.vbs" />
165:    <script language="VBScript" src="..\Functions\CalculateSDControlFlagsFunction.vbs" />
166:    <script language="VBScript" src="..\Functions\SetSDControlFlagsFunction.vbs" />
167:
168:    <script language="VBScript" src="..\Functions\DecipherACEFunction.vbs" />
169:    <script language="VBScript" src="..\Functions\CalculateACEFunction.vbs" />
170:
171:    <script language="VBScript" src="..\Functions\AddACEFunction.vbs" />
172:    <script language="VBScript" src="..\Functions\DelACEFunction.vbs" />
173:    <script language="VBScript" src="..\Functions\CreateDefaultSDFunction.vbs" />
174:
175:    <script language="VBScript" src="..\Functions\CreateTrusteeFunction.vbs" />
176:    <script language="VBScript" src="..\Functions\ReOrderACEFunction.vbs" />
```

```
177:    <script language="VBScript" src="..\Functions\ExtractUserIDFunction.vbs" />
178:    <script language="VBScript" src="..\Functions\ExtractUserDomainFunction.vbs" />
179:    <script language="VBScript" src="..\Functions\ConvertStringInArrayFunction.vbs" />
180:    <script language="VBScript" src="..\Functions\ConvertArrayInStringFunction.vbs" />
181:
182:    <script language="VBScript" src="..\Functions\DisplayFormattedSTDProperty Function.vbs" />
183:    <script language="VBScript" src="..\Functions\DisplayFormattedPropertyFunction.vbs" />
184:    <script language="VBScript" src="..\Functions\TinyErrorHandler.vbs" />
185:
186:    <reference object="ADs" version="1.0"/>
187:
188:    <!-- ***** Windows Server 2003 only ***** -->
189:    <object progid="ADsSecurityUtility" id="objADsSecurity"/>
190:
191:    <!-- ***** Windows 2000 only ***** -->
192:    <!-- <object progid="ADsSecurity" id="objADsSecurity"/> -->
193:
194:    <object progid="ADSIHelper.SDConversions" id="objADSIHelper"/>
195:
196:    <object progid="WbemScripting.SWbemLocator" id="objWMILocator" reference="true"/>
197:    <object progid="WbemScripting.SWbemNamedValueSet" id="objWMINamedValueSet" />
198:
199:    <!-- ***** Windows Server 2003 only ***** -->
200:    <object progid="WbemScripting.SWbemDateTime" id="objWMIDateTime" />
201:
202:    <!-- ***** Windows 2000 only *****-->
203:    <!-- <object progid="SWbemDateTime.WSC" id="objWMIDateTime" /> -->
204:
205:    <script language="VBscript">
206:    <![CDATA[
...:
210:    ' -----------------------------------------------------------------------------
211:    Const cComputerName = "LocalHost"
212:    Const cWMICIMv2NameSpace = "root/cimv2"
213:    Const cWMIADNameSpace = "root\directory\LDAP"
...:
261:    ' -----------------------------------------------------------------------------
262:    ' Parse the command line parameters
263:    If WScript.Arguments.Named.Count = 0 Then
264:       WScript.Arguments.ShowUsage()
265:       WScript.Quit
266:    End If
267:
268:    strFileSystem = WScript.Arguments.Named("FileSystem")
269:    strShare = WScript.Arguments.Named("Share")
270:    strADsObjectDN = WScript.Arguments.Named("ADObject")
271:    strADsUserDN = WScript.Arguments.Named("E2KMailbox")
272:    strRegistryKey = WScript.Arguments.Named("RegistryKey")
273:    strWMINameSpace = WScript.Arguments.Named("WMINameSpace")
...:
495:    strUserID = WScript.Arguments.Named("User")
496:    If Len(strUserID) = 0 Then strUserID = ""
497:
498:    strPassword = WScript.Arguments.Named("Password")
499:    If Len(strPassword) = 0 Then strPassword = ""
500:
501:    strComputerName = WScript.Arguments.Named("Machine")
502:    If Len(strComputerName) = 0 Then strComputerName = cComputerName
503:
504:    strSIDResolutionDC = WScript.Arguments.Named("SIDResolutionDC")
```

```
 505:     If Len(strSIDResolutionDC) = 0 Then strSIDResolutionDC = strComputerName
 506:
 507:  Select Case intSDType
 508:' +-----------------------------------------------------------------------------+
 509:' | File or Folder                                                              |
 510:' +-----------------------------------------------------------------------------+
 511:        Case cFileViaWMI
 512:' WMI technique retrieval ------------------------------------------------------
 ...:
 584:
 585:        Case cFileViaADSI
 586:' ADSI technique retrieval -----------------------------------------------------
 ...:
 644:
 645:' +-----------------------------------------------------------------------------+
 646:' | Share                                                                       |
 647:' +-----------------------------------------------------------------------------+
 648:        Case cShareViaWMI
 649:' WMI technique retrieval ------------------------------------------------------
 ...:
 722:
 723:        Case cShareViaADSI
 724:' ADSI technique retrieval -----------------------------------------------------
 725:            ' Security descriptor access not implemented via ADSI under Windows 2000.
 726:
 727:            ' Windows Server 2003 only ------------------------------------------
 ...:
 787:
 788:' +-----------------------------------------------------------------------------+
 789:' | Active Directory object                                                     |
 790:' +-----------------------------------------------------------------------------+
 791:        Case cActiveDirectoryViaWMI
 792:' WMI technique retrieval ------------------------------------------------------
 ...:
 860:
 861:        Case cActiveDirectoryViaADSI
 862:' ADSI technique retrieval -----------------------------------------------------
 ...:
 933:
 934:' +-----------------------------------------------------------------------------+
 935:' | Exchange 2000 mailbox                                                       |
 936:' +-----------------------------------------------------------------------------+
 937:        Case cExchange2000MailboxViaWMI
 938:' WMI technique retrieval ------------------------------------------------------
....:
1006:
1007:        Case cExchange2000MailboxViaADSI
1008:' ADSI technique retrieval -----------------------------------------------------
....:
1077:
1078:        Case cExchange2000MailboxViaCDOEXM
1079:' CDOEXM technique retrieval ---------------------------------------------------
....:
1147:
1148:' +-----------------------------------------------------------------------------+
1149:' | Registry key                                                                |
1150:' +-----------------------------------------------------------------------------+
1151:        Case cRegistryViaWMI
1152:' WMI technique retrieval ------------------------------------------------------
1153:            ' Security descriptor access not implemented via WMI.
```

```
1154:
1155:          Case cRegistryViaADSI
1156:' ADSI technique retrieval -----------------------------------------------------------------
....:
1213:
1214:' +---------------------------------------------------------------------------+
1215:' | CIM repository namespace                                                   |
1216:' +---------------------------------------------------------------------------+
1217:          Case cWMINameSpaceViaWMI
1218:' WMI technique retrieval ------------------------------------------------------------------
....:
1288:
1289:          Case cWMINameSpaceViaADSI
1290:' ADSI technique retrieval -----------------------------------------------------------------
1291:               ' Security descriptor access not implemented via ADSI.
1292:    End Select
1293:
1294:    ]]>
1295:    </script>
1296:  </job>
1297:</package>
```

Sample 4.2 is the framework used by **WMIManageSD.Wsf** to manage security descriptors. We will examine all functions included (lines 155 through 184) and the code contained in this framework (lines 507 through 1292) in the following sections. Sample 4.2 is organized in a "Select Case" structure. Each "Case" corresponds to the management of a security descriptor with a specific access method. We have a "Case" section for:

- Security descriptor from files and folders accessed by WMI (lines 511 through 584)

- Security descriptor from files and folders accessed by ADSI (lines 585 through 644)

- Security descriptor from shares accessed by WMI (lines 648 through 722)

- Security descriptor from shares accessed by ADSI (lines 723 to 787)

- Security descriptor from Active Directory objects accessed by WMI (lines 791 through 860)

- Security descriptor from Active Directory objects accessed by ADSI (lines 861 through 933)

- Security descriptor from Exchange 2000 mailboxes accessed by WMI (lines 937 through 1006)

- Security descriptor from Exchange 2000 mailboxes accessed by ADSI (lines 1007 through 1077)

- Security descriptor from Exchange 2000 mailboxes accessed by CDOEXM (lines 1078 through 1147)

- Security descriptor from registry keys accessed by WMI (lines 1151 through 1154)

- Security descriptor from registry keys accessed by ADSI (lines 1155 through 1213)

- Security descriptor from CIM repository namespaces accessed by WMI (lines 1217 through 1288)

- Security descriptor from CIM repository namespaces accessed by ADSI (lines 1289 through 1292)

Before trying to change the content of a security descriptor, let's first see how we can retrieve a security descriptor from a manageable instance and how we can decipher it. Since WMI represents real-world objects with some specific classes, we must examine the technique used to retrieve the security descriptor, based on the nature and the class capabilities representing the real-world object. Let's start with the file system objects first.

4.6.1   Connecting to file and folder security descriptors

4.6.1.1   Connecting to files and folders with WMI

Accessing file and folder security descriptors with WMI involves establishing the WMI connection to the **Root\CIMv2** namespace (Sample 4.3), since it contains the *Win32_LogicalFileSecuritySetting* class, which exposes a method to retrieve the security descriptor. This connection is completed from line 513 through 520. At line 515, the addition of the **SeSecurityPrivilege** privilege to the **SWBemLocator** object is required to access the SACL part of the security descriptor.

To execute the Sample 4.3 code portion, the following command lines must be used:

```
C:\>WMIManageSD.Wsf /FileSystem:C:\MyDirectory
C:\>WMIManageSD.Wsf /FileSystem:C:\MyDirectory\MyFile.Txt
```

Sample 4.3   *Connecting to files and folders with WMI (Part I)*

```
...:
...:
...:
508:' +-------------------------------------------------------------------------+
509:' | File or Folder                                                          |
510:' +-------------------------------------------------------------------------+
```

```
511:          Case cFileViaWMI
512:' WMI technique retrieval ----------------------------------------------------
513:              objWMILocator.Security_.AuthenticationLevel = wbemAuthenticationLevelDefault
514:              objWMILocator.Security_.ImpersonationLevel = wbemImpersonationLevelImpersonate
515:              objWMILocator.Security_.Privileges.AddAsString "SeSecurityPrivilege", True
516:
517:              Set objWMIServices = objWMILocator.ConnectServer(strComputerName, _
518:                                                    cWMICIMv2NameSpace, _
519:                                                    strUserID, _
520:                                                    strPassword)
...:
523:              Set objSD = GetSecurityDescriptor (objWMIServices, _
524:                                      strFileSystem, _
525:                                      intSDType)
526:          If boolAddAce Then
527:              Set objSD = AddACE (objWMIServices, strSIDResolutionDC, _
528:                          strUserID, strPassword, _
529:                          objSD, _
530:                          strTrustee, _
531:                          intACEType, _
532:                          intACEMask, _
533:                          intACEFlags, _
534:                          intACLtype, _
535:                          vbNull, _
536:                          vbNull, _
537:                          intSDType)
538:          End If
539:
540:          If boolDelAce Then
541:              Set objSD = DelACE (objWMIServices, strSIDResolutionDC, _
542:                          strUserID, strPassword, _
543:                          objSD, _
544:                          strTrustee, _
545:                          intACLtype, _
546:                          intSDType)
547:          End If
548:
549:          If boolOwner Then
550:              Set objSD = SetSDOwner(strSIDResolutionDC, strUserID, strPassword, _
551:                              objSD, strOwner, intSDType)
552:          End If
553:
554:          If boolGroup Then
555:              Set objSD = SetSDGroup(strSIDResolutionDC, strUserID, strPassword, _
556:                              objSD, strGroup, intSDType)
557:          End If
558:
559:          If boolSDControlFlags Then
560:              Set objSD = SetSDControlFlags(objSD, intSDControlFlags, intSDType)
561:          End If
562:
563:          If boolAddAce Or boolDelAce Or boolOwner Or boolGroup Or boolSDControlFlags Then
564:              If boolAddAce Or boolDelAce Then
565:                  Set objSD = ReOrderACE(objWMIServices, objSD, intSDType)
566:              End If
567:
568:              SetSecurityDescriptor objWMIServices, _
569:                              objSD, _
570:                              strFileSystem, _
571:                              intSDType
```

```
572:              End If
573:
574:              If boolViewSD Then
575:                  WScript.Echo
576:                  DecipherWMISecurityDescriptor objSD, _
577:                                                intSDType, _
578:                                                "", _
579:                                                boolDecipher
580:              End If
...:
585:          Case cFileViaADSI
...:
...:
...:
```

Once the WMI connection completes, the script invokes a series of sub-functions:

- Lines 523 through 525 read the security descriptor from the selected file or folder with the GetSecurityDescriptor() function.

- Lines 526 through 538 add an ACE in the security descriptor with the AddAce() function, if specified to do so on the command line.

- Lines 540 through 547 remove an ACE to the security descriptor with the DelAce() function, if specified to do so on the command line.

- Lines 549 through 552 set the owner from the security descriptor with the SetSDOwner() function, if specified to do so on the command line.

- Lines 554 through 557 set the group in the security descriptor with the SetSDGroup(), if specified to do so on the command line.

- Lines 559 through 561 set the security descriptor control flags with the SetSDControlFlags() function, if specified to do so on the command line.

- Lines 564 through 566 reorder the security descriptor ACE in the discretionary ACL with the ReOrderAce() function, if an ACE addition or removal is performed.

- Lines 568 through 571 update the security descriptor on the selected file or folder with the SetSecurityDescriptor() function.

- Lines 576 through 579 decipher and display the security descriptor settings with the DecipherWMISecurityDescriptor() function, if specified to do so on the command line. Note that this function can be replaced by the DecipherADSISecurityDescriptor() function, based on the object model used to represent the security descriptor. In this particular example, the file or folder security descriptor accessed with the WMI access method is represented in the WMI object model. So, the security descriptor deciphering will be completed with the DecipherWMISecurityDescriptor() function.

Note that the code structure is always the same for any security descriptor type (i.e., files, Active Directory objects, CIM repository namespace) and access method technique (WMI or ADSI). As we will see further, only the WMI or the ADSI connection logic, with some parameters passed to the subfunctions, will vary. The subfunctions (i.e., AddAce(), DelAce(), ReOrderAce(), etc.) will manage the security descriptor specifics according to their nature and format. For instance, in Sample 4.3, the WMI security descriptor access method retrieves the security descriptor in a WMI representation, which implies the use of a *Win32_SecurityDescriptor* instance. In order to properly manipulate this security descriptor representation in the subfunctions, it is necessary to pass the WMI connection made to the **Root\CIMv2** namespace to the subfunctions, since this namespace contains the *Win32_SecurityDescriptor*, *Win32_ACE*, and *Win32_Trustee* class definitions.

4.6.1.2   *Connecting to files and folders with ADSI*

When the security descriptor is represented in the ADSI object model, it is not necessary to pass an object representing the connection to the entity owning the security descriptor. Sample 4.4 illustrates this approach. We retrieve the exact same structure as Sample 4.3 ("Connecting to files and folders with WMI [Part I]"), while the access method to the file or the folder security descriptor is made with ADSI. In this case, no specific connection is made to the file or folder, because it uses a different tactic to get access to the entity owning the security descriptor. Based on the operating system, the script will use:

- The **ADsSecurityUtility** object instantiated at line 189 in Sample 4.2 ("The **WMIManageSD.Wsf** framework to manage security descriptors from the command line"), if you run under Windows XP or Windows Server 2003. This object is only available under Windows XP and Windows Server 2003 and is implemented by the ADSI **IADsSecurityUtility** interface.

- The **ADsSecurity** object instantiated at line 192 in Sample 4.2, if you run under Windows NT or Windows 2000. Note that the **ADsSecurity** object requires the registration of the **ADsSecurity.DLL**, which is available from the Windows 2000 Resource Kit (or the ADSI SDK for Windows NT 4.0). It is very important to know that the **ADsSe-curity.DLL** is not designed to retrieve the SACL part of a security descriptor. This is a limitation of the **ADsSecurity.DLL**.

As shown in Sample 4.4, the first parameter of the GetSecurityDescriptor() function is set to Null (line 587). The ADSI security descriptor access method for a file or a folder via ADSI does not need an object representing the connection to the examined file or folder, because the **ADsSecurityUtility** or **ADsSecurity** object uses an encapsulated logic running in the user security context. Because the ADSI access technique retrieves the security descriptor in an ADSI representation and not in a WMI presentation, there is no need to access the **Root\CIMv2** namespace. Therefore, any subsequent subfunction calls (i.e., AddAce(), DelAce(), ReOrderAce(), etc.) use a Null parameter for the WMI connection settings. Next, the security descriptor deciphering will be handled by DecipherADSISecurityDescriptor() function (lines 638 through 640).

The following command lines will invoke the Sample 4.4 code portion:

```
C:\>WMIManageSD.Wsf /FileSystem:C:\MyDirectory /ADSI+

C:\>WMIManageSD.Wsf /FileSystem:C:\MyDirectory\MyFile.Txt /ADSI+
```

Sample 4.4   *Connecting to files and folders with ADSI (Part II)*

```
...:
...:
...:
585:          Case cFileViaADSI
586:' ADSI technique retrieval -------------------------------------------------------
587:              Set objSD = GetSecurityDescriptor (vbNull, _
588:                                                 strFileSystem, _
589:                                                 intSDType)
590:          If boolAddAce Then
591:              Set objSD = AddACE (vbNull, vbNull, vbNull, vbNull, _
592:                                  objSD, _
593:                                  strTrustee, _
594:                                  intACEType, _
595:                                  intACEMask, _
596:                                  intACEFlags, _
597:                                  intACLtype, _
598:                                  vbNull, _
599:                                  vbNull, _
600:                                  intSDType)
601:          End If
602:
603:          If boolDelAce Then
604:              Set objSD = DelACE (vbNull, vbNull, vbNull, vbNull, _
605:                                  objSD, _
606:                                  strTrustee, _
607:                                  intACLtype, _
608:                                  intSDType)
609:          End If
```

```
610:
611:                 If boolOwner Then
612:                     Set objSD = SetSDOwner(vbNull, vbNull, vbNull, _
613:                                               objSD, strOwner, intSDType)
614:                 End If
615:
616:                 If boolGroup Then
617:                     Set objSD = SetSDGroup(vbNull, vbNull, vbNull, _
618:                                               objSD, strGroup, intSDType)
619:                 End If
620:
621:                 If boolSDControlFlags Then
622:                     Set objSD = SetSDControlFlags(objSD, intSDControlFlags, intSDType)
623:                 End If
624:
625:                 If boolAddAce Or boolDelAce Or boolOwner Or boolGroup Or boolSDControlFlags Then
626:                     If boolAddAce Or boolDelAce Then
627:                         Set objSD = ReOrderACE(vbNull, objSD, intSDType)
628:                     End If
629:
630:                     SetSecurityDescriptor vbNull, _
631:                                       objSD, _
632:                                       strFileSystem, _
633:                                       intSDType
634:                 End If
635:
636:                 If boolViewSD Then
637:                     WScript.Echo
638:                     DecipherADSISecurityDescriptor objSD, _
639:                                           intSDType, _
640:                                           boolDecipher
641:                 End If
...:
644:
...:
...:
...:
```

4.6.2   Connecting to file system share security descriptors

4.6.2.1   *Connecting to file system shares with WMI*

As with files and folders, the WMI logic to access a share security descriptor is exactly the same (see Sample 4.3, "Connecting to files and folders with WMI [Part I]"). Once the WMI connection to the **Root\CIMv2** namespace is established (lines 650 through 656 in Sample 4.5), the parameters passed to the subfunctions managing the security descriptor are the same. This similarity comes from two factors:

■ The security descriptor access method is based on WMI.

■ The security descriptor is represented by a *Win32_SecurityDescriptor* instance, which implies the use of the DecipherWMISecurity-

Descriptor() function to decipher the security descriptor (lines 714 through 717).

Of course, as we manage a share security descriptor, we must note some small differences as well:

- The GetSecurityDescriptor() takes a share name instead of a file or folder path (line 663).

- The modification of the security descriptor owner, group, or control flags is not applicable to a share security descriptor (lines 685 through 699).

- The SACL is not supported on a security descriptor share.

Once these differences are taken into consideration (commented out lines 685 through 699), the code logic for a share is exactly the same as before. The following command line will invoke the Sample 4.5 code portion:

```
C:\>WMIManageSD.Wsf /Share:MyDirectory
```

Sample 4.5   *Connecting to shares with WMI (Part III)*

```
...:
...:
...:
644:
645:' +--------------------------------------------------------------------------------------+
646:' | Share                                                                                |
647:' +--------------------------------------------------------------------------------------+
648:        Case cShareViaWMI
649:' WMI technique retrieval ----------------------------------------------------------------
650:            objWMILocator.Security_.AuthenticationLevel = wbemAuthenticationLevelDefault
651:            objWMILocator.Security_.ImpersonationLevel = wbemImpersonationLevelImpersonate
652:
653:            Set objWMIServices = objWMILocator.ConnectServer(strComputerName, _
654:                                                              cWMICIMv2NameSpace, _
655:                                                              strUserID, _
656:                                                              strPassword)
...:
659:            Set objSD = GetSecurityDescriptor (objWMIServices, _
660:                                                strShare, _
661:                                                intSDType)
662:            If boolAddAce Then
663:               Set objSD = AddACE (objWMIServices, strSIDResolutionDC, _
664:                                   strUserID, strPassword, _
665:                                   objSD, _
666:                                   strTrustee, _
667:                                   intACEType, _
668:                                   intACEMask, _
669:                                   intACEFlags, _
670:                                   intACLtype, _
671:                                   vbNull, _
672:                                   vbNull, _
```

```
673:                                  intSDType)
674:              End If
675:
676:              If boolDelAce Then
677:                  Set objSD = DelACE (objWMIServices, strSIDResolutionDC, _
678:                                      strUserID, strPassword, _
679:                                      objSD, _
680:                                      strTrustee, _
681:                                      intACLtype, _
682:                                      intSDType)
683:              End If
684:
685:              ' Not supported for a share security descriptor.
686:              '
687:              ' If boolOwner Then
688:              '    Set objSD = SetSDOwner(strSIDResolutionDC, strUserID, strPassword, _
689:              '                       objSD, strOwner, intSDType)
690:              ' End If
691:              '
692:              ' If boolGroup Then
693:              '    Set objSD = SetSDGroup(strSIDResolutionDC, strUserID, strPassword, _
694:              '                       objSD, strGroup, intSDType)
695:              ' End If
696:              '
697:              ' If boolSDControlFlags Then
698:              '    Set objSD = SetSDControlFlags(objSD, intSDControlFlags, intSDType)
699:              ' End If
700:
701:              If boolAddAce Or boolDelAce Or boolOwner Or boolGroup Or boolSDControlFlags Then
702:                  If boolAddAce Or boolDelAce Then
703:                      Set objSD = ReOrderACE(objWMIServices, objSD, intSDType)
704:                  End If
705:
706:                  SetSecurityDescriptor objWMIServices, _
707:                                        objSD, _
708:                                        strShare, _
709:                                        intSDType
710:              End If
711:
712:              If boolViewSD Then
713:                  WScript.Echo
714:                  DecipherWMISecurityDescriptor objSD, _
715:                                                intSDType, _
716:                                                "", _
717:                                                boolDecipher
718:              End If
...:
723:        Case cShareViaADSI
...:
...:
...:
```

4.6.2.2 Connecting to file system shares with ADSI

Connecting to a share security descriptor with ADSI is only possible under Windows XP or Windows Server 2003, because the ADSI **ADsSecurityUtility** object is only available for these platforms (see Sample 4.6). The **ADsSecurity.DLL** is not designed for this purpose. Since we use the ADSI

ADsSecurityUtility object to retrieve the security descriptor, it is not necessary to establish a connection to the manageable entity. Basically, it follows the same logic as Sample 4.4 ("Connecting to files and folders with ADSI [Part II]") but with the same restrictions as the WMI techniques: Owner, group, control flags, and SACL updates are not applicable to a share. The retrieved security descriptor is represented in the ADSI object model, which implies the use of the DecipherADSISecurityDescriptor() function (lines 781 through 783). If you run under Windows Server 2003 or Windows XP, you can use the following command line to execute this portion of the script:

```
C:\>WMIManageSD.Wsf /Share:MyDirectory /ADSI+
```

Sample 4.6   *Connecting to shares with ADSI (Part IV)*

```
...:
...:
...:
723:        Case cShareViaADSI
724:' ADSI technique retrieval ------------------------------------------------------
725:            ' Security descriptor access not implemented via ADSI under Windows 2000.
726:
727:            ' Windows Server 2003 only -----------------------------------------------
728:            Set objSD = GetSecurityDescriptor (vbNull, _
729:                                               strShare, _
730:                                               intSDType)
731:        If boolAddAce Then
732:            Set objSD = AddACE (vbNull, vbNull, vbNull, vbNull, _
733:                               objSD, _
734:                               strTrustee, _
735:                               intACEType, _
736:                               intACEMask, _
737:                               intACEFlags, _
738:                               intACLtype, _
739:                               vbNull, _
740:                               vbNull, _
741:                               intSDType)
742:        End If
743:
744:        If boolDelAce Then
745:            Set objSD = DelACE (vbNull, vbNull, vbNull, vbNull, _
746:                               objSD, _
747:                               strTrustee, _
748:                               intACLtype, _
749:                               intSDType)
750:        End If
751:
752:            ' Not supported for a share security descriptor.
753:            '
754:            ' If boolOwner Then
755:            '     Set objSD = SetSDOwner(vbNull, vbNull, vbNull, _
756:            '                           objSD, strOwner, intSDType)
757:            ' End If
758:            '
```

```
759:         ' If boolGroup Then
760:         '     Set objSD = SetSDGroup(vbNull, vbNull, vbNull, _
761:         '                            objSD, strGroup, intSDType)
762:         ' End If
763:         '
764:         ' If boolSDControlFlags Then
765:         '     Set objSD = SetSDControlFlags(objSD, intSDControlFlags, intSDType)
766:         ' End If
767:
768:         If boolAddAce Or boolDelAce Or boolOwner Or boolGroup Or boolSDControlFlags Then
769:             If boolAddAce Or boolDelAce Then
770:                 Set objSD = ReOrderACE(vbNull, objSD, intSDType)
771:             End If
772:
773:             SetSecurityDescriptor vbNull, _
774:                                   objSD, _
775:                                   strShare, _
776:                                   intSDType
777:         End If
778:
779:         If boolViewSD Then
780:             WScript.Echo
781:             DecipherADSISecurityDescriptor objSD, _
782:                                            intSDType, _
783:                                            boolDecipher
784:         End If
...:
787:
...:
...:
...:
```

4.6.3 Connecting to Active Directory object security descriptors

4.6.3.1 *Connecting to Active Directory objects with WMI*

Connecting to an Active Directory object with WMI follows the same rules as Sample 4.3 ("Connecting to files and folders with WMI [Part I]"). However, we must connect to the **Root\Directory\LDAP** CIM repository namespace, instead of the **Root\CIMv2** namespace (lines 769 through 799), in order to get access to the WMI classes representing Active Directory object classes. As mentioned previously in section 4.4 ("Which access technique to use? Which security descriptor representation do we obtain?"), the WMI security descriptor access method of an Active Directory object retrieves the security descriptor in a binary format. The conversion of the security descriptor to an ADSI security descriptor representation is made in the GetSecurityDescriptor() function. This is why, even if the security descriptor access method is based on WMI, the subsequent subfunctions (i.e., AddAce() at line 806, DelAce() at line 819, and ReOrderAce() at line 842, to name a few) do not use the WMI connection settings. Instead, these functions manipulate the security descriptor in its ADSI representation. This implies that the security descriptor deciphering technique will be handled by the DecipherADSISecurityDescriptor() function (lines 853 through 855).

Another point to note is the format of the Active Directory distinguished name. Because the script can retrieve any object type from Active Directory, and because WMI requires the class of the object, it is mandatory to specify the object class on the command line. This must be done as follows:

```
C:\>WMIManageSD.Wsf /ADObject:"user;CN=MyUser,CN=Users,DC=LissWare,DC=Net"
```

The script will properly decode the class and the **distinguishedName** in the GetSecurityDescriptor() function.

Sample 4.7 *Connecting to Active Directory objects with WMI (Part V)*

```
...:
...:
...:
787:
788:' +-----------------------------------------------------------------------------+
789:' | Active Directory object                                                     |
790:' +-----------------------------------------------------------------------------+
791:        Case cActiveDirectoryViaWMI
792:' WMI technique retrieval ------------------------------------------------------
793:            objWMILocator.Security_.AuthenticationLevel = wbemAuthenticationLevelDefault
794:            objWMILocator.Security_.ImpersonationLevel = wbemImpersonationLevelImpersonate
795:
796:            Set objWMIServices = objWMILocator.ConnectServer(strComputerName, _
797:                                                             cWMIADNameSpace, _
798:                                                             strUserID, _
799:                                                             strPassword)
...:
802:            Set objSD = GetSecurityDescriptor (objWMIServices, _
803:                                                strADsObjectDN, _
804:                                                intSDType)
805:            If boolAddAce Then
806:              Set objSD = AddACE (vbNull, vbNull, vbNull, vbNull, _
807:                                  objSD, _
808:                                  strTrustee, _
809:                                  intACEType, _
810:                                  intACEMask, _
811:                                  intACEFlags, _
812:                                  intACLtype, _
813:                                  strObjectType, _
814:                                  strInheritedObjectType, _
815:                                  intSDType)
816:            End If
817:
818:            If boolDelAce Then
819:              Set objSD = DelACE (vbNull, vbNull, vbNull, vbNull, _
820:                                  objSD, _
821:                                  strTrustee, _
```

```
822:                              intACLtype, _
823:                              intSDType)
824:          End If
825:
826:          If boolOwner Then
827:              Set objSD = SetSDOwner(vbNull, vbNull, vbNull, _
828:                                     objSD, strOwner, intSDType)
829:          End If
830:
831:          If boolGroup Then
832:              Set objSD = SetSDGroup(vbNull, vbNull, vbNull, _
833:                                     objSD, strGroup, intSDType)
834:          End If
835:
836:          If boolSDControlFlags Then
837:              Set objSD = SetSDControlFlags(objSD, intSDControlFlags, intSDType)
838:          End If
839:
840:          If boolAddAce Or boolDelAce Or boolOwner Or boolGroup Or boolSDControlFlags Then
841:              If boolAddAce Or boolDelAce Then
842:                  Set objSD = ReOrderACE(vbNull, objSD, intSDType)
843:              End If
844:
845:              SetSecurityDescriptor objWMIServices, _
846:                                    objSD, _
847:                                    strADsObjectDN, _
848:                                    intSDType
849:          End If
850:
851:          If boolViewSD Then
852:              WScript.Echo
853:              DecipherADSISecurityDescriptor objSD, _
854:                                             intSDType, _
855:                                             boolDecipher
856:          End If
...:
861:      Case cActiveDirectoryViaADSI
...:
...:
...:
```

4.6.3.2 *Connecting to Active Directory objects with ADSI*

To retrieve the security descriptor of an Active Directory object with ADSI (see Sample 4.8), it is necessary to connect to the desired Active Directory object first. This can be done in the current user security context (lines 871 and 872) or with different credentials (lines 864 through 869). The connection security context is determined by the presence of the /UserID switch on the command line, which determines the content of the **strUserID** variable. Under Windows 2000, we do not use the **ADsSecurity** object method, even if it can retrieve the security descriptor from an Active Directory object. Coding the logic directly with the ADSI base objects, instead of using another COM object encapsulating its own logic, gives us more control over the coding. Moreover, this technique is applicable to any platform

(Windows 2000, Windows Server 2003, Windows XP). This is why we must perform the connection to the Active Directory object. In the case of a file, a folder, or a share, this is done by the logic encapsulated in the **ADsSecurityUtility** or **ADsSecurity** objects.

Once the connection is established, the script invokes the GetSecurityDescriptor() function with the object referring to the Active Directory object connection (line 875). The **distinguishedName** of the object is also passed to the function (line 876). The following command line will execute this portion of the script:

```
C:\>WMIManageSD.Wsf /ADObject:"CN=MyUser,CN=Users,DC=LissWare,DC=Net" /ADSI+
```

Note that with the ADSI access method, we do not provide the object class with the **distinguishedName**, as done with the WMI access method. ADSI is able to determine the object class by itself. Once the security descriptor is retrieved (line 875), since it is represented in the ADSI object model, the subsequent functions do not need the connection parameters, unlike the case with WMI. The security descriptor is deciphered with the DecipherADSISecurityDescriptor() function (lines 926 through 928).

Sample 4.8   *Connecting to Active Directory objects with ADSI (Part VI)*

```
...:
...:
...:
861:          Case cActiveDirectoryViaADSI
862:' ADSI technique retrieval ---------------------------------------------------------------
863:          If Len (strUserID) Then
864:              Set objNS = GetObject("LDAP:")
865:              Set objADsObject = objNS.OpenDSObject("LDAP://" & strComputerName & _
866:                                                    "/" & strADsObjectDN, _
867:                                                    strUserID, _
868:                                                    strPassword, _
869:                                                    ADS_SECURE_AUTHENTICATION)
870:          Else
871:              Set objADsObject = GetObject("LDAP://" & strComputerName & "/" & _
872:                                           strADsObjectDN)
873:          End If
874:
875:          Set objSD = GetSecurityDescriptor (objADsObject, _
876:                                             strADsObjectDN, _
877:                                             intSDType)
878:          If boolAddAce Then
879:            Set objSD = AddACE (vbNull, vbNull, vbNull, vbNull, _
880:                                objSD, _
881:                                strTrustee, _
882:                                intACEType, _
883:                                intACEMask, _
884:                                intACEFlags, _
885:                                intACLtype, _
886:                                strObjectType, _
887:                                strInheritedObjectType, _
```

```
888:                              intSDType)
889:              End If
890:
891:              If boolDelAce Then
892:                  Set objSD = DelACE (vbNull, vbNull, vbNull, vbNull, _
893:                                      objSD, _
894:                                      strTrustee, _
895:                                      intACLtype, _
896:                                      intSDType)
897:              End If
898:
899:              If boolOwner Then
900:                  Set objSD = SetSDOwner(vbNull, vbNull, vbNull, _
901:                                        objSD, strOwner, intSDType)
902:              End If
903:
904:              If boolGroup Then
905:                  Set objSD = SetSDGroup(vbNull, vbNull, vbNull, _
906:                                        objSD, strGroup, intSDType)
907:              End If
908:
909:              If boolSDControlFlags Then
910:                  Set objSD = SetSDControlFlags(objSD, intSDControlFlags, intSDType)
911:              End If
912:
913:              If boolAddAce Or boolDelAce Or boolOwner Or boolGroup Or boolSDControlFlags Then
914:                  If boolAddAce Or boolDelAce Then
915:                      Set objSD = ReOrderACE(vbNull, objSD, intSDType)
916:                  End If
917:
918:                  SetSecurityDescriptor objADsObject, _
919:                                        objSD, _
920:                                        strADsObjectDN, _
921:                                        intSDType
922:              End If
923:
924:              If boolViewSD Then
925:                  WScript.Echo
926:                  DecipherADSISecurityDescriptor objSD, _
927:                                                 intSDType, _
928:                                                 boolDecipher
929:              End If
...:
933:
...:
...:
...:
```

4.6.4 Connecting to Exchange 2000 mailbox security descriptors

To get access to the security descriptor set on an Exchange 2000 mailbox, it is possible to use three techniques: WMI, ADSI, or CDOEXM. Although all techniques can retrieve and view the security descriptor settings, only the CDOEXM technique can perform an update of the Exchange 2000 security descriptor correctly, because the CDOEXM technique is the only one updating the security descriptor located in the Exchange 2000 store. We will deal with this aspect when updating the Exchange 2000 security descriptor in section 4.14.4.3 ("Updating Exchange 2000 mailbox security descriptors with CDOEXM").

4.6.4.1 *Connecting to Exchange 2000 mailbox security descriptor with WMI*

Sample 4.9 illustrates the WMI technique. Basically, this is exactly the same as the technique used to retrieve the security descriptor from an Active Directory object, simply because the Exchange 2000 mailbox security descriptor is available from Active Directory. The only difference resides in the object class that is accessed, since only **user** objects can have an Exchange 2000 mailbox. That's the reason why the **distinguishedName** given on the command line does not require the object class anymore. For instance, the following command line will retrieve the Exchange 2000 mailbox security descriptor with WMI:

```
C:\>WMIManageSD.Wsf /E2KMailbox:"CN=MyUser,CN=Users,DC=LissWare,DC=Net"
```

However, the GetSecurityDescriptor() function will look for a specific attribute containing the Exchange 2000 mailbox security descriptor. We will see this in detail when examining the GetSecurityDescriptor() function as it accesses an Exchange 2000 mailbox security descriptor in section 4.7.4. Except for this difference encapsulated in the GetSecurityDescriptor() function, Sample 4.9 is the same as Sample 4.7 ("Connecting to Active Directory objects with WMI [Part V]").

Sample 4.9   *Connecting to Exchange 2000 mailbox information with WMI (Part VII)*

```
...:
...:
...:
933:
934:' +-----------------------------------------------------------------------------+
935:' | Exchange 2000 mailbox                                                       |
936:' +-----------------------------------------------------------------------------+
937:        Case cExchange2000MailboxViaWMI
938:' WMI technique retrieval ----------------------------------------------------
939:            objWMILocator.Security_.AuthenticationLevel = wbemAuthenticationLevelDefault
940:            objWMILocator.Security_.ImpersonationLevel = wbemImpersonationLevelImpersonate
941:
942:            Set objWMIServices = objWMILocator.ConnectServer(strComputerName, _
943:                                                    cWMIADNameSpace, _
944:                                                    strUserID, _
945:                                                    strPassword)
...:
948:            Set objSD = GetSecurityDescriptor (objWMIServices, _
949:                                        strADsUserDN, _
950:                                        intSDType)
```

```
951:                    If boolAddAce Then
952:                        Set objSD = AddACE (vbNull, vbNull, vbNull, vbNull, _
953:                                            objSD, _
954:                                            strTrustee, _
955:                                            intACEType, _
956:                                            intACEMask, _
957:                                            intACEFlags, _
958:                                            intACLtype, _
959:                                            vbNull, _
960:                                            vbNull, _
961:                                            intSDType)
962:                    End If
963:
964:                    If boolDelAce Then
965:                        Set objSD = DelACE (vbNull, vbNull, vbNull, vbNull, _
966:                                            objSD, _
967:                                            strTrustee, _
968:                                            intACLtype, _
969:                                            intSDType)
970:                    End If
971:
972:                    If boolOwner Then
973:                        Set objSD = SetSDOwner(vbNull, vbNull, vbNull, _
974:                                               objSD, strOwner, intSDType)
975:                    End If
976:
977:                    If boolGroup Then
978:                        Set objSD = SetSDGroup(vbNull, vbNull, vbNull, _
979:                                               objSD, strGroup, intSDType)
980:                    End If
981:
982:                    If boolSDControlFlags Then
983:                        Set objSD = SetSDControlFlags(objSD, intSDControlFlags, intSDType)
984:                    End If
985:
986:                    If boolAddAce Or boolDelAce Or boolOwner Or boolGroup Or boolSDControlFlags Then
987:                        If boolAddAce Or boolDelAce Then
988:                            Set objSD = ReOrderACE(vbNull, objSD, intSDType)
989:                        End If
990:
991:                        SetSecurityDescriptor objWMIServices, _
992:                                              objSD, _
993:                                              strADsUserDN, _
994:                                              intSDType
995:                    End If
996:
997:                    If boolViewSD Then
998:                        WScript.Echo
999:                        DecipherADSISecurityDescriptor objSD, _
1000:                                                       intSDType, _
1001:                                                       boolDecipher
1002:                    End If
....:
1007:           Case cExchange2000MailboxViaADSI
....:
....:
....:
```

4.6.4.2   *Connecting to Exchange 2000 mailbox security descriptor with ADSI*

As with Sample 4.8 ("Connecting to Active Directory objects with ADSI [Part VI]"), Sample 4.10 follows the exact same logic. The security descriptor specificities are treated in the subfunctions. The following command line executes the Sample 4.10 code portion:

```
C:\>WMIManageSD.Wsf /E2KMailbox:"CN=MyUser,CN=Users,DC=LissWare,DC=Net" /ADSI+
```

Sample 4.10   *Connecting to Exchange 2000 mailbox information with ADSI (Part VIII)*

```
....:
....:
....:
1007:        Case cExchange2000MailboxViaADSI
1008:' ADSI technique retrieval --------------------------------------------------------------
1009:            If Len (strUserID) Then
1010:                Set objNS = GetObject("LDAP:")
1011:                Set objADsObject = objNS.OpenDSObject("LDAP://" & strComputerName, _
1012:                                                  strUserID, _
1013:                                                  strPassword, _
1014:                                                  ADS_SECURE_AUTHENTICATION)
1015:            Else
1016:                Set objADsObject = GetObject("LDAP://" & strComputerName & "/" & strADsUserDN)
1017:            End If
1018:
1019:            Set objSD = GetSecurityDescriptor (objADsObject, _
1020:                                          strADsUserDN, _
1021:                                          intSDType)
1022:        If boolAddAce Then
1023:            Set objSD = AddACE (vbNull, vbNull, vbNull, vbNull, _
1024:                                 objSD, _
1025:                                 strTrustee, _
1026:                                 intACEType, _
1027:                                 intACEMask, _
1028:                                 intACEFlags, _
1029:                                 intACLtype, _
1030:                                 vbNull, _
1031:                                 vbNull, _
1032:                                 intSDType)
1033:        End If
1034:
1035:        If boolDelAce Then
1036:            Set objSD = DelACE (vbNull, vbNull, vbNull, vbNull, _
1037:                                 objSD, _
1038:                                 strTrustee, _
1039:                                 intACLtype, _
1040:                                 intSDType)
1041:        End If
1042:
1043:        If boolOwner Then
1044:            Set objSD = SetSDOwner(vbNull, vbNull, vbNull, _
1045:                                 objSD, strOwner, intSDType)
1046:        End If
1047:
1048:        If boolGroup Then
1049:            Set objSD = SetSDGroup(vbNull, vbNull, vbNull, _
```

```
1050:                                       objSD, strGroup, intSDType)
1051:                   End If
1052:
1053:                   If boolSDControlFlags Then
1054:                       Set objSD = SetSDControlFlags(objSD, intSDControlFlags, intSDType)
1055:                   End If
1056:
1057:                   If boolAddAce Or boolDelAce Or boolOwner Or boolGroup Or boolSDControlFlags Then
1058:                       If boolAddAce Or boolDelAce Then
1059:                           Set objSD = ReOrderACE(vbNull, objSD, intSDType)
1060:                       End If
1061:
1062:                       SetSecurityDescriptor objADSObject, _
1063:                                             objSD, _
1064:                                             strADsUserDN, _
1065:                                             intSDType
1066:                   End If
1067:
1068:                   If boolViewSD Then
1069:                       WScript.Echo
1070:                       DecipherADSISecurityDescriptor objSD, _
1071:                                                      intSDType, _
1072:                                                      boolDecipher
1073:                   End If
....:
1078:          Case cExchange2000MailboxViaCDOEXM
....:
....:
....:
```

4.6.4.3   Connecting to Exchange 2000 mailbox security descriptor with CDOEXM

CDOEXM provides objects and interfaces for the management of many Exchange 2000 components. For instance, with CDOEXM you can configure Exchange Servers and stores, mount and dismount stores, and create and configure mailboxes. CDOEXM is more than an extension for ADSI; it is also an extension for Collaboration Data Object for Exchange 2000 (CDOEX). At the server level, CDOEXM retrieves specific information about the server itself, as well as the Storage Groups present on the server and stores created in the Storage Groups. From an Active Directory user object point of view, CDOEXM exposes properties and methods to manage the Exchange 2000 mailbox. CDOEXM is an important companion to ADSI and CDOEX when working with Exchange 2000. Our unique interest for the CDOEXM technique for the script purpose resides in its capability to update the security descriptor in the Exchange store (see section 4.13.4.3, "Updating Exchange 2000 mailbox security descriptors with CDOEXM").

Sample 4.11 refers to the CDOEXM security descriptor access technique. Basically, this is the same technique as Sample 4.10, since CDOEXM acts as an extension for ADSI. Again, the security descriptor specificities are managed in the GetSecurityDescriptor() function. The following command line executes the Sample 4.11 code portion:

```
C:\>WMIManageSD.Wsf /E2KMailbox:"CN=MyUser,CN=Users,DC=LissWare,DC=Net" /E2KStore+
```

Sample 4.11   *Connecting to Exchange 2000 mailbox information with CDOEXM (Part IX)*

```
....:
....:
....:
1078:          Case cExchange2000MailboxViaCDOEXM
1079:' CDOEXM technique retrieval -----------------------------------------------------------------
1080:          If Len (strUserID) Then
1081:              Set objNS = GetObject("LDAP:")
1082:              Set objADsObject = objNS.OpenDSObject("LDAP://" & strADsUserDN, _
1083:                                           strUserID, _
1084:                                           strPassword, _
1085:                                           ADS_SECURE_AUTHENTICATION)
1086:          Else
1087:              Set objADsObject = GetObject("LDAP://" & strADsUserDN)
1088:          End If
1089:          Set objSD = GetSecurityDescriptor (objADsObject, _
1090:                                      strADsUserDN, _
1091:                                      intSDType)
1092:          If boolAddAce Then
1093:              Set objSD = AddACE (vbNull, vbNull, vbNull, vbNull, _
1094:                              objSD, _
1095:                              strTrustee, _
1096:                              intACEType, _
1097:                              intACEMask, _
1098:                              intACEFlags, _
1099:                              intACLtype, _
1100:                              vbNull, _
1101:                              vbNull, _
1102:                              intSDType)
1103:          End If
1104:
1105:          If boolDelAce Then
1106:              Set objSD = DelACE (vbNull, vbNull, vbNull, vbNull, _
1107:                              objSD, _
1108:                              strTrustee, _
1109:                              intACLtype, _
1110:                              intSDType)
1111:          End If
1112:
1113:          If boolOwner Then
1114:              Set objSD = SetSDOwner(vbNull, vbNull, vbNull, _
1115:                                  objSD, strOwner, intSDType)
1116:          End If
1117:
1118:          If boolGroup Then
1119:              Set objSD = SetSDGroup(vbNull, vbNull, vbNull, _
1120:                                  objSD, strGroup, intSDType)
1121:          End If
1122:
1123:          If boolSDControlFlags Then
1124:              Set objSD = SetSDControlFlags(objSD, intSDControlFlags, intSDType)
1125:          End If
```

```
1126:
1127:                    If boolAddAce Or boolDelAce Or boolOwner Or boolGroup Or boolSDControlFlags Then
1128:                        If boolAddAce Or boolDelAce Then
1129:                            Set objSD = ReOrderACE(vbNull, objSD, intSDType)
1130:                        End If
1131:
1132:                        SetSecurityDescriptor objADsObject, _
1133:                                              objSD, _
1134:                                              strADsUserDN, _
1135:                                              intSDType
1136:                    End If
1137:
1138:                    If boolViewSD Then
1139:                        WScript.Echo
1140:                        DecipherADSISecurityDescriptor objSD, _
1141:                                                       intSDType, _
1142:                                                       boolDecipher
1143:                    End If
....:
1147:
....:
....:
....:
```

4.6.5   Connecting to registry keys security descriptor

4.6.5.1   Connecting to registry keys with WMI

The connection to the registry with WMI is possible with the use of the
StdRegProv class in the **Root\Default** namespace. Although this class
exposes the *CheckAccess* method to verify if the user invoking this method
possesses some specified permissions, it is not currently possible to retrieve a
structural representation of a registry key security descriptor (in the WMI
object model, the ADSI object model, or in a binary format). The only way
is to use the ADSI **ADsSecurityUtility** or **ADsSecurity** objects, which refer
to an ADSI security descriptor access technique.

4.6.5.2   Connecting to registry keys with ADSI

The logic developed for Sample 4.4 ("Connecting to files and folders with
ADSI [Part II]") and Sample 4.6 ("Connecting to shares with ADSI [Part
IV]") applies for Sample 4.12, since it makes use of the **ADsSecurityUtility**
object (Windows Server 2003 or Windows XP only) or the **ADsSecurity**
object (Windows 2000 or before). As already mentioned, keep in mind that
ADsSecurity object does not give access to the SACL component of the
security descriptor. The following command line executes the Sample 4.12
code portion:

```
C:\>WMIManageSD.Wsf /RegistryKey:HKLM\SOFTWARE\Microsoft /ADSI+
```

Sample 4.12   *Connecting to registry keys with ADSI (Part X)*

```
....:
....:
....:
1147:
1148:' +--------------------------------------------------------------------------------+
1149:' | Registry key                                                                   |
1150:' +--------------------------------------------------------------------------------+
1151:        Case cRegistryViaWMI
1152:' WMI technique retrieval --------------------------------------------------------------
1153:                ' Security descriptor access not implemented via WMI.
1154:
1155:        Case cRegistryViaADSI
1156:' ADSI technique retrieval -------------------------------------------------------------
1157:                Set objSD = GetSecurityDescriptor (vbNull, _
1158:                                                    strRegistryKey, _
1159:                                                    intSDType)
1160:            If boolAddAce Then
1161:                Set objSD = AddACE (vbNull, vbNull, vbNull, vbNull, _
1162:                                    objSD, _
1163:                                    strTrustee, _
1164:                                    intACEType, _
1165:                                    intACEMask, _
1166:                                    intACEFlags, _
1167:                                    intACLtype, _
1168:                                    vbNull, _
1169:                                    vbNull, _
1170:                                    intSDType)
1171:            End If
1172:
1173:            If boolDelAce Then
1174:                Set objSD = DelACE (vbNull, vbNull, vbNull, vbNull, _
1175:                                    objSD, _
1176:                                    strTrustee, _
1177:                                    intACLtype, _
1178:                                    intSDType)
1179:            End If
1180:
1181:            If boolOwner Then
1182:                Set objSD = SetSDOwner(vbNull, vbNull, vbNull, _
1183:                                objSD, strOwner, intSDType)
1184:            End If
1185:
1186:            If boolGroup Then
1187:                Set objSD = SetSDGroup(vbNull, vbNull, vbNull, _
1188:                                objSD, strGroup, intSDType)
1189:            End If
1190:
1191:            If boolSDControlFlags Then
1192:                Set objSD = SetSDControlFlags(objSD, intSDControlFlags, intSDType)
1193:            End If
1194:
1195:            If boolAddAce Or boolDelAce Or boolOwner Or boolGroup Or boolSDControlFlags Then
1196:                If boolAddAce Or boolDelAce Then
1197:                    Set objSD = ReOrderACE(vbNull, objSD, intSDType)
1198:                End If
1199:                SetSecurityDescriptor vbNull, _
```

```
1200:                                  objSD, _
1201:                                  strRegistryKey, _
1202:                                  intSDType
1203:            End If
1204:
1205:            If boolViewSD Then
1206:                WScript.Echo
1207:                DecipherADSISecurityDescriptor objSD, _
1208:                                    intSDType, _
1209:                                    boolDecipher
1210:            End If
....:
1213:
....:
....:
....:
```

4.6.6   Connecting to CIM repository namespace security descriptors

4.6.6.1   Connecting to CIM repository namespaces with WMI

With WMI, it is possible to retrieve the security descriptor of a CIM repository namespace (see Sample 4.13). However, the retrieved security descriptor is in a binary form. The GetSecurityDescriptor() function will convert the security descriptor to an ADSI security descriptor representation. With the WMI access method, to get access to the namespace security descriptor, the GetSecurityDescriptor() function requires the **SWBemServices** object created when connecting to the CIM repository namespace (lines 1222 through 1225). It is important to note that the script does not connect to the **Root\CIMv2** namespace anymore, but it connects to the namespace for which the security descriptor must be retrieved. Since the security descriptor is represented in the ADSI object model after its conversion from the binary form, the subsequent subfunctions (AddAce() at line 1232 through 1241, DelAce() at line 1245 through 1249, or ReOrderAce() at line 1270, to name a few) do not require the connection object to the managed entity.

Note that as with a share, the *owner, group*, and security descriptor *controls* update is not supported for a CIM repository namespace (lines 1252 through 1266).

Sample 4.13   *Connecting to CIM repository namespaces with WMI (Part XI)*

```
....:
....:
....:
1213:
1214:' +--------------------------------------------------------------------+
1215:' | CIM repository namespace                                            |
1216:' +--------------------------------------------------------------------+
```

```
1217:          Case cWMINameSpaceViaWMI
1218:' WMI technique retrieval --------------------------------------------------------------
1219:              objWMILocator.Security_.AuthenticationLevel = wbemAuthenticationLevelDefault
1220:              objWMILocator.Security_.ImpersonationLevel = wbemImpersonationLevelImpersonate
1221:
1222:              Set objWMIServices = objWMILocator.ConnectServer(strComputerName, _
1223:                                                               strWMINameSpace, _
1224:                                                               strUserID, _
1225:                                                               strPassword)
....:
1228:              Set objSD = GetSecurityDescriptor (objWMIServices, _
1229:                                                 strWMINameSpace, _
1230:                                                 intSDType)
1231:          If boolAddAce Then
1232:             Set objSD = AddACE (vbNull, vbNull, vbNull, vbNull, _
1233:                                 objSD, _
1234:                                 strTrustee, _
1235:                                 intACEType, _
1236:                                 intACEMask, _
1237:                                 intACEFlags, _
1238:                                 intACLtype, _
1239:                                 vbNull, _
1240:                                 vbNull, _
1241:                                 intSDType)
1242:          End If
1243:
1244:          If boolDelAce Then
1245:             Set objSD = DelACE (vbNull, vbNull, vbNull, vbNull, _
1246:                                 objSD, _
1247:                                 strTrustee, _
1248:                                 intACLtype, _
1249:                                 intSDType)
1250:          End If
1251:
1252:          ' Not supported for a CIM repository namespace security descriptor.
1253:          '
1254:          ' If boolOwner Then
1255:          '    Set objSD = SetSDOwner(vbNull, vbNull, vbNull, _
1256:          '                           objSD, strOwner, intSDType)
1257:          ' End If
1258:          '
1259:          ' If boolGroup Then
1260:          '    Set objSD = SetSDGroup(vbNull, vbNull, vbNull, _
1261:          '                           objSD, strGroup, intSDType)
1262:          ' End If
1263:          '
1264:          ' If boolSDControlFlags Then
1265:          '    Set objSD = SetSDControlFlags(objSD, intSDControlFlags, intSDType)
1266:          ' End If
1267:
1268:          If boolAddAce Or boolDelAce Or boolOwner Or boolGroup Or boolSDControlFlags Then
1269:             If boolAddAce Or boolDelAce Then
1270:                Set objSD = ReOrderACE(vbNull, objSD, intSDType)
1271:             End If
1272:
1273:             SetSecurityDescriptor objWMIServices, _
1274:                                   objSD, _
1275:                                   strWMINameSpace, _
1276:                                   intSDType
1277:          End If
```

```
1278:
1279:                   If boolViewSD Then
1280:                       WScript.Echo
1281:                       DecipherADSISecurityDescriptor objSD, _
1282:                                                      intSDType, _
1283:                                                      boolDecipher
1284:                   End If
....:
1289:               Case cWMINameSpaceViaADSI
1290:' ADSI technique retrieval -------------------------------------------------------
1291:                   ' Security descriptor access not implemented via ADSI.
1292:     End Select
1293:
1294:     ]]>
1295:     </script>
1296:   </job>
1297:</package>
```

4.6.6.2   Connecting to CIM repository namespaces with ADSI

Accessing a CIM repository namespace security descriptor is not possible with ADSI and therefore is not supported by the script. The only valid access method is implemented by WMI.

4.7   Accessing the security descriptor set on manageable entities

Now that we have a connection to the manageable entity, we are in a position to retrieve its associated security descriptor. Of course, since the access methods vary, the techniques to read the security descriptor also vary. Moreover, its encoded form, once retrieved, may also vary. This totally relies on the Microsoft ADSI and WMI capabilities. In this section, we will examine the coding techniques used with their conditions of use. The goals of Samples 4.14 through 4.24, which implement the GetSecurityDescriptor() function, are to always return a security descriptor in a manageable form, which means returning an ADSI or a WMI representation of the retrieved security descriptor.

4.7.1   Retrieving file and folder security descriptors

4.7.1.1   Retrieving file and folder security descriptors with WMI

To retrieve the structural representation of a security descriptor from a file or a folder, the *Win32_LogicalFileSecuritySetting GetSecurityDescriptor* method must be used.

It is important to note that the *GetEffectivePermission* method available from the *CIM_DataFile* class (but defined on the parent class, called *CIM_*

LogicalFile) determines whether the caller has the aggregated permissions specified by the permission argument, not only on the file system object but also on the share the file or directory resides on. At no time does this method retrieve a structural representation of the security descriptor.

The use of the *Win32_LogicalFileSecuritySetting GetSecurityDescriptor* method requires a WMI connection to the **Root\CIMv2** namespace. This connection is already executed in Sample 4.3 ("Connecting to files and folders with WMI [Part I]"), which calls the GetSecurityDescriptor() function.

In the case of a WMI security descriptor access method, the parameters of the GetSecurityDescriptor() function represent (Sample 4.14, line 9):

- An **SWBemServices** object representing the WMI connection to the **Root\CIMv2** namespace (contained in the **objConnection** variable).

- A string containing the file or folder path (contained in the **strSource** variable).

- A value representing the security descriptor access method type (contained in the **intSDType** variable), which determines the security descriptor retrieval technique through a **Select Case** statement (line 21). This value is defined in the **SecurityInclude.vbs** included at line 155 of Sample 4.2 ("The **WMIManageSD.Wsf** framework to manage security descriptors from the command line"). The **Select Case** statement determines the execution of lines 26 through 42 for a WMI security descriptor access method for a file or a folder.

With the **SWBemServices** object, the script retrieves an **SWBemObject** object representing an instance of the file specified by the file path name (lines 29 and 30). Next, the script invokes the *GetSecurityDescriptor* method of the *Win32_LogicalFileSecuritySetting* class to retrieve the security descriptor (line 33). Since the retrieved security descriptor is represented in a *Win32_SecurityDescriptor* instance, no further processing is necessary. The GetSecurityDescriptor() function ends its execution by returning the **SWBemObject** object representing the security descriptor instance (line 295).

Sample 4.14   *Retrieving file and folder security descriptors with WMI (Part I)*

```
 .:
 .:
 .:
8:' --------------------------------------------------------------------------------
9:Function GetSecurityDescriptor (objConnection, strSource, intSDType)
..:
21:    Select Case intSDType
```

```
 22:' +--------------------------------------------------------------------------------+
 23:' | File or Folder                                                                 |
 24:' +--------------------------------------------------------------------------------+
 25:          Case cFileViaWMI
 26:' WMI retrieval technique ----------------------------------------------------------
 27:               WScript.Echo "Reading File or Folder security descriptor via WMI from '" & _
 28:                            strSource & "'."
 29:               Set objWMIInstance = objConnection.Get("Win32_LogicalFileSecuritySetting='" & _
 30:                                           strSource & "'")
 ..:
 33:               intRC = objWMIInstance.GetSecurityDescriptor (objSD)
 34:               If intRC Then
 35:                   WScript.Echo vbCRLF & "Failed to get File or Folder " & _
 36:                                "security descriptor from '" & strSource & "'."
 37:                   WScript.Quit (1)
 38:               End If
 ..:
 42:' Here objSD contains a security descriptor in the WMI object model.
 43:.
...:
291:          Case Else
292:
293:     End Select
294:
295:     Set GetSecurityDescriptor = objSD
...:
299:End Function
```

4.7.1.2   Retrieving file and folder security descriptors with ADSI

To retrieve a file or folder security descriptor with ADSI (see Sample 4.15), we must distinguish if the script runs under Windows Server 2003, Windows XP, Windows 2000, or Windows NT. As mentioned in section 4.6.1.2 ("Connecting to files and folders with ADSI"), under Windows Server 2003 or Windows XP, the script uses the **ADsSecurityUtility** object. The *SecurityMask* property of this object specifies which component of the security descriptor must be retrieved with the *GetSecurityDescriptor* method

Table 4.7   *The ADsSecurityUtility Constants*

Security Descriptor Info	
Name	**Value**
ADS_SECURITY_INFO_OWNER	0x1
ADS_SECURITY_INFO_GROUP	0x2
ADS_SECURITY_INFO_DACL	0x4
ADS_SECURITY_INFO_SACL	0x8
Security Descriptor format	
Name	**Value**
ADS_SD_FORMAT_IID	1
ADS_SD_FORMAT_RAW	2
ADS_SD_FORMAT_HEXSTRING	3
Security Descriptor path	
Name	**Value**
ADS_PATH_FILE	1
ADS_PATH_FILESHARE	2
ADS_PATH_REGISTRY	3

invoked at line 55. The *SecurityMask* property requires a bitwise value, as defined in Table 4.7. By default, only the owner, the group, and the DACL components are retrieved. Because the **ADsSecurityUtility** *GetSecurityDescriptor* method can retrieve a security descriptor from a file, a file system share, or a registry key, this method requires parameters to:

- Specify the path of the entity to retrieve the security descriptor (line 55).

- A constant (as defined in Table 4.7) to determine the nature of the specified path to retrieve (line 56).

- A constant (as defined in Table 4.7) to determine the format of the retrieved security descriptor (line 57).

Sample 4.15   *Retrieving file and folder security descriptors with ADSI (Part II)*

```
..:
..:
..:
43:
44:          Case cFileViaADSI
45:' ADSI retrieval technique -------------------------------------------------------
46:             WScript.Echo "Reading File or Folder security descriptor via ADSI from '" & _
47:                          strSource & "'."
48:
49:             ' Windows Server 2003 only -----------------------------------------------
50:             objADsSecurity.SecurityMask = ADS_SECURITY_INFO_OWNER Or _
51:                                           ADS_SECURITY_INFO_GROUP Or _
52:                                           ADS_SECURITY_INFO_DACL ' Or _
53:                                           ' ADS_SECURITY_INFO_SACL
54:
55:             Set objSD = objADsSecurity.GetSecurityDescriptor(strSource, _
56:                                                   ADS_PATH_FILE, _
57:                                                   ADS_SD_FORMAT_IID)
58:
59:             ' Windows 2000 only -----------------------------------------------------
60:             ' Set objSD = objADsSecurity.GetSecurityDescriptor("FILE://" & strSource)
61:
62:             If Err.Number Then
63:                WScript.Echo vbCRLF & "Failed to get File or Folder " & _
64:                             "security descriptor from '" & strSource & "'."
65:                WScript.Quit (1)
66:             End If
67:
68:' Here objSD contains a security descriptor in the ADSI object model.
69:
...:
291:          Case Else
292:
293:    End Select
294:
295:    Set GetSecurityDescriptor = objSD
...:
299:End Function
```

Under Windows 2000 (or Windows NT), the script uses the **ADsSecurity** object implemented by the **ADsSecurity.DLL**. This object also exposes a *GetSecurityDescriptor* method. However, the method requires one single parameter, which is the path of the entity to retrieve the security descriptor. The method uses a "FILE://" pointer to determine that the given path is a file or folder path (line 60). The **ADsSecurity** object does not retrieve the SACL component of a security descriptor and does not expose any *SecurityMask* property (or equivalent) to do so. Because both **ADsSecurityUtility** and **ADsSecurity** objects do not require a connection to the examined file or folder, this parameter is set to Null when calling the GetSecurityDescriptor() function (see Sample 4.4, line 587).

Once completed, the retrieved security descriptor is represented in the ADSI object model, as opposed to the WMI security descriptor access method, which returns a security descriptor in the WMI object model (see Sample 4.14, "Retrieving file and folder security descriptor with WMI [Part I]"). We take advantage of the variant variable type used in scripts to return different types of objects from the same function.

Note: By design, with the **ADsSecurityUtility** object it is possible to retrieve the security descriptor with its SACL component on the condition that the statement of line 53 is specified (ADS_SECURITY_INFO_SACL flag). Another requirement to retrieve the SACL of a security descriptor is that the SE_SECURITY_NAME privilege (also called **SeSecurityPrivilege** or the "Manage auditing and security log" privilege in the GPO) must be granted to the thread/process requesting access to the SACL. Despite the fact that you could run the script as a member of the Administrators group (which has the SE_SECURITY_NAME privilege enabled by default at the account level—see http://msdn.microsoft.com/library/en-us/security/security/sacl_access_right.asp), it is not granted by default at the thread/process level. Therefore, it is necessary for the thread/process to explicity enable this privilege as well. Unfortunately, at writing time, a bug located in the **ADsSecurityUtility** object of Windows Server 2003 and Windows XP does not allow the retrieval of the SACL component, even if the object has been designed for this purpose and even if the statement of line 53 is specified. If you execute the script with the ADS_SECURITY_INFO_SACL flag, the following error message will be returned:

```
A required privilege is not held by the client.
```

Actually, the **ADsSecurityUtility** object retrieving the security descriptor does not grant the ADS_SECURITY_INFO_SACL privilege. Therefore, it makes it impossible to retrieve the SACL component of the security descriptor.

Due to the timing issues, it is more than likely that Microsoft won't fix this bug for the release code of Windows Server 2003. However, it is possible to use a work-around by developing a small fix. I shared this issue with my colleague, André Larbière from HP Belgium/Luxembourg, and after thinking about different approaches he developed a COM object that could be invoked during the script execution to enable the missing SE_ SECURITY_NAME privilege. We won't enter into the details of the COM object development here, but we will see how it can be used from the **WMIManageSD.Wsf** script to work around this problem. Actually, its use is pretty simple. It requires three modifications. The first modification concerns the Sample 4.2 header, where the instantiation of the object enabling the SE_SECURITY_NAME privilege is added at line 195 (**User-Right.Control** object):

```
...:
...:
...:
186:    <reference object="ADs" version="1.0"/>
187:
188:    <!-- ***** Windows Server 2003 only ***** -->
189:    <object progid="ADsSecurityUtility" id="objADsSecurity"/>
190:
191:    <!-- ***** Windows 2000 only ***** -->
192:    <!-- <object progid="ADsSecurity" id="objADsSecurity"/> -->
193:
194:    <object progid="ADSIHelper.SDConversions" id="objADSIHelper"/>
195:    <object progid="UserRight.Control" id="objADSIPriv"/>
196:    <object progid="WbemScripting.SWbemLocator" id="objWMILocator" reference="true"/>
197:    <object progid="WbemScripting.SWbemNamedValueSet" id="objWMINamedValueSet" />
198:
199:    <!-- ***** Windows Server 2003 only ***** -->
200:    <object progid="WbemScripting.SWbemDateTime" id="objWMIDateTime" />
201:
202:    <!-- ***** Windows 2000 only *****-->
203:    <!-- <object progid="SWbemDateTime.WSC" id="objWMIDateTime" /> -->
204:
205:    <script language="VBscript">
206:    <![CDATA[
...:
...:
...:
```

Next, we must make use of the **UserRight.Control** object in the **WMIManageSD.Wsf** script to enable the required privilege. The method exposed by this object to enable the privilege is only used where the **ADsSecurityUtility** object is referenced. This concerns several portions of the script code:

- Sample 4.15 ("Retrieving file and folder security descriptor with ADSI [Part II]") and Sample 4.23 ("Retrieving registry keys security descriptor with ADSI [Part X]"), both located in the GetSecurityDe-scriptor() function.

- Sample 4.52 ("Updating file and folder security descriptor with ADSI [Part II]") and Sample 4.60 ("Updating registry keys security descriptor with ADSI [Part X]"), both located in the SetSecurityDescriptor() function.

All samples are subject to the same modification. The following code shows how the script is modified based on Sample 4.15 ("Retrieving file and folder security descriptor with ADSI [Part II]"). The original code is as follows:

```
..:
..:
..:
48:
49:     ' Windows Server 2003 only -------------------------------------------------
50:     objADsSecurity.SecurityMask = ADS_SECURITY_INFO_OWNER Or _
51:                                   ADS_SECURITY_INFO_GROUP Or _
52:                                   ADS_SECURITY_INFO_DACL ' Or _
53:                                   ' ADS_SECURITY_INFO_SACL
54:
55:     Set objSD = objADsSecurity.GetSecurityDescriptor(strSource, _
56:                                                      ADS_PATH_FILE, _
57:                                                      ADS_SD_FORMAT_IID)
58:
..:
..:
..:
```

and must be changed to (lines 54 and 58 in bold):

```
..:
..:
..:
48:
49:     ' Windows Server 2003 only -------------------------------------------------
50:     objADsSecurity.SecurityMask = ADS_SECURITY_INFO_OWNER Or _
51:                                   ADS_SECURITY_INFO_GROUP Or _
52:                                   ADS_SECURITY_INFO_DACL ' Or _
53:                                   ADS_SECURITY_INFO_SACL
54:     objADSIPriv.Enable "SeSecurityPrivilege"
55:     Set objSD = objADsSecurity.GetSecurityDescriptor(strSource, _
56:                                                      ADS_PATH_FILE, _
57:                                                      ADS_SD_FORMAT_IID)
58:     objADSIPriv.Disable "SeSecurityPrivilege"
..:
..:
..:
```

Basically, this object is performing the exact same thing as the WMI **wbemPrivilegeSecurity** constant: It grants the SE_SECURITY_NAME privilege (also called **SeSecurityPrivilege**) to the process/thread. Note that the privilege is enabled before reading the security descriptor and disabled once it has been read.

If you don't plan to use this work-around (i.e., because you don't need to retrieve the SACL), to avoid this problem line 53 must be commented out. In such a case, only the WMI technique is able to retrieve the SACL of a file or folder security descriptor. If you do not need to retrieve the SACL of a file or a folder security descriptor, the native ADSI method is perfectly applicable without this work-around.

4.7.2   Retrieving file system share security descriptors

4.7.2.1   *Retrieving file system share security descriptors with WMI*

Regarding the file system shares, the *Win32_Share* class exposes (only under Windows Server 2003 or Windows XP) the *GetAccessMask* method to gather information about the share security settings. The *GetAccessMask* method returns the access rights of the share held by the user or group on whose behalf the instance is created. Unfortunately, this method does not return a structural representation of the share security descriptor.

On the other hand, the *Win32_LogicalShareSecuritySetting* class exposes an equivalent method as the *GetSecurityDescriptor* method of the *Win32_LogicalFileSecuritySetting* class. This method retrieves a structural representation of the share security descriptor. Sample 4.16 illustrates this logic. The script retrieves an instance of the *Win32_LogicalShareSecuritySetting* class in an **SWBemObject** object (lines 77 and 78). When a share is created, it is not necessarily created with a security descriptor. In such a case, the share always has a default security setting, even if no security descriptor exists. The default security grants everyone full control. Note that it is the default behavior under Windows NT 4.0 and Windows 2000. However, under Windows XP and Windows Server 2003, the default is everyone read-only. Because the *Win32_LogicalShareSecuritySetting* instance can only be retrieved with the condition that a security descriptor is set, the script manages the situation by testing the error return code of the instance retrieval (lines 79 and 80).

If no instance of this class can be retrieved, it likely means that no specific security is set, which implies the creation of a default security descriptor (line 80) by calling the CreateDefaultSD() function. This function will be examined later in section 4.8 ("Creating a default security descriptor"). If the file system share has a security descriptor set, the script invokes the *GetSecurityDescriptor* method and retrieves the security descriptor in a *Win32_SecurityDescriptor* instance (line 85). The end result is the representation of the file system share security descriptor in the WMI object model (line 295).

Sample 4.16   *Retrieving file system share security descriptors with WMI (Part III)*

```
 ..:
 ..:
 ..:
 69:
 70:' +--------------------------------------------------------------------------------+
 71:' | Share                                                                          |
 72:' +--------------------------------------------------------------------------------+
 73:          Case cShareViaWMI
 74:' WMI retrieval technique --------------------------------------------------------
 75:            WScript.Echo "Reading Share security descriptor via WMI from '" & _
 76:                         strSource & "'."
 77:            Set objWMIInstance = objConnection.Get("Win32_LogicalShareSecuritySetting='" &
 78:                                            strSource & "'")
 79:          If Err.Number = wbemErrNotFound Then
 80:              Err.Clear
 81:              Set objSD = CreateDefaultSD (objConnection, intSDType)
 82:          Else
 83:              If Err.Number Then ErrorHandler (Err)
 84:
 85:              intRC = objWMIInstance.GetSecurityDescriptor (objSD)
 86:              If intRC Then
 87:                  WScript.Echo vbCRLF & "Failed to get Share security descriptor from '" &
 88:                               strSource & "'."
 89:                  WScript.Quit (1)
 90:              End If
 91:          End If
 ..:
 95:' Here objSD contains a security descriptor in the WMI object model.
 96:
...:
291:          Case Else
292:
293:    End Select
294:
295:    Set GetSecurityDescriptor = objSD
...:
299:End Function
```

4.7.2.2   Retrieving file system share security descriptors with ADSI

To retrieve a security descriptor from a file system share via ADSI, the overall logic is basically the same. However, in the details, we must consider some peculiarities:

- It is only possible to retrieve a share security descriptor under Windows Server 2003 (or Windows XP), since these platforms implement the ADSI **ADsSecurityUtility** object.

- Managing the *owner*, the *group*, and the SACL components is not applicable to a share.

Once these restrictions are clearly identified, the script logic is pretty simple (see Sample 4.17). With the *GetSecurityDescriptor* method (line 103) and its correct parameters (as defined in Table 4.7), the script will retrieve the security descriptor in the ADSI object model. If there is no security descriptor set on the share because it uses the default security, then the script creates a default ADSI security descriptor (line 109). Once completed, the GetSecurityDescriptor() function returns the ADSI security descriptor (line 295).

Sample 4.17   *Retrieving file system share security descriptors with ADSI (Part IV)*

```
..:
..:
..:
96:
97:            Case cShareViaADSI
98:' ADSI retrieval technique -------------------------------------------------------
99:            WScript.Echo "Reading Share security descriptor via ADSI from '" & _
100:                        strSource & "'."
101:
102:            ' Windows Server 2003 only -------------------------------------------
103:            Set objSD = objADsSecurity.GetSecurityDescriptor(strSource, _
104:                                                ADS_PATH_FILESHARE, _
105:                                                ADS_SD_FORMAT_IID)
106:
107:            If Err.Number Then
108:                Err.Clear
109:                Set objSD = CreateDefaultSD (vbNull, intSDType)
110:            End If
111:
112:' Here objSD contains a security descriptor in the ADSI object model.
113:
...:
291:        Case Else
292:
293:    End Select
294:
295:    Set GetSecurityDescriptor = objSD
...:
299:End Function
```

4.7.3   Retrieving Active Directory object security descriptors

4.7.3.1   *Retrieving Active Directory object security descriptors with WMI*

The access to a security descriptor of an Active Directory object with WMI is a little bit more challenging. The GetSecurityDescriptor() function requires an **SWBemServices** object, which represents a connection to the CIM repository namespace giving access to Active Directory. As we have seen before, this connection is performed in Sample 4.7 ("Connecting to

Active Directory objects with WMI [Part V]"). Next, the **distinguished-Name** of the desired object must be correctly parsed. As a reminder, the script command-line parameters executing this portion of the code would be as follows:

```
C:\>WMIManageSD.Wsf /ADObject:"user;CN=MyUser,CN=Users,DC=LissWare,DC=Net"
```

At line 119, the script invokes the ConvertStringInArray() function to split the Active Directory object class from the object **distinguishedName**. Once complete, the returned array contains the Active Directory object class in element 0 and the **distinguishedName** in element 1. With this information, the script retrieves an instance of the specified Active Directory object (lines 132 through 134). For instance, the previous command line will create the following WMI path:

```
ds_user.ADSIPath='LDAP://CN=MyUser,CN=Users,DC=LissWare,DC=Net'")
```

Once the Active Directory object instance is retrieved in an **SWBemObject** object, the script gets access to all attributes of the Active Directory object as represented by WMI. The security descriptor of an Active Directory object is contained in the **nTSecurityDescriptor** attribute. Doing so, the script reads the value of the *DS_nTSecurityDescriptor* property exposed by WMI. Unfortunately, things are not so easy, because the security descriptor contained in this **SWBemObject** object property is in the form of an **SWBemNamedValue** object. This **SWBemNamedValue** object exposes a property called *Value*, which contains the security descriptor in a binary array (line 144). To get the security descriptor in a usable form, the script invokes the *ConvertRawSDToAdsiSD* method exposed by the **ADSIHelper** object (line 144). The **ADSIHelper** object is instantiated in Sample 4.2 at line 194. We will come back to the **ADSIHelper** object in section 4.9 ("The security descriptor conversion"). The end result is a security descriptor represented in the ADSI object model. In this particular case, we have a mixed situation, since the script uses a WMI access method, which, in the end, returns an ADSI security descriptor (line 295).

Sample 4.18   *Retrieving Active Directory object security descriptors with WMI (Part V)*

```
...:
...:
...:
113:
114:' +------------------------------------------------------------------------------+
115:' | Active Directory object                                                      |
116:' +------------------------------------------------------------------------------+
117:          Case cActiveDirectoryViaWMI
118:' WMI retrieval technique -----------------------------------------------------------
119:              arrayADInfo = ConvertStringInArray (strSource, ";")
```

```
120:                    If Ubound(arrayADInfo) <> 1 Then
121:                        WScript.Echo "The Active Directory class and object distinguished name " & _
122:                                     "must be specified as follow:" & vbCRLF & vbCRLF & _
123:                                     "/ADObject:""Objectclass;CN=MyObject," & _
124:                                     "CN=Users,DC=LissWare,DC=Net"""
125:                        WScript.Quit (1)
126:                    End If
127:
128:                    WScript.Echo "Reading " & LCase(arrayADInfo(0)) & " Active Directory " & _
129:                                 "object security descriptor via WMI from 'LDAP://" & _
130:                                 arrayADInfo(1) & "'."
131:
132:                    Set objWMIInstance = objConnection.Get("ds_" & LCase(arrayADInfo(0)) & _
133:                                                           ".ADSIPath='LDAP://" & _
134:                                                           arrayADInfo(1) & "'")
...:
137:                    Set objSD = objWMIInstance.DS_nTSecurityDescriptor
138:                    If Err.Number Then
139:                        Err.Clear
140:                        WScript.Echo vbCRLF & "Failed to get Active Directory object " & _
141:                                     "security descriptor from 'LDAP://" & strSource & "'."
142:                        WScript.Quit (1)
143:                    Else
144:                        Set objSD = objADSIHelper.ConvertRawSDToAdsiSD (objSD.Value)
145:                        If Err.Number Then ErrorHandler (Err)
146:                    End If
...:
150:' Here objSD contains a security descriptor in the ADSI object model.
151:
...:
291:            Case Else
292:
293:    End Select
294:
295:    Set GetSecurityDescriptor = objSD
...:
299:End Function
```

4.7.3.2   *Retrieving Active Directory object security descriptors with ADSI*

Retrieving a security descriptor from an Active Directory object with ADSI is, of course, a more natural technique, since ADSI is especially designed for Active Directory accesses. Despite this fact, there are some things we must still take into consideration. Sample 4.19 illustrates this technique. Although the script uses ADSI, it is required to have a connection to the Active Directory object (called an object binding in the LDAP world). This object binding is established in Sample 4.8 ("Connecting to Active Directory objects with ADSI [Part VI]") and passed in the **objConnection** variable to the GetSecurityDescriptor() function. Basically, this object represents the Active Directory object in the ADSI object model. From this object, the script retrieves the **ntSecurityDescriptor** attribute (line 161). To retrieve the SACL component, the script must initialize the *SetOption* property of this object (lines 156 through 159). The *SetOption* property works in the same way as the *SecurityMask* property of the **ADsSecurityUtility** object. There is no difference between the two properties, but the *SetOption* property is exposed by the ADSI representation of the Active Directory object. Once completed, the GetSecurityDescriptor() function returns an ADSI representation of the Active Directory object security descriptor (line 295).

Sample 4.19   *Retrieving Active Directory object security descriptors with ADSI (Part VI)*

```
...:
...:
...:
151:
152:          Case cActiveDirectoryViaADSI
153:' ADSI retrieval technique ------------------------------------------------------------
154:              WScript.Echo "Reading Active Directory object security descriptor " & _
155:                       "via ADSI from 'LDAP://" & strSource & "'."
156:              objConnection.SetOption ADS_OPTION_SECURITY_MASK, ADS_SECURITY_INFO_OWNER Or _
157:                                                                 ADS_SECURITY_INFO_GROUP Or _
158:                                                                 ADS_SECURITY_INFO_DACL Or _
159:                                                                 ADS_SECURITY_INFO_SACL
160:
161:              Set objSD = objConnection.Get("ntSecurityDescriptor")
162:              If Err.Number Then
163:                  Err.Clear
164:                  WScript.Echo vbCRLF & "Failed to get Active Directory object " & _
165:                          "security descriptor from 'LDAP://" & strSource & "'."
166:                  WScript.Quit (1)
167:              End If
168:
169:' Here objSD contains a security descriptor in the ADSI object model.
170:
...:
291:          Case Else
292:
293:      End Select
294:
295:      Set GetSecurityDescriptor = objSD
...:
299:End Function
```

4.7.4   Retrieving Exchange 2000 mailbox security descriptors

4.7.4.1   *Retrieving Exchange 2000 mailbox security descriptors with WMI*

Retrieving the Exchange 2000 mailbox security descriptor with WMI (Sample 4.20) follows the same logic as retrieving an Active Directory object security descriptor (Sample 4.18). However, only **user** objects are accessed, and, instead of reading the *DS_nTSecurityDescriptor* property of the **SWBemObject** object representing the Active Directory object instance, the script must read the *DS_msExchMailboxSecurityDescriptor* property (line 182). As in Sample 4.18 ("Retrieving Active Directory object security descriptors with WMI [Part V]"), the security descriptor is finally retrieved in a binary array and must be converted with the help of the *ConvertRawSDToAdsiSD* method exposed by the **ADSIHelper** object (line 189). Once completed, the GetSecurityDescriptor() function returns an ADSI security descriptor representation accessed by WMI (line 295).

Sample 4.20   *Retrieving Exchange 2000 mailbox security descriptors with WMI (Part VII)*

```
...:
...:
...:
170:
171:' +-----------------------------------------------------------------------------+
172:' | Exchange 2000 mailbox                                                       |
173:' +-----------------------------------------------------------------------------+
174:           Case cExchange2000MailboxViaWMI
175:' WMI retrieval technique -----------------------------------------------------
176:              WScript.Echo "Reading Exchange 2000 mailbox security descriptor " & _
177:                           "via WMI from 'LDAP://" & strSource & "'."
178:              Set objWMIInstance = objConnection.Get("ds_user.ADSIPath='LDAP://" & _
179:                                   strSource & "'")
...:
182:              Set objSD = objWMIInstance.DS_msExchMailboxSecurityDescriptor
183:              If Err.Number Then
184:                 Err.Clear
185:                 WScript.Echo vbCRLF & "Failed to get Exchange 2000 mailbox " & _
186:                                      "security descriptor from 'LDAP://" & strSource & "'."
187:                 WScript.Quit (1)
188:              Else
189:                 Set objSD = objADSIHelper.ConvertRawSDToAdsiSD (objSD.Value)
190:                 If Err.Number Then ErrorHandler (Err)
191:              End If
...:
195:' Here objSD contains a security descriptor in the ADSI object model.
196:
...:
291:           Case Else
292:
293:    End Select
294:
295:    Set GetSecurityDescriptor = objSD
...:
299:End Function
```

4.7.4.2   *Retrieving Exchange 2000 mailbox security descriptors with ADSI*

Retrieving an Exchange 2000 mailbox security descriptor with ADSI is as simple as retrieving an Active Directory object security descriptor. Instead of accessing the **ntSecurityDescriptor** attribute, the script must retrieve the **msExchMailboxSecurityDescriptor** attribute (Sample 4.21, line 206). To ensure that all components of the security descriptor are retrieved, the script initializes the *SetOption* property of the Active Directory object (lines 201 through 204).

Sample 4.21   *Retrieving Exchange 2000 mailbox security descriptors with ADSI (Part VIII)*

```
...:
...:
...:
196:
197:            Case cExchange2000MailboxViaADSI
198:' ADSI retrieval technique --------------------------------------------------------
199:            WScript.Echo "Reading Exchange 2000 mailbox security descriptor " & _
200:                         "via ADSI from 'LDAP://" & strSource & "'."
201:            objConnection.SetOption ADS_OPTION_SECURITY_MASK, ADS_SECURITY_INFO_OWNER Or _
202:                                                              ADS_SECURITY_INFO_GROUP Or _
203:                                                              ADS_SECURITY_INFO_DACL Or _
204:                                                              ADS_SECURITY_INFO_SACL
205:
206:            Set objSD = objConnection.Get("msExchMailboxSecurityDescriptor")
207:            If Err.Number Then
208:                Err.Clear
209:                WScript.Echo vbCRLF & "Failed to get Exchange 2000 mailbox " & _
210:                             "security descriptor from 'LDAP://" & strSource & "'."
211:                WScript.Quit (1)
212:            End If
213:
214:' Here objSD contains a security descriptor in the ADSI object model.
215:
...:
291:            Case Else
292:
293:    End Select
294:
295:    Set GetSecurityDescriptor = objSD
...:
299:End Function
```

4.7.4.3   *Retrieving Exchange 2000 mailbox security descriptors with CDOEXM*

If Exchange 2000 Service Pack 2 is installed, it is possible to retrieve the Exchange 2000 mailbox security descriptors with CDOEXM. Since CDOEXM acts as an extension for ADSI, the coding technique is very similar to the ADSI coding in Sample 4.21. However, instead of accessing the security descriptor stored in the Active Directory, the CDOEXM method accesses the security descriptor stored in the Exchange store. Actually, both security descriptors are the same, but the Active Directory security descriptor is the mirror of the one in the Exchange store. This will be very important when updating the Exchange 2000 mailbox security descriptors (see section 4.13.4.3, "Updating Exchange 2000 mailbox security descriptors with CDOEXM").

To get the mailbox security descriptor, the script reads the *MailboxRights* property exposed by the **IExchangeMailbox** CDOEXM interface (line 220). The end result is a security descriptor in the ADSI object model (line 295).

Sample 4.22   *Retrieving Exchange 2000 mailbox security descriptors with CDOEXM (Part IX)*

```
...:
...:
...:
215:
216:         Case cExchange2000MailboxViaCDOEXM
217:' CDOEXM retrieval technique -----------------------------------------------------
218:              WScript.Echo "Reading Exchange 2000 mailbox security descriptor " & _
219:                           "via CDOEXM from 'LDAP://" & strSource & "'."
220:              Set objSD = objConnection.MailboxRights
221:              If Err.Number Then
222:                   Err.Clear
223:                   WScript.Echo vbCRLF & "Failed to get Exchange 2000 mailbox " & _
224:                               "security descriptor from 'LDAP://" & strSource & "'."
225:                   WScript.Quit (1)
226:              End If
227:
228:' Here objSD contains a security descriptor in the ADSI object model.
229:
...:
291:         Case Else
292:
293:    End Select
294:
295:    Set GetSecurityDescriptor = objSD
...:
299:End Function
```

4.7.5   Retrieving registry key security descriptors with ADSI

In Chapter 3 (section 3.3.3, "Registry providers"), we saw that WMI implements a WMI *Registry* provider to support the *StdRegProv* class. Unfortunately, this class does not implement a method to retrieve a structural representation of a security descriptor. The only method that gives information about the registry key security is the *CheckAccess* method. This method verifies that the user invoking the method possesses the specified permissions. Although useful, this WMI method does not suit the needs of the **WMIManageSD.Wsf** script. We must use an alternate tactic implemented by ADSI to retrieve the desired information.

To retrieve a registry key security descriptor with ADSI (see Sample 4.23), we must determine if the script runs under Windows XP, Windows Server 2003, Windows 2000, or Windows NT. The selected platform determines the use of the **ADsSecurityUtility** object of Windows XP and Windows Server 2003 (lines 243 through 251) or the **ADsSecurity** object of Windows 2000 and Windows NT 4.0 (line 254). Under Windows Server 2003, to retrieve the SACL component of the security descriptor, the *SecurityMask* property of the **ADsSecurityUtility** must be initialized (lines 244 through 247). Once complete, the script retrieves the registry key security descriptor by invoking the *GetSecurityDescriptor* method of the **ADsSecurityUtility** object (lines 249 through 251). The method uses the required parameters, as specified in Table 4.7 ("The **ADsSecurityUtility** Constants").

Sample 4.23   *Retrieving registry key security descriptors with ADSI (Part X)*

```
...:
...:
...:
229:
230:' +------------------------------------------------------------------------------------+
231:' | Registry key                                                                       |
232:' +------------------------------------------------------------------------------------+
233:          Case cRegistryViaWMI
234:' WMI retrieval technique ----------------------------------------------------------------
235:
236:' Here we can't retrieve a security descriptor via this access method.
237:
238:          Case cRegistryViaADSI
239:' ADSI retrieval technique ---------------------------------------------------------------
240:              WScript.Echo "Reading registry security descriptor " & _
241:                           "via ADSI from '" & strSource & "'."
242:
243:              ' Windows Server 2003 only  -----------------------------------------------
244:              objADsSecurity.SecurityMask = ADS_SECURITY_INFO_OWNER Or _
245:                                            ADS_SECURITY_INFO_GROUP Or _
246:                                            ADS_SECURITY_INFO_DACL ' Or _
247:                                          ' ADS_SECURITY_INFO_SACL
248:
249:              Set objSD = objADsSecurity.GetSecurityDescriptor(strSource, _
250:                                                               ADS_PATH_REGISTRY, _
251:                                                               ADS_SD_FORMAT_IID)
252:
253:              ' Windows 2000 only --------------------------------------------------------
254:              ' Set objSD = objADsSecurity.GetSecurityDescriptor("RGY://" & strSource)
255:
256:              If Err.Number Then
257:                  WScript.Echo vbCRLF & "Failed to get registry security descriptor " & _
258:                               "from '" & strSource & "'."
259:                  WScript.Quit (1)
260:              End If
261:
262:' Here objSD contains a security descriptor in the ADSI object model.
263:
...:
291:          Case Else
```

```
292:
293:    End Select
294:
295:    Set GetSecurityDescriptor = objSD
...:
299:End Function
```

Since the **ADsSecurityUtility** object is subject to a bug under Windows Server 2003 and Windows XP, don't forget to refer to section 4.7.1.2 ("Retrieving file and folder security descriptors with ADSI"). If the workaround explained in that section is not used, and since the WMI technique is not able to retrieve a structural representation of a registry key security decriptor, there will be no way to retrieve the SACL of registry key security descriptors from the scripting world with the current ADSI COM objects.

Under Windows 2000 (or Windows NT), the *GetSecurityDescriptor* method of the **ADsSecurity** object is invoked (line 254). As mentioned before, no SACL component can be retrieved with this object. Once finished, the GetSecurityDescriptor() function returns the registry key security descriptor in the ADSI object model (line 295).

4.7.6   Retrieving CIM repository namespace security descriptors with WMI

To retrieve the security descriptor of a CIM repository namespace, the script must refer to a WMI system class called *__SystemSecurity*. As usual, to get access to an instance of a class, the script must connect to its corresponding CIM repository namespace. In this case, the script will be connected to the namespace from which we must retrieve the security descriptor. This connection is made in Sample 4.13 ("Connecting to CIM repository namespaces with WMI [Part XI]"), which provides an **SWBemServices** object to the GetSecurityDescriptor() function. From this connection, Sample 4.24 retrieves an instance of the *__SystemSecurity* class (line 271). Note that the *__SystemSecurity* class is a singleton class, which makes sense, since WMI implements one security descriptor per namespace. To get the namespace security descriptor, the *__SystemSecurity* class exposes the *GetSD* method (line 274). Unfortunately, things are not straightforward. The retrieved security descriptor has the format of a binary array, which forces the script to convert it to an ADSI security descriptor with the help of the **ADSIHelper** object (line 280). As a reminder, the **ADSIHelper** object is instantiated in Sample 4.2 at line 194. We will come back to the **ADSIHelper** object in section 4.9 ("The security descriptor conversion"). Once completed, the GetSecurityDescriptor() function returns a CIM repository namespace security descriptor retrieved with WMI but formatted as an ADSI security descriptor (line 295).

Sample 4.24   *Retrieving CIM repository namespace security descriptors with WMI (Part XI)*

```
...:
...:
...:
263:
264:' +------------------------------------------------------------------------------------+
265:' | CIM repository namespace                                                           |
266:' +------------------------------------------------------------------------------------+
267:          Case cWMINameSpaceViaWMI
268:' WMI retrieval technique ------------------------------------------------------------
269:              WScript.Echo "Reading CIM repository namespace security descriptor via WMI from '" & _
270:                          strSource & "'."
271:              Set objWMIInstance = objConnection.Get("__SystemSecurity=@")
...:
274:              intRC = objWMIInstance.GetSD (arrayBytes)
275:              If intRC Then
276:                 WScript.Echo vbCRLF & "Failed to get CIM repository namespace security " & _
277:                             "descriptor from '" & strSource & "'."
278:                 WScript.Quit (1)
279:              Else
280:                 Set objSD = objADSIHelper.ConvertRawSDToAdsiSD (arrayBytes)
281:                 If Err.Number Then ErrorHandler (Err)
282:              End If
283:
284:' Here objSD contains a security descriptor in the ADSI object model.
285:
286:          Case cWMINameSpaceViaADSI
287:' ADSI retrieval technique -----------------------------------------------------------
288:
289:' Here we can't retrieve a security descriptor via this access method.
290:
291:          Case Else
292:
293:     End Select
294:
295:     Set GetSecurityDescriptor = objSD
...:
299:End Function
```

4.8   Creating a default security descriptor

In Sample 4.16 ("Retrieving file system share security descriptors with WMI [Part III]") and Sample 4.17 ("Retrieving file system share security descriptors with ADSI [Part IV]"), we saw that it was necessary to create a default security descriptor by invoking the CreateDefaultSD() function (Sample 4.25). This is necessary because a file system share does not necessarily have a security descriptor defined. Because the file system share has a default behavior when no security descriptor is set, the script provides the

Figure 4.17
The default share security descriptor.

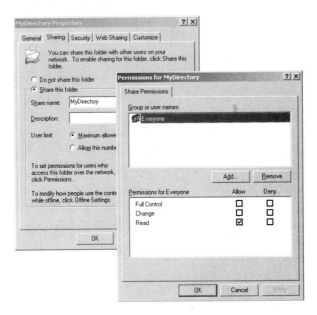

exact same default security descriptor as the one supposed to be present. So, when examining a share, this avoids any confusion for situations where no security descriptor is set for a share. Windows Explorer behaves in the same way, since it shows a security descriptor set on the share (Figure 4.17). If a script tries to retrieve the security descriptor, the code will return an error stating that no security descriptor is available. Therefore, Sample 4.25 creates the corresponding security descriptor.

It is important to note that the file system share is the only situation where a default security descriptor is created if it is missing. This is the reason why Sample 4.25 creates a default security descriptor only for file system share security descriptors accessed with WMI (lines 36 through 58) or ADSI (lines 60 through 84). All other situations expect to find a security descriptor. If there is no security descriptor set with all other manageable entities, then the script will return an error claiming that no security descriptor is available. This situation is shown in Samples 4.14 through 4.24.

As shown in Sample 4.25 (lines 38 through 58), when the security descriptor must be returned in the WMI object model, the scripts uses the **SWBemServices** object to create three new instances: one instance from the *Win32_SecurityDescriptor* class (line 38), one from the *Win32_ACE* class (line 39), and one instance from the *Win32_Trustee* class (line 40). These three new instances are the required instances to create a new security descriptor in the WMI object model. However, creating these instances is not enough. Each of them must be properly initialized. Sample 4.25 executes this task from line 42 through 58 for the WMI object model. From line 42 through 46, the script creates the trustee for the "Everyone" group. The trustee creation requires the SID of the group. Because the "Everyone" group is a built-in group available from all Windows installations, it can be created immediately with its very well known SID (S-1-1-0) in its string representation (line 44) and in its binary form (line 45).

Sample 4.25   *Create a default security descriptor for a share*

```
 .:
 .:
 .:
 8:' -------------------------------------------------------------------------------------
 9:Function CreateDefaultSD (objWMIServices, intSDType)
..:
18:    Select Case intSDType
..:
22:           Case cFileViaWMI
..:
27:           Case cFileViaADSI
..:
32:' +-----------------------------------------------------------------------------------+
33:' | Share                                                                             |
34:' +-----------------------------------------------------------------------------------+
35:           Case cShareViaWMI
36:' WMI creation technique ----------------------------------------------------------------
37:
38:               Set objNewSD = objWMIServices.Get("Win32_SecurityDescriptor").SpawnInstance_()
39:               Set objNewACE = objWMIServices.Get("Win32_ACE").SpawnInstance_()
40:               Set objNewTrustee = objWMIServices.Get("Win32_Trustee").SpawnInstance_()
41:
42:               objNewTrustee.Domain = Null
43:               objNewTrustee.Name = "Everyone"
44:               objNewTrustee.SIDString = "S-1-1-0"
45:               objNewTrustee.SID = Array (1,1,0,0,0,0,0,1,0,0,0,0)
46:               objNewTrustee.SidLength = 12
47:
48:               objNewACE.Trustee = objNewTrustee
49:               objNewACE.AceType = ACCESS_ALLOWED_ACE_TYPE
50:               objNewACE.AccessMask = FILE_SHARE_FULL_ACCESS Or _
51:                                      FILE_SHARE_CHANGE_ACCESS Or _
52:                                      FILE_SHARE_READ_ACCESS
53:               objNewACE.AceFlags = 0
54:
55:               objNewSD.DACL = Array (objNewAce)
56:               objNewSD.ControlFlags = SE_SELF_RELATIVE Or SE_DACL_PRESENT
57:
58:               ' Here objNewSD contains a security descriptor in the WMI object model.
59:
60:           Case cShareViaADSI
61:' ADSI creation technique ----------------------------------------------------------------
62:
63:               ' Windows Server 2003 only
64:               Set objNewSD = CreateObject ("SecurityDescriptor")
65:               Set objNewACL = CreateObject ("AccessControlList")
```

```
66:                       Set objNewACE = CreateObject ("AccessControlEntry")
67:
68:                       objNewACE.Trustee = "Everyone"
69:                       objNewACE.AceType = ACCESS_ALLOWED_ACE_TYPE
70:                       objNewACE.AccessMask = FILE_SHARE_FULL_ACCESS Or _
71:                                               FILE_SHARE_CHANGE_ACCESS Or _
72:                                               FILE_SHARE_READ_ACCESS
73:                       objNewACE.AceFlags = 0
74:
75:                       objNewACL.AddAce objNewAce
76:
77:                       objNewSD.DiscretionaryACL = objNewACL
78:                       objNewSD.Revision = 1
79:                       objNewSD.Control = SE_SELF_RELATIVE Or SE_DACL_PRESENT
..:
84:                       ' Here objNewSD contains a security descriptor in the ADSI object model.
..:
94:               Case cActiveDirectoryViaADSI
..:
102:              Case cExchange2000MailboxViaWMI
...:
107:              Case cExchange2000MailboxViaADSI
...:
112:              Case cExchange2000MailboxViaCDOEXM
...:
120:              Case cRegistryViaWMI
...:
125:              Case cRegistryViaADSI
...:
133:              Case cWMINameSpaceViaWMI
...:
138:              Case cWMINameSpaceViaADSI
...:
145:      End Select
146:
147:      Set CreateDefaultSD = objNewSD
...:
151:End Function
```

Next, the script initializes the rights that are necessary to grant full control access to the "Everyone" group (lines 48 through 58). Note that under Windows XP and Windows Server 2003, the default access on a share for the "Everyone" group is read-only (FILE_SHARE_READ_ACCESS flag). These values are defined in the **SecurityInclude.vbs** included at line 155 in Sample 4.2 ("The **WMIManageSD.Wsf** framework to manage security descriptors from the command line"). We will see later, in section 4.11.4 ("Deciphering the Access Control Entries"), how to select the values to create some specific rights. Once complete, the CreateDefaultSD() function returns a WMI security descriptor representation of the rights set on a file system share, as shown in Figure 4.17.

When the security descriptor must be returned in the ADSI object model, the script follows the same logic. However, it uses the ADSI object model, which means that it creates the ADSI objects representing an ADSI security descriptor (lines 64 through 66). So, it creates a security descriptor (line 64), an Access Control List (line 65), and an Access Control Entry (line 66). Once created, the script initializes the various values to grant the required right to the "Everyone" group, as shown in Figure 4.17.

An important point to note here is about the values defining the rights. Even if the security descriptor can be represented in the ADSI object model or in the WMI object model, it is interesting to see that the assigned values are always the same. This means that the values used to decipher a security descriptor remain a constant, independent of the object model used. This is an important point to remember when we decipher the security descriptor in section 4.10 ("Deciphering the security descriptor").

4.9   The security descriptor conversion

We have seen situations where the security descriptor is not directly retrieved in the WMI or in the ADSI object model. Sometimes, the security descriptor is represented as a binary array, which does not represent a usable form from a script. In such a case, it is necessary to convert the binary security descriptor to a usable object model. We mentioned that ADSI represents a good alternative to convert the binary security descriptor into the ADSI object model compared with the low-level programming that Win32 APIs require. Moreover, this approach is much simpler than digging into the low-level API programming. As a reminder, this conversion to get an ADSI security descriptor is necessary for:

- Sample 4.18, "Retrieving Active Directory object security descriptors with WMI (Part V)"

- Sample 4.20, "Retrieving Exchange 2000 mailbox security descriptors with WMI (Part VII)"

- Sample 4.24, "Retrieving CIM repository namespace security descriptors with WMI (Part XI)"

We will see further that a conversion is also necessary to update the security descriptor for:

- Sample 4.55, "Updating Active Directory object security descriptors with WMI (Part V)"

- Sample 4.57, "Updating Exchange 2000 mailbox security descriptors with WMI (Part VII)"

- Sample 4.61, "Updating CIM repository namespace security descriptors with WMI (Part XI)"

For the variable type conversion facility, the security descriptor conversion is encapsulated into a COM object called **ADSIHelper**. This ActiveX DLL object is written in Visual BASIC v6.0 (VB6), which allows the use of type definitions for variables. This comes from the fact that the ADSI technique used for the conversion requires a precise type as input parameter. Since scripting languages do not have explicit type definitions (Variant), this makes VB6 a good candidate for such programming while maintaining simplicity of use. The **ADSIHelper** object exposes two methods:

- *ConvertRawSDToAdsiSD*, which converts the binary security descriptor to an ADSI representation. The code is shown in Sample 4.26.

- *ConvertAdsiSDToRawSD*, which converts the ADSI security descriptor to a binary format. The code is shown in Sample 4.27.

Here again, we must determine if we are running under Windows Server 2003 (or Windows XP) or Windows 2000 (or Windows NT). Under Windows Server 2003 (or Windows XP), the **ADSIHelper** ActiveX DLL uses the **ADsSecurityUtility** object to convert the security descriptor (lines 25 through 33). It uses the *ConvertSecurityDescriptor* method exposed by the **ADsSecurityUtility** object. This method can convert a binary security descriptor to an ADSI security descriptor and vice versa (Sample 4.26, lines 31 through 33, and Sample 4.27, lines 72 through 74). The method uses the values defined in Table 4.7 ("The **ADsSecurityUtility** constants"). Because the values required by these conversion techniques must use a formal type, it makes it easier to program this logic under VB6 than a script, which only uses the Variant type.

Sample 4.26   *Converting the binary security descriptor to an ADSI representation*

```
1:Option Explicit
2:
3:Public Function ConvertRawSDToAdsiSD(ByVal arrayBytes As Variant) As IADsSecurityDescriptor
4:
5:' Windows Server 2003 only
6:Dim objADsSecurity As New ADsSecurityUtility
7:
8:' Windows 2000 only
9:' Dim objPropertyValue As New PropertyValue
10:
11:Dim objADsSD As IADsSecurityDescriptor
12:Dim byteSD() As Byte
13:Dim intIndice As Integer
14:
15:    On Error Resume Next
16:
17:    ' We must convert the variant array to a byte array.
18:    ' Otherwise, doesn't work ... (type conversion problem)
19:    ReDim byteSD(UBound(arrayBytes))
```

```
20:
21:     For intIndice = 0 To UBound(arrayBytes)
22:          byteSD(intIndice) = arrayBytes(intIndice)
23:     Next
24:
25:     ' Windows Server 2003 only -----------------------------------------------
26:     objADsSecurity.SecurityMask = ADS_SECURITY_INFO_OWNER Or _
27:                                   ADS_SECURITY_INFO_GROUP Or _
28:                                   ADS_SECURITY_INFO_DACL Or _
29:                                   ADS_SECURITY_INFO_SACL
30:
31:     Set objADsSD = objADsSecurity.ConvertSecurityDescriptor(byteSD, _
32:                                                     ADS_SD_FORMAT_RAW, _
33:                                                     ADS_SD_FORMAT_IID)
34:
35:     ' Windows 2000 only ------------------------------------------------------
36:     ' objPropertyValue.PutObjectProperty ADSTYPE_OCTET_STRING, (byteSD)
37:     ' Set objADsSD = objPropertyValue.GetObjectProperty(ADSTYPE_NT_SECURITY_DESCRIPTOR)
38:
39:     If Err.Number Then
40:        ErrorHandler "ConvertRawSDToAdsiSD", _
41:                 "Unable to convert raw Security Descriptor to an ADSI Security Descriptor", _
42:                 Err, _
43:                 True
..:
45:        Exit Function
46:     End If
47:
48:     Set ConvertRawSDToAdsiSD = objADsSD
49:
50:End Function
51:
..:
..:
..:
```

Under Windows 2000 (or Windows NT), the **ADSIHelper** ActiveX DLL uses the **PropertyValue** ADSI object exposed by the ADSI **IADsPropertyValue** interface (lines 36 and 37). The ActiveX DLL creates the **PropertyValue** object (line 9) and uses its *PutObjectProperty* method to assign the binary security descriptor as value (line 36). With the help of the ADSI cache and the ADSI property conversion mechanisms, the ActiveX DLL reads the assigned value by requesting an ADSI security descriptor format (line 37). The end result is that an ADSI security descriptor is returned from the ActiveX DLL. Note that this technique is also applicable under Windows Server 2003 (or Windows XP). Here, the **ADsSecurityUtility** object is only used to demonstrate some of the new ADSI capabilities provided by Windows Server 2003 and Windows XP.

The conversion of an ADSI security descriptor to a binary security descriptor follows the exact same logic (see Sample 4.27). Only the conversion types requested are inverted when compared with Sample 4.26.

Sample 4.27   *Converting the ADSI security descriptor to a binary format*

```
..:
..:
..:
51:
52:Public Function ConvertAdsiSDToRawSD(objVariantADsSD As Variant) As Variant()
53:
54:' Windows Server 2003 only
55:Dim objADsSecurity As New ADsSecurityUtility
56:
57:' Windows 2000 only
58:' Dim objPropertyValue As New PropertyValue
59:
60:Dim arrayBytes() As Variant
61:Dim byteSD() As Byte
62:Dim intIndice As Integer
63:
64:    On Error Resume Next
65:
66:    ' Windows Server 2003 only --------------------------------------------------
67:    objADsSecurity.SecurityMask = ADS_SECURITY_INFO_OWNER Or _
68:                                  ADS_SECURITY_INFO_GROUP Or _
69:                                  ADS_SECURITY_INFO_DACL Or _
70:                                  ADS_SECURITY_INFO_SACL
71:
72:    byteSD = objADsSecurity.ConvertSecurityDescriptor(objVariantADsSD, _
73:                                                      ADS_SD_FORMAT_IID, _
74:                                                      ADS_SD_FORMAT_RAW)
75:
76:    ' Windows 2000 only -----------------------------------------------------------
77:    ' objPropertyValue.PutObjectProperty ADSTYPE_NT_SECURITY_DESCRIPTOR, (objVariantADsSD)
78:    ' byteSD = objPropertyValue.GetObjectProperty(ADSTYPE_OCTET_STRING)
79:
80:    If Err.Number Then
81:        ErrorHandler "ConvertAdsiSDToRawSD", _
82:                     "Unable to convert ADSI Security Descriptor to a raw Security Descriptor", _
83:                     Err, _
84:                     True
85:        ConvertAdsiSDToRawSD = Null
86:        Exit Function
87:    End If
88:
89:    ' We must convert the byte array to a variant array.
90:    ' Otherwise, doesn't work ... (type conversion problem)
91:    ReDim arrayBytes(UBound(byteSD))
92:
93:    For intIndice = 0 To UBound(byteSD)
94:        arrayBytes(intIndice) = byteSD(intIndice)
95:    Next
96:
97:    ConvertAdsiSDToRawSD = arrayBytes
98:
99:End Function
100:
...:
...:
...:
```

4.10   Deciphering the security descriptor

To decipher the security descriptor, it is important to consider the object model used for its representation, because the object model organization will heavily influence the algorithm. As we have seen, sometimes we have a security descriptor represented in the WMI object model; sometimes we have a security descriptor represented in the ADSI object model. This implies that both object models referenced from Samples 4.3 through 4.13 must be handled in the script. Actually, the following portions of the code use a WMI deciphering technique:

- Sample 4.3, "Connecting to files and folders with WMI (Part I)"

- Sample 4.5, "Connecting to shares with WMI (Part III)"

All other portions of the code use an ADSI deciphering technique (see Sample 4.29):

- Sample 4.4, "Connecting to files and folders with ADSI (Part II)"

- Sample 4.6, "Connecting to shares with ADSI (Part IV)"

- Sample 4.7, "Connecting to Active Directory objects with WMI (Part V)"

- Sample 4.8, "Connecting to Active Directory objects with ADSI (Part VI)"

- Sample 4.9, "Connecting to Exchange 2000 mailbox information with WMI (Part VII)"

- Sample 4.10, "Connecting to Exchange 2000 mailbox information with ADSI (Part VIII)"

- Sample 4.11, "Connecting to Exchange 2000 mailbox information with CDOEXM (Part IX)"

- Sample 4.12, "Connecting to registry keys with ADSI (Part X)"

- Sample 4.13, "Connecting to CIM repository namespaces with WMI (Part XI)"

4.10.1   Deciphering the WMI security descriptor representation

Let's start with the WMI deciphering technique. Sample 4.28 shows the logic used to decipher a WMI security descriptor representation. As we have seen at the beginning of this chapter, in Figure 4.11, the *Win32_Security-*

Descriptor instance contains some *Win32_Trustee* instances (i.e., the group and the owner component) and usually one or two collections of *Win32_ACE* instances (i.e., DACL and SACL components), which in turn contain other *Win32_Trustee* instances (i.e., Trustee). With this peculiarity and the information about the nature of a WMI property (CIM type), it is possible to make use of a recursive algorithm. Each time the code encounters an object instance when it examines an instance property, the routine will call itself to decipher the instance.

Sample 4.28 *Deciphering a WMI security descriptor representation*

```
 .:
 .:
 .:
 8:' -------------------------------------------------------------------------------
 9:Function DecipherWMISecurityDescriptor (objWMIInstance, _
10:                                        intSDType, _
11:                                        ByVal strIndent, _
12:                                        boolDecipher)
..:
19:       WScript.Echo strIndent & "+- " & _
20:                    objWMIInstance.Path_.Class & " " & _
21:                    String (90 - Len (objWMIInstance.Path_.Class) - Len (strIndent), "-")
22:
23:       Set objWMIPropertySet = objWMIInstance.Properties_
24:       For Each objWMIProperty In objWMIPropertySet
25:          If Not IsNull (objWMIProperty.Value) Then
26:             If objWMIProperty.CIMType = wbemCimtypeObject Then
27:                If objWMIProperty.IsArray Then
28:
29:                   ' This is an array, we deal with the Win32_ACE
30:                   DisplayFormattedProperty Null, _
31:                                            strIndent & "| " & objWMIProperty.Name, _
32:                                            "(Win32_ACE)", _
33:                                            Null
34:                   For Each varElement In objWMIProperty.Value
35:                      DecipherWMISecurityDescriptor varElement, _
36:                                                    intSDType, _
37:                                                    strIndent & "| ", _
38:                                                    boolDecipher
39:                   Next
40:                Else
41:
42:                   ' This is not an array, we deal with a Win32_Trustee
43:                   DisplayFormattedProperty Null, _
44:                                            strIndent & "| " & objWMIProperty.Name, _
45:                                            "(Win32_Trustee)", _
46:                                            Null
47:                   DecipherWMISecurityDescriptor objWMIProperty.Value, _
48:                                                 intSDType, _
49:                                                 strIndent & "| ", _
50:                                                 boolDecipher
51:                End If
52:             Else
53:                Select Case Ucase (objWMIProperty.Name)
```

```
54:' Win32_SecurityDescriptor --------------------------------------------------------
55:                    Case "CONTROLFLAGS"
56:                        If boolDecipher Then
57:                            DisplayFormattedProperty objWMIInstance, _
58:                                    strIndent & "| " & objWMIProperty.Name, _
59:                                    DecipherSDControlFlags (objWMIProperty.Value), _
60:                                    Null
61:                        Else
62:                            DisplayFormattedProperty objWMIInstance, _
63:                                    strIndent & "| " & objWMIProperty.Name, _
64:                                    "&h" & Hex (objWMIProperty.Value), _
65:                                    Null
66:                        End If
67:' Win32_ACE ----------------------------------------------------------------------
68:                    Case "ACCESSMASK"
69:                        If boolDecipher Then
70:                            DisplayFormattedProperty objWMIInstance, _
71:                                    strIndent & "| " & objWMIProperty.Name, _
72:                                    DecipherACEMask (intSDType, objWMIProperty.Value), _
73:                                    Null
74:                        Else
75:                            DisplayFormattedProperty objWMIInstance, _
76:                                    strIndent & "| " & objWMIProperty.Name, _
77:                                    "&h" & Hex (objWMIProperty.Value), _
78:                                    Null
79:                        End If
80:                    Case "ACEFLAGS"
81:                        If boolDecipher Then
82:                            DisplayFormattedProperty objWMIInstance, _
83:                                    strIndent & "| " & objWMIProperty.Name, _
84:                                    DecipherACEFlags (intSDType, objWMIProperty.Value), _
85:                                    Null
86:                        Else
87:                            DisplayFormattedProperty objWMIInstance, _
88:                                    strIndent & "| " & objWMIProperty.Name, _
89:                                    "&h" & Hex (objWMIProperty.Value), _
90:                                    Null
91:                        End If
92:                    Case "ACETYPE"
93:                        If boolDecipher Then
94:                            DisplayFormattedProperty objWMIInstance, _
95:                                    strIndent & "| " & objWMIProperty.Name, _
96:                                    DecipherACEType (intSDType, objWMIProperty.Value), _
97:                                    Null
98:                        Else
99:                            DisplayFormattedProperty objWMIInstance, _
100:                                    strIndent & "| " & objWMIProperty.Name, _
101:                                    "&h" & Hex (objWMIProperty.Value), _
102:                                    Null
103:                        End If
104:' Win32_Trustee --------------------------------------------------------------------
105:                    Case "SID"
106:                        DisplayFormattedProperty objWMIInstance, _
107:                                strIndent & "| " & objWMIProperty.Name, _
108:                                ConvertArrayInString (objWMIProperty.Value, ",", False), _
109:                                Null
110:' Default --------------------------------------------------------------------------
111:                    Case Else
112:                        DisplayFormattedProperty objWMIInstance, _
113:                                strIndent & "| " & objWMIProperty.Name, _
```

```
114:                                    objWMIProperty.Name, _
115:                                    Null
116:                        End Select
117:            End If
118:          End If
119:    Next
120:
121:    WScript.Echo strIndent & "+-" & _
122:                        String (90 - Len (strIndent) + 2, "-")
...:
126:End Function
```

Sample 4.28 starts by enumerating all properties of the *Win32_Security-Descriptor* (lines 24 through 119). Then the code checks for a value in the first property retrieved from the collection (line 25). If there is a value, the property type is examined, and, if the property contains an object instance (line 26), the script code verifies whether this property is an array (line 27). Since we know the WMI representation of a security descriptor, when the code discovers an array of objects, we know that we are dealing with one or more *Win32_ACE* instances, since it is the only property containing objects in an array (lines 29 through 39). If this is not an array (lines 42 through 50), then, based on our knowledge of the WMI security descriptor representation, we know that it's a *Win32_Trustee* instance. In both cases, because we deal with an instance, the DecipherWMISecurityDescriptor() function is recursively called (lines 35 through 38 or lines 47 through 50).

In case the property is not an object instance, the code displays its corresponding values (lines 53 through 116). Because the *Win32_SecurityDescriptor* instance with the various *Win32_Trustee* and *Win32_ACE* instances do not have properties using the same name, we can use the **Select Case** statement to convert and display the property accordingly. For instance, the *ControlFlags* property can be displayed without any bit flag interpretation (lines 62 through 65). If the **/Decipher+** switch is specified on the command line, its value can be deciphered (lines 57 through 60). The same logic applies for the *AccessMask*, the *AceFlags*, and the *AceType* properties (lines 68, 80, and 92). If the *SID* property must be displayed (line 105), since it contains a binary array, it is first converted to a comma-delimited string with the ConvertArrayInString() function, and then it is displayed (lines 112 through 115). Any other property is displayed by the default selection of the **Select Case** statement (lines 111 through 116).

As an end result, the next command line will display the security descriptor, as follows:

```
1:   C:\>WMIManageSD.Wsf /FileSystem:C:\MyDirectory
2:   Microsoft (R) Windows Script Host Version 5.6
3:   Copyright (C) Microsoft Corporation 1996-2001. All rights reserved.
4:
```

```
 5:    Reading File or Folder security descriptor via WMI from 'C:\MyDirectory'.
 6:
 7:    +- Win32_SecurityDescriptor ----------------------------------------------------------------
 8:    | ControlFlags: .......................... &hB814
 9:    | DACL: .................................. (Win32_ACE)
10:    | +- Win32_ACE ------------------------------------------------------------------------------
11:    | | AccessMask: .......................... &h1F01FF
12:    | | AceFlags: ............................ &h3
13:    | | AceType: ............................. &h0
14:    | | Trustee: ............................. (Win32_Trustee)
15:    | | +- Win32_Trustee -----------------------------------------------------------------------
16:    | | | Domain: ............................ BUILTIN
17:    | | | Name: .............................. Administrators
18:    | | | SID: ............................... 1,2,0,0,0,0,0,5,32,0,0,0,32,2,0,0
19:    | | | SidLength: ......................... 16
20:    | | | SIDString: ......................... S-1-5-32-544
21:    | | +---------------------------------------------------------------------------------------
22:    | +----------------------------------------------------------------------------------------
23:    | +- Win32_ACE ------------------------------------------------------------------------------
24:    | | AccessMask: .......................... &h1200A9
25:    | | AceFlags: ............................ &h2
26:    | | AceType: ............................. &h0
27:    | | Trustee: ............................. (Win32_Trustee)
28:    | | +- Win32_Trustee -----------------------------------------------------------------------
29:    | | | Domain: ............................ LISSWARENET
30:    | | | Name: .............................. MyGroup
31:    | | | SID: ............................... 1,5,0,0,0,...,246,207,122,236,255,136,223,4,0,0
32:    | | | SidLength: ......................... 28
33:    | | | SIDString: ......................... S-1-5-21-3533506287-3489020660-2298473594-1247
34:    | | +---------------------------------------------------------------------------------------
35:    | +----------------------------------------------------------------------------------------
36:    | Owner: ................................. (Win32_Trustee)
37:    | +- Win32_Trustee ---------------------------------------------------------------------------
38:    | | Domain: ............................. BUILTIN
39:    | | Name: ............................... Administrators
40:    | | SID: ................................ 1,2,0,0,0,0,0,5,32,0,0,0,32,2,0,0
41:    | | SidLength: .......................... 16
42:    | | SIDString: .......................... S-1-5-32-544
43:    | +----------------------------------------------------------------------------------------
44:    | SACL: .................................. (Win32_ACE)
45:    | +- Win32_ACE ------------------------------------------------------------------------------
46:    | | AccessMask: .......................... &h10000
47:    | | AceFlags: ............................ &h43
48:    | | AceType: ............................. &h2
49:    | | Trustee: ............................. (Win32_Trustee)
50:    | | +- Win32_Trustee -----------------------------------------------------------------------
51:    | | | Domain: ............................ BUILTIN
52:    | | | Name: .............................. Administrators
53:    | | | SID: ............................... 1,2,0,0,0,0,0,5,32,0,0,0,32,2,0,0
54:    | | | SidLength: ......................... 16
55:    | | | SIDString: ......................... S-1-5-32-544
56:    | | +---------------------------------------------------------------------------------------
57:    | +----------------------------------------------------------------------------------------
58:    +------------------------------------------------------------------------------------------
```

As we can see, the script also takes care of the WMI security descriptor display, since it encloses the various components between dashed lines to obtain a pseudographical representation.

4.10.2 Deciphering the ADSI security descriptor representation

To decipher an ADSI security descriptor representation, things are easier, since no recursive algorithm is used. Sample 4.29 implements the logic. Compared with Sample 4.28 ("Deciphering a WMI security descriptor representation"), the coding technique is more literal. For each ADSI COM object used to represent the security descriptor components, and for each of their properties, the code displays the corresponding value one by one. Essentially, Sample 4.29 makes use of the DisplayFormattedSTDProperty() function to format the output. This function has the exact same role as the DisplayFormattedProperty() function developed in Chapter 1 (Sample 1.6), but the DisplayFormattedSTDProperty() function is not related to a particular object model. It is a generic function to display information in the same way as the DisplayFormattedProperty() function (which is WMI related).

Sample 4.29 starts to display the properties of the **SecurityDescriptor** object (lines 23 through 33). Next, it continues with the **AccessControlEntry** object collection stored in the Discretionary ACL (lines 35 through 44). The code displays each property of the ACE in the DACL in a loop (lines 46 through 97). Then, it repeats the exact same logic applied to the ACE in the SACL (lines 109 through 172).

Sample 4.29   *Deciphering an ADSI security descriptor representation*

```
  .:
  .:
  .:
  8:' -------------------------------------------------------------------------------
  9:Function DecipherADSISecurityDescriptor (objSD, intSDType, boolDecipher)
  ..:
 19:    WScript.Echo strIndent & "+- ADSI Security Descriptor " & _
 20:                 String (66 - Len (strIndent), "-")
 21:
 22:    ' Open Security Descriptor data -------------------------------------------
 23:    DisplayFormattedSTDProperty  strIndent & "| Owner", objSD.Owner, Null
 24:    DisplayFormattedSTDProperty  strIndent & "| Group", objSD.Group, Null
 25:    DisplayFormattedSTDProperty  strIndent & "| Revision", objSD.Revision, Null
 26:    If boolDecipher Then
 27:        DisplayFormattedSTDProperty  strIndent & "| Control", _
 28:                                     DecipherSDControlFlags (objSD.Control), _
 29:                                     Null
 30:    Else
 31:        DisplayFormattedSTDProperty  strIndent & "| Control", _
 32:                                     "&h" & Hex(objSD.Control), Null
 33:    End If
 34:
 35:    intACECount = 0
```

```
36:     Set objACL = objSD.DiscretionaryAcl
37:     intACECount = objACL.AceCount
38:     If intACECount And Err.Number = 0 Then
39:         ' Open Discretionary ACL data ------------------------------------------------
40:         strIndent = strIndent & "|"
41:         WScript.Echo strIndent & "+- ADSI DiscretionaryAcl " & _
42:                     String (69 - Len (strIndent), "-")
43:
44:         strIndent = strIndent & "|"
45:
46:         For Each objACE In objACL
47:             ' Open ACE Data ----------------------------------------------------------
48:             WScript.Echo strIndent & "+- ADSI ACE " & _
49:                         String (82 - Len (strIndent), "-")
50:
51:             If boolDecipher Then
52:                 DisplayFormattedSTDProperty  strIndent & "| AccessMask", _
53:                                              DecipherACEMask (intSDType, objACE.AccessMask), _
54:                                              Null
55:             Else
56:                 DisplayFormattedSTDProperty  strIndent & "| AccessMask", _
57:                                              "&h" & Hex(objACE.AccessMask), Null
58:             End If
59:
60:             If boolDecipher Then
61:                 DisplayFormattedSTDProperty  strIndent & "| AceFlags", _
62:                                              DecipherACEFlags (intSDType, objACE.AceFlags), _
63:                                              Null
64:             Else
65:                 DisplayFormattedSTDProperty  strIndent & "| AceFlags", _
66:                                              "&h" & Hex(objACE.AceFlags), Null
67:             End If
68:
69:             If boolDecipher Then
70:                 DisplayFormattedSTDProperty  strIndent & "| AceType", _
71:                                              DecipherACEType (intSDType, objACE.AceType), _
72:                                              Null
73:             Else
74:                 DisplayFormattedSTDProperty  strIndent & "| AceType", _
75:                                              "&h" & Hex(objACE.AceType), Null
76:             End If
77:
78:             If boolDecipher Then
79:                 DisplayFormattedSTDProperty  strIndent & "| AceFlagType", _
80:                                              DecipherACEFlagType (intSDType, objACE.Flags), _
81:                                              Null
82:             Else
83:                 DisplayFormattedSTDProperty  strIndent & "| AceFlagType", _
84:                                              "&h" & Hex(objACE.Flags), Null
85:             End If
86:
87:             DisplayFormattedSTDProperty  strIndent & "| ObjectType", _
88:                                          objACE.ObjectType, Null
89:             DisplayFormattedSTDProperty  strIndent & "| InheritedObjectType", _
90:                                          objACE.InheritedObjectType, Null
91:             DisplayFormattedSTDProperty  strIndent & "| Trustee", _
92:                                          objACE.Trustee, Null
93:
94:             ' Close ACE Data ---------------------------------------------------------
95:             WScript.Echo strIndent & "+-" & _
```

```
 96:                         String (90 - Len (strIndent) + 2, "-")
 97:       Next
 98:
 99:       strIndent = Mid (strIndent, 1, Len (strIndent) - 1)
100:
101:       ' Close Discretionary ACL data ------------------------------------------------
102:       WScript.Echo strIndent & "+-" & _
103:                         String (90 - Len (strIndent) + 2, "-")
104:       strIndent = Mid (strIndent, 1, Len (strIndent) - 1)
105:    Else
106:       Err.Clear
107:    End If
108:
109:    intACECount = 0
110:    Set objACL = objSD.SystemACL
111:    intACECount = objACL.AceCount
112:    If intACECount And Err.Number = 0 Then
113:       ' Open System ACL data ---------------------------------------------------------
114:       strIndent = strIndent & "|"
115:       WScript.Echo strIndent & "+- ADSI SystemAcl " & _
116:                         String (76 - Len (strIndent), "-")
117:
118:       strIndent = strIndent & "|"
119:
120:       For Each objACE In objACL
...:
162:       Next
163:
164:       strIndent = Mid (strIndent, 1, Len (strIndent) - 1)
165:
166:       ' Close System ACL data --------------------------------------------------------
167:       WScript.Echo strIndent & "+-" & _
168:                         String (90 - Len (strIndent) + 2, "-")
169:       strIndent = Mid (strIndent, 1, Len (strIndent) - 1)
170:    Else
171:       Err.Clear
172:    End If
173:
174:    ' Close Security Descriptor data -------------------------------------------------
175:    WScript.Echo strIndent & "+-" & _
176:                         String (90 - Len (strIndent) + 2, "-")
177:
178:End Function
```

The end result with an ADSI representation is almost the same as the WMI representation. The difference resides in the SACL representation. The following sample output is a Folder security descriptor accessed under Windows 2000 with the **ADsSecurity.DLL**. As we have seen before, the **ADsSecurity.DLL** ActiveX component doesn't support the SACL access. Therefore, it is not displayed. The output obtained is as follows:

```
 1:    C:\>WMIManageSD.Wsf /FileSystem:C:\MyDirectory /ADSI+
 2:    Microsoft (R) Windows Script Host Version 5.6
 3:    Copyright (C) Microsoft Corporation 1996-2001. All rights reserved.
 4:
 5:    Reading File or Folder security descriptor via ADSI from 'C:\MyDirectory'.
 6:
```

```
 7:   +- ADSI Security Descriptor --------------------------------------------------
 8:   | Owner: .............................. BUILTIN\Administrators
 9:   | Group: .............................. LISSWARENET\Domain Users
10:   | Revision: ........................... 1
11:   | Control: ............................ &h9004
12:   |+- ADSI DiscretionaryAcl ----------------------------------------------------
13:   ||+- ADSI ACE ---------------------------------------------------------------
14:   ||| AccessMask: ........................ &h1F01FF
15:   ||| AceFlags: .......................... &h3
16:   ||| AceType: ........................... &h0
17:   ||| AceFlagType: ....................... &h0
18:   ||| Trustee: ........................... BUILTIN\Administrators
19:   ||+--------------------------------------------------------------------------
20:   ||+- ADSI ACE ---------------------------------------------------------------
21:   ||| AccessMask: ........................ &h1200A9
22:   ||| AceFlags: .......................... &h2
23:   ||| AceType: ........................... &h0
24:   ||| AceFlagType: ....................... &h0
25:   ||| Trustee: ........................... LISSWARENET\MyGroup
26:   ||+--------------------------------------------------------------------------
27:   |+----------------------------------------------------------------------------
28:   +-----------------------------------------------------------------------------
```

4.11   Deciphering the security descriptor components

Retrieving the security descriptor components, such as the Access Control List and the Access Control Entries of the Discretionary ACL and the System ACL, is the very first step of the security descriptor deciphering. As shown in the two previous WMI and ADSI output representations, some properties contain numeric values. A closer look at these values shows that every bit composing the values has a specific meaning for the property. The interpretation of the properties represents the second step of the deciphering. In this section, we will decipher each value available from a security descriptor.

4.11.1   Deciphering the Owner and Group properties

The *Owner* and *Group* properties in the WMI object model are represented by a *Win32_Trustee* instance in an **SWBemObject** object. Therefore, Sample 4.28 ("Deciphering a WMI security descriptor representation"), by its recursive logic, naturally detects that the *Group* and *Owner* properties of the *Win32_SecurityDescriptor* class contain a *Win32_Trustee* instance. No particular deciphering technique is necessary. The *Win32_Trustee* instance is deciphered inside the DecipherWMISecurityDescriptor() in Sample 4.28. The following output sample shows the *Win32_Trustee* instances contained in a WMI *Owner* security descriptor representation coming from a folder (lines 69 through 76).

```
 1:   C:\>WMIManageSD.Wsf /FileSystem:C:\MyDirectory /Decipher+
 2:   Microsoft (R) Windows Script Host Version 5.6
 3:   Copyright (C) Microsoft Corporation 1996-2001. All rights reserved.
 4:
 5:   Reading File or Folder security descriptor via WMI from 'C:\MyDirectory'.
 6:
 7:   +- Win32_SecurityDescriptor -------------------------------------------------
 8:   | ControlFlags: ......................... &hB414
..:
68:   | +--------------------------------------------------------------------------
69:   | Owner: .............................. (Win32_Trustee)
70:   | +- Win32_Trustee ----------------------------------------------------------
71:   | | Domain: ........................... BUILTIN
72:   | | Name: ............................. Administrators
73:   | | SID: .............................. 1,2,0,0,0,0,0,5,32,0,0,0,32,2,0,0
74:   | | SidLength: ........................ 16
75:   | | SIDString: ........................ S-1-5-32-544
76:   | +--------------------------------------------------------------------------
..:
..:
..:
```

When the security descriptor is represented in the ADSI object model, things are easier. The *Group* and the *Owner* properties of a security descriptor contain a literal string representing the trustee (i.e., Domain\User), which is displayed by the DecipherADSISecurityDescriptor() function in Sample 4.29 ("Deciphering an ADSI security descriptor representation"). If some SID resolution problems occur, the property could return a SID instead of a literal string representing the trustee. The following output sample shows the trustees contained in an ADSI security descriptor representation coming from a folder (line 8 for the trustee contained in the *Owner* property and line 9 for the trustee contained in the *Group* property).

```
 1:   C:\>WMIManageSD.Wsf /FileSystem:C:\MyDirectory /Decipher+ /ADSI+
 2:   Microsoft (R) Windows Script Host Version 5.6
 3:   Copyright (C) Microsoft Corporation 1996-2001. All rights reserved.
 4:
 5:   Reading File or Folder security descriptor via ADSI from 'C:\MyDirectory'.
 6:
 7:   +- ADSI Security Descriptor -------------------------------------------------
 8:   | Owner: .............................. BUILTIN\Administrators
 9:   | Group: .............................. LISSWARENET\Domain Users
10:   | Revision: ........................... 1
11:   | Control: ............................ &h9404
..:
..:
..:
```

4.11.2 Deciphering the security descriptor Control Flags

The security descriptor *Control Flags* property (called *ControlFlags* with WMI and *Control* with ADSI; see Table 4.3, "The WMI and ADSI Secu-

Table 4.8   *The Security Descriptor Control Flags Values*

SE_GROUP_DEFAULTED	0x2	A default mechanism, rather than the original provider of the security descriptor, provided the security descriptor's group SID. To set this flag, use the SetSecurityDescriptorGroup function.
SE_OWNER_DEFAULTED	0x1	A default mechanism, rather than the original provider of the security descriptor, provided the security descriptor's owner security identifier (SID). To set this flag, use the SetSecurityDescriptorOwner function.
SE_DACL_DEFAULTED	0x8	Indicates a security descriptor with a default DACL. For example, if an object's creator does not specify a DACL, the object receives the default DACL from the creator's access token. This flag can affect how the system treats the DACL, with respect to ACE inheritance. The system ignores this flag if the SE_DACL_PRESENT flag is not set. This flag is used to determine how the final DACL on the object is to be computed and is not stored physically in the security descriptor control of the securable object. To set this flag, use the SetSecurityDescriptorDacl function.
SE_SACL_DEFAULTED	0x20	A default mechanism, rather than the original provider of the security descriptor, provided the SACL. This flag can affect how the system treats the SACL, with respect to ACE inheritance. The system ignores this flag if the SE_SACL_PRESENT flag is not set. To set this flag, use the SetSecurityDescriptorSacl function.
SE_DACL_PRESENT	0x4	Indicates a security descriptor that has a DACL. If this flag is not set, or if this flag is set and the DACL is NULL, the security descriptor allows full access to everyone. This flag is used to hold the security information specified by a caller until the security descriptor is associated with a securable object. Once the security descriptor is associated with a securable object, the SE_DACL_PRESENT flag is always set in the security descriptor control. To set this flag, use SetSecurityDescriptorDacl.
SE_SACL_PRESENT	0x10	Indicates a security descriptor that has a SACL. To set this flag, use the SetSecurityDescriptorSacl function.
SE_DACL_PROTECTED	0x1000	Windows 2000/XP: Prevents the DACL of the security descriptor from being modified by inheritable ACEs. To set this flag, use the SetSecurityDescriptorControl function.
SE_SACL_PROTECTED	0x2000	Windows 2000/XP: Prevents the SACL of the security descriptor from being modified by inheritable ACEs. To set this flag, use the SetSecurityDescriptorControl function.
SE_DACL_AUTO_INHERIT_REQ	0x0100	Requests that the provider for the object protected by the security descriptor automatically propagate the DACL to existing child objects. If the provider supports automatic inheritance, it propagates the DACL to any existing child objects, and sets the SE_DACL_AUTO_INHERITED bit in the security descriptors of the object and its child objects.
SE_SACL_AUTO_INHERIT_REQ	0x0200	Requests that the provider for the object protected by the security descriptor automatically propagate the SACL to existing child objects. If the provider supports automatic inheritance, it propagates the SACL to any existing child objects, and sets the SE_SACL_AUTO_INHERITED bit in the security descriptors of the object and its child objects.
SE_DACL_AUTO_INHERITED	0x0400	Windows 2000/XP: Indicates a security descriptor in which the DACL is set up to support automatic propagation of inheritable ACEs to existing child objects. For Windows 2000 ACLs that support auto inheritance, this bit is always set. It is used to distinguish these ACLs from Windows NT 4.0 ACLs that do not support auto-inheritance. Protected servers can call the ConvertToAutoInheritPrivateObjectSecurity function to convert a security descriptor and set this flag. This bit is not set in security descriptors for Windows NT versions 4.0 and earlier, which do not support automatic propagation of inheritable ACEs.
SE_SACL_AUTO_INHERITED	0x0800	Windows 2000/XP: Indicates a security descriptor in which the SACL is set up to support automatic propagation of inheritable ACEs to existing child objects. The system sets this bit when it performs the automatic inheritance algorithm for the object and its existing child objects. Protected servers can call the ConvertToAutoInheritPrivateObjectSecurity function to convert a security descriptor and set this flag. This bit is not set in security descriptors for Windows NT versions 4.0 and earlier, which do not support automatic propagation of inheritable ACEs.
SE_SELF_RELATIVE	0x8000	Indicates a security descriptor in self-relative format with all the security information in a contiguous block of memory. If this flag is not set, the security descriptor is in absolute format. For more information, see Absolute and Self-Relative Security Descriptors.

rity Descriptor Exposed Methods and Properties") is helpful in determining the presence of the various security descriptor subcomponents, such as the DACL and SACL. With the introduction of Windows 2000, the security descriptor inheritance is also determined by this property. Each bit in the value has a specific meaning, summarized in Table 4.8.

Based on these values, the *Control Flags* bits must be deciphered with a bitwise operation, since each label in Table 4.8 corresponds to a specific bit setting in the value. For instance, Figure 4.18 shows flags that are turned ON or OFF when the *Control Flags* value equals 0xB814 (flags turned ON are in bold).

Figure 4.18
*The Control Flags
bitwise values.*

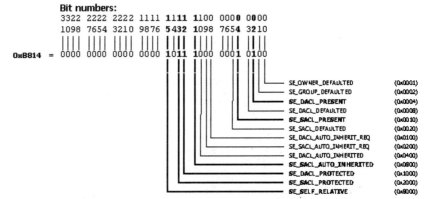

Based on the flag values, Sample 4.30 deciphers the various bits of the property.

Sample 4.30   *Deciphering the security descriptor Control Flags property*

```
 .:
 .:
 .:
 8:' -------------------------------------------------------------------------------------
 9:Function DecipherSDControlFlags (intControlFlags)
 ..:
15:    strTemp = "&h" & Hex (intControlFlags)
16:
17:    If (intControlFlags And SE_OWNER_DEFAULTED) Then
18:        strTemp = strTemp & "," & "SE_OWNER_DEFAULTED"
19:    End If
20:    If (intControlFlags And SE_GROUP_DEFAULTED) Then
21:        strTemp = strTemp & "," & "SE_GROUP_DEFAULTED"
22:    End If
23:    If (intControlFlags And SE_DACL_PRESENT) Then
24:        strTemp = strTemp & "," & "SE_DACL_PRESENT"
25:    End If
26:    If (intControlFlags And SE_DACL_DEFAULTED) Then
27:        strTemp = strTemp & "," & "SE_DACL_DEFAULTED"
28:    End If
29:    If (intControlFlags And SE_SACL_PRESENT) Then
30:        strTemp = strTemp & "," & "SE_SACL_PRESENT"
31:    End If
32:    If (intControlFlags And SE_SACL_DEFAULTED) Then
33:        strTemp = strTemp & "," & "SE_SACL_DEFAULTED"
34:    End If
35:    If (intControlFlags And SE_DACL_AUTO_INHERIT_REQ) Then
36:        strTemp = strTemp & "," & "SE_DACL_AUTO_INHERIT_REQ"
37:    End If
38:    If (intControlFlags And SE_SACL_AUTO_INHERIT_REQ) Then
39:        strTemp = strTemp & "," & "SE_SACL_AUTO_INHERIT_REQ"
40:    End If
41:    If (intControlFlags And SE_DACL_AUTO_INHERITED) Then
42:        strTemp = strTemp & "," & "SE_DACL_AUTO_INHERITED"
43:    End If
```

```
44:     If (intControlFlags And SE_SACL_AUTO_INHERITED) Then
45:         strTemp = strTemp & "," & "SE_SACL_AUTO_INHERITED"
46:     End If
47:     If (intControlFlags And SE_DACL_PROTECTED) Then
48:         strTemp = strTemp & "," & "SE_DACL_PROTECTED"
49:     End If
50:     If (intControlFlags And SE_SACL_PROTECTED) Then
51:         strTemp = strTemp & "," & "SE_SACL_PROTECTED"
52:     End If
53:     If (intControlFlags And SE_SELF_RELATIVE) Then
54:         strTemp = strTemp & "," & "SE_SELF_RELATIVE"
55:     End If
56:
57:     DecipherSDControlFlags = ConvertStringInArray (strTemp, ",")
58:
59:End Function
```

Basically, the code performs a Boolean operation on the *Control Flags* value to determine the state of the bits corresponding to the flags listed in Table 4.8. If the bit is ON, the code constructs a comma-delimited string with the different bit labels from Table 4.8 (lines 15 through 55). Most values contained in a security descriptor or in one of its components use a similar deciphering technique. Only the flags used to decipher the value are different. Once completed, the comma-delimited string is converted to an array (line 57). The obtained output result would be as follows:

```
1:     C:\>WMIManageSD.Wsf /FileSystem:C:\MyDirectory /Decipher+
2:     Microsoft (R) Windows Script Host Version 5.6
3:     Copyright (C) Microsoft Corporation 1996-2001. All rights reserved.
4:
5:     Reading File or Folder security descriptor via WMI from 'C:\MyDirectory'.
6:
7:     +- Win32_SecurityDescriptor -------------------------------------------------------------
8:     | ControlFlags: ......................... &hB814
9:                                                SE_DACL_PRESENT
10:                                               SE_SACL_PRESENT
11:                                               SE_SACL_AUTO_INHERITED
12:                                               SE_DACL_PROTECTED
13:                                               SE_SACL_PROTECTED
14:                                               SE_SELF_RELATIVE
..:
..:
..:
```

The DecipherSDControlFlags() function is called by Sample 4.28 ("Deciphering a WMI security descriptor representation" at line 59) and Sample 4.29 ("Deciphering an ADSI security descriptor representation" at line 28). Note that both the WMI and ADSI deciphering functions call the DecipherSDControlFlags() function if the command-line parameter **/Decipher+** is specified. Independent of the object model representing the security descriptor, it makes sense to have the same meaning for the values in the properties.

The *Control Flags* property determines two behaviors of the security descriptor in regard to the inherited ACE:

- How the security descriptor behaves in regard to the ACE inherited from a parent object (i.e., Parent folder in the file system or Container in Active Directory). The SE_DACL_PROTECTED and SE_SACL_PROTECTED flags determine this first behavior.

- How the ACE defined in the security descriptor is inherited by the child objects (i.e., Subfolder in the file system or a child object in Active Directory). The SE_DACL_AUTO_INHERIT_REQ and the SE_SACL_AUTO_INHERIT_REQ flags determine this second behavior.

Since these flags are quite important for a security descriptor management, it could be useful to manage the SE_DACL_PROTECTED, SE_SACL_PROTECTED, the SE_DACL_AUTO_INHERIT_REQ, and the SE_SACL_AUTO_INHERIT_REQ flags. In order to configure these flags from the command line, it is necessary to calculate the new *Control Flags* value from the labels given on the command line. Sample 4.31 makes this calculation. Other *Control Flags* bits, listed in Table 4.8, are set by the script itself when necessary and are not configurable from the command line. This is why the array defined between lines 20 and 23 only contains the four flags just mentioned.

Sample 4.31   *Calculate the security descriptor controls value*

```
 .:
 .:
 .:
 8:' -----------------------------------------------------------------------------------
 9:Function CalculateSDControlFlags (arraySDControlFlags)
 ..:
20:    arraySDControlFlagsData = Array ("SE_DACL_PROTECTED", SE_DACL_PROTECTED, _
21:                            "SE_SACL_PROTECTED", SE_SACL_PROTECTED, _
22:                            "SE_DACL_AUTO_INHERIT_REQ", SE_DACL_AUTO_INHERIT_REQ, _
23:                            "SE_SACL_AUTO_INHERIT_REQ", SE_SACL_AUTO_INHERIT_REQ)
24:
25:    For Each strSDControlFlags in arraySDControlFlags
26:        boolFlagFound = False
27:        For intIndice = 0 To UBound (arraySDControlFlagsData) Step 2
28:            If Ucase (strSDControlFlags) = Ucase (arraySDControlFlagsData(intIndice)) Then
29:                intSDControlFlags = intSDControlFlags + arraySDControlFlagsData(intIndice + 1)
30:                boolFlagFound = True
31:                Exit For
32:            End If
33:        Next
34:        If boolFlagFound = False Then
35:            WScript.Echo "Invalid SD control flags '" & strSDControlFlags & "'."
36:            WScript.Quit (1)
37:        End If
```

```
38:     Next
39:
40:     CalculateSDControlFlags = intSDControlFlags
41:
42:End Function
```

The flag labels given on the command line are passed in the form of an array as a parameter of the CalculateSDControlFlags() function (line 9). Next, another array is created (lines 20 through 23), which contains the flags accepted on the command line. To validate the flags given on the command line and calculate the final value, two loops are enclosed together (lines 25 through 38 and 27 through 33). If there is a match between the flag label given on the command line and the authorized list (line 28), its corresponding value is calculated (line 29). In case of invalid flag syntax, the loop detects that no match occurred and the script execution terminates (lines 34 through 37). For all flag labels given on the command line, the routine will follow the exact same logic. This logic is not related to the security descriptor *Control Flags* property. This algorithm is also used with the **/ACEType** and the **/ACEMask** switches in the CalculateACEType() CalculateACEMask() functions, respectively.

The CalculateSDControlFlags() function is only used when the *Control Flags* property is updated in the security descriptor. We will see later in section 4.12.3 ("Updating the security descriptor Control Flags") how this new value is updated in the security descriptor and how it is saved back to the secured entity.

Note that some security descriptors do not support ACE inheritance. This is, for instance, the case for every security descriptor of the Windows NT platform and for the file system share security descriptor (any platform). However, an ACE of a security descriptor from a parent CIM repository namespace is always inherited. This setting is not modifiable from the user interface.

4.11.3   Deciphering the Access Control Lists

Based on the security descriptor object model, the ACL is represented differently. A WMI security descriptor representation has a very basic representation of an ACL, since it is implemented in the form of an array exposed by the *DACL* and the *SACL* properties. Each array element contains a *Win32_ACE* instance. If an ACE must be added or removed from an ACL, the array must be manipulated accordingly. There is no WMI class explicitly representing an ACL.

An ADSI security descriptor representation is slightly different, since the *DiscretionaryACL* and *SystemACL* properties retrieve an **AccessControlList** object exposed by the **IADsAccessControlList** interface. This interface exposes ACEs as a collection. The interface also exposes methods to add and remove ACEs from the collection, which makes the ACE management in an ADSI ACL easier.

In both cases, there is no specific function to decipher an ACL. ACLs are retrieved in Sample 4.28 ("Deciphering a WMI security descriptor representation," lines 29 through 39) and Sample 4.29 ("Deciphering an ADSI security descriptor representation," lines 36 and 110).

For both object models, we will see the scripting technique to use to manage an ACE in an ACL in sections 4.12.4 ("Adding an ACE") and 4.12.5 ("Removing an ACE").

4.11.4 Deciphering the Access Control Entries

At the beginning of this chapter (see section 4.4.1, "The security descriptor WMI representation"), we saw that a security descriptor ACE is made up of six properties:

- The *ACE Trustee* property

- The *ACE Type* property

- The *ACE Flags* property

- The *ACE AccessMask* property

- The *ACE ObjectType* property

- The *ACE InheritedObjectType* property

However, the ADSI object model shows an additional property: the *ACE FlagType* property. The *ACE FlagType* property is used to determine the presence of a GUID number in the *ACE ObjectType* and *ACE Inherited-ObjectType* properties. This property is not a security descriptor component, but it is a property exposed by the ADSI security descriptor structural representation to signify the presence of a GUID number in *ObjectType* and/or *InheritedObjectType* ADSI properties.

As we can see, ACE properties are the same for any security descriptor regardless of its origin. On the other hand, property values and meanings may vary with the origin of the security descriptor (i.e., file system, registry, Active Directory). The best example is the *ACE AccessMask* property. The flags used to decipher an *ACE AccessMask* part of a file security descriptor will be totally different from an *ACE AccessMask* part of an Active Directory security descriptor. In this section, we will discover how to decipher all ACE properties in relation to their origins. Some property deciphering techniques are common to all security descriptors (i.e., *ACE Trustee*, *ACE Type*); other property deciphering techniques will be unique to the origin of the security descriptor.

4.11.4.1   *Deciphering the ACE Trustee property*

As with the *Owner* and *Group* properties, the *ACE Trustee* property in the WMI object model is represented by a *Win32_Trustee* instance in an **SWBemObject** object. Therefore, Sample 4.28 ("Deciphering a WMI security descriptor representation"), by its recursive logic, naturally detects that the *Trustee* property of the *Win32_ACE* instance contains a *Win32_Trustee* instance. No particular bitwise deciphering technique is necessary. The *Win32_Trustee* instance is deciphered inside the DecipherWMISecurityDescriptor() in Sample 4.28.

When the security descriptor is represented in the ADSI object model, things are easier. The *Trustee* property contains a literal string representing the trustee (i.e., Domain\User). Therefore, Sample 4.29 ("Deciphering an ADSI security descriptor representation") makes a simple display of the string without further processing.

4.11.4.2   *Deciphering the ACE Type property*

The aim of the *ACE Type* property is to determine:

- If the ACE trustee part of the same ACE is granted for the rights specified in the *ACE AccessMask*.

- If the ACE trustee part of the same ACE is denied for the rights specified in the *ACE AccessMask*.

- If the ACE trustee part of the same ACE is audited for the rights specified in the *ACE AccessMask*.

Note that an ACE can only be used for one purpose at a time: granting, denying, or auditing. So, the *ACE Type* property does not use any bitwise operation for the deciphering, since only one of the three values can be assigned for one single ACE.

Sample 4.32 shows the DecipherACEType() function, which is called by Sample 4.28 ("Deciphering a WMI security descriptor representation") at line 96 and Sample 4.29 ("Deciphering an ADSI security descriptor representation") at line 71. This demonstrates that the object model does not influence the interpretation of the value.

Sample 4.32   *Deciphering the ACE Type property*

```
.:
.:
.:
8:' --------------------------------------------------------------------------------------
9:Function DecipherACEType (intSDType, intACEType)
..:
15:    strTemp = "&h" & Hex (intACEType)
16:
17:    Select Case intSDType
18:          Case cFileViaWMI, cFileViaADSI, _
19:               cShareViaWMI, _
20:               cShareViaADSI, _
21:               cRegistryViaADSI, _
22:               cWMINameSpaceViaWMI
23:               Select Case intACEType
24:                     Case ACCESS_ALLOWED_ACE_TYPE
25:                          strTemp = strTemp & "," & "ACCESS_ALLOWED_ACE_TYPE"
26:                     Case ACCESS_DENIED_ACE_TYPE
27:                          strTemp = strTemp & "," & "ACCESS_DENIED_ACE_TYPE"
28:                     Case SYSTEM_AUDIT_ACE_TYPE
29:                          strTemp = strTemp & "," & "SYSTEM_AUDIT_ACE_TYPE"
30:                     Case SYSTEM_ALARM_ACE_TYPE
31:                          strTemp = strTemp & "," & "SYSTEM_ALARM_ACE_TYPE"
32:                     Case Else
33:
34:               End Select
35:
36:          Case cActiveDirectoryViaWMI, cActiveDirectoryViaADSI, _
37:               cExchange2000MailboxViaWMI, cExchange2000MailboxViaADSI, _
38:               cExchange2000MailboxViaCDOEXM
39:               Select Case intACEType
40:                     Case ADS_ACETYPE_ACCESS_ALLOWED
41:                          strTemp = strTemp & "," & "ADS_ACETYPE_ACCESS_ALLOWED"
42:                     Case ADS_ACETYPE_ACCESS_DENIED
43:                          strTemp = strTemp & "," & "ADS_ACETYPE_ACCESS_DENIED"
44:                     Case ADS_ACETYPE_SYSTEM_AUDIT
45:                          strTemp = strTemp & "," & "ADS_ACETYPE_SYSTEM_AUDIT"
46:                     Case ADS_ACETYPE_ACCESS_ALLOWED_OBJECT
47:                          strTemp = strTemp & "," & "ADS_ACETYPE_ACCESS_ALLOWED_OBJECT"
48:                     Case ADS_ACETYPE_ACCESS_DENIED_OBJECT
49:                          strTemp = strTemp & "," & "ADS_ACETYPE_ACCESS_DENIED_OBJECT"
50:                     Case ADS_ACETYPE_SYSTEM_AUDIT_OBJECT
51:                          strTemp = strTemp & "," & "ADS_ACETYPE_SYSTEM_AUDIT_OBJECT"
52:                     Case Else
53:
54:               End Select
55:
56:          Case cRegistryViaWMI, cWMINameSpaceViaADSI
57:
58:          Case Else
59:
```

```
60:      End Select
61:
62:      DecipherACEType = ConvertStringInArray (strTemp, ",")
63:
64:End Function
65:
..:
..:
..:
```

Sample 4.32 deciphers the *ACE Type* property according to the origin of the security descriptor. If the security descriptor does not originate from Active Directory, the code between lines 23 and 34 is executed. If the security descriptor is from Active Directory, the code between lines 39 and 54 is executed. As examples, for a non-Active Directory security descriptor, we will have an *ACE Type* (lines 18 through 34):

- Granting Access with the ACCESS_ALLOWED_ACE_TYPE flag.

- Denying Access with the ACCESS_DENIED_ACE_TYPE flag.

- Auditing Access with the SYSTEM_AUDIT_ACE_TYPE flag.

For instance, lines 38 and 54 show the *ACE Type* of a folder security descriptor.

```
1:   C:\>WMIManageSD.Wsf /FileSystem:C:\MyDirectory /Decipher+ /ADSI+
2:   Microsoft (R) Windows Script Host Version 5.6
3:   Copyright (C) Microsoft Corporation 1996-2001. All rights reserved.
4:
5:   Reading File or Folder security descriptor via ADSI from 'C:\MyDirectory'.
..:
16:  |+- ADSI DiscretionaryAcl ------------------------------------------------------------
17:  ||+- ADSI ACE ------------------------------------------------------------------------
18:  ||| AccessMask: ......................... &h1F01FF
..:
37:  ||| AceType: ............................ &h0
38:                                            ACCESS_ALLOWED_ACE_TYPE
39:  ||| AceFlagType: ........................ &h0
40:  ||| Trustee: ............................ BUILTIN\Administrators
41:  ||+---------------------------------------------------------------------------------
42:  ||+- ADSI ACE ------------------------------------------------------------------------
43:  ||| AccessMask: ......................... &h1200A9
..:
51:  ||| AceFlags: ........................... &h2
..:
53:  ||| AceType: ............................ &h0
54:                                            ACCESS_ALLOWED_ACE_TYPE
55:  ||| AceFlagType: ........................ &h0
56:  ||| Trustee: ............................ LISSWARENET\MyGroup
57:  ||+---------------------------------------------------------------------------------
58:  |+-----------------------------------------------------------------------------------
59:  +-------------------------------------------------------------------------------------
```

If the security descriptor originates from Active Directory, we will have an *ACE Type* (lines 36 through 54):

- Granting Access with the ADS_ACETYPE_ACCESS_ALLOWED flag.

- Denying Access with the ADS_ACETYPE_ACCESS_ALLOWED flag.

- Auditing Access with the ADS_ACETYPE_SYSTEM_AUDIT flag.

For instance, lines 34 and 47 show the *ACE Type* of an Active Directory security descriptor.

```
1:   C:\>WMIManageSD.Wsf /ADObject:"CN=MyUser,CN=Users,DC=LissWare,DC=Net" /Decipher+ /ADSI+
2:   Microsoft (R) Windows Script Host Version 5.6
3:   Copyright (C) Microsoft Corporation 1996-2001. All rights reserved.
4:
5:   Reading AD object security descriptor via ADSI from LDAP://CN=MyUser,CN=Users,...

7:   +- ADSI Security Descriptor ------------------------------------------------------------------
8:   | Owner: ............................ BUILTIN\Administrators
9:   | Group: ............................ LISSWARENET\Alain.Lissoir
10:  | Revision: ......................... 1
11:  | Control: .......................... &h8C14
..:
17:  |+- ADSI DiscretionaryAcl ------------------------------------------------------------------
18:  ||+- ADSI ACE ------------------------------------------------------------------------------
19:  ||| AccessMask: ...................... &hF01BD
..:
31:  ||| AceFlags: ........................ &h2
..:
33:  ||| AceType: ......................... &h0
34:                                          ADS_ACETYPE_ACCESS_ALLOWED
35:  ||| AceFlagType: ..................... &h0
36:  ||| Trustee: ......................... BUILTIN\Administrators
37:  ||+---------------------------------------------------------------------------------------
38:  ||+- ADSI ACE ------------------------------------------------------------------------------
39:  ||| AccessMask: ...................... &h20014
..:
43:  ||| AceFlags: ........................ &h3
..:
46:  ||| AceType: ......................... &h0
47:                                          ADS_ACETYPE_ACCESS_ALLOWED
48:  ||| AceFlagType: ..................... &h0
49:  ||| Trustee: ......................... LISSWARENET\MyUser
..:
..:
..:
```

If the security descriptor originates from the Active Directory and the ACE refers to Active Directory Extended Rights, we will have an *ACE Type* (lines 36 through 54):

- Granting Access with the ADS_ACETYPE_ACCESS_ALLOWED_ OBJECT flag.

- Denying Access with the ADS_ACETYPE_ACCESS_ALLOWED_
  OBJECT flag.

- Auditing Access with the ADS_ACETYPE_SYSTEM_AUDIT_
  OBJECT flag.

For instance, lines 126 and 141 show the *ACE Type* of an Active Directory security descriptor for an Extended Right. Note the presence of a GUID for the *ACE ObjectType* property at lines 130 and 145.

```
   1:   C:\>WMIManageSD.Wsf /ADObject:"CN=MyUser,CN=Users,DC=LissWare,DC=Net" /Decipher+ /ADSI+
   2:   Microsoft (R) Windows Script Host Version 5.6
   3:   Copyright (C) Microsoft Corporation 1996-2001. All rights reserved.
   4:
   5:   Reading AD object security descriptor via ADSI from 'LDAP://CN=MyUser,CN=Users,...
   6:
   7:   +- ADSI Security Descriptor -----------------------------------------------------------
   8:   | Owner: ............................... BUILTIN\Administrators
   9:   | Group: ............................... LISSWARENET\Alain.Lissoir
  10:   | Revision: ............................ 1
  11:   | Control: ............................. &h8C14
  ..:
  17:   |+- ADSI DiscretionaryAcl -------------------------------------------------------------
  18:   ||+- ADSI ACE -------------------------------------------------------------------------
 ...:
 119:   ||+- ADSI ACE -------------------------------------------------------------------------
 120:   ||| AccessMask: ......................... &h10
 ...:
 122:   ||| AceFlags: ........................... &h12
 ...:
 125:   ||| AceType: ............................ &h5
 126:                                            ADS_ACETYPE_ACCESS_ALLOWED_OBJECT
 127:   ||| AceFlagType: ....................... &h3
 ...:
 130:   ||| ObjectType: ......................... {037088F8-0AE1-11D2-B422-00A0C968F939}
 131:   ||| InheritedObjectType: ............... {BF967ABA-0DE6-11D0-A285-00AA003049E2}
 132:   ||| Trustee: ........................... BUILTIN\Pre-Windows 2000 Compatible Access
 133:   ||+-----------------------------------------------------------------------------------
 134:   ||+- ADSI ACE -------------------------------------------------------------------------
 135:   ||| AccessMask: ......................... &h10
 ...:
 137:   ||| AceFlags: ........................... &h12
 ...:
 140:   ||| AceType: ............................ &h5
 141:                                            ADS_ACETYPE_ACCESS_ALLOWED_OBJECT
 142:   ||| AceFlagType: ....................... &h3
 ...:
 145:   ||| ObjectType: ......................... {59BA2F42-79A2-11D0-9020-00C04FC2D3CF}
 146:   ||| InheritedObjectType: ............... {BF967ABA-0DE6-11D0-A285-00AA003049E2}
 147:   ||| Trustee: ........................... BUILTIN\Pre-Windows 2000 Compatible Access
 148:   ||+-----------------------------------------------------------------------------------
 ...:
 ...:
 ...:
```

We will see in section 4.11.4.5.3 ("The Active Directory object ACE AccessMask property") how to manipulate the Active Directory *ACE Access-Mask* property with Extended Rights.

4.11.4.3   *Deciphering the ACE Flags property*

The *ACE Flags* property determines the inheritance of an ACE. Do not confuse this property with the *Control Flags* property, which works at the security descriptor level, while the *ACE Flags* property works at the ACE level. The *ACE Flags* property determines how child objects inherit an ACE (i.e., Subfolder in the file system or a child object in Active Directory).

The DecipherACEFlags() function is called by Sample 4.28 ("Deciphering a WMI security descriptor representation") at line 84 and Sample 4.29 ("Deciphering an ADSI security descriptor representation") at line 62, which demonstrates once more that the object model does not influence the interpretation of the value.

As opposed to the *ACE Type* deciphering technique, the *ACE Flags* property is deciphered with a bitwise operation, because several bits determine how the ACE must be inherited. Even if the logic to decipher is always the same for any security descriptor, the origin determines the *ACE Flags* values to use to decipher. Table 4.9 lists the inheritance flags to use when the security has an origin other than Active Directory (i.e., files or folders, registry)

Table 4.10 lists the flags controlling ACE inheritance when the security descriptor comes from the Active Directory (i.e., Active Directory user object).

Moreover, the ACE inheritance capabilities rely on the security descriptor origin. For instance, a File System share security descriptor doesn't

Table 4.9   *The Security Descriptor Inheritance Flags*

OBJECT_INHERIT_ACE	0x1	Noncontainer objects contained by the primary object inherit the entry.
CONTAINER_INHERIT_ACE	0x2	Other containers that are contained by the primary object inherit the entry.
NO_PROPAGATE_INHERIT_ACE	0x4	The OBJECT_INHERIT_ACE and CONTAINER_INHERIT_ACE flags are not propagated to an inherited entry.
INHERIT_ONLY_ACE	0x8	The ACE does not apply to the primary object to which the ACL is attached, but objects contained by the primary object inherit the entry.
INHERITED_ACE	0x10	Only under Windows 2000, Windows XP, and Windows Server 2003, it indicates that the ACE was inherited. The system sets this bit when it propagates an inherited ACE to a child object.
SUCCESSFUL_ACCESS_ACE_FLAG	0x40	Used with system-audit ACEs in a SACL to generate audit messages for successful access attempts.
FAILED_ACCESS_ACE_FLAG	0x80	Used with system-audit ACEs in a SACL to generate audit messages for failed access attempts.
VALID_INHERIT_FLAGS	0x1F	Indicates whether the inherit flags are valid. The system sets this bit.

Table 4.10   *The Security Descriptor Inheritance Flags (Active Directory)*

ADS_ACEFLAG_INHERIT_ACE	0x2	Child objects will inherit this access-control entry (ACE). The inherited ACE is inheritable unless the ADS_ACEFLAG_NO_PROPAGATE_INHERIT_ACE flag is set.
ADS_ACEFLAG_NO_PROPAGATE_INHERIT_ACE	0x4	The system will clear the ADS_ACEFLAG_INHERIT_ACE flag for the inherited ACEs of child objects. This prevents the ACE from being inherited by subsequent generations of objects.
ADS_ACEFLAG_INHERIT_ONLY_ACE	0x8	Indicates an inherit-only ACE that does not exercise access control on the object to which it is attached. If this flag is not set, the ACE is an effective ACE that exerts access control on the object to which it is attached.
ADS_ACEFLAG_INHERITED_ACE	0x10	Indicates whether or not the ACE was inherited. The system sets this bit.
ADS_ACEFLAG_VALID_INHERIT_FLAGS	0x1F	Indicates whether the inherit flags are valid. The system sets this bit.
ADS_ACEFLAG_SUCCESSFUL_ACCESS	0x40	Generates audit messages for successful access attempts, used with ACEs that audit the system in a system access-control list (SACL).
ADS_ACEFLAG_FAILED_ACCESS	0x80	Generates audit messages for failed access attempts, used with ACEs that audit the system in a SACL.

implement the concept of inheritance, while an Active Directory security descriptor does. When we decipher the *ACE AccessMask* property, we will see how to set up the ACE inheritance, since it determines how *ACE Access-Mask* is applied.

The DecipherACEFlags() function deciphering the *ACE Flags* is illustrated in Sample 4.33.

Sample 4.33   *Deciphering the ACE Flags property*

```
..:
..:
..:
65:
66:' --------------------------------------------------------------------------------
67:Function DecipherACEFlags (intSDType, intACEFlags)
..:
73:     strTemp = "&h" & Hex (intACEFlags)
74:
75:     Select Case intSDType
76:           Case cFileViaWMI, cFileViaADSI, _
77:                cShareViaWMI, _
78:                cShareViaADSI, _
79:                cRegistryViaADSI, _
80:                cWMINameSpaceViaWMI
81:                If (intACEFlags And OBJECT_INHERIT_ACE) Then
82:                    strTemp = strTemp & "," & "OBJECT_INHERIT_ACE"
83:                End If
84:                If (intACEFlags And CONTAINER_INHERIT_ACE) Then
85:                    strTemp = strTemp & "," & "CONTAINER_INHERIT_ACE"
86:                End If
87:                If (intACEFlags And NO_PROPAGATE_INHERIT_ACE) Then
88:                    strTemp = strTemp & "," & "NO_PROPAGATE_INHERIT_ACE"
89:                End If
..:
99:                If (intACEFlags And SUCCESSFUL_ACCESS_ACE_FLAG) Then
100:                   strTemp = strTemp & "," & "SUCCESSFUL_ACCESS_ACE_FLAG"
```

```
101:                End If
102:                If (intACEFlags And FAILED_ACCESS_ACE_FLAG) Then
103:                    strTemp = strTemp & "," & "FAILED_ACCESS_ACE_FLAG"
104:                End If
105:
106:        Case cActiveDirectoryViaWMI, cActiveDirectoryViaADSI, _
107:                cExchange2000MailboxViaWMI, cExchange2000MailboxViaADSI, _
108:                cExchange2000MailboxViaCDOEXM
109:                If (intACEFlags And ADS_ACEFLAG_OBJECT_INHERIT_ACE) Then
110:                    strTemp = strTemp & "," & "ADS_ACEFLAG_OBJECT_INHERIT_ACE"
111:                End If
112:                If (intACEFlags And ADS_ACEFLAG_CONTAINER_INHERIT_ACE) Then
113:                    strTemp = strTemp & "," & "ADS_ACEFLAG_CONTAINER_INHERIT_ACE"
114:                End If
115:                If (intACEFlags And ADS_ACEFLAG_NO_PROPAGATE_INHERIT_ACE) Then
116:                    strTemp = strTemp & "," & "ADS_ACEFLAG_NO_PROPAGATE_INHERIT_ACE"
117:                End If
...:
127:                If (intACEFlags And ADS_ACEFLAG_SUCCESSFUL_ACCESS) Then
128:                    strTemp = strTemp & "," & "ADS_ACEFLAG_SUCCESSFUL_ACCESS"
129:                End If
130:                If (intACEFlags And ADS_ACEFLAG_FAILED_ACCESS) Then
131:                    strTemp = strTemp & "," & "ADS_ACEFLAG_FAILED_ACCESS"
132:                End If
133:
134:        Case cRegistryViaWMI, cWMINameSpaceViaADSI
135:
136:        Case Else
137:
138:    End Select
139:
140:    DecipherACEFlags = ConvertStringInArray (strTemp, ",")
141:
142:End Function
143:
...:
...:
...:
```

The following output shows the *ACE Flags* values from lines 34 through 36 and at lines 51 and 52.

```
1:   C:\>WMIManageSD.Wsf /FileSystem:C:\MyDirectory /Decipher+ /ADSI+
2:   Microsoft (R) Windows Script Host Version 5.6
3:   Copyright (C) Microsoft Corporation 1996-2001. All rights reserved.
4:
5:   Reading File or Folder security descriptor via ADSI from 'C:\MyDirectory'.
6:
7:   +- ADSI Security Descriptor -------------------------------------------------
8:   | Owner: ............................... BUILTIN\Administrators
9:   | Group: ............................... LISSWARENET\Domain Users
10:  | Revision: ............................ 1
11:  | Control: ............................. &h9404
..:
16:  |+- ADSI DiscretionaryAcl ---------------------------------------------------
17:  ||+- ADSI ACE ---------------------------------------------------------------
18:  ||| AccessMask: ......................... &h1F01FF
..:
34:  ||| AceFlags: ........................... &h3
```

```
35:                                             OBJECT_INHERIT_ACE
36:                                             CONTAINER_INHERIT_ACE
37:   ||| AceType: .......................... &h0
..:
39:   ||| AceFlagType: ...................... &h0
40:   ||| Trustee: ......................... BUILTIN\Administrators
41:   ||+------------------------------------------------------------------------------
42:   ||+- ADSI ACE ------------------------------------------------------------------
43:   ||| AccessMask: ........................ &h1200A9
..:
51:   ||| AceFlags: ......................... &h2
52:                                             CONTAINER_INHERIT_ACE
53:   ||| AceType: .......................... &h0
..:
55:   ||| AceFlagType: ...................... &h0
56:   ||| Trustee: ......................... LISSWARENET\MyGroup
57:   ||+------------------------------------------------------------------------------
58:   |+-------------------------------------------------------------------------------
59:   +--------------------------------------------------------------------------------
```

4.11.4.4   Deciphering the ACE FlagType property

The *ACE FlagType* is only used when the *ACE ObjectType* or *ACE Inherited-ObjectType* properties contain a GUID number. Only Sample 4.29 ("Deciphering an ADSI security descriptor representation") at line 80 calls the DecipherACEFlagType() function. The security descriptor WMI representation supports the display of a GUID number but does not use an *ACE FlagType* property. This property is a peculiarity of the ADSI object model representation. We will see in section 4.11.4.5.3 ("The Active Directory object ACE AccessMask property") how to interpret the GUID number. Except for these peculiarities, the *ACE FlagType* coding and deciphering technique are always the same (see Sample 4.34).

Sample 4.34   *Deciphering the ACE FlagType property*

```
...:
...:
...:
143:
144:' --------------------------------------------------------------------------------
145:Function DecipherACEflagType (intSDType, intACEFlagType)
...:
151:     strTemp = "&h" & Hex (intACEFlagType)
152:
153:     Select Case intSDType
154:          Case cFileViaWMI, cFileViaADSI, _
155:               cShareViaWMI, _
156:               cShareViaADSI, _
157:               cActiveDirectoryViaWMI, cActiveDirectoryViaADSI, _
158:               cExchange2000MailboxViaWMI, cExchange2000MailboxViaADSI, _
159:               cExchange2000MailboxViaCDOEXM, _
160:               cRegistryViaADSI, _
161:               cWMINameSpaceViaWMI
162:               If (intACEflagType And ADS_FLAG_OBJECT_TYPE_PRESENT) Then
```

```
163:                   strTemp = strTemp & "," & "ADS_FLAG_OBJECT_TYPE_PRESENT"
164:              End If
165:              If (intACEFlagType And ADS_FLAG_INHERITED_OBJECT_TYPE_PRESENT) Then
166:                   strTemp = strTemp & "," & "ADS_FLAG_INHERITED_OBJECT_TYPE_PRESENT"
167:              End If
168:
169:          Case cRegistryViaWMI, cWMINameSpaceViaADSI
170:
171:          Case Else
172:
173:      End Select
174:
175:      DecipherACEFlagType = ConvertStringInArray (strTemp, ",")
176:
177:End Function
178:
...:
...:
...:
```

The following output sample shows the *ACE FlagType* values from line 157 through 159 and 172 through 174.

```
 1:   C:\>WMIManageSD.Wsf /ADObject:"CN=MyUser,CN=Users,DC=LissWare,DC=Net" /Decipher+ /ADSI+
 2:   Microsoft (R) Windows Script Host Version 5.6
 3:   Copyright (C) Microsoft Corporation 1996-2001. All rights reserved.
 4:
 5:   Reading AD object security descriptor via ADSI from 'LDAP://CN=MyUser,CN=Users,...
 6:
 7:   +- ADSI Security Descriptor ------------------------------------------------------------
 8:   | Owner: ............................. BUILTIN\Administrators
 9:   | Group: ............................. LISSWARENET\Alain.Lissoir
10:   | Revision: .......................... 1
11:   | Control: ........................... &h8C14
..:
17:   |+- ADSI DiscretionaryAcl ---------------------------------------------------------------
149:  ||+- ADSI ACE ---------------------------------------------------------------------------
150:  ||| AccessMask: ...................... &h10
...:
152:  ||| AceFlags: ........................ &h12
...:
155:  ||| AceType: ......................... &h5
...:
157:  ||| AceFlagType: ..................... &h3
158:                                         ADS_FLAG_OBJECT_TYPE_PRESENT
159:                                         ADS_FLAG_INHERITED_OBJECT_TYPE_PRESENT
160:  ||| ObjectType: ...................... {BC0AC240-79A9-11D0-9020-00C04FC2D4CF}
161:  ||| InheritedObjectType: ............. {BF967ABA-0DE6-11D0-A285-00AA003049E2}
162:  ||| Trustee: ......................... BUILTIN\Pre-Windows 2000 Compatible Access
163:  ||+-----------------------------------------------------------------------------------
164:  ||+- ADSI ACE ---------------------------------------------------------------------------
165:  ||| AccessMask: ...................... &h10
...:
167:  ||| AceFlags: ........................ &h12
...:
170:  ||| AceType: ......................... &h5
...:
172:  ||| AceFlagType: ..................... &h3
173:                                         ADS_FLAG_OBJECT_TYPE_PRESENT
```

```
174:                                            ADS_FLAG_INHERITED_OBJECT_TYPE_PRESENT
175:    ||| ObjectType: .......................... {4C164200-20C0-11D0-A768-00AA006E0529}
176:    ||| InheritedObjectType: ................. {BF967ABA-0DE6-11D0-A285-00AA003049E2}
177:    ||| Trustee: ........................... BUILTIN\Pre-Windows 2000 Compatible Access
178:    ||+--------------------------------------------------------------------------------
...:
...:
...:
```

4.11.4.5   *Deciphering the ACE AccessMask property*

To decipher security descriptors, the script makes use of the DecipherACE-Mask() function. The DecipherACEMask() is divided into several samples due to the fact that there is always a specific set of flags to use for each security descriptor origin. The DecipherACEMask() function is illustrated in Samples 4.35 through 4.40 in the following sections.

This DecipherACEMask() function is called by Sample 4.28 ("Deciphering a WMI security descriptor representation") at line 72 and Sample 4.29 ("Deciphering an ADSI security descriptor representation") at line 53.

4.11.4.5.1   The files and folders ACE AccessMask property

To decipher a file or a folder *ACE AccessMask*, it is necessary to use the flag values listed in Table 4.11.

The column headings in this table represent the settings in the user interface. The left column lists the flags that must be used to decipher or set an *ACE AccessMask* value for a file or a folder, while the top row shows the user interface selection.

In Figure 4.19, the user interface shows a folder security descriptor. We see that the "Read & Execute" right is granted to "Everyone." In Table 4.11, in the column "Read & Execute," we see that each time there is a cross in the cell the corresponding flag is set. In such a case, we have the following flags:

- FOLDER_LIST_DIRECTORY
- FILE_READ_EA
- FOLDER_TRAVERSE
- FILE_READ_ATTRIBUTES
- FILE_READ_CONTROL
- FILE_SYNCHRONIZE

To ease flag use, some flags are generic. They are made from a combination of several flags. So, instead of using all previously listed flags, the "Read

Table 4.11 *The Files and Folders ACE AccessMask Values*

Granted & denied rights	Value	Full Control	Modify	Read & Execute	List Folder Contents	Read	Write	Traverse Folder / Execute File	List Folder / Execute Data	Read Attributes	Read Extended Attributes	Create Files / Write Data	Create Folders / Append Data	Write Attributes	Write Extended Attributes	Delete Subfolders and Files	Delete	Read Permissions	Change Permissions	Take Ownership
ACEType																				
ACCESS_ALLOWED_ACE_TYPE (Allowed access ACE)	0x0																			
ACCESS_DENIED_ACE_TYPE (Denied access ACE)	0x1	X[1]	X[1]	X[1]	X[1]	X[1]	X[1]	X[1]	X[1]	X[1]	X[1]	X[1]	X[1]	X[1]	X[1]	X[1]	X[1]	X[1]	X[1]	X[1]
SYSTEM_AUDIT_ACE_TYPE (System Audit ACE)	0x2																			
ACEMask																				
FILE_GENERIC_EXECUTE	0x1200A9			X																
FILE_GENERIC_READ	0x120089				X															
FILE_GENERIC_WRITE	0x100116					X														
FILE_ALL_ACCESS	0x1F01FF	X																		
FILE_APPEND_DATA (FOLDER_ADD_SUBDIRECTORY)	0x000004	X	X				X						X							
FILE_DELETE	0x010000	X	X														X			
FILE_DELETE_CHILD	0x000040	X														X				
FILE_EXECUTE (FOLDER_TRAVERSE)	0x000020	X	X	X	X			X												
FILE_READ_ATTRIBUTES	0x000080	X	X	X	X	X				X										
FILE_READ_CONTROL	0x020000	X	X	X	X	X												X		
FILE_READ_DATA (FOLDER_LIST_DIRECTORY)	0x000001	X	X	X	X	X			X											
FILE_READ_EA	0x000008	X	X	X	X	X					X									
FILE_SYNCHRONIZE	0x100000	X	X	X	X	X	X	X	X	X	X	X	X	X	X	X	X	X	X	X
FILE_WRITE_ATTRIBUTES	0x000100	X	X				X							X						
FILE_WRITE_DAC	0x040000	X																	X	
FILE_WRITE_DATA (FOLDER_ADD_FILE)	0x000002	X	X				X					X								
FILE_WRITE_EA	0x000010	X	X				X								X					
FILE_WRITE_OWNER	0x080000	X																		X

(1) **Windows NT 4.0/Windows 2000:** The **ADsSecurity.DLL** from the ADSI Resource Kit does not retrieve the SACL object from the registry.
Windows XP/Windows Server 2003: Unfortunately, a bug in the ADsSecurityUtility interface prevents the retrieval of the SystemACL. Microsoft doesn't plan to fix this bug in the RTM code for timing issues. WMI offers an acceptable work-around for file and folders only. For the registry key, there is no work-around available unless you use the UserRight.Control developed to work around this problem. (See section 4.7.1.2, "Retrieving file and folder security descriptors with ADSI.")

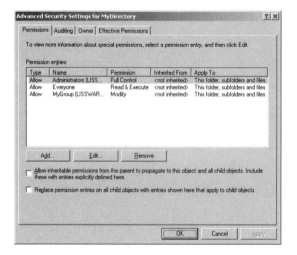

Figure 4.19 *The files and folders security descriptor user interface.*

& Execute" right can be summarized by the use of the FILE_GENERIC_ EXECUTE flag. For the files and folders, there are three generic flags listed in Table 4.11 (FILE_GENERIC_EXECUTE, FILE_GENERIC_READ, and FILE_GENERIC_WRITE).

To decipher the *ACE AccessMask* property, the logic is always the same. Sample 4.35 shows the bitwise operations executed with the flags listed in Table 4.11. Again, we see that the deciphering technique applies for an *ACE AccessMask* coming from a WMI security descriptor or an ADSI security descriptor representation.

Sample 4.35   *Deciphering the ACE AccessMask property for files and folders*

```
...:
...:
...:
178:
179:' --------------------------------------------------------------------------------
180:Function DecipherACEMask (intSDType, intACEMask)
...:
186:    strTemp = "&h" & Hex (intACEMask)
187:
188:    Select Case intSDType
189:          Case cFileViaWMI, cFileViaADSI
190:              If (intACEMask = FILE_ALL_ACCESS) Then
191:                  strTemp = strTemp & "," & "(FILE_ALL_ACCESS)"
192:              End If
193:              If (intACEMask = FILE_GENERIC_EXECUTE) Then
194:                  strTemp = strTemp & "," & "(FILE_GENERIC_EXECUTE)"
195:              End If
196:              If (intACEMask = FILE_GENERIC_READ) Then
197:                  strTemp = strTemp & "," & "(FILE_GENERIC_READ)"
198:              End If
199:              If (intACEMask = FILE_GENERIC_WRITE) Then
200:                  strTemp = strTemp & "," & "(FILE_GENERIC_WRITE)"
201:              End If
202:              If (intACEMask And FILE_READ_DATA) Then
203:                  strTemp = strTemp & "," & "FILE_READ_DATA " & _
204:                                          "(FOLDER_LIST_DIRECTORY for a Folder)"
205:              End If
206:              If (intACEMask And FILE_WRITE_DATA) Then
207:                  strTemp = strTemp & "," & "FILE_WRITE_DATA " & _
208:                                          "(FOLDER_ADD_FILE for a Folder)"
209:              End If
210:              If (intACEMask And FILE_APPEND_DATA) Then
211:                  strTemp = strTemp & "," & "FILE_APPEND_DATA " & _
212:                                          "(FOLDER_ADD_SUBDIRECTORY for a Folder)"
213:              End If
...:
245:              If (intACEMask And FILE_SYNCHRONIZE) Then
246:                  strTemp = strTemp & "," & "FILE_SYNCHRONIZE"
247:              End If
248:
...:
...:
...:
```

To distinguish the security descriptor origin, the DecipherACEMask() function uses a **Select Case** statement, where each case corresponds to a deciphering of an *ACE AccessMask* value from a specific security descriptor origin.

The execution of the following command line will completely decipher the security descriptor shown in Figure 4.19.

```
 1:  C:\>WMIManageSD.wsf /FileSystem:C:\MyDirectory /Decipher+
 2:  Microsoft (R) Windows Script Host Version 5.6
 3:  Copyright (C) Microsoft Corporation 1996-2001. All rights reserved.
 4:
 5:  Reading File or Folder security descriptor via WMI from 'C:\MyDirectory'.
 6:
 7:  +- Win32_SecurityDescriptor ------------------------------------------------------
 8:  | ControlFlags: .......................... &hBC14
 9:                                             SE_DACL_PRESENT
10:                                             SE_SACL_PRESENT
11:                                             SE_DACL_AUTO_INHERITED
12:                                             SE_SACL_AUTO_INHERITED
13:                                             SE_DACL_PROTECTED
14:                                             SE_SACL_PROTECTED
15:                                             SE_SELF_RELATIVE
16:  | DACL: ................................ (Win32_ACE)
17:  | +- Win32_ACE -------------------------------------------------------------------
18:  | | AccessMask: .......................... &h1F01FF
19:                                             (FILE_ALL_ACCESS)
20:                                             FOLDER_LIST_DIRECTORY
21:                                             FOLDER_ADD_FILE
22:                                             FOLDER_ADD_SUBDIRECTORY
23:                                             FILE_READ_EA
24:                                             FILE_WRITE_EA
25:                                             FOLDER_TRAVERSE
26:                                             FILE_DELETE_CHILD
27:                                             FILE_READ_ATTRIBUTES
28:                                             FILE_WRITE_ATTRIBUTES
29:                                             FILE_DELETE
30:                                             FILE_READ_CONTROL
31:                                             FILE_WRITE_DAC
32:                                             FILE_WRITE_OWNER
33:                                             FILE_SYNCHRONIZE
34:  | | AceFlags: ........................... &h3
35:                                             OBJECT_INHERIT_ACE
36:                                             CONTAINER_INHERIT_ACE
37:  | | AceType: ........................... &h0
38:                                             ACCESS_ALLOWED_ACE_TYPE
39:  | | Trustee: ........................... (Win32_Trustee)
40:  | | +- Win32_Trustee ------------------------------------------------------------
41:  | | | Domain: ........................... BUILTIN
42:  | | | Name: ............................. Administrators
43:  | | | SID: .............................. 1,2,0,0,0,0,0,5,32,0,0,0,32,2,0,0
44:  | | | SidLength: ........................ 16
45:  | | | SIDString: ........................ S-1-5-32-544
46:  | | +------------------------------------------------------------------------------
47:  | +--------------------------------------------------------------------------------
48:  | +- Win32_ACE -------------------------------------------------------------------
49:  | | AccessMask: .......................... &h1200A9
50:                                             (FILE_GENERIC_EXECUTE)
```

```
51:                                                 FOLDER_LIST_DIRECTORY
52:                                                 FILE_READ_EA
53:                                                 FOLDER_TRAVERSE
54:                                                 FILE_READ_ATTRIBUTES
55:                                                 FILE_READ_CONTROL
56:                                                 FILE_SYNCHRONIZE
57:    | | AceFlags: ........................... &h3
58:                                                 OBJECT_INHERIT_ACE
59:                                                 CONTAINER_INHERIT_ACE
60:    | | AceType: ........................... &h0
61:                                                 ACCESS_ALLOWED_ACE_TYPE
62:    | | Trustee: ........................... (Win32_Trustee)
63:    | | +- Win32_Trustee -----------------------------------------------------------------------
64:    | | | Name: ........................... Everyone
65:    | | | SID: ............................. 1,1,0,0,0,0,0,1,0,0,0,0
66:    | | | SidLength: ....................... 12
67:    | | | SIDString: ....................... S-1-1-0
68:    | | +-----------------------------------------------------------------------------------------
69:    | +-------------------------------------------------------------------------------------------
70:    | +- Win32_ACE -----------------------------------------------------------------------------
71:    | | AccessMask: ........................ &h1301BF
72:                                                 FOLDER_LIST_DIRECTORY
73:                                                 FOLDER_ADD_FILE
74:                                                 FOLDER_ADD_SUBDIRECTORY
75:                                                 FILE_READ_EA
76:                                                 FILE_WRITE_EA
77:                                                 FOLDER_TRAVERSE
78:                                                 FILE_READ_ATTRIBUTES
79:                                                 FILE_WRITE_ATTRIBUTES
80:                                                 FILE_DELETE
81:                                                 FILE_READ_CONTROL
82:                                                 FILE_SYNCHRONIZE
83:    | | AceFlags: ........................... &h3
84:                                                 OBJECT_INHERIT_ACE
85:                                                 CONTAINER_INHERIT_ACE
86:    | | AceType: ........................... &h0
87:                                                 ACCESS_ALLOWED_ACE_TYPE
88:    | | Trustee: ........................... (Win32_Trustee)
89:    | | +- Win32_Trustee -----------------------------------------------------------------------
90:    | | | Domain: ........................... LISSWARENET
91:    | | | Name: ........................... MyGroup
92:    | | | SID: ............................. 1,5,0,0,0,...,207,122,236,255,136,223,4,0,0
93:    | | | SidLength: ....................... 28
94:    | | | SIDString: ....................... S-1-5-21-3533506287-3489020660-2298473594-1247
95:    | | +-----------------------------------------------------------------------------------------
96:    | +-------------------------------------------------------------------------------------------
97:    | Owner: ............................... (Win32_Trustee)
98:    | +- Win32_Trustee -------------------------------------------------------------------------
99:    | | Domain: ........................... BUILTIN
100:   | | Name: ............................. Administrators
101:   | | SID: .............................. 1,2,0,0,0,0,5,32,0,0,0,32,2,0,0
102:   | | SidLength: ........................ 16
103:   | | SIDString: ........................ S-1-5-32-544
104:   | +-------------------------------------------------------------------------------------------
105: +---------------------------------------------------------------------------------------------
```

As we have seen, the *ACE AccessMask* inheritance is defined by the *ACE Flags* property. Although the deciphering technique is the same for any security descriptor (see Sample 4.33, "Deciphering the *ACE Flags*

Table 4.12   *The Files and Folders ACE Flags Values*

ACEFlags		This folder only	This folder, subfolders, and files	This folder and subfolders	This folder and files	Subfolders and files only	Subfolders only	Files only	Audit Successful access	Audit Failed access
Inheritance & Audit			**(Folders only)**							
NONE	0x0	X								
CONTAINER_INHERIT_ACE	0x2		X	X		X	X			
INHERIT_ONLY_ACE	0x8					X	X	X		
INHERITED_ACE[1]	0x10									
NO_PROPAGATE_INHERIT_ACE	0x4									
OBJECT_INHERIT_ACE	0x1		X		X	X		X		
VALID_INHERIT_FLAG[1]	0x1F									
SUCCESSFUL_ACCESS_ACE_FLAG	0x40								X	
FAILED_ACCESS_ACE_FLAG	0x80									X

(1) Set by the system.

property"), the flag values used and their combinations to decipher or set the *ACE Flags* property are dependent on the security descriptor origin, since the origin determines the inheritance capabilities.

Table 4.12 summarizes the flag values in regard to the inheritance settings that can be set from the user interface shown in Figure 4.20. The previous security descriptor deciphering output of Figure 4.19 shows the *ACE Flags* settings for the configured inheritance.

To set up a security descriptor in a folder similar to the one shown in Figure 4.19, the script must be executed several times, since it sets only one ACE at a time. Of course, Tables 4.11 ("The files and folders *ACE Access-Mask* values") and 4.12 ("The files and folders *ACE Flags* values") can be used to determine these settings. In such a case, the following command lines will set up the settings in Figure 4.19:

```
 1:   WMIManageSD.wsf /FileSystem:C:\MyDirectory /Trustee:REMOVE_ALL_ACE /DelAce+
 2:
 3:   WMIManageSD.wsf /FileSystem:C:\MyDirectory /Trustee:BUILTIN\Administrators
 4:                   /ACEType:ACCESS_ALLOWED_ACE_TYPE
 5:                   /ACEMask:FILE_ALL_ACCESS
 6:                   /ACEFlags:OBJECT_INHERIT_ACE,CONTAINER_INHERIT_ACE
 7:                   /AddAce+
 8:
 9:   WMIManageSD.wsf /FileSystem:C:\MyDirectory /Trustee:Everyone /DelAce+
10:
11:   WMIManageSD.wsf /FileSystem:C:\MyDirectory /Trustee:LissWareNET\Everyone
12:                   /ACEType:ACCESS_ALLOWED_ACE_TYPE
13:                   /ACEMask:FILE_GENERIC_EXECUTE
14:                   /ACEFlags:OBJECT_INHERIT_ACE,CONTAINER_INHERIT_ACE
```

```
15:                     /AddAce+
16:
17:   WMIManageSD.wsf /FileSystem:C:\MyDirectory /Trustee:LissWareNET\MyGroup
18:                     /ACEType:ACCESS_ALLOWED_ACE_TYPE
19:                     /ACEMask:FOLDER_LIST_DIRECTORY,
20:                             FOLDER_ADD_FILE,FOLDER_ADD_SUBDIRECTORY,FILE_READ_EA,FILE_WRITE_EA,
21:                             FOLDER_TRAVERSE,FILE_READ_ATTRIBUTES,FILE_WRITE_ATTRIBUTES,
22:                             FILE_DELETE,FILE_READ_CONTROL,FILE_SYNCHRONIZE
23:                     /ACEFlags:OBJECT_INHERIT_ACE,CONTAINER_INHERIT_ACE /AddAce+
```

Please take a few minutes to compare the command-line settings with the previous output and the content of Tables 4.11 and 4.12.

At line 1, the script removes all available ACEs. We will see in section 4.12.5 ("Removing an ACE") that the end result of this operation sets a full access right to "Everyone" on the secured object. Although it is possible to remove all ACEs one by one to obtain the desired configuration, this makes the work more complicated, because it forces us to know which ACE has to be removed. By removing all ACE entries at once, we start the security

Figure 4.20
The files and folders inheritance user interface.

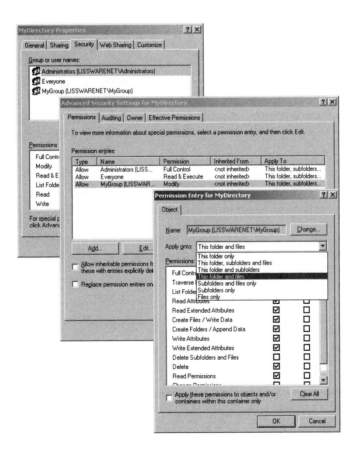

descriptor configuration from a clear and known situation. From line 3 through 7, the script configures the "Administrators" group with a full access right. If the user configuring the security descriptor is part of the "Administrators" group (which is supposed to be in this example), then the "Everyone" group can be removed (line 9). Of course, as shown in Figure 4.19, the "Everyone" group has a "Read & Execute" access. This configuration is set up from line 11 through 15. Although it is technically possible to edit the ACE properties of the deleted ACE at line 9, this requires more granularity in terms of management capabilities to change existing ACE-specific properties. For the sake of simplicity, the script manages the ACE security descriptor at the ACE level for an existing ACE, not at the ACE property level. Finally, from line 17 through 23, the script grants the "Modify" right to the "MyGroup" group. Once completed, we obtain the security settings shown in Figure 4.19. We will see in section 4.13 ("Updating the security descriptor") how the security descriptor is saved back to the secured entity (which is a folder in this example).

The script accesses the security descriptor via WMI and therefore uses the WMI *Security* provider and its related class methods implementing the security descriptor access. In the case of a file or a folder, it is possible to use ADSI as the access method. Therefore, the switch **/ADSI+** must be specified. Keep in mind the restrictions that apply to the SACL access when using ADSI (see Table 4.4).

Now, if you compare the results obtained when deciphering the Figure 4.19 configuration with the command-line switches used previously, you will see that the exact same settings are used. Basically, each time you need to configure a security descriptor, it is a good idea to configure the desired result via the user interface first. Next, run the script to decipher the desired result and reuse this output to customize the command-line switches to automate the security configuration settings. We will see other examples with other security descriptors later. The logic is always the same. Only some flags related to a specific security descriptor must be adapted (file, share, Active Directory objects, etc.).

4.11.4.5.2   The File System share ACE AccessMask property

To decipher a File System share *ACE AccessMask*, it is necessary to use the flag values listed in Table 4.13.

Deciphering the File System share *ACE AccessMask* is quite easy, since there are only three flags used. Sample 4.36 is the continuation of Sample 4.35 ("Deciphering the *ACE AccessMask* property for files and folders") and

Table 4.13 *The File System Share ACE AccessMask Values*

Granted & denied rights		Standard View		
		Full Control	Change	Read
ACEType				
ACCESS_ALLOWED_ACE_TYPE	0x0	X	X	X
ACCESS_DENIED_ACE_TYPE	0x1			
ACEMask				
FILE_SHARE_FULL_ACCESS	0x0C0040	X		
FILE_SHARE_CHANGE_ACCESS	0x010116	X	X	
FILE_SHARE_READ_ACCESS	0x1200A9	X	X	X

shows how to decipher a File System share *ACE AccessMask* with the values
listed in Table 4.13.

Sample 4.36 *Deciphering the ACE AccessMask property for File System shares*

```
...:

...:
...:
248:
249:          Case cShareViaWMI, cShareViaADSI
250:              If (intACEMask And FILE_SHARE_FULL_ACCESS) Then
251:                  strTemp = strTemp & "," & "FILE_SHARE_FULL_ACCESS"
252:              End If
253:              If (intACEMask And FILE_SHARE_CHANGE_ACCESS) Then
254:                  strTemp = strTemp & "," & "FILE_SHARE_CHANGE_ACCESS"
255:              End If
256:              If (intACEMask And FILE_SHARE_READ_ACCESS) Then
257:                  strTemp = strTemp & "," & "FILE_SHARE_READ_ACCESS"
258:              End If
259:
...:
...:
...:
```

Based on that code, an execution of the script from the command line
produces the following output if a File System share security is configured,
as shown in Figure 4.21.

```
1:   C:\>WMIManageSD.wsf /Share:MyDirectory /Decipher+
2:   Microsoft (R) Windows Script Host Version 5.6
3:   Copyright (C) Microsoft Corporation 1996-2001. All rights reserved.
4:
5:   Reading Share security descriptor via WMI from 'MyDirectory'.
6:
7:   +- Win32_SecurityDescriptor ------------------------------------------------
8:   | ControlFlags: ......................... &h8004
9:                                            SE_DACL_PRESENT
10:                                           SE_SELF_RELATIVE
11:  | DACL: ................................. (Win32_ACE)
```

```
12:   | +- Win32_ACE ------------------------------------------------------------------------
13:   | | AccessMask: ......................... &h1F01FF
14:   |                                         FILE_SHARE_FULL_ACCESS
15:   |                                         FILE_SHARE_CHANGE_ACCESS
16:   |                                         FILE_SHARE_READ_ACCESS
17:   | | AceFlags: ........................... &h0
18:   | | AceType: ............................ &h0
19:   |                                         ACCESS_ALLOWED_ACE_TYPE
20:   | | Trustee: ............................ (Win32_Trustee)
21:   | | +- Win32_Trustee ------------------------------------------------------------------
22:   | | | Domain: ........................... BUILTIN
23:   | | | Name: ............................. Administrators
24:   | | | SID: .............................. 1,2,0,0,0,0,0,5,32,0,0,0,32,2,0,0
25:   | | | SidLength: ........................ 16
26:   | | | SIDString: ........................ S-1-5-32-544
27:   | | +----------------------------------------------------------------------------------
28:   | +------------------------------------------------------------------------------------
29:   | +- Win32_ACE ------------------------------------------------------------------------
30:   | | AccessMask: ......................... &h1200A9
31:   |                                         FILE_SHARE_READ_ACCESS
32:   | | AceFlags: ........................... &h0
33:   | | AceType: ............................ &h0
34:   |                                         ACCESS_ALLOWED_ACE_TYPE
35:   | | Trustee: ............................ (Win32_Trustee)
36:   | | +- Win32_Trustee ------------------------------------------------------------------
37:   | | | Name: ............................. Everyone
38:   | | | SID: .............................. 1,1,0,0,0,0,0,1,0,0,0,0
39:   | | | SidLength: ........................ 12
40:   | | | SIDString: ........................ S-1-1-0
41:   | | +----------------------------------------------------------------------------------
42:   | +------------------------------------------------------------------------------------
43:   | +- Win32_ACE ------------------------------------------------------------------------
44:   | | AccessMask: ......................... &h1301BF
45:   |                                         FILE_SHARE_CHANGE_ACCESS
46:   |                                         FILE_SHARE_READ_ACCESS
47:   | | AceFlags: ........................... &h0
48:   | | AceType: ............................ &h0
49:   |                                         ACCESS_ALLOWED_ACE_TYPE
50:   | | Trustee: ............................ (Win32_Trustee)
51:   | | +- Win32_Trustee ------------------------------------------------------------------
52:   | | | Domain: ........................... LISSWARENET
53:   | | | Name: ............................. MyGroup
54:   | | | SID: .............................. 1,5,0,0,0,...,207,122,236,255,136,223,4,0,0
55:   | | | SidLength: ........................ 28
56:   | | | SIDString: ........................ S-1-5-21-3533506287-3489020660-2298473594-1247
57:   | | +----------------------------------------------------------------------------------
58:   | +------------------------------------------------------------------------------------
59:   +--------------------------------------------------------------------------------------
```

The *ACE Flags* property, although exposed by the WMI and the ADSI object model, is not applicable to a File System share, since the concept of inheritance does not exist for such a security descriptor type. This is why the value is always set to zero (lines 17, 32, and 47).

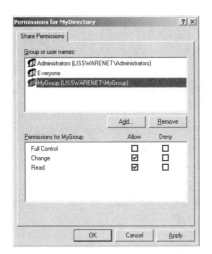

Figure 4.21
*The File System
share security
descriptor user
interface*

To configure a security descriptor equivalent to the one shown in Figure 4.21, the following command lines must be used:

```
 1:   C:\>WMIManageSD.wsf /Share:MyDirectory /Trustee:REMOVE_ALL_ACE /DelAce+
 2:   C:\>WMIManageSD.wsf /Share:MyDirectory /Trustee:BUILTIN\Administrators
 3:                                          /ACEType:ACCESS_ALLOWED_ACE_TYPE
 4:                                          /ACEMask:FILE_SHARE_FULL_ACCESS,
 5:                                                   FILE_SHARE_CHANGE_ACCESS,
 6:                                                   FILE_SHARE_READ_ACCESS
 7:                                          /ACEFlags:NONE /AddAce+
 8:   C:\>WMIManageSD.wsf /Share:MyDirectory /Trustee:Everyone /DelAce+
 9:   C:\>WMIManageSD.wsf /Share:MyDirectory /Trustee:LissWareNET\Everyone
10:                                          /ACEType:ACCESS_ALLOWED_ACE_TYPE
11:                                          /ACEMask:FILE_SHARE_READ_ACCESS
12:                                          /ACEFlags:NONE /AddAce+
13:   C:\>WMIManageSD.wsf /Share:MyDirectory /Trustee:LissWareNET\MyGroup
14:                                          /ACEType:ACCESS_ALLOWED_ACE_TYPE
15:                                          /ACEType:ACCESS_ALLOWED_ACE_TYPE
16:                                          /ACEMask:FILE_SHARE_CHANGE_ACCESS,
17:                                                   FILE_SHARE_READ_ACCESS
18:                                          /ACEFlags:NONE /AddAce+
19:   C:\>WMIManageSD.wsf /Share:MyDirectory /Decipher+
```

As for a folder, setting up the security descriptor of a File System share requires one execution per ACE configuration. Even if flag values are taken from Table 4.13, the logic is exactly the same as before. Note the *ACE Flags* set to "NONE," since inheritance is not supported for a File System share. As with a file or a folder, the WMI security descriptor access method is used, since no **/ADSI+** switch is specified.

4.11.4.5.3   The Active Directory object ACE AccessMask property

Managing the *ACE AccessMask* property of an Active Directory security descriptor is probably one of the most complex properties to handle. For Active Directory, we must first distinguish the standard rights from the Extended Rights. The standard rights are part of the system and cannot be modified.

However, because some directory-enabled applications may require the creation of some specific rights for the aim of the application, Active Directory offers a way to create new rights to protect Active Directory objects and attributes with more granularity. These rights are called the Active Directory Extended Rights and make use of the *ACE ObjectType* property. Of course, as we will see in section 4.11.4.5.3.2 ("Understanding the ACE InheritedObjectType property"), the use of an Extended Right is detected by also deciphering other ACE properties.

To decipher the standard Active Directory rights, the technique is still the same as before. A series of flags, defined in Tables 4.14 and 4.15, must be used to perform the deciphering bitwise operations.

Sample 4.37, which is part of the DecipherACEType() function, implements this logic. Due to the large number of rights, only a portion of the code is represented.

Sample 4.37   *Deciphering the ACE AccessMask property for Active Directory objects*

```
...:
...:
...:
259:
260:        Case cActiveDirectoryViaWMI, cActiveDirectoryViaADSI
261:            If (intACEMask = ADS_RIGHT_GENERIC_READ) Then
262:                strTemp = strTemp & "," & "(ADS_RIGHT_GENERIC_READ)"
263:            End If
264:            If (intACEMask = ADS_RIGHT_GENERIC_WRITE) Then
265:                strTemp = strTemp & "," & "(ADS_RIGHT_GENERIC_WRITE)"
266:            End If
267:            If (intACEMask = ADS_RIGHT_GENERIC_EXECUTE) Then
268:                strTemp = strTemp & "," & "(ADS_RIGHT_GENERIC_EXECUTE)"
269:            End If
270:            If (intACEMask = ADS_RIGHT_GENERIC_ALL) Then
271:                strTemp = strTemp & "," & "(ADS_RIGHT_GENERIC_ALL)"
272:            End If
...:
316:            If (intACEMask And ADS_RIGHT_DS_CONTROL_ACCESS) Then
317:                strTemp = strTemp & "," & "ADS_RIGHT_DS_CONTROL_ACCESS"
318:            End If
319:
...:
...:
...:
```

Table 4.14   *The Active Directory Object ACE AccessMask Values—Standard View*

Granted & denied rights		Full Control	Read	Write	Create All Child Objects	Delete All Child Objects	Allowed to Authenticate	Change Password	Receive As	Reset Password	Send As	Read Account Restrictions	Write Account Restrictions	Read General Information	Write General Information	Read Group Membership	Write Group Membership	Read Logon Information	Write Logon Information	Read Personal Information	Write Personal Information	Read Phone and Mail Options	Write Phone and Mail Options	Read Public Information	Write Public Information
		Standard					*Extended*																		
ACEType																									
ADS_ACETYPE_ACCESS_ALLOWED	0x0	X	X	X	X	X																			
ADS_ACETYPE_ACCESS_DENIED	0x1	X	X	X	X	X																			
ADS_ACETYPE_SYSTEM_AUDIT	0x2	X	X	X	X	X																			
ADS_ACETYPE_ACCESS_ALLOWED_OBJECT	0x5						X	X	X	X	X	X	X	X	X	X	X	X	X	X	X	X	X	X	X
ADS_ACETYPE_ACCESS_DENIED_OBJECT	0x6						X	X	X	X	X	X	X	X	X	X	X	X	X	X	X	X	X	X	X
ADS_ACETYPE_SYSTEM_AUDIT_OBJECT	0x7						X	X	X	X	X	X	X	X	X	X	X	X	X	X	X	X	X	X	X
ACEMask																									
ADS_RIGHT_GENERIC_ALL	0x10000000	X																							
ADS_RIGHT_GENERIC_EXECUTE	0x20000000		X																						
ADS_RIGHT_GENERIC_READ	0x80000000		X																						
ADS_RIGHT_GENERIC_WRITE	0x40000000			X																					
ADS_RIGHT_ACCESS_SYSTEM_SECURITY	0x1000000																								
ADS_RIGHT_ACTRL_DS_LIST	0x4	X	X																						
ADS_RIGHT_DELETE	0x10000	X																							
ADS_RIGHT_DS_CONTROL_ACCESS	0x100	X					X	X	X	X	X														
ADS_RIGHT_DS_CREATE_CHILD	0x1	X			X																				
ADS_RIGHT_DS_DELETE_CHILD	0x2	X				X																			
ADS_RIGHT_DS_DELETE_TREE	0x40	X																							
ADS_RIGHT_DS_LIST_OBJECT	0x80	X	X																						
ADS_RIGHT_DS_READ_PROP	0x10	X	X									X		X		X		X		X		X		X	
ADS_RIGHT_DS_SELF	0x8	X																							
ADS_RIGHT_DS_WRITE_PROP	0x20	X		X									X		X		X		X		X		X		X
ADS_RIGHT_READ_CONTROL	0x20000	X	X																						
ADS_RIGHT_SYNCHRONIZE	0x100000	X																							
ADS_RIGHT_WRITE_DAC	0x40000	X																							
ADS_RIGHT_WRITE_OWNER	0x80000	X																							

Table 4.14   *The Active Directory Object ACE AccessMask Values—Standard View (continued)*

Granted & denied rights — Standard View

ObjectType	Full Control	Read	Write	Create All Child Objects	Delete All Child Objects	Allowed to Authenticate	Change Password	Receive As	Reset Password	Send As	Read Account Restrictions	Write Account Restrictions	Read General Information	Write General Information	Read Group Membership	Write Group Membership	Read Logon Information	Write Logon Information	Read Personal Information	Write Personal Information	Read Phone and Mail Options	Write Phone and Mail Options	Read Public Information	Write Public Information
{68B1D179-0D15-4D4f-AB71-46152E79A7BC}						X																		
{AB721A53-1E2F-11D0-9819-00AA0040529B}							X																	
{AB721A56-1E2F-11D0-9819-00AA0040529B}								X																
{00299570-246D-11D0-A768-00AA006E0529}									X															
{AB721A54-1E2F-11D0-9819-00AA0040529B}										X														
{E45795B2-9455-11D1-AEBD-0000F80367C1}																								
{59BA2F42-79A2-11D0-9020-00C04FC2D3CF}											X													
{59BA2F42-79A2-11D0-9020-00C04FC2D3CF}												X												
{BC0AC240-79A9-11D0-9020-00C04FC2D4CF}													X											
{BC0AC240-79A9-11D0-9020-00C04FC2D4CF}														X										
{77B5B886-944A-11D1-AEBD-0000F80367C1}															X									
{77B5B886-944A-11D1-AEBD-0000F80367C1}																X								
{E48D0154-BCF8-11D1-8702-00C04FB96050}																								
{037088F8-0AE1-11D2-B422-00A0C968F939}																	X							
{037088F8-0AE1-11D2-B422-00A0C968F939}																		X						
{4C164200-20C0-11D0-A768-00AA006E0529}																			X					
{4C164200-20C0-11D0-A768-00AA006E0529}																				X				
{5F202010-79A5-11D0-9020-00C04FC2D4CF}																					X			
{5F202010-79A5-11D0-9020-00C04FC2D4CF}																						X		
{E45795B3-9455-11D1-AEBD-0000F80367C1}																							X	
{E45795B3-9455-11D1-AEBD-0000F80367C1}																								X

ACEFlagType																								
ADS_FLAG_OBJECT_TYPE_PRESENT[1] (0x1)						X	X	X	X	X	X	X	X	X	X	X	X	X	X	X	X	X	X	X
ADS_FLAG_INHERITED_OBJECT_TYPE_PRESENT[1] (0x2)						X	X	X	X	X	X	X	X	X	X	X	X	X	X	X	X	X	X	X

(1) Only used when the ADSI object model is used to represent the security descriptor.

Table 4.15   *The Active Directory Object ACE AccessMask Values—Advanced View*

Granted & denied rights		Full Control	List Contents	Read All Properties	Write All Properties	Delete	Delete Subtree	Read Permissions	Modify Permissions	Modify Owner	All Validated Writes	All Extended Rights	Create All Child Objects	Delete All Child Objects	Allowed to authenticate	Change Password	Receive As	Reset Password	Send As
ACEType						**Standard**											**Extended**		
ADS_ACETYPE_ACCESS_ALLOWED	0x0																		
ADS_ACETYPE_ACCESS_DENIED	0x1	X	X	X	X	X	X	X	X	X	X	X	X	X					
ADS_ACETYPE_SYSTEM_AUDIT	0x2																		
ADS_ACETYPE_ACCESS_ALLOWED_OBJECT	0x5																		
ADS_ACETYPE_ACCESS_DENIED_OBJECT	0x6														X	X	X	X	X
ADS_ACETYPE_SYSTEM_AUDIT_OBJECT	0x7																		
ACEMask																			
ADS_RIGHT_GENERIC_ALL	0x10000000	X																	
ADS_RIGHT_GENERIC_EXECUTE	0x20000000																		
ADS_RIGHT_GENERIC_READ	0x80000000																		
ADS_RIGHT_GENERIC_WRITE	0x40000000																		
ADS_RIGHT_ACCESS_SYSTEM_SECURITY	0x1000000																		
ADS_RIGHT_ACTRL_DS_LIST	0x4	X	X												X	X	X	X	X
ADS_RIGHT_DELETE	0x10000	X				X													
ADS_RIGHT_DS_CONTROL_ACCESS	0x100	X										X							
ADS_RIGHT_DS_CREATE_CHILD	0x1	X											X						
ADS_RIGHT_DS_DELETE_CHILD	0x2	X												X					
ADS_RIGHT_DS_DELETE_TREE	0x40	X					X												
ADS_RIGHT_DS_LIST_OBJECT	0x80	X																	
ADS_RIGHT_DS_READ_PROP	0x10	X		X															
ADS_RIGHT_DS_SELF	0x8	X									X								
ADS_RIGHT_DS_WRITE_PROP	0x20	X			X														
ADS_RIGHT_READ_CONTROL	0x20000	X						X											
ADS_RIGHT_SYNCHRONIZE	0x100000																		
ADS_RIGHT_WRITE_DAC	0x40000	X							X										
ADS_RIGHT_WRITE_OWNER	0x80000	X								X									
ObjectType																			
{68B1D179-0D15-4D4f-AB71-46152E79A7BC}															X				
{AB721A53-1E2F-11D0-9819-00AA0040529B}																X			
{AB721A56-1E2F-11D0-9819-00AA0040529B}																	X		
{00299570-246D-11D0-A768-00AA006E0529}																		X	
{AB721A54-1E2F-11D0-9819-00AA0040529B}																			X
ACEFlagType																			
ADS_FLAG_OBJECT_TYPE_PRESENT[1]	0x1														X	X	X	X	X
ADS_FLAG_INHERITED_OBJECT_TYPE_PRESENT[1]	0x2																		

(1) Only used when the ADSI object model is used to represent the security descriptor.

Active Directory objects can inherit an ACE from parent objects. Therefore, some flags define how the ACE inheritance behaves. These flags are summarized in Table 4.16.

When configuring ACE inheritance, it is possible to specify that the ACE inheritance will only apply on a particular Active Directory object class. This inheritance makes use of the *ACE InheritedObjectType* property, which contains a GUID number. To understand how to set up the *ACE InheritedObjectType* property, it is best to understand how Active Directory Extended Rights work first. This will help us to discover the links that exist between Active Directory classes, Active Directory attributes, and Active Directory rights. It is important to note that Active Directory Extended

Table 4.16   *The Active Directory Objects ACE Flags Values*

Inheritance & Audit		This object only	This object and all child objects	Child objects only	Audit Successful access	Audit Failed access
ACEFlags						
NONE	0x0	X				
ADS_ACEFLAG_INHERIT_ACE	0x2		X	X		
ADS_ACEFLAG_INHERIT_ONLY_ACE	0x8			X		
ADS_ACEFLAG_INHERITED_ACE[1]	0x10					
ADS_ACEFLAG_NO_PROPAGATE_INHERIT_ACE	0x4					
ADS_ACEFLAG_VALID_INHERIT_FLAGS[1]	0x1F					
ADS_ACEFLAG_SUCCESSFUL_ACCESS	0x40				X	
ADS_ACEFLAG_FAILED_ACCESS	0x80					X

(1) can only be set by the system.

Rights and ACE inheritance on specific object classes are two different things, but they use the same type of information for their configuration. This explains why it is easier to discover the Active Directory Extended Rights first.

4.11.4.5.3.1 Understanding the ACE ObjectType property

Having a good knowledge of the different Naming Contexts that Active Directory implements and how they are structured is important with respect to the origin of the GUID number contained in the *ACE ObjectType* property.

All Active Directory objects support a standard set of access rights, listed in Table 4.14. You can use these access rights in the *ACE AccessMask* of an object's security descriptor to control access at the object level. However, some objects' classes may require an access control not supported by the standard access rights. In such a case, Active Directory allows you to extend the standard access control mechanism to perform a more granular control on some Active Directory objects and attributes. An Active Directory Extended Right is an Active Directory object created from the **controlAccessRight** object class. All Active Directory Extended Rights are located in the "CN=Extended-Rights" container of the Active Directory Configuration naming context. To correctly decipher an ACE of an Active Directory Extended Right, we must distinguish between different Extended Rights types. The type is determined by the **validAccesses** attribute value defined in each **controlAccessRight** object created in the "CN=Extended-Rights" container. There are three Extended Rights types:

- **The Extended Rights enforced by Active Directory:** These Extended Rights are enforced by Active Directory to grant (or deny) a read or write operation to an Active Directory property set. A **validAccesses** attribute value of 0x30 (ADS_RIGHT_DS_READ_ PROP or ADS_RIGHT_DS_WRITE_PROP) defines this type of Extended Rights. They have an *ACE Type* set to one of these three values: ADS_ACETYPE_ACCESS_ALLOWED_OBJECT, ADS_ ACETYPE_ACCESS_DENIED_OBJECT, or ADS_ACETYPE_ SYSTEM_AUDIT_OBJECT. The *ACE AccessMask* value is equal to a logical combination of the ADS_RIGHT_DS_READ_PROP and ADS_RIGHT_DS_WRITE flags (see Table 4.14).

- **The Extended Rights enforced by applications:** These rights are enforced by applications, which could be, for instance, Exchange 2000, Outlook 2000, or the system itself but not Active Directory. A **validAccesses** attribute value of 0x100 (ADS_RIGHT_DS_CONTROL_AC- CESS) defines this type of Extended Rights. They have an *ACE Type* set to one of these three values: ADS_ACETYPE_ACCESS_ALLOWED_ OBJECT, ADS_ACETYPE_ACCESS_DENIED_OBJECT, or ADS_ ACETYPE_SYSTEM_AUDIT_OBJECT. They have an *ACE Access- Mask* value equal to the ADS_RIGHT_DS_CONTROL_ACCESS flag value (see Table 4.14).

- **The Extended Rights enforced by the system to perform extra check- ing:** These Extended Rights are called the "Validated Writes." These rights are used by the system to perform a value check or validation before writing a value to a property on an object. The value checking or validation goes beyond what is required by the Active Directory schema. This type of right uses a value of 0x8 (ADS_RIGHT_DS_ SELF) in the **validAccesses** attribute. They have an *ACE Type* set to one of these three values: ADS_ACETYPE_ACCESS_ALLOWED_ OBJECT, ADS_ACETYPE_ACCESS_DENIED_OBJECT, or ADS_ ACETYPE_SYSTEM_AUDIT_OBJECT. They have an *ACE Access- Mask* value equal to the ADS_RIGHT_DS_SELF flag value.

Figure 4.22 shows an example of the three Extended Rights types. On the left, we have the "Personal Information" right, which is enforced by Active Directory (**validAccesses** = 0x30). In the center, we have the "Send As" right, which is enforced by an application (**validAccesses** = 0x100). On the right, we have the "Add/Remove self as member" right, which is only enforced by the system itself (**validAccesses** = 0x08).

To continue, we will use the three rights in Figure 4.22 as examples. Because rights are always related to an Active Directory object, Extended

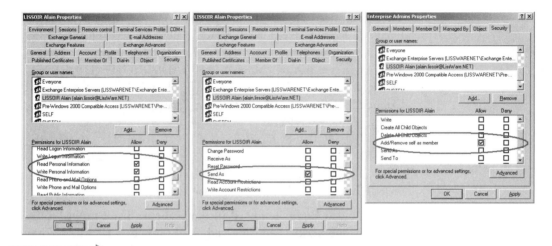

Figure 4.22   *The Extended Rights enforced by Active Directory (left), enforced by applications (center), and enforced by the system (right).*

Rights have a link with the Active Directory object classes they apply to. For instance, the Extended Rights in Figure 4.22 ("Personal Information" and "Send As") are linked with the Active Directory **user** class defined in the Active Directory schema, because they apply to objects created from the **user** class. The same rule applies for the "Add/Remove self as member" right, but it is linked with the **group** class. The link between the Extended right and the **user** class or the **group** class is made with an attribute available from the **controlAccessRight** object, called the **appliesTo** attribute. The **appliesTo** attribute may contain one or more GUID numbers, where each GUID number is the value contained in the **schemaIDGUID** attribute of the class that the Extended Rights relates to. For instance, the "Personal Information" Extended Right has several GUID numbers in the **appliesTo** attribute (Figure 4.23, left pane), where each of them is coming from the **schemaIDGUID** attribute of the corresponding classes (Figure 4.23, right pane) for the **user** class.

Although the format of the GUID number in the **schemaIDGUID** attribute is in binary, it is the same GUID number. Figure 4.24 illustrates the logic to use to convert a binary GUID number to a string GUID number and vice versa.

If we look for the same information for the "Send As" Extended Right, we find the same type of relationship (see Figure 4.25). The same rule will apply if you look at the GUID number stored in the **schemaIDGUID** attribute of the **group** class.

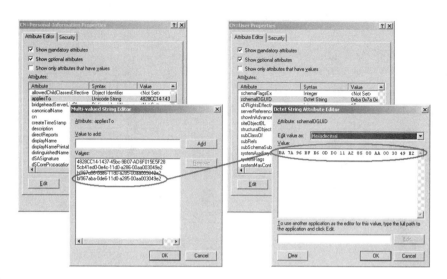

Figure 4.23   *The appliesTo GUID numbers of the "Personal Information" Extended Right in liaison with the schemaIDGUID attribute of the classSchema object.*

The aim of the "Personal Information" Extended Right (and of all Extended Rights using a **validAccesses** attribute value equal to 0x30) is to protect some Active Directory attributes associated with the class that the Extended Right refers to. This means that a relationship between Extended Rights and some Active Directory attributes also exists. To establish the link between an Extended Right and the set of attributes it protects, an Extended Right of this type (**validAccesses** = 0x30) uses another GUID number, which is stored in the **rightsGUID** attribute of the **controlAccess-Right** object. Any attributes that can be protected by the Extended Right refer to the Extended Right GUID number by storing the value in its **attributeSecurityGUID** attribute (see Figure 4.26). The **attributeSecuri-**

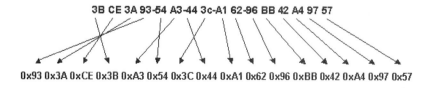

Figure 4.24   *Converting a GUID string to a GUID number and vice versa.*

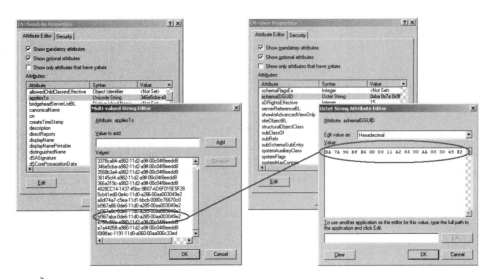

Figure 4.25   *The appliesTo GUID numbers of the "Send As" Extended Right in liaison with the schemaIDGUID attribute of the classSchema object.*

tyGUID attribute is part of the **attributeSchema** object defining the attribute in the Active Directory Schema.

Finally, Figure 4.27 summarizes the links between Extended Rights (**controlAccessRight**), Active Directory object classes (**classSchema**), and

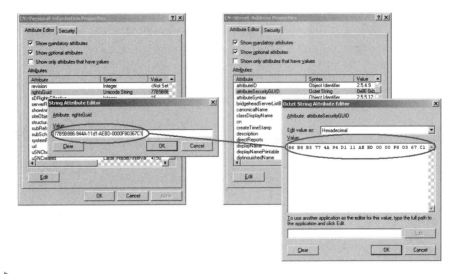

Figure 4.26   *The attributeSecurityGUID attribute of the attributeSchema object contains the rightsGUID GUID number of the "Personal Information" Extended Right.*

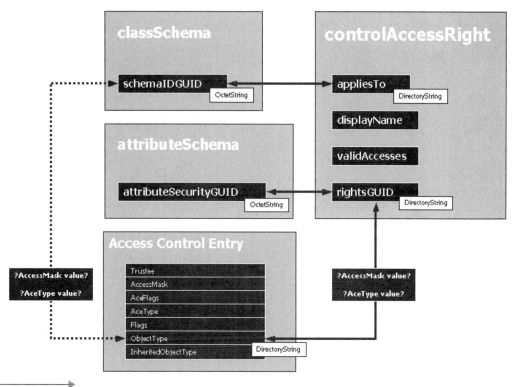

Figure 4.27   *The Extended Rights attributes links.*

attribute definitions (**attributeSchema**). Figure 4.27 also shows that the *ACE ObjectType* property of a security descriptor using an Extended Right refers to the GUID number value stored in the **rightsGUID** attribute of the **controlAccessRight** object. However, we will see later in this section that the GUID number could come from the **schemaIDGUID** attribute of a **classSchema** object. This is why we have a dashed line in Figure 4.27.

When Extended Rights use a **validAccesses** attribute value of 0x100, they do not refer to any particular attribute, since this type of right is enforced at the application level, which means that it is the responsibility of the application to validate the right (i.e., Exchange 2000 and Outlook 2000 validate the "Send As" Extended Right). The last type (**validAccesses** = 0x8) is enforced by the system and is used to lock write operations to some Active Directory attributes (i.e., "Validated write to DNS host name" right applying to the **computer** class). Table 4.17 summarizes the Extended Rights names and GUID numbers available under Windows Server 2003 and Exchange 2000 SP3 with the classes and attributes they apply to.

Table 4.17   *Extended Rights Available in Active Directory under Windows Server 2003 (Exchange 2000 Extended Rights Included)*

Extended Right Display Name	GUID number (rightsGUID)	Type	Related classes	Protected attributes
Account Restrictions	{4c164200-20c0-11d0-a768-00aa006e0529}	0x30	inetOrgPerson computer user	accountExpires msDS-User-Account-Control-Computed pwdLastSet userAccountControl userParameters
Add GUID	{440820ad-65b4-11d1-a3da-0000f875ae0d}	0x100	domainDNS	
Add PF to admin group	{ce4d81a8-afe6-11d2-aa04-00c04f8eedd8}	0x100	msExchAdminGroup	
Add/Remove Replica In Domain	{9923a32a-3607-11d2-b9be-0000f87a36b2}	0x100	domainDNS	
Add/Remove self as member	{bf9679c0-0de6-11d0-a285-00aa003049e2}	0x8	group	
Administer information store	{d74a8762-22b9-11d3-aa62-00c04f8eedd8}	0x100	msExchStorageGroup msExchServersContainer msExchPublicMDB msExchPseudoPFAdmin msExchPrivateMDB msExchPFTree msExchOrganizationContainer msExchExchangeServer msExchConfigurationContainer msExchAdminGroupContainer msExchAdminGroup	
Allocate Rids	{1abd7cf8-0a99-11d1-adbb-00c04fd8d5cd}	0x100	nTDSDSA	
Allowed to Authenticate	{68b1d179-0d15-4d4f-ab71-46152e79a7bc}	0x100	inetOrgPerson user computer	
Apply Group Policy	{edacfd8f-ffb3-11d1-b41d-00a0c968f939}	0x100	groupPolicyContainer	
Change Domain Master	{014bf69c-7b3b-11d1-85f6-08002be74fab}	0x100	crossRefContainer	
Change Infrastructure Master	{cc17b1fb-33d9-11d2-97d4-00c04fd8d5cd}	0x100	infrastructureUpdate	
Change Password	{ab721a53-1e2f-11d0-9819-00aa0040529b}	0x100	inetOrgPerson computer user	
Change PDC	{bae50096-4752-11d1-9052-00c04fc2d4cf}	0x100	domainDNS	
Change Rid Master	{d58d5f36-0a98-11d1-adbb-00c04fd8d5cd}	0x100	rIDManager	
Change Schema Master	{e12b56b6-0a95-11d1-adbb-00c04fd8d5cd}	0x100	dMD	
Check Stale Phantoms	{69ae6200-7f46-11d2-b9ad-00c04f79f805}	0x100	nTDSDSA	
Create Inbound Forest Trust	{e2a36dc9-ae17-47c3-b58b-be34c55ba633}	0x100	domainDNS	
Create named properties in the information store	{d74a8766-22b9-11d3-aa62-00c04f8eedd8}	0x100	msExchStorageGroup msExchServersContainer msExchPublicMDB msExchPrivateMDB msExchPFTree msExchOrganizationContainer msExchExchangeServer msExchConfigurationContainer msExchAdminGroupContainer msExchAdminGroup	

Table 4.17   *Extended Rights Available in Active Directory under Windows Server 2003 (Exchange 2000 Extended Rights Included) (continued)*

Extended Right Display Name	GUID number (rightsGUID)	Type	Related classes	Protected attributes
Create public folder	{cf0b3dc8-afe6-11d2-aa04-00c04f8eedd8}	0x100	msExchPFTree msExchOrganizationContainer msExchConfigurationContainer msExchAdminGroupContainer msExchAdminGroup	
Create top level public folder	{cf4b9d46-afe6-11d2-aa04-00c04f8eedd8}	0x100	msExchPFTree msExchOrganizationContainer msExchConfigurationContainer msExchAdminGroupContainer msExchAdminGroup	
DNS Host Name Attributes	{72e39547-7b18-11d1-adef-00c04fd8d5cd}	0x30	computer	dNSHostName msDS-AdditionalDnsHostName
Do Garbage Collection	{fec364e0-0a98-11d1-adbb-00c04fd8d5cd}	0x100	nTDSDSA	
Domain Administer Server	{ab721a52-1e2f-11d0-9819-00aa0040529b}	0x100	samServer	
Domain Password & Lockout Policies	{c7407360-20bf-11d0-a768-00aa006e0529}	0x30	domainDNS domain	lockOutObservationWindow lockoutDuration lockoutThreshold maxPwdAge minPwdAge minPwdLength pwdHistoryLength pwdProperties
Enable Per User Reversibly Encrypted Password	{05c74c5e-4deb-43b4-bd9f-86664c2a7fd5}	0x100	domainDNS	
Enroll	{0e10c968-78fb-11d2-90d4-00c04f79dc55}	0x100	pKICertificateTemplate	
Enumerate Entire SAM Domain	{91d67418-0135-4acc-8d79-c08e857cfbec}	0x100	samServer	
Exchange administrator	{8e48d5a8-b09e-11d2-aa06-00c04f8eedd8}	0x100	msExchAdminGroup	
Exchange full administrator	{8e6571e0-b09e-11d2-aa06-00c04f8eedd8}	0x100	msExchAdminGroup	
Exchange public folder read-only administrator	{8ff1383c-b09e-11d2-aa06-00c04f8eedd8}	0x100	msExchAdminGroup	
Exchange public folder service	{90280e52-b09e-11d2-aa06-00c04f8eedd8}	0x100	msExchAdminGroup	
Execute Forest Update Script	{2f16c4a5-b98e-432c-952a-cb388ba33f2e}	0x100	crossRefContainer	
General Information	{59ba2f42-79a2-11d0-9020-00c04fc2d3cf}	0x30	inetOrgPerson user	adminDescription codePage countryCode displayName objectSid primaryGroupID sAMAccountName sAMAccountType sDRightsEffective showInAdvancedViewOnly sIDHistory uid comment

Table 4.17 *Extended Rights Available in Active Directory under Windows Server 2003 (Exchange 2000 Extended Rights Included) (continued)*

Extended Right Display Name	GUID number (rightsGUID)	Type	Related classes	Protected attributes
Generate Resultant Set of Policy (Logging)	{b7b1b3de-ab09-4242-9e30-9980e5d322f7}	0x100	domainDNS organizationalUnit	
Generate Resultant Set of Policy (Planning)	{b7b1b3dd-ab09-4242-9e30-9980e5d322f7}	0x100	domainDNS organizationalUnit	
Group Membership	{bc0ac240-79a9-11d0-9020-00c04fc2d4cf}	0x30	inetOrgPerson user	memberOf member
Logon Information	{5f202010-79a5-11d0-9020-00c04fc2d4cf}	0x30	inetOrgPerson user	badPwdCount homeDirectory homeDrive lastLogoff lastLogon lastLogonTimestamp logonCount logonHours logonWorkstation profilePath scriptPath userWorkstations
Mail-enable public folder	{cf899a6a-afe6-11d2-aa04-00c04f8eedd8}	0x100	msExchPFTree msExchOrganizationContainer msExchConfigurationContainer msExchAdminGroupContainer msExchAdminGroup	
Manage Replication Topology	{1131f6ac-9c07-11d1-f79f-00c04fc2dcd2}	0x100	dMD configuration domainDNS	
Migrate SID History	{ba33815a-4f93-4c76-87f3-57574bff8109}	0x100	domainDNS	
Modify public folder ACL	{d74a8769-22b9-11d3-aa62-00c04f8eedd8}	0x100	msExchPseudoPFAdmin msExchPFTree	
Modify public folder admin ACL	{d74a876f-22b9-11d3-aa62-00c04f8eedd8}	0x100	msExchPseudoPFAdmin msExchPFTree msExchOrganizationContainer msExchConfigurationContainer msExchAdminGroupContainer msExchAdminGroup	
Modify public folder deleted item retention	{cffe6da4-afe6-11d2-aa04-00c04f8eedd8}	0x100	msExchPseudoPFAdmin msExchPFTree msExchAdminGroup	
Modify public folder expiry	{cfc7978c-afe6-11d2-aa04-00c04f8eedd8}	0x100	msExchPseudoPFAdmin msExchPFTree msExchAdminGroup	
Modify public folder quotas	{d03a086e-afe6-11d2-aa04-00c04f8eedd8}	0x100	msExchPseudoPFAdmin msExchPFTree msExchAdminGroup	

Table 4.17   *Extended Rights Available in Active Directory under Windows Server 2003 (Exchange 2000 Extended Rights Included) (continued)*

Extended Right Display Name	GUID number (rightsGUID)	Type	Related classes	Protected attributes
Modify public folder replica list	{d0780592-afe6-11d2-aa04-00c04f8eedd8}	0x100	msExchStorageGroup msExchServersContainer msExchPublicMDB msExchPseudoPFAdmin msExchPFTree msExchOrganizationContainer msExchExchangeServer msExchConfigurationContainer msExchAdminGroupContainer msExchAdminGroup	
Monitor Active Directory Replication	{98340fb-7c5b-4cdb-a00b-2ebdfa115a96}	0x100	dMD configuration domainDNS	
Open Address List	{a1990816-4298-11d1-ade2-00c04fd8d5cd}	0x100	addressBookContainer	
Open Connector Queue	{b4e60130-df3f-11d1-9c86-006008764d0e}	0x100	site	
Open mail send queue	{d74a8774-22b9-11d3-aa62-00c04f8eedd8}	0x100	msExchStorageGroup msExchServersContainer msExchPublicMDB msExchPrivateMDB msExchOrganizationContainer msExchExchangeServer msExchAdminGroupContainer msExchAdminGroup	
Other Domain Parameters (for use by SAM)	{b8119fd0-04f6-4762-ab7a-4986c76b399a}	0x30	domainDNS	domainReplica forceLogoff modifiedCount oEMInformation serverRole serverState uASCompat
Peek Computer Journal	{4b6e08c3-df3c-11d1-9c86-006008764d0e}	0x100	mSMQConfiguration	
Peek Dead Letter	{4b6e08c1-df3c-11d1-9c86-006008764d0e}	0x100	mSMQConfiguration	
Peek Message	{06bd3201-df3e-11d1-9c86-006008764d0e}	0x100	mSMQQueue	

Table 4.17   *Extended Rights Available in Active Directory under Windows Server 2003 (Exchange 2000 Extended Rights Included) (continued)*

Extended Right Display Name	GUID number (rightsGUID)	Type	Related classes	Protected attributes
Personal Information	{77b5b886-944a-11d1-aebd-0000f80367c1}	0x30	inetOrgPerson computer contact user	streetAddress homePostalAddress assistant info c facsimileTelephoneNumber internationalISDNNumber l publicDelegates mSMQDigests mSMQSignCertificates personalTitle otherFacsimileTelephoneNumber otherHomePhone homePhone otherIpPhone ipPhone primaryInternationalISDNNumber otherMobile mobile otherTelephone otherPager pager physicalDeliveryOfficeName thumbnailPhoto postOfficeBox postalAddress postalCode preferredDeliveryMethod registeredAddress st street telephoneNumber teletexTerminalIdentifier telexNumber primaryTelexNumber userCert userSharedFolder userSharedFolderOther userSMIMECertificate x121Address userCertificate
Phone and Mail Options	{e45795b2-9455-11d1-aebd-0000f80367c1}	0x30	inetOrgPerson group user	

Table 4.17   *Extended Rights Available in Active Directory under Windows Server 2003 (Exchange 2000 Extended Rights Included) (continued)*

Extended Right Display Name	GUID number (rightsGUID)	Type	Related classes	Protected attributes
Public Information	{e48d0154-bcf8-11d1-8702-00c04fb96050}	0x30	inetOrgPerson, computer, user	notes, allowedAttributes, allowedAttributesEffective, allowedChildClasses, allowedChildClassesEffective, altSecurityIdentities, cn, company, department, d, escription, displayNamePrintable, division, mail, givenName, initials, legacyExchangeDN, manager, msDS-AllowedToDelega
Read metabase properties	{be013017-13a1-41ad-a058-f156504cb617}	0x100	msExchServersContainer, protocolCfgSharedServer, msExchOrganizationContainer, msExchExchangeServer, msExchAdminGroupContainer, msExchAdminGroup, dMD	
Reanimate Tombstones	{45ec5156-db7e-47bb-b53f-dbeb2cd03c40f}	0x100	configuration, domainDNS	
Recalculate Hierarchy	{0bc1554e-0a99-11d1-adbb-00c04fd8d5cd}	0x100	nTDSDSA	
Recalculate Security Inheritance	{62dd28a8-7f46-11d2-b9ad-00c04f79f805}	0x100	nTDSDSA	
Receive As	{ab721a56-1e2f-11d0-9819-00aa0040529b}	0x100	msExchServersContainer, msExchPublicMDB, protocolCfgSMTPServer, msExchPrivateMDB, msExchOrganizationContainer, mTA, msExchExchangeServer, msExchAdminGroupContainer, msExchAdminGroup, inetOrgPerson, computer, user	
Receive Computer Journal	{4b6e08c2-df3c-11d1-9c86-006008764d0e}	0x100	mSMQConfiguration	
Receive Dead Letter	{4b6e08c0-df3c-11d1-9c86-006008764d0e}	0x100	mSMQConfiguration	
Receive Journal	{06xd3203-df3e-11d1-9c86-006008764d0e}	0x100	mSMQConfiguration	
Receive Message	{06xd3200-df3e-11d1-9c86-006008764d0e}	0x100	mSMQQueue	
Refresh Group Cache for Logons	{9432c620-033c-4db7-8b58-14ef6d0bf477}	0x100	nTDSDSA	

Table 4.17 *Extended Rights Available in Active Directory under Windows Server 2003 (Exchange 2000 Extended Rights Included) (continued)*

Extended Right Display Name	GUID number (rightsGUID)	Type	Related classes	Protected attributes
Remote Access Information	{037088f8-0ae1-11d2-b422-00a0c968f939}	0x30	inetOrgPerson user	msNPAllowDialin msNPCallingStationID msRADIUSCallbackNumber msRADIUSFramedIPAddress msRADIUSFramedRoute msRADIUSServiceType tokenGroups tokenGroupsGlobalAndUniversal tokenGroupsNoGCAcceptable
Remove PF from admin group	{d0b86510-afe6-11d2-aa04-00c04f8eedd8}	0x100	msExchAdminGroup	
Replicating Directory Changes	{1131f6aa-9c07-11d1-f79f-00c04fc2dcd2}	0x100	dMD configuration domainDNS	
Replicating Directory Changes All	{1131f6ad-9c07-11d1-f79f-00c04fc2dcd2}	0x100	dMD configuration domainDNS	
Replication Synchronization	{1131f6ab-9c07-11d1-f79f-00c04fc2dcd2}	0x100	dMD configuration domainDNS	
Reset Password	{00299570-246d-11d0-a768-00aa006e0529}	0x100	inetOrgPerson computer user	
Send As	{ab721a54-1e2f-11d0-9819-00aa0040529b}	0x100	msExchServersContainer msExchPublicMDB publicFolder protocolCfgSMTPServer msExchPrivateMDB msExchOrganizationContainer mTA msExchExchangeServer msExchAdminGroupContainer msExchAdminGroup group contact inetOrgPerson computer user	

Table 4.17   *Extended Rights Available in Active Directory under Windows Server 2003 (Exchange 2000 Extended Rights Included) (continued)*

Extended Right Display Name	GUID number (rightsGUID)	Type	Related classes	Protected attributes
Send Message	{06bd3202-df3e-11d1-9c86-006008764d0e}	0x100	msMQ-Group msSMQQueue	
Send To	{ab721a55-1e2f-11d0-9819-00aa0040529b}	0x100	group	
Unexpire Password	{ccc2dc7d-a6ad-4a7a-8846-c04e3cc53501}	0x100	domainDNS	
Update Password Not Required Bit	{280f369c-67c7-438e-ae98-1d46f3c6f541}	0x100	domainDNS	
Update Schema Cache	{be2bb760-7f46-11d2-b9ad-00c04f79f805}	0x100	dMD	
Validated write to DNS host name	{72e39547-7b18-11d1-adef-00c04fd8d5cd}	0x8	computer	dNSHostName msDS-AdditionalDnsHostName
Validated write to service principal name	{f3a64788-5306-11d1-a9c5-0000f80367c1}	0x8	computer	
View information store status	{d74a8756-22b9-11d3-aa62-00c04f8eed8}	0x100	msExchStorageGroup msExchServersContainer msExchPublicMDB msExchPseudoPFAdmin msExchPrivateMDB msExchPFTree msExchOrganizationContainer msExchExchangeServer msExchConfigurationContainer msExchAdminGroupContainer msExchAdminGroup	
Web Information	{e45795b3-9455-11d1-aebd-0000f80367c1}	0x30	inetOrgPerson contact user	wWWHomePage url

Each time, an "ACE" refers to an Extended Right, the *ACE ObjectType* GUID number must be searched in this table to find the corresponding Extended Rights name. Table 4.17 can also be used to determine which Extended Right protects a specific attribute of a specific Active Directory object. This should ease the process of determining which right must be set to secure a specific attribute. For instance, based on Table 4.17, we know that the "Personal Information" Extended Right protects the **street** and **telephoneNumber** attributes, among others.

To understand how to decipher this type of ACE, let's take examples from Figure 4.22. We see that a user called "LISSOIR Alain" is granted to read and change his personal information (left). At the same time, he is also granted the "Send As" right (center), and he can add or remove himself from the "Enterprise Admins" group.

By using the **WMIManageSD.Wsf** script with the following command line, deciphering this Active Directory security descriptor produces the following output:

```
  1:  C:\>WMIManageSD.Wsf /ADObject:"CN=LISSOIR Alain,CN=Users,DC=..." /Decipher+ /ADSI+
  2:  Microsoft (R) Windows Script Host Version 5.6
  3:  Copyright (C) Microsoft Corporation 1996-2001. All rights reserved.
  4:
  5:  Reading AD object security descriptor via ADSI from 'LDAP://CN=LISSOIR Alain,CN=Users,DC=...
  6:
  7:  +- ADSI Security Descriptor -----------------------------------------------------------
  8:  | Owner: .............................. LISSWARENET\Domain Admins
  9:  | Group: .............................. LISSWARENET\Domain Admins
 10:  | Revision: ........................... 1
 11:  | Control: ............................ &h9C14
 ..:
 18:  |+- ADSI DiscretionaryAcl ------------------------------------------------------------
 19:  ||+- ADSI ACE ----------------------------------------------------------------------
 ..:
 38:  ||+---------------------------------------------------------------------------------
...:
186:  ||+- ADSI ACE ----------------------------------------------------------------------
187:  ||| AccessMask: ......................... &h100
188:                                            ADS_RIGHT_DS_CONTROL_ACCESS
189:  ||| AceFlags: ........................... &h0
190:  ||| AceType: ........................... &h5
191:                                            ADS_ACETYPE_ACCESS_ALLOWED_OBJECT
192:  ||| AceFlagType: ........................ &h1
193:                                            ADS_FLAG_OBJECT_TYPE_PRESENT
194:  ||| ObjectType: ........................ {AB721A54-1E2F-11D0-9819-00AA0040529B}
195:  ||| Trustee: ........................... LISSWARENET\Alain.Lissoir
196:  ||+-------------------------------------------------------------------------------
197:  ||+- ADSI ACE ----------------------------------------------------------------------
198:  ||| AccessMask: ......................... &h30
199:                                            ADS_RIGHT_DS_READ_PROP
200:                                            ADS_RIGHT_DS_WRITE_PROP
201:  ||| AceFlags: ........................... &h0
202:  ||| AceType: ........................... &h5
```

```
203:                                        ADS_ACETYPE_ACCESS_ALLOWED_OBJECT
204:    ||| AceFlagType: ........................ &h1
205:                                        ADS_FLAG_OBJECT_TYPE_PRESENT
206:    ||| ObjectType: ........................ {77B5B886-944A-11D1-AEBD-0000F80367C1}
207:    ||| Trustee: ........................... LISSWARENET\Alain.Lissoir
208:    ||+-------------------------------------------------------------------------------
...:
232:    |+----------------------------------------------------------------------------------
233:    +-----------------------------------------------------------------------------------
...:
...:
...:
```

From line 186 through 196, the "Send As" Extended Right is granted to trustee "Alain.Lissoir" as:

- The *ACE Type* has a value equal to ADS_ACETYPE_ACCESS_ALLOWED_OBJECT (line 191).

- The *ACE AccessMask* has a value equal to ADS_RIGHT_DS_CONTROL_ACCESS ACE (line 188).

- The *ACE ObjectType* property has a GUID number corresponding to the "Send As" Extended Right (line 194). Check Table 4.17 to find the Extended Right GUID number with its corresponding display name.

In the same way, from line 197 through 208, the "Personal Information" Extended Right is granted to trustee "Alain.Lissoir" to read and write the personal information as:

- The *ACE Type* has a value equal to ADS_ACETYPE_ACCESS_ALLOWED_OBJECT (line 203).

- The *ACE AccessMask* has a value equal to ADS_RIGHT_DS_READ_PROP + ADS_RIGHT_DS_WRITE_PROP (lines 199 and 200).

- The *ACE ObjectType* property has a GUID number corresponding to the "Personal Information" Extended Right (line 206). Check Table 4.17 to find the Extended Right GUID number with its corresponding display name.

For the "Add/Remove self as member" Extended Right, the same logic applies with different values.

```
1:    C:\>WMIManageSD.Wsf /ADObject:"CN=Enterprise Admins,CN=Users,DC=..." /Decipher+ /ADSI+
2:    Microsoft (R) Windows Script Host Version 5.6
3:    Copyright (C) Microsoft Corporation 1996-2001. All rights reserved.
4:
5:    Reading AD object security descriptor via ADSI from 'LDAP://CN=Enterprise Admins,CN=...'.
6:
```

```
  7:  +- ADSI Security Descriptor --------------------------------------------------------
  8:  | Owner: ............................. LISSWARENET\Domain Admins
  9:  | Group: ............................. LISSWARENET\Domain Admins
 10:  | Revision: .......................... 1
 11:  | Control: ........................... &h9C14
 ..:
 18:  |+- ADSI DiscretionaryAcl ----------------------------------------------------------
 19:  ||+- ADSI ACE ------------------------------------------------------------------------
 ..:
 38:  ||+---------------------------------------------------------------------------------
...:
174:  ||+- ADSI ACE ------------------------------------------------------------------------
175:  ||| AccessMask: ........................ &h8
176:                                           ADS_RIGHT_DS_SELF
177:  ||| AceFlags: .......................... &h2
178:                                           ADS_ACEFLAG_CONTAINER_INHERIT_ACE
179:                                           ADS_ACEFLAG_VALID_INHERIT_FLAGS
180:  ||| AceType: ........................... &h5
181:                                           ADS_ACETYPE_ACCESS_ALLOWED_OBJECT
182:  ||| AceFlagType: ....................... &h1
183:                                           ADS_FLAG_OBJECT_TYPE_PRESENT
184:  ||| ObjectType: ........................ {BF9679C0-0DE6-11D0-A285-00AA003049E2}
185:  ||| Trustee: ........................... LISSWARENET\Alain.Lissoir
186:  ||+---------------------------------------------------------------------------------
...:
224:  |+---------------------------------------------------------------------------------
225:  +-----------------------------------------------------------------------------------
```

From line 174 through 186, the right "Add/Remove self as member" is granted to trustee "Alain.Lissoir" as:

- The *ACE Type* has a value equal to ADS_ACETYPE_ACCESS_ALLOWED_OBJECT (line 181).

- The *ACE AccessMask* has a value equal to ADS_RIGHT_DS_SELF (line 176).

- The *ACE ObjectType* property has a GUID number corresponding to the "Add/Remove self as member" Extended Right (line 184). Check Table 4.17 to find the Extended Right GUID number with its corresponding display name.

When the *ACE AccessMask* property has a value coming from a combination of the ADS_RIGHT_DS_CREATE_CHILD and ADS_RIGHT_DS_DELETE_CHILD flags, the *ACE ObjectType* property contains a GUID number, but it does not refer to an Extended Right. In this case, the GUID number refers to the **schemaIDGUID** of an Active Directory **class-Schema** object and defines a permission that grants or denies a trustee the right to create or delete objects of the referred class type. The dashed line in Figure 4.27 represents this link. Figure 4.28 shows an example of such a right on the "CN=Users" container.

If we decipher the ACE, we obtain the following result:

```
 1:  C:\>WMIManageSD.Wsf /ADObject:"CN=Users,DC=LissWare,DC=Net" /Decipher+ /ADSI+
 2:  Microsoft (R) Windows Script Host Version 5.6
 3:  Copyright (C) Microsoft Corporation 1996-2001. All rights reserved.
 4:
 5:  Reading AD object security descriptor via ADSI from 'LDAP://CN=Users,DC=LissWare,DC=Net'.
 6:
 7:  +- ADSI Security Descriptor ----------------------------------------------------------
 8:  | Owner: ............................. LISSWARENET\Domain Admins
 9:  | Group: ............................. LISSWARENET\Domain Admins
10:  | Revision: .......................... 1
11:  | Control: ........................... &h8C14
..:
17:  |+- ADSI DiscretionaryAcl -----------------------------------------------------------
18:  ||+- ADSI ACE -----------------------------------------------------------------------
..:
29:  ||+---------------------------------------------------------------------------------
...:
105: ||+- ADSI ACE -----------------------------------------------------------------------
106: ||| AccessMask: ........................ &h3
107:                                          ADS_RIGHT_DS_CREATE_CHILD
108:                                          ADS_RIGHT_DS_DELETE_CHILD
109: ||| AceFlags: .......................... &h2
110:                                          ADS_ACEFLAG_CONTAINER_INHERIT_ACE
111:                                          ADS_ACEFLAG_VALID_INHERIT_FLAGS
112: ||| AceType: ........................... &h5
113:                                          ADS_ACETYPE_ACCESS_ALLOWED_OBJECT
114: ||| AceFlagType: ....................... &h1
115:                                          ADS_FLAG_OBJECT_TYPE_PRESENT
116: ||| ObjectType: ........................ {35BE884C-A982-11D2-A9FF-00C04F8EEDD8}
117: ||| Trustee: ........................... LISSWARENET\Alain.Lissoir
118: ||+---------------------------------------------------------------------------------
...:
437: |+----------------------------------------------------------------------------------
438: +-----------------------------------------------------------------------------------
```

Figure 4.28
The ACE ObjectType property used to grant or deny the creation or deletion of objects from a particular class.

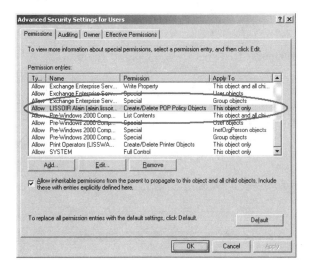

From line 105 through 118, the right "Create/Delete POP Policy Objects" is granted to trustee "Alain.Lissoir" as:

- The *ACE Type* has a value equal to ADS_ACETYPE_ACCESS_ALLOWED_OBJECT (line 113).

- The *ACE AccessMask* has a value equal to ADS_RIGHT_DS_CREATE_CHILD + ADS_RIGHT_DS_DELETE_CHILD (lines 107 and 108).

- The *ACE ObjectType* property has a GUID number corresponding to the **schemaIDGUID** of a **classSchema** object, which is the **msExch-ProtocolCfgPOPPolicy** object class (line 116). Check Table 4.18 to find the **schemaIDGUID** GUID number and determine the corresponding Active Directory class.

Because *ACE ObjectType* deciphering logic could be confusing, Table 4.19 summarizes the logic to follow to decipher this property.

The table must be read from left to right, column by column. For instance, it should be read as follows:

When the *ACE Type* property contains one of the values listed below ... (column 1)

`ADS_ACETYPE_ACCESS_ALLOWED_OBJECT`

`ADS_ACETYPE_ACCESS_DENIED_OBJECT`

`ADS_ACETYPE_SYSTEM_AUDIT_OBJECT`

... and if the "ACE AccessMask" property contains ... (column 2)

`ADS_RIGHT_DS_READ_PROP  (0x10)`

... then is that an Extended Right? (column 3)

Yes!

In such a case, the GUID number in the *ACE ObjectType* value refers ... (column 4)

> *the GUID number from the **rightsGUID** attribute of the **controlAccessRight** object,*

> *... which contains a **validAccesses** value of ... (column 5)*

`ADS_RIGHT_DS_READ_PROP Or ADS_RIGHT_DS_WRITE_PROP (0x30)`

Table 4.18   *The schemaIDGUID GUID Number with iTs Class Names*

Display Name	Object Class	schemaIDGUID
* objects	msExchDomainContentConfig	{ab3a1ad1-1df5-11d3-aa5e-00c04f8eedd8}
account objects	account	{2628a46a-a6ad-4ae0-b854-2b12d9fe6f9e}
aCSPolicy objects	aCSPolicy	{7f561288-5301-11d1-a9c5-0000f80367c1}
aCSResourceLimits objects	aCSResourceLimits	{2e899b04-2834-11d3-91d4-0000f87a57d4}
aCSSubnet objects	aCSSubnet	{7f561289-5301-11d1-a9c5-0000f80367c1}
Active Directory Service objects	nTDSService	{19195a5f-6da0-11d0-afd3-00c04fd930c9}
ADC Connection Agreement objects	msExchConnectionAgreement	{ee64c93a-a980-11d2-a9ff-00c04f8eedd8}
ADC Schema Map Policy objects	msExchSchemaMapPolicy	{348af8f2-a982-11d2-a9ff-00c04f8eedd8}
ADC Service objects	msExchActiveDirectoryConnector	{e605672c-a980-11d2-a9ff-00c04f8eedd8}
Address List objects	addressBookContainer	{3e74f60f-3e73-11d1-a9c0-0000f80367c1}
Address Template objects	addressTemplate	{5fd4250a-1262-11d0-a060-00aa006c33ed}
Address Type objects	addrType	{a8df74ab-c5ea-11d1-bbcb-0080c76670c0}
Addressing Policy objects	msExchAddressingPolicy	{e7211f02-a980-11d2-a9ff-00c04f8eedd8}
Administrative Group objects	msExchAdminGroup	{e768a58e-a980-11d2-a9ff-00c04f8eedd8}
Administrative Groups objects	msExchAdminGroupContainer	{e7a44058-a980-11d2-a9ff-00c04f8eedd8}
Administrative Role objects	msExchAdminRole	{e7f2edf2-a980-11d2-a9ff-00c04f8eedd8}
Advanced Security objects	msExchAdvancedSecurityContainer	{8cc8fb0e-b09e-11d2-aa06-00c04f8eedd8}
applicationEntity objects	applicationEntity	{3fdfee4f-47f4-11d1-a9c3-0000f80367c1}
applicationProcess objects	applicationProcess	{5fd4250b-1262-11d0-a060-00aa006c33ed}
applicationSettings objects	applicationSettings	{f780acc1-56f0-11d1-a9c6-0000f80367c1}
applicationSiteSettings objects	applicationSiteSettings	{19195a5c-6da0-11d0-afd3-00c04fd930c9}
applicationVersion objects	applicationVersion	{ddc790ac-af4d-442a-8f0f-a1d4caa7dd92}
builtinDomain objects	builtinDomain	{bf967a81-0de6-11d0-a285-00aa003049e2}
categoryRegistration objects	categoryRegistration	{7d6c0e9d-7e20-11d0-afd6-00c04fd930c9}
cc:Mail Connector objects	msExchccMailConnector	{e85710b6-a980-11d2-a9ff-00c04f8eedd8}
Certificate Template objects	pKICertificateTemplate	{e5209ca2-3bba-11d2-90cc-00c04fd91ab1}
Certification Authority objects	certificationAuthority	{3fdfee50-47f4-11d1-a9c3-0000f80367c1}
Chat Network objects	msExchChatNetwork	{e934cb68-a980-11d2-a9ff-00c04f8eedd8}
Chat Protocol objects	msExchChatProtocol	{e9621816-a980-11d2-a9ff-00c04f8eedd8}
classRegistration objects	classRegistration	{bf967a82-0de6-11d0-a285-00aa003049e2}
classStore objects	classStore	{bf967a84-0de6-11d0-a285-00aa003049e2}
comConnectionPoint objects	comConnectionPoint	{bf967a85-0de6-11d0-a285-00aa003049e2}
Computer objects	computer	{bf967a86-0de6-11d0-a285-00aa003049e2}
Computer Policy objects	msExchComputerPolicy	{ed2c752c-a980-11d2-a9ff-00c04f8eedd8}
Conference Site objects	msExchConferenceSite	{eddce330-a980-11d2-a9ff-00c04f8eedd8}
Conference Sites objects	msExchConferenceContainer	{ed7fe77a-a980-11d2-a9ff-00c04f8eedd8}
configuration objects	configuration	{bf967a87-0de6-11d0-a285-00aa003049e2}
Connection objects	nTDSConnection	{19195a60-6da0-11d0-afd3-00c04fd930c9}
connectionPoint objects	connectionPoint	{5cb41ecf-0e4c-11d0-a286-00aa003049e2}
Connections objects	msExchConnectors	{eee325dc-a980-11d2-a9ff-00c04f8eedd8}
Contact objects	contact	{5cb41ed0-0e4c-11d0-a286-00aa003049e2}
Container objects	container	{bf967a8b-0de6-11d0-a285-00aa003049e2}
country objects	country	{bf967a8c-0de6-11d0-a285-00aa003049e2}
cRLDistributionPoint objects	cRLDistributionPoint	{167758ca-47f3-11d1-a9c3-0000f80367c1}
crossRef objects	crossRef	{bf967a8d-0de6-11d0-a285-00aa003049e2}
crossRefContainer objects	crossRefContainer	{ef9e60e0-56f7-11d1-a9c6-0000f80367c1}
Data Conference Server (T.120 MCU) objects	msExchMCU	{038680ec-a981-11d2-a9ff-00c04f8eedd8}
Data Conference Technology Provider (T.120 MCU) objects	msExchMCUContainer	{03aa4432-a981-11d2-a9ff-00c04f8eedd8}
device objects	device	{bf967a8e-0de6-11d0-a285-00aa003049e2}
dfsConfiguration objects	dfsConfiguration	{8447f9f2-1027-11d0-a05f-00aa006c33ed}
dHCPClass objects	dHCPClass	{963d2756-48be-11d1-a9c3-0000f80367c1}
Directory objects	dSA	{3fdfee52-47f4-11d1-a9c3-0000f80367c1}
Directory Replication Connector objects	msExchReplicationConnector	{99f58682-12e8-11d3-aa58-00c04f8eedd8}
Directory Synchronization objects	localDXA	{a8df74b5-c5ea-11d1-bbcb-0080c76670c0}
Directory Synchronization Requestor objects	dXRequestor	{a8df74ae-c5ea-11d1-bbcb-0080c76670c0}
Directory Synchronization Server Connector objects	dXServerConn	{a8df74af-c5ea-11d1-bbcb-0080c76670c0}
Directory Synchronization Site Server objects	dXASiteServer	{a8df74b0-c5ea-11d1-bbcb-0080c76670c0}
Display Template objects	displayTemplate	{5fd4250c-1262-11d0-a060-00aa006c33ed}
displaySpecifier objects	displaySpecifier	{e0fa1e8a-9b45-11d0-afdd-00c04fd930c9}
dnsNode objects	dnsNode	{e0fa1e8c-9b45-11d0-afdd-00c04fd930c9}
dnsZone objects	dnsZone	{e0fa1e8b-9b45-11d0-afdd-00c04fd930c9}
document objects	document	{39bad96d-c2d6-4baf-88ab-7e4207600117}
documentSeries objects	documentSeries	{7a2be07c-302f-4b96-bc90-0795d66885f8}
Domain Controller Settings objects	nTDSDSA	{f0f8ffab-1191-11d0-a060-00aa006c33ed}
domain objects	domain	{19195a5a-6da0-11d0-afd3-00c04fd930c9}
Domain objects	domainDNS	{19195a5b-6da0-11d0-afd3-00c04fd930c9}
Domain Policy objects	domainPolicy	{bf967a99-0de6-11d0-a285-00aa003049e2}
domainRelatedObject objects	domainRelatedObject	{8bfd2d3d-efda-4549-852c-f85e137aedc6}
dSUISettings objects	dSUISettings	{09b10f14-6f93-11d2-9905-0000f87a57d4}

Table 4.18   *The schemaIDGUID GUID Number with iTs Class Names (continued)*

Display Name	Object Class	schemaIDGUID
Dynamic RAS Connector objects	rASX400Link	{a8df74d4-c5ea-11d1-bbcb-0080c76670c0}
dynamicObject objects	dynamicObject	{66d51249-3355-4c1f-b24e-81f252aca23b}
Encryption Configuration objects	encryptionCfg	{a8df74b1-c5ea-11d1-bbcb-0080c76670c0}
Exchange Add-In objects	addIn	{a8df74aa-c5ea-11d1-bbcb-0080c76670c0}
Exchange Admin Extension objects	adminExtension	{a8df74ac-c5ea-11d1-bbcb-0080c76670c0}
Exchange Configuration Container objects	msExchConfigurationContainer	{d03d6858-06f4-11d2-aa53-00c04fd7d83a}
Exchange Container objects	msExchContainer	{006c91da-a981-11d2-a9ff-00c04f8eedd8}
Exchange Organization objects	msExchOrganizationContainer	{366a319c-a982-11d2-a9ff-00c04f8eedd8}
Exchange Policies objects	msExchPoliciesContainer	{3630f92c-a982-11d2-a9ff-00c04f8eedd8}
Exchange Protocols objects	msExchProtocolCfgProtocolContainer	{90f2b634-b09e-11d2-aa06-00c04f8eedd8}
Exchange Server objects	msExchExchangeServer	{01a9aa9c-a981-11d2-a9ff-00c04f8eedd8}
Exchange Server Policy objects	msExchExchangeServerPolicy	{e497942f-1d42-11d3-aa5e-00c04f8eedd8}
Exchange Servers objects	msExchServersContainer	{346e5cba-a982-11d2-a9ff-00c04f8eedd8}
Extended Right objects	controlAccessRight	{8297931e-86d3-11d0-afda-00c04fd930c9}
fileLinkTracking objects	fileLinkTracking	{dd712229-10e4-11d0-a05f-00aa006c33ed}
fileLinkTrackingEntry objects	fileLinkTrackingEntry	{8e4eb2ed-4712-11d0-a1a0-00c04fd930c9}
Foreign Security Principal objects	foreignSecurityPrincipal	{89e31c12-8530-11d0-afda-00c04fd930c9}
friendlyCountry objects	friendlyCountry	{c498f152-dc6b-474a-9f52-7cdba3d7d351}
FRS Member objects	nTFRSMember	{2a132586-9373-11d1-aebc-0000f80367c1}
FRS Replica Set objects	nTFRSReplicaSet	{5245803a-ca6a-11d0-afff-0000f80367c1}
FRS Settings objects	nTFRSSettings	{f780acc2-56f0-11d1-a9c6-0000f80367c1}
FRS Subscriber objects	nTFRSSubscriber	{2a132588-9373-11d1-aebc-0000f80367c1}
FRS Subscriptions objects	nTFRSSubscriptions	{2a132587-9373-11d1-aebc-0000f80367c1}
fTDfs objects	fTDfs	{8447f9f3-1027-11d0-a05f-00aa006c33ed}
Gateway objects	mailGateway	{a8df74b7-c5ea-11d1-bbcb-0080c76670c0}
Group objects	group	{bf967a9c-0de6-11d0-a285-00aa003049e2}
groupOfNames objects	groupOfNames	{bf967a9d-0de6-11d0-a285-00aa003049e2}
groupOfUniqueNames objects	groupOfUniqueNames	{0310a911-93a3-4e21-a7a3-55d85ab2c48b}
groupPolicyContainer objects	groupPolicyContainer	{f30e3bc2-9ff0-11d1-b603-0000f80367c1}
GroupWise Connector objects	msExchGroupWiseConnector	{91eaaac4-b09e-11d2-aa06-00c04f8eedd8}
HTTP Protocol objects	msExchProtocolCfgHTTPContainer	{9432cae6-b09e-11d2-aa06-00c04f8eedd8}
HTTP Virtual Directory objects	msExchProtocolCfgHTTPVirtualDirectory	{8c3c5050-b09e-11d2-aa06-00c04f8eedd8}
HTTP Virtual Server objects	protocolCfgHTTPServer	{a8df74c2-c5ea-11d1-bbcb-0080c76670c0}
IMAP Policy objects	msExchProtocolCfgIMAPPolicy	{35f7c0bc-a982-11d2-a9ff-00c04f8eedd8}
IMAP Protocol objects	msExchProtocolCfgIMAPContainer	{93da93e4-b09e-11d2-aa06-00c04f8eedd8}
IMAP Sessions objects	msExchProtocolCfgIMAPSessions	{99f58672-12e8-11d3-aa58-00c04f8eedd8}
IMAP Virtual Server objects	protocolCfgIMAPServer	{a8df74c5-c5ea-11d1-bbcb-0080c76670c0}
indexServerCatalog objects	indexServerCatalog	{7bfdcb8a-4807-11d1-a9c3-0000f80367c1}
InetOrgPerson objects	inetOrgPerson	{4828cc14-1437-45bc-9b07-ad6f015e5f28}
Information Store objects	msExchInformationStore	{031b371a-a981-11d2-a9ff-00c04f8eedd8}
infrastructureUpdate objects	infrastructureUpdate	{2df90d89-009f-11d2-aa4c-00c04fd7d83a}
Instant Messaging Global Settings objects	msExchIMGlobalSettingsContainer	{9f116eb8-284e-11d3-aa68-00c04f8eedd8}
Instant Messaging Protocol objects	msExchProtocolCfgIMContainer	{9f116ea3-284e-11d3-aa68-00c04f8eedd8}
Instant Messaging Virtual Server objects	msExchProtocolCfgIMVirtualServer	{9f116eb4-284e-11d3-aa68-00c04f8eedd8}
IntelliMirror Group objects	intellimirrorGroup	{07383086-91df-11d1-aebc-0000f80367c1}
IntelliMirror Service objects	intellimirrorSCP	{07383085-91df-11d1-aebc-0000f80367c1}
Internet Message Formats objects	msExchContentConfigContainer	{ab3a1acc-1df5-11d3-aa5e-00c04f8eedd8}
Inter-Site Transport objects	interSiteTransport	{26d97376-6070-11d1-a9c6-0000f80367c1}
Inter-Site Transports Container objects	interSiteTransportContainer	{26d97375-6070-11d1-a9c6-0000f80367c1}
ipsecBase objects	ipsecBase	{b40ff825-427a-11d1-a9c2-0000f80367c1}
ipsecFilter objects	ipsecFilter	{b40ff826-427a-11d1-a9c2-0000f80367c1}
ipsecISAKMPPolicy objects	ipsecISAKMPPolicy	{b40ff828-427a-11d1-a9c2-0000f80367c1}
ipsecNegotiationPolicy objects	ipsecNegotiationPolicy	{b40ff827-427a-11d1-a9c2-0000f80367c1}
ipsecNFA objects	ipsecNFA	{b40ff829-427a-11d1-a9c2-0000f80367c1}
ipsecPolicy objects	ipsecPolicy	{b7b13121-b82e-11d0-afee-0000f80367c1}
Key Management Server objects	msExchKeyManagementServer	{8ce334ec-b09e-11d2-aa06-00c04f8eedd8}
leaf objects	leaf	{bf967a9e-0de6-11d0-a285-00aa003049e2}
Licensing Site Settings objects	licensingSiteSettings	{1be8f17d-a9ff-11d0-afe2-00c04fd930c9}
linkTrackObjectMoveTable objects	linkTrackObjectMoveTable	{ddac0cf5-af8f-11d0-afeb-00c04fd930c9}
linkTrackOMTEntry objects	linkTrackOMTEntry	{ddac0cf7-af8f-11d0-afeb-00c04fd930c9}
linkTrackVolEntry objects	linkTrackVolEntry	{ddac0cf6-af8f-11d0-afeb-00c04fd930c9}
linkTrackVolumeTable objects	linkTrackVolumeTable	{ddac0cf4-af8f-11d0-afeb-00c04fd930c9}
locality objects	locality	{bf967aa0-0de6-11d0-a285-00aa003049e2}
lostAndFound objects	lostAndFound	{52ab8671-5709-11d1-a9c6-0000f80367c1}
Mail Recipient objects	mailRecipient	{bf967aa1-0de6-11d0-a285-00aa003049e2}
meeting objects	meeting	{11b6cc94-48c4-11d1-a9c3-0000f80367c1}
Message Delivery Configuration objects	msExchMessageDeliveryConfig	{ab3a1ad7-1df5-11d3-aa5e-00c04f8eedd8}
Message Gateway for cc:Mail objects	mailConnector	{a8df74b6-c5ea-11d1-bbcb-0080c76670c0}
Message Transfer Agent objects	mTA	{a8df74a7-c5ea-11d1-bbcb-0080c76670c0}

Table 4.18   *The schemaIDGUID GUID Number with iTs Class Names (continued)*

Display Name	Object Class	schemaIDGUID
mHSMonitoringConfig objects	mHSMonitoringConfig	{a8df74bb-c5ea-11d1-bbcb-0080c76670c0}
Microsoft Exchange System Objects objects	msExchSystemObjectsContainer	{0bffa04c-7d8e-44cd-968a-b2cac11d17e1}
Monitoring Link Configuration objects	mHSLinkMonitoringConfig	{a8df74b9-c5ea-11d1-bbcb-0080c76670c0}
Monitoring Server Configuration objects	mHSServerMonitoringConfig	{a8df74bd-c5ea-11d1-bbcb-0080c76670c0}
msCOM-Partition objects	msCOM-Partition	{c9010e74-4e58-49f7-8a89-5e3e2340fcf8}
msCOM-PartitionSet objects	msCOM-PartitionSet	{250464ab-c417-497a-975a-9e0d459a7ca1}
msDS-App-Configuration objects	msDS-App-Configuration	{90df3c3e-1854-4455-a5d7-cad40d56657a}
msDS-AppData objects	msDS-AppData	{9e67d761-e327-4d55-bc95-682f875e2f8e}
msDS-AzAdminManager objects	msDS-AzAdminManager	{cfee1051-5f28-4bae-a863-5d0cc18a8ed1}
msDS-AzApplication objects	msDS-AzApplication	{ddf8de9b-cba5-4e12-842e-28d8b66f75ec}
msDS-AzOperation objects	msDS-AzOperation	{860abe37-9a9b-4fa4-b3d2-b8ace5df9ec5}
msDS-AzRole objects	msDS-AzRole	{8213eac9-9d55-44dc-925c-e9a52b927644}
msDS-AzScope objects	msDS-AzScope	{4feae054-ce55-47bb-860e-5b12063a51de}
msDS-AzTask objects	msDS-AzTask	{1ed3a473-9b1b-418a-bfa0-3a37b95a5306}
msExchAddressListServiceContainer objects	msExchAddressListServiceContainer	{b1fce95a-1d44-11d3-aa5e-00c04f8eedd8}
msExchBaseClass objects	msExchBaseClass	{d8782c34-46ca-11d3-aa72-00c04f8eedd8}
msExchCalendarConnector objects	msExchCalendarConnector	{922180da-b09e-11d2-aa06-00c04f8eedd8}
msExchCertificateInformation objects	msExchCertificateInformation	{e8977034-a980-11d2-a9ff-00c04f8eedd8}
msExchChatBan objects	msExchChatBan	{e8d0a8a4-a980-11d2-a9ff-00c04f8eedd8}
msExchChatChannel objects	msExchChatChannel	{e902ba06-a980-11d2-a9ff-00c04f8eedd8}
msExchChatUserClass objects	msExchChatUserClass	{e9a0153a-a980-11d2-a9ff-00c04f8eedd8}
msExchConnector objects	msExchConnector	{89652316-b09e-11d2-aa06-00c04f8eedd8}
msExchCTP objects	msExchCTP	{00aa8efe-a981-11d2-a9ff-00c04f8eedd8}
msExchCustomAttributes objects	msExchCustomAttributes	{00e629c8-a981-11d2-a9ff-00c04f8eedd8}
msExchDynamicDistributionList objects	msExchDynamicDistributionList	{018849b0-a981-11d2-a9ff-00c04f8eedd8}
msExchGenericPolicy objects	msExchGenericPolicy	{e32977cd-1d31-11d3-aa5e-00c04f8eedd8}
msExchGenericPolicyContainer objects	msExchGenericPolicyContainer	{e32977c3-1d31-11d3-aa5e-00c04f8eedd8}
msExchIMFirewall objects	msExchIMFirewall	{9f116ebe-284e-11d3-aa68-00c04f8eedd8}
msExchIMRecipient objects	msExchIMRecipient	{028502f4-a981-11d2-a9ff-00c04f8eedd8}
msExchMailboxManagerPolicy objects	msExchMailboxManagerPolicy	{36f94fcc-ebbb-4a32-b721-1cae42b2dbab}
msExchMailStorage objects	msExchMailStorage	{03652000-a981-11d2-a9ff-00c04f8eedd8}
msExchMDB objects	msExchMDB	{03d069d2-a981-11d2-a9ff-00c04f8eedd8}
msExchMonitorsContainer objects	msExchMonitorsContainer	{03f68f72-a981-11d2-a9ff-00c04f8eedd8}
msExchMultiMediaUser objects	msExchMultiMediaUser	{1529cf7a-2fdb-11d3-aa6d-00c04f8eedd8}
msExchOVVMConnector objects	msExchOVVMConnector	{91ce0e8c-b09e-11d2-aa06-00c04f8eedd8}
msExchPrivateMDBProxy objects	msExchPrivateMDBProxy	{b8d47e54-4b78-11d3-aa75-00c04f8eedd8}
msExchProtocolCfgHTTPFilter objects	msExchProtocolCfgHTTPFilter	{8c7588c0-b09e-11d2-aa06-00c04f8eedd8}
msExchProtocolCfgHTTPFilters objects	msExchProtocolCfgHTTPFilters	{8c58ec88-b09e-11d2-aa06-00c04f8eedd8}
msExchProtocolCfgIM objects	msExchProtocolCfgIM	{9f116ea7-284e-11d3-aa68-00c04f8eedd8}
msExchProtocolCfgSharedContainer objects	msExchProtocolCfgSharedContainer	{939ef91a-b09e-11d2-aa06-00c04f8eedd8}
msExchProtocolCfgSMTPIPAddress objects	msExchProtocolCfgSMTPIPAddress	{8b7b31d6-b09e-11d2-aa06-00c04f8eedd8}
msExchProtocolCfgSMTPIPAddressContainer objects	msExchProtocolCfgSMTPIPAddressContainer	{8b2c843c-b09e-11d2-aa06-00c04f8eedd8}
msExchPseudoPF objects	msExchPseudoPF	{cec4472b-22ae-11d3-aa62-00c04f8eedd8}
msExchPseudoPFAdmin objects	msExchPseudoPFAdmin	{9ae2fa1b-22b0-11d3-aa62-00c04f8eedd8}
msExchPublicFolderTreeContainer objects	msExchPublicFolderTreeContainer	{3582ed82-a982-11d2-a9ff-00c04f8eedd8}
msExchSNADSConnector objects	msExchSNADSConnector	{91b17254-b09e-11d2-aa06-00c04f8eedd8}
msieee80211-Policy objects	msieee80211-Policy	{7b9a2d92-b7eb-4382-9772-c3e0f9baaf94}
MSMail Connector objects	mSMailConnector	{a8df74be-c5ea-11d1-bbcb-0080c76670c0}
MSMQ Configuration objects	mSMQConfiguration	{9a0dc344-c100-11d1-bbc5-0080c76670c0}
MSMQ Enterprise objects	mSMQEnterpriseSettings	{9a0dc345-c100-11d1-bbc5-0080c76670c0}
MSMQ Group objects	msMQ-Group	{46b27aac-aafa-4ffb-b773-e5bf621ee87b}
MSMQ Queue Alias objects	msMQ-Custom-Recipient	{876d6817-35cc-436c-acea-5ef7174dd9be}
MSMQ Queue objects	mSMQQueue	{9a0dc343-c100-11d1-bbc5-0080c76670c0}
MSMQ Routing Link objects	mSMQSiteLink	{9a0dc346-c100-11d1-bbc5-0080c76670c0}
MSMQ Settings objects	mSMQSettings	{9a0dc347-c100-11d1-bbc5-0080c76670c0}
MSMQ Upgraded User objects	mSMQMigratedUser	{50776997-3c3d-11d2-90cc-00c04f91ab1}
msPKI-Enterprise-Oid objects	msPKI-Enterprise-Oid	{37cfd85c-6719-4ad8-8f9e-8678ba627563}
msPKI-Key-Recovery-Agent objects	msPKI-Key-Recovery-Agent	{26ccf238-a08e-4b86-9a82-a8c9ac7ee5cb}
msPKI-PrivateKeyRecoveryAgent objects	msPKI-PrivateKeyRecoveryAgent	{1562a632-44b9-4a7e-a2d3-e426c96a3acc}
mS-SQL-OLAPCube objects	mS-SQL-OLAPCube	{09f0506a-cd28-11d2-9993-0000f87a57d4}
mS-SQL-OLAPDatabase objects	mS-SQL-OLAPDatabase	{20af031a-ccef-11d2-9993-0000f87a57d4}
mS-SQL-OLAPServer objects	mS-SQL-OLAPServer	{0c7e18ea-ccef-11d2-9993-0000f87a57d4}
mS-SQL-SQLDatabase objects	mS-SQL-SQLDatabase	{1d08694a-ccef-11d2-9993-0000f87a57d4}
mS-SQL-SQLPublication objects	mS-SQL-SQLPublication	{17c2f64e-ccef-11d2-9993-0000f87a57d4}
mS-SQL-SQLRepository objects	mS-SQL-SQLRepository	{11d43c5c-ccef-11d2-9993-0000f87a57d4}
mS-SQL-SQLServer objects	mS-SQL-SQLServer	{05f6c878-ccef-11d2-9993-0000f87a57d4}
msTAPI-RtConference objects	msTAPI-RtConference	{ca7b9735-4b2a-4e49-89c3-99025334dc94}
msTAPI-RtPerson objects	msTAPI-RtPerson	{53ea1cb5-b704-4df9-818f-5cb4ec86cac1}
msWMI-IntRangeParam objects	msWMI-IntRangeParam	{50ca5d7d-5c8b-4ef3-b9df-5b66d491e526}

Table 4.18 *The schemaIDGUID GUID Number with iTs Class Names (continued)*

Display Name	Object Class	schemaIDGUID
msWMI-IntSetParam objects	msWMI-IntSetParam	{292f0d9a-cf76-42b0-841f-b650f331df62}
msWMI-MergeablePolicyTemplate objects	msWMI-MergeablePolicyTemplate	{07502414-fdca-4851-b04a-13645b11d226}
msWMI-ObjectEncoding objects	msWMI-ObjectEncoding	{55dd81c9-c312-41f9-a84d-c6adbdf1e8e1}
msWMI-PolicyTemplate objects	msWMI-PolicyTemplate	{e2bc80f1-244a-4d59-acc6-ca5c4f82e6e1}
msWMI-PolicyType objects	msWMI-PolicyType	{595b2613-4109-4e77-9013-a3bb4ef277c7}
msWMI-RangeParam objects	msWMI-RangeParam	{45fb5a57-5018-4d0f-9056-997c8c9122d9}
msWMI-RealRangeParam objects	msWMI-RealRangeParam	{6afe8fe2-70bc-4cce-b166-a96f7359c514}
msWMI-Rule objects	msWMI-Rule	{3c7e6f83-dd0e-481b-a0c2-74cd96ef2a66}
msWMI-ShadowObject objects	msWMI-ShadowObject	{f1e44bdf-8dd3-4235-9c86-f91f31f5b569}
msWMI-SimplePolicyTemplate objects	msWMI-SimplePolicyTemplate	{6cc8b2b5-12df-44f6-8307-e74f5cdee369}
msWMI-Som objects	msWMI-Som	{ab857078-0142-4406-945b-34c9b6b13372}
msWMI-StringSetParam objects	msWMI-StringSetParam	{0bc579a2-1da7-4cea-b699-807f3b9d63a4}
msWMI-UintRangeParam objects	msWMI-UintRangeParam	{d9a799b2-cef3-48b3-b5ad-fb85f8dd3214}
msWMI-UintSetParam objects	msWMI-UintSetParam	{8f4beb31-4e19-46f5-932e-5fa03c339b1d}
msWMI-UnknownRangeParam objects	msWMI-UnknownRangeParam	{b82ac26b-c6db-4098-92c6-49c18a3336e1}
msWMI-WMIGPO objects	msWMI-WMIGPO	{05630000-3927-4ede-bf27-ca91f275c26f}
NNTP Protocol objects	msExchProtocolCfgNNTPContainer	{94162eae-b09e-11d2-aa06-00c04f8eedd8}
NNTP Virtual Server objects	protocolCfgNNTPServer	{a8df74cb-c5ea-11d1-bbcb-0080c76670c0}
Notes Connector objects	msExchNotesConnector	{04c85e62-a981-11d2-a9ff-00c04f8eedd8}
Offline Address List objects	msExchOAB	{3686cdd4-a982-11d2-a9ff-00c04f8eedd8}
organization objects	organization	{bf967aa3-0de6-11d0-a285-00aa003049e2}
Organizational Unit objects	organizationalUnit	{bf967aa5-0de6-11d0-a285-00aa003049e2}
organizationalPerson objects	organizationalPerson	{bf967aa4-0de6-11d0-a285-00aa003049e2}
organizationalRole objects	organizationalRole	{a8df74bf-c5ea-11d1-bbcb-0080c76670c0}
packageRegistration objects	packageRegistration	{bf967aa6-0de6-11d0-a285-00aa003049e2}
person objects	person	{bf967aa7-0de6-11d0-a285-00aa003049e2}
physicalLocation objects	physicalLocation	{b7b13122-b82e-11d0-afee-0000f80367c1}
pKIEnrollmentService objects	pKIEnrollmentService	{ee4aa692-3bba-11d2-90cc-00c04fd91ab1}
POP Policy objects	msExchProtocolCfgPOPPolicy	{35be884c-a982-11d2-a9ff-00c04f8eedd8}
POP Protocol objects	msExchProtocolCfgPOPContainer	{93f99276-b09e-11d2-aa06-00c04f8eedd8}
POP Sessions objects	msExchProtocolCfgPOPSessions	{99f58676-12e8-11d3-aa58-00c04f8eedd8}
POP Virtual Server objects	protocolCfgPOPServer	{a8df74ce-c5ea-11d1-bbcb-0080c76670c0}
Printer objects	printQueue	{bf967aa8-0de6-11d0-a285-00aa003049e2}
Private Information Store objects	msExchPrivateMDB	{36145cf4-a982-11d2-a9ff-00c04f8eedd8}
Private Information Store Policy objects	msExchPrivateMDBPolicy	{35db2484-a982-11d2-a9ff-00c04f8eedd8}
protocolCfg objects	protocolCfg	{a8df74c0-c5ea-11d1-bbcb-0080c76670c0}
protocolCfgHTTP objects	protocolCfgHTTP	{a8df74c1-c5ea-11d1-bbcb-0080c76670c0}
protocolCfgIMAP objects	protocolCfgIMAP	{a8df74c4-c5ea-11d1-bbcb-0080c76670c0}
protocolCfgLDAP objects	protocolCfgLDAP	{a8df74c7-c5ea-11d1-bbcb-0080c76670c0}
protocolCfgNNTP objects	protocolCfgNNTP	{a8df74ca-c5ea-11d1-bbcb-0080c76670c0}
protocolCfgPOP objects	protocolCfgPOP	{a8df74cd-c5ea-11d1-bbcb-0080c76670c0}
protocolCfgShared objects	protocolCfgShared	{a8df74d0-c5ea-11d1-bbcb-0080c76670c0}
protocolCfgSMTP objects	protocolCfgSMTP	{33f98980-a982-11d2-a9ff-00c04f8eedd8}
Public Folder objects	publicFolder	{f0f8ffac-1191-11d0-a060-00aa006c33ed}
Public Folder Top Level Hierarchy objects	msExchPFTree	{364d9564-a982-11d2-a9ff-00c04f8eedd8}
Public Information Store objects	msExchPublicMDB	{3568b3a4-a982-11d2-a9ff-00c04f8eedd8}
Public Information Store Policy objects	msExchPublicMDBPolicy	{354c176c-a982-11d2-a9ff-00c04f8eedd8}
Query Policy objects	queryPolicy	{83cc7075-cca7-11d0-afff-0000f80367c1}
RAS MTA Transport Stack objects	rASStack	{a8df74d3-c5ea-11d1-bbcb-0080c76670c0}
Recipient Policies objects	msExchRecipientPolicyContainer	{e32977d2-1d31-11d3-aa5e-00c04f8eedd8}
Recipient Policy objects	msExchRecipientPolicy	{e32977d8-1d31-11d3-aa5e-00c04f8eedd8}
Recipient Update Service objects	msExchAddressListService	{e6a2c260-a980-11d2-a9ff-00c04f8eedd8}
Remote Storage Service objects	remoteStorageServicePoint	{2a39c5bd-8960-11d1-aebc-0000f80367c1}
remoteDXA objects	remoteDXA	{a8df74d5-c5ea-11d1-bbcb-0080c76670c0}
remoteMailRecipient objects	remoteMailRecipient	{bf967aa9-0de6-11d0-a285-00aa003049e2}
Replication Connectors objects	msExchReplicationConnectorContainer	{99f5867e-12e8-11d3-aa58-00c04f8eedd8}
residentialPerson objects	residentialPerson	{a8df74d6-c5ea-11d1-bbcb-0080c76670c0}
rFC822LocalPart objects	rFC822LocalPart	{b93e3a78-cbae-485e-a07b-5ef4ae505686}
rIDManager objects	rIDManager	{6617188d-8f3c-11d0-afda-00c04fd930c9}
rIDSet objects	rIDSet	{7bfdcb89-4807-11d1-a9c3-0000f80367c1}
room objects	room	{7860e5d2-c8b0-4cbb-bd45-d9455beb9206}
Routing Group Connector objects	msExchRoutingGroupConnector	{899e5b86-b09e-11d2-aa06-00c04f8eedd8}
Routing Group objects	msExchRoutingGroup	{35154156-a982-11d2-a9ff-00c04f8eedd8}
Routing Groups objects	msExchRoutingGroupContainer	{34de6b40-a982-11d2-a9ff-00c04f8eedd8}
RPC Services objects	rpcContainer	{80212842-4bdc-11d1-a9c4-0000f80367c1}
rpcEntry objects	rpcEntry	{bf967aac-0de6-11d0-a285-00aa003049e2}
rpcGroup objects	rpcGroup	{88611bdf-8cf4-11d0-afda-00c04fd930c9}
rpcProfile objects	rpcProfile	{88611be1-8cf4-11d0-afda-00c04fd930c9}
rpcProfileElement objects	rpcProfileElement	{f29653cf-7ad0-11d0-afd6-00c04fd930c9}

Table 4.18   *The schemaIDGUID GUID Number with iTs Class Names (continued)*

Display Name	Object Class	schemaIDGUID
rpcServer objects	rpcServer	{88611be0-8cf4-11d0-afda-00c04fd930c9}
rpcServerElement objects	rpcServerElement	{f29653d0-7ad0-11d0-afd6-00c04fd930c9}
rRASAdministrationConnectionPoint objects	rRASAdministrationConnectionPoint	{2a39c5be-8960-11d1-aebc-0000f80367c1}
rRASAdministrationDictionary objects	rRASAdministrationDictionary	{f39b98ae-938d-11d1-aebd-0000f80367c1}
samDomain objects	samDomain	{bf967a90-0de6-11d0-a285-00aa003049e2}
samDomainBase objects	samDomainBase	{bf967a91-0de6-11d0-a285-00aa003049e2}
samServer objects	samServer	{bf967aad-0de6-11d0-a285-00aa003049e2}
Schedule+ Free/Busy Connector objects	msExchSchedulePlusConnector	{b1fce946-1d44-11d3-aa5e-00c04f8eedd8}
Schema Attribute objects	attributeSchema	{bf967a80-0de6-11d0-a285-00aa003049e2}
Schema Container objects	dMD	{bf967a8f-0de6-11d0-a285-00aa003049e2}
Schema Object objects	classSchema	{bf967a83-0de6-11d0-a285-00aa003049e2}
secret objects	secret	{bf967aae-0de6-11d0-a285-00aa003049e2}
securityObject objects	securityObject	{bf967aaf-0de6-11d0-a285-00aa003049e2}
securityPrincipal objects	securityPrincipal	{bf967ab0-0de6-11d0-a285-00aa003049e2}
Server LDAP Protocol objects	protocolCfgLDAPServer	{a8df74c8-c5ea-11d1-bbcb-0080c76670c0}
Server objects	server	{bf967a92-0de6-11d0-a285-00aa003049e2}
Server Protocols objects	protocolCfgSharedServer	{a8df74d1-c5ea-11d1-bbcb-0080c76670c0}
Servers Container objects	serversContainer	{f780acc0-56f0-11d1-a9c6-0000f80367c1}
Service objects	serviceAdministrationPoint	{b7b13123-b82e-11d0-afee-0000f80367c1}
serviceClass objects	serviceClass	{bf967ab1-0de6-11d0-a285-00aa003049e2}
serviceConnectionPoint objects	serviceConnectionPoint	{28630ec1-41d5-11d1-a9c1-0000f80367c1}
serviceInstance objects	serviceInstance	{bf967ab2-0de6-11d0-a285-00aa003049e2}
Shared Folder objects	volume	{bf967abb-0de6-11d0-a285-00aa003049e2}
simpleSecurityObject objects	simpleSecurityObject	{5fe69b0b-e146-4f15-b0ab-c1e5d488e094}
Site Addressing objects	siteAddressing	{a8df74d9-c5ea-11d1-bbcb-0080c76670c0}
Site Connector objects	siteConnector	{a8df74da-c5ea-11d1-bbcb-0080c76670c0}
Site HTTP Protocol objects	protocolCfgHTTPSite	{a8df74c3-c5ea-11d1-bbcb-0080c76670c0}
Site IMAP Protocol objects	protocolCfgIMAPSite	{a8df74c6-c5ea-11d1-bbcb-0080c76670c0}
Site LDAP Protocol objects	protocolCfgLDAPSite	{a8df74c9-c5ea-11d1-bbcb-0080c76670c0}
Site Link Bridge objects	siteLinkBridge	{d50c2cdf-8951-11d1-aebc-0000f80367c1}
Site Link objects	siteLink	{d50c2cde-8951-11d1-aebc-0000f80367c1}
Site MTA Configuration objects	mTACfg	{a8df74a8-c5ea-11d1-bbcb-0080c76670c0}
Site NNTP Protocol objects	protocolCfgNNTPSite	{a8df74cc-c5ea-11d1-bbcb-0080c76670c0}
Site objects	site	{bf967ab3-0de6-11d0-a285-00aa003049e2}
Site POP Protocol objects	protocolCfgPOPSite	{a8df74cf-c5ea-11d1-bbcb-0080c76670c0}
Site Protocols objects	protocolCfgSharedSite	{a8df74d2-c5ea-11d1-bbcb-0080c76670c0}
Site Replication Service objects	msExchSiteReplicationService	{99f5867b-12e8-11d3-aa58-00c04f8eedd8}
Site Settings objects	nTDSSiteSettings	{19195a5d-6da0-11d0-afd3-00c04fd930c9}
Site SMTP Protocol objects	protocolCfgSMTPSite	{32f0e47a-a982-11d2-a9ff-00c04f8eedd8}
Sites Container objects	sitesContainer	{7a4117da-cd67-11d0-afff-0000f80367c1}
SMTP Connector objects	msExchRoutingSMTPConnector	{89baf7be-b09e-11d2-aa06-00c04f8eedd8}
SMTP Domain objects	protocolCfgSMTPDomain	{33d82894-a982-11d2-a9ff-00c04f8eedd8}
SMTP Domains objects	protocolCfgSMTPDomainContainer	{33bb8c5c-a982-11d2-a9ff-00c04f8eedd8}
SMTP Policy objects	msExchProtocolCfgSMTPPolicy	{359f89ba-a982-11d2-a9ff-00c04f8eedd8}
SMTP Protocol objects	msExchProtocolCfgSMTPContainer	{93bb9552-b09e-11d2-aa06-00c04f8eedd8}
SMTP Routing Sources objects	protocolCfgSMTPRoutingSources	{3397c916-a982-11d2-a9ff-00c04f8eedd8}
SMTP Sessions objects	protocolCfgSMTPSessions	{8ef628c6-b093-11d2-aa06-00c04f8eedd8}
SMTP Turf List objects	msExchSMTPTurfList	{0b836da5-3b20-11d3-aa6f-00c04f8eedd8}
SMTP Virtual Server objects	protocolCfgSMTPServer	{3378ca84-a982-11d2-a9ff-00c04f8eedd8}
Storage Group objects	msExchStorageGroup	{3435244a-a982-11d2-a9ff-00c04f8eedd8}
storage objects	storage	{bf967ab5-0de6-11d0-a285-00aa003049e2}
Subnet objects	subnet	{b7b13124-b82e-11d0-afee-0000f80367c1}
Subnets Container objects	subnetContainer	{b7b13125-b82e-11d0-afee-0000f80367c1}
subSchema objects	subSchema	{5a8b3261-c38d-11d1-bbc9-0080c76670c0}
System Attendant objects	exchangeAdminService	{a8df74b2-c5ea-11d1-bbcb-0080c76670c0}
System Policies objects	msExchSystemPolicyContainer	{32412a7a-22af-479c-a444-624c0137122e}
System Policy objects	msExchSystemPolicy	{ba085a33-8807-4c6c-9522-2cf5a2a5e9c2}
TCP (RFC1006) MTA Transport Stack objects	rFC1006Stack	{a8df74d7-c5ea-11d1-bbcb-0080c76670c0}
TCP (RFC1006) X.400 Connector objects	rFC1006X400Link	{a8df74d8-c5ea-11d1-bbcb-0080c76670c0}
top objects	top	{bf967ab7-0de6-11d0-a285-00aa003049e2}
TP4 MTA Transport Stack objects	tP4Stack	{a8df74db-c5ea-11d1-bbcb-0080c76670c0}
TP4 X.400 Connector objects	tP4X400Link	{a8df74dc-c5ea-11d1-bbcb-0080c76670c0}
transportStack objects	transportStack	{a8df74dd-c5ea-11d1-bbcb-0080c76670c0}
Trusted Domain objects	trustedDomain	{bf967ab8-0de6-11d0-a285-00aa003049e2}
typeLibrary objects	typeLibrary	{281416e2-1968-11d0-a28f-00aa003049e2}
User objects	user	{bf967aba-0de6-11d0-a285-00aa003049e2}
Video Conference Technology Provider objects	msExchIpConfContainer	{99f5866d-12e8-11d3-aa58-00c04f8eedd8}
Virtual Chat Network objects	msExchChatVirtualNetwork	{ea5ed15a-a980-11d2-a9ff-00c04f8eedd8}
X.25 MTA Transport Stack objects	x25Stack	{a8df74de-c5ea-11d1-bbcb-0080c76670c0}
X.25 X.400 Connector objects	x25X400Link	{a8df74df-c5ea-11d1-bbcb-0080c76670c0}
x400Link objects	x400Link	{a8df74e0-c5ea-11d1-bbcb-0080c76670c0}

Table 4.19   *Summary of the GUID Number Origins for the ACE ObjectType Property*

When the *ACE Type* property contains one of the values listed below ...	... and if the *ACE AccessMask* property contains ...		... then is that an Extended Right?	In such a case, the GUID number in the *ACE ObjectType* value refers ...	... which contains a validAccesses value of ...	
ADS_ACETYPE_ACCESS_ALLOWED_OBJECT	ADS_RIGHT_DS_CONTROL_ACCESS	0x100	Yes	the GUID number of the **rightsGUID** attribute of the **controlAccessRight** object, (1)	ADS_RIGHT_DS_CONTROL_ACCESS	0x100
OR						
	ADS_RIGHT_DS_READ_PROP	0x10	Yes	the GUID number of the **rightsGUID** attribute of the **controlAccessRight** object, (1)	ADS_RIGHT_DS_READ_PROP Or ADS_RIGHT_DS_WRITE_PROP	0x30
	AND/OR					
	ADS_RIGHT_DS_WRITE_PROP	0x20				
ADS_ACETYPE_ACCESS_DENIED_OBJECT	ADS_RIGHT_DS_SELF	0x8	Yes	the GUID number of the **rightsGUID** attribute of the **controlAccessRight** object, (1)	ADS_RIGHT_DS_SELF	0x8
OR						
ADS_ACETYPE_SYSTEM_AUDIT_OBJECT	ADS_RIGHT_DS_CREATE_CHILD	0x1	No	the GUID number of the **schemaIDGUID** attribute of the **classSchema** object, (2)	N/A	
	AND/OR					
	ADS_RIGHT_DS_DELETE_CHILD	0x2				

(1) See table 4.17 for **rightsGUID** attribute values of the **controlAccessRight** objects.
(2) See table 4.18 for **schemaIDGUID** attribute values of the **classSchema** objects.

To customize the three Extended Rights samples shown in Figure 4.22, the following command lines must be used:

- For the "Personal Information" Extended Right:

```
1:    C:\>WMIManageSD.Wsf /ADObject:"CN=LISSOIR Alain,CN=Users,DC=LissWare,DC=Net"
2:                        /Trustee:LissWareNET\Alain.Lissoir
3:                        /ACEType:ADS_ACETYPE_ACCESS_ALLOWED_OBJECT
4:                        /ACEMask:ADS_RIGHT_DS_READ_PROP,
5:                               ADS_RIGHT_DS_WRITE_PROP
6:                        /ACEFlags:None
7:                        /ObjectType:{77B5B886-944A-11D1-AEBD-0000F80367C1}
8:                        /AddAce+ /ADSI+
```

- For the "Send As" Extended Right:

```
1:    C:\>WMIManageSD.Wsf /ADObject:"CN=LISSOIR Alain,CN=Users,DC=LissWare,DC=Net"
2:                        /Trustee:LissWareNET\Alain.Lissoir
3:                        /ACEType:ADS_ACETYPE_ACCESS_ALLOWED_OBJECT
4:                        /ACEMask:ADS_RIGHT_DS_CONTROL_ACCESS
5:                        /ACEFlags:None
6:                        /ObjectType:{AB721A54-1E2F-11D0-9819-00AA0040529B}
7:                        /AddAce+ /ADSI+
```

- For the "Add/Remove self as member" Extended Right:

```
1:    C:\>WMIManageSD.Wsf /ADObject:"CN=Enterprise Admins,CN=Users,DC=LissWare,DC=Net"
2:                        /Trustee:LissWareNET\Alain.Lissoir
3:                        /ACEType:ADS_ACETYPE_ACCESS_ALLOWED_OBJECT
4:                        /ACEMask:ADS_RIGHT_DS_SELF
5:                        /ACEFlags:ADS_ACEFLAG_CONTAINER_INHERIT_ACE
6:                        /ObjectType:{BF9679C0-0DE6-11D0-A285-00AA003049E2}
7:                        /AddAce+ /ADSI+
```

To customize the ACE inheritance shown in Figure 4.28 ("The *ACE ObjectType* property used to grant or deny the creation or deletion of objects from a particular class"), the following command line must be used:

```
1:    C:\>WMIManageSD.Wsf /ADObject:"CN=Users,DC=LissWare,DC=Net"
2:                        /Trustee:LissWareNET\Alain.Lissoir
3:                        /ACEType:ADS_ACETYPE_ACCESS_ALLOWED_OBJECT
4:                        /ACEMask:ADS_RIGHT_DS_CREATE_CHILD,
5:                               ADS_RIGHT_DS_DELETE_CHILD
6:                        /ACEFlags:ADS_ACEFLAG_CONTAINER_INHERIT_ACE
7:                        /ObjectType:{35BE884C-A982-11D2-A9FF-00C04F8EEDD8}
8:                        /AddAce+ /ADSI+
```

Since we manipulate a security descriptor coming from Active Directory, the ADSI security descriptor access method is used. The **/ADSI+** switch is specified for every command line. Note that the WMI access method can also be used for this example, since we manage the DACL of the security descriptor. However, as we have seen in section 4.4.4 ("Which access technique to use? Which security descriptor representation do we obtain?"), the

SACL access of an Active Directory security descriptor via WMI is not supported.

The command-line input is always based on the various deciphering outputs previously seen and the content of:

- Table 4.14, "The Active Directory Object *ACE AccessMask* Values— Standard View"

- Table 4.15, "The Active Directory Object *ACE AccessMask* Values— Advanced View"

- Table 4.16, "The Active Directory Objects *ACE Flags* Values"

- Table 4.17, "Extended Rights Available in Active Directory under Windows Server 2003 (Exchange 2000 Extended Rights Included)"

- Table 4.18, "The **schemaIDGUID** GUID Number with Its Class Names"

- Table 4.19, "Summary of the GUID Number Origins for the *ACE ObjectType* Property"

4.11.4.5.3.2 Understanding the ACE InheritedObjectType property   As discussed when we examined the *ACE Flags* property (section 4.11.4.3), objects contained in subcontainers can inherit ACEs. However, with Active Directory, there are situations where only a specific class of object will inherit an ACE. Figure 4.29 shows an example of this configuration.

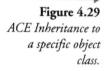

Figure 4.29
ACE Inheritance to a specific object class.

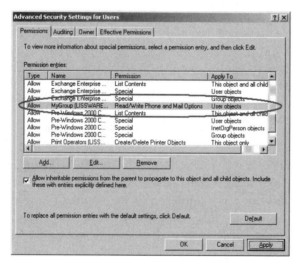

The group "MyGroup" is granted to read and write the phone and mail options on all user objects. If we decipher the ACE, we obtain the following result:

```
 1:   C:\>WMIManageSD.Wsf /ADObject:"CN=Users,DC=LissWare,DC=Net" /Decipher+ /ADSI+
 2:   Microsoft (R) Windows Script Host Version 5.6
 3:   Copyright (C) Microsoft Corporation 1996-2001. All rights reserved.
 4:
 5:   Reading AD object security descriptor via ADSI from 'LDAP:// CN=Users,DC=LissWareNET,...'.
 6:
 7:   +- ADSI Security Descriptor ------------------------------------------------------------
 8:   | Owner: ............................ LISSWARENET\Domain Admins
 9:   | Group: ............................ LISSWARENET\Domain Admins
10:   | Revision: ......................... 1
11:   | Control: .......................... &h8C14
..:
17:   |+- ADSI DiscretionaryAcl -----------------------------------------------------------
18:   ||+- ADSI ACE -----------------------------------------------------------------------
..:
33:   ||+--------------------------------------------------------------------------------
...:
121:  ||+- ADSI ACE -----------------------------------------------------------------------
122:  ||| AccessMask: .......................... &h30
123:                                              ADS_RIGHT_DS_READ_PROP
124:                                              ADS_RIGHT_DS_WRITE_PROP
125:  ||| AceFlags: ............................ &hA
126:                                              ADS_ACEFLAG_CONTAINER_INHERIT_ACE
127:                                              ADS_ACEFLAG_INHERIT_ONLY_ACE
128:                                              ADS_ACEFLAG_VALID_INHERIT_FLAGS
129:  ||| AceType: ............................. &h5
130:                                              ADS_ACETYPE_ACCESS_ALLOWED_OBJECT
131:  ||| AceFlagType: ......................... &h3
132:                                              ADS_FLAG_OBJECT_TYPE_PRESENT
133:                                              ADS_FLAG_INHERITED_OBJECT_TYPE_PRESENT
134:  ||| ObjectType: .......................... {E45795B2-9455-11D1-AEBD-0000F80367C1}
135:  ||| InheritedObjectType: ................. {BF967ABA-0DE6-11D0-A285-00AA003049E2}
136:  ||| Trustee: ............................. LISSWARENET\MyGroup
137:  ||+-------------------------------------------------------------------------------
...:
456:  |+--------------------------------------------------------------------------------
457:  +---------------------------------------------------------------------------------
```

From line 121 through 137, the "Phone and Mail options" Extended Right is granted to the trustee "MyGroup" for read and write operations as:

- The *ACE Type* has a value equal to ADS_ACETYPE_ACCESS_ ALLOWED_OBJECT (line 130).

- The *ACE AccessMask* has a value equal to ADS_RIGHT_DS_READ_ PROP + ADS_RIGHT_DS_WRITE_PROP (lines 123 and 124).

- The *ACE ObjectType* property has a GUID number corresponding to the "Phone and Mail options" Extended Right (line 134). Table 4.17 lists the Extended Rights GUID numbers with their corresponding display names.

- Because it applies to the user objects only, the *ACE InheritedObject-Type* property is set with the GUID number stored in the **schemaID-GUID** of the **user** class (line 135). To find the name of the class with the GUID number, refer to Table 4.18.

To customize this inheritance with the script, as shown in Figure 4.29, the following command line must be used:

```
 1:   C:\>WMIManageSD.Wsf /ADObject:"CN=Users,DC=LissWare,DC=Net"
 2:                        /Trustee:LissWareNET\MyGroup
 3:                        /ACEType:ADS_ACETYPE_ACCESS_ALLOWED_OBJECT
 4:                        /ACEMask:ADS_RIGHT_DS_READ_PROP,
 5:                               ADS_RIGHT_DS_WRITE_PROP
 6:                        /ACEFlags:ADS_ACEFLAG_CONTAINER_INHERIT_ACE,
 7:                               ADS_ACEFLAG_INHERIT_ONLY_ACE
 8:                        /ObjectType:{E45795B2-9455-11D1-AEBD-0000F80367C1}
 9:                        /InheritedObjectType:{BF967ABA-0DE6-11D0-A285-00AA003049E2}
10:                        /AddAce+ /ADSI+
```

As usual, the switch parameters can be taken from a deciphering output or from the various tables related to the Active Directory security descriptors (Tables 4.14 through 4.19).

Before moving to the next security descriptor type, it is interesting to note that the script offers limited support about the GUID numbers management. Actually, it is possible to extend the script in such a way that it accepts the Extended Rights and Active Directory classes display names instead of those ugly GUID numbers. Based on these names, it is always possible to retrieve their corresponding GUID numbers. This will certainly make the script easier to use. However, this logic must be implemented by performing some LDAP search operations on top of ADSI. Since we are focusing on the WMI scripting techniques, this ADSI scripting logic is beyond the scope of this book. However, this could represent a nice extension to have for a day-to-day use of the script.

4.11.4.5.4   The Exchange 2000 mailbox ACE AccessMask property

When an Exchange 2000 mailbox is created, the mailbox security descriptor is initially stored in the **msExchMailboxSecurityDescriptor** attribute of the Active Directory **user** object. The **msExchMailboxSecurityDescriptor** attribute can be accessed via ADSI or WMI, but, again, the *ACE AccessMask* deciphering technique is independent of the access method and the object model representing the security descriptor. Even if the mailbox security descriptor is stored in Active Directory, the deciphering technique is much simpler than the deciphering technique used for an Active Directory object security descriptor. Sample 4.38 uses the same logic as any other standard rights but with a different set of flags.

Sample 4.38   *Deciphering the ACE AccessMask property for Exchange 2000 mailboxes*

```
...:
...:
...:
319:
320:        Case cExchange2000MailboxViaWMI, cExchange2000MailboxViaADSI, _
321:             cExchange2000MailboxViaCDOEXM
322:             If (intACEMask And E2K_MB_FULL_MB_ACCESS) Then
323:                 strTemp = strTemp & "," & "E2K_MB_FULL_MB_ACCESS"
324:             End If
325:             If (intACEMask And E2K_MB_SEND_AS) Then
326:                 strTemp = strTemp & "," & "E2K_MB_SEND_AS"
327:             End If
328:             If (intACEMask And E2K_MB_EXTERNAL_ACCOUNT) Then
329:                 strTemp = strTemp & "," & "E2K_MB_EXTERNAL_ACCOUNT"
330:             End If
331:             If (intACEMask And E2K_MB_DELETE) Then
332:                 strTemp = strTemp & "," & "E2K_MB_DELETE"
333:             End If
334:             If (intACEMask And E2K_MB_READ_PERMISSIONS) Then
335:                 strTemp = strTemp & "," & "E2K_MB_READ_PERMISSIONS"
336:             End If
337:             If (intACEMask And E2K_MB_CHANGE_PERMISSIONS) Then
338:                 strTemp = strTemp & "," & "E2K_MB_CHANGE_PERMISSIONS"
339:             End If
340:             If (intACEMask And E2K_MB_TAKE_OWNERSHIP) Then
341:                 strTemp = strTemp & "," & "E2K_MB_TAKE_OWNERSHIP"
342:             End If
343:
...:
...:
...:
```

Table 4.20   *The Exchange 2000 Mailbox ACE AccessMask Values*

Granted & denied rights		Standard View					
		Delete Mailbox storage	Read permissions	Change permissions	Take ownership	Full mailbox access	Associated external account
ACEType							
ADS_ACETYPE_ACCESS_ALLOWED	0x0						
ADS_ACETYPE_ACCESS_DENIED	0x1	X	X	X	X	X	X
ADS_ACETYPE_SYSTEM_AUDIT	0x2						
ACEMask							
E2K_MB_CHANGE_PERMISSIONS	0x40000			X			
E2K_MB_DELETE	0x10000	X					
E2K_MB_EXTERNAL_ACCOUNT	0x4						X
E2K_MB_FULL_MB_ACCESS	0x1					X	X
E2K_MB_READ_PERMISSIONS	0x20000		X				
E2K_MB_SEND_AS	0x2						
E2K_MB_TAKE_OWNERSHIP	0x80000				X		

Table 4.21   *The Exchange 2000 Mailbox ACE Flags Values*

Inheritance & Audit		This object only	Inherit only	This object and subcontainers	This object and children objects	Subcontainers only	Children objects only	This object, subcontainers, and children objects	Subcontainers and children objects	Audit Successful access	Audit Failed access
ACEFlags											
NONE	0x0	X									
ADS_ACEFLAG_OBJECT_INHERIT_ACE[2]	0x1				X		X	X	X		
ADS_ACEFLAG_CONTAINER_INHERIT_ACE[2]	0x2			X		X		X	X		
ADS_ACEFLAG_INHERIT_ONLY_ACE[1]	0x8	X				X	X		X		
ADS_ACEFLAG_INHERITED_ACE[1]	0x10										
ADS_ACEFLAG_NO_PROPAGATE_INHERIT_ACE	0x4										
ADS_ACEFLAG_VALID_INHERIT_FLAGS[1]	0x1F	X	X	X	X	X	X	X	X		
ADS_ACEFLAG_SUCCESSFUL_ACCESS	0x40									X	
ADS_ACEFLAG_FAILED_ACCESS	0x80										X

(1) can only be set by the system.

(2) These two values are not defined in the ADS_ACEFLAG_ENUM. The
ADS_ACEFLAG_CONTAINER_INHERIT_ACE is actually defined as the ADS_ACEFLAG_INHERIT_ACE
value (0x2). The ADS_ACEFLAG_OBJECT_INHERIT_ACE value is not defined but the 0x1 value is required
to correctly decipher the Exchange 2000 ACE inheritance.

The Exchange 2000 mailbox flags with their corresponding user interface settings are summarized in Table 4.20.

Table 4.21 lists the *ACE Flags* to define ACE inheritance for an Exchange 2000 mailbox.

The mailbox security settings shown in Figure 4.30 can be deciphered with the following command line. The output would be as follows:

```
 1:   C:\>WMIManageSD.Wsf /E2KMailbox:"CN=LISSOIR Alain,CN=Users,..." /Decipher+ /ADSI+
 2:   Microsoft (R) Windows Script Host Version 5.6
 3:   Copyright (C) Microsoft Corporation 1996-2001. All rights reserved.
 4:
 5:   Reading Exchange 2000 mailbox security descriptor via ADSI from 'LDAP://CN=LISSOIR...'.
 6:
 7:   +- ADSI Security Descriptor ------------------------------------------------------------
 8:   | Owner: ............................... LISSWARENET\Alain.Lissoir
 9:   | Group: ............................... LISSWARENET\Alain.Lissoir
10:   | Revision: ............................ 1
11:   | Control: ............................. &h8004
12:                                            SE_DACL_PRESENT
13:                                            SE_SELF_RELATIVE
14:   |+- ADSI DiscretionaryAcl --------------------------------------------------------------
15:   ||+- ADSI ACE --------------------------------------------------------------------------
16:   ||| AccessMask: ........................ &h20003
17:                                            E2K_MB_FULL_MB_ACCESS
```

```
18:                                    E2K_MB_SEND_AS
19:                                    E2K_MB_READ_PERMISSIONS
20:   ||| AceFlags: .......................... &h2
21:                                    ADS_ACEFLAG_CONTAINER_INHERIT_ACE
22:                                    ADS_ACEFLAG_VALID_INHERIT_FLAGS
23:   ||| AceType: ........................... &h0
24:                                    ADS_ACETYPE_ACCESS_ALLOWED
25:   ||| AceFlagType: ....................... &h0
26:   ||| Trustee: ........................... NT AUTHORITY\SELF
27:   ||+-----------------------------------------------------------------------------
28:   |+------------------------------------------------------------------------------
29:   +-------------------------------------------------------------------------------
```

Lines 15 through 26 show the ACE configuration for the security settings shown in Figure 4.30. The *ACE AccessMask* is composed of the flags
listed in Table 4.20, while the *ACE Flags* property is made up of the flags
from Table 4.21.

To customize the Exchange 2000 security descriptor, as shown in Figure
4.30, the following command line can be used:

```
1:   C:\>WMIManageSD.Wsf /E2KMailbox:"CN=LISSOIR Alain,CN=Users,DC=LissWare,DC=Net"
2:                       /Trustee:"NT AUTHORITY\SELF"
3:                       /ACEType:ADS_ACETYPE_ACCESS_ALLOWED
4:                       /ACEMask:E2K_MB_FULL_MB_ACCESS,
5:                               E2K_MB_SEND_AS,
6:                               E2K_MB_READ_PERMISSIONS
7:                       /ACEFlags:ADS_ACEFLAG_CONTAINER_INHERIT_ACE
8:                       /AddAce+ /ADSI+
```

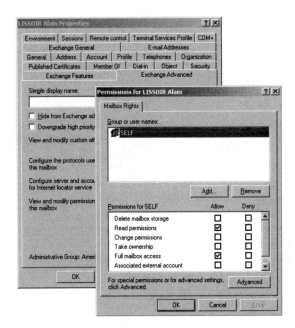

Figure 4.30
*The default
Exchange 2000
mailbox security
just after creation
from the MMC.*

It is important to note that the script sets the security on the mailbox. It doesn't create a mail-enabled or mailbox-enabled Active Directory object. In this example, we use the ADSI security descriptor access method. However, as we have seen in section 4.4.4 ("Which access technique to use? Which security descriptor representation do we obtain?"), the WMI and CDOEXM method can be used as well. The access method depends on certain conditions, which we will discuss in section 4.13.4 ("Updating Exchange 2000 mailbox").

4.11.4.5.5   The registry key ACE AccessMask property

The registry *ACE AccessMask* deciphering technique is no more complicated than any other *ACE AccessMask*. It follows the same coding and deciphering rules as seen previously. As usual, the set of flags to use to decipher the *ACE AccessMask* is dedicated to the registry. Table 4.22 summarizes the various user interface settings possible, with their corresponding values.

Table 4.23 shows the *ACE Flags* used to control the ACE inheritance in a registry hive.

Table 4.22   *The Registry Key ACE AccessMask Values*

Granted & denied rights		Standard View		Advanced View									
		Read	Full Control	Query Value	Set Value	Create Subkey	Enumerate Subkeys	Notify	Create Link	Delete	Write DAC	Write Owner	Read Control
ACEType													
ADS_ACETYPE_ACCESS_ALLOWED	0x0	X[1]	X[1]	X[1]	X[1]	X[1]	X[1]	X[1]	X[1]	X[1]	X[1]	X[1]	X[1]
ADS_ACETYPE_ACCESS_DENIED	0x1												
ADS_ACETYPE_SYSTEM_AUDIT	0x2												
ACEMask													
REG_GENERIC_FULL_CONTROL	0xF003F		X										
REG_GENERIC_READ	0x20019	X											
REG_CREATE_LINK	0x20		X						X				
REG_CREATE_SUBKEYS	0x4		X			X							
REG_DELETE	0x10000		X							X			
REG_ENUMERATE_SUBKEYS	0x8	X	X				X						
REG_NOTIFY	0x10	X	X					X					
REG_QUERY_VALUE	0x1	X	X	X									
REG_READ_CONTROL	0x20000	X	X										X
REG_SET_VALUE	0x2		X		X								
REG_WRITE_DAC	0x40000		X								X		
REG_WRITE_OWNER	0x80000		X									X	

(1) **Windows NT 4.0/Windows 2000:** The **ADsSecurity.DLL** from the ADSI Resource Kit does not retrieve the SACL object from the registry.
Windows XP/Windows Server 2003: Unfortunately, a bug in the ADsSecurityUtility interface prevents the retrieval of the SystemACL. Microsoft doesn't plan to fix this bug in the RTM code for timing issues. WMI offers an acceptable work-around for file and folders only. For the registry key, there is no work-around available unless you use the UserRight.Control developed to work around this problem. (See section 4.7.1.2, "Retrieving file and folder security descriptors with ADSI.")

Table 4.23   *The Registry Key ACE Flags Values*

Inheritance		This key only	This key and subkeys	Subkeys only
ACEFlags				
NONE	0x0	X		
CONTAINER_INHERIT_ACE	0x2		X	X
INHERIT_ONLY_ACE	0x8			X

Based on the flags of Table 4.22, Sample 4.39 deciphers the *ACE Access-Mask* property. There is nothing new to explain about the logic, since the coding technique remains the same.

Sample 4.39   *Deciphering the ACE AccessMask property for registry keys*

```
...:
...:
...:
343:
344:        Case cRegistryViaADSI
345:            If (intACEMask = REG_GENERIC_FULL_CONTROL) Then
346:                strTemp = strTemp & "," & "(REG_GENERIC_FULL_CONTROL)"
347:            End If
348:            If (intACEMask = REG_GENERIC_READ) Then
349:                strTemp = strTemp & "," & "(REG_GENERIC_READ)"
350:            End If
351:
352:            If (intACEMask And REG_QUERY_VALUE) Then
353:                strTemp = strTemp & "," & "REG_QUERY_VALUE"
354:            End If
355:            If (intACEMask And REG_SET_VALUE) Then
356:                strTemp = strTemp & "," & "REG_SET_VALUE"
357:            End If
358:            If (intACEMask And REG_CREATE_SUBKEYS) Then
359:                strTemp = strTemp & "," & "REG_CREATE_SUBKEYS"
360:            End If
...:
379:            If (intACEMask And REG_WRITE_OWNER) Then
380:                strTemp = strTemp & "," & "REG_WRITE_OWNER"
381:            End If
382:
...:
...:
...:
```

If we take the configuration settings of Figure 4.31, the script output obtained is as follows:

```
  1:   C:\>WMIManageSD.Wsf /RegistryKey:HKLM\SYSTEM\CurrentControlSet\Services\SNMP /Decipher+
  2:   Microsoft (R) Windows Script Host Version 5.6
  3:   Copyright (C) Microsoft Corporation 1996-2001. All rights reserved.
  4:
  5:   Reading registry security descriptor via ADSI from 'HKLM\SYSTEM\CurrentContr...'.
  6:
  7:   +- ADSI Security Descriptor ------------------------------------------------------------
  8:   | Owner: ............................... BUILTIN\Administrators
  9:   | Group: ............................... NT AUTHORITY\SYSTEM
 10:   | Revision: ............................ 1
 11:   | Control: ............................. &h8404
 12:                                            SE_DACL_PRESENT
 13:                                            SE_DACL_AUTO_INHERITED
 14:                                            SE_SELF_RELATIVE
 15:   |+- ADSI DiscretionaryAcl --------------------------------------------------------------
 16:   ||+- ADSI ACE --------------------------------------------------------------------------
 17:   |||   AccessMask: ......................... &h30019
 18:                                            REG_QUERY_VALUE
 19:                                            REG_ENUMERATE_SUBKEYS
 20:                                            REG_NOTIFY
 21:                                            REG_DELETE
 22:                                            REG_READ_CONTROL
 23:   |||   AceFlags: .......................... &h2
 24:                                            CONTAINER_INHERIT_ACE
 25:   |||   AceType: ........................... &h0
 26:                                            ACCESS_ALLOWED_ACE_TYPE
 27:   |||   AceFlagType: ....................... &h0
 28:   |||   Trustee: ........................... LISSWARENET\Alain.Lissoir
 29:   ||+-----------------------------------------------------------------------------------
...:
153:   |+-----------------------------------------------------------------------------------
154:   +------------------------------------------------------------------------------------
```

The highlighted trustee in Figure 4.31 has a full read access to the registry hive. It is also able to delete registry keys below the selected hive. The ACE is deciphered from line 16 through 29 with the flag values of Tables 4.22 and 4.23. To configure the same ACE with the **WMIManageSD.Wsf** script, the following command line must be used:

```
  1:   C:\>WMIManageSD.Wsf /RegistryKey:HKLM\SYSTEM\CurrentControlSet\Services\SNMP
  2:                       /Trustee:LissWareNET\Alain.Lissoir
  3:                       /ACEType:ACCESS_ALLOWED_ACE_TYPE
  4:                       /ACEMask:REG_QUERY_VALUE,
  5:                              REG_ENUMERATE_SUBKEYS,
  6:                              REG_NOTIFY,
  7:                              REG_DELETE,
  8:                              REG_READ_CONTROL
  9:                       /ACEFlags:CONTAINER_INHERIT_ACE
 10:                       /AddAce+ /ADSI+
```

The only access method available to read and update the security descriptor is exposed by ADSI. Therefore, the **/ADSI+** switch must be specified in this example.

Figure 4.31   *The registry hive security descriptor user interface.*

4.11.4.5.6   The CIM repository namespace ACE AccessMask property

Deciphering the *ACE AccessMask* of a CIM repository namespace is the same as deciphering any other *ACE AccessMask*. Only the flag values are different. Table 4.24 lists the possible configuration settings.

Regarding the *ACE Flags* to configure the ACE inheritance, you can refer to Table 4.25.

As an example, Figure 4.32 shows the default security settings of the **Root\CIMv2** namespace.

Table 4.24   *The CIM Repository Namespace Key ACE AccessMask Values*

Granted & denied rights			Advanced View							
			Execute methods	Full Write	Partial Write	Provider Write	Enable Account	Remote Enable	Read Security	Edit Security
ACEType										
ADS_ACETYPE_ACCESS_ALLOWED	0x0		x	x	x	x	x	x	x	x
ADS_ACETYPE_ACCESS_DENIED	0x1									
ADS_ACETYPE_SYSTEM_AUDIT	0x2		N/A[1]							
ACEMask										
WBEM_ENABLE	0x1						x			
WBEM_FULL_WRITE_REP	0x4			x						
WBEM_METHOD_EXECUTE	0x2	x								
WBEM_PARTIAL_WRITE_REP	0x8			x	x					
WBEM_READ_CONTROL	0x20000								x	
WBEM_REMOTE_ACCESS	0x20							x		
WBEM_WRITE_DAC	0x40000									x
WBEM_WRITE_PROVIDER	0x10			x		x				
(1) SACL is not supported in the WMI CIM repository.										

By using the script, the DecipherACEMask() function executes the code segment shown in Sample 4.40.

Sample 4.40   *Deciphering the ACE AccessMask property for CIM repository namespaces*

```
...:
...:
...:
382:
383:        Case cWMINameSpaceViaWMI
384:             If (intACEMask And WBEM_ENABLE) Then
385:                strTemp = strTemp & "," & "WBEM_ENABLE"
386:             End If
387:             If (intACEMask And WBEM_METHOD_EXECUTE) Then
388:                strTemp = strTemp & "," & "WBEM_METHOD_EXECUTE"
389:             End If
390:             If (intACEMask And WBEM_FULL_WRITE_REP) Then
391:                strTemp = strTemp & "," & "WBEM_FULL_WRITE_REP"
392:             End If
393:             If (intACEMask And WBEM_PARTIAL_WRITE_REP) Then
394:                strTemp = strTemp & "," & "WBEM_PARTIAL_WRITE_REP"
395:             End If
396:             If (intACEMask And WBEM_WRITE_PROVIDER) Then
397:                strTemp = strTemp & "," & "WBEM_WRITE_PROVIDER"
398:             End If
399:             If (intACEMask And WBEM_REMOTE_ACCESS) Then
400:                strTemp = strTemp & "," & "WBEM_REMOTE_ACCESS"
401:             End If
402:             If (intACEMask And WBEM_WRITE_DAC) Then
403:                strTemp = strTemp & "," & "WBEM_WRITE_DAC"
404:             End If
405:             If (intACEMask And WBEM_READ_CONTROL) Then
406:                strTemp = strTemp & "," & "WBEM_READ_CONTROL"
407:             End If
408:
409:        Case cRegistryViaWMI, cWMINameSpaceViaADSI
410:
```

```
411:          Case Else
412:
413:     End Select
414:
415:     DecipherACEMask = ConvertStringInArray (strTemp, ",")
416:
417:End Function
```

Table 4.25   *The CIM Repository Namespace Key ACE Flags Values*

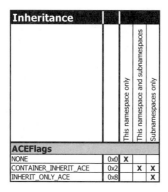

Inheritance				
		This namespace only	This namespace and subnamespaces	Subnamespaces only
ACEFlags				
NONE	0x0	X		
CONTAINER_INHERIT_ACE	0x2		X	X
INHERIT_ONLY_ACE	0x8			X

As a result, the right settings in Figure 4.32 are deciphered as follows:

```
 1:   C:\>WMIManageSD.Wsf /WMINameSpace:Root\CIMv2 /Decipher+
 2:   Microsoft (R) Windows Script Host Version 5.6
 3:   Copyright (C) Microsoft Corporation 1996-2001. All rights reserved.
 4:
 5:   Reading CIM repository namespace security descriptor via WMI from 'Root\CIMv2'.
 6:
 7:   +- ADSI Security Descriptor ------------------------------------------------------------
 8:   | Owner: ............................... BUILTIN\Administrators
 9:   | Group: ............................... BUILTIN\Administrators
10:   | Revision: ............................ 1
11:   | Control: ............................. &h8004
12:                                           SE_DACL_PRESENT
13:                                           SE_SELF_RELATIVE
14:   |+- ADSI DiscretionaryAcl --------------------------------------------------------------
15:   ||+- ADSI ACE --------------------------------------------------------------------------
16:   ||| AccessMask: ......................... &h1F
17:                                           WBEM_ENABLE
18:                                           WBEM_METHOD_EXECUTE
19:                                           WBEM_FULL_WRITE_REP
20:                                           WBEM_PARTIAL_WRITE_REP
21:                                           WBEM_WRITE_PROVIDER
22:   ||| AceFlags: ........................... &hA
23:                                           CONTAINER_INHERIT_ACE
24:                                           INHERIT_ONLY_ACE
25:   ||| AceType: ............................ &h0
26:                                           ACCESS_ALLOWED_ACE_TYPE
27:   ||| AceFlagType: ........................ &h0
28:   ||| Trustee: ............................ LISSWARENET\Alain.Lissoir
29:   ||+-----------------------------------------------------------------------------------
..:
61:   |+-------------------------------------------------------------------------------------
62:   +--------------------------------------------------------------------------------------
```

Figure 4.32
*The Root\CIMv2
namespace security
descriptor user
interface.*

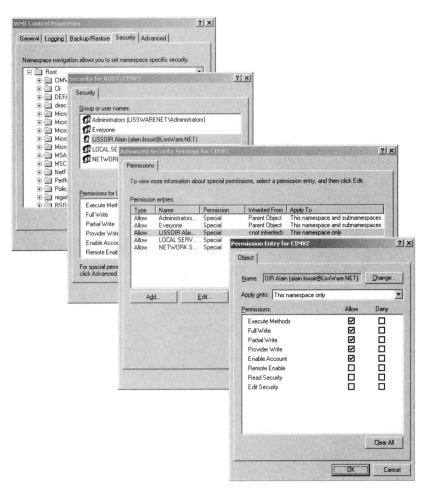

From line 15 through 29, the ACE for the highlighted trustee in Figure
4.32 is deciphered with the flags coming from Tables 4.24 and 4.25. To
configure the same ACE with the **WMIManageSD.Wsf** script, the following command line must be used:

```
 1:    C:\>WMIManageSD.Wsf /WMINameSpace:Root\CIMv2
 2:                        /Trustee:LissWareNET\Alain.Lissoir
 3:                        /ACEType:ACCESS_ALLOWED_ACE_TYPE
 4:                        /ACEMask:WBEM_ENABLE,
 5:                                 WBEM_METHOD_EXECUTE,
 6:                                 WBEM_FULL_WRITE_REP,
 7:                                 WBEM_PARTIAL_WRITE_REP,
 8:                                 WBEM_WRITE_PROVIDER
 9:                        /ACEFlags:CONTAINER_INHERIT_ACE,INHERIT_ONLY_ACE
10:                        /AddAce+
```

The only access method available to read and update the security descriptor is exposed by WMI via the *GetSD* and *SetSD* methods of the _*SystemSecurity* singleton system class (see sections 4.7.6 and 4.13.6). Therefore, no /ADSI+ switch is specified in this example.

4.12 Modifying the security descriptor

In the previous sections we have seen how to access a security descriptor on a secured entity and how to decipher the security descriptor. Although we saw some of the command-line parameters to use to update the security descriptor based on deciphering results and various tables, we did not discover the scripting technique to effectively modify the various security descriptor components. The purpose of this section is to explain how the security descriptor modification is coded, based on the parameters given on the command line.

4.12.1 Updating the security descriptor Owner

The scripting technique used to update the *Owner* property of the security descriptor differs, based on the security descriptor object model used. With the ADSI object model, the owner is nothing other than a single property containing the "Domain\UserID" owner. However, with the WMI object model, the owner is an instance of the *Win32_Trustee* class and requires some extra logic to create the instance. Sample 4.41 shows the SetSD-Owner() function, which includes the script code for the two object models.

Sample 4.41   *Updating the security descriptor owner*

```
 .:
 .:
 .:
 8:' --------------------------------------------------------------------------------
 9:Function SetSDOwner(strSIDResolutionDC, strUserID, strPassword, _
10:                    objSD, strTrustee, intSDType)
..:
14:    Select Case intSDType
15:' Here we have an ADSI security descriptor representation
16:         Case cFileViaADSI, _
17:              cShareViaADSI, _
18:              cActiveDirectoryViaWMI, cActiveDirectoryViaADSI, _
19:              cExchange2000MailboxViaWMI, cExchange2000MailboxViaADSI, _
20:              cExchange2000MailboxViaCDOEXM, _
21:              cRegistryViaADSI, _
22:              cWMINameSpaceViaWMI
23:
24:              objSD.Owner = strTrustee
25:
```

```
26:' Here we have a WMI security descriptor representation
27:        Case cFileViaWMI, _
28:             cShareViaWMI
29:
30:             objSD.Owner = CreateTrustee (strTrustee, _
31:                                          strSIDResolutionDC, _
32:                                          strUserID, _
33:                                          strPassword)
34:
35:' Here we can't retrieve a security descriptor via this access method.
36:        Case cRegistryViaWMI, cWMINameSpaceViaADSI
37:
38:    End Select
39:
40:    WScript.Echo "Security descriptor owner updated to '" & strTrustee & "'."
41:
42:    Set SetSDOwner = objSD
43:
44:End Function
```

From line 16 through 24, the owner is stored in the *Owner* property of the ADSI **SecurityDescriptor** object (line 24). With the ADSI object model, the update of the security descriptor owner is pretty straightforward, since it assigns a literal string to the *Owner* property.

To update the security descriptor owner with the WMI object model (lines 27 through 33), the script must first create an instance of the *Win32_Trustee* class. This instance is created in the CreateTrustee() function (lines 30 through 33). The CreateTrustee() function is shown in Sample 4.42.

Sample 4.42   *Creating a Win32_Trustee instance*

```
.:
.:
.:
8:' -----------------------------------------------------------------------------------------
9:Function CreateTrustee (strTrustee, strSIDResolutionDC, strUserID, strPassword)
..:
17:    objWMILocator.Security_.AuthenticationLevel = wbemAuthenticationLevelDefault
18:    objWMILocator.Security_.ImpersonationLevel = wbemImpersonationLevelImpersonate
19:
20:    Set objWMIServices = objWMILocator.ConnectServer(strSIDResolutionDC, ""Root\CIMv2"", _
21:                                         strUserID, strPassword)
..:
24:    Set objTrustee = objWMIServices.Get("Win32_Trustee").SpawnInstance_()
25:
26:    objTrustee.Domain = ExtractUserDomain (strTrustee)
27:    objTrustee.Name = ExtractUserID (strTrustee)
28:
29:    Set objWMIInstances = objWMIServices.ExecQuery ("Select SID From Win32_Account Where " & _
30:                                         "Name='" & objTrustee.Name & "'")
..:
33:    If objWMIInstances.Count = 1 Then
34:        For Each objWMIInstance In objWMIInstances
```

```
35:             objTrustee.SIDString = objWMIInstance.SID
36:
37:             Set objSID = objWMIServices.Get("Win32_SID.SID='" & objWMIInstance.SID & "'")
38:
39:             objTrustee.SID = objSID.BinaryRepresentation
40:             objTrustee.SidLength = objSID.SidLength
..:
43:      Next
44:    Else
45:       WScript.Echo "WMI Trustee '" & strTrustee & "' not found on SIDResolutionDC '" & _
46:                    strSIDResolutionDC & "'."
47:       WScript.Quit (1)
48:    End If
..:
54:    Set CreateTrustee = objTrustee
..:
58:End Function
```

This function is slightly more complex, because an instance of the
Win32_Trustee class requires the SID of the user. Because the SID of the
user must be resolved against the domain hosting that user, the Cre-
ateTrustee() function requires some extra parameters:

- **Trustee:** This parameter contains the "Domain\UserID" for which
  the *Win32_Trustee* must be created.

- **SIDResolutionDC:** This parameter contains the Fully Qualified
  Domain Name (FQDN) of the domain controller to be used for the
  SID resolution. It should be a domain controller hosting the domain
  name given in the trustee. By default, if no SIDResolutionDC is
  given, the localhost is used. If the script is executed on a system not
  hosting the trustee in its local SAM (or domain if it is a domain controller), the **/SIDResolutionDC** parameter must be given. In such a
  case, it must be the FQDN of the domain controller able to resolve
  the SID for the specified "Domain\UserID." If the trustee could not
  be resolved to a SID, the *Win32_Trustee* instance creation will fail.
  So, make sure that the selected CIM repository (the default one or
  the one specified by the **/SIDResolutionDC** switch) always knows
  the passed "UserID" for the associated "Domain." Note that when
  the security descriptor is represented in the ADSI object model, the
  SID resolution is performed inside the ADSI COM object managing
  the trustee, which makes the task a little bit easier, but this requires
  that the workstation is well connected to the right domain to resolve
  the trustee (directly or via trusts).

- **UserID:** This parameter is the UserID that WMI uses for the WMI
  remote connection. It corresponds to the UserID given with the **/User**
  switch. If the switch is not specified, the security context of the user

executing the script is used to perform the WMI connection to the SIDResolutionDC. In such a case, you must make sure that this user has access, via WMI, to the required system in the **Root\CIMv2** namespace.

- **Password:** This parameter is the password to be used with the UserID performing the WMI remote connection.

From line 17 through 21, the script performs a WMI connection to resolve the trustee to a SID. Once completed, a new instance of the *Win32_Trustee* class is created (line 24). Next, the domain name (line 26) and the user name (line 27) of the trustee are assigned to the corresponding *Win32_Trustee* class properties. To find the SID corresponding to the user name, the script performs a WQL query (lines 29 and 30). If there is one valid response from the WQL query (line 33), the result is enumerated (lines 34 through 43), and the string representation of the SID is saved in the *Win32_Trustee* instance (line 35). In case of a SID resolution problem, the script displays an error message and stops its execution (lines 44 through 48).

Because a *Win32_Trustee* instance also requires a binary representation of the SID, lines 37 through 40 retrieve some extra SID information with another WQL query (line 37). This query is based on the *Win32_SID* class, which uses the SID string representation as one of its properties. Once found, the script assigns the remaining *Win32_Trustee* properties with the binary SID information (lines 39 and 40). Next, the CreateTrustee() function returns the *Win32_Trustee* instance, which is assigned to the *Owner* property of the *Win32_SecurityDescriptor* instance at line 30 of Sample 4.41.

To produce the result shown in Figure 4.33, the command line to use to update the security descriptor owner is as follows:

```
1:   C:\>WMIManageSD.Wsf /ADObject:"CN=LISSOIR Alain,CN=Users,DC=LissWare,DC=Net"
2:                       /Owner:LissWareNET\Alain.Lissoir /ADSI+
```

4.12.2   Updating the security descriptor Group

The logic used to update the *Group* property is the same as that used to update the *Owner* property (see Sample 4.43). Via ADSI, the *Group* property is directly assigned with the "Domain\Group" value (line 24). Via WMI, Sample 4.43 makes use of the CreateTrustee() function previously explained (see Sample 4.42).

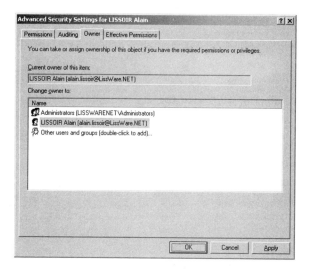

Figure 4.33
*An Active
Directory security
descriptor owner.*

Sample 4.43   *Updating the security descriptor group*

```
 .:
 .:
 .:
 8:' --------------------------------------------------------------------------------------
 9:Function SetSDGroup(strSIDResolutionDC, strUserID, strPassword, _
10:                   objSD, strTrustee, intSDType)
..:
14:    Select Case intSDType
15:' Here we have an ADSI security descriptor representation
16:          Case cFileViaADSI, _
17:               cShareViaADSI, _
18:               cActiveDirectoryViaWMI, cActiveDirectoryViaADSI, _
19:               cExchange2000MailboxViaWMI, cExchange2000MailboxViaADSI, _
20:               cExchange2000MailboxViaCDOEXM, _
21:               cRegistryViaADSI, _
22:               cWMINameSpaceViaWMI
23:
24:               objSD.Group = strTrustee
25:
26:' Here we have a WMI security descriptor representation
27:          Case cFileViaWMI, _
28:               cShareViaWMI
29:
30:               objSD.Group = CreateTrustee (strTrustee, _
31:                                            strSIDResolutionDC, _
32:                                            strUserID, _
33:                                            strPassword)
34:
35:' Here we can't retrieve a security descriptor via this access method.
36:          Case cRegistryViaWMI, _
37:               cWMINameSpaceViaADSI
38:
39:    End Select
```

```
40:
41:    WScript.Echo "Security descriptor group updated to '" & strTrustee & "'."
42:
43:    Set SetSDGroup = objSD
44:
45:End Function
```

4.12.3   Updating the security descriptor Control Flags

The security descriptor *Control Flags* property contains several flags (see Table 4.8, "The security descriptor *Control Flags* values"). However, the script does not allow the modification of all flags, since the script already manages some of them internally. The flags that can be specified from the command line are:

- SE_DACL_PROTECTED
- SE_SACL_PROTECTED
- SE_DACL_AUTO_INHERIT_REQ
- SE_SACL_AUTO_INHERIT_REQ

As shown in Table 4.8, these flags are controlling the security descriptor behavior regarding the inherited ACE. For instance, if the security descriptor is protected against inherited ACE, which means that inherited ACE is not inherited by the security descriptor (SE_DACL_PROTECTED=ON), we have a configuration similar to the one shown in Figure 4.34 (right pane). Note that the user interface check box is unchecked when the SE_ DACL_PROTECTED flag is turned ON.

During a *Control Flags* modification (SE_DACL_PROTECTED=OFF to SE_DACL_PROTECTED=ON, or as shown in Figure 4.34, left and

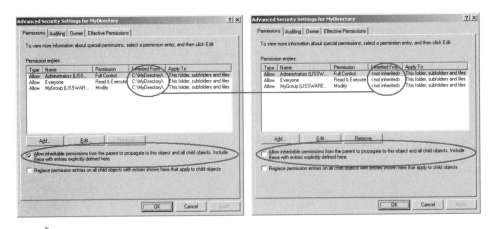

Figure 4.34   *The Control Flags configuration.*

right panes) by script via ADSI or WMI, the inherited ACEs are not inherited anymore and become directly applied ACE (or noninherited ACE).

The next command line turns to ON the SE_DACL_PROTECTED flag, since it is currently turned OFF (left pane of Figure 4.34):

```
1:   C:\>WMIManageSD.Wsf /FileSystem:C:\MyDirectory /SDControls:SE_DACL_PROTECTED
2:   Microsoft (R) Windows Script Host Version 5.6
3:   Copyright (C) Microsoft Corporation 1996-2001. All rights reserved.
4:
5:   Reading File or Folder security descriptor via WMI from 'C:\MyDirectory'.
6:   ACL inheritance protection is OFF and will be turned ON.
7:   Setting File or Folder security descriptor via WMI to 'C:\MyDirectory'.
```

Now the SE_DACL_PROTECTED is turned ON (right pane of Figure 4.34).

If the script is run a second time with the same parameters, the bit corresponding to the SE_DACL_PROTECTED flag is switched back to OFF.

```
1:   C:\>WMIManageSD.Wsf /FileSystem:C:\MyDirectory /SDControls:SE_DACL_PROTECTED
2:   Microsoft (R) Windows Script Host Version 5.6
3:   Copyright (C) Microsoft Corporation 1996-2001. All rights reserved.
4:
5:   Reading File or Folder security descriptor via WMI from 'C:\MyDirectory'.
6:   ACL inheritance protection is ON and will be turned OFF.
7:   Setting File or Folder security descriptor via WMI to 'C:\MyDirectory'.
```

As a consequence (see Figure 4.35), the inherited ACEs are added to the noninherited ACEs.

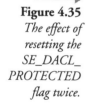

Figure 4.35
The effect of resetting the SE_DACL_PROTECTED flag twice.

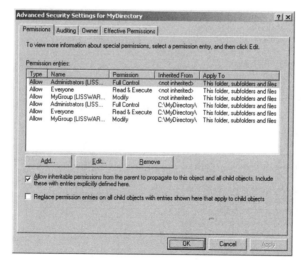

The manipulation of all *Control Flags* bits is basically the same. Whenever the security descriptor is represented in the ADSI or WMI object models, Sample 4.44 uses the same logic as previously. Because the *Control Flags* property is named *Control* in the ADSI object model and named *ControlFlags* in the WMI object model, the script code must take the object model used into consideration to assign the new value, despite the fact the logic is the same (lines 23 through 27 for the ADSI object model, lines 35 through 39 for the WMI object model).

Sample 4.44   *Updating the security descriptor control flags*

```
. :
. :
. :
8:' -------------------------------------------------------------------------------
9:Function SetSDControlFlags(objSD, intSDControlFlags, intSDType)
..:
13:    Select Case intSDType
14:' Here we have an ADSI security descriptor representation
15:        Case cFileViaADSI, _
16:            cShareViaADSI, _
17:            cActiveDirectoryViaWMI, cActiveDirectoryViaADSI, _
18:            cExchange2000MailboxViaWMI, cExchange2000MailboxViaADSI, _
19:            cExchange2000MailboxViaCDOEXM, _
20:            cRegistryViaADSI, _
21:            cWMINameSpaceViaWMI
22:
23:            If (objSD.Control And intSDControlFlags) = intSDControlFlags Then
24:                WScript.Echo "ACL inheritance protection is OFF and will be turned ON."
25:            Else
26:                WScript.Echo "ACL inheritance protection is ON and will be turned OFF."
27:            End If
28:
29:            objSD.Control = objSD.Control Xor intSDControlFlags
30:
31:' Here we have a WMI security descriptor representation
32:        Case cFileViaWMI, _
33:            cShareViaWMI
34:
35:            If (objSD.ControlFlags And intSDControlFlags) = intSDControlFlags Then
36:                WScript.Echo "ACL inheritance protection is OFF and will be turned ON."
37:            Else
38:                WScript.Echo "ACL inheritance protection is ON and will be turned OFF."
39:            End If
40:
41:            objSD.ControlFlags = objSD.ControlFlags Xor intSDControlFlags
42:
43:' Here we can't retrieve a security descriptor via this access method.
44:        Case cRegistryViaWMI, _
45:            cWMINameSpaceViaADSI
46:
47:    End Select
48:
49:    Set SetSDControlFlags = objSD
50:
51:End Function
```

4.12.4   Adding an ACE

To manipulate ACEs in security descriptors, it is necessary to look at the ACL. Since ACLs are represented differently in the ADSI and WMI object models, the script must handle them differently. The next two sections will explain the logic used for the ACE additions in the ADSI and WMI object models, respectively. The code snippets are direct applications of sections 4.11.3 ("Deciphering the Access Control Lists") and 4.11.4 ("Deciphering the Access Control Entries") as examples of configuring ACEs to make use of the **/AddACE+** switch.

The AddACE() function is executed when the **/AddACE+** switch is specified on the command line. For example:

```
C:\>WMIManageSD.Wsf /WMINameSpace:Root\MyNameSpace
                    /Trustee:BUILTIN\Administrators /ACEType:ACCESS_ALLOWED_ACE_TYPE
                    /ACEMask:WBEM_ENABLE,
                             WBEM_METHOD_EXECUTE,
                             WBEM_WRITE_PROVIDER,
                             WBEM_REMOTE_ACCESS
                    /ACEFlags:CONTAINER_INHERIT_ACE
                    /AddAce+
```

4.12.4.1   Adding an ACE in the ADSI object model

The AddACE() function shown in Samples 4.45 and 4.46 implements the logic to add ACEs in the ADSI and WMI object models. The function is divided into two parts: one for the ADSI object model (Sample 4.45) and the second one (Sample 4.46) for the WMI object model. Because the new ACE is built and added in the function, the function exposes several parameters:

- **objWMIServices:** This parameter is an **SWBemServices** object representing the WMI connection to the local CIM repository. This parameter is only used to create a new instance of the *Win32_ACE* class when the security descriptor is represented in the WMI object model. For the ADSI object model, this parameter can be set to Null.

- **SIDResolutionDC, UserID, and Password:** These parameters are the ones used by the CreateTrustee() function (Sample 4.42, "Creating a *Win32_Trustee* instance"). They are only used when the security descriptor is represented in the WMI object model. For the ADSI object model, these parameters can be set to Null (see Sample 4.4, "Connecting to files and folders with ADSI [Part II]," line 591).

- **objSD:** This parameter is the structural representation of the security descriptor in the ADSI or WMI object model.

- **Trustee, ACEType, AccessMask, ACEFlags, ACLType, ObjectType,**
  and **InheritedObjectType:** These parameters are the new ACE properties. These parameters are used both in the ADSI and WMI object
  models. Note that the *ObjectType* and *InheritedObjectType* parameters
  are only used when the security descriptor is an Active Directory
  security descriptor.

- **SDType:** This parameter determines the security descriptor access
  method, which implicitly determines the object model.

Sample 4.45   *Adding ACE in the ADSI object model (Part I)*

```
 .:
 .:
 .:
 8:' --------------------------------------------------------------------------------------------
 9:Function AddACE(objWMIServices, strSIDResolutionDC, strUserID, strPassword, _
10:          objSD, strTrustee, intACEType, intAccessMask, intACEFlags, intACLType, _
11:          strObjectType, strInheritedObjectType, intSDType)
 ..:
21:    Select Case intSDType
22:' Here we have an ADSI security descriptor representation
23:         Case cFileViaADSI, _
24:             cShareViaADSI, _
25:             cActiveDirectoryViaWMI, cActiveDirectoryViaADSI, _
26:             cExchange2000MailboxViaWMI, cExchange2000MailboxViaADSI, _
27:             cExchange2000MailboxViaCDOEXM, _
28:             cRegistryViaADSI, _
29:             cWMINameSpaceViaWMI
30:
31:          Select Case intACLType
32:              Case cDACL
33:                  Set objACL = objSD.DiscretionaryAcl
34:              Case cSACL
35:                  Set objACL = objSD.SystemAcl
36:              Case Else
37:                  Exit Function
38:          End Select
39:
40:          Set objNewACE = CreateObject("AccessControlEntry")
41:
42:          objNewACE.Trustee = strTrustee
43:          objNewACE.AceType = intACEType
44:          objNewACE.AccessMask = intAccessMask
45:          objNewACE.AceFlags = intACEFlags
46:
47:          Select Case intSDType
48:              Case cActiveDirectoryViaWMI, cActiveDirectoryViaADSI, _
49:
50:                  If Len (strObjectType) Then
51:                     objNewACE.ObjectType = strObjectType
52:                     objNewACE.Flags = objNewACE.Flags Or _
53:                                  ADS_FLAG_OBJECT_TYPE_PRESENT
54:                  End If
55:
56:                  If Len (strInheritedObjectType) Then
```

```
57:                              objNewACE.InheritedObjectType = strInheritedObjectType
58:                              objNewACE.Flags = objNewACE.Flags Or _
59:                                        ADS_FLAG_INHERITED_OBJECT_TYPE_PRESENT
60:                         End If
61:
62:              Case cFileViaADSI, _
63:                   cExchange2000MailboxViaWMI, cExchange2000MailboxViaADSI, _
64:                   cExchange2000MailboxViaCDOEXM, _
65:                   cRegistryViaADSI, _
66:                   cWMINameSpaceViaWMI
67:
68:          End Select
69:
70:          objACL.AddAce objNewACE
71:
72:          Select Case intACLType
73:                 Case cDACL
74:                      objSD.DiscretionaryAcl = objACL
75:                      objSD.Control = objSD.Control Or SE_DACL_PRESENT
76:                 Case cSACL
77:                      objSD.SystemAcl = objACL
78:                      objSD.Control = objSD.Control Or SE_SACL_PRESENT
79:          End Select
80:
81:          Wscript.Echo "Trustee '" & strTrustee & _
82:                  "' has been added to security descriptor."
..:
..:
..:
```

Sample 4.45 starts by extracting the ACL from the ADSI security descriptor. Based on the **ACLType** parameter, the Discretionary ACL or the System ACL is extracted (lines 31 through 38). Next, it builds the new ACE by creating a new instance of the **AccessControlEntry** ADSI object (line 40) and assigns the ACE properties (lines 42 through 45). If the security descriptor is an Active Directory security descriptor, then the **ObjectType** and/or the **InheritedObjectType** parameters are assigned (lines 47 through 68). These two parameters contain GUID numbers, as explained in sections 4.11.4.5.3.1 ("Understanding the ACE ObjectType property") and 4.11.4.5.3.2 ("Understanding the ACE InheritedObjectType property"). Because this portion of the script manages the ADSI security descriptor representation, it must set the *ACE FlagType* property of the ADSI **AccessControlEntry** object to save the GUID values back to the security descriptor.

Next, the new ACE is added to the ACL (line 70), and the ACL is stored back in the security descriptor according to the **ACLType** parameter (lines 72 through 79).

4.12.4.2   Adding an ACE in the WMI object model

In the WMI object model, the overall logic is exactly the same as the ADSI object model. However, instead of manipulating the ACE from a collection

(ACL), Sample 4.46 manipulates an array containing ACEs. As before, it extracts the ACL from the WMI security descriptor according to the **ACLType** parameter (lines 92 through 99). Next, it creates a new ACE with the use of the **SWBemServices** object (line 101) and assigns the various ACE properties (lines 103 through 109). Note the use of the CreateTrustee() function (Sample 4.42, "Creating a *Win32_Trustee* instance") to assign the WMI ACE *Trustee* property. Once completed, the new ACE is added to the ACL (lines 111 through 119). Next, the ACL is stored back to the security descriptor according to the **ACLType** parameter (lines 123 through 130).

Sample 4.46   *Adding ACE in the WMI object model (Part II)*

```
..:
..:
..:
87:
88:' Here we have a WMI security descriptor representation
89:          Case cFileViaWMI, _
90:               cShareViaWMI
91:
92:          Select Case intACLType
93:               Case cDACL
94:                    arrayACL = objSD.DACL
95:               Case cSACL
96:                    arrayACL = objSD.SACL
97:               Case Else
98:                    Exit Function
99:          End Select
100:
101:         Set objNewACE = objWMIServices.Get("Win32_ACE").SpawnInstance_()
102:
103:         objNewACE.Trustee = CreateTrustee (strTrustee, _
104:                                            strSIDResolutionDC, _
105:                                            strUserID, _
106:                                            strPassword)
107:         objNewACE.AceType = intACEType
108:         objNewACE.AccessMask = intAccessMask
109:         objNewACE.AceFlags = intACEFlags
110:
111:         ' If ACL already contains some ACE, make sure we don't destroy them ...
112:         If IsArray (arrayACL) Then
113:            intIndice = UBound(arrayACL)
114:            ReDim Preserve arrayACL (intIndice + 1)
115:            Set arrayACL (intIndice + 1) = objNewACE
116:         Else
117:            ReDim arrayACL (0)
118:            Set arrayACL (0) = objNewACE
119:         End If
...:
123:         Select Case intACLType
124:               Case cDACL
125:                    objSD.DACL = arrayACL
126:                    objSD.ControlFlags = objSD.ControlFlags Or SE_DACL_PRESENT
```

```
127:                       Case cSACL
128:                           objSD.SACL = arrayACL
129:                           objSD.ControlFlags = objSD.ControlFlags Or SE_SACL_PRESENT
130:              End Select
131:
132:              Wscript.Echo "Trustee '" & strTrustee & _
133:                          "' has been added to security descriptor."
134:
135:' Here we do not have a security descriptor available via these access methods.
136:        Case cRegistryViaWMI, cWMINameSpaceViaADSI
137:
138:    End Select
...:
142:End Function
```

4.12.5 Removing an ACE

Since the script must manage ACLs in two different object models to remove an ACE from an ACL, the coding technique will be different. Moreover, the logic to remove an ACE from an ACL is totally different from ACE additions. The next two sections cover this functionality in the DelACE() function with the ADSI object model (Sample 4.47) and the WMI object model (Sample 4.48).

The DelACE() function is executed when the **/DelACE+** switch is specified on the command line. For example:

```
C:\>WMIManageSD.Wsf /Share:MyDirectory /Trustee:Everyone /DelAce+
```

4.12.5.1 *Removing ACE in the ADSI object model*

Basically, the DelACE() input parameters are almost the same as the Add-ACE() parameters. However, the DelACE() function does not require all ACE details. Only the **Trustee** is necessary. Simply said, the function browses all ACEs in the ACL and removes any ACE that has a matching **Trustee**. Of course, if a trustee is granted with many different rights (which means that it could exist in many different ACEs), all ACEs matching that trustee will be removed. If a more granular removal technique is required, then the match must be made on more ACE properties than on the **Trustee**, which will require more command-line parameters not supported by the **WMIManageSD.Wsf** script in its current version.

Note that it is possible to use a special keyword (**REMOVE_ALL_ACE**) assigned to the **Trustee** parameter of the DelACE() function to remove all ACEs present in the ACL. In such a case, after this removal, the script grants the "Everyone" Full Control right to make sure that the object is still accessible. Granting "Everyone" Full Control is equal to suppressing the concept of controlling the access. From a human point of view, this makes sense, but from a computer point of view, removing all access controls means no access at all. That's why this trustee is added. Note that this right is only set for a DACL. In the case of a SACL, no default ACE is created. The ACL of a SACL will be emptied.

Now that we understand the DelACE() function features, let's see how the coding works (see Sample 4.47).

Sample 4.47   *Removing ACE in the ADSI object model (Part I)*

```
 . :
 . :
 . :
 8:' --------------------------------------------------------------------------------------------
 9:Function DelACE(objWMIServices, strSIDResolutionDC, strUserID, strPassword, _
10:              objSD, strTrustee, intACLType, intSDType)
..:
..:
..:
26:    Select Case intSDType
27:' Here we have an ADSI security descriptor representation
28:          Case cFileViaADSI, _
29:              cShareViaADSI, _
30:              cActiveDirectoryViaWMI, cActiveDirectoryViaADSI, _
31:              cExchange2000MailboxViaWMI, cExchange2000MailboxViaADSI, _
32:              cExchange2000MailboxViaCDOEXM, _
33:              cRegistryViaADSI, _
34:              cWMINameSpaceViaWMI
35:
36:              Select Case intACLType
37:                    Case cDACL
38:                        Set objACL = objSD.DiscretionaryAcl
39:                    Case cSACL
40:                        Set objACL = objSD.SystemAcl
41:                    Case Else
42:                        Exit Function
43:              End Select
44:
45:              ' Only proceed an ACE removal, if there is at least one available ...
46:              If objACL.AceCount Then
47:                  If Ucase(strTrustee) = "REMOVE_ALL_ACE" Then
48:                      For Each objACE In objACL
49:                          objACL.RemoveAce (objACE)
50:                      Next
51:
52:                      If objACL.AceCount = 0 Then
53:                          Select Case intACLType
54:                              Case cDACL
55:                                  Set objNewACE = CreateObject("AccessControlEntry")
56:
57:                                  objNewACE.Trustee = "Everyone"
58:                                  objNewACE.AceType = ADS_ACETYPE_ACCESS_ALLOWED
59:                                  objNewACE.AccessMask = ADS_RIGHT_GENERIC_ALL
60:                                  objNewACE.AceFlags = CONTAINER_INHERIT_ACE Or _
61:                                                       OBJECT_INHERIT_ACE
62:
63:                                  Wscript.Echo "All ACE removed, Trustee '" & _
```

```
 64:                                          objNewACE.Trustee & _
 65:                                     "' (Full Control) has been created."
 66:
 67:                             objACL.AddAce objNewACE
 68:
 69:                             objSD.Control = objSD.Control Or _
 70:                                         SE_DACL_PRESENT
...:
 73:                     Case cSACL
 74:                             objSD.Control = objSD.Control And _
 75:                                         (NOT SE_SACL_PRESENT)
 76:                 End Select
 77:             End If
 78:
 79:             boolRemoveAce = True
 80:         Else
 81:             For Each objACE In objACL
 82:                 If Ucase(objACE.Trustee) = Ucase(strTrustee) Then
 83:                     If (objACE.AceFlags And INHERITED_ACE) = INHERITED_ACE Then
 84:                         Wscript.Echo "Trustee '" & objACE.Trustee & _
 85:                                         "' is inherited and therefore can't be removed."
 86:                     Else
 87:                         Wscript.Echo "Trustee '" & strTrustee & _
 88:                                     "' has been removed from security descriptor."
 89:                         objACL.RemoveAce (objACE)
 90:
 91:                         If objACL.AceCount = 0 Then
 92:                             Select Case intACLType
 93:                                 Case cDACL
 94:                                     Set objNewACE = CreateObject("AccessControlEntry")
 95:
 96:                                     objNewACE.Trustee = "Everyone"
 97:                                     objNewACE.AceType = ADS_ACETYPE_ACCESS_ALLOWED
 98:                                     objNewACE.AccessMask = ADS_RIGHT_GENERIC_ALL
 99:                                     objNewACE.AceFlags = CONTAINER_INHERIT_ACE Or _
100:                                                     OBJECT_INHERIT_ACE
101:
102:                                     Wscript.Echo "All ACE removed, Trustee '" & _
103:                                                 objNewACE.Trustee & _
104:                                                 "' (Full Control) has been created."
105:
106:                                     objACL.AddAce objNewACE
107:
108:                                     objSD.Control = objSD.Control Or _
109:                                                 SE_DACL_PRESENT
...:
112:                                 Case cSACL
113:                                     objSD.Control = objSD.Control And _
114:                                                 (NOT SE_SACL_PRESENT)
115:                             End Select
116:                         End If
117:
118:                         boolRemoveAce = True
119:                     End If
120:                 End If
121:             Next
122:         End If
123:
124:         If objACL.AceCount = 0 Then
125:             Wscript.Echo "All ACE removed."
```

```
126:              End If
127:
128:              Select Case intACLType
129:                      Case cDACL
130:                              objSD.DiscretionaryAcl = objACL
131:                      Case cSACL
132:                              objSD.SystemAcl = objACL
133:              End Select
134:          Else
135:              WScript.Echo "No existing ACE to remove."
136:              WScript.Quit(1)
137:          End If
...:
...:
...:
```

As with the AddACE() function, the DelACE() function first retrieves the DACL or the SACL, based on the **ACLType** parameter (lines 36 through 43). Once complete, the DelACE() function is divided into two parts for each object model:

1. **Removing all ACEs (lines 47 through 79):** This part makes use of the **REMOVE_ALL_ACE** keyword to remove all available ACEs. The script enumerates all ACEs to remove instead of creating a new ACL (lines 48 through 50). Recreating a new ACL will force the version number of the ACL to be set in the ADSI object model. To keep the logic totally generic, the script keeps the ACL object intact by removing only ACEs. Since the **AccessControl-List** object exposes the *RemoveACE* method, this makes the coding technique quite easy (line 49). Of course, creating a brand new ACL is also a valid technique. Next, if the ACL is emptied (line 52), the script checks if the ACL comes from a DACL (line 54) or a SACL (line 73). In case of a DACL, a default ACE is created (lines 55 through 70). At lines 69 and 70, the script sets the security descriptor *Control Flags* according to the DACL presence. At lines 74 and 75, the script sets the SACL presence to OFF in the security descriptor *Control Flags*, since a default ACE is only created for a DACL. Note that inherited ACEs are not removed by ADSI. They continue to appear as inherited ACEs. If they must be removed, the SE_DACL_PROTECTED flag must be first set to ON, or the parent object defining the inherited ACE must be modified accordingly.

2. **Removing a specific ACE based on the Trustee name (lines 81 through 121):** In such a case, the script enumerates all ACEs (lines 81 through 121), but if the **Trustee** DelACE() function parameter matches the *Trustee* property of an examined ACE (line

82), then the ACE is removed (line 89). Note that inherited ACEs are not removed (lines 83 through 85). Once the ACE is removed, and if the DACL does not contain any ACE, a default ACE based on the "Everyone" trustee is created (lines 93 through 109), as done in the first part of the code. Next, the security descriptor *Control Flags* is set accordingly (lines 108 and 109, lines 113 and 114).

4.12.5.2   *Removing ACE in the WMI object model*

The ACE removal in the WMI object model follows the same logic as the ACE removal in the ADSI object model. Of course, as mentioned previously, instead of manipulating a collection of ACEs in an ACL, Sample 4.48 manipulates items in an array, where the array represents the ACL and array items represent ACEs.

Sample 4.48   *Removing ACE in the WMI object model (Part II)*

```
...:
...:
...:
140:
141:' Here we have a WMI security descriptor representation
142:          Case cFileViaWMI, _
143:               cShareViaWMI
144:
145:          Select Case intACLType
146:               Case cDACL
147:                    arrayACL = objSD.DACL
148:               Case cSACL
149:                    arrayACL = objSD.SACL
150:               Case Else
151:                    Exit Function
152:          End Select
153:
154:          ' Only proceed an ACE removal, if there is at least one available ...
155:          If IsArray(arrayACL) Then
156:             If UCase (strTrustee) = "REMOVE_ALL_ACE" Then
157:                If UBound(arrayACL) = 0 Then
...:
...:
...:
158:          Select Case intACLType
159:               Case cDACL
160:                    Set objNewACE = objWMIServices.Get("Win32_ACE").SpawnInstance_()
161:
162:                    objNewACE.Trustee = CreateTrustee ("Everyone", _
163:                                                        strSIDResolutionDC, _
164:                                                        strUserID, _
165:                                                        strPassword)
166:                    objNewACE.AceType = ADS_ACETYPE_ACCESS_ALLOWED
167:                    objNewACE.AccessMask = ADS_RIGHT_GENERIC_ALL
168:                    objNewACE.AceFlags = CONTAINER_INHERIT_ACE Or _
```

```
169:                                      OBJECT_INHERIT_ACE
170:
171:                    Wscript.Echo "All ACE removed, Trustee 'Everyone' " & _
172:                              "(Full Control) has been created."
173:
174:                    ReDim arrayNewACL (0)
175:                    Set arrayNewACL (0) = objNewACE
176:
177:                    objSD.ControlFlags = objSD.ControlFlags Or _
178:                                      SE_DACL_PRESENT
...:
181:                Case cSACL
182:                    objSD.ControlFlags = objSD.ControlFlags And _
183:                                      (NOT SE_SACL_PRESENT)
184:          End Select
...:
...:
...:
185:               End If
186:
187:               boolRemoveAce = True
188:            Else
189:
190:               strDomainName = ExtractUserDomain (strTrustee)
191:               strUserName = ExtractUserID (strTrustee)
192:
193:               intIndice2 = 0
194:               For intIndice1 = 0 To UBound(arrayACL)
195:                   Set objACE = arrayACL(intIndice1)
196:                   Set objTrustee = objACE.Trustee
197:                   If Ucase(objTrustee.Name) = Ucase(strUserName) Then
198:                      If (objACE.AceFlags And INHERITED_ACE) = INHERITED_ACE Then
199:                          Wscript.Echo "Trustee '" & strTrustee & _
200:                                    "' is inherited and therefore can't be removed."
201:
202:                          ReDim Preserve arrayNewACL(intIndice2)
203:                          Set arrayNewACL(intIndice2) = objACE
204:                          intIndice2 = intIndice2 + 1
205:                      Else
206:                          Wscript.Echo "Trustee '" & strTrustee & _
207:                                    "' has been removed from security descriptor."
208:
209:                          If UBound(arrayACL) = 0 Then
...:
...:
...:
210:            Select Case intACLType
211:                Case cDACL
212:                    Set objNewACE = objWMIServices.Get("Win32_ACE").SpawnInstance_()
213:
214:                    objNewACE.Trustee = CreateTrustee ("Everyone",
215:                                                    strSIDResolutionDC, _
216:                                                    strUserID, _
217:                                                    strPassword)
218:                    objNewACE.AceType = ADS_ACETYPE_ACCESS_ALLOWED
219:                    objNewACE.AccessMask = ADS_RIGHT_GENERIC_ALL
220:                    objNewACE.AceFlags = CONTAINER_INHERIT_ACE Or _
221:                                      OBJECT_INHERIT_ACE
222:
223:                    Wscript.Echo "All ACE removed,Trustee 'Everyone'" & _
```

```
224:                                "(Full Control) has been created."
225:
226:                      ReDim arrayNewACL (0)
227:                      Set arrayNewACL (0) = objNewACE
228:
229:                      objSD.ControlFlags = objSD.ControlFlags Or _
230:                                       SE_DACL_PRESENT
...:
233:               Case cSACL
234:                      objSD.ControlFlags = objSD.ControlFlags And _
235:                                       (NOT SE_SACL_PRESENT)
236:             End Select
...:
...:
...:
237:                          End If
238:
239:                        boolRemoveAce = True
240:                     End If
241:                   Else
242:                     ReDim Preserve arrayNewACL(intIndice2)
243:                     Set arrayNewACL(intIndice2) = objACE
244:                     intIndice2 = intIndice2 + 1
245:                   End If
...:
249:               Next
250:             End If
251:
252:             intAceCount = Ubound(arrayNewACL)
253:             If Err.Number = 9 Then
254:                Err.Clear
255:
256:               Wscript.Echo "All ACE removed."
257:
258:               Select Case intACLType
259:                      Case cDACL
260:                          objSD.DACL = Null
261:                      Case cSACL
262:                          objSD.SACL = Null
263:               End Select
264:             Else
265:               Select Case intACLType
266:                      Case cDACL
267:                          objSD.DACL = arrayNewACL
268:                      Case cSACL
269:                          objSD.SACL = arrayNewACL
270:               End Select
271:             End If
272:           Else
273:             WScript.Echo "No existing ACE to remove."
274:             WScript.Quit(1)
275:           End If
276:
277:' Here we can't retrieve a security descriptor via this access method.
278:        Case cRegistryViaWMI, _
279:             cWMINameSpaceViaADSI
280:
281:     End Select
282:
283:     If boolRemoveAce = False Then
```

```
284:        WScript.Echo "WARNING: Implicit ACE for Trustee '" & strTrustee & _
285:                    "' NOT found in security descriptor."
286:        WScript.Quit(1)
287:    End If
288:
289:    Set DelACE = objSD
290:
291:End Function
```

Although the overall logic used in the WMI object model is the same as the logic used in the ADSI object model, in the coding details there are some important differences. From a global standpoint, we still have two parts with the same purpose as for the ADSI object model:

1.   Removing all ACEs (lines 156 through 187)

2.   Removing a specific ACE based on the Trustee name (lines 188 through 250)

Because the ACL in the WMI object model is represented by an array, instead of manipulating the original array content another array is populated with the ACEs that are not removed. When all ACEs are removed in a DACL, this new array is initialized with the default ACE based on the "Everyone" trustee (lines 160 through 180). When removing a specific ACE, the inherited ACEs are not removed and are copied to the new array (lines 198 through 204). The same applies for ACEs that do not match the **Trustee** DelACE() function input parameter (lines 242 through 244). Basically, when an ACE is removed from the original ACL, it is not copied to the new array. Before completion, the script checks if the new array is initialized with some ACEs (line 252). If there is no ACE, the UBound() function returns an error (line 253). In such a case, the DACL or the SACL (based on the **ACLType** parameter) is set to Null (lines 258 through 270). If the new array is initialized with one or more ACEs, no error is returned and the DACL or SACL property is assigned with this new array (lines 265 through 270).

4.12.6   Reordering ACEs

When ACEs are added or removed from an ACL, it is quite important to properly reorder ACEs, because, in some cases, adding an ACE at the top of an ACL could create undesired security access. This ordering is also called the canonical order. When editing permissions with the ACL editor (i.e., from the Windows Explorer), it is important to note that the editor saves the updated rights in canonical order. Therefore, to avoid any security troubles, it is important to perform the same ordering from the **WMIManage-SD.Wsf** script. The ACEs in an ACL must be sorted into these five groups:

- Access-denied ACEs, which apply to the object itself

- Access-denied ACEs, which apply to a child of the object, such as a property set or property

- Access-allowed ACEs, which apply to the object itself

- Access-allowed ACEs, which apply to a child of the object, such as a property set or property

- All inherited ACEs

The ADSI and WMI object models do not support a method to properly order ACEs in an ACL. This implies that a customized logic must handle the ACE ordering. Sample 4.49 implements the logic in the ADSI object model, while Sample 4.50 implements the logic in the WMI object model. Both samples uses a logic inspired from Microsoft Knowledge Base article Q269159.

4.12.6.1 *Reordering ACEs in the ADSI object model*

The overall idea of the logic is to store ACEs in several temporary ACLs (one per category). Once completed, these temporary ACLs are read in the requested order and each ACE is stored in a new ACL. The end result is that this new ACL contains all ACEs in the required order.

Sample 4.49 *Reordering ACE in the ADSI object model (Part I)*

```
 .:
 .:
 .:
 8:' --------------------------------------------------------------------------------------
 9:Function ReOrderACE(objWMIServices, objSD, intSDType)
 .:
39:     Select Case intSDType
40:' Here we have an ADSI security descriptor representation
41:         Case cFileViaADSI, _
42:              cShareViaADSI, _
43:              cActiveDirectoryViaWMI, cActiveDirectoryViaADSI, _
44:              cExchange2000MailboxViaWMI, cExchange2000MailboxViaADSI, _
45:              cExchange2000MailboxViaCDOEXM, _
46:              cRegistryViaADSI, _
47:              cWMINameSpaceViaWMI
48:
49:              ' Only the DACL is re-ordered
50:              Set objACL = objSD.DiscretionaryAcl
51:
52:              If objACL.AceCount Then
53:                  Set objNewACL = CreateObject("AccessControlList")
```

```
54:                    Set objImplicitDenyACL = CreateObject("AccessControlList")
55:                    Set objImplicitDenyObjectACL = CreateObject("AccessControlList")
56:                    Set objImplicitAllowACL = CreateObject("AccessControlList")
57:                    Set objImplicitAllowObjectACL = CreateObject("AccessControlList")
58:                    Set objInheritedACL = CreateObject("AccessControlList")
59:
60:                    For Each objACE In objACL
61:                        If ((objACE.AceFlags And ADS_ACEFLAG_INHERITED_ACE) = _
62:                                            ADS_ACEFLAG_INHERITED_ACE) Or _
63:                           ((objACE.AceFlags And INHERITED_ACE) = INHERITED_ACE) Then
64:                            objInheritedACL.AddAce objACE
65:                        Else
66:                           Select Case objACE.AceType
67:                                Case ADS_ACETYPE_ACCESS_DENIED,ACCESS_DENIED_ACE_TYPE
68:                                     objImplicitDenyACL.AddAce objACE
69:                                Case ADS_ACETYPE_ACCESS_DENIED_OBJECT
70:                                     objImplicitDenyObjectACL.AddAce objACE
71:                                Case ADS_ACETYPE_ACCESS_ALLOWED,ACCESS_ALLOWED_ACE_TYPE
72:                                     objImplicitAllowACL.AddAce objACE
73:                                Case ADS_ACETYPE_ACCESS_ALLOWED_OBJECT
74:                                     objImplicitAllowObjectACL.AddAce objACE
75:                                Case Else
76:                                    ' Bad objACE
77:                           End Select
78:                        End If
79:                    Next
80:
81:                    ' Implicit Deny ACE.
82:                    For Each objACE In objImplicitDenyACL
83:                        objNewACL.AddAce objACE
84:                    Next
85:
86:                    ' Implicit Deny ACE Objects.
87:                    For Each objACE In objImplicitDenyObjectACL
88:                        objNewACL.AddAce objACE
89:                    Next
90:
91:                    ' Implicit Allow ACE.
92:                    For Each objACE In objImplicitAllowACL
93:                        objNewACL.AddAce objACE
94:                    Next
95:
96:                    ' Implicit Allow ACE Objects.
97:                    For Each objACE In objImplicitAllowObjectACL
98:                        objNewACL.AddAce objACE
99:                    Next
100:
101:                    ' Inherited ACE.
102:                    For Each objACE In objInheritedACL
103:                        objNewACL.AddAce objACE
104:                    Next
105:
106:                    objNewACL.AclRevision = objACL.AclRevision
107:
108:                    objSD.DiscretionaryAcl = objNewACL
...:
118:                End If
119:
...:
...:
...:
```

At line 50, the ReOrderACE() function extracts the ACL from the DACL. Note that the SACL is not considered, since the ACE order is only important for security accesses. Next, if ACEs are contained in the DACL (line 52), the script creates five new ACL objects: one for the new ordered ACL (line 53) and one new ACL for each category (lines 54 through 58). For each ACE in the ACL, the script enumerates all ACEs and stores each of them in its corresponding ACL category based on its type (lines 60 through 79). Once complete, the new ACL is built from each ACL category created (lines 81 through 104). The end result is a list of ACEs properly ordered. Before returning, the new ACL is stored back to the DACL (line 108).

4.12.6.2   *Reordering ACEs in the WMI object model*

The ACE reordering under the WMI object model is the same as the ACE ordering in the ADSI object model. Of course, since ACLs under WMI are represented by an array, the code manipulates items in different arrays (one per category). Except for this difference, the logic of Sample 4.50 is exactly the same as Sample 4.49.

Sample 4.50   *Reordering ACE in the WMI object model (Part II)*

```
...:
...:
...:
119:
120:' Here we have a WMI security descriptor representation
121:          Case cFileViaWMI, _
122:               cShareViaWMI
123:
124:               ' Only the DACL is re-ordered
125:               arrayACL = objSD.DACL
126:
127:               If IsArray (arrayACL) Then
128:                   For intIndice = 0 To UBound(arrayACL)
129:                       If ((arrayACL(intIndice).AceFlags And ADS_ACEFLAG_INHERITED_ACE) = _
130:                                                ADS_ACEFLAG_INHERITED_ACE) Or _
131:                          ((arrayACL(intIndice).AceFlags And INHERITED_ACE)=INHERITED_ACE) Then
132:                           intInheritedACL = intInheritedACL + 1
133:                           ReDim Preserve arrayInheritedACL(intInheritedACL)
134:                           Set arrayInheritedACL(intInheritedACL) = arrayACL(intIndice)
135:                       Else
...:
136: Select Case arrayACL(intIndice).AceType
137:        Case ADS_ACETYPE_ACCESS_DENIED,ACCESS_DENIED_ACE_TYPE
138:            intImplicitDenyACL = intImplicitDenyACL + 1
139:        ReDim Preserve arrayImplicitDenyACL(intImplicitDenyACL)
140:            Set arrayImplicitDenyACL(intImplicitDenyACL) = arrayACL(intIndice)
141:        Case ADS_ACETYPE_ACCESS_DENIED_OBJECT
142:            intImplicitDenyObjectACL = intImplicitDenyObjectACL + 1
```

```
143:                ReDim Preserve arrayImplicitDenyObjectACL(intImplicitDenyObjectACL)
144:                Set arrayImplicitDenyObjectACL(intImplicitDenyObjectACL) = arrayACL(intIndice)
145:          Case ADS_ACETYPE_ACCESS_ALLOWED,ACCESS_ALLOWED_ACE_TYPE
146:                intImplicitAllowACL = intImplicitAllowACL + 1
147:                ReDim Preserve arrayImplicitAllowACL(intImplicitAllowACL)
148:                Set arrayImplicitAllowACL(intImplicitAllowACL) = arrayACL(intIndice)
149:          Case ADS_ACETYPE_ACCESS_ALLOWED_OBJECT
150:                intImplicitAllowObjectACL = intImplicitAllowObjectACL + 1
151:                ReDim Preserve arrayImplicitAllowObjectACL(intImplicitAllowObjectACL)
152:                Set arrayImplicitAllowObjectACL(intImplicitAllowObjectACL) = arrayACL(intIndice)
153:          Case Else
154:                ' Bad ACE
155: End Select
...:
156:                     End If
157:                Next
158:
159:                ' Implicit Deny ACE.
160:                If intImplicitDenyACL Then
161:                    For intIndice = 1 To Ubound(arrayImplicitDenyACL)
162:                        ReDim Preserve arrayNewACL(intNewACL)
163:                        Set arrayNewACL(intNewACL) = arrayImplicitDenyACL(intIndice)
164:                        intNewACL = intNewACL + 1
165:                    Next
166:                End If
167:
168:                ' Implicit Deny ACE Objects.
169:                If intImplicitDenyObjectACL Then
170:                    For intIndice = 1 To Ubound(arrayImplicitDenyObjectACL)
171:                        ReDim Preserve arrayNewACL(intNewACL)
172:                        Set arrayNewACL(intNewACL) = arrayImplicitDenyObjectACL(intIndice)
173:                        intNewACL = intNewACL + 1
174:                    Next
175:                End If
176:
177:                ' Implicit Allow ACE.
178:                If intImplicitAllowACL Then
179:                    For intIndice = 1 To Ubound(arrayImplicitAllowACL)
180:                        ReDim Preserve arrayNewACL(intNewACL)
181:                        Set arrayNewACL(intNewACL) = arrayImplicitAllowACL(intIndice)
182:                        intNewACL = intNewACL + 1
183:                    Next
184:                End If
185:
186:                If intImplicitAllowObjectACL Then
187:                    ' Implicit Allow ACE objects.
188:                    For intIndice = 1 To Ubound(arrayImplicitAllowObjectACL)
189:                        ReDim Preserve arrayNewACL(intNewACL)
190:                        Set arrayNewACL(intNewACL) = arrayImplicitAllowObjectACL(intIndice)
191:                        intNewACL = intNewACL + 1
192:                    Next
193:                End If
194:
195:                If intInheritedACL Then
196:                    ' Inherited ACE.
197:                    For intIndice = 1 To Ubound(arrayInheritedACL)
198:                        ReDim Preserve arrayNewACL(intNewACL)
199:                        Set arrayNewACL(intNewACL) = arrayInheritedACL(intIndice)
200:                        intNewACL = intNewACL + 1
201:                    Next
```

```
202:                End If
203:
204:                    objSD.DACL = arrayNewACL
205:                End If
206:
207:' Here we do not have a security descriptor available via this access method.
208:        Case cRegistryViaWMI, _
209:             cWMINameSpaceViaADSI
210:
211:    End Select
212:
213:    Set ReOrderACE = objSD
214:
215:End Function
```

4.13   Updating the security descriptor

Now that the security descriptors can be read from protected entities via WMI or ADSI, their components, such as the *Control Flags*, can be updated; ACEs can be added and removed from DACL or SACL, but security descriptors must be saved back to the protected entities to make the security change effective. Because the security descriptor access methods differ if they come from a file, Active Directory, or a CIM repository namespace, the object model used to save security descriptors will be the same as the one used to read the security descriptor. Of course, even if the object model remains the same to save the security descriptor, the invoked method will be different. In the next sections, we will see how the security descriptor can be saved back to a protected entity in regard to its origin and the object model used.

4.13.1   Updating file and folder security descriptors

In section 4.7.1 ("Retrieving file and folder security descriptor"), both object models offered an access method to read a security descriptor. To save the security descriptor back to the file system, both object models will be considered in the same way.

4.13.1.1   Updating file and folder security descriptors with WMI

In Chapter 2, when we worked with the *CIM_LogicalFile* class supported by the *Win32* provider, although we didn't use all methods, we discussed the methods exposed by this class (see Table 2.17, "The *CIM_LogicalFile* Methods") to change the security permissions. We had:

- The *ChangeSecurityPermissions* or *ChangeSecurityPermissionsEx* methods: These methods change the security permissions for the logical file specified in the object path. If the logical file is a folder, then

ChangeSecurityPermissions will act recursively, changing the security permissions of all files and subfolders the folder contains.

- The *TakeOwnerShip* or *TakeOwnerShipEx* methods: These methods obtain ownership of the logical file specified in the object path. If the logical file is actually a directory, then *TakeOwnerShip* acts recursively, taking ownership of all the files and subdirectories the directory contains. We already demonstrated the *TakeOwnerShipEx* method in Chapter 2, with Sample 2.36.

On the other hand, the *Win32_LogicalFileSecuritySetting* class, supported by the *Security* provider, exposes two methods to retrieve and update the security descriptor:

- *GetSecurityDescriptor* method: Retrieves a structural representation of the object's security descriptor.

- *SetSecurityDescriptor* method: Replaces a structural representation of the object's security descriptor.

Although the methods from the *Win32_LogicalFileSecuritySetting* and *CIM_LogicalFile* classes seem to be redundant, they are not! The *CIM_LogicalFile ChangeSecurityPermissions* method is able to change one or several security descriptor subcomponents (owner, group, Discretionary ACL, or System ACL) recursively in a File System directory tree. On the other hand, the *Win32_LogicalFileSecuritySetting SetSecurityDescriptor* method replaces the complete structural representation of a security descriptor of a file or a directory object represented by a *Win32_LogicalFileSecuritySetting* instance (see Sample 4.51).

Sample 4.51   *Updating file and folder security descriptors with WMI (Part I)*

```
. :
. :
. :
 8:' ---------------------------------------------------------------------------
 9:Function SetSecurityDescriptor (objConnection, objSD, strSource, intSDType)
. .:
21:     SetSecurityDescriptor = False
22:
23:     Select Case intSDType
24:' +-------------------------------------------------------------------------+
25:' | File or Folder                                                          |
26:' +-------------------------------------------------------------------------+
27:            Case cFileViaWMI
28:' WMI update technique -----------------------------------------------------
29:
30:' Here objSD contains a security descriptor in the WMI object model.
31:
```

```
32:                    WScript.Echo "Setting File or Folder security descriptor via WMI to '" & _
33:                                 strSource & "'."
34:
35:            ' Set objWMIInstance = objConnection.Get("CIM_LogicalFile='" & strSource & "'")
..:
38:            ' intRC = objWMIInstance.ChangeSecurityPermissionsEx (objSD, _
39:            '                                                     13, _
40:            '                                                     Null, _
41:            '                                                     Null, _
42:            '                                                     True)
43:
44:            Set objWMIInstance = objConnection.Get("Win32_LogicalFileSecuritySetting='" &
45:                                 strSource & "'")
..:
48:            intRC = objWMIInstance.SetSecurityDescriptor (objSD)
49:
50:            If intRC Then
51:               WScript.Echo vbCRLF & "Failed to set File or Folder security " & _
52:                                    "descriptor to '" & strSource & "' (" & intRC & ")."
53:            Else
54:               SetSecurityDescriptor = True
55:            End If
..:
..:
..:
```

By default, the code replaces the structural representation of the security descriptor (lines 44 through 48). However, the commented out lines 35 through 42 show the coding technique to use if you do want to make a recursive replacement with the *ChangeSecurityPermissionsEx* method of the *CIM_LogicalFile* class. Note that the *ChangeSecurityPermissionsEx* method does not necessarily replace the whole security descriptor. A set of flags, listed in Table 4.26, determines which part of the security descriptor needs to be replaced.

Nothing forces you to use the *ChangeSecurityPermissionsEx* method. By default, the script makes use of the *SetSecurityDescriptor* method exposed by the *Win32_LogicalFileSecuritySetting* class. Eventually, the script can process the recursion itself. Of course, this logic must be developed in the script code, but the Microsoft Knowledge Base article Q266461 shows an example for the File System security descriptor. In its current version, the SetSe-

Table 4.26   *The ChangeSecurityPermissionsEx Method Flags for the Security Descriptor Recursive Update*

ChangeSecurityPermissionsEx flags	Bit	Value
Change_Owner_Security_Information	0	1
Change_Group_Security_Information	1	2
Change_Dacl_Security_Information	2	4
Change_Sacl_Security_Information	3	8

curityDescriptor() function does not support the recursive application of a security descriptor, but the script can easily be expanded.

4.13.1.2   *Updating file and folder security descriptors with ADSI*

Through ADSI, under Windows Server 2003 (or Windows XP), the script makes use of the **IADsSecurityUtility** interface. This interface was already used in section 4.7.1.2 ("Retrieving file and folder security descriptors with ADSI") and follows the same logic to save the security descriptor back to the File System. Of course, a different method must be used, as shown in Sample 4.52 (lines 73 through 76). Under Windows 2000 (or Windows NT 4.0), the **ADsSecurity** object is used to save the security descriptor (line 79).

The ADSI techniques do not expose functionality to recursively save the security descriptor, although WMI does with the *ChangeSecurityPermissions-Ex* method. To accomplish this, it is necessary to recursively browse the File System hierarchy, as described in the Microsoft Knowledge Base article Q266461.

Sample 4.52   *Updating file and folder security descriptors with ADSI (Part II)*

```
..:
..:
..:
58:
59:          Case cFileViaADSI
60:' ADSI update technique ---------------------------------------------------------
61:
62:' Here objSD contains a security descriptor in the ADSI object model.
63:
64:              WScript.Echo "Setting File or Folder security descriptor via ADSI to '" & _
65:                      strSource & "'."
66:
67:              ' Windows Server 2003 only ---------------------------------------------
68:              objADsSecurity.SecurityMask = ADS_SECURITY_INFO_OWNER Or _
69:                                            ADS_SECURITY_INFO_GROUP Or _
70:                                            ADS_SECURITY_INFO_DACL ' Or _
71:                                            ' ADS_SECURITY_INFO_SACL
72:
73:              objADsSecurity.SetSecurityDescriptor strSource, _
74:                                                   ADS_PATH_FILE, _
75:                                                   objSD, _
76:                                                   ADS_SD_FORMAT_IID
77:
78:              ' Windows 2000 only --------------------------------------------------
79:              ' objADsSecurity.SetSecurityDescriptor objSD, "FILE://" & strSource
80:
81:          If Err.Number Then
82:              Err.Clear
83:              WScript.Echo vbCRLF & "Failed to set File or Folder security " & _
84:                           "descriptor to '" & strSource & "' (" & intRC & ")."
```

```
85:                  Else
86:                      SetSecurityDescriptor = True
87:                  End If
88:
..:
..:
..:
```

Since the **ADsSecurityUtility** object is subject to a bug under Windows Server 2003 and Windows XP, don't forget to refer to section 4.7.1.2 ("Retrieving file and folder security descriptors with ADSI"). If the work-around explained in that section is not used, then it will be impossible to save the updated SACL security descriptor back to the file system.

4.13.2   Updating File System share security descriptors

When a File System share security descriptor is read (see section 4.7.2, "Retrieving file system share security descriptor"), it is not always certain that a security descriptor is available from the share. In such a case, when no security descriptor is available, a default security descriptor is created based on the "Everyone" trustee. To save the security descriptor back to the File System share, we will see that some care must be taken.

4.13.2.1   *Updating share security descriptors with WMI*

With the WMI object model it is necessary to retrieve an instance of the File System share in an **SWBemObject** to update the security descriptor (see Sample 4.53).

Sample 4.53   *Updating share security descriptors with WMI (Part III)*

```
..:
..:
..:
88:
89:' +-------------------------------------------------------------------------------+
90:' | Share                                                                         |
91:' +-------------------------------------------------------------------------------+
92:          Case cShareViaWMI
93:' WMI update technique ----------------------------------------------------------
94:
95:' Here objSD contains a security descriptor in the WMI object model.
96:
97:              WScript.Echo "Setting Share security descriptor " & _
98:                      "via WMI to '" & strSource & "'."
99:
100:             Set objWMIInstance = objConnection.Get("Win32_LogicalShareSecuritySetting='" &
101:                                 strSource & "'")
102:             If Err.Number = wbemErrNotFound Then
103:                 Err.Clear
104:                 Set objWMIInstance = objConnection.Get("Win32_Share='" & strSource & "'")
```

```
...:
107:                    intRC = objWMIInstance.SetShareInfo (0, "", objSD)
108:                    If intRC Then
109:                       WScript.Echo vbCRLF & "Failed to set Share security descriptor to '" & _
110:                                   strSource & "' (" & intRC & ")."
111:                    Else
112:                       SetSecurityDescriptor = True
113:                    End If
114:                 Else
115:                    If Err.Number Then ErrorHandler (Err)
116:
117:                    intRC = objWMIInstance.SetSecurityDescriptor (objSD)
118:                    If intRC Then
119:                       WScript.Echo vbCRLF & "Failed to set Share security descriptor to '" & _
120:                                   strSource & "' (" & intRC & ")."
121:                    Else
122:                       SetSecurityDescriptor = True
123:                    End If
124:                 End If
...:
...:
...:
```

The *Win32_LogicalShareSecuritySetting* class can be used to retrieve an instance of the File System share but with the condition that the share has a security descriptor set (lines 100 and 101). If no security descriptor exists, a **wbemErrNotFound** error will be returned, even if the share is well defined (line 102). In such a case the *SetSecurityDescriptor* method of the *Win32_ LogicalShareSecuritySetting* class can't be used to save the security descriptor. At that time, the script must retrieve an instance of the File System share by using another class: the *Win32_Share* class (line 104) discussed in Chapter 2 with Sample 2.65. This class exposes the *SetShareInfo* method (line 107). The third input parameter of this method requires a structural WMI representation of the security descriptor (made from the *Win32_SecurityDescriptor* class). This technique saves to the File System share the updated or created security descriptor (see Sample 4.25, "Create a default security descriptor for a share").

4.13.2.2 *Updating share security descriptors with ADSI*

To update the File System share security descriptor with ADSI, it is mandatory to run under Windows Server 2003 (or Windows XP) and make use of the **IADsSecurityUtility** interface, as shown in Sample 4.54. Under Windows 2000 (or Windows NT 4.0), there is no way to update a File System share security descriptor with ADSI.

However, things are easier with ADSI than they are with WMI, since it is not necessary in the ADSI object model to retrieve an instance of the share to update the security descriptor (lines 137 through 140). Only the

SetSecurityDescriptor method of the **IADsSecurityUtility** interface needs to be used.

Sample 4.54   *Updating share security descriptors with ADSI (Part IV)*

```
...:
...:
...:
127:
128:          Case cShareViaADSI
129:' ADSI update technique --------------------------------------------------------------
130:
131:' Here objSD contains a security descriptor in the ADSI object model.
132:
133:              WScript.Echo "Setting Share security descriptor via ADSI to '" & _
134:                           strSource & "'."
135:
136:              ' Windows Server 2003 only --------------------------------------------
137:              objADsSecurity.SetSecurityDescriptor strSource, _
138:                                       ADS_PATH_FILESHARE, _
139:                                       objSD, _
140:                                       ADS_SD_FORMAT_IID
141:
142:              If Err.Number Then
143:                 Err.Clear
144:                    WScript.Echo vbCRLF & "Failed to set Share security descriptor to '" & _
145:                          strSource & "' (" & intRC & ")."
146:              Else
147:                 SetSecurityDescriptor = True
148:              End If
149:
...:
...:
...:
```

4.13.3   Updating Active Directory object security descriptors

In section 4.7.3 ("Retrieving Active Directory object security descriptors"), the script retrieves the security descriptor via WMI and ADSI. To update the security descriptor back to Active Directory the script will also use the WMI and ADSI techniques.

4.13.3.1   *Updating Active Directory object security descriptors with WMI*

Updating the security descriptor in Active Directory is little bit more complex than the previous security descriptor update mechanisms. This logic is implemented in Sample 4.55. First, the script must retrieve an instance of the Active Directory object secured by the security descriptor to update (lines 158 through 165). As with the security descriptor access in Sample 4.18 ("Retrieving Active Directory object security descriptors with WMI

[Part V]"), the script invokes the ConvertStringInArray() function to split the Active Directory object class from the object **distinguishedName** (line 158).

Sample 4.55   *Updating Active Directory object security descriptors with WMI (Part V)*

```
...:
...:
...:
149:
150:' +-------------------------------------------------------------------------------+
151:' | Active Directory object                                                       |
152:' +-------------------------------------------------------------------------------+
153:          Case cActiveDirectoryViaWMI
154:' WMI update technique ----------------------------------------------------------
155:
156:' Here objSD contains a security descriptor in the ADSI object model.
157:
158:          arrayADInfo = ConvertStringInArray (strSource, ";")
159:          WScript.Echo "Setting " & LCase(arrayADInfo(0)) & _
160:                       " Active Directory object security descriptor " & _
161:                       "via WMI to 'LDAP://" & arrayADInfo(1) & "'."
162:
163:          Set objWMIInstance = objConnection.Get("ds_" & LCase(arrayADInfo(0)) & _
164:                                        ".ADSIPath='LDAP://" & _
165:                                        arrayADInfo(1) & "'")
...:
168:          arrayBytes = objADSIHelper.ConvertAdsiSDToRawSD (objSD)
...:
171:          Set objTempSD = objWMIInstance.DS_nTSecurityDescriptor
...:
174:          objTempSD.Value = arrayBytes
175:          Set objWMIInstance.DS_nTSecurityDescriptor = objTempSD
176:
177:          objWMINamedValueSet.Add "__PUT_EXTENSIONS", True
178:          objWMINamedValueSet.Add "__PUT_EXT_CLIENT_REQUEST", True
179:          objWMINamedValueSet.Add "__PUT_EXT_PROPERTIES", _
180:                          Array ("DS_nTSecurityDescriptor")
181:
182:          objWMIInstance.Put_ wbemChangeFlagUpdateOnly Or wbemFlagReturnWhenComplete, _
183:                          objWMINamedValueSet
184:      If Err.Number Then
185:          Err.Clear
186:          WScript.Echo vbCRLF & "Failed to set Active Directory object " & _
187:                      "security descriptor to 'LDAP://" & strSource & "'."
188:      Else
189:          SetSecurityDescriptor = True
190:      End If
...:
...:
...:
```

Because the WMI security descriptor method retrieves a security descriptor in a raw form, the WMI security descriptor update method must set the security descriptor in the same format. This requires a conversion of the security descriptor from its ADSI form to a binary form. This conversion is made with the help of the ActiveX DLL (line 168) used during the read operation of the security descriptor. During the read operation of the security descriptor (see Sample 4.18), we saw that the security descriptor is contained in an **SWBemNamedValue** object assigned to the *DS_nTSecurityDescriptor* property of the **SWBemObject** representing the Active Directory object instance. Because the script saves the updated security descriptor back to the Active Directory, it sets the value of the **SWBemNamedValue** object (line 174) to the *DS_nTSecurityDescriptor* property (line 175). Now that the security descriptor of the **SWBemObject** object representing the Active Directory object is updated, this WMI instance must be updated back to the Active Directory. Here, the script uses a WMI partial update technique (lines 177 through 183). We already used the partial-instance update technique in Chapter 3 (section 3.6.1.1, "Creating and updating objects in Active Directory"). Actually, it is impossible to save the complete Active Directory object instance at once, because some of the Active Directory attributes defined in this instance can only be set by the system itself. This means that if we try to save the complete instance back to Active Directory without a partial-instance update, Active Directory will reject the update, since it will consider this update as a violation of the rules enforced by the directory schema (constraint violation). Therefore, the script uses the partial-instance update mechanism and specifies that only the **ntSecurityDescriptor** Active Directory attribute (lines 179 through 180), represented by the *DS_nTSecurityDescriptor* WMI property, must be updated.

4.13.3.2   *Updating Active Directory object security descriptors with ADSI*

Updating an Active Directory security descriptor with ADSI is much simpler than the WMI technique (see Sample 4.56). To ensure that all security descriptor components are saved (i.e., DACL, SACL), the *SetOption* property is initialized accordingly (lines 201 through 204). Next, the security descriptor is placed back into the **nTSecurityDescriptor** attribute (line 206) and committed back to the Active Directory (line 209).

Sample 4.56   *Updating Active Directory object security descriptors with ADSI (Part VI)*

```
...:
...:
...:
193:
194:          Case cActiveDirectoryViaADSI
195:' ADSI update technique -------------------------------------------------------------
196:
197:' Here objSD contains a security descriptor in the ADSI object model.
198:
```

```
199:                 WScript.Echo "Setting Active Directory object security " & _
200:                         "descriptor via ADSI to 'LDAP://" & strSource & "'."
201:                 objConnection.SetOption ADS_OPTION_SECURITY_MASK, ADS_SECURITY_INFO_OWNER Or _
202:                                                                    ADS_SECURITY_INFO_GROUP Or _
203:                                                                    ADS_SECURITY_INFO_DACL Or _
204:                                                                    ADS_SECURITY_INFO_SACL
205:
206:                 objConnection.Put "ntSecurityDescriptor", objSD
...:
209:                 objConnection.SetInfo
210:                 If Err.Number Then
211:                     Err.Clear
212:                     WScript.Echo vbCRLF & "Failed to set Active Directory object " & _
213:                             "security descriptor to 'LDAP://" & strSource & "'."
214:                 Else
215:                     SetSecurityDescriptor = True
216:                 End If
217:
...:
...:
...:
```

4.13.4   Updating Exchange 2000 mailbox security descriptors

Updating the Exchange 2000 mailbox security descriptor requires some specific considerations. With the initial release of Exchange 2000 and with Service Pack 1, the use of ADSI and CDOEXM to manage the mailbox security descriptor was quite limited. All of the information required to create an Exchange 2000 mailbox is initially stored in the Active Directory. By initializing a specific set of attributes associated with a user object, it is possible to create a mailbox using ADSI. Although not officially supported by Microsoft, this is technically possible (at least until Exchange 2000 Service Pack 3). The supported Microsoft solution is to use the CDOEXM extension to create the mailbox. Basically, CDOEXM abstracts the set of attributes required via the *CreateMailbox* method exposed by the **IMailbox-Store** CDOEXM interface. This gives the guarantee of a reliable code, even if Microsoft changes the underlying logic of the mailbox creation in the future. Put simply, the ADSI technique can be seen as a raw mailbox creation process, while the CDOEXM technique can be seen as a logic encapsulated in a COM object.

Despite this nice abstraction layer, until Exchange 2000 Service Pack 2, the original CDOEXM version does not expose any attributes or methods to update mailbox security. Instead, CDOEXM configures a default security for the mailbox, which is not always the one required by Administrators. One possible solution is to use ADSI and access the **msExchMailboxSecurityDescriptor** attribute to initialize the Exchange

2000 mailbox security descriptor as required. But this technique has its limitations, since it only works well for new mailboxes, not existing mailboxes. Why? When an Exchange 2000 mailbox is created, the information required for the definition of the mailbox is stored in the Active Directory. Actually, the physical mailbox, the one in the Exchange 2000 Store, is not created immediately. This "physical" mailbox is created only when the user connects to the new mailbox or when mail is delivered to it. At that time, the mailbox is really created in the Exchange Store, and its security is set from the **msExchMailboxSecurityDescriptor** attribute in the Exchange 2000 Store.

The Active Directory **msExchMailboxSecurityDescriptor** becomes a copy of the real security descriptor set in the store and it only mirrors its value. In this case, ADSI can't be used anymore to change the mailbox security, since it does not provide access to the security descriptor in the store. Any change to the **msExchMailboxSecurityDescriptor** attribute will not be reflected in the Store. So, this solution only works for brand new mailboxes before they are "physically" created in the Exchange Store. Actually, the **msExchMailboxSecurityDescriptor** has two purposes:

- The attribute is a placeholder used to store the security information that will be written to the mailbox security descriptor in the Exchange store when the "physical" mailbox is created.

- Since the attribute is replicated in the Exchange organization, it allows the mailbox permissions to be accessible to all Exchange servers that are connected to different GCs. The evaluation of the "Send as" permission (Extended Right) requires the mailbox permissions to be accessible by all Exchange servers.

Since the Exchange 2000 Service Pack 2, it is possible to update the mailbox security descriptor in the Exchange Store using a new property, called *MailboxRights*, which is exposed by the **IMailboxStore** CDOEXM interface. Since CDOEXM acts as an ADSI extension, this property is associated with the ADSI **IADsUser** interface.

Based on this technical explanation, we can conclude that the Exchange 2000 mailbox security descriptor can be read with any access method (WMI, ADSI, CDOEXM), but it can only be updated with:

- WMI, if the mailbox is not physically created in the Exchange 2000 Store.

- ADSI, if the mailbox is not physically created in the Exchange 2000 Store.

- CDOEXM, if the mailbox is physically created or not in the Exchange 2000 Store. However, Exchange 2000 Service Pack 2 is required!

Now that the update conditions of the Exchange 2000 mailbox security descriptor are clear, let's see how this can be coded in a script.

4.13.4.1   *Updating Exchange 2000 mailbox security descriptors with WMI*

The Exchange 2000 mailbox security descriptor update follows the exact same logic as the update of an Active Directory object security descriptor. The only difference is in the attribute to be updated. For an Active Directory object, the script updated the *DS_nTSecurityDescriptor* of the **SWBemObject** representing the Active Directory object (see Sample 4.55). For the Exchange 2000 mailbox security descriptor, the script updates the *DS_msExchMailboxSecurityDescriptor* property of the **SWBemObject** representing the Active Directory user object (see Sample 4.57). For the rest, we use the same four steps:

- Retrieval of the Active Directory user object instance (lines 228 and 229)

- Conversion of the security descriptor to a binary format (line 232)

- Assignment of the **SWBemNamedValue** object assigned to the *DS_msExchMailboxSecurityDescriptor* property (lines 235 to 239)

- Partial update of the WMI instance representing the Active Directory user object (lines 241 through 247)

Sample 4.57   *Updating Exchange 2000 mailbox security descriptors with WMI (Part VII)*

```
...:
...:
...:
217:
218:' +------------------------------------------------------------------------------+
219:' | Exchange 2000 mailbox                                                        |
220:' +------------------------------------------------------------------------------+
221:         Case cExchange2000MailboxViaWMI
222:' WMI update technique ---------------------------------------------------------
223:
224:' Here objSD contains a security descriptor in the ADSI object model.
225:
226:             WScript.Echo "Setting Exchange 2000 mailbox security " & _
227:                          "descriptor via WMI to 'LDAP://" & strSource & "'."
228:             Set objWMIInstance = objConnection.Get("ds_user.ADSIPath='LDAP://" & _
229:                                              strSource & "'")
...:
232:             arrayBytes = objADSIHelper.ConvertAdsiSDToRawSD (objSD)
...:
```

```
235:                    Set objTempSD = objWMIInstance.DS_msExchMailboxSecurityDescriptor
...:
238:                    objTempSD.Value = arrayBytes
239:                    Set objWMIInstance.DS_nTSecurityDescriptor = objTempSD
240:
241:                    objWMINamedValueSet.Add "__PUT_EXTENSIONS", True
242:                    objWMINamedValueSet.Add "__PUT_EXT_CLIENT_REQUEST", True
243:                    objWMINamedValueSet.Add "__PUT_EXT_PROPERTIES", _
244:                                        Array ("DS_msExchMailboxSecurityDescriptor")
245:
246:                    objWMIInstance.Put_ wbemChangeFlagUpdateOnly Or wbemFlagReturnWhenComplete, _
247:                                        objWMINamedValueSet
248:              If Err.Number Then
249:                    Err.Clear
250:                    WScript.Echo vbCRLF & "Failed to set Exchange 2000 mailbox " & _
251:                                        "security descriptor to 'LDAP://" & strSource & "'."
252:              Else
253:                    SetSecurityDescriptor = True
254:              End If
...:
...:
...:
```

4.13.4.2   *Updating Exchange 2000 mailbox security descriptors with ADSI*

As with the ADSI update technique of a security descriptor from an Active Directory object, the update of a security descriptor of an Exchange 2000 mailbox follows the same logic and coding technique. However, instead of updating the **nTSecurityDescriptor** attribute, Sample 4.58 updates the **msExchMailboxSecurityDescriptor** attribute (lines 270 and 273).

Sample 4.58   *Updating Exchange 2000 mailbox security descriptors with ADSI (Part VIII)*

```
...:
...:
...:
257:
258:          Case cExchange2000MailboxViaADSI
259:' ADSI update technique ---------------------------------------------------------
260:
261:' Here objSD contains a security descriptor in the ADSI object model.
262:
263:                WScript.Echo "Setting Exchange 2000 mailbox security " & _
264:                             "descriptor via ADSI to 'LDAP://" & strSource & "'."
265:                objConnection.SetOption ADS_OPTION_SECURITY_MASK, ADS_SECURITY_INFO_OWNER Or _
266:                                                               ADS_SECURITY_INFO_GROUP Or _
267:                                                               ADS_SECURITY_INFO_DACL Or _
268:                                                               ADS_SECURITY_INFO_SACL
269:
270:                objConnection.Put "msExchMailboxSecurityDescriptor", objSD
...:
273:                objConnection.SetInfo
274:              If Err.Number Then
275:                    Err.Clear
276:                    WScript.Echo vbCRLF & "Failed to set Exchange 2000 mailbox " & _
277:                                        "security descriptor to 'LDAP://" & strSource & "'."
```

```
278:              Else
279:                 SetSecurityDescriptor = True
280:              End If
281:
...:
...:
...:
```

4.13.4.3   Updating Exchange 2000 mailbox security descriptors with CDOEXM

The CDOEXM mailbox security descriptor update technique is the only one able to update the security descriptor when the Exchange 2000 mailbox is physically created in the Exchange 2000 Store. As mentioned before, the Exchange 2000 Service Pack 2 is required. Basically, instead of directly updating the **msExchMailboxSecurityDescriptor** attribute (see Sample 4.58) with the line:

```
objConnection.Put "msExchMailboxSecurityDescriptor", objSD
```

the CDOEXM property, acting as an extension for ADSI, is assigned with the updated security descriptor as follows:

```
objConnection.MailboxRights = Array (objSD)
```

Behind the scenes, the logic encapsulated in the CDOEXM object will update the security descriptor in the Active Directory and at the same time in the Exchange 2000 Store. Sample 4.59 shows the complete code in the context of the script. As we can see, the code modification to support the CDOEXM is very small and the overall logic looks like the ADSI update method. This facility comes mainly from the fact that CDOEXM acts as an extension for ADSI.

Sample 4.59   *Updating Exchange 2000 mailbox security descriptors with CDOEXM (Part IX)*

```
...:
...:
...:
281:
282:          Case cExchange2000MailboxViaCDOEXM
283:' CDOEXM update technique ------------------------------------------------------------
284:
285:' Here objSD contains a security descriptor in the ADSI object model.
286:
287:              WScript.Echo "Setting Exchange 2000 mailbox security " & _
288:                           "descriptor via CDOEXM to 'LDAP://" & strSource & "'."
289:              objConnection.MailboxRights = Array (objSD)
290:
291:              objConnection.SetInfo
292:              If Err.Number Then
293:                 Err.Clear
294:                 WScript.Echo vbCRLF & "Failed to set Exchange 2000 mailbox " & _
295:                              "security descriptor to 'LDAP://" & strSource & "'."
```

```
296:                    Else
297:                        SetSecurityDescriptor = True
298:                    End If
299:
...:
...:
...:
```

4.13.5   Updating registry key security descriptors with ADSI

To read a registry key security descriptor, we must determine if we are running under Windows NT 4.0, Windows 2000, Windows XP, or Windows Server 2003 (see section 4.7.5, "Retrieving registry key security descriptors with ADSI"). As we have seen, under Windows 2000 (or Windows NT 4.0), we can use the **ADsSecurity.DLL** ActiveX to read a registry security descriptor. Under Windows XP or Windows Server 2003, we should use the **IADsSecurityUtility** interface to read the security descriptor from the registry. To update the security descriptor to a registry key, the logic follows the same rule. By default, Sample 4.60 implements the Windows XP/Windows Server 2003 logic (lines 316 through 325), but the commented out lines can be swapped to run the script under Windows NT 4.0/Windows 2000 (line 328). Under Windows XP/Windows Server 2003, the *Security-Mask* is set up to ensure that all components of the security descriptor are saved back to the registry (lines 317 through 320).

Sample 4.60   *Updating registry key security descriptors with ADSI (Part X)*

```
...:
...:
...:
299:
300:' +----------------------------------------------------------------------------------+
301:' | Registry key                                                                     |
302:' +----------------------------------------------------------------------------------+
303:            Case cRegistryViaWMI
304:' WMI update technique ------------------------------------------------------------
305:
306:' Here we can't retrieve a security descriptor via this access method.
307:
308:            Case cRegistryViaADSI
309:' ADSI update technique ------------------------------------------------------------
310:
311:' Here objSD contains a security descriptor in the ADSI object model.
312:
313:                WScript.Echo "Setting registry security descriptor via ADSI to '" & _
314:                             strSource & "'."
315:
316:                ' Windows Server 2003 only ------------------------------------------
317:                objADsSecurity.SecurityMask = ADS_SECURITY_INFO_OWNER Or _
318:                                              ADS_SECURITY_INFO_GROUP Or _
319:                                              ADS_SECURITY_INFO_DACL ' Or _
320:                                            ' ADS_SECURITY_INFO_SACL
```

```
321:
322:                 objADsSecurity.SetSecurityDescriptor strSource, _
323:                                            ADS_PATH_REGISTRY, _
324:                                            objSD, _
325:                                            ADS_SD_FORMAT_IID
326:
327:           ' Windows 2000 only ------------------------------------------------------
328:           ' objADsSecurity.SetSecurityDescriptor objSD, "RGY://" & strSource
329:
330:           If Err.Number Then
331:              Err.Clear
332:              WScript.Echo vbCRLF & "Failed to set registry security descriptor to '" & _
333:                           strSource & "'."
334:           Else
335:              SetSecurityDescriptor = True
336:           End If
337:
...:
...:
...:
```

Since the **ADsSecurityUtility** object is subject to a bug under Windows Server 2003 and Windows XP, don't forget to refer to section 4.7.1.2 ("Retrieving file and folder security descriptors with ADSI"). If the workaround explained in that section is not used, and since the WMI technique is not able to update a structural representation of a registry key security decriptor, there will currently be no way to update the SACL of a registry key security descriptor from the scripting world with the current ADSI COM objects.

4.13.6 Updating CIM repository namespace security descriptors with WMI

When reading a CIM repository namespace security descriptor, we always retrieve the security descriptor in a raw format. Therefore, the script converts it into an ADSI structural representation (see section 4.7.6, "Retrieving CIM repository namespace security descriptors with WMI," Sample 4.24). To update the security descriptor back to a CIM repository namespace, the security descriptor must be converted back to a raw format from its ADSI structural representation. Sample 4.61 illustrates the logic.

Sample 4.61   *Updating CIM repository namespace security descriptors with WMI (Part XI)*

```
...:
...:
...:
337:
338:' +---------------------------------------------------------------------------+
339:' | CIM repository namespace                                                  |
340:' +---------------------------------------------------------------------------+
341:          Case cWMINameSpaceViaWMI
```

```
342:' WMI update technique -------------------------------------------------------------
343:
344:' Here objSD contains a security descriptor in the ADSI object model.
345:
346:               WScript.Echo "Setting CIM repository namespace security descriptor via WMI to '" & _
347:                            strSource & "'."
348:               Set objWMIInstance = objConnection.Get("__SystemSecurity=@")
...:
351:               arrayBytes = objADSIHelper.ConvertAdsiSDToRawSD (objSD)
...:
354:               intRC = objWMIInstance.SetSD (arrayBytes)
355:               If intRC Then
356:                  WScript.Echo vbCRLF & "Failed to set CIM repository namespace security " & _
357:                               "descriptor to '" & strSource & "'."
358:               Else
359:                  SetSecurityDescriptor = True
360:               End If
361:
362:           Case cWMINameSpaceViaADSI
363:' ADSI update technique ------------------------------------------------------------
364:
365:' Here we can't retrieve a security descriptor via this access method.
366:
367:           Case Else
368:
369:      End Select
370:
371:End Function
```

First, the script retrieves an instance of the *__SystemSecurity* singleton class (line 348). Next, it converts the ADSI security descriptor structural representation to a raw format (line 351) with the help of the **ADSIHelper** object (see section 4.9, "The security descriptor conversion"). Then it uses the *SetSD* method exposed by the *__SystemSecurity* class to update the security descriptor.

4.14 How WMI scripters are affected by the Microsoft security push

In early 2002, Microsoft took a huge security initiative to make the Windows platform more secure. This initiative requested all Microsoft developers to review their code for any type of potential problems that could lead to a security breach into the existing Operating Systems. This initiative implied that all new developments were put on hold for awhile until the security review of existing source codes was completed. Of course, Windows Server 2003 inherits the benefit of this security initiative, since some of its existing structures have been updated based on the discoveries. As far as WMI under Windows Server 2003 is concerned, Microsoft made some changes or enhancements at the WMI COM/DCOM level. Of course, most of these changes concern WMI C++ programmers dealing with the WMI COM low-level interfaces. However, some of these changes impact the WMI scripting as well:

- One of the WMI COM/DCOM modifications impacts the WMI asynchronous scripting. Actually, Microsoft added one new feature under Windows Server 2003 to enforce security of the WMI asynchronous calls.

- The security descriptor set on a CIM repository namespace can't be set to NULL.

- The ADSI WMI Extension is removed under Windows Server 2003.

- A new built-in group, called the Windows Authorizations Access Group (WAAG), has been added.

4.14.1   Asynchronous scripting

To understand the impact of the security initiative on the asynchronous scripting, it is necessary to look at some of the mechanisms involved at the COM/DCOM level when WMI asynchronous operations or events are involved. However, we will not delve into the details of the COM/DCOM interfaces to explain this. Instead, we will give a high-level overview of the mechanism and how a script making use of an asynchronous call can be affected.

Generally speaking, when a WMI client application performs asynchronous operations or events, it first connects to the WMI process **WinMgmt.Exe** (see Figure 4.36, arrow 1). During this first step, the WMI client passes a sink to **WinMgmt.Exe** to allow **WinMgmt.Exe** to call the sink routine implemented by the client later on.

When working at the COM/DCOM level, the WMI client application has control of the authentication level for the **WinMgmt.Exe** outgoing calls (see the first book, *Understanding WMI Scripting*, Chapter 4, sections 4.3.3, "The security settings of the moniker," and 4.4.1, "Establishing the WMI connection"). In such a case, **WinMgmt.Exe** retrieves the WMI client security settings when called, and always attempts to call back the client sink routine with the same authentications level (see Figure 4.36, arrow 2). For obvious security reasons, it is always recommended that clients perform a security access check when the sink routine is invoked. However, when the WMI client is a WMI script or cannot control the security settings of the process or when the environment is pre-Windows 2000 (using NTLM), the machine LocalSystem does not have a network identity and it is impossible

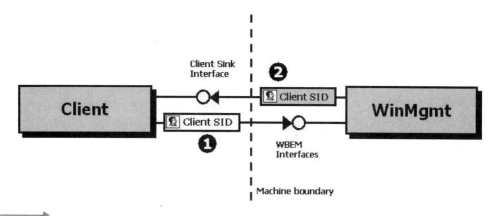

Figure 4.36   *A WMI client application performing an asynchronous operation.*

to control the security level of the callback. In such a case another action takes place, which utilizes **UnSecApp.Exe** (see Figure 4.37). Note that this slightly different action is also applicable for other applications, such as MMC snap-ins.

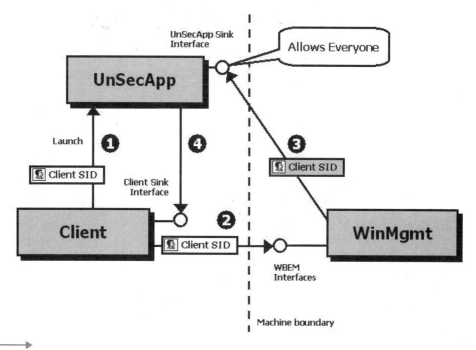

Figure 4.37   *A WMI client application performing an asynchronous operation where UnSecApp.Exe is involved.*

When a WMI script invokes an asynchronous operation, the WMI COM underlying mechanism starts **UnSecApp.Exe** in a separate process on the client (see Figure 4.37, arrow 1). Once started, **UnSecApp.Exe** passes its own sink to the client. Next, when the WMI script initiates the asynchronous call to **WinMgmt.Exe**, it passes the **UnSecApp.Exe** sink along with the call (see Figure 4.37, arrow 2). Therefore, during the **WinMgmt.Exe** callback, the sink utilized is the **UnSecApp.Exe** sink (see Figure 4.37, arrow 3). Because the WMI script can't enforce the callback security as a COM/DCOM WMI client (as shown in Figure 4.36), to get this callback working the **UnSecApp.Exe** accepts callbacks from everyone. Once the callback is accepted by **UnSecApp.Exe**, it returns the asynchronous call information back to the WMI script (see Figure 4.37, arrow 4). It is important to note that **UnSecApp.Exe** is only involved during the asynchronous operations. Therefore, synchronous and semisynchronous operations do not use the same mechanism.

When using asynchronous operations or event notifications in this implementation (Windows NT 4.0, Windows 2000, and Windows XP), it is recommended you take some precautions:

- If you can implement a logic that does not use asynchronous calls for your scripts, consider this option as the best option from a security standpoint. Therefore, you should always try to consider a synchronous or semisynchronous scripting technique when possible.

- If you must absolutely use an asynchronous scripting technique, make sure that the script does not perform some critical operations in the event sink (i.e., system shutdown) in a too powerful security context (i.e., administrative security context). If you implement an asynchronous scripting technique, it is a good idea to implement access checks in the client code as well. Obviously, as a preventive approach, it is best that you don't let scripts execute in the security context of an administrator whenever possible.

- Despite the previous recommendations, if you must perform some critical operations in the event sink in an administrative security context, as we will discuss in the next section, under Windows Server 2003 you can activate a lockdown mechanism, which Microsoft implements to secure the **WinMgmt.Exe** callbacks. Note that at writing time, there is no plan to implement a similar mechanism for the previous Operating System versions.

4.14.1.1   *How the lockdown mechanism of Windows Server 2003 works*

Under Windows Server 2003, Microsoft created a wrapper for **UnSec-App.Exe**. This wrapper plays the role of a security broker between the WMI client and the **WinMgmt.Exe** to validate the callbacks executed on the **UnSecApp.Exe** sink.

However, by default, this wrapper is disabled to ensure a backward compatibility with the WMI asynchronous applications previously developed. If the environment requires a stronger security, it is possible to enable the wrapper in two ways:

- **By programming:** This is only possible for the WMI COM/DCOM applications. In such case, the wrapper behavior can be determined by application, which means that one WMI client application could require authenticating the callbacks, while another will run with the default settings (Everyone).

- **By changing a registry key:** This is the technique to use for the WMI scripts, because there is no way from the scripting environment to determine the wrapper behavior. It is important to note that if the registry key is modified to enable the wrapper to only accept the authenticated calls, the setting is global for all applications (see Figure 4.38). There is no granularity available.

The registry key to change is located in the registry hive HKLM\SOFT-WARE\Microsoft\WBEM\CIMOM, where the *UnsecappAccessControlDefault* value must be changed as follows:

- To allow anonymous calls (default), the *UnsecappAccessControlDefault* value must be set to 0.

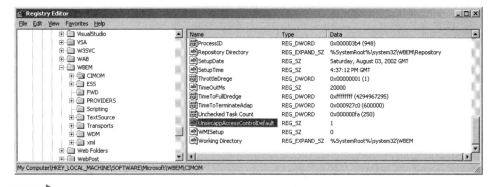

Figure 4.38   *The registry activating the new lockdown mechanism of Windows Server 2003.*

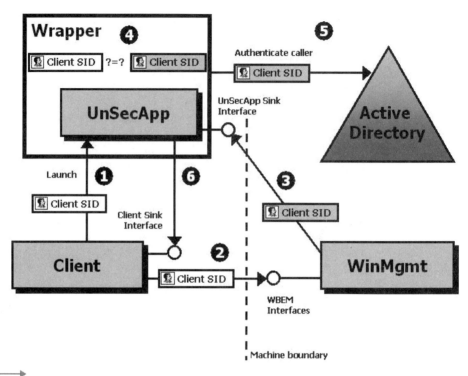

Figure 4.39   *A WMI client application performing an asynchronous operation where UnSecApp.Exe is involved and when the Windows Server 2003 lockdown mechanism is activated.*

- To allow authenticated calls (global setting), the *UnsecappAccessControlDefault* value must be set to 1. Althought the default registry key value is set to 0, it is recommended to set it to 1 if you plan to use asynchronous calls in your applications or scripts.

Once enabled, the wrapper intercepts every callback to **UnSecApp.Exe** in order to verify the identity of the component performing the callback, which should normally be **WinMgmt.Exe** (see Figure 4.39). Actually, the wrapper extracts the SID of the client application from the security token when the initial call of the client application is executed (see Figure 4.39, arrow 1). When the callback to **UnSecApp.Exe** is performed (see Figure 4.39, arrow 3), the wrapper intercepts the callback as well to extract the SID of the caller. The extraction of the SID implies a call against Active Directory, which validates the SID existence of the caller. Next, the SID of the caller is compared with the SID of the client (see Figure 4.39, arrow 4) and if they match, **UnSecApp.Exe** executes the callback to the client application (see Figure 4.39, arrow 6).

As long as the script runs in an authenticated security context, the activation doesn't affect the operation. However, if the callback is delivered under a different identity, the callback will not be returned to the sink routine, and **UnSecApp.Exe** will place an entry into the event log. However, the activation of the registry key setting could only affect applications in pre-Windows 2000 environments due to the lack of LocalSystem identity.

Note: LocalSystem in a Kerberos environment has an identity in an Active Directory environment like any other users. For instance, this allows the Windows services to run in the machine security context rather than a specific domain user. In NTLM environments, LocalSystem has local credentials only and cannot be resolved in a domain, which therefore doesn't provide a network identity.

4.14.2   Setting the security descriptor of a CIM repository namespace

When creating a namespace in the CIM repository, the only element of information required is the name of the namespace, since the name of the namespace is used as a key property of the instance representing the namespace. However, every namespace is protected by a security descriptor, which is inherited from the parent namespace at creation time. Since the security of a namespace could be different from the one set on the parent, it is possible to set a different security descriptor (i.e., by using the *SetSD* method exposed by the *__SystemSecurity* system class). Since the security initiative, it is now impossible to set a security descriptor to null.

If by any chance the security descriptor is set to null on a namespace, the namespace will inherit the security of the parent namespace, since the "non-inheritance" option is not set. However, by eliminating the ability to set a null security descriptor, Microsoft wants to prevent anyone from deliberately removing the namespace security descriptor. Therefore, this initiative is purely preventive.

4.14.3   The ADSI WMI Extension

In Chapter 5 of the first book, *Understanding WMI Scripting*, we see how the ADSI WMI Extension can be used from scripts. This extension is available under Windows NT 4.0 (if ADSI and WMI are installed), Windows 2000, and Windows XP. Under Windows Server 2003 with the security push initiative, this extension has been removed from the Operating System. At writing time, the availability of this extension as a separate download is still under discussion at Microsoft. Actually, Microsoft decided to remove this extension from the Operating System for two reasons:

- One of the drivers during the security push was to leave only enabled components that are intensively used. Since the ADSI WMI Extension was not heavily used, Microsoft decided to remove it from the Operating System to reduce the potential surface of attacks.

- Although the ADSI WMI Extension is not subject to any particular security thread, Microsoft decided to remove it, since it requires high-level privileges to run.

4.14.4 The Windows Authorizations Access Group (WAAG)

The Windows Authorizations Access Group (WAAG) is a new built-in security group introduced in Windows Server 2003. The members of this group are allowed to look up group membership for a particular user. For example, the idea is that user "Alain Lissoir" should not be able to look up other users in the Active Directory and find out that they are members of some selected group of people created by someone else. Therefore, under Windows Server 2003, looking up group membership for another user has to be explicitly granted to users by adding them to the WAAG group in the domain. How is this group related to WMI? Actually, when someone creates a subscription (i.e., for a permanent event consumer), WMI needs to verify if the user who creates the subscriptions has the rights to do that. This verification process enumerates all group membership for the users and therefore the account under which this enumeration is done must be included in WAAG built-in group.

4.15 Summary

In this chapter, besides the IIS configuration regarding WMI and the WMI security changes driven by the security push initiative, we discussed how security descriptors are structured and how they can be deciphered, based on:

- The selected Operating System (Windows NT 4.0/Windows 2000 versus Windows XP/Windows Server 2003)

- The security descriptor origin (file, folders, Active Directory, etc.)

- The security descriptor object model representation (WMI versus ADSI)

The management of the security descriptor clearly shows the limitation of WMI in respect to some secured objects. The complementary nature of ADSI and CDOEXM are, of course, a great help in offering good management coverage of most common security descriptors. However, this requires an extended knowledge of these two technologies, which complicates the scripting techniques. Hopefully, to minimize the learning curve of WMI, ADSI, and CDOEXM, the **WMIManageSD.Wsf** script is generic enough to easily extend its security descriptor management capabilities to support other securable objects, on the condition that some COM components are available to offer a scriptable access.

5

The Optional Windows Components and Application WMI Providers

5.1 Objective

Throughout Chapters 2, 3, and 4 of this book dedicated to WMI, we discovered a lot of classes with their associated WMI providers. This discovery was a long process and showed some of the infinite management capabilities offered by WMI. However, the WMI providers and classes discovered in these chapters only focused on the core Operating System components. At no time were optional components, such as Terminal Services or Internet Information Server, considered. Similarly, Microsoft desktop and server applications, such as Office 2000, Internet Explorer, Exchange 2000, and SQL Server 2000, were not considered. Last but not least, management software, such as Insight Manager, Microsoft Operation Manager, and HP OpenView, were not considered either. The aim of this chapter is to give a brief overview of the WMI capabilities of these various applications. Reading the previous chapters brought you the necessary background to master the WMI scripting techniques. This implies that the remaining challenge is to understand the WMI capabilities of these applications. This is why this chapter will describe the WMI capabilities supported by the applications, without a specific focus on the scripting technique itself. Therefore, we will not systematically develop scripts for each feature, since the scripts will use the exact same scripting techniques as the ones provided throughout the previous chapters.

5.2 WMI and some additional Windows services

5.2.1 Network Load-Balancing service

Available under Windows Server 2003 and Windows 2000 Server, the *Network Load-Balancing* provider consists of two WMI providers registered in

Table 5.1   *The Network Load-Balancing Providers Capabilities*

Provider Name	Provider Namespace	Class Provider	Instance Provider	Method Provider	Property Provider	Event Provider	Event Consumer Provider	Support Get	Support Put	Support Enumeration	Support Delete	Windows Server 2003	Windows XP	Windows 2000 Server	Windows 2000 Professional	Windows NT 4.0
Network Load Balancing Providers																
NlbsNicProv	Root/MicrosoftNLB		X	X				X	X	X		X		X		
Microsoft|NLB_Provider|V1.0	Root/MicrosoftNLB		X	X				X	X	X	X	X		X		

the **Root\MicrosoftNLB** namespace: the *NlbsNicProv* provider, implemented as an instance and method provider, and the *Microsoft|NLB_Provider|V1.0* provider, also implemented as an instance and method provider (see Table 5.1).

These two WMI providers support the classes listed in Table 5.2.

Table 5.2   *The Network Load-Balancing Providers Classes*

Name	Type	Description
MicrosoftNLB_Cluster	Dynamic	Represents an instance of a Network Load-Balancing cluster. Only nodes that have remote control enabled contribute to the ClusterState property as reported in this class and respond to the methods invoked from this class.
MicrosoftNLB_ClusterSetting	Dynamic	Represents data that identifies the Network Load-Balancing cluster to which a node belongs.
MicrosoftNLB_ExtendedStatus	Dynamic	Used by the Network Load-Balancing provider to report error codes specific to Network Load Balancing.
MicrosoftNLB_Node	Dynamic	Represents an instance of a node within a Network Load-Balancing cluster.
MicrosoftNLB_NodeSetting	Dynamic	Represents the configuration data specific to a node.
MicrosoftNLB_PortRuleDisabled	Dynamic	Represents a port rule on a single node whose filtering mode is set to "Disable." Do not use this class unless you need to manage Windows 2000 clusters. Always use MicrosoftNLB_PortRuleEx for managing port rules if possible.
MicrosoftNLB_PortRuleEx	Dynamic	The MicrosoftNLB_PortRuleEx WMI class represents a port rule on a node. The provider will only return the instances for this class that correspond to the node upon which it resides. Consequently, to configure a node, the client must explicitly connect to that node
MicrosoftNLB_PortRuleFailover	Dynamic	Represents a Network Load-Balancing port rule set to single-host filtering mode. Do not use this class unless you need to manage Windows 2000 clusters. Always use MicrosoftNLB_PortRuleEx for managing port rules if possible.
MicrosoftNLB_PortRuleLoadbalanced	Dynamic	Represents a Network Load-Balancing port rule set to multiple-host filtering mode. Do not use this class unless you need to manage Windows 2000 clusters. Always use MicrosoftNLB_PortRuleEx for managing port rules if possible.
MicrosoftNLB_ClusterClusterSetting	Association	Associates an instance of the MicrosoftNLB_Cluster class to an instance of the MicrosoftNLB_ClusterSetting class.
MicrosoftNLB_NodeNodeSetting	Association	Associates an instance of the MicrosoftNLB_Node class to an instance of the MicrosoftNLB_NodeSetting class.
MicrosoftNLB_NodeSettingPortRule	Association	Associates an instance of the MicrosoftNLB_NodeSetting class to instances of classes derived from MicrosoftNLB_PortRule.
MicrosoftNLB_ParticipatingNode	Association	Associates an instance of the MicrosoftNLB_Cluster class with participating MicrosoftNLB_Node class instances.
MicrosoftNLB_PortRule	Abstract Class	MicrosoftNLB_PortRule is an abstract base class from which classes that represent port rules are derived. Do not use this class unless you need to manage Windows 2000 clusters. Use MicrosoftNLB_PortRuleEx.
NlbsNic	Dynamic	Allows the management of the NLB network adapter settings through a set of WMI static methods.

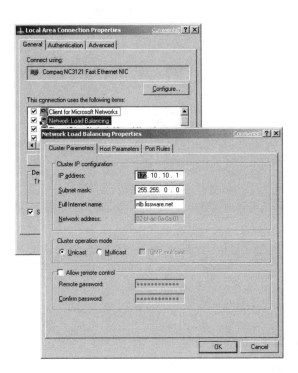

Figure 5.1
The NLB network adapter user interface.

The *NlbsNicProv* provider only supports the *NlbsNic* class, which exposes a series of static methods (*Static* Qualifier set to true) to manage the NLB adapter configuration. Basically, the methods can retrieve and set the configuration parameters available from the user interface in the network settings (see Figure 5.1).

Note that the *NlbsNic* class does not expose any properties. All information must be retrieved and set through the methods listed in Table 5.3.

Sample 5.1 shows how to proceed to retrieve information about the NLB network configuration settings.

Table 5.3   *The NlbsNic Class Static Methods*

Name	Description
ControlCluster	Changes local operational status of cluster or port.
GetClusterConfiguration	Gets extended cluster configuration information.
GetCompatibleAdapterGuids	Gets the list of GUIDs of adapters compatible with NLBand the number of adapters currently bound to NLB.
QueryConfigurationUpdateStatus	Queries status of a pending asynchronous cluster configuration update.
RegisterManagementApplication	Registers a management application with NLB.
UnregisterManagementApplication	Unregisters a management application with NLB.
UpdateClusterConfiguration	Asynchronously updates cluster configuration.

Sample 5.1   *Retrieving NLB network configuration settings*

```
 1:<?xml version="1.0"?>
 .:
 8:<package>
 9: <job>
..:
13:   <runtime>
..:
17:   </runtime>
18:
19:   <script language="VBScript" src="..\Functions\TinyErrorHandler.vbs" />
20:
21:   <object progid="WbemScripting.SWbemLocator" id="objWMILocator" reference="true"/>
22:
23:   <script language="VBscript">
24:   <![CDATA[
..:
28:   Const cComputerName = "LocalHost"
29:   Const cWMINameSpace = "root\MicrosoftNLB"
..:
62:   ' -----------------------------------------------------------------------------
63:   ' Parse the command line parameters
64:   strUserID = WScript.Arguments.Named("User")
65:   If Len(strUserID) = 0 Then strUserID = ""
..:
80:   Set objWMIClass = objWMIServices.Get ("NlbsNIC")
81:   If Err.Number Then ErrorHandler (Err)
82:
83:   intRC = objWMIClass.GetCompatibleAdapterGuids(arrayAdapterGuids, intNumBoundToNlb)
84:   If intRC Then
85:      WScript.Echo "Error getting Compatible Adapter GUID. (" & intRC & ")"
86:      WScript.Quit (1)
87:   End If
88:
89:   For intIndice = 0 To intNumBoundToNlb - 1
90:      WScript.Echo "Adapter GUID #" & intIndice + 1 & ": ................ " & _
91:                   arrayAdapterGuids (intIndice)
92:
93:      intRC = objWMIClass.GetClusterConfiguration (arrayAdapterGuids (intIndice), _
94:                                                   strFriendlyName, _
95:                                                   intGeneration, _
96:                                                   arrayNetworkAddresses, _
97:                                                   boolNLBBound, _
98:                                                   strClusterNetworkAddress, _
99:                                                   strClusterName, _
100:                                                  strTrafficMode, _
101:                                                  arrayPortRules, _
102:                                                  intHostPriority, _
103:                                                  strDedicatedNetworkAddress, _
104:                                                  intClusterModeOnStart, _
105:                                                  boolPersistSuspendOnReboot, _
106:                                                  boolRemoteControlEnabled, _
107:                                                  intHashedRemoteControlPassword)
108:      If intRC Then
109:         WScript.Echo "Error getting Cluster Configuration. (" & intRC & ")"
110:         WScript.Quit (1)
111:      End If
112:
113:      WScript.Echo "Adapter friendly name: .......... " & strFriendlyName
114:      WScript.Echo "Generation: ..................... " & intGeneration
115:      For Each varTemp In arrayNetworkAddresses
```

```
116:               WScript.Echo "Network address(es): ............ " & varTemp
117:          Next
118:          WScript.Echo "NLB bound: ..................... " & boolNLBBound
119:          WScript.Echo "Cluster network address: ........ " & strClusterNetworkAddress
120:          WScript.Echo "Cluster name: ................... " & strClusterName
121:          WScript.Echo "Traffic mode: ................... " & strTrafficMode
122:          For Each varTemp In arrayPortRules
123:               WScript.Echo "Rules: ......................... " & varTemp
124:          Next
125:          WScript.Echo "Host priority: .................. " & intHostPriority
126:          WScript.Echo "Dedicated network address: ...... " & strDedicatedNetworkAddress
127:          WScript.Echo "Cluster mode on startup: ........ " & intClusterModeOnStart
128:          WScript.Echo "Persist suspend on reboot: ...... " & boolPersistSuspendOnReboot
129:          WScript.Echo "Remote control enabled: ......... " & boolRemoteControlEnabled
130:          WScript.Echo "Hashed remote control password: .. " & intHashedRemoteControlPassword
131:     Next
...:
137:     ]]>
138:     </script>
139:   </job>
140:</package>
```

To retrieve NLB network settings, the first thing to do is to retrieve the adapter GUID (lines 83 through 87). This can be done with the *GetCompatibleAdapterGuids* static method exposed by the *NlbsNIC* class (line 83). Once the adapter GUID is known, it can be used to retrieve the cluster configuration with the *GetClusterConfiguration* static method. This method returns the information in a set of variables passed in the method parameters (lines 93 through 107). Once the *GetClusterConfiguration* static method is successfully invoked, the script displays the content of the variables with respect to their types (lines 113 through 130). The execution of Sample 5.1 shows the following output:

```
 1:   C:\>ViewNLBSSettings.wsf
 2:   Microsoft (R) Windows Script Host Version 5.6
 3:   Copyright (C) Microsoft Corporation 1996-2001. All rights reserved.
 4:
 5:   Adapter GUID #1: ................ {8C4CECDF-1D96-4E2E-9B0C-066BFA705E0A}
 6:   Adapter friendly name: .......... Local Area Connection
 7:   Generation: ..................... 1
 8:   Network address(es): ............ 10.10.10.3/255.0.0.0
 9:   NLB bound: ...................... True
10:   Cluster network address: ........ 172.10.10.1/255.255.0.0
11:   Cluster name: ................... nlb.lissware.net
12:   Traffic mode: ................... UNICAST
13:   Rules: .......................... ip=255.255.255.255 protocol=BOTH start=0 end=65535
                                        mode=MULTIPLE affinity=SINGLE
14:   Host priority: .................. 1
15:   Dedicated network address: ...... 10.10.10.3/255.0.0.0
16:   Cluster mode on startup: ........ 1
17:   Persist suspend on reboot: ...... False
18:   Remote control enabled: ......... False
19:   Hashed remote control password: .. 0
```

We recognize some of the information shown in Figure 5.1, such as the cluster IP address (line 10) or the cluster traffic mode (line 12).

The *NlbsNIC* class exposes many other methods (see Table 5.3). For instance, the *ControlCluster* method can be used to control the cluster state, while the *UpdateClusterConfiguration* method can be used to update the cluster configuration settings. Because this method asynchronously updates the configuration settings (*note:* do not confuse with the asynchronous scripting techniques), it is possible to get the update status by invoking the *QueryConfigurationUpdateStatus* method. This summarizes the capabilities of the *NblsNIC* class supported by the *NlbsNICProv* provider. As usual, **WMI CIM Studio** or the **LoadCIMinXL.Wsf** script (see Sample 4.32 in the appendix) can be used to retrieve information about these classes with their methods.

The *Microsoft\NLB_Provider\V1.0* provider supports all the other classes listed in Table 5.2. These classes represent the node and cluster configuration settings as well but in an object model typical to the CIM repository class representation (instances, associations, etc.). For instance, since a cluster is always made of nodes, and since nodes and clusters have some specific configuration settings, the object model implemented in the CIM repository is made up of associations.

If we start looking from the *MicrosoftNLB_Node* class, we can see that this class is associated with (see Figure 5.2):

- The *MicrosoftNLB_NodeSetting* class via *MicrosoftNLB_NodeNodeSetting* association class

- The *MicrosoftNLB_Cluster* class with *MicrosoftNLB_ParticipatingNode* association class

As part of the node settings, we also have the port rules defining the IP filtering rules. Therefore, the *MicrosoftNLB_NodeSetting* class is associated

Figure 5.2
The NLB class associations.

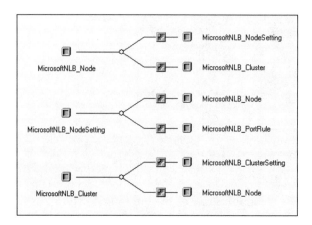

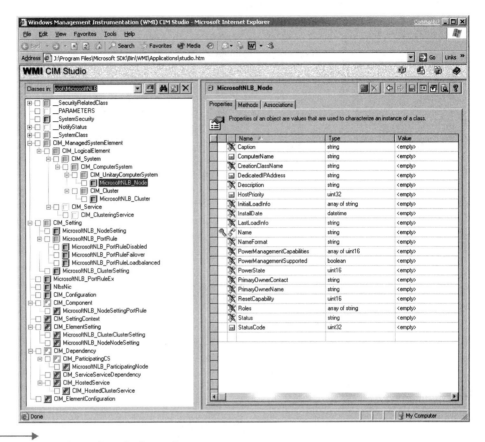

Figure 5.3   *The Node and Cluster classes.*

with the *MicrosoftNLB_PortRule* class, which has three subclasses: *MicrosoftNLB_PortRuleDisabled*, *MicrosoftNLB_PortRuleFailover*, and *MicrosoftNLB_PortRuleLoadbalanced*. In the same way, the *MicrosoftNLB_ Cluster* is associated with the *MicrosoftNLB_ClusterSetting* class. This object model is shown with **WMI CIM Studio** (see Figure 5.3).

It is important to note that since no event provider is implemented, this means that any WMI event subscriptions require the **WITHIN** statement in the WQL event query.

5.2.2   Cluster service

Registered in the **Root\MSCluster** namespace, the WMI Cluster support is implemented with three WMI providers, as shown in Table 5.4. These providers are available under Windows Server 2003 only.

Table 5.4 *The Cluster Providers Capabilities*

Provider Name	Provider Namespace	Class Provider	Instance Provider	Method Provider	Property Provider	Event Provider	Event Consumer Provider	Support Get	Support Put	Support Enumeration	Support Delete	Windows Server 2003	Windows XP	Windows 2000 Server	Windows 2000 Professional	Windows NT 4.0
Cluster Providers																
Cluster Event Provider	Root/MSCluster					X						X				
MS_CLUSTER_CLASS_PROVIDER	Root/MSCluster	X						X		X		X				
MS_CLUSTER_PROVIDER	Root/MSCluster		X	X				X	X	X	X	X				

In total more than 30 classes are supported by these providers. The supported classes are listed in Table 5.5.

An interesting point concerns the presence of the *Cluster* WMI event provider. As shown in Table 5.5, this provider supports seven extrinsic event classes, which can be used to track any cluster state modifications. All extrinsic event classes are derived from the *MSCluster_Event* superclass. Therefore, a WQL query such as

```
Select * From MSCluster_Event
```

will detect all changes supported by the event provider and related to the cluster.

Among the 30 classes in Table 5.5, the most interesting ones from a management perspective are the *MSCluster_Node, MSCluster_Cluster, MSCluster_Service, MSCluster_ResourceGroup,* and *MSCluster_Resource.* For instance, with the *MSCluster_Node* class, it is possible to enable the cluster node event log replication at the node level by configuring the *EnableEventLogReplication* property. With the *MSCluster_Cluster SetQuorumResource* method, it is possible to define the quorum resources and customize the Admin extension resources. The *MSCluster_Service AddNode* and *EvictNode* methods allow the addition and the removal of cluster nodes. This class also allows the start and stop of the cluster service, since it is a class derived from the *CIM_Service* superclass. And, last but not least, with the *MSCluster_ResourceGroup* and *MSCluster_Resource* classes, it is possible to bring a cluster resource on-line or off-line. It is also possible to move a resource to another cluster node. As usual, by using **WMI CIM Studio** or the **Load-CIMinXL.Wsf** script, you can gather more information about the class properties and the methods they expose.

Table 5.5   *The Cluster Providers Classes*

Name	Type	Description
MSCluster_Cluster	Dynamic	Represents a cluster.
MSCluster_Network	Dynamic	Represents cluster networks, which define a network as a connection between network interfaces on the same subnet.
MSCluster_NetworkInterface	Dynamic	Represents the network interface used by the cluster.
MSCluster_Node	Dynamic	Represents a cluster node.
MSCluster_Resource	Dynamic	Represents a cluster resource.
MSCluster_ResourceGroup	Dynamic	Represents a cluster group.
MSCluster_ResourceType	Dynamic	Represents a resource type.
MSCluster_Service	Dynamic	Represents a Cluster service is a Windows NT/Windows 2000 component used to control server cluster activities on a single node.
MSCluster_ClusterToNetwork	Association	Represents the networks the cluster uses for communication.
MSCluster_ClusterToNetworkInterface	Association	Represents the network interfaces the cluster has installed on the nodes it manages.
MSCluster_ClusterToNode	Association	Association class that provides access to the nodes in a cluster.
MSCluster_ClusterToQuorumResource	Association	Represents the cluster quorum resource.
MSCluster_ClusterToResource	Association	Represents the resources in a cluster.
MSCluster_ClusterToResourceGroup	Association	Provides access to the groups in a cluster.
MSCluster_ClusterToResourceType	Association	Represents the groups in the cluster.
MSCluster_NetworkToNetworkInterface	Association	Represents the network interfaces connected to a network.
MSCluster_NodeToActiveGroup	Association	Represents the groups active on a node.
MSCluster_NodeToActiveResource	Association	Represents the resources active on a node.
MSCluster_NodeToHostedService	Association	Represents a service managed by the cluster as a resource.
MSCluster_NodeToNetworkInterface	Association	Represents the network interfaces connected to a node.
MSCluster_ResourceGroupToPreferredNode	Association	Represents a list of the resource groups and their preferred nodes list.
MSCluster_ResourceGroupToResource	Association	Represents the resources in a group.
MSCluster_ResourceToDependentResource	Association	Represents the dependencies of a resource.
MSCluster_ResourceToPossibleOwner	Association	Represents a list of the resources and their possible owner nodes.
MSCluster_ResourceTypeToResource	Association	Represents resources of a particular type.
MSCluster_Event	Extrinsic Event	Represents a cluster event.
MSCluster_EventGroupStateChange	Extrinsic Event	Represents a group state change event.
MSCluster_EventObjectAdd	Extrinsic Event	Represents an add object event. An add object event is generated when a cluster object is added to the cluster.
MSCluster_EventObjectRemove	Extrinsic Event	Represents a remove object event. A remove object event is generated when a cluster object is removed from the cluster.
MSCluster_EventPropertyChange	Extrinsic Event	Represents a property change event. A property change event is generated when a cluster object property is changed.
MSCluster_EventResourceStateChange	Extrinsic Event	Represents a resource state change event.
MSCluster_EventStateChange	Extrinsic Event	Represents a state change event. A state change event is generated when the state of a cluster changes.

Because a cluster consists of various components, the WMI classes are linked together with a collection of association classes. For instance, Figure 5.4 illustrates the associations in place for the *MSCluster_Cluster* class.

5.2.3   Terminal Server service

To support the WMI management of Terminal Services under Windows Server 2003, several providers are registered in the **Root\CIMv2** namespace. Basically, there is one WMI provider per management function supported from WMI. This huge number of providers makes the situation

Figure 5.4
*The MSCluster_*
Cluster class
associations.

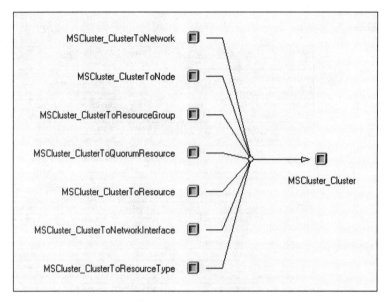

a little bit confusing compared with the two previous Windows services. Therefore, we will examine this service in more detail.

Each provider supports one class from Table 5.6. You can determine the provider that supports a selected class by simply looking at the provider

Table 5.6   *The Terminal Server Providers Capabilities*

Provider Name	Provider Namespace	Class Provider	Instance Provider	Method Provider	Property Provider	Event Provider	Event Consumer Provider	Support Get	Support Put	Support Enumeration	Support Delete	Windows Server 2003	Windows XP	Windows 2000 Server	Windows 2000 Professional	Windows NT 4.0
Terminal Server Providers																
Win32_WIN32_TERMINAL_Prov	Root/CIMV2	X	X					X	X	X	X	X	X			
Win32_WIN32_TERMINALSERVICE_Prov	Root/CIMV2	X	X					X	X	X	X	X	X			
Win32_WIN32_TERMINALSERVICESETTING_Prov	Root/CIMV2	X	X					X	X	X	X	X	X			
Win32_WIN32_TERMINALSERVICETOSETTING_Prov	Root/CIMV2	X	X					X	X	X	X	X	X			
Win32_WIN32_TERMINALTERMINALSETTING_Prov	Root/CIMV2	X						X	X	X	X	X	X			
Win32_WIN32_TSACCOUNT_Prov	Root/CIMV2	X	X					X	X	X	X	X	X			
Win32_WIN32_TSCLIENTSETTING_Prov	Root/CIMV2	X	X					X	X	X	X	X	X			
Win32_WIN32_TSENVIRONMENTSETTING_Prov	Root/CIMV2	X	X					X	X	X	X	X	X			
Win32_WIN32_TSGENERALSETTING_Prov	Root/CIMV2	X	X					X	X	X	X	X	X			
Win32_WIN32_TSLOGONSETTING_Prov	Root/CIMV2	X	X					X	X	X	X	X	X			
Win32_WIN32_TSNETWORKADAPTERLISTSETTING_Prov	Root/CIMV2	X	X					X	X	X	X	X	X			
Win32_WIN32_TSNETWORKADAPTERSETTING_Prov	Root/CIMV2	X	X					X	X	X	X	X	X			
Win32_WIN32_TSPERMISSIONSSETTING_Prov	Root/CIMV2	X	X					X	X	X	X	X	X			
Win32_WIN32_TSREMOTECONTROLSETTING_Prov	Root/CIMV2	X	X					X	X	X	X	X	X			
Win32_WIN32_TSSESSIONDIRECTORY_Prov	Root/CIMV2	X	X					X	X	X	X	X	X			
Win32_WIN32_TSSESSIONDIRECTORYSETTING_Prov	Root/CIMV2	X	X					X	X	X	X	X	X			
Win32_WIN32_TSSESSIONSETTING_Prov	Root/CIMV2	X	X					X	X	X	X	X	X			

name, since the provider name contains the class name. For instance, the *Win32_WIN32_TERMINALSERVICETOSETTING_Prov* provider supports the *Win32_TerminalServiceToSetting* class. Of course, this is a peculiarity of the *Terminal Services* providers naming convention. Previously, to determine which supported a selected class, you would check the *Provider* Qualifier of the class. Even if there is one provider per class, this doesn't change anything from a scripting point of view. This WMI model is mainly designed to customize the Terminal Services configuration settings. The only interesting point to note is that none of the providers is implemented as an event provider, which implies the use of the **WITHIN** statement when monitoring Terminal Services settings. The supported classes are shown in Table 5.7.

With these classes, you can manage the settings available from the "Terminal Services Configuration" MMC. With the *Win32_TerminalServiceSetting* class, you can manage the settings shown in the "Server Settings" folder

Table 5.7   *The Terminal Server Providers Classes*

Name	Type	Description
Win32_Terminal	Dynamic	The Win32_Terminal class is the element of the TerminalSetting association where groups such as: General, Logon, Session, Environment, Remote Control, Client, Network Adapter, and Permission are several configuration setting classes.
Win32_TerminalService	Dynamic	The Win32_TerminalService class provides Terminal Service load-balancing indicators.
Win32_TerminalServiceSetting	Dynamic	The Win32_TerminalServiceSetting class defines the configuration for TerminalServerSetting. This includes capabilities such as Terminal Server Mode, Licensing, Active Desktop, Permissions Capability,Deletion of Temporary folders, and Temporary folders per session.
Win32_TSAccount	Dynamic	The Win32_TSAccount class allows deleting an existing account on the Win32_Terminal class and Modify exisiting Permissions.
Win32_TSClientSetting	Dynamic	The Win32_TSClientSetting class defines the configuration for Win32_Terminal. This includes capabilities such as Connection policy, printer, drive, clipboard mappings, color depth, and connection settings.
Win32_TSEnvironmentSetting	Dynamic	The Win32_TSEnvironmentSetting class defines the configuration for Win32_Terminal. This includes capabilities such as Initial program policy.
Win32_TSGeneralSetting	Dynamic	The Win32_TSGeneralSetting includes capabilities such as Protocol, Transport, Comment, Windows authentication, and Encryption Level.
Win32_TSLogonSetting	Dynamic	The Win32_TSLogonSetting class allows configuring logon settings such as Username, Domain, and Password.
Win32_TSNetworkAdapterListSetting	Dynamic	The Win32_TSNetworkAdapterListSetting class enumerates IP address, GUID, and Name of the Network Adapter.
Win32_TSNetworkAdapterSetting	Dynamic	The Win32_TSNetworkAdapterSetting class defines the configuration for Win32_Terminal. This includes capabilities such as Network Adapter, Maximum Connections, etc.
Win32_TSPermissionsSetting	Dynamic	The Win32_TSPermissionsSetting class allows granting permissions to new accounts and restoring default permissions on the terminal.
Win32_TSRemoteControlSetting	Dynamic	The Win32_TSRemoteControlSetting class defines the configuration for Win32_Terminal. This includes capabilities such as Remote Control policy.
Win32_TSSessionDirectory	Dynamic	The Win32_TSSessionDirectory class defines the configuration for Win32_TSSessionDirectorySetting. This includes capabilities such as Session Directory store, Cluster Name, and Server IP address.
Win32_TSSessionSetting	Dynamic	The Win32_TSSessionSetting class defines the configuration for Win32_Terminal. This includes capabilities such as Time-limits, Disconnection, and Reconnection actions.
Win32_TerminalServiceToSetting	Association	The Win32_TerminalServiceToSetting class is an association with Win32_TerminalService as the Element and Win32_TerminalServiceSetting as the Setting property that includes Terminal Server Mode,Licensing, Active Desktop, Permissions Capability, Deletion of Temporary folders, and Temporary folders per session.
Win32_TerminalTerminalSetting	Association	The Win32_TerminalTerminalSetting class represents an association between a Terminal and its configuration settings.
Win32_TSSessionDirectorySetting	Association	The Win32_TSSessionDirectorySetting class is an association with Win32_TerminalService as the Element and Win32_TSSessionDirectory as the Setting property that includes Terminal Server Session Directory Location, Cluster Name, and SessionDirectoryActive properties.

Figure 5.5
The Terminal
Services
Configuration
MMC.

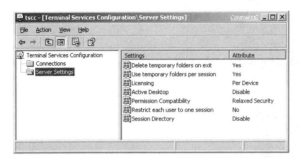

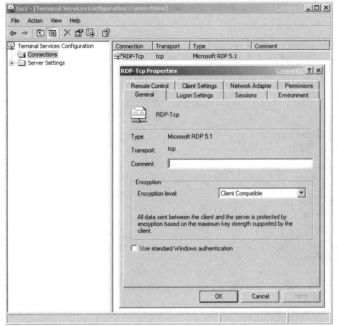

(see Figure 5.5, Server Settings view—top). With all other classes you can manage the settings of the connection transport visible in the "Connections" folder (see Figure 5.5, Connections view—bottom).

5.2.3.1   The Terminal Server configuration

To configure the Terminal Server settings, the *Win32_TerminalServiceSetting* class exposes several methods. Each method corresponds to a setting of the "Server Settings."

As shown in the Sample 5.2 code snippet, the license mode can be changed with the *ChangeMode* method (line 267) and the corresponding value shown in Table 5.8.

Sample 5.2 *Changing the license mode*

```
...:
...:
...:
264:
265:         ' License Mode -------------------------------------------------------------------
266:         If boolChangeLicenseMode Then
267:             intRC = objWMIInstance.ChangeMode (intChangeLicenseMode)
...:
270:             If intRC = 0 Then
271:                 WScript.Echo "TS license mode settings configured."
272:             Else
273:                 WScript.Echo "Failed to configure license mode settings (" & intRC & ")."
274:             End If
275:         End If
276:
...:
...:
...:
```

The same logic applies to change the other server settings shown in Figure 5.5, Server Settings view. However, a specific method must be used for each. Therefore the *Win32_TerminalServiceSetting* class exposes the *SetAllowTSConnections*, *SetHomeDirectory*, *SetProfilePath*, *SetSingleSession*, and *SetTimeZoneRedirection* methods. The corresponding values listed in Table

Table 5.8 *The Win32_TerminalServiceSetting Customization Values*

License Mode	Value	Win32_TerminalServiceSetting Method/Property
Admin	1	
PerDevice	2	*ChangeMode()* method
PerSession	3	
Personal	4	
Security Mode		
Full	0	*UserPermission* property
Relaxed	1	
TS Connections		
Allow	1	*SetAllowTSConnections()* method
Deny	0	
Home Directory		
	C:\MyHomePath	*SetHomeDirectory()* method
Profile Path		
	C:\MyProfilePath	*SetProfilePath()* method
Delete Temp Folders		
Enabled	1	*SetPolicyPropertyName()* method
Disabled	0	
Use Temp Folders		
Enabled	1	*SetPolicyPropertyName()* method
Disabled	0	
Single Session		
Enabled	1	*SetSingleSession()* method
Disabled	0	
Time Zone Redirection		
Enabled	1	*SetTimeZoneRedirection()* method
Disabled	0	

5.8 must be used as the method parameter. In some cases, to customize the *Win32_TerminalServiceSetting* instance, it is necessary to update a property. This is the case for the security mode. In such a case, the script must set the *UserPermission* property (see Sample 5.3, lines 279 through 281) with the corresponding value (see Table 5.8).

Sample 5.3   *Changing the security mode*

```
...:
...:
...:
276:
277:        ' Security Mode ----------------------------------------------------------------
278:        If boolSecurityMode Then
279:            objWMIInstance.UserPermission = intSecurityMode
280:            objWMIInstance.Put_ (wbemChangeFlagCreateOrUpdate Or _
281:                                 wbemFlagReturnWhenComplete)
...:
284:            WScript.Echo "TS security mode configured."
285:        End If
286:
...:
...:
...:
```

A final peculiarity concerning the *Win32_TerminalServiceSetting* class is the modification of the temporary folder settings (see Sample 5.4). These settings must be set with the *SetPolicyPropertyName* method (lines 325 and 326, lines 338 and 339), which accepts two parameters: The first parameter corresponds to the property name to configure, and the second parameter corresponds to the value assigned to the selected property name.

Sample 5.4   *Changing the temporary folder settings*

```
...:
...:
...:
322:
323:        ' Delete Temp Folders --------------------------------------------------------
324:        If boolDeleteTempFolders Then
325:            intRC = objWMIInstance.SetPolicyPropertyName ("DeleteTempFolders", _
326:                                                          intDeleteTempFolders)
...:
329:            If intRC = 0 Then
330:                WScript.Echo "TS Delete Temp Folders setting configured."
331:            Else
332:                WScript.Echo "Failed to configure Delete Temp Folders setting(" & intRC & ")."
333:            End If
334:        End If
335:
336:        ' Use Temp Folders -----------------------------------------------------------
337:        If boolUseTempFolders Then
338:            intRC = objWMIInstance.SetPolicyPropertyName ("UseTempFolders", _
339:                                                          intUseTempFolders)
...:
```

```
342:                    If intRC = 0 Then
343:                        WScript.Echo "TS Use Temp Folders setting configured."
344:                    Else
345:                        WScript.Echo "Failed to configure Use Temp Folders setting(" & intRC & ")."
346:                    End If
347:                End If
348:
...:
...:
...:
```

5.2.3.2   The Terminal Server connections configuration

To manage the Terminal Services connections settings, all other classes from Table 5.7 must be used. Even if the overall logic is the same as for the "Server Settings" with the *Win32_TerminalServiceSetting* class, the Terminal Services connections settings are a bit more complex to set up due to the number of configuration possibilities. In any case, the first action is to retrieve the connection settings instance. By default the "RDP-tcp" connection is the only connection setting instance available (see Figure 5.5, Connections view).

5.2.3.2.1   Enabling/disabling the Terminal Server connections

Enabling or disabling the connection settings is the easiest configuration to perform, since it involves the invocation of the *Enable* method of the *Win32_Terminal* class (see Sample 5.5). A parameter value of 1 enables the connection settings instance, while a parameter value of 0 disables it (line 594). This action corresponds to a right click on the connection name available in the MMC and selecting "Enable connection" or "Disable connection" (in the "All tasks" submenu).

Sample 5.5   *Enabling/disabling the Terminal Services connections*

```
...:
...:
...:
587:
588:    ' Enable/Disable ------------------------------------------------------------
589:    If boolTerminalEnable Then
590:        Set objWMIInstance = objWMIServices.Get ("Win32_Terminal='" & _
591:                                          strTerminalName & "'")
592:        If Err.Number Then ErrorHandler (Err)
593:
594:        intRC = objWMIInstance.Enable (intTerminalEnable)
...:
597:        If intRC = 0 Then
598:            If intTerminalEnable = 1 Then
599:               WScript.Echo "TS enabled."
600:            Else
601:               WScript.Echo "TS disabled."
602:            End If
```

```
603:      Else
604:          WScript.Echo "Failed to enable/disable Terminal Server (" & intRC & ")."
605:      End If
606:  End If
607:
...:
...:
...:
```

5.2.3.2.2   The Terminal Services remote control settings

To configure the remote control connection settings, the *RemoteControl* method exposed by the *Win32_TSRemoteControlSetting* class must be invoked. To properly customize all combinations available from the user interface (see Figure 5.6), it is necessary to set up the *RemoteControlPolicy* property before any other settings.

To set up the various combinations, the two parameters (the *RemoteControl* method parameter and the *RemoteControlPolicy* property) must combine different values. Table 5.9 shows the various combinations for both values with their corresponding settings.

Sample 5.6 shows the coding logic to update the *RemoteControlPolicy* property (lines 614 through 616) and invoke the *RemoteControl* method (lines 619 and 620) if the policy is enabled.

Figure 5.6
The Terminal Services remote control configuration.

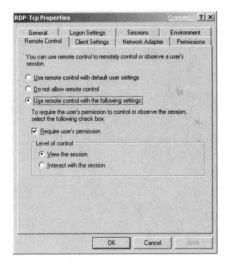

Table 5.9   *The Terminal Services Remote Control Configuration Values*

	LevelOfControl	RemoteControlPolicy
Use remote control with default user settings	0	1
Do not allow remote control	0	0
Use remote control with the following settings		
Require user's permission is **checked**		
View the session	3	0
Interact with the session	1	0
Require user's permission is **unchecked**		
View the session	4	0
Interact with the session	2	0

Sample 5.6   *Configuring the Terminal Services remote control settings*

```
...:
...:
...:
607:
608:    ' Remote Control --------------------------------------------------------------
609:    If boolRemoteControl Then
610:        Set objWMIInstance = objWMIServices.Get ("Win32_TSRemoteControlSetting='" & _
611:                                        strTerminalName & "'")
...:
614:        objWMIInstance.RemoteControlPolicy = intRemoteControlPolicy
615:        objWMIInstance.Put_ (wbemChangeFlagCreateOrUpdate Or _
616:                            wbemFlagReturnWhenComplete)
...:
619:        If intRemoteControlPolicy = 0 Then
620:            intRC = objWMIInstance.RemoteControl (intLevelOfControl)
...:
622:        End If
623:
624:        If intRC = 0 Then
625:            WScript.Echo "TS Remote Control policy configured."
626:        Else
627:            WScript.Echo "Failed to configure the Remote Control policy (" & intRC & ")."
628:        End If
629:    End If
630:
...:
...:
...:
```

5.2.3.2.3   The Terminal Services network adapter and connection limit settings

To set up the connection limit, it is necessary to update the *MaximumConnections* property exposed by the *Win32_TSNetworkAdapterSetting* instance representing the Terminal Services network adapter and connection limit settings (see Figure 5.7).

Figure 5.7
*The Terminal
Service connection
limit settings.*

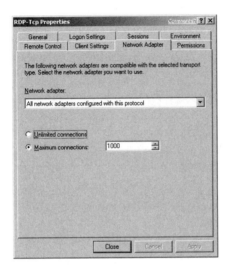

A value of 4,294,967,295 (which is 2^32 – 1, the biggest unsigned integer on 32 bits) sets the connection limit to unlimited. Any other value determines the connection limit in seconds. Sample 5.7 illustrates the coding logic (lines 637 through 639).

Sample 5.7   *Configuring the Terminal Services maximum connection settings*

```
...:
...:
...:
630:
631:    ' Maximum TS connections --------------------------------------------------------
632:    If boolMaximumConnections Then
633:        Set objWMIInstance = objWMIServices.Get ("Win32_TSNetworkAdapterSetting='" & _
634:                                          strTerminalName & "'")
...:
637:        objWMIInstance.MaximumConnections = longMaximumConnections
638:        objWMIInstance.Put_ (wbemChangeFlagCreateOrUpdate Or _
639:                        wbemFlagReturnWhenComplete)
...:
642:        If longMaximumConnections = cNoConnectionLimit Then
643:            WScript.Echo "TS has no connections limit configured."
644:        Else
645:            WScript.Echo "TS has " & longMaximumConnections & " connections limit configured."
646:        End If
647:    End If
648:
649:    ' Adapter ------------------------------------------------------------------------
650:    If boolAdapter Then
651:        Set objWMIInstance = objWMIServices.Get ("Win32_TSNetworkAdapterSetting='" & _
652:                                          strTerminalName & "'")
...:
655:        If UCase (strIPAddress) = "ALL" Then
656:            intRC = objWMIInstance.SelectAllNetworkAdapters
```

```
...:
658:      Else
659:          intRC = objWMIInstance.SelectNetworkAdapterIP (strIPAddress)
...:
661:      End If
662:
663:      If intRC = 0 Then
664:          WScript.Echo "TS adapter configured."
665:      End If
666:    End If
667:
...:
...:
...:
```

From the *Win32_TSNetworkAdapterSetting* instance it is also possible to determine which adapter is compatible with the selected Terminal Services Transport. To set up all adapters, the *SelectAllNetworkAdapters* method must be invoked (line 656). To select a specific network adapter, the *SelectNetworkAdapterIP* method must be invoked with the adapter IP address as a parameter (line 659).

5.2.3.2.4   The Terminal Services encryption and authentication settings

To configure the encryption level, the *SetEncryptionLevel* method exposed by the *Win32_TSGeneralSetting* class must be invoked. To configure the authentication method, the *WindowsAuthentication* property exposed by the *Win32_TSGeneralSetting* instance must be updated.

Figure 5.8 shows the various settings available, while Table 5.10 contains the miscellaneous values.

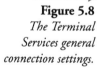

Figure 5.8
The Terminal Services general connection settings.

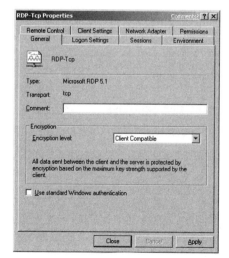

Table 5.10 *The Terminal Services Encryption and Authentication Level Values*

	MinEncryptionLevel	WindowsAuthentication
High	3	
Client Compatible	2	
Use standard Windows Authentication **checked**		1
Use standard Windows Authentication **unchecked**		0

Sample 5.8 illustrates the coding logic.

Sample 5.8 *Configuring the Terminal Services encryption and authentication levels*

```
...:
...:
...:
667:
668:    ' Encryption level -------------------------------------------------------
669:    If boolEncryptionLevel Then
670:        Set objWMIInstance = objWMIServices.Get ("Win32_TSGeneralSetting='" & _
671:                                        strTerminalName & "'")
...:
674:        intRC = objWMIInstance.SetEncryptionLevel(intEncryptionLevel)
...:
677:        WScript.Echo "TS encryption level configured."
678:    End If
679:
680:    ' Windows Authentication -------------------------------------------------
681:    If boolWinAuthentication Then
682:        Set objWMIInstance = objWMIServices.Get ("Win32_TSGeneralSetting='" & _
683:                                        strTerminalName & "'")
...:
686:        objWMIInstance.WindowsAuthentication = intWinAuthentication
687:        objWMIInstance.Put_ (wbemChangeFlagCreateOrUpdate Or _
688:                            wbemFlagReturnWhenComplete)
...:
691:        If intRC = 0 Then
692:            WScript.Echo "TS Windows authentication configured."
693:        End If
694:    End If
695:
...:
...:
...:
```

5.2.3.2.5 The Terminal Services client settings

To set up the Terminal Services default client settings, various methods and properties exposed by the *Win32_TSClientSetting* class must be used. Figure 5.9 shows the settings available.

The number of values that could be set to customize the Terminal Services default client settings is quite confusing, because it is sometimes necessary to update a property directly by assigning a new value; at other times, it may be necessary to invoke a method instead (see Table 5.11).

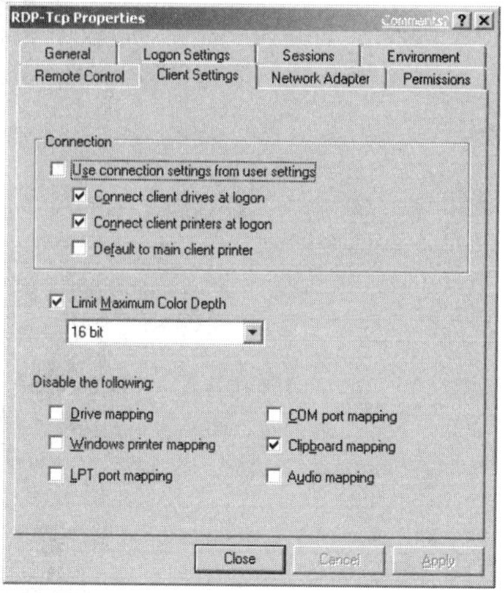

Figure 5.9
The Terminal Services default client settings.

Table 5.11   *The Terminal Services Default Client Settings Values*

	ConnectionPolicy
Use connection settings from user settings **unchecked**	0
Use connection settings from user settings **checked**	1
	ConnectClientDrivesAtLogon
Connect client drives at logon **unchecked**	0
Connect client drives at logon **checked**	1
	ConnectPrinterAtLogon
Connect client printers at logon **unchecked**	0
Connect client printers at logon **checked**	1
	DefaultToClientPrinter
Default to main client printer **unchecked**	0
Default to main client printer **checked**	1
	ColorDepthPolicy
Limit color depth **unchecked**	1
Limit color depth **checked**	0
	ColorDepth
8-bit	1
15-bit	2
16-bit	3
24-bit	4
	DriveMapping
Drive mapping **unchecked**	0
Drive mapping **checked**	1
	WindowsPrinterMapping
Windows printer mapping **unchecked**	0
Windows printer mapping **checked**	1
	LPTPortMapping
LPT port mapping **unchecked**	0
LPT port mapping **checked**	1
	COMPortMapping
COM port mapping **unchecked**	0
COM port mapping **checked**	1
	ClipboardMapping
Clipboard mapping **unchecked**	0
Clipboard mapping **checked**	1
	AudioMapping
Audio mapping **unchecked**	0
Audio mapping **checked**	1

By updating the *ConnectionPolicy* property exposed by the *Win32_TSClientSetting* class, a script will perform the exact same change as selecting the "Use connection settings from user settings" check box. Sample 5.9 shows the coding logic.

Sample 5.9   *Configuring the Terminal Services client connection policy settings*

```
...:
...:
...:
695:
696:     ' User Connection settings --------------------------------------------------------
697:     If boolConnUserSettings Then
698:         Set objWMIInstance = objWMIServices.Get ("Win32_TSClientSetting='" & _
699:                                       strTerminalName & "'")
...:
702:         objWMIInstance.ConnectionPolicy = intConnUserSettings
703:         objWMIInstance.Put_ (wbemChangeFlagCreateOrUpdate Or _
704:                         wbemFlagReturnWhenComplete)
...:
707:         If intConnUserSettings = 0 Then
708:             intRC = objWMIInstance.ConnectionSettings (intConnClientDrivesAtLogon, _
709:                                       intConnClientPrintersAtLogon, _
710:                                       intDefaultToMainClientPrinter)
...:
712:         End If
713:
714:         If intRC = 0 Then
715:             WScript.Echo "TS user connection settings configured."
716:         Else
717:             WScript.Echo "Failed to configure user connection settings (" & intRC & ")."
718:         End If
719:     End If
720:
...:
...:
...:
```

If the "Use connection settings from user settings" check box is unchecked, a client connection policy must be defined. Therefore, the three check boxes in the "Connection" frame (See Figure 5.9) can be configured. This is the reason why Sample 5.9 invokes the *ConnectionSettings* method exposed by the *Win32_TSClientSetting* class and sets the state of the three check boxes (lines 708 through 710).

Regarding the color depth policy, the overall logic is the same as for the client connection policy. Sample 5.10 shows the logic. To define the color depth policy, the *SetColorDepthPolicy* method must be invoked with a parameter value defining the check box state (line 727). Table 5.11 lists the miscellaneous values to use. If the color depth policy is enabled, the color depth must be set by invoking the *SetColorDepth* method, with a parameter value corresponding to the number of bits defining the color depth (line 731).

Sample 5.10   *Configuring the Terminal Services client color depth policy settings*

```
...:
...:
...:
720:
721:     ' Color depth settings ----------------------------------------------------------------
722:     If boolColorDepth Then
723:         Set objWMIInstance = objWMIServices.Get ("Win32_TSClientSetting='" & _
724:                                             strTerminalName & "'")
...:
727:         intRC = objWMIInstance.SetColorDepthPolicy (intColorDepth)
...:
730:         If intColorDepth = 0 Then
731:             intRC = objWMIInstance.SetColorDepth (intColorDepthBit)
...:
733:         End If
734:
735:         If intRC = 0 Then
736:             WScript.Echo "TS color depth settings configured."
737:         Else
738:             WScript.Echo "Failed to configure color depth settings (" & intRC & ")."
739:         End If
740:     End If
741:
...:
...:
...:
```

The final settings concerning the client connection settings concern the resource mappings. These settings correspond to the drive, Windows printer, LPT port, COM port, clipboard, and audio mapping (see Figure 5.9). Here, the logic is a little bit different, since there is no dedicated property or method to use for each setting. To configure these parameters, the *SetClientProperty* method exposed by the *Win32_TSClientSetting* class must be used. Sample 5.11 shows the logic to use for the LPT port mapping, but the technique is the same for all mappings. Basically, the first method parameter contains the property name and the second parameter a Boolean value defining the state (line 748). You can check the *Win32_TSClientSetting* class properties to determine the mapping properties to use during the method invocation.

Sample 5.11   *Configuring the Terminal Services client mapping settings*

```
...:
...:
...:
741:
742:     ' LPT Resource mapping -------------------------------------------------------------
743:     If Len (boolLPTMapping) Then
744:         Set objWMIInstance = objWMIServices.Get ("Win32_TSClientSetting='" & _
745:                                             strTerminalName & "'")
...:
```

```
748:        intRC = objWMIInstance.SetClientProperty ("LPTPortMapping", boolLPTMapping)
...:
751:        If intRC = 0 Then
752:            WScript.Echo "TS LPT port mapping configured."
753:        Else
754:            WScript.Echo "Failed to configure LPT port mapping (" & intRC & ")."
755:        End If
756:    End If
757:
...:
...:
...:
```

5.2.3.2.6   The Terminal Services environment settings

To configure the environment settings of the Terminal Services connection, the *Win32_TSEnvironmentSetting* class must be used. The first setting concerns the initial program policy (see Figure 5.10), which allows the startup of a specific application at logon time.

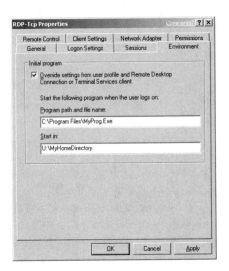

Figure 5.10
The Terminal Services connection environment settings.

As shown in Sample 5.12, to define the initial program policy the *InitialProgramPolicy* property must be updated (lines 844 and 845) accordingly to the values listed in Table 5.12. If the policy is enabled, the *InitialProgram* method exposed by the *Win32_TSEnvironmentSetting* class must be invoked (lines 849 through 852), with two parameters containing the program name and the initial program path, respectively.

Sample 5.12   *Configuring the Terminal Services connection environment settings*

```
   ...:
   ...:
   ...:
   837:
   838:    ' Initial program -------------------------------------------------------------
   839:    If boolInitialProgram Then
   840:       Set objWMIInstance = objWMIServices.Get ("Win32_TSEnvironmentSetting='" & _
   841:                                       strTerminalName & "'")
   ...:
   844:          objWMIInstance.InitialProgramPolicy = intInitialProgramPolicy
   845:          objWMIInstance.Put_ (wbemChangeFlagCreateOrUpdate Or _
   846:                            wbemFlagReturnWhenComplete)
   ...:
   849:          If intInitialProgramPolicy = 0 Then
   850:             intRC = objWMIInstance.InitialProgram (strInitialProgramName, strInitialProgramPath)
   ...:
   852:          End If
   853:
   854:          If intRC = 0 Then
   855:             WScript.Echo "TS initial program configured."
   856:          Else
   857:             WScript.Echo "Failed to configure initial program (" & intRC & ")."
   858:          End If
   859:    End If
   860:
   861:    ' Display Wallpaper -------------------------------------------------------------
   862:    If boolDisplayWallPaper Then
   863:       Set objWMIInstance = objWMIServices.Get ("Win32_TSEnvironmentSetting='" & _
   864:                                       strTerminalName & "'")
   ...:
   867:          intRC = objWMIInstance.SetClientWallPaper (intDisplayWallPaper)
   ...:
   870:          If intRC = 0 Then
   871:             WScript.Echo "TS display wallpaper configured."
   872:          Else
   873:             WScript.Echo "Failed to configure display wallpaper (" & intRC & ")."
   874:          End If
   875:    End If
   876:
   ...:
   ...:
   ...:
```

Table 5.12   *The Terminal Services Connection Environment Policy Settings*

TS environment settings	InitialProgramPolicy
Override settings from user profile and Remote Desktop Connection or Terminal Services Client **unchecked**	1
Override settings from user profile and Remote Desktop Connection or Terminal Services Client **checked**	0

The wallpaper setting is set with the *SetClientWallPaper* method exposed by the *Win32_TSEnvironmentSetting* class. This method sets the *ClientWallPaper* property exposed by the same class. When the *SetClientWallPaper* method parameter is set to 1, the *ClientWallPaper* property is set to 1 as well and forces the display of the wallpaper on the client desktop.

5.2.3.2.7 The Terminal Services connection logon settings

The *Win32_TSLogonSetting* class configures the Terminal Services connection logon settings shown in Figure 5.11.

Figure 5.11
The Terminal Services connection logon settings.

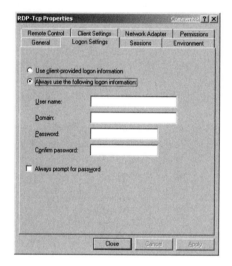

As shown in Sample 5.13, to configure the client logon policy the *ClientLogonInfoPolicy* property exposed by the *Win32_TSLogonSetting* class must be updated (lines 883 through 885). If the policy is enabled, the logon parameters must be defined with the *ExplicitLogon* method exposed by the *Win32_TSLogonSetting* class (lines 888 through 893). The values to use are listed in Table 5.13.

Table 5.13   *The Terminal Services Connection Logon Values*

	ClientLogonInfoPolicy
Use client-provided logon information	1
Always use the following logon information	0
	PromptForPassword
Always prompt for password **unchecked**	0
Always prompt for password **checked**	1

Sample 5.13   *Configuring the Terminal Services connection logon settings*

```
...:
...:
...:
876:
877:    ' Logon as -------------------------------------------------------------------------
878:    If boolClientLogon Then
879:        Set objWMIInstance = objWMIServices.Get ("Win32_TSLogonSetting='" & _
880:                                                 strTerminalName & "'")
...:
883:        objWMIInstance.ClientLogonInfoPolicy = intClientLogonPolicy
884:        objWMIInstance.Put_ (wbemChangeFlagCreateOrUpdate Or _
885:                             wbemFlagReturnWhenComplete)
...:
888:        If intClientLogonPolicy= 0 Then
889:            intRC = objWMIInstance.ExplicitLogon (strLogonUser, _
890:                                                  strLogonDomain, _
891:                                                  strLogonPassword)
...:
893:        End If
894:
895:        If intRC = 0 Then
896:            WScript.Echo "TS client logon information configured."
897:        Else
898:            WScript.Echo "Failed to configure client logon information (" & intRC & ")."
899:        End If
900:    End If
901:
902:    ' Prompt password ------------------------------------------------------------------
903:    If boolPromptPassword Then
904:        Set objWMIInstance = objWMIServices.Get ("Win32_TSLogonSetting='" & _
905:                                                 strTerminalName & "'")
...:
908:        intRC = objWMIInstance.SetPromptForPassword (intPromptPassword)
...:
911:        If intRC = 0 Then
912:            WScript.Echo "TS prompt password configured."
913:        Else
914:            WScript.Echo "Failed to configure prompt password (" & intRC & ")."
915:        End If
916:    End If
917:
...:
...:
...:
```

To determine if the user must be prompted for the password, the *Set-PromptPassword* method exposed by the *Win32_TSLogonSetting* class must be invoked (line 908). A value of 1 will prompt the user for the password.

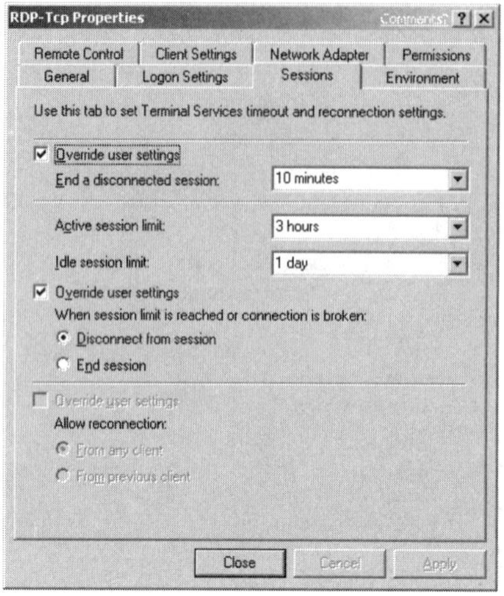

Figure 5.12
The Terminal Services connection session settings.

5.2.3.2.8   The Terminal Services connection session settings

The *Win32_TSSessionSetting* class exposes properties to configure the Terminal Services connection session settings shown in Figure 5.12.

The overall logic shown in Sample 5.14 is the same as before. The Terminal Services session policy must be defined first (lines 924 through 926) by updating the *TimeLimitPolicy* property exposed by the *Win32_TSSessionSetting* class. The value to use is shown in Table 5.14. If the policy is enabled, the *TimeLimit* method exposed by the *Win32_TSSessionSetting*

Table 5.14   *The Terminal Services Connection Session Values*

	TimeLimitPolicy
Override user settings **unchecked**	0
Override user settings **checked**	1
	DisconnectedSessionLimit
End a disconnected session	
Never	0
n minutes	Delay in Min * 60 * 1000
	ActiveSessionLimit
Active session limit	
Never	0
n minutes	Delay in Min * 60 * 1000
	IdleSessionLimit
Idle session limit	
Never	0
n minutes	Delay in Min * 60 * 1000
	BrokenConnectionPolicy
Override user settings **unchecked**	1
Override user settings **checked**	0
	BrokenConnectionAction
Disc. From session	0
End session	1
	ReconnectionPolicy
Override user settings **checked**	1

class will define the *DisconnectedSessionLimit* (line 930), *ActiveSessionLimit* (line 937), and *IdleSessionLimit* (line 944) properties. The values to use are listed in Table 5.14.

Sample 5.14   *Configuring the Terminal Services connection session settings*

```
...:
...:
...:
917:
918:     ' User Session settings ------------------------------------------------------
919:     If boolUserTimeLimitSettings Then
920:        Set objWMIInstance = objWMIServices.Get ("Win32_TSSessionSetting='" & _
921:                                          strTerminalName & "'")
...:
924:        objWMIInstance.TimeLimitPolicy = intUserTimeLimitPolicy
925:        objWMIInstance.Put_ (wbemChangeFlagCreateOrUpdate Or _
926:                          wbemFlagReturnWhenComplete)
...:
929:        If intUserTimeLimitPolicy = 0 Then
930:           intRC = objWMIInstance.TimeLimit ("DisconnectedSessionLimit", intEndDiscSession)
...:
933:           If intRC Then
934:              WScript.Echo "Failed to configure disconnected session limit (" & intRC & ")."
935:           End If
936:
937:           intRC = objWMIInstance.TimeLimit ("ActiveSessionLimit", intActiveSessionLimit)
...:
940:           If intRC Then
941:              WScript.Echo "Failed to configure Active session limit (" & intRC & ")."
942:           End If
943:
944:           intRC = objWMIInstance.TimeLimit ("IdleSessionLimit", intIdleSessionLimit)
...:
947:           If intRC Then
948:              WScript.Echo "Failed to configure idle session limit (" & intRC & ")."
949:           End If
950:        End If
951:
952:        WScript.Echo "TS user session settings configured."
953:     End If
954:
955:     ' Broken Session ------------------------------------------------------
956:     If boolBrokenSession Then
957:        Set objWMIInstance = objWMIServices.Get ("Win32_TSSessionSetting='" & _
958:                                          strTerminalName & "'")
...:
961:        objWMIInstance.BrokenConnectionPolicy = intBrokenConnectionPolicy
962:        objWMIInstance.Put_ (wbemChangeFlagCreateOrUpdate Or _
963:                          wbemFlagReturnWhenComplete)
...:
966:        If intBrokenConnectionPolicy = 0 Then
967:           intRC = objWMIInstance.BrokenConnection (intBrokenConnectionAction)
...:
969:        End If
970:
971:        If intRC = 0 Then
```

```
972:          WScript.Echo "TS broken connection action settings configured."
973:      Else
974:          WScript.Echo "Failed to configure broken connection action settings (" & intRC & ")."
975:      End If
976:  End If
977:
...:
...:
...:
```

The same logic applies for the broken session policy. The *BrokenConnectionPolicy* property exposed by the *Win32_TSSessionSetting* class must be set first (lines 961 through 963). If the policy is enabled, the *BrokenConnectionAction* property must be set with the *BrokenConnection* method (line 967).

5.2.3.2.9 The Terminal Services connection permissions settings

As we have seen in Chapter 4, managing the security often implies the manipulation of a security descriptor. However, to modify the Terminal Services connection permissions settings, it is necessary to invoke specific methods exposed by the *Win32_TSPermissionsSetting* class (see Figure 5.13).

The *Win32_TSPermissionsSetting* class exposes the *AddAccount* method, which takes two parameters: the Domain\UserID account name and the permission value, which defines the right granted for the given account name (see Table 5.15, "Values" column).

To restore the default permissions, the *Win32_TSPermissionsSetting* class exposes the *RestoreDefaults* method. To delete an account granted on the

Figure 5.13
The Terminal Services connection permission settings.

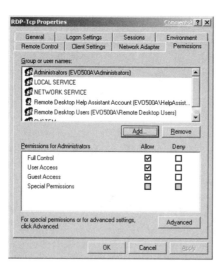

Table 5.15   *The Terminal Services Permission Values and Masks*

TS permissions settings	Values	Masks
Guest	0	32
User and Guest	1	417
Full control, User and Guest	2	983999

Terminal Services connection settings, the *Delete* method exposed by the *Win32_TSAccount* class must be used. If the granted permissions must be modified, the *Win32_TSAccount* class exposes the *ModifyPermissions* and *ModifyAuditPermissions* methods. Both methods require an access mask (see Table 5.15, "Masks" column) and a Boolean value to determine if the access mask is granted or denied.

5.2.4   Windows Driver Model provider

The *Windows Driver Model* (WDM) provider is available from Windows 2000 and later. This provider gives access to WMI information exposed by drivers that are WDM enabled. WDM is an operating system interface through which hardware components (device drivers) provide information exposed by WMI (see Table 5.16). Actually, the *WDM* provider is made up of two providers registered in the **Root\WMI** namespace:

- A class, instance, and method provider called *WMIProv*

- An event provider called *WMIEventProv*

We will not go into the details of the WDM operating system interface. However, to retrieve information from the WDM-enabled drivers, WDM drivers must expose WMI information loaded in the CIM repository. To

Table 5.16   *The WDM Providers Capabilities*

Provider Name	Provider Namespace	Class Provider	Instance Provider	Method Provider	Property Provider	Event Provider	Event Consumer Provider	Support Get	Support Put	Support Enumeration	Support Delete	Windows Server 2003	Windows XP	Windows 2000 Server	Windows 2000 Professional	Windows NT 4.0
WDM Provider																
WMIProv	Root/WMI	X	X	X				X	X	X		X	X	X	X	
WMIProv	Root/MicrosoftNLB	X	X	X				X	X	X		X				
WMIEventProv	Root/WMI					X						X	X	X		
WMIEventProv	Root/MicrosoftNLB					X						X				

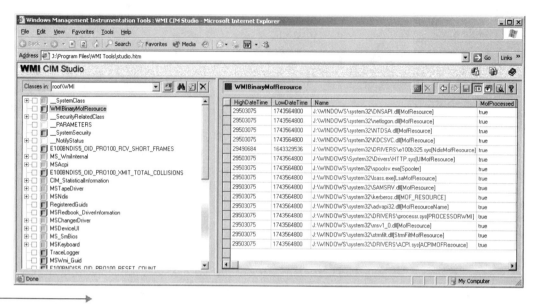

Figure 5.14   *The WMIBinaryMofResource class instances.*

determine the list of drivers exposing information in the CIM repository, it is possible to request instances of the *WMIBinaryMofResource* class (see Figure 5.14).

The most interesting classes supported by the instance provider are summarized in Table 5.17.

Since an event provider is also available, an extrinsic event class can be used in the WQL event queries. The event class is called *WMIEvent* and is used as a parent class to define a collection of extrinsic event classes (see Figure 5.15).

To give a first example of the *WDM* providers classes use, we can reuse the **GetCollectionOfInstances.wsf** script (see Sample 1.5, "Listing all instances of a class with their properties formatted") and request all instances of the *MSDiskDriver_Geometry* class.

```
C:\>GetCollectionOfInstances.wsf MSDiskDriver_Geometry /Namespace:Root\WMI
Microsoft (R) Windows Script Host Version 5.6
Copyright (C) Microsoft Corporation 1996-2001. All rights reserved.


Active: ...............................  TRUE
BytesPerSector: .......................  512
Cylinders: ............................  5169
*InstanceName: ........................  IDE\DiskMAXTOR_6L040J2_...__A93.0500\3631... 2020202020_0
MediaType: ............................  12
SectorsPerTrack: ......................  63
TracksPerCylinder: ....................  240
```

Table 5.17 *The WDM Providers Classes*

Name	Description
MSAcpi_ThermalZoneTemperature	ThermalZone temperature information
MSAcpiInfo	ACPI Table data
MSChangerParameters	Changer Parameters
MSChangerProblemDeviceError	Changer Errors
MSChangerProblemEvent	Changer Problem Warning
MSDeviceUI_FirmwareRevision	Firmware Revision
MSDiskDriver_Geometry	Disk Geometry
MSDiskDriver_Performance	Disk performance statistics
MSIde_PortDeviceInfo	Scsi Address
MSKeyboard_ClassInformation	Keyboard class driver information
MSKeyboard_ExtendedID	Keyboard port extended ID
MSKeyboard_PortInformation	Keyboard port driver information
MSMCAEvent_CPUError	MCA CPU Error Event
MSMCAEvent_InvalidError	MCA Unknown Error Event
MSMCAEvent_MemoryError	MCA Memory Error Event
MSMCAEvent_MemoryPageRemoved	Memory page has been removed
MSMCAEvent_PCIBusError	MCA PCI Bus Error Event
MSMCAEvent_PCIComponentError	MCA PCI Platform Component Error Event
MSMCAEvent_PlatformSpecificError	MCA Platform Specific Error Event
MSMCAEvent_SMBIOSError	MCA SMBIOS Error Event
MSMCAEvent_SwitchToCMCPolling	CMC handling switched from interrupt driver to polling
MSMCAEvent_SwitchToCPEPolling	CPE handling switched from interrupt driver to polling
MSMCAEvent_SystemEventError	MCA Platform IPMI System Eventlog Error Event
MSMCAInfo_RawCMCEvent	This contains a CMC event
MSMCAInfo_RawCorrectedPlatformEvent	This contains a Corrected Platform event
MSMCAInfo_RawMCAData	This contains the raw MCA logs
MSMCAInfo_RawMCAEvent	This contains a MCA event
MSMouse_ClassInformation	Mouse class driver information
MSMouse_PortInformation	Mouse port driver information
MSNdis_CurrentLookahead	NDIS Current Lookahead
MSNdis_CurrentPacketFilter	NDIS Current Packet Filter
MSNdis_DeviceWakeOnMagicPacketOnly	This control decides whether the network device should wake up the system only on receiving a Magic packet
MSNdis_DriverVersion	NDIS Driver Version
MSNdis_EnumerateAdapter	NDIS Enumerate Adapter
MSNdis_HardwareStatus	NDIS Hardware Status
MSNdis_LinkSpeed	NDIS Link Speed
MSNdis_MacOptions	NDIS MAC Options
MSNdis_MaximumFrameSize	NDIS Maximum Frame Size
MSNdis_MaximumLookahead	NDIS Maximum Lookahead Supported
MSNdis_MaximumSendPackets	NDIS Maximum Send Packets
MSNdis_MaximumTotalSize	NDIS Maximum Packet Total Size
MSNdis_MediaConnectStatus	NDIS Media Connect Status
MSNdis_MediaInUse	NDIS Media Types In Use
MSNdis_MediaSupported	NDIS Media Types Supported
MSNdis_NdisEnumerateVc	NDIS Enumerate VC
MSNdis_NotifyAdapterArrival	NDIS Notify Adapter Arrival
MSNdis_NotifyAdapterRemoval	NDIS Notify Adapter Removal
MSNdis_NotifyVcArrival	NDIS Notify VC Arrival
MSNdis_NotifyVcRemoval	NDIS Notify VC Removal
MSNdis_PhysicalMediumType	NDIS Physical Medium Type
MSNdis_ReceiveBlockSize	NDIS Receive Block Size
MSNdis_ReceiveBufferSpace	NDIS Receive Buffer Space
MSNdis_ReceiveError	NDIS Receive Errors
MSNdis_ReceiveNoBuffer	NDIS Receive No Buffer
MSNdis_ReceivesOk	NDIS Receives OK
MSNdis_StatusDevicePowerOff	NDIS Device Power Off Notification
MSNdis_StatusDevicePowerOn	NDIS Device Power On Notification
MSNdis_StatusLinkSpeedChange	NDIS Status Link Speed Change
MSNdis_StatusMediaConnect	NDIS Status Media Connect
MSNdis_StatusMediaDisconnect	NDIS Status Media Disconnect
MSNdis_StatusMediaSpecificIndication	NDIS Status Media Specific Indication
MSNdis_StatusProtocolBind	NDIS Protocol Bind Notification
MSNdis_StatusProtocolUnbind	NDIS Protocol Unbind Notification
MSNdis_StatusResetEnd	NDIS Status Reset End
MSNdis_StatusResetStart	NDIS Status Reset Start
MSNdis_TransmitBlockSize	NDIS Transmit Block Size
MSNdis_TransmitBufferSpace	NDIS Transmit Buffer Space
MSNdis_TransmitsError	NDIS Transmit Errors
MSNdis_TransmitsOk	NDIS Transmits OK
MSNdis_VendorDescription	NDIS Vendor Description
MSNdis_VendorDriverVersion	NDIS Vendor's Driver Version
MSNdis_VendorID	NDIS Vendor ID
MSNdis_VlanIdentifier	NDIS VLAN Identifier

Table 5.17   *The WDM Providers Classes (continued)*

Name	Description
MSPower_DeviceEnable	The control sets whether the device should dynamically power on and off while the system is working.
MSPower_DeviceWakeEnable	This control indicates whether the device should be configured to wake a sleeping system.
MSRedbook_DriverInformation	Digital Audio Filter Driver Information (redbook)
MSRedbook_Performance	Digital Audio Filter Driver Performance Data (redbook)
MSSerial_CommInfo	Serial Communications Information
MSSerial_CommProperties	Communication properties for serial port
MSSerial_HardwareConfiguration	Hardware configuration for serial port
MSSerial_PerformanceInformation	Performance information for serial port
MSSerial_PortName	Serial Port Name
MSSmBios_RawSMBiosTables	Raw SMBIOS Tables
MSSmBios_SMBiosEventlog	Raw SMBIOS Eventlog
MSSmBios_Sysid1394List	List of 1394 SYSIDS
MSSmBios_SysidUUIDList	List of UUID SYSIDS
MSTapeDriveParam	Tape Drive Parameters
MSTapeDriveProblemEvent	Tape Drive Problem Warning
MSTapeMediaCapacity	Tape Media Capacity
MSTapeProblemDeviceError	Device Errors
MSTapeProblemIoError	IO Read Write Errors
MSTapeSymbolicName	Tape Symbolic Name
ProcessorCStateEvent	Processor CStates Event
ProcessorMethods	Methods to alter Processor Performance States
ProcessorPerformance	Processor Information
ProcessorPerfStateEvent	Processor Performance State Change Event
ProcessorStatus	Processor Performance Information
ProcessorTransitionEvent	Processor Transition Event

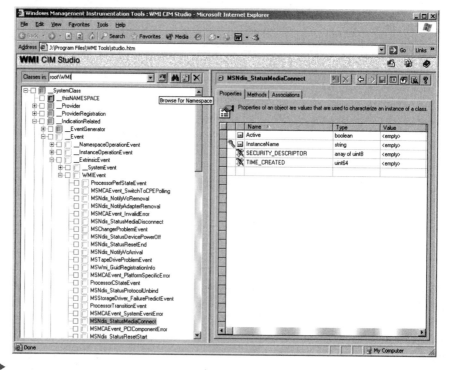

Figure 5.15   *The WMIEvent extrinsic event class.*

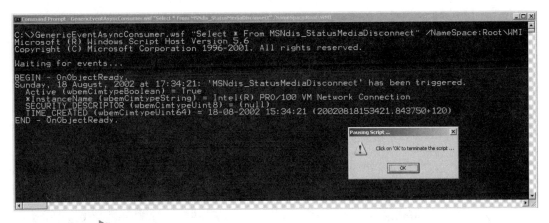

Figure 5.16   *Detecting network cable disconnections with the MSNdis_StatusMediaDisconnect extrinsic event class.*

Actually, the *MSDiskDriver_Geometry* class exposes a subset of the information retrieved by the *Win32_DiskDrive* class.

As a second example, we can also detect network cable disconnections/reconnections. To do so, we must work with the *MSNdis_StatusMediaDisconnect* class, which is a subclass of the *WMIEvent* extrinsic event class. If we reuse Sample 6.17 ("A generic script for asynchronous event notification") in the appendix, when a network cable disconnection occurs, the script returns an event notification, as shown in Figure 5.16.

By requesting instances of the *MSNdis_MediaConnectStatus* class, it is possible to retrieve the state of all network connections available in the system.

```
C:\>GetCollectionOfInstances.wsf MSNdis_MediaConnectStatus /Namespace:Root\WMI
Microsoft (R) Windows Script Host Version 5.6
Copyright (C) Microsoft Corporation 1996-2001. All rights reserved.


Active: ................................. TRUE
*InstanceName: ......................... WAN Miniport (Network Monitor)
NdisMediaConnectStatus: ................. 0

Active: ................................. TRUE
*InstanceName: ......................... WAN Miniport (IP)
NdisMediaConnectStatus: ................. 0

Active: ................................. TRUE
*InstanceName: ......................... Intel(R) PRO/100 VM Network Connection
NdisMediaConnectStatus: ................. 0
```

When the *NdisMediaConnectStatus* property is set to 0, the network is connected. When the property is set to 1, the network is disconnected.

5.3   WMI and some (server) products

5.3.1   Internet Information Server provider

The *Internet Information Server* (IIS) provider is available with IIS 6.0, which comes with Windows Server 2003. It is made up of one single provider implemented as a method, instance, and class provider. It is available from the **Root\MicrosoftIISv2** namespace (see Table 5.18).

This provider supports a collection of WMI classes whose purpose is to expose the information contained in the IIS metabase. The IIS metabase is nothing more than a database containing all IIS configuration settings. This information is stored in a collection of objects and properties defining the various settings supported by IIS. Of course, if we have objects and properties in the metabase, it means we have a schema defining those objects and properties. Therefore, as in any schema implementation, we also have objects with properties (part of the schema) defining objects and properties that can be stored in the metabase. These objects are called the Schema Management Objects. We will not go into the IIS metabase schema discovery, since this would detract from the WMI focus, but it is important to know that WMI classes reflect the IIS metabase schema definitions, whose object instances are represented by WMI instances. This is the reason why the *IIS* provider is implemented as a class provider (to retrieve the IIS metabase schema definitions as WMI classes) and an instance provider (to retrieve the IIS metabase data stored in the IIS metabase objects).

Understanding how WMI maps the IIS metabase is not an easy thing. So, let's take a concrete example. For instance, the IIS metabase schema contains definitions for the **IISWebServer** metabase class and its related

Table 5.18   *The Internet Information Server Provider*

Provider Name	Provider Namespace	Class Provider	Instance Provider	Method Provider	Property Provider	Event Provider	Event Consumer Provider	Support Get	Support Put	Support Enumeration	Support Delete	Windows Server 2003	Windows XP	Windows 2000 Server	Windows 2000 Professional	Windows NT 4.0
IIS Provider																
IIS__PROVIDER	Root/MicrosoftIISv2	X	X	X				X	X	X	X	X				

properties, such as the **ServerBindings** property. Therefore, the CIM repository contains some equivalent WMI classes and properties to expose the same information through WMI. In this specific example (see Figure 5.17), we will have an *IISWebServer* WMI class made from the *CIM_ManagedSystemElement* superclass (left-center position). However, the CIM repository object model is slightly different from the IIS metabase object model. For example, the *IISWebServer* WMI class doesn't have a property called *ServerBindings*. Instead, the *IISWebServer* WMI class has an association with the *IISWebServerSetting* WMI class made from the *CIM_Setting* superclass (right upper-corner position), which exposes a WMI class property called *ServerBindings*. The association between the *IISWebServer* and *IISWebServerSetting* WMI classes is made with the *IIsWebServer_IIsWebServerSetting* association class made from the *CIM_ElementSetting* class (center-top position).

The *ServerBindings* property of the *IISWebServerSetting* WMI class contains a WMI instance of an object made from the *ServerBinding* class

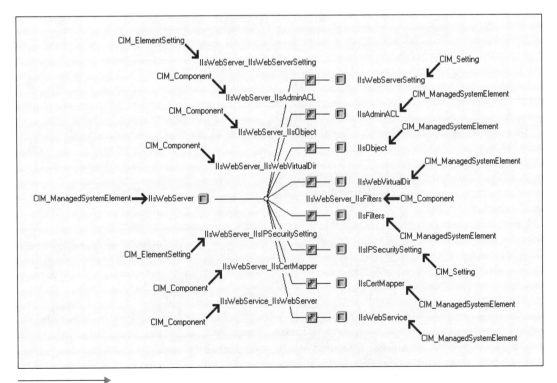

Figure 5.17   *The IISWebServer class associations with their respective superclasses.*

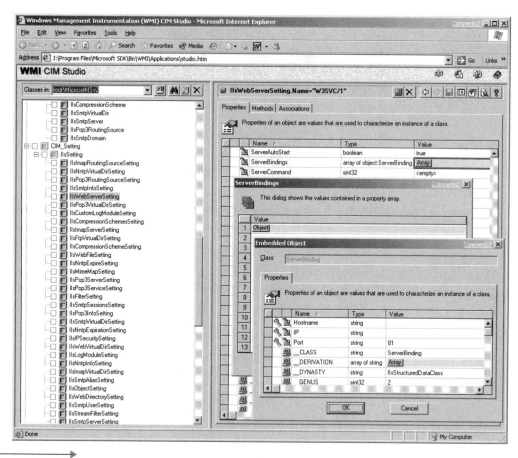

Figure 5.18   *The ServerBindings property and ServerBinding instance.*

(which is made from the *IIsStructuredDataClass* superclass), as shown with **WMI CIM Studio** in Figure 5.18.

As we can see in Figure 5.17, the *IISWebServer* WMI class has some other associations. All associations are made from association classes derived from the *CIM_ElementSetting* or *CIM_Component* superclasses. On the other hand, all associated classes are made from the *CIM_Setting* or *CIM_ManagedSystemElement* superclasses. Next, when a WMI class exposing IIS settings requires a structured representation, the property that should expose the structured information actually exposes an instance made from a class derived from the *IIsStructuredDataClass* superclass (i.e., *ServerBinding* class). This indicates that all IIS WMI classes are always made from five superclasses (see Figure 5.17):

- **The *CIM_ManagedSystemElement* class:** The *CIM_ManagedSystem-Element* class contains subclasses that correspond to node definitions of the metabase Schema. For example, an *IIsWebServer* WMI instance corresponds to the **IIsWebServer** node of the IIS metabase, which represents an instance of an IIS Web server. As another example, the *IIsWebVirtualDir* instance corresponds to the **IIsWebVirtualDir** node of the IIS metabase, which represents an instance of a Web virtual directory. The *IIsWebServer* WMI instance and the *IIsWebVirtualDir* instance expose read-only properties and methods, whereas the associated instances made from the *CIM_Setting* subclasses contain the writeable properties for the nodes. For example, the *IIsWebServer* class derived from the *CIM_ManagedSystemElement* class exposes read-only properties for an IIS Web server as well as methods that can modify some properties of the *IIsWebServerSetting* class instance and manage the IIS Web Server (i.e., start or stop the Web server).

  On the other hand, the *IIsWebServerSetting* class properties (derived from the *CIM_Setting* class and associated with the *IISWebServer* class) can be updated to modify the IIS Web server settings (see Figure 5.19).

- **The *CIM_Setting* class:** The classes derived from the *CIM_Setting* superclass expose properties corresponding to the metabase node properties that can be set at those nodes. The associated classes derived from the *CIM_ManagedSystemElement* class expose methods that manipulate the node properties. As previously mentioned, the *IIsWebServerSetting* class (derived from the *CIM_Setting* superclass) and the *IIsWebServer* class (derived from the CIM_*ManagedSystem-Element* class) refer to Web sites on your Web server, where the *IIsWebServer* class contains the read-only properties of a Web site and

Figure 5.19
The associations of the CIM_ ManagedSystem-Element superclass.

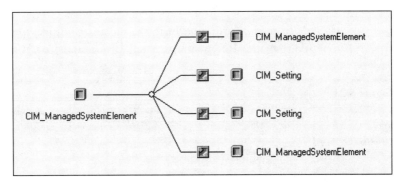

Figure 5.20
*The associations of
the CIM_Setting
superclass.*

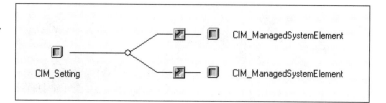

the *IIsWebServerSetting* class contains the writeable properties of a Web site (see Figure 5.20).

- **The *IIsStructuredDataClass* class:** The classes derived from the *IIsStructuredDataClass* class contain properties whose data requires a structured representation. For example, the *ServerBindings* property in the metabase is a string whose format is "IP:Port:Hostname." In the WMI representation, a *ServerBinding* class is available with three properties corresponding to the IP address, the port number, and the host name. In Figure 5.18, a class such as the *IIsWebServerSetting* class (made from the *CIM_Setting* class) contains a property called *ServerBindings,* which is an array of *ServerBinding* class instances.

- **The *CIM_Component* class:** The classes created from this association superclass map each class made from the *CIM_ManagedSystemElement* superclass to another class made from the *CIM_ManagedSystemElement* superclass. As with any association classes, the properties of these classes are references to the two associated classes (see Figure 5.21).

- **The *CIM_ElementSetting* class:** The classes created from this association class associate each class made from the *CIM_ManagedSystemElement* superclass to its matching class made from the *CIM_Setting* superclass. The properties of these classes are references to the two associated classes (see Figure 5.22).

To read information from the metabase with scripts, it is possible to use ADSI in the IIS: namespace (all IIS versions) or WMI (IIS 6.0 only). A

Figure 5.21
*The CIM_
Component class
with its references.*

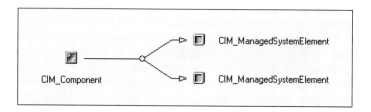

Figure 5.22
*The CIM_*
ElementSetting
class with its
references.

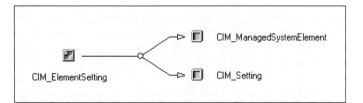

script reading the **IISWebServer ServerBindings** property with ADSI will look as follows:

```
1:    Set objIISWebServer = GetObject ("IIS://LocalHost/W3SVC/1")
2:
3:    arrayServerBindings = objIISWebServer.Get ("ServerBindings")
4:
5:    For Each varServerBinding In arrayServerBindings
6:        WScript.Echo "ServerBindings: '" & varServerBinding & "'"
7:    Next
```

At line 1, the "W3SVC/1" represents the IIS Web server instance to be accessed via ADSI. Next, the script requests the **ServerBindings** property from the object representing the Web service instance (line 3). From line 5 through 7, the "For Each" loop enumerates all values found in the **Server-Bindings** property.

The **ADSUTIL.VBS** script from an IIS installation (check %System-Drive%\Inetpub\AdminScripts folder) uses ADSI to access the IIS metabase. For example, to read the **IISWebServer ServerBindings** property with **ADSUTIL.VBS**, we should use the following command line:

```
C:\>adsutil.vbs GET W3SVC/1/ServerBindings
Microsoft (R) Windows Script Host Version 5.6
Copyright (C) Microsoft Corporation 1996-2001. All rights reserved.

ServerBindings                 : (LIST) (1 Items)
  ":81:"
```

In addition to being able to retrieve all properties stored in the IIS metabase, **ADSUTIL.VBS** also allows most configuration settings and operations handled by the "Internet Information Services" MMC from the command line.

With WMI, to retrieve the **ServerBindings** of the **IISWebServer** "W3SVC/1" node from the metabase, we should retrieve the *IISWebServer-Settings* WMI instance (which is actually associated with the *IISWebServer* WMI class and contains the Web server configuration settings). This is illustrated in Sample 5.15. However, for information completeness, the code enumerates all properties of the *IISWebServerSettings* WMI instance, which explains why it is slightly longer than the ADSI example.

Sample 5.15   *Viewing the IISWebServer ServerBindings property with WMI*

```
 1:<?xml version="1.0"?>
 .:
 8:<package>
 9:  <job>
..:
13:    <runtime>
..:
17:    </runtime>
18:
19:    <script language="VBScript" src="..\Functions\DisplayFormattedPropertiesFunction.vbs" />
20:    <script language="VBScript" src="..\Functions\DisplayFormattedPropertyFunction.vbs" />
21:    <script language="VBScript" src="..\Functions\TinyErrorHandler.vbs" />
22:
23:    <object progid="WbemScripting.SWbemLocator" id="objWMILocator" reference="true"/>
24:
25:    <script language="VBscript">
26:    <![CDATA[
..:
30:    Const cComputerName = "LocalHost"
31:    Const cWMINameSpace = "root\MicrosoftIISv2"
32:    Const cWMIClass = "IISWebServer"
..:
59:    objWMILocator.Security_.AuthenticationLevel = wbemAuthenticationLevelDefault
60:    objWMILocator.Security_.ImpersonationLevel = wbemImpersonationLevelImpersonate
61:
62:    Set objWMIServices = objWMILocator.ConnectServer(strComputerName, cWMINameSpace, _
63:                                          strUserID, strPassword)
..:
66:    Set objWMIWebServerInstances = objWMIServices.InstancesOf (cWMIClass)
..:
69:    For Each objWMIWebServerInstance In objWMIWebServerInstances
70:        DisplayFormattedProperties objWMIWebServerInstance, 0
71:
72:        Set objWMIAssociatedInstances = objWMIServices.ExecQuery _
73:                                ("Associators Of {IISWebServer='" & _
74:                                objWMIWebServerInstance.Name & "'}")
75:        For Each objWMIAssociatedInstance In objWMIAssociatedInstances
76:            DisplayFormattedProperties objWMIAssociatedInstance, 2
77:        Next
..:
79:    Next
..:
85:    ]]>
86:    </script>
87:  </job>
88:</package>
```

Sample 5.15 does not use any new scripting techniques. However, it exploits the *IISWebServer* class associations in place to retrieve all required information. First, the script retrieves all instances of the *IISWebServer* WMI class (line 66) to enumerate all instances retrieved (lines 69 through

77). For each instance of the *IISWebServer* class, the script requests all existing associations (lines 72 through 74), as shown in Figure 5.17. This is done with the help of the WQL data query:

```
Associators Of {IISWebServer='W3SVC/1'}
```

To restrict the list of associations to the *IISWebServerSetting* class, the following WQL data query can be used:

```
"Associators Of {IISWebServer='W3SVC/1'} Where AssocClass=IIsWebServer_IIsWebServerSetting"
```

Next all instances are enumerated to display all their properties (lines 75 through 77). The display of the properties is performed in the DisplayFormattedProperties() function. This function acts recursively if a property, such as the *ServerBindings* property of the *IISWebServerSetting* class, exposes an object instance. Therefore, the output will be as follows for the first IIS Web server instance:

```
  1:   C:\>ViewIISSettings.wsf
  2:   Microsoft (R) Windows Script Host Version 5.6
  3:   Copyright (C) Microsoft Corporation 1996-2001. All rights reserved.
  4:
  5:
  6:   - IIsWebServer ------------------------------------------------------------
  7:   AppIsolated: ........................... 2
  8:   AppPackageID: ..........................
  9:   AppPackageName: ........................
 10:   *Name: ................................. W3SVC/1
 11:   ServerState: ........................... 2
 12:
 13:     - IIsWebServerSetting --------------------------------------------------
 14:     AccessExecute: ....................... FALSE
 15:     AccessFlags: ......................... 1
...:
146:     EnableDocFooter: ..................... FALSE
147:     EnableReverseDns: .................... FALSE
148:     FrontPageWeb: ........................ FALSE
149:
150:       - HttpCustomHeader ---------------------------------------------------
151:       *Keyname: ..........................
152:
153:
154:       - HttpError ----------------------------------------------------------
155:       *HandlerLocation: .................. J:\WINDOWS\help\iisHelp\common\400.htm
156:       *HandlerType: ...................... FILE
157:       *HttpErrorCode: .................... 400
158:       *HttpErrorSubcode: ................. *
...:
334:       - HttpError ----------------------------------------------------------
335:       *HandlerLocation: .................. J:\WINDOWS\help\iisHelp\common\500-15.htm
336:       *HandlerType: ...................... FILE
337:       *HttpErrorCode: .................... 500
338:       *HttpErrorSubcode: ................. 15
339:
340:     HttpExpires: ......................... D, 0x15180
341:     HttpPics: ............................
```

```
...:
379:      MaxEndpointConnections: ................ 255
380:
381:        - MimeMap -----------------------------------------------------------------
382:        *Extension: ........................
383:
384:      *Name: .............................. W3SVC/1
385:      NetLogonWorkstation: ................... 0
386:      NotDeletable: .......................... FALSE
...:
396:      RevocationFreshnessTime: .............. 128
397:      RevocationURLRetrievalTimeout: ......... 0
398:
399:        - ScriptMap ---------------------------------------------------------------
400:        *Extensions: ........................ .asp
401:        *Flags: ............................. 1
...:
556:        - SecureBinding -----------------------------------------------------------
557:        *IP: ...............................
558:        *Port: .............................. 443:
559:
560:      ServerAutoStart: ...................... TRUE
561:
562:        - ServerBinding -----------------------------------------------------------
563:        *Hostname: .........................
564:        *IP: ...............................
565:        *Port: .............................. 80
566:
567:      ServerComment: ........................ Default Web Site
568:      ServerListenBacklog: .................. 40
...:
577:      UseHostName: .......................... FALSE
578:      Win32Error: ........................... 0
579:
580:  - IIsWebServer -------------------------------------------------------------------
581:  AppIsolated: ............................. 2
582:  AppPackageID: ............................
583:  AppPackageName: ..........................
584:  *Name: ................................... W3SVC/2
585:  ServerState: ............................. 2
...:
...:
...:
```

We recognize from line 562 through 565 the properties of the *Server-Binding* class instance. Of course, Sample 5.15 retrieves all available properties. To just retrieve the **IISWebServer ServerBindings** property, such as we did with ADSI, the code to use will look as follows:

```
 1:  Set objWMIServices = GetObject ("winmgmts:root\MicrosoftIISv2")
 2:
 3:  Set objWMIWebServerInstance = objWMIServices.Get ("IISWebServerSetting='W3SVC/1'")
 4:  arrayWMIServerBindings = objWMIWebServerInstance.ServerBindings
 5:
 6:  For Each objWMIServerBindingInstance In arrayWMIServerBindings
 7:      WScript.Echo objWMIServerBindingInstance.Port
 8:      WScript.Echo objWMIServerBindingInstance.Hostname
 9:      WScript.Echo objWMIServerBindingInstance.IP
10:  Next
```

Even if it is possible to perform many IIS metabase configurations through ADSI or WMI, the ADSI metabase access method has some limitations compared with the WMI access method. For example, the WMI access method implicitly offers all advantages of the WMI architecture, such as the WQL queries, the standard WMI COM API object model and instrumentation (i.e., Event notifications), and the CIM repository object model capabilities to associate entities. ADSI doesn't have these features. On the other hand, it is important to note that only ADSI allows you to extend the IIS metabase. However, once the extensions are created, the IIS WMI provider can return existing schema extensions. This can be done because the *IIS* provider is also implemented as a class provider.

Even if the IIS metabase object model is slightly different from the WMI class object model, it is clear that a good knowledge of the IIS metabase is an indispensable foundation in understanding the meaning of each WMI class representing manageable IIS entities. The **Root\MicrosoftIISv2** namespace contains more than 300 WMI classes related to the IIS management, which makes it impossible to review them one by one in this section. Moreover, all these classes reflect the IIS metabase schema. However, with the Internet Information Server 6.0 in Windows Server 2003, Microsoft has created a very nice *IIS* Provider Tutorial. It is available from the Internet Information Server MMC by selecting "Help" and "Help Topics." This tutorial is located in the "Programmatic Administration Guide" and is entitled the "IIS WMI Provider Tutorial." It is also possible to access the tutorial directly from the IISMMC.CHM help file located in the %SystemRoot%\System32\Help directory. For anyone interested in delving into the IIS management from WMI, this tutorial is worth reading! Of course, you can also continue to use the **LoadCIMinXL.Wsf** (see Sample 4.32 in the appendix) to retrieve detailed information about the IIS WMI classes.

5.3.2   Exchange 2000

With the release of Exchange 2000, Microsoft included three WMI providers: *ExchangeRoutingTableProvider, ExchangeQueueProvider,* and *Exchange-ClusterProvider,* which provide an easy way for any application to access Exchange 2000 management information. Each of the three providers relates to a specific component set of Exchange 2000:

- The *ExchangeRoutingTableProvider* runs on top of the routing API.

- The *ExchangeQueueProvider* runs on top of the queue API.

- The *ExchangeClusterProvider* runs on top of the cluster API.

Table 5.19   *The Exchange 2000 WMI Providers*

Provider Name	Provider Namespace	Class Provider	Instance Provider	Method Provider	Property Provider	Event Provider	Event Consumer Provider	Support Get	Support Put	Support Enumeration	Support Delete	Exchange 2000 RTM	Exchange 2000 SP1	Exchange 2000 SP2
Exchange 2000 Providers														
Exchange Queue provider	Root/CIMv2/Applications/Exchange	X								X		X	X	
Exchange Cluster provider	Root/CIMv2/Applications/Exchange	X								X		X	X	
Exchange Routing Table provider	Root/CIMv2/Applications/Exchange	X						X	X	X		X	X	
Exchange Message Tracking Log provider	root/MicrosoftExchangeV2	X					X	X	X	X				X
Exchange DS Access provider	root/MicrosoftExchangeV2	X					X		X					X

Each of these providers delivers information with a set of classes available in the **Root\CIMv2\Applications\Exchange** namespace to ease the notification and diagnostics of some problems that may occur in Exchange 2000. With the release of Service Pack 2, Exchange 2000 delivers two additional WMI providers:

- The *Exchange Message Tracking* provider runs on top of the message tracking API.

- The *Exchange DS Access* provider runs on top of the DSAccess API.

These two providers expose a set of classes available from the **Root\MicrosoftExchangeV2** WMI namespace (see Table 5.19).

The release of Exchange 2000 Service Pack 3 does not add anything new regarding WMI.

Note that none of these providers is implemented as event providers. This will imply the use of the **WITHIN** statement when executing WQL event queries. Moreover, as we will see in the following text, none of the classes supported by these providers is associated with any other classes. They are implemented as standalone classes providing information about some specific Exchange components.

5.3.2.1   The Routing Table provider

The *Exchange Routing Table* WMI provider works on top of the Exchange Transport Core. You may think that the purpose of this provider is to access available existing routes from the routing table of Exchange 2000, but you'd be wrong. Rather, its purpose is as follows:

- To publish the status of the local Exchange 2000 server in the routing table, based on the monitoring conditions configured with the Exchange System Manager (ESM).

- To retrieve the status of other Exchange 2000 servers in the organization from the routing table, based on the monitoring conditions configured with the ESM.

- To publish the status of the Exchange 2000 local connectors in the routing table.

- To retrieve the status of other Exchange 2000 connectors present in the organization from the routing table.

The routing table is used as a transport to publish the local status of the server and the local connector states in the organization. To perform this task, the *Exchange Routing Table* provider implements a dedicated way of access to and from the routing table only for the System Attendant. Every Exchange 2000 server in the organization is publishing its state in the routing table in this way. This means that it is possible for one server to get the status of all the servers and connectors in the enterprise as they are seen from that server. To distinguish the information retrieved between the server and the connectors, the *Exchange Routing Table* provider implements two WMI classes: *ExchangeServerState* and *ExchangeConnectorState*. Each of these classes has a specific set of properties.

The states retrieved from the *ExchangeServerState* class are based on the monitoring conditions set with the ESM. Different information states are available from this class for the critical components of an Exchange 2000 server installation. The ESM allows an Administrator to configure a set of conditions determining a state for the monitored com-

Figure 5.23
The Exchange System Manager monitoring settings.

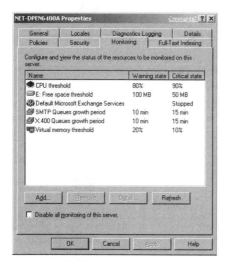

ponent (see Figure 5.23). With the ESM, it is possible to define a monitoring condition with a corresponding state for:

- The queues

- The disk space available on any disk in the system

- The memory usage

- The CPU usage for a "warning" and/or a "critical" threshold

- Any Windows 2000 services relevant to Exchange 2000

The *ExchangeConnectorState* class is based on the same principle as the *ExchangeServerState* class. The class provides a monitoring capability of the connectors configured in an Exchange organization. The state is published in the routing table. When this class is interrogated from the ESM or by a script, the class offers a list of the connectors available from the routing table with their corresponding status. Using this class, it is possible to know the current state of all the connectors in the Exchange 2000 organization as seen from that server (see Figure 5.24).

The set of properties exposed by the *ExchangeServerState* class can be retrieved with the **LoadCIMinXL.Wsf** script (see Sample 4.32 in the appendix). If we reuse the **GetCollectionOfInstances.wsf** script (see Sample

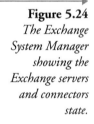

Figure 5.24
The Exchange System Manager showing the Exchange servers and connectors state.

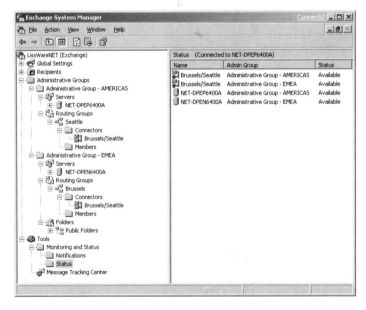

1.5, "Listing all instances of a class with their properties formatted"), we obtain the following output for the *ExchangeServerState* class:

```
 1:   C:\>GetCollectionOfInstances.wsf ExchangeServerState
                            /NameSpace:Root\CIMV2\Applications\Exchange
 2:   Microsoft (R) Windows Script Host Version 5.6
 3:   Copyright (C) Microsoft Corporation 1996-2001. All rights reserved.
 4:
 5:
 6:   ClusterState: ........................... 1
 7:   ClusterStateString: ..................... OK
 8:   CPUState: ............................... 1
 9:   CPUStateString: ......................... OK
10:   DisksState: ............................. 1
11:   DisksStateString: ....................... OK
12:   *DN: .................................... CN=NET-DPEN6400A,CN=Servers,
                                               CN=Administrative Group - EMEA,
                                               CN=Administrative Groups,CN=LissWareNET,
                                               CN=Microsoft Exchange,CN=Services,
                                               CN=Configuration,DC=LissWare,DC=NET
13:   GroupDN: ................................ CN=Seattle,CN=Routing Groups,
                                               CN=Administrative Group - EMEA,
                                               CN=Administrative Groups,CN=LissWareNET,
                                               CN=Microsoft Exchange,CN=Services,
                                               CN=Configuration,DC=LissWare,DC=NET
14:   GroupGUID: .............................. {088D875C-335A-4429-807F-B8B257CE15DE}
15:   GUID: ................................... {B5ED627E-E59A-4A43-8B6C-F71E5F2CEC6E}
16:   MemoryState: ............................ 1
17:   MemoryStateString: ...................... OK
18:   Name: ................................... NET-DPEN6400A
19:   QueuesState: ............................ 1
20:   QueuesStateString: ...................... OK
21:   ServerMaintenance: ...................... FALSE
22:   ServerState: ............................ 1
23:   ServerStateString: ...................... OK
24:   ServicesState: .......................... 1
25:   ServicesStateString: .................... OK
26:   Unreachable: ............................ FALSE
27:   Version: ................................ 6132
```

Table 5.20 lists the *ExchangeServerState* class properties.

5.3.2.2   *The Queue provider*

The WMI *Queue* provider is based on the Queue API. The scope of this provider is local to the Exchange 2000 server. The provider implements two WMI classes:

- The *ExchangeLink* class to retrieve information about the Exchange links directly from the Queue API

- The *ExchangeQueue* class to retrieve information about the Exchange queues directly from the Queue API

Table 5.20   *The ExchangeServerState Class Properties*

Name	Description
ClusterState Property	When the ExchangeServerState instance represents a clustered Exchange server, the ClusterState property specifies the state of the clustered resources on that server.
ClusterStateString Property	When the ExchangeServerState instance represents a clustered Exchange server, the ClusterStateString property specifies the state of the cluster resources on that server.
CPUState Property	The CPUState property specifies the current state of the CPU on the Exchange server. This is the same state information shown on the Monitoring and Status Properties page of the Exchange System Manager.
CPUStateString Property	The CPUStateString property specifies the current state of the CPU on the Exchange server.
DisksState Property	The DisksState property specifies the current state of the disk storage on the computer running Exchange 2000 Server.
DisksStateString Property	The DisksStateString property specifies the current state of the disk storage on the computer running Exchange 2000 Server.
DN Property	The DN property specifies the Microsoft Active Directory distinguished name (DN) of the Exchange server object.
GroupDN Property	The GroupDN property specifies the DN of the Exchange 2000 Server routing group in Active Directory.
GroupGUID Property	The GroupGUID property specifies the globally unique identifier (GUID) of the Exchange 2000 Server routing group in Active Directory.
GUID Property	The GUID property specifies the GUID of the Exchange 2000 Server server object in Active Directory.
MemoryState Property	The MemoryState property specifies the current state of the memory on the computer running Exchange 2000 Server.
MemoryStateString Property	The MemoryStateString property specifies the current state of the memory on the computer running Exchange 2000 Server.
Name Property	The Name property specifies the name of the computer running Exchange 2000 Server.
QueuesState Property	The QueuesState property specifies the current state of the queues on the computer running Exchange 2000 Server.
QueuesStateString Property	The QueuesStateString property specifies the current state of the queues on the computer running Exchange 2000 Server.
ServerMaintenance Property	The ServerMaintenance property, when TRUE, specifies that the notifications set up in the Exchange 2000 Server System Manager Monitoring and Status page have been disabled.
ServerState Property	The ServerState property specifies the current state of the computer running Exchange 2000 Server.
ServerStateString Property	The ServerStateString property specifies the current state of the computer running Exchange 2000 Server.
ServicesState Property	The ServicesState property specifies the current state of the monitoring services running on the Exchange 2000 Server computer.
ServicesStateString Property	The ServicesStateString property specifies the current state of the monitoring services running on the Exchange 2000 Server computer.
Unreachable Property	The Unreachable property, when TRUE, specifies that the Exchange 2000 Server computer is currently unreachable.
Version Property	The Version property indicates the version of the Exchange server.

For both classes, most of the properties are the ones exposed by the Queue API.

From a scripting and management perspective, for both classes, the most interesting data is the *IncreasingTime* property. The Queue API does not provide this property directly. This is a property calculated by the WMI *Queue* provider (see Figure 5.25).

The *IncreasingTime* value represents the length of time, while the number of messages in the Link/Queue has not decreased. The time is returned in milliseconds. To monitor this property, it is important to understand how the calculation is made. Two important factors influence how to monitor the value:

- The sampling frequency (Tx interval in Figure 5.25)

- The *IncreasingTime* value threshold to determine a critical situation

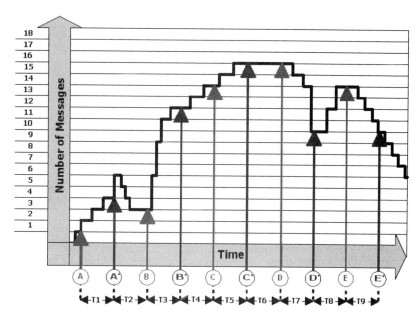

Figure 5.25
The IncreasingTime property behavior from the ExchangeLink and ExchangeQueue classes.

Each time a sample is taken, the *IncreasingTime* property is calculated and a new value is determined. The first polling interval (A in Figure 5.25) always returns an *IncreasingTime* value of zero, because it is the first sample read. But when the second polling interval occurs (A′ in Figure 5.25), the *IncreasingTime* value will be equal to the T1 interval, because the number of messages has not decreased between A and A′.

When the next polling interval occurs (B in Figure 5.25), the *Increasing-Time* value will be equal to zero, because the number of messages has decreased between A′ and B. It is important to note that the number of messages has decreased below the prior measured level. If the number of message levels does not decrease below the prior level, the *IncreasingTime* value is equal to T1 + T2. If the number of messages decreases to below the prior level, then the *IncreasingTime* value is set to zero.

For the same situation, if the polling interval is changed to measure at point A for the first sample and at point C for the second sample, the *IncreasingTime* value will not be equal to zero, because the number of messages has not been detected as decreasing below the number of messages measured at point A. The *IncreasingTime* value will be equal to T1 + T2 + T3 + T4.

Furthermore, if the polling is done between:

■ A and B: *IncreasingTime* is equal to T1 + T2.

- B and C: *IncreasingTime* is equal to T1 + T2 + T3 + T4.

- C and D: *IncreasingTime* is equal to T1 + T2 + T3 + T4 + T5 + T6.

- D and E: *IncreasingTime* is equal to zero.

   Now, if the polling is done in the following way:

- A and A′:   *IncreasingTime* is equal to T1.

- A′ and B: *IncreasingTime* is equal to zero.

- B and B′:   *IncreasingTime* is equal to T3.

- B′ and C: *IncreasingTime* is equal to T3 + T4.

- C and C′:   *IncreasingTime* is equal to T3 + T4 + T5.

- C′ and D: *IncreasingTime* is equal to T3 + T4 + T5 + T6.

- D and D′:   *IncreasingTime* is equal to zero.

- D′ and E: *IncreasingTime* is equal to T8.

- E and E′:   *IncreasingTime* is equal to zero.

By changing the sampling frequency, we see that the *IncreasingTime* value can be very different. With the slowest sampling frequency, we miss the decreasing period between A and B. With the fastest polling frequency, this decreasing period is detected. Now, it is important to look at this behavior in a real-time scale.

If we suppose that the Tx interval is equal to one minute, the alert threshold for the *IncreasingTime* value is set on 30,000 ms (30 s), and the polling interval is set every Tx (every one minute), you will get a notification at point A′. This will be useless, because the queue has decreased between A′ and B. It is clear that you don't want to be notified for such a situation. In a production environment the number of messages can increase suddenly for one minute (or more), but the number of messages can decrease rapidly in the next few minutes. In such a case, you get an alert for a noncritical situation.

Now, if we suppose that the Tx interval is equal to one hour, the alert threshold for the *IncreasingTime* value is set on 14,400,000 ms (4 h), and the polling interval is set every Tx (every one hour), you will only get a notification at point D. This is a better situation, because you are notified for a nondecreasing situation after four hours. On the other hand, it is a little bit too long to be notified, because this situation may hide a real problem.

The key is to find a compromise between the polling intervals to detect quickly any nondecreasing situations without getting an alert for increasing situations that are temporary. A best practice is to choose, for instance, to poll every 10 s and an *IncreasingTime* threshold value of 1,800,000 ms (30 min). In this situation, the flow represented in Figure 5.25 will never generate an alert. Only real nondecreasing situations longer than a half-hour will be detected with a precision of 10 s.

Again, you can use the **LoadCIMinXL.Wsf** script (see Sample 4.32 in the appendix) to discover the *ExchangeLink* and *ExchangeQueue* class properties. To get a notification if the *IncreasingTime* reaches a fixed value, the following WQL event query can be used:

```
 1:   C:\>GenericEventAsyncConsumer.wsf "Select * From __InstanceModificationEvent Within 5
                                         Where TargetInstance ISA 'ExchangeQueue' And
                                         TargetInstance.IncreasingTime > 10000"
                                         /Namespace:root\CIMV2\Applications\Exchange
 2:   Microsoft (R) Windows Script Host Version 5.6
 3:   Copyright (C) Microsoft Corporation 1996-2001. All rights reserved.
 4:
 5:   Waiting for events...
 6:
 7:   BEGIN - OnObjectReady.
 8:   Saturday, 22 June, 2002 at 09:33:17: '__InstanceModificationEvent' has been triggered.
 9:     PreviousInstance (wbemCimtypeObject)
10:       CanEnumAll (wbemCimtypeBoolean) = True
11:       CanEnumFailed (wbemCimtypeBoolean) = True
12:       CanEnumFirstNMessages (wbemCimtypeBoolean) = True
13:       CanEnumFrozen (wbemCimtypeBoolean) = True
14:       CanEnumInvertSense (wbemCimtypeBoolean) = True
15:       CanEnumLargerThan (wbemCimtypeBoolean) = True
16:       CanEnumNLargestMessages (wbemCimtypeBoolean) = False
17:       CanEnumNOldestMessages (wbemCimtypeBoolean) = False
18:       CanEnumOlderThan (wbemCimtypeBoolean) = True
19:       CanEnumRecipient (wbemCimtypeBoolean) = True
20:       CanEnumSender (wbemCimtypeBoolean) = True
21:       GlobalStop (wbemCimtypeBoolean) = False
22:       IncreasingTime (wbemCimtypeUint32) = 5227
23:      *LinkName (wbemCimtypeString) = CurrentlyUnreachableLink
24:       MsgEnumFlagsSupported (wbemCimtypeUint32) = -1073741505
25:       NumberOfMessages (wbemCimtypeUint32) = 1
26:      *ProtocolName (wbemCimtypeString) = SMTP
27:      *QueueName (wbemCimtypeString) = net-dpep6400a.Emea.LissWare.NET
28:       SizeOfQueue (wbemCimtypeUint64) = 243
29:       Version (wbemCimtypeUint32) = 4
30:       VirtualMachine (wbemCimtypeString) = NET-DPEN6400A
31:      *VirtualServerName (wbemCimtypeString) = 1
32:     SECURITY_DESCRIPTOR (wbemCimtypeUint8) = (null)
33:     TargetInstance (wbemCimtypeObject)
34:       CanEnumAll (wbemCimtypeBoolean) = True
35:       CanEnumFailed (wbemCimtypeBoolean) = True
36:       CanEnumFirstNMessages (wbemCimtypeBoolean) = True
37:       CanEnumFrozen (wbemCimtypeBoolean) = True
38:       CanEnumInvertSense (wbemCimtypeBoolean) = True
39:       CanEnumLargerThan (wbemCimtypeBoolean) = True
40:       CanEnumNLargestMessages (wbemCimtypeBoolean) = False
41:       CanEnumNOldestMessages (wbemCimtypeBoolean) = False
42:       CanEnumOlderThan (wbemCimtypeBoolean) = True
```

```
43:        CanEnumRecipient (wbemCimtypeBoolean) = True
44:        CanEnumSender (wbemCimtypeBoolean) = True
45:        GlobalStop (wbemCimtypeBoolean) = False
46:        IncreasingTime (wbemCimtypeUint32) = 10415
47:        *LinkName (wbemCimtypeString) = CurrentlyUnreachableLink
48:        MsgEnumFlagsSupported (wbemCimtypeUint32) = -1073741505
49:        NumberOfMessages (wbemCimtypeUint32) = 1
50:        *ProtocolName (wbemCimtypeString) = SMTP
51:        *QueueName (wbemCimtypeString) = net-dpep6400a.Emea.LissWare.NET
52:        SizeOfQueue (wbemCimtypeUint64) = 243
53:        Version (wbemCimtypeUint32) = 4
54:        VirtualMachine (wbemCimtypeString) = NET-DPEN6400A
55:        *VirtualServerName (wbemCimtypeString) = 1
56:      TIME_CREATED (wbemCimtypeUint64) = (null)
57:    END - OnObjectReady.
```

As we can see, the *IncreasingTime* value is higher than 10 s between the **PreviousInstance** (line 22) and the **TargetInstance** (line 46). Tables 5.21 and 5.22 list the *ExchangeLink* and *ExchangeQueue* properties, respectively.

5.3.2.3   *The Cluster provider*

The *Cluster* provider implements the *ExchangeClusterResource* class directly, based on the cluster service. The State property contains the state of the Exchange 2000 Cluster group. This class is similar in function to the *ExchangeServerState*, but it works at the cluster level instead of the server level. Table 5.23 lists the *ExchangeClusterResource* properties.

5.3.2.4   *The Message Tracking Logs provider*

When "Message Tracking" is enabled on an Exchange 2000 server, all messages that go through this server are logged in a shared directory. The content of this directory can be examined with the Exchange System Manager, via the "Message Tracking Center," as shown in Figure 5.26.

With the tracking center, it is possible to track messages by sender, target recipients, server name, and message ID. It is also possible to select a window time (start date, end date) for the selection.

Before Exchange 2000 Service Pack 2, this was the only easy way to retrieve this information. Once Service Pack 2 is installed, it is possible to retrieve the same information with WMI.

The *Message Tracking Logs* WMI provider is called the *ExchangeMessageTrackingProvider* and gives access in read-only mode to the messages logged in the "Exchange Message Tracking" system. This provider supports one single class, called the *Exchange_MessageTrackingEntry* class (see Tables 5.24 and 5.25), which is a template representing a message tracking entry. With

Table 5.21   *The ExchangeLink Properties*

Name	Description
ActionFreeze Property	The ActionFreeze property, when TRUE, specifies that the link supports freezing messages in its queues. The ActionFreeze property corresponds to the sixth bit (0x00000020) of the SupportedLinkActions property.
ActionKick Property	The ActionKick property, when TRUE, specifies that the link can trigger its queues to retry transmitting waiting messages immediately, instead of waiting for the default protocol timeout before retrying the transmission. The ActionKick property corresponds to the first bit (0x00000001) of the SupportedLinkActions property.
ActionThaw Property	The ActionThaw property, when TRUE, specifies that the link supports thawing messages in its queues. Thawing a queue is also known as "unfreezing" that queue. The ActionThaw property corresponds to the seventh bit (0x00000040) of the SupportedLinkActions property.
ExtendedStateInfo Property	The ExtendedStateInfo property specifies the text description of the current link status.
GlobalStop Property	The GlobalStop property specifies whether the link is currently stopped.
IncreasingTime Property	The IncreasingTime property specifies the amount of time, in milliseconds, that the number of messages waiting to be transferred by the link has been increasing.
LinkDN Property	The LinkDN property specifies the Active Directory globally unique identifier (GUID) of the connector object that generated the link.
LinkName Property	The LinkName property specifies the name of the link.
NextScheduledConnection Property	The NextScheduledConnection property specifies the date and time when a connection will be attempted to transfer waiting messages.
NumberOfMessages Property	The NumberOfMessages property specifies the number of messages that are waiting for transmission across the link.
OldestMessage Property	The OldestMessage property specifies the date and time that the oldest message that is still waiting to be transmitted was received into the link.
ProtocolName Property	The ProtocolName property specifies the transmission protocol for the link.
SizeOfQueue Property	The SizeOfQueue property specifies the total size of the messages in the link, in bytes.
StateActive Property	The StateActive property, when TRUE, specifies that the link is active. The StateActive property corresponds to first bit (0x00000001) of the StateFlags property.
StateFlags Property	The StateFlags property specifies the state of the link. The individual bits of this property are available as the link State... and Type... properties of this class.
StateFrozen Property	The StateFrozen property indicates whether the link is currently frozen. The StateFrozen property corresponds to the sixth bit (0x00000020) of the StateFlags property.
StateReady Property	The StateReady property, when TRUE, specifies that the link is ready to accept new messages. The StateReady property corresponds to the second bit (0x00000002) of the StateFlags property.
StateRemote Property	The StateRemote property, when TRUE, specifies that the destination for messages in this link is on a remote server, instead of the messages being delivered to a local store. The StateRemote property corresponds to the fifth bit (0x00000010) of the StateFlags property.
StateRetry Property	The StateRetry property, when TRUE, specifies that the link is retrying a transmission that was unsuccessful. The StateRetry property corresponds to the third bit (0x00000004) of the StateFlags property.
StateScheduled Property	The StateScheduled property, when TRUE, specifies that the link is scheduled for periodic activation, as compared with asynchronous, on-demand activation. The StateScheduled property corresponds to the fourth bit (0x00000008) of the StateFlags property.
SupportedLinkActions Property	The SupportedLinkActions property specifies the actions supported by the link. The individual bits of this property are available as the Action... properties in this class.
TypeCurrentlyUnreachable Property	The TypeCurrentlyUnreachable property, when TRUE, specifies that the link holds messages for destinations that currently cannot be reached. The TypeCurrentlyUnreachable property corresponds to the thirteenth bit (0x00001000) of the StateFlags property.
TypeDeferredDelivery Property	The TypeDeferredDelivery property, when TRUE, specifies that the link holds mail that is awaiting a trigger to start transmission. The TypeDeferredDelivery property corresponds to the fourteenth bit (0x00002000) of the StateFlags property.
TypeInternal Property	The TypeInternal property indicates that the link is used for internal message processing. The TypeInternal property corresponds to the fifteenth bit (0x00004000) of the StateFlags property.
TypeLocalDelivery Property	The TypeLocalDelivery property, when TRUE, specifies that the link handles local mail delivery. The TypeLocalDelivery property corresponds to the tenth bit (0x00000200) of the StateFlags property.
TypePendingCategorization Property	The TypePendingCategorization property, when TRUE, specifies that the link is resolving addresses against entries in Active Directory. The TypePendingCategorization property corresponds to the twelfth bit (0x00000800) of the StateFlags property.
TypePendingRouting Property	The TypePendingRouting property, when TRUE, specifies that the link is determining the routing of the next message that is waiting to be transmitted. The TypePendingRouting property corresponds to the eleventh bit (0x00000400) of the StateFlags property.
TypePendingSubmission Property	The TypePendingSubmission property, when TRUE, specifies that the link handles messages that have not yet been submitted to the routing engine. The TypePendingSubmission property corresponds to the sixteenth bit (0x00008000) of the StateFlags property.
TypeRemoteDelivery Property	The TypeRemoteDelivery property, when TRUE, specifies that the link is currently handling a remote message delivery. The TypeRemoteDelivery property corresponds to the ninth bit (0x00000100) of the StateFlags property.
Version Property	The Version property specifies the version number of the underlying link control software.
VirtualMachine Property	The VirtualMachine property specifies the name of the virtual machine that is the source of the link.
VirtualServerName Property	The value of the VirtualServerName property is the integer number of the virtual machine that is the source of the link. This number is the Microsoft Active Directory® common name (CN) for the virtual server object.

Table 5.22   *The ExchangeQueue Properties*

Name	Description
CanEnumAll Property	The CanEnumAll property, when TRUE, specifies that the queue can enumerate all of the messages that it has waiting for transmission. The CanEnumAll property corresponds to the thirty-first bit (0x40000000) of the MsgEnumFlagsSupported property.
CanEnumFailed Property	The CanEnumFailed property, when TRUE, specifies that the queue can enumerate the messages that it has waiting for transmission that it was unable to transfer. The CanEnumFailed property corresponds to the ninth bit (0x00000100) of the MsgEnumFlagsSupported property.
CanEnumFirstNMessages Property	The CanEnumFirstNMessages property, when TRUE, specifies that the queue can enumerate the first N messages that it has waiting for transmission. The CanEnumFirstNMessages property corresponds to the first bit (0x00000001) of the MsgEnumFlagsSupported property.
CanEnumFrozen Property	The CanEnumFrozen property, when TRUE, specifies that the queue can enumerate messages that it has waiting for transmission that have been frozen. The CanEnumFrozen property corresponds to the sixth bit (0x00000020) of the MsgEnumFlagsSupported property.
CanEnumInvertSense Property	The CanEnumInvertSense property, when TRUE, specifies that the queue can enumerate messages that it has waiting for transmission that do not match the criteria requested. For example, requesting the oldest messages while inverting the request sense would return the newest messages. The CanEnumInvertSense property corresponds to the thirty-second bit (0x80000000) of the MsgEnumFlagsSupported property.
CanEnumLargerThan Property	The CanEnumLargerThan property, when TRUE, specifies that the queue can enumerate the messages that it has waiting for transmission that are larger than a specified value. The CanEnumLargerThan property corresponds to the fourth bit (0x00000008) of the MsgEnumFlagsSupported property.
CanEnumNLargestMessages Property	The CanEnumNLargestMessages property, when TRUE, specifies that the queue can enumerate the specified number of the largest messages that it has waiting for transmission. The CanEnumNLargestMessages property corresponds to the seventh bit (0x00000040) of the MsgEnumFlagsSupported property.
CanEnumNOldestMessages Property	The CanEnumNOldestMessages property, when TRUE, specifies that the queue can enumerate the specified number of the oldest messages that it has waiting for transmission. The CanEnumNOldestMessages property corresponds to the eighth bit (0x00000080) of the MsgEnumFlagsSupported property.
CanEnumOlderThan Property	The CanEnumOlderThan property, when TRUE, specifies that the queue can enumerate the messages that it has waiting for transmission that arrived before a specified date and time. The CanEnumOlderThan property corresponds to the fifth bit (0x00000010) of the MsgEnumFlagsSupported property.
CanEnumRecipient Property	The CanEnumRecipient property, when TRUE, specifies that the queue can enumerate the recipients of messages that it has waiting for transmission. The CanEnumRecipient property corresponds to the fourth bit (0x00000004) of the MsgEnumFlagsSupported property.
CanEnumSender Property	The CanEnumSender property, when TRUE, specifies that the queue can enumerate the senders of messages that it has waiting for transmission. The CanEnumSender property corresponds to the second bit (0x00000002) of the MsgEnumFlagsSupported property.
GlobalStop Property	The GlobalStop property specifies whether the queue is currently stopped.
IncreasingTime Property	The IncreasingTime property specifies the amount of time, in milliseconds, that the number of messages waiting to be transferred by the queue has been increasing.
LinkName Property	The LinkName property specifies the name of the link in which this queue is contained.
MsgEnumFlagsSupported Property	The MsgEnumFlagsSupported property specifies a bit-mapped set of flags that indicate what types of objects can be enumerated. The individual bits of this property are available as the queue CanEnum... properties in th class.
NumberOfMessages Property	The NumberOfMessages property specifies the number of messages that are waiting for transmission by the queue.
ProtocolName Property	The ProtocolName property specifies the transmission protocol for the queue.
QueueName Property	The QueueName property specifies the name of the queue.
SizeOfQueue Property	The SizeOfQueue property specifies the total size of all messages in the queue, in bytes.
Version Property	The Version property specifies the version number of the Exchange software.
VirtualMachine Property	The VirtualMachine property specifies the name of the virtual machine that is the source of the link.
VirtualServerName Property	The value of the VirtualServerName property is the integer number of the virtual machine that is the source of the queue. This number is the Microsoft Active Directory common name (CN) for the virtual server object.

Table 5.23   *The ExchangeClusterResource Properties*

Name	Description
Name Property	The Name property returns the name of the Exchange cluster resource.
Owner Property	The Owner property for a cluster resource specifies the cluster node of which the resource is a part.
State Property	The State property specifies the current state of the cluster resource.
Type Property	The Type property specifies the resource type.
VirtualMachine Property	The VirtualMachine property returns the name of the virtual machine that owns this resource.

Figure 5.26
The "Message Tracking" user interface.

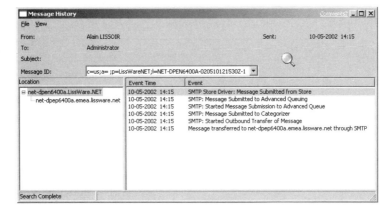

Table 5.24   *The Exchange_MessageTrackingEntry Class Properties*

Name	Description
KeyID	The KeyID property uniquely identifies the message to which the log entry pertains.
AttemptedPartnerServer	The AttemptedPartnerServer property indicates the server to which Exchange tried to send a message, but was unable to complete the transfer.
ClientIP	The ClientIP property indicates the Transmission Control Protocol/Internet Protocol (TCP/IP) address of the messaging client that originally submitted the message.
ClientName	The ClientName property indicates the name of the messaging client application that submitted the message.
Cost	The Cost property indicates the relative effort required to transfer the message. There are no specific units used in this property. Higher values indicate slower network connections must be used, or a greater number of transfers is required to transfer the message.
DeliveryTime	The DeliveryTime property indicates the date and time, in coordinated universal time (UTC), when the message was transferred successfully from the computer running Microsoft Exchange 2000 Server.
Encrypted	The Encrypted property indicates, when TRUE, that the message is encrypted.
EntryType	The EntryType property indicates what occurred to cause the message tracking log entry to be created.
ExpansionDL	The ExpansionDL property indicates the name of the Exchange distribution list that was expanded. After the distribution list is expanded, the message recipient list includes the names of the individual members of that distribution list.
LinkedMessageID	The LinkedMessageID property provides a string that can be used to retrieve message tracking log entries for the message after it has been transferred.
MessageID	The MessageID property indicates the identifier string for the message. The identifier may be assigned by the messaging client application or by the computer running Exchange 2000 Server.
OriginationTime	The OriginationTime property indicates the date and time, in UTC, when the message was created by the messaging client application.
PartnerServer	The PartnerServer property indicates the server to which Exchange transferred the message.
Priority Property	The Priority property specifies the importance of the message, as displayed by the messaging client application. "Urgent" "Normal" "Not Urgent"
RecipientAddress	The RecipientAddress property is an array that specifies the email addresses of each message recipient.
RecipientCount	The RecipientCount property indicates how many recipients are in the recipients list for the message.
RecipientStatus	The RecipientStatus property is an array that indicates the status of an individual message recipient.
SenderAddress	The SenderAddress property specifies the email address of the message sender.
ServerIP	The ServerIP property indicates the TCP/IP protocol address of the computer running Exchange 2000 Server.
ServerName	The Server property indicates the computer name of the computer running Exchange 2000 Server that created the message tracking log entry.
Size	The Size property indicates the message size, including attachments, in bytes.
Subject	The Subject property indicates the subject of the message, as found in the Subject: message header.
SubjectID	The SubjectID property specifies an identifier created by the messaging client application.
TimeLogged	The TimeLogged property indicates the date and time, in UTC, when the message tracking log entry was created.
Version	The Version property indicates the version of the service that created the message tracking log entry.

Table 5.25   *The Exchange_MessageTrackingEntry EntryType Property Meaning*

Values	Description
0	Message received through X400
1	tevtProbeTransferIn
3	Report received
4	Message submitted
5	tevtProbeSubmission
6	tevtProbeTransferOut
7	Message transferred out
8	Report transferred out
9	Message delivered
10	Report delivered
18	tevtStartAssocByMTSUser
23	tevtReleaseAssocByMTSUser
26	Distribution list expanded
28	Message redirected
29	Message rerouted
31	Server downgraded by MTA
33	Report absorbed
34	Report generated
43	Unroutable report discarded
50	Message deleted by Administrator
51	Probe deleted by Administrator
52	Report deleted by Administrator
1000	Message delivered locally
1001	Message transferred in over backbone
1002	Message transferred out over backbone
1003	Message transferred out over gateway
1004	Message transferred in over gateway
1005	Report transferred in over gateway
1006	Report transferred out over gateway
1007	Report generated
1010	SMTP: Message queued outbound
1011	SMTP: Message transferred out
1012	SMTP: Inbound message received
1013	SMTP: Inbound message transferred
1014	SMTP: Message rerouted
1015	SMTP: Report transferred in
1016	SMTP: Report transferred out
1017	SMTP: Report generated
1018	SMTP: Report absorbed
1019	SMTP: Message submitted to Advanced Queuing
1020	SMTP: Started outbound transfer of message
1021	SMTP: Message sent to badmail directory
1022	SMTP: Advanced Queue failure
1023	SMTP: Message delivered locally
1024	SMTP: Message submitted to Categorizer
1025	SMTP: Started message submission to Advanced Queue
1026	SMTP: Advanced Queue failed to deliver message
1027	SMTP Store Driver: Message submitted from Store
1028	SMTP Store Driver: Message delivered locally to Store
1029	SMTP Store Driver: Message submitted to MTA
1030	SMTP: Non-delivery report (NDR) generated
1031	SMTP: Message transferred out

the **GetCollectionOfInstances.wsf** script (see Sample 1.5, "Listing all instances of a class with their properties formatted"), it is possible to list all instances of the *Exchange_MessageTrackingEntry* class.

```
1:   C:\>GetCollectionOfInstances.wsf Exchange_MessageTrackingEntry
                 /NameSpace:Root\MicrosoftExchangeV2 /Machine:net-dpep6400a.emea.LissWare.NET
2:   Microsoft (R) Windows Script Host Version 5.6
3:   Copyright (C) Microsoft Corporation 1996-2001. All rights reserved.
4:
5:   ClientIP: ............................. 10.10.10.3
6:   ClientName: ........................... net-dpen6400a.LissWare.NET
7:   DeliveryTime: ......................... 0
8:   Encrypted: ............................ FALSE
```

```
 9:    EntryType: ............................ 1019
10:    InstallDate: .......................... 10-05-2002 12:15:01
11:    *KeyID: ...............................
                         \\net-dpep6400a.Emea.LissWare.NET\NET-DPEP6400A.log\20020510.log,2082
12:    MessageID: ............................
                         8C05225BE6E2A5438AF2FC417C0D60BB2C8F@net-dpen6400a.LissWare.NET
13:    OriginationTime: ...................... 10-05-2002 12:15:31
14:    Priority: ............................. 0
15:    RecipientAddress: ..................... Administrator@LissWare.NET
16:    RecipientCount: ....................... 1
17:    RecipientStatus: ...................... 0
18:    SenderAddress: ........................ Alain.Lissoir@LissWare.NET
19:    ServerIP: ............................. 192.10.10.3
20:    ServerName: ........................... net-dpep6400a.Emea.LissWare.NET
21:    Size: ................................. 3339
22:    TimeLogged: ........................... 10-05-2002 12:15:31
23:    Version: .............................. Version: 6.0.3590.0
24:
25:    ClientIP: ............................. 10.10.10.3
26:    ClientName: ........................... net-dpen6400a.LissWare.NET
27:    DeliveryTime: ......................... 0
28:    Encrypted: ............................ FALSE
29:    EntryType: ............................ 1025
30:    InstallDate: .......................... 10-05-2002 12:15:31
31:    *KeyID: ...............................
                         \\net-dpep6400a.Emea.LissWare.NET\NET-DPEP6400A.log\20020510.log,2361
32:    MessageID: ............................
                         8C05225BE6E2A5438AF2FC417C0D60BB2C8F@net-dpen6400a.LissWare.NET
33:    OriginationTime: ...................... 10-05-2002 12:15:31
34:    Priority: ............................. 0
35:    RecipientAddress: ..................... Administrator@LissWare.NET
36:    RecipientCount: ....................... 1
37:    RecipientStatus: ...................... 0
38:    SenderAddress: ........................ Alain.Lissoir@LissWare.NET
39:    ServerIP: ............................. 192.10.10.3
40:    ServerName: ........................... net-dpep6400a.Emea.LissWare.NET
41:    Size: ................................. 3339
42:    TimeLogged: ........................... 10-05-2002 12:15:31
43:    Version: .............................. Version: 6.0.3590.0
44:
..:
84:
85:    DeliveryTime: ......................... 1
86:    Encrypted: ............................ FALSE
87:    EntryType: ............................ 1028
88:    InstallDate: .......................... 10-05-2002 12:15:31
89:    *KeyID: ...............................
                         \\net-dpep6400a.Emea.LissWare.NET\NET-DPEP6400A.log\20020510.log,3198
90:    MessageID: ............................
                         8C05225BE6E2A5438AF2FC417C0D60BB2C8F@net-dpen6400a.LissWare.NET
91:    OriginationTime: ...................... 10-05-2002 12:15:31
92:    Priority: ............................. 0
93:    RecipientAddress: ..................... Administrator@LissWare.NET
94:    RecipientCount: ....................... 1
95:    RecipientStatus: ...................... 0
96:    SenderAddress: ........................ Alain.Lissoir@LissWare.NET
97:    ServerName: ........................... net-dpep6400a.Emea.LissWare.NET
98:    Size: ................................. 3339
99:    TimeLogged: ........................... 10-05-2002 12:15:32
```

Figure 5.27
The "DSAccess"
user interface.

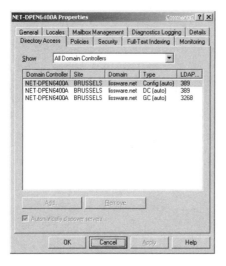

5.3.2.5   The DSAccess provider

The *DSAccess* component of Exchange 2000 manages access to the Active Directory for various Exchange components. *DSAccess* also caches Active Directory requests to improve performance. Because the Active Directory is a critical component of Exchange 2000, it is important to closely monitor which Active Directory server(s) Exchange 2000 is using. Having too many Exchange 2000 servers working with the same Active Directory server(s) may seriously impact overall system performance. As shown in Figure 5.27, once Service Pack 2 is installed, the Exchange System Manager displays which Active Directory Domain Controller is being used by the Exchange 2000 server.

Besides this user interface extension, Microsoft also implemented a WMI provider, called *ExchangeDsAccessProvider*, supporting one WMI class called the *Exchange_DSAccessDC* class. Basically, this provider, with its supported class, retrieves the same set of information. However, due to the WMI capabilities, it is possible to monitor the *DSAccess* state—something that is not possible from the Exchange System Manager. By reusing the **GetCollectionOfInstances.wsf** script (see Sample 1.5, "Listing all instances of a class with their properties formatted"), the following output shows the list of properties exposed by the *Exchange_DSAccessDC* class.

```
1:    C:\>GetCollectionOfInstances.wsf Exchange_DSAccessDC /NameSpace:Root\MicrosoftExchangeV2
2:    Microsoft (R) Windows Script Host Version 5.6
3:    Copyright (C) Microsoft Corporation 1996-2001. All rights reserved.
4:
5:
```

```
 6:    ConfigurationType: ....................... 1
 7:    DirectoryType: ........................... 0
 8:    InstallDate: ............................. 01-01-2000
 9:    IsFast: .................................. TRUE
10:    IsInSync: ................................ TRUE
11:    IsUp: .................................... TRUE
12:    LDAPPort: ................................ 389
13:    *Name: ................................... net-dpen6400a.LissWare.NET
14:    *Type: ................................... 0
15:
16:    ConfigurationType: ....................... 1
17:    DirectoryType: ........................... 0
18:    InstallDate: ............................. 01-01-2000
19:    IsFast: .................................. TRUE
20:    IsInSync: ................................ TRUE
21:    IsUp: .................................... TRUE
22:    LDAPPort: ................................ 389
23:    *Name: ................................... net-dpen6400a.LissWare.NET
24:    *Type: ................................... 1
25:
26:    ConfigurationType: ....................... 1
27:    DirectoryType: ........................... 0
28:    InstallDate: ............................. 01-01-2000
29:    IsFast: .................................. TRUE
30:    IsInSync: ................................ TRUE
31:    IsUp: .................................... TRUE
32:    LDAPPort: ................................ 3268
33:    *Name: ................................... net-dpen6400a.LissWare.NET
34:    *Type: ................................... 2
```

Table 5.26 lists the *Exchange_DSAccessDC* properties.

Table 5.26   *The Exchange_DSAccessDC Class Properties*

Name	Description
Name	The Name property specifies the computer name of the domain controller. When creating new DSAccessDC instances, or when retrieving a specific DSAccessDC instance, the Name property is required.
Type	The DirectoryType property indicates the role that the domain controller plays in the Exchange system. "Configuration Domain Controller" "Local Domain Controller" "Global Catalog"
AsyncConnectionCount	The AsyncConnectionCount indicates the number of asynchronous (non-blocking) connections currently open between the computer running Exchange 2000 Server and the domain controller.
ConfigurationType	The ConfigurationType property indicates whether the instance describes a domain controller that was detected automatically, or one that was specified manually. "Manual" "Automatic"
DirectoryType	The DirectoryType property indicates whether the domain controller is an Active Directory or an Exchange Server 5.5 directory service. "Active Directory" "Exchange 5.5 Directory"
IsFast	The IsFast property indicates, when TRUE, that the domain controller response time has been less than two seconds.
IsInSync	The IsInSync property indicates whether the domain controller is synchronized with the Global Catalog server and with the Configuration domain controller.
IsUp	The IsUp property indicates whether the domain controller was available the last time Exchange attempted to access it.
LDAPPort	The LDAPPort property specifies the Transmission Control Protocol/Internet Protocol (TCP/IP) port on which the domain controller listens for Lightweight Directory Access Protocol (LDAP) requests.
SyncConnectionCount	The SyncConnectionCount indicates the number of synchronous (blocking) connections currently open between the computer running Exchange 2000 Server and the domain controller.

With the script in Sample 6.17 ("A generic script for asynchronous event notification") in the appendix, the following command-line sample can be used to receive a notification for any changes that occur to any instances of the *Exchange_DSAccessDC* class. Note the presence of the **WITHIN** statement, since none of the Exchange WMI providers is implemented as event providers. The WQL event query will look as follows:

```
Select * From __InstanceModificationEvent Within 5 Where TargetInstance ISA 'Exchange_DSAccessDC'
```

5.3.3 SQL Server 2000

When installing SQL Server 2000, no WMI support is provided with the installation. To add the WMI management capabilities to your SQL Server installation, another setup from the folder "\x86\Other\WMI," located on the SQL Server 2000 CD, must be executed. This setup creates the **Root\MicrosoftSQLServer** namespace and registers the unique WMI SQL provider implemented as an instance and method provider in the CIM repository (see Table 5.27).

During the setup, a collection of WMI classes is created in the **Root\MicrosoftSQLServer** namespace that maps manageable instances of SQL Server 2000. The SQL Server WMI classes model objects, such as databases and tables, with their associated settings. The SQL Server WMI implementation provides several management capabilities, including:

- Create, change, or delete managed objects, such as creating or deleting a database. For instance, to create a database, the *Create* method of the *MSSQL_Database* class must be invoked. However, to delete a database, the WMI instance of the database must be retrieved, and then the *Delete_* method of the **SWBemObject** object representing the database instances must be invoked.

- Administer managed objects, such as backing up databases and logs. For instance, invoking the *SQLBackup* method of the *MSSQL_SQLServer* class will perform a backup of the SQL server.

- Retrieve information on specific managed objects, such as determining whether full-text indexing is enabled on a table. This can be done easily by reading the *FullTextIndexActive* property of the *MSSQL_Table* instance.

- Query managed objects that meet a specific criterion, such as listing all encrypted stored procedures. This can be performed with some traditional WQL data queries.

Table 5.27 *The WMI SQL Provider Capabilities*

Provider Name	Provider Namespace	Class Provider	Instance Provider	Method Provider	Property Provider	Event Provider	Event Consumer Provider	Support Get	Support Put	Support Enumeration	Support Delete
MS SQL Provider											
MicrosoftSQLServer 2000	Root/MicrosoftSQLServer		X	X				X	X	X	X

- Execute methods defined for managed objects. For instance, to rebuild indexes from a table it is necessary to invoke the *RebuildIndex* method of the *MSSQL_Table* class.

- Generate events when a managed object is created, changed, or deleted, such as sending an event when a database option is changed. This can be done easily with a WQL event query. However, since the SQL WMI provider is not implemented as an event provider, the WQL event query requires the use of the **WITHIN** statement.

- Enumerate managed objects. As another example, to list all tables in a database it is necessary to retrieve all *MSSQL_Table* instances associated with the *MSSQL_Database* instance.

- Describe relationships between managed objects. For instance, to identify which logins are authorized to access a database it is necessary to enumerate *MSSQL_Login* instances associated with the *MSSQL_Database* instance via the *MSSQL_DatabaseLogin* association class.

Besides these functionalities, there are two interesting points to note:

- The SQL Server 2000 WMI implementation maps over the SQL Distributed Management Objects API (SQL-DMO) but does not support the management of the SQL replication.

- The SQL Server 2000 WMI implementation can also be used with SQL Server 7.0.

The SQL WMI classes supported are listed in Table 5.28.

It is important to mention that the **Root\MicrosoftSQLServer** namespace doesn't only contain SQL server classes. It also contains classes from the **Root\CIMv2** namespace. Actually, the **Root\MicrosoftSQLServer** namespace contains a registration of the WMI *View* provider (see Chapter 3, section 3.9.1) to make classes such as *Win32_Service* and *Win32_Process*

Table 5.28   *The WMI SQL Classes*

Name	Type	Description
MSSQL_BackupDevice	Dynamic	The MSSQL_BackupDevice class represents backup devices known to the SQL Server installation.
MSSQL_Check	Dynamic	The MSSQL_Check class represents the attributes of a SQL Server integrity constraint.
MSSQL_Column	Dynamic	The MSSQL_Column class represents columns in a SQL Server table.
MSSQL_ConfigValue	Dynamic	The MSSQL_ConfigValue class represents the SQL Server configuration values. Some SQL Server configuration options do not take effect until the SQL Server service has been stopped and restarted. You can force the server to immediately accept changes in some options by using the ReconfigureWithOverride method. The DynamicReconfigure property indicates whether the ConfigValue object requires a restart.
MSSQL_Database	Dynamic	The MSSQL_Database class represents a SQL Server database. Each SQL Server installation can contain one or more databases.
MSSQL_DatabaseFile	Dynamic	The MSSQL_DatabaseFile class is an extension to the CIM_DataFile class. It contains properties that are relevant to an operating system file that is also a file storing SQL Server database data.
MSSQL_DatabaseRole	Dynamic	The DatabaseRole object represents the properties of a SQL Server database role. SQL Server database roles establish groups of users with similar security attributes. Database permissions can be granted by role, simplifying database security planning and administration.
MSSQL_DatabaseSetting	Dynamic	The MSSQL_DatabaseSetting class represents the settings for a database. These settings control the access to and the behavior of the database.
MSSQL_Default	Dynamic	The MSSQL_Default object represents the attributes of a SQL Server default. Defaults provide data to columns and user-defined data types when no other data is available on an INSERT statement execution. Unlike DRI defaults, represented by the MSSQL_DRIDefault class, the defaults represented by the MSSQL_Default class can be bound to one or more columns and datatypes.
MSSQL_DRIDefault	Dynamic	The MSSQL_DRIDefault class represents the properties of a Microsoft SQL Server column default. Defaults provide data to columns and user-defined data types when no other data is available on an INSERT statement execution. Unlike other defaults, the Declarative Referential Integrity defaults are associated with one and only one column.
MSSQL_ErrorLog	Dynamic	The MSSQL_ErrorLog class represents the error logs used by the SQL Server installation.
MSSQL_ErrorLogEntry	Dynamic	The MSSQL_ErrorLogEntry class represents the entries in a SQL Service error log.
MSSQL_FileGroup	Dynamic	The MSSQL_FileGroup class represents the groups of operating system files used to store a database. A SQL Server filegroup categorizes the operating system files containing data from a single SQL Server database to simplify database administration tasks, such as backup. A filegroup cannot contain the operating system files of more than one database, though a single database can contain more than one filegroup.
MSSQL_ForeignKey	Dynamic	The MSSQL_ForeignKey class represents the foreign keys defined for a SQL Server database table.
MSSQL_FullTextCatalog	Dynamic	The MSSQL_FullTextCatalog class represents a single Microsoft Search persistent data store. Microsoft Search enables full-text queries on data maintained by Microsoft SQL Server. The service both builds the indexes providing full-text query capability and participates in query resolution by providing result data during a full-text query. Index data is maintained within a full-text catalog.
MSSQL_FullTextCatalogService	Dynamic	The MSSQL_FullTextCatalogService class represents the Microsoft Search full-text indexing service. The Microsoft Search full-text indexing service enables full-text queries on data maintained by SQL Server. Microsoft Search both builds the indexes providing full-text query capability and participates in query resolution by providing result data during a full-text query.
MSSQL_Index	Dynamic	The MSSQL_Index class represents an index for a SQL Server table. A SQL Server index optimizes access to data in SQL Server tables. Indexes are also used to enforce some constraints, such as UNIQUE and PRIMARY KEY constraints.
MSSQL_IndexTableInformation	Dynamic	The MSSQL_IndexTableInformation class represents the information regarding the age and structure of the index statistical information.
MSSQL_IntegratedSecuritySetting	Dynamic	The MSSQL_IntegratedSecuritySetting class represents the security settings of a SQL Server installation. This setting affects all login connections to SQL Server regardless of the login authentication type.
MSSQL_LanguageSetting	Dynamic	The MSSQL_LanguageSetting class represents the properties of an installed SQL Server language record. Language record identifiers categorize system messages so that error and status information can be presented as localized text. A language record specifies the format for dates displayed in system messages.
MSSQL_Login	Dynamic	The MSSQL_Login class represents the login authentication records present in a SQL Server installation.
MSSQL_PrimaryKey	Dynamic	The MSSQL_PrimaryKey class represents a primary key of a table. A primary key must also be a candidate key of the table.
MSSQL_Process	Dynamic	The MSSQL_Process class represents SQL Server processes. Note that these are not the same as an operating system's notion of a process. These are the processes identified by the SQL Server and assigned a SQL Server process ID by SQL Server.
MSSQL_RegistrySetting	Dynamic	The MSSQL_RegistrySetting class represents the installation and run-time parameters of SQL Server stored in the registry.
MSSQL_Rule	Dynamic	The MSSQL_Rule class represents a single Microsoft SQL Server data-integrity rule. SQL Server offers several mechanisms for ensuring data integrity. A SQL Server rule is a Transact-SQL condition_expression syntax element that defines a data-integrity constraint. A rule can be bound to a column or user-defined data type.

Table 5.28   *The WMI SQL Classes (continued)*

Name	Type	Description
MSSQL_SQLServer	Dynamic	The MSSQL_SQLServer class represents a SQL Server installation. There will be one instance of this class for each installation of SQL Server on the computer system.
MSSQL_SQLServerRole	Dynamic	The MSSQL_SQLServerRole class represents a SQL Server security role not constrained to operation within a single database. Roles are used to establish groups of users, in order to make it convenient to set permissions for a group of users.
MSSQL_StoredProcedure	Dynamic	The MSSQL_StoredProcedure class represents standard as well as extended stored procedure defined in a SQL Server database. SQL Server stored procedures can contain input and output parameters and can return the results of one or more SELECT statements or a single long integer. In order to create an instance of a new stored procedure, the Text properties need to be specified along with the key properties of the class. The Text property specifies the Transact-SQL script that defines the stored procedure.
MSSQL_StoredProcedureParameter	Dynamic	The MSSQL_StoredProcedureParameter class represents the input and output parameters of a SQL Server stored procedure.
MSSQL_SystemDatatype	Dynamic	The MSSQL_SystemDatatype class represents base data type defined in Microsoft SQL Server.
MSSQL_Table	Dynamic	The MSSQL_Table class represents a table in the SQL Server database.
MSSQL_TransactionLog	Dynamic	The MSSQL_TransactionLog class represents the transaction log of a Microsoft SQL Server database. A SQL Server transaction log maintains a record of modifications to the Operating System files containing the data of an SQL Server database. The transaction log provides data-recovery assistance in the event of system failure and an SQL Server database has at least one operating system file that stores transaction log records. A transaction log can be written to more than one operating system file. Each SQL Server database maintains its own transaction log and the operating system file or files that store log records cannot be shared with another database.
MSSQL_Trigger	Dynamic	The MSSQL_Trigger class represents a trigger. SQL Server supports using triggers as a kind of stored procedure. Triggers are executed when a specified data modification, such as an attempt to delete a row, is attempted on the table on which the trigger is defined.
MSSQL_UniqueKey	Dynamic	The MSSQL_UniqueKey object represents a unique key in a database. All candidate keys that are not the primary key are unique keys.
MSSQL_User	Dynamic	The User object exposes the attributes of a single Microsoft SQL Server database user.
MSSQL_UserDatatype	Dynamic	The MSSQL_UserDatatype class represents a data type defined by a user.
MSSQL_UserDefinedFunction	Dynamic	The MSSQL_UserDefinedFunction class represents a user-defined function in the SQL Server database.
MSSQL_View	Dynamic	The MSSQL_View class represents view tables in the database.
MSSQL_BaseDatatype	Association	The MSSQL_BaseDatatype class represents an association between a user-defined datatype and the system datatype from which it is derived.
MSSQL_ColumnDatatype	Association	The MSSQL_ColumnDatatype class associates a column its data type.
MSSQL_ColumnDefault	Association	The MSSQL_ColumnDefault class associates a column to the default for the column.
MSSQL_ColumnDRIDefault	Association	The MSSQL_ColumnDRIDefault class associates a column to a DRI default.
MSSQL_ColumnRule	Association	The MSSQL_ColumnRule class represents an association between a column and a rule bound to the column.
MSSQL_DatabaseCandidateKey	Association	The MSSQL_DatabaseCandidateKey class represents an association between a database and a candidate key that is present in one of the tables in the database. This association allows an application to perform a single traversal to find the candidate keys in a database
MSSQL_DatabaseDatabaseRole	Association	The MSSQL_DatabaseDatabaseRole class associates database role to the database within which the role is defined.
MSSQL_DatabaseDatabaseSetting	Association	The MSSQL_DatabaseDatabaseSetting class associates a SQL Server database to an instance of the MSSQL_DatabaseSetting class that contains the settings for the database.
MSSQL_DatabaseDatatype	Association	The MSSQL_DatabaseDatatype class associates a database to the datatypes defined within the database.
MSSQL_DatabaseDefault	Association	The MSSQL_DatabaseDefault association associates a database to the defaults defined within the database.
MSSQL_DatabaseFileDataFile	Association	The MSSQL_DatabaseFileDataFile class associates a CIM_DataFile class to the MSSQL_DatabaseFile class that contains database file-specific properties of an Operating System file.
MSSQL_DatabaseFileGroup	Association	The MSSQL_DatabaseFileGroup class represents an association between a database and the file group that contains the operating system files that store the data for the database.
MSSQL_DatabaseFullTextCatalog	Association	The MSSQL_DatabaseFullTextCatalog class represents an association between a database and a full-text catalog that stores index data used for full-text queries against the database.
MSSQL_DatabaseLogin	Association	The MSSQL_DatabaseLogin class represents an association between a database and a login that is mapped to a user defined in the database. This association allows an application to perform a single traversal to find the logins mapped to the users defined in the database.
MSSQL_DatabaseOwnerLogin	Association	The MSSQL_DatabaseOwnerLogin class represents an association between a database and the login mapped to the user that owns the database.
MSSQL_DatabaseRoleDatabasePermission	Association	The MSSQL_DatabaseRoleDatabasePermission class represents the permissions that a database role has for the database in which it is defined. The instances of this class represent only the permission that has been explicitly granted or denied to the user object. For example, if a database role has permissions to access a database by virtue of being a member of another database role, then there will not be a permission association instance between the role and the database.

Table 5.28   *The WMI SQL Classes (continued)*

Name	Type	Description
MSSQL_DatabaseRoleStoredProcedurePermission	Association	The MSSQL_DatabaseRoleStoredProcedurePermission class represents the permissions that a database role has for a stored procedure. The instances of this class represent only the permission that has been explicitly granted or denied to the user object. For example, if a database role has permissions to access the stored procedure by virtue of being a member of another database role, then there will not be a permission association instance between the role and the stored procedure.
MSSQL_DatabaseRoleTablePermission	Association	The MSSQL_DatabaseRoleTablePermission class represents the permissions that a database role has for a table. The instances of this class represent only the permissions that have been explicitly granted or denied to the user object. For example, if a database role has permissions to access the table by virtue of being a member of another database role, then there will not be a permission association instance between the role and the table.
MSSQL_DatabaseRoleUserDefinedFunctionPermission	Association	The MSSQL_DatabaseRoleUserDefinedFunctionPermission class represents the permissions that a database role has for a table. The instances of this class represent only the permissions that have been explicitly granted or denied to the user object. For example, if a database role has permissions to access the user-defined function by virtue of being a member of another database role, then there will not be a permission association instance between the role and the user-defined function.
MSSQL_DatabaseRoleViewPermission	Association	The MSSQL_DatabaseRoleViewPermission class represents the permissions that a database role has for a view. The instances of this class represent only the permissions that have been explicitly granted or denied to the user object. For example, if a database role has permissions to access the view by virtue of being a member of another database role, then there will not be a permission association instance between the role and the view.
MSSQL_DatabaseRule	Association	The MSSQL_DatabaseRule class represents an association between a database and the rules defined within the database.
MSSQL_DatabaseStoredProcedure	Association	The MSSQL_DatabaseStoredProcedure class represents an association between the database and a stored procedure defined within the database.
MSSQL_DatabaseTable	Association	The MSSQL_DatabaseTable class represents an association between a database and a table contained within the database.
MSSQL_DatabaseTransactionLog	Association	The MSSQL_DatabaseTransactionLog class represents an association between the database and the transaction log for the database.
MSSQL_DatabaseUser	Association	The MSSQL_DatabaseUser class represents an association between a database and a user defined for the database.
MSSQL_DatabaseUserDefinedFunction	Association	The MSSQL_DatabaseUserDefinedFunction class represents an association between a database and a user-defined function defined within the database.
MSSQL_DatabaseView	Association	The MSSQL_DatabaseView class represents an association between a database and a view contained within the database.
MSSQL_DBMSObjectOwner	Association	The MSSQL_DBMSObjectOwner class represents an association between a SQL database object and the user who owns the object.
MSSQL_ErrorLogDataFile	Association	The MSSQL_ErrorLogDataFile class represents an association between a SQL Server error log, and the operating system file used to store the error log.
MSSQL_ErrorLogErrorLogEntry	Association	The MSSQL_ErrorLogErrorLogEntry class represents an association between an error log and an entry in the error log.
MSSQL_FileGroupDatabaseFile	Association	The MSSQL_FileGroupDatabaseFile class represents an association between a database file group and an operating system files that is part of the group.
MSSQL_FullTextWin32Service	Association	The MSSQL_FullTextWin32Service represents an association between an instance of MSSQL_FullTextCatalogService and the corresponding instance of the Win32_Service.
MSSQL_IndexColumn	Association	The MSSQL_IndexColumn class represents an association between an index and a column that participates in the index.
MSSQL_IndexFileGroup	Association	The MSSQL_IndexFileGroup class represents an association between an index and a file group that stores the index.
MSSQL_IndexStatistics	Association	The MSSQL_IndexStatistics class represents an association between an index and the statistical information stored with the index.
MSSQL_KeyColumn	Association	The MSSQL_KeyColumn class represents an association between a key and a column that is part of the key.
MSSQL_KeyFileGroup	Association	The MSSQL_KeyFileGroup class represents an association between a key and the file group used to store the key.
MSSQL_LoginDefaultDatabase	Association	The MSSQL_LoginDefaultDatabase class represents an association between a login and the default database for the login.
MSSQL_LoginWin32Group	Association	The MSSQL_LoginWin32Group class represents an association between a login and the Win32 user group used for authentication by the login.
MSSQL_LoginWin32UserAccount	Association	The MSSQL_LoginWin32UserAccount class represents an association between a login and the Win32 user account used for authentication by the login.
MSSQL_MemberDatabaseRole	Association	The MSSQL_MemberDatabaseRole class represents an association between two database roles, one being a member of the other.
MSSQL_MemberLogin	Association	The MSSQL_MemberLogin class represents an association between a SQL Server role and a login that is a member of the role.
MSSQL_MemberUser	Association	The MSSQL_MemberUser class represents an association between a database role and a user that is a member of the role.
MSSQL_ReferencedKey	Association	The MSSQL_ReferencedKey class represents an association between a foreign key and the candidate key that the foreign key references.
MSSQL_ReferencedTable	Association	The MSSQL_ReferencedTable class represents an association between a foreign key and the table that contains the primary key referenced by the foreign key.
MSSQL_SQLServerBackupDevice	Association	The MSSQL_SQLServerBackupDevice class represents an association between a SQL Server installation and a backup device known to SQL Server.

Table 5.28 *The WMI SQL Classes (continued)*

Name	Type	Description
MSSQL_SQLServerConfigValue	Association	The MSSQL_SQLServerConfigValue class represents an association between a SQL Server installation and the configured value settings for the installation.
MSSQL_SQLServerDatabase	Association	The MSSQL_SQLServerDatabase class represents an association between a SQL Server installation and a database that is part of the installation.
MSSQL_SQLServerErrorLog	Association	The MSSQL_SQLServerErrorLog represents an association between a SQL Server installation and the error log used by the installation.
MSSQL_SQLServerIntegratedSecuritySetting	Association	The MSSQL_SQLServerIntegratedSecuritySetting class represents an association between a SQL Server installation and its security settings.
MSSQL_SQLServerLanguageSetting	Association	The MSSQL_SQLServerLanguageSetting class represents an association between a SQL Server installation and its language settings.
MSSQL_SQLServerLogin	Association	The MSSQL_SQLServerLogin class represents an association between a SQL server and a login defined within the SQL Server.
MSSQL_SQLServerRegistry	Association	The MSSQL_SQLServerRegistry class represents an association between a SQL Server installation and its registry setting.
MSSQL_SQLServerServerRole	Association	The MSSQL_SQLServerServerRole class represents an association between a SQL server and server roles defined within the SQL server.
MSSQL_SQLServerSQLServerConnectionSetting	Association	The MSSQL_SQLServerSQLServerConnectionSetting class represents an association between a SQL Server installation and the settings used by the SQL Server provider to connect to the SQL Server.
MSSQL_SQLServerUser	Association	The MSSQL_SQLServerUser class represents an association between a SQL Server and a database user. This association allows an application to perform a single traversal to find the database users in a SQL Server and the login that they are mapped to.
MSSQL_StoredProcedureStoredProcedureParameter	Association	The MSSQL_StoredProcedureStoredProcedureParameter class associates a stored procedure to a parameter used in the stored procedure.
MSSQL_TableCheck	Association	The MSSQL_TableCheck class represents an association between a table and the checks defined for the table.
MSSQL_TableColumn	Association	The MSSQL_TableColumn class represents an association between a table and a column contained in the table.
MSSQL_TableFileGroup	Association	The MSSQL_TableFileGroup class represents an association between a table and the file groups used to store the table.
MSSQL_TableIndex	Association	The MSSQL_TableIndex class represents an association between a table and an index defined for the table.
MSSQL_TableKey	Association	The MSSQL_TableKey class represents an association between a table and a key defined for the table.
MSSQL_TableTextFileGroup	Association	This class associates a table with the file group that is used to store the variable-length data in the table.
MSSQL_TableTrigger	Association	The MSSQL_TableTrigger class represents an association between a table and a trigger defined for the table.
MSSQL_TransactionLogDataFile	Association	The MSSQL_TransactionLogDataFile class represents an association between SQL Server transaction log and the Operating System file that is used to store the log.
MSSQL_UserDatabasePermission	Association	The MSSQL_UserDatabasePermission class represents the permissions granted to a user for a database. The instances of this class represent only the permission that has been explicitly granted or denied to the user object. For example, if a user has permissions to access a database by virtue of being a member of a certain database role, then there will not be a permission association instance between the user and the database.
MSSQL_UserDatatypeDefault	Association	The MSSQL_UserDatatypeDefault class represents an association between a user-defined datatype and the rule bound to the column.
MSSQL_UserDatatypeRule	Association	The MSSQL_UserDatatypeRule class represents an association between a user-defined datatype and the rule bound to the column.
MSSQL_UserLogin	Association	The MSSQL_UserLogin class represents an association between a database user and the login used to authenticate the user.
MSSQL_UserStoredProcedurePermission	Association	The MSSQL_UserStoredProcedurePermission class represents the permissions granted to a user for a stored procedure. The instances of this class represent only the permission that has been explicitly granted or denied to the user object. For example, if a user has permissions to access a stored procedure by virtue of being a member of a certain database role, then there will not be a permission association instance between the user and the stored procedure.
MSSQL_UserTablePermission	Association	The MSSQL_UserTablePermission class represents the permissions granted to a user for a table. The instances of this class represent only the permission that has been explicitly granted or denied to the user object. For example, if a user has permissions to access a table by virtue of being a member of a certain database role, then there will not be a permission association instance between the user and the table.
MSSQL_UserUserDefinedFunctionPermission	Association	The MSSQL_UserUserDefinedFunctionPermission class represents the permissions granted to a user for a stored procedure. The instances of this class represent only the permission that has been explicitly granted or denied to the user object. For example, if a user has permissions to access a user defined function by virtue of being a member of a certain database role, there will not be a permission association instance between the user and the user defined function.
MSSQL_UserViewPermission	Association	The MSSQL_UserViewPermission class represents the permissions granted to a user for a view. The instances of this class represent only the permission that has been explicitly granted or denied to the user object. For example, if a user has permissions to access a view by virtue of being a member of a certain database role, then there will not be a permission association instance between the user and the view.

Table 5.28   *The WMI SQL Classes (continued)*

Name	Type	Description
View Classes		
CIM_DataFile	Dynamic	CIM_DataFile is a type of logical file that is a named collection of data or executable code.
CIM_LogicalFile	Dynamic	The CIM_LogicalFile class represents a named collection of data (this can be executable code) located in a file system on a storage extent.
CIM_Service	Dynamic	A logical element that contains the information necessary to represent and manage the functionality provided by a device and/or software feature. A service is a general-purpose object to configure and manage the implementation of functionality. It is not the functionality itself.
Win32_BaseService	Dynamic	The Win32_BaseService class represents executable objects that are installed in a registry database maintained by the Service Control Manager. The executable file associated with a service can be started at boot time by a boot program or by the system. It can also be started on-demand by the Service Control Manager. Any service or process that is not owned by a specific user, and that provides an interface to some functionality supported by the computer system, is a descendent (or member) of this class. Example: The dynamic host configuration protocol (DHCP) client service on a Windows NT/Windows 2000 computer system.
Win32_Group	Dynamic	The Win32_Group class represents data about a group account. A group account allows access privileges to be changed for a list of users. Example: Marketing2.
Win32_Process	Dynamic	The Win32_Process class represents a sequence of events on a Win32 system. Any sequence consisting of the interaction of one or more processors or interpreters, some executable code, and a set of inputs, is a descendent (or member) of this class. Example: A client application running on a Win32 system.
Win32_Service	Dynamic	The Win32_Service class represents a service on a Win32 computer system. A service application conforms to the interface rules of the Service Control Manager (SCM) and can be started by a user automatically at system boot through the Services control panel utility, or by an application that uses the service functions included in the Win32 API. Services can execute even when no user is logged on to the system.
Win32_UserAccount	Dynamic	The Win32_UserAccount class contains information about a user account on a Win32 system.
Win32_GroupUser	Association	The Win32_GroupUser class represents an association between a group and an account that is a member of that group.

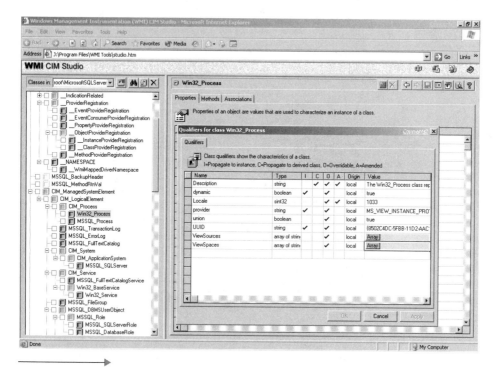

Figure 5.28   *The Win32_Process View class in the Root\MicrosoftSQLServer namespace.*

from the **Root\CIMv2** namespace available in the **Root\Microsoft-SQLServer** (see bottom of Table 5.28). Figure 5.28 shows the view class Qualifiers for the *Win32_Process* class.

5.4   WMI and some Windows applications

5.4.1   Microsoft Office

Both Office 2000 and Office XP come with their WMI instance providers. Office 2000 registers a provider called **OffProv** in the **Root\MSAPPS** namespace, while Office XP registers a provider called **OffProv10** in the **Root\MSAPPS10** namespace (see Table 5.29).

Both providers support a set of classes representing management information about Office. Office XP comes with some additional classes compared with Office 2000. Table 5.30 shows the classes available under Office 2000 and Office XP.

As shown in Table 5.29, the information about Office instances can't be updated. For instance, if you need to determine if a Word document is open, you can request the instances of the *Win32_WordDocument* class. The output would be as follows:

```
1:   C:\>GetCollectionOfInstances.wsf Win32_WordDocument /Namespace:Root\MSAPPS
2:   Microsoft (R) Windows Script Host Version 5.6
3:   Copyright (C) Microsoft Corporation 1996-2001. All rights reserved.
4:
5:
6:   CreateDate: ............................ 20010118112800.******+***
7:   *Name: ................................. MyWordDocument.doc
8:   Path: .................................. C:\My Documents\MyWordDocument.doc
9:   Size: .................................. 295
```

Table 5.29   *The Office Provider Capabilities*

Provider Name	Provider Namespace	Class Provider	Instance Provider	Method Provider	Property Provider	Event Provider	Event Consumer Provider	Support Get	Support Put	Support Enumeration	Support Delete
Office 2000 and XP Providers											
OffProv (Office 2000)	Root/MSAPPS		X					X		X	
OffProv10 (Office XP)	Root/MSAPPS10		X					X		X	

Table 5.30   *The Office 2000 and Office XP Classes*

Office 2000	Office XP
N/A	Win32_Access10AlternateStartupFileLoc
N/A	Win32_Access10ComAddin
N/A	Win32_Access10ComAddins
N/A	Win32_Access10DefaultFileLoc
N/A	Win32_Access10JetComponents
N/A	Win32_Access10StartupFolder
Win32_AccessDatabase	Win32_AccessDatabase
Win32_AccessProject	Win32_AccessProject
Win32_AccessSummary	Win32_AccessSummary
N/A	Win32_ADOCoreComponents
N/A	Win32_Excel10AlternateStartupFileLoc
N/A	Win32_Excel10DefaultFileLoc
N/A	Win32_Excel10StartupFolder
Win32_ExcelActiveWorkbook	Win32_ExcelActiveWorkbook
Win32_ExcelActiveWorkbookNotable	Win32_ExcelActiveWorkbookNotable
Win32_ExcelAddIn	Win32_ExcelAddIn
Win32_ExcelAddIns	Win32_ExcelAddIns
Win32_ExcelChart	Win32_ExcelChart
Win32_ExcelCharts	Win32_ExcelCharts
N/A	Win32_ExcelComAddin
N/A	Win32_ExcelComAddins
Win32_ExcelSheet	Win32_ExcelSheet
Win32_ExcelSummary	Win32_ExcelSummary
Win32_ExcelWorkbook	Win32_ExcelWorkbook
Win32_FrontPageActivePage	Win32_FrontPageActivePage
Win32_FrontPageActiveWeb	Win32_FrontPageActiveWeb
Win32_FrontPageAddIn	Win32_FrontPageAddIn
Win32_FrontPageAddIns	Win32_FrontPageAddIns
Win32_FrontPagePageProperty	Win32_FrontPagePageProperty
Win32_FrontPageSummary	Win32_FrontPageSummary
Win32_FrontPageTheme	Win32_FrontPageTheme
Win32_FrontPageThemes	Win32_FrontPageThemes
Win32_FrontPageWebProperty	Win32_FrontPageWebProperty
N/A	Win32_JetCoreComponents
Win32_OdbcCoreComponent	Win32_OdbcCoreComponent
Win32_OdbcDriver	Win32_OdbcDriver
N/A	Win32_OfficeWatsonLog
Win32_OleDbProvider	Win32_OleDbProvider
N/A	Win32_OutlookAlternateStartupFile
N/A	Win32_OutlookComAddin
N/A	Win32_OutlookComAddins
N/A	Win32_OutlookDefaultFileLocation
N/A	Win32_OutlookStartupFolder
Win32_OutlookSummary	Win32_OutlookSummary
N/A	Win32_PowerPoint10AlternateStartupLoc
N/A	Win32_PowerPoint10ComAddin
N/A	Win32_PowerPoint10ComAddins
N/A	Win32_PowerPoint10DefaultFileLoc
N/A	Win32_PowerPoint10Font
N/A	Win32_PowerPoint10Fonts
N/A	Win32_PowerPoint10Hyperlink
N/A	Win32_PowerPoint10Hyperlinks
N/A	Win32_PowerPoint10PageNumber
N/A	Win32_PowerPoint10PageSetup
N/A	Win32_PowerPoint10SelectedTable
N/A	Win32_PowerPoint10StartupFolder
N/A	Win32_PowerPoint10Table
N/A	Win32_PowerPoint10Tables
Win32_PowerPointActivePresentation	Win32_PowerPointActivePresentation
Win32_PowerPointPresentation	Win32_PowerPointPresentation
Win32_PowerPointSummary	Win32_PowerPointSummary
N/A	Win32_Publisher10ActiveDocument
N/A	Win32_Publisher10ActiveDocumentNoTable
N/A	Win32_Publisher10AlternateStartupFileLocation
N/A	Win32_Publisher10CharacterStyle
N/A	Win32_Publisher10COMAddIn
N/A	Win32_Publisher10COMAddIns
N/A	Win32_Publisher10DefaultFileLocation
N/A	Win32_Publisher10Font
N/A	Win32_Publisher10Fonts
N/A	Win32_Publisher10Hyperlink
N/A	Win32_Publisher10Hyperlinks
N/A	Win32_Publisher10MailMerge

Table 5.30 *The Office 2000 and Office XP Classes (continued)*

Office 2000	Office XP
	N/A Win32_Publisher10PageNumber
	N/A Win32_Publisher10PageSetup
	N/A Win32_Publisher10ParagraphStyle
	N/A Win32_Publisher10Sections
	N/A Win32_Publisher10SelectedTable
	N/A Win32_Publisher10StartupFolder
	N/A Win32_Publisher10Styles
	N/A Win32_Publisher10Table
	N/A Win32_Publisher10Tables
Win32_PublisherSummary	Win32_PublisherSummary
	N/A Win32_RDOCoreComponents
Win32_ServerExtension	Win32_ServerExtension
Win32_Transport	Win32_Transport
Win32_WebConnectionError	Win32_WebConnectionError
Win32_WebConnectionErrorMessage	Win32_WebConnectionErrorMessage
Win32_WebConnectionErrorText	Win32_WebConnectionErrorText
Win32_WordActiveDocument	Win32_Word10ActiveDocument
Win32_WordActiveDocumentNotable	Win32_Word10ActiveDocumentNotable
Win32_WordAddin	Win32_Word10Addin
	N/A Win32_Word10AlternateStartupFileLocation
Win32_WordCharacterStyle	Win32_Word10CharacterStyle
	N/A Win32_Word10DefaultFileLocation
Win32_WordDocument	Win32_Word10Document
Win32_WordField	Win32_Word10Field
Win32_WordFields	Win32_Word10Fields
Win32_WordFileConverter	Win32_Word10FileConverter
Win32_WordFileConverters	Win32_Word10FileConverters
Win32_WordFont	Win32_Word10Font
Win32_WordFonts	Win32_Word10Fonts
Win32_WordHeaderAndFooter	Win32_Word10HeaderAndFooter
Win32_WordHyperlink	Win32_Word10Hyperlink
Win32_WordHyperlinks	Win32_Word10Hyperlinks
Win32_WordMailMerge	Win32_Word10MailMerge
Win32_WordPageNumber	Win32_Word10PageNumber
Win32_WordPageSetup	Win32_Word10PageSetup
Win32_WordParagraphStyle	Win32_Word10ParagraphStyle
Win32_WordSections	Win32_Word10Sections
Win32_WordSelectedTable	Win32_Word10SelectedTable
Win32_WordSettings	Win32_Word10Settings
	N/A Win32_Word10StartupFileLocation
Win32_WordStyles	Win32_Word10Styles
Win32_WordSummary	Win32_Word10Summary
Win32_WordTable	Win32_Word10Table
Win32_WordTables	Win32_Word10Tables
Win32_WordTemplate	Win32_Word10Template
	N/A Win32_WordComAddin
	N/A Win32_WordComAddins

5.4.2 Internet Explorer

Internet Explorer 5.0 (and later) provides a WMI instance provider called **IEINFO5**. This provider supports a collection of classes representing the configuration settings of Internet Explorer. These classes are available in the **Root\CIMV2\Applications\MicrosoftIE** namespace (see Table 5.31).

As with the *Office* provider, the *Internet Explorer* provider doesn't support update of the configuration settings. Therefore, it is a read-only mode provider (see Table 5.32).

The *MicrosoftIE_LanSettings* class exposes the same information as the *Win32_Proxy* class. However, with the *SetProxySetting* method exposed by the *Win32_Proxy* class, it is possible to update the Proxy LAN settings. You

Table 5.31   *The Internet Explorer Provider Capabilities*

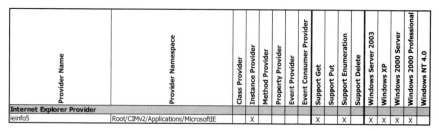

Provider Name	Provider Namespace	Class Provider	Instance Provider	Method Provider	Property Provider	Event Provider	Event Consumer Provider	Support Get	Support Put	Support Enumeration	Support Delete	Windows Server 2003	Windows XP	Windows 2000 Server	Windows 2000 Professional	Windows NT 4.0
Internet Explorer Provider																
ieinfo5	Root/CIMv2/Applications/MicrosoftIE	X						X		X		X	X	X	X	

can refer to Chapter 3 (Sample 3.13, "Managing the Windows Proxy LAN settings") for more information about the *Win32_Proxy* class.

For instance, if you need to know the certificates available from Internet Explorer, you can request the instances of the *MicrosoftIE_Certificate* class. The output would be as follows:

```
 1:   C:\>GetCollectionOfInstances.wsf MicrosoftIE_Certificate
                                /Namespace:Root\CIMv2\Applications\MicrosoftIE
 2:   Microsoft (R) Windows Script Host Version 5.6
 3:   Copyright (C) Microsoft Corporation 1996-2001. All rights reserved.
 4:
 5:
 6:   *IssuedBy: ............................ Hewlett-Packard Primary
                                             Class 2 Certification Authority
 7:   *IssuedTo: ............................ Alain Lissoir
 8:   SignatureAlgorithm: ..................... md5RSA
 9:   *Type: ................................ Personal
10:   Validity: ............................. 21-05-2002 to 22-05-2003
11:
12:   *IssuedBy: ............................ Administrator
13:   *IssuedTo: ............................ Administrator
14:   SignatureAlgorithm: ..................... sha1RSA
15:   *Type: ................................ Personal
16:   Validity: ............................. 01-08-2002 to 31-07-2005
17:
18:   *IssuedBy: ............................ Administrator
19:   *IssuedTo: ............................ Administrator
20:   SignatureAlgorithm: ..................... sha1RSA
21:   *Type: ................................ Personal
22:   Validity: ............................. 01-08-2002 to 08-07-2102
```

Table 5.32   *The Internet Explorer WMI Classes*

Name	Description
MicrosoftIE_Summary	Retrieves the various settings of Internet Explorer, such as the active printer, the build number, Java Virtual Machine version, Service Pack levels and fixes, version, etc.
MicrosoftIE_ConnectionSettings	Retrieves the Dial-up connection settings of Internet Explorer.
MicrosoftIE_Object	Retrieves information about the various ActiveX, Codecs, Objects added to Internet Explorer.
MicrosoftIE_Publisher	Retrieves Internet Explorer publisher information.
MicrosoftIE_LanSettings	Retrieves the LAN connection settings of Internet Explorer.
MicrosoftIE_FileVersion	Retrieves Internet Explorer files information (date, version, etc.).
MicrosoftIE_Certificate	Retrieves Internet Explorer certificates information.
MicrosoftIE_ConnectionSummary	Retrieves Internet Explorer connection summary.
MicrosoftIE_Cache	Retrieves Internet Explorer cache settings.
MicrosoftIE_Security	Retrieves Internet Explorer security settings.

As another example, if you need to determine the file version used by Internet Explorer, you can request the instances of the *MicrosoftIE_FileVersion* class. The output would be as follows:

```
 1:  C:\>GetCollectionOfInstances.wsf MicrosoftIE_FileVersion
                              /Namespace:Root\CIMv2\Applications\MicrosoftIE
 2:  Microsoft (R) Windows Script Host Version 5.6
 3:  Copyright (C) Microsoft Corporation 1996-2001. All rights reserved.
 4:
 5:
 6:  Company: ............................... Microsoft Corporation
 7:  Date: .................................. 20011112140000.******+***
 8:  *File: ................................. actxprxy.dll
 9:  *Path: ................................. J:\WINDOWS\system32
10:  Size: .................................. 96
11:  Version: ............................... 6.0.3590.0
12:
13:  Company: ............................... Microsoft Corporation
14:  Date: .................................. 20011112140000.******+***
15:  *File: ................................. advpack.dll
16:  *Path: ................................. J:\WINDOWS\system32
17:  Size: .................................. 89
18:  Version: ............................... 6.0.3590.0
19:
20:  Company: ............................... Microsoft Corporation
21:  Date: .................................. 20011112140000.******+***
22:  *File: ................................. asctrls.ocx
23:  *Path: ................................. J:\WINDOWS\system32
24:  Size: .................................. 87.5
25:  Version: ............................... 6.0.3590.0
26:
27:  Company: ............................... Microsoft Corporation
28:  Date: .................................. 20011112140000.******+***
29:  *File: ................................. browselc.dll
30:  *Path: ................................. J:\WINDOWS\system32
31:  Size: .................................. 61.5
32:  Version: ............................... 6.0.3590.0
..:
..:
..:
```

5.5 WMI and some Enterprise Management software

Most management software available today on the market utilizes WMI information. By developing scripts on top of the WMI COM API and discovering what WMI information is available from Windows 2000, Windows Server 2003, or Windows XP, we learned how to use WMI information from scripts. The great thing about WMI is that it abstracts the management information for all WMI information types, which means that management information accessed from scripts can be accessed in the same way from any other types of information. Therefore, all WMI information knowledge acquired throughout this book is directly applicable to any Enterprise Management software supporting WMI information utilization.

Considering Enterprise Management software as some powerful WMI consumers is just a partial view of the WMI capabilities offered by some software solutions. Actually, most Enterprise Management software also provides information through WMI, implementing WMI providers and Common Information Model (CIM) class extensions in order to provide management data. Of course, the WMI information available depends heavily on the software implementation. Today, all major management solutions for the Windows platform rely on WMI, such as Microsoft Operations Manager (http://www.microsoft.com/mom), Systems Management Server (http://www.microsoft.com/smserver/default.asp), IBM's Tivoli solution portfolio (http://www-3.ibm.com/software/tivoli/), Hewlett-Packard's OpenView (http://www.openview.hp.com), Computer Associates Unicenter (http://www.cai.com/products), and even Compaq Insight Manager (http://www.compaq.com/manage). Unfortunately, it will be impossible to review the WMI capabilities of all Enterprise Management software available on the market today. Therefore, we will only consider the following Enterprise Management software:

- Compaq Insight Manager and Management Agents (now called Insight Manager after the HP/Compaq merger)

- Microsoft Operation Manager (MOM)

- HP OpenView Operations for Windows (OVOW)

Moreover, only the WMI provider aspects of the software solution will be considered, since they are the most interesting information to know about in order to utilize the WMI information they provide. If you use another management software solution, please contact your Enterprise Management software vendor to gather more information on this subject.

5.5.1 Insight Management Agents

The Insight Management Agents were developed by Compaq to manage the Compaq server's hardware. The complete management solution, also known under the name "Compaq Insight Manager," is made up of a management console and a series of agents.

Information retrieved by the agents can be very useful, because sometimes hardware will obscure things from the Operating System. For example, Windows can see logical drives created on a SmartArray controller but has no information about the physical drives or the RAID level. The Insight

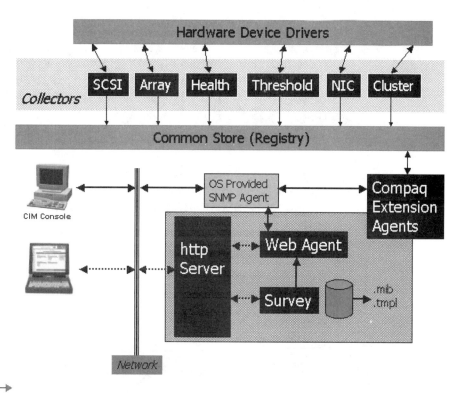

Figure 5.29 *The Insight Management Web-enabled Agents architecture of CIM, version 7 SP1.*

Management Agents provide information about this and many other aspects of a ProLiant. The management console consolidates the information collected by the Insight Management Agents. The architecture of the Insight Management Agents, coming with "Insight Manager version 7 SP1," is based on SNMP and HTTP and does not currently act as WMI providers. Although there is a WMI consumer component in the agents that does provide some limited information about Windows, no hardware-specific information is exposed through WMI with this version (see Figure 5.29). This data is routinely retrieved via SNMP.

In Chapter 3, section 3.7.5.2, we saw how to integrate and access standard SNMP information (SNMPv1 and SNMPv2) from WMI. We also examined how private MIB information can be integrated (Cisco MIB) and how SNMP traps can be received. By applying this knowledge and integrating the SNMP information of the Insight Management Agents in WMI, we can use the same techniques to retrieve this information with WMI scripts (or any other WMI consumers). As a result, the Agents SNMP information of Insight Manager version 7 SP1 is accessed through the Windows WMI *SNMP* providers.

Because the Insight Agent SNMP information is part of a private MIB, it is obvious that we may find some specific SNMP information that is not defined in the standard RFC 1213. This Enterprise MIB information is defined in a set of MIB files available via download from the Management Toolkit or on the management CD in the ProLiant Essentials Value Pack included with every ProLiant.

To access the enterprise MIB information from WMI, it is necessary to load the MIB file information into the WMI CIM repository. This can be done using the **SMI2SMIR.Exe** MIB to MOF converter provided with WMI.

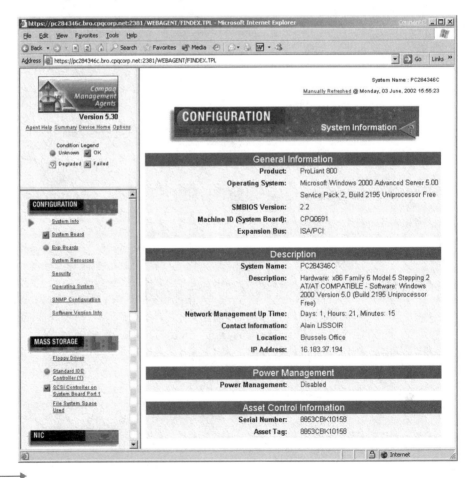

Figure 5.30   *The Insight Management Agents information.*

Table 5.33   *Insight SNMP MIB Files*

MIB Filename	Description	Compaq Insight Manager Support
CPQAPLI.MIB	Compaq Appliance MIB	v 4.70
CPQCLUS.MIB	Compaq Cluster MIB	v 4.21
CPQCMC.MIB	Compaq/Powerware/Rittal MIB	v 5.30
CPQCR.MIB	ClusteredRaid MIB (Shrewsbury)	v 4.50
CPQFCA.MIB	Compaq Fibre Channel MIB	v 3.60
CPQHLTH.MIB	Compaq System Health MIB	v 2.x
CPQHOST.MIB	Compaq Host MIB	v 2.x
CPQIDA.MIB	Compaq Drive Array MIB	v 2.x
CPQIDE.MIB	Compaq IDE MIB	v 2.51
CPQNIC.MIB	Compaq NIC MIB	v 4.20
CPQRACK.MIB	Compaq Rack MIB	v 5.30
CPQRECOV.MIB	Compaq Recovery Server MIB	v 2.50
CPQSCSI.MIB	Compaq SCSI MIB	v 2.x
CPQSINFO.MIB	Compaq System Information MIB	v 2.x
CPQSM2.MIB	Compaq Remote Insight MIB	v 2.51
CPQSTAT.MIB	Compaq External Status MIB	v 3.50
CPQSTDEQ.MIB	Compaq Standard Equipment MIB	v 2.x
CPQSTSYS.MIB	Compaq Storage System MIB	v 2.x
CPQTHRSH.MIB	Compaq Threshold MIB	v 2.x
CPQUPS.MIB	Compaq UPS MIB	v 2.x
SVRCLU.MIB	Compaq Common Cluster Management MIB	v 4.70
SVRNTC.MIB	Digital Microsoft Windows Cluster MIB	v 4.70

The Insight Agents have a lot of enterprise MIB information, so let's take a very easy example. Figure 5.30 shows some information that is specific to ProLiant hardware. The figure shows the system type with its serial number and its asset tag.

To retrieve this information from WMI via SNMP, we must a use a private MIB file. The required MIB file is called "CPQSINFO.MIB." You can check Table 5.33 for a complete list of the SNMP MIB files. To successfully convert the "CPQSINFO.MIB" MIB file into a MOF file, we also need the "CPQHOST.MIB" and "RFC1213.MIB" MIB files, since they contain definitions used in "CPQSINFO.MIB." The conversion to a MOF file can be created as follows:

```
C:\>SMI2SMIR /m 0 /g CPQSINFO.MIB CPQHOST.MIB Rfc1213.MIB > CPQSINFO.MOF

SMI2SMIR : Version <UnknownVersion> : MIB definitions compiled from "CPQSINFO.MIB"

SMI2SMIR : Syntax Check successful on "CPQSINFO.MIB"

SMI2SMIR : Version <UnknownVersion> : MIB definitions compiled from "CPQHOST.MIB"

SMI2SMIR : Syntax Check successful on "CPQHOST.MIB"

SMI2SMIR : Version <UnknownVersion> : MIB definitions compiled from "Rfc1213.MIB"

SMI2SMIR : Syntax Check successful on "Rfc1213.MIB"

SMI2SMIR : Semantic Check successful on "CPQSINFO.MIB"

SMI2SMIR: Generated MOF successfully
```

Once the MOF file is generated, it is ready to be loaded in the WMI
CIM repository with **MOFComp.Exe**, as follows:

```
C:\>Mofcomp.Exe CPQSINFO.MOF
Microsoft (R) 32-bit MOF Compiler Version 5.1.3590.0
Copyright (c) Microsoft Corp. 1997-2001. All rights reserved.
Parsing MOF file: CPQSINFO.MOF
MOF file has been successfully parsed
Storing data in the repository...
Done!
```

Once completed, the selected namespace to access the Insight Management Agents should show the WMI classes representing the Insight Management Agents information. Ensure that the Insight Management Agents
are properly installed and that the SNMP host is available on the network
during this operation (see Figure 5.31).

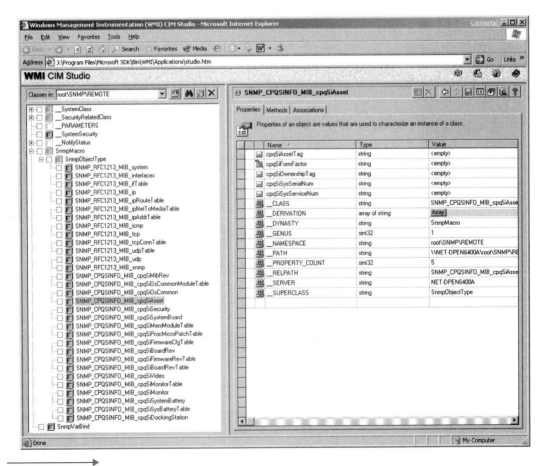

Figure 5.31   *Some Insight Management Agents SNMP classes in the CIM repository.*

If we reuse a sample script developed in Chapter 1 (Sample 1.4, "Listing a single instance of a class with its properties formatted") to retrieve the instances of the *SNMP_CPQSINFO_MIB_cpqSiAsset* class, we should obtain an output similar to this one:

```
 1:  C:\>GetSingleInstance.wsf SNMP_CPQSINFO_MIB_cpqSiAsset
 2:  Microsoft (R) Windows Script Host Version 5.6
 3:  Copyright (C) Microsoft Corporation 1996-2001. All rights reserved.
 4:
 5:
 6:  - SNMP_CPQSINFO_MIB_cpqSiAsset --------------------------------------------------
 7:  cpqSiAssetTag: ......................... 8853CBK10158
 8:  cpqSiFormFactor: ........................ tower
 9:  cpqSiOwnershipTag: ...................... 2020202020202020202020202020202020...
10:  cpqSiSysSerialNum: ...................... 8853CBK10158
```

We recognize the serial number (line 10) and the asset tag (line 7) from Figure 5.30. Of course, we only compiled one single MOF file. To create all MOF files representing the complete Insight Manager v7 SP1 private MIB, you can use the following batch file:

```
SMI2SMIR /m 0 /g MIBS\CPQSINFO.MIB MIBS\CPQHOST.MIB MIBS\RFC1213.MIB > CPQSINFO.MOF
SMI2SMIR /m 0 /g MIBS\CPQAPLI.MIB MIBS\CPQHOST.MIB MIBS\RFC1213.MIB > CPQAPLI.MOF
SMI2SMIR /m 0 /g MIBS\CPQCLUS.MIB MIBS\CPQHOST.MIB MIBS\RFC1213.MIB > CPQCLUS.MOF
SMI2SMIR /m 0 /g MIBS\CPQCMC.MIB MIBS\CPQHOST.MIB MIBS\RFC1213.MIB > CPQCMC.MOF
SMI2SMIR /m 0 /g MIBS\CPQCR.MIB MIBS\CPQHOST.MIB MIBS\RFC1213.MIB > CPQCR.MOF
SMI2SMIR /m 0 /g MIBS\CPQFCA.MIB MIBS\CPQSTSYS.MIB MIBS\CPQHOST.MIB MIBS\RFC1213.MIB
             > CPQFCA.MOF
SMI2SMIR /m 0 /g MIBS\CPQHLTH.MIB MIBS\CPQSINFO.MIB MIBS\CPQHOST.MIB MIBS\RFC1213.MIB
             > CPQHLTH.MOF
SMI2SMIR /m 0 /g MIBS\CPQHOST.MIB MIBS\RFC1213.MIB > CPQHOST.MOF
SMI2SMIR /m 0 /g MIBS\CPQIDA.MIB MIBS\CPQHOST.MIB MIBS\RFC1213.MIB > CPQIDA.MOF
SMI2SMIR /m 0 /g MIBS\CPQIDE.MIB MIBS\CPQHOST.MIB MIBS\RFC1213.MIB > CPQIDE.MOF
SMI2SMIR /m 0 /g MIBS\CPQNIC.MIB MIBS\CPQSTDEQ.MIB MIBS\CPQSINFO.MIB MIBS\CPQHOST.MIB
             MIBS\RFC1213.MIB > CPQNIC.MOF
SMI2SMIR /m 0 /g MIBS\CPQRACK.MIB MIBS\CPQHOST.MIB MIBS\RFC1213.MIB > CPQRACK.MOF
SMI2SMIR /m 0 /g MIBS\CPQRECOV.MIB MIBS\CPQHOST.MIB MIBS\RFC1213.MIB > CPQRECOV.MOF
SMI2SMIR /m 0 /g MIBS\CPQSCSI.MIB MIBS\CPQHOST.MIB MIBS\RFC1213.MIB > CPQSCSI.MOF
SMI2SMIR /m 0 /g MIBS\CPQSINFO.MIB MIBS\CPQHOST.MIB MIBS\RFC1213.MIB > CPQSINFO.MOF
SMI2SMIR /m 0 /g MIBS\CPQSM2.MIB MIBS\CPQHOST.MIB MIBS\RFC1213.MIB > CPQSM2.MOF
SMI2SMIR /m 0 /g MIBS\CPQSTAT.MIB MIBS\CPQHOST.MIB MIBS\RFC1213.MIB > CPQSTAT.MOF
SMI2SMIR /m 0 /g MIBS\CPQSTDEQ.MIB MIBS\CPQHOST.MIB MIBS\RFC1213.MIB > CPQSTDEQ.MOF
SMI2SMIR /m 0 /g MIBS\CPQSTSYS.MIB MIBS\CPQHOST.MIB MIBS\RFC1213.MIB > CPQSTSYS.MOF
SMI2SMIR /m 0 /g MIBS\CPQTHRSH.MIB MIBS\CPQHOST.MIB MIBS\RFC1213.MIB > CPQTHRSH.MOF
SMI2SMIR /m 0 /g MIBS\CPQUPS.MIB MIBS\CPQHOST.MIB MIBS\RFC1213.MIB > CPQUPS.MOF
SMI2SMIR /m 0 /g MIBS\ETHER.MIB > ETHER.MOF
SMI2SMIR /m 0 /g MIBS\SVRCLU.MIB > SVRCLU.MOF
SMI2SMIR /m 0 /g MIBS\SVRNTC.MIB > SVRNTC.MOF
SMI2SMIR /m 0 /g MIBS\TOKEN.MIB > TOKEN.MOF
```

Once all generated MOF files are loaded in the CIM repository, only the MIBs that the correlation mechanism can resolve will be visible in the CIM repository. You can get more information about the created classes from Table 5.34.

Table 5.34　*Insight Management Agents WMI Classes Created from the MIB Files*

WMI Class name	Description
SNMP_CPQSTDEQ_MIB_cpqSeMibRev	The major and minor revision level of the MIB with the overall condition (1:other, 2:ok, 3:degraded, 4:failed).
SNMP_CPQSTDEQ_MIB_cpqSeOsCommon	The Insight Agent's polling frequency. The frequency, in seconds, at which the Insight Agent requests information from the device driver. A frequency of zero (0) indicates that the Insight Agent retrieves the information upon request of a management station; it does not poll the device driver at a specific interval.
SNMP_CPQSTDEQ_MIB_cpqSeOsCommonModuleTable	A table of software modules that provide an interface to the device this MIB describes. A description of a software module that provides an interface to the device this MIB describes.
SNMP_CPQSTDEQ_MIB_cpqSeCpuTable	A list of the CPUs (processors) in the system. The main processor (if such a concept is valid for this machine) should be the first entry in the table. A description of a CPU (processor) in the system.
SNMP_CPQSTDEQ_MIB_cpqSeCpuCacheTable	A list of the CPU caches in the system. A description of a CPU caches in the system.
SNMP_CPQSTDEQ_MIB_cpqSeFpuTable	A list of the FPUs (floating-point coprocessors) in the system. A description of an FPU in the system. The fpuUnitIndex of any entry in this table will equal the cpuUnitIndex of the corresponding CPU in the cpqSeCpu table.
SNMP_CPQSTDEQ_MIB_cpqSeMemory	The amount of base memory and the total amount of memory in kilobytes. A kilobyte is 1024 bytes.
SNMP_CPQSTDEQ_MIB_cpqSeEisaInitTable	A list of EISA function port initialization entries. A description of an EISA function port initialization.
SNMP_CPQSTDEQ_MIB_cpqSeEisaSlotTable	A list of EISA slot information entries. A description of an EISA slot.
SNMP_CPQSTDEQ_MIB_cpqSeEisaIntTable	A list of EISA function interrupt configuration entries. A description of an EISA function interrupt configuration.
SNMP_CPQSTDEQ_MIB_cpqSeEisaPortTable	A list of EISA function port I/O configuration entries. A description of an EISA function port I/O configuration.
SNMP_CPQSTDEQ_MIB_cpqSeEisaFreeFormTable	A list of EISA function free form entries. A description of an EISA function free form.
SNMP_CPQSTDEQ_MIB_cpqSeEisaDmaTable	A list of EISA function DMA configuration entries. A description of an EISA function DMA configuration.
SNMP_CPQSTDEQ_MIB_cpqSeEisaFunctTable	A list EISA function information entries. A description of an EISA function.
SNMP_CPQSTDEQ_MIB_cpqSeEisaMemTable	A list of EISA function memory configuration entries. A description of an EISA function memory configuration.
SNMP_CPQSTDEQ_MIB_cpqSeOptRomTable	A table of option ROM descriptions. An option ROM description.
SNMP_CPQSTDEQ_MIB_cpqSeRom	The BIOS ROM data area, System ROM version information for the redundant ROM image (this will be left blank if the system does not support a redundant ROM) and the system ROM version information.
SNMP_CPQSTDEQ_MIB_cpqSeKeyboard	A description of the keyboard.
SNMP_CPQSTDEQ_MIB_cpqSeVideo	A description of the video system in the computer. This may include the manufacturer, board name, modes supported, etc..
SNMP_CPQSTDEQ_MIB_cpqSeSerialPortTable	A table of serial port descriptions. A description of a serial port.
SNMP_CPQSTDEQ_MIB_cpqSeParallelPortTable	A table of parallel port descriptions. A description of a parallel port.
SNMP_CPQSTDEQ_MIB_cpqSeFloppyDiskTable	A table of floppy drive descriptions. A floppy drive description.
SNMP_CPQSTDEQ_MIB_cpqSeFixedDiskTable	A table of ST-506 interface accessible fixed disk descriptions. A fixed disk description.
SNMP_CPQSTDEQ_MIB_cpqSePciFunctTable	A list of PCI function information entries. A description of the functions in each PCI slot.
SNMP_CPQSTDEQ_MIB_cpqSePciSlotTable	A list of PCI slot information entries. A description of a PCI slot.
SNMP_CPQSTDEQ_MIB_cpqSePciMemoryTable	A list of PCI base memory entries. A description of the base memory usage in each function.
SNMP_CPQSINFO_MIB_cpqSiMibRev	The major and minor revision level of the MIB with the overall condition (1:other, 2:ok, 3:degraded, 4:failed).
SNMP_CPQSINFO_MIB_cpqSiOsCommonModuleTable	A table of software modules that provide an interface to the device this MIB describes. A description of a software module that provides an interface to the device this MIB describes.
SNMP_CPQSINFO_MIB_cpqSiOsCommon	The Insight Agent's polling frequency. The frequency, in seconds, at which the Insight Agent requests information from the device driver. A frequency of zero (0) indicates that the Insight Agent retrieves the information upon request of a management station, it does not poll the device driver at a specific interval.
SNMP_CPQSINFO_MIB_cpqSiAsset	Contains miscellaneous information about the system, such as the customer changeable identifier (asset) that is set to the system serial number at the time of manufacture, the form factor of the system, the serial number of the system unit, and the service number of the system unit.
SNMP_CPQSINFO_MIB_cpqSiSecurity	Contains miscellaneous information about the system security, such as the state of the diskette boot control feature or the current configuration of the Compaq Smart Cover sensor.
SNMP_CPQSINFO_MIB_cpqSiSystemBoard	Contains miscellaneous information about the system board, such as the state of the auxiliary input (pointing) device or the current condition of the correctable memory.
SNMP_CPQSINFO_MIB_cpqSiMemModuleTable	A table of memory module descriptions. A memory module description.
SNMP_CPQSINFO_MIB_cpqSiProcMicroPatchTable	This table lists the set of processor microcode patches that the system ROM contains. During post, the ROM will apply the appropriate patches to the CPU microcode. Scan this table to ensure that a patch is being applied to a processor. An entry describing one microcode patch contained in the system ROM.
SNMP_CPQSINFO_MIB_cpqSiFirmwareCfgTable	Table of soft switches and symbols maintained by the firmware. May be operating system and/or option-specific and will certainly be system-specific. This list is intended to be easily extensible and support arbitrary datatypes. It includes such switches as powerup options, default dump device, etc. Note: The string comparison for svrFwSymbolName is case insensitive. Each entry represents one variable or symbol maintained by or stored by some instance of firmware in the system.
SNMP_CPQSINFO_MIB_cpqSiBoardRev	The previous and current board revision configuration date in MM/DD/YY format. This is the date that the EISA Configuration Utility was used to define the current configuration.
SNMP_CPQSINFO_MIB_cpqSiFirmwareRevTable	A table of firmware revision descriptions. A firmware revision description.
SNMP_CPQSINFO_MIB_cpqSiBoardRevTable	A table of board revision descriptions. A board revision description.
SNMP_CPQSINFO_MIB_cpqSiVideo	The manufacturer, model description and technical information of the video display.
SNMP_CPQSINFO_MIB_cpqSiMonitorTable	A table of all video monitor descriptions connected to this system. A video monitor description.
SNMP_CPQSINFO_MIB_cpqSiMonitor	This value specifies the overall condition of the system's monitor(s).

Table 5.34   *Insight Management Agents WMI Classes Created from the MIB Files (continued)*

WMI Class name	Description
SNMP_CPQSINFO_MIB_cpqSiSystemBattery	This value specifies the overall condition of all of the system batteries.
SNMP_CPQSINFO_MIB_cpqSiSysBatteryTable	A table of System Batteries. A system battery description.
SNMP_CPQSINFO_MIB_cpqSiDockingStation	Docking station miscellaneous information such as the asset tag, the serial number, status, and model.
SNMP_CPQSCSI_MIB_cpqScsiMibRev	The major and minor revision level of the MIB with the overall condition (1:other, 2:ok, 3:degraded, 4:failed).
SNMP_CPQSCSI_MIB_cpqScsiOsCommonModuleTable	A table of software modules that provide an interface to the device this MIB describes. A description of software modules that provide an interface to the device this MIB describes.
SNMP_CPQSCSI_MIB_cpqScsiOsCommon	The Insight Agent's polling frequency. The frequency, in seconds, at which the Insight Agent requests information from the device driver. A frequency of zero indicates that the Insight Agent retrieves the information upon request of a management station; it does not poll the device driver at a specific interval.
SNMP_CPQSCSI_MIB_cpqScsiCntlrTable	Compaq SCSI Controller Table. Compaq SCSI Controller Table Entry.
SNMP_CPQSCSI_MIB_cpqScsiPhyDrvTable	Compaq SCSI Physical Drive Table. Compaq SCSI Physical Drive Entry.
SNMP_CPQSCSI_MIB_cpqScsiTargetTable	Compaq SCSI Target Table. Compaq SCSI Target Entry.
SNMP_CPQHLTH_MIB_cpqHeMibRev	The major and minor revision level of the MIB with the overall condition (1:other, 2:ok, 3:degraded, 4:failed).
SNMP_CPQHLTH_MIB_cpqHeThermalFanTable	A table of fan descriptions. A fan description.
SNMP_CPQHLTH_MIB_cpqHeFltTolFanTable	A table of Fault-Tolerant Fan Entries. A Fault-Tolerant Fan Entry.
SNMP_CPQHLTH_MIB_cpqHeTemperatureTable	A table of Temperature Sensor Entries. A Temperature Sensor Entry.
SNMP_CPQHLTH_MIB_cpqHeThermal	Miscellaneous information about the thermal envrionment, such as the overall condition of the system's thermal environment or the status of the fan(s) in the system.
SNMP_CPQHLTH_MIB_cpqHeSysUtilPciTable	A table of PCI utilization numbers for a whole aggregate PCI bus or a specific device on that bus. PCI utilization entry.
SNMP_CPQHLTH_MIB_cpqHeSysUtil	The EISA bus utilization as a percentage of the theoretical maximum during the last hour, the last 30 minutes, the last 5 minutes, and the last minute. The total time (in minutes) the system has been in full operation (while the server health supporting software was running) is also available.
SNMP_CPQHOST_MIB_cpqHoMibRev	The major and minor revision level of the MIB with the overall condition (1:other, 2:ok, 3:degraded, 4:failed).
SNMP_CPQHOST_MIB_cpqHoInfo	A further description of the host OS.
SNMP_CPQHOST_MIB_cpqHoCpuUtilTable	A table of CPU utilization entries. A description of a CPU's utilization.
SNMP_CPQHOST_MIB_cpqHoFileSysTable	A table of file system descriptions. A file system description.
SNMP_CPQHOST_MIB_cpqHoIfPhysMap	The overall condition of all interfaces.
SNMP_CPQHOST_MIB_cpqHoIfPhysMapTable	A table of interface to physical hardware mappings. A mapping of an interface table entry to physical hardware.
SNMP_CPQHOST_MIB_cpqHoSystemStatus	This item indicates how many code server shares are currently configured on the system. The date/time when the agents were last loaded. The globally unique identifier of this server. If the OS cannot determine a unique ID, it will default the variable to contain all 0's. The management station can then perform a SET to this variable to provide the unique ID.
SNMP_CPQIDE_MIB_cpqIdeMibRev	The major and minor revision level of the MIB with the overall condition (1:other, 2:ok, 3:degraded, 4:failed).
SNMP_CPQIDE_MIB_cpqIdeOsCommonModuleTable	A table of software modules that provide an interface to the device this MIB describes. A description of software modules that provide an interface to the device this MIB describes.
SNMP_CPQIDE_MIB_cpqIdeOsCommon	The Insight Agent's polling frequency. The frequency, in seconds, at which the Insight Agent requests information from the device driver. A frequency of zero indicates that the Insight Agent retrieves the information upon request of a management station; it does not poll the device driver at a specific interval.
SNMP_CPQIDE_MIB_cpqIdeIdentTable	Compaq IDE Drive Identification Table. Compaq IDE Identification Table Entry.

This technique is applicable to any Insight Management Agents version. However, the Insight Management Agents also expose some performance data through WMI in the **Root\Default** namespace. Table 5.35 shows the list of classes and their related properties with the Agents version exposing that information. The ones marked with "< 5.5" were first exposed via WMI in version 5.5 but were also previously exposed through the BMC Legacy Patrol software.

All classes are derived from the *CPQ_System_Performance* superclass (see Figure 5.32).

Table 5.35   *The Insight Management Agents Performance Classes*

System Object	CPQ_System	Counter available from Agent version
System performance properties supported are:		
System Up Time	SystemUpTime	< 5.5
Total Threads	TotalThreads	< 5.5
Context Switch Rate	ContextSwitchRate	< 5.5
Processor Queue Length	CPUQueueLength	< 5.5
Total Processes	Processes	5.5
Registry In Use Percent	RegistryUsage	5.5
Server Object	**CPQ_Server**	
Server performance properties supported are:		
Network Utilization	TotalByteRate	< 5.5
Server Sessions	ServerSessions	< 5.5
Access Permission Errors	AccessPermissionsErrors	< 5.5
Access Granted Errors	GrantedAccessErrors	< 5.5
Logon Errors	LogonErrors	< 5.5
Sessions Errored-Out	SessionsErroredOut	5.5
Context Block Queue Rate	ContextBlockQueueRate	5.5
Processor Object	**CPQ_Processor**	
Processor performance properties supported are:		
Interrupts Per Second	InterruptRate	< 5.5
Processor Time Percent	CpuTimePercent	< 5.5
Processor User Time Percent	CpuUserTimePercent	< 5.5
Processor Privileged Time Percent	PrivilegedCpuTimePercent	< 5.5
Percent DPC Time	PercentDPCTime	6.2
Percent Interrupt Time	PercentInterruptTime	6.2
Memory Object	**CPQ_Memory**	
Memory performance properties supported are:		
Available Memory	AvailableBytes	< 5.5
Pages Rate	PageRate	< 5.5
Pages Input Rate	PageInputRate	< 5.5
Pages Output Rate	PageOutputRate	5.5
Page Fault Rate	PageFaultRate	< 5.5
Cache Faults Rate	CacheFaultRate	< 5.5
Page Reads/Sec	PageReadsPersec	6.2
Page Writes/Sec	PageWritesPersec	6.2
Pool Nonpaged Bytes	PoolNonpagedBytes	6.2
Cache Bytes	CacheBytes	6.2
Paging File Object	**CPQ_PagingFile**	
Paging File performance properties supported are:		
Paging File Instance Name	PagingFile	< 5.5
Paging File Usage Percent	PageFileUsagePercent	< 5.5
Cache Object	**CPQ_Cache**	
Cache performance properties supported are:		
Copy Read Hits Percent	CopyReadHitsPercent	< 5.5
Cache Copy Reads Rate	CopyReadRate	< 5.5
Physical Disk Object		
For each physical disk instance:		
Disk Instance Name	PhysicalDisk	< 5.5
Average Disk Queue Length	DiskQueueLength	< 5.5
Disk Busy Time Percent	DiskTimePercent	< 5.5
Disk Bytes/Sec	DiskBytesPersec	6.2
Disk Transfers/Sec	DiskTransfersPersec	6.2
Disk Reads/Sec	DiskReadsPersec	6.2
Disk Writes/Sec	DiskWritesPersec	6.2
Disk Read Bytes/Sec	DiskReadBytesPersec	6.2
Disk Write Bytes/Sec	DiskWriteBytesPersec	6.2
Current Disk Queue Length	CurrentDiskQueueLength	6.2

Table 5.35   *The Insight Management Agents Performance Classes (continued)*

Logical Disk Object	CPQ_LogicalDisk	
Logical Disk performance properties supported are:		
Disk Instance Name	LogicalDisk	< 5.5
Disk Free Space	FreeMegabytes	< 5.5
Disk Free Space Percent	FreeSpacePercent	< 5.5
Average Disk Queue Length	DiskQueueLength	< 5.5
Disk Busy Time Percent	DiskTimePercent	< 5.5
Network Interface Object	**CPQ_NetworkInterface**	
Network Interface performance properties supported are:		
Controller Name	NetworkInterface	< 5.5
Total Byte Rate	TotalByteRate	< 5.5
Packet Rate	PacketRate	< 5.5
Output Queue Length	OutputQueueLength	< 5.5
Packet Outbound Errors	PacketOutboundErrs	5.5
Packet Receive Errors	PacketReceiveErrs	5.5
Current Bandwidth	CurrentBandwidth	5.5
Bytes Sent/Sec	BytesSentPersec	6.2
Bytes Received/Sec	BytesReceivedPersec	6.2
Packets Sent/Sec	PacketsSentPersec	6.2
Packets Received/Sec	PacketsReceivedPersec	6.2
TCP Object	**CPQ_Tcp**	
TCP performance properties supported are:		
Active Connections	ConnectionsActive	< 5.5
Established Connections	ConnectionsEstablished	< 5.5
Segments Rate	SegmentsRate	< 5.5
Retransmitted Segment Rate	SegmentsRetransmitRate	< 5.5
Connection Failures	ConnectionFailures	< 5.5
Process Object	**CPQ_Process**	
Process performance properties supported are:		
Process Name	Process	< 5.5
Thread Count	ThreadCount	< 5.5
Private Bytes	PrivateBytes	< 5.5
Page File Bytes	PageFileBytes	< 5.5
Working Set	WorkingSet	< 5.5
Processor Time Percent	CpuTimePercent	< 5.5
Processor Privileged Time Percent	PrivilegedTimePercent	< 5.5
Page Fault Rate	PageFaultRate	< 5.5

Figure 5.32

The CPQ_System_Performance superclass with its subclasses, as shown in WMI CIM Studio.

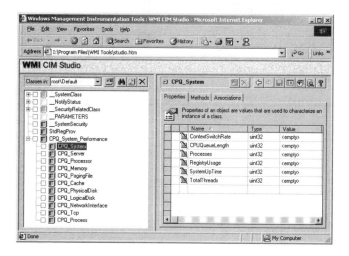

5.5.2 Microsoft Operation Manager

When Microsoft Operation Manager (MOM) is installed, the WMI provider coming with the product is not installed by default. In the MOM installation directory ("C:\Program Files\Microsoft Operation Manager 2000\One Point"), there is a MOF file called OM.MOF. You must compile the **OM.MOF** file with **MOFComp.Exe** to get the *MOM* provider and its unique extrinsic event class registered in the CIM repository.

Once completed, a new namespace is created, called **Root\MCS**. The *MOM* provider is implemented as an event provider, which means that WQL event queries don't need to use the **WITHIN** statement. The WQL event query will look as follows:

```
Select * From OM_Alert
```

The *OM_Alert* extrinsic event class represents the alerts generated on the MOM console. The aim of this provider with its unique class is to notify WMI event subscribers interested in receiving notifications for the MOM alerts. The *OM_Alert* class exposes the properties listed in Table 5.36.

The biggest interest of the *OM_Alert* extrinsic event class resides in the possibility to interface any other management products with MOM. Of course, this is only possible on the condition that management products support WMI data utilization. For instance, a company can decide to use MOM to manage and monitor the Microsoft environment, while the gen-

Table 5.36   *The OM_Alert Extrinsic Event Class with the MOM SP1 Classes*

MOM Provider classes (RTM)	
Class	**Description**
OM_Alert	One Point Operations Manager Alert
MOM Provider classes (SP1)	
Class	**Description**
MSFT_Alert	Represents a MOM alert and it provides access to details about the alert's status and other properties.
MSFT_AlertHistory	Represents a MOM alert history and it provides access to details about the alert's status and other properties.
MSFT_AlertResolutionState	Represents a MOM alert and it provides access to details about the alert's status and other properties.
MSFT_Computer	Represents a MOM computer in the managed MOM environment.
MSFT_ComputerGroup	Represents a MOM computer group.
MSFT_MicrosoftOperationsManager	Represents information about the MOM software (installed date, version).
MSFT_TodayStatistics	Provides daily sums for several of the most important measurements in the network environment Microsoft Operations Manager is monitoring.
MSFT_Script	Represents a MOM script with all its parameters.
MSFT_AlertHistoryToAlertResolutionState	Associates an alert history with its state.
MSFT_AlertToAlertResolutionState	Associates an alert with its state.
MSFT_AlertToAlertHistory	Associates an alert with history.
MSFT_AlertToComputer	Associates an alert with a computer.
MSFT_ComputerToComputerGroup	Associates a computer with a computer group.
MSFT_ScriptToComputerGroup	Associates a script to a computer group.

erated alerts are forwarded to another enterprise management software having WMI data utilization capabilities. In such a case, the enterprise management software will utilize alerts generated from the *OM_Alert* class.

When the MOM Service Pack 1 is installed, another WMI provider extends the management capabilities and the information set available from MOM through WMI. This new WMI provider exposes alerts, alert history, computers, computer groups, and "computer to computer group" associations. However, by default, as with the previous *MOM* provider, it is not registered by default in the CIM repository

Once the Service Pack 1 is installed, the MOM installation directory ("C:\Program Files\Microsoft Operation Manager 2000\One Point") contains a MOF file called **MOMWMI.MOF**. Once the registration with **MOFCOMP.EXE** is completed, it creates a new namespace called Root\MOM, containing classes listed in Table 5.36.

5.5.3 HP OpenView Operations for Windows

Understanding the WMI capabilities and the WMI information exposed by HP OpenView Operations for Windows v7 (OVOW v7) is invaluable for people who want to develop automated tasks, applications, or scripts integrating with OVOW v7. OVOW v7 provides the first and only service management engine based completely on the WBEM/WMI specification. The use of WMI/WBEM permits extensive customization of the OpenView Operations Management Server via scripting and automation tools— a capability used heavily by lights-out and highly automated enterprises.

There are hundreds of WMI classes, and it is impossible to review all the possibilities offered by the OVOW v7 WMI implementation in a few pages. Most classes available are used by OVOW for internal functions, such as supporting OVOW interconsole synchronization of events, status, and actions. Therefore, external WMI consumers are not officially supported. It is important to understand that even if the features presented in this section are fully functional, HP does not officially support them, because they rely on some internal WMI functions of the OVOW v7 architecture. These WMI internal functions are subject to change without notice with the next release of OVOW.

Despite this restriction, some aspects can be very useful in the field and deserve closer examination. For instance, the application of some typical tasks, such as programmatically acknowledging alerts or monitoring changes to some alerts, demonstrates how OVOW v7 can easily be extended with the use of a standard management interface such as WMI.

Therefore, we will concentrate on a very typical WMI class exposed by the OVOW v7 WMI implementation and used heavily by the OVOW console: the *OV_Message* class.

When installing OVOW v7 in a Windows 2000 system, the setup process creates three new namespaces in the CIM repository:

- **Root\HewlettPackard\OpenView**
- **Root\HewlettPackard\OpenView\Console**
- **Root\HewlettPackard\OpenView\Data**

By default, only administrators have full access to WMI namespaces. However, the OVOW setup modifies the default security on the **Root\HewlettPackard\OpenView\Data** namespace to allow access to members of the Local Administrators, HP-OVE-ADMINS, and HP-OVE-OPERATORS groups.

All namespaces contain one or more WMI providers, as summarized in Table 5.37.

Table 5.37   *The HP OpenView Providers Capabilities*

Provider Name	Class Provider	Instance Provider	Method Provider	Property Provider	Event Provider	Event Consumer Provider	Support Get	Support Put	Support Enumeration	Support Delete
Root\HewlettPackard\OpenView										
storeprov_PermEventConsumer						X				
Root\HewlettPackard\OpenView/Console										
OVConsoleEvents			X		X					
Root\HewlettPackard\OpenView/Data										
AdsProv		X							X	
DnsProv		X							X	
NetProv		X							X	
NnmProv		X							X	
OV_ActionRequest_InstanceProvider		X	X				X	X	X	X
OV_ActionResponseEvent_Provider					X					
OV_Message_InstanceCreationAndDeletionEvent_Provider					X					
OV_Message_InstanceProvider		X	X				X		X	
OV_Message_NumberOfAnnotationsChangeEvent_Provider					X					
OV_Message_SeverityChangeEvent_Provider					X					
OV_Message_StateChangeEvent_Provider					X					
OV_Message_TextChangeEvent_Provider					X					
OV_MessageAction_InstanceProvider		X	X				X			
OV_MessageAction_StateChangeEvent_Provider					X					
OvAutoDeploy_PermEventConsumer						X				
OvEpStatusEventProvider					X					
OvEpStatusInstProvider		X					X		X	
pppprov		X		X			X		X	
RegPropProv				X			X	X		
StoreInstanceProv		X		X			X	X	X	X
storeprov_PermEventConsumer						X				
UnmAgtProv		X							X	

As we can see in Table 5.37, OVOW v7 brings several instance providers, event providers, event consumer providers, method providers, and one property provider. Some providers also combine several roles. Each provider supports a set of WMI classes that mostly represent OVOW manageable objects, such as managed nodes, services, node groups, and console messages.

As an example, we can track OVOW v7 alerts displayed on the OVOW console (see Figure 5.33) to trigger the execution of a script. With the script Sample 6.17 ("A generic script for asynchronous event notification") in the appendix, we can easily track alerts via this WMI alert consumer script. Of course, in this case, we use a script as a WMI consumer, but this can be any other WMI consumer application, such as another Enterprise Management System, able to consume WMI alerts. To track all new messages displayed at the OVOW console, we should start the script with the following WQL event query:

```
Select * From __InstanceCreationEvent Where TargetInstance ISA 'OV_Message'
```

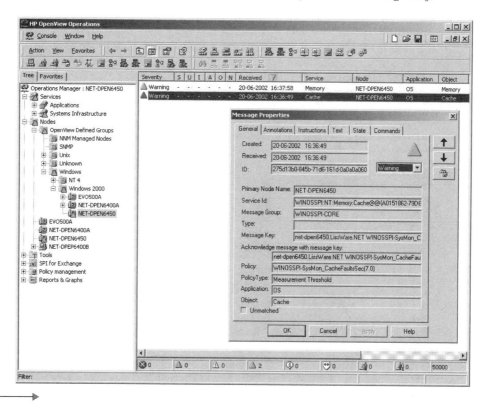

Figure 5.33   *The HP OpenView Operations for Windows console showing alerts.*

The WQL query makes use of the __*InstanceCreationEvent* intrinsic event class, which captures any instance creation event of the *OV_Message* WMI class. The *OV_Message* class is a template representing the OVOW v7 alerts. With this WQL event query, the script receives a notification each time a new alert is available from the OVOW console. By observing the displayed data, you will see that the information exactly matches the alert information shown in Figure 5.33.

```
 1: C:\>GenericEventAsyncConsumer.wsf "Select * From __InstanceCreationEvent
                          Where TargetInstance ISA 'OV_Message'"
                          /Namespace:root\HewlettPackard\OpenView\Data
 2: Microsoft (R) Windows Script Host Version 5.6
 3: Copyright (C) Microsoft Corporation 1996-2001. All rights reserved.
 4:
 5: Waiting for events...
 6:
 7: BEGIN - OnObjectReady.
 8: Thursday, 20 June, 2002 at 16:36:49: '__InstanceCreationEvent' has been triggered.
 9:    TargetInstance (wbemCimtypeObject)
10:       AcknowledgeAfterTroubleTicket = False
11:       AgentId = 059bbdd0-7eed-71d6-1e0e-0a0a0a060000
12:       Application = OS
13:       AutomaticAction = (null)
14:       ConditionId = 00000000000000000000000000000000000
15:       CreateTroubleTicketInterface = False
16:       DoNotification = False
17:       *Id = 275d13b0-845b-71d6-161d-0a0a0a060000
18:       InstructionAvailable = False
19:       IsProxied = False
20:       LogOnly = False
21:       MessageGroup = WINOSSPI-CORE
22:       MessageKey = net-dpen6450.LissWare.NET WINOSSPI-SysMon_CacheFaultsSec
23:       MessageKeyRelation = net-dpen6450.LissWare.NET WINOSSPI-SysMon_CacheFaultsSec
24:       NodeName = {A0151862-79D6-47F9-8952-97F563F29429}
25:       NumberOfAnnotations = 0
26:       Object = Cache
27:       OperatorAction = (null)
28:       OriginalId = 00000000000000000000000000000000000
29:       OriginalServiceId = WINOSSPI:NT:Memory:Cache@@<$MSG_NODE_ID>
30:       OriginalText = Monitor WINOSSPI-SysMon_CacheFaultsSec: Threshold:... Value: 77.17
31:       ServiceId = WINOSSPI:NT:Memory:Cache@@{A0151862-79D6-47F9-8952-97F563F29429}
32:       Severity = 4
33:       Source = WINOSSPI-SysMon_CacheFaultsSec(7.0)
34:       SourceType = 8
35:       State = 2
36:       Text = Object: Memory, Counter: Cache Faults/sec: The threshold of 15 ...
37:       TimeCreated = 20-06-2002 16:36:49 (20020620163649.000000+120)
38:       TimeOfStateChange = 20-06-2002 16:36:49 (20020620163649.000000+120)
39:       TimeReceived  = 20-06-2002 16:36:49 (20020620163649.000000+120)
40:       Type (wbemCimtypeString) =
41:       Unmatched (wbemCimtypeBoolean) = False
42:       UsedNotificationInterfaces (wbemCimtypeString) =
43:       UserOfStateChange (wbemCimtypeString) =
44: END - OnObjectReady.
..:
50: Finished.
```

If we closely examine the *OV_Message* WMI class (), we can see that besides the 34 properties exposed by the class, there are also 16 methods available. Table 5.38 was generated with the **LoadCIMinXL.Wsf** script (see Sample 4.32 in the appendix).

Table 5.38   *The OV_Message Class*

Properties	Syntax	Access	Description
AcknowledgeAfterTroubleTicket	boolean	Read	If trouble ticket generation succeeds, acknowedge the message
AgentId	string	Read	The "Agent ID" that uniquely identifies the agent (different than the "Node ID") - used to support NAT and DHCP environments
Application	string	Read	The "Application" that created the message. Similar in many respects to the Windows Event Log "Source" field.
AutomaticAction	object:OV_MessageAction	Read	If an automatic action is assigned to the event, this object is valid.
ConditionId	string	Read	The "Condtion" id (a GUID) of the rule that triggered the event
CreateTroubleTicketInterface	boolean	Read	True if this event should generate a new trouble ticket
DoNotification	boolean	Read	True if this event should generate an e-mail message, SMS or page
Id (key)	string	Read	The internal ID of the message. This is the key for the OV_Message table, and can be used to directly retrieve a message object.
InstructionAvailable	boolean	Read	True if instruction text is available
IsProxied	boolean	Read	True if proxied through a secondary node. Not currently used
LogOnly	boolean	Read	True if the event is to be written to the log (acknowledged) browser without display to the console
MessageGroup	string	Read	A grouping to classify the message - arbitrary
MessageKey	string	Read	A unique "Key" to identify the message. Used to keep only the most recent message displayed in the browser. Also used for "paired" events (good acknowleged bad)
MessageKeyRelation	string	Read	The message key that will be acknowledged when this message is received. Can contain wildcards and pattern matches.
NodeName	string	Read	The ID of the node in the OV_ManagedNode table. This is not the display name of the node, but the GUID representing the node in the OV_ManagedNode table. Query or GetObject from OV_ManagedNode against objMessage.NodeName to get the Caption or PrimaryNodeName values.
NumberOfAnnotations	sint32	Read	Number of available annotations on a message
Object	string	Read	The "Object" of the message. Similar in many respects to the Windows Event Log "Category" field.
OperatorAction	object:OV_MessageAction	Read	Exists if an operator-initiated action is available for this message
OriginalId	string	Read	The original message ID generating this event
OriginalServiceId	string	Read	The original service ID assigned to the event
OriginalText	string	Read	The original text of the event
ServiceId	string	Read	The ID of the service that this message belongs to. This is not the display name of the service, but the internal ID representing the service in the OV_Service table. Query or GetObject from the OV_Service against objMessage.ServiceID to get the Caption or Description properties.
Severity	sint32	Read	Defines the severity of the message ("Unknown=1", "Normal=2", "Warning=4", "Minor=8", "Major=16", "Critical=32")
Source	string	Read	Origin of the message.
SourceType	sint32	Read	Defines the message source type ("Unknown=0x2000", "MPE Console=0x2001", "Open Message Interface=0x2002", "Logfile Entry | Windows Event Log=0x2004", "Measurement Threshold=0x2008", "SNMP Interceptor=0x2010", "Message Stream Interface=0x2020", "Reserved=0x2040", "Reserved=0x2080", "Scheduled Command=0x2100", "Measurement Threshold=0x2200", "Windows Management Interface=0x2400")
State	sint32	Read	Defines the state of the message ("Undefined=1", "Unowned=2", "Owned=3", "Acknowledged=4", "Node Deleted=5", "Deleted=6")
Text	string	Read	The text of the message as displayed to the user.
TimeCreated	datetime	Read	The time the event was created at the node
TimeOfStateChange	datetime	Read	The time when the state of the message was last changed (owned, disowned, acknowledged)
TimeReceived	datetime	Read	The time the event was received at the management server
Type	string	Read	The internal type of the message, assigned by the policy creator. This is often used in Manager of Manager environments to selectively route messages around.
Unmatched	boolean	Read	If the event didn't match any conditions of the policy, but the "send unmatched" option was enabled on the node.
UsedNotificationInterfaces	string	Read	Indicates if the notification interface was used
UserOfStateChange	string	Read	The NT/AD username of the user that performed the last state change (own,disown, acknowledge, unacknowledge)

Table 5.38   *The OV_Message Class (continued)*

Methods	Parameters	Syntax	Description
GetInstruction	**Output:**		
	Instruction	string	Gets the instruction text for this event.
	ReturnValue	sint32	
ChangeText	**Input:**		
	NewText	string	Sets new text for an existing message, and fires a TextChange event
	Output:		
	ReturnValue	sint32	
ChangeSeverity	**Input:**		
	NewSeverity	sint32	Modifies the message severity ("Unknown", "Normal", "Warning", "Minor", "Major", "Critical")
	Output:		
	ReturnValue	sint32	
Acknowledge	**Output:**		
	ReturnValue	sint32	Marks the message as acknowledged (resolved/superceded)
Unacknowledge	**Output:**		
	ReturnValue	sint32	Marks the message as unacknowledged (unresolved problem report)
Own	**Output:**		
	ReturnValue	sint32	Marks the message as "Owned". The caller of the method is the owner.
Disown	**Output:**		
	ReturnValue	sint32	Marks the messages as "Unowned".
GetAnnotation	**Input:**		
	AnnotationNumber	sint32	Gets a textual annotation to the message. Annotations are available to all operators that can view the message. OV_Message can have any number of annotations attached. It serves as a useful mechanism of tracking updates and changes of an ongoing problem report.
	Output:		
	Annotation	object:OV_MessageAnnotation	
	ReturnValue	sint32	
ModifyAnnotation	**Input:**		
	AnnotationNumber	sint32	Modifies a textual annotation to the message.
	NewText	string	
	Output:		
	ReturnValue	sint32	
DeleteAnnotation	**Input:**		
	AnnotationNumber	sint32	Deletes a textual annotation to the message.
	Output:		
	ReturnValue	sint32	
AddAnnotation	**Input:**		
	Text	string	Adds a textual annotation to the message.
	Output:		
	ReturnValue	sint32	
AcknowledgeMessages	**Input:**		
	MessageIDs	string	Marks a collection of messages as acknowledged (resolved/superceded)
	Output:		
	MassOperationResults	object:OV_Message_MassOperationResult	
	ReturnValue	sint32	
UnacknowledgeMessages	**Input:**		
	MessageIDs	string	Unmarks a collection of messages as unacknowledged (unresolved problem report)
	Output:		
	MassOperationResults	object:OV_Message_MassOperationResult	
	ReturnValue	sint32	
OwnMessages	**Input:**		
	MessageIDs	string	Marks a collection of messages as "Owned". The caller of the method is the owner.
	Output:		
	MassOperationResults	object:OV_Message_MassOperationResult	
	ReturnValue	sint32	
DisownMessages	**Input:**		
	MessageIDs	string	Marks a collection of messages as "Unowned".
	Output:		
	MassOperationResults	object:OV_Message_MassOperationResult	
	ReturnValue	sint32	
CountMessages	**Input:**		
	WhereClause	string	For future use, not currently supported.
	Output:		
	Count	sint32	
	ReturnValue	sint32	

The methods exactly match the selection we get by right-clicking on the alerts in the OVOW console. For example, some of these methods are *Acknowledge, AcknowledgeMessages, Disown, DisownMessages, Own, OwnMessages, Unacknowledge, UnacknowledgeMessages, AddAnnotation,* and *ChangeSeverity.* In the same way, by using another set of WMI classes, such as *OV_Message_SeverityChangeEvent, OV_Message_StateChangeEvent,*

OV_Message_TextChangeEvent, *OV_Message_NumberOfAnnotationsChange-Event*, and *OV_MessageAction_StateChangeEvent*, it is possible to track the alert state modifications. These extrinsic event classes are very easy to use, since you just need to run the **GenericEventAsyncConsumer.wsf** script with a different WQL event query. For example, to track the alert severity changes, you use the *OV_Message_SeverityChangeEvent* event class in the following WQL event query:

```
Select * From OV_Message_SeverityChangeEvent
```

Since the *OV_Message* class, with its related *OV_Message_InstancePro-vider* WMI provider, is used to implement the features to manage the OVOW v7 console messages, it is possible to create a script managing messages from the command line.

Before digging into the code details, let's see the command-line parameters exposed by the script. Basically, the script exposes most methods supported by the *OV_Message* class as a command-line parameter.

```
C:\>OVOWMessageManager.wsf
Microsoft (R) Windows Script Host Version 5.6
Copyright (C) Microsoft Corporation 1996-2001. All rights reserved.

Usage: OVOWMessageManager.wsf MessageID /Action:value
                             [/AnnotationNumber:value] [/Annotation:value]
                             [/Severity:value] [/Text:value] [/WQLQuery:value]
                             [/Machine:value] [/User:value] [/Password:value]
Options:

MessageID        : OVOW Message(s) ID.
Action           : Determines the OVOW Message action to perform.
AnnotationNumber : Specifies the annotation number.
Annotation       : Specifies the annotation text.
Severity         : Specifies the message severity.
Text             : Specifies the text message. (Used with ChangeText)
WQLQuery         : Specifies WQL Query for the messages to list.
Machine          : Determines the WMI system to connect to.
User             : Determines the UserID to perform the remote connection.
Password         : Determines the password to perform the remote connection.
Examples:

    OVOWMessageManager.wsf /Action:List
    OVOWMessageManager.wsf /Action:List
                        /WQLQuery:"Select * From OV_Message Where Severity=4"
    OVOWMessageManager.wsf 60ad8ae0-9014-71d6-08a8-0a0a0a060000 /Action:View
    OVOWMessageManager.wsf 60ad8ae0-9014-71d6-08a8-0a0a0a060000 /Action:Acknowledge
    OVOWMessageManager.wsf 60ad8ae0-9014-71d6-08a8-0a0a0a060000,
                        098fd400-7ef0-71d6-0b88-0a0a0a060000
                        /Action:AcknowledgeMessages
    OVOWMessageManager.wsf 60ad8ae0-9014-71d6-08a8-0a0a0a060000
                        /Action:Unacknowledge
    OVOWMessageManager.wsf 60ad8ae0-9014-71d6-08a8-0a0a0a060000,
                        098fd400-7ef0-71d6-0b88-0a0a0a060000
                        /Action:UnacknowledgeMessages
    OVOWMessageManager.wsf 60ad8ae0-9014-71d6-08a8-0a0a0a060000 /Action:Own
```

```
OVOWMessageManager.wsf 60ad8ae0-9014-71d6-08a8-0a0a0a060000,
                       098fd400-7ef0-71d6-0b88-0a0a0a060000
                       /Action:OwnMessages
OVOWMessageManager.wsf 60ad8ae0-9014-71d6-08a8-0a0a0a060000
                       /Action:Disown
OVOWMessageManager.wsf 60ad8ae0-9014-71d6-08a8-0a0a0a060000,
                       098fd400-7ef0-71d6-0b88-0a0a0a060000
                       /Action:DisownMessages
OVOWMessageManager.wsf 60ad8ae0-9014-71d6-08a8-0a0a0a060000
                       /Action:AddAnnotation
                       /Annotation:"This is my message annotation"
OVOWMessageManager.wsf 60ad8ae0-9014-71d6-08a8-0a0a0a060000
                       /Action:GetAnnotation /AnnotationNumber:1
OVOWMessageManager.wsf 60ad8ae0-9014-71d6-08a8-0a0a0a060000
                       /Action:ModifyAnnotation
                       /AnnotationNumber:1
                       /Annotation:"This is my updated message annotation"
OVOWMessageManager.wsf 60ad8ae0-9014-71d6-08a8-0a0a0a060000
                       /Action:DeleteAnnotation
                       /AnnotationNumber:1
OVOWMessageManager.wsf 60ad8ae0-9014-71d6-08a8-0a0a0a060000
                       /Action:ChangeSeverity /Severity:Unknown
OVOWMessageManager.wsf 60ad8ae0-9014-71d6-08a8-0a0a0a060000
                       /Action:ChangeSeverity /Severity:Normal
OVOWMessageManager.wsf 60ad8ae0-9014-71d6-08a8-0a0a0a060000
                       /Action:ChangeSeverity /Severity:Warning
OVOWMessageManager.wsf 60ad8ae0-9014-71d6-08a8-0a0a0a060000
                       /Action:ChangeSeverity /Severity:Minor
OVOWMessageManager.wsf 60ad8ae0-9014-71d6-08a8-0a0a0a060000
                       /Action:ChangeSeverity /Severity:Major
OVOWMessageManager.wsf 60ad8ae0-9014-71d6-08a8-0a0a0a060000
                       /Action:ChangeSeverity /Severity:Critical
OVOWMessageManager.wsf 60ad8ae0-9014-71d6-08a8-0a0a0a060000
                       /Action:ChangeText /Text:"This is my new text"
OVOWMessageManager.wsf 60ad8ae0-9014-71d6-08a8-0a0a0a060000
                       /Action:GetInstruction
```

Although there are 16 methods exposed by the *OV_Message* class, we will see that most methods use the same scripting techniques. As shown in Sample 5.16, the first lines are devoted to the external functions inclusion (lines 63 through 69), constants declaration (lines 79 through 81), XML command-line parameters parsing (lines 130 through 213), and the WMI connection (lines 225 through 229).

Sample 5.16   *The script initialization phase*

```
1:<?xml version="1.0"?>
.:
8:<package>
9:  <job>
..:
13:    <runtime>
..:
61:    </runtime>
62:
63:    <script language="VBScript" src=".\Functions\DecodeOVOWManagedNodeFunction.vbs" />
```

```
64:    <script language="VBScript" src=".\Functions\DecodeOVOWMessageFunction.vbs" />
65:    <script language="VBScript" src=".\Functions\OVOWErrorHandler.vbs" />
66:    <script language="VBScript" src=".\Functions\ConvertStringInArrayFunction.vbs" />
67:    <script language="VBScript" src=".\Functions\DisplayFormattedPropertiesFunction.vbs" />
68:    <script language="VBScript" src=".\Functions\DisplayFormattedPropertyFunction.vbs" />
69:    <script language="VBScript" src=".\Functions\TinyErrorHandler.vbs" />
70:
71:    <object progid="WbemScripting.SWbemLocator" id="objWMILocator" reference="true"/>
72:    <object progid="WbemScripting.SWbemDateTime" id="objWMIDateTime" />
73:
74:    <script language="VBscript">
75:    <![CDATA[
..:
79:    Const cComputerName = "LocalHost"
80:    Const cWMINameSpace = "Root/HewlettPackard/OpenView/Data"
81:    Const cWMIClass = "OV_Message"
...:
129:   ' -- COMMAND LINE PARSING --------------------------------------------------
130:   If WScript.Arguments.Named.Count Then
131:       Select Case Ucase(WScript.Arguments.Named("Action"))
132:              Case "LIST"
133:                     strWQLQuery = WScript.Arguments.Named("WQLQuery")
134:                     If Len(strWQLQuery) = 0 Then
135:                         strWQLQuery = "Select * From " & cWMIClass
136:                     End If
137:                     boolList = True
138:              Case "VIEW"
139:                     boolView = True
...:
203:       End Select
204:   End If
205:
206:   If boolList = False Then
207:       If WScript.Arguments.Unnamed.Count = 0 Then
208:          WScript.Arguments.ShowUsage()
209:          WScript.Quit
210:       Else
211:          arrayWMIOVMessages = ConvertStringInArray (WScript.Arguments.Unnamed.Item(0), ",")
212:       End If
213:   End If
...:
224:   ' -- WMI CONNECTION --------------------------------------------------------
225:   objWMILocator.Security_.AuthenticationLevel = wbemAuthenticationLevelDefault
226:   objWMILocator.Security_.ImpersonationLevel = wbemImpersonationLevelImpersonate
227:
228:   Set objWMIServices = objWMILocator.ConnectServer(strComputerName, cWMINameSpace, _
229:                                          strUserID, strPassword)
...:
...:
...:
```

Once the initialization phase is completed, based on the command-line parameters given, a specific section of the script will be executed. Let's start with the /**Action:List** switch. Basically, this switch displays the OVOW v7 messages in the same way as the OVOW console. This switch produces the following output (the output is divided into two blocks, since it is larger than the page).

```
C:\>OVOWMessageManager.wsf /Action:List
Microsoft (R) Windows Script Host Version 5.6
Copyright (C) Microsoft Corporation 1996-2001. All rights reserved.

1269 message(s) to list.

OVOW Messages
================================================================================== →
                                                                                   →
                                                                                   →
Severity      State         Time received                  Object     Application →
---------------------------------------------------------------------------------- →
  Normal Acknowledged 20020613190429.000000+120                None HP OpenView Operations →
  Warning      Unowned 20020613190727.000000+120 opcmona (Monitor Agent) HP OpenView Operations →
  Warning Acknowledged 20020613191226.000000+120                Memory              OS →
  Normal Acknowledged 20020613191319.000000+120            OvDnsDscr HP OpenView Operations →
  Normal Acknowledged 20020614090237.000000+120                None HP OpenView Operations →
                                                                                   →
→  ===========================================================================
→
→                    Node name      OS Version                     Message ID
→  -------------------------------------------------------------------------
→  NET-DPEN6450.LissWare.NET Windows 2000(5.0)  9f56fcd0-7eef-71d6-05bf-0a0a0a060000
→  NET-DPEN6450.LissWare.NET Windows 2000(5.0)  098fd400-7ef0-71d6-0b88-0a0a0a060000
→  NET-DPEN6450.LissWare.NET Windows 2000(5.0)  bc12ae40-7ef0-71d6-0b88-0a0a0a060000
→  NET-DPEN6450.LissWare.NET Windows 2000(5.0)  db5686a0-7ef0-71d6-05bf-0a0a0a060000
→  NET-DPEN6450.LissWare.NET Windows 2000(5.0)  6b8258d0-7f64-71d6-11fd-0a0a0a060000
```

We recognize the different characteristics (severity, state, time received, etc.) of an OVOW message, as shown in Figure 5.33. Sample 5.17 shows how to code the logic retrieving the OVOW message list.

Sample 5.17   *Retrieving a collection of OV_Message instances*

```
...:
...:
...:
232:     ' -- LIST -----------------------------------------------------------------
233:     If boolList Then
234:         Set objWMIOVMessages = objWMIServices.ExecQuery (strWQLQuery)
...:
237:         WScript.Echo objWMIOVMessages.Count & " message(s) to list." & vbCRLF
238:
239:         If objWMIOVMessages.Count Then
240:             WScript.Echo "OVOW Messages "  & String (193, "=") & vbCRLF
241:             WScript.Echo "      Severity              State" & _
242:                          "              Time received" & _
243:                          "                                Object" & _
244:                          "                    Application" & _
245:                          "                  Node name" & _
246:                          "              OS Version" & _
247:                          "                        Message ID"
248:             WScript.Echo String (207, "-")
249:
250:             For Each objWMIOVMessage In objWMIOVMessages
251:                 strSeverity = DecodeOVOWMessageSeverity (objWMIOVMessage.Severity) & _
252:                               "(" & objWMIOVMessage.Severity & ")"
253:                 strState = DecodeOVOWMessageState (objWMIOVMessage.State) & _
254:                            "(" & objWMIOVMessage.State & ")"
```

```
255:
256:                     Set objWMIManagedNode = objWMIServices.Get ("OV_ManagedNode.Name='" & _
257:                                                  objWMIOVMessage.NodeName & "'")
258:                     If Err.Number Then
259:                         strPrimaryNodeName = "<ERROR>"
260:                     Else
261:                         strPrimaryNodeName = objWMIManagedNode.PrimaryNodeName
262:                         strOSType = DecodeOVOWManagedNodeOSType (objWMIManagedNode.OSType) & "(" & _
263:                                 DecodeOVOWManagedNodeOSVersion (objWMIManagedNode.OSVersion) & ")"
264:                     End If
265:
266:                     WScript.Echo String (15 - Len (strSeverity), " ") & _
267:                             strSeverity & " " & _
...:
280:                             String (36 - Len (objWMIOVMessage.Id), " ") & _
281:                             objWMIOVMessage.Id
282:
283:                     Set objWMIManagedNode = Nothing
284:             Next
285:         Else
286:             WScript.Echo "No information available." & vbCRLF
287:         End If
...:
290:     End If
291:
...:
...:
...:
```

The first operation consists of retrieving a collection of instances by executing a WQL data query (line 234). The WQL data query is defined during the command parsing processing (lines 133 through 137 in Sample 5.16). The default WQL data query used is (line 135):

```
Select * From OV_Message
```

Of course, it is possible to specify another data query by using the /WQL-Query: switch on the command line (line 133). For example, a valid command line would be:

```
C:\>OVOWMessageManager.wsf /Action:List /WQLQuery:"Select * From OV_Message Where Severity=4"
```

where the severity number corresponds to the severity level listed in Table 5.39.

Once the WQL data query is completed, the script displays a header (lines 240 through 248) and enumerates all instances of the *OV_Message* class available for the specified WQL data query (lines 250 through 284). For each instance listed, Sample 5.17 retrieves and displays a specific set of properties:

- **The Severity level** (lines 251 and 252) is decoded with the DecodeO-VOWMessageSeverity() function included at line 64. The DecodeO-

Table 5.39   *The OV_Message and OV_ManagedNode Property Value Meanings*

Severity	
Unknown	1
Normal	2
Warning	4
Minor	8
Major	16
Critical	32

State	
Undefined	1
Unowned	2
Owned	3
Acknowledged	4
Node Deleted	5
Deleted	6

SystemType	
Alpha Family	35
Other	1
PA-RISC Family	144
Pentium Compatible	11
Power PC Family	27
SPARC Family	80

SourceType	
Unknown	0x2000
MPE Console	0x2001
Open Message Interface	0x2002
Logfile Entry | Windows Event Log	0x2004
Measurement Threshold	0x2008
SNMP Interceptor	0x2010
Message Stream Interface	0x2020
Reserved	0x2040
Reserved	0x2080
Scheduled Command	0x2100
Measurement Threshold	0x2200
Windows Management Interface	0x2400

OSType	
AIX	9
HPUX	8
LINUX	36
SNMP	65535
Solaris	29
Tru64	6
Unknown	0
Windows 2000	58
Windows NT	18
Windows XP	101
Windows Server 2003	102

OSVersion	
4.0	18000
2.6	29010
7	29020
8	29030
Red Hat 6.X	36206
Red Hat 7.X	36207
SuSE 6.X	36306
SuSE 7.X	36307
Turbo 6.X	36406
Turbo 7.X	36407
5.0	58000
V1	65535000

VOWMessageSeverity() function uses the information shown in Table 5.39 to determine the corresponding severity text.

- **The Message State** (lines 253 and 254) is decoded with the Decode-OVOWMessageState() function, also included at line 64. The DecodeOVOWMessageState() function uses information from Table 5.39 to determine the corresponding state text.

- **The Managed Node instance** (lines 256 and 257) is retrieved by requesting an instance of the *OV_ManagedNode* class with the node identifier exposed by the *NodeName* property of the *OV_Message* class. An *OV_ManagedNode* instance represents a managed node (i.e., computer) in the OVOW world. The node identifier is nothing other than a GUID number generated by OVOW v7 for each node configured or discovered in OVOW.

- **The Managed Node name** (line 261) corresponds to the DNS or WINS node name and is available from the *PrimaryNodeName* property exposed by the *OV_ManagedNode* class.

- **The Managed Node OS type and version** (lines 262 and 263) are, respectively, decoded with the DecodeOVOWManagedNode-OSType() and DecodeOVOWManagedNodeOSVersion() functions included at line 63. The DecodeOVOWManagedNodeOSType() and DecodeOVOWManagedNodeOSVersion() functions use the information in Table 5.39 to determine the text corresponding to the OS type and version values.

- **The Message ID** (lines 280 and 281) is the unique identifier of the message. Its value is a GUID number generated by OVOW. The script retrieves the message identifier by reading the ID property value exposed by the *OV_Message* class. The message identifier will be required to manage the various message attributes (*severity*, *state*, *annotation*, etc.)

From line 266 through 281, the script displays all these properties in a series of formatted columns.

It is possible to see all properties of an OVOW console message by referencing its GUID number (visible with the **/Action:List** switch) and the use of the **/Action:View** switch. For example, the following command line will show all properties of the OVOW message using the message identifier: 5bc2e7a0-7f66-71d6-09ae-0a0a0a060000:

```
 1:  C:\>OVOWMessageManager.wsf 5bc2e7a0-7f66-71d6-09ae-0a0a0a060000 /Action:View
 2:  Microsoft (R) Windows Script Host Version 5.6
 3:  Copyright (C) Microsoft Corporation 1996-2001. All rights reserved.
 4:
 5:  AcknowledgeAfterTroubleTicket: ........... FALSE
 6:  AgentId: ............................. 059bbdd0-7eed-71d6-1e0e-0a0a0a060000
 7:  Application: ......................... OS
 8:  ConditionId: ......................... 00000000000000000000000000000000000000
 9:  CreateTroubleTicketInterface: ........... FALSE
10:  DoNotification: ....................... FALSE
11:  *Id: ................................. 5bc2e7a0-7f66-71d6-09ae-0a0a0a060000
12:  InstructionAvailable: .................. FALSE
13:  IsProxied: ........................... FALSE
14:  LogOnly: ............................. FALSE
15:  MessageGroup: ........................ WINOSSPI-CORE
16:  MessageKey: .......................... net-dpen6450.LissWare.NET
                                            WINOSSPI-SysMon_CacheFaultsSec
17:  MessageKeyRelation: ................... net-dpen6450.LissWare.NET
                                            WINOSSPI-SysMon_CacheFaultsSec
18:  NodeName: ............................ {A0151862-79D6-47F9-8952-97F563F29429}
19:  NumberOfAnnotations: .................. 1
20:  Object: .............................. Cache
21:  OriginalId: .......................... 00000000000000000000000000000000000000
22:  OriginalServiceId: ................... WINOSSPI:NT:Memory:Cache@@<$MSG_NODE_ID>
23:  OriginalText: ........................ Monitor WINOSSPI-SysMon_CacheFaultsSec:
                                            Threshold: Scripting Value: 26.03
24:  ServiceId: ........................... WINOSSPI:NT:Memory:Cache@@{A0151862-79D6-...9429}
25:  Severity: ............................ Critical
26:  Source: .............................. WINOSSPI-SysMon_CacheFaultsSec(7.0)
27:  SourceType: .......................... 8
28:  State: ............................... Acknowledged
29:  Text: ................................ Object: Memory, Counter: Cache Faults/sec:
30:                                         The threshold of 20 has been crossed at 26!
31:  TimeCreated: ......................... 20020614091425.000000+120
32:  TimeOfStateChange: .................... 20020614091934.000000+120
33:  TimeReceived: ........................ 20020614091425.000000+120
```

```
34:     Type: ....................................
35:     Unmatched: .............................. FALSE
36:     UsedNotificationInterfaces: ..............
37:     UserOfStateChange: ...................... SYSTEM
```

The logic to display this information is not really different from the logic used for the **/Action:List** switch, and the output is similar to the one obtained with the **GenericEventAsyncConsumer.wsf** script used previously. This is illustrated in Sample 5.18.

Sample 5.18   *Retrieving all properties of an OV_Message instance*

```
...:
...:
...:
291:
292:     ' -- VIEW -------------------------------------------------------------
293:     If boolView Then
294:         Set objWMIOVMessage = objWMIServices.Get (cWMIClass & "='" & _
295:                                                 arrayWMIOVMessages (0) & "'")
...:
298:         Set objWMIPropertySet = objWMIOVMessage.Properties_
299:         For Each objWMIProperty In objWMIPropertySet
300:             Select Case objWMIProperty.Name
301:                 Case "AutomaticAction"
302:                     If IsObject (objWMIProperty.Value) Then
303:                         DisplayFormattedProperty objWMIOVMessage, _
304:                                 objWMIProperty.Name, _
305:                                 "Automatic Action", _
306:                                 Null
307:
308:                         Set objWMIMessageAction = objWMIProperty.Value
309:                         DisplayFormattedProperties objWMIMessageAction, 2
310:                         Set objWMIMessageAction = Nothing
311:                         WScript.echo
312:                     End If
313:                 Case "OperatorAction"
314:                     If IsObject (objWMIProperty.Value) Then
315:                         DisplayFormattedProperty objWMIOVMessage, _
316:                                 objWMIProperty.Name, _
317:                                 "Operator Action", _
318:                                 Null
319:
320:                         Set objWMIMessageAction = objWMIProperty.Value
321:                         DisplayFormattedProperties objWMIMessageAction, 2
322:                         Set objWMIMessageAction = Nothing
323:                         WScript.echo
324:                     End If
325:                 Case "Severity"
326:                     DisplayFormattedProperty objWMIOVMessage, _
327:                             objWMIProperty.Name, _
328:                             DecodeOVOWMessageSeverity (objWMIOVMessage.Severity), _
329:                             Null
330:                 Case "SourceType"
331:                     DisplayFormattedProperty objWMIOVMessage, _
332:                             objWMIProperty.Name, _
333:                             DecodeOVOWMessageSourceType (objWMIOVMessage.SourceType), _
```

```
334:                            Null
335:                Case "State"
336:                    DisplayFormattedProperty objWMIOVMessage, _
337:                            objWMIProperty.Name, _
338:                            DecodeOVOWMessageState (objWMIOVMessage.State), _
339:                            Null
340:                Case Else
341:                    DisplayFormattedProperty objWMIOVMessage, _
342:                            objWMIProperty.Name, _
343:                            objWMIProperty.Name, _
344:                            Null
345:            End Select
346:        Next
347:        Set objWMIPropertySet = Nothing
348:
349:        Set objWMIOVMessage = Nothing
350:    End If
351:
...:
...:
...:
```

First, the script retrieves the instance corresponding to the message ID given on the command line (lines 294 and 295). Since we can specify several message IDs separated by a column on the command line, the script converts all message IDs given in an array. This operation is completed during the command-line parsing at line 211 in Sample 5.16. This is why line 295 refers to the element zero of the array. Once done, the script enumerates all properties available from the *OV_Message* class. If a property requires a specific decoding, the **Select Case** statement will handle that for each property listed in the case. For example, we will recognize the decoding functions used previously for the severity and state properties. The *Source-Type* property follows the same logic and is decoded by invoking the DecodeOVOWMessageSourceType() included at line 64. The *Automatic-Action* and *OperatorAction* properties are slightly different, since they expose an instance of the *OV_MessageAction* class. Instances of this class expose information about actions that must be performed in relation to the console message (automatic or operator actions). Since an *OV_MessageAction* instance is contained in these two properties, another set of properties is available. Therefore, the script invokes the DisplayFormattedProperties() function to display all its properties. Behind the scenes, the DisplayFormattedProperties() invokes the DisplayFormattedProperty() function to display the property values. These two functions are included at lines 67 and 68, respectively.

As previously mentioned, the *OV_Message* class also exposes a series of methods allowing the management of OVOW messages. From a scripting point of view, we can classify the methods into two categories:

- The methods related to one specific instance of an OVOW message. These methods are: *Acknowledge, Unacknowledge, Own, Disown, Add-Annotation, GetAnnotation, ModifyAnnotation, DeleteAnnotation, ChangeSeverity, ChangeText, GetInstruction,* and *CountMessages.*

- The methods not specifically related to one particular OVOW message but to a series of OVOW messages. These methods are: *AcknowledgeMessages, UnacknowledgeMessages, OwnMessages,* and *DisownMessages.*

As with the **/Action:View** command-line parameter, the management of a specific *OV_Message* instance starts with the retrieval of the *OV_Message* instance corresponding to the message ID specified on the command line. Some command-line examples managing an OVOW message are:

```
C:\>OVOWMessageManager.wsf 60ad8ae0-9014-71d6-08a8-0a0a0a060000 /Action:Acknowledge
C:\>OVOWMessageManager.wsf 60ad8ae0-9014-71d6-08a8-0a0a0a060000 /Action:Unacknowledge
C:\>OVOWMessageManager.wsf 60ad8ae0-9014-71d6-08a8-0a0a0a060000 /Action:Own
C:\>OVOWMessageManager.wsf 60ad8ae0-9014-71d6-08a8-0a0a0a060000 /Action:Disown
```

The scripting technique is always the same for any of these command-line parameters. Sample 5.19 shows the code used to acknowledge an OVOW message. Only the invoked method differs if you want to unacknowledge, own, or disown an OVOW message.

Sample 5.19   *Managing a specific OV_Message instance*

```
...:
...:
...:
352:    ' -- ACKNOWLEDGE -----------------------------------------------------------
353:    If boolAcknowledge Then
354:        Set objWMIOVMessage = objWMIServices.Get (cWMIClass & "='" & _
355:                                          arrayWMIOVMessages (0) & "'")
...:
358:        intRC = objWMIOVMessage.Acknowledge()
359:        If intRC Then
360:            OVOWErrorHandler (intRC)
361:        Else
362:            WScript.Echo "Message acknowledge successfully completed."
363:        End If
...:
366:    End If
367:
...:
...:
...:
```

The technique is pretty easy. The first step retrieves an instance of the OVOW message using the message ID given on the command line (lines 354 and 355). Next, the corresponding *OV_Message* method is invoked (line 358). If an error occurs, the OVOWErrorHandler() function is invoked to display the corresponding error message. This function is included at line 65.

Other methods, such as *AddAnnotation, GetAnnotation, ModifyAnnotation, DeleteAnnotation, ChangeSeverity, ChangeText, GetInstruction,* and *CountMessages,* follow the same logic. However, these methods require some extra parameters. For example, to change the message severity, the **/Action:ChangeSeverity** switch must be given with the **/Severity:Minor** switch to specify the severity level (see Sample 5.20). The severity level is converted to its corresponding value (see Table 5.39) during the command-line parsing parameters. An example command line would be:

```
C:\>OVOWMessageManager.wsf 60ad8ae0-9014-71d6-08a8-0a0a0a060000
                                /Action:ChangeSeverity /Severity:Minor
```

Sample 5.20   *Changing the OVOW message severity level*

```
...:
...:
...:
547:
548:    ' -- CHANGE SEVERITY --------------------------------------------------------
549:    If boolChangeSeverity Then
550:       Set objWMIOVMessage = objWMIServices.Get (cWMIClass & "='" & _
551:                                       arrayWMIOVMessages (0) & "'")
...:
554:       intRC = objWMIOVMessage.ChangeSeverity(intSeverity)
555:       If intRC Then
556:          OVOWErrorHandler (intRC)
557:       Else
558:          WScript.Echo "Message ChangeSeverity successfully completed."
559:       End If
...:
562:    End If
563:
...:
...:
...:
```

After retrieving the *OV_Message* instance corresponding to the message ID given on the command line (lines 550 and 551), the script invokes the *ChangeSeverity* method with the desired severity level (line 554) input parameter. Next, the error handling is processed, as previously.

A final peculiarity in the scripting technique concerns the *GetAnnotation* method invocation—not especially in the command-line parameters, such as:

```
C:\>OVOWMessageManager.wsf 60ad8ae0-9014-71d6-08a8-0a0a0a060000
                                /Action:GetAnnotation /AnnotationNumber:1
```

but more in the way that the annotation is returned by WMI. Sample 5.21 shows this.

Sample 5.21   *Retrieving the OVOW message annotation*

```
...:
...:
...:
491:
492:   ' -- GET ANNOTATION ---------------------------------------------------------------
493:   If boolGetAnnotation Then
494:      Set objWMIOVMessage = objWMIServices.Get (cWMIClass & "='" & _
495:                                          arrayWMIOVMessages (0) & "'")
...:
498:      intRC = objWMIOVMessage.GetAnnotation(intAnnotationNumber, _
499:                                     objWMIMessageAnnotation)
500:      If intRC Then
501:         OVOWErrorHandler (intRC)
502:      Else
503:         If Len (objWMIMessageAnnotation.Text) Then
504:            WScript.Echo "Message annotation: " & vbCRLF & vbCRLF & _
505:                         objWMIMessageAnnotation.Text & vbCRLF
506:         Else
507:            WScript.Echo "Message Annotation not available." & vbCRLF
508:         End If
509:         WScript.Echo "Message GetAnnotation successfully completed."
510:      End If
...:
513:   End If
514:
...:
...:
...:
```

Once the OVOW message instance is retrieved (lines 494 and 495), the *GetAnnotation* method is invoked (lines 498 and 499). This method requires two parameters: one input parameter, which corresponds to the annotation number, and one output parameter, which is returned as an instance of the *OV_MessageAnnotation* class. Once this instance is retrieved, the script checks that the annotation text is not null by examining the length of the text property (line 503) and displaying the annotation text (lines 504 and 505) if it is available.

Instead of managing OVOW messages one by one, it is possible to acknowledge, unacknowledge, own, or disown a collection of messages. Some command-line examples are:

```
C:\>OVOWMessageManager.wsf 60ad8ae0-9014-71d6-08a8-0a0a0a060000,098fd400-7ef0-71d6-0b88-0a0a0a060000
                        /Action:AcknowledgeMessages
C:\>OVOWMessageManager.wsf 60ad8ae0-9014-71d6-08a8-0a0a0a060000,098fd400-7ef0-71d6-0b88-0a0a0a060000
                        /Action:UnacknowledgeMessages
C:\>OVOWMessageManager.wsf 60ad8ae0-9014-71d6-08a8-0a0a0a060000,098fd400-7ef0-71d6-0b88-0a0a0a060000
                        /Action:OwnMessages
```

```
C:\>OVOWMessageManager.wsf 60ad8ae0-9014-71d6-08a8-0a0a0a060000,098fd400-7ef0-71d6-0b88-0a0a0a060000
                /Action:DisownMessages
```

Because these *OV_Message* invoked methods do not refer to a particular OVOW message, the methods performing these actions are implemented as a static method (*static* qualifier set to true). Therefore, these methods must be invoked from an instance of a class (which means in this case an instance of the *OV_Message* class) and not from an instance of a real manageable entity (which means in this case, an instance of the *OV_Message* class created with a message ID). Sample 5.22 shows how to proceed.

Sample 5.22   *Managing a series of OV_Message instances*

```
...:
...:
...:
367:
368:     ' -- ACKNOWLEDGE MESSAGES -----------------------------------------------------
369:     If boolAcknowledgeMessages Then
370:         Set objWMIClass = objWMIServices.Get (cWMIClass)
...:
373:         intRC = objWMIClass.AcknowledgeMessages(arrayWMIOVMessages)
374:         If intRC Then
375:             OVOWErrorHandler (intRC)
376:         Else
377:             WScript.Echo "Messages acknowledge successfully completed."
378:         End If
...:
381:     End If
382:
...:
...:
...:
```

Instead of retrieving an instance corresponding to an OVOW message ID, the script retrieves an instance of the class only (line 370). Next, it invokes the *AcknowledgeMessages* method, which requires an array containing all message IDs of the OVOW messages that must be acknowledged (line 373). During the command-line parameters parsing, all message IDs given on the command line (and separated by a column) are stored in an array (line 211 in Sample 5.16). This technique is exactly the same for the *UnacknowledgeMessages*, *OwnMessages*, and *DisownMessages* methods.

5.6   WMI and the .NET Framework

The .NET Framework programming environment is an extensive subject. Even if we only consider the relationship that exists between WMI and the .NET Framework, this topic represents enough information to at least dedicate an entire chapter in this book. However, in this book, we have considered the WMI scripting aspect without considering the programming aspects from languages such as C, C++, or Visual BASIC. Looking at the .NET Framework implies that we leave the scripting world to enter the world of programming with languages such as C# or VB.NET. Therefore, we will just give a brief overview of the .NET Framework WMI capabilities, since this topic is beyond the scope of this book. Some basic knowledge about the .NET Framework architecture, its concepts, and its usage from **Visual Studio.NET** are required.

5.6.1   The .NET Framework WMI information access

In this book, we have exclusively used the **SWbemScripting** COM objects to access WMI information from scripts. However, from C or C++ applications, it is also possible to access the same WMI information by using the native WMI COM interfaces, known as the **IWbem** interfaces. Once the .NET Framework is part of the system, another technology is available to applications accessing WMI information. The .NET WMI object model exposed by the *System.Management* and the *System.Management.Instrumentation* .NET namespaces are designed to support the utilization and the providing of WMI information:

- The *System.Management* **namespace**: This .NET namespace contains .NET classes that provide access to a rich set of management information and management events about the system, devices, and applications instrumented to the WMI. Applications and services can query for interesting management information, using .NET classes derived from *ManagementObjectSearcher* and *ManagementQuery* classes, or subscribe to a variety of management events using the *ManagementEventWatcher* class. Simply said, the *System.Management* namespace offers the required functionality for the WMI clients to access management data.

- The *System.Management.Instrumentation* **namespace**: This .NET namespace provides the .NET classes necessary to instrument applications for management and expose their management information and events through WMI to potential consumers. Consumers can then easily manage, monitor, and configure these applications acting as WMI information providers. The management data is available for WMI scripts or any other applications. Simply said, the *System.Management.Instrumentation* namespace offers the required functionality for WMI applications to provide management information (managed code) to potential WMI clients. It offers an alternate route for developing WMI providers to the C and C++ COM interfaces.

These two .NET namespaces are totally independent from each other. For instance, if an application provides information with the *System.Management.Instrumentation* namespace, this does not limit the visibility of the instrumentation to the *System.Management* classes, which means that the information provided can be utilized by any other WMI information types (i.e., WMI COM API). On the other hand, if you use the *System.Management* classes, this will allow you to access any WMI information, not just the instrumentation written using the *System.Management.Instrumentation* namespace.

Using the .NET Framework technology to access WMI information implies that we use a programming object model different from the one used for scripting. Does it mean that all material we learned before is not applicable anymore? Well, from a coding technique point of view, it is clear that a completely new object model must be relearned, since it imposes a new coding technique besides the new .NET languages adaptations. However, since the .NET Framework acts as a WMI consumer relying on the existing WMI infrastructure (i.e., WMI COM objects, CIMOM, CIM repository), all WMI classes and information provided under Windows NT, Windows 2000, Windows Server 2003, and Windows XP remain valid. This is where we clearly see the advantage of the abstraction layer that the CIM repository and the CIM Object Manager provide!

Besides the new WMI .NET object model, version 1.00 of the .NET Framework acted as a WMI provider as well. It brought a new WMI provider, called *NetFrameworkv1Provider* provider. Known as the Configuration provider, it supported a collection of WMI classes to manage the .NET Framework and its components. However, subsequent versions of the .NET Framework do not include this provider anymore.

Basically, the .NET Framework is an addition to the existing WMI infrastructure. It is an add-on from a WMI application programming point of view (to develop WMI consumers and providers) and from a .NET Framework manageability point of view (since it brings a WMI provider to manage the .NET application configuration settings).

Figure 5.34 shows the three WMI tiers and identifies how the *System.Management* namespace is layered on WMI: Microsoft Windows Forms (Windows Forms), Web Forms (ASP.NET), and management applications can act as clients that access the WMI instrumentation. At the same time, management providers can be either existing codes, which wrap system or

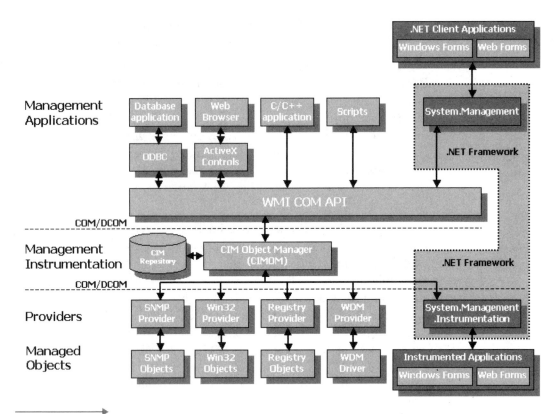

Figure 5.34   *The .NET Framework and the WMI architecture.*

application instrumentation, or Windows Forms and Web Forms/ASP.NET applications, which expose management instrumentation about themselves to other clients by using the *System.Management.Instrumentation* namespace.

In this section, we will only cover the WMI information utilization aspect supported by the *System.Management* namespace.

5.6.2   Accessing WMI information from Visual Studio.NET

Before doing a brief overview of the .NET coding technique regarding the WMI information access, it is interesting to note that Microsoft provides a WMI-based management extension to the **Visual Studio.NET Server Explorer** tool. This component adds two new nodes to the **Visual Studio.NET Server Explorer** tool:

- **The Management Data node:** Management Data allows the application developer to browse and modify WMI data as well as invoke methods.

- **The Management Events node:** Management Events enable the application developer to register for WMI events.

This add-on can be downloaded from http://www.microsoft.com/downloads/release.asp?ReleaseID=31155. Once installed, you can start the **Visual Studio.NET Server Explorer** tool by pressing Ctrl+Alt+S. Then you can browse the "Management Classes" node and, for instance, select the "Disk Volumes" node and expand the tree until you get the drive list shown in Figure 5.35.

By selecting the C: drive, you will recognize the information exposed by the *Win32_LogicalDisk* class (display name "Disk Volumes" for the C: instance). Note that the **Server Explorer** tool doesn't show the real class name; rather, it shows the class display name. The class display name corre-

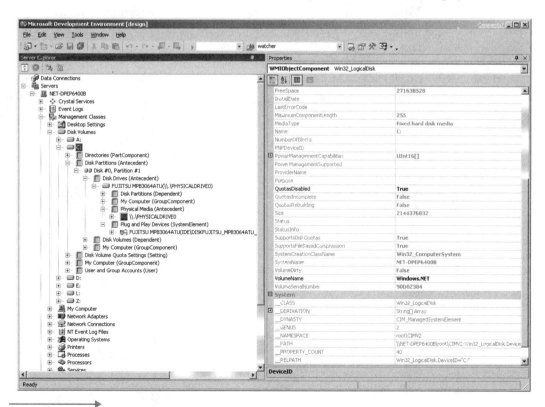

Figure 5.35   *The WMI-based management extension to the Visual Studio.NET Server Explorer tool.*

sponds to the value stored in the **displayname** Qualifier available from the WMI class definition. This could be confusing the first time, since you likely worked with real class names rather than class display names (especially in the WMI COM environment). As shown in Figure 5.35, the *Win32_DiskVolume* class has a "Disk Volumes" display name, where "Disk Volumes" is the value assigned to the **displayname** Qualifier of the *Win32_ DiskVolume* class.

By expanding the "Disk Volumes," the **Server Explorer** shows all existing instances of the class (i.e., A:, C:, D:, and E:). Next, if you expand one instance of the *Win32_LogicalDisk* class (i.e., C:), the **Server Explorer** will show all class display names of instances associated with the expanded instance (i.e., directories, partitions, volume quota, etc.). Behind the scenes, **Server Explorer** uses the association classes defined in the CIM repository to establish the link. Moreover, **Server Explorer** allows you to see the properties of a class or instance and execute methods from classes (static methods) or instances (nonstatic methods). If you plan to execute a method, the **Visual Studio.NET Server Explorer** tool will prompt you for the method input parameters. Once the method executes, it will show you the method execution result with the eventual output parameters. However, by default, not all classes from the CIM repository are visible from the **Visual Studio.NET Server Explorer** tool. By right-clicking on the Management Data node and selecting Add Class from the context menu, you get the dialog shown in Figure 5.36.

Figure 5.36
Browsing WMI namespaces for classes.

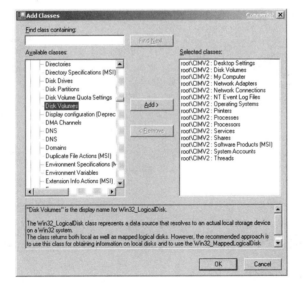

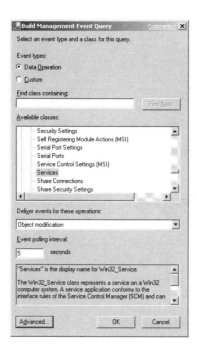

Figure 5.37
Event subscription from Visual Studio.NET.

This window allows you to search and browse in the CIM repository across all namespaces and class names. Again, this window shows the class display names, but note that the real class name is visible in the description at the bottom of the window.

With this extension, it is also possible to subscribe to WMI events. For this, you need to right-click on the "Management Events" node and select the "Add Event Query" selection. At that time, the window shown in Figure 5.37 appears.

First, you must select a class from the "Available Classes" window. In Figure 5.37, the "Services" display name corresponds to the *Win32_Service* class. Once the class display name is selected and the condition of event delivery selected with an eventual polling interval, the event query configured in Figure 5.37 will correspond to the following WQL event query:

```
Select * From __InstanceModificationEvent Within 5 Where TargetInstance ISA 'Win32_Service'
```

Once a modification occurs to one of the Windows services, **Visual Studio.NET** will show the instance modification, as shown in Figure 5.38 in the "Output" window (bottom of the screen).

To summarize, we can say that the WMI-based management extension to the **Visual Studio.NET Server Explorer** tool is an updated, integrated,

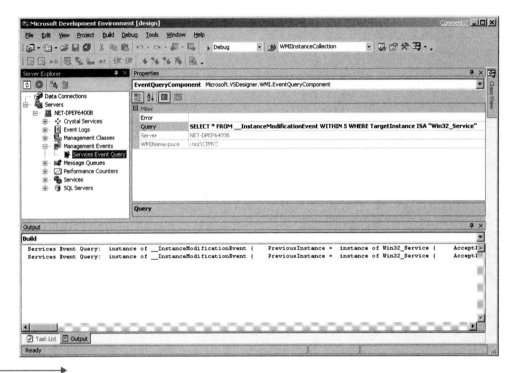

Figure 5.38   *Viewing events from Visual Studio.NET.*

and combined version of **WMI CIM Studio**, **WMI Object Browser**, and **WBEMTEST.Exe** tools.

5.6.3   Accessing WMI information from a .NET language

Even if the object model is different from the one we used in the scripting environment, the type of functionality provided by the .NET *System.Management* classes is similar to the one provided by the WMI COM interfaces. All properties and methods exposed by the WMI COM interfaces have their equivalents in the *System.Management* classes. As before, the event subscriptions and method executions are available as well. Of course, because the .NET Framework abstracts WMI COM interfaces with the *System.Management* and the *System.Management.Instrumentation* classes, it is clear that an adapted coding technique from a language such as C# or VB.NET is required. We won't cover all aspects and details of .NET programming in C# or VB.NET here. Since .NET is an entirely new implementation in several strategic areas, I encourage you to gather more information about this subject, which is mainly available from the Microsoft .NET Framework SDK. Today, there are loads of publications available on this matter as well. However, through some small examples, we will quickly see that the functionality level you get from the .NET *System.Management* classes is similar to the one you have from the WMI COM API. If you master the capabilities of the WMI COM API (and you should, as you arrive at the end of this book), it will be quite easy to reproduce logics developed in VBScript or Jscript from WSH with a .NET language and the *System.Management* classes.

Because the startup is always the most painful step, let's examine a very basic WMI sample in C#, performing a WMI connection and listing all properties of all instances of the *Win32_Service* class (see Sample 5.23).

Sample 5.23 *Connecting and retrieving all Windows Services instances with their properties with the System.Management classes with C#*

```
 1:   using System;
 2:   using System.Management;
 3:
 4:   class Constants
 5:           {
 6:              public const string UserID = "LISSWARENET\\Administrator";
 7:              public const string Password = "password";
 8:              public const string ComputerName = "net-dpen6400a.LissWare.NET";
 9:              public const string NameSpace = "Root\\CIMv2";
10:              public const string WMIClass = "Win32_Service";
11:           }
12:
13:   class WMISample
14:        {
15:        public static int Main(string[] args)
16:            {
17:              ConnectionOptions options = new ConnectionOptions();
18:              options.Username = Constants.UserID;
19:              options.Password = Constants.Password;
20:              options.Authentication = AuthenticationLevel.Default;
21:              options.Impersonation = ImpersonationLevel.Impersonate;
22:
23:              ManagementScope scope = new ManagementScope();
24:              scope.Path = new ManagementPath("\\\\" + Constants.ComputerName +
25:                                              "\\" + Constants.NameSpace);
26:              scope.Options = options;
27:
28:              try {
29:                  scope.Connect();
30:                  }
31:              catch (Exception Err)
32:                  {
33:                  Console.WriteLine("Failed to connect: " + Err.Message);
34:                  return 1;
35:                  }
36:
```

```
37:           ManagementClass WMIClass = new ManagementClass(Constants.WMIClass);
38:           WMIClass.Scope = scope;
39:
40:           ManagementObjectCollection WMIInstanceCollection = WMIClass.GetInstances();
41:
42:           foreach (ManagementObject WMIInstance in WMIInstanceCollection)
43:               {
44:                   Console.WriteLine();
45:                   PropertyDataCollection.PropertyDataEnumerator propertyEnumerator =
46:                                           WMIInstance.Properties.GetEnumerator();
47:                   while (propertyEnumerator.MoveNext())
48:                       {
49:                           PropertyData property = (PropertyData)propertyEnumerator.Current;
50:                           Console.WriteLine(property.Name + " = " + property.Value);
51:                       }
52:               }
53:           return 0;
54:           }
55:       }
```

Sample 5.23 executes the following WMI operations:

- **Performs a WMI remote connection** (lines 17 through 35): The remote connection parameters are stored in an object called **options** made from the *ConnectionOptions* .NET class (line 17). Each parameter of this object holds one parameter for the connection. For instance, the *username* and *password* properties contain the credentials (lines 18 and 19), while the *authentication* and *impersonation* properties determine the WMI authentication and impersonation mode, respectively (lines 20 and 21). Next, the system name and the WMI namespace to access are specified in a **ManagementScope** object created from the *ManagementScope* class (lines 23 through 25). The **ManagementScope** object information is completed with the connection parameters previously created (line 26). Once done, the WMI connection is executed (line 29). In case of error, the exception is handled with a "Try ... catch" C# statement (lines 28 through 35). All connection parameters are defined in constants. These values are available from the *Constants* .NET class defined from line 4 through 11.

- **Retrieves the list of Windows Services available** (lines 37 and 40): Before retrieving all Windows Services available, the code sample creates a **ManagementClass** object from the *ManagementClass* .NET class (line 37). This object represents the WMI class given in reference during the object creation, which is the *Win32_Service* WMI class defined as a constant at line 10. With the **ManagementClass** object, the C# code requests all instances of the *Win32_Service* WMI class by invoking the *GetInstance()* .NET method (line 40). Note that the **ManagementClass** object knows about the connection details, since it reuses the **ManagementScope** object created for the connection (line 38). Because the connection is previously established (line 29) and because the *ManagementClass* object reuses the same **ManagementScope** object, the connection is not recreated and the connection channel is reused. The *GetInstance()* .NET method invocation creates a new **ManagementObjectCollection** object (line 40), which contains a collection of all Windows Services instances available from the connected system.

- **For each Windows service in the collection, the code retrieves all properties with their values** (lines 42 through 52): To display the Windows services available, the **ManagementObjectCollection** object must be enumerated. Therefore, a loop performs this enumeration (lines 42 through 52). For each Windows service instance we have in the collection, the C# code retrieves the property list available from the instance by creating a **PropertyDataCollection.PropertyDataEnumerator** object (lines 45 and 46). Next, for each property we have in this new collection, the code enumerates each property one by one (lines 47 through 51) and retrieves the property in a **PropertyData** object (line 49) to display its name and its corresponding value (line 50).

As we can see in Sample 5.23, we perform a task we already did many times from WSH. From a functional point of view, there is no difference. However, the coding and the object references are totally different. This makes sense, since we use another language (i.e., C#) and programming object model.

We can also submit WQL queries as we did from the WMI COM interfaces. Sample 5.24 uses the same structure to retrieve the same set of information as Sample 5.23. However, instead of invoking the *GetInstances()* .NET method, it performs a WQL data query.

Sample 5.24   *Connecting and retrieving all Windows Services instances with their properties with a WQL data query with the System.Management classes with C#*

```
1:   using System;
2:   using System.Management;
3:
4:   class Constants
5:       {
6:       public const string UserID = "LISSWARENET\\Administrator";
7:       public const string Password = "password";
8:       public const string ComputerName = "net-dpen6400a.LissWare.NET";
9:       public const string NameSpace = "Root\\CIMv2";
```

```
10:          public const string WQLQuery = "Select * From Win32_Service";
11:          }
12:
13:   class WMISample
14:          {
15:          public static int Main(string[] args)
16:                 {
..:
37:                 ManagementObjectSearcher WMIInstanceSearcher = new ManagementObjectSearcher();
38:                 WMIInstanceSearcher.Query = new ObjectQuery(Constants.WQLQuery);
39:                 WMIInstanceSearcher.Scope = scope;
40:
41:                 ManagementObjectCollection WMIInstances = WMIInstanceSearcher.Get();
42:
43:                 foreach (ManagementObject WMIInstance in WMIInstances)
44:                        {
..:
53:                        }
54:                 return 0;
55:                 }
56:          }
```

The first modification concerns line 10. This line defines the WQL data query in a new constant. On line 38, this constant is referenced to create an **ObjectQuery** object made from the *ObjectQuery* .NET class. Next, this object is stored in a new **ManagementObjectSearcher** object (line 38) created previously (line 37) from the *ManagementObjectSearcher* .NET class. As in Sample 5.23, the **ManagementObjectSearcher** object reuses the **ManagementScope** object created previously (skipped lines 16 through 37) to establish the WMI connection (line 39). Next, a **ManagementObjectCollection** object is created (line 41). Instead of creating this object from the *GetInstance()* .NET method, it is created by invoking the WMI search with the *Get()* .NET method exposed by the **ManagementObjectSearcher** object. The search is based on the WQL data query assigned to the **ManagementObjectSearcher** object (line 38). Next, as before, the C# code enumerates all instances available with their properties and values (lines 43 through 53).

If we talk about WQL data queries, we should talk about WQL event queries as well. This is the purpose of Sample 5.25, which performs an asynchronous WQL event query.

Sample 5.25   *Connecting and performing a WQL event query to display Windows Services instances subject to a modification with the System.Management classes with C#*

```
1:   using System;
2:   using System.Management;
3:
4:   class Constants
5:          {
6:          public const string UserID = "LISSWARENET\\Administrator";
```

```
 7:                    public const string Password = "password";
 8:                    public const string ComputerName = "net-dpen6400a.LissWare.Net";
 9:                    public const string NameSpace = "Root\\CIMv2";
10:                    public const string WQLQuery = "SELECT * FROM __InstanceModificationEvent" +
11:                                              "WITHIN 5 " +
12:                                              "WHERE TargetInstance ISA \"Win32_Service\"";
13:               }
14:
15:    class WMISample
16:         {
17:         public static int Main(string[] args)
18:              {
..:
30:                    WQLEventQuery WQLEventQuery = new WqlEventQuery();
31:                    WQLEventQuery.QueryString = Constants.WQLQuery;
32:
33:                    ManagementEventWatcher WMIEventWatcher = new ManagementEventWatcher();
34:                    WMIEventWatcher.Scope = scope;
35:                    WMIEventWatcher.Query = WQLEventQuery;
36:
37:                    WMIEventHandler WMIHandler = new WMIEventHandler();
38:                    WMIEventWatcher.EventArrived +=
39:                              new EventArrivedEventHandler(WMIHandler.Arrived);
40:
41:               try {
42:                    WMIEventWatcher.Start();
43:                    }
44:               catch (Exception Err)
45:                    {
46:                    Console.WriteLine("Failed to connect: " + Err.Message);
47:                    return 1;
48:                    }
49:
50:               Console.WriteLine("Waiting for events ...");
51:
52:               while (!WMIHandler.IsArrived)
53:                    {
54:                    System.Threading.Thread.Sleep(1000);
55:                    }
56:
57:               WMIEventWatcher.Stop();
58:
59:               return 0;
60:               }
61:         }
62:
63:         public class WMIEventHandler
64:               {
65:               private bool isArrived = false;
66:
67:               public void Arrived(object sender, EventArrivedEventArgs EventArgs)
68:                    {
69:                    ManagementBaseObject WMIInstance =
70:                              (ManagementBaseObject)(EventArgs.NewEvent["TargetInstance"]);
71:
72:                    Console.WriteLine("Event triggered ...\n" );
73:                    PropertyDataCollection.PropertyDataEnumerator propertyEnumerator =
74:                              WMIInstance.Properties.GetEnumerator();
75:                    while (propertyEnumerator.MoveNext())
76:                         {
```

```
77:                        PropertyData property = (PropertyData)propertyEnumerator.Current;
78:                        Console.WriteLine(property.Name + " = " + property.Value);
79:                        }
80:
81:                        isArrived = true;
82:                   }
83:
84:           public bool IsArrived
85:                   {
86:                   get
87:                     {
88:                     return isArrived;
89:                     }
90:                   }
91:               }
```

This last .NET C# example is slightly more complex. As with previous examples, Sample 5.25 starts by creating the **ConnectionOptions** and **ManagementScope** objects (lines 19 through 28). Next, it creates the **WQLEventQuery** object holding the WQL event query (lines 30 and 31) defined as a constant in the *Constants* class (lines 10 through 12). To briefly demonstrate the versatility of the *System.Management* classes, the WQL query can be assigned to the **WQLEventQuery** object in many different ways. In Sample 5.24, we used one coding technique (line 38). In Sample 5.25, we use the following assignment, where we split the object creation from the WQL query assignment:

```
WQLEventQuery WQLEventQuery = new WqlEventQuery();
WQLEventQuery.QueryString = Constants.WQLQuery;
```

However, in the *System.Management* namespace object model, the WQL query can also be specified parameter by parameter:

```
WQLEventQuery WQLEventQuery = new WqlEventQuery("__InstanceModificationEvent", new TimeSpan(0,0,5),
                           "TargetInstance ISA 'Win32_Service'");
```

Or, eventually, the WQL query parameters can be assigned to their respective properties one by one:

```
WQLEventQuery WQLEventQuery = new WqlEventQuery();
WQLEventQuery.EventClassName = "__InstanceModificationEvent";
WQLEventQuery.Condition = "TargetInstance ISA 'Win32_Service'";
WQLEventQuery.WithinInterval = new TimeSpan(0,0,5);
```

All these WQL query assignments produce the exact same result: They create a **WQLEventQuery** object made from the *WQLEventQuery* .NET class containing the WQL query defined in the *Contants* .NET class. This small example shows how versatile the object model can be and how it can be confusing for beginners as well!

Next, the portion of code preparing the ground for the asynchronous event monitoring starts with the creation of a **ManagementEventWatcher** object (lines 33 through 39). This object contains the connection settings (line 34) and the **WQLEventQuery** object (line 35). Since the monitoring is asynchronous, a **WMIEventHandler** object is created (line 37) from the *WMIEventHandler* .NET class defined further in the code (lines 63 through 91). This class implements the event sink routine handling WMI event notifications. We will come back to this class creation later in this section.

Once the **ManagementEventWatcher** object is created (line 33), in addition to the **ManagementScope** and **WQLEventQuery** objects information, the **ManagementEventWatcher** object needs to know which routine is used as the event handler. Therefore, based on the event type, the **ManagementEventWatcher** object is initialized with a pointer to the event routine. The event types can be:

- **EventArrived:** Occurs when a new event arrives.

- **Stopped:** Occurs when a subscription to an event is canceled.

```
38:              WMIEventWatcher.EventArrived +=
39:                      new EventArrivedEventHandler(WMIHandler.Arrived);
```

For people not used to the C# notation, the VB.NET notation may make more sense:

```
AddHandler WMIEventWatcher.EventArrived, AddressOf WMIHandler.Arrived
```

Next, the event watching is started (line 42) by invoking the *Start()* method of the **ManagementEventWatcher** object. Since the WMI connection is performed during the event watching startup process, the statement is enclosed in a "Try ... catch" C# statement to manage exceptions (lines 41 through 48). Next, the C# code will wait until an event arrives (lines 52 through 55). The *IsArrived* property is exposed by the *WMIEventHandler* .NET class created within the C# code (lines 84 through 90).

The last piece of code to examine concerns the event handler itself (lines 63 through 91). The event handler is triggered for the **EventArrived** event. Therefore, a subfunction, which must be named *Arrived()*, is created inside the .NET class (lines 67 to 82). Two .NET objects are passed as parameters along the event notification:

- **Sender** object: This object contains information about the event sender. For instance, with this object it is possible to retrieve information contained in the **WMIEventWatcher** object created in the first part of the code. This could be done as follows inside the event handler routine:

```
ManagementEventWatcher WMIEventWatcher = (ManagementEventWatcher) sender;
Console.WriteLine(WMIEventWatcher.Query.QueryString);
```

- **EventArgs** object: This object contains information about the event itself and is made from the *EventArrivedEventArgs* .NET class. This object exposes two properties: the *Context* property and the *NewEvent* property. The *NewEvent* property gets information about the WMI event notification. Therefore, to retrieve information about the WMI instance subject to the *__InstanceModificationEvent*, the C# code retrieves, via the WMI *TargetInstance* property exposed by the WMI instance event notification, the *Win32_Service* instance subject to the changes (line 69 and 70). This instance is stored in a **Management-BaseObject** object made from the *ManagementBaseObject* .NET class.

```
68:        ManagementBaseObject WMIInstance =
69:            (ManagementBaseObject)(EventArgs.NewEvent["TargetInstance"]);
```

Once the **ManagementBaseObject** object is available, Sample 5.25 proceeds as previous samples: It enumerates all properties with their values of the WMI instance (lines 72 through 82). Once the enumeration is completed, the *IsArrived* property exposed by the *WMIEventHandler* .NET class is updated (line 81), which makes the main routine of Sample 5.25 exiting from its loop at lines 52 through 55. Then the event watcher is stopped (line 57) before the C# code terminates (line 59).

5.7   Summary

Today, most applications released by Microsoft are WMI enabled. Even if we only reviewed some of the most important applications produced by Microsoft, there are many other applications supporting WMI that we didn't talk about, such as Host Integration Server (Microsoft SNA Server), System Management Server (SMS), or Services For Unix 3.0 for some existing products. At writing time, some new products, still under development, will also make an extensive usage of a WMI. To give some examples:

- Exchange Server 2003 extends the current Exchange 2000 WMI capabilities for administration purposes.

- Automated Deployment Service provides a new set of WMI classes for its administration and automation purposes.

- Windows System Resource Manager makes use of the SMTP event consumer for alerting purposes.

- Microsoft Meta-Directory Service 3.0 provides a new set of WMI classes for its administration and its internal instrumentation.

To give another example in the area of the Enterprise management software, HP OpenView Operations for Windows or Microsoft Operation Manager utilize WMI information to manage Windows at the enterprise level while providing WMI information at the same time for manageability and customization. Today, it is inconceivable that management applications in the Windows space are not WMI enabled. WMI is the foundation of a solid enterprise management solution for everyone in charge of managing or administering Windows platforms today.

5.8   Useful Internet URLs

Management (WMI) Extensions for Visual Studio .NET RTM Server Explorer

```
http://www.microsoft.com/downloads/release.asp?ReleaseID=31155
```

6

A Look Into the Future of WMI Scripting

Discussing the future of any technology is always a challenge, since so many things may change between the moment you write down where you think the technology will go and the time you see the final implementation. However, by looking at what we have today and the way Microsoft analyzes the feedback it has received from customers, we can arrive at some "best guesses."

The current scripting infrastructure, implemented by WSH 5.6, is powerful enough to perform most tasks required by administrators. Leveraging the WSH 5.6 infrastructure via various COM object models, such as ADSI and WMI, to gain access to the system settings and monitoring provides administrators with a powerful set of tools. However, learning these technologies is not particularly easy for administrators, especially for those who do not want to be programmers. As explained in the WMI examples in this book, you need to know, understand, and master many interfaces and other components to harness all the power offered by the WSH/WMI combination. More specifically, to play with WMI, you must learn:

- The CIM repository mechanisms, to understand their organization and how to get access to the classes representing real-world manageable entities.

- The WMI providers capabilities, since they determine the classes capabilities (i.e., update, enumeration, events).

- The classes contained in the CIM repository, since they represent the template of the real-world manageable entities.

- The WMI COM object model or the .NET Framework classes, to understand how to get access to the management data from a coded logic in a script or a C# program.

- A scripting or programming language (i.e., VBScript, JSCript, VB.NET, C#), to create the core logic of the tasks (i.e., structure, loops, statements, etc.).

If you look at these technologies from a high-level perspective, you realize that you must understand and master a large number of concepts and technologies to effectively script on top of WMI. Actually, this is the root of many of the new ideas, and where the foundation for the future of the Windows management layers may come from, since Microsoft wants to simplify the amount of knowledge required to work with the management data available on the Windows platforms.

6.1   The .NET Framework and scripting

Although the .NET Framework is a well-determined Microsoft strategy today and represents a step forward in simplification, you still need to understand some of the underlying mechanisms that WMI takes advantage of, such as the CIM repository and the nature of the classes (i.e., instance class, event class). The .NET Framework *System.Management* and *System.Management.Instrumentation* namespaces deliver a new management programming object model, which is more consistent than the isolated islands of interfaces implemented by COM technologies, such as is the case when WMI is combined with ADSI or CDOEXM to do some Exchange management. Unfortunately, we already know that the current .NET Framework classes do not represent all the manageable elements of a Windows platform, since most features rely on the existing COM plumbing. As such, there are still many interfaces that need to be provided before we will be able to write code to manage every facet of the Windows operating system. Keep in mind that "managing" implies the concepts of "configuration," "monitoring," and "alerting." In this sense, the current .NET Framework classes still have their limitations, since most information exposed by the .NET classes relies on WMI.

To improve matters, Microsoft is considering the development of a new Windows management layer, which will include the current WMI implementation, as well as some new implementations to cover areas not yet contained in WMI. Since the access method to the management data will be .NET based, the transparency of the access method will be handled behind the scenes by the .NET Framework abstraction layer. Regardless of how the management data is retrieved (via the existing WMI implementation or some new technologies still not fully defined), the Windows management layer will provide the information in an abstracted way. The goal of such an implementation is to hide the complexity that you cannot skip today if you are willing to use WMI. The new abstraction layer, acting as a management infrastructure service, will ideally be more object oriented when compared with the current implementation, which requires too much effort to work with. Of course, one can say that the current implementation is already object oriented, since we deal with COM objects all the time! So, where is the difference? In an ideal object-oriented world, a developer doesn't normally deal with the infrastructure implementation as we do with WMI. The essence of objects available through the model should provide the necessary information without having to deal with its core implementation. From that perspective, WMI is far from an ideal object-oriented programming environment. This is a major focus for Microsoft as it drives for future simplification. Bear in mind that this vision is a generic representation of how things could be. There is no implementation available in any form at the time of this writing. In fact, these statements are purely the vision of things that may be realized over a two- to three-year time frame.

Another aspect is the scripting environment itself. Today, we have two directions clearly defined in Microsoft technologies: the programming model, based on the .NET Framework class model and the new line of .NET Server products such as Windows Server 2003, and a set of next-generation servers to replace current versions of products such as Exchange and SQL that will be built on the .NET framework. The question we must ask is: Where do scripting technologies fit?

The aim of scripting technologies is to fill a gap between the pure programming world only used by "real programmers" and the user interface mostly used by support teams, help desks, and administrators. However, most enterprise administrators need to automate tasks in their day-to-day work, but they are not programmers and don't want to be one. Even if the .NET Framework class model offers most of the features to create managed code and manage the Windows environment, it does not necessarily represent a viable solution for enterprise administrators. In fact, you very rarely find administrators who install **Visual Studio.NET** and start learning languages such as C# or VB.NET just to write a few lines of code to automate simple or repetitive management tasks. In addition, any good operating system always provides a shell with a scripting language to develop coded logic (i.e., the Korn and C shells for the UNIX platform or REXX for IBM systems). Therefore, Microsoft needs to fill a space in its operating system that offers the advantages of the scripting environments, as we know them today, and exploits the power of the .NET environment at the same time.

6.2   Windows scripting environments

Under the current Windows Operating System platform, we have two important scripting environments implemented by **CMD.EXE** and WSH. **CMD.EXE** uses the old-fashioned CMD (command-line) commands, while WSH is purely COM/DCOM based. When looking at the Microsoft .NET strategy, how do the CMD and WSH environments fit into the .NET Framework, which uses a completely different run-time environment? This current .NET Framework run-time environment is currently not designed to support scripts, or at least in a way we know scripting today. This is where Microsoft is still determining many options they can pursue over the next two to three years.

We have a good realization about many of the shortcomings of the existing scripting environment. For the CMD environment, limitations exist, such as not being able to access system management data without the use of an external executable or script that acts as a "black box." For WSH, we have another set of limitations, such as the use of non-strongly-typed languages such as VBScript and the inability to invoke any .NET Framework features or Win32 APIs (unless you use PERL with a third-party scripting engine that supports Win32 API calls). Another confusing problem is the need to use different COM technologies to retrieve management data (i.e., ADSI, CDOEXM, WMI, to name a few). In addition, these COM technologies sometimes overlap each other (i.e., you can start and stop Windows services with WMI, but you can do this as well from ADSI), which creates additional confusion.

Although there is no concrete architecture or components today to address these limitations and leverage the actual scripting technologies via the power of the .NET framework, Microsoft would like to eliminate most of the limitations that exist in the current environments while maintaining the advantages that the scripting technologies offer today. In this respect, the golden rule is "simplicity"! In other words, the technology must be easy to learn and use.

Looking into the future, we could predict that Microsoft will get rid of the current CMD shell, since it is the origin of many limitations. A new CMD shell built on top of the .NET framework could replace the current version. This development may also imply that we will see a new WSH environment. Currently, WSH is based on a COM/DCOM-based architecture, but we know that Microsoft is basing any new development on top of the .NET framework, so it is clear that the "new" WSH will certainly not be the same as today. It is more than likely that a new shell will support a more powerful command-line language while supporting one or more scripting languages. It is also possible that the new shell will support both graphical and text interfaces to make script writing and execution easier. For instance, with WSH today, any administrator can start Notepad, write a few lines in Jscript or VBScript, and launch the script to begin executing. This is an ease of access to programmatic control that most programming languages don't support, and Microsoft is conscious of the advantages delivered by such an implementation. However, it will take time before we get to a Windows platform that is 100 percent .NET enabled, and, because of this, we can be almost certain that the current COM/DCOM WSH and WMI architectures will not vary enormously over the next two to three years.

6.3   Final thoughts

Of course, all these probable changes may discourage people from getting to know WSH and WMI in their current form, but you should always remember that the technology of today solves today's problems and the technology of tomorrow is not yet available. Since Windows Server 2003 (and before) is based on COM/DCOM, the current WSH and WMI implementation will remain in use for many years, which reinforces the importance of investing in scripting technologies and WMI today, even if Microsoft is considering where a new architecture for scripting might bring us in the future.

Appendix

Scripts listed in this section are fully documented in *Understanding WMI Scripting* (ISBN 1555582664) along with the WMI aspects and the scripting techniques they use. Beyond the learning curve they represent, they also offer useful functionalities to pursue our WMI discovery process. That's the reason why they are used many times throughout this second volume dedicated to WMI. The most experienced people in WMI, using this second volume on a standalone basis, can refer to this section to gather more information about these scripts. Again, the scripts are given for reference only. People interested in getting more information about the scripts must refer to *Understanding WMI Scripting* (ISBN 1555582664).

Sample 4.6   *Retrieving all instances of the Win32_Service class with their properties*

```
1:<?xml version="1.0"?>
 .:
8:<package>
9:    <job>
..:
13:       <object progid="WbemScripting.SWbemLocator" id="objWMILocator" reference="true"/>
14:
15:       <script language="VBscript">
16:       <![CDATA[
..:
20:       Const cComputerName = "LocalHost"
21:       Const cWMINameSpace = "root/cimv2"
22:       Const cWMIClass = "Win32_Service"
..:
27:       objWMILocator.Security_.AuthenticationLevel = wbemAuthenticationLevelDefault
28:       objWMILocator.Security_.ImpersonationLevel = wbemImpersonationLevelImpersonate
29:       Set objWMIServices = objWMILocator.ConnectServer(cComputerName, cWMINameSpace, "", "")
30:       Set objWMIInstances = objWMIServices.InstancesOf (cWMIClass)
31:
32:       For Each objWMIInstance in objWMIInstances
33:           WScript.Echo objWMIInstance.Name & " (" & objWMIInstance.Description & ")"
34:           WScript.Echo "    AcceptPause=" & objWMIInstance.AcceptPause
35:           WScript.Echo "    AcceptStop=" & objWMIInstance.AcceptStop
36:           WScript.Echo "    Caption=" & objWMIInstance.Caption
37:           WScript.Echo "    CheckPoint=" & objWMIInstance.CheckPoint
```

```
38:        WScript.Echo "    CreationClassName=" & objWMIInstance.CreationClassName
39:        WScript.Echo "    Description=" & objWMIInstance.Description
40:        WScript.Echo "    DesktopInteract=" & objWMIInstance.DesktopInteract
41:        WScript.Echo "    DisplayName=" & objWMIInstance.DisplayName
42:        WScript.Echo "    ErrorControl=" & objWMIInstance.ErrorControl
43:        WScript.Echo "    ExitCode=" & objWMIInstance.ExitCode
44:        WScript.Echo "    InstallDate=" & objWMIInstance.InstallDate
45:        WScript.Echo "    Name=" & objWMIInstance.Name
46:        WScript.Echo "    PathName=" & objWMIInstance.PathName
47:        WScript.Echo "    ProcessId=" & objWMIInstance.ProcessId
48:        WScript.Echo "    ServiceSpecificExitCode=" & objWMIInstance.ServiceSpecificExitCode
49:        WScript.Echo "    ServiceType=" & objWMIInstance.ServiceType
50:        WScript.Echo "    Started=" & objWMIInstance.Started
51:        WScript.Echo "    StartMode=" & objWMIInstance.StartMode
52:        WScript.Echo "    StartName=" & objWMIInstance.StartName
53:        WScript.Echo "    State=" & objWMIInstance.State
54:        WScript.Echo "    Status=" & objWMIInstance.Status
55:        WScript.Echo "    SystemCreationClassName=" & objWMIInstance.SystemCreationClassName
56:        WScript.Echo "    SystemName=" & objWMIInstance.SystemName
57:        WScript.Echo "    TagId=" & objWMIInstance.TagId
58:        WScript.Echo "    WaitHint=" & objWMIInstance.WaitHint
59:    Next
..:
64:    ]]>
65:    </script>
66:   </job>
67:</package>
```

Sample 4.14 *Setting one read/write property of a Win32_Registry class instance directly*

```
1:<?xml version="1.0"?>
 .:
8:<package>
9:  <job>
..:
13:      <object progid="WbemScripting.SWbemLocator" id="objWMILocator" reference="true"/>
14:
15:      <script language="VBscript">
16:      <![CDATA[
..:
20:      Const cComputerName = "LocalHost"
21:      Const cWMINameSpace = "root/cimv2"
22:      Const cWMIClass = "Win32_Registry"
23:      Const cWMIInstance = "Microsoft Windows.NET Server|J:\WINDOWS|\Device\Harddisk0\Partition8"
..:
28:      objWMILocator.Security_.AuthenticationLevel = wbemAuthenticationLevelDefault
29:      objWMILocator.Security_.ImpersonationLevel = wbemImpersonationLevelImpersonate
30:      Set objWMIServices = objWMILocator.ConnectServer(cComputerName, cWMINameSpace, "", "")
31:      Set objWMIInstance = objWMIServices.Get (cWMIClass & "='" & cWMIInstance & "'")
32:
33:      WScript.Echo objWMIInstance.Name & " (" & objWMIInstance.Description & ")"
34:
35:      Wscript.Echo "Current registry size is: " & objWMIInstance.ProposedSize  & " MB."
36:
37:      objWMIInstance.ProposedSize = objWMIInstance.ProposedSize + 10
38:      objWMIInstance.Put_ (wbemChangeFlagUpdateOnly Or wbemFlagReturnWhenComplete)
39:
40:      Wscript.Echo "Current registry size is: " & objWMIInstance.ProposedSize  & " MB."
```

```
..:
45:    ]]>
46:    </script>
47:  </job>
48:</package>
```

Sample 4.15   *Setting one read/write property of a Win32_Registry class instance indirectly*

```
1:<?xml version="1.0"?>
.:
8:<package>
9:  <job>
..:
13:    <object progid="WbemScripting.SWbemLocator" id="objWMILocator" reference="true"/>
14:
15:    <script language="VBscript">
16:    <![CDATA[
..:
20:    Const cComputerName = "LocalHost"
21:    Const cWMINameSpace = "root/cimv2"
22:    Const cWMIClass = "Win32_Registry"
23:    Const cWMIInstance = "Microsoft Windows.NET Server|J:\WINDOWS|\Device\Harddisk0\Partition8"
..:
29:    objWMILocator.Security_.AuthenticationLevel = wbemAuthenticationLevelDefault
30:    objWMILocator.Security_.ImpersonationLevel = wbemImpersonationLevelImpersonate
31:    Set objWMIServices = objWMILocator.ConnectServer(cComputerName, cWMINameSpace, "", "")
32:    Set objWMIInstance = objWMIServices.Get (cWMIClass & "='" & cWMIInstance & "'")
33:
34:    WScript.Echo objWMIInstance.Name & " (" & objWMIInstance.Description & ")"
35:
36:    Set objWMIPropertySet = objWMIInstance.Properties_
37:
38:    Wscript.Echo "Current registry size is: " & objWMIPropertySet.Item("ProposedSize") & " MB."
39:
40:    objWMIPropertySet.Item("ProposedSize") = objWMIPropertySet.Item("ProposedSize") + 10
41:    objWMIInstance.Put_ (wbemChangeFlagUpdateOnly Or wbemFlagReturnWhenComplete)
42:
43:    Wscript.Echo "Current registry size is: " & objWMIPropertySet.Item("ProposedSize") & " MB."
..:
50:    ]]>
51:    </script>
52:  </job>
53:</package>
```

Sample 4.30   *A generic routine to display the SWbemPropertySet object*

```
.:
6:' --------------------------------------------------------------------------------------------
7:Function DisplayProperties (objWMIInstance, intIndent)
..:
14:    Set objWMIPropertySet = objWMIInstance.Properties_
15:    For Each objWMIProperty In objWMIPropertySet
16:
17:        boolCIMKey = objWMIProperty.Qualifiers_.Item("key").Value
18:        If Err.Number Then
19:            Err.Clear
```

```
20:          boolCIMKey = False
21:      End If
22:      If boolCIMKey Then
23:          strCIMKey = "*"
24:      Else
25:          strCIMKey = ""
26:      End If
27:
28:      If Not IsNull (objWMIProperty.Value) Then
29:          If objWMIProperty.CIMType = wbemCimtypeObject Then
30:              If objWMIProperty.IsArray Then
31:                  For Each varElement In objWMIProperty.Value
32:                      WScript.Echo Space (intIndent) & strCIMKey & objWMIProperty.Name & _
33:                              " (" & GetCIMSyntaxText (objWMIProperty.CIMType) & ")"
34:                      DisplayProperties varElement, intIndent + 2
35:                  Next
36:              Else
37:                  WScript.Echo Space (intIndent) & strCIMKey & objWMIProperty.Name & _
38:                          " (" & GetCIMSyntaxText (objWMIProperty.CIMType) & ")"
39:                  DisplayProperties objWMIProperty.Value, intIndent + 2
40:              End If
41:          Else
42:              If objWMIProperty.IsArray Then
43:                  For Each varElement In objWMIProperty.Value
44:                      WScript.Echo Space (intIndent) & strCIMKey & objWMIProperty.Name & _
45:                              " (" & GetCIMSyntaxText (objWMIProperty.CIMType) & ") = " & _
46:                              varElement
47:                  Next
48:              Else
49:                  If objWMIProperty.Name = "TIME_CREATED" Then
50:                      objWMIDateTime.SetFileTime (objWMIProperty.Value)
51:
52:                      WScript.Echo Space (intIndent) & strCIMKey & objWMIProperty.Name & _
53:                              " (" & GetCIMSyntaxText (objWMIProperty.CIMType) & ") = " & _
54:                              objWMIDateTime.GetVarDate (True) & _
55:                              " (" & objWMIDateTime.Value & ")"
56:                  Else
57:                      If objWMIProperty.CIMType = wbemCimtypeDatetime Then
58:                          objWMIDateTime.Value = objWMIProperty.Value
59:
60:                          WScript.Echo Space (intIndent) & strCIMKey & objWMIProperty.Name & _
61:                                  " (" & GetCIMSyntaxText (objWMIProperty.CIMType) & ") = " & _
62:                                  objWMIDateTime.GetVarDate (True) & _
63:                                  " (" & objWMIProperty.Value & ")"
64:                      Else
65:                          WScript.Echo Space (intIndent) & strCIMKey & objWMIProperty.Name & _
66:                                  " (" & GetCIMSyntaxText (objWMIProperty.CIMType) & ") = " & _
67:                                  objWMIProperty.Value
68:                      End If
69:                  End If
70:              End If
71:          End If
72:      Else
73:          WScript.Echo Space (intIndent) & strCIMKey & objWMIProperty.Name & _
74:                  " (" & GetCIMSyntaxText (objWMIProperty.CIMType) & ") = (null)"
75:      End If
76:  Next
..:
79:End Function
80:
```

```
 81:' -----------------------------------------------------------------------------------------
 82:Function GetCIMSyntaxText (intCIMType)
 83:
 84:    Select Case intCIMType
 85:            ' Signed 16-bit integer
 86:           Case 2
 87:                 GetCIMSyntaxText = "wbemCimtypeSint16"
 88:            ' Signed 32-bit integer
 89:           Case 3
 90:                 GetCIMSyntaxText = "wbemCimtypeSint32"
 91:            ' 32-bit real number
 92:           Case 4
 93:                 GetCIMSyntaxText = "wbemCimtypeReal32"
 94:            ' 64-bit real number
 95:           Case 5
 96:                 GetCIMSyntaxText = "wbemCimtypeReal64"
 97:            ' String
 98:           Case 8
 99:                 GetCIMSyntaxText = "wbemCimtypeString"
100:            ' Boolean value
101:           Case 11
102:                 GetCIMSyntaxText = "wbemCimtypeBoolean"
103:            ' CIM object
104:           Case 13
105:                 GetCIMSyntaxText = "wbemCimtypeObject"
106:            ' Signed 8-bit integer
107:           Case 16
108:                 GetCIMSyntaxText = "wbemCimtypeSint8"
109:            ' Unsigned 8-bit integer
110:           Case 17
111:                 GetCIMSyntaxText = "wbemCimtypeUint8"
112:            ' Unsigned 16-bit integer
113:           Case 18
114:                 GetCIMSyntaxText = "wbemCimtypeUint16"
115:            ' Unsigned 32-bit integer
116:           Case 19
117:                 GetCIMSyntaxText = "wbemCimtypeUint32"
118:            ' Signed 64-bit integer
119:           Case 20
120:                 GetCIMSyntaxText = "wbemCimtypeSint64"
121:            ' Unsigned 64-bit integer
122:           Case 21
123:                 GetCIMSyntaxText = "wbemCimtypeUint64"
124:            ' Date/time value
125:           Case 101
126:                 GetCIMSyntaxText = "wbemCimtypeDatetime"
127:            ' Reference to a CIM object.
128:           Case 102
129:                 GetCIMSyntaxText = "wbemCimtypeReference"
130:            ' 16-bit character
131:           Case 103
132:                 GetCIMSyntaxText = "wbemCimtypeChar16"
133:    End Select
134:
135:End Function
```

Sample 4.31 *Browsing the namespaces to find class definitions*

```
 1:<?xml version="1.0"?>
 .:
 8:<package>
 9:  <job>
..:
13:    <runtime>
..:
18:    </runtime>
19:
20:    <script language="VBScript" src="..\Functions\DisplayInstanceProperties.vbs" />
21:    <script language="VBScript" src="..\Functions\TinyErrorHandler.vbs" />
22:
23:    <object progid="WbemScripting.SWbemLocator" id="objWMILocator" reference="true"/>
24:    <object progid="WbemScripting.SWbemDateTime" id="objWMIDateTime" />
25:
26:    <script language="VBscript">
27:    <![CDATA[
..:
31:    Const cComputerName = "LocalHost"
32:    Const cWMINameSpace = "Root"
33:    Const cWMINamespaceClass = "__NAMESPACE"
34:    Const cWMIClass = "__EventProviderRegistration"
..:


40:    ' -----------------------------------------------------------------------------
41:    ' Parse the command line parameters
42:    If WScript.Arguments.Unnamed.Count = 0 Then
43:       strWMIClass = InputBox ("Enter the WMI Class to examine: ", _
44:                               "WMI Class:", _
45:                               cWMIClass)
46:
47:       If Len (strWMIClass) = 0 Then
48:          WScript.Arguments.ShowUsage()
49:          WScript.Quit
50:       End If
51:    Else
52:       strWMIClass = WScript.Arguments.Unnamed.Item(0)
53:    End If
54:    strWMIClass = Ucase (strWMIClass)
55:
56:    strUserID = WScript.Arguments.Named("User")
57:    If Len(strUserID) = 0 Then strUserID = ""
58:
59:    strPassword = WScript.Arguments.Named("Password")
60:    If Len(strPassword) = 0 Then strPassword = ""
61:
62:    strComputerName = WScript.Arguments.Named("Machine")
63:    If Len(strComputerName) = 0 Then strComputerName = cComputerName
64:
65:    DisplayNameSpaces cWMINameSpace, strWMIClass, strUserID, strPassword, strComputerName
66:
67:    ' -----------------------------------------------------------------------------
68:    Function DisplayNameSpaces (ByVal strWMINameSpace, _
69:                                ByVal strWMIClass, _
70:                                ByVal strUserID, _
71:                                ByVal strPassword, _
```

```
 72:                               ByVal strComputerName)
 ..:
 82:          objWMILocator.Security_.AuthenticationLevel = wbemAuthenticationLevelDefault
 83:          objWMILocator.Security_.ImpersonationLevel = wbemImpersonationLevelImpersonate
 84:          Set objWMIServices = objWMILocator.ConnectServer(strComputerName, _
 85:                                                            strWMINameSpace, _
 86:                                                            strUserID, _
 87:                                                            strPassword)
 ..:
 90:          Set objWMIInstance = objWMIServices.Get (strWMIClass)
 91:          If Err.Number Then
 92:             Err.Clear
 93:          Else
 94:             WScript.Echo strWMINameSpace
 95:             DisplayProperties objWMIInstance, 2
 ..:
 97:          End If
 98:
 99:          Set objWMINSInstances = objWMIServices.InstancesOf (cWMINamespaceClass, _
                                                                   wbemQueryFlagShallow)
100:          For Each objWMINSInstance in objWMINSInstances
101:             DisplayNameSpaces strWMINameSpace & "/" & objWMINSInstance.Name, _
102:                               strWMIClass, strUserID, strPassword, strComputerName
103:          Next
...:
108:      End Function
109:
110:      ]]>
111:      </script>
112:   </job>
113:</package>
```

Sample 4.32 ➤ *A Windows Script File self-documenting the CIM repository classes in an Excel sheet*

```
  1:<?xml version="1.0"?>
  .:
  8:<package>
  9:  <job>
 ..:
 13:      <runtime>
 ..:
 31:      </runtime>
 32:
 33:      <script language="VBScript" src="..\Functions\TinyErrorHandler.vbs" />
 34:
 35:      <object progid="WbemScripting.SWbemLocator" id="objWMILocator" reference="true"/>
 36:      <object progid="EXCEL.application" id="objXL"/>
 37:      <object progid="WScript.Shell" id="WshSHell"/>
 38:
 39:      <script language="VBscript">
 40:      <![CDATA[
 ..:
 44:      Const cLevelClassOnly = 1
 45:      Const cLevelClassWithProps = 2
 46:      Const cLevelClassWithPropsAndMethods = 3
 47:      Const cLevelClassWithPropsAndMethodsWithInParams = 4
 48:      Const cLevelClassWithPropsAndMethodsWithInOutParams = 5
 49:      Const cLevelClassWithPropsQAndMethodsQWithParamsQ = 6
```

```
 50:
 51:      Const Black = 1
 52:      Const Silver = 15
 53:      Const Aqua1 = 42
 54:      Const Aqua2 = 8
 55:      Const White1 = 2
 56:      Const White2 = 40
 57:      Const White3 = 19
 58:      Const Yellow = 27
 59:
 60:      Const cOriginPosition = 9
 61:      Const cQualifierPosition = 10
 62:
 63:      Const cComputerName = "LocalHost"
 64:      Const cWMINameSpace = "Root/CIMv2"
 ..:
 81:      ' --------------------------------------------------------------------------------
 82:      ' Parse the command line parameters
 83:      If WScript.Arguments.Unnamed.Count = 0 Then
 84:         strWMIClass = InputBox ("Enter the WMI Class to examine: ", _
 85:                                 "WMI Class:", _
 86:                                 "Win32_Service")
 87:
 88:         If Len (strWMIClass) = 0 Then
 89:            WScript.Arguments.ShowUsage()
 90:            WScript.Quit
 91:         End If
 92:      Else
 93:         strWMIClass = WScript.Arguments.Unnamed.Item(0)
 94:      End If
 95:      ' strWMIClass = Ucase (strWMIClass)
 96:
 97:      strUserID = WScript.Arguments.Named("User")
 98:      If Len(strUserID) = 0 Then strUserID = ""
 99:
100:      strPassword = WScript.Arguments.Named("Password")
101:      If Len(strPassword) = 0 Then strPassword = ""
102:
103:      strComputerName = WScript.Arguments.Named("Machine")
104:      If Len(strComputerName) = 0 Then strComputerName = cComputerName
105:
106:      strWMINameSpace = WScript.Arguments.Named("NameSpace")
107:      If Len(strWMINameSpace) = 0 Then strWMINameSpace = cWMINameSpace
108:      strWMINameSpace = UCase (strWMINameSpace)
109:
110:      intExplorationDepth = Cint (WScript.Arguments.Named("Level"))
111:      If intExplorationDepth = 0 Then
112:         intExplorationDepth = cLevelClassWithPropsAndMethodsWithInOutParams
113:      End If
114:
115:      boolSubClass = WScript.Arguments.Named("Sub")
116:      boolOrigin = Not WScript.Arguments.Named("Origin")
117:
118:      ' --------------------------------------------------------------------------------
119:      ' Prepare an Excel worksheet
120:      ' Make it visible, don't hide it because for the save, the user will be prompted!
121:      objXL.Visible = True
122:
123:      ' Open Excel and start an empty workbook
124:      objXL.Workbooks.Add
```

```
125:
126:      ' Put the cursor on the A1 cell
127:      objXL.ActiveSheet.range("A1").Activate
128:      objXL.ActiveSheet.Name = Mid (strWMIClass, 1, 31)
129:
130:      objXL.Columns("A:Z").Font.Name = "Tahoma"
131:      objXL.Columns("A:Z").IndentLevel = 0
132:      objXL.Columns("A:Z").VerticalAlignment = 2
133:
134:      If intExplorationDepth > cLevelClassWithPropsAndMethodsWithInOutParams Then
135:
136:         ' Format the XL Sheet
137:         objXL.Columns("A:I").ColumnWidth = 5
138:         objXL.Columns("J").ColumnWidth = 22
139:         objXL.Columns("K").ColumnWidth = 16
140:         objXL.Columns("L").ColumnWidth = 22
141:         objXL.Columns("M:Z").ColumnWidth = 7
142:         objXL.Rows("1").Orientation = 90
143:         objXL.Rows("1").VerticalAlignment = 3
144:         objXL.Rows("1").HorizontalAlignment = 3
145:
146:         objXL.Range("A" & objXL.ActiveCell.Row & ":Z" & objXL.ActiveCell.Row).Font.Bold = True
147:         objXL.Range("A" & objXL.ActiveCell.Row & ":Z" & objXL.ActiveCell.Row).Font.Size = 16
148:
149:         intX = cOriginPosition
150:         ' Origin
151:         objXL.Activecell.Offset(0, intX).Value = "Origin"
152:
153:         intX = cQualifierPosition
154:         ' Name
155:         objXL.Activecell.Offset(0, intX).Value = "Qualifier Name"
156:         ' Value
157:         objXL.Activecell.Offset(0, intX + 1).Value = "Value"
158:         ' Amended
159:         objXL.Activecell.Offset(0, intX + 2).Value = "Amended"
160:         ' Local
161:         objXL.Activecell.Offset(0, intX + 3).Value = "Local"
162:         ' Overridable
163:         objXL.Activecell.Offset(0, intX + 4).Value = "Overridable"
164:         ' Propagates to instance
165:         objXL.Activecell.Offset(0, intX + 5).Value = "Propagates to instance"
166:         ' Propagates to subclass
167:         objXL.Activecell.Offset(0, intX + 6).Value = "Propagates to subclass"
168:
169:         intX = 0
170:         objXL.Activecell.Offset(1, 0).Activate
171:      End If
172:
173:      ' -------------------------------------------------------------------------
174:      ' Connect to WMI
175:      objWMILocator.Security_.AuthenticationLevel = wbemAuthenticationLevelDefault
176:      objWMILocator.Security_.ImpersonationLevel = wbemImpersonationLevelImpersonate
177:      Set objWMIServices = objWMILocator.ConnectServer(strComputerName, _
178:                                                         strWMINameSpace, _
179:                                                         strUserID, _
180:                                                         strPassword)
...:
183:      DisplayClasses intX, objWMIServices, strWMIClass
...:
187:      ' -------------------------------------------------------------------------
```

```
188:    objXL.ActiveSheet.range("A1").Activate
189:
190:    ' Save & Close the Workbook. If file exists, user will be prompted.
191:    objXL.Workbooks.Application.ActiveWorkbook.SaveAs _
192:        (WshShell.CurrentDirectory & "\" & objXL.ActiveSheet.Name)
193:    objXL.Workbooks.close
194:    objXL.Quit
195:
196:    ' --------------------------------------------------------------------------------
197:    Function DisplayClasses (ByVal intX, ByVal objWMIServices, ByVal strWMIClass)
...:
209:        Set objWMIInstance = objWMIServices.Get (strWMIClass, wbemFlagUseAmendedQualifiers)
...:
212:        If intExplorationDepth > cLevelClassOnly Then
213:            ' Format the XL sheet
214:            objXL.Range("A" & objXL.ActiveCell.Row & ":Z" & _
                                objXL.ActiveCell.Row).Font.Bold = True
215:            objXL.Range("A" & objXL.ActiveCell.Row & ":Z" & _
                                objXL.ActiveCell.Row).Font.Size = 18
216:            objXL.Range("A" & objXL.ActiveCell.Row & ":Z" & _
                                objXL.ActiveCell.Row).Font.ColorIndex = White1
217:            objXL.Range("A" & objXL.ActiveCell.Row & ":Z" & _
                                objXL.ActiveCell.Row).Interior.ColorIndex = Black
218:
219:            ' List the classes
220:            ' Class
221:            objXL.Activecell.Offset(0, 0).Value = "Class"
222:            objXL.Activecell.Offset(1, 0).Activate
223:        End If
224:
225:        WScript.Echo Space (intX) & strWMIClass
226:        objXL.Activecell.Offset(0, intX).Value = strWMIClass
227:
228:        If intExplorationDepth > cLevelClassOnly Then
229:            ' Format the XL sheet
230:            objXL.Range("A" & objXL.ActiveCell.Row & ":Z" & _
                                objXL.ActiveCell.Row).Interior.ColorIndex = Aqua1
231:        End If
232:
233:        If intExplorationDepth > cLevelClassWithPropsAndMethodsWithInOutParams Then
234:            DisplayQualifiers (objWMIInstance.Qualifiers_)
235:        End If
236:
237:        objXL.Activecell.Offset(1, 0).Activate
238:
239:        If intExplorationDepth > cLevelClassOnly Then
240:            Set objWMIPropertySet = objWMIInstance.Properties_
241:            If objWMIPropertySet.Count Then
242:                intX = intX + 1
243:
244:                ' Format the XL Sheet
245:                objXL.Range("A" & objXL.ActiveCell.Row & ":Z" & _
                                    objXL.ActiveCell.Row).Font.Bold = True
246:                objXL.Range("A" & objXL.ActiveCell.Row & ":Z" & _
                                    objXL.ActiveCell.Row).Font.Size = 14
247:                objXL.Range("A" & objXL.ActiveCell.Row & ":Z" & _
                                    objXL.ActiveCell.Row).Interior.ColorIndex = Silver
248:
249:                ' List the properties of the Class
250:                ' Properties
```

```
251:                    objXL.Activecell.Offset(0, intX).Value = "Properties"
252:                    objXL.Activecell.Offset(1, 0).Activate
253:
254:            For Each objWMIProperty In objWMIPropertySet
255:
256:                If (objWMIProperty.Origin = strWMIClass) Or boolOrigin Then
257:                    objXL.Activecell.Offset(0, intX).Value = objWMIProperty.Name
258:                    objXL.Range("A" & objXL.ActiveCell.Row & ":Z" & _
                                    objXL.ActiveCell.Row).Interior.ColorIndex = Aqua2
259:                    If intExplorationDepth < cLevelClassWithPropsQAndMethodsQWithParamsQ Then
260:                        objXL.Activecell.Offset(0, intX + 3).Value = _
                                    objWMIProperty.Qualifiers_.Item("CIMTYPE").Value
261:
262:                        boolCIMKey = objWMIProperty.Qualifiers_.Item("key").Value
263:                        If Err.Number Then
264:                            Err.Clear
265:                            boolCIMKey = False
266:                        End If
267:                        If boolCIMKey Then
268:                            objXL.Activecell.Offset(0, intX + 4).Value = "(Key)"
269:                        End If
270:
271:                        boolCIMRead = objWMIProperty.Qualifiers_.Item("read").Value
272:                        If Err.Number Then
273:                            Err.Clear
274:                            boolCIMRead = False
275:                        End If
276:
277:                        boolCIMWrite = objWMIProperty.Qualifiers_.Item("write").Value
278:                        If Err.Number Then
279:                            Err.Clear
280:                            boolCIMWrite = False
281:                        End If
282:
283:                        If boolCIMRead ANd boolCIMWrite Then
284:                            objXL.Activecell.Offset(0, intX + 5).Value = "Read/Write"
285:                        Else
286:                            If boolCIMRead Then
287:                                objXL.Activecell.Offset(0, intX + 5).Value = "Read"
288:                            End If
289:                            If boolCIMWrite Then
290:                                objXL.Activecell.Offset(0, intX + 5).Value = "Write"
291:                            End If
292:                        End If
293:
294:                        strDescription = objWMIProperty.Qualifiers_.Item("Description").Value
295:                        If Err.Number Then
296:                            Err.clear
297:                        Else
298:                            objXL.Activecell.Offset(0, intX + 6).Value = strDescription
299:                            objXL.Activecell.Offset(0, intX + 6).WrapText = False
300:                        End If
301:
302:                    End If
303:                    If intExplorationDepth >
                                cLevelClassWithPropsAndMethodsWithInOutParams Then
304:                        objXL.Activecell.Offset(0, cOriginPosition).Value = _
                                objWMIProperty.Origin
305:                        DisplayQualifiers (objWMIProperty.Qualifiers_)
306:                    End If
```

```
307:
308:                         objXL.Activecell.Offset(1, 0).Activate
309:                 End If
310:             Next
311:         End If
...:
314:         If intExplorationDepth > cLevelClassWithProps Then
315:             Set objWMIMethodSet = objWMIInstance.Methods_
316:             If objWMIMethodSet.Count Then
317:                 ' Format the XL Sheet
318:                 objXL.Range("A" & objXL.ActiveCell.Row & ":Z" & _
                                    objXL.ActiveCell.Row).Font.Bold = True
319:                 objXL.Range("A" & objXL.ActiveCell.Row & ":Z" & _
                                    objXL.ActiveCell.Row).Font.Size = 14
320:                 objXL.Range("A" & objXL.ActiveCell.Row & ":Z" & _
                                    objXL.ActiveCell.Row).Interior.ColorIndex = Silver
321:
322:                 ' List the methods of the Class
323:                 ' Properties
324:                 objXL.Activecell.Offset(0, intX).Value = "Methods"
325:                 objXL.Activecell.Offset(1, 0).Activate
326:
327:                 For Each objWMIMethod In objWMIMethodSet
328:                     If (objWMIMethod.Origin = strWMIClass) Or boolOrigin Then
329:                         objXL.Activecell.Offset(0, intX).Value = objWMIMethod.Name
330:                         objXL.Range("A" & objXL.ActiveCell.Row & ":Z" & _
                                            objXL.ActiveCell.Row).Interior.ColorIndex = White2
331:                         If intExplorationDepth >
                                            cLevelClassWithPropsAndMethodsWithInOutParams Then
332:                             objXL.Activecell.Offset(0, cOriginPosition).Value = _
                                            objWMIMethod.Origin
333:                             DisplayQualifiers (objWMIMethod.Qualifiers_)
334:                         Else
335:                             strDescription = objWMIMethod.Qualifiers_.Item("Description").Value
336:                             If Err.Number Then
337:                                 Err.clear
338:                             Else
339:                                 objXL.Activecell.Offset(0, intX + 6).Value = strDescription
340:                                 objXL.Activecell.Offset(0, intX + 6).WrapText = False
341:                             End If
342:                         End If
343:                         objXL.Activecell.Offset(1, 0).Activate
344:
345:                         If intExplorationDepth > cLevelClassWithPropsAndMethods Then
346:                             Set objWMIObject = objWMIMethod.InParameters
347:                             Set objWMIPropertySet = objWMIObject.Properties_
348:                             If Err.Number = 0 Then
349:                                 intX = intX + 1
350:
351:                                 ' Format the XL Sheet
352:                                 objXL.Range("A" & objXL.ActiveCell.Row & ":Z" & _
                                                objXL.ActiveCell.Row).Font.Bold = True
353:                                 objXL.Range("A" & objXL.ActiveCell.Row & ":Z" & _
                                                objXL.ActiveCell.Row).Font.Size = 10
354:                                 objXL.Range("A" & objXL.ActiveCell.Row & ":Z" & _
                                                objXL.ActiveCell.Row).Interior.ColorIndex = Silver
355:
356:                                 ' List the methods of the Class
357:                                 ' Parameters
358:                                 objXL.Activecell.Offset(0, intX).Value = "Input parameter(s)"
```

```
359:                          If intExplorationDepth >
                                    cLevelClassWithPropsAndMethodsWithInOutParams Then
360:                              DisplayQualifiers (objWMIObject.Qualifiers_)
361:                          End If
362:                          objXL.Activecell.Offset(1, 0).Activate
363:
364:                          For Each objWMIProperty In objWMIPropertySet
365:
366:                              If (objWMIProperty.Origin = strWMIClass) Or boolOrigin Then
367:                                  objXL.Activecell.Offset(0, intX).Value = _
                                          objWMIProperty.Name
368:                                  objXL.Range("A" & objXL.ActiveCell.Row & ":Z" & _
                                          objXL.ActiveCell.Row).Interior.ColorIndex = White3
369:                                  If intExplorationDepth =
                                          cLevelClassWithPropsAndMethodsWithInParams Or _
370:                                      intExplorationDepth =
                                          cLevelClassWithPropsAndMethodsWithInOutParams Then
371:                                      objXL.Activecell.Offset(0, intX + 2).Value = _
                                  objWMIProperty.Qualifiers_.Item("CIMTYPE").Value
372:                                      strDescription = _
                                          objWMIProperty.Qualifiers_.Item("Description").Value
373:                                      If Err.Number Then
374:                                          Err.clear
375:                                      Else
376:                                          objXL.Activecell.Offset(0, intX + 5).Value = _
                                              strDescription
377:                                          objXL.Activecell.Offset(0, intX + 5).WrapText = _
                                              False
378:                                      End If
379:                                  End If
380:                                  If intExplorationDepth >
                                          cLevelClassWithPropsAndMethodsWithInOutParams Then
381:                                      objXL.Activecell.Offset(0, cOriginPosition).Value = _
                                          objWMIProperty.Origin
382:                                      DisplayQualifiers (objWMIProperty.Qualifiers_)
383:                                  End If
384:                                  objXL.Activecell.Offset(1, 0).Activate
385:                              End If
386:
387:                          Next
388:                          intX = intX - 1
389:                      Else
390:                          Err.Clear
391:                      End If
...:
394:                  End If
395:
396:                  If intExplorationDepth >
                          cLevelClassWithPropsAndMethodsWithInParams Then
397:                      Set objWMIobject = objWMIMethod.OutParameters
398:                      Set objWMIPropertySet = objWMIObject.Properties_
399:                      If Err.Number = 0 Then
400:                          intX = intX + 1
401:
402:                          ' Format the XL Sheet
403:                          objXL.Range("A" & objXL.ActiveCell.Row & ":Z" & _
                                  objXL.ActiveCell.Row).Font.Bold = True
404:                          objXL.Range("A" & objXL.ActiveCell.Row & ":Z" & _
                                  objXL.ActiveCell.Row).Font.Size = 10
405:                          objXL.Range("A" & objXL.ActiveCell.Row & ":Z" & _
```

```
                                          objXL.ActiveCell.Row).Interior.ColorIndex = Silver
406:
407:                              ' List the methods of the Class
408:                              ' Parameters
409:                              objXL.Activecell.Offset(0, intX).Value = "Output parameter(s)"
410:                              If intExplorationDepth >
                                      cLevelClassWithPropsAndMethodsWithInOutParams Then
411:                                  DisplayQualifiers (objWMIObject.Qualifiers_)
412:                              End If
413:                              objXL.Activecell.Offset(1, 0).Activate
414:
415:                              For Each objWMIProperty In objWMIPropertySet
416:
417:                                  If (objWMIProperty.Origin = strWMIClass) Or boolOrigin Then
418:                                      objXL.Activecell.Offset(0, intX).Value = _
                                              objWMIProperty.Name
419:                                      objXL.Range("A" & objXL.ActiveCell.Row & ":Z" & _
                                              objXL.ActiveCell.Row).Interior.ColorIndex = Yellow
420:                                      If intExplorationDepth =
                                          cLevelClassWithPropsAndMethodsWithInOutParams Then
421:                                          objXL.Activecell.Offset(0, intX + 2).Value = _
                                              objWMIProperty.Qualifiers_.Item("CIMTYPE").Value
422:                                          strDescription = _
                                              objWMIProperty.Qualifiers_.Item("Description").Value
423:                                          If Err.Number Then
424:                                              Err.clear
425:                                          Else
426:                                              objXL.Activecell.Offset(0, intX + 5).Value = _
                                                      strDescription
427:                                              objXL.Activecell.Offset(0, intX + 5).WrapText = _
                                                      False
428:                                          End If
429:                                      End If
430:                                      If intExplorationDepth >
                                          cLevelClassWithPropsAndMethodsWithInOutParams Then
431:                                          objXL.Activecell.Offset(0, cOriginPosition).Value = _
                                              objWMIProperty.Origin
432:                                          DisplayQualifiers (objWMIProperty.Qualifiers_)
433:                                      End If
434:                                      objXL.Activecell.Offset(1, 0).Activate
435:                                  End If
436:
437:                              Next
438:                              intX = intX - 1
439:                          Else
440:                              Err.Clear
441:                          End If
...:
444:                      End If
445:                  End If
446:
447:              Next
448:          End If
...:
450:      End If
...:
454:      intX = intX - 1
455: End If
456:
457: If boolSubClass Then
```

```
458:            Set objWMISubClasses = objWMIServices.SubClassesOf (strWMIClass, _
459:                                                wbemQueryFlagShallow)
460:            For Each objWMISubClass in objWMISubClasses
461:                DisplayClasses intX + 1, objWMIServices, objWMISubClass.Path_.RelPath
462:            Next
...:
464:        End If
465:
466:    End Function
467:
468:    ' -------------------------------------------------------------------------------
469:    Function DisplayQualifiers (objWMIQualifiers)
...:
478:        intX = cQualifierPosition
479:
480:        For Each objWMIQualifier In objWMIQualifiers
481:            objXL.Activecell.Offset(1, 0).Activate
482:            objXL.Activecell.Offset(0, intX).Value = objWMIQualifier.Name
483:            If IsArray (objWMIQualifier.Value) Then
484:                For Each varElement In objWMIQualifier.Value
485:                    If Len (objXL.Activecell.Offset(0, intX + 1).Value) = 0 Then
486:                        objXL.Activecell.Offset(0, intX + 1).Value = varElement
487:                    Else
488:                        objXL.Activecell.Offset(0, intX + 1).Value = _
                                        objXL.Activecell.Offset(0, intX + 1).Value & _
489:                                    Chr(10) & _
490:                                    varElement
491:                    End If
492:                    If Ucase (objWMIQualifier.Name) = "DESCRIPTION" Then
493:                        objXL.Activecell.Offset(0, intX + 1).WrapText = False
494:                    End If
495:                Next
496:            Else
497:                objXL.Activecell.Offset(0, intX + 1).Value = objWMIQualifier.Value
498:                If Ucase (objWMIQualifier.Name) = "DESCRIPTION" Then
499:                    objXL.Activecell.Offset(0, intX + 1).WrapText = False
500:                End If
501:            End if
502:
503:            ' Amended
504:            objXL.Activecell.Offset(0, intX + 2).Value = objWMIQualifier.IsAmended
505:            ' Local
506:            objXL.Activecell.Offset(0, intX + 3).Value = objWMIQualifier.IsLocal
507:            ' Overridable
508:            objXL.Activecell.Offset(0, intX + 4).Value = objWMIQualifier.IsOverridable
509:            ' Propagates to instance
510:            objXL.Activecell.Offset(0, intX + 5).Value = objWMIQualifier.PropagatesToInstance
511:            ' Propagates to subclass
512:            objXL.Activecell.Offset(0, intX + 6).Value = objWMIQualifier.PropagatesToSubclass
513:        Next
514:
515:    End Function
516:
517:    ]]>
518:    </script>
519:  </job>
520:</package>
```

Sample 6.14 *A generic script for synchronous event notification*

```
 1:<?xml version="1.0"?>
 .:
 8:<package>
 9:  <job>
..:
13:    <runtime>
..:
19:    </runtime>
20:
21:    <script language="VBScript" src="..\Functions\TinyErrorHandler.vbs" />
22:    <script language="VBScript" src="..\Functions\DisplayInstanceProperties.vbs" />
23:
24:    <object progid="WbemScripting.SWbemLocator" id="objWMILocator" reference="true"/>
25:    <object progid="WbemScripting.SWbemDateTime" id="objWMIDateTime"/>
26:
27:    <script language="VBscript">
28:    <![CDATA[
..:
32:    ' -------------------------------------------------------------------------------------------
33:    Const cComputerName = "LocalHost"
34:    Const cWMINameSpace = "root/cimv2"
..:
48:    ' -------------------------------------------------------------------------------
49:    ' Parse the command line parameters
50:    If WScript.Arguments.Unnamed.Count < 1 Then
51:       WScript.Arguments.ShowUsage()
52:       WScript.Quit
53:    Else
54:       strWQLQuery = WScript.Arguments.Unnamed.Item(0)
55:    End If
56:
57:    strUserID = WScript.Arguments.Named("User")
58:    If Len(strUserID) = 0 Then strUserID = ""
59:
60:    strPassword = WScript.Arguments.Named("Password")
61:    If Len(strPassword) = 0 Then strPassword = ""
62:
63:    strComputerName = WScript.Arguments.Named("Machine")
64:    If Len(strComputerName) = 0 Then strComputerName = cComputerName
65:
66:    strWMINameSpace = WScript.Arguments.Named("NameSpace")
67:    If Len(strWMINameSpace) = 0 Then strWMINameSpace = cWMINameSpace
68:    strWMINameSpace = UCase (strWMINameSpace)
69:
70:    objWMILocator.Security_.ImpersonationLevel = wbemImpersonationLevelImpersonate
71:    objWMILocator.Security_.Privileges.Add wbemPrivilegeSecurity
72:    Set objWMIServices = objWMILocator.ConnectServer(strComputerName, strWMINameSpace, _
73:                                                     strUserID, strPassword)
..:
76:    Set objWMIEvent = objWMIServices.ExecNotificationQuery (strWQLQuery)
..:
79:    WScript.Echo "Waiting for events ..."
80:
81:    Set objWMIEventInstance = objWMIEvent.NextEvent
82:    If Err.Number then
83:       WScript.Echo "0x" & Hex(Err.Number) & " - " & Err.Description & " (" & Err.Source & ")"
```

```
 84:    Else
 85:       WScript.Echo
 86:       WScript.Echo FormatDateTime(Date, vbLongDate) & " at " & _
 87:                    FormatDateTime(Time, vbLongTime) & ": '" & _
 88:                    objWMIEventInstance.Path_.Class & "' has been triggered."
 89:       DisplayProperties objWMIEventInstance, 2
 90:    End If
 ..:
 97:    WScript.Echo "Finished."
 98:
 99:    ]]>
100:    </script>
101:    </job>
102:</package>
```

Sample 6.17 *A generic script for asynchronous event notification*

```
  1:<?xml version="1.0"?>
  .:
  8:<package>
  9:  <job>
 ..:
 13:    <runtime>
 ..:
 19:    </runtime>
 20:
 21:    <script language="VBScript" src="..\Functions\TinyErrorHandler.vbs" />
 22:    <script language="VBScript" src="..\Functions\DisplayInstanceProperties.vbs" />
 23:    <script language="VBScript" src="..\Functions\PauseScript.vbs" />
 24:
 25:    <object progid="WbemScripting.SWbemLocator" id="objWMILocator" reference="true"/>
 26:    <object progid="WbemScripting.SWbemDateTime" id="objWMIDateTime" />
 27:
 28:    <script language="VBscript">
 29:    <![CDATA[
 ..:
 33:    ' -----------------------------------------------------------------------------
 34:    Const cComputerName = "LocalHost"
 35:    Const cWMINameSpace = "root/cimv2"
 ..:
 49:    ' -----------------------------------------------------------------------------
 50:    ' Parse the command line parameters
 51:    If WScript.Arguments.Unnamed.Count = 0 Then
 52:       WScript.Arguments.ShowUsage()
 53:       WScript.Quit
 54:    Else
 55:       strWQLQuery = WScript.Arguments.Unnamed.Item(0)
 56:    End If
 57:
 58:    strUserID = WScript.Arguments.Named("User")
 59:    If Len(strUserID) = 0 Then strUserID = ""
 60:
 61:    strPassword = WScript.Arguments.Named("Password")
 62:    If Len(strPassword) = 0 Then strPassword = ""
 63:
 64:    strComputerName = WScript.Arguments.Named("Machine")
 65:    If Len(strComputerName) = 0 Then strComputerName = cComputerName
 66:
```

```
67:    strWMINameSpace = WScript.Arguments.Named("NameSpace")
68:    If Len(strWMINameSpace) = 0 Then strWMINameSpace = cWMINameSpace
69:    strWMINameSpace = UCase (strWMINameSpace)
70:
71:    Set objWMISink = WScript.CreateObject ("WbemScripting.SWbemSink", "SINK_")
72:
73:    objWMILocator.Security_.ImpersonationLevel = wbemImpersonationLevelImpersonate
74:    objWMILocator.Security_.Privileges.AddAsString "SeSecurityPrivilege", True
75:    Set objWMIServices = objWMILocator.ConnectServer(strComputerName, strWMINameSpace, _
76:                                          strUserID, strPassword)
..:
79:    objWMIServices.ExecNotificationQueryAsync objWMISink, strWQLQuery,, wbemFlagSendStatus
..:
82:    WScript.Echo "Waiting for events..."
83:
84:    PauseScript "Click on 'Ok' to terminate the script ..."
85:
86:    WScript.Echo vbCRLF & "Cancelling event subscription ..."
87:    objWMISink.Cancel
..:
92:    WScript.Echo "Finished."
93:
94:    ' -------------------------------------------------------------------------------------
95:    Sub SINK_OnCompleted (iHResult, objWBemErrorObject, objWBemAsyncContext)
96:
97:        Wscript.Echo
98:        Wscript.Echo "BEGIN - OnCompleted."
99:        Wscript.Echo "END   - OnCompleted."
100:
101:   End Sub
102:
103:   ' -------------------------------------------------------------------------------------
104:   Sub SINK_OnObjectReady (objWbemObject, objWbemAsyncContext)
105:
106:       Wscript.Echo
107:       Wscript.Echo "BEGIN - OnObjectReady."
108:       WScript.Echo FormatDateTime(Date, vbLongDate) & " at " & _
109:                    FormatDateTime(Time, vbLongTime) & ": '" & _
110:                    objWbemObject.Path_.Class & "' has been triggered."
111:
112:       DisplayProperties objWbemObject, 2
113:
114:       Wscript.Echo "END - OnObjectReady."
115:
116:   End Sub
117:
118:   ' -------------------------------------------------------------------------------------
119:   Sub SINK_OnProgress (iUpperBound, iCurrent, strMessage, objWbemAsyncContext)
120:
121:       Wscript.Echo
122:       Wscript.Echo "BEGIN - OnProgress."
123:       Wscript.Echo "END   - OnProgress."
124:
125:   End Sub
126:
127:   ]]>
128:   </script>
129:   </job>
130:</package>
```

Samples 6.18–6.21 *Monitoring, managing, and alerting script for the Windows services*

```
 1:<?xml version="1.0"?>
 .:
 8:<package>
 9: <job>
..:
13:    <runtime>
..:
18:    </runtime>
19:
20:    <script language="VBScript" src="..\Functions\TinyErrorHandler.vbs" />
21:    <script language="VBScript" src="..\Functions\PauseScript.vbs" />
22:    <script language="VBScript" src="..\Functions\LoopSvcStartupRetry.vbs" />
23:    <script language="VBScript" src="..\Functions\GenerateHTML.vbs" />
24:    <script language="VBScript" src="..\Functions\SendMessageExtendedFunction.vbs" />
25:
26:    <object progid="WbemScripting.SWbemLocator" id="objWMILocator" reference="true"/>
27:    <object progid="WbemScripting.SWbemNamedValueSet" id="objWMIInstanceSinkContext"/>
28:    <object progid="WbemScripting.SWbemDateTime" id="objWMIDateTime" />
29:
30:    <script language="VBscript">
31:    <![CDATA[
..:
35:    ' ------------------------------------------------------------------------------
36:    Const cComputerName = "LocalHost"
37:    Const cWMINameSpace = "root/cimv2"
38:    Const cWMIClass = "Win32_Service"
39:    Const cWMIQuery = "Select * from __InstanceModificationEvent
                                     Within 10 Where TargetInstance ISA 'Win32_Service'"
40:
41:    Const cPauseBetweenRestart = 2
42:    Const cRestartLimit = 3
43:
44:    Const cTargetRecipient = "Alain.Lissoir@LissWare.NET"
45:    Const cSourceRecipient = "WMISystem@LissWare.NET"
46:
47:    Const cSMTPServer = "10.10.10.201"
48:    Const cSMTPPort = 25
49:    Const cSMTPAccountName = ""
50:    Const cSMTPSendEmailAddress = ""
51:    Const cSMTPAuthenticate = 0' 0=Anonymous, 1=Basic, 2=NTLM
52:    Const cSMTPUserName = ""
53:    Const cSMTPPassword = ""
54:    Const cSMTPSSL = False
55:    Const cSMTPSendUsing = 2              ' 1=Pickup, 2=Port, 3=Exchange WebDAV
..:
61:    Class clsMonitoredService
62:          Public strServiceName
63:          Public intServiceRetryCounter
64:    End Class
..:
78:    ' ------------------------------------------------------------------------------
79:    ' Parse the command line parameters
80:    If WScript.Arguments.Unnamed.Count = 0 Then
81:       WScript.Arguments.ShowUsage()
82:       WScript.Quit
83:    Else
```

```
84:        For intIndice = 0 To WScript.Arguments.Unnamed.Count - 1
85:            ReDim Preserve clsService(intIndice)
86:            Set clsService(intIndice) = New clsMonitoredService
87:            clsService(intIndice).strServiceName =
                              Ucase(WScript.Arguments.Unnamed.Item(intIndice))
88:            clsService(intIndice).intServiceRetryCounter = 0
89:        Next
90:    End If
91:
92:    strUserID = WScript.Arguments.Named("User")
93:    If Len(strUserID) = 0 Then strUserID = ""
94:
95:    strPassword = WScript.Arguments.Named("strPassword")
96:    If Len(strPassword) = 0 Then strPassword = ""
97:
98:    strComputerName = WScript.Arguments.Named("Machine")
99:    If Len(strComputerName) = 0 Then strComputerName = cComputerName
100:
101:    Set objWMISink = WScript.CreateObject ("WbemScripting.SWbemSink", "SINK_")
102:
103:    objWMILocator.Security_.AuthenticationLevel = wbemAuthenticationLevelDefault
104:    objWMILocator.Security_.ImpersonationLevel = wbemImpersonationLevelImpersonate
105:    Set objWMIServices = objWMILocator.ConnectServer(strComputerName, cWMINameSpace, _
106:                                               strUserID, strPassword)
...:
109:    For intIndice = 0 To UBound (clsService)
110:
111:        Set objWMIInstance = objWMIServices.Get (cWMIClass & "='" & _
112:                                clsService(intIndice).strServiceName & "'")
113:
114:        boolSvcStatus = LoopServiceStartupRetry (objWMIInstance, intIndice)
115:        If boolSvcStatus = False Then
116:            WScript.Quit
117:        End If
118:
119:        If Len(strWMIQuery) = 0 Then
120:            strWMIQuery = "TargetInstance.Name='" & clsService(intIndice).strServiceName & "'"
121:        Else
122:            strWMIQuery = strWMIQuery & " Or " & _
123:                       "TargetInstance.Name='" & _
124:                       clsService(intIndice).strServiceName & "'"
125:        End If
126:
127:        WScript.Echo "Adding '" & clsService(intIndice).strServiceName & _
128:                   "' to subscription to monitor '" & cWMIClass & "'." & vbCRLF
129:
130:        objWMIInstanceSinkContext.Add Cstr(clsService(intIndice).strServiceName), intIndice
131:    Next
132:
133:    strWMIQuery = cWMIQuery & " And TargetInstance.State='Stopped' And (" & strWMIQuery & ")"
134:
135:    objWMIServices.ExecNotificationQueryAsync objWMISink, _
136:                                     strWMIQuery, _
137:                                           , _
138:                                           , _
139:                                           , _
140:                                     objWMIInstanceSinkContext
...:
143:    WScript.Echo "Waiting for events..."
144:
```

```
145:     PauseScript "Click on 'Ok' to terminate the script ..."
146:
147:     WScript.Echo vbCRLF & "Cancelling event subscription ..."
148:     objWMISink.Cancel
...:
153:     WScript.Echo "Finished."
154:
155:     ' -------------------------------------------------------------------------------------
156:     Sub SINK_OnCompleted (iHResult, objWBemErrorObject, objWBemAsyncContext)
...:
160:         Wscript.Echo
161:         Wscript.Echo "BEGIN - OnCompleted."
162:         Wscript.Echo "END   - OnCompleted."
163:
164:     End Sub
165:
166:     ' -------------------------------------------------------------------------------------
167:     Sub SINK_OnObjectReady (objWbemObject, objWbemAsyncContext)
...:
175:         Wscript.Echo
176:         Wscript.Echo "BEGIN - OnObjectReady."
177:         WScript.Echo FormatDateTime(Date, vbLongDate) & " at " & _
178:                      FormatDateTime(Time, vbLongTime) & ": '" & _
179:                      objWbemObject.Path_.Class & "' has been triggered."
180:
181:         Select Case objWbemObject.Path_.Class
182:             Case "__InstanceModificationEvent"
183:                 Set objWMIInstance = objWbemObject
184:             Case "__AggregateEvent"
185:                 Set objWMIInstance = objWbemObject.Representative
186:             Case Else
187:                 Set objWMIInstance = Null
188:         End Select
189:
190:         If Not IsNull (objWMIInstance) Then
191:             boolSvcStatus = LoopServiceStartupRetry (objWMIInstance.TargetInstance, _
192:                 objWbemAsyncContext.Item (objWMIInstance.TargetInstance.Name).Value)
193:
194:             If boolSvcStatus = False Then
195:                 If SendMessage (cTargetRecipient, _
196:                                 cSourceRecipient, _
197:                                 objWMIInstance.TargetInstance.SystemName & " - " & _
198:                                     FormatDateTime(Date, vbLongDate) & _
199:                                     " at " & _
200:                                     FormatDateTime(Time, vbLongTime), _
201:                                 GenerateHTML (objWMIInstance.PreviousInstance, _
202:                                               objWMIInstance.TargetInstance) , _
203:                                 "") Then
204:                     WScript.Echo "Failed to send email to '" & cTargetRecipient & "' ..."
205:                 End If
206:             End If
207:         End If
...:
211:         Wscript.Echo "END - OnObjectReady."
212:
213:     End Sub
214:
215:     ' -------------------------------------------------------------------------------------
216:     Sub SINK_OnProgress (iUpperBound, iCurrent, strMessage, objWbemAsyncContext)
...:
```

```
220:        Wscript.Echo
221:        Wscript.Echo "BEGIN - OnProgress."
222:        Wscript.Echo "END   - OnProgress."
223:
224:    End Sub
225:
226:    ]]>
227:   </script>
228:  </job>
229:</package>
```

Index

Abstract classes, 20
Access Control Entries (ACEs)
    access-allowed, 711
    access-denied, 711
    ACE AccessMask property, 626–27, 637–91
    ACE Flags property, 632–35
    ACE FlagType property, 626, 635–37
    ACE InheritedObjectType property, 651, 678–80
    ACE ObjectType property, 648, 652–78
    ACE Trustee property, 627
    ACE Type property, 627–32
    adding, in ADSI object model, 499–701
    adding, in WMI object model, 701–3
    deciphering, 626–91
    defined, 545
    defined in security descriptor, 624
    elements, 546
    Extended Rights reference, 666
    inheritance, customizing, 677
    inheritance control, 632
    inheritance support, 625
    inheritance to specific object class, 678
    inherited, 624, 696, 711
    properties, 626
    properties, changing, 644
    removing, 643, 703–10
    removing, in ADSI object model, 703–7
    removing, in WMI object model, 707–10
    reordering, 710–15
    reordering, in ADSI object model, 711–13
    reordering, in WMI object model, 713–15
AccessControlEntry object, 548, 616, 701
AccessControlList object, 548
Access Control Lists (ACLs)
    deciphering, 625–26
    defined, 545
    Discretionary (DACL), 545
    editor, 710
    System (SACL), 546, 551
ACE AccessMask property, 626–27, 637–91
    Active Directory object, 648–80
    Active Directory object values, 649–52
    CIM repository namespace, 687–91
    equal value, 667, 668, 670, 679
    Exchange 2000 mailbox, 680–84
    Exchange 2000 mailbox values, 681
    files and folders, 637–44
    files and folders values, 642
    file system share, 644–47
    file system share values, 645
    inheritance, 641
    registry key, 684–87
    registry key values, 684
    See also Access Control Entries (ACEs)
ACE Flags property, 632–35
    deciphering, 632, 633–34
    defined, 632
    for Exchange 2000 mailbox, 682
    file system share and, 646
    inheritance flags, 632–33
    values, 634–35
    See also Access Control Entries (ACEs)
ACE FlagType property, 626
    deciphering, 635–36
    defined, 635
    values, 636–37
    See also Access Control Entries (ACEs)
ACE InheritedObjectType property, 651, 678–80
    setting, 680
    understanding, 678–80

ACE ObjectType property, 648
   deciphering logic, 670
   to grant/deny object creation/deletion, 669
   GUID number, 667, 668, 670, 679
   GUID number origins summary, 676
   understanding, 652–78
   See also Access Control Entries (ACEs)
ACE Trustee property, 627
ACE Type property, 627–32
   Active Directory Extended Rights and, 630–31
   for Active Directory security descriptor, 630
   aim, 627
   bitwise operation, 627
   deciphering, 627–32
   equal value, 667, 668, 670, 679
   function, 627–29
   for non-Active Directory security descriptor, 629
   values, 670
   See also Access Control Entries (ACEs)
Active Directory
   classes, 373, 375, 376
   creating in, 378–81
   Domain Controller, 153
   group memberships, monitoring, 383–86
   mapping, 375
   msExchMailboxSecurityDescriptor, 725
   Naming Contexts, 652
   objects, creating, 378–79
   organizationalPerson class, 373, 374
   person class, 373, 374
   querying, 381
   replication state, 397–99, 401–2
   rights, 652
   rights, deciphering, 648
   schema, 373, 375
   search depth, 382
   searching in, 381–83
   security descriptor inheritance flags, 633
   top class, 373, 374
   updating in, 378–81
   user class, 373, 374, 376
Active Directory Extended Rights
   ACE reference to, 666
   ACE Type property and, 630–31
   "Add/Remove self as member," 677
   attributes links, 657
   defined, 652
   enforced by Active Directory, 653
   enforced by applications, 653

   enforced by system to perform extra checking, 653
   example, 653, 654
   GUID number, 655
   list of, 658–65
   location, 652
   name, 666
   "Personal Information," 677
   "Send As," 677
   understanding, 651–52
   under Windows Server 2003, 658–65
   validAccess attribute value, 657
Active Directory object ACE AccessMask property,
    648–80
   deciphering, 648
   flag values, 652
   management, 648
   values (advanced view), 651
   values (standard view), 649–50
Active Directory object security descriptors, 571–75
   with ADSI connection, 573–75
   connecting to, 571–75
   registry keys retrieval with, 600–602
   retrieving, 594–97
   retrieving with ADSI, 596–97
   retrieving with WMI, 594–96
   updating, 721–24
   updating, with ADSI, 723–24
   updating, with WMI, 721–23
   with WMI connection, 571–73
Active Directory providers, 211
   activity in log file, 391
   capabilities, 372
   classes, 377
   debugging, 391–94
   defined, 212
   DS_LDAP_Class_Containment class, 376, 377
   DS_LDAP_Instance_Containment class, 376, 377
   Level registry key for, 392
   RootDSE class, 377
   trace logging of, 391
   See also WMI providers
Active Directory Replication provider, 394–405
   capabilities, 394
   classes, 394
   defined, 394
   implementation, 395
   location, 394
   MSAD_DomainController class, 395, 400
   MSAD_NamingContext class, 399

MSAD_ReplCursor class, 400
MSAD_ReplNeighbor class, 401
MSAD_ReplPendingOp class, 399
Active Directory Service Interfaces. *See* ADSI
Active Directory Trust Monitoring provider, 211
Active Server Page. *See* ASP scripts
AddAce() function, 564, 571, 699–701
    AccessMask parameter, 700
    ACEFlags parameter, 700
    ACEType parameter, 700
    ACLType parameter, 700, 701, 702
    InheritedObjectType parameter, 700
    ObjectType parameter, 700
    objSD parameter, 699
    objWMIServices parameter, 699
    Password parameter, 699
    SDType parameter, 700
    SIDResolutionDC parameter, 699
    Trustee parameter, 700
    UserID parameter, 699
ADSIHelper object, 595, 598
    ActiveX DLL, 608, 609
    defined, 608
    methods, 608
ADSI object model
    adding ACEs in, 699–701
    removing ACEs in, 703–7
    reordering ACEs in, 711–13
ADSI security descriptor representation, 544, 547–49
    ACLs, deciphering, 626
    Active Directory objects connection with, 573–75
    Active Directory objects retrieval with, 596–97
    Active Directory update with, 723–24
    CIM repository namespaces connection with, 585
    conversion, 607–9
    deciphering, 616–19
    Exchange 2000 mailbox connection with, 578–79
    Exchange 2000 mailbox retrieval with, 598–99
    Exchange 2000 mailbox update with, 727–28
    file/folder connection with, 565–67
    file/folder retrieval with, 587–92
    file/folder update with, 718–19
    file system share connection with, 569–71
    file system share retrieval with, 593–94
    file system share update with, 720–21
    logical structure, 548
    registry keys connection with, 581–83
ADSI WMI Extension, 737–38
ADsSecurity.DLL, 589, 618, 729

ADsSecurity object, 565, 566, 573, 581
    GetSecurityDescriptor method, 602
    SecurityMask property, 601
ADsSecurityUtility object, 565, 569, 570, 581, 587, 589
    bug, 602, 719
    ConvertSecurityDescriptor method, 608
    for security descriptor conversion, 608
    SecurityMask property, 597
ADSUTIL.VBS script, 781
Application WMI providers, 741–860
    Cluster, 747–49
    Exchange 2000, 785–802
    IIS, 776–85
    Internet Explorer, 811–13
    Microsoft Office, 809–11
    Network Load-Balancing, 741–47
    OVOW, 825–43
    SQL Server 2000, 802–9
    Terminal Server, 749–71
    WDM, 771–75
    See also WMI providers
Arrays
    intKeyTypes, 239
    strSubKeys, 236, 239
ASP scripts
    anonymous/basic authentication, 538
    authentication settings, 536–39
    configuration under Windows 2000+, 537–38
    configuration under Windows NT, 536–37
    running, 536
Association view classes
    creation, 516
    defined, 509
    listing, 514–15
    output, 517
    Win32_DiskQuota class and, 516
Asynchronous event notification, 883–84
Asynchronous scripting, 732–37
    access checks and, 734
    precautions, 734
AttributeSchema object, 655–56
Authentication
    anonymous/basic, 538
    definition locations, 539
    passport/digest, 537–38
    settings, 536–38
    WIA, 537
    See also Security
AutoDiscovery/AutoPurge (ADAP), 492

Battery information retrieval, 74–76
Boot.INI file, 166–67
   item ordering, 167
   item ordering, respecting, 166
BrowseRegistry() function, 233, 235
BrowseRegistryValues() function, 235, 236

CalculateACEMask() function, 625
CalculateACEType() function, 625
CalculateSDControlFlags() function, 625
CheckIfRSOPLoggingModeData() function, 307
CHKDSK utility, 37
   executing, via WMI, 37–39
   on remote computer, 37
CIM_Component class, 780
CIM_DataFile class, 132, 134
CIM_Directory class
   methods, 134
   output, 126–27
CIM_ElementSetting class, 780, 781
CIM_LogicalFile class, 125
   ChangeSecurityPermissionsEx method, 715–16, 717
   ChangeSecurityPermissions method, 715–16, 717
   Compress method, 139
   Copy method, 138
   defined, 134
   Delete method, 139
   equal manipulation of files/directories, 135
   methods, 135
   Rename method, 138
   TakeOwnerShip method, 139, 716
   UnCompress method, 139
CIM_ManagedSystemElement class, 779
CIM repository
   access for WMI-ASP, 541
   browsing, 8
   Cisco Flash SNMP classes in, 466
   classes, self-documenting, 873–81
   namespace, 12, 571
   namespace access, 530
   private MIB in, 464–65
   Registry provider registration in, 7
CIM repository namespace ACE AccessMask property,
      687–91
   deciphering, 688–89
   flag values, 689
   values, 688
CIM repository namespace security descriptors
   ADSI connection, 585

retrieving, 602–3
setting, 737
updating, 730–31
user interface, 690
WMI connection, 583–85
See also Security descriptors
CIM_Setting class, 779–80
Cisco Internetwork Operating System (IOS), 457, 463
   Cisco router 2503 loaded with, 457
   loaded in flash memory, 464
Classes
   abstract, 20
   Active Directory providers, 377
   Active Directory Replication provider, 394
   Association view, 509
   Clock provider, 320
   Cluster providers, 749
   COM component, 105–13
   computer system hardware, 31–105
   desktop information, 113–21
   DFS provider, 344
   Disk Quota provider, 330
   DNS provider, 424–25
   driver, 122–24
   file system, 124–39
   Forwarding providers, 518
   input device, 31–33
   instances vs., 6
   Internet Explorer provider, 812
   IP routing providers, 416
   job scheduler, 183–91
   Join view, 509, 510–11
   Kernel Job Object providers, 247
   mass storage, 33–40
   Microsoft Office providers, 810–11
   modem device, 77–82
   motherboard, controller, port, 40–49
   multimedia audio/visual, 146–47
   networking, 147–54
   networking device, 49–73
   Network Load Balancing (NLB) providers, 742
   NT Event Log providers, 219
   operating system, 105–209
   operating system settings, 154–71
   page file, 139–46
   power device, 74–77
   printing device, 82–96
   process, 171–83
   registry, 183

Registry providers, 225
Resultant Set of Policies (RSOP) providers, 287–88
security descriptor, 544
Security provider, 552
service, 191–97
Shadow Copy providers, 353
share, 197–201
SNMP providers, 452, 453
SQL provider, 804–8
start menu, 201–2
System Restore provider, 311
as templates, 27
Terminal Server providers, 751
TrustMon provider, 252
Union view, 509, 513–14
user account, 202–9
video and monitor, 96–105
WBEM provider, 213
Win32 providers, 29, 30
Windows Driver Model (WDM) provider, 773–74
Windows Installer provider, 268–69, 270–72
Windows Product Activation provider, 261
See also specific classes
ClassSchema object, 656
    defined, 656
    schemaIDGUID attribute, 657, 668
Clock provider, 319–23
    capabilities, 320
    classes, 320
    defined, 319
    Win32_LocalTime class, 321–23
    Win32_UTCTime class, 320–21, 323
Cluster provider, 794
Cluster Service providers, 211, 747–49
    capabilities, 748
    classes, 749
    defined, 747
    MSCluster_Cluster class, 748, 749, 750
CMD.EXE, 864
Collaboration Data Objects for Exchange Management
        (CDOEXM), 550, 575–76
    companions, 579
    Exchange 2000 mailbox connection with, 579–81
    Exchange 2000 mailbox retrieval with, 599–600
    Exchange 2000 mailbox update with, 728–29
    IExchangeMailbox interface, 600
    IMailboxStore, 725
COM
    API, 785, 813, 851

components, 106
information, 106–7
instances, 107
objects, 6
COM component classes, 105–13
    defined, 105
    list of, 105
    Win32_ClassicCOMClassSetting class, 109
    Win32_DCOMApplicationAccessAllowedSetting
        class, 113
    Win32_DCOMApplicationLaunchAllowedSetting
        class, 113
    Win32_DCOMApplicationSetting class, 109, 111,
        112
    Win32_SID class, 113
    See also Operating system classes
COM/DCOM-based architecture, 864, 865
Command-line parsing, 62
Common Information Model (CIM), 814
Compaq Insight Manager, 814
Computer Associates Unicenter, 814
Computer system hardware classes, 31–105
    input device, 31–33
    mass storage, 33–40
    modem device, 77–82
    motherboard, controller, port, 40–49
    networking device, 49–73
    power device, 74–77
    printing device, 82–96
    video and monitor, 96–105
    See also Win32 providers
Configuration Change provider, 326–28
    capabilities, 327
    implementation, 326
    Win32_SystemConfigurationChangeEvent class,
        326–27
ConsumerClassNames property, 9, 10
ControlAccessRight object, 652, 654
    appliesTo attribute, 654
    rightsGUID attribute, 655, 657
Control Flags, 620–25
    bits, 621, 624
    bits manipulation, 698
    bitwise values, 622
    configuration, 696
    deciphering, 622–23
    defined, 545
    flag specification, 696
    labels, 625

Control Flags *(cont'd.)*
  modification, 696–97
  naming, 698
  SE_DACL_PROTECTED, 697
  updating, 696–98
  validating, 625
  value calculation, 624–25
  values, 621
  See also Security descriptors
ConvertArrayString() function, 614
ConvertStringInArray() function, 72, 188
ConvertStringInArrayFunction.vbs, 62
Cooked Counter provider, 486
Core OS components event providers, 319–29
  Clock, 319–23
  Configuration Change, 326–28
  defined, 212
  power management, 323–25
  shutdown, 325–26
  Volume Change, 328–29
  See also WMI providers
Core OS components providers, 213–319
  defined, 212
  Kernel Job Object, 246–51
  NT Event Log, 218–24
  Registry, 224–41
  RSOP, 281–309
  Session, 241–46
  System Restore, 309–19
  TrustMon, 251–58
  WBEM, 213–18
  Windows Installer provider, 267–81
  Windows Proxy, 258–60
  WPA, 260–67
  See also WMI providers
Core OS file system components providers,
      329–72
  defined, 212
  DFS, 344–52
  Disk Quota, 329–44
  Shadow Copy, 352–72
  See also WMI providers
CreateDefaultSD() function, 592, 603
CreateTrustee() function, 693–94
  Password parameter, 694
  SIDResolutionDC parameter, 693
  Trustee parameter, 693
  UserID parameter, 693–94
Current time, getting, 321–23

DCOM security settings, 112
DecipherACEFlags() function, 632
DecipherACEFlagType() function, 635–36
DecipherACEMask() function
  defined, 637
  Select Case statement, 640
DecipherACEType() function, 627–29, 649
DecipherADSISecurityDescriptor() function, 564, 620
Deciphering security descriptors, 611–19
  ACE AccessMask property, 637–91
  ACE Flags property, 632–35
  ACE FlagType property, 635–37
  ACEs, 626–91
  ACE Trustee property, 627
  ACE Type property, 627–32
  ACLs, 625–26
  ADSI representation, 616–19
  components, 619–91
  Control Flags property, 620–25
  Group property, 619–20
  Owner property, 619–20
  WMI representation, 611–15
  See also Security descriptors
DecipherSDControlFlags() function, 623
DecipherWMISecurityDescriptor() function, 564, 565,
      567–68, 572, 619
DecodeIPRouteFunction.vbs file, 420
DecodeOVOWManagedNodeOSType() class, 836
DecodeOVOWManagedNodeOSVersion() function,
      836
DecodeOVOWMessageSeverity() function, 835–36
DecodeOVOWMessageSourceType() function, 839
DecodeOVOWMessageState() function, 836
Default security descriptors
  creating, 603–7
  share, 604, 605–6
  See also Security descriptors
DelACE() function, 564, 571
  code, 704–6
  defined, 703
  functioning, 706
  input parameters, 703
  remove all ACEs part, 706
  remove a specific ACE part, 706–7
  Trustee parameter, 703, 710
  See also Access Control Entries (ACEs)
Desktop information classes, 113–21
  defined, 113
  list of, 113

Win32_Desktop class, 113–14
Win32_Environment class, 115–21
Win32_TimeZone class, 115
Win32_UserDesktop class, 144
See also Operating system classes
DFS provider, 344–52
    capabilities, 344
    classes, 344
    defined, 344
    Win32_DfsNode class, 344, 345, 348, 349, 350,
        351, 352
    Win32_DfsNodeTarget class, 344, 348
    Win32_DfsTarget class, 344, 348, 349, 351, 352
    See also Distributed File System (DFS)
Directories
    copying, 136–38
    deleting, 136–38
    manipulation of, 135
    renaming, 136–38
Discretionary ACL (DACL), 546
Disk drive information, gathering, 127–28, 129–30
Disk partitions
    hosting logical disks, 130
    information, gathering, 127–29
Disk Quota provider, 124, 131, 329–44
    capabilities, 329
    classes, 330
    defined, 329
    Win32_DiskQuota class, 330, 332, 339, 341, 343
    Win32_QuotaSetting class, 330, 331, 332, 338
    Win32_VolumeQuotaSetting class, 331
Disk quotas
    configuring, per user, 339–41
    creating, 339–41
    default, configuring, 332, 334–38
    default, per volume, 332
    default settings, 330
    deleting, 339–41, 343–44
    enabling, 336
    limit, 338, 341
    managing, 355
    retrieving, 331, 355
    updating, 339–41, 343
    viewing, 339–41
    Windows Explorer management interface, 333
Disk services management, 357
DisplayFormattedProperty() function, 23, 58, 434, 616
DisplayFormattedPropertyFunction.vbs, 23, 24
    code, 24–26

for displaying two properties, 58
    parameters, 24
DisplayFormattedSTDProperty() function, 616
DisplayInstanceProperties.vbs, 23
DisplayNameSpaces() function, 11, 12, 13
DisplayProviderClasses() function, 14
DistinguishedName object, 722
Distributed File System (DFS)
    configuration example, 348
    creating, 346–48, 350–51
    defined, 344
    deleting, 346–48, 350–51
    domain-based, 344
    modifying, 346–48, 350–51
    Root, 344
    viewing, 346–48, 350–51
    See also DFS provider
DMA resource usage, 45
DNS
    alias, creating, 428
    association classes, 428
    boot method, 436
    cache, clearing, 446
    classes, 426–27, 430
    domain class, 426, 427
    forwarders, 436
    information, viewing, 434–36
    log level, 436
    records class, 427, 450
    records management, 446–47
DNS provider, 211, 212, 423–50
    availability, 424
    capabilities, 424
    classes, 424–25
    defined, 423
    implementation, 425
    MicrosoftDNS_Atype class, 449
    MicrosoftDNS_Cache class, 426, 446
    MicrosoftDNS_CNAMEType class, 449
    MicrosoftDNS_Domain class, 426
    MicrosoftDNS_
        DomainResourceRecordContainment class,
        426
    MicrosoftDNS_ResourceRecord class, 426–27,
        448–50
    MicrosoftDNS_RootHints class, 426
    MicrosoftDNS_Server class, 426, 427, 431–37
    MicrosoftDNS_ServerDomainContainment class,
        426

DNS provider *(cont'd.)*
    MicrosoftDNS_Zone class, 426, 427, 439–46
    See also Network components providers
DNS servers
    class, 426
    listening IP addresses, 437
    management, 431–34
    property values, 437
    recursion, 436–37
    round-robin, 437
    scavenging, 436
    slave, 436
    starting, 436
    stopping, 436
DNS zones, 437–46
    creating, 443–44
    deleting, 445
    managing, 440–43
    pausing, 445
    record retrieval and, 447
    refreshing, 445
    reloading, 445
    resuming, 445
    Root Hints, 446
    saving, 446
    secondary addresses, reconfiguring, 445
    type, updating, 444–45
    update, forcing, 445
    viewing, 438–39
Domain Naming Master FSMO, 391
Domains, joining/unjoining, 163
Driver classes, 122–24
    defined, 122
    list of, 122
    Win32_SystemDriver class, 122–23
    Win32_VXD class, 123–24
    See also Operating system classes
DSAccess provider, 800–802
    defined, 800
    ExchangeDSAccessDC class, 800–802
    See also Exchange 2000 providers
DSClass_To_DNInstance class, 388
DS_LDAP_Class_Containment class, 376
DS_LDAP_Instance_Containment class
    associations, 377
    defined, 376
DSProvider.LOG file, 392–93
    defined, 392
    information, 392–93

DsReplicaConsistencyCheck() API, 403
Dynamic-Link Libraries (DLLs), 6

Environment variables
    creating, 116–18, 119
    deleting, 116–18, 121
    instances, 119, 120, 121
    reading, 116–18, 118–19
    updating, 116–18, 120–21
_EventConsumerProviderRegistration system class,
        9, 10, 13
Event consumer providers, 4–6
    ConsumerClassNames property, 9, 10
    defined, 4
    examples, 6
    registration, 4
    See also WMI providers
Event Correlator providers, 525–26
    defined, 525
    list of, 525
    resource, 526
Event notification
    asynchronous, 883–84
    synchronous, 882–83
_EventProviderRegistration system class, 9, 10, 13
Event providers, 4
    defined, 4
    EventQueryList property, 9, 10
    implementation, 6
    registration, 4, 5
    supported WQL queries, 9
    See also specific providers; WMI providers
Exchange 2000, 27
Exchange 2000 mailbox ACE AccessMask property,
        680–84
    deciphering, 681
    flag values, 682
    values, 681
Exchange 2000 mailbox security descriptors,
        576–81
    ADSI connection, 578–79
    CDOEXM connection, 579–81
    connecting to, 576–81
    retrieving, 597–600
    retrieving with ADSI, 598–99
    retrieving with CDOEXM, 599–600
    retrieving with WMI, 597–98
    storage, 680
    updating, 726–29

updating, with ADSI, 727–28
updating, with CDOEXM, 728–29
updating, with WMI, 726–27
WMI connection, 576–77
See also Security descriptors
Exchange 2000 providers, 785–802
    capabilities, 786
    Cluster, 794
    defined, 785
    DSAccess, 800–802
    ExchangeClusterResource class, 794, 796
    ExchangeConnectorState class, 787, 788
    Exchange_DSAccessDC class, 800–802
    ExchangeLink class, 789, 793, 794
    ExchangeMessageTrackingEntry class, 794–98
    ExchangeQueue class, 789, 793, 794
    ExchangeServerState class, 787–90
    Message Tracking Logs, 794–800
    Queue, 789–94
    Routing Table, 786–89
    types of, 785
ExchangeClusterResource class, 794, 796
ExchangeConnectorState class, 787, 788
Exchange_DSAccessDC class, 800–802
    defined, 800
    instances, 802
    properties, 801
ExchangeLink class, 789, 793, 794
    defined, 789
    IncreasingTime property, 790–94
    properties, 795
ExchangeMessageTrackingEntry class,
            794–98
    defined, 794
    EntryType property, 798
    instances, 798
    properties, 797
ExchangeQueue class, 789, 793, 794
    defined, 789
    IncreasingTime property, 790–94
    properties, 796
Exchange Routing Table provider, 786–89
    defined, 786
    purpose, 786–87
    See also Exchange 2000 providers
ExchangeServerState class, 787–90
    output, 789
    properties, 790
    states, 787

File/folder ACE AccessMask property, 637–44
    deciphering, 639
    flags, 637
    values, 638
File/folder security descriptors, 567–71
    connecting to, 562–67
    connection with ADSI, 565–67
    connection with WMI, 562
    Flags property values, 642
    inheritance user interface, 643
    retrieval with ADSI, 587–92
    retrieval with WMI, 585–87
    retrieving, 585–92
    updating, 715–19
    updating, with ADSI, 718–19
    updating, with WMI, 715–18
    user interface, 638
    See also Security descriptors
FILELIST.XML, 310
Files
    copying, 136–38
    deleting, 136–38
    page, 140–42, 144–45
    renaming, 136–38
File size
    alert, 134
    current, 134
    watching, 133–34
File system classes, 124–39
    defined, 124
    list of, 125
    Win32_DikPartition class, 127
    Win32_Directory class, 125
    Win32_DiskDriveToDiskPartition class, 129
    Win32_DiskQuota class, 124, 131
    Win32_QuotaSetting class, 124, 131
    Win32_ShortcutFile class, 124
    Win32_VolumeQuotaSetting class, 124, 131
    See also Operating system classes
File system share ACE AccessMask property, 644–47
    deciphering, 645
    flags, 644, 645
    output, 645–46
    values, 645
    See also ACE AccessMask property
File system share security descriptors, 567–71
    ACE Flags property and, 646
    with ADSI connection, 569–71
    connecting to, 567–71

File system share security descriptors *(cont'd.)*
   default, 604
   retrieving, 592–94
   retrieving with ADSI, 593–94
   retrieving with WMI, 592–93
   updating, 719–21
   updating, with ADSI, 720–21
   updating, with WMI, 719–20
   user interface, 647
   with WMI connection, 567–69
   See also Security descriptors
Flexible Single Master Operations (FSMO) roles
   active, 387
   Domain Naming Master, 391
   Infrastructure Master, 390
   modifications, 387
   monitoring, 387–91
   PDC Emulator, 390
   RID Master, 391
   Schema Owner, 391
FORMAT.COM command, 369
Forwarding providers, 517–25
   capabilities, 517
   classes, 518
   consumer, 517–19
   defined, 517
   event, 517–19
   MSFT_FCExecutedTraceEvent class, 523, 524
   MSFT_FCTargetTraceEvent class, 523, 524
   MSFT_ForwardingConsumer class, 518–22
   types of, 517
Fully Qualified Domain Name (FQDN), 459

GenerateHTML() function, 386
GenericEventAsyncConsumer.wsf script, 522
GetCollectionOfInstances.wsf
   defined, 26
   reusing, 146, 148
   using, 27
GetSecurityDescriptor() function, 564, 568, 571, 576,
      583, 594
GetSIDFromUserID() function, 207–8
GetSingleInstance.wsf, 20–21
   defined, 26
   using, 27
Group class, 654
Group Policies Management Console (GPMC), 284
Group Policy Objects (GPOs), 281
   appliance filtering, 283

application order, 293
applied at site level, 292
container location, 282
container name, 304
creation, 308
deletion, 308
Domain, 292
enforcing automatic startup, 291, 293
information levels, 305–6
infrastructure, 284
link information, 307
Local, 292
order of, 282
RSOP_GPO instance information, 305
RSOP information retrieval from, 295–96, 297,
      299–303, 307–8
rules list information, 305–6
Site, 292
SOM information, 306–7
status, 294
Group property
   deciphering, 619–20
   defined, 545
   representation, 619
   updating, 694–96
   via ADSI, 694
   via WMI, 694–95
   See also Security descriptors
Groups
   associated instances of, 204
   membership, 530
   membership, retrieving, 205
GUID number
   in ACE ObjectType value, 670
   appliesTo, 655, 656
   conversion, 655
   corresponding, retrieving, 680
   Extended Rights, 655, 679
   format, 654
   origins summary, 676
   schemaIDGUID, 671–75

Helper providers, 508–26
   defined, 213
   Event Correlator, 525–26
   Forwarding, 517–25
   View, 508–17
   See also WMI providers

High-performance providers, 6, 486–502
    aim, 486
    capabilities, 486
    Cooked Counter, 486
    defined, 486
    Performance Counter, 486
    Win32_PerfFormattedData classes, 489–92
    Win32_PerfFormattedData_Tcpip_
        NetworkInterface class, 493–94, 497
    Win32_PerfRawData class, 486, 487–88, 489
    See also Performance providers
HP OpenView, 814

IADsSecurityUtility interface, 718, 720, 721, 725, 729
IBM Tivoli solution portfolio, 814
IEINFO5, 811
IIS provider, 776–85
    capabilities, 776
    CIM_Component class, 780
    CIM_ElementSetting class, 780, 781
    CIM_ManagedSystemElement class, 779
    CIM_Setting class, 779–80
    defined, 776
    IIsStructuredDataClass class, 780
    IISWebServerSetting class, 777
    See also Internet Information Server (IIS)
IIsStructuredDataClass class, 780
IISWebServer class, 776–77
    associations, 777
    instances, 783
    ServerBindings property, 777, 781, 782, 783, 784
IISWebServerSetting class, 777
Infrastructure Master FSMO, 390
Inherited ACEs, 624, 696, 711
Input device classes, 31–33
    defined, 31
    Win32_Keyboard class, 31
    Win32_PointingDevice class, 31–32
    See also Computer system hardware classes
Insight Management Agents, 814–23
    defined, 814–15
    enterprise MIB information, 817
    information, 816
    information collected by, 815
    performance classes, 822–23
    SNMP classes, 818
    SNMP information, 816
    WMI classes created from MIB files, 820–21
Insight SNMP MIB files, 817

_InstanceProviderRegistration system class, 13
Instance providers, 3
    defined, 3
    implementation, 6
    provider qualifier, 9
    registration, 3
    See also WMI providers
Instances
    environment variables, 119, 120, 121
    listing all, with properties formatted, 22–23
    listing single, with properties formatted, 21–22
    QFE, 162
    video controller, 100
    WMI, locating, 8
    WMI provider registration, locating, 11, 12–13,
        14–15
    See also specific classes
Internet Explorer provider, 811–13
    capabilities, 812
    classes, 812
    defined, 811
    MicrosoftIE_Certificate class, 812
    MicrosoftIE_FileVersion class, 813
    MicrosoftIE_LanSettings class, 811
    read-only mode, 811
Internet Information Server (IIS), 536
    anonymous access with, 540
    authentication definition locations, 539
    customizing, 539–44
    provider, 211
    See also IIS provider
IPConfig.Exe utility, 58
IP routing providers, 211, 415–23
    capabilities, 415
    classes, 416
    defined, 415
    types of, 415
    Win32_ActiveRoute class, 417, 422
    Win32_IP4PersistedRouteTable class, 416,
        422, 423
    Win32_IP4RouteTable class, 416, 420, 422, 423
    Win32_IP4RouteTableEvent class, 416
    See also Network components providers
IPv4 routes
    adding, 418–19, 420–22
    deleting, 418–19, 422–23
    persistent, 416–17
    viewing, 418–19

Job scheduler classes, 183–91
    defined, 183
    list of, 183
    Win32_CurrentTime class, 184
    Win32_ScheduledJob class, 184, 185, 188, 190
    See also Operating system classes; Scheduled jobs
Join view classes
    created, 512
    defined, 509
    listing, 510–11
Jscript, 275

Kerberos environment, LocalSystem, 737
Kernel Job Object providers, 246–51
    capabilities, 246
    classes, 247
    defined, 246
    Win32_NamedJobObjectActgInfo class, 250
    Win32_NamedJobObject class, 247, 250
    Win32_NamedJobObjectLimitSetting class, 250
    Win32_NamedObjectProcess class, 250
Knowledge Consistency Checker (KCC), 403
    execution, forcing, 403
    triggering, 404

LDAP
    querying Active Directory with, 383
    query operation, 382
LoadCIMinXL.wsf script, 20, 30, 785, 829
    defined, 26
    using, 27, 30
LocateProviders.wsf script
    defined, 26
    using, 27
Logical disks
    disk partitions hosting, 130
    information, gathering, 127–28, 130–31

ManagementBaseObject object, 858
ManagementClass object, 852, 853
ManagementEventWatcher object, 856–57
Management Information Base (MIB)
    files, 451–52
    Insight SNMP files, 817
    private, conversion, 481
    SNMP definitions, 454
    SNMP private information, accessing, 463–67
ManagementObjectSearcher object, 854
ManagementScope object, 852, 853, 856

Mass storage classes, 33–40
    defined, 33
    list of, 33
    Win32_LogicalDisk class, 33–40
    See also Computer system hardware classes
Memory, information gathering, 44
Message Tracking Logs provider, 794–99
    defined, 794
    ExchangeMessageTrackingEntry class, 794–98
    user interface, 797
    See also Exchange 2000 providers
_MethodProviderRegistration system class, 13
Method providers
    defined, 4
    provider qualifier, 9
    registration, 4, 5
    See also WMI providers
Methods. *See specific classes and methods*
MicrosoftDNS_Atype class, 449
MicrosoftDNS_Cache class, 426, 446
MicrosoftDNS_CNAMEType class, 449
MicrosoftDNS_Domain class, 426
MicrosoftDNS_DomainResourceRecordContainment
        class, 426
MicrosoftDNS_ResourceRecord class, 426–27
    CreateFromTextRepresentation method, 449
    defined, 448
MicrosoftDNS_RootHints class, 426
MicrosoftDNS_Server class, 426, 427
    BootMethod property, 436
    EventLogLevel property, 436
    Forwarders property, 436
    IsSlave property, 436
    ListenAddresses property, 437
    methods, 431–34
    NoRecursion property, 436–37
    properties, 436
    RoundRobin property, 437
    StartScavenging method, 436
    StartService method, 436
    StopService method, 436
MicrosoftDNS_ServerDomainContainment class, 426
MicrosoftDNS_Zone class, 426, 427
    AllowUpdate method, 445
    ChangeZoneType method, 444–45
    CreateZone method, 443–44
    ForceRefresh method, 445
    instances, 439
    PauseZone method, 445

property values, 444
ReloadZone method, 445
ResetSecondaries method, 445
WriteBackRootHintDatafile method, 446
WriteBackZone method, 446
Microsoft_DomainTrustStatus class, 252
MicrosoftIE_Certificate class, 812
MicrosoftIE_FileVersion class, 813
MicrosoftIE_LanSettings class, 811
Microsoft_LocalDomainInfo class, 252, 256
Microsoft Office providers, 809–11
    capabilities, 809
    classes, 810–11
    defined, 809
    OffProv, 809
    OffProv10, 809
    See also Application WMI providers
Microsoft Operations Manager, 814, 824–25
    installation directory, 824, 825
    OM_Alert class, 824
    Service pack 1, 825
Microsoft_TrustProvider class, 252, 253, 256
Modem device classes, 77–82
    defined, 77
    list of, 73
    modem information retrieval, 78–80
    Win32_POTSModem class, 77, 78
    See also Computer system hardware classes
MOFCOMP.EXE, 463, 480, 508, 522, 818
MOF files
    compiling, 463
    loading, 466
    namespace creation with, 460, 461, 509
    to register Performance Monitor provider, 503–4
Motherboard, controller, port classes, 40–49
    defined, 40
    hardware components, 40
    hardware resource information retrieval, 42–43, 44,
        45, 47–49
    list of, 41–42
    Win32_DMAChannel class, 40, 46, 47
    Win32_IRQResource class, 40
    Win32_PCMCIAController class, 40
    Win32_PhysicalMemory class, 40
    Win32_Processor class, 40
    See also Computer system hardware classes
MSAD_DomainController class, 395, 400
    ExecuteKCC method, 403
    instances, 395

MSAD_NamingContext class, 399
MSAD_ReplCursor class, 400
MSAD_ReplNeighbor class, 401
    information display from, 401–2
    SyncNamingContext method, 404
MSAD_ReplPendingOp class, 399
MSCluster_Cluster class, 748, 749, 750
MSDiskDriver_Geometry class, 772, 775
MSFT_FCExecutedTraceEvent class, 523, 524
MSFT_FCTargetTraceEvent class, 523, 524
MSFT_ForwardingConsumer class, 518–22
    Authenticate parameter, 521
    Encryption parameter, 521
    ForwardingQoS parameter, 521
    IncludeSchema parameter, 521
    instances, creating, 518–19, 520
    MaximumQueueSize parameter, 521
    support, 518
    target machine, 518
    TargetSD parameter, 522
    Targets parameter, 522
MSFT_SomFilter class, 306
MSNdis_MediaConnectStatus class, 775
MSNdis_StatusMediaDisconnect class, 775
MSSQL_Database class, 802, 803
MSSQL_DatabaseLogin class, 803
MSSQL_SQLServer class, 802
Multimedia audio/visual class, 146–47
    defined, 146
    properties and methods, 146
    Win32_CodecFile class, 146–47
    See also operating system classes

Namespaces
    browsing, 12
    browsing, for class definitions, 872–73
    browsing, for classes, 848
    CIM repository, 530, 571
    CIMv2, 509, 514, 541, 571, 583
    creation with MOF file, 460, 461
    MicrosoftDNS, 431
    MicrosoftIISv2, 509, 785
    MicrosoftSQLServer, 802, 803
    MSCluster, 747
    .NET, 844–45
    Policy, 296
    Root, 12, 530, 535
    RSOP, 285–86, 296
    RSOP User, 307

Namespaces *(cont'd.)*
    SNMP, 451
    Subscription, 517
    System.Management, 844, 862
    System.Management.Instrumentation, 844–45, 846,
        862
    View, 511, 514
.NET classes
    ConnectionOptions, 852
    Constants, 852, 856
    EventArrivedEventArgs, 858
    ManagementClass, 852, 853
    ManagementScope, 852
    System.Management, 850, 856
    System.Management.Instrumentation, 850
    WMIEventHandler, 857, 858
    WQLEventQuery, 856
NetDiagnostics class, 412–14
    defined, 412
    scripting with, 413–14
    Win32_PingStatus class and, 414
.NET Framework, 843–58
    abstraction layer, 862
    class model, 863
    defined, 845
    languages adaptation, 845
    object model, 845
    power of, 864
    scripting and, 862–63
    System.Management.Instrumentation namespace,
        844–45, 846, 862
    System.Management namespace, 844, 862
    WMI architecture and, 846
    WMI information access, 844–46
Network adapter configuration, 62–65, 66–68
    code, 62–65, 66–68
    command-line parameters, 66
    DisableIPSec, 72
    EnableDHCP, 69
    EnableIPFilterSec, 70
    EnableIPSec, 72
    EnableIPSecFilter, 72
    EnableStatic, 71
    EnableWINS, 70
    ReleaseDHCPLease, 69
    ReleaseDHCPLeaseAll, 69–70
    ReNewDHCPLease, 70
    ReNewDHCPLeaseAll, 70
    SetDeadGWDetect, 70, 72

    SetDNSSuffixSearchOrder, 70
    SetGateways, 71–72
    SetIPConnectionMetric, 71
Network adapters
    associated instances of, 53
    enabled, 52
    listing, 51–52
    name, finding, 51
    settings, 757–59
Network components providers, 405–86
    defined, 212
    DNS, 423–50
    IP routing, 415–23
    Network Diagnostic, 412–15
    Ping, 405–12
    SNMP, 450–86
    See also WMI providers
NetworkConnectionStatus() function, 52
Network Diagnostic provider, 412–15
    capabilities, 412
    defined, 412
    NetDiagnostics class, 412–14
    testing connectivity with, 413–14
Networking classes, 147–54
    defined, 147
    list of, 147
    Win32_ActiveRoute class, 147
    Win32_IP4PersistedRouteTable class, 147
    Win32_IP4RouteTable class, 147
    Win32_IP4RouteTableEvent class, 147
    Win32_NetworkClient class, 148
    Win32_NetworkConnection class, 148
    Win32_NetworkProtocol class, 150
    Win32_NTDomain class, 152–53
    Win32_PingStatus class, 147
    See also Operating system classes
Networking device classes, 49–73
    defined, 49
    list of, 49
    network device information retrieval, 49–50, 51–52,
        54, 55–57
    Win32_NetworkAdapter class, 51, 54
    Win32_NetworkAdapterConfiguration class, 49, 55
    Win32_NetworkProtocol class, 55, 57
    See also Computer system hardware classes
Network Load Balancing (NLB) providers, 211, 741–47
    capabilities, 742
    class associations, 746
    classes, 742

configuration settings, 744–45
defined, 741–42
NlbsNic class, 743, 746
NlbsNic class, 743
    ControlCluster method, 746
    GetClusterConfiguration method, 745
    UpdateClusterConfiguration method, 746
NotePad.Exe, 175, 181
NotificationMapper class, 473, 475
NT Event Log
    backing up, 219
    configuration, viewing/updating, 221–24
    files, 218
    overwrite policy, 224
NT Event Log providers, 218–24
    capabilities, 218, 218–19
    classes, 219
    defined, 218
    operation support, 218
    Win32_NTEventlogFile class, 220–24
    Win32_NTLogEvent class, 219–20

ObjectClass objects, 381
ObjectQuery object, 854
OffProv, 809
OffProv10, 809
OM_Alert class, 824
OpenView Operations for Windows. See OVOW
Operating system classes, 105–209
    COM component, 105–13
    defined, 105
    desktop information, 113–21
    driver, 122–24
    file system, 124–39
    job scheduler, 183–91
    multimedia audio/visual, 146–47
    networking, 147–54
    operating system settings, 154–71
    page file, 139–46
    process, 171–83
    registry, 183
    service, 191–97
    share, 197–201
    start menu, 201–2
    user account, 202–9
    See also Win32 providers
Operating systems
    application time slice, 169–70
    configuring, 157–58

date and time, 169–70
file dump values, 169
properties, viewing, 159–60
rebooting, 169–70
recovery options, change, 169
recovery parameters, 167–68
shutdown values, 170
Operating system settings classes, 154–71
    defined, 154
    list of, 155
    Win32_ComputerSystem class, 152, 154, 159, 160,
        163
    Win32_OperatingSystem class, 154
    Win32_OSRecoveryConfiguration class, 154
    Win32_QuickFixEngineering class, 154
    See also Operating system classes
Options object, 852
OV_ManagedNode class, 836
OV_MessageAction class, 839
OV_MessageAnnotation class, 842
OV_Message class, 826
    defined, 828
    instance management, 840, 843
    instances, retrieving, 834–35
    methods, 830, 832
    properties, 829
    properties, retrieving, 838–39
OVOW, 27, 825–43
    console, 826
    console showing alerts, 827
    defined, 825
    message annotation, retrieving, 842
    message characteristics, 834
    message collections, 842–43
    message display, 833
    message IDs, 843
    message management, 839
    message severity level, changing, 841
    OV_MessageAction class, 839
    OV_MessageAnnotation class, 842
    OV_Message class, 826, 828
    OV_MessageNode class, 836
    provider capabilities, 826
    providers, 827
    script initialization phase, 832–33
Owner property
    deciphering, 619–20
    defined, 644
    representation, 619

Owner property *(cont'd.)*
    updating, 691–94
    See also Security descriptors

Page file classes, 139–46
    defined, 139
    list of, 140
    Win32_PageFile class, 139, 143, 144
    Win32_PageFileUsage class, 143
    See also Operating system classes
Page files
    creating, 140–42, 144
    deleting, 140–42, 145
    updating, 140–42, 144–45
    viewing, 140–43
PDC Emulator FSMO, 390
Performance Counter provider, 486
Performance counters
    data capture, at regular intervals, 497–99, 501–2
    incrementing, 502
    instance data, saving, 502
    retrieval performance, 500
Performance Monitor
    counters, retrieving, 504–5
    counters, viewing, 506–7
    counters availability, 507
Performance Monitoring provider, 502–7
    capabilities, 503
    ClassContext qualifier, 506
    defined, 502
    MOF file to register, 503–4
    PropertyContext qualifier, 506
    Provider qualifier, 506
    registration, 503
Performance providers, 486–507
    defined, 212
    high-performance, 486–502
    Performance Monitoring, 502–7
    See also WMI providers
PING.Exe utility, 406, 412
Ping provider, 212, 405–12
    capabilities, 406
    defined, 405
    Win32_PingStatus class, 405, 407, 408, 411
    See also Network components provider
Power device classes, 74–77
    battery information retrieval, 74–76
    defined, 74
    list of, 74

Win32_PowerManagementEvent class, 74
    See also Computer system hardware classes
Power management
    events, 325
    event type values, 325
Power Management provider, 212, 323–25
    capabilities, 324
    defined, 323
    Win32_PowerManagementEvent class, 323, 325
Printer drivers
    adding, 83, 94
    information retrieval, 89
    instance creation, 94
    managing, 85–87
    removing, 83, 94, 95
    viewing, 87–88
Printers
    adding, 83, 90–91
    connections, adding, 90–91
    default, 93
    deleting, 92–93
    information retrieval, 89
    managing, 85–87, 92–93
    pausing/resuming, 83
    removing, 83
    renaming, 92–93
    viewing, 87–88
Printing device classes, 82–96
    defined, 82
    list of, 82
    Win32_Printer class, 82, 83, 89
    Win32_PrinterDriver class, 89
    Win32_PrinterJob class, 83, 89
    See also Computer system hardware classes
Print jobs
    canceling, 83
    deleting, 96
    information retrieval, 89
    managing, 85–87, 95
    names, 95
    pausing/resuming, 83
    sample output, 96
    viewing, 87–88
Privileges, 531–34
Process classes, 171–83
    defined, 171
    list of, 171
    Win32_Process class, 171, 174, 175, 176

Win32_ProcessStartup class, 176–78
    See also Operating system classes
Processes
    creating, 172–73, 177
    killing, 172–73, 178–79
    OnCompleted sink routine and, 180–81
    OnObjectReady sink routine and, 179
    viewing, 172–73, 174–75
Properties
    displaying, 58
    See also specific classes and properties
Property providers, 3–4
    defined, 3
    implementation, 6
    provider qualifier, 9
    registration, 3
    Registry, 4
    See also WMI providers
PropertyValue object, 609
Provider qualifier, 9
    retrieving, 15
    use of, 20
Provider registration
    class provider, 2
    event consumer provider, 4
    event provider, 4, 5
    instance provider, 3
    instances, locating, 11, 12–13, 14–15
    method provider, 4, 5
    NT Event Log event provider, 5
    property, 3–4
    system classes, 2
    Win32 method provider, 5

Queue provider, 789–94
    defined, 789
    ExchangeLink class, 789, 793, 794
    ExchangeQueue class, 789, 793, 794
    See also Exchange 2000 providers
Quick Fix Engineering (QFE), 162

Registries
    browsing, 229–33, 236, 237–39
    change detection, 225
    creating information in, 229–32, 233–34, 240–41
    deleting information in, 229–32, 234–35
    hive type identification, 228
    key monitoring, 227
    key value, 234

searching/replacing information in, 229–32, 236, 237–39
    search/replace operations, 228
    tree, 234
    updating information in, 240–41
    value parsing, 239–40
    value reading, 239
    values display, 235, 240
Registry class, 183
Registry key ACE AccessMask property, 684–87
    deciphering, 685
    flag values, 685
    values, 684
RegistryKeyChangeEvent class, 226
Registry keys security descriptor, 581–83
    ADSI connection, 581–83
    retrieving, 600–602
    retrieving with ADSI, 600–602
    retrieving with WMI, 600
    updating, 729–30
    user interface, 687
    WMI connection, 581
    See also Security descriptors
Registry providers, 4, 6, 234–41
    capabilities, 225
    classes, 225
    event provider, 225
    registration, 7
    registration in CIM repository, 7
    RegistryKeyChangeEvent class, 226
    RegistryTreeChangeEvent class, 226
    RegistryValueChangeEvent class, 226
    StdRegProv class, 225
    types of, 224
RegistryTreeChangeEvent class, 226
RegistryValueChangeEvent class, 226
ReOrderAce() function, 564, 571, 713
Reordering ACEs, 710–15
    in ADSI object model, 711–13
    group sorting, 711
    in WMI object model, 713–15
    See also Access Control Entries (ACEs)
ReplaceString() function, 228, 239–40
Replication state
    inbound, viewing, 401–2
    managing, 397–99
    viewing, 397–99
Restore points
    creating, 309, 315–16

Restore points *(cont'd.)*
  defined, 309
  event type for, 316
  identifying, 316
  restoring, 317
  type definition, 316
  viewing, 313–14
  See also System Restore
Restore status, 317
Resultant Set of Policies (RSOP)
  analyzing, 284
  associated instances information, 304
  calculation, 282
  classes/methods, 285
  defined, 281
  information, retrieving, 295–96, 297, 299–303,
     307–8
  information display, 301
  information examination, 300
  instance information, 303–4
  instances, 301
  namespaces, 285–86
  representation, 308
  sessions, 299
  subnamespaces, 286, 287
Resultant Set of Policies (RSOP) providers, 211,
     281–309
  classes, 287–88
  list of, 282
  location, 282
  Logging mode, 285, 294
  modes, 284–85
  Planning mode, 284–85
  RSOP_GPLink class, 307
  RSOP_IEAKPolicySetting class, 289, 290
  RSOP_PolicySetting class, 289
  RSOP_SecuritySettings class, 293
  RSOP_SOM class, 307
  RSOP_SystemService class, 292, 294, 309
  WITHIN statement and, 308
RID Master FSMO, 391
RootDSE class, 377
Root namespace, 12, 530
  default security settings on, 535
  defined, 12
  See also Namespaces
ROUTE.Exe, 418
RSOP_GPLink class, 307
RSOP_IEAKPolicySetting class, 289, 290

RsopLoggingModeProvider class, 286, 296–97
  CreateSession method, 286
  RsopDeleteSession method, 301
RSOP_PolicySetting class, 289
RSOP_SecuritySettings class, 293
RSOP_SOM class, 307
RSOP_SystemService class, 292, 294, 309

Scheduled jobs
  creating, 185–87, 190
  deleting, 185–87, 191
  viewing, 185–87, 189
  See also Job scheduler classes
SchemaIDGUID attribute, 657, 668
  defined, 656
  GUID number, 671–75
  See also ClassSchema object
Schema Owner FSMO, 391
Scope of Management (SOM), 296, 306–7
Scripting
  asynchronous, 732–37
  .NET Framework and, 862–63
  security, 529–739
  Windows environment, 864–65
SearchString() function, 228, 239
Security
  anonymous authentication and, 538
  configuration, 529–35
  configuration under Windows 2000+, 537–38
  configuration under Windows NT, 536–37
  connection settings, 530
  default settings on Root namespace, 535
  privileges, 531–34
  scripting, 529–739
SecurityDescriptor object, 616, 692
Security descriptors
  accessing, 546–47
  accessing, on manageable entities, 585–603
  access method, 567
  access technique decision, 549–51
  ACL, 545
  Active Directory object, connecting, 571–75
  Active Directory object, retrieving, 594–97
  Active Directory object, updating, 721–24
  Active Directory objects, 561
  ADSI representation, 547–49
  CIM repository namespace, connecting, 583–85
  CIM repository namespace, retrieving, 602–3
  CIM repository namespace, setting, 737

CIM repository namespace, updating, 730–31
CIM repository namespaces, 562
classes, 544
control, 545
Control Flags property, 620–25, 696–98
controls value calculation, 624–25
conversion, 607–9
deciphering, 611–19
default, creating, 603–7
Exchange 2000 mailbox, connecting, 575–81
Exchange 2000 mailbox, retrieving, 597–600
Exchange 2000 mailbox, updating, 726–29
Exchange 2000 mailboxes, 561–62
file/folder, connecting, 562–67
file/folder, retrieving, 585–92
file/folder, updating, 715–19
files/folders, 561
file system share, connecting, 567–71
file system share, retrieving, 592–94
file system share, updating, 719–21
Folder, 618–19
format, 547
Group property, 545, 619–20, 694–96
logical structure (ADSI), 548
logical structure (WMI), 545
management, 544–51
modifying, 691–715
object model representation, 739
origin, 738
Owner property, 544, 619–20, 691–94
registry keys, 562
registry keys, connecting, 581–83
registry keys, retrieving, 600–602
registry keys, updating, 729–30
representations, 550
returned in ADSI object model, 606
revision level, 548–49
from shares, 561
updating, 691–98, 715–31
Win32_ACE class, 614
Win32_SecurityDescriptor class, 544, 604, 611
Win32_Trustee class, 544
WMI representation, 544–46
SecurityInclude.vbs, 606
Security provider, 551–55
    capabilities, 552
    classes, 552
    defined, 551–52
    implementation, 551

support, 552
Win32_LogicalFileSecuritySetting class, 552, 553, 554, 555
Win32_LogicalShareSecuritySetting class, 555
Win32_SecuritySettingOfLogicalFile class, 552
Win32_SID class, 553, 554
Select Case statement, 81, 614
SendAlert() function, 406
SendMessage() function, 386
Server Explorer tool, 846–49
    defined, 846
    display names/instances, 848
    illustrated, 847
    method input parameters prompt, 848
    nodes, 847
    starting, 847
    See also Visual Studio.NET
Service classes, 191–97
    defined, 191
    list of, 191
    Win32_BaseService class, 191, 194, 197
    Win32_Service class, 191–97
    See also Operating system classes
Session providers, 241–46
    capabilities, 241
    classes, 241
    defined, 241
    Win32_ServerConnection class, 242, 243, 246
    Win32_ServerSession class, 242, 243, 246
    Win32_SessionConnection class, 242
    Win32_SessionShare class, 242
Sessions
    deleting, 246
    RSOP, 299
    viewing, with associations, 243–45
SetRegistryValue() function, 234, 240
SetSDControlFlags() function, 564
SetSDGroup() function, 564
SetSDOwner() function, 564, 691
SetSecurityDescriptor() function, 564, 717–18
Shadow copies
    creating, 359–60
    deleting, 360
    managing, 352, 357
    viewing, 362–63
Shadow Copy providers, 352–72
    capabilities, 353
    classes, 353
    defined, 352–53

Shadow Copy providers *(cont'd.)*
    Win32_ShadowCopy class, 354, 358, 359, 360, 361,
        363
    Win32_ShadowStorage class, 354, 361, 363, 370,
        371–72
    Win32_Volume class, 353, 354, 355, 360, 361, 363,
        365, 367
Shadow storage
    associating, 361
    specific volume for, 363
    viewing, 362–63
Share classes, 197–201
    defined, 197
    list of, 197
    Win32_ServerConnection class, 201
    Win32_ServerSession class, 201
    Win32_Share class, 198, 202
    See also Operating system classes
Shutdown provider, 325–26
    capabilities, 325
    defined, 325
    Win32_ComputerShutdownEvent class, 325
SID
    retrieving, from UserID, 207–8
    retrieving UserID from, 208–9
Simple Network Management Protocol. *See* SNMP;
        SNMP providers
SINK_OnCompleted() routine, 179, 181, 182, 183
SINK_OnObjectReady() routine, 134, 179, 183
SMI2SMIR.Exe, 463, 465, 482
SNMP
    AgentAddress qualifier, 454–55, 459
    AgentReadCommunityName qualifier, 455
    AgentTransport qualifier, 455–56
    commands, sending, 480–85
    configuration, 480
    data, reading, 480
    data access, 454–63
    data access organization, 467–70
    data access through remote computer, 470
    debugging output level, 485
    devices, MOF file for creating dedicated namespace
        for, 461–63
    enabling, on Cisco router, 458
    manageable entities, 452
    Module Information Repository, 453
    obtaining localhost IP addresses with, 456–57
    obtaining remote device IP addresses with, 458–59
    private MIB information access, 463–67

    providers, debugging, 485–86
    proxy namespace qualifiers, 255
    SMI, 451
    write operations, 480
SnmpColdStartNotification class, 472, 473
SNMP Module Information Registry (SMIR), 451
SNMP_OLD_CISCO_TS_MIB_lts class, 481–82, 484
    defined, 481
    illustrated, 481
    instances, creating, 482
SNMP providers, 450–86
    capabilities, 451
    classes, 452, 453
    defined, 450
    dynamic, 453
    installing, 450–51
    NotificationMapper class, 473, 475
    registration instances, 453
    SEEP, 471
    SnmpColdStartNotification class, 472, 473
    SNMP_OLD_CISCO_TS_MIB_lts class, 481–82,
        484
    SnmpV1Notification class, 473
    SnmpV2Notification class, 473, 474
    SnmpVarBind class, 473, 474, 477–79
    SREP, 471
    under Windows Server 2003, 451
    See also Network components providers
SNMPREG.MOF, 460
SNMP traps
    coldStart, 472
    enterprise-nonspecific, 471
    enterprise-specific, 471
    generic, 471
    of notifications, 453
    receiving, 471–80
    types of, 471
SnmpV1Notification class, 473
SnmpV2Notification class, 473, 474
SnmpVarBind class, 473, 474
    DisplayProperties() function and, 477
    DisplaySNMPBindings() function and, 478–79
    encoding types, 479–80
    instances, displaying, 477, 478–79
    properties, 479
SplitArrayInTwoArrays() function, 62
SQL provider, 802–9
    capabilities, 803
    classes, 804–8

defined, 802–3
SQL Server 2000, 27
Start menu classes, 201–2
    defined, 201
    list of, 201
    Win32_LogicalProgramGroup class, 201–2
    Win32_LogicalProgramGroupOrItem class, 202
    See also Operating system classes
StdRegProv class, 225
    CreateKey method, 234
    defined, 225
    DeleteKey method, 235
    DeleteValue method, 235
    EnumKey method, 236
    EnumValues method, 239
    instantiation, 232
    methods, 227–28
    as static class, 232
Structure of Management Information (SIM), 451
SWBemDateTime object, 323
SWBemLastError object, 392, 484, 485
SWBemLocator object, 562
SWBemNamedValueSet object, 463, 469, 470, 484,
    595, 723
SWBemObject object, 197, 314
    Delete_method, 93, 96, 121, 146, 190, 360
    DS_msExchMailboxSecurityDescriptor property,
    726
    DS_nTSecurityDescriptor property, 723, 726
    Put_ method, 92, 119, 120, 121, 169
SWBemPropertySet object, 476, 869–71
SWBemRefresher object, 500, 502
SWBemScripting objects, 844
SWBemServices object, 14, 15, 470
SWBemSink object, 501
Switches
    /Action, 118, 345
    /Action:ChangeSeverity, 841
    /Action-Create, 118
    /Action:List, 120, 217, 317, 833
    /Action:View, 840
    /Action:ViewNodes, 348, 349
    /Action:ViewRootNodes, 348
    /AddPrinters+, 87
    /ADSI+, 644, 647, 677, 686, 691
    /BaseKey, 232
    /ComputerRSOPOnly+, 298
    /CounterName, 497, 500
    /DaysOfMonth, 188

/DaysOfWeek, 188
/Decipher+, 614
/DelACE+, 703
/Delete, 190, 243, 246
/DisplayRegValue+, 235
/DomainInfo+, 256
/Env, 118, 120
/Executable, 174
/ForegroundApplicationBoost, 170
/GPOFullInfo+, 304, 305
/InstanceName, 497
/Interval, 502
/List+, 51, 188
/List:PrintJobs, 96
/Machine, 277
/NewRSOPSession+, 297, 299
/PackageName, 278
/PackageVersion, 278
/Password, 277
/PauseBeforeTerminate, 182
/Persistent+, 422, 423
/PingAddress, 414
/PingPort, 415
/Portable+, 76
/ProxyAddress, 260
/Raw, 500
/Rename, 165
/RepIPendingOp+, 399
/ReplNeighbor, 402
/ServiceType, 195
/SetDateTime, 170
/Severity:Minor, 841
/ShadowCopyID, 360
/SoftwareFeatures+, 275
/Terminate, 182
/TerminateCode, 178, 182
/UnJoin+, 164
/User, 277
/UserID, 573
/UserRSOP, 297
/UserRSOPOnly+, 298
/Verbose+, 407
/ViewProxy+, 260
/WQLQuery, 835
Synchronous event notification, 882–83
System ACL (SACL), 546, 551
System.Management.Instrumentation namespace,
    844–45, 846, 862
System.Management namespace, 844, 862

System Management Server (SMS), 858
System Monitor application, 502
System Restore
    changes, 309
    compression, 310
    defined, 309
    disk space requirement, 309
    disk space use percentage, 311
    feature exploitation, 312
    monitoring, disabling, 311, 314–15
    monitoring, enabling, 314–15
    operations, 309
    parameters, updating, 318–19
    restore point, 309
    standby mode, 309
    wizard, 309, 310
SystemRestore class, 311, 313, 314, 315, 317
    CreateRestorePoint method, 315
    defined, 311
    Disable method, 314
    Enable method, 314
    GetLastRestoreStatus method, 317
    instances, 313
    Restore method, 317
SystemRestoreConfig class, 311
    properties, 319
    using, 318–19
System Restore provider, 309–19
    capabilities, 310
    classes, 311
    implementation, 310
    SystemRestore class, 311, 313, 314, 315, 317
    SystemRestoreConfig class, 311, 318, 319
_SystemSecurity class
    GetSD method, 691
    SetSD method, 691, 731
Systems Management Server, 814

Terminal Server providers
    capabilities, 750
    classes, 751
    defined, 749–50
    Win32_GeneralSetting class, 759
    Win32_Terminal class, 755
    Win32_TerminalServiceToSetting class, 751, 752
    Win32_TSAccount class, 771
    Win32_TSClientSetting class, 760–63
    Win32_TSEnvironmentSetting class, 764–66
    Win32_TSLogonSetting class, 766–67

Win32_TSNetworkAdapterSetting class, 757–59
Win32_TSPermissionSetting class, 770
Win32_TSRemoteControlSettings class, 756
Win32_TSSessionSetting class, 768–70
Terminal Services, 749–71
    client color depth policy settings, 763
    client mapping settings, 763–64
    client settings, 760–64
    configuration MMC, 752, 752–55
    connection environment policy settings, 765
    connection limit settings, 758
    connection logon settings, 766–67
    connection permission settings, 770–71
    connections, enabling/disabling, 755–56
    connections configuration, 755–71
    connection session settings, 768–70
    default client settings, 761
    encryption/authentication settings, 759–60
    environment settings, 764–66
    general connection settings, 759
    network adapter settings, 757–59
    remote control configuration, 756–57
    remote control configuration values, 757
Time Service provider, 153
TrustMon provider, 251–58
    capabilities, 252
    classes, 252
    defined, 251
    Microsoft_DomainTrustStatus class, 252
    Microsoft_LocalDomainInfo class, 252, 256
    Microsoft_TrustProvider class, 252, 253, 256
Trusts
    status change detection, 256
    verifying, 254–56

UnionDrives_C class, 513
Union view classes
    creation, 515–16
    defined, 509
    listing, 513
    See also View provider
UnSecApp.Exe, 734
    callback, 736
    event log entry, 737
    sink, 735
    wrapper, 735
Updating security descriptors, 691–98, 715–31
    Active Directory object, 721–24
    Active Directory object, with ADSI, 723–24

Active Directory object, with WMI, 721–23
    CIM repository namespace, 730–31
    Control Flags, 696–98
    Exchange 2000 mailbox, 724–29
    Exchange 2000 mailbox, with ADSI, 727–28
    Exchange 2000 mailbox, with CDOEXM, 728–29
    Exchange 2000 mailbox, with WMI, 726–27
    file/folder, 715–19
    file/folder, with ADSI, 718–19
    file/folder, with WMI, 715–18
    file system share, 719–21
    file system share, ADSI, 720–21
    file system share, with WMI, 719–20
    Group property, 694–96
    Owner property, 691–94
    registry key, 729–30
    See also Security descriptors
User account classes, 202–9
    defined, 202
    list of, 203
    Win32_Account class, 202, 204
    Win32_Group class, 202, 204, 205
    Win32_SystemAccount class, 202
    Win32_UserAccount class, 202, 207, 208
    See also Operating system classes
User class, 654
    link with Extended right, 654
    schemaIDGUID attribute, 680
UserID
    retrieving, from SID, 208–9
    retrieving SID from, 207–8
UserRight.Control object, 590

Video adapter
    hardware resources list, 103
    information retrieval, 100–103
Video and monitor classes, 96–105
    defined, 96
    desktop monitor information retrieval, 97–99
    list of, 97
    Win32_DesktopMonitor class, 97
    Win32_DisplayConfiguration class, 96
    Win32_DisplayControllerConfiguration class, 96–97
    Win32_VideoConfiguration class, 96
    Win32_VideoController class, 99
    Win32_VideoSettings class, 99
    See also Computer system hardware classes
Video controller, associated instances, 100

View provider, 508–17
    Association view classes, 509, 514–15
    capabilities, 509
    defined, 508
    Join view classes, 509, 510–11
    qualifiers, 510
    registering, 508
    UnionDrives_C class, 513
    Union view classes, 509, 513–14
Visual Studio.NET, 844, 863
    event subscription, 849
    instance modification, 849
    Management Data node, 847, 848
    Management Events node, 847, 849
    Management (WMI) Extensions for, 858
    Server Explorer tool, 846–49
    viewing events from, 850
    WMI information access from, 846–50
Volume Change event provider, 328–29
    capabilities, 328
    defined, 328
    Win32_VolumeChangeEvent class, 328, 329

WBEM provider, 213–18
    capabilities, 214
    classes, 213
    instance, 214
    Win32_MethodParameterClass class, 213–14
    Win32_WMIElementSetting class, 213–14
Win32_Account class, 202, 204, 554
Win32_ACE class, 614
Win32_ActiveRoute class, 147, 417, 422
Win32_AllocatedResource class, 54
Win32_BaseService class, 122, 191, 194, 197
    Change method, 196
    Create method, 194
    defined, 191
    Delete method, 197
    See also Service classes
Win32_Battery class, 324
Win32_ClassicCOMClassSetting class, 109
Win32_CodecFile class, 146–47
    defined, 146
    Group property, 146
    instances, 146–47
    See also Multimedia audio/visual class
Win32_ComputerShutdownEvent class, 325
Win32_ComputerSystem class, 152
    collection, 159

Win32_ComputerSystem class *(cont'd.)*
   defined, 154
   definition, 163
   DomainRole property, 160
   instances, 159
   JoinDomainOrWorkGroup method, 163
   property modifications, 165
   Rename method, 165
   UnJoinDomainOrWorkGroup method, 164
   Win32_WindowsProductActivation class
      association, 261
Win32_CurrentProbe class, 324
Win32_CurrentTime class, 184, 320
Win32_DCOMApplicationAccessAllowedSetting class,
      113
Win32_DCOMApplicationLaunchAllowedSetting class,
      113
Win32_DCOMApplicationSetting class
   associations, 112
   defined, 109
   instances, 111
   settings, 109–11
   See also COM component classes
Win32_Desktop class, 113–14
   associations, 114
   defined, 113
   See also Desktop information classes
Win32_DesktopMonitor class, 97
Win32_DfsNode class, 344, 345, 348, 349, 350, 351,
      352
   Create method, 344, 351
   instance creation, 351
   instance deletion, 352
   instance properties, 349
   instances, 345, 348, 350
   State property, 352
   Timeout property, 351
Win32_DfsNodeTarget class, 348
   associations, 345, 348
   illustrated, 345
Win32_DfsTarget class, 344, 348, 349, 351, 352
   instance properties, 349
   instances, 348
   property modifications, 351
   State property, 352
Win32_DikPartition class
   associations, 127
   defined, 127
   instances, 128, 129, 130

Win32_Directory class, 125
Win32_DiskDrive class, 127, 129
Win32_DiskDriveToDiskPartition class, 129
Win32_DiskQuota class, 124, 131, 330, 332
   associations, 330
   Association View class and, 516
   instances, 331, 343
   path, 343
   for quota configuration, 332
   for quota configuration per user, 339
   references, 341
Win32_DisplayConfiguration class, 96
Win32_DisplayControllerConfiguration class, 96–97
Win32_DMAChannel class, 40
   instances, 46
   instances, retrieving, 47
Win32_Environment class, 115–21
   command-line parameters, 115–16
   defined, 115
   operations, 116
   See also Desktop information classes
Win32_GeneralSetting class, 759
Win32_Group class, 202, 204, 205
   associations, 204, 205
   defined, 202
   instances, 204
   See also User account classes
Win32_IP4PersistedRouteTable class, 147
   associations, 416–17
   associations, verifying, 423
   instances, creating, 422
Win32_IP4RouteTable class, 147, 423
   instances, 416, 420
   instances, creating, 420
   instances, deleting, 422
Win32_IP4RouteTableEvent class, 147, 416
Win32_IRQResource class, 40, 47
Win32_Keyboard class, 31
Win32_LocalTime class, 321–23
Win32_LogicalDisk class, 33–40, 127, 330, 341
   Chkdsk method, 37, 39
   class associations, 33, 34
   defined, 33
   for monitoring free space, 34–35
   VolumeSerialNumber property, 366
   Win32_Volume class vs., 354
   WQL query conditions, 36
   See also Mass storage classes
Win32_LogicalFile class, 138–39

Win32_LogicalFileSecuritySetting class, 552, 553, 554, 555
   associations, 552, 553
   file system object, 554
   GetSecurityDescriptor method, 585–86, 716
   security settings, 553
   SetSecurityDescriptor method, 716, 717, 720
Win32_LogicalProgramGroup class, 201–2
Win32_LogicalProgramGroupOrItem class, 202
Win32_LogicalShareSecuritySetting class, 555, 592
Win32_LogonSession class, 149–50
   associations, 150
   defined, 149
Win32_MappedLogicalDisk class, 149
Win32_MethodParameterClass class, 176–77, 213–14
Win32_NamedJobObjectActgInfo class, 250
Win32_NamedJobObject class, 171, 247, 250
Win32_NamedJobObjectLimitSetting class, 250
Win32_NamedObjectProcess class, 250
Win32_NetworkAdapter class, 51, 150–51
   associations, 151
   Index property, 54
   name property and, 51
   See also Networking device classes
Win32_NetworkAdapterConfiguration class, 49
   command-line parameter and method correspondence, 65
   command-line parameters, 66
   defined, 55
   DisableIPSec method, 72, 73
   EnableDHCP method, 69
   EnableIPSecFilter method, 70, 72, 73
   EnableIPSec method, 72
   EnableStatic method, 71
   EnableWINS method, 70
   Index property, 55
   instance, retrieving, 55, 66
   methods, 58–60
   network adapter configuration, 62–65, 66–68
   parameters input, 62
   parameters required by, 60
   ReleaseDHCPLeaseAll method, 69
   ReleaseDHCPLease method, 69
   ReNewDHCPLeaseAll method, 70
   ReNewDHCPLease method, 70
   SetDeadGWDetect method, 70, 72
   SetDNSSuffixSearchOrder method, 70
   SetGateways method, 71–72
   SetIPConnectionMetric method, 71
   string to array conversion, 62
   See also Networking device classes
Win32_NetworkClient class, 148
Win32_NetworkConnection class, 148
Win32_NetworkProtocol class, 55, 57, 150
Win32_NTDomain class, 152–53
Win32_NTEventlogFile class, 220–24
   capabilities, 221
   defined, 220
   sample use, 221–24
Win32_NTLogEvent class, 219–20
   associations, 219
   output, 220
Win32_OperatingSystem class
   collection, 159
   defined, 154
   instances, 159
Win32_OSRecoveryConfiguration class
   collection, 159
   defined, 154
   instances, 159
Win32_PageFile class
   defined, 139
   instances, 143, 144
   Name property, 143
   See also Page file classes
Win32_PageFileUsage class, 143
Win32_PCMCIAController class, 40
Win32_PerfFormattedData classes, 489–92
   as calculated performance counter, 493
   list of, 489–91
   naming conventions, 492
Win32_PerfFormattedData_Tcpip_NetworkInterface class, 493–94, 497
   instance name, 497
   instances, 497
   properties, 494
Win32_PerfRawData classes, 486, 487–88, 489
   list of, 487–88
   naming convention, 492
Win32_PhysicalMemory class, 40
Win32_PingStatus class, 147
   with asynchronous timer, 408–10
   availability, 408
   instances, creating, 405
   instantiation, 408
   NetDiagnostics class and, 414
   properties, displaying, 407

Win32_PointingDevice class, 31–32
    output, 31–32
    practical application, 32
    See also Input device classes
Win32_PortableBattery class, 324
Win32_POTSModem class, 77, 78
    associations, 77
    properties enumeration, 78
    See also Modem device classes
Win32_PowerManagementEvent class, 323–24, 325
    availability, 323–24
    relationship, 74
Win32_Printer class, 82–83
    AddPrinterConnection method, 83
    AddPrinterDriver method, 83, 94
    associations, 82–83
    CancelAllJobs method, 83
    defined, 89
    DMTF date/time value, 90
    instance creation, 83, 91
    instance deletion, 83
    Pause method, 83
    Resume method, 83
    StartTime property, 90
    UntilTime property, 90
Win32_PrinterDriver class, 89
Win32_PrinterJob class, 83, 89
Win32_Process class
    asynchronous method execution, 179
    Create method, 176, 177, 181
    defined, 171
    executable name and, 174
    GetOwner method, 175
    GetOwnerSID method, 175
    instances, 176
    Terminate method, 178, 180, 181
    See also Process classes
Win32_Processor class, 40
Win32_ProcessStartup class, 176–78
    as abstract class, 176
    instances, 176, 178
    properties, 177
    See also Process classes
Win32_Product class, 269, 272, 275, 277, 278, 281
    Admin method, 278
    Advertise method, 278
    associations, 275
    Install method, 278
    instances, 275, 281

    key, 281
    methods, 227
Win32 providers, 29–209
    capabilities, 30
    classes, 30
    class support, 29
    computer system hardware classes, 31–105
    defined, 29
    implementation, 29–30
    method, registration, 5
    operating system classes, 105–209
    summary, 209
_Win32Provider system class
    ComponentID property, 108
    instances, 8
Win32_Proxy class, 258, 260
Win32_QuickFixEngineering class, 154
Win32_QuotaSetting class, 124, 131, 330, 331, 332, 338
    associations, 330
    instances, 331
    instances, updating, 338
    using, 332
Win32_Registry class, 183
    setting read/write property (directly), 868–69
    setting read/write property (indirectly), 869
Win32_ScheduledJob class, 188, 190
    Create method exposed by, 190
    DaysOfMonth parameter, 185, 187, 188
    DaysOfWeek parameter, 185, 187, 188
    defined, 184
    instances, 188
    methods, 184
    properties, 188
    See also Job scheduler classes
Win32_SecurityDescriptor class, 544
    Group property, 619–20
    instances, 604, 611
    Owner property, 619
Win32_SecuritySettingOfLogicalFile class, 552
Win32_ServerConnection class, 201, 242, 243, 246
Win32_ServerSession class, 201, 242, 243, 246
Win32_Service class, 30, 191–97
    defined, 191
    instances, 194
    retrieving all instances of, 867–68
    See also Service classes
Win32_SessionConnection class, 242
Win32_SessionShare class, 242

Win32_ShadowCopy class, 354, 360, 361
    Create method, 359
    defined, 354
    instances, 354, 358
    instances, retrieving, 363
    instances, viewing, 358
    viewing, 358
Win32_ShadowStorage class, 354, 361, 363, 370,
        371–72
    associations, 363
    Create method, 360–61
    defined, 354
    instances, creating, 370
    instances, removing, 371–72
    instances, retrieving, 370
    instances, updating, 371
    MaxSpace property, 370
    properties, 354–55
Win32_Share class, 198, 202
    Create method, 198
    defined, 198
    Delete method, 198
    SetShareInfo method, 198, 201, 720
    See also Share classes
Win32_ShortcutFile class, 124
Win32_SID class, 113
Win32_SoftwareFeature class, 275
Win32_SystemAccount class, 202
Win32_SystemConfigurationChangeEvent class,
        326–27
Win32_SystemDriver class, 122–23
    defined, 122
    output, 122–23
    properties and methods, 122
    See also Driver classes
Win32_Terminal class, 755
Win32_TerminalServiceToSetting class, 751, 752
    ChangeMode method, 752
    instances, customizing, 754
    SetAllowTSConnections method, 753
    SetHomeDirectory method, 753
    SetPolicyPropertyName method, 754
    SetProfilePath method, 753
    SetSingleSession method, 753
    SetTimeZoneRedirection method, 753
Win32_TimeZone class, 115
Win32_Trustee class, 544
    instance binary representation requirement, 694
    instances, creating, 692–93

instance SID requirement, 693
Win32_TSAccount class, 771
Win32_TSClientSetting class, 760–63
    ConnectionPolicy property, 762
    ConnectionSettings method, 762
    SetClientProperty method, 763
    SetColorDepth method, 762
    SetColorDepthPolicy method, 762
Win32_TSEnvironmentSetting class, 764–66
Win32_TSLogonSetting class, 766–67
Win32_TSNetworkAdapterSetting class, 757–59
    MaximumConnections property, 757
    SelectAllNetworkAdapters method, 759
    SelectNetworkAdapterIP method, 759
Win32_TSPermissionSetting class, 770
Win32_TSRemoteControlSetting class, 756
Win32_TSSessionSetting class, 768–70
    ActiveSessionLimit property, 769
    BrokenConnectionAction property, 770
    BrokenConnectionPolicy property, 770
    defined, 768
    DisconnectedSessionLimit property, 769
    IdleSessionLimit property, 769
    TimeLimit method, 768
    TimeLimitPolicy property, 768
Win32_UninterruptiblePowerSupply class, 324
Win32_UserAccount class, 114, 115, 202, 207, 208
    defined, 202
    instances, 208
    in user name conversion, 207
    See also User account classes
Win32_UserDesktop class, 144
Win32_UTCTime class, 320–21, 323
Win32_VideoConfiguration class, 96
Win32_VideoController class
    defined, 99
    properties list, 103
Win32_VideoSettings class, 99
Win32_VolumeChangeEvent class, 328, 329
    defined, 328
    EventType property, 329
    use, 328
Win32_Volume class, 353, 354, 355
    associating shadow storage with, 361
    associations, 355
    Chkdsk method, 365–66
    DefragAnalysis method, 367–68
    Format method, 369–70
    illustrated, 355

Win32_Volume class *(cont'd.)*
instances, 360, 361, 363, 365
SerialNumber property, 367
Win32_LogicalDisk class vs., 354
Win32_VolumeQuotaSetting class, 124, 131, 331
Win32_VXD class, 123–24
Win32_WindowsProductActivation class, 261, 265–66
methods, 266
operations supported by, 265
SetProductKey method, 266–67
Win32_ComputerSystem class association, 261
Win32_WMIElementSetting class, 213–14
Win32_WMISetting class
properties exposure, 215
as singleton class, 217
Windows Authorization Access Group (WAAG), 732, 738
defined, 738
group, 738
Windows Driver Model (WDM) provider, 771–75
capabilities, 771
classes, 773–74
defined, 771
MSDiskDriver_Geometry class, 772, 775
MSNdis_MediaConnectStatus class, 775
MSNdis_StatusMediaDisconnect class, 775
Windows Installer
actions, 280–81
Admin Installation, 277, 278
Advertisement, 277
Installation, 277, 278
Microsoft Support Tools, 276
package management, 273–75, 277–80
power, 277
Windows Installer provider
actions classes, 268
adding, under Windows Server 2003, 268
associations classes, 269
checks classes, 269
classes, 268–69, 270–72
core classes, 269
defined, 267
external association classes, 269
installing, 267
settings classes, 269
Win32_Product class, 269, 272, 275, 277, 278, 281
Windows Integrated Authentication (WIA), 537
Windows management layer, 863

Windows Product Activation provider, 211, 260–67
capabilities, 260
classes, 261
defined, 260
methods, 261
Win32_WindowsProductActivation class, 261, 265–66
Windows Product Activation (WPA)
action verification, 266
code, 263–65
execution, 262
information display, 265
information management, 260
See also Windows Product Activation provider
Windows Proxy provider, 258–60
capabilities, 258
defined, 258
Win32_Proxy class, 258, 260
Windows scripting environments, 864–65
Windows Server 2003
Active Directory Extended Rights and, 658–65
lockdown mechanism, 735–37
registry activating lockdown mechanism, 735
SNMP providers and, 451
Terminal Services, 749–71
Windows services
alerting, 885–88
connecting, 851–52, 853–54
creating, 193
deleting, 193
displaying, with WQL event query, 854–56
instances, creating, 195–96
instances, deleting, 197
instances, modifying, 196
instances, viewing, 194
managing, 885–88
monitoring, 885–88
parameters, 195
retrieving, 851–52, 853–54
updating, 193
WinMgmt.Exe, 253, 732, 734
callbacks, 734
stopping/restarting, 253
WITHIN statement, 27, 30, 281, 425, 751
WMI
access methods, 529–30
Active Directory objects connection with, 571–73
Active Directory objects retrieval with, 594–96
Active Directory object update with, 721–23

adding ACEs in, 701–3
ASP and, 536–44
CIM repository namespace connection with,
       583–85
CIM repository namespace retrieval with, 602–3
COM API, 785, 813, 851
deciphering ACLs and, 625
Exchange 2000 mailbox connection with, 576–77
Exchange 2000 mailbox retrieval with, 597–98
Exchange 2000 mailbox update, 726–27
file/folder connection with, 562–65
file/folder retrieval with, 585–87
file/folder update with, 715–18
file system share connection with, 567–69
file system share retrieval with, 592–93
file system share update with, 719–20
information types, 813
.NET Framework and, 843–58
privileges, 531–34
registry keys connection with, 581
registry keys retrieval with, 600
removing ACEs in, 707–10
reordering ACEs in, 713–15
SDK, 8
security configuration, 529–35
security descriptor management, 544–51
security descriptor representation, deciphering,
       611–15
security scripting, 529–739
settings, updating, 215–17
WMI-ASP scripts, 539
    CIM repository accessed by, 541
    Win32_Service class, 541, 542–44
WMIBinaryMofResource class, 772
WMI CIM Studio, 20, 30, 482
WMI client applications
    asynchronous operation, 733
    asynchronous operation with UnSecApp.Exe, 733,
       736
WMIEventHandler object, 857
WMIEventWatcher object, 857
WMI filters, 284
    defined, 283
    illustrated example, 283
WMI logging level, 218
WMIManageSD.Wsf script, 556, 558, 561, 590, 600,
       606, 666, 686, 739
WMI provider discovery, 8–20
    helpers for, 20–26

summary, 27–28
system classes, 1
WMI providers, 211–527
    Active Directory, 37–394
    Active Directory Replication, 394–405
    application, 741–860
    capabilities, 8, 16–19
    categories, 212
    class, 2–3
    Clock, 319–23
    Cluster, 747–49
    Configuration Change, 326–28
    core OS components, 212, 213–319
    core OS components event, 212, 319–29
    core OS file system components, 212, 329–72
    DFS, 344–52
    Disk Quota, 124, 131, 329–44
    DNS, 211, 423–50
    event consumer, 4–6
    Event Correlator, 525–26
    Exchange 2000, 785–802
    Forwarding, 517–25
    helper, 213, 508–26
    high-performance, 6, 486–502
    IIS, 776–85
    instance, 3
    Internet Explorer, 811–13
    IP routing, 415–23
    Kernel Job Object, 246–51
    list, 16–19
    listing, 8–9
    method, 4
    Microsoft Office, 809–11
    most important, 16–19
    network components, 212, 405–86
    Network Diagnostic, 412–15
    Network Load-Balancing, 741–47
    NT Event Log, 218–24
    OVOW, 825–43
    performance, 212, 486–507
    Performance Monitoring, 502–7
    Ping, 405–12
    power management, 323–25
    primary role, 6
    property, 3–4
    registration system classes, 2
    Registry, 224–41
    retrieving information about, 1
    RSOP, 281–309

WMI providers *(cont'd.)*
  Security, 551–55
  Session, 241–46
  Shadow Copy providers, 352–72
  shutdown, 325–26
  SNMP, 450–86
  SNMP class registration, 2
  SQL Server 2000, 802–9
  summary, 526
  System Restore, 309–19
  Terminal Server, 749–71
  trace logging of, 391
  TrustMon, 251–58
  types of, 1–8
  View, 508–17
  Volume Change, 328–29
  WBEM, 213–18
  WDM, 771–75
  Windows Installer provider, 267–81
  Windows Proxy, 258–60
  WPA, 260–67

WMISystemRestore.Wsf script, 312, 317
Workgroups, joining/unjoining, 163
Workstations, renaming, 163
WQLEventQuery object, 856, 857
WSHRemote, 111